DATE DUE

			PRINTED IN U.S.A.

Literature Criticism from 1400 to 1800

Guide to Gale Literary Criticism Series

For criticism on	Consult these Gale series
Authors now living or who died after December 31, 1959	*CONTEMPORARY LITERARY CRITICISM (CLC)*
Authors who died between 1900 and 1959	*TWENTIETH-CENTURY LITERARY CRITICISM (TCLC)*
Authors who died between 1800 and 1899	*NINETEENTH-CENTURY LITERATURE CRITICISM (NCLC)*
Authors who died between 1400 and 1799	*LITERATURE CRITICISM FROM 1400 TO 1800 (LC)* *SHAKESPEAREAN CRITICISM (SC)*
Authors who died before 1400	*CLASSICAL AND MEDIEVAL LITERATURE CRITICISM (CMLC)*
Black writers of the past two hundred years	*BLACK LITERATURE CRITICISM (BLC)*
Authors of books for children and young adults	*CHILDREN'S LITERATURE REVIEW (CLR)*
Dramatists	*DRAMA CRITICISM (DC)*
Hispanic writers of the late nineteenth and twentieth centuries	*HISPANIC LITERATURE CRITICISM (HLC)*
Native North American writers and orators of the eighteenth, nineteenth, and twentieth centuries	*NATIVE NORTH AMERICAN LITERATURE (NNAL)*
Poets	*POETRY CRITICISM (PC)*
Short story writers	*SHORT STORY CRITICISM (SSC)*
Major authors from the Renaissance to the present	*WORLD LITERATURE CRITICISM, 1500 TO THE PRESENT (WLC)*

ISSN 0740-2880

Volume 40

Literature Criticism from 1400 to 1800

Critical Discussion of the Works
of Fifteenth-, Sixteenth-, Seventeenth-, and
Eighteenth-Century Novelists, Poets, Playwrights,
Philosophers, and Other Creative Writers

Jelena O. Krstović, Editor

Suzanne Dewsbury, Associate Editor

GALE

DETROIT · NEW YORK · TORONTO · LONDON

STAFF

Jelena O. Krstović, *Editor*

Dana Barnes, Daniel G. Marowski, *Contributing Editors*
Michelle Lee, Suzanne Dewsbury *Associate Editors*
Ira Mark Milne, *Assistant Editor*
Aarti Stephens, *Managing Editor*

Susan M. Trosky, *Permissions Manager*
Kimberly F. Smilay, *Permissions Specialist*
Sarah Chesney, Steve Cusack, Kelly A. Quinn, *Permissions Associates*

Victoria B. Cariappa, *Research Manager*
Julia C. Daniel, Tamara C. Nott, Tracie A. Richardson, Cheryl L. Warnock, *Research Associates*

Mary Beth Trimper, *Production Director*
Deborah Milliken, *Production Assistant*

Pamela A. Reed, *Photography Coordinator*
Randy Bassett, *Image Database Supervisor*
Mike Logusz, Robert Duncan, *Imaging Specialists*

This book is printed on acid-free paper that meets the minimum requirements of American National Standard for Information Sciences—Permanence Paper for Printed Library Materials, ANSI Z39.48-1984.

Library of Congress Catalog Card Number 94-29718
ISBN 0-7876-1249-9
ISSN 0740-2880
Printed in the United States of America

10 9 8 7 6 5 4 3 2 1

Contents

Preface   vii

Acknowledgments   xi

Preface

L *iterature Criticism from 1400 to 1800 (LC)* presents critical discussion of world authors of the fifteenth through eighteenth centuries. The literature of this period reflects a turbulent time of radical change that saw the rise of modern European drama, the birth of the novel and personal essay forms, the emergence of newspapers and periodicals, and major achievements in poetry and philosophy. Many of these historical forces continue to influence modern art and society. *LC,* therefore, provides valuable insight into the art, life, thought, and cultural transformations that took place during these centuries.

Scope of the Series

LC provides an introduction to the great poets, dramatists, novelists, essayists, and philosophers of the fifteenth through eighteenth centuries, and to the most significant interpretations of these authors' works. Because criticism of this literature spans nearly six hundred years, an overwhelming amount of scholarship confronts the student. *LC* organizes this material into volumes addressing specific historical and cultural topics, for example, "Literature of the Spanish Golden Age," or "Literature and the New World." Every attempt is made to reprint the most noteworthy, relevant, and educationally valuable essays available.

Readers should note that there is a separate Gale reference series devoted exclusively to Shakespearean studies. Although belonging properly to the period covered in *LC,* William Shakespeare has inspired such a tremendous and ever-growing corpus of secondary material that the editors have deemed it best to give his works extensive coverage in a separate series, *Shakespearean Criticism.*

Each author entry in *LC* presents a survey of critical response to a topic or an author's oeuvre. Early criticism is offered to indicate initial responses, later selections document any rise or decline in literary reputations, and retrospective analyses provide students with modern views. The size of each author entry is a relative reflection of the scope of criticism available in English. Every attempt has been made to identify and include the seminal essays on each author's work and to include recent commentary providing modern perspectives.

The need for *LC* among students and teachers of literature and history was suggested by the proven usefulness of Gale's *Contemporary Literary Criticism (CLC), Twentieth-Century Literary Criticism (TCLC),* and *Nineteenth-Century Literature Criticism (NCLC),* which excerpt criticism of works by nineteenth- and twentieth-century authors. There is no duplication of critical material in any of these literary criticism series. Major authors may appear more than once in one or more of the series because of the great quantity of critical material available and because of their relevance to a variety of thematic topics.

Thematic Approach

Beginning with Volume 12, the authors in each volume of *LC* are organized around such themes as specific literary or philosophical movements, writings surrounding important political and historical events, the philosophy and art associated with eras of cultural transformation, and the literature of specific social or ethnic groups. Each volume contains a topic entry providing a historical and literary overview, and several author entries which examine major representatives of the featured period.

Organization of the Book

Each entry consists of the following elements: author or thematic heading, introduction, list of principal works, annotated works of criticism (each preceded by a bibliographical citation), and a bibliography of further reading. Also, most author entries contain author portraits and other illustrations.

- The **Author Heading** consists of the author's name (the most commonly used form), followed by birth and death dates. (If an author wrote consistently under a pseudonym, the pseudonym is used in the author heading, with the real name given in parentheses on the first line of the biographical and critical introduction.) Also located here are any name variations under which an author wrote, including transliterated forms for authors whose native languages use nonroman alphabets. Uncertain birth or death dates are indicated by question marks. Topic entries are preceded by a **Thematic Heading,** which simply states the subject of the entry.

- The **Biographical and Critical Introduction** contains background information that concisely introduces the reader to the author or topic.

- Most *LC* author entries include **Portraits** of the author. Many entries also contain illustrations of materials pertinent to an author's career, including author holographs, title pages, letters, or representations of important people, places, and events in an author's life.

- The **List of Principal Works** is ordered chronologically, by date of first book publication, identifying the genre of each work. In the case of foreign authors whose works have been translated into English, the title and date (if available) of the first English-language edition are given in brackets following the foreign-language listing. Unless otherwise indicated, dramas are dated by first performance, not first publication.

- **Criticism** is arranged chronologically in each author entry to provide a useful perspective on changes in critical evaluation over time. For the purpose of easy identification, the critic's name and the date of first composition or publication of the critical work are given at the beginning of each piece of criticism. Unsigned criticism is preceded by the title of the source in which it appeared. All titles by the author featured in the critical entry are printed in boldface type. Publication information (such as publisher names and book prices) and some parenthetical numerical references (such as footnotes or page and line references to specific editions of works) have been occasionally deleted to provide smoother reading of the text. Footnotes that appear with previously published pieces of criticism are reprinted at the end of each essay or excerpt. In the case of excerpted criticism, only those footnotes that pertain to the excerpted text are included.

- Critical essays are prefaced by **Annotations** as an additional aid to students using *LC*. These explanatory notes provide information such as the importance of a work of criticism, the commentator's individual approach to literary criticism, and a brief summary of the reprinted essay. In some cases, these notes cross-reference the work of critics within the entry who agree or disagree with each other.

- A complete **Bibliographical Citation** of the original essay or book precedes each piece of criticism.

- An annotated bibliography of **Further Reading** appears at the end of each entry and suggests resources for additional study. In some cases, significant essays for which the editors could not obtain reprint rights are included here.

Cumulative Indexes

Each volume of *LC* includes a cumulative **Author Index** listing all the authors that have appeared in the following sources published by Gale: *Contemporary Literary Criticism, Twentieth-Century Literary Criticism, Nineteenth-Century Literature Criticism, Literature Criticism from 1400 to 1800, and Classical and Medieval Literature Criticism,* along with cross-references to the Gale series *Short Story Criticism, Poetry Criticism, Children's Literature Review, Authors in the News, Contemporary Authors, Contemporary Authors Autobiography Series, Contemporary Authors Bibliographical Series, Dictionary of Literary Biography, Concise Dictionary of Literary Biography, Something about the Author, Something about the Author Autobiography Series, and Yesterday's Authors of Books for Children.* Readers will welcome this cumulative author index as a useful tool for locating an author within the various series. The index, which includes authors' birth and death dates, is particularly valuable for those authors who are identified with a certain period but whose death dates cause them to be placed in another, or for those authors whose careers span two periods. For example, F. Scott Fitzgerald is found in *TCLC,* yet a writer often associated with him, Ernest Hemingway, is found in *CLC.*

Beginning with Volume 12, *LC* includes a cumulative **Topic Index** that lists all literary themes and topics treated in *LC, NCLC, TCLC,* and the *CLC* Yearbook. Each volume of *LC* also includes a cumulative **Nationality Index** in which authors' names are arranged alphabetically under their respective nationalities and followed by the numbers of the volumes in which they appear.

Each volume of *LC* also includes a cumulative **Title Index,** an alphabetical listing of all literary works discussed in the series. Each title listing includes the corresponding volume and page numbers where criticism may be located. Foreign-language titles that have been translated followed by the tiles of the translation—for example, *El ingenioso hidalgo Don Quixote de la Mancha (Don Quixote).* Page numbers following these translated titles refer to all pages on which any form of the titles, either foreign-language or translated, appear. Titles of novels, dramas, nonfiction books, and poetry, short story, or essay collections are printed in italics, while individual poems, short stories, and essays are printed in roman type within quotation marks.

A Note to the Reader

When writing papers, students who quote directly from any volume in the Literary Criticism Series may use the following general format to footnote reprinted criticism. The first example pertains to material drawn from periodicals, the second to material reprinted from books.

> T. S. Eliot, ᴧJohn Donne,@ *The Nation and the Athenaeum,* 33 (9 June 1923), 321-32; excerpted and reprinted in *Literature Criticism from 1400 to 1800,* Vol. 10, ed. James E. Person, Jr. (Detroit: Gale Research, 1989), pp. 28-9.

> Clara G. Stillman, *Samuel Butler: A Mid-Victorian Modern* (Viking Press, 1932); excerpted and reprinted in *Twentieth-Century Literary Criticism,* Vol. 33, ed. Paula Kepos (Detroit: Gale Research, 1989), pp. 43-5.

Suggestions Are Welcome

Since the series began, features have been added to *LC* in response to various suggestions, including a nationality index, a Literary Criticism Series topic index, and thematic organization of entries.

Readers who wish to suggest new features, themes or authors to appear in future volumes, or who have other suggestions or comments are cordially invited to write to the editor (fax: 313 961-6599).

Acknowledgments

The editors wish to thank the copyright holders of the excerpted criticism included in this volume and the permissions managers of many book and magazine publishing companies for assisting us in securing reproduction rights. We are also grateful to the staffs of the Detroit Public Library, the Library of Congress, the University of Detroit Mercy Library, Wayne State University Purdy/Kresge Library Complex, and the University of Michigan Libraries for making their resources available to us. Following is a list of the copyright holders who have granted us permission to reproduce material in this volume of. Every effort has been made to trace copyright, but if omissions have been made, please let us know.

PHOTOGRAPHS AND ILLUSTRATIONS APPEARING IN *LC,* VOLUME 40, WERE RECEIVED FROM THE FOLLOWING SOURCES:

Preromanticism

INTRODUCTION

Preromanticism refers to the period in European literature that occurred between the Augustan age and the era of Romanticism, covering the years from approximately the middle of the eighteenth century to the early 1790s. In this period rigid notions about style and the absolute authority of religion and science began to yield to an emphasis on personal thoughts and feelings, often triggered by observation of nature. The search for meaning led within, to the probing of the mind and a focus on the inner self, and to an individual, personal interpretation of the world.

While controversy has abounded in many aspects of discussion of Preromanticism, there are some areas of general agreement, including subject matter. The scholar Bertrand H. Bronson has offered a list of favorite topics of the Preromantics: "Country Pleasures, Times of the Day, Seasons of the Year; Abstractions—Fancy, Solitude, Sleep, Death—inviting description, evoking feeling, tempting the moral comment." Bronson also quotes Josephine Miles's example of an ideal poetic sentence for the time, a construction she based on statistical count and analysis of the works of the Preromantic poets: "Rise, fair day, before the eyes and soul of man." Bronson points out the use of the invocatory form of the verb and "the tendency to apostrophize and implore" as characteristic of the period.

The Preromantics also highly stressed the idea of originality in writing. Many poets of this period felt restricted by the precedents established by classic works of the past and the prevalent attitude that the greatest literature had already been written. Walter Jackson Bate has argued that it was because of having to face the question "What is there left to write?" that the Preromantics so emphasized the ideals of originality and sincerity. No one championed these ideals more than Edward Young, who extolled subjectivity in his *Conjectures on Original Composition* (1759), urging that poets look within for originality and not attempt to copy the ancients. Nature served an important role in realizing these goals; for example, in James Thomson's nature poetry, the poet experiences the world primarily through his senses and eventually comes to realize his part in it. According to Margaret Sherwood, Thomson's work represents "a new self-consciousness in regard to nature. . . . Here is beauty, no longer an abstract conception of fitness of organism to its use, but a joy, brought home through the senses, which stir feeling and mild reflection." Some scholars have gone so far as to state that the concept of the self was "invented" shortly after the middle of the eighteenth century, and that before that people thought of themselves mainly according to their set roles in society rather than as individuals. According to John O. Lyons, this self "first was treated as the whole organic complex of the perceiving being in sympathetic relation to the world around it. Such a concept of the self was expressed in the concern with the passions, the minute perception of human motive, and the reality of nature, for it assumed the efficacy of inductive science."

Yet the emphasis on self did not create self-centeredness to the detriment of others. To the contrary, the Preromantics believed that the person who sought self-knowledge would became more sympathetic to the suffering of others. Feelings were emphasized to such an extent that man began to relate to nature and animals on a different level than in previous times, to actually feel akin to them and sympathize with them. In the immensely popular "novels of sensibility" there was great emphasis on sentiment and sympathy, with plot being little more than a means of setting up a context for these feelings. Howard Mumford Jones has described the standard themes in novels of sensibility as "undeserved poverty, divine benevolence, or virtue in distress." He has enumerated some of the plot devices of this genre as "the orphan of mysterious but noble parentage, attempts at seduction or rape, imprisonment in jail or convent," forced exile, and many others, often shared with Gothic horror novels. Interest in the uniqueness of individuals also extended into respect for folk culture, and an area that gained great attention was the collection and preservation of folk songs. Robert Burns, for example, devoted much of his later life to transcribing and editing old Scottish airs. The Preromantic period also saw an unprecedented demand for histories and biographies; personal details that would previously have been thought outside the proper scope of literature were now deemed acceptable.

The use of the term Preromanticism has been adamantly debated by scholars. Some prefer to call the period the age of sensibility, others the post-Augustan era, while others deny that it should be considered a separate period at all, viewing it as simply occurring late in the Augustan era. Bronson and other critics have pointed out the problems in defining the terms Augustan and Romantic, and therefore the difficulties in attempting to define either "post-Augustan" or "Preromantic." Even though Augustan and Romantic are theoretically opposites, in practice, "post-Augustan" and "Preromantic" are often used interchangeably. In arguing against the term Preromantic, Northrop Frye has written: "Not only did the 'pre-romantics' not know that the Romantic movement was going to succeed them, but there has probably never been a case on record of a poet's having regarded a later poet's work as the fulfillment of his own." Many scholars have pointed out, however, that the terms Romantic and Romanticism were not used by the writers in question themselves, but are of later origin, and the same is true of the term Preromanticism. A lively debate continues regarding Preromanticism, as does critical interest in the writers and works associated with the period.

OVERVIEWS

Margaret Sherwood (essay date 1934)

SOURCE: "Some Phases of Development of Thought in the World of Letters in the Eighteenth Century," in *Undercurrents of Influence in English Romantic Poetry*, AMS Press, 1971, pp. 28-113.

[*In the following excerpt from a work originally published in 1934, Sherwood describes how eighteenth-century authors reacted against prevailing religious and scientific notions through a new emphasis on subjectivism.*]

The great flowering of poetry in the so-called romantic period of the late eighteenth and the early nineteenth centuries in England was not a sudden portent; growth was swift, but not sudden. More and more the student turns back to the eighteenth century to study origins, trace influences, search out undercurrents of thought, that he may better understand that rich, complex, modern product. Throughout a great part of this century groping for fuller life is revealed in the form and in the content of the poetry that is written; wandering in that world of letters of the mid-eighteenth century is like wandering in the forest when spring draws near, when one hears a faint murmur and rustle of life, everywhere an air of expectancy, of awaiting. As the century goes on there is increasingly a reaching out for fuller existence, a release of human nature from the bonds of convention, a slow liberation of emotion, imagination, and the deeper powers of the human mind. Such conditions prevail only when great ideas are stirring beneath the surface, waiting to emerge.

Today our thought and our imaginative insight are dominated by evolutionary conceptions; our tendency is to interpret all aspects of man's life in terms of growth and development; to think of the past as indis-

solubly bound up with the present; we are constantly questioning, in every department of thinking, how things came to be. Our literature, our scholarship, our philosophy, our psychology reflect these habits of mind. It is of singular interest to turn back to a period when these ideas did not prevail, to try to trace, in the minds of a few thinkers, incipient stages of these tendencies, to follow the deepening life of the thought of man as his very vocabulary changes from abstract rationalistic terms to terms of growth; fascinating to question whether the tendency which developed into the historical method in the humanities, into the evolutionary conception in science, may not have manifested itself in minor forms, in subtler ways; to question literature here and there to see in how far it reveals the slow changing of the very texture of man's thought, as a consciousness of process, of life opening out endlessly, replaces the desire for abstract finalities of judgment. Back of all the varied apprehensions of growth, of life in things, lies the ground idea of our modern thought, of the oneness of the universe, which finds its spiritual counterpart in the idea of the close interrelatedness of all human lives, society as one; as the idea of physical development, evolution, finds its counterpart in the idea of spiritual evolution. In searching for glimmerings of these ideas in the period to which we turn, no claim is made that the writers in question were the first to suggest them. This is a dangerous assertion to make in regard to any idea, and especially in regard to evolutionary ideas, which go back to the very dawn of man's thought, in Greece.

In the early eighteenth century certain reactionary tendencies begin to appear against the prevailing modes of thought of the preceding century. We of the complex present have difficulty in finding our way back into the simplicity and objectivity of seventeenth century thought, in its dominant trend. One knew where one was in that period; law was law, and conformity was expected of the right-minded citizen. The dogmas of church and of state had the authority of long tradition; science was establishing its creed of unquestionable law throughout the physical universe; kings were upon their thrones, the critics upon theirs, and absolute power in carrying out decrees was as evident in the world of literature as in the political world. It was not, outwardly, a world of perplexity, of mystery; all was clear and above-board. Whatever your private reserves, your duty was not to thread your way through intricate mazes of speculation in regard to the ultimate realities, or in regard to matters of right and wrong. Reason was adequate to reach the truth of things; duty was conformity, at least of one's outer or official self, to an objective standard; one gave official consent to creeds established by law. Wandering back to that world of hard, definite mountain outlines and unshaded plains, we should feel as lost in it as did Sir Thomas Browne, with that questioning mind: "I love to lose myself in a mystery; to pursue my reason to an O Altitudo!" . . ."

Where there is an obscurity too deep for our reason, 'tis good to sit down with a description, periphrasis, or adumbration."

His distinctive figure, standing in the market-place at Norwich, with a look of whimsical thoughtfulness upon his face, might well symbolize that human instinct that will not down, that is forever alert in periods of dogmatic certainties as in others, searching beyond the found. He was not alone in that seventeenth century in pursuing thought to an *O Altitudo!* but he and his like were not the dominant voices. The seventeenth century had its mystics; the outcast philosopher Spinoza had achieved that which would compel future generations to think more deeply; the thought of Plato and of Plotinus was creeping in through the influential Cambridge group, to become more and more potent in the minds of certain thinkers in later days,—the subtlest and the most pervasive influence helping bring about the romantic movement in literature and in philosophy.

But the dominant note was the note of outer authority. Periods of over-assurance are weather breeders; too clear a sky is a sure token of mysteriously dispersed clouds that gather quickly, and over-confident assertion is the mother of doubt. The coming of new moods, new mental attitudes, new inquiries that meant, in time, the breaking of the certainties, was but natural sequence; submerged currents of thought and feeling began to emerge; men reached out to new ways of conceiving and interpreting life; questioning of every kind of authority went hand in hand with search for deeper truth than any formula, political, scientific, philosophic had yet found. The slow approach of revolution in every department of thought ended, toward the close of the eighteenth century in a period that was revolution indeed. Contemplation of that outer world of illimitable spaces and certain movements that had been gloriously revealed by seventeenth century science was not enough; men became increasingly conscious of realities that the laws of physics did not reach. Reason was supreme, but, in the skepticism of Hume, reason began to doubt itself, inquiring into the nature of the instrument by which these outer facts were known. The trend of speculative thought turned from without to within. In philosophy came a curiosity and desire to probe the nature of the mind, a movement that, toward the end of the century, in the philosophy of Kant, transferred the seat of authority from outer law to the human mind itself. The drift of interest in the world of letters was from objective to subjective; many were filled with longing to explore their own inner experience and that of others, to make conquest of the world within. From that standard of impersonality in the pseudo-classic canon of literature, that endeavor to present, in rendering human experience, only the typical, that which is true of all men, men passed to a belief in the profound significance of the personal reaction to life, the interpretation of the world as individually possessed; passed,

too, from a conception of a law of form, imposed from without, to a conception of individual shaping power, working, imaginatively, from within. In science itself came a movement that, toward the end of the century, brought, not abandonment of the idea of universal law, but discovery that man must dig more deeply into the hidden nature of things to find reality of law; and the static conceptions of the seventeenth century began to give way to a tentative conception of the dynamic, of law at work within the universe, in incessant activity and change, the beginning of the modern idea of evolution. Dogmatic theology trembled, as it trembles still, at the thought of God, changing from that of a power, sitting apart in a long seventh day of rest, to that of a power still mysteriously working within.

Yet seventeenth century philosophy, seventeenth century science alike had their own awe-inspiring sublimities, which stimulated the minds and imaginations of men in ways which we have only partially divined. The vast oneness of all that is was a dominant seventeenth century affirmation; in metaphysics as in science, philosopher and scientist were groping toward the infinite along different trails. Spinoza in his *Ethic* (1677), affirmed the one absolutely infinite substance, God, as the only existence; while the scientific discoveries, the Copernican-Galilean revelation of the vastness of the universe, and of the laws that govern it, stretched the mind of man toward the infinite of the world of matter. To Galileo's proved vision of a vast system, one in its working, in which earth was only an atom, no longer the center of the universe, was added knowledge more significant still. Men's thought was different after Newton discovered the law of gravitation and, in his *Principia* (1687), revealed the interdependence of all that is, body answering body by virtue of an inner bond, reaching from inmost center to inmost center, known in its working but not in its ultimate nature, every atom affecting every other atom. No more important idea was ever launched; it deeply influenced thought, and not scientific thought alone.

Swiftly on the trail of the scientists' "what" followed, as usual, the speculation and affirmation of those who must know "why." Contemplation of the working of the laws of the universe revealed to certain thinkers that the old conception of God, inherited from the Hebrew people, was not great enough for the God manifest in the laws ruling through infinite space. These laws had been clearly demonstrated; the Deists, holding their reason adequate to solve all problems, imagined that they could demonstrate as clearly the God who made the law. Working back to the creator from the created, they claimed that no further revelation of him was necessary than that made manifest in his works. Out of questions regarding the nature of the universe, ruled, in both scientific and in theological thought, by power from outside, developed fierce debate. There was consternation in theological circles over the newly-discovered truths of science; in England the Deist controversy made up an important part of the thought of the late seventeenth and the early eighteenth centuries, centering in the question of a God revealed through nature, versus a God revealed through Scripture; natural law versus supernatural happenings. Hard blows were given and received; and, as in "battles long ago," "much slaughter was of people on both parties"; "and either smote other in middes of their shields." "Then they stood together and gave many sad strokes on divers places of their bodies, and the blood brast out on many sides and places." The theologians were rather the victors, but, as is usual in the irony of life, their victory was loss; in grasping the weapons of their opponents, in over-rationalizing the religion they were defending, they went far toward deadening the very springs of faith in the Church they served. Out of the perplexity and turmoil of these troubled times emerged thought and feeling which were to have vast consequences in the literature of a later period. . . .

Bertrand H. Bronson (lecture date 1971)

SOURCE: "The Retreat from Reason," in *Studies in Eighteenth-Century Culture,* edited by Harold E. Pagliaro, The Press of Case Western Reserve University, 1972, pp. 225-38.

[*In the following essay, originally delivered as a lecture in 1971, Bronson examines the eighteenth-century attack on reason as it led up to Preromanticism.*]

Lest I stumble, and because the time is short, I will state at once the propositions I would try to illustrate in what follows. As generalities, they are unlikely to excite disagreement, and the interest must lie in the fluctuations of thought and feeling that differentiate those generations, chronologically viewed.

1. At the opening of the eighteenth century there is a weakening of conviction of the importance of man's personal relation to God the Father.

2. There is a depersonalizing of external nature, from the cooperative universal Mother to universal, unalterable physical laws.

3. There is a shrinkage of assurance of the potency of man's rational powers, no longer seen as "infinite in faculty," yet a keener sense of reliance on them.

As the century passes its meridian, values are gradually rescaled and redefined, roughly as follows:

4. Nature in a "state of nature" is preferred to nature domesticated.

5. Irregularity enforces a lawless appeal that surpasses rational ordering.

6. Sudden irrational conversion and conviction of salvation by faith returns to religion.

7. Emotional assurance tends to supplant the appeal to reason as expressed in logical trains of thought.

It may be laid down as an axiom, as Dr. Johnson would say, that everything had already begun before we realized. In the context of the moment, this truth if pursued would take me back straightway into the seventeenth century, where I have no wish to go, further than to acknowledge that the beginnings are there, Pyrrhonism and all.

About 1700 there was an unusually pervasive sense of the opening of a century as a true beginning: almost the birth of a "brave new world." The shadows and superstitions of the past were being dispersed by Newton's universal light, swept away like ghosts:

> 'Tis well an Old Age is out,
> And time to begin a New.[1]

As Newton had disclosed the laws of celestial mechanics, Locke had found a key to the inner world, which could open the mechanics of the mind—or a clue, a method, if not a key. The new revelations, fortunately, did not require the sacrifice of cherished beliefs. Locke and Newton were devout. God was still Creator and Lord of all, and the natural universe bore witness to His power and glory: "The works of Nature everywhere sufficiently evidence a Deity," declared Locke. "The spangled heavens proclaim their great Original," sang Addison. But now the old ideal system of orders, each hierarchically ascending, and bound together in mutual cooperative obedience to divine command, needed reformulation in less spiritual terms—the political order in Britain having already been reconstituted by the simple stroke of an ax. The new world-view still assumed a Divine Author, but shifted the focus of attention, in Tuveson's phrase, from *why* to *how* He did it.

The prevailing optimism of the age rested in the conviction that the physical universe was based on natural laws which could be discovered—gradually—by man, and understood as being fixed, regular, unalterable procedures; not beyond the capacity of human mentality to grasp as principles, though too vast to be comprehended as a whole, and too complicated to be known except piecemeal; but not supernatural, not outside or alien to intellectual process as we know it. Underlying this confidence is faith—faith in the Creator, faith in the stability of Nature, and faith in rationality as humanly conceived. The supreme expression of this confidence is paragraph IX of the first Epistle of Pope's *Essay on Man,* beginning:

> All are but parts of one stupendous whole,
> Whose body Nature is, and God the soul.

Because of its very lack of philosophical originality, Pope's statement is a paradigm of its century's characteristic attitude toward the Cosmos; it was so widely accepted as to be translated into twenty languages, and into some of them many times. Catholics, Protestants, and deists could join in adopting it, punctuating or footnoting to suit themselves.

But when God said, "Let Newton be!" a part of His meaning perhaps was, "If undisturbed, he will look after things so competently that I can afford to relax." If, in other words, the physical universe was so perfectly organized as Newton had made manifest, it needed no divine tinkering to keep it going—had needed, did, and would need none. This thought, of course, had far-reaching implications that could be chilling. How could man know that he was an object of any concern or interest to a God so impalpable and aloof? It was easy to believe in a divine original, a *causa causans;* but revelation might be *essential* to convince us any longer of our own importance. On the other hand, the deist position was a great simplifier, liberating those who embraced it from a load of worrying theological dogma. The climate of optimism, an inherited feeling-tone common to the age, and not directly subverted by the new world-view, remained emotionally operative.

If there was a slackening in man's communion with a personal God as the Age of Enlightenment began, two concomitants—and perhaps, partly, consequences—were: (1) the elevation of Nature as a surrogate for a present, immanent Deity; and (2) a closer scrutiny of the thinking process. Descartes had failed to break out of the octopus-like stranglehold of seventeenth-century Pyrrhonism to any objective truth ("I thought, then perhaps I was," in Pierre-Daniel Huet's wicked paraphrase of 1689). But Locke had begun to collect the evidence of what seems normally to be going on in our minds, and this appeared to be a hopeful method and a stimulating exercise. Perhaps God had, after all, provided us with the necessary tools for acquiring knowledge suited to existence on this "isthmus of a middle state."

Following the hopeful track, Shaftesbury, Locke's too-bright pupil, discovered that man is naturally virtuous, sociable, beauty-loving. And why not? For proof, one need only consult one's uncorrupted responses to the positives and negatives of experience, and find where one's instinctive preferences lie. For Shaftesbury, to cultivate and possess the social affections completely is, in his words, "to live according to Nature, and the Dictates and Rules of supreme Wisdom. This is Morality, Justice, Piety, and natural Religion." It is only necessary, for everyone's good, to restrain the "self-affections." Shaftesbury, Basil Willey declares, is the *typical* English moralist of the "Enlightenment"; and Hume notices that he first occasions the distinction

between two theories of morals, "that which derives them from Reason, and that which derives them from 'an immediate feeling and finer internal sense.'"

Already, then, in the century's first decade, the breeze is setting toward "immediate, undefinable perception" as a more dependable criterion than reason, in moral discriminations as in questions of art. This tendency picks up strength from the academic authority and respectability of Hutcheson, who systematized Shaftesbury's elegant rhapsodizing. Sorley has neatly summarized his work in a sentence: "Hutcheson maintained the disinterestedness of benevolence; he assimilated moral and aesthetic judgments; he elaborated the doctrine of the moral sense . . . ; and he identified virtue with universal benevolence: in the tendency towards general happiness he found the standard of goodness."[2]

To make the emotions a basis of ethics is something like inverting Pope's dictum to read, "Passion the card, while Reason trims the sail." To accept it, one must have faith in natural instincts, must believe in the morality of Nature, and that human nature, as servant of that divinity, is most moral when likest to her. Shaftesbury's impassioned invocation exemplifies the faith: "O Glorious *Nature*! supremely Fair, and soveraignly Good! All-loving, and All-lovely, All-divine! . . . O mighty Nature! Wise Substitute of *Providence*! impower'd *Creatress*! . . . Thee I invoke, and Thee alone adore."[3] The date of this outburst is 1709. It could be part of the youthful Goethe's pantheistic hymn "Ganymed" ("Wie im Morgenglanze Du rings mich anglühst, Frühling, Geliebter!"), the pitch of exaltation is so close. How wholeheartedly Thomson would have endorsed this natural morality I must leave to Professor Cohen to determine. *The Seasons* is descriptive rather than prescriptive; but in general, Nature and God are not indistinguishable in Thomson, however harmonious; and I suspect that he would not have subscribed to the ethics of cultural primitivism. Nevertheless, the doctrine of the moral sense, as taught by Shaftesbury and Hutcheson, was potent, both at home and abroad. It suited an age of sensibility, and increasingly as the century wore on. Anyone who has leafed through the amazing compilation of Margaret Fitzgerald, *First Follow Nature,* and the equally surprising survey by Lois Whitney of primitivistic popular fiction must realize how inescapable the sympathetic theme of rural felicity soon became.[4]

In contrast, Johnson placed the Golden Age firmly in pre-lapsarian days. His suspicions of hypothetical subsequent golden ages in conditions of pastoral life were confirmed by sociological enquiry in the Highlands and Western Islands, of which he gave a remarkably fair-minded and dispassionate report. Apart from human hardships and deprivations, his reaction to wild Nature deserves to be recalled in this connection:

Regions mountainous and wild, thinly inhabited, and little cultivated, make a great part of the earth, and he that has never seen them, must live unacquainted with much of the face of nature, and with one of the great scenes of human existence . . . ; the imaginations excited by the view of unknown and untravelled wilderness are not such as arise in the artificial solitude of parks and gardens, a flattering notion of self-sufficiency, a placid indulgence of voluntary delusions, a secure expansion of the fancy, or a cool concentration of the mental powers. The phantoms which haunt a desert are want, and misery, and danger; the evils of dereliction rush upon the thoughts; man is made unwillingly acquainted with his own weakness, and meditation shews him only how little he can sustain, and how little he can perform.[5]

Very different was the purely aesthetic response of Gray to untouched natural grandeur. Extremely different were the sentiments and operations on Nature of the landscape gardeners of the age, whether Pope, or Shenstone, or Jago, or Capability Brown, or Repton. Pope had said,

> But treat the Goddess like a modest fair,
> Nor over-dress, nor leave her wholly bare;
> Let not each beauty ev'ry where be spy'd,
> Where half the skill is decently to hide.[6]

In fact, for such as these nature was something of a commodity to be altered at will and exploited to suit man's immediate taste and enjoyment. The point of view was not, any more than Johnson's, indicative of union with Nature. Rather, it was basically utilitarian, and exclusive of objectionable society. Only that part of external Nature was required that could serve as the club-house grounds. There were members privileged to use the grounds for health and pleasure, and others who worked on them for a livelihood, furthering thereby the aesthetic enjoyment of the members.

It is clear that the aesthetic tastes of the members were changing rapidly as the century proceeded. There was a growing appetite for more challenging, more esoteric, excitements than domesticated nature could supply. A clear preference was developing for the irregular—even the disorderly and wild.

A. R. Humphreys makes a startling generalization in his admirable little book on Shenstone: "The attack on geometry is perhaps the most significant fact of eighteenth-century aesthetics."[7] Certainly, the statement could be amply illustrated in the arts of gardening, architecture, and interior decoration. As the decades pass, we can observe everywhere a relinquishing of mathematical rule, exact equations, right lines; and everywhere a liberation of fancy. There is nothing serpentine—or even symmetrical—about a subterranean grotto: "Would not this, Dr. Johnson, make a pretty, cool place in summer?" "Madam, I think it would—for a toad." Crudely put, the movement is from reason to imagination, from rational to whimsical. Simultaneously, the temperature gradually rises, the pitch of excitement increases—more often to hot tears than to laughter.

The signs of a will to escape from common daylight are everywhere. Into the Past, through Gothicizing (Strawberry Hill, Abbotsford, Fonthill Abbey) and bogus ruins in landscaping (Sanderson Miller, Shenstone's ruined Priory). "It is not every one that can build a ruin," declares Gilpin, "to suggest Time—Decay—Evanescence of Joy."

> LORD OGLEBY: Your Ruins, did you say, Mr. Sterling?
>
> STERLING: Ay, ruins, my Lord! and they are reckoned very fine ones too. You would think them ready to tumble on your head. It has just cost me a hundred and fifty pounds to put my ruins in thorough repair.[8]

Into the Distant and Strange: the craze of the 'fifties for Chinoiseries (designs for Chinese buildings; Oriental gardening; Chinese bridges, pagodas, furniture—Garrick's Chinese bed—tableware [china!], wall-paper). To the pursuit of the Primitive, of the South Seas and Savannahs—a contemporary human Past. The increasing delight in irrational forms, in nature, from the Sublime of "mountain gloom and glory" to the less ecstatic Picturesque ("artful wildness to perplex the scene"); in art, the cult of the restless and wayward Rococo. Away with straight lines and right angles—Nature abhors them! Follow the involuted curves till the eye is mazed and the mind takes flight.

Midway in the century came Hume. And, intellectually speaking, Hume is the watershed. Up to him, as Basil Willey has noted, it is possible to hold that Reason and Nature go hand in hand. Although, as Douglas White in his recent book *Pope and the Contest of Controversy*[9] takes pains to emphasize, the emotions, or Passions, in Pope's view of human nature, play a dominant, motivating role; yet Reason, in its function of comparing and judging alternative values and purposes, still serves as a brake on headlong, thoughtless impulse:

> Self-love, the spring of motion, acts the soul;
> Reason's comparing balance rules the whole.
> Man, but for that, no action could attend,
> And, but for this, were active to no end.[10]

Reason's business is "to check, delib'rate, and advise." Its restraint is essential. But now comes Hume to prove that it is utterly impossible to get outside our own perceptions to an objective reality, even so far as to verify in a single instance the relation of cause and effect. "Our reason," he says, "neither does, nor is it possible it ever shou'd, upon any supposition, give us an assurance of the continu'd and distinct existence of body. That opinion must be entirely owing to the imagination." "By the very completeness of his destructive efficacy," as Basil Willey remarks, Hume " ... showed that man cannot live by Reason alone."[11] And if we are driven to admit the utter inadequacy of reason to cope with the most elementary phenomena of human existence, we must choose one of two alternatives: either to give up our trust in it, or to pretend that the truth is false, and go on believing in the fiction. But if any considerable number of people were actually convinced "that our perceptions are not possest of any independent existence," it is obvious that our confidence in rationality would be irreparably weakened, and that we should at the very least be thrown back upon a greater reliance upon our natural feelings and common-sense conclusions. This at any rate did occur. Although Hume's absolute philosophical skepticism is unacceptable to the normal mind, it cannot but shake our confidence that we are standing on terra firma. And I, moreover, am ready to suppose that there is some obscure connection between the simultaneous emergence of the extreme Pyrrhonism of Hume's treatise, and the revival of religious faith manifest in the tidal wave of the Wesleys' and Whitefield's Methodism. Driven to a complete dead-end, we turn back to escape. As Hume himself writes, "Nature is obstinate, and will not quit the field, however strongly attack'd by reason." If not brute instinct, we must trust the extra-rational, "believing where we cannot prove," and dismissing, like Rochester a century earlier,

Reason, an *ignis fatuus* in the mind,
Which, leaving light of nature, sense, behind,

leads its misguided follower on a grotesque pursuit of the dancing vapor,

Till, spent, it leaves him to eternal night.[12]

Intellectual convictions probably played a relatively small part in directing the current of thought and feeling. If we look at the poetry and fiction of the century, we can observe the same tendencies as were noticed in the physical arts: a freer and usually more irresponsible play of fancy, though not yet full-fledged Romantic Imagination; a growing refusal to be regulated by precedent; a desire to range; and a taste for higher seasoning. Instances spring to mind: fiction with an odd angle of vision—a lapdog, a guinea, a sofa; fantastical travel-books and imaginary voyages, St. Pierre's *Paul et Virginie,* Paltock's *Peter Wilkins;* Sterne's psychological capers on prostrate Locke; *The Man of Feeling; The Castle of Otranto; Vathek;* Gothic romances by the score. In the last-named, the supernatural element, an injection of irrational dread. Patricia Spacks has traced the far-reaching effects in eighteenth-century poetry of the powerful appeal of fear of the supernatural in her significant study *The Insistence of Horror*.[13] She brings out the fact that, whereas earlier in the century the treatment of the supernatural is habitually deprecatory, in the latter half it is made evident that our "secret terrours and apprehensions" of the unearthly cannot be dismissed as unimportant, they are so deeply rooted in the human psyche.

Other evidences of emotional involvement with the past and the distant are of course widespread in poetry of the age. The so-called Antiquarian Revival had important results for poetic practice and theory: Joseph Warton's manifesto that Invention and and Imagination are the chief sinews of a poet, repudiating Dryden and Pope; Thomas Warton's celebration of feudal society as the most poetically satisfying material: "We have parted," he declared, "with extravagancies that are above propriety, with incredibilities that are more acceptable than truth, and with fictions that are more valuable than reality."[14] After this, Percy's interest in the bards and in primitive and early popular poetry; melancholy Ossian; anachronistic Chatterton. Pursuit of the geographically distant was more successful in prose than in verse. But the same urge was behind it as underlay the interest in the past: the perspective of distance from the present-and-immediate excited and fed the imagination. Warton's *Oriental Eclogues,* Gray's interest in Welsh and Norse poetry and poetics, Collins' in Scottish superstition show how the distances, spatial and temporal, interact.

All these manifestations were more or less timid ventures into the unknown, forays on the frontiers of the rational and familiar world. What to do with what some may think the main business of our announced subject, the out-and-out irrational (or the suprarational), I do not know. Smart, in *Jubilate Agno,* quite obviously has crossed boundaries into a country with strange laws, though not too far to be visited by familiar beings. But the light slants from a surprising angle on everything. Take a cat or a mouse as instances. They do not resemble Chaucer's cat and mouse, which obey the habits of their kind, the cat in occupying the most comfortable seat or in chasing the mouse, the mouse in running away. Smart's Jeoffrey the cat is by now too well known to need more than naming; but his mouse also deserves consideration, because his timidity has probably never before been seen in quite so favorable a light: "For," says Smart, "the mouse is a creature of great personal valor." Suddenly we find ourselves in Brobdingnag with Gulliver. . . . As the monkey replied to the elephant, "I can't help it if I's puny: I been sick."

William Blake is a still more dangerous case, more frightening to me because he seems to be on his way to Olympus, if not already arrived, and I cannot follow him in that rarefied atmosphere. We know, I think, that when he set out on his earthly pilgrimage, his feet were in firm contact with his place and time. We know what books he read and whom he talked to. So that we have good reason to regard him as a phenomenon of his age. But I will not undertake to explain him, nor to situate him within the context we have been considering.

> Non ragioniam dell'uom, ma guarda e passa!

At my commencement, the last proposition was: "Emotional conviction tends to supplant the appeal to Reason as expressed in logical trains of thought." But that Blake speaks with a private "symbolic logic," I do most powerfully and potently believe—on hearsay.

As for Cowper, who might have completed the triumvirate of the transcendentally enlightened, he was—I cannot think unfortunately—not often seized, in his fits of manic depression, with a *cacoethes scribendi*. He summed up his despair in words of blinding *clarity*:

> No voice divine the storm allay'd,
>   No light propitious shone;
> When, snatch'd from all effectual aid,
>   We perish'd, each alone:
> But I, beneath a rougher sea,
> And whelm'd in deeper gulphs than he.[15]

In the end, I suspect, we are driven to rest uneasily in a conviction of the irrationality of the totally rational. And with this point of view we shall find Johnson in staunch agreement. His dislike of scholastic reasoning was inveterate, as we see in his treatment of Harris ("a prig, and a bad prig"), or system-builders like Berkeley ("I refute him thus"), or dogmatists like Monboddo, or brandishers of the "terrific" or "bugbear" style like Petvin ("when speculation has done its worst, two and two still make four"). "Perhaps," as Imlac once remarked, "if we speak with rigorous exactness, no human mind is in its right state. There is no man whose imagination does not sometimes predominate over his reason, who can regulate his attention wholly by his will, and whose ideas will come and go at his command."[16] Although Johnson was impatient with nature-as-guide-ers, with those he called "feelers," and with ultra-sensibilitarians, he never forgot how small a part reason, or rationality, played in the conduct of mundane daily living, or how little likely even the wisest planning was to be justified in the sequel. Man, he insisted, is not endowed with either the faculties or the knowledge to make the wisest choices, being uncertain of the future.

In May of 1778, Boswell had a conversation with Lord March-mont, some of which he set down:

> I know not how it came in that somebody did not act by reason. "Who does?" said Lord Marchmont. "Do you know the man who does? No man but one

in Bedlam." Said I, "By what principle then *do* we act?" Said my Lord, "Why, by a variety of motives: by habits, by passion, by a liability to impressions." He said a brahmin said of human life, "The Creator meant to have a comedy." "But," said Lord Marchmont, . . . "No audience would bear such a comedy." He said our finding that we do not act by reason should teach us to be humble, to remember what we are—poor worms."[17]

Boswell was puzzled; but in the main Johnson would have agreed. Twenty years earlier, he had set down a memorable conversation between Rasselas and his sister Nekayah:

> "I cannot," protested Rasselas, "forbear to flatter myself that prudence and benevolence will make marriage happy. . . . Whenever I shall seek a wife, it shall be my first question, whether she be willing to be led by reason?" "Thus it is, said Nekayah, that philosophers are deceived. There are a thousand familiar disputes which reason never can decide; questions that elude investigation, and make logick ridiculous; cases where something must be done, and where little can be said. Consider the state of mankind, and enquire how few can be supposed to act upon any occasions, whether small or great, with all the reasons of action present to their minds. Wretched would be the pair above all names of wretchedness, who should be doomed to adjust by reason every morning all the minute detail of a domestick day."[18]

Johnson's fundamental distrust of systematic rationality may shed at least a flickering light on his unquenchable hilarity over his friend Bennet Langton's making his will. Neither Boswell nor Chambers, who had executed it, could perceive any reason for for Johnson's immoderate laughter, which Boswell unforgettably describes. Johnson creates an elaborate imaginary picture of Langton's triumphal return to his country estate, bearing his trophy and displaying it as he proceeds, with the appropriate explanatory monologue to innkeepers by the way. He carried this play of fancy to such a pitch of Falstaffian exuberance that his host was impatient to be rid of him. Even then, says Boswell,

> Johnson could not stop his merriment, but continued it all the way till we got without the Temple-gate. He then burst into such a fit of laughter, that he appeared to be almost in a convulsion; and, in order to support himself, laid hold of one of the posts at the side of the foot pavement, and sent forth peals so loud, that in the silence of the night his voice seemed to resound from Temple-bar to Fleet-ditch.[19]

The scene has frightening overtones. Such cosmic mirth seems so far beyond the occasion that gave rise to it as to belong rather to a Ninth Symphony, to Olympus, to a volcanic eruption. But one jocular exclamation of

Johnson's to Chambers echoes in the mind: "I trust you have had more conscience than to make him say, 'being of sound understanding;' ha, ha, ha!" Is it the laughter of Democritus?

> To thee were solemn toys or empty shew:
> The robes of pleasure and the veils of woe
> All aid the farce, and all thy mirth maintain,
> Whose joys are causeless, or whose griefs are
>   vain.[20]

But who is to say whether tears or laughter is the more appropriate?

Notes

[1] John Dryden, *The Secular Masque,* lines 90-91.

[2] William Ritchie Sorley, *A History of English Philosophy* (New York and London, 1921), p. 161.

[3] "The Moralists," in *Characteristics of Men, Manners, Opinions, Times, etc.,* 2 vols., ed. J. M. Robertson (London, 1900), II, 98.

[4] Fitzgerald, New York, 1947; Whitney, *Primitivism and the Idea of Progress in English Popular Literature of the Eighteenth Century* (Baltimore, 1934).

[5] *A Journey to the Western Isles of Scotland,* ed. Mary Lascelles (New Haven and London, 1971), pp. 40-41.

[6] Pope, "Epistle to Burlington," lines 51-54.

[7] Humphreys, *William Shenstone: An Eighteenth-Century Portrait* (Cambridge, 1937), p. 48.

[8] George Colman the Elder and David Garrick, *The Clandestine Marriage,* II, i.

[9] White, Chicago, 1970.

[10] *An Essay on Man,* II, lines 59-62.

[11] *The Eighteenth Century Background* (London, 1940), p. 111.

[12] "A Satyr against Reason and Mankind," lines 12-13, 24.

[13] Spacks, Cambridge, Mass., 1962.

[14] *The History of English Poetry,* 3 vols. (London, 1774-81), II, 463.

[15] "The Cast-Away," lines 61-66.

[16] *Rasselas,* chap. 44.

[17] *Boswell in Extremes,* ed. C. McC. Weis and F. A. Pottle (New York, 1970), p. 335.

[18] *Rasselas,* chap. 29.

[19] Boswell, *Life of Johnson,* May 10, 1773.

[20] Johnson, "The Vanity of Human Wishes," lines 65-68.

Peckham describes the chief characteristics of a shift in the eighteenth-century frame of mind:

. . . [The] shift in European thought was a shift from conceiving the cosmos as a static mechanism to conceiving it as a dynamic organism: static—in that all the possibilities of reality were realized from the beginning of things or were implicit from the beginning, and that these possibilites were arranged in a complete series, a hierarchy from God down to nothingness—including the literary possibilites from epic to Horatian ode, or lyric; a mechanism—in that the universe is a perfectly running machine, a watch usually. (A machine is the most common metaphor of this metaphysic.) Almost as important as these concepts was that of uniformitarianism, implicit both in staticism and mechanism, whenever these two are separated, as frequently happens. That is, everything that change produces was to be conceived as a part to fit into the already perfectly running machine; for all things conformed to ideal patterns in the mind of God or in the non-material ground of phenomena. . . .

Now this mighty static metaphysic world, which had governed perilously the thoughts of men since the time of Plato, collapsed of its own internal inconsistencies in the late eighteenth century—or collapsed for some people. . . .

The new metaphor is not a machine; it is an organism. . . .

The universe is alive. It is not something made, a perfect machine; it grows. Therefore change becomes a positive value, not a negative value; change is not man's punishment, it is his opportunity. . . . [The] artist is original because he is the instrument whereby a genuine novelty, an emergent, is introduced into the world, not because he has come with the aid of genius a little closer to previously existent pattern, natural and divine. . . .

Morse Peckham, "Toward a Theory of Romanticism," PMLA, Vol. LXVI, no. 2, March, 1951.

Roland Mortier (essay date 1972)

SOURCE: "'Sensibility,' 'Neoclassicism,' or 'Preromanticism'?" in *Eighteenth- Century Studies: Presented to Arthur M. Wilson,* edited by Peter Gay, The University Press of New England, 1972, pp. 153-64.

[*In the following essay Mortier examines some key aspects of Preromanticism in France.*]

The ambiguities and the contradictions of the notion of *preromanticism* have been underlined time and again. If we were to accept this historical category, the so-called "Century, or Age of Enlightenment," would extend in France at the most over about forty years: starting in 1715 (with the death of Louis XIV), it would end, if we are to believe Paul Van Tieghem, in 1755.[1] Deprived of Dederot and Rousseau, of all its emotional, "sensitive," or affective content,[2] the age of Enlightenment fades in this way into a desiccated rationalism, which in its turn (in the minds of detractors) could be identified with Voltaire. In that case, Bayle and Laclos would be excluded from a period of which they were, each in his own way, illustrious examples.

One might, at least, limit these annexationist aims (of which romanticism itself, we must acknowledge, is quite innocent), and restrict the preromantic wave in France to the last third of the eighteenth century. Baculard d'Arnaud, Loaisel de Tréogate, Ramond de Carbonnières, Letourneur, Mercier, and Bernardin de Saint-Pierre are called to the witness stand and testify in its behalf. But would not this be giving short shrift to Chénier, Parny, Condorcet, Chamfort, Laclos, Volney, Beaumarchais, the abbé Delille, even to Sade, who are certainly their equals as far as literary quality and historical significance are concerned?

In such a debate, it is really too easy to pit name against name, challenger against challenger. Representativeness is too subjective a criterion to allow the establishment of sound periodization. All told, what most clearly invalidates the notion of "preromanticism," is that in the only period during which factual arguments could be put forward in its favor, the undeniable irruption of sensibility coincides with a vigorous rebirth of classicism. The so-called preromantic era is the very one which other historians, with just as much right, call the neoclassical age. Faced with this paradox, must we renounce all attempts at synthesis, consider all period divisions as utopian visions? That would be giving up a bit too quickly, and throwing out the baby with the bath.

The last third of the eighteenth century (and we could add to it the years of the Consulate and the Empire) doubtless constitutes an entity endowed with characteristic features. The ambiguity stems from the desire on either side to reduce these features to a single one, to go from the complex to the singular, and to trim the luxuriant growth into straight lines.

In the realm of the fine arts—from architecture to the decorative arts—this is obvious. The end of the eighteenth century is stamped in its essence with a concern for rigor, purity, bareness, simple and noble truth ("edle

Einfalt und stille Grösse," in Winckelmann's phrase). The easy grace, the fragile artifices of rococo, are denounced as so many expressions of decadence and perversion. It is not mere chance that the Revolution, in its harsh and pure phase, should choose to be Roman and to drape itself in Brutus's toga. David was to supplant Boucher and his adulterated charms. Houdon was to represent Voltaire and Diderot in the antique style. The latter proposed that Pigalle glorify Voltaire by sculpting him in the nude at the age of seventy-six. Bouchardon made a statue of Louis XV as a Roman emperor. The rococo style, with its languid curves, gave way to stark and grandiose creations. The desire for monumentality prevailed over the search for refinement and over the somewhat precious charm of the decoration of the *"petits appartements."* The gigantic projects of a Ledoux and a Boullée, almost cubist in their soberness, set their powerful stamp on the end of the century.

With the injustice of all reactions, criticism rejected the *"fêtes galantes,"* the boudoir scenes, Crébillon's and Voisenon's racy and adulterated sensuality, the false ingenuousness of Greuze's young maids *en bloc,* and it did so in the name of an aesthetics which called itself moral, civic, virile before openly asserting itself as republican. Antiquity was no longer offered as an example in the name of the sacrosanct doctrine of imitation or of a preeminence as evident as it was *a priori,* but because it proposed models of noble simplicity, of constant fidelity to nature and truth.

It would be wrong, however, to confine the end of the century as a whole to the severity of David's style or to the icy perfection of Canova's people. Spartan rigor is not a common denominator that can account satisfactorily for the manifold tendencies of a time that was rich and contradictory, like all creative periods in the history of man's genius.

The success of the word *preromantic,* made fashionable and founded in theory by Paul Van Tieghem,[3] has made us forget, or neglect, a fact that Louis Bertrand had stressed in his book which despite its age is still unique of its kind, *La fin du classicisme et le retour à l'antique dans la seconde moitié du XVIIIᵉ siècle et les premières années du XIXᵉ, en France* (Paris, 1897). Studying the literature of the Directoire and the Empire he noted with surprise: "The strangest thing is that these ultra-romantic lucubrations are contemporary with the most narrowly classical works," (p. 356) and he cited Nodier and Raynouard, Creuzé de Lesser and the abbé Delille.

We could obviously remove the contradiction by opposing these two currents as the end of one taste and the birth of another. According to this hypothesis two irreconcilable tendencies, then, coexisted for a few decades, one superimposed on the other. This would have resulted in a fuzzy, hybrid zone in which two styles and two periods crossed each other, an end point and a point of departure.

The trouble with such an interpretation, whose undeniable merit is that it is clear, simple, and didactic, is that it does not fit the facts. Chénier, Madame de Staël, Chateaubriand, just like Diderot in the preceding generation, did not feel an inner conflict between the penchant for emotion and the taste for rigor; they strove to reconcile them. The young Romantics laid claim to Chénier. In the realm of painting the group of the "bearded" or the "primitives" dressed in the Greek style, indulged in the mystique of hierophants, and called David a "Vanloo," or "rococo" (Bertrand, p. 316).

They worshipped "high taste," the "severe style," but this excludes neither emotion nor pathos. Chénier's Hellenism—had it been known around 1800—would no doubt have seemed slightly too alexandrine, and insufficiently "antique." But they also raved about "Erse" poetry, about Ossian, about the barbaric song of the Edda revealed by P.-H. Mallet, just as they rediscovered the Gothic style, or Shakespeare, and created from nothing the fascination of mountains or scientific fantasy.

Is all this as contradictory as some would have it? We would be going up a blind alley if we tried to reduce the complexity of the period to a matter of themes and motives. We will limit ourselves to two of them to be concrete and remain within the bounds of our subject; ruins on the one hand, tombs on the other.

The theme of ruins must not be identified *a priori* with a romantic or even preromantic sensibility (whatever historical extension one may wish to give its definition).[4] It appears after 1330, with Petrarch, in a humanistic perspective which is itself part of the vast aspiration toward the "restauratio" or "renovatio" of antique Rome. Ruins are a pretext for meditating on a past splendor whose remains, however dilapidated, fragmentary, degraded by time, are still an object of admiration and wonder. Melancholy is only a passing reaction that soon fades before the exaltation of Roman prestige and the dream of its complete restoration. This is the theme of "Roma quanta fuit, ipsa ruina docet," that was later amplified and enhanced by Du Bellay.

Not until Hubert Robert and his most eloquent expounder, the Diderot of the *Salons,* can we see a "poetry of the ruins" come into being, associated with twilight, solitude, meditation on the flight of time, and the precariousness of love.[5]

Far from pursuing that path, in 1791 Volney was to bring the theme of ruins back into the orbit of historical and philosophical reflection; he was nearer on this point to Montesquieu, Voltaire, or d'Holbach than to the exalted reveries of the *Salon* of 1767. The ghostly landscape of the forest of columns that antique Palmyra had become, led him to meditate on the causes of the fall of empires.

The literary motif of ruins, far from necessarily including nostalgia and lyricism, can adapt itself to the most diverse uses. It may, as for Diderot, be associated with intimate reveries, with an enthusiastic response to the sublime, with exaltation and the cry of the soul. In that case, in good logic, the preromantic élan should be dated about twenty-five years before the grave neoclassical meditation, and the schema too commonly adopted by literary histories should be reversed.[6]

Sepulchral inspiration also lends itself to different if not always contradictory variations.[7] On the English side, we note the recurrent appearance of the old Puritan theme of "Memento mori" and "Pulvis es, et in pulverem reverteris," so abundantly explored since the Middle Ages in didactic moralism and dances of death. Edward Young's *Night Thoughts* (1742-1745) are in the line of a constant that had generously supplied baroque art with ideas and images. As Louis Cazamian beautifully put it: "The spirit of Milton's *Penseroso,* and not that of the *Allegro,* sets the tone for landscape literature in the eighteenth century. . . . " (*Histoire de la littérature anglaise,* [Paris, 1925], p. 801). Young says nothing different from what religious orators and apologists repeat almost everywhere, but he says it with a contagious emotion which stirs tragic shudders. *Night Thoughts* nevertheless takes the form of an oratorical and discursive work, whose language is abstract and whose structure is wholly cerebral—in brief a very classical "machine" which does not substantially differ from Pope's poetry. Young is more an apologist than a poet, and only *a posteriori* did he appear as an ancestor—a very dubious one—of romantic sensibility. In France, in Italy, in Spain, in Germany, in the countries where religion was powerfully institutionalized and rationalized, this Puritan threnody on the vanity of happiness, the rewards of suffering and the quandary of unbelief, was felt as a rejuvenated and renewed form of the old Christian pessimism, somewhat neglected during the eighteenth century in favor of a desperately finalistic and reassuring theodicy.

Young's popularity corresponds to the transformation of religious sensibility which appears in parallel fashion in the *Profession de foi du Vicaire savoyard* (the only work of Rousseau's, we should note, that Voltaire always unreservedly admired). Should we, then, proclaim this as romanticism? We would be forgetting a bit too quickly that the eighteenth century, generally held to be irreligious, was also the source of modern religiosity which is subjective, lyrical, individualist, and very distant from the faith of a Bossuet, a Pascal, or a Malebranche.

It is much better, therefore, to abide by the chronological framework that we have set ourselves, which is that of the end of the century. Now, if "sepulchral" works abounded at that time,[8] they were hardly distinguished by their romantic character. Their most evident meaning tends to be either moral, or civic or national.[9] The most significant example is no doubt Ugo Foscolo's famous poem *Dei Sepolcri* (1807). That this same Foscolo is also the author of the *Ultime lettere di Jacopo Ortis* should have reminded us of the coexistence in the same mind of sentimental impulses oriented toward morose delectation, and an ardent patriotism exalted by the French Revolution. *Dei Sepolcri*, like Alessandro Verri's *Notti Romane* and Pindemonte's *Cimeteri*, is a moral amplification on national grandeur, the cult of the dead which, furthermore, merges with that of great men and with the passion for liberty.

Far from belonging to a "lugubrious" inspiration (Van Tieghem, 37), such poetry perpetuates the austere civic and moral inspiration that imbued, in another register, David's *Marat assassiné* (1793). For Foscolo, just as for David, "fia santo e lagrimato il sangue per la patria versato."

The use of the tomb in neoclassical architecture is one of the most revealing traits of its inspiration. Boullée's imagination is obsessed with cenotaphs. They combine the ideas both of grandeur and of perpetuity: conical or pyramidal, they tend towards an almost abstract bareness that is supposed to suggest their eternity as well as their kinship with the colossal creations of Assyria and Egypt.

The visionary architects of the neoclassical age were, in the final analysis, poets.[10] In 1784 Boullée conceived an extraordinary spherical cenotaph in honor of Newton, the hero of modern science who discovered the mathematical formula for the movement of the universe.[11] "Sublime spirit! Vast and profound genius! Divine being!" he exclaimed. "Oh Newton! if, by the breadth of your enlightenment and the sublimity of your genius, you determined the shape of the earth, I have conceived the project of enclosing you in your discovery. It is in a way enclosing you with yourself." Light and shadow effects were to give this sphere a strange appearance, capable of suggesting the mystery of the cosmos. "Yes," Boullée wrote, "I believe that our buildings, especially public ones, ought, in some fashion, to be poems."[12]

The same Boullée imagined gigantic cemeteries, with a pyramidal portal, watched over by sphinxes which were to be transformed, by night, into "shadow architecture." Diderot wrote, in the *Salon* of 1767: "A palace must be in ruins to become an object worthy of interest." Hubert Robert had applied this formula to the letter when he represented the Grande Galerie of the Louvre in a ruined state. As for Boullée, he created from nothing what he called a "buried architecture" and the example he gave was a *monument funéraire* whose low and sinking lines suggested absorption and burial.

In short, whether we consider painting, architecture, or literature, neoclassicism and sensibility, far from being exclusive or divergent, live happily together in the grand conceptions of the end of the eighteenth century. Ledoux dreams of building vast classical palaces astride a stream, on top of a cave (château of Eguière) or facing Alpine peaks (the episcopal palace at Sisteron).

Ledoux realized in the purest neoclassical style some of Rousseau's fantasies and at times foreshadowed the ground plan of the phalansteries. His project for the city of Chaux comprised a Panaretheon and a Coenobium in the heart of the forest.

The architect executes on paper the scientific and technical feats that Chénier was to exalt in *L'Amérique* and in *Hermès*. Possessed by the demon of the absolute, he draws the perfect city, the temple of Love, the palace of Concord, the house of Unity. As against this, Delille the poet exalts Ledoux's project in the fifth canto of *L'Imagination* (1806):

> A l'honneur des Français, que n'eût point ajouté
> Le généreux projet de ta vaste cité!
> Là serait le bonheur; là de la race humaine
> Le monde eût admiré le plus beau phénomène.

But no architect's phantasmagoria more eloquently points to the unconscious of the time than the extraordinary *"Rendez-vous de Bellevue, à la pointe du rocher"* imagined by Lequeu, which unites in unbelievable confusion a small-scale Greek temple, a Renaissance tower, and a Gothic gate. The same Lequeu also imagined the romantic underground passage with hidden galleries, threatening machinery, secret corridors designed for initiation rites, that seem to foreshadow Kafka's *Penal Colony*, while in fact he quite simply referred to a few pages of the abbé Terrasson's *Séthos*, illustrating in a puerile fashion an initiation to heroism and duty.[13]

We have come a long way indeed from the graces and volutes of the rococo. The second half of the century of "Enlightenment" turned to the ancients for a lesson in grandeur, a model of rigor and majesty, and—as Peter Gay has so well demonstrated in his book *The Enlightenment: An Interpretation. The Rise of Modern Paganism* (1966)—a vision of the world which is at once grandiose, coherent, and secular in opposition to the prestige of Christian tradition.

Here is imaginary antiquity, in which memories of Plutarch mingle with those of Seneca, and which the Revolution would attempt to relive. But the enlightened age projected into this antiquity its obsessions, anxieties, and impulses. As Hugh Honour says in a recent book that excellently synthesizes the givens of the problem (*Neo-Classicism,* London: Penguin, 1968, p. 186): "The Neo-classical movement contained within itself the seeds of most of the Romantic forces that were to destroy it." Therefore he concludes his work with a brilliant analysis of Ingres's picture, *Oedipe et le Sphinx* (1808), that marks the internal split which was then forming: "A new vision of antiquity is here beginning to emerge—very different from the cool, calm land of liberty and reason described by Winckelmann and painted by David. In this grim mountain cleft there is no sign of eternal springtime. The dark irrational gods are once more closing in." (Honour, p. 190)

But we would then have to admit, at the outset, that antiquity for the neoclassicists was only this cool, calm land of liberty and reason. We have seen from the examples of Diderot, Chénier, and Boullée, that the return to antiquity could include the thrust of emotion, the throb of dreams, the call of the cosmic, the meditation on eternity and time. An attentive study of the facts reveals, we can see, that far from being incompatible, neoclassicism and sensibility were enriched by mutual contributions, that they were nurtured from the same source,[14] which became dissociated only after 1825, when this unity—precarious and confused no doubt, yet rich and varied as life itself—was to burst apart. . . .

Notes

[1] *Le Romantisme dans la littérature européenne* (Paris, 1948), 40: "French preromanticism appears to us as made up at first of two successive waves, that of Diderot and Rousseau which was formed after 1755, and that of their successors . . . who came into the picture after 1769 . . ." It is significant that in his posthumous book on *Le Sentiment de la nature dans le préromantisme européen* (Paris, 1960), Paul Van Tieghem no longer speaks of a preromantic current or period in the eighteenth century, but only of preromantic writers.

[2] This kind of restrictive definition has been wittily called "definition by larceny" by Peter Gay, precisely in connection with the notion of "preromanticism." See *The Party of Humanity: Essays in the French Enlightenment* (New York, 1964), 253-254.

[3] Later synthesized by André Monglond in the domain of French language. (*Le Préromantisme français,* 2 vols. [Grenoble, 1930].)

[4] Which we plan to study separately, from Joachim du Bellay to the Romantics, in a work to be published later.

[5] See Hubert Burda, *Die Ruine in den Bildern Hubert Roberts* (München, 1967).

[6] The internal evolution of Diderot's esthetics takes the same direction: if the exaltation of unbridled sensibility in the *Entretiens entre Dorval et moi* (written in 1756) corresponds quite well to "preromanticism" as defined by Van Tieghem and developed by Monglond, one should consider as "classical" the preeminence given to lucidity and intelligence in *Le Paradoxe sur le comédien* (written between 1769 and 1778).

[7] In his study on *Le "Plaisir des tombeaux" au XVIIIe siècle* (*R.L.C.* avril-juin 1938, pp. 287-311), R. Michéa already clearly contrasted a protestant movement, coming from England, to a Latin conception in which the cult of the dead merges with that of the fatherland.

[8] The sepulchral craze, around 1800, is much more than a literary theme. A veritable collective obsession could be discerned in it. We refer the reader, on this point, to Lionello Sozzi's remarkable study, *I "Sepolcri" e le discussioni francesi negli anni del Direttorio e del Consolato,* in "Giornale Storico della Letteratura Italiana," vol. CXLIV (1967), 567-588.

[9] The numerous texts quoted by Lionello Sozzi *all point in both directions.*

[10] They were literally revealed by Emil Kaufmann in his monograph *Three Revolutionary Architects* (Transactions of the American Philosophical Society, N.S., t. 42, 1952). In fact, Kaufmann had devoted articles and studies in German to them since 1929. A synthesis of these works was published in 1955 under the title *Architecture in the Age of Reason: Baroque and Post-Baroque in England, Italy, France* (Cambridge, Mass.), and was translated into French in 1963 under the title *L'Architecture au siècle des lumières.*

[11] Praise of Newton was always written in an exalted style at the end of the eighteenth century. The botanist André-Joseph Canolle, another instance of the convergence between poetry and the scientific spirit at that time, wrote in his *Délices de la solitude, puisés dans l'étude et la contemplation de la nature* ([Paris, 2d ed., 1799], p. 59), in the chapter on *Emblêmes de l'amour* "O genius of Newton! borne on your audacious wings I rise to the heavens amidst those globes whose immense ellipses you have centered in the sphere of our knowledge. Thence, through the eyes of your sublime understanding, I see these luminous bodies which command the respect of even the boldest imaginations, move according to the same laws that rule our hearts." One will not fail to be struck by the analogy between the tone of this passage and that of Chénier in *L'Invention* or in *L'Amérique,* as well as by the similarity between this theory of love-as-attraction and the conceptions developed some time later by Charles Fouri-

er. So true it is that the literary study of that time is still to be undertaken.

[12] In E.-L. Boullée, *Essai sur l'art,* ed. J.-M. Pérouse de Montclos (Paris, 1968), 47 and 137. The commentator notes (138, n. 116) that there had been at least three other projects for a "Cenotaph to Newton" before 1800.

[13] All these projects, which, for the most part, are still in their author's portfolios, were the subject of a traveling exhibition (Bibliothèque Nationale de Paris, Metropolitan Museum, etc.) and they appear in the copious catalog *Visionary Architects* (University of St. Thomas, Houston, 1968.)

[14] Similar conclusions are to be found in *Neo-classicism: Virtue, Reason and Nature,* by Rémy G. Saisselin (Intro. to *Neo-Classicism: Style and Motif,* Cleveland Museum of Art Exhibition, 1964, p. 3) and in *Le Néo-classicisme,* by François-Georges Pariset (*Information d'Histoire de l'Art* [Paris, 1959], nʳ 2, p. 47). . . .

DEFINING THE PERIOD

Bertrand H. Bronson (essay date 1953)

SOURCE: "The Pre-Romantic or Post-Augustan Mode," in *ELH: A Journal of English Literary History*, Vol. 20, No. 1, March, 1953, pp. 15-28.

[*In the following excerpt Bronson details why no individual post-Augustan poet adequately exemplifies the Preromantic period.*]

The topic that confronts us is one that carries doubt in its very face. "Pray," asks Christian, "who are your Kindred, if a man may be so bold?" "Almost the whole Town," answers By-ends; "and in particular, my Lord Turnabout, my Lord Time-server, my Lord Fair-spech. . . . Also Mr. Smooth-man, Mr. Facing-bothways, Mr. Any-thing; and the Parson of our Parish, Mr. Two-tongues, was my Mothers own Brother by my Father's side: And to tell you the truth, I am become a Gentleman of good Quality, yet my Great Grandfather was but a Waterman, looking one way, and rowing another: and I got most of my estate by the same occupation."

Our critical terminology is notoriously loose, and I am not too envy-ridden that it has fallen to my colleagues on either side—more timely-happy than myself—to clarify the meaning of the terms *Augustan* and *Romantic*. I, at least, can take their meanings for granted, in so far as they stand conventionally for opposite attitudes and aims.

But, if "Romantic" can and does bear as many meanings as Mr. Lovejoy has taught us to acknowledge, what dubious significance may lurk in the term "pre-Romantic"! "Pre-" in the sense of anticipating, of early, of premature? "Pre-" as preparative, as leading to, as germ-laden, as exhibiting the incipient stages of a disease about to become rampant and epidemic? Or "pre-" merely in a chronological sense, as occurring, whatever its nature, in the period before Romanticism burst forth, when, presumably, all those implicated meanings of the term, like a swarm of bees, clustered most thickly, or were most fully realized? Obviously, we are in a measure precluded from adopting either of the two first senses until the main term has been satisfactorily defined.

Similarly, the term "post-Augustan" gives us pause. Accepting the general implications of Augustanism just now so magisterially displayed, what should we presume to be the content of a "post-Augustan" era? Is it the fag-end of the day, "as after sunset fadeth in the west"? Is it a sequel imitative, or reactive, standing in some effective or consequential relation? or, again, is it merely a phenomenon casually subsequent in time? Unless the last, the answer here must emerge from further inquiry: it cannot be definitively foreseen.

A causal connection, if assumed to exist in either direction, is a severe curb on free discussion. These given terms of reference deny us any ground of our own, any independent room. Our space and our building have meaning only as they look before and after. We are assigned in advance to either a vestibule or a lean-to, without opportunity for a side-long glance. What is still more unwelcome, we know not which it is:—only that the space is the same, whatever it be called. Augustan and Romantic are opposites, we have been taught: yet, apparently, "post-Augustan" is interchangeable with "pre-Romantic," for they cover the same plot of literary ground. The choice of terms depends on our discovering whether we are coming or going, and which is which. Unless perhaps an interrogation point was omitted in the title, which might then have been intended to force a verdict: "Post-Augustan *or* pre-Romantic?"—or should we now add, "Post-Augustan *and/or* pre-Romantic?"

In this dilemma, it may be wiser for a time to abandon altogether the terms in question, and seek for an independent name among the materials within our boundaries. Simply, then, who are the major voices in poetry, the bulk of whose effort falls inside the period we wish, with their help, to define? Let us answer: Edward Young, Johnson, Collins, Gray, the younger Wartons, Akenside, Smart, Shenstone, Macpherson, Goldsmith, Churchill, Chatterton, Cowper, Burns, with, at the one end, Thomson, and, at the other, Crabbe and Blake. Merely to call the roll is to advertise the difficulty of finding common denominators for talents so divergent in aim, so various in style, so unequal in attainment. If we search among them for an eponym, several names drop at once from candidacy. No one is likely to plead for Akensidian, Smartian, Shenstonian, Macphersonian, Chattertonian, Blakean as the normative modes. Akenside might perhaps be a typical figure,—if we could ever remember by the end of the paragraph what he had been saying! Smart's pious rhapsodizing (at its best approaching the insane, as George Sherburn has dryly remarked) is too special to be representative, either in style or in content. Shenstone achieves his masterpiece in the neo-Spenserian mode, and does nothing else in verse but what others do better. Macpherson writes cadenced prose, loosely regularized by an insistent three-stress rhythm ("The wind and the rain are past: calm is the noon of day. The clouds are divided in heaven") so obsessive that one is almost upset by his occasional departures from it. Quite a number of younger spirits abandoned their minds to imitation in that mode, but all regained their composure before committing more than a nuisance. Next, Chatterton is neo-Tudor, and inimitable, and apart: a dark star. And then Blake, who neither belonged to a school nor established one,—unless in the 20th century. And lastly, to the foregoing we may as well add Burns, who, though himself the culmination of an impressive tradition, moves into the main current of English poetic traffic only to be lost in it, indistinguishable from the crowd.

None of these, I think, will serve adequately as eponym for the Age. No more, perhaps, will some with greater claims to be called representative figures. And first, the greatest name of all, which has lent itself to the Age more often than any other. We shall not have to deliberate long before deciding that the epithet *Johnsonian* will hardly do to characterize the poetic mode of his era. For one reason, of course, Johnson's work in poetry was almost all done before 1750, and does not typify at all the bulk of poetic achievement in the second half of the century. For another, although Johnson was a true poet, his major poems are too conventional to set a fashion, and too few to dominate the conventions within which he writes. That is to say, other poets writing in the classical tradition are not deflected by Johnson away from Pope or Dryden. He found the established norm quite congenial, and his innovations within it (if we can call them such) are below the conscious level. But his finest work in couplets displays a density of emotional statement closer, one may almost feel, to the Jacobean than to the Augustan poetic habit. There is a weight of content in his characteristic passages that Dryden would have worked out by expansion, and Pope by simplification. Observe, writes Johnson,

> How nations sink, by darling schemes oppress'd,
> When vengeance listens to the fool's request.
> Fate wings with ev'ry wish th'afflictive dart,

Each gift of nature, and each grace of art:
With *fatal* heat impetuous courage glows,
With *fatal* sweetness elocution flows:—
Impeachment stops the speaker's pow'rful
　　breath,
And restless fire precipitates on death.

This is poetry for reading, not for hearing. If we reversed the first couplet, thus:—

> When vengeance listens to the fool's request,
> [See] nations sink, by darling schemes
> 　　oppress'd,—

the logic of cause and effect would become clearer, though at the sacrifice of rhetorical point. Yet we should still have to excogitate that the vengeance here meant is a nemesis lying ironically in wait to trip each of us by means of his most cherished desire, granting it only to destroy us; to appreciate how whole nations, involved in their unwise leaders' darling schemes, have collapsed in ruin, frightful demonstrations of the vanity of human wishes. *Vengeance, listens, fool's,* and *request* must all be drawn out in their particular senses before the meaning of that line is clear. And an equal compactness, with-holding the facilitating connective elements, is evident in the couplet that immediately succeeds:

> Fate wings with ev'ry wish th'afflictive dart,
> Each gift of nature, and each grace of art.

Here, the syntax is at first baffling: it is not apparent that the object of the verb intervenes between three parallel prepositional phrases, so that what the poet is saying is this: Our every desire, our every personal endowment, whether a natural gift or an acquired and cultivated skill, is employed by fate to feather the arrows of affliction by which we ourselves are brought down.

Such lines as these exhibit pressures that are surely Johnson's own. Whether it could be claimed that they reflect also the characteristic perplexities of the age, I doubt. I doubt equally whether the larger structures of Johnson's thought—such passages as the famous address to the young scholar, where the six parallel couplets, like sequent combers, drive grandly forward to break at last on that inexorable negative ("should thy soul indulge . . . Should Reason guide . . . Should no false Kindness . . . Should tempting Novelty . . . Should Beauty . . . Should no Disease . . . :—

> *Yet hope not* life from grief or danger free,
> *Nor* think the doom of man revers'd for thee:")—

I doubt, I say, whether such massively insistent and sustained rhetorical statement can be found elsewhere in the poetry of that day or later. This, then, is the

Johnsonian mode, or part of it,—and not the mode of the Age. On the other hand, there are doubtless sufficient echoes of the Augustan equilibrium. Compare the restrictive balance of Johnson's

> See nations slowly wise and meanly just
> To buried merit raise the tardy bust

with Pope's

> A Being darkly wise, and rudely great.

Or, in another key, Johnson's

> What are acres? What are houses?
> Only dirt, or wet or dry.

Collins, to continue, will not provide us with a paradigm. "A solitary song-bird," asserted Swinburne, "among many pipers and pianists." Surely not that; but probably few of his generation would have chosen him their spokesman. Johnson, as we know, who thought of him kindly and took some trouble over him, disapproved both of his choice of subject and his manner in poetry. Loving the supernatural, Collins, he thought, went "in quest of mistaken beauties" of allegorical description and neglected "sentiment," which latter we may take to refer to the products of rational observation. He also found Collins' style objectionable: his diction labored and injudicious and unmusical, his phrasing wilfully perverse.

There is a deeper meaning than the one intended, in Johnson's phrase for Collins: "a literary adventurer." All his short life as a poet—it ended before he was thirty—Collins was looking for a sustaining subject, and hero-worshipping. Always hoping to graduate, he never truly left school. He continued to think of himself as an "admiring youth" under tutelage, and to look to others for the right sentiments and the proper attitudes. Any one who glances at the *Odes* in their first edition must be struck by the collegiate air of the book:—its combination of brashness and timidity, so smacking of insecurity mixed with vaulting ambition. From the title-page with its Pindaric motto to the last couplet of the concluding *Passions* ode, the reliance on Authority is all-pervasive. For example, in the opening ode (to Pity) "*Pella's* Bard" is glossed thus: "*Euripides,* of whom *Aristotle* pronounces, on a Comparison of him with *Sophocles,* That he was the greater Master of the tender Passions . . ." Collins calls upon "Her, whose Lovelorn Woe" etc., explaining in a note: "The . . . Nightingale, for which *Sophocles* seems to have entertain'd a peculiar Fondness." And, concluding the Ode for Music, entitled *The Passions,* he addresses Music in a paragraph which, considering Handel's achievement and reputation by that date, betrays an abject flight from experience:

> 'Tis said, and I believe the Tale,
> Thy humblest *Reed* could more prevail,
> Had more of strength, diviner Rage,
> Than all which charms this laggard Age . . .
> O bid our vain Endeavours cease,
> Revive the just Designs of *Greece,*
> Return in all thy simple State!

Now this is either the cant of the Schools, sheer learned humbug, or stony insensibility. Since we cannot but assume the poet's familiarity with Handel, whom his friends the Wartons greatly admired, it is charitable to attribute this passage to youthful bigotry. It is an example of Collins' failure to escape from the library. He saw, not Nature only, but Art and Life as well, through the spectacles of books. Genius he certainly was, but his inspiration was usually vicarious. His Pegasus sprang from a desk, seldom from a ground of values independently possessed. Therefore, description was safer than sentiment. "His greatest fault"—again Johnson has the right word—"was irresolution." Although he subscribed to the Wartons' youthful manifesto that poetry should be rescued from "the fashion of moralizing" and restored to "its right channel" of imaginative invention, the poets whom he most admired—Sophocles, Pindar, Spenser, Shakespeare, Milton—were not afraid of substantial sentiment; and the three young Wykehamists were ready to settle for less extreme objectives than they at first declared. Even Collins, the most daring of the triumvirate, could write couplets like the following:

> Each rising Art by slow Gradation moves,
> Toil builds on Toil, and Age on Age improves,

and like

> O blest in all that Genius gives to charm,
> Whose Morals mend us, and whose Passions
>   warm!

The poet in Joseph Warton died also in his twenties, to be succeeded by the moderate critic, as would probably have been Collins' case, to judge by the projects reported. Although, at twenty, in their own conceit mad for trackless wastes and assorted grisliness, or for tiger-hunts in Georgia with virtuous Indian swains, they managed to resist these impulses; and the Warton brothers pretty well tired out their Miltonic muses by one or two trips to the charnel-house in a Chippendale chair. Thomas's muse was sturdier than his brother's; but it can hardly be claimed, interesting as they are, that either of them was able to develop a style of his own. They were imitators, not creators; and whatever is best in their verses mirrors Milton.

The poetry of Gray, on the contrary, reflects a multitude, but mirrors none. Gray, George Sherburn has said, "typifies the transitional poet who loved tradition yet courted novelty." We should wish to qualify this pronouncement, which says a great deal in little space. Gray loved tradition*s*: he was a connoisseur of them. No one had a more discerning eye, a more discriminating ear, a keener relish for what was essential in a tradition. It might be the sublime pomp of the Pindaric ode—what quickened and brought it to fruition, what lingered after it down the centuries; it might be the majesty of Milton's achievement, gathering into itself what was great in Greek, Roman, Italian, and English poetry; it might be the tragic terror of northern traditions, Scandinavian or British. In whatever direction, he probed for the quintessential, delighting to *report*— to bring home—the special virtues of each kind. Therefore, the object of his search was novelty only indirectly: not novelty for its own sake, but rather, excellence far-sought and far-brought: the distillation of a wide and deep learning in the retort of a refined, sensitive intelligence. The lines of his odes glow and glitter with this distillation. He did not so much court novelty as encounter it by chance in the combining of earlier proprieties. If Gray typifies the transitional poet, he exalts the class to a status above that of the established schools. He did not realize his ideal, but where are his competitors in kind?

Over Goldsmith's pleasant, but for the most part unimportant verse, we need not linger. Easier by far than Johnson's, at its most serious it aims at a kindred goal, and it is appropriate that Johnson should have rounded off the conclusion of "The Traveller" with his own couplets. Their noticeably more involuted complexity lends the needed climactic weight without disturbing the tone. In "The Deserted Village," less ambitious but more felicitous, Goldsmith hits a mean of formal familiarity, of comfortable precision, of politeness in the truest sense, that in verse perfectly answers Johnson's commendation of Addison's prose as a model of the middle style. That it can be equalled elsewhere in the century is doubtful; but that it was elsewhere even attempted may also be doubted. Pope is much too self-conscious for this; Crabbe is not by any means self-conscious enough. Cowper, who can be at once familiar and polite in short metres or in prose letters, is prone in his couplets to be too shrill and insistent; while the blank verse of "The Task" puts in rather for Thomsonian laurels. Yet Cowper's variety and range, of matter and manner, light, or satiric, or Miltonic, his lively and articulate interest in, and sensitive reflection of, so many of the topics of his time, religious, political, social, or literary, might make him a strong contender for the most typical figure, without his ever establishing a mode.

If we have now run through our list without finding any one to set up as the inclusive exemplar of his age in poetry, it becomes apparent that we shall have to reinstate them all as partial representatives, each characteristic in greater or less degree, and in his own

fashion. But perhaps, fascinated by the diversity of the procession, we may be charged with being guilty of a half-hearted effort to find the underlying community.

That elements of such a community exist I scarcely doubt. Josephine Miles, in an extraordinarily original and interesting analysis of the common language of poets in the 1740's—among whom more than half of our list appear—has even found it possible to construct an ideal poetic sentence for the lot. They would unite in saying,

> Rise, fair day, before the eyes and soul of
> man,

and therein, according to Miss Miles, "would combine generally and gently the abstract and the visual in [their] moral imperative. This was [their] major vocabulary, the fair day, in its natural and airy setting; the eye, soul, hand, heart of man in youth and power; above, heaven and God. It was a world viewed, felt, and considered, and its great poetizing power was to bring more and more of what it considered and felt into view."[1]

The elements of Miss Miles's sentence are based in every part on demonstrable evidence. These were the words,—the nouns, the adjective, and the verb,—most commonly used by the poets of the mid-century, according to statistical count. The verb in its imperative or invocatory form we have all noted: the constant tendency to apostrophize and implore, until we are prompted to borrow Goldsmith's unconscious parody of the habit:

> O!—But let Exclamation cease!

or fretfully to coin an impromptu etymology for the name, *Ode*. We could all, with a little thought, make a brief table of tricks and topics favorite among poets of the period. It would include heads like: Country Pleasures, Times of the Day, Seasons of the Year; Abstractions—Fancy, Solitude, Sleep, Death,—inviting description, evoking feeling, tempting the moral comment. As John Dyer put it:

> Thus is nature's vesture wrought,
> To instruct our wand'ring thought;
> Thus she dresses green and gay,
> To disperse our cares away.

To some of us, one of the most interesting questions is the relative power of the abstract and general to excite emotional vibrations, and the way in which the process works. This is a problem both too large and too limiting for present discussion. Personification has attracted some attention of late;[2] but it is clear that abstraction maintains its purchase on the feelings far beyond the limits of allegorical suggestion. Ian Jack has recently shown how much 'grandeur of generality' Johnson gains by his special, 'generic,' use of the definite article[3] (and the indefinite may be added):

> Dart the quick taunt, and edge the piercing gibe

or

> Against your fame with fondness hate combines,
> The rival batters, and the lover mines.

And compare

> New sorrow rises as the day returns,
> A sister sickens, or a daughter mourns.

Close examination of what I shall denominate "the abstractive correlative" might carry us a long way toward understanding the basic appeals of eighteenth-century poetry.

An amusing if minor manifestation of this affective side of generalizing technique is the special little thrill of delight evoked by the deft use of a philosophic or scientific term in a context where one would not have expected it. A very familiar instance is Cowper's

> O for a lodge in some vast wilderness,
> Some boundless *contiguity* of shade!

Goldsmith loves the same word and uses it in both his major poems, once thus:

> To scape the pressure of contiguous pride.

Another example from Goldsmith's "The Traveller" is this:

> And love's and friendship's finely pointed dart
> Fall blunted from each *indurated* heart.

Again, Goldsmith's

> With daring aims *irregularly* great.

Or Thomson's notorious

> And *ventilated* states renew their bloom.

Or Matthew Green's engaging

> *Tarantulated* by a tune

and his

> The *consanguinity* of sound.

Somewhat antiseptic is Cowper's

> The stable yields a stercoraceous heap. . . .

But we must beware of emulating Little Jack Horner.

The delightful shock of abstract vs. concrete issues with an almost seventeenth-century air from Smart's "quick peculiar quince"; and, in general,—and not forgetting Pope's "Die of a rose in aromatic pain"—this habit may have significant affiliations with the previous century. Certainly, no one ever understood its musical possibilities better than Sir Thomas Browne. Perhaps, then, on one side, this trait is affined to the impulse to recover the Past, the same force that caused poets to break out in a rash of Allegro-Penserosiads and Spenseriantics.

Goldsmith's "daring aims irregularly great" may stand to remind us of a far-reaching inclination, backed by explicit theory, to set much store by the beauty of irregularity. The aesthetic implications of this impulse in landscape, in architecture, in literature, for the shift from classicism toward the romantic position, have been sufficiently outlined by Lovejoy, who quotes, among much other evidence, Gilpin's remark:

> Regularity and exactness excite no pleasure in the imagination unless they are made use of to contrast with something of an opposite kind.[4]

Approval of irregularity might favor the arrival of sublimity, and lead eventually to an Ode on Intimations of Immortality; but it did not by any means relieve this generation of the duty of propriety of language in the kind of writing attempted. This was still a matter of the utmost importance. It accounts among other things for the difference in style between Gray's Odes and his *Elegy*. "The style of elegy," wrote Shenstone, "should imitate the voice and language of grief; or if a metaphor of dress be more agreeable, it should be simple and diffuse, and flowing as a mourner's veil."[5]

Miss Miles has indicated that the flow of the poetic current was more and more toward the visible and sensory, away from the abstract and moral, as the century progressed. If this be so, what we have noticed as arresting abstraction is perhaps an atavistic streak in the temper of the time. But it cannot be merely vestigial in its import if, as we are suggesting, its antiquarian aura links it at some points to that Revival of the Past in terms of which some sturdy critics have mainly read the Romantic Movement.

To be reminded of Browne is to remind ourselves that a stylistic device like the one singled out here may be just as much at home in prose as in poetry. And, in general, I suppose it may fairly be contended that what is typical in the age under survey is as clearly visible in its prose as in the work of its poets—possibly more clearly. This is to suggest that what we discover here is a community of matter—or a common view of things—rather than a primary community of manner. What the poets were looking for was not so much a fresh poetical rhetoric that could be prescriptively established—a dominating, authoritative idiom to supplant the Augustan,—as a set of fresh topics to stimulate poetic invention and feeling. Their sensibilities were in the main similarly aligned to the new appeals. But they were generally agreed that they did not want to repudiate the heritage of the recent past: only, they did not want to be confined by it. They wished to extend their range of feeling and utterance; and, in their effort to do so, manner tended to become a little less controlling than heretofore. They were inclined to allow more scope for the development of a heterogeneous poetic utterance. As to style, they came to prefer eclectic habits, to scatter their allegiances. We shall hardly succeed, therefore, in isolating any widely typical post-Augustan or pre-Romantic Mode in Poetry. For it is this very *uncommittedness* which defines the period at which we have been glancing.

In one of its most important rôles, the term *Mode* has musical significance. As we know, the medieval, ecclesiastical modes began, around the turn of the sixteenth to seventeenth century, to prove inadequate to bear the new pressures for musical expression, secular and harmonic. The old diatonic patterns came to seem more and more unwieldy and inflexible, and were gradually loosened by the introduction of more frequent chromaticism, the modern major-minor harmonic coloring eventually supplanting the earlier modality. But the Elizabethan composers were fascinated by the contrast, and delighted in heightening the colors in a crowded interplay of opposed systems. They were close enough to the old to know it in their bones; and they were not as yet so much surrendering its values as renewing their sense of them by experimentally challenging and then reasserting them. The challenge was not hostile, but affectionate. Consequently, one finds in their music a characteristically nostalgic and disturbing beauty:—at the hour of farewell, as it were, a premonition of homesickness. Much of the tonal iridescence of these composers comes from their impaired but not severed allegiance to the Modes.

Something of the same kind of interest attaches to the poetry of the mid-eighteenth century. Probably we should acknowledge as a rule that there is always more of the previous age in each succeeding period than in our anxiety to sharpen distinctions we are usually ready to admit. More of the Augustan in the next era, more of the post-Augustan (to call it so) in the Romantic. The period under present scrutiny is, at any rate, too close to the triumphs of Dryden and Pope to be able to forget them, and it is generally well-mannered and decorous—over-decorous, some would say. But it is also discontented, restless, uncommitted, unwilling to stay,

yet undetermined to go. These opposing tensions give it a waywardness, an unpredictability, that are continually engaging one's surprised attention. Its variety is as hard to fix as the changes of the natural scene which so beguiled it; and if driven into a corner, we should have to declare that its historic function is to unmodify. Its mode, so to say, is prismatic. It is the time, in short, wherein are to be found coexisting Thomson's spaciousness, Johnson's massiveness, Collins' incorporeality, the Warton's bi-partisanship, Gray's eclecticism, Young's commiseration, Akenside's reasonableness, Smart's enthusiasm, Shenstone's placidity, Macpherson's rant, Churchill's unmannerliness, Goldsmith's amenity, Chatterton's atavism—rootless in Time as Collins in Space,—Cowper's humanity, Burns's pride and passion, Crabbe's sobriety, Blake's extravagance. Each of these qualities finds its own expression in a verbal idiom conditioned in part by outer, but more and more by inner, leading. As Polonius would have it, "For the Law of Writ, and the Liberty, these are the only men."

Notes

[1] Josephine Miles, *The Primary Language of Poetry in the 1740's and 1840's* (Univ. of Calif. Publications in English, XIX, No. 2, 1950), p. 222.

[2] See particularly, Earl R. Wasserman, "The Inherent Values of Eighteenth-Century Personification," *PMLA,* LXV (1950), pp. 435-63.

[3] Ian Jack, *Augustan Satire* (Oxford, 1952), pp. 142f.

[4] A. O. Lovejoy, *Essays in the History of Ideas* (Baltimore, 1948), p. 158 ("The First Gothic Revival and the Return to Nature," an essay first published in *MLN,* 1932, pp. 414-446).

[5] William Shenstone, *Works,* ed. 1768, I, 20 ("A Prefatory Essay on Elegy").

Northrop Frye (lecture date 1955)

SOURCE: "Towards Defining an Age of Sensibility," in *ELH: A Journal of English Literary History*, Vol. 23, No. 2, June, 1956, pp. 144-52.

[*In the following excerpt from a lecture delivered in 1955, Frye asserts that in the age of sensibility poets emphasized their work as process, not product.*]

The period of English literature which covers roughly the second half of the eighteenth century is one which has always suffered from not having a clear historical or functional label applied to it. I call it here the age of sensibility, which is not intended to be anything but a label. This period has the "Augustan" age on one side of it and the "Romantic" movement on the other, and it is usually approached transitionally, as a period of reaction against Pope and anticipation of Wordsworth. The chaos that results from treating this period, or any other, in terms of reaction has been well described by Professor Crane in a recent article in the Toronto Quarterly. What we do is to set up, as the logical expression of Augustanism, some impossibly pedantic view of following rules and repressing feelings, which nobody could ever have held, and then treat any symptom of freedom or emotion as a departure from this. Our students are thus graduated with a vague notion that the age of sensibility was the time when poetry moved from a reptilian Classicism, all cold and dry reason, to a mammalian Romanticism, all warm and wet feeling.

As for the term "pre-romantic," that, as a term for the age itself, has the peculiar demerit of committing us to anachronism before we start, and imposing a false teleology on everything we study. Not only did the "pre-romantics" not know that the Romantic movement was going to succeed them, but there has probably never been a case on record of a poet's having regarded a later poet's work as the fulfilment of his own. However, I do not care about terminology, only about appreciation for an extraordinarily interesting period of English literature, and the first stage in renewing that appreciation seems to me the gaining of a clear sense of what it is in itself.

Some languages use verb-tenses to express, not time, but the difference between completed and continuous action. And in the history of literature we become aware, not only of periods, but of a recurrent opposition of two views of literature. These two views are the Aristotelian and the Longinian, the aesthetic and the psychological, the view of literature as product and the view of literature as process. In our day we have acquired a good deal of respect for literature as process, notably in prose fiction. The stream of consciousness gets careful treatment in our criticism, and when we compare Arnold Bennett and Virginia Woolf on the subject of Mrs. Brown we generally take the side of Virginia Woolf. So it seems that our age ought to feel a close kinship with the prose fiction of the age of sensibility, when the sense of literature as process was brought to a peculiarly exquisite perfection by Sterne, and in lesser degree by Richardson and Boswell.

All the great story-tellers, including the Augustan ones, have a strong sense of literature as a finished product. The suspense is thrown forward until it reaches the end, and is based on our confidence that the author knows what is coming next. A story-teller does not break his illusion by talking to the reader as Fielding does, because we know from the start that we are listening to Fielding telling a story—that is, Johnson's arguments about illusion in drama apply equally well to prose fiction of Fielding's kind. But when we turn

to *Tristram Shandy* we not only read the book but watch the author at work writing it: at any moment the house of Walter Shandy may vanish and be replaced by the author's study. This does break the illusion, or would if there were any illusion to break, but here we are not being led into a story, but into the process of writing a story: we wonder, not what is coming next, but what the author will think of next.

Sterne is, of course, an unusually pure example of a process-writer, but even in Richardson we find many of the same characteristics. Johnson's well-known remark that if you read Richardson for the story you would hang yourself indicates that Richardson is not interested in a plot with a quick-march rhythm. Richardson does not throw the suspense forward, but keeps the emotion at a continuous present. Readers of *Pamela* have become so fascinated by watching the sheets of Pamela's manuscript spawning and secreting all over her master's house, even into the recesses of her clothes, as she fends off assault with one hand and writes about it with the other, that they sometimes overlook the reason for an apparently clumsy device. The reason is, of course, to give the impression of literature as process, as created on the spot out of the events it describes. And in the very beginning of *Boswell in London* we can see the boy of twenty-one already practising the art of writing as a continuous process from experience. When he writes of his adventure with Louisa he may be writing several days after the event, but he does not use his later knowledge.

In poetry the sense of literature as a finished product normally expresses itself in some kind of regularly recurring metre, the general pattern of which is established as soon as possible. In listening to Pope's couplets we have a sense of continually fulfilled expectation which is the opposite of obviousness: a sense that eighteenth-century music also often gives us. Such a technique demands a clear statement of what sound-patterns we may expect. We hear at once the full ring of the rhyming couplet, and all other sound-patterns are kept to a minimum. In such a line as:

> And strains from hard-bound brains eight lines
> a year,

the extra assonance is a deliberate discord, expressing the difficulties of constipated genius. Similarly with the alliteration in:

> Great Cibber's brazen, brainless brothers
> stand,

and the fact that these are deliberate discords used for parody indicates that they are normally not present. Johnson's disapproval of such devices in serious contexts is written all over the *Lives of the Poets*.

When we turn from Pope to the age of sensibility, we get something of the same kind of shock that we get when we turn from Tennyson or Matthew Arnold to Hopkins. Our ears are assaulted by unpredictable assonances, alliterations, inter-rhymings and echolalia:

> Mie love ys dedde,
> Gon to hys death-bedde . . .

> With brede ethereal wove,
> O'erhang his wavy bed . . .

> The couthy cracks begin when supper's o'er,
> The cheering bicker gars them glibly gash . . .

> But a pebble of the brook
>   Warbled out these metres meet . . .

In many of the best-known poems of the period, in Smart's *Song to David,* in Chatterton's elegies, in Burns's songs and Blake's lyrics, even in some of the Wesley hymns, we find a delight in refrain for refrain's sake. Sometimes, naturally, we can see the appropriate literary influences helping to shape the form, such as the incremental repetition of the ballad, or Old Norse alliteration in *The Fatal Sisters.* And whatever may be thought of the poetic value of the Ossianic poems, most estimates of that value parrot Wordsworth, and Wordsworth's criticisms of Ossian's imagery are quite beside the point. The vague generalized imagery of Ossian, like the mysterious resonant names and the fixed epithets, are part of a deliberate and well unified scheme. *Fingal* and *Temora* are long poems for the same reason that *Clarissa* is a long novel: not because there is a complicated story to be told, as in *Tom Jones* or an epic of Southey, but because the emotion is being maintained at a continuous present by various devices of repetition.

The reason for these intensified sound-patterns is, once again, an interest in the poetic process as distinct from the product. In the composing of poetry, where rhyme is as important as reason, there is a primary stage in which words are linked by sound rather than sense. From the point of view of sense this stage is merely free or uncontrolled association, and in the way it operates it is very like the dream. Again like the dream, it has to meet a censor-principle, and shape itself into intelligible patterns. Where the emphasis is on the communicated product, the qualities of consciousness take the lead: a regular metre, clarity of syntax, epigram and wit, repetition of sense in antithesis and balance rather than of sound. Swift speaks with admiration of Pope's ability to get more "sense" into one couplet than he can into six: concentration of sense for him is clearly a major criterion of poetry. Where the emphasis is on the original process, the qualities of subconscious association take the lead, and the poetry becomes hypnotically repetitive, oracular, incantatory,

dreamlike and in the original sense of the word charming. The response to it includes a subconscious factor, the surrendering to a spell. In Ossian, who carries this tendency further than anyone else, the aim is not concentration of sense but diffusion of sense, hence Johnson's remark that anybody could write like Ossian if he would abandon his mind to it. Literature as product may take a lyrical form, as it does in the sublime ode about which Professor Maclean has written so well, but it is also the conception of literature that makes the longer continuous poem possible. Literature as process, being based on an irregular and unpredictable coincidence of sound-patterns, tends to seek the brief or even the fragmentary utterance, in other words to centre itself on the lyric, which accounts for the feeling of a sudden emergence of a lyrical impulse in the age of sensibility.

The "pre-romantic" approach to this period sees it as developing a conception of the creative imagination, which became the basis of Romanticism. This is true, but the Romantics tended to see the poem as the *product* of the creative imagination, thus reverting in at least one respect to the Augustan attitude. For the Augustan, art is posterior to nature because nature is the art of God; for the Romantic, art is prior to nature because God is an artist; one deals in physical and the other in biological analogies, as Professor Abrams' *Mirror and the Lamp* has shown. But for the Romantic poet the poem is still an artefact: in Coleridge's terms, a secondary or productive imagination has been imposed on a primary imaginative process. So, different as it is from Augustan poetry, Romantic poetry is like it in being a conservative rhetoric, and in being founded on relatively regular metrical schemes. Poe's rejection of the continuous poem does not express anything very central in Romanticism itself, as nearly every major Romantic poet composed poems of considerable, sometimes immense, length. Poe's theory is closer to the practice of the age of sensibility before him and the *symbolistes* after him.

In the age of sensibility most of the long poems, of course, simply carry on with standard continuous metres, or exploit the greater degree of intensified recurrent sound afforded by stanzaic forms, notably the Spenserian. But sometimes the peculiar problems of making associative poetry continuous were faced in a more experimental way, experiments largely ignored by the Romantics. Oracular poetry in a long form often tends to become a series of utterances, irregular in rhythm but strongly marked off one from the other. We notice in Whitman, for instance, that the end of every line has a strong pause—for when the rhythm is variable there is no point in a run-on line. Sometimes this oracular rhythm takes on at least a typographical resemblance to prose, as it does in Rimbaud's *Saison en Enfer,* or, more frequently, to a discontinuous blend of prose and verse in which the sentence, the paragraph and the line are much the same unit. The chief literary influence for this rhythm has always been the translated Bible, which took on a new impetus in the age of sensibility; and if we study carefully the rhythm of Ossian, of Smart's *Jubilate Agno* and of the Blake Prophecies, we can see three very different but equally logical developments of this semi-Biblical rhythm.

Where there is a strong sense of literature as aesthetic product, there is also a sense of its detachment from the spectator. Aristotle's theory of catharsis describes how this works for tragedy: pity and fear are detached from the beholder by being directed towards objects. Where there is a sense of literature as process, pity and fear become states of mind without objects, moods which are common to the work of art and the reader, and which bind them together psychologically instead of separating them aesthetically.

Fear without an object, as a condition of mind prior to being afraid of anything, is called *Angst* or anxiety, a somewhat narrow term for what may be almost anything between pleasure and pain. In the general area of pleasure comes the eighteenth-century conception of the sublime, where qualities of austerity, gloom, grandeur, melancholy or even menace are a source of romantic or penseroso feelings. The appeal of Ossian to his time on this basis needs no comment. From here we move through the graveyard poets, the Gothic-horror novelists and the writers of tragic ballads to such *fleurs du mal* as Cowper's *Castaway* and Blake's Golden Chapel poem in the Rossetti MS.

Pity without an object has never to my knowledge been given a name, but it expresses itself as an imaginative animism, or treating everything in nature as though it had human feelings or qualities. At one end of its range is the apocalyptic exultation of all nature bursting into human life that we have in Smart's *Song to David* and the ninth Night of *The Four Zoas*. Next comes an imaginative sympathy with the kind of folklore that peoples the countryside with elemental spirits, such as we have in Collins, Fergusson, Burns and the Wartons. Next we have the curiously intense awareness of the animal world which (except for some poems of D. H. Lawrence) is unrivalled in this period, and is expressed in some of its best realized writing: in Burns's *To a Mouse,* in Cowper's exquisite snail poem, in Smart's superb lines on his cat Geoffrey, in the famous starling and ass episodes in Sterne, in the opening of Blake's *Auguries of Innocence*. Finally comes the sense of sympathy with man himself, the sense that no one can afford to be indifferent to the fate of anyone else, which underlies the protests against slavery and misery in Cowper, in Crabbe and in Blake's *Songs of Experience*.

This concentration on the primitive process of writing is projected in two directions, into nature and into history. The appropriate natural setting for much of the poetry of sensibility is nature at one of the two poles of process, creation and decay. The poet is attracted by the ruinous and the mephitic, or by the primeval and "unspoiled"—a picturesque subtly but perceptibly different from the Romantic picturesque. The projection into history assumes that the psychological progress of the poet from lyrical through epic to dramatic presentations, discussed by Stephen at the end of Joyce's *Portrait,* must be the historical progress of literature as well. Even as late as the preface to Victor Hugo's *Cromwell* this asumption persists. The Ossian and Rowley poems are not simple hoaxes: they are pseudepigrapha, like the Book of Enoch, and like it they take what is psychologically primitive, the oracular process of composition, and project it as something historically primitive.

The poetry of process is oracular, and the medium of the oracle is often in an ecstatic or trance-like state: autonomous voices seem to speak through him, and as he is concerned to utter rather than to address, he is turned away from his listener, so to speak, in a state of rapt self-communion. The free association of words, in which sound is prior to sense, is often a literary way of representing insanity. In Rimbaud's terrifyingly accurate phrase, poetry of the associative or oracular type requires a "dérèglement de tous les sens." Hence the qualities that make a man an oracular poet are often the qualities that work against, and sometimes destroy, his social personality. Far more than the time of Rimbaud and Verlaine is this period of literature a period of the *poète maudit*. The list of poets over whom the shadows of mental breakdown fell is far too long to be coincidence. The much publicized death of Chatterton is certainly one of the personal tragedies of the age, but an easier one to take than the kind of agony which is expressed with an almost definitive poignancy by Smart in *Jubilate Agno:*

> For in my nature I quested for beauty, but God,
> God, hath sent me to sea for pearls.

It is characteristic of the age of sensibility that this personal or biographical aspect of it should be so closely connected with its central technical feature. The basis of poetic language is the metaphor, and the metaphor, in its radical form, is a statement of identity: "this is that." In all our ordinary experience the metaphor is non-literal: nobody but a savage or a lunatic can take metaphor literally. For Classical or Augustan critics the metaphor is a condensed simile: its real or common-sense basis is likeness, not identity, and when it obliterates the sense of likeness it becomes barbaric. In Johnson's strictures on the music and water metaphor of Gray's *Bard* we can see what intellectual abysses, for him, would open up if metaphors ever passed beyond the stage of resemblance. For the Romantic critic, the identification in the metaphor is ideal: two images are identified within the mind of the creating poet.

But where metaphor is conceived as part of an oracular and half-ecstatic process, there is a direct identification in which the poet himself is involved. To use another phrase of Rimbaud's, the poet feels not "je pense," but "on me pense." In the age of sensibility some of the identifications involving the poet seem manic, like Blake's with Druidic bards or Smart's with Hebrew prophets, or depressive, like Cowper's with a scapegoat figure, a stricken deer or castaway, or merely bizarre, like Macpherson's with Ossian or Chatterton's with Rowley. But it is in this psychological self-identification that the central "primitive" quality of this age really emerges. In Collins's *Ode on the Poetical Character,* in Smart's *Jubilate Agno,* and in Blake's *Four Zoas,* it attains its greatest intensity and completeness.

In these three poems, especially the last two, God, the poet's soul and nature are brought into a white-hot fusion of identity, an imaginative fiery furnace in which the reader may, if he chooses, make a fourth. All three poems are of the greatest complexity, yet the emotion on which they are founded is of a simplicity and directness that English literature has rarely attained again. With the 1800 edition of *Lyrical Ballads,* secondary imagination and recollection in tranquillity took over English poetry and dominated it until the end of the nineteenth century. The primitivism of Blake and Smart revived in France with Rimbaud and Gérard de Nerval, but even this development had become conservative by the time its influence reached England, and only in a few poems of Dylan Thomas, and those perhaps not his best, does the older tradition revive. But contemporary poetry is still deeply concerned with the problems and techniques of the age of sensibility, and while the latter's resemblance to our time is not a merit in it, it is a logical enough reason for re-examining it with fresh eyes.

NEW DIRECTIONS IN POETRY AND PROSE
Walter Jackson Bate (essay date 1946)

SOURCE: "The Growth of Individualism: The Premise of the Association of Ideas," in *From Classic to Romantic: Premises of Taste in Eighteenth-Century England,* Cambridge, Mass.: Harvard University Press, 1946, pp. 129-59.

[*In the following excerpt from his highly influential work* From Classic to Romantic, *Bate describes how a new emphasis on feelings led poets to experiment with sympathy, synaesthesia, suggestiveness, and sublimity.*]

"Poetry," said Wordsworth, "is the history, or science, of the feelings"; for it is the "heart" which seeks "the light of truth." A rather general reliance on feeling as a valid means of insight and communication accompanied the earlier stages of the increased relativism which, in varying guises and degrees, has tended to dominate western art since the latter part of the eighteenth century. It is an ironic commonplace of intellectual history that one of the major sources of the romantic stress on feeling was ultimately the mechanistic psychology of the seventeenth and eighteenth centuries. Empiricism, having disposed of the mind as a strictly rational instrument, was increasingly forced to fall back on the immediate feeling of the individual. "What is commonly, and in a popular sense, called reason," said Hume, "is nothing but a general and a calm passion which takes a comprehensive and distant view of its object"; and "what we call *strength of mind,*" for example, is only "the prevalence of the calm passions above the violent." Despite the admittedly extreme position of Hume, it is significant that even those who opposed him, such as the members of the Scottish "Common-Sense" School, urged an intuitionalism which had a strongly emotional tinge. In general, the copious British writing of the eighteenth century on sentiment or feeling, and on the use which intuition makes of it, simply anticipated Kant—who of course drew heavily on it in his earlier work—in its desire to find or reconstruct some general basis for knowledge, morality, and art.

As it reflected and abided by this general empirical tendency, English aesthetic criticism increasingly verged towards the subjective emotionalism which had been advocated or implied by the *je ne sais quoi* "School of Taste" and by Shaftesbury and his ardent following. Stemming from Shaftesbury, a modified confidence in an "inner sense" passed almost imperceptibly, especially through the Scottish school of moralists and critics, into much of later eighteenth-century British thought. But what had before been rather confusedly and impulsively advanced by critics of the *je ne sais quoi* faith and by the early Shaftesburyans now received psychological support. Associationism, in particular, tended to give such a support by breaking down the barrier between "thought" and "feeling": by considering thought and conviction as an intricately interrelated series of feelings and responses on the part of the human mechanism to an external stimulus. A parallel tendency had already begun in France, with the importation of Locke's sensationalism. "How many excellent philosophers," said La Mettrie, in his *Man as a Machine,* "have now shown that thought is but a faculty of feeling!" Whether the position was taken that the emotional response to the good and the beautiful is the function of an innate sense, which is unerring in its insight; or whether, in another extreme, this response was viewed as simply the accumulated result of habit and experience, and as merely the sole means of cognition possible under the circumstances, a general standpoint gradually assumed is that which Goethe permitted Faust to utter in the often-abused statement, "Feeling is all."

Feeling transcends what is usually regarded as "reason," not only because it offers a more spontaneous vitality of realization, but also because it is aware of nuances of significance and of interrelationship to which the logical process is impervious. Certain realities, stated a Scottish writer, John Gregory, necessarily defy strictly mental cognition; there is, for example, "a correspondence between certain external forms of Nature, and certain affections of the Mind, that may be *felt*, but cannot be explained." Abraham Tucker, again, maintained that we can only "reason *about*" such a phenomenon as "force"; and the implication of his entire conception of the imagination is that, because of its fluidity and elusiveness compared with the fixed character of human "reason," such an aspect of nature as "force" cannot be known and divulged except by a feeling through direct experience. The primary characteristic of empirical reality is flux and change; the reasoning process *abstracts* and *categorizes* conclusions from this flux, and bestows on them an artificial rigidity and a static order of its own. It is in this sense that Wordsworth referred to the intellect as "meddling," and that Keats stated "I am certain of nothing but the holiness of the Heart's affections and the truth of Imagination. . . . I have never yet been able to perceive how anything can be known for truth by consequitive reasoning." By "feeling," said the noted German prophet of romanticism, August Wilhelm von Schlegel, one becomes aware of the subtlest and most fluid interrelationships between objects or between ideas: "The ancient art and poetry rigorously separate things which are dissimilar; the romantic delights in indissoluble mixtures." Classicism conceives the world as exhibiting the harmonious legislation of law and order, and as

> reflecting in itself the eternal images of things. Romantic poetry, on the other hand, is the expression of a secret attraction to a chaos which lies concealed . . . and is perpetually striving after new and marvellous births. . . . The former is more simple, clear, and like to nature in the self-existent perfection of its works; the latter . . . approaches more to the secret of the universe. For Conception can only comprise each object separately, but nothing in truth can ever exist separately and by itself; *Feeling* perceives all in all at one and the same time.[1]

II

The evolution of the romantic stress on feeling as a means of effective insight may be characteristically illustrated by the increasing rôle assigned to sympathy in both moral and aesthetic theory. It is one of the common tenets of English romantic criticism that the

imagination is capable, through an effort of sympathetic intuition, of identifying itself with its object; and, by means of this identification, the sympathetic imagination grasps, through a kind of direct experience and feeling, the distinctive nature, identity, or "truth" of the object of its contemplation. The critical opinions of Wordsworth, Coleridge, and several minor critics frequently reveal this assumption. Hazlitt, as Mr. Bullitt has shown, made it the basis not only of his conception of the imagination but of his ethics, and there is reason to believe that Keats did likewise.

As it finally matured in English romantic thought, and in so far as it was applied to purely aesthetic ends, this conception of sympathy bears certain similarities to the more restricted and specific doctrine of *Einfühlung*, which was developed in Germany at the close of the last century and to which the term "empathy" has since been devoted in English. In British romantic thought generally, however, sympathy had a broad moral application, and played an important part in the attempt to re-establish a bond of union not only among mankind but also between man and external nature. As such, its ramifications were numerous and varied, and extended from its influence on the sober ethics of some of the early-nineteenth-century Scottish school to its predominance in the brilliant interpretation, by Hazlitt and occasionally Keats, of Shakespeare and of the poetic function generally; from its presence in Wordsworth's calm and meditative regard for nature to its subjectively nostalgic and almost nihilistic expression in Byron's occasional identification of himself with the ocean, the storm, and the mountains, or in Shelley's yearning to merge himself in the West Wind. Like other aspects of the romantic emphasis on feeling as a primary means of aesthetic and moral insight and communication, the conception of sympathy as a guiding principle took rise, on the one hand, from the innate sensibility hypothesized by Shaftesbury and his more moderate Scottish followers, and, on the other hand, from empirical associationism.

A belief in the importance of the artist's capacity to enter totally into his subject, with a resulting obliteration of his own identity, is occasionally found in early English neo-classicism. One writer, for example, in the latter half of the seventeenth century, had dwelt upon Shakespeare's ability to "metamorphose" himself into his characters. Shaftesbury, somewhat later, almost anticipated the language of Keats's famous contention that the true poet "has no character . . . no identity," but that he becomes "annihilated" in the characters of those about him and concerns himself with revealing their essential natures. For Shaftesbury, too, considered that in the conception and portrayal of his subject the poet is, ideally speaking, "annihilated," and is "no certain man, nor has any certain or genuine character." In addition to this sort of anticipation of what was later to become a pervasive assumption in much general aesthetic theory, there is also a pronounced tendency, among a few of the earlier intuitional moralists of the eighteenth century, to regard sympathy as an important aid to the "moral sense." For example, James Arbuckle, an admiring disciple of Shaftesbury, considered moral action impossible without the capacity to enter sympathetically into others: man is ultimately controlled by feeling rather than reason; and we may consequently "see the Wisdom of our Creator in giving us this imagining *Faculty,* and such a Facility of placing ourselves in Circumstances different from those we are really in, to enforce our Duty upon us, not only by Reason, but by Passion and powerful Inclination."[2]

The emerging of this moral conception, among some of the benevolists, received a sudden and marked impetus from empiricism; and Hume, who demolished reason as an ethical guide and yet discovered no distinct "moral sense," resolved almost all moral response into sympathy. It is significant that even Johnson admitted that "all joy or sorrow for the happiness or calamities of others is produced by an act of the imagination, that realizes the event . . . by placing us, for a time, in the condition of him whose fortune we contemplate; so that we feel . . . whatever emotions would be excited by the same good or evil happening to ourselves." Yet sympathy, like any other emotional capacity, was regarded by Johnson as at best a means of enforcing the rational grasp of the universal. Adam Smith particularized and extended the doctrine of sympathy which Hume had advanced; and the design of his *Theory of Moral Sentiments* (1759) is the complete substitution of sympathy for the "moral sense" as man's internal monitor, and the elaboration of it as an all-embracing principle. Moral judgment, for Smith, involved a sympathetic participation with those who would be affected by the external consequences, good or bad, of an act; but it equally necessitated an awareness, through sympathy with the executor of the act, both of the "intention or affection of the heart" from which he acts, and of the specific situation, bodily or mental, which helps to prompt that intention. Although he emphasized the instinctiveness of such sympathetic understanding, and even regarded it as divinely implanted, Smith also recognized the contributing influence of habit and custom. He consequently admitted that a large relativity in sympathetic reaction is bound to result—a relativity determined by the associations which experience teaches and by the inherent sensitivity and capacity of the individual nature. Smith, finally, did not identify his internal monitor with the imagination, but he stressed at the outset the complete inability of the sympathy to function without the imagination:

As we have no immediate experience of what other men feel, we can form no idea of the manner in which they are affected, but by conceiving what we ourselves should feel in the like situation. Though our brother is on the rack, as long as we ourselves are at our ease, our senses will never inform us of what he suffers. They never did and never can carry us beyond our persons, and it is by the imagination that we can form any conception of what are his sensations.[3]

The influence of the *Theory of Moral Sentiments* on British moral thought was suggestive rather than directing. Many contemporary Scottish moralists emphasized the rôle of sympathy as a greatly contributing though by no means sole principle of morality, and, like Dugald Stewart, agreed that the imagination is of fundamental importance to any exercise of sympathy. Among Scottish literary critics, moreover, the book enjoyed a far more widespread vogue. The *Theory of Moral Sentiments* is in some respects hardly more than an indication of a growing moral and aesthetic tendency. Yet the book elaborated and even crystallized some of the assumptions of this tendency, particularly the interworking of sympathy with the imagination; and it is of some significance that the development of the sympathetic imagination as an aesthetic doctrine came largely from a group of Scottish critics who almost agreed with Archibald Alison's estimate of the *Moral Sentiments* as "the most eloquent work on the subject of Morals that Modern Europe has produced," and who felt with James Beattie that "the philosophy of Sympathy ought also to form a part of the science of Criticism."

Among critics who ultimately stem from the "moral sense" school, there is a strong inclination to maintain the intimate connection between imagination and "sensibility," and to assume, as John Ogilvie did, that "in proportion to the degree in which one takes place, will be always the poignancy and edge of the other." Extreme sensibility, and a consequent "enthusiasm" on the part of the poet, whether they were psychologically a part of imaginative action itself or whether they were externally complementary in their working with it, were especially necessary for the complete self-absorption of the poet in the object of his concern, and for the sympathetic understanding which he achieves by means of this absorption.[3]

The general eighteenth-century principle that, in order to comprehend and represent nature, one must posses above all an extensive knowledge of human nature in its various ramifications is naturally assumed as a necessary qualification for genuine sympathy. As Beattie, echoing Adam Smith, pointed out, we sympathize with what we know; and the wider our knowledge and experience, the wider is the scope of our sympathy and the juster and more accurate it is in perceiving the character and significance of its object. Yet the broadest knowledge of mankind, Beattie added, would not have enabled a poet like Blackmore to portray such characters as Homer's Achilles, Shakespeare's Othello, or Milton's Satan; for the hapless Blackmore was not endowed with that "sensibility" which "must first of all engage him warmly in his subject." The poet who aspires for lasting reputation "must not only study nature, and know the reality of things; but he must possess . . . sensibility, to enter with ardent enthusiasm into every part of his subject, so as to transfuse into his work a pathos and energy sufficient to raise corresponding emotions in his reader." Indeed, it is sensibility and "enthusiastic delight" which make fruitful and even possible the knowledge won from experience; enthusiasm rivets the attention; "He best shall paint them"—he quotes from Pope—"who can feel them most"; for close and accurate observation of nature, sustained over any period of time, "is to be expected from those only who take pleasure in it." And in one of his later works Beattie even maintained that sympathy was not only indispensable to poetic creation, but that, together with "liveliness" and "distinct apprehension" of imagination, it comprises "taste" itself; and if a reader lack "sympathy, it will be impossible for him to receive any true pleasure from a good poem, however skilled he may be in language and versification, and however well acquainted with the ordinary appearances of nature."

III

In successful sympathetic identification, whether directed to a moral or an aesthetic end, the necessary qualifications, on the one hand, of instinctive sensibility and imaginative fervor, and, on the other, of extensive acquaintance with human nature, are not to be viewed as separate in their use; they together comprise a single intuition, immediate and inevitable in its procedure, but none the less sagacious and informed. The distinctively British yoking of empiricism and intuitionalism, so frequently present in the whole of British philosophy, was especially assumed by critics who emphasized the importance of sympathetic participation. "Exquisite sensibility" and "the most copious imagination," said John Ogilvie, must be extensively schooled and disciplined by study and practical experience. This union of feeling, imagination, and experience constitutes "discernment," by means of which the poet is capable of

> entering deeply into the characters of those with whom he is conversant. He gains a facility of reading in the countenance those sensations, however closely concealed, that actuate the heart; and of collecting from casual, loose, and unsupported assertions thrown out apparently at random . . . such significant and distinguishing criteria as are decisive of their justness, propriety, and importance.[4]

However variously it may have shown itself in their works, said Ogilvie, "this facility of entering deeply into the feelings of the heart distinguishes principally those authors who will always stand in the highest rank of eminence"; and he would have agreed with Beattie that the verdict of time illustrates that no work of art "can give lasting delight to a moral being, but that which awakens sympathy." This faculty of identification is necessary not only in the creation of art, but also for taste itself. The general disposition of a critic of genuine taste is

> characterized by no circumstance more remarkably than its power of entering into a character when supplied with slight materials, and such as an ordinary mind would wholly overlook. . . . Thus it is that a discerning critic, attentive to the first dawning of genius, will discover in a few loose thoughts thrown out without much connection, the characters of an accurate or comprehensive understanding; and from a few strokes in the same manner of pathos or of description, will judge of the future extent, fertility, and even of the characteristical bias of imagination.[5]

But "discernment," whatever the elements that constitute it, is a single and integrated intuition: in seizing upon the interior workings of the mind and feelings of the person with whom it has become identified, it follows them "through all their windings, and the effects arising from each, however complicated," with an automatic immediacy; and it achieves a coalesced unity which cannot be grasped rationally or "by considering separately each particular part, however necessary to constitute a whole."

The instinctive working of sympathy and its prevalence in one form or another were further substantiated by British associationism. "Since the mind," said Joseph Priestley, "perceives, and is conscious of nothing, but the ideas that are present to it, it must, as it were, *conform* itself to them": dependent as it is upon sensation alone, it adapts itself to the character of what is immediately before it, and does it

> so instantaneously and mechanically, that no person whatever hath reflection . . . to be upon his guard against some of the most useless and ridiculous effects of it. What person, if he saw another upon a precipice and in danger of falling, could help starting back, and throwing himself into the same posture as he would do if he himself were going to fall? At least he would have a strong propensity to do it. And what is more common than to see persons in playing at bowls, lean their own bodies, and writhe them into every possible attitude, according to the course they would have their bowl to take? . . . The more vivid are a man's ideas, and the greater is his general sensibility, the more intirely, and with the greater facility, doth he adapt himself to the situations he is viewing.[6]

For not only are ideas associated with each other; but, as many British associationists showed, ideas, sensations, sentiments, and even muscular motions may all be as easily interrelated with each other by association; and indeed, the difference between an idea and a feeling is little more than a difference in intensity of realization. Thus one critic cited the manner in which Achilles' anger arises, at the thought of his injury, as revealing Homer's understanding of "a close linked connexion of ideas and sensations." Just as a certain idea, added Erasmus Darwin, may be association evoke the passion of anger, and this in turn the appropriate muscular response; so, by a kind of reverse process, if we assume

> the attitude that any passion naturally occasions, we soon in some degree acquire that passion; hence when those that scold indulge themselves in loud oaths, and violent action of the arms, they increase their anger by the mode of expressing themselves; and on the contrary the counterfeited smile of pleasure in disagreeable company soon brings along with it a portion of the reality.

This method of "entering into the passions of others is rendered of very extensive use by the pleasure we take in imitation." Though it may vary in degree, intelligence, and scope, a propensity to imitation of some sort is universally instinctive to the human mind; and it is simply from the same capacity, said Darwin, which underlies

> our aptitude for imitation, [that there] arises what is generally understood by the word of sympathy, so well explained by Dr. Smith of Glasgow. Thus the appearance of a cheerful countenance gives us pleasure, and of a melancholy one makes us sorrowful. Yawning and sometimes vomiting are thus propagated by sympathy, and some people of delicate fibres, at the presence of a spectacle of misery, have felt pain in the same parts of their own bodies, that were diseased or mangled in the other. Amongst the writers of antiquity, Aristotle thought this aptitude to imitation an essential property of the human species, and calls man an imitative animal.[7]

The insistence, by the more mechanistic associationists, that sympathy is an instinctive human response also manifests a growing critical attempt to find a more spontaneous and a more comprehensive means of grasping the distinctive character of a particular, whether it be an object or a person, and then of portraying it through some sort of "expression." In his *Essay on Taste* (1759), Alexander Gerard spoke of an innate "sensibility of heart," by means of which, in poetry and drama, we identify ourselves with the characters "and sympathize with every change in their condition." Hume had always maintained that sympathy "is nothing but the conversion of an idea into an impression by the force of the imagination": if the imagination and the capacity for sensibility are strong enough, in other words, an idea becomes more intensely and therefore more emotionally realized; and this impression, when

felt with sufficient vivacity, is in turn fused and transformed into the state of feeling or the general condition which was originally observed. In much the same way, Alexander Gerard implied that sympathy is a kind of general propensity of imagination and feeling which prepares the observer "for readily catching, as by infection, any passion": this propensity or "force of sympathy enlivens our *ideas* of the passions infused by it to such a pitch, as in a manner *converts* them to the passions themselves." These passions, raised in the beholder by the sympathetic observation of the passions of others, in turn catch and dominate his imagination, the performance of which is then comparable to that of a magnetic field:

> As the magnet selects from a quantity of matter the ferruginous particles, which happen to be scattered through it, without making an impression on other substances; so imagination, by a similar sympathy, equally inexplicable, draws out from the whole compass of nature such ideas as we have occasion for, without attending to any others.[8]

The previous chapter cited the manner in which, according to Gerard, a "passion" or a dominant association draws to itself, by an instinctive infallibility, all that is congruous or pertinent to its object, cause, or general character, and modifies these subordinate associations and directs them to a new and coalesced unity. The function of sympathy is that it serves as the basis, the medium, through which the passions or dominant associations operate in this almost magnetic creation or response; and according as sympathy has been broadened and rectified by experience and knowledge, those passions admitted, and the manner of their working, will be intellectually, morally, or aesthetically just and fruitful. This standpoint was later assumed even more by Richard Payne Knight, who took it for granted that practically all aesthetic pleasure arises from some aspect of "internal sympathy," and who especially maintained that it is "only by sympathy" that the emotions can in any way be connected with "taste."

IV

Sympathy, as an aesthetic conception, hardly tended to sanction an indiscriminate naturalism in art. The strongest sympathies, said Knight, are evoked by what we most admire. Thus, "it is not with the agonies of a man writhing in the pangs of death, that we sympathize, on beholding the celebrated group of Laocoön and his sons; . . . but it is with the energy and fortitude of mind, which those agonies call into action and display."[9] Similarly, the characters portrayed, he later stated, must be such that either liking or esteem is in some way present; it is solely with certain "energies of mind" of which we approve, and which are revealed by the character under generally significant circumstances, that any lasting sympathy can be had; and if such characters are completely absent, a dramatic work of art fails to call forth any genuine or widespread interest and, despite whatever merit it may otherwise have, becomes a temporary amusement.

At the same time, however, the doctrine of sympathy lent a strong encouragement to a certain verisimilitude of particular representation. For we also, said Beattie, sympathize with what we know: we realize what we see in the concrete more vividly than what we hear described; and accordingly a marked contrast was often drawn by some of the critics of the period between "representation" and "description." "Our sympathy," said Lord Kames, "is not raised by description. . . . It is this imperfection, . . . in the bulk of our plays, that confines our stage almost entirely to Shakespeare." "Naturalness" can be achieved, added Hugh Blair, only if the artist possesses "the power of entering deeply into the character he draws, of becoming for a moment the very person whom he exhibits, and of assuming all his feelings"; and he cited various dramas of the period as examples of the complete lack of this quality, and of the consequent use of the dialogue as a means of "describing" the characters rather than "representing" them. Homer was occasionally cited as the outstanding example of a sympathetic discernment strong enough to represent "natural" characters; but there was more disposition to agree with James Beattie, who considered that Shakespeare possessed so powerful a capacity to enter into his characters that, had he not employed comic admixture, his tragedies would have been too intense for any "person of sensibility" to watch. Shakespeare, said Elizabeth Montagu, had "the art of the Dervise, in the Arabian tales, who could throw his soul into the body of another man, and be at once possessed of his sentiments, adopt his passions, and rise to all the functions and feelings of his situation." Such statements foreshadow Keats's famous designation of Shakespeare as a man of great "negative capability," and Hazlitt's statement of him that

> He was nothing in himself; but he was all that others were, or that they could become. He not only had in himself the germs of every faculty and feeling, but he could follow them by anticipation, intuitively, into all their conceivable ramifications, through every change of fortune, or conflict of passion, or turn of thought. . . . He had only to think of anything in order to become that thing, with all the circumstances belonging to it.[10]

Sympathy, then, is elicited by the "natural" particular and not by what is generally or abstractly described. Yet in its conception of the particular, sympathetic understanding, since momentary reactions are only partial disclosures of a character, is not confined to the present: sentiments, associations, and motives will always depend on the antecedent state of mind, and the sympathetic imagination will grasp this progressive interworking in the characters which are its subject; in its portrayal of distress, for example, it will suggest, as Gerard said, "such circumstances of former prosperity as aggravate the present distress"—for this very aggravation is a part of the distinctive nature of the distress as it now is. Such imaginative projection, then, will "blend" together the past and present, and, said Ogilvie, perceive and exhibit the natural outlets, however small, which a disposition in the character will take, and "the influence of habit, prepossession, . . . and other such causes as contribute to form a variety of minds particularly investigated." For employing as it does the automatic "coalescing" capacity of association, sympathetic projection may be assumed to detect these aspects, ramifications, and disclosures of character, not as piecemeal or intellectually anatomized phenomena, but as being intrinsically centered in the concrete particular with which it has identified itself.

Romanticism extended the feeling of sympathy to a participation in external nature as well. "If a Sparrow comes before my Window," said Keats, "I take part in its existence and pick about the Gravel"; and he also spoke of the poet as

> the man who with a bird,
> Wren, or Eágle, finds his way to
> All its instincts.

The feeling for animals, however, was less definitely sympathetic than Keats would indicate, and tended to be an outflow of vague fellow-feeling rather than actual identification. We may recall, if a bit unfairly, such unfortunately extreme examples as Coleridge's address to the ass—"I hail thee *Brother*"—or Wordsworth's Peter Bell, who repents through sympathy with an ass, and asks

> When shall I be as good as thou?
> Oh! would, poor beast, that I had now
> A heart but half as good as thine!

It was in this more general and sentimental vein that the feeling for animals was occasionally reflected in the later eighteenth century. An associationist critic, Thomas Percival, felt, for example, that Dyer's unfortunate poem on sheep and the wool trade, *The Fleece* (1757), often neglected opportunities to exploit sympathy to its most exquisite pitch. Percival, who reminds one of such earlier benevolists as John Gilbert Cooper, said he had been "informed that, after the dam has been shorn, and turned into the fold to her lambs, they become estranged to her, and that a scene of reciprocal distress ensues; which a man of lively imagination, and tender feelings, might render highly interesting and pathetic." Lawrence Sterne, he added, would not have neglected such an opportunity; and Percival, who perhaps would have shared Walt Whitman's desire to "turn and live with the animals," became so moved by the prospect that he himself composed and inserted in his criticism the missing scene written "in the manner of Sterne."

Moreover, said Beattie, "We sympathize . . . even with things inanimate. To lose a staff we have long worn, to see in ruins a house in which we have long lived, may affect us . . . though in point of value the loss be nothing." Sympathy with the inanimate arises if we possess a "lively conception" of its significance or end. "Things inanimate," Wordsworth later said, can "speak to social reason's inner sense, With inarticulate language." It is in this respect that he achieved a gayety of spirits in the "jocund company" of the daffodils; and that during his youth, as he wrote in the *Prelude,* he

> was mounting now
> To such community with highest truth—
> A track pursuing, not untrod before,
> From strict analogies by thought supplied
> Or consciousnesses not to be subdued.
> To every natural form, rock, fruit, or flower,
> Even the loose stones that cover the highway,
> I gave a moral life: *I saw them feel,*
> *Or linked them to some feeling.*

A less effusive but more mechanically mimetic identification with the inanimate may extend to such phenomena as force or even form. "Sublimity," for example, has at all times the general association of power, whether magnitude, grandeur, or simply strength of emotion be the means by which it is communicated. Through a kind of identification with objects which have this association of great power, the consequent "expansion of mind" in the beholder results in a feeling of "noble pride." We may recall Richard Wagner's later almost empathic interpretation of the sublime in his essay on Beethoven. The mind, given expanse, finds its own power and that in which it participates combined. For since Lockean sensationalism has taught us that the mind is conscious only of the ideas that are present to it, the mind must, said Priestley, "conform" itself to them:

> and even the idea it hath of its own extent . . . must enlarge or contract with its field of view. By this means also, a person, for the time, enters into, adopts, and is actuated by the sentiments that are presented to his mind. . . . From this principle . . . ideas of our *own* greatness, dignity, and importance, are the result of our contemplating large and grand objects. This will be conspicuous when we consider the sublime.[11]

And these feelings of pride, of dignity, of expansion, elicited through identification, are projected upon the object or force and help to give it the character of sublimity. Moreover, aesthetic susceptibility to what we designate as "form" in classical sculpture, said Richard Payne Knight, arises as much from "mental sympathies" as does the pleasure from more individualistic portrayal: however general and ideal the representation, and however lacking may be individual "expression," the observer associates certain postures and general contours with specific "passions and dispositions of mind"; through his associations, his sympathies are elicited and read, so to speak, into the original aesthetic form.

Yet there is also an awareness that an associative identification may be achieved with even simple form as such. Keats, for example, later said that he could almost project himself into a moving billiard-ball, and conceive, as though these qualities were his own, its combined "roundness, smoothness and volubility and the rapidity of its motion." . . .

V

Whether it was applied to a virtual associative identification, or to an inner mechanical and mimetic conformity with an object or sound, or whether it revealed itself as merely as vague and frankly subjective outflow of sentiment, the development of the conception of sympathy may be cited as distinctively illustrating the manner in which empirical associationism befriended and combined with emotional intuitionalism. It may also serve, at least in some of its aspects, as a very characteristic example of the attempt to find, in the welter of individual and subjective response, some valid means of both moral and aesthetic understanding—a means, moreover, by which the direct impression of experience could be drawn upon. But if feeling transcends the logical process by sympathetically detecting and realizing qualities in the external world, it can also discern and satisfy more subjective values and reactions which are no less real. Analogies, for example, need not conform to strictly rational demands: what might logically appear as the most diverse phenomena may excite the same feeling and consequently form analogies which, though they obviously exist to the human organism alone, are none the less true and valid simply because they *are* human responses. The employment of these analogies in art is thus not only justifiable; it may even be said to reveal a certain truth about the nature of subjective feeling itself and also to show a fuller significance, in human terms, in any phenomenon which is portrayed.

One of the most characteristic indications of this romantic attitude was a growing concern with what has since been called "synaesthesia": perceptions which come by means of different senses may strike a common emotional note; it is the subjective emotion which is important rather than the perception; and greater subtlety and richer scope may be attained in any art by exploiting this communality of impression and overcoming the division of the senses. The interworking of the senses, as an aesthetic goal, attained considerable vogue on the continent during the nineteenth century: Wagner's *Gesammtkunst,* or "art-work of the future," in which the separate arts are to be fused together, is characteristic of it; and Irving Babbitt has illustrated its extensive appearance in France and the occasionally amusing extremes it reached there.

Synaesthesia was almost as extensive but far more moderate in English romanticism; and its use in English poetry was rather to give, as it were, an additional dimension to an image by bringing to bear the further interpretation of another sense. Thus, Keats may use such phrases as "embalmèd darkness," "shadows of melodious utterance," "the *touch of scent,*" or "bowers of *fragrant* and enwreathèd *light.*" Or he may make incense almost tangible by calling it "soft" and by picturing it as "hanging":

> I cannot see what flowers are at my feet
> Nor what *soft incense hangs* upon the boughs.

The poet, said Coleridge, must command "what Bacon calls the *vestigia communia* of the senses, the latency of all in each, and more especially as by a magical *penna duplex,* the excitement of vision by sound and the exponents of sound." Similarly, Hazlitt defined "gusto" as a powerful vitality of feeling which, when called forth, pervades and dominates the senses with a synthetic and unifying control: it is possessed by an artist when "the impressions made on one sense excite by affinity those of another"; and Hazlitt complained of Claude Lorraine's landscapes that "they do not interpret one sense by another . . . that is, his eye wanted imagination: it did not sympathize with his other faculties. He saw the atmosphere, but did not *feel* it."[12]

Synaesthesia, at least in England, was one of the many progeny of eighteenth-century British associationism. Sir Isaac Newton, at the beginning of the century, had attempted to coördinate mathematically the colors refracted by a prism with the notes of the octave. In France, not long after, Father Castel, who decided that there was nothing like carrying a matter to its logical conclusion, built his intriguing color-clavichord. Thus the note *do,* because of an intrinsic "majesty," was equated with blue; *re,* because of a rural, sprightly quality, with green; and *sol,* which he considered a warlike and angry note, with red. We are told that the persevering Castel even considered performing concerts of perfumes by means of a clavichord of scent-boxes. Shortly after the middle of the century, synaesthesia was treated with occasional seriousness in England. Locke had told of a blind man who likened scarlet to the sound of a trumpet. The story had since been often repeated as an illustration of the imagination's potentialities for error; but it was now sometimes quoted with commendation of the blind man's perspicacity! Several associationists began to discuss the emotional

interrelation of sight, sound, and touch. A familiar example is Edmund Burke's inclusion of smoothness as one of the properties of the beautiful; for there is a "chain," he said, "in all our sensations; they are all but different sorts of *feelings* calculated . . . to be affected after the same manner." . . .

VI

The emotions of man have common ground: the intensity set up by one provides easy access for the admission of a further emotion; and grief, love, anger, hate, and fear may all easily pass into each other. The border line between feelings, indeed, is so thin as to be almost hypothetical. The framework of the passions, as Hume had said,

> is not like a wind instrument, which, in running over all the notes, immediately loses the sound when the breath ceases; but rather resembles a string-instrument, where, after each stroke, the vibrations still retain some sound. . . . Each stroke will not produce a clear and distinct note of passion, but the one passion will always be mixed . . . with the other.[15]

This conception of the interworking and interfluctuation, so to speak, of the passions was extended by several associationist critics; and one may note, in such extensions, an emergence of the romantic confidence that, whereas reason, in Schlegel's words, "can only comprise each object separately, . . . *Feeling* perceives all in all at one and the same time," and hence is susceptible to certain analogies which could not otherwise be descried. There seems to be a general assumption that, with one feeling inevitably exciting another by affinity, man's emotional nature is almost a kind of sounding board: that an impression may there give rise to a general reverberation, as it were, which will in turn, by a kind of reverse procedure, again find outward analogy and expression in other, externally different perceptions and inclinations. The development of this general premise would not only account for such ramifications as associational synaesthesia or as the subjectively felt analogies between sensations and emotions themselves; it would also be one of the contributing elements to the common romantic emphasis on "suggestiveness."

At least one aspect of the evolution of the conception of "sublimity" pertinently illustrates the progressive working towards "suggestiveness," The state of elevation or transport which Longinus had postulated as characteristic of the sublime was one which had as its end the insight into the ideal or the universal. Empiricism, with its confidence in sensation alone, quickly sanctioned a tendency to regard sublimity as simply an exhilaration which is evoked by contemplating what is large enough to challenge conception to its fullest exertion. The influence of Locke's sensationalism on

Addison's conception of "greatness" is characteristic: by the sight of great magnitude, the imagination is "flung into a pleasing astonishment," and both mind and the emotions—since their condition is determined by their objects—are thus completely released from "restraint."

By the middle of the century, sublimity had become almost synonymous with the highest possible emotion which could be aroused. It was with this belief that Edmund Burke, in his famous work on *The Origin of Our Ideas of the Sublime and Beautiful* (1757), made terror a basis of sublimity; for whatever "operates in a manner analogous to terror . . . is productive of the strongest emotion which the mind is capable of feeling." A less frankly sensationalistic and certainly a less terror-ridden interpretation quickly ensued. Sublimity might be equated with "magnitude," "majesty," or "grandeur"; or more often, among the associationists, with anything which suggested "force" or "power." But in almost all cases the sublime, as one writer said, "dilates and expands the mind, and puts its grasp to trial"; and it is conceded to be that which displays—and demands from the beholder—the most vigorous response of imagination and feeling. Familiar illustrations of this sublime vigor are Homer, Shakespeare, Milton, and the Bible, especially the books of Isaiah and Job. A number of patriotic Scots, moreover, never failed to instance also Macpherson's Ossianic forgeries, which swept much of Europe and were dear to the heart of Napoleon, but which Reynolds cited as an example of the "false sublime" and Johnson thought could have been written by "many men, many women, and many children."

The frequent opposing of sublimity to the artificial, the sophisticated, and the weakly regular may be exemplified by such works as William Duff's *Essay on Original Genius* (1767). "The sublime," said Duff, "is the proper walk of a great Genius, in which it delights to range, and in which alone it can display its powers to advantage, or put forth its strength." Any emotion which is capable of attaining genuine elevation partakes of sublimity when it is sufficiently intense and searching; hence writers from Duff to Knight streesed the intimate connection between the sublime and the pathetic; and Knight added that, when felt with enough vitality, all sympathetic identification is sublime. But "it is one thing," as Burke said, "to make an image clear, and another to make it affecting to the imagination"; and whatever may constitute sublimity, it is always strongly favored by a certain amount of "obscurity." "We yield to sympathy," added Burke, "what we refuse to description." In Homer's one opening line about the wrath of Achilles, said Ogilvie, he suggests a "hero unbridled, furious, implacable, resentful"; but in the *Aeneid,* Virgil "poens his subject with a detail of circumstances which . . . strike not the mind so forcibly

when taken together as the single stroke of his inimitable rival."

For the vitality and vigor with which the sublime is felt arises less from sensation than from an energetically subjective activity of the mind; and whatever "increases this exercise or employment of Imagination," stated Alison, "increases also the *emotion* of beauty or sublimity." The unstated and indefinite encourages this exercise. A thunderstorm, continued Alison, is customarily considered sublime; "but there is a low and feeble sound which precedes it, more sublime in reality than all the uproar of the storm itself." The premonition of what is to come, either in nature or in a work of art, tempts a creative and independent reaction from the observer, reader, or hearer: it incites a deeper tension, in which are concentrated and resolved all felt anticipations and images which he can associate with what is to follow. It is largely because it excites a more energetic response of imagination and feeling that the sublime is profounder in effect than the beautiful. For art can most successfully elicit feeling and secure a consequent sympathetic understanding only when, disregarding entrance by piecemeal perception of detail, it penetrates at once to the emotional frame, and, arousing there "a strong working of mind," as Coleridge later said, effects a complete "substitution of a sublime *feeling* of the unimaginable for a mere image."

VII

Suggestiveness also becomes a necessary means in proportion to the degree that an aesthetic object is employed for "expression" rather than "*im*pression." For expression strives, through suggestion, to disclose what is beyond the formal quality of the object. It thus transcends the limitations of what could at any one time be known through an intrinsic presentation; and by doing so, it achieves a superior scope and variety, and a more multiform plexus of potential meaning. Its use in humanistic classicism is less pronounced, and is also channeled towards a determined end: the suggestion, for example, in classical sculpture, of a potential readiness for all possible rounded and liberal activities is a suggestion which is always subdued to an ideal decorum and consonance; and its implication of the universal is combined with an almost imposed clarity of purpose and form. The romantic employment of expression is more restless: it reveals a decreased confidence in the intrinsic value of immediate aesthetic form; and it seeks less to declare the harmony and order of the determined or the given than to awaken an inference or feeling of the undetermined or the undeclared. In its attempt to evoke inference rather than to impose form, and thus to appeal directly to the individual associations or feelings of the beholder, romantic suggestiveness had several later ramifications, which might vary from the occasional nineteenth-century cult of "magic" and "wonder"—the romantic period, said Theodore Watts-Dunton, was "the renascence of wonder"—to the hardly less subjective but highly intellectualized symbolism which somewhat succeeded it. As it is most successfully present in English romanticism, however, the use of suggestion, though primarily emotional and even subjective in its effect, tended to be centripetal instead of extreme or deliberate.

In addition to the greater number of ideas and of nuances of feeling which suggestiveness, by going beyond the object, can excite, the very activity of mind which is aroused is one of the primary satisfactions which art can give. "Nothing more powerfully excites any affection," Hume had stated, "than to conceal some part of its object, by throwing it into a kind of shade, which, at the same time that it shows enough to prepossess us in favor of the object, leaves still some work for the imagination." Critics of the later eighteenth century frequently insisted that resemblance must never be too exact in art. Much of aesthetic pleasure, said Adam Smith, is determined by the very "degree of disparity between the imitating and the imitated object": imitation fruits and flowers, for example, please far less than a mere picture of them, and painted statues have less appeal than unpainted ones. By summoning up an active response of imagination and feeling, moreover, an augmented vitality of realization is made possible. Erasmus Darwin, speaking of the importance of suggestiveness, mentioned a sketch of "a shrivelled hand stretched through an iron grate in the stone floor of a prison-yard, to reach at a mess of porrage, which affected me with more horrid ideas of the distress of the prisoner in the dungeon below than could have been perhaps produced by an exhibition of the whole person."[16]

Similarly, in poetry, metaphors must not be too close, nor descriptions too detailed. Darwin cited the brief, pathetic statement of Lear: "Pray you, undo this button. Thank you, Sir." Here the "oppression at the bosom of the dying King is made visible, not described in words." By the use of "the language of suggestion," wrote Richard Edgeworth, "Agamemnon hiding his face at the sacrifice of his daughter expresses little to the eye, but much to the imagination." Or in the line, "Springs upward like a Pyramid of fire," Milton, said Beattie, evokes a conception, all at one instant, both of Satan's enormous size and refulgent appearance and of motion so swift "as to appear a continued track of light, and lessening to the view according to the increase of distance, till it end in a point, and then disappear."

Indeed, because of its capacity for immediate penetration, poetry is often stressed by some of the later associationists as superior to the visual arts. "The Painter addresses himself to the Eye," said Alison; "the Poet speaks to the Imagination"; and the statement was something of a commonplace by the end of the century. The

"presence of genius," Coleridge later maintained, is not shown by

> elaborating a picture: we have had many specimens of this sort of work in modern poems, where all is so dutchified, if I may use the word, by the most minute touches, that the reader naturally asks why words, and not painting, are used. . . . The power of poetry is, by a single word, perhaps, *to instil energy into the mind, which compels the imagination to produce the picture.* Prospero tells Miranda,

> One midnight,
> Fated to the purpose, did Antonio open
> The gates of Milan; and i' the dead of darkness,
> The ministers for the purpose hurried thence
> Me, and thy *crying* self.

Here, by introducing a single happy epithet, "crying," . . . a complete picture is presented to the mind, and in the production of such pictures the power of genius consists.[17]

For man's inner reservoir of feeling, perpetually animated by the ready creative impulse of the imagination, responds, when given a suggestive fillip, with a faithful re-creation of its own which is more vitally appreciated and more sympathetically comprehended than any merely passive and externally noted observation could be. And, in its act of re-creation, it achieves an intensity of conception from which the extraneous and the discordant "evaporate," and which is therefore able to divine certain relations, qualities, and energies hitherto unapparent. "The excellence of every art," said Keats, "is its intensity, capable of making all disagreeables evaporate from their being in close relationship with Beauty and Truth." In the unity of creative insight which this intensity produces, the complete meaning and character of its object stand revealed as a sudden "swelling into reality"—a reality, Keats said, which is "all ye know on earth," and which, because it is the true, the vital, the significant, is also seen as the beautiful.

Notes

[1] August Wilhelm von Schlegel, *Lectures on Dramatic Art and Literature* (1809-1811), Lect. xxii.

[2] James Arbuckle, *Collection of Letters and Essays* (1722), I, 33-34 (No. 4).

[3] Adam Smith, *Theory of Moral Sentiments* (2nd ed., 1762), p. 2.

[4] John Ogilvie, *Philosophical and Critical Observations on the Nature, Characters, and Various Species of Composition* (1774), I, 178, 282-283, and *passim.*

[5] *Ibid.,* I, 220-221.

[6] Joseph Priestley, *Course of Lectures on Oratory and Criticism* (1777), pp. 126-127.

[7] Erasmus Darwin, "Of Instinct," *Zoonomia* (1794-1796), I, 146-147.

[8] Alexander Gerard, *Essay on Taste* (1759), pp. 173-174.

[9] Richard Payne Knight, "Of the Passions," *An Analytical Inquiry into the Principles of Taste* (2nd ed., 1805), p. 335.

[10] William Hazlitt, *Lectures on the English Poets* (1818-1819), *Works* (ed. Howe, 1931-1934), V, 47-48.

[11] Joseph Priestley, *A Course of Lectures on Oratory and Criticism* (1777), pp. 126-127.

[12] Hazlitt, "On Gusto," *Works* (ed. Howe, 1931-1934), IV, 78-79. . . .

[15] Hume, "Dissertation on the Passions" (1757), *Works* (1854), IV, 191.

[16] Darwin, *Botanic Garden* (1789-1791), II, 125-126.

[17] Coleridge, *Shakespearean Criticism* (ed. Raysor, Cambridge, Mass.: 1930), II, 174.

W. J. Bate (essay date 1965)

SOURCE: "The English Poet and the Burden of the Past, 1660-1820," in *Aspects of the Eighteenth Century*, edited by Earl R. Wasserman, The Johns Hopkins Press, 1965, pp. 245-64.

[*In the following excerpt Bate discusses ways in which eighteenth-century English poets dealt with the "burden of the past"—the intimidation of obviously superior earlier poetry—by following the new Preromantic ideals of originality and sincerity.*]

I

The theme of this essay could be expressed by a remark Johnson quotes from Pliny in one of the *Ramblers* (No. 86): "The burthen of government is increased upon princes by the virtues of their immediate predecessors." And Johnson goes on to add: "He that succeeds a celebrated writer, has the same difficulties to encounter."

I have often wondered whether we could find any more comprehensive way of taking up the whole of English poetry from the middle seventeenth century down to the present—or for that matter the modern history of the arts as a whole—than by exploring the effects of this accumulating anxiety and the question it so direct-ly presents to the poet or artist: What is there left to do? Yet this is not a subject we seem tempted to pursue. As critics or historians, we too often tend to focus on one of two things. We either concentrate on the writer's "subjects" (what he is obviously writing *about,* or what he says elsewhere is concerning him), or, if we prefer to be more indirect or subtle and try to look beneath the surface, we concentrate on what interests us and what we therefore feel should be interesting or motivating him, whether it be a "climate of ideas" or psychoanalytic preoccupations.

Unlike the poet, the critic or historian always has a subject matter—literature itself (or the other arts). And as for finding a new "idiom" in which to express himself, any difficulties in doing so are not only rudimentary in comparison but usually unnecessary. Relatively unbothered by any sharp personal experience of the same sort, we continue to remain oblivious because of the natural pride and embarrassed silence of the writer himself. The writer or artist may be self-revealing enough in other ways. But when his anxiety has to do with the all-important matter of his craft, and his achievement or impotence there, he naturally prefers to wrestle with it privately or to express it only indirectly. The subject, in other words, is not one for which we can compile a clean-cut reading list. We begin to sense its importance only when we look between the lines, or follow closely the life of writer after writer, or weigh the context of self-defensive manifestoes or fatalistic excuses in eras of militant transition in style, and, above all, when we note the nagging apprehension, from generation to generation, that the poet is somehow becoming increasingly powerless to attain (or is in some way being forbidden to try to attain) the scope and power of the earlier poetry that he so deeply admires.

We need, as historians, to keep in mind what it means to artists and writers to come immediately after a great creative era. We need to keep in mind the natural anxieties, the intimidations, the temptations to paralysis, their understandable desire to establish themselves, and the appeal of different procedures from those they have been accustomed to admire. The burden of the past upon the writers of eighteenth-century England is an immensely fruitful subject—fruitful for understanding the general situation, in some ways the nature of the achievement, not only of this period but also of the Romantics, the Victorians, and the twentieth century. We could, in fact, make a very good argument that this remorseless deepening of self-consciousness, before the rich and intimidating legacy of the past, becomes the greatest single problem that modern art (art, that is to say, since the close of the seventeenth century) has had to face, and that it will become so increasingly in the future.

In comparison, most of the "ideas" or preoccupations that we extract (as conflicts, goals, or anxieties) and then picture as so sharply pressing on the mind of the artist are often less directly urgent. We need, as Johnson often reminds us, to remember that the critic or historian of the arts as well as the artist himself have very different vocations, however much their interests overlap or intertwine. The critic or historian of the arts, as we have said, can always find a subject matter. He may have his own anxieties and uncertainties. But he is at least not in competition with Shakespeare or Milton, Dryden or Pope, Wordsworth or Keats. The poet, on the other hand, is unavoidably aware, in a very direct and concrete sense, of previous writers, and never so much as when he tries to establish a difference; and he is keenly aware of them in a way that he is not (if he is writing in the early eighteenth century) of Newton, Locke, or Shaftesbury. Newtonian philosophy, ideals of order and decorum, or Shaftesburian benevolence may all have concerned eighteenth-century poets. It is taken for granted that they have an important place in our consideration of what the English poetry of the eighteenth century became. The point is merely that these poets also had one very direct problem that was at least as absorbing to them, and often far more so: the stark problem of what and how to write.

So with the English Romantics. Keats, who certainly faced enough personal difficulties, would become really despondent (except after his fatal illness began) only when, as he told his friend Richard Woodhouse, he felt that "there was nothing original to be written in poetry; that its riches were already exhausted—and all its beauties forestalled." Goethe rejoiced that he was not born an Englishman and did not have to compete with the achievement of Shakespeare. The situation is the same when we move on to the Victorians or to the first half of the twentieth century: these writers, we say, were faced with a difficult situation, which we then proceed briskly to document—the decline of faith, the lack of certainty in moral as well as religious values. All this is true (and is true of certain earlier eras). But the pessimism we explain with such a cumbersome machinery of ideas has often an even sharper, more immediate spur—the nagging questions: what is there left to write? and how, as craftsmen, do we get not only new subjects but a new idiom? A great deal of modern literature—and criticism—is haunted, as Spender says, by the thought of a "Second Fall of Man," and almost everything has been blamed: the Renaissance loss of the medieval unity of faith, Baconian science, British empiricism, Rousseau, the French Revolution, industrialism, nineteenth-century science, universities and academicism, the growing complexity of ordinary life, the spread of mass media. But whatever else enters into the situation, the principal explanation is the writer's loss of self-confidence as he compares what he feels able to do with the rich heritage of past art and literature. Scientists, we notice, are not affected with this despondency. And we do not account for that interesting exception, or for any number of other exceptions that enter into the picture, if we try to attribute it to mere insensitivity.

II

If you took up English neoclassicism solely in the light of what we call the "history of ideas," it could still remain one of the great unresolved puzzles of literary history. No explanation for it—at least no explanation why it caught on so quickly and firmly after 1660—would satisfy anyone for very long except the person who provides it.

Let me hurry to say that I am not speaking of English neoclassic *theory*—that is of neoclassic critical writing. It is only too easy, if we confine ourselves to the history of critical theory, to trace an ancestral line through Sidney and Ben Jonson down to the Restoration (the history of critical theory is by definition a history of *ideas*). And if we want more help, we have merely to turn to the intellectual history of England during the sixteenth and seventeenth centuries and we can find any number of ideas, if not ancestral at least collateral, to enrich our genealogical chart. But once the glow of discovery has faded, the result is not really very persuasive except to the confirmed Hegelian, of which there are twentieth as well as nineteenth-century varieties. Our consciences begin to remind us that, as historians of ideas, we are naturally swayed by special interests. We have a vocational interest in presupposing that there is a relatively clean-cut influence of "ideas" on artists, meaning, by "ideas," concepts that we, as historians, have abstracted from a large, diverse period of human life, and which may very well have struck our attention only because they are so susceptible of genealogy. Of course we all say—and say it quite sincerely—that what we are really interested in is the *reciprocal* influence of ideas and art. But it is so difficult to put neatly the influence of art, in all its diversity, on the climate of ideas. To the orderly mind of the historian, this task is as elusive, or as unmanageably messy, as having to describe and categorize the influence of people on ideas. We find ourselves feeling that it is better to leave all that for some future, more leisurely consideration. Hence, in our actual practice if not in ultimate ideal, we lean radically toward the simplicities of thinking in terms of a one-way traffic.

A sense of all this begins to nag the conscience after we trace our genealogies of ideas in order to explain English neoclassicism: the rephrasing, by sixteenth- and seventeenth-century critics, of classical ideals; the premium on decorum, refinement, regularity, and the ways in which they are particularized; the confidence in method; the influence of mathematics. Are these ideas, these concepts and values, that we have abstracted, not progenitors after all of the actual neoclassic literature to come, but only midwives, escorts, even (to quote Eliot) "attendant persons"? Putting it another way: were these particular concepts and ideas such that they would have been left undeveloped, would have fallen on deaf ears, unless there had also been *other* considerations, equally or perhaps more important?

We know very well, for example, that English literature itself, from the time of Elizabeth down into the middle seventeenth century, showed a diversity that has been unrivaled since the most fertile days of Athens. We also know that it showed, at its best, a power or intensity in its diversity (in idiom, in metaphor, in cadence) that has haunted English literature ever since that time. And this literature was written at the same time as those more theoretical works to which we are looking for the ancestry of English neoclassicism. We know that the intensity and diversity of that literature (or, putting it more truthfully, an intensity both of, and within, diversity) far outweighs our thin sketch of theoretical or merely critical concepts through the Elizabethan and Jacobean eras. To put it bluntly: it is not at all from English life and English experience in its widest sense, from the time of Elizabeth through that of Cromwell, that a really developed neoclassicism came so suddenly. We know perfectly well that systematized and pervasive neoclassicism is very much a French product, and that it was in fact viewed as that (whether with respect, restiveness, or antagonism) by the English themselves, from Dryden, Rymer, and Temple down to Hazlitt and Francis Jeffrey, a century and a half later.

Then why did English neoclassicism occur? We are always being reminded that these values of the "New Classicism" of France never sat too easily on the English mind. Of course they did not. In fact, they were always being qualified by native English attitudes; and (though we have recently tended to exaggerate the amount) there was a good deal of open dissent. But this makes the matter all the more curious: Why should it have flourished so rapidly when there was this much tendency to dissent and qualify? There is, in fact, nothing else in the whole of the long literary history of England quite like this brisk transition. There is no other instance, after the invention of printing, where you find a settled group of literary premises and aims imported almost bodily, adopted with such dispatch, and then transformed into orthodoxy, or near-orthodoxy, for so long a time (a full seventy or eighty years), despite a large undercurrent that runs counter to it. Of the three really great transitions in English poetry since the Elizabethans and Jacobeans, this is the first. The second is found in the large shift that took place in the late eighteenth and early nineteenth centuries, and the third in the radical change of idiom and mode during the first half of the twentieth century. But the second of these transitions, to which we apply the loose word "romantic," was the reverse in almost every way from what we are considering now. To begin with, it was slower and longer prepared for in the actual writing (as distinct from critical theory) that preceded it. It emerged

from within the neoclassic stronghold, opening the walls one by one. To a large extent it was demonstrably— even dramatically—a nationalistic movement in England (as it was in another, more pronounced way, in Germany). When we turn to our own era, we have to admit that the transition to the new poetic idiom of the early and middle twentieth century was rapid, and that it was analogous to the neoclassic transition in speed as well as in other ways. On the other hand, this radical modern change was less metaphysically rationalized; in some ways it was closer to its own immediate past (the English romantics) than Pope ever was to Shakespeare or Milton; nor was it—despite the influence of the French Symbolists and of others—a continental importation: too much else, by that time, was already going on within the English-speaking world generally.

III

To the England of the Restoration and the early eighteenth century, the mature and sophisticated neoclassicism of France had an irresistible appeal. It gave them a chance to be different from their own immediate English predecessors while at the same time, it offered a counterideal that was impressively—almost monolithically—systematized. French neoclassicism appeared to have answers ready for almost any kind of objection to it. And most of the answers had this further support: they inevitably referred—or pulled the conscience back— to the premises of "reason" and of ordered nature that the English themselves were already sharing, though not perhaps in the same spirit as the French. To dismiss an argument that led directly back to "reason" was something they were not at all prepared to do. Even the more articulate writers still lacked the vocabulary to express any hesitations they might have felt. And in any case, had not their own English Newton already helped to disclose the universal architecture, and to an extent that no Frenchman had done?—Newton, as James Thomson later said, "whom God / To mortals lent to trace his boundless works."

But to the English—if not the French at this particular time—there was a built-in conflict in what this welcome new body of ideals carried. On the one hand, they found themselves embracing the classical ideal that really great art was *general;* and this, by definition, seemed to imply that great art naturally concerns itself with the most widely applicable subjects and in doing so reaches a wide audience. Yet at the same time this new classical art, this neoclassicism of France, openly cultivated what the English eighteenth century (and, in a curious way, the English romantics) called "refinement." The French could meet and absorb this challenge; the English could not. "Refinement," in this new systematized model of how to proceed, could be admitted as both new and desirable. But the ideal of "generality" brought back to the English mind their own past creative achievement—Shakespeare and Milton especially. Critics could tell them that Waller and Denham had brought to English poets the new, cherished values of "refinement"—cleanliness, smoothness, urbanity, and sophistication. But, after admitting this, where was the "generality" (generality in the grander sense of the word—"the *grandeur* of generality," to use Johnson's phrase)? Dryden—however bland, self-controlled, self-confident, and, in the best sense of the word, negligent—had himself slightly chafed beneath this dichotomy. He swung back and forth. But always, in thinking of the rich English past, he was aware of "the giants before the flood" (we see this in the *Essay of Dramatic Poesy:* the dice there are secretly loaded on the side of his great English progenitors), and, in speaking of Shakespeare, he could say enviously that "All the images of nature were *still present* to him." Pope also would speak differently at different times. But one thing that remained with him was that early advice from William Walsh: "Mr. Walsh . . . used to tell me that there was *one way left of excelling;* for though we had several great poets, we never had any one great poet that was correct; and he desired me to make that my study and aim." Pope could say that "Nature and Homer were the same"; he could himself translate Homer; and he could contemplate writing a blank-verse epic on a legendary British hero. Nevertheless this gifted poet—certainly one of the eight or ten greatest in the entire history of English letters—settled in practice for the more specialized (and newer) quality of "refinement"; this at least, for the English poet, remained as "one way left of excelling."

But whatever Pope's individual success (and that itself created a further problem for still later poets) the classical ideal of generality, of scope in subject and breadth of appeal, continued to bring back the question: what has happened to the "greater genres," to epic and dramatic tragedy? That question, and all it implies, was to haunt the English poet henceforth. Take just three instances, purposely selected because each writer is so masculinely vigorous and independent. Johnson, loathing any cant about "decline" or anything else that reflected on man's freedom—Johnson who was "always angry," as he said, "whenever he heard earlier periods extolled at the expense of the modern"—could still permit Imlac to say that, whatever, the nation and language and however different the explanations offered, "it is commonly observed that the early writers are in possession of nature, and their followers of art: that the first excel in strength and invention, and the latter in elegance and refinement." Keats could compare the ancients and the Elizabethans to "Emperors of vast Provinces," while by contrast "each of the moderns like an Elector of Hanover keeps his petty state." And, to glance ahead another hundred years, there are those lines of Yeats:

> Shakespearean fish swam the sea, far away
>   from land;

> Romantic fish swam in nets coming to the hand;
> What are all those fish that lie gasping on the
>   strand?

IV

By the middle of the eighteenth century, after a hundred years of the English neoclassic adventure in the arts, we find an almost universal suspicion that something had somehow gone wrong. And nothing could be historically more shortsighted and parochial than to associate that feeling, as has so often been done, merely with a budding "romanticism" restive against "neoclassic restriction." The uneasiness went far deeper and afflicted those who sympathized with the stylistic mode, or modes, of neoclassic poetry. This is especially true by the second half of the century. Who are the conservatives who leap to mind? They are men like Burke, who hungered for amplitude and the "sublime," or the classically minded Reynolds, who found himself, as he grew older, thinking of Michelangelo and longing for the scope and power associated with the lost "sublime." As conservatives in poetry we think of Johnson and Goldsmith. Yet there is that illuminating moment when Boswell tells Johnson of a dispute between the Augustan-minded Goldsmith and Robert Dodsley the publisher. Goldsmith had maintained that there was no

> poetry produced in this age. Dodsley appealed to his own Collection, and maintained, that though you could not find a palace like Dryden's "Ode on St. Cecilia's Day," you had villages composed of very pretty houses; and he mentioned particularly "The Spleen." JOHNSON. "I think Dodsley gave up the question. He and Goldsmith said the same thing; only he said it in a softer manner than Goldsmith did; for he acknowledged that there was no poetry, nothing that towered above the common mark."

These conservatives are simply thinking and reacting in the vein typified by Sir William Temple, two or three generations before: that of an intelligent and well-read Englishman who has been brought up on the classics, and who is looking for the exemplification of broad classical values in the literature of his own day. (To say this is not to deny that Temple also said some silly things. It is easy to pick holes in what he says about literature; but we, as historians, have the accumulated labors of two and a half centuries of criticism and scholarship to permit us our superiority.)

Whatever else can be said of the spate of critical writing that suddenly begins in the middle of the eighteenth century, we can describe it as an attempt (however confused) to reground the entire thinking about poetry in the light of one overwhelming fact: the obviously superior originality and at least an apparently greater immediacy and universality of subject and appeal in the poetry of earlier periods. The regrounding brought with it the fear—more openly expressed than ever before in history—that literature and the other arts as well were threatened with decline.[1] This was not at all the result of reading Vico (of whom few had heard) or of reading reflections by others who had read Vico. Nor is the matter disposed of by saying that "progress" is a "romantic" idea and that thoughts of the "Golden Age" or of historical cycles are natural to a neoclassical period. Least of all do we show much insight when we mutter that this apprehension is an old one and cite once again the sixteenth-and seventeenth-century writers who dwell on the "decay of nature." The sort of anxiety of which we are now speaking is very different from the idea of the "decay of nature." In fact, the people who felt it most strongly were those who believed most in progress in other ways—for whom the decline in the arts was the unfortunate by-product of the increase in knowledge, communication, taste, and general civilization. And in any case we should remember that the practicing writer is quite capable of falling into apprehensions without the aid of the philosopher—especially when the cards appear to be stacked against him. This has been possible for a very long time. I think of the poignant epigram left by an Egyptian writer of 2000 B.C. (Khakheperresenb): "Would I had phrases that are not known, utterances that are strange, in new language that hath not been used, free from repetition, not an utterance which hath grown stale, which men of old have spoken."

Several diagnoses were advanced, many of them dovetailing with the discussion of other matters. There were the outright primitivists (so often discussed apart from this pressing, personal concern on the part of the writer). Earlier, more primitive folk, as Thomas Blackwell said in his *Enquiry into the Life and Writings of Homer* (1735), "lived naturally": their passions were simple, direct and intense; their conversation did not consist of "the Prattle, and little pretty Forms that enervate a polished Speech" in the later periods of a culture. This approach continues without interruption and with increasing sophistication until it culminates in Wordsworth's great preface to the *Lyrical Ballads* at the end of the century. It can be hopeful (as it is in Wordsworth)—assuming that we are free, if we want, to get back to the "essential passions." But more often it assumes that the door is closed. The best example I can think of is William Duff's *Essay of Original Genius* (1767), the concluding chapter of which bears the long title (here abbreviated): "That Original Poetic Genius Will in General Be Displayed in Its Ultimate Vigour in the Early . . . Periods of Society . . . and That It Will Seldom Appear in a Very Great Degree in Cultivated Life."

Other diagnoses, which included a fair admixture of the primitivistic spirit, focused on specific factors. An example is John Brown's *Dissertation on the Rise,*

Union, and Power, the Progressions, Separations, and Corruptions of Poetry and Music (1763). The tendency of the arts to "divide" and specialize was also applied to language itself. Few of the rhetorics and general studies of language, during the later eighteenth century, failed to note that metaphor and with it poetic "suggestiveness" in general are gradually lost as a language becomes more exact and denotative through use and through the growth of a more analytic writing. Before long everyone was agreeing. Typically, when a small discussion group was founded in Manchester (The Literary and Philosophical Society of Manchester), one of the papers in their first volume (1781-83) could stress that a language was more poetic in its earlier stages; that poetic feeling later becomes "minced into finer portions," and that therefore a "strong poetic character may be expected to decline, as Taste improves."

Still others, in searching for an explanation, found it in the self-consciousness and timidity created by the growth of criticism—a growth considered inevitable as a culture grows older and a part of the price paid for the spread of literacy. Sir William Temple had implied as much. But it is now, in the mid-eighteenth century, that the thought is really grasped at, in the hope of finding some simple explanation. There is the well-known remark in Joseph Warton's *Essay on Pope* (1756)—well-known because even Johnson thought it one that "deserves great attention": "In no polished nation, after criticism has been much studied, and the rules of writing established, has any very extraordinary work ever appeared." This is a central point in Goldsmith's *Enquiry into the Present State of Polite Learning* (1759), and Goldsmith did much to popularize it. Yet the idea, however common, is never treated too seriously (partly, of course, because critics—who would naturally be the ones to pursue the idea—were not eager to argue against the basis of what they themselves spent their time pursuing).

The real interest of this attitude appears indirectly: that is, in its underlying sense of how much intimidation may have to do with the writer's fluency and what he tries to attain. And Edward Young, in the *Conjectures on Original Composition* (1759), faces the whole matter of intimidation directly, though he is thinking less about the effect of criticism than about the intimidating pressures, on the practicing writer, of great models of the past—those great models on whom the present writer has naturally been educated. Young's approach appears at first to be far more interesting and valuable. The disappointment comes in Young's rather easy conclusion of what the writer should do about it. In effect Young suggests that the writer pull himself up by his own bootstraps. Let us imitate the general spirit of the past writers we admire (their boldness, their openness, their range) but keep selecting our own means of working toward it: He that imitates the *Iliad* is not imitating Homer.

V

Meanwhile the essence of the problem was being put by David Hume, though relatively few people cared to dwell on it. In his essay "Of the Rise and Progress of the Arts and Sciences," he considers different facets of the subject and then advances his "fourth observation": "That when the arts and sciences come to perfection in any state, from that moment they naturally, or rather necessarily, decline, and seldom or never revive in that nation where they formerly flourished." The observation, he admits, is theoretically puzzling and seems to be "contrary to reason."

Is not the answer that "a noble emulation is the source of every excellence"? If, in a period just before us, an art seems to have attained a "perfection," this very achievement, pressing on the artist that follows, will "extinguish emulation, and sink the ardor of generous youth." Hume does not elaborate at the moment on what happens when emulation proves so difficult. But in his essay "Of Simplicity and Refinement" (where he states that "the excess of refinement is now more to be guarded against than ever") he goes a little further: after an art has reached a high level, "the endeavor to *please by novelty* leads men wide of simplicity and nature."

There are two points made by Hume, whose uncanny perceptions in so many other ways have continued to arouse or bedevil our thinking since his time. First, he implies that decline is inevitable (and not for any Spenglerian reason—Hume is no post-Hegelian believer in the determinism of the *Zeitgeist*—but rather for empirical reasons that have to do with the way that human nature insists on behaving). But we need not linger on this matter of inevitability: Hume was no dogmatist; he could quickly change his position when given additional facts to consider. The second point is the important one: that, because of the spirit of emulation—because of the need of the artist to feel that he has a chance before the accumulated "perfection of the past"—he is in danger either of giving up, or else of manicuring the past, or, finally, of searching, in compensation, for novelty for its own sake.

In bringing up this directly human problem of emulation, Hume resurrects some remarks by Velleius Paterculus, written about the year 30 A.D. (*Historiae Romanae*, I. xvii): when we feel ourselves unable to excel (or even to equal) the great predecessors immediately before us, hope and emulation languish; we gradually resign the pursuit in which they have excelled and try to seek out a new one. This is one of those instances when an idea or attitude, expressed by a long-forgotten writer, becomes alive once again and is repeated in a

new context because it seems to make sense. Velleius touched home to very few people before Hume; but henceforth we find him briefly quoted or echoed by those who knew or had read Hume, such as Lord Kames or Archibald Alison. The speculations of men like Kames or Alison, however, are limited and indirect, revealing a general, unlocalized suspicion that they are unwilling to apply to literature in any detail. Kames, for example, in his *Sketches of the History of Man* (1774), cites the effect of Newton on mathematics in Great Britain since Newton's day—the whole study of it has since languished. Kames also speculates about the ultimate effect of the great painters of the Italian Renaissance, and compares Raphael, Michelangelo, and Titian to large oaks that intercept new plants from the "sunshine of emulation."

I suspect that one reason this large problem of the burden of the past and of its effect on emulation was not followed up, but rather bruited around as a premise, is because it was most clearly seen by men who were fundamentally conservative (in the broad sense of the word): by men who valued the gains in general insight (and, if you will, "progress" and "refinement") that had been won since the Middle Ages and the Renaissance. All of these men, however different in other ways, are the reverse of nostalgic primitivists—they include not only Johnson, Burke, and Goldsmith, but also such men as Hume and Voltaire. For Hume, however radical his ultimate effect as a philosopher, in most respects wanted to conserve what he conceived to be the gains of his age. So did Voltaire, in another way. Being independent and original people themselves, and at the same time hoping to conserve recently attained values, they especially felt the tensions, the contradictions, the embarrassments. It can be seriously argued that the most truly original ideas that have persisted from the eighteenth century (leaving aside Rousseau)—ideas that have since been developed or merely repeated—have come from men who, in general spirit, wished to conserve the gains of the time and its immediate past. Themselves so energetic, so appreciative of the appeal of novelty ("No man," said Johnson, "ever yet became great by imitation."), these men were especially clairvoyant in recognizing to what the pressure for novelty at all costs could eventually lead. So with Voltaire, whose essay on taste written for the *Encyclopédie* (1757) was soon translated and widely read in England. If a period of art immediately behind us has little to be said for it, the pressure to be different can be valuable. But if "artists through the apprehension of being regarded as mere imitators" feel it necessary to "strike out into new and uncommon paths" after a really great period of art, the direction is probably going to be downward. And Richard Hurd, in ending his long *Discourse on Poetical Imitation*, felt himself justified in one general conclusion that "they who have a comprehensive view of the history of letters, in their general periods, . . . will hardly dispute": that though many other causes may contribute to decline, "yet the *principal,* ever, is this *anxious dread of imitation* in polite and cultivated writers."

VI

Meanwhile, in its restive attempt to lift the burden of the past, or at least to shift it a little to one side, the English eighteenth century had struck back at its own most recent inheritance (neoclassicism) with two relatively new ideals (new at least for art) that were henceforth to haunt almost every English writer, and in time almost every Western European and American artist: the ideals of *originality* and *sincerity.*

Like most compensatory ideals that become rigid through anxiety, they only complicated the problem further (and, for that matter, also conflicted with each other). That is, they quickly became the sort of ideals that you can neither live with nor live without. You cannot openly deny them. You cannot afford to come out and say that you want to be "unoriginal" or "insincere." Yet if you are never to write a line unless you are convinced that you are totally "sincere," then when do you start? You can be sure that something is going to happen both to your fluency and your range. David Perkins, in his new book, *Wordsworth and the Poetry of Sincerity,* has brilliantly and sympathetically shown the dilemma that Wordsworth inherited and then—through his own individual success—powerfully deepened. Similarly, if you are exhorted to be "original" at all costs, then how to you take even the first step—especially if what you have been taught most to admire is represented by great predecessors from whom you must distinguish yourself, and, even worse, if your "original" departure from those admired models must spring from an "originality" that is itself "sincere"?

This was the fearful legacy of the great Romantics who come at the close of the eighteenth century—who in this, as in so many other ways, are so much the children of the eighteenth century: a legacy that consisted not of just one but a whole series of conflicting demands. To begin with, you were exhorted to be "original" at all costs, and yet reminded that you could not be "original" about the most important things.[2] Twenty-five centuries of past poetry had virtually insured that. You were told that the "inner life" still remained to be explored, and yet the whole character of your education and idealism was dominated by the great past examples of objective art (above all, poetic drama); and the "inner life" seemed by contrast hopelessly specialized in appeal as well as fraught with all the dangers of self-absorption. At the same time, as the eighteenth century passed into the nineteenth, the critical intelligence of England and Scotland was turning, with more delicacy and more historical understanding than ever before, to the great works of the English Renaissance—the Elizabethans and Jacobeans. Hazlitt,

with sharp impatience, weighed the modern movement against that rich past. The title of his little essay, "Why the Arts Are Not Progressive," suggests a point of view that persists through almost every critical work he wrote, and which is all the more persuasive because of his robust liberalism: Where are the greater "genres"— the direct turning to "nature," with simplicity and confidence—that we find dawning so splendidly in Chaucer and then reaching a high norm from the time of Shakespeare to the middle seventeenth century? Coleridge, in his own way, was ending with an ideal of poetry by which, as he "freely" admitted, he was himself no poet—an ideal that looked back to the great poetic dramas of another era. The interesting thing, as we pass the year 1800, is that it is the major figures (or the near-major figures) who betray this anxiety. Among reviewers, it is the best of them, Francis Jeffrey, who especially looks for a poetry (or, if not a poetry, at least a prose fiction) that will give back to us a literature that will have something of the older range and strength of the epic and poetic drama. Thomas Love Peacock was not a major critic. But he was a realistic and shrewd man. His *Four Ages of Poetry* put, with distilled irony, the helplessness of his contemporaries if they really wanted to write poetry comparable to that of the envied past. After a primitive "iron" age comes the "golden" age (the great days of Greece, in the ancient world; or the era of Shakespeare in the English Renaissance). Then the Silver Age takes over— Rome, and Augustan England. And what is now about to appear is an Age of Brass.

VII

Was there no way of getting out of this self-created prison? For of course it *was* self-created. How the oriental artist, during all those centuries that he followed his craft, would have stared—or laughed—if told that these past artists by whom, and through whom, he had been taught should suddenly represent territory that was *verboten:* that he had studied them only in order to be different! Take any of the great past eras we say we admire: Would not the Greek artist, the Renaissance artist, be complimented if he was told he could be virtually mistaken for his greatest predecessors; and, if he was able to go still further than they, did he not assume that it would be through assimilating the virtues and techniques of his predecessors while perhaps capping them with just a little more? Was it not a sufficient triumph even to recapture a few of the virtues of our greatest predecessors, as Sir Joshua Reynolds said in his last discourse to the students at the Royal Academy?—that last discourse in which he disowned his earlier willingness to abide by "the taste of the times in which I live" and said that, "however unequal I feel myself to that attempt, were I now to begin the world again, I would tread in the steps of that great master [Michelangelo] . . . [since] to catch the slightest of his perfections would be glory and distinction enough." It requires no heroic effort to be different from the great.

Nature—life in all its diversity—is still constantly before us. Cannot we *force* ourselves to turn directly toward it? And some of the Romantics tried to do just that. I quote, because it is so short, a remark from a letter of the painter John Constable (October 31, 1820): "In the early ages of the fine arts, the productions were more affecting and sublime"; and why? Only because "the artists, being without human exemplars, *were forced to have recourse to nature.*" "Force yourselves to have that recourse" was, in effect, the advice of two of the greatest men of letters that the eighteenth century produced—Johnson and Goethe. Over and over again, though Johnson allowed Imlac in *Rasselas* to admit that "the first writers took possession of the most striking objects," he himself kept stressing that "there are qualities in . . . nature *yet* undiscovered, and combinations in the powers of art yet untried." Granted (in fact it is tautological) that over-all characteristics remain the same. But the poet can still observe the "alterations" that "time is always making in the modes of life." The complaint "that all topics are pre-occupied" is repeated only by the timid or by the militantly conservative, a complaint "by which some discourage others and some themselves." And Goethe could point out the mistake of the new "subjective" writer who concentrates solely on expressing his individual feelings in the frantic hope of being "original." He will have his reward. He has "soon talked out his little *internal* material, and is at last ruined by *mannerism,*" by mere repetition of what his small inner fountain provides, while the poet who turns directly to nature, to external reality, will tap a perennial fountain of subject matter and, in doing so, become "inexhaustible and forever new." To some extent, that salutary counsel was followed.[3] The Romantics opened up the subjective world; but they did so greatly, and with profound and wide appeal, because some of them could simultaneously cling to the other ideal.

But problems still remained—problems that sharply anticipate these that we now face a century later. Take just one. Assume that you can still pull yourself up by your bootstraps and can energetically and freshly begin, by some miracle, to write in the "larger *genres*" of poetry—the epic, poetic drama, or at least analogous equivalents. There is still the fact that your audiences, your readers, are different now from what they were in the past. At least they threaten to be so. Even if they, and the critics who assail you, could somehow put "originality" out of their minds (which they will not), and could be as open as they enthusiastically say that Shakespeare's audience was, is it not also a fact that this more literate modern audience, living in its more complex world, has been deriving its "imaginative exercise"— its *katharsis,* to use Aristotle's term—from literature itself, from the large accumulated heritage of imaginative

literature? Hazlitt shrewdly raised that question. The Aristotelian *katharsis* that comes in seeing a great tragedy (with us it too often comes in merely *reading* great tragedies) "substitutes an *artificial and intellectual* interest for real passion." It does this automatically. But in that case could we not say that

> Tragedy, like Comedy, must therefore defeat itself; for its patterns must be drawn from the living models within the breast, from feeling or from observation; and the materials of Tragedy cannot be found among a people, who are the habitual spectators of Tragedy, whose interests and passions are not their own, but ideal, remote, sentimental, and abstracted. It is for this reason chiefly, we conceive, that the highest efforts of the Tragic Muse are in general the earliest; where the strong impulses of nature are not lost in the refinements and glosses of art.

And John Wilson could develop, from this premise, a question that would strike home to every poet of the time (and still more to every poet since). The human imagination, when both fed and challenged constantly by a rich but unsystematized life, may move freely and instinctively into the "larger genres," in its hope to convey or understand its experience. But if the habitual, daily use of our imaginations (no longer submitting to *real* life and constantly dwelling in the mesh of it) turns largely for compensatory nourishment and exercise to past poetry, shall we not end with merely a lyric—or, if not a lyric, at least a shorter-breathed— poetry, a poetry produced largely from the soil of past poetry?

VIII

And yet, with all the strikes against them, the greater Romantics still succeeded (astonishingly so when we remember that, in England, we are dealing with only some twenty-five years, in a nation with about a twenty-fifth of the population of the English-speaking world now). To try even to touch on what each of them did would demand another essay—perhaps another ten essays. If we were forced to put it quickly and to overlook completely the step-by-step drama of each writer's life (and it is from this that we could learn what, in Johnson's phrase about biography, we could "put to use"), I suppose we could still draw a few morals. And whatever morals we draw, we come back to the heart of the eighteenth century. For in its rather traumatic reconsideration of what next to do (and this is the first of the periods that have followed the Renaissance—and thus the first to face the situation we ourselves face now), the eighteenth century was to some extent self-corrective. While it created further embarrassments for itself and for the century and a half that has followed, an important part of it never lost its hold upon essentials but rather came, after struggle and self-division, to a deeper appreciation of them. Perhaps the greatest lesson it learned from comparing its own experience with the larger past was the value of bold-ness; not the boldness of negativism, of grudgingly withholding one's assent, of talking out of the side of the mouth as we seek to establish our identities or reach into our pockets for our mite of "originality." None of us, as Goethe said, is really very "original" but gets most of what he attains in his short life from others. The boldness desired involves a direct facing up to what we admire, and then trying to be like it (the old Greek ideal of education, of *paideia,* of trying to be like the excellence, or *arête,* that we have come to admire—whatever our self-defensive protests). It is like that habit of Keats of beginning each large new effort by rereading *Lear* and of keeping always close at hand that engraving of Shakespeare which he found in the lodging house in the Isle of Wight when he went off to begin *Endymion;* in a sense, what this typifies was true of them all: true at least of the greatest artists (Wordsworth, looking constantly back as he did to Milton; Beethoven, who in his last days kept rereading the scores of Handel; Goethe, who constantly returned to the Greeks or to Shakespeare). In effect, they end-ed—at their best—in violating the taboo that they in-herited and that so many of their contemporaries were strengthening.

IX

To reduce that taboo to size, to get ourselves out of this self-created prison, to heal or overcome this need-less self-division, has been the greatest single problem for modern art. And in saying this, we are also speak-ing of something even larger—the freedom of man (that freedom so indispensable to achievement) to follow openly and directly what he most values: what he has been taught to value, what he secretly or openly wish-es he had done or could do.

For the brute fact remains that in *no other* aspect of life (only in the arts during the last two centuries, and hardly ever in the arts before then) do you have a situation where the whole procedure of what to do with your life, your vocation, your craft—the whole process of learning and achievement—is crazily split down the middle by two opposing demands. On the one hand, we have the natural human response to great examples that, from childhood up, are viewed as pro-totypes (in statecraft, science, religion, or anything else—including even the hero worship and desire for emulation in gangsters). In no case do you have this natural response of the human heart and mind exer-cised through education, encouraged, and gradually absorbed into the conscience and bloodstream—and, at the same time have suddenly blocking it a *second* injunction: the injunction that you are forbidden to be very closely like these examples. In no other case are you simultaneously enjoined to admire and at the same time to try, at all costs, *not* to follow closely what you admire, not merely in any of the details but in over-all

procedure, in general object, in any of the broader conventions of mode, vocabulary, or idiom. Yet here, in the arts this split is widening with every generation, and not only widening but dramatized, with a helpless and blind militancy on each side.

The essence of neurosis is conflict. It becomes espe-cially so when you face obviously conflicting demands: when the pressures (or what we imagine the pressures to be) are ones that enjoin us to move in two differ-ent—in fact, two *opposing*—directions at once. And what do you do then? I think of the fable of the don-key that starved when he was confronted, on each side, with two equally distant bales of hay. The arts stutter, stagger, pull back into paralysis and indecision before such a conflict of demand. As such they mirror the greatest single cultural problem we face, assuming that we physically survive: that is how to use a heritage, when we know and admire so much about it, how to grow by means of it, how to acquire our "identities," how to be ourselves.

As we now try to reground our thinking, to discover what next to do, we have the salutary example of the greatest writers of that short period a century and a half ago that came at the close of the eighteenth century. Naturally any number of problems have increased, or been newly created, since their time. An example of the latter is the disastrous modern split between "pop-ular" and "sophisticated" art that has become so great in the middle twentieth century—a split where each tries to be as unlike the other as possible. But in many ways we are better off.

X

. . . My concern here is to illustrate the perennial rel-evance of the eighteenth century. This brilliant, and on the whole honest, era was the first of the modern pe-riods to follow the Renaissance. It was the first in any number of respects to face dramatically what we our-selves face today.

Notes

[1] See the article of John D. Scheffer, "The Idea of Decline in Literature and the Fine Arts in Eighteenth-Century England," *Modern Philology,* XXXIV (1936-37), 155-78.

[2] Francis Jeffrey is characteristic—all the more so because (despite some of his remarks on Wordsworth) he was in general so warm a champion of the new effort in literature. Here is just one excerpt (from his review of Scott's *Lady of the Lake*): "As the elements of poetical emotion are necessarily limited, so it was natural for those who first sought to excite it, to avail themselves of those subjects, situations, and images, that were most obviously calculated to produce that effect . . . after-poets were in a very different situation.

They could neither take the most general topics of interest, nor treat them with the [same] ease and difference . . . because this was precisely what had been done. . . ."Jeffrey then takes up the alternatives that appear to be shaping up: an increasing and more detailed realism in the study and presentation of character; a more careful (but more "limited") exploration of the emotional life; or, thirdly, a self-conscious "distortion" of object and idiom, either by "affectation" of an obvious sort or through "dissecting" a subject—or a "narrow corner" of it—"with such curious and microscopic accuracy" that its "original form" is "no longer discernible to the eyes of the uninstructed." Elsewhere Jeffrey speculates that the promising new genre of the novel will give us something of what we find in the great dramatic poetry of the Elizabethans and Jacobeans. We sometimes have the feeling, as we look through Jeffrey's reviews, that we are reading an earlier version of Edmund Wilson's essay, "Is Verse a Dying Technique?" And Keats himself, "cowering," as he said, "under the wings of great Poets," occasionally wonder whether epic poems (though he himself was about to begin one—*Hyperion*) were not "splendid impositions" on the modern world.

[3] The routine historian of criticism or historian of ideas shows only his own parochialism when he tries to "periodize" the great. Greatness, when it reaches a certain level, finds itself meeting the great of other eras in what Keats calls "an immortal freemasonry." Johnson has far more in common with the great English Romantics—with the greatest writers in the English language since the Romantics—than with the minor figures of his day. He also bears that same relation to the past (he is in some ways, as Whitehead says, "of the essence of the seventeenth century").

Howard Mumford Jones (essay date 1974)

SOURCE: "Sensibility," in *Revolution & Romanticism*, Cambridge, Mass.: The Belknap Press of Harvard University Press, 1974, pp. 81-115.

[*In the following excerpt Jones explores some of the characteristics of the novel of sensibility and its relation to Preromanticism.*]

. . . The term sensibility (*sensibilité*) and the term sentimentalism, often equated with it, together with their cognate adjectives, are as vague, broad, and disputable as romanticism itself, and the movement (dare one call it the program?) of sensibility touched philosophy, theology, poetry, nonfictional prose, the drama, and the novel in various ways, nor does painting escape (for example, Greuze's domestic scenes, which were intended to touch the feeling heart). Harder to isolate but nonetheless an influential cultural element in the age was musical sentimentality, notably evident in airs composed to be played or sung in the salon or the drawing room. The harp became a "romantic" instrument, and writers not versed in musical history were likely to equip suffering heroines with harps which they could not possibly carry into the wild, wild woods wherein this sad sisterhood produced effusions of their own or songs alleged to be traditional "ballads." . . .

The appeal of sensibility in Western culture everywhere was to the feeling heart, and standard approaches involved undeserved poverty, divine benevolence, or virtue in distress. Evil or wickedness was caused, so to speak, by misunderstanding of purpose in a benevolent universe. Wrote Leibniz:

> The order of things, which to our confused senses appears as that of space, of time, and of cause and effect, vanishes in the clear light of thought, and gives way to an intellectual order in the mind of the Creator or God. . . . the things of the world, which are created in complete harmony with one another, continue to manifest this harmony or mutual agreement.

The failure of a right education of the moral sense and of a belief that virtue and beauty are interchangeable, or, in sum, the substitution of egotism for benevolence, creates or permits evil to develop in the soul. But such is the eventual appeal of goodness even to the hardened heart that in the long run the reprobate—for example, Lovelace in *Clarissa Harlowe* or the hypocritical Joseph Surface in Sheridan's *The School for Scandal*—will either repeat or be driven by exposure from society. . . .

Poets of all the nations overflowed with sensibility—for example, James Thomson, whose *The Seasons,* published at intervals from 1726 to 1730, had an enormous vogue. Thomson's universe is not without its horrors: in "Winter" a "swain disastered" perishes in the snow close to his wife, his children, his friends, and "the fire fair-blazing and the vestment warm"; in "Summer" "all-conquering Heat" causes "all the world without, unsatisfied and sick" to "toss" at noon, and "the Thunder holds his black tremendous throne"; in "Autumn," wherein

> The meteor sits, and shows the narrow path
> That winding leads through pits of death,

"a proud city, populous and rich" is seized by an earthquake and

>   convulsive hurl'd
> Sheer from the black foundation, stench-
>   involved,
> Into a gulf of blue sulphureous flame.

But since it would be dissonant to sing "the cruel raptures of the savage kind," Thomson turns to a shepherd on the grassy turf in the midst of his many-bleating flock, "of various cadence"; passes on to a tribute to Wealth, Commerce, Liberty, Law, and God—

> Inspiring God! who, boundless Spirit all,
> And unremitting Energy pervades,
> Adjusts, sustains, and agitates the whole.

God is especially tender of the feeling heart. When Musidora, in "Summer," goes bathing in a woodland stream, she is spied upon by Damon, who, however, behaves in the most exemplary manner:

> What shall he do? In sweet confusion lost,
> And dubious flutterings, he a while remain'd:
> A pure ingenuous elegance of soul,
> A delicate refinement, known to few,
> Perplex'd his breast, and urg'd him to retire:
> But love forbade.

Having satisfied his voyeurism to the full, Damon writes this note to Musidora, which he throws on the river bank:

> "Bathe on, my fair,
> Yet unbeheld save by the sacred eye
> Of faithful love: I go to guard thy haunt,
> To keep from thy recess each vagrant foot,
> And each licentious eye."

Not unnaturally the naked Musidora reads this document "with wild surprise" and flies

> to find those robes
> Which blissful Eden knew not.

After she gets dressed, she pens a note which she hangs on a beech tree. Her epistle coyly concludes:

> " . . . the time may come you need not fly."

Comment on this mixture of sex and sensibility would be superfluous. The age thought it all very fine, and if there are green serpents, rattlesnakes, "the lively-shining leopard," keen hyenas, and man-eating lions in the tropics (as there are in "Summer"), this is all part of God's mysterious yet benevolent plan. A concluding "Hymn" leads us into the right way where "Universal Love" smiles all around,

> From seeming evil still educing good.

As Thomson remarks at the very end: "I lose Myself in Him . . . Come then, expressive Silence, muse his Praise." Public "Liberty" somehow also gets involved.

So far as the general reading public is concerned, the most influential branch of this kind of writing was probably the novel of sensibility. Such works were innumer-

able, but there is only room to list some leading titles and to discuss one or two of them. Here again the problem of categorization is virtually insoluble. It does not seem to me, for example, that Prévost's *Manon Lescaut* (1732), sentimental enough to have occasioned at least three major operas, comes under our classification, since "virtue" is absent from the lives of a young man without moral principle and a heroine whose main notion of success is to have a good time with males. At the other end of the temporal spectrum I assume that Jane Austen's *Sense and Sensibility,* begun in 1797 and published in 1811, marks an important turn in the vogue of the fiction of sensibility. The sentimental of course we have always with us.

Some of the devices of this eighteenth-century fictional genre—the orphan of mysterious but noble parentage, attempts at seduction or rape, imprisonment in jail or convent, enforced exile of the "Don't-darken-my-doors-again" variety, deserving poverty, the restoration of the rightful (and virtuous) heir to estates hitherto possessed by the villain—such topics were transferred to (sometimes from) the Gothic tale of terror. Novels of sensibility flooded Europe. Leading titles include Marivaux's unfinished *La Vie de Marianne* (1736-1742), known in English as *The Virtuous Orphan;* Richardson's widely disseminated *Pamela; or, Virtue Rewarded* (1740-1741), and his *Clarissa Harlowe* (1747-1748), one of the great English novels; Rousseau's *Julie, ou La Nouvelle Héloïse* (1761), the subtitle of which is usually overlooked: *Lettres de deux amants, habitants d'une petite ville au pied des Alpes* (inaccurate in fact but pointing to the relation between sensibility and "Nature"); Henry Brooke's *The Fool of Quality* (1760-1762); Goldsmith's *The Vicar of Wakefield* (1766); Sterne's *A Sentimental Journey through France and Italy* (1768), which, like Rousseau, transforms erotic emotion into sensibility; Henry Mackenzie's *The Man of Feeling* (1771), which *begins* with chapter xi; and Goethe's *Die Leiden des jungen Werthers* (1774), which according to legend led sensitive young men to commit suicide and certainly increased the vogue of Ossian. A special niche should be kept for Bernardin de Saint-Pierre's *Paul et Virginie* (1786), the heroine of which drowns rather than take off her heavy clothing in order to be rescued from the sea by a naked sailor. I omit, perhaps wrongly, Marmontel's three volumes of *Contes moraux* (1765); I omit the first American novel, William Hill Brown's *The Power of Sympathy* (1789), aimed, like *Clarissa,* "to expose the dangerous Consequences of Seduction"; I omit Mrs. Inchbald and Mrs. Opie and other virtuous members of a mob of scribbling women; and I omit many shapeless German fictions that belong to this general category.

In their monumental *Samuel Richardson: A Biography* (Clarendon Press, 1971) T. C. Duncan Eaves and Ben D. Kimpel quote a letter dated December 8, 1741, from

Aaron Hill to Richardson, written to smoke out the true author of *Pamela*. Part of the epistle runs:

> Who could have dreamt, he should find, under the modest Disguise of a *Novel*, all the *Soul* of Religion, Good-breeding, Discretion, Good-nature, Wit, Fancy, Fine Thought, and Morality?—I have done nothing but read it to others, and hear others again read it, to me, ever since it came into my Hands; and I find I am likely to do nothing else, for I know not how long yet to come: because, if I lay the Book down, it comes after me.—When it has dwelt all Day long upon the Ear, It takes Possession, all Night, of the Fancy. . . . Yet, I confess, there is *One*, in the World, of whom I think with still greater Respect, than of PAMELA: and That is, of the wonderful AUTHOR OF PAMELA.

The letter is illuminating. It exhibits the fascination this novel had for its readers, it hints at the connection between God and nature ("the *Soul* of Religion," in Hill's phrase) and virtuous feeling, and above all it assumes as a matter of course that the aim of sensibility is to reinforce the value patterns of the genteel. Indeed, one of the curious elements in this genre of fiction is the emotional attachment to social status displayed by the leading personages. The vicar of Wakefield, having been jailed, rejoices that on his release his parishioners still respect him as a minister. Pamela wants to rise from a serving maid to a lady of assured social position. Marianne in the Marivaux novel is forever fearful that somebody in good society will discover that she lives or has lived in a linendraper's establishment. Harley in *The Man of Feeling* rescues a girl from a brothel but the girl proves to be the daughter of a genteel officer. The vast majority of the characters in *Clarissa* are "respectable," and so are those in *La Nouvelle Héloïse*—even Saint-Preux, though of "humble origin," is, like Werther, an educated young man, capable of becoming the friend of Lord Edward Bomston.

It is a nice question in emotional arithmetic whether, in proportion to the lengths of the books that contain them, Marivaux's Marianne or Mackenzie's Harley weeps more often; both novels are among the wettest in Europe. It is a more important question to ponder whether weeping, which expressed everything from rapture to indignation, was common in eighteenth-century literature only, or found also in actual life. And it is an even more important problem, though an insoluble one, whether this excess of lachrymosity may not have produced by an understandable reaction the brutal indifference of a great many "virtuous" French revolutionaries to the terrors and the massacres they thought necessary to support the revolution.

The plots of most of these sentimental masterpieces can be reduced to three or four sentences and have little interest in themselves. Treatment is everything,

and one may select *La Vie de Marianne*, translated by Mrs. Mary Collyer as *The Virtuous Orphan* in 1743 (Mrs. Collyer "improved" the original French, omitted parts of the text, and invented an ending). [I have used the fine edition edited by William Harlin McBurney and Michael Francis Shugrue and printed by the Southern Illinois University Press (Carbondale and Edwardsville), 1965.] Marianne, daughter of a noble family, loses her parents, who are robbed and murdered in an attack on a stagecoach. As a child she is brought up by some virtuous villagers, but has to leave them, and under the care of a naive priest is confided to the protection of a rich hypocrite named de Climal, who lodges her with a linen-draper and, a combination of Tartuffe and Pecksniff, tries to seduce her. She attracts the attention of a handsome hero, de Valville, nephew of de Climal, moves in and out of convents, is once kidnapped through the influence of the de Valville family, and almost loses her lover to her bosom friend, Mlle Varthon. But Marianne has during her numerous mishaps won the admiration of Mme de Valville, the mother of her lover. In Mrs. Collyer's version all ends happily. But as Dr. Johnson said of Richardson's fiction, only a fool would read these volumes for the story: it is the climate of sensibility that matters.

Mrs. Collyer was obviously of this opinion. In her introduction she writes:

> The reflections [mostly by Marianne] have nothing in them studied and forced, but are the language of the heart, the fruits of experience, dictated immediately by the circumstances of the person who makes them. The sentiments throughout have an uncommon delicacy and beauty in them; they do honor to morality, and ought to be cherished by everyone who would be truly polite [note the emphasis on status], and throw a luster and an attractive quality on his virtues . . .

Marianne tells her own story for the benefit of a single correspondent, and she writes, "The remembrance of these things brings tears into my eyes; and I am obliged, dear Madame, to break off, in order to dissipate the too painful ideas which crowd into my mind." When she discovers she has been put into a linen-draper's establishment she says: "Had I fallen from some superior region, I could not have been more chagrined than I was at my present situation. Persons whose sentiments are delicate are sooner cast down than others; their hearts are more sensible, their souls more tender than the rest of the world, and those humane dispositions, that make them more sensible of the superior, the God-like pleasure of doing good, here add an emphasis to every misery." Marianne learns to call Mme de Valville "Maman" and thus describes her:

> She had a greater attachment to the moral virtues than to the peculiar duties of Christianity, regarded more the punctilious exercises of instrumental religion

than she complied with them, honored more the very devout than she thought of being so herself, loved God more than she feared Him, and conceived of His justice and goodness in a manner almost peculiar to herself and, from the benevolent dispositions of her own tender heart, justly inferred what must be those in the tender Parent of mankind who had fixed them there.

On his deathbed the repentant de Climal asks Marianne's forgiveness and adjures here: "Be virtuous in spite of all opposition, and you will find that 'to be good is to be happy.' It will raise you above many of the miseries of life, give you charms that time will not be able to efface, and render you forever lovely, forever blessed."

And so on and so on. When Marianne takes from Mlle Varthon a love letter which the fickle de Valville has written to Mlle Varthon, who has become Marianne's friend and knows nothing of de Valville's expressed affection for Marianne, "I took it up with a trembling hand and durst not at first look upon those characters which had before often filled me with delight. At last, however, I cast a look upon it, and wet it with my tears." And when Marianne is at last recognized by an uncle through the agency of the inexpressibly benevolent M. de Rosand, the scene runs as follows:

> Advancing hastily to me, "Oh, my dear niece," cried he, taking me in his arms and embracing me, "thou dear remains of my lost brother!" This tender exclamation at first softened me to such a degree that I was unable to speak to him. At last recovering myself, "Dear Sir," cried I, looking upon him with a tender kind of pleasure, "you are the first, the only person I know of my kindred. How happy do I think myself in being related to you!" While I was speaking M. Dorsin and another person were coming in; but how great, how inexpressible was my surprise when, lifting my eyes and looking over my uncle's shoulder, I saw a person whom I had long before thought dead—my dear friend, my indulgent [foster-] parent, M. de Rosand! I started, gave a shriek, stood motionless, while a flood of tender ideas flowed into my mind. My uncle meanwhile retired a few steps, and M. de Rosand held me in his arms while joy tied both our tongues.

> At last he cried out, "Oh, my child!" Here the tears trickled down his aged cheeks, and he was too full to say more.

> "Oh, my father!" then cried I and stopped too and clasped my arms about him. The tears gushed from my eyes, which, while he kissed me, mingled with his. Sure there never was a more tender interview! What a pleasing painful transport! Our minds, Madame, are capable of receiving only a certain degree of pleasure, and all beyond that is pain. Our passions are confused sensations which, when violent, swell

the heart. Its emotions become turbulent, and the excess of our delight we find nearly allied to pain.

In the next pages "my uncle and M. Dorsin" are "bathed in tears," Marianne, finding herself very weak and "almost ready to faint," sits down, everybody sits down, the repentant de Valville turns up, having thoughtfully brought along a coach, and various hostile relatives appear. But the uncle invites everybody to dinner, and Marianne, assured of her social status, informs an inimical old lady, "The honor of a virtuous mind is derived from itself and can receive no addition from the accidental advantages of birth or fortune, nor can the want of them render a person truly valuable worthy of reproach." Some days after her wedding ("the porter's whistle informed us that company was at the gate, which proved to be several persons of quality"), Marianne is commanded to tell her life story to the Queen of France. Cinderella cannot ask for more.

The rest of the vast library of fictional sensibility is much like *La Vie de Marianne*. Clarissa, to be sure, is made of sterner stuff, but like Charles II she is an unconscionable time dying, and her emotional state seems to be due less to the physiological shock of having been raped than to the feeling that, in refusing to marry the detestable Mr. Solmes, she has been an undutiful daughter. The letters of Saint-Preux and Julie are bathed in rapture, desolation, melancholy, and longing; Julie, dying, desires Saint-Preux to bring up her children. *The Man of Feeling* produces sentences of this type: "There was a tear in her eye,—the sick man kissed it off in its bud, smiling through the dimness of his own," and Harley dies when he discovers that Miss Walton, whom he adores, returns his affection. The narrator then tells us: "I sometimes visit his grave, I sit in the hollow of the tree. It is worth a thousand homilies: every noble feeling rises within me! every beat of my heart awakens a virtue!"

. . . Saint-Preux may have been a new type in European literature, the weak hero loved by woman, and he anticipates the Byronism that is to come, just as Werther's indignation at being patronized by persons of higher rank anticipates Robespierre's egalitarianism. Talleyrand once said that the French Revolution was born out of vanity. But it was nourished by this immense sea of passion—religious, erotic, nostalgic, self-pitying—emotionalism as fundamental to the age of the Enlightenment as the Enlightenment itself.

THE FOCUS ON THE SELF
Christopher Fox (essay date 1988)

SOURCE: "Some Problems of Perspective," in *Locke and the Scriblerians: Identity and Consciousness in*

Early-Eighteenth-Century Britain, University of California Press, 1988, pp. 7-26.

[*In the following excerpt Fox examines changing views regarding personal identity and consciousness during the late eighteenth century.*]

> You *deny that we have any Consciousness at all, that we continue the same individual Being at differ-ent times*. If so; it can be to no great Purpose for us to dispute about any Thing; For, before you receive my Reply, you may happen possibly to be entirely changed into another Substance; and, the next time you write, may deny that you have any Conscious-ness at all, that you continue the same individual Being who wrote this remarkable Sentence.
> —*Samuel Clarke to Anthony Collins, November 1707*

A good starting point would be to ask why the early eighteenth-century discussion of identity and consciousness has not been better known. That personal identity was a concern of eighteenth-century writers has not, of course, been denied by literary scholars. Ever since Ian Watt pointed some years ago to the age's difficulties in "defining the individual person," critical attention has increasingly focused on the issue and its impact on literature.[1] And subsequent studies have contributed significantly to our knowledge of the problem, particularly in the later eighteenth century. But the same studies have tended to ignore the emergence of the problem, and the amount of concern over it, in the early part of the century. They have also tended to downplay or even dismiss the importance here of Shaftesbury's tutor, John Locke, the first one in modern times to pose the question of identity-of-person. And even when scholars have located this question in Locke, they have often failed to see the revolutionary nature of Locke's approach—something not missed in the age of Pope.

There are a number of possible reasons for this neglect, some quite understandable. Chief among them is a tendency to see Locke himself as a noncontroversial and "safe" writer, whose doctrines were readily embraced by his contemporaries. Ignoring Locke's treatment of personal identity, scholars have tended instead to see the problem originating later, with Hume. Still another reason rests in our modern preoccupation with the self-in-consciousness, which tends to blind us to how strange this concept seemed when Locke introduced it. This same preoccupation also makes it difficult to perceive other ways of looking at the self, particularly the old theological vision of the self-as-substance, which Locke's theory had threatened and which his critics were determined to defend. Though there may be other reasons for the neglect of the early eighteenth-century discussion, these, I think, are the main ones.

The first rests in a prevalent historical misconception of the age's response to Locke himself. The rapid (and seemingly unimpeded) success of his new "way of ideas" tends to ease us into the belief that everything Locke said was immediately accepted. "On all questions of psychology," Ernst Cassirer assures us, "Locke's authority remained practically unchallenged throughout the first half of the eighteenth century." Donald Greene similarly speaks of the age "when Locke reigned virtually unchallenged," and Willey and Miller concur.[2]

True as such statements are about the extraordinary influence of Locke's work, they do obscure the important fact that many of his ideas were highly controversial. A necessary corrective balance is offered by the historical perspective of John Yolton and Kenneth Maclean. In the best existing survey of the relation of Locke to eighteenth-century literature, Maclean tells us that during the early decades of the century Locke's "philosophy was almost unanimously condemned in pulpit and pamphlet." In a study of the eighteenth-century response to Locke's *Essay* Yolton does not simply agree with this statement; he substantiates it. In a selective survey of the mass of pamphlets, sermons, and books Locke's work provoked, Yolton persuasively argues that Locke's "doctrines had a disturbing effect upon the traditional moral and religious beliefs" of his age and that he was indeed considered "one of the more dangerous . . . writers of the day."[3] One doctrine that disturbed Locke's contemporaries was his theory of personal identity, which first appeared in the second edition of the *Essay* in 1694. And our received notions of the philosopher's unchallenged authority should not obscure the fact that all the way from Edward Stillingfleet's *Doctrine of the Trinity* in 1696 to Joseph Butler's "Of Personal Identity" in 1736—and thereafter, in the work of Hume—Locke's theory was under almost continual attack in Pope's lifetime.

A second reason for the neglect of this early discussion may rest in the seemingly revolutionary nature of Hume's destruction of the abiding self in *A Treatise of Human Nature* (1739-1740). Even the best scholars, enchanted by the dazzling argument of the brilliant and suasive Scotsman, have often overlooked the earlier context. Leo Braudy, for example, in a fine essay on Richardson, dismisses the importance of Locke's theory and finds his context in Hume, who "does not demand the same fixity of personal identity." Yet it is precisely this "fixity of personal identity" that Locke's theory had threatened to the core. In her excellent *Imagining a Self*, Patricia Meyer Spacks likewise finds a context in Hume, certainly a valid one for the later writers she discusses. But when she suggests at one point that Thomas Reid and Joseph Butler "both write in the shadow of Hume," she may be overemphasizing Hume at the expense of Locke. Hume himself speaks about the "nature of *personal identity,* which has become so great a question in philosophy, especially of late years in *England*."[4] When Hume says this, he is pointing to nearly fifty years of debate on the issue, a debate originated by Locke. In his own commonsensical manner, Reid is certainly responding in part to Hume. But Reid also penned a chapter titled "Of Mr. Locke's Account of our Personal Identity," tracing the "strange consequences" of that theory, among them this: "if personal identity," as Locke had argued, "consisted in consciousness, it would certainly follow, that *no man is the same person any two moments of his life*."[5] Butler, writing three years before Hume, is explicitly reacting to "strange perplexities" about "the meaning of that identity or sameness of person" which Locke's theory had raised and to the implications drawn from that theory by Anthony Collins in an early debate with Samuel Clarke (1706-1708). Locke's "hasty observations," says Butler,

> have been carried to a strange length by others, whose notion, when traced and examined to the bottom, amounts, I think, to this: '*That personality is not a permanent, but a transient thing:* that it lives and dies, begins and ends continually: that no one can any more remain one and the same person two moments together, than two successive moments can be one and the same moment: that our substance is indeed continually changing; but whether this be so or not, is, it seems, nothing to the purpose; *since it is not substance, but consciousness alone, which constitutes personality;* which consciousness, being successive, cannot be the same in any two moments, nor consequently the personality constituted by it.'[6]

Butler's assessment of the conclusion Collins drew from Locke is, on the whole, quite accurate. This same debate over "personality" between Clarke and Collins also becomes the subject of an elaborate parody in *The Memoirs of Scriblerus.* More important now is Butler's—and, for that matter, Reid's—pinpointing of the source of the "strange perplexities" about personal identity, not in Hume and the later age, but in Locke.

Butler's comment also points to another reason why the early context has gone unnoticed: our modern preoccupation with "consciousness," which tends to obscure the revolutionary nature of Locke's theory and, at the same time, to blind us to other ways of looking at the self. That "personality is not a permanent, but a transient thing" and that it has a great deal to do with "consciousness" does not seem strange at all to us, the heirs of Proust and Woolf. But it seemed radical to Butler. Conversely, Butler's own position (implied above and asserted later) that personality is permanent and is made so by *substance* does seem strange and should remind us that people once felt differently about such things.

To understand Butler's negative response to the self-in-consciousness, it would help to examine some other contemporary texts. The first, published eight years

before Butler's comment, has been variously attributed to Zachary Mayne or, more recently, Charles Mayne. In the introduction to this significant and neglected work, titled *An Essay on Consciousness,* the author tells us in 1728:

> There [is] no Account whatever of *Consciousness,* either now extant, or whereof even the Memory hath been preserved to us, by the bare mention of its Title, in the Catalogues of Books and Treatises reported to be lost; nor so much as any Notice taken of it, in the most elaborate Discourses concerning the Mind . . . unless occasionally, or where the doing of it was in a manner unavoidable.

The writer goes on to assert that he is the first one ever to consider "consciousness" fully and "to put the candid Reader in Mind before-hand, that all the most favourable Allowances imaginable are to be made to a Work or Performance which is wholly new in its kind, or to the *very first Essay on a Subject*."[7] These statements in 1728 suggest, rightly, that the word *consciousness* and the concept behind it are "wholly new" at the time. Though the author's boast to be the first ever to analyze consciousness can be disputed, his claim as to the use of the word in his title appears to be nearly correct. In fact, outside of several minor uses of the word itself, the earliest written use of the term *consciousness* in the language is by John Locke. And in the sense of the "totality of the impressions, thoughts, and feelings, which make up a person's conscious being," Locke *is* the first. The *OED,* significantly, cites the earliest written occurrence of *consciousness* in this sense as book 2, chapter 27 of the *Essay concerning Human Understanding.* For it is in this chapter, "Of Identity and Diversity," that Locke sets forth his theory of personal identity and argues "that *self* is not determined by Identity . . . of Substance . . . but only by Identity of consciousness."[8]

Locke's use of the word in that context appears to be original. The received idea (passed down for decades by A. C. Fraser's popular and now dated edition of the *Essay*) holds that the word *consciousness* in Locke is a post-Cartesian import, borrowed from the French.[9] Yet, as late as 1808, in a translation of Dugald Stewart, Pierre Prévost states that "*Consciousness* is an English word for which I confess I have not found a particular equivalent in our language."[10] A century earlier, the first French translator of Locke's *Essay* had real difficulty with the term. In a long note to Locke's chapter on identity (2.27.9), Pierre Coste first cites Cicero's *conscientia* ("moral awareness," "knowledge of oneself") to suggest the connotations of *consciousness.* Coste then gives an elaborate explanation of the steps he has taken to translate Locke's term correctly, by "diverting" the French word *conscience* "from its ordinary sense, in order to give it one which has never been given it in our Language":

The English word is *consciousness*. . . . In French we do not have, in my opinion, any words but *sentiment & conviction* which answer, in any significant way, to this idea. But in many points of this Chapter they express very imperfectly the thought of Mr. Locke, which makes personal identity absolutely dependent on the act of the man *quo sibi est conscious.* . . . After having mused for some time on the means of remedying this inconvenience, I have never found a better way than availing myself of the term *Conscience* to explain this act. This is why I will take care to have this word printed in Italic, so that the reader will always remember to attach this idea [to the word]. And to make one better distinguish between this sense and that one ordinarily gives to the word, there occurred to me a device. . . . it is to write *conscience* in two words joined by a dash, in this manner, *con-science*. But, one will say, that is a strange license, of diverting a word from its ordinary sense, in order to give it one which has never been given it in our Language. . . . I confess that in a Work that was not like this . . . such a liberty would be inexcusable. But in a Philo-sophical Discourse one not only may, but must employ new words . . . when one has no aim but to explicate the *precise* thought of the author.[11]

Coste concludes by suggesting that, in French, Malebranche had come closest to Locke's meaning with a use of *conscience* in the *Recherche de la vérité* (1674-1678). Whether Locke and Malebranche were working from similar premises is debatable. Important here is that Malebranche never uses *conscience* in conjunction with personal identity. Nor do his earliest English translators, in rendering the work, change *conscience* into "consciousness."[12] Coste was highly regarded in the philosophical circles of his own country; his translation of Locke ran through numerous editions, was well received by Bayle and Leibniz (among others), and was used by the Abbé Du Bos to introduce the *Essay* to the French court.[13] If Coste were satisfied with *conscience* as an equivalent of "consciousness," why did he feel the need to alter the word? The very bulk of Coste's note, his laborious attempts to get at Locke's concept of "consciousness"—through Latin, through the various senses of *sentiment* and *conviction,* through hyphenation, through italicization—all strongly suggest that any easy identification of *conscience* with "consciousness" is a dubious one at best. The same factors also point to the originality of Locke.[14]

Coste's comments, along with those in *An Essay on Consciousness,* may help us understand Butler's adverse response to any suggestion that "consciousness alone" constitutes the "personality." Like so many early critics of Locke's theory, Butler is reacting to what is to him (though not to us) a thoroughly new and radical view of the self. That this same view does not seem strange to us accounts for a tendency to underestimate the importance of Locke's theory.

This same preoccupation with consciousness, which makes it easy to underestimate Locke, also makes it difficult to understand the position Butler and other contemporaries are attempting to defend. Butler's argument against the Lockean self-in-consciousness is that the personality is instead a "permanent" entity and is made so by "substance." On the face of it, this position probably seems as strange to us as Locke's did to Butler. What does Butler mean by saying that the self is "permanent"? Or by his use of that strange word *substance?* These are hard questions to answer, involving a context difficult for the modern scholar to reconstruct. But we need to examine the background here, because this age-old vision of the self-as-substance is crucial to our understanding of the problem and the Scriblerians' response.

Though the substantial self has a number of antecedents in the classical world, its medieval and Cartesian context is most important here. Amélie Rorty points out that the "idea of a person as a unified center of choice and action, the unit of legal and theological responsibility," is central to Christian belief. "If judgment summarizes a life, as it does in the Christian drama, then that life must have a unified location."[15] That location had been defined for the Middle Ages by Boethius: *persona . . . est naturae rationabilis indiuidua substantia* ("A person is the individual substance of a rational nature"). According to Étienne Gilson, this definition remained largely intact during the formative years of Christian thought. As late as 1710, in his *Tractatus . . . de Persona. Or, A Treatise of the Word Person,* John Clendon affirms that "This *Boethius* was a Gentleman of Quality, had been Consul of *Rome,* and was nevertheless so great a Philosopher and Divine, that his Definition of a Person hath been Authentick, and in Effect held ever since."[16]

On this view, the individual is made up of both mind and body, material and immaterial substance. The immaterial substance or soul is by no means the whole person in this construct, but it *is* that indivisible and immortal part of him which assures his personal continuity and ontological permanence. As John Smith asserts in 1660, *"no Substantial and Indivisible thing ever perisheth."*[17] In *Nosce Teipsum* (1599), John Davies attests to the survival of the substantial self, an entity that will outlast "Time itself":

> As then the Soul a substance hath alone,
> Besides the Body in which she is confined;
> So hath she not a body of her own,
> But is a spirit, and immaterial mind. . . .
> Heaven waxeth old, and all the spheres above
> Shall one day faint, and their swift motion stay:
> And Time itself in time shall cease to move:
> Only the Soul survives, and lives for aye.[18]

That this soul as "substance" will live "for aye" (and

therefore insure one's personal continuity) is affirmed in 1678 by Ralph Cudworth, who assures us that the soul's "*Substantiality* is so Demonstrable; from whence it follows" that the self will not "perish or vanish into Nothing."[19] As Gilson puts it: "firmly based . . . on the substantiality of the intellect and the immortality it carries with it, the Christian individual" was thus "invested with all the dignity of a permanent being, indestructible, distinct from every other in his very permanence."[20]

If the substantial self provides us with metaphysical certainty of our own persistence as a "permanent being," it also assures us that we will be held accountable for our actions. Since all moral accountability (both in this world and in the next) depends upon a person's remaining the same, the substantial self thus serves an ethical function as well. As Samuel Clarke was later to remark, it "facilitates the Belief of . . . a future Retribution, by securing a Principle of *Personal Individuality,* upon which the Justice of all Reward or Punishment is entirely grounded."[21]

Descartes challenged the medieval establishment. But he did little to threaten the substantial vision of the self or its ontological and ethical assurances. In fact, as a well-known passage in the *Discourse on Method* indicates, Descartes supported the substantialist position:

> But immediately I noticed that while I was trying thus to think everything false, it was necessary that I, who was thinking this, was something. And observing that this truth *'I am thinking therefore I exist'* was so firm and sure that all the most extravagant suppositions of the sceptics were incapable of shaking it, I decided that I could accept it without scruple as the first principle of the philosophy I was seeking.

> Next I examined attentively what I was. I saw that while I could pretend that I had no body and that there was no world and no place for me to be in, I could not for all that pretend that I did not exist. I saw on the contrary that from the mere fact that I thought of doubting the truth of other things, it followed quite evidently and certainly that I existed; whereas if I had merely ceased thinking . . . I should have had no reason to believe that I existed. From this I knew I was a substance whose whole essence or nature is . . . to think.[22]

Descartes here moves from the question of his existence (the *cogito*) to the nature of that existence (the *substantia cogitans*). He begins by asserting that the self is "something" that thinks and therefore exists, and he ends by affirming, without question, that its nature is substantial. As *Meditations* 2 and 6 make clear, two points are important here to Descartes: first, when he thinks, he must exist; second, should he cease to think, he might cease to exist. From these two points follow the conclusions that he must *always* be thinking and that this alone presupposes an underlying, "indi-

visible" self or soul, "a substance whose whole essence or nature" is to think.[23] "By regarding a thinking event as inseparable from a spiritual substance," one historian of philosophy tells us, Descartes "assumed that it is dependent upon a persisting self." And from this "rationalistic standpoint," another concludes, "the problem of personal identity never really arose."[24] Thus, in not questioning the presence of the substantial self—of a "something" underlying and unifying the diversity of experience—Descartes carried on the old theological vision: a vision that assured the individual of his ontological permanence at the same time it secured his moral accountability.

With this context in mind, we can return to Butler's position and understand it more clearly. When Butler claims that the personality is "permanent" and is made so by "substance," he is defending the orthodox theological conception of the self. When Locke argues "that *self* is not determined by Identity . . . of Substance . . . but only by Identity of consciousness," he is shattering that old substantial vision. And what Locke offered in its place did not provide, in his critics' eyes, the same ontological and ethical assurance that the person persists as a permanent being. As they saw it, the new concept of "Identity of consciousness" led instead to an opposite conclusion: that the self is, in Butler's words, "not a permanent, but a transient thing."

Working out of an essay on Pirandello by Joseph Wood Krutch, Ernest Lee Tuveson arrived some years ago at a similar estimate of the import of Locke's theory. In his Pirandello study, Krutch had outlined a vision of the personality central to most classical and all Christian ethics, of "a fully conscious unity," a "soul captain," which "is an ultimate, even *the* ultimate continuous reality persisting through time": in short, the substantial self. Krutch then described what he considered a modern phenomenon whereby this "hard-core" character, "persisting through time," is replaced by a totally "fluid" entity, existing only from "moment to moment." Tuveson, however, locates the source of this shift not in modern times but two centuries earlier, in Locke. The dramatic ramification of Locke's theory, says Tuveson, is that no "unchanging soul is necessary to constitute the personality." As a result, "the personality itself" becomes "a shifting thing; it exists, not throughout a lifetime as an essence, but hardly from hour to hour."[25]

Tuveson remains one of the few moderns to see this as an implication of Locke's critique of the substantial self and his attempt to place personal identity in consciousness. But a point that still needs to be made— and a point clearly reflected above in Butler's statement—is the extent to which Locke's own contemporaries took this to be an implication. One of the central issues of the early debate is whether the self is something static, substantial, and knowable, or something fluid, shifting, and inscrutable; whether the personality is a permanent or a transient thing. To his early supporters, Locke had rid discussions of personality of an occult term, *immaterial substance.* To his early critics, Locke had severed substance from selfhood and had paved the way for the denial of the abiding self, a denial which appears to come earlier than Hume. Working out of Locke's theory, Anthony Collins told Samuel Clarke in 1708: "no Man has the same . . . Consciousness to Day that he had Yesterday." Indeed, we "are not conscious, that we continue a Moment the same individual numerical Being." Clarke's response perhaps best suggests the orthodox reaction to the new view of the self-inconsciousness: "[Y]ou make *individual Personality* to be a mere *external imaginary Denomination,* and nothing at all in reality."[26]

As we explore the early discussion of identity and consciousness, we cannot then let our received ideas of Locke's unchallenged authority, or the seemingly revolutionary nature of Hume's theory, or our own modern bias in favor of the self-in-consciousness blind us to just how radical *this* notion was when Locke first proposed it.

We also cannot deny the Scriblerians' interest in such developments. The evidence points the other way. That Pope and other members of the Scriblerus group were widely informed of philosophical trends cannot be denied. Dugald Stewart praised Dr. John Arbuthnot in particular for his analysis of the philosophical "errors of his contemporaries." Similar praise was accorded Arbuthnot in his own time by George Berkeley, who dined with Swift at Arbuthnot's quarters in St. James Palace and afterwards described the doctor (whether justly or not) as "my first proselyte." In the same letter of 1713, Berkeley calls Arbuthnot "a great philosopher."[27] In a letter to Swift the following year, Arbuthnot suggests the truth of such praise, by turning his wit upon the author of *The Principles of Human Knowledge* himself: "Poor philosopher Berkeley; has now the idea of health, which was very hard to produce in him, for he had an idea of a strange feaver upon him so strong that it was very hard to destroy it by introducing a contrary one."[28]

Despite Swift's expressed contempt for matters theoretical, he, too, was conversant with current philosophical issues. As his *Remarks* on Tindal's *Rights of the Christian Church* suggest, Swift also took an interest—and not a wholly uncritical one at that—in the current controversy over Locke's *Essay.* Since "our modern Improvement of Human Understanding," Swift says at one point, "instead of desiring a Philosopher to describe or define a Mouse-trap, or tell me what it is; I must gravely ask, what is contained in the Idea of a Mouse-trap?" Like a number of fellow clerics, Swift seems to have been suspicious of the religious ramifications of the "refined Way of Speaking . . . intro-

duced by Mr. *Locke,*" especially when this "new Way of putting Questions to a Man's Self" was applied by a Toland or a Tindal to orthodox Christian doctrine.[29]

Pope has been called the "first major English poet to write for a generation that had begun to think in terms of 'the way of ideas.'"[30] And of the members of the Scriblerus group, Pope appears to have been the most sympathetic to Locke. Pope owned a copy of the fourth edition of Locke's *Essay* (1700). Talks with Joseph Spence suggest that Pope had also studied it. In these conversations, Pope frequently commends Locke's style and especially the closeness of his reasoning, which Pope found superior to that of any of the French writers or even "any one of the ancients."[31] Despite his admiration of the philosopher, Pope too knew about the controversial import of the *Essay.* He was aware, for instance, of an earlier attempt to ban Locke's book at Oxford.[32]

That Pope and his friends also knew about Locke's theory of personal identity is evident in the Scriblerus papers. Kenneth Maclean says that an "interested antipathy for philosophy may well have been the cornerstone upon which Arbuthnot, Swift, and the young Pope founded the Scriblerus Club, whose records . . . abound in elaborate parodies of the fine points of the *Essay concerning Human Understanding.*" Later, after locating one such parody (and there are others) of Locke's chapter "Of Identity and Diversity," Maclean adds that "one is greatly impressed with the knowledge of the *Essay* that such thorough satire implies." Maclean is not the first to point to this parody. In 1751, William Warburton notes the Scriblerians' specific use of book 2, chapter 27, and elsewhere accuses Pope and his friends of some unfair "representation of what is said in the *Essay*"—a tendency, Warburton adds, which these "wanton wits" shared with more "serious writers" of the age.[33]

Not only do the Scriblerians parody Locke's theory, they also pick up much of the debate surrounding it. This includes a burlesque version of the most detailed discussion of identity and consciousness in early eighteenth-century Britain, the pamphlet war between Samuel Clarke and Anthony Collins. The Scriblerians' response to this and other Lockean controversies will be our topic in Part III.

Before exploring the Scriblerians' response, we will first look at the larger discussion. This is the function of Part II, which examines the discussion of identity and consciousness in early eighteenth-century Britain. We will first consider Locke's controversial theory, then central themes in the ensuing debate, conducted in the wide-ranging philosophical, literary, and theological circles of Pope's time.

That personal identity was considered a theological issue should not surprise us, especially when we recall that sameness of person insured eschatological accountability. But other factors also historically linked this concept with theological concerns. Boethius's influential definition of "person" appears in his *Treatise against Eutyches and Nestorius* (ca. 512), a defense of Christ's two natures and the related doctrines of the Resurrection and Incarnation. It is safe to say that prior to Locke, nearly all theoretical discussions of "person" tend to be concerned chiefly with theological doctrines rather than with the "personality" in any distinctively modern sense. For example, Augustine's central examination of "person" in the early books of *De Trinitate* considers the question only insofar as it helps us comprehend the Persons of the Godhead. (As a modern commentator points out, the "nature of the human person is relevant" to Augustine "only as an image or incomplete analogy of the divine trinity.")[34] In the *Summa,* Aquinas later places the issue within the context of the Resurrection and considers such questions as the possibility of this event in the case of a cannibal. How can the same man rise with the same body in this instance, asks Saint Thomas, when this man has consumed the flesh of other men? Such a culinary preference, he concludes, is only accidental, not essential. The substantial soul that informs the cannibal's body will remain after death and by a "conjunction to a soul numerically the same the man will be restored to matter numerically the same."[35] The doctrine, in this instance, is upheld.

The tendency to consider identity primarily within the context of theological doctrines persists up to the time of Locke's theory at the end of the seventeenth century, and well into the next. Robert Boyle, for example, in *Some Physico-Theological Considerations about the Possibility of the Resurrection* (1675) discusses the issue of corporeal identity at the Resurrection, given the rather grim fact of bodily decomposition. Though Boyle's investigation presents "one of the more extensive discussions of the concept of identity prior to Locke," the real issue here is the doctrine, not identity. The orthodox belief in the substantial self is assumed a priori, and whether the person remains the same, accountable agent is never under question, as it was soon to be with Locke. Boyle knows that "whatever duly organized portion of matter [the human soul] is united to, it therewith constitutes the same man" and thus "the import of the *resurrection* is fulfilled."[36]

Boyle's interest in the subject helps us understand why, historically, when Locke's theory appeared, it immediately became enmeshed in debates over the Trinity and the Resurrection. Or why the earliest references to his theory of personal identity occur in works like William Sherlock's *A Defence of Dr. Sherlock's Notion of a Trinity in Unity* (1694) and Matthew Tindal's *Reflexions . . . touching the Doctrine of the Trinity* (1695). Another, more immediate reason is suggested by Yol-

ton and shown in Swift's *Remarks* on Tindal's *Rights:* namely, that Locke's *Essay* was often appropriated by others and applied to orthodox articles of faith.[37] The concern with the traditional doctrines of the Trinity and the Resurrection—and the alleged threat to them by Locke's new theory—runs throughout the early eighteenth-century debate. The great controversy between Bishop Edward Stilling-fleet and Locke himself, for example, was sparked by the bishop's attack on Locke in *A Discourse in Vindication of the Doctrine of the Trinity* (1696). Nearly thirty years later, Winch Holdsworth would preach *A Sermon . . . in which the Cavils . . . of Mr. Locke and others, against the Resurrection of the Same Body, are examin'd* (1720); and Henry Felton would follow with a popular Easter sermon at Oxford on *The Resurrection of the same Numerical Body . . . in which Mr. Lock's Notions of Personality and Identity are confuted* (1725).

These critics of the religious impact of Locke's theory were not alone.[38] Locke was interested in the same concerns, and his chapter on personal identity is partly embedded in the traditional theological context I have sketched. The *Essay* itself, as Locke's *Epistle to the Reader* tells us, began as an attempt to arrive at a way of dealing with important *"Difficulties"* in *"Morality and Divinity, those parts of Knowledge, that Men are most concern'd to be clear in."*[39] It must have peeved the author of the *Essay* to be accused of confusing the very issues he had sought to clarify, among them the question of identity and the doctrine of the Resurrection.

We will occasionally look at this strand of the contemporary controversy. But my chief interest in exploring the early discussion is less in these doctrinal matters than in some questions Locke raised in new and exciting ways (among these, the startling possibility that the same man could, at different times, be different persons). Such questions have a direct bearing on the Scriblerians and broader implications for an age witnessing the rise of a new way of looking at the personality and the decline of an old one.

Notes

[1] Ian Watt, *The Rise of the Novel* (Berkeley and Los Angeles: University of California Press, 1957), p. 18. For literary studies that do recognize Locke's importance see especially John A. Dussinger, *The Discourse of the Mind in Eighteenth-Century Fiction* (The Hague: Mouton, 1974), pp. 31-43; and Ernest Lee Tuveson, *The Imagination as a Means of Grace: Locke and the Aesthetics of Romanticism* (Berkeley and Los Angeles: University of California Press, 1960).

[2] Ernst Cassirer, *The Philosophy of the Enlightenment,* trans. Fritz C. A. Koelln and James P. Pettegrove (Princeton: Princeton University Press, 1951), p. 99; and Donald Greene, "Augustinianism and Empiricism: A

Note on Eighteenth-Century English Intellectual History," *Eighteenth-Century Studies* 1 (1967-1968): 52. For similar statements: Perry Miller, *Errand into the Wilderness* (New York: Harper, 1964), p. 168; and Basil Willey, *The Seventeenth Century Background* (Garden City: Doubleday, 1953), pp. 264-65.

[3] Kenneth Maclean, *John Locke and English Literature of the Eighteenth Century* (New Haven: Yale University Press, 1936), pp. 5-6; and John W. Yolton, *John Locke and the Way of Ideas* (Oxford: Clarendon Press, 1956), p. ix.

[4] Leo Braudy, "Penetration and Impenetrability in *Clarissa*," in *New Approaches to Eighteenth-Century Literature: Selected Papers from the English Institute,* ed. Phillip Harth (New York: Columbia University Press, 1974), p. 182; Patricia Meyer Spacks, *Imagining a Self: Autobiography and Novel in Eighteenth-Century England* (Cambridge, Mass.: Harvard University Press, 1976), p. 3; David Hume, *A Treatise of Human Nature,* ed. L. A. Selby-Bigge, rev. P. H. Nidditch (2d ed., Oxford: Clarendon Press, 1978), p. 259.

Because the *Treatise* is such a remarkable book, we also tend to forget that in the first decade of its existence the work itself received surprisingly little attention. (This of course would change in the 1760s and thereafter, with the major critiques of Beattie and others.) Quoting Pope, to whom he sent a copy of the *Treatise,* Hume tells us in *My Own Life:* "Never literary attempt was more unfortunate than my Treatise of Human Nature. It fell *dead-born from the press,* without reaching such distinction, as even to excite a murmur among the zealots." Though this statement "by no means tells the whole story," says Hume's modern biographer, "the immediate reception of the *Treatise* was certainly not such as to lend him encouragement." See Hume's *Philosophical Works,* ed. Thomas H. Green and Thomas H. Grose, 4 vols. (1882-1886; reprint ed., Darmstadt: Scientia Verlag, 1964), 3:2; and Ernest Campbell Mossner, *The Life of David Hume* (Austin: University of Texas Press, 1954), p. 116.

[5] Thomas Reid, *Essays on the Intellectual Powers of Man* (1785; reprint ed., New York: Garland Publishing, 1971), pp. 333, 336 (my italics).

[6] That Butler is directly alluding to Collins's use of Locke is indicated by Butler's own note to this comment: "See an *Answer to Dr. Clarke's Third Defence.*" See "Of Personal Identity," *The Works of Joseph Butler,* ed. W. E. Gladstone, 2 vols. (Oxford: Clarendon Press, 1896), 1:387, 392 (my italics), and 392n.

[7] *Two Dissertations Concerning Sense and the Imagination. With an Essay on Consciousness* (London, 1728), pp. 141, 143 (my italics). Nearly a century ago, commenting on this work, Noah Porter noted that it "is surprising that this first and important contribu-

tion . . . has not been better known." With the exception of a Garland reprint (1976), this is still the case. The reprint does not provide an introduction to the *Essay,* nor does it confront the issue of authorship. (The work was not attributed to Mayne until 1824; and Porter later suggested that the author is "probably" the son of a Zachary Mayne who died in 1694. Yet that Mayne had no son of this name. More recently, the work has been attributed to Charles Mayne, though the evidence for his authorship appears, at present, to be slight.) A new edition is being prepared by James G. Buickerood and the present author. See Noah Porter, "Philosophy in Great Britain and America: A Supplementary Sketch," appended to his translation of Friedrich Ueberweg's *A History of Philosophy,* 2 vols. (New York: Scribner's, 1890), 2:368. A computer search of the *Eighteenth-Century Short Title Catalogue* shows only two other works between 1700 and 1800 with the word *consciousness* in a main title: an obscure sermon published in 1727, and a one-page apology in 1770. Both are inconsequential.

[8] John Locke, *An Essay Concerning Human Understanding,* ed. P. H. Nidditch (Oxford: Clarendon Press, 1975), p. 345. Hereafter, references in the text to the *Essay* are to this edition and will be given in Arabic numbers in the order book, chapter, section: e.g., 2.27.23. In an extended consideration of some book and chapter, where it is obvious that I am discussing the same chapter, I give only section numbers.

[9] See Alexander Campbell Fraser, ed., *An Essay Concerning Human Understanding* (1894; reprint ed., New York: Dover, 1959), 1:448-49n.

[10] "*Consciousness* est un mot anglais, auquel j'avoue que je ne trouve point d'équivalent dans notre langue." See *Élémens de la Philosophie de l'Esprit Humain. Par Dugald Stewart,* trans. Pierre Prévost, 2 vols. (Geneva, 1808), "Préface du Traducteur," 1: xix-xx. For difficulties in finding a French equivalent for the English *consciousness,* see also note 11 below and the Continental review of *An Essay on Consciousness* (London, 1728) in *Bibliotheque Raisonnée des Ouvrages des Savans de l'Europe* 2 (1729): 293-311, especially 308-11.

[11] Pierre Coste, trans., *Essai Philosophique Concernant L'Entendement Humain par M. Locke* (5th ed., Amsterdam and Leipzig, 1755), pp. 264-65n. The original reads:

> Le mot Anglois est *consciousness.* . . . En François nous n'avons à mon avis que les mots de *sentiment* & de *conviction* qui répondent en quelque sorte à cette idée. Mais en plusieurs endroits de ce Chapitre ils ne peuvent qu'exprimer fort imparfaitement la pensée de Mr. *Locke,* qui fait absolument dépendre

l'identité personnelle de cet acte de l'Homme *quo sibi est conscius*. . . . Après avoir songé quelque tems aux moyens de remédier à cet inconvénient, je n'en ai point trouvé de meiileur [*sic*] que de me servir du terme de *Conscience* pour exprimer cet acte même. C'est pourquoi j'aurai soin de le faire imprimer en Italique, afin que le Lecteur se souvienne d'y attacher toujours cette idée. Et pour faire qu'on distingue encore mieux cette signification d'avec celle qu'on donne ordinairement à ce mot, il m'est venu dans l'esprit un expédient. . . . c'est d'écrire *conscience* en deux mots joints par un tiret, de cette manière, *con-science*. Mais, dira t-on, voilà une étrange licence, de détourner un mot de sa signification ordinaire, pour lui en attribuer une qu'on ne lui a jamais donnée dans notre Langue. . . . J'avoue que dans un Ouvrage qui ne seroit pas, comme celui-ci, de pur raisonnement, une pareille liberté seroit tout-à-fait inexcusable. Mais dans un Discours Philosophique non seulement on peut, mais on doit employer des mots nouveaux . . . lorsqu'on n'en a point qui expriment l'idée *précise* de l'Auteur.

The same note appears, in slightly altered form, in the first edition (1700).

[12] Coste, *Essai,* p. 265n, refers the reader to book 3, part 2, chapter 7, section 4 of the *Recherche,* a section titled "Comment on connaît son âme." Right at the beginning of this section, Malebranche says:

Il n'en est pas de même de l'ame, nous ne la connoissons point par son idée: nous ne la voïons point en Dieu: nous ne la connoissons que par *conscience*.

Malebranche's most recent translators render it this way:

Such is not the case with the soul, [which] we do not know through its idea—we do not see it in God; we know it only through *consciousness*.

The earliest English translators, however, do not make this switch. *Conscience* remains "conscience"; and the word *consciousness* is conspicuously absent. The earliest English translator, for instance, tells us:

It is not so with the Soul, we do not know it by its Idea: We do not see it in God; we only know it by *Conscience*.

The second translator, Thomas Taylor, likewise says:

But 'tis not so in point of the Soul; we know her not by her Idea; we see her not in GOD; we know her only by Conscience.

See Nicolas Malebranche, *Recherche de la vérité,* ed. Geneviève Rodis-Lewis, 3 vols. (Paris: J. Virn, 1945-1962), 1: 451; *The Search after Truth,* trans. Thomas M. Lennon and Paul J. Olscamp (Columbus: Ohio State University Press, 1980), p. 237; *Malebranch's Search*

After Truth . . . Done out of French from the last Edition, [trans. Richard Sault], 2 vols. (London, 1694-1695), 1: 57; and *Father Malebranche's Treatise Concerning the Search After Truth,* trans. Thomas Taylor (London, 1694), p. 125. I thank James Buickerood for calling this to my attention.

[13] See Yolton, *Way of Ideas,* pp. 22-24. Coste began his translation in 1696 under the encouragement of Jean Le Clerc, editor of the highly respected *Bibliothèque Universelle;* Coste completed it at Oates, where he served from 1697 on as a tutor to the Mashams and a secretary to Locke himself. See Maurice Cranston, *John Locke: A Biography* (New York: Macmillan, 1957), p. 438; and Locke, *Essay,* ed. Nidditch, pp. xxxiv-xxxvi. Information about Locke and Coste also appears in Joseph Spence, *Observations, Anecdotes, and Characters of Books and Men,* ed. James M. Osborn, 2 vols. (Oxford: Clarendon Press, 1966), 2: 560, No. 1502.

[14] One name absent from Coste's note is Descartes. This is surprising, for the usual story has it that Descartes essentially invented the concept of consciousness. If consciousness was so important to Descartes, why does Coste fail to mention him? Is it because Descartes himself never really defined the term and rarely used it? Perhaps so. Some years ago, Alfred Balz noted that the standard story needs to be revised, for it is "difficult . . . to credit Descartes himself with this doctrine." What was important to Descartes was the soul's "capacity of reasoning . . . not self-consciousness." See Alfred G. A. Balz, *Cartesian Studies* (New York: Columbia University Press, 1951), pp. 29, 40. Coste's failure to mention Descartes may also be connected with another point: that in seventeenth-century *French* translations of Descartes's Latin, his uses of the Latin *conscientia* are most often rendered as "sentiment" or "connoissance"; the word *conscience* is, apparently, used just once. On this point, see Robert McRae, "Descartes' Definition of Thought," in *Cartesian Studies,* ed. R. J. Butler (Oxford: Basil Blackwell, 1972), p. 55n. In the history of the concept of consciousness, Locke's place is (one suspects) more important than usually noticed.

[15] Amélie Oskenberg Rorty, "A Literary Postscript: Characters, Persons, Selves, Individuals," in *The Identities of Persons,* ed. Amélie Oskenberg Rorty (Berkeley and Los Angeles: University of California Press, 1976), p. 309. For earlier concepts of the substantial self, see especially Sir Ronald Syme's *Tacitus,* 2 vols. (Oxford: Clarendon Press, 1958), 1: 420-21; and R. G. Collingwood, *The Idea of History* (Oxford: Clarendon Press, 1946), pp. 42-45.

[16] Boethius, *The Theological Tractates,* trans. H. F. Stewart and E. K. Rand (London: Loeb Classical Library, 1918), p. 92; Étienne Gilson, "Christian Person-

alism," in *The Spirit of Mediaeval Philosophy,* trans. A. C. H. Downes (New York: Scribner's, 1940), p. 201; and John Clendon, *Tractatus Philosophico-Theologicus de Persona. Or, A Treatise of the Word Person* (London, 1710), p. 94.

[17] John Smith, *A Discourse Demonstrating the Immortality of the Soul,* in his *Select Discourses* (London, 1660), p. 66.

[18] Sir John Davies, *Nosce Teipsum,* in *Silver Poets of the Sixteenth Century,* ed. Gerald Bullet (London: Everyman, 1947), pp. 362, 397.

[19] Ralph Cudworth, *The True Intellectual System of the Universe* (London, 1678), p. 868.

[20] Gilson, "Christian Personalism," p. 203.

[21] Samuel Clarke, *The Works of Samuel Clarke,* 4 vols. (London, 1738), 3:851.

[22] René Descartes, *Philosophical Writings,* trans. John Cottingham, Robert Stoothoff, and Dugald Murdoch, 2 vols. (Cambridge, England: Cambridge University Press, 1985), 1: 127.

[23] In the *Second Meditation,* Descartes posits: "Thinking? At last I have discovered it—thought; this alone is inseparable from me. I am, I exist—that is certain. But for how long? For as long as I am thinking. For it could be that were I totally to cease from thinking, I should totally cease to exist." In the *Sixth Meditation,* he argues "that there is a great difference between the mind and the body, inasmuch as the body is by its very nature always divisible, while the mind is utterly indivisible." See the *Philosophical Writings,* 2:18, 59.

[24] Wolfgang von Leyden, *Seventeenth-Century Metaphysics: An Examination of Some Main Concepts and Theories* (New York: Barnes and Noble, 1968), p. 111; and Henry E. Allison, "Locke's Theory of Personal Identity: A Re-Examination," in *Locke on Human Understanding: Selected Essays,* ed. I. C. Tipton (Oxford: Clarendon Press, 1977), p. 106.

[25] Joseph Wood Krutch, *"Modernism" in Modern Drama: A Definition and an Estimate* (Ithaca: Cornell University Press, 1953), p. 83; and Tuveson, *Imagination,* pp. 27-29.

[26] Anthony Collins, *An Answer to Mr. Clarke's Third Defence,* in *Works of Clarke,* 3:870; and Samuel Clarke, *A Third Defence of An Argument Made Use of in a Letter to Mr. Dodwell,* in Clarke, *Works of Clarke,* 3:844. Also see Clarke's comments in *A Fourth Defence of An Argument Made Use of in a Letter to Mr. Dodwell,* in Clarke, *Works of Clarke,* 3:902.

[27] Dugald Stewart, *The Collected Works,* ed. Sir William Hamilton, 11 vols. (Edinburgh, 1854), 1: 604; and *Berkeley and Percival,* ed. B. Rand (Cambridge, England: Cambridge University Press, 1914), pp. 114, 121, 123. When Berkeley called Arbuthnot "a great philosopher" we must also remember the possibility that he may have meant "natural philosopher," or what we call a scientist.

[28] *The Correspondence of Jonathan Swift,* ed. Sir Harold Williams, 5 vols. (Oxford: Clarendon Press, 1963-1965), 2:137.

[29] See Swift's *Remarks upon a Book, Intitled, The Rights of the Christian Church,* in *The Prose Works of Jonathan Swift,* ed. Herbert Davis, 14 vols. (Oxford: Basil Blackwell, 1938-1968), 2:80. That Swift employed the controversy over Locke has been argued by Rosalie Colie, Irvin Ehrenpreis, and W. B. Carnochan. Though the first two studies nominally deal with personal identity, they actually take up the related, though different, issue of defining the essence of "man" as "species"—a point Carnochan's book clarifies. See Rosalie L. Colie, "Gulliver, the Locke-Stillingfleet Controversy, and the Nature of Man," *History of Ideas News Letter* 2 (1956): 58-62; Irvin Ehrenpries, "The Meaning of Gulliver's Last Voyage," in *Swift: A Collection of Critical Essays,* ed. Ernest Lee Tuveson (Englewood Cliffs, N. J.: Prentice-Hall, 1964), pp. 123-42; and W. B. Carnochan, *Lemuel Gulliver's Mirror for Man* (Berkeley and Los Angeles: University of California Press, 1968), esp. pp. 130-31, 150-53. Also see Ricardo Quintana, *Two Augustans: John Locke, Jonathan Swift* (Madison: University of Wisconsin Press, 1978).

[30] Ernest Lee Tuveson, "*An Essay on Man* and 'The Way of Ideas,'" *English Literary History* 26 (1959): 368-69.

[31] On Pope's copy of Locke's *Essay,* see Maynard Mack, "Pope's Books: A Biographical Survey with a Finding List," in *English Literature in the Age of Disguise,* ed. Maximillian Novak (Berkeley and Los Angeles: University of California Press, 1977), p. 271, item no. 105. For Pope's comments on Locke, see Spence's *Anecdotes,* 1:92, no. 212; 170-71, nos. 388-89; p. 217, no. 510; p. 226, no. 535.

[32] In a note to *The Dunciad,* Pope tells us that in "the year 1703 there was a meeting of the heads of Oxford to censure Mr. Locke's Essay on Human Understanding, and to forbid the reading of it." As Maurice Cranston shows, the details of this censure were shadowy, even to Locke himself. Locke's friends were, however, able to establish that such meetings did in fact take place in November 1703; that they were directed primarily at Locke's *Essay* and Le Clerc's *Logic;* and that the attempt failed. See *The Twickenham Edition of the Works of Alexander Pope,* ed. John Butt, 11 vols.

(New Haven: Yale University Press, 1939-1969), vol. 5, *The Dunciad,* ed. James Sutherland (3d ed., 1963), p. 36an. Also see Cranston, *John Locke,* pp. 466-69.

[33] Maclean, *John Locke and English Literature,* pp. 10-11, 101; and William Warburton, *The Works of Alexander Pope, Esq.,* 9 vols. (London, 1751), 6:127, 129. See also Robert A. Erickson, "Situations of Identity in *The Memoirs of Martinus Scriblerus,*" *Modern Language Quarterly* 26 (1965): 388-400; and A. C. Fraser's edition of Locke's *Essay,* 1:455n.

[34] A. C. Lloyd, "On Augustine's Concept of a Person," in *Augustine: A Collection of Critical Essays,* ed. R. A. Markus (New York: Anchor, 1972), p. 191. Also see p. 197.

[35] Thomas Aquinas, *Summa contra Gentiles: Book Four,* trans. Charles J. O'Neil (Notre Dame, Ind.: University of Notre Dame Press, 1975), chapters 80-81, pp. 301, 303.

[36] Robert Boyle, *Some Physico-Theological Considerations about the Possibility of the Resurrection,* in *Selected Philosophical Papers of Robert Boyle,* ed. M. A. Stewart (Manchester: Manchester University Press, 1979), pp. xxiii, 206. That in the early eighteenth century the problem was still seen as closely related to traditional doctrines is suggested by Isaac Watts's careful note to his attack on Locke's theory in 1733: "This discourse is entirely confined to personality among creatures, and has no reference to divine personality here." ("Of Identity and Diversity," in *Philosophical Essays on Various Subjects . . . with Some Remarks on Mr. Locke's Essay on the Human Understanding* [London, 1733], in *The Works,* ed. George Burder, 6 vols. [London, 1810-1811], 5:624n.)

[37] On the connection between Locke and the Deists, see Yolton, *Way of Ideas,* esp. pp. 126-48, 167-81. One question that could use more exploration is the connection between Locke's theory in 1694 and the Trinitarian controversy of the same decade.

[38] Other works that take up Locke's theory within the traditional context of these theological concerns include, for example, Henry Lee, *Anti-Scepticism: Or, Notes upon each Chapter of Mr. Lock's Essay concerning Humane Understanding* (London, 1702); [Samuel Bold], *A Discourse concerning the Resurrection of the Same Body* (London, 1705); Will Lupton, *The Resurrection of the Same Body: A Sermon Preach'd before the University of Oxford* (Oxford, 1711); Winch Holdsworth's sequel to his anti-Lockean sermon of 1720, *A Defence of the Doctrine of the Resurrection of the Same Body . . . in which the Character, Writings, and Religious Principles of Mr. Lock . . . are Distinctly considered* (London, 1727); Catherine Trotter [Cockburn], *A Letter to Dr. Holdsworth, in Vindication of*

Mr. Locke (London, 1726); Henry Felton, *The Universality . . . of the Resurrection, being a Sequel to that wherein Personal Identity is asserted* (London, 1733); and Isaac Watts, "The Resurrection of the Same Body," in *Philosophical Essays on Various Subjects* (1733), in *The Works,* 5:576-80.

[39] Locke, *Essay,* p. 11. Yolton has shown that it was Locke's interest in solving such problems that initially led to the formation of his new way of ideas. See Yolton, *Way of Ideas,* esp. p. viii.

FURTHER READING

Arthos, John. *The Language of Natural Description in Eighteenth-Century Poetry.* 1949. Reprint. New York: Octagon Books, 1970, 463 p.

> Discusses the influence of natural science on eighteenth-century descriptive poetry, tracing the ways various poets shaped and transcended the conventional terminology of scientific description.

Bogel, Fredric V. *Literature and Insubstantiality in Later Eighteenth-Century England.* Princeton, N.J.: Princeton University Press, 1984, 226 p.

> Discusses many of the Preromantic writers in the context of the literature of sensibility.

Butler, Marilyn. *Romantics, Rebels and Reactionaries: English Literature and Its Background 1760-1830.* Oxford: Oxford University Press, 1982, 213 p.

> Discusses Romantic and Preromantic writers and artists in historical context, focusing on their "rebellious" aspect.

———. "Romanticism in England." In *Romanticism in National Context,* edited by Roy Porter and Mikulas Teich, pp. 37-48. Cambridge: Cambridge University Press, 1988.

> Argues that the Preromantics and Romantics understood the interconnectedness of literary history and political history.

Butt, John. "Conclusion: The Quest for Energy." In *The Mid-Eighteenth Century,* edited by Geoffrey Carnell, pp. 495-513. Oxford: Clarendon Press, 1979.

> Summarizes the spirit of the late eighteenth-century writers, emphasizing their enthusiasm and regard for original genius.

Draper, John W. "The Funeral Elegy and the Rise of English Romanticism." In his *The Funeral Elegy and the Rise of English Romanticism,* pp. 314-31. New York: New York University Press, 1929.

> Uses the funeral elegy as an index of social change, seeing it as a reflection of sentimentalism and individualism.

Harth, Phillip, ed. *New Approaches to Eighteenth-Century Literature*. New York: Columbia University Press, 1974, 217 p.

> Collection of essays including studies of the problem of genre and on the interrelatedness of literary forms.

Hudson, Nicholas. "'Oral Tradition': The Evolution of an Eighteenth-Century Concept." In *Tradition in Transition: Women Writers, Marginal Texts, and the Eighteenth-Century Canon*, edited by Alvaro Ribeiro and James G. Basker, pp. 161-76. Oxford: Clarendon Press, 1996.

> Examines the controversy surrounding, and the eventual acceptance of, the notion of oral tradition.

Lyons, John O. "Out of the Void." In his *The Invention of the Self: The Hinge of Consciousness in the Eighteenth Century*. Carbondale : Southern Illinois University Press, 1978, 268 p.

> Analyzes the "invention of the self" during the Preromantic period and its effect on historical writing, travel literature, pornography, and charcterization in fictional works.

Monk, Samuel H. *The Sublime: A Study of Critical Theories in XVIII-Century England*. 1935. Reprint. Ann Arbor: Ann Arbor Paperbacks, The University of Michigan Press, 1960, 250 p.

> Standard critical overview of the background and treatment of the idea of the sublime in the eighteenth and nineteenth centuries.

Stephen, Leslie. "General Conditions of Thought." In his *History of English Thought in the Eighteenth Century*, pp. 435-59. New York: G. P. Putnam's Sons, 1876.

> Explores the impetuses behind sentimentalism and naturalism and explains why neither literary reaction satisfactorily resolved the deficiencies of the period leading up to Romanticism.

Tillotson, Geoffrey. "The Manner of Proceeding in Certain Eighteenth- and Early-Nineteenth-Century Poems." In his *Augustan Studies*, pp. 111-46. London: University of London, The Athlone Press, 1961.

> Analyzes the importance of word order in poetry and prose.

Wesling, Donald. "Augustan Form: Justification and Break-up of a Period Style." *Texas Studies in Literature & Language* 22, No. 3 (Fall 1980): 394-428.

> Describes and defines the Augustan form, and discusses what it represented to the Romantic writers.

Williams, Anne. *Prophetic Strain: The Greater Lyric in the Eighteenth Century*. Chicago: University of Chicago Press, 1984, 185 p.

> Explores the lyric's usurpation of verse in the eighteenth century, and the concurrent development of Romanticism.

Robert Burns

1759-1796

(Born Robert Burnes) Scottish poet and lyricist.

The following entry contains critical essays on Burns's relationship to Preromanticism. For further information on Burns, see *LC*, vols. 3 and 29.

INTRODUCTION

The national poet of Scotland, Burns is revered as the "heaven-taught ploughman" who expressed the soul of a nation in the language of the common man and sang of universal humanity. Burns worked on more than three hundred songs, and it is largely due to his revival of the lyric that he is considered a Preromantic. He made the Scots dialect acceptable in elevated, serious poetry, and his depiction of rural Scottish life and manners marked a radical departure from the stately and decorous subjects typical of eighteenth-century poetry. His frank expression of his love for women, drink, and bawdy lyrics contributed to his image as a natural man, honest and spontaneous. Burns is admired for his compassion, which extended even to the lowliest animals, his humor, his patriotism, and his fervent championship of the innate freedom and dignity of humanity. In present times Burns's works remain an important part of the popular culture of Scotland, and his "Auld Lang Syne" is sung around the world every New Year's Eve.

Biographical Information

Burns was born in Alloway, near Ayr in southwestern Scotland, to an impoverished tenant farmer and his illiterate wife. Although Burns was largely self-taught, he was not in reality the "noble savage" some later biographers made him out to be. Burns received formal schooling whenever possible, and it was during a three-year period of regular attendance in a one-room schoolhouse, as a student of John Murdock, that Burns was exposed to a large body of English literature which included William Shakespeare, John Milton, the Augustans John Dryden, Joseph Addison, and Alexander Pope (including his translation of Homer), and the Preromantics James Thomson, Thomas Gray, and William Shenstone. Further, Burns's father, William Burnes (whose famous son later altered the spelling of the family name), instructed him at home, and Burns ardently read any book he could borrow. Burns's family moved from one rented farm to another during his childhood, at each place enduring the hard work of farming in poor soil and suffering the extreme financial difficulties exacerbated by high rents. Excessive toil during his childhood is blamed in part for Burns's eventual early death. At fifteen, Burns fell in love with a girl with whom he was working, and it was this love that caused Burns to first write a lyric. He later recalled this episode: "Among her other love-inspiring qualifications, she sang sweetly; and 'twas her favorite reel to which I attempted giving an embodied vehicle in rhyme." Burns was to follow this method for his writing for the rest of his life. He would always hear a melody in his head while creating lyrics; never would the lyrics be set down first. Some of his poetry began to circulate in manuscript form in the early 1780s. By 1785 and 1786 Burns had written nearly all of his best poems, all of them in Scots. Burns credited the creation of his finest poetry, that dealing with country life, to the inspiration he gained from reading the Scottish vernacular poets Allan Ramsay and Robert Fergusson. In 1786, with aid from friends, he published *Poems, Chiefly in the Scottish Dialect*. Published in the town of Kilmarnock, the edition was an overnight sensation and quickly sold out. The second edition, published in Edinburgh the following year, brought critical acclaim and fame to Burns. It was in this city that, for a season, Burns was feted and much admired by the literati and the doctors, lawyers, and dignitaries of the city. Some scholars argue that Burns's reputation as a self-taught peasant led him to a dead end; Burns could not grow while attempting to match the image expected of him. It is only "Tam o' Shanter," his later narrative masterpiece, that makes this argument difficult. The latter part of Burns's creative career was devoted to collecting and revising the vast body of Scottish folk songs transmitted orally from generation to generation—work that continued, legend has it, to the last moments of his life. Although Burns was badly in need of money, he refused any payment for his work, considering his efforts to be his patriotic duty to Scotland. In 1796, at the age of 37, Burns died from rheumatic heart disease.

Major Works

While the theme of freedom—political, religious, personal, and sexual—dominates Burns's poetry and songs, the themes of love and fellowship also recur. The poem "For A' That and A' That" is an implicitly political assertion of Burns's beliefs in equality and freedom. His outrage over what he considered the false and restricting doctrine of the Scottish church is clear in such satirical poems as "Holy Willie's Prayer" and "The Holy Fair." "Holy Willie's Prayer" concerns a self-professed member of the elect who, through his own narration, inadvertently exposes his hypocrisy and ethical deficiencies. "The Holy Fair," a lively, highly descriptive account of a religious gathering, contrasts the dour, threatening view of life espoused by the Calvinist preachers with the reality of life as it is actually lived. The simple celebrants, after dutifully and respectfully attending to the sermons, continue their pleasurable everyday pursuits—the enjoyment of conviviality, drink, and romance—which are ever present in Burns's work. Burns's many love poems and songs touchingly express the human experience of love in all its phases: the sexual love of "The Fornicator"; the more mature love of "A Red, Red Rose"; the happiness of a couple grown old together in "John Anderson, My Jo." Whatever the subject, critics find in Burns's verses a riotous celebration of life, an irrepressible joy in living. Burns's characters are invariably humble, their stories told against the background of the Scottish rural countryside. Although natural surroundings figure prominently in his work, Burns differed from the succeeding Romantic poets in that he had little interest in nature itself, which in his poetry serves but to set the scene for human activity and emotion. In 1787 Burns met James Johnson, the editor of *The Scots Musical Museum*. This meeting set off Burns's enthusiasm (he referred to himself as "absolutely craz'd" over the prospect) for restoring, recov-

ering, and collecting old folk songs of Scotland, an ambitious task that was to occupy Burns for the rest of his life. According to James Kinsley, Burns "assimilated the whole musical tradition of Scotland, going over the airs till he discovered their character, their mood, and their potentiality as settings for songs." Burns also wrote many verse epistles. Although each was addressed to only one correspondent, it was understood that members of a select circle would hear at least some of the content, and that much of this content would also reach Burns's opponents. Thus these writings were both private and semi-public. Not collected until after Burns's death, the verse epistles are invaluable for their revelations of Burns's innermost hopes and fears and for their wide range of expression.

Critical Reception

Although the initial publication of Burns's poems in 1786 was immensely successful, critics were soon to write more on what they considered to be Burns's moral defects (he had been arrested as a fornicator) than on his verses. In 1808 Francis Jeffrey attacked Burns as being contemptuous of prudence and decency, although he continued in the same review to assert that Burns was a "great and original genius." Sentimental poems such as "The Cotter's Saturday Night" and "To a Mountain Daisy" received the most favorable attention; Burns's earthier pieces, when not actually repressed, were tactfully ignored. "The Jolly Beggars," now considered one of his best poems, was rejected for years on the ground that it was coarse and contained low subject matter. Although these assessments held sway until well into the nineteenth century, more recent critics have taken opposing views, with some of Burns's more sentimental writings being taken as bathetic and false. Burns's English and primarily-English verses have long been found disappointing, with many critics calling them badly imitative and urging that they be completely ignored. Burns himself acknowledged that he lacked the command of English that he had for his native tongue. Other critics find that Burns's combination of two dialects results in an intriguing synthesis as many times two different meanings for a given word add depth to the poem in question. Burns spelled many words in English to reflect Scots pronunciation, and this can lead to confusion over the exact proportion of the two dialects. Although the epistles are not Burns's most important works, G. Scott Wilson has asserted that: "The verse-epistles which Burns wrote between 1784 and 1786 are, with the possible exception of Pope's Horatian epistles, the finest examples of the style in Scots or English." Stopford A. Brooke has written that Burns's intellectual genius was most displayed in his outspoken wit. "In satire of this kind—the fierce, stinging, witty, merciless satire, the naked mockery, the indignant lash—he stands alone. No one has ever done the same kind of thing so well—and those who felt the whip deserved it." In addition to lauding Burns as a poet, Ralph Waldo Emerson praised him as having struck more telling blows against false theology than Martin Luther.

PRINCIPAL WORKS

Poems, Chiefly in the Scottish Dialect (poetry) 1786
* *The Scots Musical Museum.* 6 vols. (songs) 1787-1803
** *A Select Collection of Original Scottish Airs for the Voice.* 8 vols. (songs) 1793-1818
The Works of Robert Burns (poetry) 1800
The Poems and Songs of Robert Burns. 3 vols. (poetry, songs) 1968
The Letters of Robert Burns 2 vols. (letters) 1985
The Songs of Robert Burns (songs) 1993

* This collection contains some two hundred songs and fragments written or edited by Burns.

** This collection contains some seventy songs by Burns, most altered by later editors.

CRITICISM

Stopford A. Brooke (essay date 1920)

SOURCE: "Robert Burns," in *Naturalism in English Poetry*, E. P. Dutton & Company, 1920, pp. 113-34.

[*In the following essay Brooke praises Burns as the first writer to achieve naturalism in his Scottish poems, the restorer of passion to poetry, and the master of sincerity, pathos, and stinging satire.*]

Robert Burns, of whom Scotland is justly proud, was the child of his own country, and his poetic ancestors were not English, but Scottish. When I say that—and I shall enlarge on it afterwards—I exclude the poetry he wrote in ordinary English, in which he did not use his native dialect. These poems, in verse, diction and manner, are full of English echoes, and derive from Shenstone, Gray and others of that time. The only distinctive element they have is that now and then the irrepressible genius of the man, his rustic, national individuality, bursts, like a sudden gush of clear water, for a line or two, out of the dull expanse of his imitative verse. He should have done, with all impulses on his own part to write in English, and with all requests from others to do so, what David did with Saul's armour, put it off when he had worn it once and

said, "I cannot go with these—I have not proved them."

Poets should cling to their natural vehicle, to their native song. When Burns put on English dress, his singing robes slipped off him, his genius moved in fetters, he lost his distinction, his wit ran away, his passion was not natural; above all, the lovely charm of his words—their pleasant surprises, their delicate shades of expression, even their subtle melodies like the melodies of Nature herself, of the wind in the trees, of the brook over the pebbles, of the wild whispering of the sea, deserted him. It is wise to skip almost everything that he wrote in English, for there he was encumbered by alien traditions; and the traditions were those of the conventional poetry, and amazingly foreign to his genius.

There were two other elements in his poetry which were foreign to his fresh Naturalism, to his genius. The first of these was his tendency to personification. That smacked of the past poetry both English and Scottish. Dunbar, Lyndsay and Ramsay used this as much as Spenser or Gray. And Burns, though his poetry was like a new day, could not quite, any more than Coleridge, get rid of this remnant of yesterday.

The second thing was his habit of moralising in poetry, of drawing lessons for life not indirectly, but directly, from Nature, from human events. I cannot quite trace this habit to the previous Scottish poets. I believe it came to Burns from Gray. Sometimes it is as well done as it is by Gray, sometimes with even a greater freshness, as in the two admirable poems on turning up the nest of the field mouse with the plough, and on seeing a louse climbing a lady's bonnet in church. At other times, though the moralising is well expressed, it is not naturally expressed. It sounds as if he had taken it from some one else, as if it belonged to the old didactic strain, not to the new world of poetry, the gate of which he threw open. It is a reversion, not a creation of his own. And, as poetry, though not as a piece of sermon, it is somewhat wearying. We miss it in the freshness of the new wind which had begun to blow, and we miss the new Naturalism. At these two points Burns had clinging to him some of the rags of the past. At this last point he is rather the English than the Scottish poet. His greatest power, that which made him different from all the poets of his time, that which introduced into the time at which he wrote an element which revolutionised its lyric singing, was his absolute naturalness, the opposite and the enemy of convention in poetry. He bubbled up into poetry like a springing well into an arid plain, and the plain grew fertile as the well made itself into a stream and watered the desert. We have seen how Cowper began that in England in the natural quietudes of the "Task," and in a few deeply felt lyrics. But Cowper's character and circumstances forbade the unchastened naturalness of Burns, who immediately followed his own impulse without a thought of what the world would say; who flashed the impulse of the moment into verse; to whom everything was a subject, but who chose the last subject which occurred to him when he had a more eager impulse than usual; who never asked why or what he should sing;

> For me, an aim I never fash—
> I rhyme for fun.

As it came he took the world, as the moment came he made his poem. The circumstance of the moment flew into verse. He lived and wrote; loving and ranting, laughing and weeping, slashing his foes and flattering his friends, wooing and loving and sorrowing; praying and cursing; now with the Jolly Beggars, now with Mary in Heaven, in the alehouse, in the church, by the brookside in the summer, on the hills in the drifting snow, by the dark sea in storm; dancing and half-drunk at the Holy Fair and Halloween, or sitting douce and grave in the religious quiet of the Cottar's Saturday Night. Everything seemed to suit his hand, and naturalness was at the root of all. He sang as the bird sings on the bough. The long struggle for Naturalism, which we have followed from the time of Pope till now, received its first complete realisation in the Scottish poetry of Burns. This, of course, is the same as saying that he was sincere. He had that great quality. No one can ever doubt, as he reads any poem of Burns, that he is saying in it exactly what he felt. Nothing is reconsidered; no mask is worn; there is no thought of what the world would say, no modifications on that account. We touch the very life of the man at the moment, the very truth—and, when we are weary of the quantity of insincere poetry which we read, or of poetry over-wrought by art, to read Burns is a mighty consolation. And, indeed, it is almost a lesson in the high moralities. We understand better what Truth means, what a loveliness, as of the ideal world, it bestows on work in which it shines. That is so true that it glorifies poems in Burns which the dainty Philistines think coarse.

But naturalness and sincerity do not make a poet. There are hundreds who possess these qualities who could not make a verse, nor sing them into a song. Along with them there must be the natural gift, the shaping power of imagination, the executive hand of the born artist. And I am not sure that any of our poets possessed this natural gift, *i.e.,* within his range, which was not that of the greater poets, in richer fullness than Burns. Other poets begin with inferior work and somewhat slowly reach their excellence. They have to train their powers. Burns leaped at once into his proper excellence. His masterpieces were nearly all written in the first six months of his poetical life, and they were masterpieces in three or four different kinds of poetry. There was no need to correct or

polish them, to recompose, or to lay them aside. They gushed out like a fountain, clear and full, from the living rock—their shaping, their melody, their passion, their subject-matter alive and natural, needing no work, no change, born like a flower of the field.

"Within his range," remember; and that range was limited. Were I not to guard what I have said by this phrase, I might seem to equal him with the greater poets who move on the higher planes of thought, and travel over larger lands towards infinite horizons. Burns cannot be classed with them, but, all the same, he is often more natural and sincere than they, and his natural gift, so far as it was capable of going, was more spontaneous than theirs. Theirs needed care and work to bring to excellence, his did not.

When we find naturalness and sincerity combined in a man, we find the testing-stones of his character. However other parts of his character or his circumstances may influence him, these two qualities will lead our judgments concerning him into rightness. For want of recognising these two qualities in him, Burns has been rudely or foolishly praised or blamed by men. His naturalness, left uncontrolled and hurried on into excess by the strength of his passions, led him astray into weakness; and with women into folly, vanity and sensuality. But his sincerity in all he did, even in wrong—his deep sincerity with himself, should lead us to judge him gently, and humbly as well as firmly, in wonder whether we should have done only half as well, had we had his nature and his genius. And so Wordsworth felt concerning him—Wordsworth who had almost a Puritan morality. No tenderer, humbler verses were ever written than he wrote about Burns. So also felt Carlyle, so felt R. L. Stevenson. Others have been more priggish in their judgments, but even they are fascinated. Fascination is the word. The weaknesses, the follies, the sins of Burns do not die; they must be felt and condemned; but they earn the pardon of some because of their passionate naturalness, and of others because of his rare and noble sincerity.

But I do not speak here of his character. Enough and to spare has been written about that. The critics who write about Burns cannot keep off that subject! They spend, like Carlyle, like Stevenson, like Professor Shairp, three-fourths of their essays on the moral and psychological questions which arise out of his career; and they shove the literature of the man into the background. It seems a wonderful novelty for them—living in the midst of a conventional society, and reading for the most part books which smack of the literary cliques, and of the temporary drifts of the time—to come across a man who lived as natural a life as we may suppose Adam lived, and felt like a child born on the original Aryan steppe—doing, thinking and feeling, even after he had been to Edinburgh, just exactly what his will urged him, at the moment, to do. There is a naïveté in the suppressed astonishment of the critics over this phenomenon which always amuses me. Carlyle makes a whole series of sermonettes about Burns. Even Stevenson preaches, with an air, it is true, of detachment, but with a judicial note, flavoured with a self-conceited legality, which offends me. As to Shairp and many others, their moralities are almost Pharisiac. None of them seems to feel, as he writes, that Burns was as far above them as a star is above the earth; and that, naughty as he was, he was, even through all his follies and weaknesses, wiser at heart than they.

I turn to him as a poet. He had, in his best poetry, no English ancestors. All his poetic ancestry was in Scotland. He was the culmination of a long line of poets who wrote in the Lowlands, and who derived more than half of their special qualities from the Celtic blood so largely infused into the whole country which lay between Edinburgh and Glasgow, between the Border and the valleys of the Forth and the Clyde. The characteristics which are distributed through James I., Barbour, Henryson, Dunbar, Douglas, Ramsay and Ferguson, appear also in Burns, and glorified. He was their climax. He inherited them, and they were Scottish, not English, and, for the most part, Celtic, not Teutonic—Celtic in their love of Nature, their rollicking humour, their hot, frank and satiric abuse, their nationality, their isolated individuality, their pathetic power, and their quick passion for women. At every one of these points English poetry is of a different temper, manner and tradition—and Burns is less an English poet than Theocritus or Catullus. He is outside of the tradition. That is the reason why, when he attempted to write in "the English," he made such a mess of it.

Being of this descent, he was not unworthy of it. He concentrated into his work all the qualities and excellences of the poets who preceded him. He was the flowering of this tree that, rooted in the Lowlands, had grown into a noble expansion through the summers and winters of four centuries. I might trace in Burns the elements of Henryson, Barbour, or Dunbar brought to their best shaping and life, were not that too long a criticism for this place; but take his closer predecessors, take Ramsay and Ferguson. Their work is fairly good here and there. Its elements are in a great part the elements of Burns. But there is as much difference between their shaping and his of these elements, and of the class of subjects into which they and he enter, as there is between the chatter of a sparrow and the song of the nightingale. He is the poet, the flowering of their song. Nothing so good was before him, and nothing so good after him, nothing half so sincere, half so natural or half so passionate.

As such he was, of couse, national. Carlyle, who ought to have known better, seems to think that the poetry

of Scottish nationality was only born into a full life in Burns. Burns himself fell into that error. Scottish poetry, even when, as with the first James, it derived impulse from England, clung pertinaciously to its own country. The Chaucerian poems of Scotland reject the conventional landscape of Chaucer and insert that of their own land. Whatever English form the Scottish poets used they reanimated with the spirit of Scotland. The ballads are alive with national feeling. The greater Makers are no exception. Barbour is on fire with national feeling, he hates the English. Dunbar's "Golden Targe" thrills with it, and his "Thistle and the Rose" sings little of the Rose and much of the Thistle. Douglas paints hour by hour the landscape of his own low hills in May and winter. Not an expression, not a picture is even touched by England. Alexander Scott, like the others, personifies his native land with a steadfast and moral patriotism. Ramsay, Ferguson, before Burns—a shoal of inferior poets after him, bubble with nationality.

But Burns threw around it a passion and a beauty of imaginative words, a charm of personification, which it had never had before, and never has had since.

"The Poetic Genius of my country found me, as the prophetic bard Elijah did Elisha—at the plough, and threw her inspiring mantle over me. She bade me sing the loves, the joys, the rural scenes and rural pleasures, in my native tongue. I tuned my wild, artless notes as she inspired."

He keeps himself throughout to the scenery, the subjects, the heroes, the warlike struggles, the rustic life, the women of his own land. His Muse is wholly untravelled. Carlyle said he had "a resonance in his bosom for every note of human feeling"—it is far too large a statement, but what there is of human feeling is all Scottish. The Muse of Scotland appears to him— let us read some of that vision. It well illustrates all I say; it is almost the best criticism of his own poetry.

The Muse tells how she loved him from his birth and listened to his

> rudely carrolled, chiming phrase,
> 　in uncouth rhymes.

And then she sketches him as the poet, and all the elements of his genius:

> I saw thee seek the sounding shore,
> Delighted with the dashing roar;
> And when the North his fleecy store
> 　Drove through the sky,
> I saw grim Nature's visage hoar
> 　Struck thy young eye.
>
> Or when the deep green-mantled earth
> Warm cherished every floweret's birth,

And joy and music pouring forth
  In every grove,
I saw thee eye the general mirth
  With boundless love.

When ripened fields, and azure skies,
Called forth the reapers' rustling noise,
I saw thee leave their evening joys,
  And lonely stalk,
To vent thy bosom's swelling rise
  In pensive walk.

When youthful love, warm-blushing, strong,
Keen-shivering shot thy nerves along—
Those accents, grateful to thy tongue,
  The adorèd Name—
I taught thee how to pour in song
  To soothe thy flame.

I saw thy pulses' maddening play
Wild send thee Pleasure's devious way,
Misled by Fancy's meteor ray,
  By Passion driven,
And yet the light that led astray
  Was light from Heaven.

Nor must we leave Burns without hearing some of the lines written to William Simpson; the last verse of which found a still nobler representation in **"Scots, wha hae wi' Wallace bled,"** composed as he rode against the fierce wind and rain over the lonely moors of Galloway, silent and grim with patriotic passion. This is national enough:

  Ramsay and famous Ferguson
  Gied Forth an' Tay a lilt aboon
  Yarrow an' Tweed to monie a tune
    Owre Scotland rings,
  While Irwin, Lugar, Ayr an' Doon,
    Naebody sings.

  The Ilissus, Tiber, Thames an' Seine,
  Glide sweet in monie a tunefu' line!
  But, Willie, set your fit to mine,
    An' cock your crest;
  We'll gar our streams an' burnies shine
    Up wi' the best.

  We'll sing auld Coila's plains and fells,
  Her moors red-brown wi' heather bells,
  Her banks an' braes, her dens an' dells,
    Where glorious Wallace
  Oft bare the gree, as story tells,
    Frae Southron billies.

  At Wallace' name, what Scottish blood
  But boils up in a spring-tide flood?
  Oft have our fearless fathers strode
    By Wallace' side:

  Still pressing onwards, red-wat-shod,
    Or glorious died.

On the other side, there is not unfrequently felt in his poetry the influence, like a perfume wafted from cultivated fields far away, which flits with the wind over a wild moorland, of the half-classical, half-courtly note of the Augustan school. Along with this there is also a touch of chivalrous sentiment such as might be derived from the Scottish sentiments for the Stuarts. These two elements steal strangely in among the rustic songs, and especially among the love-songs. To the first we owe the conventions of Sol and Phœbus, and others of the same kind. To it also we owe certain artificial love-poems which read as if they were written by the Caroline poets. Moreover, an element of reflective morality on life, and another of deistic religion, carried, at times, into a personal relation to God by the natural passion of Burns, seem to belong to this influence.

To the second, to the Cavalier element (and Burns read the Cavalier songs), we may owe a few of the finest of his songs, not especially about the Stuarts—his Jacobite songs are commonplace—but about those Scots who carried their love of fighting, their hatred of England and their sword into a foreign service. The best of these I quote, and nothing better was ever done in this way. The gathering night, the wet wind on the sea, the lonely spirit of the exile, his cavalier spirit, his passionate love, his battle-courage, his presentment of death, are all woven together into a lyric whole:

  Go fetch to me a pint o' wine,
    An' fill it in a silver tassie,
  That I may drink, before I go,
    A service to my bonnie lassie.
  The boat rocks at the pier o' Leith,
    Fu' loud the wind blows frae the ferry,
  The ship rides by the Berwick-law,
    And I maun leave my bonnie Mary.

  The trumpets sound, the banners fly,
    The glittering spears are rankèd ready;
  The shouts o' war are heard afar,
    The battle closes thick and bloody;
  But it's no the roar o' sea or shore
    Wad mak me langer wish to tarry;
  Nor shout o' war that's heard afar—
    It's leaving thee, my bonnie Mary!

These are the modifications of his dominant nationality.

Next, right down from the Celtic spirit, comes the ranting, roaring wit of Burns, and secondly, the savage brilliancy of his satire—what the old Scottish poets called "flyting." Of the first there is no finer example in the language than **"The Jolly Beggars."** Villon never did anything more real, more vital, more keenly in the subject. It never flags for a moment. Every man and woman in it is alive to the last rag on their bodies; and coarse as they are, it is impossible, so vivid is their humanity, to help feeling kindly to them, even to regret not being with them for a time. Their jollity seems to redeem their naughtiness. It is a masterpiece. So is, in a less reckless society, **"Tam O' Shanter."** Every one knows that poem. Its mirth, its philosophy, its strange touches of moral sentiment, its spiritualisation of drunkenness, its visions of the invisible, its happy turns of wit, its admirable phrases, its amazing dash and rush from end to end, all mingled into harmony, linked easily together, the changes never seeming out of place, the style always right, make it one of the joys of literature. Wit has seldom been more gay, the force of life has seldom been so unbroken; it races in full tide through every line.

He was capable, however, of a more delicate humour, which chiefly played round the quips and cranks and wiles of love affairs. The best example of this, having, beyond the event, to do with a common, almost a universal element in human nature, is **"Duncan Gray cam' here to woo,"**—a thing shaped as well as a lyric girl, nothing in it which ought to be out, nothing out which ought to be in. Other poems of the same happy, lively, soft humour, play like children through his book of songs. He was a kindly creature; his heart was open to all humanity. He loved the world; and nowhere is this wide affectionateness shown more than in his gay poems of humour. I think it was this affectionateness in the man, this universal love, which made his humour so natural, so unforced, so unwearying. We never hear a laboured or a conventional note in it. It is as fresh as his passion. However, he was splendidly capable of savage satiric wit. And on this side he descends from the Celtic spirit. **"The Holy Fair," "The Ordination,"** the **"Address to the Unco' Guid," "Holy Willie's Prayer," "Death and Doctor Hornbrook,"** are scathing, outspoken, unsparing slaughters in verse. They are, perhaps, the things in his poetry which most display his intellectual genius. In satire of this kind—the fierce, stinging, witty, merciless satire, the naked mockery, the indignant lash—he stands alone. No one has ever done the same kind of thing so well— and those who felt the whip deserved it. But these satirical poems are not to be compared, as poetry, to the songs. They are first in their own class, but their class is not a high one. They seem also to be exceptions to his general kindliness. But they are partly modified by the laughing wit that runs through them; and what they attack was the only thing that Christ spoke harshly of—want of love, cruelty, condemnation of the weak, combined with hypocrisy. Just indignation was at the root of his satire, the indignation of loving kindness with a religion and a morality of damnation.

It is said that humour and pathos are closely connected, that the true humorist is capable of the most pathetic expression. However that may be, Burns, when he felt deeply, was a master of pathos. He had, like the Celt, the sorrow of his wit and the wit of his sorrow. His melancholy was as profound as his flashing humour was bright; and he passed in a moment from one to the other. This was the Celtic nature in him. It is strange to turn from **"The Jolly Beggars"** to **"Mary Morison,"** from **"The Holy Fair"** to **"Mary in Heaven,"** from **"Duncan Gray"** to **"The Banks of Doon."** Their contrasts illustrate the range of Burns, but the contrasts are very great.

I do not care to criticise or dwell upon the beauty of these pathetic things. It is best to read them, to leave them to make their own impression.

To read these poems is to realise how passionately he could love and enshrine his love; and Burns, in that progress of Naturalism of which we have been speaking, restored to our poetry, after a long interval, the passionate love-poem. It can scarcely be said to have existed since the days of Dryden. But now, like a Princess that had slept a hundred years, it woke up at the kiss of a Prince of Poetry, and broke out into singing and sang a hundred songs about herself, and her whims and vagaries, her joys and sorrows, her gaiety and melancholy, her profound happiness and exaltation in passionate feeling. It was like a naked tree bursting into a million leaves—a grey meadow suddenly starred with a multitude of flowers.

And this sprang out of the heart of a peasant, as I may well call Burns, though he was a small farmer's son. It was underived from other poets, though we can trace its rise in Ramsay and Ferguson. It was pure Scotland, for Burns had not read the Elizabethan songs. It was unassisted by any literary class, for the best of the love-lyrics were made before he went to Edinburgh; not was there a soul in Edinburgh capable of writing one of them. It rose fresh from the natural earth and the life of those who lived by the earth; born while the poet drove the plough and reaped the corn and milked the cow and watched the sheep. The Muse was tired of didactic philosophy and satire, of refined and classic verse, of faded sentiment; she had enough of Crabbe's stern miseries, of Cowper's unimpassioned softness, of the slow river and the stately grove, of the sandy shore and the grey waves. She wanted something fresh, living, intense in feeling; she wanted frank natural passion, and scenery to match its wildness and its strength, the dashing torrent and the lonely moor, the dark lake and the long-ridged hills, the larks singing in the solitudes, the chasing clouds and sunlight on the mountain side, the birches rustling in the glen, the wild storm that drifted the deep snow. And she made Burns and gave him the passion of Nature and man:

> Gie me ane spark of Nature's fire,
> That's a' the learning I desire;
> Then,though I trudge through dirt and mire,
>   At plough or cart;
> My Muse, though hamely in attire,
>   May touch the heart.

And the love-poetry was not of cavalier and lady, of gentlefolk in society or in the settled life of English counties, but of the poor in their cottages, and in the scattered huts upon the moor:

> Love hath he found in huts where poor men
>   lie.

He sings the old man and his wife going down life's hill together to the far-off land beyond death, the merry-hearted girls who meets her lover at the fair, the lovers trysting by the mill-stream and where the corn-rigs are bonny; where the rye stands tall, and where the hazels grow by the stream in the meadows, where at even the sheep are called home, where broom and the gowan and the bluebell are listening to the linnet, everywhere within that wild soft Lowland country, where, among its crossing glens, Nith and Callawater stray, till all Nature as she lives in this pastoral country is closely interwoven with the love of maid and man. He sings the lighter forms of love, its moments, its fleeting passion. He sings the love of a lifetime, its steadiness, its honour and its serious passion. He sings the passion of the sorrows of love, its partings, its misfortunes, its despairs, its rapture. Almost every note is touched, and for the most part with an honest sincerity and manliness which is enchanting. Read **"The Birks of Aberfeldy,"** read **"I love my Jean,"** read:

> O, my love's like a red, red rose,
>   That's newly sprung in June:
> O, my love's like the melodie
>   That's sweetly played in tune.

And read, for joy and nature and delight in loving, **"O Saw ye Bonnie Lesly,"** and then, for the pity and passion of pitiful love, listen to **"Highland Mary"**—the love that might have saved him and that fate denied him.

I have said that he wove together Nature and lovers. His way with Nature was to weave her into the life of man. She is not loved for her own sake only, as Wordsworth and Shelley loved her. She is loved, but along with man and woman, as Gray and Collins loved her, but far more than they. The love of Nature has grown up to fuller stature since their time. It is almost as fresh, as natural in Burns as it is in Wordsworth, but it has no philosophy, and Nature in it has no separate life of her own. The love of Nature is gathered in Burns solely around the scenery of the dales and low flowing hills and meadows and clear streams and birch and hazel and thorn of the Lowland valleys—a scenery which has, in its half wild, half cultivated aspect, a special sentiment of its own—curiously and charmingly special. To visit it and know its spirit would be to enjoy better the poetry of Burns, for the spirit of its life breathes from poem to poem like an ethereal force. I can feel that, though I have never lived among its soft appeals. It caught the childish heart of Burns. Its natural charm moved the first impulses of his art, till he passed from Nature and the emotion she awakened, to the life of the human heart. Nature was the threshold, man was the temple:

> The Muse—nae Poet ever found her
> Till by himsel' he learned to wander
> Adown some trotting burn's meander,
>   An' no think lang;
> O! sweet to stray and pensive ponder
>   A heartfelt sang.

Always Nature was second, humanity first—the background, sometimes used like a theatrical property, for the human act and passion he sung. But for the most part, the scenery comes naturally into the piece and is harmonised with its humanity. And always when the love and sorrow and joy are most deep, the landscape is most delightful and true. But it is never touched with the deep spirit of ideal beauty; it is never alive with a life of its own; it never has a soul that speaks to us. That was to come. It had not yet been born.

Yet, as he mingled together Nature and man, and especially the animal life of Nature, he illustrated his thoughts of human life by what he saw in Nature; and transferred to flowers and birds the deep affection he had for mankind. A sudden tenderness wakens in him for the life of flower or animal, because their pain images the pain of man, their morning joy his joy. When his plough crushes the daisy, he speaks of it as if he had crushed a child:

> Wee, modest, crimson-tippèd flower!
> Thou'st met me in an evil hour,
> For I maun crush amang the stowre
>   Thy slender stem:
> To spare thee now is past my power,
>   Thou bonnie gem.

There he slips out of this close intimacy with pure Nature into human life, and compares the daisy's fate with helpless maid and luckless bard, and finally with his own fate. It never is Nature for herself alone.

As quick and tender is his love for animals. The birds sing in every song. Nothing can be more wisely doggish than the characters of Cæsar and Luath in **"The Twa Dogs,"** that close, vital piece of rustic life, where the cottar's life and dwelling and homely phrases and pains are painted with intense and joyous reality. **"The**

Death of Mailie" lives in the life of the sheep; nor is the **"Farmer's Salutation to his Old Mare"** less kindly, less alive, less sympathetic. The man and his animal comrade have been together like John Anderson and his wife:

> Monie a sair darg we twa hae wrought
> An' wi' the weary warl' fought!
> An' monie an anxious day, I thought
>   We wad be beat!
> Yet here to crazy age we're brought,
>   Wi' something yet.
>
> An' think na', my auld, trusty servan',
> That now perhaps thou's less deservin',
> An' thy auld days may end in starvin',
>   For my last fou,
> A heapit stimpart, I'll reserve ane
>   Laid by for you.
>
> We've worn to crazy years thegither;
> We'll toyte about wi' ane anither;
> Wi' tentie care I'll flit thy tether
>   To some hain'd rig,
> Where ye may nobly rax your leather,
>   Wi' sma' fatigue.

This was the pleasant fashion in which, like Cowper, he re-introduced, with the sincerest feeling, the affection of man for the animal world and the comradeship between them, as a subject for poetry; and none of all the poets who followed him in this has done it with more naturalness. When his coulter turns up the nest of the field mouse, he talks to it as to a hurt child. He has harmed a fellow creature:

> I'm truly sorry man's dominion
> Has broken Nature's social union,
> An' justifies the ill opinion
>   Which makes thee startle
> At me, thy poor, earth-born companion,
>   An' fellow-mortal!

That will be the note of a really civilised society. It is not the note of our half-barbarous condition.

The last quality of his poetry which I instance is its strong personal note. I said that Cowper brought back, in this new Naturalism, personal revelation into English poetry. Burns did the same thing in Scotland. He paints himself just as he is, with the finest sincerity, with no dressing up for public. The lectures the critics give him for his aimless and uncontrolled life he gives to himself; and in far clearer and better words than they use. If a poet, recognised to be a quite true person, describes his character and its faults as they are, and draws quite justly and sternly the moral of them, the public might let him alone and the moralist critics might cease to preach. They only weary the

publicans and sinners, and double the conceit of the Pharisees. There is no need for their long-winded dissertations. We know Burns through and through from himself, and I sometimes wish he were now alive in order to satirise these gentlemen who make him the text of their sermons. If you want to see and feel the man—if you want to take a moral warning from his life—or to learn from him how to live apart from the world and wisely—collect his personal statements—read them together—and the very living, thinking, loving, failing, noble creature will stand by your side, exactly, minutely, as he was in the centre of his spirit.

He painted other men as clearly as he painted himself, whenever he cared to do this work. He had a wonderful, keen eye for the outside of all the types of men he met, he had just as keen an eye for their souls whether they were bad or good. And the words, the fiery phrases with which he described what he saw, were as vital, as lucid, as sharp as his sight. The execution was as clear as the conception. Words were his servants. He said to them: "Do this," and they did it. We know the whole of his society, their houses, their way of life, their dress, their pleasures, their amusements at the fair, on the farm, at the meeting-house; when they preach and drink and dance, and read the evening prayer, and wander with their sweethearts by the river. We can build all the different types, and the full type also itself of that society into our mind. No poetry is more individualising. But beyond the range of the society he knew his poetry does not travel. His range as a poet is then limited. The greater world of thoughts and passions was not for him; nor its mightier doings. Even in his own world of lyric poetry, he is almost entirely limited to the love-lyric. Into that far wider world of the lyric, whither we have been led by the poets that followed him, he did not come. His circle as a poet was then small, but within it he was excellent. And one thing was the source of his excellence. It was the deep charity of his nature. No one ever loved his fellows, and the natural world with them, better than he. He lives not only by his style, as some have said, but because the spirit of his style was Love, and the master of his imagination was Love:

> Deep in the general heart of man
>   His power survives.

Christina Keith (essay date 1956)

SOURCE: "The Background of Burns: Eighteenth-Century Scotland," in *The Russet Coat: A Critical Study of Burns's Poetry and of Its Background*, Robert Hale & Company, 1956, pp. 7-27.

[*In the following excerpt Keith describes Scotland's Golden Age, a time of nationalism and rich intellec-*

tual life; Edinburgh's reception of and influence on Burns; and why Burns's limited reading and self-education caused him to focus on satire and song.]

The eighteenth century, into which Burns had the amazing good fortune to be born, was Scotland's Golden Age, when everywhere her latent talents were unfolding, and the sun rose towards the high meridian of her literary achievement. Not only that—it was the bright breathing-space between two centuries of religious intolerance—in different ways, both equally repellent. With the close of the nightmare seventeenth century, the Killing Times were over. No longer did the Edinburgh crowds mill round the gallows in the Grass-market for a sight of the latest Convenanter sent there 'to glorify God'. No longer were the dragoons out riding the Ayrshire mosses after hunted men. The era of the Covenant was over. . . . And the nineteenth century of materialism and Disruption, rending the land from the Solway to the Pentland with legalistic disputes, had not yet begun so that, in this Golden Age, Scotland had a breathing-space to think, for once, of other things than religion. It was this lighter mental atmosphere, already by Burns' birth in 1759 well-established over the whole realm, that made his literary achievement possible. . . . For this was the century of Boswell and Hume, of the raciest biography and the most original philosophy, of the revolutionary economics of queer Adam Smith,—the century too of the captivating old songs, 'John cum kiss me now', 'Guidwife, count the lawin' ', 'De'il tak' the wars'—of the merry Scots country dances, alike in a village barn or in a fashionable Edinburgh oyster-cellar—the century of the finest claret and the best law—of the infinite variety on the road from His Grace's magnificent chaise and four with its postillions and powdered footmen, to the blue-clad beggar with his badge—of chapmen like Patrick Walker with the most breath-taking broadsheets in their pack—of the first ships on the Clyde—of the beautiful old Edinburgh silver and the spacious Regency squares—of surgery and medicine such as carried Edinburgh's name far over the Seven Seas—of a New Town with the most brilliant talk in Europe—before the blighting nineteenth century fell, hushing all laughter on the Sabbath and silencing all talk but what bore on the Free Kirk or the Established, and strangling all thought, like an iron curtain between living things and the sun. The eighteenth century was Scotland's Golden Age.

For even at its outset, the atmosphere was lightened. The heavy air that had hung thick round the Laigh Parliament House in Edinburgh, where dripped the thumbscrew and the boot still red with the blood of tortured Covenanters—that heavy air was blown to the four airts. And if it were a quarrel nearly as violent as the religious strife itself that now dispelled it, it may well be that nothing less could have cleared that foul air. But in the raging contentions over the famous—or

infamous—Treaty of Union of 1707, torture, arraignment, persecution itself were alike swept into the limbo of the forgotten past, to disappear for ever from contemporary Scottish thought. The atmosphere had lightened. . . . Tho' it was a tornado that cleared the air. Not since Bannockburn—and that was 1314—had Scotland been so conscious of her national identity, as now in 1707. And conscious of it, only, it would appear, at the moment of losing it, for henceforth her destinies were to be merged in those of the larger kingdom to the South. Fury at such monstrous annihilation—for it seemed no less to the man in the street—stung the country wide awake, intensifying and sharpening those elements in the national character that, by long disuse, had been growing blunted or even indistinguishable. But now they were pin-pointed. Never had men been so Scotch before. In the redoubtable thistle, reposing on Queen Anne's bosom on that last Scots coin struck on the eve of the Union, every prickle stuck out. . . . From the point of view of our poet, this process is of great importance. For the facets of Scots individuality were now being chiselled sharp and clear so that men in Aberdeen—the cool and uncovenanted Aberdeen—could realise their kinship with—say—dour Presbyterians in Edinburgh or simple country folk as in Thomas Boston's remote parish of Ettrick, or worldly merchants stepping it high on the Trongate of Glasgow. Nationality now transcended parochialisms. All were Scots now. A public was thus being created that would recognise Burns to be not now a merely local figure, but of an appeal throughout Scotland. He was indeed the first Scots writer to be of national significance. . . . More than that, his subjects also were being prepared for him. For, had Burns come to Ayrshire in the seventeenth century, he would have found only folk like the pious John Brown of Priesthill, whom Clavers' dragoons shot down, or the fanatic Peden the Prophet skulking in dens and caves, or the ardent young Richard Cameron, the Red Rebel of Airdsmoss, all of them men fired to utter sincerity by one idea and so, incapable of being satirised. But, with this tide of nationalism spreading—even as the flood-tide of religion ebbed—other sorts came now into view—the tinkers on the road, the topers in the howffs, Holy Willie in his pew in Mauchline Kirk. And, unlike their seventeenth-century predecessors, these were universals—folk to be found as readily anywhere else. Thus, by the middle of the eighteenth century, the public and the material were alike ready for the satirist's pen. . . . But, by then, other changes too had taken place. For, after the Union with its bitterness had unified the country, as nothing else could have done, came a major event that extended, as it were, that country's cultural frontiers. In 1715 Jacobite Scotland rose for James the Old Chevalier. And Jacobite Scotland was largely, if not entirely, Scotland north of the Highland Line—country Aberdeenshire, in fact ('The Standard on the Braes o' Mar') under Mar himself, the Gordons of Huntly and the Earl Marischal. Here then, for the first time, a Gaelic-speaking area in the Highlands aligned itself with Southern Scotland, if only on behalf of such a sorry personage as 'Mr. Melancholy', heir to the long line of Stuart kings at Holyrood. But tho' it was only country Aberdeenshire so far—and the more distant areas of the Highlands and Islands remained in the '15 totally unaffected—it was still the first direct infusion of different blood and different traditions into the make-up of Scottish nationality. After the '15, Scotland no longer consisted merely of the cities, the Lowlands and a strip of the East Coast with its ancient towns of Arbroath—Montrose—Dundee. After the '15, if you spoke of Scotland, you had to think of the Hinterland too, that vague, mountainous, unpredictable region of which the wilds of Aberdeenshire were but the gateway—those menacing fastnesses behind the mists—the Bens and over the trackless moors—those also were now equally Scotland. The horizon of the nation had widened, as throughout the eighteenth century it was to widen still more. . . . But the process came too late for Burns. Of East Coast blood himself (the most practical blood in Scotland) and born in agricultural Ayrshire, he never assimilated this new, strange element in the national character. For him Scotland was always—the beggars, the topers, the churchgoers of the Lowlands and the girls you met with them, the woods and burns they walked beside. It was left for Scott, nurtured from boyhood on Border romance (at Smailholm Tower, on Tweedside, or riding the mosses at Carter Fell) to seize on and interpret the kindred spirit of the Highlands and relate it to the national character, as one component part of it. But for Burns neither Highland Ben nor Border Peel, tho' he visited both in his journeyings, held any meaning. He was stone-cold to both. It is this limitation of outlook that has to be considered when one comes to assess his personality and his title to speak for all Scotland. . . . And after the '15 came the '45, a Rising on a much grander scale and involving, especially after Culloden, the whole of the Highlands as far North as John o' Groats, as far West as Barra. With the Prince hiding in moor and cave or threading his way between the Outer Isles, and the English redcoats hot after him, not a Highlander now but was conscious of the antithesis between Scots and English. Not a Highlander but knew he was part of Scotland now. The lines from Holyrood now ran straight out to Benbecula and reached to far Strathnaver. Edinburgh at long last was the nerve-centre of the whole kingdom. What the hated Union had begun in 1707, the White Rose and its aftermath completed in the '45. For the first time, the whole of geographical Scotland was one united nation. . . . If rather a dull one. It was a good thing Burns didn't come in the first half of the eighteenth century, for there would have been no brilliant capital to welcome him. With no persecutions truly, Edinburgh in the early 1700's had now no pageantry either. With the last Scots Parliament sitting in 1707, the

ancients in the dark Closes off the High Street might well talk of the magnificence they had once seen at that very Close-mouth when, year by year, the gorgeous procession of the Riding of the Parliament would sweep through the Canongate from royal Holyrood—Commissioners of the Burghs and Shires, periwigged Judges and their train, peers of Scotland in scarlet and ermine on their gaily caparisoned horses with their lacqueys in gold and silver coats, resplendent Bishops and the two Archbishops in brilliant vestments, trumpeters and heralds and pursuivants, the Sword of State, the Sceptre and the Crown—with the lawn sleeves of the Bishop of Edinburgh reaching out from a window high above, to bless them all as they passed. The Riding of the Parliament! Back into Scotland's remotest history it ran—the jingling of the bridles, the blast of the trumpets rousing the long-dead centuries. But all that was over. With the stroke of the pen in 1707 finished and done with. No need to crouch in the Closes now, or listen for a phantom bridle jingling up the causeway. Nothing in scarlet and ermine would ever pass that way again. . . . So, the political Scotland over and done with, it had to be a social Scotland now. New lights were riding on the horizon now. And, with the lighter air, new interests were springing up. You could sing a song now. And it needn't be one of those 'Gude and Godlie Ballates' either that the Kirk had tried to impose. But older songs than those. And bolder. Jollier songs altogether, like those in 'Cockelbie's Sow' that uproarious old poem of the fifteenth century, or in 'The Complaynt of Scotland' of 1549, when Mary Queen of Scots was but a child of six, and Scotland still carefree. Gay songs of Robin Hood or Johnny Armstrong, the Border reiver, or wild songs of 'The Red Harlaw'. Some, it is true, had got lost in the interval, but snatches of others still survived, enough to show that even in the worst shadow of the Reformation, someone must still have been humming them beneath his breath. . . . And now, old Scots songs became the rage. Old Scots poems too. What with the weary Kirk and that black Geneva gown, it was many a long day since Scotland had had her fill of either. But she took it now. In 1706, on the eve of the hated Union, Watson's Collection (the first of many) came out, of *Comic and Serious Scots Poems*. Here you could read the famous 'Christis Kirk on the Green' of King James I, that delectable poem of villagers on high holiday, or Sempill's popular mock-elegy 'The Piper of Kilbarchan', or Montgomerie's notable allegory 'The Cherrie and the Slae', a dull poem perhaps but with a ravishing metre. Burns pored over all three. . . . By 1724 there was more. Allan Ramsay the poet gathered all the old songs he could find into his *Tea-Table Miscellany* that Edinburgh devoured. The very cosiness of its title emphasises the difference between the comfortable eighteenth century and the bad old days of the Covenanters. Was not Edinburgh sitting at her tea-table now, instead of glowering up at a scaffold? But Scotland couldn't have enough of her old songs. By the mid-century there was a flood of them. *The Lark* ('my constant vademecum', Burns) in 1740 held nearly 500 of them—Scots and English too—with a glossary to help you out with the old Scots words. And 'The Charmer' came out after that, with more, and 'The Linnet', 'The Thrush', 'The Robin'—the whole country was singing. From castle to cot, the songs went everywhere. Most important of all, they were in Burns' pocket as, a lad of sixteen, he guided his plough, and in his head—ringing by day and by night.

And the songs weren't the only let-up either. There were books and plays. By 1725 you could borrow a book that was not ecclesiastical from Allan Ramsay's pleasant library in the High Street, and by 1736—wonder of wonders!—you could even see a play. The Drama was coming back! Tho' it was only the inoffensive and now well-known *Gentle Shepherd,* and the modest hall which showed it, had incontinently—under the fury of the Kirk—to shut up shop, but—Edinburgh had seen it! And with the turn of the century in 1759 the spark had become a fire. Here was the whole town crowding to the new Theatre Royal to see that wild success *Douglas*—the play that turned every Scottish head that saw it. A Scotsman—and a minister of the Kirk, at that!—John Home, had written it, and here—in open defiance of the fuming Edinburgh Presbytery—here was another, the most distinguished cleric in Scotland, the unsnubbable 'Jupiter' Carlyle, actually leaning out of his box 'neath the gay Canongate candles, to applaud it. The spark had become a fire! By 1781 you might call it a furnace. The immortal Mrs. Siddons was playing in town. And the General Assembly itself—that august Parliament of the Kirk—had perforce to rearrange its sessions (or there mightn't have been a Geneva gown present!) so as not to clash with her performances. Truly the wheel had come full circle—since the long shadows by the gallows in the Grassmarket.

Excursus on Drama

Tho' it wasn't as surprising as all that. For Scotland has always been, in her way, a dramatic nation. Not, of course, in the way of great tragedy, which is fundamentally alien to her temper,—for even her great novelists fail in tragic themes, Scott's *Bride of Lammermoor* and Stevenson's ambitious *Weir of Hermiston* alike falling flat. But in the drama of low life, Scotland, like Holland, finds herself. Here, like Holland (also afflicted with a stern Reformation and also finding relief from it in a similar way, in the alehouse studies of Jan Steen)—here, like Holland then, she excels. Give her a pot-house scene or the rollicking merriment of the road, and no one can do it better. In this sphere, the nation's dramatic history has been continuous. It began, as far as can be traced, in the early fourteenth century with the *Tale of Rauf Colzear,* a collier who, entertaining an unknown foreigner, knocks him about

in the wildest horse-play—only to discover on his return visit, coals and all, to Paris, that it is Charlemagne, the King himself, he has been buffeting about—a situation fraught with the authentic appeal of its descendant, the Pantomime Transformation Scene. *Cockelbie's Sow* too has just as lively vignettes, with a harlot feasting her jovial friends on the proceeds of the sow's sale—for a threepenny bit! While, all through the (still un-Reformed) fourteenth and fifteenth centuries went on the immensely popular miracle-plays and pageants,—presenting Bible-stories of the most sensational kind (by choice)—like Daniel in the lions' den, or Herodias dancing for John the Baptist's head, with the head actually being struck off. You couldn't have it too thrilling! It was in the towns, naturally, you'd see most of this play-acting. Here is the city of Aberdeen, in 1445, performing in the open air 'the secret drama of the Halie Blude' (Holy Blood)—and in the next century the City of Edinburgh's official welcome to Marie of Guise (mother of Mary Queen of Scots)[1] takes the form of a pageant and a play. A few years later, on Good Friday morning in Stirling, they put on 'a drama against the Papists' by a certain Friar Kyllour before King James V himself. And you might have thought the Reformation, that stopped so many interesting things, would have put a stop to this fun too. But at first it did not. For here, on a July day in 1571 (eleven years after Scotland had been 'converted') is no less a personage than John Knox himself listening to a play at the University of St. Andrews. It wasn't a mild play either, for he saw '*The Castle of Edinburgh,* according to Mr. Knox's doctrine, being besieged and taken, and the captain, with one or two with him, hanged in effigy'. So writes the engaging James Melville, himself a young St. Andrews' student at the time. Even six years later at Perth, play-acting was still rampant. They were staging the Corpus Christi play,—that 'idolatrous and superstitious fancy' as it was now called—on a June day in the open. Now, however, the Kirk had had time to get going and the rash players were threatened with her excommunication. . . . Aligned with these Bible stories is the famous *Christis Kirk on the Green* (a wild success for three centuries and the direct spiritual ancestor of Burns' Holy Fair) where the jollification takes in the whole village and is as rough and riotous as either Rauf Colzear or Cockelbie's Sow. It is not till the eve of Flodden, in the flush of the Renaissance, that sophistication comes in, with the Court poet Dunbar and his incredible 'Twa Mariit Wemen and the Wedo' on that summer midnight over the roses and the wine—a dramatic interlude as outspoken as anything in the Heptameron of La Reine Margot, its contemporary in France—. Sophisticated too is, a little later, Lyndesay's drama of the *Three Estates.* And with that—like a thunderbolt—in the sixteenth century, descends the terrible Reformation. But even then, the dramatic instinct is not wholly quenched. Oddly enough, John Knox himself is the best witness to it, in those parts of his *History* like the brilliant dialogues between himself and the Queen—in his realistic account of Cardinal Beaton's murder—in his eyewitness tale of the sacking of St. Giles—all of them good 'theatre'. Nor, in the dreary Killing Time that followed, did drama utterly die. Driven underground, it is true, but here is Patrick Walker the chapman, up and down the road. And if you buy his broadsheets, as they did like wildfire alike on Edinburgh streets and lonely Galloway moors, you'll get every kind of a thrill that you could ask of the tensest drama—the thud of the dragoons riding across the mosses after John Brown, the jingle of Clavers' bridle and the curt order to shoot, the wild eyes of Peden the Prophet, as he sat in mortal danger, at your ingle-cheek. But now, in the Golden eighteenth century drama was free again. And down in country Ayrshire Burns was to write his **'Jolly Beggars'** and later, at Ellisland, his exhilarating **'Tam o' Shanter'**. Sudden and unheralded as these two pieces may appear, there is in reality nothing of suddenness about them. Like the 'small white rose of Scotland' itself, their roots strike deep and far—sunk profoundly in the nation's past. . . . And after Burns' day, the drama of low life still went on. In the strait-laced nineteenth century, it is true, it was again driven underground—but now, Neil Munro's Para Handy stories, Joe Corrie's tense 'one-act'ers, the Repertory Theatres in Glasgow—Perth—Dundee,—the Drama Festivals over the whole land, are one and all in the tradition. Scotland's dramatic instinct, over the centuries has been continuous.

Eighteenth-Century Scotland's Books

But if the theatre, in the late eighteenth century, was making the most notable come-back, it was by no means the only one. Scotland itself was crackling with life—intellect stirring in all directions. Tho' it was, unexpectedly enough, from the Highlands that the first sheet-lightning broke, with the publication of Macpherson's famous Ossian in 1762. Ossian indeed carried Scotland's name to every library table in Europe, and to every literary salon—starting the rage for sentiment that was to last for half a century and issue in Goethe's Werther and Scott's own early work, *Lenore*. Were the Highlands—it was the universal query now— really as Ossian showed them, misty mountains and mournful heroines—tears and laments and phantom heroes? No one knew but it made you weep to think they were. If hard-headed folk like Mme. de Staël in worldly Paris (not to speak of Napoleon later) choked with sobs over Ossian's plaints, no wonder that inexperienced young Robert Burns in stolid Ayrshire didn't quite know what to make of this queer Highlander. Over Henry Mackenzie's *Man of Feeling* (published nearly ten years later in 1771) 'a book I prize next to the Bible' he was clearer. It, at any rate, was Scotch of the brand he knew and written by a plain Edinburgh man. Nothing here about mountains or mist, tho' plenty still about tears. Burns, untaught by wider reading (for 'prizing the Bible' didn't mean reading it. It was not until his accident in Edinburgh in 1787 that he took to that, getting as far as Joshua) and inexperienced in the great masters, lapped its easy pathos up. And while the mawkish sentiment of both these prize best-sellers must have been bad for any young poet— accounting, later on, for such things as the fulsomeness of **'Edina'** and the worst sentimental patches of **'The Cottar'**—they probably did him no more harm than that. For, reflecting at the mature age of twenty-eight in his autobiographical letter to Moore, on the books that had given him the most pleasure, of all he'd ever read, Burns singles out an astonishing couple—(1) an obscure *Life of Hannibal,* author unnamed and (2) the *History of Sir William Wallace* (himself an Ayrshire man) in a bowdlerised version, then current, of Blind Harry—from which it can safely be assumed that Robin's was not a bookish mind. Unimpressionable with regard to scenery, he was just as unreceptive to the written word. When he came to his life-work, the songs, he had fortunately shaken off both Ossian and Mackenzie. . . . Tho' there were books then being written in his Scotland, that were well worth reading. Edinburgh knew them all. Apart from the two best-sellers, there was the Glasgow-born novelist Smollett whose latest work *Humphrey Clinker* (1771) brought his Southern readers to the beauties of Loch Lomond and later, if somewhat less flatteringly, up Edinburgh's own historic High Street. In Theology, if you liked it—and Edinburgh did!—there was a new and broad-minded kind purveyed by the admirable Dr. Blair of the High Kirk, author of those *Sermons* that even George III wished to read. In History there was Robertson, Principal of the University, for the first time bringing the *History of Scotland* in pleasant, and still readable narrative to Londoners that had never looked at a Scots historian before. In Philosophy—ah! here Scotland had once again a native-born son, David Hume, as completely at home in Paris as her sons like Duns Scotus had been in older days. Even more so, perhaps. For Hume not only wrote his *Treatise of Human Nature* that the Sorbonne studied, but knew Paris's fashionable world too in his friendship with a delightful French Marquise—and moved, as to the manner born, among the candles and music of Versailles. And in a quiet corner of the Canongate, sat shy Adam Smith whose epoch-making *Wealth of Nations* in 1776 had just introduced the world to the new and portentous subject of Economics. It was a society bred on books like these—the books Burns never read— that was being prepared to welcome him, as no Edinburgh society before or since would have welcomed a raw Ayrshire poet. For what would the fanatic seventeenth century have done to the brazen author of **'The Holy Fair'**, or the narrow Disruption nineteenth confronted with the blasphemy of **'Holy Willie's Prayer'**? But the broad-minded eighteenth, at a first glance in 1786, asked him—straight from the plough—

to dine with the cream of their own intellectual company, and unhesitatingly set the cachet of immortality—then in their gift—to the hitherto provincial *Kilmarnock Edition* so that, when in 1787 the first *Edinburgh Edition* of his poems came out, London (that had left the *Kilmarnock* unheeded) printed it at once, with Dublin—Philadelphia—New York—following suit. It was eighteenth-century Edinburgh 'made' Burns.

Eighteenth-Century Edinburgh

The Capital that welcomed him, the Edinburgh that had been growing up now from 1769 on, was the city that is still the delight of Europe—that New Town of those splendid streets and squares, with their spacious, uncrowded magnificence and their long, alluring vistas carrying the eye far over the Forth into the distant mountains of the North. Robert Adam was at work, planning the elegance and perfect proportions of Charlotte Square: in the drawing-rooms of Moray Place—but a stone's-throw away—there were again mantelpieces and ceilings of a delicacy and curious carving that recalled the art of the sixteenth century in town-houses such as that of Marie of Guise, the Queen-Regent, in the old, dark Edinburgh High Street. . . . And by the close of the eighteenth century, Raeburn was painting men like the Highland chief, The Mac-Nab, in full—and no longer forbidden—Highland dress, or the eminent Sir John Sinclair, Founder of the Board of Agriculture, or the homely and wise Dr. Adam, Rector of the High School, or the sinister hanging Judge, Lord Braxfield—even as young Allan Ramsay earlier painted the fine Scots ladies in their delicate satins and pearly lace, with roses as exquisitely poised on hair or bosom as ever was the Pompadour's—so that the eye to-day can picture the people who moved in those drawing-rooms or walked in those pleasant squares. A wonderful Edinburgh—and a brilliant Scotland!

For if Edinburgh in the second half of the eighteenth century seethed with intellectual life, it wasn't only Edinburgh, but country Scotland as well. Boswell, touring it with Dr. Johnson in 1773, has left it on record that in the rudest country inn, as at Glenmoriston, he'd come across books like *The Spectator* (which you would never nowadays in any Scots inn at all!). In Dunvegan, over in lonely Skye, on every window-sill the Doctor could finger a classical tome. In the ministers' manses he saw the walls lined with authors of the standing of Bossuet or Massillon. And the very rustics knew their Latin. While in the wilds of the excessively practical Nor'-East he came upon eccentrics like Lord Monboddo arguing with almost Oxford learning about the Homeric problem or the Origin of Man. And if you think Boswell is carefully choosing his evidence, you've only to look at Sir John Sinclair's *First Statistical Account,* published, it is true, at the close of the eighteenth century in 1798, but written of an era at least ten years earlier, to find Boswell's account elaborated in detail. Not a parish in rural Scotland but was alive with interest in the Arts. The brilliance of the Capital was reflected in a thousand facets in village and hamlet and town. Never had Scotland been so well-educated before. Never has she been so well-educated since. It was on to a stage like this, before an audience as many-sided and as gifted that Burns came forward in the second half of the eighteenth century to make his trials.

Burns Against His Literary Background

Educated he was, if only self-educated, but without the discipline of Church learning which Knox, for example, a trained priest, had had. With it, or because of it, Knox was able to write that long and fascinating *History of the Reformation.* Without it, Burns, never having had the advantage of any mental discipline whatsoever, can write nothing long at all. His interest soon flags—his répertoire a series of occasional pieces. By contrast, again, with Knox, who had seen and lived in other countries, Burns, who had done neither, is, in outlook, provincial. He sees nothing but Ayrshire. By contrast, further, with Fergusson, his immediate predecessor (and to some extent, model) who had had a University education, Burns' outlook is illiterate. For while Fergusson, with his University behind him, is sensible of his own ignorance and will write only of what he knows, 'The Leith Races', 'The Farmer's Ingle', Burns, without any University standard, is totally unaware of it. Never once does it dawn on him there is anything more to know, so that he will write with equal confidence an epigram on a translation of Martial (whom he did not know) and a poem on Hallowe'en (which he did). . . . And when one comes to the perennial stuff of poetry—things like the Charlemagne legend, or the even more famous story of King Arthur and the Round Table, that had embroidered and enriched the fabric of all European literatures (Scots literature among them) from the fifteenth century on—all that is but a blank page to Burns. He knows nothing of it. Nor of that wealth of classical mythology that, with a single word, can light torches of poetic fire to illumine and glorify the surrounding scene. Yet Dunbar before him has the trick of it, and the modern Scots Renaissance School ('Babylon blaws doun in stour'—Wm. Soutar) after him. But Burns? No: alone of Scots poets, he claims no link with the immemorial background of European poetic thought. He alone knows no Muses. His poetry, therefore, rings no bells. There is a thinness about it that, if you come to it from any other poet, strikes you at once. It is all on the surface. That is all that Robin sees. And sometimes—you will say—a very good surface too. But in the Edinburgh of Hume's *Treatises* and Robertson's *History* and Adam Smith's *Wealth of Nations*—even of Smollett's *Humphrey Clinker*—they looked for something more. And Edinburgh opinion—even kindly Edinburgh opinion—was quick to notice that the young man from Ayrshire was over-sure of himself. A clever tongue—and ideas—but he made no allowances at all, in this exceptionally gifted Capital, for anybody else having either. It is a shallowness that is apparent also, if inevitably, in his work. . . . For, apart from Ossian and Mackenzie, Burns had read little. Fergusson and Allan Ramsay, to be sure—some Shenstone, Pope, Sterne—Thomson's *Winter*—Beattie—nearly all of them his own contemporaries, or near-contemporaries. Yet it is not from these, but from writers of an earlier age, breathing a different air and looking at life from a different angle, that a man broadens his mind. But to these, Burns, not being a bookish person, was allergic. So that, without the breadth of mind this kind of education gives, he came to believe—for all his window-dressing of the brotherhood of Man (borrowed from the contemporary slogans of the French Revolution) that Virtue resided only in the class he knew. 'The birkie ca'd a lord' never had a trace of it. And Robin becomes—to his own disaster—Scotland's first class-conscious poet. . . . And, as it is assuredly from the Past, its standards and its art, that a man acquires a knowledge of Beauty, Burns, being thus insensitive to the Past (for his mental interest, like his physical, took in only what was nearest to him, as the mouse, the mountain daisy, the girl just then on the doorstep)—Burns therefore never attained to this, for a poet, most vital knowledge. So that he writes, as readily, abominations like 'the tenebrific scene', as gems like

> whiles glitter'd to the nightly rays
> wi bickerin', dancin' dazzle.

He has no aesthetic criterion. . . . His appeal to the ear also traverses but the range of everyday things— the only things that interested him—like the hisses in the **'Holy Fair'**, the reel in **'Tam o' Shanter'**, the staggering lines in **'Death and Dr. Hornbook'**. A witchery potent, no doubt, and at times both instant and compelling—but a witchery of the street. For he cannot lift you, like Milton or Tennyson, those masters of verbal harmonies, into the sonorous music of the spheres. . . . And being thus insensitive to the past, it further follows there is little appeal in Burns' work to the imagination. When the Kirk (the only traditional institution to which he responded) is behind him, her imagery does indeed colour his thought, which elsewhere is but plain statement, unrelieved by literary figures of any kind. . . . In the main, then, his appeal—ironically enough, like that of the Kirk he hated—is neither to the imagination nor to the ear, but to the intellect. But, luckily for him, Scotland has always been a country that looked to the intellect for enjoyment. Even from the time of Barbour, author of the earliest known Scots poem 'The Brus', emphasis falls largely on the intellect, for Barbour was not only Archdeacon of Aberdeen, but an Oxford scholar too.

And the galaxy of poets at the Renaissance Court of James IV were not only poets, but men of learning as well—Henryson, author of the delightful pastoral 'Robin and Makyn' but also a learned Benedictine at Dunfermline Abbey, Dunbar of 'The Golden Targe' an Oxford man again and as a Franciscan, trained in the Church's lore, Gavin Douglas, first European translator of Virgil's *Aeneid*. Even when the writer is not himself of much learning, the appeal is still the same, as in Davie Lyndesay's 'Three Estates', making a direct bid to the intellect, in its powerful political satire. To this traditional bias in favour of the intellect rather than the senses, the Reformation only added strength, for Knox, author, it is true, of the famous *History,* is even better known as the planner of Scotland's austere and highbrow modern education. In the seventeenth century, the great Samuel Rutherfurd of the magnificent *Letters* and the rebellious *Lex Rex*—the foremost author of his time in Scotland—was to be found in the Chair of Latin in Edinburgh University and later as Principal of St. Mary's College, St. Andrews. While in the eighteenth Hume—Boswell—Adam Smith—were all of them definitely preoccupied with learning. And if Burns, who now took up their mantle, was Scotland's first unlearned writer, the appeal of his work was nevertheless—paradoxically enough— the same as theirs, and in line with his country's long tradition. As firmly as Knox himself, Burns aimed at the intellect. Tho', being as he was, without the ancient learning, he—more than any of his predecessors—was thrown on his own resources to do it.

These were, however, considerable. He was possessed of a native wit, keen and sharp, that made him see through shams, and a tongue, the match of it, to pillory them. And not having the learning of his forebears to trick out and adorn the wit, he must needs polish that wit itself till, sharp as a surgeon's knife, it cut right through to the bone. You might miss a point of Dunbar's for the aureate gods and goddesses nearly smothering it. Nobody in this world ever missed a point of Burns's. With nothing to shade it, it is diamond-clear. . . . And having great natural parts, he did not transmogrify the rural life he saw around him, into such stylised woodenness as Ramsay's 'Gentle Shepherd'. He looked directly at his world and drew from that. Moreover, the Cottar, tho' clearly drawn from life, is not a transcript either, but an artistic whole. Burns could create. . . . He had, further, an imagination that,—since it could not feed on the famous mythology of the past—had perforce to feed on something within its own range, as—the superstitions of the Kirk, the twa dogs, the mountain daisy. Within that range, it is both original and sincere and can move an audience as it will. When, however, it is flung beyond that range and faced with the historic past or the glorious present of Edinburgh, it fails dismally, as in the artificial **'Edina'** which moves nobody. The quality, indeed, of Burns' imagination is sharply real-ist. For while Scott at the mouth of an old Close in the High Street would see the centuries roll back in vivid and romantic cavalcade, Burns—at the same point— never saw anything but a tavern, and a chair to carry him to Clarinda. And no visitor, great or small, of all the millions that, down the ages, have paused o'er the city, ever saw less of Edinburgh's beauty. Robin, indeed, looked through it blankly, as he did through Highland Ben and Border Peel. For him they had, all three, no existence. . . . And he had, finally, a gift that only came to him late in life, after much trial and error—an artistic skill that became, in his best songs, well-nigh impeccable. Here, with a self-criticism as remarkable as it is unexpected, in a man of his hot blood, he pruned and cut, cut and pruned, till only the rounded bud remained—the glowing heart of the song, crystal-clear and brief as the rose itself. And the song, with the certainty of an eagle's wing, carried the emotion he desired, straight to the listener's heart. . . . With these gifts and these deficiencies, Burns had really no choice in the form his work took. Apart from the epistle (which has more the character of versified prose, but to which he gave a new life by making it the vehicle of his own rich personality) there are only two literary forms that demand no background and no mental breadth for their successful practice—the satire and the song. With the wit, and the tongue—you can write satire. From Rome down, who wrote it first, it needs only these and concentration upon its immediate object. The song, again, is all the better for no background and demands the same kinds of heat and concentration as the satire, but in a positive—not negative—direction. To the song, then, and the satire, by his very limitations, Burns was, of necessity, driven. Of these forms and of these only, he made a complete success.

So that, on the momentous November evening in 1786 when, an unknown young man of twenty-seven, he first rode into Edinburgh, he was not as empty-handed as he seemed. He had, indeed, considerable assets. Already to his credit stood the *Kilmarnock Edition*. And in the *Kilmarnock* was **'The Cottar's Saturday Night'** that he himself considered his best work, and for satires, that scathing **'Holy Fair'** and for epistles, some of the best he was ever to write, like that gay one to James Smith

And large, before Enjoyment's gale,
  Let's tak' the tide—

And for songs, that **'Corn-Rigs'** (the only good one) that would ensure him a place, if not at the head, at least among the first half-dozen of his country's lyrists. And, for humour, the incomparable **'Address to the De'il'**. Up his sleeve (written, but not published) there was the blistering **'Holy Willie's Prayer'**, that most perfect example of satire in our tongue, and the highly original cantata of **'The Jolly Beggars'**. All in

all, Burns came to Edinburgh with a full quiver. Had he never written another word, he would still take his place, on his satires, as a classic of English literature. . . . Apart from his poetic achievement, Burns came to Edinburgh in the prime of manhood, with his mind razor-sharp to the characters of those around him. Had he not proved it, with the beggars in Poosie Nansie's, with the ministers and their audiences in Mauchline Kirk, pin-pointed one and all in his ruthless satire? With an eye too, to the excellences of family life. The Cottar, if over-sentimentalised, is still a recognisable picture of a well-known original. . . . And with a fund of humour for all things, high and low. Burns, that is, was now in the full tide of mastery of his craft. . . . Yet, after Edinburgh, he wrote no more satires, few of these salty epistles even, so full of urbane wisdom—nothing of low life to compare with **'The Jolly Beggars'**, nor of good life to set alongside **'The Cottar'**. At twenty-seven, the full flood of his genius seems arrested—dammed up. That wit, diamond-clear, razor-sharp, found nothing, it seems, further to cut. . . . What, then, happened to Burns in Edinburgh? It was not lack of recognition. For Edinburgh—brilliant, sophisticated Edinburgh—it is a matter of history now—took the young poet straightway to her arms, if not to her heart. Within a fortnight of his arrival, every door was opened to him. And it is likewise admitted that this tumultuous reception did not sweep him, raw as he was, off his feet. He moved through the elegant drawing-rooms, sat at wine with the learned and the travelled and the polished and talked with them as if he were sitting and talking in his rightful place, where he had always been, where he should be. And yet—found nothing to write of! But by his second visit in 1787 it had got about that the clever young Ayrshire satirist was keeping a memorandum-book, with the characters of his entertainers shatteringly—and amusingly, if you took it that way—hit off to the life. And the epigram on the dignified Lord Advocate ending

His argument he tint it . . .
But what his common sense came short,
  He eked out wi' law, man

or that on the eloquence of the Dean (the extremely popular Henry Erskine)

Like wind-driven hail it did assail,
  Or torrents owre a lin, man:
The Bench sae wise lift up their eyes,
  Hauf-wauken'd wi' the din, man

tho' neither was at the time published, may well explain why brilliant Edinburgh, on second thoughts, had appreciably cooled off. A formidable pen! But the epigrams, clever as they were, were not satire. Edinburgh might enjoy them—or fear them—but the world at large, to whom the Lord Advocate and the Dean were but names—could not savour them to the full. Whereas folk like Holy Willie or the preachers at Mauchline Fair, unlike the Dean, had a universal audience, for hypocrites are kent folk to all the world. How then came it that Burns wrote no more satire? . . . But for satire you have to know your victims—so to speak,—inside out, as Horace knew the bore of the Via Sacra on his daily walks through the lively Forum, and the travellers he would meet on the way to the coast. As Burns did too, who had lived all his life with Holy Willie at his elbow and seen Holy Fairs times without number. Whereas the men he met now at the fine Edinburgh tables, with the candle-light falling softly on polished silver and fragile cut crystal, were men he met only there—mere voices to him. They talked—or listened—but what they did to-morrow, or what they were really thinking now? Who could tell? How could any man tell? For there was an impenetrable armour of sophistication—polish—conventionality—whatever it was—about them, that kept you at arm's length and effectually prevented you from ever really knowing. Burns would plunge with a forthright Jacobin sword-thrust, and the Lord Advocate, or his like, merely lifting an eyebrow, would riposte. You couldn't even make them angry. So that satire faded out. Unlike Daddy Auld, these men never gave themselves away. So that you could only hate them—those 'elegant patricians'. And hatred filling all your mind because of the too too vivid contrast, seen now at close quarters, between what they had and what you hadn't, stifled all the laughter and the mockery that alone made Horatian satire (Burns's kind) possible. It was, perhaps, inevitable that the brilliant Have-Not, meeting the brilliant Have's, should react like this. And the hatred lasted, after Edinburgh—long after Edinburgh—till it issued in fierce thunderbolts like **'A Man's a Man for a' that'**. So maybe the fine Edinburgh tables had done their work after all. . . . For the conditions for satire were gone for ever.

But if the New Town, all unconsciously, killed something in Burns, the Old Town made amends. Over there in the High Street, in the dark, crowded Closes, with the winter dusk ancient Edinburgh of the dead-and-gone centuries seemed to come alive again. And as Burns moved out from his Lawnmarket lodging into the black street, an old song would greet his ear, 'De'il tak' the wars', or, in lighter vein, 'Saw ye my dearie, my Eppie Macnab?', or that universal favourite 'John, cum kiss me now'. From the Anchor Close? Or the Advocate's? Or even the aristocratic Canongate? From any or from all of them, for everybody was singing the old songs here. Robin knew them too, from *The Lark* that he had pored over, as a boy in Ayrshire, but here in Edinburgh you could hear them every night—in every Close—and from all sorts of people. A periwigged Judge, perhaps, like Lord Hailes, a connoisseur in all these old songs—or a sedan-chair would come past, with the brightest eyes in Scotland

flashing out at you from it—the Duchess of Gordon?—and she knew them too—or Mr. Creech (the famous bookseller)'s printer, that convivial William Smellie, founder of the Crochallan Fencibles, that riotous club that met in the Anchor Close—and the coarser the old song here, the more to the taste of the Crochallans. Burns knew that too. Or, best of all, in Libberton's Wynd, down the Cowgate way, in the dark recesses of Johnnie Dowie's Howff—far ben, in that innermost stifling cellar they called 'the Coffin'—two men would be sitting, that had all the Scots songs at their finger-tips. Here Burns would drift in oftenest, as if pulled by a magnet, for one of the two was the now famous William Herd, that poor Edinburgh clerk who had been writing down every odd scrap of old Scots song—every random line still floating in the air—all his working life, and who, like as not, had the treasure-trove with him there. The other was noteworthy too—that James Johnson on whose little music-shop in Lady Stair's Close, Burns could look down from his window in the Lawnmarket. Johnson had the authentic passion too. Songs by Scotsmen were what Johnson wanted, whether in the vernacular or no. Herd would have naught but songs in the braid Scots. Over the good Edinburgh ale and the guttering candles in Johnnie Dowie's, Burns would listen to Herd and Johnson. It was surely Destiny herself brought these two within his ken—the two of all then alive in broad Scotland, who could help him most in the work he had to do. And when the clock of St. Giles' beat out twelve, and Dowie's doors shut—as shut they aye did on the stroke—and Burns made home, under the midnight stars, to the Lawnmarket again,—the High Street, as he passed down it, would be still aglow with life—fiddles scraping and laughter pealing and the tap-tap of dancing feet. Reels and strathspeys down every Close—and as a stray cellar-door would open, you could see the lighted room within, and the whirl of gay brocade and the gallants' fine coats. And ever and on, the quick beat of the reels—the slower strathspeys. Slow them both down a beat or two, and you could set a song to them. A Scots song. And Robin knew all the tunes. Were they not, every one in that *Caledonian Pocket Companion* he'd studied all his life? . . . Night after night in Johnnie Dowie's, talking with Herd—night after night with those reels and strathspeys ringing in his head. Down in Ayrshire as a boy he'd liked the Scots songs himself, but up in the New Town the vogue had been all for the English. Tho' maybe Herd was right. Maybe the Scots ones were better—'We're a' kissed sleepin', 'Guidwife, count the lawin'! You couldn't get better than these. Like his own **'Corn-rigs were bonnie',** that he'd put in the *Kilmarnock*. And most unlike his own **'From thee, Eliza, I must go',** that he had also put. . . . Those old Scots songs. Was there anything else that could charm you—hold you—fill your whole mind like them? 'There is a certain something in the old Scotch songs, a wild happiness of thought and expression', Burns is writing from

Edinburgh in the winter of 1787. 'An engraver (Johnson) in this town has set about collecting and publishing all the Scotch songs with the music, that can be found . . . I have been absolutely crazed about it, collecting old stanzas . . . ' Absolutely crazed about it! To the two over the ale in Dowie's howff there was nothing in the whole world but just Scots songs. And to that third man now, making home under the midnight stars, to the fiddles scraping out the fey old tunes in every dark Close—to that third man now too. From then on, to his last breath in 1796, nothing in the world for Robert Burns either but Scots songs. It was eighteenth-century Edinburgh, the Old Town and the brilliant New, that together 'made' Burns.

Notes

[1] For this information I am indebted to Moffat's *The Bible in Scotland,* pp. 30-2.

L. M. Angus-Butterworth (essay date 1969)

SOURCE: "The 'Annus Mirabilis,' 1785," in *Robert Burns and the 18th-Century Revival of Scottish Vernacular Poetry,* Aberdeen University Press, 1969, pp. 169-89.

[In the following excerpt Angus-Butterworth examines the histories and inspirations of several of Burns's famous poems.]

The Cottar's Saturday Night

It has often been noticed that Burns drew his inspiration for **The Cottar's Saturday Night** from Fergusson's poem *The Farmer's Ingle,* and this as a bare statement may give the impression that one is derived from the other. Actually the connection between the two is so slight that little more than the general idea was borrowed.

We can imagine the impact made on Burns's mind by the descriptions which the earlier poet gives of the farmer's home life, and how his imagination must have been fired by the depiction of scenes which he knew much better than Fergusson. Here, indeed, was a theme so intimately within his experience that none specially designed for him could have been more fitting. But what the prentice hand of Fergusson had attempted, Burns was able to transform by his master touch.

The opening verse of **The Cottar's Saturday Night,** addressed to Robert Aiken,[1] is thought by Chambers and others to have been added after the rest of the poem was written, but forms a very appropriate introduction. The poet sets the scene, too, by quoting these lines of Gray:

Let not ambition mock their useful toil,
Their homely joys and destiny obscure;
Nor grandeur hear, with a disdainful smile
The short and simple annals of the poor.[2]

The 'homely joys' were such as Burns himself knew and loved, so that he was very much at home in describing the quiet domestic scenes. At the same time he preserves a certain detachment, so that Crawford remarks that in his account of the Cottar and his wife, 'Burns eyes the couple quizzically but not unkindly, and he chooses the artificial expressions quite deliberately, so that there shall be no doubt as to his attitude'.[3]

The resemblance between the first verse of *The Farmer's Ingle,* and Burns's second verse is worthy of notice, and if we compare them the relationship of the two poems becomes clear. The lines of Fergusson read as follows:

Whan gloamin' gray out-owre the welkin[4] keeks,[5]
Whan Bawtie ca's the owsen[6] to the byre,
Whan Thrasher John, sair dung,[7] his barn-door steeks,[8]
Whan lusty lasses at the dighting[9] tire:
What bangs fu' leal the e'ening's coming cauld,
And gars[10] snaw-tappit winter freeze in vain;
Gars dowie[11] mortals look baith blithe and bauld,
Nor fleyed[12] wi' a' the puirtith[13] o' the plain;
Begin, my Muse, and chant in hamely strain.

The corresponding verse in **The Cottar's Saturday Night** reads:

November chill blaws land wi' angry sugh;
The short'ning winter-day is near a close;
The miry beasts retreating frae the plough:
The black'ning trains o' craws to their repose:
The toil-worn cotter frae his labour goes,
This night his weekly moil is at an end,
Collects his spades, his mattocks, and his hoes,
Hoping the morn in ease and rest to spend,
And weary, o'er the moor, his course does hameward bend.

Apart from a vague similarity of subject, what strikes us at once are the wide differences in the character of the poems. The contrast of language is great. Fergusson as usual is concerned only with the vernacular. Burns, being still at an early stage in his career, was not averse to writing in English, but shows his power by alternating in places between Scots and English. His procedure may be said to consist of using English for the basic narrative, but not hesitating to introduce Scots words and phrases where these heighten the characterization or bring home his meaning more clearly. This was not a mere matter of embellishment, but a brilliant demonstration that he was bilingual. The simple sincerity of many passages disguises his consummate linguistic skill.

Another fundamental point of contrast is that whereas the rhyming in *The Farmer's Ingle* is *a b a b c d c d*, the form of stanza used in **The Cottar** is that of Spenser and also of Shenstone, namely *a b a b b c b c c*. Thus as Burns here 'maintains the perfect form of the Spenserian stanza',[14] he has adopted an English measure which was quite outside Fergusson's scope.

In what is no doubt a just assessment Angellier says: 'La distance qui sépare le plus haut effort de Fergusson, de ce qui n'est pas le chef-d'oeuvre de Burns, c'est-à-dire *Le Foyer du Fermier, du Samedi soir,* est incommensurable. Les deux pieces n'appartiennent pas aux mêmes régions. Celle de Fergusson est de petite description exacte. Elle n'a ni la grande poésie, ni la noble enthousiasme, ni la portée sociale de celle de Burns. Elle n'a en rien cette plénitude de vie.'[15]

Dr. Otto Ritter suggests in general terms, without giving direct parallels, that in **The Cottar's Saturday Night** there is to be found something of Thomson's *Winter,* Shenstone's *Schoolmistress,* Gray's *Elegy* and Goldsmith's *Deserted Village.*[16] Sutherland has observed that this was following the standard practice of the eighteenth century in heightening the perception of the reader by reminding him of poems with which he was already familiar, and that Milton himself had done this in the century before.[17] Crawford is more specific, and notes for example that the lines: ''Tis when a youthful, loving pair, / In other's arms, breathe out the tender tale / Beneath the milk-white thorn that scents the ev'ning gale', echo the reference of Shakespeare to 'the milk-white rose',[18] and Milton's lines: 'And every Shepherd tells his tale / Under the Hawthorn in the dale,'.[19]

Crawford is largely accurate in his statement that: 'The evolution of the poem is from a sombre beginning, with its portrayal of the weariness that is the aftermath of physical labour, to a concretely presented interior that merged imperceptibly into a transfiguration and sublimation of the worshipping father and his family.'[20] Part of the quality and merit of the poem is the result of this major development of the theme.

One of the prime virtues of Burns as a poet is that he devoted himself in his major works to subjects about which he had intimate knowledge. He was no stranger to the life led by the small farmer. He speaks with affection of the mother's devoted care in sewing so that her family shall appear decent in the eyes of the

world, and it is natural that he should use the braid Scots in such lines as:

> The mother wi' her needle and her sheers,
> Gars auld claes look amaist as weel's the
> new.

And a perfectly authentic note is struck in describing the courting of the daughter Jenny:

> Wi' kindly welcome, Jenny brings him ben[21];
> A strappin' youth; he takes the mother's
>   eye;
> Blithe Jenny sees the visit's no ill-ta'en;
> The father cracks[22] of horses, ploughs and
>   kye[23];
> The youngster's artless heart o'erflows wi'
>   joy,
> But blate[24] and lathefu',[25] scarce can weel
>   behave;
> The mother, wi' a woman's wiles, can spy
> What makes the youth sae bashfu' and sae
>   grave:
> Weel pleased to think her bairn's respected
>   like the lave.[26]

Thus, although the standard is not the same throughout, it is impossible to accept the view of Henley, so often superficial in his judgments, that the poem is 'of its essence sentimental and therefore pleasingly untrue'.[27] Equally unacceptable is the opinion of a Russian critic, who condemns the cottar on political grounds and suggests that, because he is a proprietor, he must belong to the past: 'And that the countryman—the cottar whom Burns depicted in the "Saturday Night"—was an owner, although a small one; he was "on his own", the master of a self-contained economic unit, and at the time of Burns no longer a typical figure in the Scottish village. Hence one cannot but feel that this represents a utopian, retrospective glance into the past.'[28]

Essentially **The Cottar's Saturday Night** is a sincere and warm-hearted tribute on the part of Burns to the simple, wholesome pleasures among which he had been brought up. It has plenty of quiet humour, but is without the sophistication which might now be considered necessary. Froude shows a just appreciation of how well this reflects Scottish life in this passage: 'Among their good qualities, the Scots have been distinguished for humour—not for venomous wit, but for kindly, genial humour, which half loves what it laughs at—and this alone shows clearly enough that those to whom it belongs have not looked too exclusively on the gloomy side of the world. I should rather say that the Scots have been an unusually happy people. Intelligent industry, the honest doing of daily work, with a sense that it must be done well, under penalties; the necessaries of life moderately provided for; and a sensible content with the situation of life in which men are born—this through the week, and at the end of it the **Cottar's Saturday Night**—the homely family, gathered reverently and peacefully together, and irradiated with a sacred presence.—Happiness! such happiness as we human creatures are likely to know upon this world, will be found there, if anywhere.'[29]

In an age when there is so much concentration upon the sordid and unpleasant in literature, it is inevitable that a wholesome and charming work like **The Cottar's Saturday Night** should be unfashionable, and should be condemned as sentimental for the same reason that kindred poems by Goldsmith and Gray are for the time being not fully appreciated. But unhealthy preoccupation with sexual depravity and the like can only be a passing phase, and meanwhile the poem continues to have countless warm admirers. One major advantage which it brought to Burns himself was his friendship with Mrs. Dunlop. Upon reading it at a time of deep sorrow in her family that lady wrote: 'The poignancy of your expression soothed my soul', and thereafter her faith in him never faltered.

The Jolly Beggars

This remarkable *tour de force* deserves careful consideration on a number of counts, and it may be appropriate to look first at the circumstances under which it was written. During the winter of 1785, Burns in company with John Richmond and James Smith, spent an evening with Johnnie Dow who, besides being a rhymester, kept a tavern in Mauchline. When the party broke up Burns and his two friends set off for home, and, in walking through the village, they passed the door of an inn or lodging-house for vagrants and beggars kept by a Mrs. Gibson, usually known as Poosie Nansie.

The establishment of Poosie Nansie and her daughter Racer Jess was a disreputable one, but on this occasion the sound of revelry was so cheerful that Burns and his companions went inside to see what kind of party was afoot. It was already the close of the evening, so that the call could only be a short one. There would probably have been danger for any person by himself to have ventured in, but for three young men to do so together was a different matter. At the time Burns was twenty-six, and to get the thing in perspective we have to realize that today the three indulging in this escapade might not long have ceased to be university students. While allowing for the poet's genius, there was an element of an undergraduate prank about the affair.

Although this chance visit to an ale-house was a brief one, a glimpse of the inmates was sufficient to fire the poetic imagination of Burns. What he actually saw may have been very limited, and that drab and squalid,

but one reason why the impression made on him was strong was because the scene was a novel one so far as he was concerned: there is nothing to indicate that he was ever in such a place before this or afterwards. He found it convenient, in fact, to forget that he ever wrote **The Jolly Beggars**, and it was not published until some few years after his death. The cantata, Italian in origin, is used in the case of **The Jolly Beggars** in the sense of a short lyrical drama set to music, with solos and choruses. Burns read the first draft to John Richmond within a few days of the event. In view of the amount of work involved this was an almost incredible achievement. In **The Jolly Beggars** he provides eight songs and choruses, and matches them to folk-airs. To link the solos together he gives descriptive passages without tunes, headed *Recitativo*.

After an introduction, six of the beggars sing songs in turn. A 'Son of Mars', to the tune *Soldier's Joy*, describes his wartime experiences and how he came by his wounds—'This here was for a wench, and that other in a trench, when welcoming the French at the sound of a drum'. His 'doxy', to the tune *Sodger Laddie*, tells of her conquests in another field—'I once was a maid tho' I cannot tell when, and still my delight is in proper young men'. Next 'Merry Andrew', to the tune *Auld Sir Symon*, shows scant respect for the great ones of church and state, opening his song with—'Sir Wisdom's a fool when he's fou; Sir Knave is a fool in a Session; he's there but a prentice, I trow, but I am a fool by profession'. A female beggar then laments her 'Highland Lad', hanged for rieving (or pillaging), to the tune *O, An' Ye Were Dead, Gudeman,* singing—'A highland lad my love was born, the lalland[30] laws he held in scorn; but he still was faithfu' to his clan, my gallant, braw John Highlandman'. She is followed by 'A pigmy Scraper wi' his fiddle', who tries to comfort her to the tune *Whistle Owre the Lave O't;* saying—'Let me ryke (reach) up to dight (wipe) that tear, an' go wi' me an' be my dear'. But 'Her charms had struck a sturdy caird (or vagrant tinker), as weel as poor gut-scraper', and he, to the air *Clout the Cauldron,* warns off 'that shrimp, that wither'd imp, with a' his noise an' cap'rin'', at the point of a rapier.

The climax of what has been described as this 'wild and glorious cantata' is now reached, when the bard, as 'a wight of Homer's craft',[31] rises to toast the fair sex, to the tune *For A' That, An' A' That,* and to lead the final chorus, to the air *Jolly Mortals, Fill your Glasses,* the refrain of this being:

> A fig for those by law protected!
> Liberty's a glorious feast!
> Courts for Cowards were erected,
> Churches built to please the Priest.

Naturally the customers of Poosie Nansie could not sing the verses which Burns afterwards wrote for them, nor could they be aware of the tunes he was afterwards to select with such skill. For that matter there is not the slightest reason for thinking that any soldier, fiddler or tinker was actually present, or that the relationship of one member of the company to another was as described by the poet. In the same way the vivid and realistic description in **Tam o' Shanter** of the warlocks and witches dancing to the sound of the bagpipes played by Old Nick is not evidence that Tam really saw anything of the kind. What there is evidence of, in both instances, is the immense creative faculty in poetry which Burns possessed.

The Jolly Beggars displays very impressively Burns's scholarship and his great knowledge of old songs. It also reveals how true his ear was, and how excellent his musical taste, in finding just the right tune to fit verses which are to be sung in character. All this is a striking achievement for a young man. Wittig says of **The Jolly Beggars** that it is: 'the fullest symposium of the Scottish tradition. There is no other compilation in which we find such a wealth of old motifs, songs, tunes, Scottish metres and echoes of the Makars, brought freshly to life in a congenial form.'[32]

Thus while this cantata is an intensely original work, which only Burns could have written, it shows the influence of literary tradition. As early as the first half of the sixteenth century a song that became popular in Scotland was *The Jolly Beggar,* attributed to King James V. Again the song 'I once was a maid . . . ', although so much more savage in content, is clearly related to the gentle lines of Allan Ramsay:

> My soger laddie's over the sea
> And he will bring gold and money to me;
> And when he comes hame, he'll make me a
>   lady;
> My blessing gang wi' my soger laddie.

In introducing the fiddler Burns again echoes Ramsay, which is something rare with him, but makes the earlier poet appear dull and pedestrian by comparison, as in the very skilful use of Italian musical terms:

> Then in an *arioso* key
> The wee Apollo
> Set off wi' *allegretto* glee
> His *ginga* solo.

The corresponding lines in Ramsay read:

> On which Apollo,
> With meikle pleasure play'd himself
> Baith jig and solo.[33]

We may notice, too, that when the fiddler says to the female beggar: 'An' go with me an' be my dear', it immediately recalls the line of Marlowe: 'Come live with me and be my Love.'[34]

In a famous passage Matthew Arnold speaks of **The Jolly Beggars** as this 'puissant and splendid production'. He also says that in it: 'there is more than hideousness and squalor, there is bestiality; yet the piece is a superb poetic success. It has breadth, truth and power which make the famous scene in Auerbach's Cellar of Goethe's *Faust* seem artificial and tame beside it, and which are only matched by Shakespeare and Aristophanes.'[35] Part of the poetic success mentioned by Arnold came about because, fine as the individual items in the poem are, the themes are closely knit into a unity, and form an artistic whole which transcends each of them in excellence.

No doubt Burns enjoyed writing **The Jolly Beggars**. It was evidently the passionate outpouring of material he had already accumulated in his mind, under the stimulus of an exceptionally interesting experience, but as a cautious and circumspect Scot he did not choose to allow its appearance to have any ill effect upon his reputation, and it was not published in complete form until 1802, six years after his death. There was then another gap before the editor George Thomson wished to stage the cantata in 1814. Thomson did not find the task easy. First he invited the Scottish composer Farquhar Graham to 'realize' a 'purified' version, but when the result was ready it proved unsatisfactory. He then approached Beethoven, rightly acting on the principle that only the best was good enough for Burns, but unfortunately the great composer did not accept the commission. Finally Sir Henry Bishop undertook the work, and the piece was staged in Edinburgh in March 1823. The result must have been satisfactory at least from a financial point of view, for Bishop received in payment a gold snuff-box, decorated with Scottish jasper and agate; a suite of Scottish damask; and two pictures.

Address to the Deil

Burns was very keenly interested in the Devil. This poem was written in 1785, and his brother Gilbert says of it: 'The curious idea of such an address was suggested to him by running over in his mind the many ludicrous accounts and representations we have from various quarters of this august personage.' This jocular burlesque of Milton's Satan was written after reading *Paradise Lost,* and at the head of it he quotes the Miltonic epigraph:

> O Prince! O Chief of many thronèd Pow'rs!
> That led th' embattl'd seraphim to war. . . .

It appears that the idea of contrasting Milton's grand conception with that of popular superstition and folklore made a strong appeal to Burns's sense of humour. Burns had evidently much the closer acquaintance with the Devil, for whereas Milton regards with awe from a respectful distance, the Scottish bard is on very familiar terms, even to the use of nick-names. But while here and in other poems, such as **Tam o' Shanter,** the personality of 'Auld Clootie'[36] is expressed in terms closely in accord with the ancient traditions of the countryside, Burns had a great love for Milton. In a letter to James Smith he says: 'Give me a spirit like my favourite hero, Milton's Satan.'

There are other references in his letters to Milton's Satan, for whom, with his usual sound taste for what was of merit in literature, he had a particular regard. He was not alone in this preference, and it has been said of *Paradise Lost* that: 'The magnificent figure of Satan is consistently more appealing than Milton's God', with the curious reversal in the poem of what Milton set out to do and what he actually accomplished.

What we are considering here has a good deal to do with character and temperament. Unlike Shakespeare, who was at one with his own age, Milton always looked backwards, as in his preoccupation with medieval theology. Burns lived in the present: 'The joy of my heart', he said, 'is to study men, their manners, and their ways,' so that it is constantly evident that his figures are of flesh and blood. Part of the merit of what he created came about because he put much of himself into his poems, and expressed his own nature. Shakespeare had the same outlook when he said:

> This above all: to thine own self be true,
> And it must follow, as the night the day,
> Thou canst not then be false to any man.

This sympathetic understanding of humanity is a fundamental feature in the works of Burns, and is an element common to all the great masters. In this he was akin to Shakespeare, who, as Dryden remarks, 'needed not the spectacles of books to read nature: he looked inward and found her there'. Again, as Stewart Perowne has said: 'There never was a less bookish playwright than Shakespeare. Be the setting what it may, it is to the flesh and blood he knew that the action and the talk is committed.'[36a]

The subject of the Devil was one in which Burns remained very interested. In 1796, only a few months before his death, he wrote an epistle **To Colonel De Peyster,** the fourth and fifth stanzas of which read:

> Then that curst carmagnole, Auld Satan,
> Watches, like baudrons by a ratton,
> Our sinfu' saul to get a claut on
>   Wi' felon ire;
> Syne, whip! his tail ye'll ne'er cast saut on
>   He's aff like fire.

> Ah Nick! Ah Nick! it is na fair,
> First showing us the tempting ware,
> Bright wines and bonie lasses rare,
>   To put us daft;
> Syne weave, unseen, thy spider snare,
>   O'Hell's damned waft!

Reid suggests that the philosophy of Burns was a rebelliously kindly one, summed up in a verse expressing the hope that even the Devil may escape damnation[37]:

> But fare you weel, auld Nickie-ben!
> O wad ye tak' a thought an men!
> Ye aiblins[38] might—I dinna ken—
> Still hae a stake
> I'm wae[39] to think upo' yon den
> Ev'n for your sake.

Death and Dr. Hornbook

Among the most remarkable of the early poems of Burns is the one entitled **Death and Dr. Hornbook.** This famous satire relates to one John Wilson, the schoolmaster of Tarbolton. To increase his income Wilson kept a grocer's shop, from which he sold drugs as well as groceries. He displayed a card in his window announcing that he would give advice free about 'common disorders'.

The poet was present at a masonic meeting at which the dominie made too ostentatious a display of his medical knowledge, sufficient in fact to fill any thoughtful person with alarm at the possible consequences of his activities. Burns, as a conscientious and far-sighted man, was immediately aware of the dangers from such a charlatan, and drew public attention to them by writing his poem at 'seed time', 1785. While publication of the poem made a considerable stir, there appears to be no foundation for the statement by Lockhart that it forced Wilson to close his shop.[40]

This satire deserves notice both as a brilliant piece of work in itself and because it is representative of others which Burns wrote in this style. In it he depicts a reveller who encounters Death on his way home. The dread figure reassures him personally, but proceeds to complain bitterly that he is being outdone in his business by an amateur who kills off people at a great rate before he has time to get to them. The following four verses, although they do not fully reveal the ingenious story, are otherwise typical. Death says:

> Whare I kill'd ane, a fair strae-death,[41]
> By loss o' blood, or want o' breath,
> This night I'm free to tak my aith,[42]
>   That Hornbook's skill
> Has clad a score i' their last claith,[43]
>   By drap and pill.

An honest wabster[44] to his trade,
Whase wife's twa nieves[45] were scarce weel
  bred,
Gat tippence-worth to mend her head,
    When it was sair[46];
The wife slade cannie[47] to her bed,
    But ne'er spak mair.

A countra laird had ta'en the batts,[48]
Or some curmurring[49] in his guts,
His only son for Hornbook sets,
    An' pays him well.
The lad, for twa guid gimmer-pets,[50]
    Was laird himsel.

A bonie lass—ye kend her name—
Some ill-brewn drink had hov'd[51] her
  wame[52];
She trusts hersel, to hide the shame,
    In Hornbook's care;
Horn sent her aff to her lang hame,
    To hide it there.

The power of poetic narrative, shown here, and of giving a lively picture in a very few words, seems almost Chaucerian in character. And although the satire is penetrating, it is tempered by kindly humour, so that the feelings of the victim were not wounded. Wilson became, in fact, one of the poet's innumerable friends, and even told Gilbert Burns that he considered the poem 'rather a compliment'. At a later date he sought the advice and help of Burns in seeking a post in a lawyer's office in Edinburgh. In his reply, written from Ellisland, the poet says: 'I am truly sorry, my dear Sir, that you find yourself so uncomfortably situated in Tarbolton; the more so, as I fear you will find on trial that the remedy you propose is worse than the disease. . . . To a gentleman who is unacquainted with the science of law, and who proposes to live merely by the drudgery of his quill, he has before him a life of many sorrows. . . . I should be very sorry any friend of mine should ever try it.'[53] Nevertheless Burns enclosed a cordial note of recommendation addressed to a leading Edinburgh lawyer whom the poet described as 'honest John Somerville'.

Holy Willie's Prayer

The amount of energy which Burns devoted to his various interests was quite extraordinary. He can almost certainly be regarded as one of those vivid personalities whose internal fires burn so brightly that an early death is practically inevitable, there being a close resemblance to such cases as those of Goldsmith, Mozart, Schubert and others. One of the many things that interested him, and which found expression in his poetry, was theological controversy. At the first sight this might seem extremely unpromising ground for a poet, but in fact there were issues which were very

live ones in Scotland at this period, and were passionately debated.

Contemporary society was sharply divided between those who supported the rigid Calvinistic creed and outlook, who were known as the 'Auld Lichts', and those who had a more rational outlook, known as the 'New Lichts'. It may be noted that one of the books found in the library of Burns was Taylor's *Original Sin,* a favourite work of the New Light party. The poet found himself drawn into the controversy when two of his friends, Gavin Hamilton (1751-1805), and Robert Aiken, became involved.

Hamilton owned the land farmed by Robert and his brother at Mossgiel, besides practising as a lawyer in Mauchline. All the records show that he was an exceptionally pleasant and kindly man of the highest character, and it was natural that he should appreciate similar qualities in the poet. A firm friendship did in fact grow up between them, with some important consequences.

Dr. Ross remarks that 'Like Burns, Hamilton was a zealous and intelligent supporter of the New Light doctrine',[54] and was therefore brought into trouble with local orthodox opinion. Perhaps because Mr. Hamilton was one of those rare people of really blameless life, he excited the envy and hatred of one afterwards immortalized by Burns as 'Holy Willie', who sought an opportunity to injure him. This dreadful fellow hid his misdeeds, including the embezzling of church funds, under a cloak of hypocrisy in the form of sour bigotry. He eventually found an opening by accusing Mr. Hamilton of being lax in church attendance and, worse still, of allowing a servant to pull kale on the Sabbath.

An accusation of this kind was then a most serious matter, and could easily ruin a professional man. The Process brought by 'Holy Willie' received a full hearing in the Presbytery of Ayr, and Mr. Hamilton had representing him as Counsel the eloquent Mr. Robert Aiken. Right finally triumphed, but it was a close thing.

Burns was deeply moved by this attack on his upright and irreproachable friend by one whose life he knew to be a slimy sham. In his **Holy Willie's Prayer** the searing fire of his anger is evident, and has been likened to the scourge of knotted cords with which the money-changers were driven from the Temple. Not only is the poem a magnificent one in itself, but much of Burns the man is revealed in it. It was written in 1785, shortly after **Death and Dr. Hornbook,** to which it is somewhat akin.

Dr. Ross says of 'Holy Willie'[55] that he was 'a great pretender for sanctity'. This 'sanctimonious and self-satisfied' man, although for a time an elder, appears to have been more often drunk than sober, and to have become increasingly voluble in his cups. Burns refers to him as 'a rather oddish bachelor, justly famed for that polemical chattering which ends in tippling orthodoxy, and for that spiritualized bawdry which becomes liquorish devotion'. It is said that eventually 'Holy Willie', returning from a carousal, fell into a ditch in a drunken stupor, and was found dead there the following morning.

Holy Willie's Prayer, described as 'a rough but most pungent satire', followed soon after the poet's **Twa Herds,** which had caused 'a roar of applause'. Both immediately gained a wide circulation in manuscript. 'Burns', says Sir Leslie Stephen, 'represents the revolt of a virile and imaginative nature against a system of belief and practice which, as he judged, had degenerated into mere bigotry and pharisaism.' In these 'satires of startling vigour' he therefore attacked bigotry and superstition. Public opinion was moving in the same direction, and Burns would have been welcome as a continuing champion of the moderate party in church affairs, had his mind not been too great for theological squabbles.

Much of the effect of **Holy Willie's Prayer** would have been lost if Burns had shown any lack of a sense of proportion, but in fact there is both biting satire and zestful humour. The poet seems to find an almost playful enjoyment in contrasting his victim's pretensions with his real nature, and does it in exquisitely ludicrous terms. At the same time there is no lack of serious thought. Burns felt contempt for hypocritical outward show because it caricatured morality which he respected and upheld. The other side of his feeling is revealed in his **Cottar's Saturday Night,** with its description of family devotions, which belongs to the same period.

Scotch Drink

An early poem, **Scotch Drink,** has caused raising of eyebrows because of the perverse idea that the mere choice of such a subject shows what a drunken reprobate Burns must have been. The facts of the case are expressed by Chambers, here as always an excellent authority: 'He was, as has been said, no lover of drink, but his social spirit had invested it with many interesting associations in his mind. Looking round for subjects, the poem of Fergusson, entitled *Caller Water,* seems to have suggested to him a similar strain on the artificial beverages of his native country.'[56]

A major theme in the poem, which was clearly a large part of its inspiration, related to the cancellation of an ancient right of the laird of Ferintosh to distil duty-free whisky. Gunnyon says: 'This poem was suggested by the withdrawal of an Act of Parliament empowering Duncan Forbes of Culloden to distil whisky on his barony of Ferintosh, free of duty, in return for services rendered to the Government. This privilege was a source of great revenue to the family; and as Ferintosh whisky was cheaper than that produced elsewhere, it became very popular, and the name Ferintosh thus became something like a synonym for whisky all over the country. Compensation for the loss of privilege, to the tune of £21,580, was awarded to the Forbes family by a jury. . . . The circumstances gave the poet his clue; and the subject was one calculated to evoke his wildest humour.'[57]

In one verse the poet says:

> Thee, Ferintosh! O sadly lost!
> Scotland lament frae coast to coast!
> Now colic-grips, an' barkin hoast,
>   May kill us a';
> For loyal Forbes' chartered boast
>   Is ta'en awa!

In this poem Burns gives as usual some fascinating glimpses into social customs in all grades of society, which his wide acquaintance gave him unusual opportunities of observing. In the following verse, for example, he compares the serving of ale in silver mugs at the tables of the wealthy, with the use among more humble folk of brisk small-beer as a favourite relish to porridge:

> Aft clad in massy siller weed,
> Wi' gentles thou erects thy head;
> Yet humbly kind in time o' need,
>   The poor man's wine,
> His wee drap parritch, or his bread
>   Thou kitchens fine.

The habit Burns had of heading his verses with quotations is extremely interesting, not only because of their often illuminating application to the particular verses, but because of the sidelights they give on his reading. **Scotch Drink** is headed with a verse from Solomon's Proverbs, a favourite source. Biblical references were frequent, but many of the authors he loved were represented, including Shakespeare, Milton, Pope, Gray and Goldsmith. In his songs the names of appropriate tunes he has chosen took the place of quotations.

A similar theme is to be found in **The Author's Ernest Cry and Prayer to the Scotch Representatives in the House of Commons,** a high-spirited poem, full of humour and irony, in which Burns rails at governmental interference with the liberties of distillers and whisky-drinkers.

The Whistle

Many of the biographers of Burns have expressed scandalized horror at what they have imagined to be his intemperate habits, while failing to produce evidence to support their supposition. It has been suggested, however, that the poet can be condemned from his own works. In particular his poem **The Whistle** has been accepted as proof of dreadful debauchery on the part of Burns. As this is regarded as an extreme case, showing Burns at his worst, it is desirable to look closely at what really happened.

The whistle in question belonged to Captain Robert Riddel, a landowner and friend of Burns, living at Friar's Carse House, immediately to the south of Ellisland. Burns tells the curious history of the whistle in these words: 'In the train of Anne of Denmark, when she came to Scotland with our James VI, there came over also a Danish gentleman of gigantic stature and great prowess, and a matchless champion of Bacchus. He had a little ebony whistle, which at the commencement of the orgies was laid on the table, and whoever was the last able to blow it, everybody else being disabled by the potency of the bottle, was to carry off the whistle as a trophy of victory. The Dane produced credentials of his victories, without a single defeat, at the courts of Copenhagen, Stockholm, Moscow, Warsaw, and several of the petty courts in Germany; and challenged the Scots Bacchanalians to the alternative of trying his prowess, or else of acknowledging their inferiority. After many overthrows on the part of the Scots, the Dane was encountered by Sir Robert Lawrie of Maxwelton, ancestor of the present worthy baronet of that name; who, after three days and three nights' hard contest, left the Scandinavian under the table,

And blew on the whistle his requiem shrill.

Sir Walter, son to Sir Robert before mentioned, afterwards lost the whistle to Walter Riddel of Glen Riddel, who had married his sister.' By 1789 the famous whistle had come by descent to Burns's neighbour, Captain Robert Riddel, who felt he would like to make it the subject of a friendly contest with two other descendants of the Scandinavian's conqueror, namely Alexander Fergusson of Craigdarroch and Sir Robert Lawrie of Maxwelton, then M.P. for Dumfriesshire.

How dreadful, many have felt, that Burns should have joined in gross debauchery of this sort. Actually he did nothing of the kind, and it is curious to note that no one condemns the three rather eminent men who were the real contestants. The part that Burns was called upon to play, as a friend of those concerned, was to act as a kind of judge and umpire. In response to a reminder, apparently sent on the evening of the dinner, he sent this note in verse, afterwards preserved at Craigdarroch House, indicating that he was delayed by his Excise duties:

> The King's poor blackguard slave am I,
> And scarce dow spare a minute;

But I'll be with you by and bye,
Or else the devil's in it!

R.B.

William Hunter, a senior member of the household at Friar's Carse, provided some years later this record of the occasion. 'Burns', he says, 'was present the whole evening. He was invited to attend the party, to see that the gentlemen drank fair, and to commemorate the day by writing a song.' Hunter continues: 'I recollect well, that when the dinner was over, Burns quitted the table, and went to a table in the same room that was placed in a window that looked south-east: and there he sat down for the night. I placed before him a bottle of rum and another of brandy, which he did not finish, but left a good deal of each when he rose from the table after the gentlemen had gone to bed. . . . When they were put to bed, Burns walked home without any assistance, not being the worse of drink.'

Hunter adds: 'When Burns was sitting at the table in the window, he had pen, ink and paper, which I brought to him at his own request. He now and then wrote on the paper, and while the gentlemen were sober, he turned round often and chatted with them, but drank none of the claret which they were drinking. . . . I heard him read aloud several parts of the poem, much to the amusement of the three gentlemen.'

Chambers remarks in connection with the above matter that Burns 'was of too social and mirth-loving a nature to refuse to join in occasional revelries, such as then too frequently occurred amongst gentlemen as well as commoners; but he liked these scenes rather in spite of, than from a love of, drinking', adding that, 'All his old Ellisland servants testify to the sobriety of his life there.'

This episode gives us an intimate and typical glimpse of the poet avoiding the excesses of his friends while remaining on cordial terms with them. It is interesting, too, to note his brilliant feat of composing the poem on the spot, showing how actively his mind was working; and of recounting the verses as they are written to auditors who were enthusiastic about them until unconsciousness supervened. And while at the close of the evening Burns walked soberly home, ready to rise out on his rounds at the crack of dawn, it was far otherwise with the contestants: it is on record, for example, that Lawrie, 'gallant Sir Robert, deep-read in old wines', never afterwards quite recovered from the effects of the contest.

Halloween

When Burns was a boy his father used to invite a poor widow, Betty Davidson, 'to spend a few months at a time with his family, both at Alloway and Mount Oliphant, where, to requite his kindness, she was most assiduous in spinning, carding, and doing all kinds of good offices that were in her power. She was of a mirthful temperament, and therefore a great favourite with the children.' The old dame had a wonderful collection of tales about witches, warlocks, ghosts and the like, and the recital of these had so strong an effect on the imagination of the poet that for ever afterwards, in his nocturnal rambles, he kept a sharp lookout in suspicious places.

The interest in such things remained with Burns, and with the passing years his knowledge of the traditional lore of witchcraft in his part of the country became unrivalled. In his poem on **Halloween** the depth of his learning is well displayed. In his introduction to it he says: 'The following poem will, by many readers, be well enough understood; but, for the sake of those who are unacquainted with the manners and traditions of the country where the scene is cast, notes are added to give some account of the principal charms and spells of that night, so big with prophecy to the peasantry in the West of Scotland. The passion of prying into futurity makes a striking part of the history of human-nature in its rude state, in all ages and nations; and it may be some entertainment to a philosophic mind, if any such should honour the author with a perusal, to see the remains of it, among the more unenlightened in our own.' The calm, detached standpoint of the poet is to be noted, for it was very rare in his day, and causes one to reflect upon the amount of credulity which survives in full vigour in our own time, nearly two centuries later, waiting for someone with a mind as impartial and philosophic as that of Burns to observe its manifestations.

The poem itself forms a valuable record of ancient customs and beliefs, and there is so much conservatism about what is essentially an oral tradition that there may be little change in the course of a millennium. At the same time there is often obscurity about the meaning of particular actions, and for that reason among others the notes that Burns gives are very helpful. Incidentally here again we find the poet in the role of a serious antiquary. To quote one note must suffice. He says: 'The first ceremony of Halloween is pulling each a stock or plant of kail. They (the lasses and lads) must go out, hand in hand, with eyes shut, and pull the first they meet with: its being big or little, straight or crooked, is prophetic of the size and shape of the grand object of all their spells—the husband or wife. If any *yird,* or earth, stick to the root, that is *tocher,* or fortune; and the taste of the *custoc,* that is, the heart of the stem, is indicative of the natural temper and disposition. Lastly the stems or, to give them their ordinary appellation, the *runts,* are placed somewhere above the head of the door; and the Christian names of the people whom chance brings into the house are, according to the priority of placing the *runts,* the names in question.'

The poem gains interest by being given a locale. Thus in a note on the line: *On Cassilis Downans dance,* Burns says that these are 'Certain little romantic, rocky green hills, in the neighbourhood of the ancient seat of the Earls of Cassilis', and of the line: *There up the cove to stray and rove,* he says that the cove is 'A noted cavern near Colean-house called the Cove of Colean, which, as well as Cassilis-Downans, is famed in country story for being a favourite haunt of fairies'.

Notes

[1] Robert Aiken of Ayr (1739-1807) was a prosperous lawyer in his native town.

[2] *The Elegy,* verse 8.

[3] Thomas Crawford, *Burns* (1960), p. 177.

[4] sky.

[5] oxen.

[6] peeps.

[7] overcome.

[8] shuts, cf. *sneck,* to latch or fasten.

[9] cleaning.

[10] makes.

[11] doleful.

[12] frightened or made afraid.

[13] poverty.

[14] J. Logie Robertson, *Furth in Field,* p. 260.

[15] F. Angellier, *Robert Burns; la vie, les oeuvres,* Paris (1893), II, 80.

[16] Otto Ritter, Dr.Phil., *Quellenstudien zu Robert Burns, 1773-1791,* Berlin (1901), p. 99.

[17] James Sutherland, *A Preface to Eighteenth-Century Poetry,* Oxford (1948), pp. 132-6, cf. also Perry, *English Literature in the 18th Century,* pp. 435 ff.

[18] *Henry IV,* Pt. II, I, i. 254.

[19] *L'Allegro,* lines 67-68.

[20] Op. cit. pp. 180-1.

[21] inside.

[22] chats, gossips.

[23] cows.

[24] bashful—hesitating.

[25] reluctant.

[26] literally what is left, i.e. the rest of people

[27] W. E. Henley, in *The Poems of Robert Burns,* edited by W. E. Henley and T. F. Henderson (1896), IV, 277.

[28] A. E. Elistratova, *Robert Burns,* Moscow (1957).

[29] J. A. Froude, *Short Studies on Great Subjects* (The Influence of the Reformation on the Scottish Character), (1867-83), II, 147.

[30] Scottish variant of Lowland.

[31] Burns observes that Homer is allowed to be the earliest ballad singer on record.

[32] K. Wittig, *The Scottish Tradition in Literature,* Edinburgh (1958), p. 211.

[33] Allan Ramsay, *Poems,* edited by Geo. Chalmers (1800), *An Elegy on Patie Birnie,* 1, 235.

[34] Christopher Marlowe (1564-93), *The Passionate Shepherd to his Love.*

[35] Matthew Arnold, 'The Study of Poetry', in *Essays in Criticism,* 2nd series (1954 edition), pp. 26 and 31-33.

[36] This Scottish name for Satan is taken from his cloven feet or *cloots.*

[36a] Stewart Perowne, O.B.E., M.A., F.S.A., in *The Times,* 6 June 1964.

[37] Op. cit. p. 155.

[38] or ablings, a Scottish form of 'able', with suf. 'lings', i.e. possibly.

[39] The Scottish form of sad or woeful.

[40] John Gibson Lockhart, *Life of Robert Burns* (1959 edition), pp. 50-51.

[41] death in a comfortable straw bed.

[42] oath.

[43] grave-cloth.

[44] weaver.

[45] fists.

[46] aching or sore.

[47] slid gently or quietly.

[48] colic.

[49] rumbling.

[50] pet-ewes.

[51] swelled.

[52] belly.

[53] 11 September 1790.

[54] John D. Ross, LL.D., *Who's Who in Burns,* published by Eneas Mackay, Stirling (1927).

[55] Actually William Fisher (1737-1809).

[56] Op. cit. I, 202.

[57] W. Gunnyon, *Burns Manuscripts in the Kilmarnock Monument* (1889), p. 121.

Frederick L. Beaty (essay date 1971)

SOURCE: *Light from Heaven: Love in British Romantic Literature*, Northern Illinois University Press, 1971, 288 p.

[*In the excerpt below Beaty analyzes Burns's use of humor in his writings about romantic love.*]

Robert Burns's distinction as a love poet stems chiefly from his ability to perceive the comic aspects of what he considered a very serious emotion. The eighteenth-century adaptation of sentiment to comedy, as well as the Scottish vernacular tradition, afforded him ample precedent for this seemingly paradoxical combination. As random comments in his letters indicate, he was obviously interested in examining the comic spirit; yet he apparently elaborated no critical manifesto of his own to explain his practice. Perhaps because he was often regarded as an inspired but untaught genius who succeeded without conscious artistry, influential critics of the early nineteenth century usually looked not to him for illustrations of their comic theories but rather to Jean Paul Richter, who had obligingly translated his own precepts into concrete examples. Not until after many of the speculations about humor had crystallized into definite concepts could Burns's achievement be fully analyzed.[1] Just as his poetry had unwittingly sanctioned in advance many of the tenets enunciated in Wordsworth's preface to *Lyrical Ballads* (1800), so too his portrayals of comic love anticipated theories of subsequent analysts and, consequently, have become increasingly meaningful in the light of critical doctrines articulated after his practice.

As Romantic critics saw it, the dichotomy between humor and wit inherited from the eighteenth century constituted one of the basic cleavages between neoclassicism and their own aesthetic of natural sensibility. In his introduction to *Lectures on the English Comic Writers,* Hazlitt made the distinction explicit: "Humour is the describing the ludicrous as it is in itself; wit is the exposing it, by comparing or contrasting it with something else. Humour is, as it were, the growth of nature and accident; wit is the product of art and fancy."[2] Whereas wit, being contrived and generally derisive, was considered the province of the mind, humor, being natural and empathic, belonged essentially to the heart. Similarly De Quincey, when he attempted to popularize Richter's philosophical theories on the comic, carefully emphasized the distinction between wit as "a purely intellectual thing" and humor as a phenomenon that brought into play "the *moral* nature" involving the will, affections, and temperament.[3] Humor in Richter's creative works, according to De Quincey, was interwoven with pathos, his gentle satire characterized by smiles rather than by scornful laughter. Subsequently Carlyle, who had assimilated much of the comic psychology in Richter's *Vorschule der Aesthetik* (1804), demeaned the irony and caricature of neoclassical satirists to a position conspicuously lower than that of humor. "True humour," Carlyle explained in his second essay on Richter, "springs not more from the head than from the heart; it is not contempt, its essence is love; it issues not in laughter, but in still smiles, which lie far deeper."[4] Through a kinship with sensibility, therefore, the ultimate justification of humor resembled that for human love: it helped unite man with mankind.

Despite objections from purists who preferred their emotions and their genres unalloyed, the analogy of love and humor was generally endorsed by Romantic critics as a valid precept for life, as well as art. Even the delicate question of whether the heart was capable of sympathetic laughter was argued affirmatively by Lamb, who differentiated between "the petrifying sneer of a demon which excludes and kills Love" and "the cordial laughter of a man which implies and cherishes it."[5] By laughing *with* rather than *at* humanity, one might enjoy himself while heightening his benevolent proclivities. And if humor was produced by what was universally comic, laughter, especially from a man sufficiently perceptive to associate the ludicrous with traits in himself, could prove highly edifying. Keats, in the letter that evolves his principle of imaginative identification, selfless sympathy, and suspended judgment

known as "negative capability," significantly progressed toward this doctrine from a statement praising the superiority of humor over wit.[6] As Keats realized, humor enabled an imaginative understanding whereby one was made to *feel* rather than (as in wit) to *start.* Furthermore, the artistic advantages of humor were seen to rest on valid psychological grounds. As both De Quincey and Carlyle pointed out in their respective analyses of Richter, humor prevented sensibility from deteriorating into maudlin sentimentality. However serious the emotion of love might be, a touch of the comic—what Bergson in his essay *Laughter* defined as "a momentary anesthesia of the heart"—contributed to a healthful perspective. The conjunction of active and passive, far from annihilating one another, restored a sane equilibrium appropriate to the Romantic goal of unified sensibilities. By its very nature life was seen to be full of incongruities, paradoxes, and frustrations imposed by mundane limitations. Yet if the dominant principle of life was (like that of its creator) love, then the force striving for unity with the infinite tended to transcend finite limitations. Hence the juxtaposition of finite and infinite, which Richter postulated as the true source of humor, contributed to the desired totality of existence.

The soundness of Romantic insight, striving for the union of reason, sentiment, intuition, and imagination, was later confirmed by professional psychologists. Sigmund Freud, who endorsed many of the Romantic theories on the comic derived from Richter, demonstrated that levity, however pleasurable, was an earnest matter, especially when it involved "broken" humor "that smiles through tears."[7] Subsequent psychologists have also explained the compatibility of love and humor in their own terms without seriously disrupting Romantic concepts. While love is customarily associated now with the integrative or self-transcending tendency and the comic spirit with the self-assertive, human emotions are usually mixed. Love, in all except its hypothetically pure instances, is sufficiently ambivalent to include some of the self-assertive. Sexual love, particularly in regard to masculine behavior, contains enough of the aggressive to invite forms of the comic that are indeed far less sympathetic than humor. Nor does laughter provoked by such instances undermine the essential seriousness, for the emotions meet on common ground.

Yet exactly how much of prevalent theory on comic love Burns was consciously aware of is difficult to ascertain. It seems likely, however, that he may have been acquainted with one of the longest treatises on the comic spirit, that by the Scottish philosopher-poet James Beattie, whose poems and essays Burns greatly admired.[8] Continuing the traditions first popularized by Addison and Steele (and later by Sterne), Beattie, in his "Essay on Laughter and Ludicrous Composition" (1776), claimed that laughter arising from innocent mirth was not only therapeutically desirable but also indicative of a benevolent, rather than a spiteful, nature. Moreover, he predicted a genre of which Burns was to become the chief poetical exponent. "As romantic love in its natural regular procedure is now become so copious a source of joy and sorrow, hope and fear, triumph and disappointment," Beattie asserted, "we might reasonably conclude, that in its more whimsical forms and vagaries it could scarce fail to supply materials for laughter."[9] His views on the *vis comica* were essentially standard, even though his terminology differed somewhat from that of other aestheticians and his specific definitions perhaps did not indicate rigid classification.[10] *Wit* he described as the "unexpected discovery of resemblance between ideas supposed dissimilar"—a kind of *discordia concors* such as Dr. Johnson saw in metaphysical analogies. *Humor* Beattie identified with the "comic exhibition of singular characters, sentiments, and imagery." Yet he certainly divided the comic spirit into two categories according to the responses it evoked: the *ridiculous* arousing contempt or disapproval, and the *ludicrous* producing an uncomplicated, risible emotion. This latter reaction was brought about by the pleasant awareness of inconsistencies—often in an unusual mixture of similarity and contrariety. As the "Essay" further analyzed it, innocent laughter could be purely "animal" if occasioned by tickling or sudden gladness and "sentimental" when it proceeded from feeling or sentiment. Since theories such as these were already formulated, Burns, who was especially sensitive to the incongruities of certain character traits in particular situations, had only to put the sentimental comic into practice.

Before fully understanding Burns's treatment of "romantic love," however, one must recognize that to him sexual attraction was the most compelling justification for existence. Complete gratification in love became virtually synonymous with the pursuit of happiness; and from this basic premise, which colored all he had to say about love, stemmed the related attitudes expressed throughout his poetry. Associated from the beginning with poetic inspiration, this "delicious Passion," as he explained to Dr. John Moore, was held "to be the first of human joys, our dearest pleasure here below."[11] His most celebrated affirmation of loyalty to the eternal feminine, **"Green grow the Rashes,"** declares that lasses alone compensate for the anxieties of life.[12] Dividing humanity into those with hearts and those without, Burns vows his preference for the simple joys of making love, one of the few inalienable rights of the poor. The basic distinction between the "warly race" obsessed with respectability and those who respond to the gadflies of feeling appears in several other poems, especially the **"Epistle"** to William Logan (I, 300-302), which contains the poet's expression of sincere delight in womankind: "I like them dearly; / God bless them a'!" Obviously Burns does not assume that a man's love need be confined to one girl. In opposition to grave Calvinistic strictures condemning earthly joys, he cites scriptural (and therefore irrefutable) authority that Solomon, traditionally the wisest of men and devotee of infinite variety, "dearly lov'd the lasses." Carrying matters a step further in poems contributed to *The Merry Muses of Caledonia,* Burns is often very explicit, sometimes by means of clever metaphors, about the unsurpassed pleasures women afford sexually. Obversely, as lines from **"To J. S*****"** (I, 178-83) indicate, he characterizes the loss of physical love as the worst blight of senility, depriving man of his greatest joy.

Quite logically, a belief so devoutly affirmed had to be translated into practice, and many of Burns's poems celebrate the following of natural inclination—a precept he advocated most convincingly from the masculine viewpoint. Despite some admissions, as in the **"Epistle to a Young Friend"** (I, 248-51), that illicit affection hardened the heart and petrified the feelings, he usually assumed that the most ardent flames of love ought to be kindled immediately because they were too often of short duration. Hence he advised his brother William: " . . . try for intimacy as soon as you feel the first symptoms of the passion."[13] Somewhat like his bard in **"Love and Liberty"** (I, 206), Burns usually regarded it a mortal sin to thwart divinely implanted instinct. Being a man entailed fulfilling the obligations of manhood, and whoever shirked them was not entitled to the name. In an attempt to refine a coarse original of his song **"The Taylor"** (II, 872-73), Burns implies this argument as explanation for the central character's behavior. Whereas in the earlier version the tailor sadistically took advantage of a sleeping maiden, in Burns's humorous redaction he attains his goal through ingratiating charm. (This alteration itself indicates how the poet frequently softened the harsh original without radically changing its import.) The profession of Burns's tailor provides him with nothing more than an entrée; his real vocation is that of a lover who "kend the way to woo." In one choice line the poet laconically sums up all that is indelicate in the earlier account, adds what is needed to conclude the anecdote, and comments on the action: "The Taylor prov'd a man O."

A much richer psychological treatment of this theme appears in the song **"Had I the wyte"** (II, 842-43). A man obviously disturbed by his recent excursion into adultery tries to allay his conscience by repeated questioning whether he ought to be blamed for his actions. Part of the humor no doubt stems from the transposition of customary roles in love—of an aggressive Lady Booby plotting the seduction of a relatively passive Joseph Andrews. But the crowning achievement in the lyric is the speaker's unwitting revelation of his own naïveté and his unwillingness to admit that the married woman had actually manipulated him. Knowing that he would not wish his valor impugned, she had shrewdly called him "a coward loon" for his reluctance to enter her house. Then perceiving his vanity and susceptibility to pity, she complained of how cruelly her absent husband treated her and thereby threw all the blame for her own actions upon a tyrannical spouse. What indeed could a sympathetic young man do but comfort and console her? In retrospect he protests:

> Could I for shame refus'd her;
> And wad na Manhood been to blame,
> Had I unkindly us'd her.

> (II, 842)

After performing his duty, he reveals some uncertainty about true manly behavior by recounting that on the following morning he tried to drown his compunction in brandy, though he continues to solicit our comforting assurance that he was not the one to blame.

A somewhat different aspect of the problem is reflected in many of Burns's autobiographical poems that poignantly describe the suffering inflicted by conventional morality on natural deeds of love. The concept of vice as a virtue carried to excess was difficult for him to comprehend when the virtue was love and when others of his acquaintance seemingly enjoyed the pleasures without concomitant pains. Nevertheless, his overall attitude was remarkably consistent in that he not only followed masculine instinct but also assumed all the parental responsibilities that his encompassing affection and limited financial means could provide. The pathos tinged with humor in poems concerning his own difficulties with unplanned parenthood no doubt reveals his mixed reactions. Probably the best illustration occurs in **"A Poet's Welcome to his love-begotten Daughter"** (I, 99-100), which concedes his great delight upon first becoming an illegitimate father. Assuring his child by Elizabeth Paton that she is just as welcome as though she had been invited, he tenderly addresses her as "Sweet fruit o' monie a merry dint" (I, 100).

Not even the pains attendant on illegitimacy could diminish the swaggering bravado he assumes in a few of his poems celebrating propagation of bastards. One reason for such boasting on his part was undoubtedly the private masculine audience to whom such poems were initially addressed. Furthermore, his defiance of ecclesiastical authorities, who in some cases had been no better than he, for the penance and fine they imposed upon him could best be expressed with mocking raillery. Though in **"A Poet's Welcome"** he merely disclaims any objection to being called "fornicator," he boldly asserts his right to that distinction in **"The Fornicator"** (I, 101-102). That Burns sincerely believed he had been made to suffer excessively is clear from his repeated comparison of himself to Biblical "men of God," who achieved ultimate salvation despite

rather cavalier attitudes toward the seventh commandment. King David and King Solomon, both famous as poets and adulterers, provided him with choice illustrations of sexual energy as the true manifestation of vitality. In **"Robert Burns' Answer"** (I, 278-80), a devil-may-care poem regarding his own ill repute, the poet argues that even though he may give women's "wames a random pouse," the manly sport of fornication should not call down great abuse from men who admire King David as one of the "lang syne saunts." Burns then concludes with a fanciful tale, the true index of his indignation, about how he made fools of the Kirk Session that assessed punishment for his transgression. According to this account, the defendant candidly admitted he would never be any better unless he were gelded; and the minister, perhaps on the analogy that an offending eye ought to be plucked out, immediately endorsed amputation of whatever proved to be a "sp'ritual foe." But instead Burns facetiously recommended putting the offending part under the guidance of the lass—a suggestion that pleased the Session "warst ava" and ended the interview.

The autobiographical poem that even the most devoted followers of Burns sometimes find difficult to justify is the **"Epistle to J. R*******"** (I, 61-63), with its elaborate metaphor of game-poaching. First must be remembered, however, the character of the individual for whose enjoyment it was originally intended. The opening lines of the **"Epistle"** characterize its recipient as "rough, rude, ready-witted R[ankine]," a man apparently well known for his rowdy festivities and exposés of hypocritical clergymen. Hence the principal anecdote was especially appropriate. Then too, the tradition of witty comparisons was so well established in Scottish vernacular poetry that Burns's analogy of poaching and promiscuous lovemaking would not have appeared so derogatory to the woman as it may seem today. As Burns put it,

> 'Twas ae night lately, in my fun,
> I gaed a rovin wi' the gun,
> An' brought a *Paitrick* to the *grun'*.

> (I, 62)

Indeed many of Burns's poems employ metaphors, such as ploughing, threshing, playing the fiddle, filling the bowl, and shooting wild birds, that were common in the Scottish tradition long before he used them. Thus in the poem addressed to Rankine the implied comparison of his affair with Elizabeth Paton, the servant girl who bore his first child, to shooting down a partridge that did not rightfully belong to him and consequently having to pay a guinea's fine in the Poacher-Court (Kirk Session) ought to be regarded as a clever and natural treatment of the subject. If it reveals a sportive flippancy toward the begetting of bastards, it is nevertheless distinct from mere locker-room braggadocio. By connecting two of the most primitive survival drives in man—hunting for food and gratifying the sexual impulse—it atavistically reveals a basic masculine desire to make a sportive pleasure of necessity.

Nevertheless, Burns's depiction of young girls who have unwisely yielded to the rapture of love shows highly sympathetic insight, sometimes mixed with restrained masculine humor, into their various plights. Portraying them without ridicule or sentimentality, he accepts their condition as an unfortunate though natural consequence of love. The "sleepy bit lassie" in **"The Taylor fell thro' the bed"** (II, 509) naïvely thought the tailor could do her no harm, and indeed he gave her such satisfaction that now she longs for his return. Slightly graver complications have ensued for the girl in **"To the Weaver's gin ye go"** (I, 382-83), who laments the loss of her happiness for granting more than her heart to a weaver lad. Though reluctant to tell what occurred, she now fears that information will soon become increasingly obvious to everyone. But the subtlest and perhaps most appealing characterization of such a girl appears in the first set of lyrics entitled **"Duncan Gray"** (I, 393). Whereas her friends can still enjoy themselves, she now has the cares of unintentional motherhood, which she with half-hearted jocularity blames on the bad girthing. While she and Duncan were riding a horse on Lammas night, she recalls, the girthing broke, and one fall followed another. Now she wistfully hopes that Duncan will keep his oath so that all (including the bad girthing) may be rectified. Also from the feminine point of view, **"The rantin dog the Daddie o't"** (I, 184) expresses the anxieties of an unwed, expectant mother who seeks assurance that Rob, the rollicking father of her child, will assume his paternal obligations. Quite understandably she finds it difficult to joke about her very serious plight, and adding to the embarrassment is her realization that she has taken in earnest what had only been poked in fun.

Burns's songs about courtship are also rich in portraits of charming young girls who, tempering good humor with common sense, know what they want and cleverly overcome obstacles to their goals. An outstanding example is the lass in the song **"O whistle, and I'll come to ye, my lad"** (II, 700-701). Since there seems to be parental objection to her lover, she gives him explicit instructions on how to reach her without letting anyone else know. And though she wants him to ignore her publicly, she nevertheless insists that he is not to court another, even in jest, for fear he may accidentally be enticed away. In **"Last May a braw wooer"** (II, 795-96) a girl less in control of the situation pretends to be virtually inaccessible and, to her dismay, almost loses the young man to a rival. With cunning, however, she proceeds to win him back and reveals her dissembling nature even in her public reasons for marrying him—not for her own

sake but, ironically, just "to preserve the poor body in life." Especially winsome is the maiden in **"I'm o'er young to Marry Yet"** (I, 384), who pleads with her suitor that at her tender age and as her mother's only child she is psychologically unprepared for marriage. But unwilling to reject his proposal completely, she suggests that should he come again next summer she will be older and perhaps ready to reconsider.

Timidity in men, on the other hand, is a topic rarely mentioned by Burns. Significantly, in his gallery of lovers the traditionally humorous bashful young men are almost nonexistent. He did, however, compose to the tune of "The Bashful Lover" lyrics entitled **"On a bank of Flowers"** (II, 514-15), portraying a lad who is shy only at first. Having chanced upon lightly clad Nelly asleep among summer flowers, Willie begins by merely gazing and wishing; but when she awakes and flees in terror, he presumably overcomes his initial hesitancy and overtakes her in the woods.

The most despicable variety of courtship in Burns's view was that which hypocritically aimed at marriage for money, and he was particularly scornful of men offering themselves as marketable commodities. **"There's a youth in this City"** (II, 525-26) pokes fun at a handsome, elegantly attired young man in search of a wealthy girl to marry. Several prospects with commendable fortunes are eager to have him, but actually he loves none of them so much as himself. A thoroughly cynical attitude toward the transience of feminine beauty is satirized in the song, **"Hey for a lass wi' a tocher"** (II, 808-9), in which a man extols woman's wealth as her only enduring attraction. Without denying the witchcraft of youthful beauty, he brazenly expresses his preference for a lass with "acres o' charms." Of course, shallow-hearted girls may also prefer silver to love. Meg o' the mill, in the second set of lyrics concerning her exploits (II, 689), foolishly jilts a desirable miller for a repulsive but rich laird. In all these instances, as in Burns's poems of social protest, wealth is deplored as a corrupting influence.

Comedy of a more playful sort is produced by refining the natural instinct of courtship into sophisticated skill—such as the fine art of seduction. In **"Extempore—to Mr. Gavin Hamilton"** (I, 236-37), a poem that strips the ornamental tinsel from many seemingly important matters and shows them as trivial, Burns relates how he applied the same technique to a female Whig. Her initial refusal to have faith in a poet, as well as his exalted reference to "Her whigship," arouses our antipathy toward a pretentious woman who deserves to be not only corrected but leveled. The poet's adroitness in the game of "love for love's sake" is so great that, despite her inevitable objections while they "grew lovingly big," he taught her "her terrors were naething." Burns concludes:

> Her whigship was wonderful pleased,
>   But charmingly tickled wi' ae thing;
> Her fingers I lovingly squeezed,
>   And kissed her and promised her—
>   naething.
>
>   (I, 237)

Whatever the consequences, seduction might be regarded as a challenging sport in which each of the two individuals, while abiding by the rules of the game, fulfills his prescribed part.

By transposing the customary roles of male and female, as Thurber has often done in our day, Burns provided another rich source of the comic, well exemplified in **"Wha is that at my bower door"** (II, 616-17). In the original song the woman is blatantly aggressive whereas the man is meekly compliant. In Burns's version, the woman, though less conniving, is still manipulator of the action and puts up only token resistance to letting her lover, Findlay, in. He, on the other hand, understands his obligations: he must argue until she deludes herself into thinking that, against her better judgment, his rhetoric has overwhelmed her. These pretenses are clear from the dialogue; the girl introduces in conditional clauses exactly what she ought to fear while Findlay counters with his assurance that each condition will be fulfilled. When he promises to abide by her last stipulation—never to tell what may transpire in her bower—there is no longer any need for him to remain outside.

Burns was also interested in burlesquing artificial conventions of courtship in his second set of lyrics entitled **"Duncan Gray"** (II, 666-68). When he sent the words of this song to George Thomson, he observed that the melody "precludes sentiment" and that "the ludicrous is its ruling feature."[14] Both Meg, with the proud disdain of a courtly lady, and Duncan, with his lachrymose despair verging on suicide, so overplay their roles that they achieve the comic of exaggeration. Excessive sentimentality in Duncan, however, produces its own reaction, for he banishes affectation by realizing the absurdity of dying for "a haughty hizzie." As he recovers his health, Meg, discovering how much his love had meant to her, grows ill pining for him. The fact that Duncan is "a lad o' grace," as well as a shrewd psychologist trained in Scottish common-sense philosophy, permits all to turn out well. Pitying Meg, who suffers as he himself once languished, he demonstrates his true worth by magnanimously refusing to cause her death. The guarded manner in which he accepts her indicates he has learned a very practical lesson in amatory psychology: nothing is quite so attractive as casual indifference.

Perhaps because of the limited range of possibilities inherent in the subject, Burns rarely approached the comical aspects of married love with the geniality and compassion required of true humor. In writing of domestic situations, he easily turned from humor to satire, and it should not be surprising that the preponderance of marriage poems are, by their very nature, sharply succinct and often epigrammatic. This antipathy toward the marital state, revealed with varying degrees of aggressiveness in the majority of his poems treating comic love, is exactly what one should expect. According to Freud's analysis, no institution in our society has been more carefully guarded by accepted morality or more vulnerable to attack than the connubial relationship.[15] The prevalence of cynical jokes deriding wedlock as bedlock illustrates the unconscious antagonism which men in particular feel toward rigid suppresion of sexual liberty. Since this hostility can be temporarily freed from the unconscious by means of some clever witticism—a "pleasure premium," that enables us to laugh at what we revere—tendentious wit aimed at marriage momentarily overcomes whatever inhibitive power exists and permits us to enjoy a release of aggression, often quite contrary to what our sober thoughts might recommend. Burns's practice would indeed tend to support Freud's theory. Regarding marriage as a mixed blessing, he was not able, as he admits in **"Yestreen I had a pint o' wine"** (II, 555-56), to resign himself wholeheartedly to its restraints. Yet his ability to identify imaginatively with either opponent in marital warfare not only relieved him of acerbity but permitted him, usually with the verbal economy of an excellent reconteur, to turn even the worst situation into a good joke.

One group of his poems about marriage emphasizes the change which a husband feels has occurred in his wife since their wedding. Stanza vi of **"Extempore—to Mr. Gavin Hamilton"** (I, 236) cogently points out how during courtship the lover sparkles and glows when "Approaching his bonie bit gay thing," but after the irrevocable ceremony he learns he has acquired a dressed-up "naething." The unfortunate man in **"O ay my wife she dang me"** (II, 881-82) has suffered considerably; yet there is something admirably winning about his resignation to fate. Though the peace and rest he anticipated in marriage were never realized, at least he has the consolation of knowing that, after enduring "pains o' hell" on earth, he is assured of bliss above. The husband in the justly admired **"Whistle o'er the lave o't"** (I, 434-35) has also had his hopes shattered, but through an amazing humor born of torment he seems to be chuckling while cataloguing his woes. All that he had associated with Maggie before the wedding has now changed to its antithesis, and but for fear Maggie would find out, he would even name the one he wishes were in her grave. Implying far more than he expresses, he refrains from elaborating on each unpleasantness and turns it into jest by whistling about what cannot be altered. No doubt the evasive and suggestive quality that makes him a fascinating conversationalist also renders him a most exasperating husband to a shrew.

A considerable number of marriage poems are concerned less with mutability than with exposing and ridiculing an intolerable wife. In so doing, they also reveal the curious relationships between the shortcomings of one spouse and the weaknesses of the other. For example, in **"The Henpeck'd Husband"** (II, 909) Burns expresses the belief that a vixen is partially the fault of a spineless, fearful husband who deserves reproach rather than pity. The anomalous situation would never occur if the husband of such a woman wisely subdued her by breaking either her spirit or her heart. The efficacy of such action is demonstrated in **"My Wife's a wanton, wee thing"** (II, 512), in which the man expresses doubt concerning his licentious wife's ability to behave unless she is controlled as a child ought to be ruled—namely, by the rod. Perhaps the only suffering husband who genuinely elicits our pity, however, is the one in **"Kellyburnbraes"** (II, 644-46). There the unfortunate man yields his termagant wife to the devil, who thereupon discovers her to be more than a match for him and his demons. Upon returning the shrew to earth, the devil admits that he had never been truly in hell until he acquired a wife.

Among several poems that disparage the husband without particularly ennobling the wife, some make light of the essentially serious affliction of impotence in advanced age. The young woman in **"What can a young lassie"** (II, 607-8) temporarily evokes our sympathy with complaints about her peevish, jealous old husband until she reveals her plan to torment him to death and then use his "auld brass" to buy herself a "new pan." The subject receives an almost poignant treatment in **"The deuk's dang o'er my daddie"** (II, 652-53), where acrid hostility between the lusty wife and her incapable spouse is mixed with remembrance of happier bygone days and nights. Two of Burns's songs deal with an equally old marital jest, cuckoldry, but they do so in a manner characteristic of his humor. The women of **"O an ye were dead Gudeman"** (II, 835) and **"We'll hide the Couper"** (II, 848-49) are openly and defiantly committing adultery with their lovers while their husbands do nothing but resign themselves to their proverbial horns. Though some compassion is naturally directed toward the poor, helpless cuckolds, the comic pleasure derived from these two lyrics stems less from a debasement of the husbands than from our fascination with the hussies' brazen determination to satisfy their desires.

Burns could hardly write of love without relating it humorously to another of his chief delights, John Barleycorn, which he recognized as a true, though unscrupulous, liberator of psychic energy. In some instances alcohol could demean its imbiber to such a ludicrous state that he became excellent material for mordantly satirical, aggressive comedy. Especially when

associated with Calvinistic moral attitudes, as in **"Holy Willie's Prayer"** (I, 74-78), tippling served to accentuate what Burns considered the irreconcilability of canon law with man's instinctive nature. Willie's anthropomorphic concept of God—capriciously unjust, vindictive, and incapable of love—reveals the speaker himself. Since his sexual drive is wholly identified with proscribed pleasure, what Burns would have called human love can never be anything but lust in Willie Fisher, who ironically justifies his own promiscuity by pleading drunkenness. Also in **"The Holy Fair"** (I, 128-37) a perversion of what ought to be the celebration of divine love in a communion service is allied with alcohol and lechery. Superstition and hypocrisy in the preaching tent combined with careless fun in an adjacent tavern justify the poet's attack on the Scottish Kirk—a corruption of faith that ideally should be characterized by good deeds, sincerity, and love. Hence he comments ironically on the man who, by letting his hand wander over the bosom of his lass during a sermon, makes a mockery of both religion and human love. As the scene moves to the tavern, he portrays a predominant mood of lechery whereby liquor alters Venus Uranus into a lusty pandemic lass. Thus what began with a hardhearted religion leads, through the stimulation of drink, to a parody of love—"houghmagandic."

With less satire and far greater humor, Burns treats the bibulous freeing of emotion more sympathetically in **"Tam o' Shanter"** (II, 557-64). Just as good Scotch drink presumably released Burns's thoughts and feelings for poetical composition, so too it heightens Tam's amiability toward both Souter Johnie and the landlady, causing him to postpone his return to a hostile, sullen wife. Unfortunately it later contributes to his admiration for an attractive witch dancing lustily in a sark so short that it barely covers, and as a result Tam is momentarily deprived of rational control. Quite unconsciously he roars out the ingenuous praise that almost undoes him. With mock-serious didacticism, Burns in the conclusion warns that the path leading from alcohol to lecherous contemplation often culminates in disaster. The negative moral lesson is, of course, a variant of the admonition in a classic naughty story pertinent to mice and ardent men. Because Tam loses his head to drink and a "cutty sark," his mare is bereft of her tail.

An entirely different attitude toward the combination of love and alcohol is found in **"Love and Liberty"** (I, 195-209), often published as **"The Jolly Beggars."** Its characters, who have a simple, intuitively acute perception of man's nature, possess no inhibitions whatever and accept the basic instincts without any concern for what is ordinarily called ethical standards. What might in polite society be condemned as obscene is from their point of view perfectly normal. Indeed the comedy of this cantata, which is universally considered Burns's masterpiece, verges on what Freud analyzed as the naïvely comical—the effect often produced in adult listeners by the spontaneous, forthright comments of children.[16] The poet's sympathy with (and at times even undisguised envy of) a segment of humanity usually thought beneath contempt is just as sincere as the beggars' irrepressible and appealing candor. Had these uninhibited outcasts been deliberately attacking institutions of the society they rejected, then some of their satirical jibes might be considered tendentious wit: the reader would have to assume that through enticement of comic pleasure they were trying to elicit his hostility against principles which he had been conditioned to respect unquestioningly, despite an unconscious dislike.[17] There are indeed occasional touches of such wit in their oblique comments on marriage, respectability, legality, and religion, particularly in the Merry Andrew's song and the final chorus; yet these bits of aggression are casually tossed off at inhabitants of a world having little contact with theirs. The supremely winning quality of the beggars is their belief in both love and liberty not in the negative sense of revolt against restraint but rather as positive virtues. The old soldier and his doxy, both of whom enjoy their present indulgence in love and drink rather than the exploits of their former military careers; the professional Merry Andrew who admits to being a fool; the female pickpocket whose Highland lover died on the gallows for defiance of Lowland laws; the small fiddler who proposes cohabitation with the pickpocket; the bold tinker who offers himself to the same "unblushing fair"; the bard who, resigning himself to the loss of one mistress because he has two others left, sings in praise of free love and freely flowing drink—all reveal in an unsophisticated way their refusal to be duped by the hypocritical cant of society.

There is something wonderfully refreshing, as Burns himself acknowledged in his commonplace book, about associating with such people.[18] Though their actual deeds may be no better than those of respectable friends, the beggars' mental attitude is more appealing because of its unpretentious honesty. They spontaneously express by both precept and example what all of us know intuitively but have been taught to renounce. The occasional intrusion of artificial diction on their vernacular, to which many critics have objected, subtly reminds us of conventional society's attempt to veneer their basic propensities; yet the beggars remain essentially loyal to all that is natural in humanity. They have indeed achieved the "happy state" described in one of Burns's favorite quotations: " . . . when souls each other draw, / When love is liberty, and nature law" (Pope's "Eloïsa to Abelard," ll. 91-92).[19] Especially when we compare the beggars' adherence to their own code of behavior with the contrasting failure of society to abide by its ethical standards, we realize the supreme humor with which the poet conceived his work.

There were inevitably nineteenth-century critics who let Burns's personal frailties and artistic improprieties prejudice their estimates of his achievement. Yet among the most objectively perceptive, his extraordinary ability to fuse the seemingly heterogeneous elements of love and comedy by means of uniquely incisive humor did not go wholly unnoticed. Lamb, who was quick to recognize in Burns some qualities he himself possessed, observed "a jocular pathos, which makes one feel in laughter."[20] After reading a collection of Burns's unpublished letters, Byron remarked: "What an antithetical mind!—tenderness, roughness—delicacy, coarseness—sentiment, sensuality—soaring and grovelling, dirt and deity—all mixed up in that one compound of inspired clay!"[21] Carlyle, equally aware of these paradoxes, especially stressed "the tenderness, the playful pathos" and perceived that the principle of love which characterized Burns's poetry "occasionally manifests itself in the shape of Humour."[22] Aside from the drollery associated with caricature, Carlyle claimed for Burns "in his sunny moods, a full buoyant flood of mirth" related to his ability to be a "brother and often playmate to all Nature." To emphasize this extraordinary ability Carlyle especially cited those poems expressing a fellow feeling with animals, presumably because mice, mares, and sheep would seem the most difficult creatures with whom a love poet could imaginatively identify himself. And while some genteel critics regarded his subject matter as crudely unpoetical, Matthew Arnold thought Burns had provided a genuine criticism of life, ironic though it was.[23] Despite a revulsion from "Scotch drink, Scotch religion, and Scotch manners," Arnold stressed the "overwhelming sense of the pathos of things" and singled out for illustration of particular merit those works he especially admired. Strangely enough, all that he selected dealt humorously with love. If such poems lacked the requisite high seriousness that excluded their author from the Victorian Valhalla of poetical heroism, it was because Burns (like Chaucer, with whom Arnold repeatedly compared him) believed that many serious observations on life could be uttered more effectively in jest than in grave solemnity.

Notes

[1] Stuart M. Tave's *The Amiable Humorist* (Chicago, 1960), which surveys comic theory of the eighteenth and early nineteenth centuries, clearly demonstrates what meager attention Romantic critics paid to Burns's humorous treatment of love.

[2] "On Wit and Humour" (1818), *The Complete Works of William Hazlitt,* ed. P. P. Howe (London, 1930-34), VI, 15.

[3] "John Paul Frederick Richter" (1821), *The Collected Writings of Thomas De Quincey,* ed. David Masson (Edinburgh, 1889-90), XI, 270.

[4] "Jean Paul Friedrich Richter" (1827), *The Works of Thomas Carlyle,* ed. H. D. Traill (London, 1896-99), XXVI, 17.

[5] "On the Genius and Character of Hogarth" (1811), *The Works of Charles and Mary Lamb,* ed. E. V. Lucas (London, 1903-1905), I, 86.

[6] *The Letters of John Keats,* ed. Hyder E. Rollins (Cambridge, Mass., 1958), I, 193. Subsequent references to Keats's letters appear in the text.

[7] *Jokes and Their Relation to the Unconscious* (1905), *The Standard Edition of the Complete Psychological Works of Sigmund Freud,* tr. and ed. James Strachey (London, 1953-64), VIII, 232.

[8] In addition to several references to Beattie's poems, he alludes to the "Essay on Truth" in "The Vision" (ll. 171-74) and was presumably acquainted with the "Essay on Poetry and Music" (*The Letters of Robert Burns,* ed. J. DeLancey Ferguson [Oxford, 1931], II, 148). Since the "Essay on Laughter" was often printed with Beattie's other essays, Burns probably knew it.

[9] *Essays* (London, 1779), p. 438.

[10] *Essays,* pp. 301-305, 380-83.

[11] *Letters,* I, 108.

[12] *The Poems and Songs of Robert Burns,* ed. James Kinsley (Oxford, 1968), I, 59-60. All subsequent references to Burns's poetry cite volume and page of this edition.

[13] *Letters,* I, 332.

[14] *Letters,* II, 135.

[15] *Jokes,* p. 110.

[16] *Jokes,* pp. 182-88.

[17] *Jokes,* pp. 90-119.

[18] *Robert Burns's Commonplace Book 1783-1785,* ed. James C. Ewing and D. Cook (Glasgow, 1938), pp. 7-8.

[19] See *Letters,* I, 8; II, 271. Cf. also Pope's *Essay on Man,* III, 207-8.

[20] Letter of 20 March 1799 to Southey, *The Letters of Charles and Mary Lamb,* ed. E. V. Lucas (London, 1935), I, 152.

[21] Journal entry for 13 December 1813, *The Works of Lord Byron: Letters and Journals,* ed. Rowland E. Prothero (London, 1898-1901), II, 376-77—hereafter cited as *LJ.*

[22] "Burns" (1828), *Works,* XXVI, 283.

[23] "The Study of Poetry" (1880), *The Works of Matthew Arnold* (London, 1903-1904), IV, 32-40.

David Murison (essay date 1975)

SOURCE: "The Language of Burns," in *Critical Essays on Robert Burns,* edited by Donald A. Low, Routledge & Kegan Paul, 1975, pp. 54-70.

[*In the following essay Murison outlines the history of the Scots dialect and examines the relationship between Scots and English in Burns's writing.*]

No small part of a poet's business is the manipulation of words, and the great poets have usually been great creators also in the use of language. But even the greatest have to work within the general limits of the language they begin with, its vocabulary, its idiom and its rhythms, and Burns is no exception. In his case the picture is complicated by the fact that for historical reasons he had two languages at his disposal, whose relations to one another have to be understood before we can appreciate his technique and achievement.

Scots and English are essentially dialects of the same original language, Anglo-Saxon, and the differences between them are far outweighed by their similarities, and, for reasons that will appear, the differences, once marked and predictable, are becoming more and more blurred as far as Scots is concerned. But differences there are, not only purely linguistic but also stylistic and thematic. There is of course a large common vocabulary, but Scots has a considerable Norse element and some Dutch, French and Gaelic not shared with English; the vowel and to a lesser extent the consonant systems are different; the grammatical forms, especially in the verbs, vary somewhat; and there are a great many subtle distinctions in syntax and idiom. These differentiae had established and consolidated themselves by the late fifteenth century, and from then on it was as possible to speak of two distinct languages, as it was of two distinct nations. But, as is well known, a series of historical accidents inhibited the growth of the northern tongue and left the field open for the ultimate triumph of the other over the whole island. The Reformation of 1560 and the circulation of the English Bible, in default of a Scots one which never materialized, gave English a spiritual prestige as the language of solemnity and dignity, for the more serious affairs of life, while Scots remained the speech of informality, of the domestic, the sentimental and, significantly enough, the comic, a dichotomy well seen in **'The Cotter's Saturday Night'**. The Union of the Crowns in 1603 took the Scottish court and the patrons of culture to London, and almost immediately the results were seen, not only in the language of literature in the works of the poets Drummond, Alexander and Mure, and prose-writers like Urquhart, but in the official documents of state and burgh, and the private papers of the nobility which become more and more anglicized as the century advances, so that English was now gaining also in social prestige at the expense of Scots.

The seventeenth century is in fact the period of transition from Scots to English, and the cope-stone to the process was put on by the Parliamentary Union of 1707, when thenceforth the laws of Scotland would be promulgated from London in the King's English and all administrative pronouncements and documentation would be in the official language of the legislature. It was the process of 1603 over again in a more thorough and final form. Scots prose now lost all status, was reduced to the level of a dialect, and in the eighteenth century hardly exists as a literary form.

In verse, however, all was not lost. The popular tradition of the Middle Ages that we find in 'Christ's Kirk on the Green', 'Peblis to the Play', 'Rauf Coilzear', 'The Wyf of Auchtermuchty', carried on through the seventeenth century, along with the ballad and folksong and such genre pieces as Sempill's elegy on 'Habbie Simson', notable for its stanza form, the verse epistle, the testament poem, and much more of the sort that was republished by the Edinburgh printer James Watson in his *Choice Collection* of 1706-11. This undoubtedly inspired Allan Ramsay to carry on in the same vein both with anthologies of medieval and contemporary poems, the *Ever Green* and the *Tea-Table Miscellany,* and with a considerable volume of work of his own. And not only was this tradition, because it was of its nature popular, in the vernacular, but also Ramsay himself adopted Scots as the first language of his poems from his own strong nationalist sympathies, later seen in his preface (in Scots) to his collection of proverbs. So it was Ramsay who laid the trail and struck the keynote for this revival of Scottish literature and language as a kind of spiritual compensation for the political eclipse which had overtaken the nation. But it was not a full-scale revival of either. In the eighteenth century as compared with the early sixteenth there was no prose in Scots of a serious, philosophical or scientific nature—the day for that was past. Poetry and its language are on a more popular and less intellectual level; there is no epic, no metaphysical verse, nothing like Dryden or Pope. The vocabulary is much more restricted and personal, more realistic and down to earth, and hence, in Scotland,

more regional, because, in the absence of a standard form of speech and of a national and literary centre, local dialects inevitably rise into prominence, as indeed happened in the north-east of Scotland with poets like Skinner, Alexander Ross and Robert and William Forbes, whose works are in some measure linguistic *tours de force*. The efforts to extend the scope and usage of Scots vocabulary, as with Gavin Douglas in 1513 and the *Complaynt of Scotland* in 1548, had long been abandoned, and of course there was none of the polishing and refining that went on in English under the Augustans.

After 1700 the unrestricted penetration of Scotland by English through the Bible and the Church, legal and bureaucratic usage, newspapers and the educational system, produced, especially among those most exposed to it, a kind of mixed informal language in which English words and forms could be grafted on to the vernacular in whatever degree the speaker or writer wished: a state of affairs not so very different from that of today, only the basic Scots vocabulary has become so much thinner and English has replaced it.

Every speaker has various 'registers' or modifications of speech, according to the company he is in or the topic he is discussing, or the atmosphere or manner in which he is discussing it, distinguishing the language of, say, sport from that of politics; though the more educated or socially exalted one is, the more the limits of variation tend to become restricted. In eighteenth-century Scotland the fluctuations were as between more or less Scots and less or more English, the beauties of American and Soho 'in-talk' not having yet struck us. In effect the Age of Enlightenment and Philosophy and the beginnings of the Industrial Revolution were being superimposed on the old feudal and rural culture of Scotland, and in speech terms this corresponds roughly to the functional demarcation line between English as the language of abstract and formal thought and Scots as the language of immediacy and intimacy at a lower intellectual pitch.

The social prestige of English, besides, steadily increased throughout the century, and a mastery of it came to be the aim of at least the upper classes, not merely in writing, as in the case of David Hume, but also in speech, for the English of Scotland was still distinct enough from that of England to be only half-intelligible, as the Scots MPs found to their mortification when they took their seats in the new Westminster. This led later to the somewhat ludicrous elocution classes run in Edinburgh by an Irishman for the Select Society 'for Promoting the Reading and Speaking of the English Language' in 1761.

It was into this confused and unstable linguistic situation that Burns was born. Both influences, Scots and English, were at work on him from his earliest youth, for he himself was the child of two diverse characters who in themselves epitomize the history and culture of Scotland. It was his father who insisted on a good education for his sons; who represented the Scotland that had descended from the Reformation by way of the Kirk, that had had its wits sharpened and its philosophy deepened on the frozen logic of the Shorter Catechism; from John Murdoch, the dominie at Alloway, Burns came to know the great works of English literature, Shakespeare, Milton, Pope and other Augustans, and was given a thorough drilling in formal English composition and style. William Burnes himself had written a short religious treatise for family use, in impeccable English.

But there was his mother too and her people and his old nurse, representing the native force in Burns, the element which is of the soil of Scotland, of the folk and their lore, their daily lives, their superstitions, their delight in the fields and woods of Ayrshire, in banks and braes and running water so characteristically Scottish, their shrewd mother-wit, their proverbs, all expressed in their pithy forceful Scots tongue. It is in fact in the blending of the two strains in the Scottish heritage, the intellectual and the traditional, that Burns and his poetry stand out as the voice of Scotland.

Besides the rigorous discipline of Murdoch's emphasis on style, we know from brother Gilbert that the young poet was reading the *Spectator* and Pope's translation of Homer[1] so that the influence of Augustan English was in full play, and there is an even more important note in his autobiographical letter to Dr Moore where he describes his close study of 'a collection of English songs'. 'I pored over them driving my cart, or walking to labour—song by song—verse by verse; carefully noting the true, tender, or sublime, from affectation and fustian; and I am convinced I owe much to this of my critic-craft, such as it is.'[2] Undoubtedly Burns's uncanny flair for the right word in the right place was in part at least the outcome of this.

Another more immediate result was the production of the Mount Oliphant period, a particularly unhappy phase of his life when he developed teenage melancholia and wrote elegies and odes all in somewhat stilted English about 'fickle Fortune', and even attempted a tragedy, of which only the dismal fragment 'All devil as I am, a damned wretch' survives.

Fortunately, about this time he picked up a copy of Ramsay's *Tea-Table Miscellany* and tried his hand at song-writing in Scots, or rather in that half-Scots half-English form that goes back to the early eighteenth or even late seventeenth century, when there was a craze for Scots songs, in London as well as in Scotland. The very first piece he ever wrote, **'Handsome Nell'**, was in this vein, and also the clever **'Tibbie, I hae seen the day'**, which is in pretty straight Scots with an English rhyme here and there, as in stanza 2.

Meanwhile his formal if fitful education was progressing; he had read Locke's *Essay concerning Human Understanding,* attended a course in trigonometry and his reading[3]

> was enlarged with the very important addition of Thomson's and Shenstone's Works. I had seen mankind in a new phasis; and I engaged several of my schoolfellows to keep up a literary correspondence with me. This last helped me much on in composition. I had met with a collection of letters by the Wits of Queen Anne's reign, and I pored over them most devoutly.

All this goes to show the strict training Burns gave himself in language, the careful weighing up of each word, the ordering of the thought, the choice of imagery as in one of his next songs, **'The Lass of Cessnock Banks'**, which is self-confessedly an exercise in the use of similes, and above all in **'Mary Morison'**, which the indefatigable Ritter has shown to be full of echoes of Shakespeare, Pope, Thomson, Shenstone, Mackenzie among others,[4] but these have been woven into a perfect conceptual unity and, what is more, rendered into Scots, despite one or two English forms like *those, poor* and *shown, canst* and *wilt,* and anglicized spellings like *trembling, thought,* and the *-ed* of the past participles. We see the same process at work again a little later in **'Corn Rigs'** and much later in **'A Red Red Rose'**. Both have motifs and phrases from earlier folk-songs both Scottish and English. **'Corn Rigs',** though pitched at a lower and earthier level, is extraordinarily deft in its use of the plainest Scots, with the exception of the one line 'I lock'd her in my fond embrace'; the whole thing reads like an ordinary conversation, and yet by sheer word-music and the evocation of the harvest moonlight produces an almost magical effect. Well might Burns say of it himself, 'The best stanza that ever I wrote, at least the one that pleases me best, and comes nearest to my *beau ideal* of poetical perfection, is this—

> I hae been blythe wi' Comrades dear; I hae been merry drinking;
> I hae been joyfu' gath'rin gear; I hae been happy thinking;
> But a' the pleasures e'er I saw, tho' three times doubl'd fairly,
> That happy night was worth them a', amang the rigs o'barley.

It was about this time (1782), however, that the vital incident occurred in Burns's poetic career. 'Meeting with Fergusson's Scotch Poems I strung anew my wildly-sounding lyre with emulating vigour.'[5] Later, in his Commonplace Book of August 1784, he links 'the excellent Ramsay and the still more excellent Fergusson' as between them inspiring him to concentrate on celebrating the scenery and life of his native Ayrshire, a theme he reiterates in verse in his **'Epistle to William Simpson'**. Burns had in fact found himself as a dedicated Scottish poet.

It was out of this that the Kilmarnock edition sprang. The models are obvious, Fergusson's dialogue between 'Plainstanes and Causey' for **'The Twa Dogs'**; 'Caller Water' for **'Scotch Drink'**; 'Leith Races' for **'The Holy Fair'**; and even more directly 'The Farmer's Ingle' for **'The Cotter's Saturday Night'**. **'The Twa Dogs'** is a remarkably successful experiment in social criticism in straight conversational Scots. Because of the restricted nature and scope of eighteenth-century Scots, there has to be a certain reduction in focus, the abstract has to be seen in terms of the concrete, the sophistication of an all-purpose language has to be forgone, but within these limits the vigour and vivacity of the concepts are hard to better and the humour adds to the verve:

> There, at Vienna, or Versailles,
> He rives his father's auld entails;
> Or by Madrid he takes the rout,
> To thrum guittarres an' fecht wi' nowt;
> Or down Italian Vista startles
> Whore-hunting amang groves o' myrtles;
> Then bowses drumlie German-water,
> To mak himsel look fair an' fatter,
> An' clear the consequential sorrows,
> Love-gifts of Carnival Signioras.

The last two lines from the Edinburgh edition, substituted for the original couplet, 'An' purge the bitter ga's an' cankers, / O' curst Venetian bores an' chancres', show a further improvement in linguistic polish and wit. **'The Holy Fair'**, one of Burns's greatest poems, shows the same masterly command of language, by turning the simplest and most natural of conversational prose into poetry. The marvellous evocation of a summer morning in stanza I in plain direct Scots, with just a nod of concession to the Augustans in the second line:

> Upon a simmer Sunday morn,
> When Nature's face is fair,
> I walked forth to view the corn
> An' snuff the callor air:
>
> The rising sun, owre Galston muirs,
> Wi' glorious light was glintan;
> The hares were hirplan down the furrs
> The lav'rocks they were chantan
> Fu' sweet that day

leads on to the well-conceived and concretely rendered vision of the three allegorical women, Supersti-

tion, Hypocrisy and Fun, and the utter naturalness of the half-recognition of the last:

> Wi' bonnet aff, quoth I, 'Sweet lass,
> I think ye seem to ken me;
> I'm sure I've seen that bonie face,
> But yet I canna name ye.'

And so on through memorable phrase and epigram, 'Screw'd up, grace-proud faces', 'Common-sense has taen the road, / An' aff, an' up the Cowgate', 'There's some are fou o' love divine, / There's some are fou o' brandy', to the broad chuckle at the end.

The same skill in manipulating colloquial Scots is seen at its best in the Epistles, modelled on the verse correspondence between Ramsay and Hamilton of Gilbertfield in the 'Habbie Simson' stanza, so well adapted to the sentential nature of folk-speech, with the frequent sardonic afterthought or phrase of finality conveyed neatly in the 'bob-wheel' at the end:

> 'But faith! he'll turn a corner jinkan, / An' cheat you yet';
> 'The last sad cape-stane of his woes; / Poor Mailie's dead';
> 'I see ye upwards cast your eyes—/ Ye ken the road';
> 'Wha does the utmost that he can, / Will whiles dae mair';
> 'A rousing whid at time to vend, / And nail't with Scripture'.

When we come to the **'Epistle to a Young Friend'**, we find a somewhat different type of Scots. The easy spontaneous style of the Epistles to John Lapraik or William Simpson is more formalized into a series of moral apothegms, still in Scots but in a strongly anglicized variety of it, a homiletic Scots such as must have been heard from many an early eighteenth-century pulpit from the old-fashioned school of preachers of the Moderate faction in the Kirk. It is not unlike Blair, and the poem probably contains more lines quoted from Burns than any other. 'Still keep something to yoursel, / Ye scarcely tell to ony'; 'The glorious privilege of being independent'; 'The fear o' Hell's a hangman's whip, / To haud the wretch in order'; 'A correspondence fix'd wi' Heav'n / Is sure a noble anchor'. The classic instance of this is in **'Tam o' Shanter'**. The narrative proceeds with gathering speed in good rich Scots (and nowhere is Burns's facility with the language in better evidence), when at a natural pause in the story he introduces the series of similes 'But pleasures are like poppies spread', which has given critics such a time of it. But surely this is simply the moral homily once again, interpolated with a certain mock solemnity and the tongue well in the cheek, and of course in English, as such homilies were bound to be.

This style in fact in different contexts reappears in **'The Cotter's Saturday Night'** and **'The Vision'**. In the former the language switches from Scots to English as the theme fluctuates between the descriptive and domestic and the stagy moralizing which the majority of critics delight in execrating. But linguistically the most significant part is when, 'the chearfu' supper done', the Scots of the chatter at table almost insensibly and by degrees slides into English as the father takes down the Bible and worship begins. This is essentially the matter of historical tradition, and the inveterate association of the Bible and liturgical language in general in Scotland with English. The setting of **'The Vision'** is not dissimilar, having the same homely vivid vernacular description of the inside of the cottage and even of Coila in the first part, and a thoroughly classical English ode in the second when he meditates on the abstractions of the social order and the function of the poet, with some good lines in it, especially the succinct and profound 'But yet the light that led astray, / Was light from Heaven', which sums up in a few words the whole problem and matter of moral philosophy. But he said more or less the same thing in his Epistles to John Lapraik and Willie Simpson more directly and simply and unaffectedly in Scots, and they are worth, and will stand, comparison with **'The Vision'** on this very point.

In **'Holy Willie's Prayer'** the same technique is employed, but with a much more serious purpose; liturgical English and down-to-earth Scots are woven together and made to alternate with consummate skill in bringing out the two facets of Willie's character so that he is condemned out of his own mouth:

> Yet I am here, a chosen sample,
> To shew thy grace is great and ample,
> I'm here, a pillar o' thy temple
>   Strong as a rock;
> A guide, a ruler and example
>   To a' thy flock. . . .
>
> Besides, I farther maun avow,
> Wi' Leezie's lass, three times I trow;
> But Lord, that Friday I was fou
>   When I cam near her,
> Or else, thou kens, thy servant true,
>   Wad never steer her.

Again a comparison of the Scots **'Mouse'** with the more Englified **'Daisy'** reinforces the general judgment that Burns, in the words of Scott,[6]

> never seems to have been completely at his ease when he had not the power of descending at pleasure into that which was familiar to his ear, and to his habits. . . . His use of English when assumed as a primary and indispensable rule of composition, the comparative penury of rhimes,

and the want of a thousand emphatic words which his habitual acquaintance with the Scottish supplied, rendered his expression confined and embarrassed.

Scott, who was much in the same boat himself, knew the lack of uninhibited fluency that comes of using a stepmother tongue.

So much for the stylistics of the Kilmarnock edition, that mixture, in varying degrees, of Scots for the particular in description and narrative, in which the poet intimately participates, and English or Englified Scots for the more reflective and philosophical passages, when the poet steps back as a commentator and adopts a persona more remote from his subject. This becomes his general practice, and even his songs, in so far as the theme permits, present the same linguistic pattern, as we shall see.

But Burns's Scots itself is worth examining more closely. The poet himself, no doubt with a view to an audience of anglicized Scots, itself a recognition of the linguistic changes in eighteenth-century Scotland, provided to his first edition a glossary, which he much enlarged in his second, of the Scots words he thought needed explanation, and to these he added notes on the pronunciation which all reciters of Burns would do well to heed. He noted also that in Scots the present participle ends in *-an* (from an earlier *-and*) and the past participle in *-t*. The first must be based on the observation of his own ears, detecting a distinction between the participle and the verbal noun which was already dying out in the central dialects of Scotland, but is historically founded and still survives in the northern and southern peripheries of Scots, though long abandoned in literary Scots. He does not apply it rigorously in his own text, and gave it up in his later work. His Scots vocabulary is copious; in his complete works he employs over 2,000 peculiarly Scots words (the average Scots speaker today would have about 500 at the most); his definitions are accurate, and not without humour: *blink*, a glance, an amorous leer, a short space of time, a smiling look, to look kindly, to shine by fits; *clachan*, a small village about a church, a hamlet; *fetch*, to stop suddenly in the draught and then come on too hastily; *hoddan*, the motion of a sage country farmer on an old cart horse; *houghmagandie*, a species of gender composed of the masculine and feminine united; *whid*, the motion of a hare running but not frighted, a lie.

He has of course the vocabulary of the farmer in *aiver, bawsont, fittie-lan, fow, icker, ket, luggie, outler, pattle, stibble-rig, stimpart, risk, thrave, thack* and *raep;* the **'Inventory'** is in fact one of many such Scots poems in the tradition of the medieval 'Wowin of Jok and Jenny' where lists of words are versified for their own sake; **'Halloween'** again is a richly dialectal catalogue of rustic folklore; the terminology of curling appears in **'Tam Samson's Elegy'**. He had an interest in words as such, as his usage and the glossary show and as his few random notes on Border dialect during his tour by the Tweed in 1787 bear out; and to Robert Anderson he admitted the advantages in having 'the *copia verborum*, the command of phraseology which the knowledge and use of the English and Scottish dialects afforded him'.[7]

His native dialect was of course that of Kyle, which is in a debatable land between the dialect region of Strathclyde and that of Galloway, and there are a few words which are specifically from that area, words like *crunt, daimen, gloamin shot, ha bible, icker, jauk, kiaugh, messan, pyle, raucle, rockin, roon, shangan, thummart, wiel, winze, wintle*, all from the rural or local poems; but, by and large, his vocabulary is eclectic, avoiding the purely provincial, and so remaining in the broad stream of traditional literary, one might even say, metropolitan Scots, such at least as had survived the seventeenth-century break-up. For this he is considerably indebted above all to Ramsay, and in part to some others of his poetical predecessors, Sempill, Skinner, Hamilton of Bangour, Ross of Lochlee, whom he mentions several times, and of course Fergusson.

Ritter and others have painstakingly accumulated instances of borrowing and adaptation[8] till one is tempted to wonder if Burns ever wrote an original line, and there is neither need nor space to detail these here. Furthermore, Burns's native command of Scots was such as to make it difficult to distinguish borrowings from spontaneous uses.

But Burns made no secret of his indebtedness to others in the free-masonry of poetry—and, of course, in the songs adaptation was his stated policy and practice—and in his use of some words the borrowings are plain and palpable. It is obvious that he knew passages of Ramsay and Fergusson by heart, and echoes of their phraseology are found in him. The rhymes 'awfu, unlawfu' and 'a winsome wench and walie' in **'Tam o'Shanter'** are straight from Ramsay's 'Tale of Three Bonnets'; Ramsay preceded him with *aspar, auld-farran, bellum, beet, Land o' Cakes, clishmaclaver, collieshangie, cooser, dink, donsie, fair fa', flewit, goave, grunzie, jockteleg, ripple, sculduddcrie, shaul, whigmaleerie, wimple;* in many cases the contexts are close enough to suggest direct borrowing. Fergusson had been at the same source himself and had passed on to Burns *bughtin time, cheek for chow, drant, doylt, glamour, gloamin, hoddan gray, lyart, oergang, rowt*. It is worth noting incidentally how the poetic quality improves with each borrowing.

Katharine Ogie (a seventeenth-century song) in Ramsay, *Tea-Table Miscellany* (1876), I, 69:

O were I but some shepherd swain!
  To feed my flock beside thee,
At boughting-time to leave the plain,
  In milking to abide thee.

Fergusson *Hallowfair,* vi:

Now, it was late in the ev'ning,
  And boughting-time was drawing near,
The lasses had stench'd their griening
  Wi' fouth o' braw apples and beer.

Burns *The Lea-Rig,* i:

.When o'er the hill the eastern star
  Tells bughtin-time is near, my jo,
And owsen frae the furrowed field
  Return sae dowf and weary, O.

To old Scots proverbs and traditional sayings Burns is indebted for 'the stalk o' carl help', 'to stand abeigh', 'sturt and strife', 'moop and mell', and *rigwoodie* from **'Tam o' Shanter'** is attested in connection with witchcraft early in the eighteenth century. Another of Burns's sources must have been the Chapbooks which circulated over the south-west at this period, particularly the ever-popular broadly humorous sketches of Dougal Graham. To Dougal, Burns certainly owes *clinkumbell* as a nickname for a kirk-beadle, most likely *fligmagairies,* and possibly also *bow-kail,* and *lallan. Fiere* in **'Auld Lang Syne'** is from the vocabulary of the ballads.

Burns then is a skilful adapter of the poetic language of his predecessors, another follower in the long if intermittent tradition coming down from the Middle Ages, of which echoes can still be heard among our moderns who write in Scots. For if there is any one quality more than another which characterizes Scottish literature it is the recurrent theme, the repeated metaphor and image, the resumed standpoint, due not only to the tenacity of the native strain in spite, or perhaps because, of alien pressure but also in no small measure to the limits imposed on it by the use of Scots. But within the tradition Burns made his own contribution to the poetic vocabulary of Scots, of which his innumerable imitators have made good use ever since, as *agley, bethankit, blellum, burnewin, catch-the-plack, glib-gabbit, hogshouther, Johnny Ged, primsie, raible, redwatshod*, of which Carlyle said, 'in this one word, a full vision of horror and carnage, perhaps too frightfully accurate for Art', *run deil, skelvy, skinking, smytrie, snick-drawing, staumrel,* not necessarily all Burns's own invention but first recorded in his works.

When we come to consider the question of the language of the later Burns, especially the Burns of the songs, we are considerably helped by

Burns's own explicit statements. To Thomson he was quite emphatic,[9]

> If you are for English verses, there is, on my part, an end of the matter. . . . These English verses gravel me to death. I have not that command of the language that I have of my native tongue.— In fact, I think my ideas are more barren in English than in Scotish.—I have been at **'Duncan Gray'**, to dress it in English, but all that I can do is deplorably stupid.—For instance—

> Song—Tune, Duncan Gray—Let not woman e'er complain.

And most readers would agree with him.

Burns's argument, constantly repeated to Thomson, is that in the music of the songs there is a pastoral simplicity, pathos or liveliness which should be matched with a similar simplicity in the words, which he associates with Scots. Even 'a sprinkling of the old Scotish' is better than nothing. In the event this turns out something like **'Ae Fond Kiss'** on paper, but when one reflects that it is in the simpler type of diction that Scots and English vocabulary coincide, and that if one follows Burns's instructions in his glossary to ignore the anglicized spelling and pronounce in the Scots manner, the poem is in effect a Scots poem with one or two Englishisms, like 'groans', rather than the other way round.

One must remember that Burns got his Scots orthography from Ramsay—one of his less happy borrowings, since Ramsay's spelling is haphazard, inconsistent and often so anglicized as to blur the distinction in phonetic values between Scots and English, as for instance in spellings like *light* for *licht; poor, moon, coost,* for *puir, mune, cuist; down* for *doun; wrath* for *wraith; how* for *hoo; hours* for *oors; arm* for *airm;* etc; *-ed,* more often than not, appears for *-it,* and *-ing* for the participle *-in,* or as Burns would have it, *-an,* but the English form is preferable to the Scots in the first verse of **'Ca' the yowes'**, to preserve the assonance with *sang* and *amang* and reproduce the prolonged ringing echo of the bird's song through the woods.

In his refashioning of older songs Burns is guided by the language of the original and as many of his models were from the seventeenth century, English as well as Scots, the language is naturally mixed in varying degrees according to the prescription given above, with the seasoning of old Scots *quantum sufficit*. If it were too thickly Scots to his mind, then 'I will vamp up the old song and make it English enough to be understood' he says to Thomson in regard to the song **'Sleep'st thou or wauk'st thou'**.[10]

But this is the exception with him rather than the rule. On one occasion at least he did the opposite by trying to write down the anglicized courtly or cavalier song of the seventeenth-century poet, Sir Robert Aytoun, 'I do confess thee sweet', with the usual involved epigrammatic style but a good song for all that, to the popular level by Scotticizing it. 'I do think I have improved the simplicity of the sentiments by giving them a Scots dress.' But here for once he misconstrued his model and his customary good taste in language failed him so that he comes second-best out of the comparison.

'Simplicity' was his motto, and in his long-protracted wranglings with George Thomson over the text as well as the music of his songs he had to tell him that he was apt to sacrifice simplicity for pathos, sentiment and point. To Thomson's constant niggling for more English, he answered bluntly 'I'll rather write a new song altogether than make this English. The sprinkling of Scotch in it, while it is but a sprinkling, gives it an air of rustic naïveté, which time will rather increase than diminish.'[11] In general he rings the changes freely within this mixed Anglo-Scots style, theme and mood being usually a determining factor. The gay extravert comic song, the social or community song, is, as one would expect, from its immediacy and concreteness, in Scots, like **'The Deil's awa wi' th' Exciseman'**, or **'Willie brewed a Peck o' Maut'**, or **'Willie Wastle'**, or **'Whistle an' I'll come to ye, my Lad'**, or **'Duncan Gray'**, or **'Contented wi' Little'**.

The same colloquial dexterity of **'The Holy Fair'** is reproduced in **'Tam Glen'** and **'Last May a Braw Wooer'**, and to this he adds sprightly wit in **'Green grow the Rashes'**, **'There was a Lad'**, **'Whistle o'er the Lave o't'**, **'The Carle o' Kellyburn Braes'**. All these are in good rich Scots. The 'pastoral simplicity' vein is worked in **'The Banks o' Doon'**, where the student of Burns's styles has the advantage of having three versions to compare, the first with the rather halting opening 'Sweet are the banks—the banks o' Doon'; the second trimmed in the direction of even greater simplicity with the starkness of the ballad in it and faint echoes of 'O waly, waly up the bank' and much the best version; and the third, the modern popular one, verbally spun out to suit a different tune from the original. It provides an object lesson in showing how Burns's taste was pretty unerring when he was left to himself, and it compares favourably too with the turgid English of **'To Mary in Heaven'** where the poet is simply attitudinizing with the same general thought and imagery.

In this type of song, though it is more personal and reflective, good idiomatic Scots is still the medium, and universality is achieved by the simplicity, and this is true of many of his other great songs, **'John Ander-**

son, my jo', 'My Luve's like a Red Red Rose', 'O a' the Airts', and 'Auld Lang Syne'. There is more English in the pensive melancholy or sentimental mood of **'Bonie Wee Thing'**, where the last verse wanders off into an Augustan conceit, or of **'O, wert thou in the Cauld Blast'**, and the graceful and courtly **'A Rosebud by my Early Walk'**. On the other hand, **'It was a' for our Rightfu' King'** for all its cavalier and Jacobite overtones is in Scots, suggesting an intensity and spontaneity of feeling which made the mother tongue inevitable, when the particular human situation is posed against the general political background. This ability to fix in the vivid concrete terms of ordinary experience a universal truth is of course Burns's strongest suit and the essential secret of his genius and popularity. We have already seen it in **'The Twa Dogs'**. In his songs it appears splendidly in **'A Man's a Man'**. It is indeed 'prose thoughts inverted into rhyme', as Burns himself said—the prose thoughts of Tom Paine's *Rights of Man,* but out of the English prose Burns has made an immortal song in plain Scots. As Snyder points out, out of 263 words in the whole poem, 240 are monosyllables. The relationship of Scots and English and the potentialities of the one as against the other in the hands of Burns could hardly be better illustrated.

'Scots wha hae', which was written about the same time, has the same background in the ferment of the French Revolution and one can hear echoes of 'La Marseillaise' in it. Here Burns is striking the attitude of the patriot, and doubtless it was intended as a kind of national anthem of a nation that may even yet find the moral courage to sing it. It is a rhetorical address to the whole people; it deals with the abstractions of liberty, nationalism and tyranny, it demands dignity and solemnity, and, at this metaphysical level, one would expect English instead of Scots. In the event Burns has compromised according to his usual formula. The grammar is English, the rhymes are Scots, the forms are mixed, *sae,* for instance, but *woe, foe;* the usage in the first two lines is not the idiomatic vernacular, as Sir James Murray remarked;[12] yet there can be no question of its success as a poem and of Burns's skill in wedding the two linguistic traditions. On a larger canvas the two traditions appear again side by side and partly fused in **'The Jolly Beggars'**. The recitativo, the intimate homely detailed description, is in Scots, the songs of the soldier and his doxy who had served so long abroad are in English; the wit of the Merry Andrew's song is conveyed in the Scots of that sort in which Burns excelled; the sentimentality of **'A Highland Lad'** is in the mixed style he normally favoured; the fiddler and the tinker, as 'gangrel bodies' of no fixed abode, sing in different degrees of Scots, conditioned partly by the tunes prescribed for them. The bard's song is similarly attuned to his literary trade, with snatches of older songs and allusions to Castalia and Helicon, but in the main in Scots. But

when the particular gives way to the general, when the individuals unite in a chorus of social criticism and formulate their philosophy of life, the language, as has often enough been noticed, turns to Augustan English in a kind of secular hymn.

Burns, like so many Scottish writers before him, took his traditions as he found them and worked within them, chiselling and polishing till his best reaches almost to perfection, and in his own line no one has ever surpassed him. His sound linguistic schooling, which was essentially classical, mediated through the Augustans, made him realize the weaknesses of a broken-down language, such as eighteenth-century Scots had become, deficient in a prose tradition and limited in abstract vocabulary. Yet, through his predecessors in both written and oral literature, he knew what it would still do and he chose it for himself because it was his own heritage. It was sound instinct in him that made him go for simplicity, and marry the language of feeling with that of thought by conceiving both in their most concrete terms. It is this that makes his language so vivid and quotable. No one has ever wrung so much humour, passion and beauty out of monosyllables as Burns, even at times magic:

> The wan moon sets behind the white wave,
>   And time is setting with me, Oh.

And in so doing he gave the old Scots tongue a new lease of life, a new dignity and a renewed worth which even today and even in spite of the Scots themselves it has not altogether lost.

Notes

[1] In Chambers-Wallace, *Life and Works of Burns* (Edinburgh, 1896), I, p. 35.

[2] J. De Lancey Ferguson, *Letters of Robert Burns* (Oxford, 1931), I, p. 109.

[3] *Ibid.,* p. 111.

[4] O. Ritter, *Quellenstudien zu Robert Burns 1773-1791* (Berlin, 1901), pp. 23-6.

[5] *Letters,* I, p. 113.

[6] Scott, in *Quarterly Review* (February 1809), p. 35.

[7] *Burns Chronicle* (1925), p. 12.

[8] Ritter, *passim.*

[9] *Letters,* II, pp. 122, 268.

[10] *Ibid.*

[11] *Ibid.,* p. 205.

[12] J. A. H. Murray, *Dialect of the Southern Counties of Scotland* (London, 1873), p. 71n.

Mary Ellen Brown (essay date 1984)

SOURCE: "The Early Period: Burns's Conscious Collecting of Folksongs," in *Burns and Tradition*, Macmillan Press, 1984, pp. 1-26, 147-50.

[*Here, Brown describes Burns as a transitional figure bridging the two spheres of oral and literate composition.*]

> (That Bards are second-sighted is nae joke,
> And ken the lingo of the sp'ritual folk;
> Fays, Spunkies, Kelpies, a', they can explain
>   them,
> An ev'n the vera deils they brawly ken
>   them.)
>
> > 'The Brigs of Ayr, a Poem'

Robert Burns is remembered as much for his personality and character as for his poetry and songs. It is rather ironic that as an individual his roots in a peasant class are extolled, even emphasised; however, as a creative artist his debts to written, élite precedents are principally cited. Both are probably somewhat extreme positions: as an individual Burns both represented and transcended his class; as a poet and songwright he followed the example of earlier writers while being simultaneously influenced by the oral literary forms which flourished in the milieu of his birth.

The stress on Burns' literary sources is a natural and explicable one: those who study Burns as literary historians and critics see him and his work through the dimension of time and often in comparison with other written work—the tangible records of the artistic endeavours of the past; and he does seem to have been the culmination of the Scottish literary tradition and to have profited from exposure to English literature. Burns himself praised a number of his predecessors and tried, in as much as was possible, to read the best of past artistry and to keep abreast of current efforts. The primary matrix in which he lived, however, was not completely a literate one: much of the artistic communication he shared with his contemporaries was oral and aural; for the ballads and folksongs he absorbed from multiple hearings[1] and the legends and other narratives which punctuated convivial conversation were a more pervasive and typical—if, unfortunately, ephemeral—part of the everyday world in which he lived than the poetry of Robert Fergusson or Thomas Gray. In a famous biographical letter to Dr Moore written after he had received acclaim as a poet, Burns described the influences he had come under when he was a boy and specifically mentions his mother and an old woman, loosely connected with the family, who provided him with an early stock of songs, tales, legends, beliefs, proverbs, and customs:

> In my infant and boyish days too, I owed much to an old Maid of my Mother's, remarkable for her ignorance, credulity and superstition.—She had, I suppose, the largest collection in the county of tales and songs concerning devils, ghosts, fairies, brownies, witches, warlocks, spunkies, kelpies, elf-candles, dead-lights, wraiths, apparitions, cantraips, giants, inchanted towers, dragons and other trumpery.[2]

The oral artistic creations, cumulatively built and recreated, passed on from generation to generation, stable in general form but varied in individual performance, were his birthright and a natural and universal part of the general society in which he lived—where traditional custom, belief, and practice dominated and overt creativity and innovation were not sought. This traditionally oriented way of life and the oral artistic communications it supported and sustained played a far more significant role in shaping and determining the directions of Burns' artistry than has been recognised.

Like all writers or creative artists, Burns was not an isolate; and he cannot be realistically divorced from the milieu in which he lived. He was a product of what had gone before and what was and his artistry often lay in uniquely blending, juxtaposing, or representing this. He was a part of a long tradition.[3] When T. S. Eliot suggests in 'Tradition and the Individual Talent' that all artists are a part of a tradition and are representatives of it, he is referring essentially to literary and élite aesthetic traditions.[4] Any artist is, as well, a product of a cultural tradition, and it is Burns' cultural tradition which has been slighted and frequently overlooked in most serious studies of the man and his work.

The rural Ayrshire into which Burns was born might be described as a modified peasant society: it was rurally based and dominated by agriculture; its people were relatively homogeneous and shared a body of knowledge, mostly oral; it was a society in many respects characterised by a preference for the old ways, for what had always been, the 'tried and true'. This society often provided the background and informing principle for Burns' writing; and the oral artistry found in such a society shaped the form, content, style, and process of much of his work. These traditional manifestations of culture—folkways or folklife and oral literature—might be broadly called *folklore*. And what follows is a documentation and illustration of the multiplicity of ways folklore affected Burns' art, exhibiting his debt to his own folkloric matrix and the traditional and repeated aspects of life, especially the oral artistic communications, which were a part of it.

This debt to his milieu and its artistry was largely unconscious and intuitive prior to 1786.[5] Edinburgh marked a transition to a far more aware and conscious artistry, to be discussed in Chapters 2 and 3, which was both antiquarian and national in inspiration. The poetry prior to Edinburgh deals primarily with folk-life,[6] with description of the rural existence, resulting sometimes in frankly occasional pieces; and Burns makes his larger comments about life against this backdrop, which was his milieu and naturally became an important part of his creative view. While Hugh MacDiarmid faults Burns for this localism,[7] it was undoubtedly essential for the establishment of his poetic voice and rarely kept Burns from suggesting a more universally applicable principle or sentiment as well. The events of 1786—the publication of the Kilmarnock edition and the visit to Edinburgh—precipated a shift away from this local poetry which drew its inspiration from the region of the poet's birth.

Burns was not an oddity in writing poems and songs.[8] He knew other local poets who shared his predilection for rhyme and exchanged verse letters with several—notably John Lapraik. The existence and prestige of poets, representing relatively defined locales, sometimes mere rhymers or village versifiers, may have its roots in the Celtic past where poet or bard stood in close relationship to priest or chieftain, being responsible for memory of the past as well as celebration of the present. Such a tradition surely continues in the often puerile laureate effusions composed to mark the special events of the present. But long ago the poet held a central position close to the seat of power and celebrated high points of the life and yearly round of activity; he spoke for as well as against the status quo, was often under protection of chieftain or priest's office, and used well-established traditional forms and structures as vessels for a contemporary message. Burns too took the forms and structures of the past and developed them by using the present: sometimes his pieces were frankly occasional and descriptive; in others his satire and social criticism worked effectively as in the days of the Celtic bards. But unlike the Celtic bard, Burns had no chieftain to protect him to sanction or approve his words.

Like the Celtic bard, Burns wrote for a local audience, which shared his interest in the geographic area and in current events and issues. That audience was known to him; it included his friends and his neighbours; and as often as not he read or recited his productions aloud to them[9] or circulated them in handwritten manuscripts. The audience he addressed—their politics, ethos—no doubt affected what lines he added or cut, amply illustrated in his lengthy correspondence with Mrs Dunlop and the manuscript versions he frequently sent her. Such flexibility reflects an attitude more akin to oral communication than to the impersonality of the written literary world where the reading public is only generally known and where the literary text is fixed and unchanging. Burns' audience always retained a specific quality for him even when he was no longer a local, but more nearly a national, poet. The principal edition of his work, the 1786 Kilmarnock edition, was essentially aimed at a relatively local audience, though, to be sure, his Preface looked beyond it. This concern with audience is characteristic of oral communication; it reflects a need for immediate response, for give and take. Burns' poetry and songs, like the traditional folk-songs and narratives, were passed on in a small, local, mostly homogeneous group.

If his audience was local and shared his world, that world found its way into his creative work as an essential ingredient in facilitating communication. He began with the common world, the familiar which he knew and to which he—as are all outstanding writers—was extraodinarily sensitive. He was not merely a describer, an ethnographer; he selected and focused on aspects of the shared world as a base from which to draw broader conclusions and generalisations about the human condition. And in transferring reality to creative work, whether destined for oral or written transmission, his own unique personality and background—albeit shaped by the common tradition—contributed to an equally individual perception of the world. Nonetheless his depiction of the world held in common with his audience lay within the recognisable parameters of general experience and formed the essential understood background which often effectively drew the readers or hearers of his work into the poem or song and provided them with a basis for the response all artistic endeavours strive for if they are indeed an effective means of communication. Burns wrote about what he knew using familiar forms and familiar language as well as familiar content. From a specific account of aspects of religious controversy rampant in Burns' day in 'The Ordination'[10] and in 'The Kirk of Scotland's Garland—a new Song' (no. 264) to a depiction of a gathering of three friends, including himself, in 'Willie brew'd a peck o' maut' (no. 268), Burns drew on his own environment for surface content. The obvious and identifiable are especially blatant in his frankly occasional and extemporary poems and songs, which, like 'At Roslin Inn' (no. 158), remark on the obvious and record an impression; they remain not as a great testimony to his poetic power, but as testimony to his spur-of-the-moment poetic ability.

The celebration of the immediate, often a shared experience, links Burns with both the earlier bardic and the later poet laureate traditions. Many of his occasional poems are said to have been off-the-cuff extemporaneous productions. Some were composed in writing and remain today incised in windows of various inns he frequented. Other works he created mentally, in memory, and later, after a long journey on horseback perhaps, put in writing.[11] The oral sound rather than the written text may well have controlled his composition.[12] His use of proverbs and sayings from oral tradition,[13] phrases from traditional songs,[14] not to mention the whole stanzas and refrains which provided the basic material for many of his songs suggests a compositional technique akin to oral formulaic composition.[15] Multiple versions of some of his works may also reflect a concept of artistic product which does not insist on fixity of text; such disregard for a definitive text links Burns to the world of traditional oral composition. In many ways, Burns was a kind of transition figure—an individual who straddled both the literate and the oral worlds, and his own method of composition reflected compositional approaches from both worlds.

He composed and wrote, of course, as all artists do—at least in part—in order to communicate, perhaps to influence. But he created as well to provide solace for himself: 'However as I hope my poor, country Muse, who, all rustic, akward [*sic*], and unpolished as she is, has more charms for me than any other of the pleasures of life beside—as I hope she will not then desert me, I may, even then, learn to be, if not happy, at least easy, and south a sang to sooth my misery.—'[16] And he created to relieve tension—as entertainment—as part of life. Creating, composing was for Burns, as for oral poets past and present, organically a part of the life he led:

> Leeze me on rhyme! it's ay a treasure,
> My chief, amaist my only pleasure,
> At hame, a-fiel, at wark or leisure,
>   The Muse, poor hizzie!
> Tho' rough an raploch be her measure,
>   She's seldom lazy.
>
> Haud tae the Muse, my dainty Davie:
> The warl' may play you [monie] a shavie;
> But for the Muse, she'll never leave ye,
>   Tho' e'er sae puir,
> Na, even tho' limpan wi' the spavie
>   Frae door tae door.
>   (ll. 37-48, no. 101)

And the use of poetic and song form, recognisably distinct from daily discourse, allowed Burns to write of love for women whom he could not ordinarily so address and to write of subjects, especially bawdry, he might not discuss in polite conversation. The functions of his art were many.

Burns' focus in his early work on local topics, his frequent use of traditional material, his acceptance of the fluidity of texts, his stress on audience and the oral socialisation of his own works, and his articulated views on the function of composition—all suggest Burns' strong and largely intuitive ties to the traditional and partially oral matrix of late eighteenth-century Ayrshire. This is not meant to diminish his relationship with the literary world: he read; he felt a debt to Allan Ramsay, to Robert Fergusson and others—both Scottish and English. And it was through the creative medium—writing and related print—he shared with them that his work lives today. But the literary and literate world was superimposed on the traditional and oral world which formed the very basis of his being. It provided him with forms and structures, content and contexts on which to build. Scottish tradition and Scottish oral artistry were his birthright.

Burns utilised various aspects of the whole gamut of traditional life and art available to him. The content of his poems and songs overtly drew upon the repeated themes, made reference to known locale as well as to facets of the shared oral art; utilised phrases, lines and stanzas extant in the tradition; described custom, practice, belief, and milieu; and repeatedly used the structures and forms of the traditional oral artistry circulating in his milieu. Not only was the content and often the structure of his work drawn from the folkloric milieu, but his very medium of communicating—the Scots vernacular—and stylistic devices such as repetition and frequent use of refrain assert his cultural heritage. And in several works he replicates the traditional matrix for artistic communication. Scottish traditional life and especially its oral and artistic forms dominated Burns' own aesthetic perspective and formed, frequently, the unconscious basis for his creativity.

Burns' most obvious debt to the oral world of which he was part is at the level of overt content. His kinship with earlier poetry and song is illustrated by his use of themes, shared with his predecessors, whether their medium was oral or written. Earlier in the eighteenth century, the Jacobite theme had certainly had definite political overtones, but as restoration of an independent Scotland and a distinctly Scottish monarch became less and less a possibility, the Jacobite theme became the accepted vehicle for popular nationalistic expression, indulged in, through composition or participation, by persons who might not have supported the Jacobite risings of the first half of the century. This romantic Jacobitism had many adherents, Burns among them, and vague references to Bonnie Prince Charlie, especially to his absence and to the implications of his overseas' residence for Scotland, occur in Burns' songs, particularly when he draws on earlier Jacobite songs and phrases to provide a link with the established tradition—'him that's far awa',[17] the White Cockade, the badge of the Stuarts,[18] **'Here's a Health to them that's awa'**.[19] While nationalism appears in various guises in Burns' work as in **'The Vision'** (no. 62) with its celebration of the power of poetry in proclaiming a Scottish nation, the theme is more often than not linked with Jacobite sentiment as in the **'Song—'**. . . .

> The small birds rejoice in the green leaves
>   returning,
> The murmuring streamlet winds clear thro'
>   the vale;
> The primroses blow in the dews of the
>   morning,
> And wild-scattered cowslips bedeck the
>   green dale:
> But what can give pleasure, or what can
>   seem fair,
> When the lingering moments are numbered
>   by Care?
> No birds sweetly singing, nor flowers gayly
>   springing,
> Can sooth the sad bosom of joyless
>   Despair.—
>
> The deed that I dared, could it merit their
>   malice,
> A KING and a FATHER to place on his throne;
> His right are these hills, and his right are
>   these vallies,
> Where wild beasts find shelter but I can
>   find none:
> But 'tis not my sufferings, thus wretched,
>   forlorn,
> My brave, gallant friends, 'tis your ruin I
>   mourn;
> Your faith proved so loyal in hot, bloody
>   trial,
> Alas, can I make it no sweeter return!
>
>   (no. 220)[20]

Additionally, this song utilises another recurring theme—the contrast of the seasons and the moods they project and reflect.[21] Playing against this theme in **'Sonnet, on the Death of Robert Riddel, Esq.** *of Glen Riddel, April 1794'*, Burns speaks of the inappropriateness of spring to his mood in this comment:

> No more, ye warblers of the wood, no more,
> Nor pour your descant, grating, on my soul:
> Thou young-eyed spring, gay in the verdant
>   stole,
> More welcome were to me grim winter's
>   wildest roar.
>
>   (ll. 1-4, no. 445)

Laments, too, were a form or kind of song Burns shared with his predecessors and contemporaries though he recognised their stereotyped nature when he wrote: 'These kind of subjects are much hackneyed; and besides, the wailings of the rhyming tribe over the ashes of the Great, are damnably suspicious, and out of all character for sincerity.—These ideas damp'd

my Muse's fire.'[22] Nonetheless he succumbed to writing laments from time to time.[23]

Since he was familiar with both oral and written artistry, it is understandable that he should have drawn from the great corporate fund such themes and topics as the *chanson de malmarié*,[24] the romantic view of the rural population implicit in such works as **'The Cotter's Saturday Night'**,[25] praise of liberty,[26] and especially glorification of love and the lasses, found notably in such songs as the famous **'I love my Jean'**. . . .

> Of a' the airts the wind can blaw,
>   I dearly like the West;
> For there the bony Lassie lives,
>   The Lassie I lo'e best:
> There's wild-woods grow, and rivers row,
>   And mony a hill between;
> But day and night my fancy's flight
>   Is ever wi' my Jean.—
>
> I see her in the dewy flowers,
>   I see her sweet and fair;
> I hear her in the tunefu' birds,
>   I hear her charm the air:
> There's not a bony flower, that springs
>   By fountain, shaw, or green;
> There's not a bony bird that sings
>   But minds me o' my Jean.—
>
>   (no. 227)

Sharing not only themes but also superficial content with both popular and oral literature and with his traditionally oriented world, Burns utilised stereotyped, pastoral names for his protagonists; see his many Elizas and Jockeys. And he referred almost as frequently to local events or persons, often women, as in his lines on Elizabeth Paton:

> 'Twas ae night lately, in my fun,
> I gaed a rovin wi' the gun,
> An' brought a *Paitrick* to the *grun'*,
>   A bonie *hen*,
> And, as the twilight was begun,
>   Thought nane wad ken.
>
> The poor, wee thing was *little hurt;*
> I *straiket* it a wee for sport,
> Ne'er thinkan they wad fash me for 't;
>   But, Deil-ma-care!
> Somebody tells the *Poacher-Court,*
>   The hale affair.
>
>   (ll. 37-48, no. 47, **'Epistle to J. R.
>   ******, Enclosing some Poems'**)

Local places too find specific inclusion—Stewart Kyle, Mauchline.[27] Additionally, Burns borrowed commonplaces, sometimes entire lines and phrases, from earlier oral and written literature as well as from life: 'An' she has twa sparkling, rogueish een';[28] 'An' durk an' pistol at her belt';[29] Now fare ye well, an' joy be wi you';[30] 'In *ploughman phrase* "GOD send you speed",/ Still daily to grow wiser.';[31] 'saut tear blin't his e'e', reminiscent of 'Sir Patrick Spens' and other ballads;[32] and proverbs, such as 'Deil tak the hindmost'.[33] Burns also picked up the sexual slang of the vernacular and subtly incorporated it into his work, using, for example, the hunting metaphor with reference to Elizabeth Paton, printed above, and in **'The Hunting Song'** (no. 190); he also used the term 'brose and butter' in his poem of that name (no. 78), referring, in the argot, to an abundance of semen. His references to traditional belief and custom are, of course, nowhere in greater concentration than in **'Halloween'** (no. 73); but they are found in many works. The devil, so familiar a figure in Scots tradition that he is called 'auld cloven Clooty', 'Auld Nick',[34] appears from time to time,[35] as does death, personified, carrying a scythe over one shoulder and a three-pronged spear over the other.[36] Burs mentions belief in second-sight, that is the ability to foresee the future, a trait often attributed to poets.[37] And as part of his local, traditional orientation he alludes to legendary figures such as King Coil, said once to have been King of Kyle.[38]

Burns' most significant and pervasive use of traditional material as the basis for his works' content is, undoubtedly, in his songs.[39] He was deeply involved with song, that artistic complex of text and tune, throughout his life. His first known work, **'O once I lov'd'** to the tune 'I am a man unmarried', written at fourteen, was a song; and his last work was a song. Thus songwriting framed his artistic life. Since, however, it became a very conscious process and his primary artistic mode after his Edinburgh stay, discussion of the songs will, for the most part, be left until Chapter 3.

The present, the local, Burns' own world is overwhelmingly obvious in the content of a group of poems often referred to as 'manners-painting'. Together these poems might well be called ethnographic or ethnoliterature, for they depict the environment from a variety of perspectives, exhibiting a multiplicity of aspects of life. Detailing various facets of life in eighteenth-century Ayrshire, these verbal pictures have served for subsequent generations as records of the life of the times: in fact, various works on eighteenth-century Scotland quote Burns as the source of their information and other publications provide corroborative parallel information.[40] I have enlarged the parameters of this group to include a number of works which contain, albeit sometimes briefly and incidentally, valuable detail about the life and times, which Burns incorporated into his works as important indicators of time and place.[41] Dealing with aspects of life which are traditional, long having been a part of the yearly round of existence, many of these poems focus on

custom, those repeated practices which dominate life; on belief; and on various aspects of life found in rural Ayrshire. In most, the description of the traditional practices provides the broad canvas on which Burns paints his conception of life and against which he outlines various aspects for particular notice. His selection of detail is not random: elements were specifically chosen to make a point and, in the works judged the best, to enable implied social comment; the descriptions served well as valid backgrounds from which to work. As early as 1783, Burns had articulated his own interest in the study of men, their manners and their ways 'and for this darling subject, I chearfully sacrifice every other consideration'.[42] 'Believe me . . . it is the only study in this world will yield solid satisfaction'.[43] This interest, widespread among the educated élite in the eighteenth century, no doubt stimulated Burns' selective descriptions of aspects of traditional life.

The bulk and most significant examples of Burns' focus on traditional life were probably written between 1784 and 1785. They include insignificant incidental detail of a man's wardrobe, refer to calendar customs such as Hogmanay and harvest home, to traditional food and drink as well as to hiring practices and welcoming gifts—to man and animal. Additionally, beliefs about witches and the devil find frequent articulation. Five extended examples should illustrate the centrality of his own traditional milieu, the way of life handed down from generation to generation, in his artistry. Here the description of ethnographic detail is not incidental, but integral.

Burns' ethnographic bent may well have reached its apogee in **'Halloween'** (no. 73), his poem dealing with the sacred night when spirits overtly walk mortal territory and under proper ritual circumstances may foretell or enable prophecy of the future. The poem is explicitly descriptive of certain elements of the calendar celebration, is prefaced by an explanatory introduction, and is copiously footnoted by Burns to explain the rituals mentioned to the uninitiated. It is perhaps a universal human desire to know and, if possible, to control the future: in different times and places, the means of doing so will, of course, differ. In eighteenth-century Ayrshire, prognosticatory customs were practised on various days—Halloween being one—in an attempt to foretell future relationships between individuals of different sexes. In Burns' poem, the participants are young people looking forward to the next rite of passage, the next radical change in their own lives, and hoping to know something about what to expect. Burns vividly describes the various rituals—performed, at least to some extent, because of belief in their efficacy: pulling up stalks of kail, of oats; throwing yarn into a kiln; eating an apple in front of a mirror; pretending to winnow; and sewing hemp. Kinsley and others from the eighteenth to twentieth centuries have shown that all of these practices were both widespread and well-known. The practice of pulling up green kail stocks is a case in point: according to Eve Blantyre Simpson, a couple—eyes shut, hand in hand—should pull stocks from the garden of an unmarried man or woman. If the stock is stout, the future will be good; if the roots have no dirt attached to them, poverty will be their lot; furthermore, the taste of the stock's kernel will indicate the future spouse's temperament.[44] Similarly, William Grant Stewart discusses this 'customary art of divination'. A couple, blindfolded, pull up a stock of kail; its qualities enable prophesy of the future mate's size and shape. If dirt adheres to the root, they will have good fortune; the taste of the stem foretells the disposition of the future mate.[45] M. Macleod Banks, and others, also record the tradition.[46] Burns' own note touches on these same points, undoubtedly indicating his own observation of this practice:

> The first ceremony of Halloween, is, pulling each a *Stock,* or plant of kail. They must go out, hand in hand, with eyes shut, and pull the first they meet with: its being big or little, straight or crooked, is prophetic of the size and shape of the grand object of all their Spells—the husband or wife. If any *yird,* or earth, stick to the root, that is *tocher,* or fortune; the taste of the *custoc,* that is, the heart of the stem, is indicative of the natural temper and disposition.[47]

All of these rituals may give valuable hints about one's future—who one will marry, whether or not the girl will be a virgin, whether present courtship will be smooth, what status or occupation the future mate will have. But **'Halloween'** would be rather a dry, anthropological account had not Burns particularised the general by peopling his celebration with willing, hopeful individuals—joined together in fun and anticipation in a calendar custom long known. Burns names spots they might visit—known in legend to be fairy rings—and he suggests the validity of the rituals when he has Grannie warn against certain practices—for, in the past, they have driven people mad, at least temporarily—and she describes one such account. A young lad, anxious to disprove her warning and simultaneously to prove himself to his assembled peers, takes it as a dare and goes out alone; but he succumbs to fear if not to madness. These are real people, come together, who interact—however disjointedly—before our eyes, making their beliefs and customs alive and functioning. The concluding stanza

> Wi' merry sangs, an' friendly cracks,
>   I wat they did na weary;
> An unco tales, an' funnie jokes,
>   Their sports were cheap an' cheary:
> Till *butter'd So'ns,* wi' fragrant lunt,
>   Set a' their gabs a steerin;

> Syne, wi' a social glass o' strunt,
>   They parted aff careerin
> Fu' blythe that night.
>
>   (ll. 244-52, no. 73)

makes it clear that the rituals were performed in a social context which included the telling of tales and jokes, the exchange of chatter, as well as a traditional dish of sowens (a mixture of oatmeal and sour milk), with butter, on this significant day of the year.

'Halloween' describes both belief and custom and the people who hold them: thus the traditional milieu is, to all extents and purposes, the subject of the poem. The preface and the epigraph from Goldsmith alert one to Burns' distanced stance—these practices are of the uneducated but worthy rural folk—and explain Burns' detached focus in the poem proper. But the description and thus the poem itself are sympathetic and there is no contrast with the ways of educated folk, essentially because Burns describes his own physical—if not mental—milieu; and he has given us a scene of multiple dimensions, having the force of reality. His own world, however limited, was the basis of his artistry; such a work as this shows his dependence on the people he knew—'their manners and their ways'. There would otherwise have been no poem.

In the song **'Tam Glen'** (no. 236), we get a far less sustained description of prognostication having to do with relationships of the sexes both on Halloween and on St. Valentine's Day. Here the belief and custom support the dominant idea of the song: that Tam Glen is the only lad for her:

> Yestreen at the Valentines' dealing;
>   My heart to my mou gied a sten;
> For thrice I drew ane without failing,
>   And thrice it was written, Tam Glen.—
>
> The last Halloween I was waukin
>   My droukit sark-sleeve, as ye ken;
> His likeness cam up the house staukin,
>   And the very grey breeks o' Tam Glen!
>
>   (ll. 21-8, no. 236)

The traditional evidences used to support her choice are only part of her argument, but they are valid within the poem's milieu. In this brief look at the rationalising of a young girl, Burns has, in referring to shared traditional practices, made her dilemma far more interesting and lifelike, exemplifying yet again his debt to the milieu of his birth.

In **'The Holy Fair'** (no. 70) Burns describes an annual event, an ingathering of Clergy and parishioners from an extended local area for worship and communion. Although the event was begun with the sacred in mind, the secular now reigns and Burns' deft flashes from scene to scene give us a look at this tradition. His selection of foci presents the events, contrasts them, and concludes that the effective reason for having such fairs is hardly the obvious religious one:

> How monie hearts this day converts,
>   O' Sinners and o' Lasses!
> Their hearts o' stane, gin night are gane
>   As saft as ny flesh is.
> There's some are fou o' *love divine;*
>   There's some are fou o' *brandy;*
> An' monie jobs that day begin,
> May end in *Houghmagandie*
>   Some ither day.
>
> (ll. 235-43, no. 70)

This is not description for description's sake; it is a selective panoramic perspective, presenting a spectrum of viewpoints, which no doubt reflect reality. But in an age when the clergy and Kirk session had so much control over the lives of the people, such non-compliance appears startling. Burns was not deceived: it was not religion man loved and clung to; rather it was secular delight. Those who deny the truth, blind to what is in front of their eyes, proclaiming the sacred holiness of the day, they are wrong; they are hypocrites. We know what such 'holy fairs' were like because of Burns' description, but we must recognise that the description was but a vehicle and perhaps an essential one for Burns' comment about the people among whom he lived. Thus, the traditions of his day, generally known to his audience, provided the shared background, and through selective and judicious choice from a wide spectrum of behaviour, he forces the reader to question with him the Holy Fair's very being.

There are many remnants today of the visual acuity pre-eminent in days of old when oral, aural, and visual were the rule and reading and writing the possession of few. For goodness knows how long shops and taverns announced their function and name in signs hung prominently to attract the cognoscenti—which in this case was virtually everyone—with known and recognised symbols, rather than words. Such signs were part of the known. In brief, hardly flattering verses, **'Versicles on Sign-posts'** (no. 244), Burns again plays against the known—a visual traditional art/craft—to satirise qualities of various unnamed individuals—such as the man too wont to smile:

> His face with smile eternal drest
> Just like the Landlord to his guest,
> High as they hang with creaking din
> To index out the country Inn—
>
> (ll. 6-9, no. 244)

But Burns' ethnography is perhaps most complete in the scene and context described in **'The Cotter's Saturday Night'** (no. 72). The technique for such description may well have come from Robert Fergusson's 'The Farmer's Ingle' and a model for comment from such English authors as Gray, whose lines appear as epigraph to the poem, but the basis of the poem is a description of the traditional and typical life around him, illustrating all humanity's inherent dignity, nowhere more obvious than among the poor of Scotland. Burns' depiction of a man—weary from six day's toil—in domestic repose must be recognised as filtered and skewed, an ideal rather than an actuality. But in the description there is much detail about life: the gear of his work, his ploughing, the indication of the coming Sabbath as a day of rest; the visitation of his children fee'd out to plough, herd, or run errands; the sharing of news while light sociable tasks like mending continue; the modest supper of porridge and cheese followed by the family worship around the fire, begun with the singing of a psalm, followed by the reading of the scripture, and culminating with the prayer. There is considerable evidence to support the accuracy of various portions of Burns' account—concerning food, religious practices, and economic circumstances. Henry Gray Graham describes the necessity earlier in the eighteenth century of daily religious worship in the home, devolving later to the Saturday-night observance of Burns' depiction.[48] Marjorie Plant describes the centrality of 'meal' in the diet, supplemented in the poem with cheese.[49] And R. H. Cromek describes the domicile of a cotter and his house, including a description of family worship which he suggests was never depicted more eloquently than by Burns.[50] Gilbert Burns recorded that Burns was inspired by the invocation 'Let us worship God' proclaiming the start of family worship. General accounts of the eighteenth century confirm the veracity of Burns' presentation of the life of the cotter, caught at the bottom of the economic heap in the agricultural upheavals of the eighteenth century which did away with much of the joint land tenure and communal work, thereby creating a classed society with the 'have-nots', sending their children out to work and yet still barely managing to survive, becoming more numerous. And the testimony—early attributed to a servant of Burns' friend and correspondent Mrs Dunlop but subsequently to others—that 'I've seen the same thing in my ain father's house mony a time, and he couldna hae described it ony ither gate' suggests the reliability of his account.[51] Another version recorded by John D. Ross tells of Burns' pleasure when he asked a Mossgiel friend how she liked his poems—'Weel, Rab, gin ye canna write something we dinna ken, dinna put aff yer time writing sic havers; I'm sure there's naething new in that; we see a' that ongauns every day o' our lives.'[52] And biographical critics have suggested that Burns was actually depicting here his own early environment—although strictly speaking William Burnes was a class above, a tenant farmer, although a poor one. Artistically Burns here combines his knowledge of English and Scottish literary traditions; but far more importantly he limns the traditional matrix, the way of life, choosing from it positive and humanising elements for comment and reflection, as well as for contrast. His own folkways provided him with the shared elements from and through which to make his point. Unwittingly on the one hand, but necessarily and predictably on the other, Burns was an ethnographer, describing the life he knew best as an integral part of his own artistry.

The traditional milieu provided more than content for his poems and songs; it also provided models for some of his verse forms and structures. He used the ballad and folksong stanza pattern, to be described in Chapter 3, throughout his life, both intuitively and consciously. Additionally, he used the traditional form for his epigrams and epitaphs which were usually topical and of questionable poetic value.

Notes

[1] August Angellier in *Robert Burns, La Vie, Les Oeuvres,* 2 vols (Paris, 1983) pointed to this when he said: 'But underneath this scholarly poetry there existed a popular poetry which was very abundant, very vigorous, very racy and very original'. See especially p. 14 of Jane Burgoyne's selected translation from Angellier in the *Burns Chronicle and Club Directory,* 1969. Other portions of the translation appeared in 1970, 1971, 1972, 1973.

[2] J. De Lancey Ferguson (ed.) *The Letters of Robert Burns,* 2 vols (Oxford: Clarendon Press, 1931), 1: 106, no. 125. Burns adopted a superior tone here in keeping with the accepted pose of the eighteenth-century man of letters. All references to Burns' letters are to Ferguson's edition. Only letter numbers will be given when the citation appears in the text proper.

[3] Most critics and students of Burns take some stance towards his relationship with previous work. Hans Hecht, *Robert Burns: The Man and His Work,* 2nd rev. ed. (London: William Hodge & Company, 1950), p. 29, suggests that Burns was the culmination of a tradition, but he speaks of a literary rather than a cultural inheritance.

[4] See T. S. Eliot, *The Sacred Wood* (London: Methuen, 1950), pp. 47-59.

[5] Angellier earlier suggested this division and I agree with him that Burns' work prior to Edinburgh was dominated by depiction of the world around him. After Edinburgh, Angellier indicates that Burns relied less on the specific incidents and more on general sentiments. I concur again but the significance of this move to generality is in Burns' nationalism.

[6] Hecht, *Robert Burns,* p. 86 discusses the Kilmarnock poems as *Heimatkunst.*

[7] For an example of Hugh MacDiarmid's view of Burns, see *Burns Today and Tomorrow* (Edinburgh: Castle Wynd Printers, 1959).

[8] See John Strawhorn, 'Burns and the Bardie Clan', *Scottish Literary Journal,* 8 (1981): 5-23 for a discussion of fellow poets.

[9] No. 180 'On scaring some Water-Fowl in Loch-Turit, a wild scene among the Hills of Oughtertyre' is said to have been read one evening after supper. See Robert Chambers and William Wallace (eds), *The Life and Works of Robert Burns,* 4 vols (New York: Longmans, Green, and Co., 1896), 2: 193. W. E. Henley and T. F. Henderson (eds), *The Poetry of Robert Burns,* 4 vols (Edinburgh: T. C. and E. C. Jack, 1896-7) mention several additional instances: see, for example, 1:328.

[10] All references to Burns' work are to James Kinsley (ed.), *The Poems and Songs of Robert Burns,* 3 vols (Oxford: Clarendon Press, 1968). Item numbers will be given hereafter in the text. 'The Ordination' is no. 85.

[11] See for example 'The Banks of Nith' (no. 229) and Burns' comment in Ferguson, *Letters,* no. 265, that it was composed as he jogged along the bank.

[12] James Cameron Ewing and Davidson Cook (eds), *Robert Burns's Commonplace Book 1783-1785* (Carbondale, Illinois: Southern Illinois University Press, 1965), p. 39. In describing the inspiration for his fragment 'Altho' my bed were in you muir' (Kinsley, *Poems and Songs,* no. 22) said to be an imitation of 'a noble old Scottish Piece called McMillan's Peggy', Burns comments: 'I have even tryed to imitate, in this extempore thing, that irregularity in the rhyme which, when judiciously done, has such a fine effect on the ear.—'

[13] 'Worth gaun a mile to see' is from 'The Humble Petition of Bruar Water to the Noble Duke of Atholl', Kinsley, *Poems and Songs,* no. 172.

[14] See 'For lake o' from '[Lines written on a Banknote]', ibid., no. 106.

[15] See the general work on this subject by Albert Lord, *The Singer of Tales* (New York: Atheneum, 1971) and a book which presents specific application of this theory to the Scottish scene, David Buchan's *The Ballad and the Folk* (London: Routledge & Kegan Paul, 1972).

[16] Ewing and Cook, *Commonplace Book,* p. 42.

[17] See Kinsley, *Poems and Songs,* no. 208—'Musing on the roaring Ocean'.

[18] Ibid., no. 306, 'The White Cockade'.

[19] Ibid., no. 391, 'Here's a Health to them that's awa'.

[20] It is perhaps interesting to note that this Jacobite verse is written in standard, literary English, indicative of the broad popularity of this theme.

[21] For other examples, see Kinsley, *Poems and Songs,* nos 3 'I dream'd I lay', 10 'Winter, A Dirge', 66 'The Braes o' Ballochmyle', 138 'Again rejoicing Nature sees', 218 'The Winter it is Past', 316 'Lament of Mary Queen of Scots on the Approach of Spring', 336 'Gloomy December'.

[22] Ferguson, *Letters,* no. 164.

[23] Kinsley, *Poems and Songs,* nos 144 'On Fergusson', 160 'On the death of Sir J. Hunter Blair', 186 'On the death of the late Lord President Dundas', 233 'A Mother's Lament for the loss of her only Son', 238 'Sketch for an Elegy', 334 'Lament for James, Earl of Glencairn', 445 'Sonnet, on the Death of Robert Riddel, Esq.'

[24] Ibid., no. 235 'Whistle o'er the lave o't'.

[25] Ibid., no. 72 'The Cotter's Saturday Night' and also no. 71 'The Twa Dogs. A Tale'.

[26] Ibid., no. 451 'Ode for General Washington's Birthday' and no. 625 'The Tree of Liberty.'

[27] Ibid., no. 44—'A fragment—When first I came to Stewart Kyle'.

[28] Ibid., no. 11, 'On Cessnock banks a lassie dwells'.

[29] Ibid., no. 81, 'The Author's Earnest Cry and Prayer, to the Right Honorable and Honorable, the Scotch Representatives in the House of Commons'.

[30] Ibid., no. 90, 'Letter to J—s T—t, GL—nc—r'.

[31] Ibid., no. 105, 'Epistle to a Young Friend'.

[32] Ibid., no. 216, 'Rattlin, roarin Willie'.

[33] Ibid., no. 136, 'To a Haggis'.

[34] Ibid., no. 119B, 'Robert Burns' Answer' to 'Epistle from a Taylor to *Robert Burns*'.

[35] Ibid., no. 54, 'Epitaph on Holy Willie'.

[36] Ibid., no. 55, 'Death and Doctor Hornbook. A True Story'.

[37] Ibid., no. 120, 'The Brigs of Ayr, a Poem. Inscribed to J. B. *********, Esq; Ayr'.

[38] Ibid., no. 71, 'The Twa Dogs. A Tale'.

[39] Hecht, *Robert Burns,* p. 217 says, 'Burns's lyric poetry . . . clings to the clear realism of its chief sources: the Scottish popular and traditional songs'.

[40] See as example Marjorie Plant, *The Domestic Life of Scotland in the Eighteenth Century* (1899; reprint ed., London: Adam & Charles Black, 1969).

[41] I include Kinsley, *Poems and Songs,* nos 40 'The Ronalds of the Bennals', 57 'Epistle to J. L*****k, An Old Scotch Bard', 67 'Third Epistle to J. Lapraik', 70 'The Holy Fair', 71 'The Twa Dogs. A Tale', 72 'The Cotter's Saturday Night', 73 'Halloween', 74 'The Mauchline Wedding', 75 'The Auld Farmer's New-year-morning Salutation to his Auld Mare, Maggie', 76 'Address to the Deil', 77 'Scotch Drink', 79 'To J. S****', 86 'The Inventory', 102 'To Mʳ Gavin Hamilton, Mauchline', 136 'To a Haggis', 140 'There was a lad', 236 'Tam Glen', 244 'Versicles on Sign-posts', 321 'Tam o' Shanter. A Tale', 514 'Poem, Addressed to Mr. Mitchell, Collector of Excise'.

[42] Ferguson, *Letters,* no. 13.

[43] Ibid., no. 10.

[44] Eve Blantyre Simpson, *Folk Lore in Lowland Scotland* (London: J. M. Dent, 1908), p. 14.

[45] William Grant Stewart, *The Popular Superstitions and Festive Amusements of the Highlanders of Scotland* (1851: reprint ed., Hatboro, Pennsylvania: Norwood Editions, 1974), p. 161.

[46] M. Macleod Banks, *British Calendar Customs: Scotland,* 3 vols (London: William Glaisher, 1937, 1939, 1941), 3: 122-4.

[47] Kinsley, *Poems and Songs,* 1: 153-4.

[48] See H. G. Graham, *The Social Life of Scotland in the Eighteenth Century,* 5th ed. (London: Adam & Charles Black, 1969), p. 336.

[49] See Plant, *Domestic Life,* pp. 97-8.

[50] R. H. Cromek, *Remains of Nithsdale and Galloway Song* (Paisley: Alexander Gardner, 1880), p. 212.

[51] James Ballantine (comp. and ed.), *Chronicle of the Hundredth Birthday of Robert Burns* (Edinburgh: A. Fullarton & Co., 1859), pp. 70-1.

[52] John D. Ross, *Burnsiana,* 5 vols (Paisley: Alexander Gardner, 1892), 1: 23-4.

Alan Bold (essay date 1991)

SOURCE: "Burns and Philosophy," in *A Burns Companion*, Macmillan, 1991, pp. 109-15, 391-99.

[*In the following excerpt Bold considers Burns's familiarity with the works and ideas of John Locke, David Hume, and other philosophers.*]

As a result of the obsequious Preface to the Kilmarnock Edition and Henry Mackenzie's influential description of the poet as a 'Heaven-taught ploughman' (CH, 70) Burns was regarded, by his early readers, as an ignorant man able, by some miracle, to produce poetry. An unsigned notice in the *General Magazine and Impartial Review* (1787) summed up the position: 'By general report we learn, that R. B. is a plough-boy, of small education' (CH, 88). In fact, by the time the Kilmarnock Edition was published, Burns had read not only the poetry of Pope and Shenstone, not only the fiction of Richardson and Fielding, but the philosophy of John Locke and Adam Smith. Before he left Lochlea in 1784, Burns had read Locke's *An Essay Concerning Human Understanding* (1690), a work regarded as the foundation of British empiricism.

The impact of Locke's *Essay* on Burns must have been profound, stimulating his insights into human nature and reinforcing his critical attitude to the kirk (religious dogmatists were disturbed by Locke's implication that reasonable discourse depended on 'determined ideas', not obscurantist religious dogma). Briefly, the *Essay* is an assault on dogmatic beliefs, a book that showed Locke to be preemiment among those David Hume described (in his Introduction to *A Treatise of Human Nature*) as 'philosophers in England, who have . . . put the science of man on a new footing, and . . . excited the curiosity of the public'. In Book I, Locke dismisses the doctrine of an innate knowledge of moral and speculative truths; in Book II he argues that experience accounts for ideas, both ideas of sensation derived from the outer senses, and ideas of reflection induced by introspection; in Book III he discusses the subjective limitations of language; in Book IV he undermines Cartesian assumptions about general truths.

Burns mentions Locke's *Essay* in his Autobiographical Letter and, writing to Mrs McLehose in January 1788, refers to 'the Great and likewise Good Mr Locke, Author of the famous essay on the human understanding' (CL, 386). Burns would have delighted in Locke's appeals to individual observation, taking this as an encouragement to remain open to natural experience rather than relying on dogma. Locke argued that the mind knows nothing but what it receives from without; so knowledge is founded on observation which the mind rearranges ('Nothing can be in the intellect which was not first in the senses'). Endorsing empirical science (in particular the achievement of 'the incomparable Mr Newton'), with its basis in observation and experiment, Locke rejected the arrogant appeal to innate ideas (of God or anything else). Reacting against scholastic essentialism, Locke drew a distinction between the real (and unknown) essence of an object and its 'nominal essence', accessible to observation. It was a philosophy attractive to a poet of Burns's inquisitive outlook. Indeed, Locke (in 'The Epistle to the Reader') encouraged the individual to regard his own intellectual quest as an end in itself:

> For the understanding, like the eye, judging of objects only by its own sight, cannot but be pleased with what it discovers, having less regret for what has escaped it, because it is unknown. Thus he who has raised himself above the alms-basket, and not content to live lazily on scraps of begged opinions, sets his own thoughts on work, to find and follow truth, will (whatever he lights on) not miss the hunter's satisfaction; every moment of his pursuit will reward his pains with some delight, and he will have reason to think his time not ill spent, even when he cannot much boast of any great acquisition.

That reference to 'scraps of begged opinions' must have been relished by Burns as putting the self-righteous in their place.

Burns was never a systematic student of philosophy but, in the course of his short life, showed a shrewd appreciation of those philosophers who confirmed what he concluded through observation and experience. By turns radical, reformist and revolutionary in politics, he was liberal in philosophy; as well as gaining an understanding of Lockean liberalism he was able, in the early summer of 1789, to enthuse over Adam Smith's *Wealth of Nations* with its emphasis on natural liberty and its insistence that productivity should take priority over pedigree, thus putting the gentry in *their* place. The Scottish intellectual climate of his time was enlightened and Burns, though raised in a farming community, expanded his intellect through reading and embraced the body of thought that stood for the Enlightenment.

In his first Common Place Book (completed by October 1785), Burns praises Adam Smith's *The Theory of Moral Sentiments* (1759), a collection of lectures influenced by the empiricist Francis Hutcheson who had taught Smith at Glasgow University and whose *Inquiry Into the Origins of Our Ideas of Beauty and Virtue* (1725) associated moral judgement with an intuitive apprehension of virtue as a pleasure. Smith considered that happiness was quantitative and endorsed Hutcheson's sentimental view of morality. Burns wrote: 'I entirely agree with that judicious philosopher Mr Smith in his excellent Theory of Moral Sentiments, that Remorse is the most painful sentiment that can embitter the human bosom' (CB, 7).

Elsewhere in the first Common Place Book, Burns expressed a Deism that was implicit in Locke's *Essay* (with its reference to 'some knowing intelligent Being . . . which whether any one will please to call God, it matters not') and current among Scottish Common Sense philosophers. Burns declared 'the grand end of human life is to cultivate an intercourse with that Being to whom we owe life' (CB, 22), a teleology that informs a letter of 1788 where he refers to 'a great unknown Being who could have no other end in giving [man] existence but to make him happy' (CL, 90). The Common Sense philosophers, suspicious of rigid Calvinism but reluctant to abandon this 'great unknown Being', were willing to defend the moderate, liberal Presbyterian tradition against the atheistic onslaughts of Hume. One of them, John Gregory, wrote to James Beattie in 1767:

> Atheism and materialism are the present fashion. If one speaks with warmth of an infinitely wise and good Being, who sustains and directs the frame of nature, or expresses his steady belief of a future state of existence, he gets hints of his having either a very weak understanding, or of being a very great hypocrite. (William Forbes, *An Account of the Life and Writings of James Beattie,* New York, 1807, p. 73)

Beattie was not only a prominent Common Sense philosopher and Professor of Moral Philosophy at Aberdeeen University; he was also a poet. Burns admired Beattie in both capacities. Beattie had, in his *Essay on the Nature and Immutability of Truth* (1770), attempted to refute Hume's scepticism; his poem *The Minstrel: or, The Progress of Genius* (1771-4) was a greatly popular work in its time. Burns praised Beattie in **'The Vision'** (1785) for his verse and for his attack on Hume:

> Hence, sweet, harmonious Beattie sung
>   His *Minstrel* lays;
> Or tore, with noble ardour stung,
>   The sceptic's bays.
>
> (62/CW, 118)

In a letter of 1788 Burns saluted Beattie as 'the immortal Author of the *Minstrel*' (CL, 364).

Burns's satire **'The Holy Fair'** (1785), pointedly depicts Common Sense distancing itself from the dogmas of an Auld Licht minister. As soon as the minister gets up to preach, Common Sense departs:

> See, up he's got the word o God,
>   An meek an mim has view'd it,
> While Common-sense has taen the road
>   An aff, an up the Cowgate
>   Fast, fast that day.
>
> (70/CW, 137)

On a parochial level, Burns personifies Common Sense as a tribute to his humane friend Dr John Mackenzie of Mauchline. However, the poem transcends the parochial level and Common Sense is regarded as the natural enemy of life-denying reactionary religion. Again, in **'The Ordination'** (1786), Burns invokes 'Curst Common-sense, that imp o Hell' as the enemy of the Auld Licht minister Mackinlay:

> And Common-sense is gaun, she says,
>   To mak to Jamie Beattie
>   Her plaint this day.
>
> (85/CW, 194)

And in **'The Brigs of Ayr'** (1786) the New Brig (the liberal voice of progression) contrasts 'common-sense' with 'Plain, dull stupidity'.

In the **'Epistle to James Tennant of Glenconner'** (1786), Burns praises both Adam Smith and Thomas Reid, the most prominent Common Sense philosopher but, humorously, suggests that Reid's philosophy only elaborates on the sagacity of the common people:

> Smith, wi his sympathetic feeling,
> An Reid, to common sense appealing.
> Philosophers have fought and wrangled,
> An meikle Greek and Latin mangled,
> Till, wi their logic-jargon tir'd
> As in the depth of science mir'd,
> To common sense they now appeal—
> What wives and wabsters see and feel!
>
> (90/CW, 200)

From personal experience and observation, as well as philosophical inclination, Burns allied himself with a sturdy commonsense and with the Scottish Common Sense philosophers. Coincidentally, Tom Paine's republican treatise of 1776, a book Burns would certainly have known about as a potent influence on the American revolution, was called *Common Sense,* thus giving the term a revolutionary connotation.

One Common Sense philosopher was personally well known to Burns. Dugald Stewart, whom Burns considered 'The most perfect character I ever saw' (cited by Snyder, 200), met the poet before he went to Edinburgh then went on walks with him in the capital. Professor of Moral Philosophy at Edinburgh University from 1785 until his retirement in 1810, Stewart was an admirer (and biographer) of the Common Sense philosopher Thomas Reid who oppposed Hume's concept of mind-dependent entities and argued in favour of a commonsense contact with mind-independent realities. Stewart's introduction to his *Outlines of Moral Philosophy* (1793) gives some indication of his approach:

> The ultimate object of philosophical inquiry is the same which every man of plain understanding proposes to himself, when he remarks the events which fall under his observation with a view to the future regulation of his conduct. The more knowledge of this kind we acquire, the better can we accommodate our plans to the established order of things, and avail ourselves of natural Powers and Agents for accomplishing our purposes. (*The Collected Works of Dugald Stewart,* ed. Sir William Hamilton, Edinburgh, 1854-60, vol. II, p. 6)

If, as is likely, Stewart expressed such ideas in conversation with Burns, the impact would have been positive for Burns also aspired to articulate the insights of 'every man of plain understanding'.

Gilbert Burns suggested that, in his Mount Oliphant period, Burns 'remained unacquainted . . . with Hume' (GN), thus implying that he subsequently read Scotland's greatest philosopher though in his capacity as a historian (since Gilbert links Hume with William Robertson). As noted above, there is a reference to Hume as 'the sceptic' in **'The Vision'** and in the **'Prologue Spoken by Mr Woods'** (on the actor's benefit night, 16 April 1787) there is, Kinsley supposes in annotating a passage on Edinburgh's cultural reputation, a 'tribute to the philosophers Hume, Dugald Stewart, and Adam Smith . . . and to Hume and Robertson as historians' (Kinsley, 1232):

> Philosophy, no idle pedant dream,
> Here holds her search by heaven-taught
>   Reason's beam:
> Here History paints with elegance and force
> The tide of Empire's fluctuating course . . .
>   (151/CW, 275)

The second line of the quotation pays no tribute to Hume who had no faith in heaven and who insisted, in *A Treatise of Human Nature,* 'Reason is, and ought only to be, the slave of the passions.' Produced for declamation in public, the phrase about 'heaven-taught Reason' sounds suspiciously like a specific disavowal of Hume the philosopher, though Hume the historian is given due credit.

Before Burns left Edinburgh and its 'heaven-taught Reason', he sent an **'Address to William Tytler'**, Tytler (1711-92) being the author of *A Historical and Critical Enquiry into the Evidence against Mary Queen of Scots* (1760), an attempt to refute the Stuart volumes (1754, 1757) of Hume's *History of England.*

On reading the *Enquiry* Hume described Tytler as 'a Scots Jacobite, who maintains the innocence of Queen Mary [and is] beyond the reach of argument or reason' (cited by Kinsley, 1233). Burns, however, described Tytler as

> Revered defender of beauteous Stuart,
> Of Stuart!—a name once respected,
> A name which to love was once mark of a
>   true heart,
> But now 'tis despis'd and neglected!
>   (152/CW, 276)

Burns advised Tytler to burn this poem as 'rather heretical' (CL, 291). Though he disapproved of Hume's treatment of Mary Queen of Scots, Burns was proud to list—in a letter of 1791 written for publication in the *Statistical Account of Scotland*—'Hume's History of the Stewarts' (CL, 587) among the books in the library of the Monkland Friendly Society.

Burns could be devious when it suited his strategy and was cautious about condemning Hume the historian in public. Hume the philosopher required different tactics: the implied rebuke of the **'Prologue Spoken by Mr Woods'** and a diplomatic silence. Though Hume had been dead for a decade when Burns arrived in Edinburgh, the sceptical philosopher was still a dangerous figure to discuss, still widely regarded as the atheistic scourge of God-fearing folk. Yet the work of Burns is in accord with Hume's naturalism and his affirmative attitude. In his Conclusion to Book I of *A Treatise of Human Nature* (which fell 'dead-born from the press' when published in 1739) Hume declared 'Human Nature is the only science of man; and yet has been hitherto the most neglected.' In Section I, Part IV of Book I of the *Treatise,* Hume said:

> Nature, by an absolute and uncontrollable necessity, has determined us to judge as well as to breathe and feel; nor can we any more forbear viewing certain objects in a stronger and fuller light, upon account of their customary connection with a present impression, than we can hinder ourselves from thinking, as long as we are awake, or seeing the surrounding bodies, when we turn our eyes towards them in broad sunshine . . . It is happy, therefore, that nature breaks the force of all sceptical arguments in time, and keeps them from having any considerable influence on the understanding.

This appeal to nature is as compelling as that of Rousseau, Hume's hostile friend. Hume may have felt that poets were 'liars by profession' but, as a man who valued passion above reason, would surely have approved of Burns. And it is difficult to believe that Burns, sometimes a liar through discretion, did not approve of Hume—the enemy of dogma, the empirical successor to Locke, the admirer of nature, the friend of Adam Smith and Dr Blacklock (to whom Hume transferred his salary as librarian of the Advocates' Library)—even though direct evidence is elusive.

Notes

Abbreviations

Poems are cited with reference to two sources: the number assigned to them in James Kinsley's three-volume *The Poems and Songs of Robert Burns* (1968) and his one-volume *Burns: Poems and Songs* (1969), available as an Oxford Paperback; and the page numbers from James A. Mackay's one-volume *The Complete Works of Robert Burns* (1986), authorised by the Burns Federation. Thus 'Tam o Shanter' (321/CW, 410-15) indicates that the poem is numbered 321 by Kinsley and printed on pp. 410-15 of Mackay's edition. . . .

CB Raymond Lamont Brown (ed.), *Robert Burns' Common Place Book* (1969).

CH Donald A. Low (ed.), *Robert Burns: The Critical Heritage* (1974).

CL James A. Mackay (ed.), *The Complete Letters of Robert Burns* (1987). . . .

CW James A. Mackay (ed.), *The Complete Works of Robert Burns* (1986). . . .

GN Gilbert's Narrative (see Appendix D). . . .

Kenneth Simpson (essay date 1994)

SOURCE: "Robert Burns: 'Heaven-taught ploughman'?," in *Burns Now*, edited by Kenneth Simpson, Canongate Academic, 1994, pp. 70-91.

[*In the following excerpt Simpson examines the myth of Burns as an uneducated peasant and the benefits and limitations such an image held for Burns.*]

It was Henry Mackenzie who, in December 1786, wrote admiringly of Burns as 'this Heaven-taught ploughman'.[1] Within a few decades Scott was claiming, 'Burns . . . had an education not much worse than the sons of many gentlemen in Scotland'.[2] Scott's version is probably closer to the mark than Mackenzie's, but each had his reasons for forming a very specific conception of Burns, just as each had a specific conception of Scotland (and the two are closely interrelated).

Mackenzie's essay in *The Lounger* was headed 'Surprising Effects of Original Genius, exemplified in the Poetical Productions of Robert Burns, An Ayrshire Ploughman'. Mackenzie, whose values epitomise the polite taste of the Edinburgh literati, laments Burns's use of 'provincial dialect' as a 'bar . . . to his fame' but notes enthusiastically 'with what uncommon penetration and sagacity this Heaven-taught ploughman, from his humble and unlettered station, has looked upon men and manners'. Mackenzie's enthusiasm is symptomatic of the desire of Scottish writers and thinkers that Scotland should lead the response to Rousseau's plea for a return to Nature on the grounds that Reason had failed man by creating a corrupt social order. Heaven's greatest gift is the values of the heart; heaven teaches natural benevolence. 'Heaven-taught' is used by Burns himself with reference to Robert Fergusson as a term of the highest praise. In **'Ode for General Washington's Birthday'** Burns addresses Scotland in these terms:

> Thee, Caledonia, thy wild heaths among,
> Famed for the martial deed, the heaven-
>   taught song,
>   To thee, I turn with swimming eyes.
>   Where is that soul of Freedom fled?
> Immingled with the mighty Dead!
> Beneath that hallowed turf where Wallace
>   lies!

Freedom is lost, but the 'heaven-taught song' endures.

It is strikingly paradoxical—and somehow typically Scottish—that while the work of the Scottish philosophers, essentially secular in its bias, was placing man at the centre of human investigation, at the same time Scottish poets were to be seen as the recipients of divine inspiration. Scottish intellectuals, intent on proving Scotland's right to cultural partnership with England, were determined to show that Scotland was in the vanguard of taste. With a strong religious tradition and sublime landscape, Scotland seemed a plausible breeding-ground for the noble savage as poet. Michael Bruce, a prime contender, had died young, while James Macpherson's undeniably massive achievement had been shown to be a forgery. The Ayrshire ploughman-poet fitted the bill perfectly. Burns was recruited to the cause of establishing Scottish pre-eminence in the vogues of noble savagery and sensibility. He enlisted readily and helped perpetuate the myth, presenting himself as follows in the Preface to his Commonplace Book:

> As he was but little indebted to scholastic education, and bred at a plough-tail, his performances must be strongly tinctured with his unpolished, rustic way of life; but as I believe, they are really his own, it may be some entertainment to a curious observer of human nature to see how a ploughman thinks, and feels, under the pressure of Love, Ambition, Anxiety, Grief with the like cares and passions, which, however diversified by the Modes, and Manners

of life, operate pretty much alike I believe, in all the Species.[3]

It is ironic that Burns's prose is often at its most formal when he is claiming in letters to his social superiors that he is an uneducated peasant. In fact these letters prove that he was a master of voice and persona. Yet the belief persisted that Burns always wrote about himself and his own experience and was incapable of anything as sophisticated as the invention of personae. His first editor, James Currie, was adamant that 'if fiction be . . . the soul of poetry, no one had ever less pretensions to the name of poet than Burns . . . the subjects on which he has written are seldom, if ever, imaginary'.[4] With help from the poet himself, the image of the untutored rustic was firmly established. It has bedevilled Burns criticism ever since.

Yet the reality was altogether different. Commenting on the work of a fellow poet, Burns challenged the description of Truth as 'the soul of every song that's nobly great', offering instead, 'Fiction is the soul of many a song that's nobly great'.[5] As one who numbered himself among 'the harum-scarum Sons of Imagination and Whim'[6], he upheld the importance of the imagination. His social life was characterised by inventiveness and self-drama, so much so that Maria Riddell pronounced him unequalled in 'the sorcery of fascinating conversation'.[7]

If Burns was indeed 'this Heaven-taught ploughman', then the Almighty's school was indeed a good school. Burns is revealed in both poems and letters as an alert observer of events in the wider world. The French king and queen are labelled 'a perjured Blockhead & an unprincipled Prostitute'.[8] Of events across the Atlantic he writes:

> I will not, I cannot, enter into the merits of the cause; but I dare say, the American Congress, in 1776, will be allowed to have been as able and as enlightened, and, a whole empire will say, as honest, as the English Convention in 1688; and that the fourth of July will be as sacred to their posterity as the fifth of November is to us.[9]

A week later he was writing to Mrs Dunlop:

> Is it not remarkable, odiously remarkable, that tho' manners are more civilized, & the rights of mankind better understood, by an Augustan Century's improvement, yet in this very reign of heavenly Hanoverianism, and almost in this very year, an empire beyond the Atlantic has had its REVOLUTION too, & for the very same maladministration & legislative misdemeanors in the illustrious and sapientipotent Family of H— as was complained of in the 'tyrannical & bloody house of Stuart'.[10]

Developments in the sciences interested him also. In one letter he writes of the soil structure of Ellisland in terms which indicate some awareness of James Hutton's infant geology, and Mrs Dunlop discusses with him experiments in chemistry and natural physics. Mrs Dunlop sends for his appraisal some poems she has written in French. They debate the respective merits of Dryden's Virgil and Pope's Homer ('I suspect the translators would have suited better had Pope and Dryden exchanged authors',[11] comments Mrs Dunlop). She sends him Ariosto and Tasso, only to remark ruefully, 'I fear you have not liked Tasso'.[12]

Burns's own letters are replete with evidence of his range of reading. To Moore he writes:

> I know very well, the novelty of my character has by far the greatest share in the learned and polite notice I have lately got; and in a language where Pope and Churchill have raised the laugh, and Shenstone and Gray drawn the tear; where Thomson and Beattie have painted the landskip, and Littleton and Collins described the heart; I am not vain enough to hope for distinguished Poetic fame.[13]

What he termed 'the history of MYSELF which he sent to Moore has references to Addison, Pope, Shakespeare, 'Tull and Dickson on Agriculture, The Pantheon, Locke's Essay on the human understanding, Stackhouse's history of the Bible, Justice's British Gardiner's directory, Boyle's lectures, Allan Ramsay's works, Taylor's scripture doctrine of original sin, a select collection of English songs, Hervey's meditations . . . Thomson's and Shenstone's works . . . Sterne and Mackenzie—Tristram Shandy and the Man of Feeling were my bosom favorites'.[14] The letters are testimony to the range and quality of Burns's education. That education helped shape both the man and the poet.

Burns wrote to Mrs Dunlop, 'I cannot for the soul of me resist an impulse of any thing like Wit'.[15] His reading helped him to give free play to such impulses. At regular social gatherings in a fairly close community the play of wit was a useful outlet for his considerable intelligence. His wide reading also introduced an element of stability and it was a source of values. It had a more practical function, too, as this remark to Mrs Dunlop suggests:

> Do you know, I pick up favorite quotations, and store them in my mind as ready armour, offensive, or defensive, amid the struggle of this turbulent existence. Of these is one, a very favorite one, from Thomson's Alfred—
>
> Attach thee firmly to the virtuous deeds
> And offices of life: to life itself,

With all its vain and transient joys, sit
   loose'.[16]

(He had already quoted these lines in a letter to her
two years earlier.) As 'Sylvander' he writes to Mrs
McLehose's 'Clarinda':

> The only *unity* (a sad word with Poets and Critics!)
> in my ideas is CLARINDA. There my heart 'reigns
> and revels'—

> 'What art thou Love! whence are those
>   charms,
>   That thus thou bear'st an universal rule!
> For thee the soldier quits his arms,
>   The king turns slave, the wise man fool.

> In vain we chase thee from the field,
>   And with cool thoughts resist thy yoke:
> Next tide of blood, Alas! we yield;
>   And all those high resolves are broke!'

> I like to have quotations ready for every occasion.
> They give one's ideas so pat, and save one the
> trouble of finding expression adequate to one's
> feelings.[17]

(If he was truly devoted to 'Clarinda', wouldn't he
have taken the trouble? Or wouldn't he at least have
found something better than those lines of turgid cliché from an anonymous song in *The Hive* (1724)?
This suggests that the Sylvander/Clarinda correspondence involved a considerable degree of posing and
play.) The letter continues:

> I think it is one of the greatest pleasures attending
> a Poetic genius, that we can give our woes, cares,
> joys, loves &c. an embodied form in verse, which,
> to me, is ever immediate ease.

Emotions need to be expressed. Having a stock of
quotations readily speeds the process and brings ease.
Poetry is here functioning essentially as catharsis.

On a deeper level, Burns found in literature the means
of clearly identifying and expressing values and attitudes which he personally held. Nationalism is a case
in point. Burns had to be circumspect as to the expression of nationalist views. Here the work of Ramsay and Fergusson was to provide useful precedent.
One of the foremost indications of the ingenuity of the
poets of the eighteenth-century vernacular revival is in
the metaphors which they find to communicate their
nationalism. 'Base foreign fashions have intervened',
claims the speaker in Ramsay's 'Tartana'. How better
to assert the national cultural identity than by attacking
foreign tastes and trends? Music provides a fertile
source. Take these stanzas from Ramsay's 'An Elegy
on Patie Birnie':

> After ilk tune he took a sowp,
> And bann'd wi' birr the corky cowp
> That to the Papists' country scowp,
>   To lear 'ha, ha's,
> Frae chiels that sing hap, stap, and lowp,
>   Wanting the b—s.

> That beardless capons are na men,
> We by their fozie springs might ken,
> But ours, he said, could vigour len'
>   To men o' wier,
> And gar them stout to battle sten
>   Withoutten fear.

The identification of culture with heroism here is significant. Fergusson's celebration of the New Year
holidays, 'The Daft Days', includes this:

> Fiddlers, your pins in temper fix,
> And roset weel your fiddlesticks;
> But banish vile Italian tricks
>   From out your *quorum;*
> Nor *fortes* wi' *pianos* mix—
>   Gie's *Tullochgorum.*

> For nought can cheer the heart sae weel,
> As can a canty Highland reel;
> It even vivifies the heel
>   To skip and dance:
> Lifeless is he wha canna feel
>   Its influence.

In these poems are two of the precedents for the
favourable comparison of Scottish melodies with Italian in stanza 13 of **'The Cotter's Saturday Night'**:

> They chant their artless notes in simple
>   guise;
> They tune their hearts, by far the noblest
>   aim:
> Perhaps *Dundee's* wild-warbling measures
>   rise,
> Or plaintive *Martyrs,* worthy of the name;
> Or noble *Elgin* beets the heaven-ward flame,
> The sweetest far of Scotia's holy lays:
> Compar'd with these, *Italian trills* are tame;
> The tickl'd ears no heart-felt raptures raise;
> Nae unison hae they, with our Creator's
>   praise.

Sometimes Burns's nationalism surfaces in the most
unexpected ways. The witches in **'Tam o' Shanter'**
have travelled the world: their collection of trophies
includes 'Five tomahawks, wi' blue red-rusted / Five
scymitars, wi' murder crusted'. But when it comes to
music and dance they are patriots to the core:

> Warlocks and witches in a dance:
> Nae cotillion, brent new frae France,

But hornpipes, jigs, strathspeys, and reels,
Put life and mettle in their heels.

Food offers another metaphor for nationalism. Behind the humorous flyting bluster of **'Address to a Haggis'** a serious claim is being made for Scottish values. Again Fergusson ('my elder brother in the Muse', Burns called him) was almost certainly the inspiration with his poem, 'To the Principal and Professors of the University of St Andrews, on their superb treat to Dr Samuel Johnson'. Fergusson claims that the university regents have spared no expense to treat Dr Johnson to all sorts of foreign delicacies. Had he been in charge, Fergusson would have provided a quite different menu:

> *Imprimis,* then, a haggis fat,
> Weel tottled in a seything pat,
> Wi' spice and ingans weel ca'd through,
> Had helped to gust the stirrah's mou',
> And placed itself in trencher clean
> Before the gilpy's glowrin een.
> *Secundo,* then, a gude sheep's head,
> Whase hide was singit, never flea'd,
> And four black trotters cled wi' girsle,
> Bedown his throat had learn'd to hirsle.
> What think ye, niest, o' gude fat brose,
> To clag his ribs? a dainty dose!
> And white and bluidy puddings routh,
> To gar the Doctor skirl, 'O Drouth!'

Fergusson goes on to infer that Scottish writing, like Scottish cuisine, is lively, and natural, and praiseworthy. The poem develops into a moving plea to the Scottish people: be true and natural Scots, for the alternative is a gloomy one—the demise of Scottish culture:

> Devall then, Sirs, and never send
> For daintiths to regale a friend;
> Or, like a torch at baith ends burning
> Your house'll soon grow mirk and
>   mourning'.

There is a subtle irony in Fergusson's making claims for the vigour of the native Scottish literary tradition by means of techniques which epitomise it at its most expressive. Similarly, in 'Elegy on the Death of Scots Music' his expressive use of standard Habbie for serious purposes shows that despite the ostensible lament Scottish cultural forms are alive and well.

Authority is almost certainly inimical to the Scottish character; hence the vigour of Ramsay's and Fergusson's reaction against the unquestioning adoption of classical and neo-classical forms, modes, and rules. But there is also a sense in which Scottish poets of the vernacular revival compensate for the loss of political independence by asserting their cultural independence through the innovative use of classical poetic forms to

render distinctly Scottish material. Here is the start of Ramsay's 'Elegy on Lucky Wood':

> O Canongate! poor eldritch hole,
> What loss, what crosses thou dost thole!
> London and death gar thee look drole,
>   And hing thy head:
> Wow, but thou hast e'en a cauld coal
>   To blaw indeed.

Burns's **'Tam Samson's Elegy'** has its antecedents in Ramsay's mock-elegies. But Burns could achieve moving and original effect within the conventional elegiac mode, as the very fine **'Elegy on Captain Matthew Henderson'** shows.

Another important respect in which Burns was influenced by the earlier poets of the vernacular revival is in the interplay of Scots and formal English. To employ both the vernacular and standard English within the one poem was a risky undertaking. The perfect modulation of the tongues was not always achieved, and sometimes the ultimate effect was not the intended one. Here is the start of Ramsay's pastoral eclogue, 'Richy and Sandy on the Death of Mr Addison':

> Richy
>
> What gars thee look sae dowf, dear Sandy,
>   say?
> Cheer up, dull fellow, take thy reed and play
> 'My apron deary', or some wanton tune:
> Be merry, lad, an' keep thy heart aboon.
>
> Sandy
>
> Na, na, it winna do; leave me to mane:
> This aught days twice o'er tell'd I'll whistle
>   nane.
>
> Richy
>
> Wow, man, that's unco' sad! Is't that yer jo
> Has ta'en the strunt? Or has some bogle-bo,
> Glowrin frae 'mang auld wa's, gi'en ye a
>   fleg?
> Or has some dauted wedder broke his leg?
>
> Sandy
>
> Naething like that, sic troubles eith were
>   borne:
> What's bogles, wedders, or what Mausy's
>   scorn?
> Our loss is meikle mair, and past remead:
> Adie, that played and sang sae sweet, is
>   dead!
>
> Richy
>
> Dead! says't thou?—Oh, haud up my heart,
>   O Pan!
> Ye gods, what laids ye lay on feckless man!

Ramsay is making a genuine attempt to claim vernacular Scots' right to a place in British literature; but it doesn't quite succeed. Burns, too, could unwittingly achieve a comic effect by the incongruous use of formal English. One suspects that he might wish to revise these lines from **'Epistle to Davie, a Brother Poet'**:

> It lightens, it brightens,
>   The tenebrific scene,
> To meet with, and greet with
>   My Davie or my Jean!

The makars had employed the juxtaposing of Scots idiom and formal English for reductive effect. It is the ideal means for deflating pomposity and pretension. In Fergusson, Burns encountered the clashing of tongues for comic and reductive effect. Typical is the conclusion of 'The Daft Days':

> Let mirth abound, let social cheer
> Invest the dawning of the year;
> Let blithesome Innocence appear,
>   To crown our joy:
> Nor envy wi' sarcastic sneer,
>   Our bliss destroy.
>
> And thou, great god of *Aqua-vitae!*
> Wha says the empire o' this city,
> Whan fou we're sometimes capernoity,
>   Be thou prepared
> To hedge us frae that black banditti,
>   The City-Guard.

Similarly, Burns is expert at undermining pretension by the strategic use of vernacular Scots as, for instance, in stanza 6 of **'Address to the Unco Guid'**:

> Ye high, exalted, virtuous Dames,
>   Ty'd up in godly laces,
> Before ye gie poor Frailty names,
>   Suppose a change o' cases;
> A dear-lov'd lad, convenience snug,
>   A treacherous inclination—
> But, let me whisper i' your lug,
>   Ye're aiblins nae temptation.

Burns's bilingualism was set to serve a range of purposes, personal as well as literary. Revealingly, after one of his visits to Edinburgh Burns wrote in exaggeratedly sustained vernacular to William Nicol, master of the High School of Edinburgh. The expressive Scots idiom seems to convey a sense of release; writing the letter has had a cathartic effect on its author.

The linguistic and cultural duality in Burns reflects in part the respective influences of his parents. Through Agnes Brown of Kirkoswald Burns had access to the native oral tradition. William Burnes, with his emphasis on the importance of both reading and correctly pronouncing English, saw clearly where the future lay.

In the English authors whom Burns read avidly there was a further rich source of personae. To varying degrees these personae corresponded with, and gave voice to, aspects of his own personality. In Pope and the *Spectator* essays Burns found the voice of the observer. To Murdoch he wrote, 'I seem to be one sent into the world, to see, and observe . . . the joy of my heart is to "Study men, their manners, and their ways"'.[18] This was a useful stance for the satirist. But for a satirist of Burns's skill and vehemence (he wrote on one occasion of 'the bloodhounds of Satire'[19]), living in a tight-knit community, one of the effects was, as David Sillar noted, to prompt 'suspicious fear'[20] among his neighbours and hence a progressive distancing of the poet from his community. The voice of the detached observer comes to challenge that of the exuberant participant for primacy of place in both Burns's poems and his letters. There are a number of letters in which Burns rails at the mob or fashionable society (including one to Peter Hill in which he clearly distinguishes the two Edinburghs). Here he protests to Mrs Dunlop:

> However respectable, Individuals in all ages have been, I have ever looked on Mankind in the lump to be nothing better than a foolish, headstrong, credulous, unthinking mob; and their universal belief has ever had extremely little weight with me.[21]

That voice is remarkably similar to that of the elderly misanthrope, Matt Bramble, in Smollett's *Humphry Clinker*. Six months earlier, Burns had written to Hill, 'I want Smollett's novels, for the sake of his incomparable humour. I already have *Roderick Random* and *Humphry Clinker*.'[22]

To one of 'the harum-scarum sons of Imagination and Whim' the lure of Sterne's *Tristram Shandy* was strong. Plainly the Shandean voice struck a chord with Burns's desire to present himself as a whimsically independent spirit. Here is part of one of the letters first published in G. Ross Roy's revised edition of the *Letters* (1985):

> Writing Sense is so damn'd, dry, hide-bound a business, I am determined never more to have anything to do with it.—I have such an aversion to right line and method, that when I can't get over the hedges which bound the highway, I zigzag across the road just to keep my hand in.[23]

In *Tristram Shandy* Burns encountered Sterne's amused demonstration in terms of fictional practice of Locke's views on understanding, association, and identity. It is evident that the flux of the human mind and the ways in which we associate fascinated Burns, and a letter to Mrs Dunlop in which he tells of the appeal which 'The Vision of Mirza' in the *Spectator* had for him traces the caprices of individual association to a spiritual source—the Soul.[24] One of Burns's greatest achievements was—out of personal need—to shape the verse-epistle into a medium for communicating mental flux. 'The self-dramatisations of the epistles', says Thomas Crawford, 'express a mind in motion, giving itself over at different times to *conflicting* principles and feelings; they mirror that mind as it grappled with a complex world. In order to body it forth, Burns had to be, in himself, and not simply in play, both Calvinist and anti-Calvinist, both fornicator and champion of chastity, both Jacobite and Jacobin, both local and national, both British and European, both anarchist and sober calculator, both philistine and anti-philistine'.[25] A mode and a form had been found that were capable of rendering complexity, even multiplicity, of self.

Of the qualities essential to the personality of the poet, Burns habitually identifies open-heartedness as the foremost. Gavin Hamilton's brother is complimented as having 'a heart that might adorn the breast of a Poet'[26]: and to Josiah Walker Burns writes, 'You know from experience the bedlam warmth of a poet's heart'[27]. Rousseau had claimed that our ancestors were naturally benign and that it was rationalist civilisation that had corrupted man, and in *Tristram Shandy* Sterne had offered man's capacity for benign emotion as a positive good. Here Burns was to find endorsement of his own belief in the values of the heart. To Murdoch he writes, on 15 January 1783:

> My favorite authors are of the sentimental kind, such as Shenstone, particularly his Elegies, Thomson, Man of feeling, a book I prize next to the Bible, Man of the World, Sterne, especially his Sentimental journey, Macpherson's Ossian, etc. these are the glorious models after which I endeavour to form my conduct[28].

Before his twenty-fourth birthday Burns has found in literature models for his behaviour as well as his writing. In Mackenzie was more than endorsement of the values of the heart: there was also the recommendation that one practise benevolence, it being not only beneficial for the victim to have relief from suffering but also rewarding for the benefactor to contemplate himself in that role. In *The Man of Feeling* the 'self-approving joy' of the age of sensibility raises its refined head. Thus in **'To a Mountain Daisy'** Burns could employ the sentimental rhetoric which Pope some seventy years earlier had used in 'Elegy to the Memory of an Unfortunate Lady'; Burns employs it to address a flower whose stem he has severed. The Edinburgh literati found Burns exemplifying what for them was a prime requisite of the peasant-poet, pathetic struggle, and they were able to view him with

benevolent condescension, rather in the manner of Burns's speaker's response to the mountain daisy. Burns paid a price for his participation in polite Edinburgh's sentimental games: in Carol McGuirk's terms it was a 'chronic anxiety'.[29]

There is one other highly significant source of endorsement of the values of the heart. Sending Moore his impressions of *Zeluco,* Burns commented, 'Original strokes, that strongly depict the human heart, is your and Fielding's province, beyond any other Novellist, I have ever perused'.[30] Moore was being complimented; Fielding's influence was very real. David Daiches has noted that Burns, 'like Fielding's Tom Jones, believed in the doctrine of the good heart and held that kindness, generosity of spirit, and fellow feeling were the central virtues'.[31] Could it be that Burns modelled some of his conduct on that of Fielding's romantic hero, Tom Jones? In their relations with women each maintains a clear distinction between idealised love and sexual needs. His passions aroused by thinking of his beloved Sophia, Tom leaps into the bushes with the first woman he encounters, who happens to be Molly Seagrim, fresh from a day's manure spreading in the fields. Similarly Burns writes a typically stylised and formal letter to 'Clarinda' in the course of which he makes reference to his having fathered a child to the maid, Jenny Clow.[32]

In terms of literary technique Fielding's influence on Burns was considerable. Both Fielding and Burns relished their abilities as stylists. One of Fielding's aims in *Tom Jones* was to check by parody the excesses of popular romance. As a consequence Tom and Sophia are at times required to act and speak like the hero and heroine of that genre (for example, the chance meeting of the lovers at the corner of the canal where previously Tom risked drowning to save Sophia's little bird). Such passages must surely have been at the back of Burns's mind when he wrote this to Wilhelmina Alexander of Ballochmyle:

The Scenery was nearly taken from real life; though I dare say, Madam, you do n't recollect it: for I believe you scarcely noticed the poetic Reveur, as he wandered by you.—I had roved out as Chance directed, on the favorite haunts of my Muse, the banks of Ayr; to view Nature in all the gayety of the vernal year.—

The Sun was flaming o'er the distant, western hills; not a breath stirred the crimson opening blossom, or the verdant spreading leaf.

'Twas a golden moment for a poetic heart.—I listened the feathered Warblers, pouring their harmony on every hand, with a congenial, kindred regard; and frequently turned out of my path lest I should disturb their little songs, or frighten them to another station.—'Surely,' said I to myself, 'he must be a wretch indeed, who, regardless of your harmonious endeavours to please him, can eye your elusive flights, to discover your secret recesses, and rob you of all the property Nature gives you; your dearest comforts, your helpless, little Nestlings.'

Even the hoary Hawthorn twig that shot across the way, what heart, at such a time, but must have been interested in its welfare, and wished it to be preserved from the rudely browsing Cattle, or the withering eastern Blast?

Such was the scene, and such the hour, when in a corner of my Prospect I spyed one of the finest pieces of Nature's workmanship that ever crowned a poetic Landskip; those visionary Bards excepted who hold commerce with aerial Beings.—

Had CALUMNY & VILLAINY taken my walk, they had, at that moment, sworn eternal peace with such an Object.—[33]

It is inconceivable that Burns, as an accomplished mimic and master-ironist, did not realise that what he was offering here was the posturings of romance.

One of the main elements in Fielding's *Tom Jones* is the comic-epic. Ordinary, even mundane, experience is presented with the elaborate formality appropriate to the classical heroic mode. In Ramsay and Fergusson Burns found that inflation and reduction were integral to the Scottish poetic tradition. Fielding, writing in a different tradition and a different genre, sanctioned the technique further. Two traditions met, the common ground being the clash of manner and matter, or formal and idiomatic language, or generalisation and detail. One episode in *Tom Jones* finds the narrator following Mr Allworthy to the top of a hill to watch the sunrise. If there is anything finer in nature, he suggests, it can only be that which Mr Allworthy represents—a being replete with benevolence. Mr Allworthy has to descend because his sister rings the breakfast-bell—from the sublime to the mundane, but doubly so because the narrator is now concerned about how to get the reader safely back down the hill of his elaborate prose without breaking his neck. Compare the following extract from a letter of Burns to Thomson in which a lengthy passage in the grand manner reaches a climax, only to be undermined:

> Do you think that the sober, gin-horse routine of existence could inspire a man with life, & love, & joy—could fire him with enthusiasm, or melt him with pathos, equal to the genius of your Book?— No! No!!!—Whenever I want to be more than ordinary *in song;* to be in some degree equal to your diviner airs; do you imagine I fast & pray for the celestial emanation?—Tout au contraire! I

have a glorious recipe, the very one that for his own use was invented by the Divinity of Healing & Poesy when erst he piped to the flocks of Admetus.—I put myself in a regimen of admiring a fine woman; & in proportion to the adorability of her charms, in proportion are you delighted with my verses.

> The lightning of her eye is the godhead of Parnassus, & the witchery of her smile the divinity of Helicon!

> To descend to the business with which I began; if you like my idea of—'when she cam ben she bobbit'—the following stanzas of mine, altered a little from what they were formerly when set to another air, may perhaps do instead of worse stanzas.[34]

Also noteworthy is a wonderfully, almost manically, exuberant letter to Cunningham in which Burns plainly relishes his expertise in the grand manner for comic effect. It includes, 'I feel, I feel the presence of Supernatural assistance! Circled in the embrace of my elbow-chair, my breast labors, like the bloated Sybil on her three-footed stool, & like her too, labors with Nonsense'.[35] Likewise, the account of the celebrations before sunrise at Ben Lomond is, simply, a *tour de force.*[36]

In the poems the reductive contrast of manner and matter is used to telling effect. For instance, this is part of the description of Moodie's preaching in **'The Holy Fair':**

> Hear how he clears the points o' Faith
>   Wi' rattlin an' thumpin!
> Now meekly calm, now wild in wrath,
>   He's stampan, an' he's jumpan!
> His lengthen'd chin, his turn'd up snout,
>   His eldritch squeel an' gestures,
> O how they fire the heart devout,
>   Like cantharidian plaisters
>   On sic a day!

In **'Elegy on the Year 1788'** international and local events are set on the one level, the former reduced, the latter inflated:

> The Spanish empire's tint a head,
> An' my auld teethless Bawtie's dead;
> The toolzie's teugh 'tween Pitt an' Fox,
> An' our gudewife's wee birdy cocks.

In **'Death and Dr Hornbook'** the process of inflation and reduction informs the whole poem. Death?— He is a pathetic figure, in need of a comforting chat and struggling to retain the vestiges of his pride. Who is to be feared now?—The monstrously incompetent pharmacist, Dr Hornbook, who has made Death redundant.

It is in Burns's other great narrative poem, **'Tam o' Shanter',** that the epic and comic-epic legacies are put to greatest effect:

> By this time he was cross the ford,
> Whare, in the snaw, the chapman smoor'd;
> And past the birks and meikle stane,
> Whare drunken Charlie brak's neck-bane;
> And thro' the whins, and by the cairn,
> Whare hunters fand the murder'd bairn;
> And near the thorn, aboon the well,
> Whare Mungo's mither hang'd hersel . . .

> Coffins stood round, like open presses,
> That shaw'd the dead in their last dresses;
> And, by some devilish cantraip slight,
> Each in its cauld hand held a light.
> By which heroic Tam was able
> To note upon the haly table,
> A murderer's banes, in gibbet-airns;
> Twa span-lang, wee, unchristen'd bairns;
> A thief, new-cutted frae a rape,
> Wi' his last gasp his gab did gape;
> Five tomahawks, wi' blude red-rusted;
> Five scymitars, wi' murder crusted;
> A garter, which a babe had strangled;
> A knife, a father's throat had mangled . . .

—What are these if not the epic catalogue set to the service of mock-Gothic horror? And the 'Heaven-taught ploughman' seems to have mastered the epic simile:

> As bees bizz out wi' angry fyke,
> When plundering herds assail their byke;
> As open pussie's mortal foes,
> When, pop! she starts before their nose;
> As eager runs the market-crowd,
> When 'Catch the thief!' resounds aloud:
> So Maggie runs, the witches follow,
> Wi' mony an eldritch skreech and hollow.

One effect of rendering ordinary beings by means of the machinery of epic is to endow them with representative significance. The elevating effect is most obvious in Fielding's *Tom Jones* in the mock-epic account of the battle in the graveyard between Molly and the villagers. The participants in the battle assume archetypal significance courtesy of the epic rhetoric which inflates and generalises; it becomes *the* village punch-up. Similarly Tam becomes mankind's representative; he is truly 'heroic Tam', and the account of his experiences has become the definitive version of man's encounter with the supernatural.

There is one other respect in which *Tom Jones* and **'Tam o' Shanter'** may be compared. Fielding creates

an identifiable narrator—identifiable in terms of personality and values. Urbane and witty, Fielding's narrator is also fallible and he certainly likes the sound of his own voice: scarce an episode passes that has not been prefaced by commentary from our ever-present guide. This pattern is repeated in **'Tam o' Shanter'**—episode, commentary, episode, commentary. The narrator is eager to place his account of Tam's experiences in the context of universalising commentary, the fruits of his worldly wisdom:

> Ah, gentle dames! it gars me greet,
> To think how many counsels sweet,
> How many lengthen'd sage advices,
> The husband frae the wife despises!

Like Fielding's narrator in *Tom Jones,* the narrator of **'Tam o' Shanter'** is capable of irony and self-irony ('But here my Muse her wing maun cour / Sic flights as far beyond her power'). But as Fielding is not synonymous with the narrator of *Tom Jones* and so subjects his narrator to authorial irony, so Burns—who is equally not the narrator of **'Tam o' Shanter'**—subjects his creation to authorial irony. **'Tam o' Shanter: A Tale'**—the sub-title is deceptively simple, and deliberately so. It is a tale of what happens to Tam; it is also a tale of someone telling a tale. *Tom Jones* is as much an account of narrator-reader relations as a story of what happens to Tom and Sophia. Sterne's *Tristram Shandy* is about the narrator's desperate and largely futile attempt to give an account of his life and opinions, enlisting the reader's help when necessary.[37] Could it be that Burns's 'tale', traditionally regarded as the culmination of the folk-tradition, may be set alongside these sophisticated experiments in narration, where what happens is important, but how it is recounted is equally important? And could it be that in that play of relationships involving poet, narrator, and Tam there is some sort of resolution—albeit temporary—of the poet's problems of identity: multiplicity of identity finds a focus in that play of relationships; paradoxically, in the controlled flux of play lies the basis of stability? It might be added that Burns's obsessive and fluctuating relationship with the Devil (who is both 'that noble personage' and 'Auld Hangie . . . Auld Nickie-Ben') has a comparable function.

Burns lived in various worlds, sometimes simultaneously. The chameleon nature and the charismatic personality made this possible; and, by and large, the linguistic ability and stylistic expertise kept pace with the multiplicity of perspective (the point is perhaps most readily demonstrated by comparing **'Tam o' Shanter'** with Burns's prose account to Grose[38] of largely the same material). Burns wrote to Moore, 'my first ambition was, and still my strongest wish is, to please my Compeers, the rustic Inmates of the Hamlet'.[39] In that sentence substance and style are plainly at loggerheads. In the preface to the Commonplace Book he observed, 'I was placed by Fortune among a class of men to whom my ideas would have been nonsense'. Some of Burns's finest poems are those in which he finds the means of communicating on various levels and to various audiences. **'To a Mouse'** is both an address to a mouse and, as Thomas Crawford has suggested, a depiction of the plight of both the peasantry and the human race. Burns's 'compeers' may well have been amused by two dogs conversing, but **'The Twa Dogs'**, echoing Goldsmith and Crabbe and showing the influence of Adam Smith, is a poem about the political and social state of man in the eighteenth century. In **'The Auld Farmer's New-Year-Morning Salutation to his Auld Mare, Maggie'** the 'rustic inmates' would hear a familiar voice—that of the peasant-farmer who gives an account of his hardships but stoically accepts his condition. Burns, ironically distanced, offers such a voice as a means of suggesting that men must begin to question their lot and challenge their condition; Enlightenment is meaningless unless it reaches such people also. **'Address to the Deil'** would be immediately accessible to those versed in the folk-tradition and Presbyterianism. It is also, though less obviously, a poem about Burns trying to identify and reconcile conflicting elements within himself, elements in whose creation both the folk-tradition and Presbyterianism have played a significant part.

How could a man of acute intelligence and notable breadth and depth of knowledge countenance the reduction of himself to the stereotype of the 'Heaven-taught ploughman'? One answer is that he responded to market forces. Robert Anderson challenged Burns with being more learned than he would acknowledge, and this was the poet's response:

> It was . . . a part of the machinery, as he called it, of his poetical character to pass for an illiterate ploughman who wrote from pure inspiration. When I pointed out some evident traces of poetical imitation in his verses, privately, he readily acknowledged his obligations . . . but in company he would not suffer his pretensions to pure inspiration to be challenged, and it was seldom done where it might be supposed to affect the success of the subscription for his *Poems*.[40]

But he responded so successfully that there was no escape; having helped create the role, he was obliged to continue to play it. The range of reading, ready absorption of material, and talent for mimicry combined in Burns to produce a range of styles, modes, and personae which he used to great creative effect. Ultimately, however, these served more than a literary function: Burns became trapped behind the personae which he had so readily created.

If since 1707 Scots have been uncertain as to their identity, then it is understandable that they should worship a poet who had such a gift for creating voices and personae. But the poet himself paid a price.

Notes

[1] *Lounger,* No. 97 (9 Dec. 1786); reprinted in Donald A. Low (ed.), *Robert Burns: The Critical Heritage* (London & Boston, 1974), 67-71.

[2] Letter to Lord Byron, 6 Nov. 1813; reprinted in Low (ed.), *Burns: Critical Heritage,* 258.

[3] *Robert Burns's Commonplace Book* 1783-1785, intro. David Daiches (London, 1965), I.

[4] 'Criticism on the writings of Burns', *The Works of Robert Burns, with an Account of his Life* (Liverpool, 1800), I, 267; reprinted in Low (ed.), *Burns: Critical Heritage,* 132.

[5] *The Letters of Robert Burns,* ed. J. DeLancey Ferguson; 2nd edn., ed. G. Ross Roy (Oxford, 1985), I, 326.

[6] *Letters,* I, 109

[7] 'Character Sketch' by 'Candidior' (Maria Riddell), *Dumfries Journal,* Aug. 1796; reprinted Low (ed.), *Burns: Critical Heritage,* 102.

[8] *Letters,* II, 334.

[9] *Letters,* I, 334-5.

[10] *Letters,* I, 337.

[11] *Robert Burns and Mrs Dunlop: Correspondence,* ed. William Wallace (London, 1898), 60.

[12] *Ibid.,* 65.

[13] *Letters,* I, 88.

[14] *Letters,* I, 138, 141.

[15] *Letters,* I, 392.

[16] *Letters,* II, 165.

[17] *Letters,* I, 207.

[18] *Letters,* I, 17.

[19] *Letters,* I, 175.

[20] *The Life and Works of Robert Burns,* ed. Robert Chambers, rev. William Wallace, 4 vols. (Edinburgh & London, 1896), I, 68-9.

[21] *Letters,* I, 349.

[22] *Letters,* I, 296.

[23] *Letters,* I, 131.

[24] *Letters,* I, 348.

[25] Thomas Crawford, *Burns: A Study of the Poems and Songs* (2nd edn., reprinted Edinburgh, 1978), 104.

[26] *Letters,* I, 152.

[27] *Letters,* I, 155.

[28] *Letters,* I, 17.

[29] Carol McGuirk, *Robert Burns and the Sentimental Era* (Athens, Georgia, 1985), 77

[30] *Letters,* II, 74.

[31] David Daiches, *God and the Poets* (Oxford, 1984), 144.

[32] *Letters,* II, 122.

[33] *Letters,* I, 63-4.

[34] *Letters,* II, 315-16.

[35] *Letters,* II, 146.

[36] *Letters,* I, 124-5.

[37] For a fuller account of Sterne's influence on Burns, see Kenneth Simpson, *The Protean Scot: The Crisis of Identity in Eighteenth-Century Scottish Literature* (Aberdeen, 1988), ch. 8.

[38] *Letters,* II, 29-31.

[39] *Letters,* I, 88.

[40] Robert Anderson to James Currie, 28 Sept. 1799, printed in *Burns Chronicle,* 1925, 12; cited Crawford, *Burns,* 198-9, n. 20.

Ian McIntyre (essay date 1995)

SOURCE: "Apotheosis," in *Dirt & Deity: A Life of Robert Burns,* HarperCollins Publishers, 1995, pp. 413-44.

[*Here, McIntyre presents a survey of critical and public reaction to Burns over the span of two hundred years.*]

. . . The critics had continued to give as much attention to the defects of Burns's moral character as to the qualities of his poetry. The publication of Cromek's *Reliques of Robert Burns* in 1808 had occasioned two influential unsigned reviews—that by Francis Jeffrey in the *Whig Edinburgh Review,* and that by Walter Scott in the first issue of the *Quarterly Review,* recently established as a rival Tory voice. Jeffrey, who was later to begin his demolition of Wordsworth's *The Excursion* with the notorious 'This will never do!' was alive to the value of a provocative opening:

> Burns is certainly by far the greatest of our poetical prodigies—from Stephen Duck down to Thomas Dermody. *They* are forgotten already; or only remembered for derision. But the name of Burns, if we are not mistaken, has not yet 'gathered all its fame'; and will endure long after those circumstances are forgotten which contributed to its first notoriety . . .

Burnsians who succumbed to apoplexy at this early point missed much that was judicious and discriminating, because it was Jeffrey's contention that to regard their hero as a prodigy was to derogate from his merits: 'We can see no propriety in regarding the poetry of Burns chiefly as the wonderful work of a peasant, and thus admiring it much in the same way as if it had been written with his toes.' Behind the acerbic and sometimes patronising manner, an informed critical intelligence was at work. Jeffrey, who stood in the urbane tradition of Addison and Johnson, was critical of what he termed the 'undisciplined harshness and acrimony' of Burns's invective, although that was not the most severe criticism he had to offer:

> The leading vice in Burns's character, and the cardinal deformity, indeed, of all his productions, was his contempt, or affectation of contempt, for prudence, decency and regularity; and his admiration of thoughtlessness, oddity, and vehement sensibility;—his belief, in short, in *the dispensing power* of genius and social feeling, in all matters of morality and common sense . . . This pitiful cant of careless feeling and eccentric genius, accordingly, has never found much favour in the eyes of English sense and morality. The most signal effect which it ever produced, was on the muddy brains of some German youth, who are said to have left college in a body to rob on the highway! because Schiller had represented the captain of a gang as so very noble a creature . . .

These were robust strictures, but Jeffrey was not less incisive in what he had to say about the humour, the pathos and the animation which he found in Burns. He paid particularly close attention to the songs. They were, he said, 'written with more tenderness, nature, and feeling than any other lyric compositions that are extant' and were likely to outlive all his other work.

His judgement that Burns was 'entitled to the rank of a great and original genius' was unqualified.[1]

Scott, in his review for the *Quarterly* a month later,[2] did not think that Cromek had performed much of a service either to the poet or the public: 'The contents of the volume before us are more properly gleanings than reliques, the refuse and sweepings of the shop, rather than the commodities which might be deemed contraband.' Like Jeffrey, he thought highly of the songs—'No poet of our tongue ever displayed higher skill in marrying melody to immortal verse'—although he also took the view that Burns's devotion to compiling and composing for musical collections was so much time and talent frittered away and a diversion from 'his grand plan of dramatic composition'.

For Scott, Burns was 'the child of passion and feeling'. The tone of his review is kindlier than Jeffrey's, but he shakes his head no less reprovingly over his recklessness:

> The extravagance of genius with which this wonderful man was gifted, being in his later and more evil days directed to no fixed or general purpose, was, in the morbid state of his health and feelings, apt to display itself in hasty sallies of virulent and unmerited severity: sallies often regretted by the bard himself; and of which, justice to the living and to the dead, alike demanded the suppression.

Scott's social and political conservatism did nothing to blunt his literary judgement, however—he dwelt at length, for instance, on the merits of that riotously subversive piece **'The Jolly Beggars'**—'for humorous description and nice discrimination of character, [it] is inferior to no poem of the same length in the whole range of English poetry'. He also had a keen eye for the strengths and weaknesses of Burns's prose style, pointing impartially to the 'meretricious ornaments' to be found in his letters to Clarinda and the mastery of the vernacular he displayed in one of his letters to William Nicol—'an attempt to read a sentence of which, would break the teeth of most modern Scotchmen'.[3]

By the time Scott's son-in-law, John Gibson Lockhart, tried his hand at a biography in 1828, he felt the need to placate the reader with a defensively worded preface: 'Some apology must be deemed necessary for any new attempt to write the *Life of Burns*.' By then Wordsworth, Coleridge and Hazlitt had all had their say and so, in *English Bards and Scotch Reviewers*, had Byron; there is even a short passage referring to Burns in *Sanditon*, the novel which Jane Austen left unfinished at her death.

Lockhart had, in fact, correctly identified the need for something less monumental than the successive edi-

tions of Currie, and his book was well received. 'All people applaud it,' Scott told him in a letter, 'a new edition will immediately be wanted'. Scott was right. The style is mellifluous and Lockhart's *Life* ran into many editions; it was only in the 1930s that it came under the beady scrutiny of modern academic scholarship: 'Inexcusably inaccurate from beginning to end, at times demonstrably mendacious,' wrote Snyder. He allowed one thing in its favour—it was the occasion of a famous review by Thomas Carlyle.[4]

Carlyle, thirty-two years old and still struggling to establish himself, had just abandoned Edinburgh for the bleak solitude of Craigenputtoch. He saw Burns's life as a tragedy of potential unfulfilled and opportunity squandered, but argued that he must for all that be ranked 'not only as a true British poet, but as one of the most considerable British men of the eighteenth century':

> An educated man stands, as it were, in the midst of a boundless arsenal and magazine, filled with all the weapons and engines which man's skill has been able to devise from the earliest time; and he works, accordingly, with a strength borrowed from all past ages. How different is *his* state who stands on the outside of that storehouse, and feels that its gates must be stormed, or remain forever shut against him! His means are the commonest or rudest; the mere work done is no measure of his strength. A dwarf behind his steam-engine may remove mountains; but no dwarf will hew them down with the pickaxe; and he must be a Titan that hurls them abroad with his arms.

Carlyle's own origins and associations were not so very different from those of Burns and nobody before or since has written about him with such passionate insight. He paid scant attention to Lockhart's text—what he produced was not really a review at all but an extended essay in biography. For him, Burns's writing was 'no more than a poor mutilated fraction of what was in him, broken glimpses of a genius that could never show itself complete'. He notes, however, the tonic effect of his work on Scottish literature as a whole: 'For a long period after Scotland became British, we had no literature . . . Theologic ink, and Jacobite blood, with gall enough in both cases, seemed to have blotted out the intellect of the country.'

The merits of the poetry interest Carlyle less than the psychological complexities of the man who wrote it:

> There is but one era in the life of Burns, and that is the earliest. We have not youth and manhood, but only youth . . . With all that resoluteness of judgement, that penetrating insight, and singular maturity of intellectual power, he never attains to any clearness regarding himself.

He acknowledges that Burns was unfortunate in some of the 'fashionable danglers after literature' he fell in with along the way, but contemplates the various difficulties he encountered in his life with a complete lack of sentimentality; in Carlyle's view, the world treated him no worse than it did Tasso or Galileo or Camoens. 'It is his inward, not his outward misfortunes that bring him to the dust.' Burns, he declares, like Byron, never came to 'moral manhood'.

His conclusion is that the Burnses, the Swifts and the Rousseaus of this world are sometimes tried 'at a tribunal far more rigid than that where the Plebiscita of common civic reputations are pronounced,' and that the result is often a condemnation that is both blind and cruel:

> Granted, the ship comes into harbour with shrouds and tackle damaged; the pilot is blameworthy; he has not been all-wise and all-powerful; but to know *how* blameworthy, tell us first whether his voyage has been round the Globe, or only to Ramsgate and the Isle of Dogs.[5]

Jeffrey, still editing the *Review* after twenty-six years, considered the article too long and diffuse and did not admire its author's Germanic English. When Carlyle received the proofs, he found that he had been drastically pruned—'the body of a quadruped with the head of a bird,' he grumbled to his wife; 'a man shortened by cutting out his thighs, and fixing the Knee-pans on the hips!' He restored the cuts and returned the proofs to Jeffrey, telling him he was free to drop the article but not to mutilate it; rather surprisingly, his editor acquiesced.[6] As things turned out, Carlyle's views on Burns carried a good deal further than either the Isle of Dogs or Ramsgate; Goethe thought so highly of the article that he translated long passages from it and published them in his collected works.

Language was initially something of a barrier to the spread of Burns's fame beyond the English-speaking world. There were several translations into French between 1825 and 1840 and articles about him began to appear in the Russian periodical press in the 1820s. (Appropriately enough there is an early translation of **'Ae Fond Kiss'** by Mikhail Lermontov, himself the descendant of a Scottish adventurer called Learmont who had entered the Russian service in the seventeenth century.) Burns's work was also greatly admired in Scandinavia, and one of the first to translate him was Henrik Wergeland, the outstanding Norwegian lyric poet of the nineteenth century.

In Canada and the United States, Burns's egalitarianism and his identification with the colonial cause had gone down well from the start. There were also many expatriate Scots who needed no prompting either to promote the work or foster the legend. Emigrant sons of Caledonia might quickly shed their Scottish accents after a few years in the land of the free, but they remained in the grip of a powerful nostalgia for the real or imagined Scotland they had left behind. From Pittsburgh, in 1852, the young Andrew Carnegie wrote home to an uncle:

> Although I cannot say sow crae just as broad as I once could I can read about Wallace, Bruce and Burns with as much enthusiasm as ever and feel proud of having been a son of old Calodonia, [*sic*] and I like to tell people when they ask, 'Are you native born?' 'No sir, I am a scotchman,' and I feel as proud as I am sure as ever Romans did when it was their boast to say, 'I am a Roman citizen.'[7]

In 1859, the hundredth anniversary of Burns's birth was widely celebrated in North America. In New York City, a centenary oration was given by the Reverend Henry Ward Beecher, then at the height of his fame as a congregational minister and moral crusader. Until his death, he told his audience, Burns's life had been a failure: 'Ever since it has been a marvelous success.' In Boston, there was a lavishly eloquent tribute from Ralph Waldo Emerson:

> Not Latimer, nor Luther struck more telling blows against false theology than did this brave singer. The Confession of Augsburg, the Declaration of Independence, the French Rights of Man, and the 'Marseillaise', are not more weighty documents in the history of freedom than the songs of Burns.

Emerson drew heady comparisons with Rabelais, Shakespeare and Cervantes. 'If I should add another name,' he continued, 'I find it only in a living country-man of Burns.' (He was a great friend and admirer of Carlyle's.) The genius of Burns was exceptional, and for a curious reason:

> The people who care nothing for literature and poetry care for Burns . . . Yet how true a poet he is! And the poet, too, of poor men, of gray hodden and the guernsey coat and the blouse . . . And as he was thus the poet of the poor, anxious, cheerful, working humanity, so had he the language of low life . . . It seemed odious to Luther that the devil should have all the best tunes; he would bring them into the churches; and Burns knew how to take from friars and gypsies, blacksmiths and drovers, the speech of the market and the street, and clothe it with melody . . . [8]

Celebrations took place in fifty-nine other locations in the United States. We know this because they were chronicled in meticulous detail by an Edinburgh artist and man of letters called James Ballantine. England did slightly better with seventy-six meetings, the Colonies notched up forty-eight and Ireland ten; the occasion was also marked by Burnsians in Copenhagen. Ballantine recorded proudly that in Scotland itself the day was celebrated by six hundred and seventy-six events:

> The utmost enthusiasm pervaded all ranks and classes. Villages and hamlets, unnoticed in statistical reports, unrecorded in Gazetteers, had their dinners, suppers, and balls. City vied with clachan, peer with peasant, philanthropist with patriot, philosopher with statesman, orator with poet, in honouring the memory of the Ploughman Bard.[9] . . .

As the nineteenth century drew to a close, the apotheosis of Burns was well-nigh accomplished. In March 1885, a marble bust was placed in Poets' Corner in Westminster Abbey. It was unveiled by Gladstone's successor as Prime Minister, Lord Rosebery, and the name of the Prince of Wales stood at the head of the subscription list. The sculptor was the Aberdonian Sir John Steell, who had executed the marble figure for the Scott Monument in Edinburgh and who had been awarded a commission some years previously for a statue of Burns in New York's Central Park—the first outside Scotland. Bronze casts of this were made, one for Dundee, one for Dunedin, one for the Thames Embankment. This too had been unveiled by Rosebery, who delivered a speech arrestingly free of the sentimentality that was so often the hallmark of such occasions:

> It was not much for him to die so young; he died in noble company, for he died at the age which took away Raphael and Byron, the age which Lord Beaconsfield has called the fatal age of 37. After all, in life there is but a very limited stock of life's breath; some draw it in deep sighs and make an end; some draw it in quick draughts and have done with it; and some draw it placidly through four-score quiet years; but genius as a rule makes quick work with it. It crowds a lifetime into a few brief years, and then passes away, as if glad to be delivered of its message to the world, and glad to be delivered from an uncongenial sphere.[10]

In the heyday of Victorian prosperity a small army of likenesses in stone and bronze sprang up in Great Britain, North America and the southern hemisphere—not only statues, but plaques and roundels, panels in high and low relief, busts in bronze and plaster and wood and Sicilian marble. James Mackay, indefatigable auditor of the world's store of Burnsiana, believes that only Christopher Columbus and (in his day) Lenin have been more widely commemorated.

A bust had been installed in the Mercantile Library in St Louis, Missouri, in 1866; on Labour Day, 1877, a statue was unveiled by the Scottish community in the Australian gold-rush town of Ballarat. Burns attracted the attention of a number of nineteenth-century Italian sculptors. Fidardo Landi, a professor in the Academy of Fine Arts in Carrara, produced several busts—one of them found its way to the public library of Fall River in Massachussets. In the Scottish capital, the statue in marble commissioned from John Flaxman in 1824 took some time to find a permanent home. Originally sited in the Burns monument on Calton Hill, it was subsequently transferred to the University Library. The Principal, however, Dr John Lee, took exception to this on the ground that Burns was not a graduate. After some wrangling it was moved to the National Gallery of Scotland; finally, in 1889, it came to rest in the entrance hall of the newly-opened National Portrait Gallery, and that is where it stands today.

Burns seated, Burns standing to attention, Burns leaning on a stick, Burns sprawled on the fork of a tree. Life-size in Adelaide, eleven feet tall in San Francisco. Burns in plaid and breeches, Burns in the Fox livery of buff and blue; bare-headed and shirt-sleeved in Barre, Vermont, in Auckland he is got up in a tail coat and a Kilmarnock bonnet. In Aberdeen his expression is stern and dignified, in Central Park it is pained; he looks earnest in Ayr, vacant in Dumfries. Burns in the act of composition, Burns gazing at the evening star, Burns holding a bunch of daisies . . . The range is truly eclectic, although inevitably some are more successful than others. 'Undoubtedly the most pretentious of all Burns monuments,' writes James Mackay of the structure unveiled in Kilmarnock in 1879—'a fusion of Scots Baronial, neo-Gothic and Italianate, with a dash of Baroque and a hint of Romanesque'.[11]

The centenary of Burns's death in 1896 was also widely marked. At the Mausoleum in Dumfries, wreaths arrived from around the world. The one sent by Burnsians in New South Wales was somewhat delayed. It had been placed inside a block of ice and conveyed to Scotland in the refrigerated hold of a ship normally used for transporting frozen meat. It finally reached Dumfries by goods train early in August, and was met by the town band and a large crowd, but although it had by this time begun to melt, the block of ice in which the wreath was entombed was still too big to be got through the gateway of the Mausoleum.

There was an ambitious exhibition in Glasgow. It was held under the patronage of Queen Victoria and of a galaxy of the great and the good—dukes and marquesses, generals and archbishops, Lord Provosts and Members of Parliament, university principals and newspaper editors. Sir John Millais, then President of the Royal Academy, was an Honorary Vice-President, as was the historian W. E. H. Lecky; literature was represented by the oddly-assorted duo of Bret Harte and Algernon Swinburne. Lord Rosebery, whose premiership had ended so miserably the year before, accepted the honorary presidency; another patron was Andrew Carnegie—for many years it was *de rigueur* in the libraries he endowed in the United States (there were more than three thousand of them) to have a bust of Burns on display.

An unwieldy general committee was established. It included, as *ex-officio* members, not only the entire executive council of the Burns Federation, founded eleven years previously, but the presidents, vice-presidents and secretaries of all the clubs affiliated to it. These already numbered seventy—the Burns Haggis Club of Alloa and the Winnipeg St Andrew's Society, the St Rollox Jolly Beggars and the Scottish Thistle Club of San Francisco . . . Happily there was also a much smaller executive committee with a strong leavening of Glasgow lawyers and businessmen, and they saw to it that the exhibition was ready by the appointed day in July.

In the six galleries of the Royal Glasgow Institute of the Fine Arts in Sauchiehall Street the committee assembled a remarkable collection. There were books and manuscripts, portraits and pictures. The Trustees of the National Gallery of Scotland in Edinburgh declined for some reason to lend the original portrait for which Burns gave sittings to Nasmyth, but the Skirving drawing in red chalk was there, and McKenzie's portrait 'Bonnie Jean and Grandchild' attracted much attention.

The book section of the exhibition was a bibliographical feast. The organisers had managed to lay their hands on 696 different editions, issued by 243 publishers in thirty-two cities and towns of the United Kingdom (which at that time included the whole of Ireland)—303 editions in Scotland, 359 in England, thirty-four in Ireland. The editors of the catalogue expressed some disappointment at having been able to round up only some seventy editions from the United States:

> Only four of the greater cities are represented, while wealthy, populous, and progressive centres like Washington, Chicago, Cincinnati, San Francisco, St. Louis, and New Orleans do not appear at all. The presence in the list of relatively small places like Salem and Wilmington may be taken as evidence that Burns has been much more widely and frequently reprinted in the United States than would appear from this collection . . . [12]

There was also a section of translations and continental editions—Burns in Bohemian, Burns in Flemish, Burns in Hungarian, Burns in medieval Latin. Germany was strongly represented, and even the Old Enemy was catered for: *Burns in English,* translated from the Scottish Dialect by Alexander Corbett, Boston, 1892.

The most popular feature of the exhibition was the display of relics. A writer in the *Twentieth Century* in 1892 had poured scorn on the credulity of Church dignitaries in Rome who venerated such objects as a bottle of the Virgin's milk or a vial of the sweat of St Michael when he contended with Satan. Such excesses were clearly not to be expected in the land of Calvin and cakes, but the editors of the catalogue deemed it prudent to issue a mild disclaimer: 'Though no hall-mark of genuineness can be claimed on the ground of admission to the Exhibition, it is not to be supposed that any large proportion of the articles shown were of the nature of counterfeits."[13]

The crowds who thronged the large gallery found much to excite their interest. Here was the poet's excise ink bottle and the Bible he had read when he was at Brow Well; here was a draught-board he and Gilbert had used at Lochlea, and here was his masonic apron and the jewel he had worn as Depute Master of the St James' Lodge at Tarbolton. There were two of his razors, his blunderbuss and several locks of his hair; there was Jean's rolling pin, and a pair of her black silk embroidered stockings. John B. Morgan had lent the bolt and two hasps from the outer door of Clarinda's house; the Kilmarnock Burns Club had lent a small egg-cup made from the old rafters of the steading at Mossgiel; J. R. S. Hunter Selkirk, LL.D., had made several items available from his collection, including 'a piece of wood which formed part of a joist on which the bed rested on which Burns died.' 'All are redolent of his humanity—scarce one of his spirituality,' wrote Duncan McNaught, the then editor of the *Burns Chronicle:*

> Burns is no abstraction to his countrymen. His poetry is embalmed in their hearts, and his overshadowing personality pervades and is ever associated with it. Hence it is that everything connected, in the remotest degree, with his earthly pilgrimage is guarded by all sorts and conditions of men with a solicitude that is apt to evoke a smile from those outwith the pale of the national feeling.[14]

The 1890s saw important advances in Burns scholarship—much of it from outside that pale. In 1893 the Frenchman Auguste Angellier of the University of Lille brought out his magisterial two-part *Life and Works.* The first volume was a searching biographical study, the second considered Burns's poetry not only in its British context, but against a broader European background. To Angellier, Burns stands out in the literature of his native land as a somewhat isolated figure. In his view, he could find congenial literary asylum in the French tradition, and he draws interesting comparisons with poets of an earlier age like François Villon and Mathurin Régnier.[15]

In Britain the centenary was marked by two substantial works. William Wallace published his extensive revision of Dr Robert Chambers' four-volume study, first published in 1851-2, and Henley and Henderson produced a new text of the poems far superior to any that had previously appeared. The flamboyant Henley (Robert Louis Stevenson, a close friend, called him 'boisterous and piratic'—he was the model for Long John Silver), enlivened this Centenary edition with a brilliantly acerbic biographical essay, as readable today as it was in the closing years of Victoria's reign.

The German academic Hans Hecht, a godson of Brahms, published his excellent short biography in 1919.[16] After that, the centre of gravity of Burns scholarship shifted to North America, and the contributions made during the 1930s by such scholars as Franklin Bliss Snyder and J. De Lancey Ferguson have not been surpassed. Ferguson's edition of the *Letters* came out in 1931 and Snyder's *Life* the following year. Ferguson's original and penetrating study, *Pride and Passion,* which appeared on the eve of the Second World War, ended on a glum note: Burns's worshippers, he concluded, were ashamed of the best part of his nature and his work, and nobody else read him at all.

Ferguson was perhaps unduly despondent; academics sometimes are. His energetic fellow-countrymen did not see reading books and erecting statues as the only ways of paying homage to the bard. In St Louis, Missouri, there was a long-established Burns Cottage Association; in 1902 it had published a report of a project to build an exact replica of Burns's cottage at the Louisiana Purchase Exposition. During the First World War a young Scot called John Reith, later to become celebrated as the first director-general of the British Broadcasting Corporation, was despatched to the United States on a weapons procurement mission. Wounded in France, and with a vivid scar on his cheek to prove it, he found himself much fêted by the local business community in Philadelphia. On one occasion he stayed overnight with a wealthy family of Scottish descent. 'Next morning I was awakened by telephone at 5.30,' he noted in his diary. 'They showed me with great pride that the grounds immediately in front of the dining room were laid out in boxwood hedges and little paths the same pattern as behind Burns' cottage at Ayr.'[17]

From 1924 onwards Burns became widely known in the Soviet Union through the translations of Samuil Marshak. A friend of Gorki's and celebrated in Russia as a children's poet, Marshak also translated Shakespeare, Blake, Edward Lear and A. A. Milne; by the time he died in 1964, his translations of Burns had sold more than a million copies.

The poems became available in Icelandic in 1924, Rumanian in 1925 and Esperanto in 1926. (The Faroese had to wait till 1945, and the Albanians until the 1960s.) Their appeal was not confined to the English-speaking world and to Europe. 'In order to understand China,' the philosopher Lin Yutang wrote in 1935, 'one needs a little detachment and a little simplicity of mind too; that simplicity of mind so well typified by Robert Burns, one of the most Scottish and yet most universal of all poets.'[18]

Interest in the life and work of Burns continued at a high level in the inter-war years, even if changed economic conditions meant that he was now less frequently immortalised in stone.[19] There was no check, however, to the commercial exploitation of the Bard. Memorabilia in porcelain and pottery had begun to appear early in the nineteenth century. Burns's friends in Dumfries commissioned a splendid three-gallon punch-bowl and four whisky jugs from Spode as early as 1819, and ceramics remained attractive to those whose enthusiasm for Burns was tempered with some aesthetic sensibility—the Globe Inn in Dumfries still possesses a delightful Staffordshire flatback figure of Tam o'Shanter and Souter Johnny, for instance, and in the middle of the nineteenth century items of salt-glazed stoneware were also produced at Portobello and other Scottish potteries. Later, the flood of souvenirs and mementoes was swollen by all manner of printed ephemera—labels for whisky bottles, calendars, match boxes and cigarette cards, beer mats, T-shirts and the lids of shortbread tins.

In the twentieth century, as in the nineteenth, Burns has been hi-jacked for a range of political purposes. The authors of the *Great Soviet Encyclopedia* wrote about him as predictably as they did about Dickens. ('Burns, who had assimilated the progressive ideas of the Enlightenment, created an original form of poetry that was modern in spirit and content . . .') A pamphlet published in Vancouver in 1926 was entitled *Robert Burns, Patriot and Internationalist*. In Scotland, whenever there has been a revival of the fortunes of the Scottish National Party, some of its less sophisticated candidates have tended to evince a loud proprietary interest. In 1989, at the first Dumfries Burns Festival, an exhibition was mounted with the title 'For a' That'. It was advertised as having two aims—to shed new light on Burns, and to get more people thinking about contemporary art. One of the paintings on display depicted a newspaper billboard which proclaimed 'Robert Burns calls for Tougher Sanctions Against South Africa'.

Earlier, in the 1950s and 60s, he was the occasion of a controversy in which, improbably, philately became caught up in politics. A month after the 160th anniversary of Burns's death in 1956, the Soviet Union, rather mysteriously, issued a special 40-kopeck postage stamp. The British Post Office was notoriously conservative in the matter of commemorative issues, and when the Burns Federation and its many allies made a case for a stamp to mark the bicentenary of the birth, they came up against a brick wall.

Four years later, when it was announced that five stamps would be issued to mark the Shakespeare quatercentenary, Scottish tempers rose; in Ayrshire, the Stevenston Branch of the Scottish National Party produced a crudely-printed label decorated with the Lion rampant which read 'BOYCOTT THE SHAKESPEARE STAMPS! "NO PRECEDENT" FOR BURNS, WHY ONE FOR HIM?' The Labour government that came to power in 1964 adopted a more liberal policy, and two Burns stamps were eventually issued in 1966—in time, somewhat raggedly, to mark the 207th anniversary.

In more recent times Burnsians have had to brace themselves against the impact of feminism. A charity event at the Kelvingrove Galleries in Glasgow in January 1992 was billed as Scotland's first women-only Burns Supper, although some of those present thought this a misnomer and argued that it should be called a Jean Armour Supper. 'We are going to make it more sophisticated,' announced one of the organisers. Champagne was served in place of whisky. A few men in kilts were allowed to be present to serve the haggis.

Notes

[1] *Edinburgh Review,* xiii (January 1809), pp. 249-76.

[2] *Quarterly Review,* i, (February 1809), pp. 19-36.

[3] Letters, 112. This is the letter written from Carlisle in June 1787. See pp. 145-6 *supra.*

[4] Snyder, p. 488.

[5] *Edinburgh Review,* xlviii, no. xcvi, December 1828.

[6] The two men were very good friends. 'A beautiful little man,' Carlyle wrote of Jeffrey in his *Reminiscences,* 'and a bright island to me and mine in the sea of things.'

[7] Letter to George Lauder dated 30th May 1852, now in the Carnegie papers in the Library of Congress. Quoted in Joseph Frazier Wall, *Andrew Carnegie,* Oxford University Press, New York, 1970, p. 101.

[8] E. W. Emerson, (ed.) *Complete Works of Ralph Waldo Emerson,* Centenary Edition, Boston and New York, 1911, vol. xi, pp. 440-3. Margaret Fuller, Emerson's associate on the transcendentalist magazine the *Dial,* waxed even more rhapsodical: 'Since

Adam,' she wrote, 'there has been none that approached nearer fitness to stand up before God and angels in the naked majesty of manhood than Robert Burns.' (Quoted in Franklyn Bliss Snyder, *Robert Burns, His Personality, His Reputation and His Art,* University of Toronto Press, 1936, p. 77.)

[9] James Ballantine (comp. and ed.) *Chronicle of the Hundredth Birthday of Robert Burns,* A. Fullarton & Co., Edinburgh, 1859, p. 430. Ballantine (1808-77) began life as a house-painter. He later became interested in the revival of glass-painting, and was commissioned to execute the stained-glass windows in the House of Lords. He was also one of the so-called Whistle-binkie poets, who published collections of sentimental songs and poems.

[10] Robert Rhodes James, *Rosebery,* Weidenfeld and Nicolson, London, 1963, p. 213.

[11] James A. Mackay, *Burnsiana,* Alloway Publishing Ltd., Ayr, 1988, p. 36.

[12] *Memorial Catalogue of the Burns Exhibition,* William Hodge & Company and T. R. Annan & Sons, Glasgow, 1898, p. 196.

[13] *Ibid.,* p. 92. A substantial number of the Burns letters which passed through the auction rooms in the 1880s and 1890s turned out to be forgeries, many of them the work of an Edinburgh man called Alexander H. Smith. This enterprising citizen (he became known as 'Antique' Smith) managed to keep one step ahead of the law for quite some time.

[14] *Ibid.,* pp. 91-2.

[15] Villon, (c. 1431-1463), thief and murderer as well as poet, would easily find a place in *The Jolly Beggars.* He is remembered especially for his *Grand Testament* and for his *Ballade des dames du temps jadis,* with its celebrated refrain, *'Mais où sont les neiges d'antan?'* The life of Régnier (1573-1613) was less violent but equally dissipated. A disciple of Ronsard and a forerunner of Molière, he was a stylish and penetrating satirist. Burns would have approved of the licence he permitted himself in his language and of many of his sentiments: *'C'est honte de vivre et de n'être amoureux'*—'it is shameful to live and not be in love.'

[16] *Robert Burns, Leben und Wirken des schottischen Volksdichters,* Carl Winter, Heidelberg. There is an excellent English translation by Jane Lymburn, first published in 1936 by William Hodge and Co. Alloway Publishing Ltd. of Ayr brought out a new edition in 1981.

[17] Entry for 16 May 1916, Reith Diaries, BBC Writ-

ten Archives Centre, Caversham.

[18] Lin Yutang, *My Country and My People,* New York, 1935. Another Chinese Burnsian, Dr. Wen Yuan-Ning, visiting Britain as a member of a Chinese goodwill parliamentary mission towards the end of the Second World War, was invited to propose the Immortal Memory in a BBC radio programme. Burns's treatment of common incidents and feelings, he said, reminded him very much of the poetry of his own country. ('Robert Burns: Songs and Poems to Celebrate the Anniversary of the Poet's Birth', BBC Home Service, 9.40 p.m., 25th January 1944.)

[19] There were exceptions. James Mackay notes that Cheyenne, Wyoming, boasts an elegant bronze on a granite pedestal, erected in 1929; it was presented by Mary Gemmell Gilchrist, the widow of one of Wyoming's most colourful cattle-barons—and a native of Ayrshire. An enormous Burns Memorial was also put up in Canberra, Australia, in 1935. (Mackay, *Burnsiana, op. cit.,* p. 46.)

FURTHER READING

Bibliography

Egerer, J. W. *A Bibliography of Robert Burns.* Carbondale: Southern Illinois University Press, 1965, 396 p.

> Impressive list documents first appearances of Burns's poetry and prose up to 1802, and most editions of his works up to 1953.

Reid, J. B., ed. *A Complete Word and Phrase Concordance to the Poems and Songs of Robert Burns.* 1889. Reprint. New York: B. Franklin, 1968, 568 p.

> With glossary of Scottish words, notes, index, and appendix of readings.

Biography

Carswell, Catherine. *The Life of Robert Burns.* London: Chatto & Windus, 1930, 467 p.

> Often scorned for its lack of documentation, a sympathetic and highly readable account of Burns's life.

Daiches, David. *Robert Burns and His World.* London: Thames and Hudson, 1971, 128 p.

> Lavishly illustrated work treats Burns's life and career; bibliography and chronology included.

Douglas, Hugh. *Robert Burns: The Tinder Heart.* Gloucestershire: Alan Sutton Publishing Ltd, 1996, 299 p.

Biography with index of poems and songs and bibliography.

Snyder, Franklyn Bliss. *The Life of Robert Burns.* 1932. Reprint. Hamden Conn.: Archon Books, 1968, 524 p.

> Highly acclaimed biography eschews anecdotal material for "verifiable fact."

Criticism

Beaty, Frederick L. "The Necessity of Marriage: Burns and Wordsworth." In his *Light From Heaven: Love in British Romantic Literature,* pp. 59-80. Dekalb: Northern Illinois University Press, 1971.

> Examines Burns's wide-ranging and sometimes contradictory views on matrimony as expressed in his poems and letters.

Crawford, Thomas. "Maturity." In his *Burns: A Study of the Poems and Songs,* pp. 217-56. Edinburgh and London: Oliver and Boyd, 1960.

> Examines "Tam o'Shanter" and Burns's democratic poems and politics.

Damrosch, Jr., Leopold. "Burns, Blake, and the Recovery of Lyric." *Studies in Romanticism* 21, no. 4 (Winter 1982): 637-60.

> Asserts that Burns's merging of his own experience with Scottish folk tradition enabled the poet "to be personal and impersonal at once."

Jack, R. D. S. and Andrew Noble, eds. *The Art of Robert Burns.* London: Vision Press, 1982, 240 p.

> Collection of essays examines Burns's lyrics, satires, poems, and epistles, as well as his careful cultivation of his image.

Kinsley, James. "The Music of the Heart." *Renaissance and Modern Studies* 8 (1964): 5-52.

> Examines Burns's "personal and passionate" interest in songs and his "patriotic mission" to recover, interpret, and compile the old folk songs of Scotland.

Low, Donald A., ed. *Robert Burns: The Critical Heritage.* London: Routledge & Kegan Paul, 1974, 447 p.

> Ambitious and invaluable collection of contemporaneous and near-contemporaneous criticism.

———. *Critical Essays on Robert Burns.* London: Routledge and Kegan Paul, 1975, 191 p.

> Important collection of essays covers Burns's life, work, and audience.

———. "Values, Voice and Verse Form." In his *Robert Burns,* pp. 31-57. Edinburgh: Scottish Academic Press, 1986.

> Considers Burns's motivation in writing selected works.

McGuirk, Carol. *Robert Burns and the Sentimental Era.*
Athens: The University of Georgia Press, 1985, 193 p.
　Considers Burns in terms of the sentimental.

Snyder, Franklin Bliss. *Robert Burns: His Personality,
His Reputation and His Art.* 1936. Reprint. Port
Washington, N.Y.: Kennikat Press, 1970, 119 p.
　Examines Burns's personality, reputation, and art.
　Snyder concludes that, although the poet was a
　national genius, his works also show evidence of
　craftsmanship.

**Additional coverage of Burns's life and career is contained in the following sources
published by Gale Research:** *Literature Criticism from 1400 to 1800,* **Vols. 3 and
29, and** *Poetry Criticism,* **Vol. 6.**

William Collins

1721-1759

English poet.

The following entry contains critical essays focusing on Collins's relationship to Preromanticism. For further information on Collins, see *LC*, Vol. 4.

INTRODUCTION

Collins is considered one of the most important transitional Preromantic figures in English poetry. While employing in his works elements of the neoclassical style used by his peers, he foreshadowed many of the themes and techniques characteristic of the Romantic period. Included among the best of the lyric poets of the eighteenth century, Collins is acclaimed for his experimentation with the ode, his descriptions of human emotions, and the vivid personifications found in his imagery.

Biographical Information

Little is known about any phase of Collins's life. His father was a haberdasher and the mayor of Chichestor. When Collins was eleven years old he was admitted into Winchester College, where he published his first poems in periodicals. Studying under the aid of a demyship (scholarship), he spent two years at Magdalen College, Oxford, and earned a Bachelor's degree in art. In 1742 he published *Persian Eclogues*, which attracted much public attention; after anonymously publishing *Verses Humbly Address'd to Sir Thomas Hanmer* in the following year, he abandoned his demyship and devoted his full energy to writing. He moved to London, where he spent lavishly and ran up large debts. After moving to the Richmond area to escape his creditors he met and became a close friend of the poet James Thomson. Under Thomson's influence Collins began to rework his poems, concentrating on the ode form. In 1746 he published *Odes on Several Descriptive and Allegoric Subjects*, a collection which is now considered his finest work, although at the time it received almost no notice. In 1749 he began his last poem, "An Ode on the Popular Superstitions of the Highlands," but in 1750 he suffered his first mental breakdown, the start of a ten-year decline during which he was not able to complete any work. In 1759 he died with "An Ode on the Popular Superstitions of the Highlands" still unfinished.

Major Works

Collins published a relatively small amount of work during his lifetime. A few newly discovered pieces which are credited as early work by Collins have been published in *Drafts and Fragments*. His first published volume, *Persian Eclogues*, owed its popularity at the time to its exotic setting and descriptions. Collins later revised these poems, republishing them under the title *Oriental Eclogues* in 1757. The work for which he is best known, *Odes on Several Descriptive and Allegoric Subjects*, contains two of his most famous poems, "Ode to Evening" and "Ode to Fear." These poems contain many of the elements which characterize his work: strong emotional descriptions, the newly worked ode form, and a personal relationship to the subject. Collins's last poem, "Ode on the Popular Superstitions of the Highlands of Scotlands," although unfinished, is considered one of his greatest works, hinting at his literary potential. His approach to the natural world, his treatment of the artistic self, and his inventive language foreshadow the nineteenth-century introspective poetry which would follow him.

Critical Reception

The central issue of contention among critics of Collins's work is whether to classify him as an eighteenth-century neoclassical poet or as a prophet for the nineteenth-century Romantic movement. Some scholars believe that he is both, embodying enough of the rationality and restraint of the earlier age to be identified with his contemporaries, while foreshadowing the Romantic period with his experiments in the ode form and the new personal element in his descriptions. Critics do agree that Collins wrote most of his important poetry between 1744 and 1746 and that *Odes on Several Descriptive and Allegoric Subjects* marks a certain maturity in his writing style. Such odes as "Pity," "Fear," "Liberty," and "Evening" reveal his intense concern with personal experience. Critics perceive this quality as a foremost attribute of Collins's verse and one which influenced not only such contemporaries as Thomas Gray, but also such nineteenth-century writers as Samuel Taylor Coleridge, William Wordsworth, and William Blake. Much has also been written about Collins's mental illness, particularly in speculation about how this influenced his skill at describing emotions. Because of the small volume of his work which has survived, Collins is perceived by many scholars as an unfortunate genius whose vast potential can only be guessed. Algernon Charles Swinburne summarized the *Odes* as "above all things, a purity of music, a clarity of style, to which I know of no parallel in English verse from the death of Andrew Marvell to the birth of William Blake."

PRINCIPAL WORKS

"Sonnet" [as Delicatulus] (poetry) 1739; published in journal *Gentleman's Magazine*

*Persian Eclogues (poetry) 1742; revised edition, 1757

**Verses Humbly Address'd to Sir Thomas Hanmer on His Edition of Shakespear's Works (poetry) 1743

Odes on Several Descriptive and Allegoric Subjects (poetry) 1746

An Ode Occasion'd by the Death of Mr. Thomson (poetry) 1749

The Passions, an Ode (poetry) 1750

The Poetical Works of Mr. William Collins: With Memoirs of the Author; and Observations on His Genius and Writings (poetry) 1765

***An Ode on the Popular Superstitions of the Highlands of Scotland, etc. (poetry) 1898

The Works of William Collins (poetry and letters) 1979

**This work was also published as *Oriental Eclogues*.

***This work was also published as *An Epistle: Addrest to Sir Thomas Hanmer, on His Edition of Shakespear's Works* in 1744.
****This work was written in 1749. A posthumous edition of the poem appeared in 1788 with revisions now generally considered spurious.

CRITICISM

Walter C. Bronson (essay date 1898)

SOURCE: An introduction to *The Poems of William Collins*, Ginn & Company, 1898, pp. xi-lxiv.

[*In the following essay, Bronson argues that Collins foreshadowed the Romantic movement and shares more with such later poets as John Keats and Percy Bysshe Shelley than with his contemporaries Alexander Pope and Samuel Johnson.*]

. . . Collins's fame was slow in coming, partly because he outran the literary taste of his age. He was a pioneer in Romanticism, and the public and the critics were not yet ready for Romanticism. Collins was a romanticist by nature, in temperament and type of mind ranging rather with Shelley and Keats than with Addison, Pope, or Johnson. But he was not wholly a romanticist; elements of a true Classicism were deep within him. And he fell upon times in which a pseudo-classical ideal predominated. The history of his poetic development is the resultant of the three forces indicated, of which the last rapidly declined, and the second remained about stationary, while the first steadily increased.

If Collins had not written a line, we should still have known that he sympathized deeply with the new movement which was beginning to transform literature in England. One evidence of this is the attitude of his friend Joseph Warton, who in the preface to his own odes affirmed the conviction that "the fashion of moralizing in verse has been carried too far," and that "invention and imagination" are "the chief faculties of a poet."[2] When it is remembered how intimate the two men were, and that their first intention had been to publish their odes jointly, we may fairly assume that the preface expressed the views of Collins as well.

From Thomas Warton we learn that Collins was fond of black-letter reading and had collected many rare old books illustrating the earlier periods of English literature.[3] His enthusiasm for the Renaissance, and his long-cherished plan of writing a history of the Revival of Learning, also indicate his sympathy with the earlier Romanticism. And, finally, Johnson's half-mournful description of his friend's romantic tendencies shows that this man, born when Pope was in the heyday of his power, and dying when Johnson ruled literary London with a bludgeon of common sense, was yet brother to Spenser, to the youthful Milton, to Chatterton and Blake, to the many ill-regulated enthusiasts and poetic dreamers of the early nineteenth century.[4]

When we turn to the poems themselves, we see in them an interesting struggle between Collins's natural romantic tendencies, his natural classic tendencies, and the literary conventions of the day.

The early minor poems all show, in varying degrees, the lyric instinct which had become so rare amid the prevailing didacticism in English verse. In the songs about Fidele and Damon the romantic elements of love, nature, and the supernatural are handled with simplicity and truth; while the introduction of folklore in the former is a prophecy of the *Ode to Fear* and the *Ode on the Popular Superstitions of the Highlands*. The obvious elements of conventionalism in these slight poems do not call for special remark.

In the *Oriental Eclogues* the struggle between conventional form and new subject-matter is patent. The artificial pastoral was not yet quite dead in England; it had been kept alive by the mighty names of Vergil, Spenser, and Milton, and recently by the example of Pope. It was, therefore, natural enough that the youthful Collins should write pastorals. What is noteworthy is that he sought for new metal to pour into the time-worn moulds, and anticipated Southey, Byron, and Moore in turning to the Orient for poetic material. The result, it must be admitted, is tame; but the mildness of the romantic flavor is easily explained. Salmon's *History of Persia,* from which Collins got his inspiration, although sensible and mildly interesting, is not imaginative or picturesque; and Collins showed that he was greatly athirst by sucking from it as much romance as he did. But even if the poet had had a richer treasury, he would not have dared to display its stores more freely. The apologetic tone of the preface is significant. Collins was evidently afraid that the "rich and figurative style" and the "elegancy and wildness of thought" might offend the taste of his readers. Romanticism was yet a timid thing in England.[5] Modern readers find the *Oriental Eclogues* less wild than wooden; for there is much that is conventional, not only in the style and verse, but even in the subject-matter and spirit. A didactic motive is apparent throughout, as in the handling of similar material by Addison and Johnson. The truism that virtue is essential to lasting love and happiness, and the hackneyed themes of pastoral love and rural delights, constitute the warp and woof of the first and third eclogues, and enter largely into the texture of the other two. Oriental love, which was to receive such sensuous treatment later at the hands of Byron and Moore, is kept within the bounds of a decent tameness. Even the fact of polygamy is politely ignored. Only one Zara weeps for the distant Hassan; and Abbas, the Persian monarch, might have been an English gentleman except for a little initial despotism

in his manner of appropriating the rustic Abra. The fine opportunities for pictorial effect in the second eclogue are imperfectly developed, although the local coloring here is the best in the series; the novel situation in the desert is made subordinate to shallow moralizing, current at the time, about the evils of "trade." Similarly, in the fourth eclogue, the scenic possibilities of midnight in devastated Circassia are largely sacrificed to commonplaces of pastoral description. In brief, the *Oriental Eclogues* are significant in the history of English Romanticism rather for their tendencies than for their achievement.

In the *Epistle Addressed to Sir Thomas Hanmer* the occasion overrode the poet. The result was the least individual of Collins's poems. The epistolary form, the conventional metre and style, the gross flattery, the half-blind estimate of Shakspere,—in all these Collins was hardly more than an amanuensis for the spirit of the age. Yet even in this poem may be detected some signs of the individuality of the man who was soon to write the *Odes Descriptive and Allegorical*. The references to Greek literature and the Renaissance are significant. The allusions to Shakspere's idyllic plays and to the fairyland of *A Midsummer-Night's Dream* and *The Tempest* remind one of the *Song from Shakespear's Cymbeline* and of the delicate Arcadian fancy in several of the odes. And the instinct for the sculpturesque and picturesque, soon to be revealed in the *Odes,* is suggested here also by the wish that painters would go to Shakspere for subjects and by the vivid sketches of two great scenes from the plays.

In the *Odes* of 1747 we pass into a new atmosphere. Here the influence of convention sinks to a subordinate place, and classic and romantic tendencies become dominant. The literary fashions of the day linger here and there in diction and phrasing, in an occasional frigid personification, and in the literary or political didacticism which underlies several of the odes; but over these matters we need not linger. The classic and the romantic elements require more detailed examination. We will begin with the latter.

In these odes Collins reveals his poetical creed by his literary allusions. Spenser and his school, Shakspere, Milton, Otway—that belated Elizabethan,—these are the gods of his idolatry among English poets; while he speaks slightingly of the then popular Waller, and implies that pathos is a lost note in the British lyre. His practice conforms to his theory. The *Odes,* in their main effect, are not intellectual and didactic, but imaginative, pictorial, and lyrical. They are not chiefly to be thought out, but to be looked at, felt, and sung. The versification is an index to the spirit of the whole. The end-stopped pentameter couplet of the *Eclogues* and the *Epistle,* a form so admirable for narration, exposition, or satire, so ill-adapted for lyric flow, has given place to a variety of measures that fitly embody the subject-matter.

But it is the subject-matter itself which most clearly shows the poet's trend toward Romanticism. Collins was, literally, a visionary. He saw visions. He lived in a world of imaginary beings, some beautiful, some terrible, some the creation of folklore and legend, and some the product of his own imagination. If the *Odes* be read rapidly, with this single point in view, it is surprising how constantly the poet's thought escapes from reality to an imaginary world. Even *The Manners,* in praise of the observation of the real world, is all compact of fancies about "wizard Passions," "giant Follies," and "magic shores." *The Passions* is didactic in intent, praising the simplicity of Greek music above the complex music of modern times. But the lesson is a picture. And in place of the historical Alexander in Dryden's similar ode, Collins painted a new Pandemonium and Elysium in one, where bedlam Passions mingle with the Loves and Graces. The political and military events of the day, passing through this poet's mind, are transformed into a dream-land peculiarly his own, where ideal figures stand out in colossal bas-relief, as in the *Ode to Mercy,* or, as in the *Ode to a Lady* and *How Sleep the Brave,* shadowy forms at once delicate and majestic mourn over the graves of the heroic dead.

But the *Ode to Fear,* the *Ode to Liberty,* and the *Ode on the Poetical Character* are richest in elements of the supernatural or semi-supernatural. In the beginning of the last-named, Collins's imagination manifestly revels in the marvellous legend of the magic girdle; he is wandering amid the mazes of *The Faerie Queene.* The description of creation, an echo from the idealism of Plato and Spenser, beats with an inward heat, an intense pleasure in the fantastic richness of the picture. And the ideal landscape with which the ode ends had its inspiration in a reverence, amounting almost to worship, for Milton as the poet of the supernatural sublime. The antistrophe of the *Ode to Liberty* shows how well Collins knew the poetic value of old legends and traditions; the fabled disruption of Britain from the mainland is thoroughly romantic in its rugged wildness and a certain element of the monstrous; while the second epode is rich with imaginative beauty deriving from old Celtic sources. The *Ode to Fear* marks the climax of the supernatural element in these *Odes* of 1747. A true imaginative shudder runs through the whole. It is conceived and expressed throughout with a vigor which shows that the poet had himself lifted "the veil between" and was looking out with pleasurable awe into the dim, vast realm of imaginative Terror and the dark Sublime. From the classic drama he selects those aspects which are most closely allied to the murkiness of the "Gothic" mind; and the conception, in the strophe, of fiends who "over Nature's wrecks and wounds preside" is essentially Teutonic, the counterpart of the Greek belief in fair spirits, the guardian divinities of mountains, trees, and running brooks.

The treatment of nature in the *Odes* is not remarkable except in the *Ode to Evening.* A French critic has recently observed that in this poem Collins anticipated the work of the modern "impressionist" school; and he points out that "the phenomena of evening, which dissolve progressively all natural form and destroy the solidity of every object," are peculiarly adapted for treatment in accordance with the doctrine of the impressionists that "things are more poetic by their aspects than by their forms, and by their colors than by their substance."[6]

But curious as this anticipation is, it concerns us more just now to ask what relation the poem bore to Collins's own environment and to the rest of his work. It must have had a close relation, although it seems so unique. It cannot have been a literary freak, a poem-child of the nineteenth century born out of due time.

What view of the matter did Collins himself probably take? It is not likely that he supposed he was doing anything unusual. And in a way he was not. It is singular that this poem, in the last stanza, is marred by worse conventionalism than can be found elsewhere in the *Odes.* Furthermore, the mood of the poem is common enough. Eventide, when all things are idealized by dimness and calm, is Nature's popular poetry, felt by the most callous, and disposing every one to pensiveness and repose. Nor does the ode show minute or subtle observation, such as distinguishes much of the nature poetry of the present century. The objects and aspects described are obvious and common. The exquisite fineness in the poem is fineness of feeling and expression, not of perception. We should not expect Collins, the dreamer and visionary, to have a particularly keen eye for the facts of the external world. And in this poem, as elsewhere, he was more dreaming than seeing; or, more accurately, he *was* seeing, but only because in this case seeing and dreaming were nearly one, nature at twilight creating a fairy world much like his own land of dreams. In other words, Collins did know and greatly love the common phenomena of evening, for the reason that they were peculiarly congenial to his mood and closely akin to that imaginary world in which his fancy loved to dwell.

As confirming this view, note how Collins mingles in the poem the facts of nature with his own and others' fancies. The sun and the hours are persons, as in old mythology. Elves, and nymphs who shed the dew, and Pensive Pleasures sweet, prepare Evening's shadowy car. Even the conventional personifications with which the poem ends show only the same tendency carried farther; fancy banishes fact altogether, and nothing is left but the group of wooden abstractions, stiffly sitting in the "sylvan shed." This sorry ending is simply a striking proof of the fact that Collins, in this poem, had no thought of making an objective study of nature, still less of founding a new school of nature poetry. He was not trying, in Wordsworth's phrase, to keep his eye "steadily on the object." Rather he was attracted instinctively to the dreamy aspects of twilight, partly for their own sake, and partly because they made so poetic a habitation for the creatures of his imagination.; and so he wrote a poem in which the two series of facts, the real and the imaginary, freely intermingled, although they never became identified. In all this there was nothing new in kind. He was simply at his old trick of dreaming again, only in this instance it was evening, instead of the wars on the continent or the literature of terror, that supplied the inspiration and part of the material.

If this be true, we should expect to find it true at the core of the poem, in the conception of evening itself. And it is true there. Throughout the ode, *Evening* and *evening* are distinct, and Collins's attention is divided between the two. Whole stanzas are given up to natural description, without the slightest immediate reference to Evening the person. At other times Evening is directly addressed, but rather frigidly and in terms which only in the most general way suggest a connection with the objective facts; as "chaste Eve," "nymph reserved," "maid composed," "calm votaress," and "meekest Eve." In a few places the relation is more intimate, and the personification more imaginative, notably in

> Prepare thy shadowy car,

and in

> marks o'er all
> Thy dewy fingers draw
> The gradual dusky veil.

But the person and the phenomena are never completely fused, as might have happened had Collins been wholly absorbed in picturing the scenes of the real world at evening time. Keats, in his ode to Autumn, was thus absorbed in catching up into words the subtle spirit of the "season of mists and mellow fruitfulness," and he has identified Autumn the person with autumn the season. Autumn in his poem is no sturdy matron with sickle and sheaf. She is the haunting spirit of the "granary floor," the "half-reaped furrow," and the oozing cider-press. She has no fixed body, but many flitting incarnations, in which "whoever seeks abroad" may catch glimpses of her very essence. In the *Ode to Evening* there is no such inner unity. Collins was at once describing the appearances of nature at his favorite hour of twilight and writing an ode to the personified spirit of the hour. The spirit was as real to him as the hour, and probably he would not have cared to identify the two. The thought of a semi-supernatural being, beautiful, ethereal, the goddess-queen of twilight, dim-flitting in delicate majesty through her shadowy realm, was of just the sort to captivate the imag-

ination of Collins. He must have loved with delicate intensity the natural phenomena of evening; but they doubtless took on additional charm when he thought of them as the drapery and chariot and dim fairyland of the mystic Spirit of Twilight. And so it probably never occurred to him that this poem on evening was materially different in motive or method from his other odes. Just as in the *Ode to Fear* he pictured an imaginary world of terror as the dwelling-place for his "mad nymph," so in the *Ode to Evening* he merely took, ready made to his hand by nature, the world of twilight as the realm of his "maid composed."

The poem has, therefore, a perfectly definite and normal relation to the qualities of Collins's mind and to his usual poetic method. Wherein, then, does its uniqueness consist? Precisely in this happy combination of delicate fancy with delicate fact, and in the singular felicity with which the elusive, dissolving appearances of twilight are described in words as magical as themselves. In short, the right subject had found the right poet.

In its relation to Romanticism the *Ode to Evening* is as remarkable in one way as the *Ode to Fear* is in another. The descriptive parts of the poem are entirely romantic in their intense though delicate passion for some of the loveliest aspects of nature, and in the fidelity, born of love, with which those aspects are delineated. It is interesting to compare the ode with the description of evening in the third eclogue:

> While ev'ning dews enrich the glitt'ring glade,
> And the tall forests cast a longer shade.[7]

The lines are as conventional as they well could be; they show memory of other poets' phrases, not observation of the real world. Contrast with them these lines from the ode:

> But when chill blust'ring winds, or driving
>   rain,
> Forbid my willing feet, be mine the hut
>   That from the mountain's side
>   Views wilds, and swelling floods,
>
> And hamlets brown, and dim-discover'd
>   spires,
> And hears their simple bell, and marks o'er all
>   Thy dewy fingers draw
>   The gradual dusky veil.

At the time when the *Persian Eclogues* were written, Collins must already have learned to know and love the sights and sounds of evening; but he had not yet felt that it was worth while, in poetry, to try to paint the appearances of nature as faithfully as possible, and that in fact anything else in descriptions of nature was hardly worth doing at all. When, in the *Ode to Evening,* he reached that point, not by theory but by instinct and by happy accident in choice of subject, he had taken a step which English poetry in general was to take some years later.

The Classicism in the poetry of Collins is, at first glance, even more apparent than the Romanticism. It is present in all the poems, from earliest to latest, but may be most conveniently studied in the *Odes* of 1747, where it reached its highest development.

Collins's love for genuine classic art receives direct expression in the *Ode to Simplicity,* which draws its inspiration from Greek literature and not from the frigid Classicism of the age of Queen Anne. The same backward look appears in the many other allusions to Greek literature, art, and history. Collins's admiration for Milton, which is shown by frequent Miltonic echoes in style even more than by direct praise, resulted naturally from the combination of the classic and the romantic in his own ideal; for Milton came nearer to realizing such an ideal than any other English poet. It was natural that a poet of Collins's tastes and literary environment, groping about for a richer poetic method, yet appreciating all that was good in the classical ideals of the day and drawn powerfully towards the truer Classicism of ancient art, should turn to the author of *Lycidas* and *Paradise Lost* as his exemplar and guide. The last of the great Elizabethans satisfied at once his love of classic finish and his hunger for richness, imagination, and lofty passion.

In practice Collins's classic instincts appear partly in a certain restraint in the handling of romantic subject-matter, which he never allows to run away with him into extravagance or disproportion. This restraint was the easier, however, because his romantic material was comparatively meagre and tame. But his Classicism appears chiefly in constant qualities of verse, style, and general manner. The *Odes* are characterized by a repose, an economy of expression, and a purity of outline which suggest Greek sculpture, the pictures of Raphael, or the tapestries of Mantegna. Even where the style is involved, as in some of the longer odes, the total effect is simple—the threads may be curiously interwoven, but the resulting figure is clear and restful; while many of the shorter odes have the snow-pure limbs of a statue fresh from the sculptor's chisel. The versification of the *Odes* is finished and careful. Collins exercised considerable freedom in the choice of stanza-forms; but, having chosen them, he adhered to them. Within the individual line he admitted but few variations, and those usually consisted merely of a shifting of accent in the first foot. A freedom in the placing of cæsuras, never degenerating into license or caprice, contributes its part to the total effect of Collins's verse at its best, an effect which may be briefly described as a combination of polish with variety, richness, and ease.

The *Ode on the Death of Mr. Thomson,* published two years and a half later than the *Odes* of 1747, bears evidence that Collins had not gone backward in his poetic development. In their sincerity and naturalness the verses are separated by a great gulf from the conventional elegy of the day. In feeling and manner they are purely lyric; something of the motion of the "lorn stream" itself flows in gentle sadness through the lines. The world of legend and fancy in which Collins loved to wander gleams out here and there—in the name of "druid" given to Thomson, in the allusion to the harp of Æolus, in the foot-note referring to Thomson's most romantic poem; while the lines

> And see, the fairy valleys fade;
> Dun night has veil'd the solemn view,

recall the *Ode to Evening* in their combination of fancy with one of the most romantic phases of nature.

But it is not till we turn to the *Ode on the Popular Superstitions of the Highlands of Scotland* that we realize how far Collins had advanced in the theory and practice of Romanticism during the three years that followed the publication of the earlier *Odes*.

Scattered through the poem are several expressions showing the belief now held by Collins about the new class of subjects for poetry. Something of the old apologetic tone lingers still. He thinks it necessary to exhort Home, "though learned," not to forget the "homelier thoughts" of the "untutored swain." He props up the cause of Romanticism by citing the examples of Tasso, Fairfax, Spenser, and Shakspere. And in one instance he adopts language still more apologetic:

> Nor need'st thou blush, that such false themes
>   engage
> Thy gentle mind, of fairer stores possest.

But it would appear that in these passages Collins was merely seeking to conciliate his opponents in poetic theory; for in other lines he shows enthusiastic faith in the poetic value of the new subject-matter, and makes a just distinction between the imaginative and the false:

> Let thy sweet Muse the rural faith sustain:
> These are the themes of simple, sure effect,
> That add new conquests to her boundless
>   reign,
> And fill, with double force, her heart-
>   commanding strain.
> In scenes like these, which, daring to depart
> From sober truth, are still to nature true.

It is evident that Collins had even come to realize that it was just this kind of food which his own genius had needed for its full development; and there is a touch of pathos in his gentle envy of Home for having the good fortune to be born in "Fancy's land," far from the barren conventionalism of literary England:

Fresh to that soil thou turn'st, whose ev'ry
   vale
Shall prompt the poet, and his song demand:
To thee thy copious subjects ne'er shall fail;
Thou need'st but take the pencil to thy hand,
And paint what all believe who own thy
   genial land.

Still more remarkable is the absence of the didactic point of view. In the *Eclogues,* and even in the *Odes* of 1747, didacticism still clung to the skirts of the poet's magic mantle. In this ode the superstitions of the Highlands are not recommended because they could be used to point a moral, but wholly for their intrinsic poetical qualities. They "call forth fresh delight to Fancy's view." These themes of "simple, sure effect" are valued because they can the "answering bosom pierce." Fairfax's poetry is praised, not because it taught truth and morality, but because "at each sound imagination glows" and the verse "fills the impassioned heart and wins the harmonious ear." Here is advance indeed since the days of the *Persian Eclogues,* when Hassan's camels were hitched to the dog-cart of a prudential morality.

Most significant of all is the imaginative abandon with which Collins throws himself into these superstitions of the North. This is particularly noticeable in the stanzas about the water-fiend and his hapless victim. Even the theory of Romanticism is for a time forgotten; and the ghost of the drowned man, with "blue-swollen face," and "shivering cold," stands before the mind's eye with all the vividness and realism of popular superstition.

This part of the ode, and the sketch of the simple inhabitants of St. Kilda, also anticipated in some degree that sympathetic and truthful portrayal of the lives of the poor which was to characterize so much of the poetry of Burns, Crabbe, and Wordsworth. The picture of island life is of course roseate compared with the stern realism of *The Parish Register* or the poetic homeliness of *Michael;* but in comparison with the conventional descriptions of rural life in the *Persian Eclogues* it shows a considerable advance in naturalness and truth.

Collins's own style and method reveal the same progress in Romanticism. The stanza is a rather shapeless and clumsy enlargement of the Spenserian; and the style at times is decidedly Spenser-like in diffuse picturesqueness or in delicate luxury of color:

For, watchful, lurking 'mid th' unrustling reed,
At those mirk hours the wily monster lies,
And listens oft to hear the passing steed,
And frequent round him rolls his sullen eyes,
If chance his savage wrath may some weak
   wretch surprise.

Yet frequent now, at midnight's solemn hour,
The rifted mounds their yawning cells unfold,
And forth the monarchs stalk with sov'reign
   pow'r,
In pageant robes, and wreath'd with sheeny
   gold,
And on their twilight tombs aërial council
   hold.

In not a few lines Collins has followed his own advice to Home to suit his style to his romantic subject-matter and "proceed in forceful sounds and colours bold." An instance occurs in the third stanza:

At ev'ry pause, before thy mind possest,
Old Runic bards shall seem to rise around,
With uncouth lyres, in many-colour'd vest,
Their matted hair with boughs fantastic
   crown'd.

The style of the poem as a whole strikes one as having more of romantic warmth and dash, and less of classical finish, than any other of Collins's odes; but, as regards the comparative lack of finish, it should be remembered that we have only an imperfect first draught.

The limitations and the distinctive quality of the Romanticism in the poetry of Collins have already been implied; but they may now be briefly stated. Many of the romantic aspects of nature, the picturesque in humble life, the picturesque in the feudal past, and the whole world of concrete human passion and struggle either are entirely absent from Collins's verse or receive only incidental and rudimentary treatment. His Romanticism was that of an idealist with strong classical tendencies, and anything which does not blend readily with the classical and the ideal could not enter his pages. It is a tempting problem what would have been his poetical development had he lived, with faculties unimpaired, for a generation longer. On the one hand, his letter in 1750, in its reference to his new ode on the music of the Grecian theatre, shows how highly he still valued "correct" composition modelled upon the Greek classics. On the other hand, so rapid had been his progress in Romanticism during the brief interval between the *Odes* of 1747 and the *Ode on the Popular Superstitions of the Highlands* that it is probable that he would have moved with ever increasing speed toward the bolder and wider Romanticism reached even in his own century by Chatterton and Blake.

The influence of Collins upon the development of the Romantic Movement in England was indefinite and slight. This was chiefly due to the loss, for more than a generation, of his most romantic poem. Had the *Ode on the Popular Superstitions of the Highlands* been given to the world in 1749 instead of in 1788, it could not have failed to exert a powerful influence upon the growth of English Romanticism; for, as Professor Phelps has remarked, "it struck a new note in English verse," and was "the first important poem" in that branch of Romanticism which dealt with "native superstitions or Teutonic mythology."[8] As it was, we can do little more than guess at the quiet effect which the published poems of Collins may have wrought upon the poets of his own and the succeeding generation. We may think that we detect the atmosphere of the **Ode to Evening** in the *Elegy Written in a Country Churchyard;* the influence of the more elaborate odes upon Gray's Pindarics; an echo of the **Oriental Eclogues** in Chatterton's *African Idylls;* possibly a trace of **The Passions** in Beattie's *Ode to Hope,* and of the **Ode on the Poetical Character** in the same poet's conception, in *The Minstrel,* of the poetic temperament. But these and like surmises are at best a scant and shadowy harvest. And when the **Ode on the Popular Superstitions of the Highlands** finally came to light, it could no longer do the work of a pioneer, but was, instead, a prophecy fulfilled; while to a later generation still, the name of Collins was a pitiful and indignant memory, not an inspiration to new deeds in poesie. Wordsworth, at the threshold of his poetic career, prayed

> that never child of song
> May know that poet's sorrows more.[9]

And Scott, looking back with the tenderness of a robust nature for a delicate and unfortunate one, recognized the kinship between himself and "Collins, ill-starred name," who loved

> to tread enchanted strand,
> And thread . . . the maze of Fairyland;
> Of golden battlements to view the gleam,
> And slumber soft by some Elysian stream.[10]

But both Wordsworth and Scott found their inspiration elsewhere than in the pages of Collins. . . .

Notes

. . . [2] "The public has been so much accustomed of late to didactic poetry alone, and essays on moral subjects, that any work where the imagination is much indulged will perhaps not be relished or regarded. The author therefore of these pieces is in some pain lest certain austere critics should think them too fanciful and descriptive. But as he is convinced that the fashion of moralizing in verse has been carried too far, and as he looks upon invention and imagination to be the chief faculties of a poet, so he will be happy if the following odes may be looked upon as an attempt to bring back poetry into its right channel."—*Odes on Several Subjects,* by Joseph Warton, London, 1746.

[3] "My lamented friend Mr. William Collins, whose odes will be remembered while any taste for true poetry remains, shewed me this piece [Skelton's *Nigramansir*] at Chichester, not many months before his death; and pointed it out as a very rare and valuable curiosity. He intended to write the history of the Restoration of Learning under Leo the Tenth, and with a view to that design had collected many scarce books."—*The History of English Poetry,* by T. Warton, section XXXIII, foot-note.

"In the dispersed library of the late Mr. William Collins, I saw a thin folio of two sheets in black letter, containing a poem in the octave stanza, entitled, *Fabyl's Ghoste,* printed by John Rastell in the year 1533."—*Ibid.,* section XLI.

"Among the books of my friend the late Mr. William Collins of Chichester, now dispersed, was a collection of short comic stories in prose, printed in the black letter under the year 1570."—*Ibid.,* section LII.

"I was informed by the late Mr. Collins of Chichester, that Shakespeare's *Tempest,* for which no origin is yet assigned, was formed on this favorite romance [*Aurelio and Isabella*]. But although this information has not proved true on examination, an useful conclusion may be drawn from it, that Shakespeare's story is somewhere to be found in an Italian novel, at least that the story preceded Shakespeare. Mr. Collins had searched this subject with no less fidelity than judgment and industry: but his memory failing in his last calamitous indisposition, he probably gave me the name of one novel for another."—*Ibid.,* section LX.

Of like purport, as showing Collins's knowledge of the Elizabethan drama, is the following: "That our poet admired Ben Jonson, we learn from Tom Davies [bookseller and would-be actor], who, speaking of the epilogue to *Every Man Out of His Humour,* at the presentation before Queen Elizabeth, observes, 'Mr. Collins, the author of several justly esteemed poems, first pointed out to me the particular beauties of this occasional address.'" (*Dramatic Miscellanies,* vol. II, p. 77.)—Dyce's *Collins,* p. 12.

[4] "He had employed his mind chiefly on the works of fiction, and subjects of fancy; and, by indulging some peculiar habits of thought, was eminently delighted with those flights of imagination which pass the bounds of nature, and to which the mind is reconciled only by a passive acquiescence in popular traditions. He loved fairies, genii, giants, and monsters; he delighted to rove through the meanders of enchantment, to gaze on the magnificence of golden palaces, to repose by the waterfalls of Elysian gardens."—*Lives of the Poets,* London, 1820, vol. XI, p. 268.

[5] See W. L. Phelps's *Beginnings of the English Romantic Movement,* passim.

[6] "*L'Ode au Soir* est en effet de la poésie impression-
iste au premier chef; d'instinct, Collins a découvert et
appliqué inconsciemment la théorie que l'on sait, et il
lui a suffi pour cela du désir d'imiter son objet aussi
étroitement que possible, car s'il est vrai que les cho-
ses sont plus poétiques par leurs aspects que par leurs
formes et par leurs couleurs que par leur substance, on
comprendra aisément comment le phénomène du soir,
qui dissout progressivement toute forme naturelle et
détruit la solidité de toute objet, s'accommode mieux
que tout autre d'être traité selon cette doctrine, qui, si
elle est douteuse dans d'autres cas, est absolument vraie
dans celui-là."—*Heures de Lecture d'un Critique,* by
Émile Montégut, Paris, 1891, pp. 213, 214.

[7] The next two lines, with their pleasant touches of
local color, were added in the second edition, which
appeared fifteen years after the first; they afford, therefore, additional proof of the change in Collins's manner of describing nature:

> What time 't is sweet o'er fields of rice to
>   stray,
> Or scent the breathing maize at setting day.

[8] *Beginnings of the English Romantic Movement,* p.
137.

[9] *Remembrance of Collins.*

[10] *The Bridal of Triermain,* Introduction. . . .

Alan D. McKillop (essay date 1923)

SOURCE: "The Romanticism of William Collins," in
Studies in Philology, Vol. XX, No. 1, January, 1923,
pp. 1-16.

[*In the essay below, McKillop discusses the importance of Collins's work to the Romantic movement.*]

By common consent William Collins is reckoned among
those writers who prepared the way for the full romantic revival, and yet it requires some care to reach a
precise estimate of his work and to calculate its trend.
In the middle decades of the eighteenth century a thousand roads led men from the neo-classical temple of
taste and wit, and we find Collins, like many others,
making his way along these various paths. When he
inscribes to John Home *An Ode on the Popular Superstitions of the Highlands of Scotland,* we know
where to have him; it is clear whence the poem derives
and whither it tends. Professor Beers has pointed out
in the work of Collins's friend James Thomson the
very passages that gave the starting point for the ode,[1]
and, as an investigator of the origins of romanticism,
finds it the most interesting of Collins's poems;[2] James
Russell Lowell long ago remarked that it contained the

whole romantic school in the germ.[3] And yet, splendid
as this poem is, it lacks the prestige it would have won
had it been published when it was written, more than
ten years before James Macpherson came forth with
Ossian. By 1789 Collins's Celtic notes could not get
all the esteem that was being lavished on the "big
bow-wow" of Macpherson. Are there other elements
in Collins which have a direct connection with the
eighteenth century revolt? His best and most famous
piece of work, the *Ode to Evening,* hardly helps us to
answer this question. In this almost perfect poem there
is nothing fragmentary, ecstatic, or malcontent. It opens
a perspective of nature in which the meditative soul
can dwell at ease and reconciled. But if we read through
at a sitting the slender collection of Collins's verse, we
find that these two poems, for the reasons indicated,
together with some short pieces of exquisitely simple
and mellow quality, such as the *Ode Written in the
Beginning of the Year 1746* and the *Ode on the Death
of Mr. Thomson,* stand somewhat apart from the rest
of his work. Must the remaining poems be put into the
lumber-room of neoclassicism, or do they offer something to the critic who is looking for romantic impulses in the middle of the eighteenth century?

In Collins's own time his unfortunate life tinged his
personality and his work with adventitious romance;
and a little more explicitness in biography or tradition,
a little more elaboration of a legend, might have put
him on the beadroll of romantic martyrs along with
Chatterton. Goldsmith struck the key thus: "The neglected author of the **Persian Eclogues,** which, however inaccurate, excel any in our language, is still alive:
happy, if *insensible* of our neglect, not *raging* at our
ingratitude."[4] These words, written in 1759, were anticipated by John Gilbert Cooper, who in his *Letters
concerning Taste* referred the reader to "a Collection
of Odes published a few Years ago by MR. WILLIAM
COLLINS, whose neglected Genius will hereafter be both
an Honour and a Disgrace to our Nation."[5] Years later
John Scott of Amwell wrote:

> Alive neglected, and when dead forgot,
>   Even COLLINS slumbers in a grave
>   unknown.[6]

To the end of the century the poet was in the opinion
of many readers "the admirable and . . . much injured
Collins."[7] Professor Bronson has proved that Collins
was not really neglected in the generation following
his death,[8] but it must be said that there has always
been a touch of the esoteric about his reputation. The
situation is well summarized in *A Dialogue in the
Shades between Churchill and Collins,* published in
the *European Magazine* in 1793.[9]

> "Collins: Where so fast, *Charles?* You might at least
> congratulate me on the honour the world has lately
> done my memory, and felicitate me upon obtaining

that fame which an insensible nation would not give me while living . . . Churchill: Your fair fame has been long established among those whom it is alone flattering to be beloved by. Your elegant Verses have always charmed, and always will, all true Poets, and all men of fine taste and delicacy of sentiment."

The early criticisms of Collins develop a kind of double tradition: the unfortunate poet is presented on the one hand as the feeble victim of extreme sensibility, and on the other as one swept away by the strength of his imagination. The first aspect may be illustrated by these lackadaisical lines:

> Poor *Collins* sung, but Nature could not
> bear—
>   The wild bard fainted in his sister's arms,
> He sigh'd and died—pale Fancy dropt a tear
>   To see her son o'erpowered by her charms.[10]

And the second by the following passage from a set of *Verses on some late English Poets:*

> O COLLINS! nobly warm and wild,
> Fair Fancy's best beloved child!
> What mad ambitious thoughts could fire
> Thy mind to seize Apollo's lyre?
> Didst thou not find those hands of thine
> Too rough to touch the chords divine?[11]

Or both aspects may be combined, as in an ode *To the Lyric Muse* published in the same year as Langhorne's edition of Collins:

> If e'er to modern days
> Descend thy genuine lays,
>   Thee *Collins,* hapless *Collins* did possess:
> Curdles my blood in every vein,
> Fear, with all his ghastly train,
> Danger with his giant stride,
> Murder fell, and Ruin wide,
> On my thick-beating heart tumultuous press—
> That Pity with her dewy lighted eyes,
> Curs'd be the wretch his memory who denies,
> Which erst he bade in numbers soft to flow,
> And pluck'd the cypress wreath for yet
>   another's woe.[12]

Dr. Johnson's downright words, in which he debits all Collins's work to extravagant romanticism, with the emphasis on imagination rather than sensibility, have been repeated by many, and notably adapted by Scott in *The Bridal of Triermain.* Collins's first editor, Dr. John Langhorne, held the same opinion independently: "A passion for whatever is greatly wild, or magnificent in the works of nature, seduces the imagination to attend to all that is extravagant, however unnatural. Milton was notoriously fond of high romance, and gothic *diableries,* and Collins, who in genius and en-

thusiasm bore no very distant resemblance to Milton, was wholly carried away by the same attachments."[13] And in two sonnets Langhorne had already described Collins as the pathetic victim of imagination:

FANCY. SONNET I.

> . . . , the hope of all my studious care,
>   The Muses' love whose blooming genius
>   won;
>   O, while the Nine for thee, their favour'd son,
> The wreathes of * * * 's living groves
>   prepare;
> Of FANCY'S too prevailing power beware!
>   Oft has she bright on life's fair morning
>   shone,
>   Oft seated HOPE on REASON'S sovereign
>   throne,
> Then clos'd the scene in darkness and despair.
> Of all her gifts, of all her powers possest,
>   Let not her flattery win thy youthful ear;
> Nor vow long faith to such a various guest,
>   False at the last, tho' now, perchance, full
>   dear:
> The casual lover with her charms is blest,
>   But woe to them her magic bands that wear!

WISDOM. SONNET II.

> Reclining in that old and honour'd shade,
>   Where MAGDALEN'S graceful tower informs
>   the sky,
>   Urging strong thought thro' contemplation
>   high,
> WISDOM in form of ADDISON was laid;
>   Who thus fair Truth's ingenuous lore
>   convey'd
> To the poor shade of COLLINS wandering by.
> The tear stood trembling in his gentle eye,
> With modest grief reluctant, while he said—
>   'Sweet Bard! belov'd by every muse in vain!
>   'With powers whose fineness wrought their
>   own decay!
>   'Ah! wherefore, thoughtless didst thou yield
>   the rein
>   'To Fancy's will, and chase her meteor ray?
>   'Ah! why forgot thy own Hyblaean strain?
>   'Peace rules the breast, where Reason rules
>   the day.'[14]

Some of the best known of the later criticisms of Collins emphasize imagination rather than pathos. He appears magnified almost beyond recognition in Nathan Drake's essay *On the Government of the Imagination; on the Frenzy of Tasso and Collins,* where he is described as "one of our most exquisite poets, and of whom, perhaps, without exaggeration it may be asserted, that he partook of the credulity and enthusiasm of Tasso, the magic wildness of Shakspeare, the sublimity of Milton, and the pathos of Ossian."[15] Sir Egerton Brydges turns the tables on those who reproached Collins for having a strong imagination: "Collins is a proof that he who gives up the reins to his own fancy may act injuriously to his own happiness; but who can deny that he stands the best chance of attaining the mantle of a poet?"[16]

Nowadays readers may find it as hard to understand why Collins's imagination should be called fiery and uncontrolled as why Gray should ever have been considered obscure. They would be inclined to agree with the blunt eighteenth century critic who wrote: "The merit of Collins lies in his tender melancholy; his defects are confusion and incorrectness of style."[17] Recently Mr. Mark Van Doren, classifying writers of odes, put Collins with the Horatians, not with the Pindars, with those who are "Attic, choice, perhaps didactic, and . . . stimulated by observation of human nature," rather than with those who are "impassioned and superlative, and . . . inspired by the spectacle of human glory."[18] Excellent as these distinctions are, it is hard to apply them to Collins. He is as far from being a Horace (witness his un-Horatian treatment of Horatian themes in *The Manners*) as he is from being a Pindar. And yet we cannot doubt that he would rather have been a Pindar than a Horace, that to him delicate conciseness and sententiousness seemed as nothing in comparison with the upward surge of imagination. After all, we must turn back to Doctor Johnson for the key to Collins's temperament and work:

> He had employed his mind chiefly upon works of fiction and subjects of fancy, and by indulging some peculiar habits of thought was eminently delighted with those flights of imagination which pass the bounds of nature, and to which the mind is reconciled only by a passive acquiescence in popular traditions. He loved fairies, genii, giants, and monsters; he delighted to rove through the meanders of inchantment, to gaze on the magnificence of golden palaces, to repose by the water-falls of Elysian gardens. This was, however, the character rather of his inclination than his genius; the grandeur of wildness and the novelty of extravagance were always desired by him, but were not always attained.[19]

The last sentence goes far toward canceling what the eighteenth century said about Collins's ungovernable imagination. It may be hard to recognize in the fantastic Gothic poet of Johnson's description the Collins whom we know, but the central truth about him is reached in this criticism, for his inclinations did indeed outreach his genius, and he aspired to a grandeur and extravagance which he achieved not more than once or twice. The way in which he sought his romantic goal is not described by Johnson, whose account refers primarily to his reading rather than to his poetry. What Collins did in his own verse was to take seriously the neoclassical commonplaces about verse and inspiration, and to try to achieve poetic ecstasy within the narrow limits set for him by the current conventional imagery. He earnestly sought "rapture" and "enthusiasm" where many a third-rate writer of Pindarics told him he might find them. It was an enterprise which was doomed to failure, and indeed no one could be more deeply conscious of his failure than he was himself—no one felt more keenly the impotence of British poetry in the middle of the eighteenth century.

Collins's merits, as well as his failure, may best be emphasized by showing how completely he was hedged about by the conventional ideas of his time. Then, as always, there was not only convention *and* revolt, but a convention *of* revolt, in poetry. If one did not care to polish couplets, there was the ode, where one was supposed to have more freedom, though as a matter of fact this form was almost as completely petrified as the didactic poem or the satire. Still it was felt that the ode left a loophole for a return to simplicity and authentic inspiration.

> While the other branches of Poetry have been gradually modelled by the rules of criticism, the Ode hath only been changed in a few external circumstances, and the enthusiasm, obscurity and exuberance which characterized it when first introduced, continue to be ranked among its capital and discriminating excellencies.[20]

The Pindaric type was still felt by conservative critics to be the ode *par excellence*.[21] But there was an alternative to the Pindaric ecstasy.

> Of the descriptive and allegorical Ode the Writings of the Ancients afford no Examples: The Choruses of their Drama bear the greatest similarity to it; and particularly those of *Euripides,* in which he is followed by Seneca. This Species of Writing is in almost every circumstance different from the *Pindarick* Ode, which has its Foundation in Fact and Reality, that Fact worked up and heightened by a studied Pomp and Grandeur of Expression; it not only admits of, but requires bold Digressions, abrupt and hasty Transitions: while the other is built intirely [*sic*] upon Fancy, and Ease and Simplicity of Diction are its peculiar Characteristics.[22]

Joseph Warton, in the Advertisement to his *Odes on Various Subjects,* considers the ode an imaginative poem, "fanciful and descriptive," and contrasts it with the current moralizing verse. In his work the ode often becomes a mere excursus, a "train" or pictorial catalogue; characteristic are the *Ode to Fancy, Against Despair, To Evening,* and *To Solitude.*[23] Collins's **Ode to Evening** is the closest thing in his work to the purely descriptive Warton ode, though its coherence, perspective, and lyric unity make it far superior to any other poem of this type. The imagery of the ode was usually bound together, however, by an abstract idea, and this of course brought the theoretically free writer of odes back into the toils of eighteenth century convention. Collins, though he tries to work both in the "descriptive and allegorical" and the Pindaric traditions, leans heavily on such abstractions, even when he could gain unity by sheer imaginative power.

The ideas about which the mid-century odes of Collins and his contemporaries centred were remarkable neither for depth nor novelty of doctrine. Most threadbare of all was the theme of the "power of music," deservedly satirized in Bonnell Thornton's "much admir'd Burlesque Ode, Written in Banter of the Odes on St. Caecilia's Day, and descriptive of several exquisite and old-fashion'd Instruments, viz. the Salt-box, the Jew's Harp, the Marrow-Bones and Cleavers, and Hurdy-Gurdy."[24] After many a degenerate and perfunctory imitator of Dryden's *Alexander's Feast* and *St. Cecilia's Day,* and Pope's ode on the same occasion, came Collins's *Passions: An Ode for Music.* To most writers of St. Cecilia verse this theme was simply a peg on which to hang versified commonplaces, such as may be found conveniently gathered in Christopher Smart's *Ode for Music on St. Cecilia's Day*—the music of the spheres; the shepherd's notes and Saint Cecilia; Waller in the role of Orpheus playing his lyre in a solitary grove at Penshurst, with Philomel answering the lay, while the waters of the Medway "weep away" to the sea; the story of Arion; the power of music over the tender and the martial emotions; the sacred music of Purcell; echoes of *L'Allegro* and *Il Penseroso.* But the idea of music was so far from being taken seriously that it usually existed side by side with the equally conventional idea of pictorial verse. Poetry painted and poetry sang. As Daniel Webb acutely remarked:

> Objects in repose, or the beauties of still-life, fall not within the province of musical imitation; nor can music take a part in the coloring of language. Our modern lyric poesy is a school for painters, not for musicians. The form of invocation, the distinctions of the strophe, the antistrophe, and chorus, are mere pretensions. To what purpose do we solicit the genius of music, while we abandon, without reserve, the plectrum for the pencil, and cast aside the lyre, as a child doth its rattle, in the moment that we proclaim it to be the object of our preference?[25]

In the *Passions* Collins follows the tableaux and the allegorical framework of *Alexander's Feast,* and tries to present the reality of music in a pictorial way.[26] So far, splendid as the poem is, it must lie exposed to the general attack on the principle *ut pictura poesis,* for the allegorical figures are mechanical rather than dramatic in their action, and are so far bound by eighteenth century convention. But after Exercise, Sport, Joy, and the rest have passed from the scene, Collins shows that music is to him the symbol of an inaccessible ideal. Dryden ends *Alexander's Feast* with a commonplace on the progress of music; after Timotheus came Cecilia, and the invention of the organ:

> The sweet enthusiast, from her sacred store,
>   Enlarged the former narrow bounds,
>   And added length to solemn sounds,
> With Nature's mother-wit, and arts unknown
>   before.

But Collins's conclusion directly contradicts these perfunctory lines of Dryden's. For Collins Greek music represents the lost inspiration of poetry, and Saint Cecilia is inferior to Timotheus. Addressing Music, he cries:

> Arise as in that elder time,
> Warm, energic, chaste, sublime!
> Thy wonders, in that godlike age,
> Fill thy recording sister's page—
> 'Tis said, and I believe the tale,
> Thy humblest reed could more prevail,
> Had more of strength, diviner rage,
> Than all which charms this laggard age,
> Ev'n all at once together found,
> Caecilia's mingled world of sound.
> O bid our vain endeavours cease,
> Revive the just designs of Greece,
> Return in all thy simple state,
> Confirm the tales her sons relate!

Although Collins uses the idea of the lost glories of Greek poetry and music in a romantic way, it must be remembered that the conception itself was a commonplace of his time. Addison remarked as a matter of course that the ancients excelled the moderns in the arts, and Warton agreed with him.[27] It was no new thing to represent the lyric muse with "Grecian form and Grecian robe."[28] Joseph Warton implores Fancy to inspire some rural bard with lays that stir the heart, and finally to

> bid Britannia rival Greece![29]

Mark Akenside, with what Hartley Coleridge called his "classical Quixotism," said that his purpose in the *Pleasures of the Imagination* was to "tune to Attic themes the British lyre,"[30] and in his ode *On Lyrick Poetry* sought inspiration for the modern English lyric from the Greek. Moreover, this praise of Greece was closely connected with the praise of freedom, just as in Collins's *Simplicity* and *Liberty.* Akenside's best ode, *To the Right Honourable Francis Earl of Huntington* (1748), professes to glorify Pindar not as a mere poet but as the champion of freedom and civic virtue.

Warton's *Ode occasioned by reading Mr. West's Translation of Pindar* is identical in thought. The meretricious ornaments of modern Latin culture were often contrasted with Greek simplicity.

> Too long have the beauties of the British muse, like
>   those of our ladies, been concealed, or spoiled, by

foreign modes and false ornaments. . . . . Let us endeavour to recover her from the tyrannical sway of fashion and prejudice, and restore her to her native rights. Let us leave to the sallow French their rouge and white paint, but let the British red and white appear in it's genuine lustre, as laid on by nature's own pencil. . . . Then shall she move forth confessed the genuine sister of the Grecian muse, and not the less beautiful for being the younger.[31]

And in exactly similar vein John Armstrong:

The *British* poetry is universally allowed, by the best judges of both, to be much superior to the *Italian;* and why should you wonder to find the music of the one country brought into competition with that of the other? The music of these islands seems to agree in character with that of the ancients; which, from the accounts we have of it, excelled in simplicity and passion. How simple the music must have been that delighted *Greece,* in the days of *Alcaeus, Sappho, Pindar,* and *Anacreon,* seems to appear from the very make of their capital instrument the Lyre.[32]

But the Greek ideal is almost never projected into the romantic and unattainable distance. Akenside writes *On the Absence of the Poetic Inclination,* but he gets his power back by the easy expedient of conjuring with the name of Milton. Panegyrists of Greece were likely to end by praising Britain, as in an *Ode to the Genius of Antient Greece* which says nevertheless:

To *Greece* no more shall *Britain* bow.[33]

Moreover these early romanticists, who, in the words of a later reviewer speaking of Thomas Warton, "possessed a classic taste with a Gothic Muse,"[34] were confused by their double allegiance. Thomas Warton, in his *Verses on Sir Joshua Reynolds' Painted Window, at New-College, Oxford,* tells how Reynolds has "broke the Gothic chain" and lured him back from his mediæval studies to Greek art, but ends by saying that it must be the artist's work

With arts unknown before, to reconcile
The willing graces to the Gothic pile.

William Mason, too, would "mingle *Attic* art with Shakespear's fire."[35] And even Collins, in the conventional ending of the **Ode to Liberty,** conceives of a hybrid shrine for the goddess:

Ev'n now, before his favour'd eyes,
In Gothic pride, it seems to rise!
Yet Graecia's graceful orders join,
Majestic thro' the mix'd design.

Yet at his best he rises above this eclecticism, which at most could only give the old poetry variegated ornaments and a new subject-matter. His singleness of purpose could not rest content with such a superficial compromise. We may conjecture that in his lost **Ode on the Music of the Grecian Theatre** he elaborated the theme of Greece as the symbol of vanished inspiration, and showed still more clearly how his Hellenism differed from that of his contemporaries.

The denial of eighteenth century complacency discovered in the conclusion of the **Passions** comes out most clearly in Collins's frequent and peculiar use of the progress formula of his time. A recent writer has pointed out how four of his odes conform to the usual pattern of the progress piece. "Collins's **'Ode to Liberty'** is, in outline and in the first half only, almost the same as Thomson's 'Liberty,' a progress from Greece through Rome, Florence, Venice, Switzerland, and Holland, to Britain."[36] Collins uses the theme of the progress of poetry "twice in truncated form, once in full—in the odes to **'Fear'** and **'Simplicity'** and in the **'Epistle to Hanmer.'**"[37] But the typical progress piece of the eighteenth century was written in the spirit of the *Aufklärung,* best expressed in Wagner's words to Faust, which have been recognized as containing a whole philosophy of history:

Es ist ein grosz Ergetzen
Sich in den Geist der Zeiten zu versetzen,
Zu schauen wie vor uns ein weiser Mann
        gedacht,
Und wie wir's dann zuletzt so herrlich weit
        gebracht.[38]

Dryden drew the same conclusion in a resonant passage that has more than mere flattery in it:

The wit of Greece, the gravity of Rome,
Appear exalted in the British loom:
The Muses' empire is restored again,
In Charles his reign, and by Roscommon's
        pen.[39]

The principle of climax, if nothing else, demanded that the progress piece favor the moderns, and show that now at last "the force of nature could no farther go." Even Gray's *Progress of Poesy,* the greatest in this kind, ends with a note of exultation. Joseph Warton's lines *To a Gentleman upon his Travels to Italy* belong to the progress type, and end thus complacently:

Nor she, mild queen, will cease to smile
On her Britannia's much lov'd isle,
Where there her best, her favorite Three were
        born,
While Theron warbles Grecian strains,
Or polished Dodington remains,
The drooping train of arts to cherish and
        adorn.

But Collins does not reach such conclusions. The conventional **Epistle Addresst to Sir Thomas Hanmer** does indeed praise Shakespeare as "the perfect boast of time." Yet at the same time Collins denies the dogma of progress in the drama.

> Each rising art by just gradation moves,
> Toil builds on toil, and age on age improves:
> The Muse alone unequal dealt her rage,
> And grac'd with noblest pomp her earliest
>   stage.

And after Shakespeare, he tells us, the "progress" of English dramatic poetry is an anticlimax:

> Yet ah! so bright her morning's op'ning ray,
> In vain our Britain hop'd an equal day!
> No second growth the western isle could bear,
> At once exhausted with too rich a year.

In the *Ode to Fear* the progress form is abandoned in the antistrophe for an imitation of *Il Penseroso,* and Collins brings his poem to an end with the idea of arrested inspiration which is never far away in his work:

> O thou whose spirit most possest
> The sacred seat of Shakespear's breast,
> By all that from thy prophet broke,
> In thy divine emotions spoke,
> Hither again thy fury deal!
> Teach me but once like him to feel,
> His cypress wreath my meed decree,
> And I, O Fear, will dwell with thee!

The *Ode to Simplicity* concludes its short historic survey with a description of the low state of Italian poetry and music:

> No more, in hall or bow'r,
> The passions own thy pow'r;
>   Love, only love, her forceless numbers
>   mean:
> For thou hast left her shrine;
> Nor olive more, nor vine,
>   Shall gain thy feet to bless the servile scene.

Similarly, while Thomson ends his *Liberty* with a survey of British civilization and a glowing prophecy of future glories, Collins, in the Second Epode of his *Liberty,* lets his imagination dwell on the shrine of Liberty that once stood in the primeval forests of Britain.

> Thy shrine in some religious wood,
> O soul-enforcing goddess, stood! . . .
> Tho' now with hopeless toil we trace
> Time's backward rolls to find its place;
> Whether the fiery-tressed Dane
> Or Roman's self o'erturn'd the fane,
> Or in what heaven-left age it fell,
> 'T were hard for modern song to tell.

In this instance, though the placing of the ideal in an inaccessible past is characteristic of Collins, the conclusion is weakened by conventional optimism of the worst kind; and the piece closes with the return of Liberty and an attendant group of abstractions to Britain's shore. But in spite of this instance all these progress pieces of Collins's show more or less clearly that his mind reverted inevitably to the idea that true poetry was remote from things present and modern. To this extent they illustrate precisely Schiller's definition of *sentimentalische Dichtung.*

The real subject of Collins's odes, then, is the concept of poetry; Simplicity, Fear, Pity, and the rest are only ancillary to an idea of inspiration which is conceived and intensely desired, but never fully realized. Accordingly, the *Ode on the Poetical Character* must be called his most characteristic poem, for it is the apotheosis of the idea of inspiration. The magic girdle of poetic power was woven on the day of creation, when God placed Fancy on his sapphire throne,—

> The whiles, the vaulted shrine around,
> Seraphic wires were heard to sound,
> Now sublimest triumph swelling,
> Now on love and mercy dwelling;
> And she, from out the veiling cloud,
> Breath'd her magic notes aloud:
> And thou, thou rich-hair'd Youth of Morn,
> And all thy subject life, was born!

The identity of poetry and music is the central thing in the creation. But even here Collins does not feel that he possesses the essence of poetry. Some romanticists of later generations have felt him to be among the highest poets because of his intensity and ardor. Swinburne once wrote: "I hold Collins as *facile principem* in the most quintessential property of a poet proper."[40] The youthful Coleridge avowed his preference for the abstract sublimity of Collins: "Now Collins's **'Ode on the Poetical Character,'**—that part of it, I should say, beginning with 'The band (as faery legends say) Was wove on that creating day,'—has inspired and whirled *me* along with greater agitations of enthusiasm than any the most *impassioned* scene in Schiller or Shakespeare, using 'impassioned' in its confined sense, for writing in which the human passions of pity, fear, anger, revenge, jealousy, or love are brought into view with their workings. Yet I consider the latter poetry as more valuable, because it gives *more general* pleasure, and I judge of all things by their utility."[41] But Collins himself feels that the primal rapture of poetry is beyond the reach of any modern:

> Where is the bard whose soul can now
> Its high presuming hopes avow?
> Where he who thinks, with rapture blind,
> This hallow'd work for him design'd?

It is by denying the presence of poetry, by despairing of his calling, that Collins often becomes a romantic poet. He does not consistently recover the true poetry which he felt was lost; he does not consistently seek to put something in place of Pindarics that will not carry the imagination, and allegorical abstractions that cannot be intensely realized. He is incorrigibly intellectual and abstract, but at the same time so ardent and sincere that he knows his abstractions are not sufficient unto themselves. When he writes of "Greece" or "music" he is not thinking so much of Greek life and literature, or of the actual art of music, as of simple, ecstatic poetry in itself. His imagination never provides his poetry with a rich content, but we have seen that it is possible to detect romantic intent in his work even when the style and the ostensible theme are pseudo-classic. His abstractness often kept him in line with eighteenth century formalism, but his ardor and sincerity bore it in upon him that his own verse was "a thing wherein we feel there is some hidden want."

Notes

[1] *A History of English Romanticism in the Eighteenth Century* (New York, 1906), 94, 114.

[2] *Ibid.,* 170.

[3] *Prose Works* (Boston, n. d.), IV, 3.

[4] *Works* (London, 1908), III, 508.

[5] Third edition (London, 1757), 47. First edition, 1754. H. O. White, "William Collins and his Contemporary Critics," *Times Literary Supplement,* Jan. 5, 1922, suggests that Goldsmith may have taken his cue from Cooper.

[6] "Stanzas written at Medhurst in Sussex, after attempting in vain to find the Burial Place of Collins, the Poet, which is said to be at Chichester." *Universal Magazine,* LXXIII (1783), 278.

[7] William Preston, "Thoughts on Lyric Poetry," *European Magazine,* XIV (1788), 174.

[8] Athenaeum Press *Collins* (Boston, n. d.) xxx-xxxix. For important additional references see H. O. White, *loc. cit.* Still other early tributes to Collins are cited and discussed below.

[9] By Thomas Clio Rickman. *European Magazine,* XXIV, 345.

[10] *Scots Magazine,* XXVIII (1766), 544.

[11] *Scots Magazine,* XXXV (1773), 486.

[12] *Scots Magazine,* XXVII (1765), 101-102.

[13] *The Poetical Works of Mr. William Collins* (London, 1765), 153.

[14] *Monthly Review,* XXX (1764), 122, 123. The sonnets are here attributed to "the Author of *The Visions of Fancy,*" that is, to Langhorne. They do not appear in the collected poems of Langhorne as given by Anderson and Chalmers, and I do not find that they have been used by Collins's editors and biographers.

[15] *Literary Hours* (Third edition, London, 1804), I, 64.

[16] *Censura Literaria* (London, 1815), III, 340-42.

[17] Robert Heron [John Pinkerton], *Letters of Literature* (London, 1785), 131.

[18] *The Poetry of John Dryden* (New York, 1920), 241.

[19] *Lives of the English Poets,* ed. George Birkbeck Hill (Oxford, 1895), III, 337, 338.

[20] John Ogilvie, "Essay on the Lyric Poetry of the Ancients," prefixed to *Poems on Several Subjects* (London, 1762), xxiv.

[21] John Brown, *Dissertation on the Rise, Union, and Power, the Progressions, Separations, and Corruptions, of Poetry and Music* (London, 1763), 197.

[22] Richard Shepherd, *Odes Descriptive and Allegorical* (London, 1761), iii.

[23] Cf. "A Dissertation on the Modern Ode," reprinted from *Lloyd's Magazine* in the *Scots Magazine,* XXV (1763), 265-68. An elaborate attack on the odes written by "the gentlemen-professors of modern-ancient poetry." "Whether the poet addresses himself to Wisdom or Folly, Mirth or Melancholy, he breaks out in a fine enthusiasm, with an 'Oh,' or, 'Hail,' or some such pathetic expression, which naturally leads him to a description, in at least fourteen lines, of the person and dwelling of no matter whom; which, with some observations upon her equipage and attendance, no matter what, make two stanzas, struck out from one word as it were; and all these beauties, according to the laws of the exactest critics, arise very naturally from the subject."

[24] Imitated in "An Irregular Balladistical Ode, Composed to be Set to Music," Noted *Monthly Review,* XXXIX (1768), 401.

[25] *Observations on the Correspondence between Poetry and Music* (London, 1769), 133, 134.

[26] John Ogilvie (*op. cit.,* lxiv), working out a theory of personification for the ode, says: "Thus Anger, Revenge, Despair, Hope, etc., can be distinguished

from each other almost as easily when they are copied by the pencil, as when *we feel their influence on our own minds, or make others observe it on our actions.*" Ogilvie no doubt has Collins's *Passions* in mind here. In Collins the allegorical figures appear in the following order: Fear, Anger, Despair, Hope, Revenge.

[27] *Adventurer,* Nos. 127, 133.

[28] "An Ode on Lyrick Poetry." *London Magazine,* XIX (1750), 228.

[29] "Ode To Fancy."

[30] Bk. I, l. 604.

[31] Thomas Sheridan, *British Education* (London, 1756), 365-66.

[32] *Miscellanies* (London, 1770), II, 154-55.

[33] *Poems, chiefly by Gentlemen of Devonshire and Cornwall* (Bath, 1792), I, 14. Original date of this poem 1760.

[34] *Critical Review,* N. S., X (1794), 20.

[35] "To the Reverend Mr. Hurd."

[36] R. H. Griffith, "The Progress Pieces of the Eighteenth Century." *Texas Review,* V (1920), 218 ff., especially 221.

[37] *Ibid.,* 224. "Collins's 'Ode to Simplicity' is an embryo 'Progress of Poesy,' and it is hardly conceivable that Gray did not thence derive a hint upon which he, without doubt, immensely improved."—Duncan C. Tovey, in Preface to *Letters of Thomas Gray* (London, 1909), I, xxiv.

[38] *Faust,* ll. 570-73.

[39] *Epistle to the Earl of Roscommon.*

[40] *Letters,* ed. Gosse and Wise (New York, 1919), II, 42.

[41] *Letters,* ed. Ernest Hartley Coleridge (London, 1895), I, 196-97.

Edward Gay Ainsworth Jr. (essay date 1937)

SOURCE: "Collins's Influence at the Turn of the Century," in *Poor Collins: His Life, His Art, and His Influence,* Cornell, 1937, pp. 256-68.

[*In the following essay, Ainsworth considers Collins's influence on William Wordsworth, Samuel Taylor Coleridge, and Robert Southey.*]

In the last years of the century . . . Collins made his first appeal to Wordsworth, Coleridge, and Southey, young and significant poets of the new romantic generation. In the works of all three poets there is definite evidence of his influence, a force which they were never to outgrow. At various times in his career Wordsworth spoke favorably of Collins. He showed considerable interest in Dyce's edition of the poet, and Dyce apparently consulted him on several points. He was particularly concerned with the Highland Ode and definitely repudiated the version in Bell's copy (the 1788 anonymous edition). He writes January 12, 1827:

> You are at perfect liberty to declare that you have rejected Bell's copy in consequence of my opinion of it; and I feel much satisfaction in being the instrument of rescuing the memory of Collins from this disgrace.[1]

He speaks again of the ode in a letter to Dyce, October 29, 1828,[2] remarking that "it was circulated through the English newspapers, in which I remember to have read it with great pleasure upon its first appearance," and noting further the source of some of the imagery, he says:

> By the bye, I am almost sure that that very agreeable line,
>
> > "Nor ever vernal tree was heard to murmur"
>
> is from Warton's account of St. Hilda.

Knight has evidently misread "tree" for "bee," "Warton" for "Martin," and "Hilda" for "Kilda"; Wordsworth is referring to *A Voyage to St. Kilda,* with which he was familiar, for he mentions the *Voyage among the Western Isles* at the head of poem XXXIV in the *Itinerary Poems of 1833.* On three occasions he gives a favorable opinion of Collins as a poet. He says in the letter to Dyce, January 12, 1827:

> These three writers, Thomson, Collins, and Dyer had more poetic imagination than any of their contemporaries unless we reckon Chatterton as of that age.

Again in his letter of October 29, 1828, he calls Collins

> An author who from the melancholy circumstances of his life, particularly the latter part of it, has a peculiar claim upon such attention as you [Dyce] have bestowed upon him and his works.

In his *Essay Supplementary to the Preface,* 1815, he comments on Collins's neglect in his lifetime and his subsequent fame:

When Thomson died, Collins breathed forth his regrets in an Elegiac Poem, in which he pronounces a poetical curse upon him who should regard with insensibility the place where the poet's remains were deposited. The poems of the mourner himself have now passed through innumerable editions, and are universally known; but if, when Collins died, the same kind of imprecation had been pronounced by a surviving admirer, small is the number whom it would not have comprehended. The notice which his poems attained during his lifetime was so small and of course the sale so insignificant, that not long before his death he deemed it right to repay the bookseller the sum which he had advanced for them, and threw the edition into the fire.

He also commented critically on the **Ode to Evening**. In a letter to Dyce, May, 1830, he writes:

A word or two about Collins. You know what importance I attach to following strictly the last copy of the text of an author; and I do not blame you for printing in the **Ode to Evening** "brawling" spring; but surely the epithet is most unsuitable to the time, the very worst, I think, that could have been chosen.[3]

When Wordsworth wrote his first poetry Collins was one of the eighteenth century poets to whom he turned. *Lines Written While Sailing in a Boat at Evening* and *Remembrance of Collins* are tributes to him, both suggestive of the **Ode on the Death of Mr. Thomson**. There are slight reminiscences of Collins in both *An Evening Walk* and *Descriptive Sketches*. Line 235 of *An Evening Walk* echoes Wordsworth's favorite line from **The Passions:**

Yet hears her song "by distance made more sweet."

which he was later to remember in *Personal Talk*, II, 24-5, when he wrote:

. . . sweetest melodies
Are those that are BY DISTANCE MADE
MORE SWEET.

Lines 280-1 of *An Evening Walk* (1820 version) recall the **Ode to Evening:**

Or clock that blind against the wanderer born
Drops at his feet and stills his DRONING
    HORN,

as do lines 291-4:

Like Una shining on her gloomy way,
The half-seen form of Twilight roams astray;
Shedding through play loop-holes mild and
    small,
Gleams that upon the lake's still bosom fall.[4]

Line 372 echoes the **Ode on the Death of Mr. Thomson:**

The boat's first motion—made with
DASHING OAR.

Other instances from *An Evening Walk* are: "EVE'S MILD HOUR invites my steps abroad," 89; "the hound, the horse's tread, and MELLOW HORN, 245; "heard by calm lakes as peeps the FOLDING STAR;" 280.

Three times in his later poetry he was to remember the poet of evening. *Miscellaneous Sonnet,* XXI (Part II) begins:

Hail Twilight, sovereign of one peaceful
    hour!

and especially in

At thy MEEK BIDDING, SHADOWY POWER!

suggests Collins. Sonnet XXXV, *Gordale*, begins in the manner and idiom of Collins:

At early dawn, or rather when the air
Glimmers with fading light and SHADOWY
    EVE
Is busiest to confer and to bereave,
Then, PENSIVE VOTARY, let thy feet repair
To Gordale chasm. . . .

And in *Miscellaneous Sonnets,* Part II, VI, *June, 1820,* he pays tribute both to Thomson and to Collins:

For I have heard the quire of Richmond hill
Chanting with indefatigable bill,
Strains that recalled to mind a distant day;
When, haply under shade of that same wood,
And scarcely conscious of the DASHING OARS
Plied steadily between those willowy shores,
The sweet-souled poet of the Season stood—.

Collins, then, exercised a slight but definite influence on the poetry of Wordsworth who remembered him with pleasure.

Upon the young Coleridge, the poet of "tumid ode and turgid stanza," Collins cast even a stronger spell. Coleridge admits his early admiration long afterwards in the *Preface to the Edition of 1832:*

The poems produced before the author's twenty-fourth year, devoted as he was to the "soft strains" of Bowles, HAVE MORE IN COMMON WITH THE PASSIONATE LYRICS OF COLLINS and the picturesque wildness of the pretended Ossian, than with the well-turned sentimentality of that Muse which the overgrateful poet has represented as his earliest inspirer.

He preferred Collins to Gray[5] and thought he had the greater genius.[6] He found part of his pleasure in Collins's poetry because it was but generally and not perfectly understood.[7] He was particularly impressed by the *Ode on the Poetical Character,* on which he twice comments. Writing to Thelwall, December 17, 1796, he confesses:

> Now Collins's *Ode on the Poetical Character*—that part of it, I should say, beginning with "The band (as fairy legends say) Was wove on that creating day,"—has . . . whirled *me* along with greater agitations of enthusiasm than any the most *impassioned* scene in Schiller or Shakespeare, using the "impassioned" in its confined sense, for writing in which the human passions of pity, fear, anger, revenge, jealousy, or love are brought into view with their workings.[8]

Again he comments in the *Preface to the Second Edition of the Poems:*

> A poem that abounds in allusions, like the "Bard" of Gray, or one that impersonates high and abstract truths, like Collins's **"Ode on the Poetical Character,"** claims not to be popular—but should be acquitted of obscurity. The deficiency is in the Reader. But this is a charge which every poet, whose imagination is warm and rapid, must expect from his *contemporaries.* Milton did not escape it; and it was adduced with virulence against Gray and Collins. We now hear no more of it: not that their poems are better understood at present than they were at their first publication; but their fame is established; and a critic would accuse himself of frigidity or inattention who should profess not to understand them.

It is further suggestive that he had planned an edition of Collins and Gray; the project is twice mentioned in his *Note Book.*[9]

The early poems of Coleridge abound in suggestions of Collins—his diction, his personification, and his imagery. Two passages in *Dura Navis* recall the *Ode to Fear.* The picture of Vengeance, 39-40:

> Whilst Vengeance drunk with human blood
>   stands by
> And smiling fires each heart and arms each
>   hand,

and the passage, 49-55:

> With trembling hands the lot I see thee draw
> Which shall, or sentence thee a victim drear,
> To that ghaunt Plague which savage knows no
>   law,
> Or, deep thy dagger in the friendly heart,
> Whilst each strong passion agitates thy breast,

> Though oft with Horror back I see thee start,
> Lo! Hunger *drives* thee to th' inhuman heart,

have Collins's tone. The epithet "meek-eyed Peace," 59, is also from Collins, though it was first Milton's.

The *Monody on the Death of Chatterton,* 1790, echoes Collins in its praise of Otway, 20, "Whom Pity's self had taught to sing." Its description of "Poverty of Giant Mien," 48, recalls the *Ode to Fear,* and the imprecation, 86-7, is again in the manner of the *Ode to Fear:*

> Grant me, like thee, the lyre to sound,
> Like thee, with fire divine to glow.

A Wish, 1792, is an unrhymed lyric, the first stanza of which faintly suggests the *Ode to Evening.* Ode, April, 1792, is like Collins throughout, but the conclusion, 31-40 particularly, suggests the *Ode to Mercy:*

> Then cease, thy frantic Tumults cease,
>   Ambition, sire of War!
> Nor o'er the mangled Corse of Peace
>   Urge on thy scythed Car.
> And oh! that Reason's voice might swell
> Wish whisper'd Airs and holy spell
>   To rouse thy gentler Sense,
> As bending o'er the chilly bloom
> The Morning wakes its soft Perfume
>   With breezy Influence.

The *Song of the Pixies,* 1796, is peculiarly in Collins's vein. In describing the fairy-folk of Devonshire, it deals with those "airy beings" whom Collins delighted to present. Stanza V is full of echoes of the *Ode to Evening:*

> When EVENING'S DUSKY CAR
>   Crown'd with her DEWY STAR
> Steals o'er the fading sky in shadowy flight;
>   On leaves of aspen trees
>   We tremble to the breeze
> Veil'd from the grosser ken of mortal sight.
>   Or, haply, at the visionary hour,
> Along our wildly-bower'd sequestered walk,
> We listen to the enamour'd rustic's talk
>   Or guide of soul-subduing power
> The glance that from the half-confessing eye
> Darts the fond question or the soft reply.

Equally suggestive of Collins are "the parting gleam" of day on Otter's Stream, 67, and the band of "sombre hours," 76-7, attendant upon Night. The picture of the train of virtues which accompany the Faery Queen of the Pixies, 96-100, is typical of Collins's personifications:

> Graceful Ease in artless stole,
> And white-robed Purity of soul,
>   With Honour's softer mien;
> Mirth of the loosely-flowing hair,

And meek-eyed Pity eloquently fair,
Whose tearful cheeks are lovely to the view,
    As snow-drop wet with dew.

The personification, diction, and manner of Collins are evident in a number of the other early poems to a leser degree. *An Effusion at Evening,* 1792, mentions the "shadowy pleasures," 7, and echoes the ***Ode to Evening*** in lines 57-8:

No more shall deck THY PENSIVE PLEASURES SWEET
With wreaths of sober hue my evening seat.

The same strain runs indefinably through *Lines on an Autumnal Evening. Translation of Wrangham's Hendecasyllabi* mentions "white-robed Truth," 1, and "meek-eyed Pity," 5. *Pantisocracy,* 8, speaks of the "wizard passions" in Collins's phrase. The figures of "Heart-fretting Fear, with pallid look aghast" and its mingled forms of Misery, 11-18, suggest again the ***Ode to Fear.*** In two of the *Sonnets on Eminent Characters* there are echoes of ***The Passions.*** In *To William Godwin,* 7-8, Coleridge quotes directly:

Thy steady eye has shot its glances keen—
And bade th' All-lovely "scenes at distance
    hail."

In *To Robert Southey,* 6-7, he echoes lines 93-4 of the same ode:

Waked by the Song doth HOPE-born FANCY
    fling
RICH SHOWERS OF DEWY FRAGRANCE FROM HER
    WING.

Lines Written at Shurton Bars, 1795, 29-30, mentions the viewless influence of "Meek Evening," and *To the Author of Poems,* 1795, 41, speaks of "Eve's mild gleam." The revised *Monody on the Death of Chatterton* mentions the "wizard passions," 147, "sober eve," 152, and "young-eyed Poesy," 154, all in Collins's characteristic idiom. *To a Young Friend,* 1796, 55, borrows "fancy-blest" from the ***Ode to Liberty.*** The influence of Collins is, then, abundantly evident in many of the poems between 1790 and 1796, a time at which the young Wordsworth was also turning to him.

In one significant instance Coleridge was to remember Collins after this date. The familiarity with ***The Passions*** so evident in the earlier poems was to manifest itself in the strange dream vision of *Kubla Khan.* The passage in Collins, 64-6:

Thro' Glades and Glooms the MINGLED MEASURE
    stole,
Or o'er some HAUNTED Stream with fond
    Delay,
    Round an HOLY Calm diffusing,

was transmuted into:

A savage place! as HOLY and enchanted
As e'er beneath a waning moon was HAUNTED
By woman wailing for her demon lover!

and was remembered again in:

Where was heard the MINGLED MEASURE
From the fountains and the caves.[10]

Perhaps, too, Coleridge remembered the fragment the ***Bell of Arragon.*** The lines:

The bell of Arragon, they say,
Spontaneous speaks the fatal day,

and

Whatever dark aërial power,
Commissioned, haunts the gloomy tower,

suggest a passage in *Christabel,* lines 198-201:

I have heard the gray-haired friar tell
How on her death-bed she did say,
That she should hear the castle-bell
Strike twelve upon my wedding-day.

It is not surprising to find Coleridge so drawn to Collins. In their love of folk-lore, in their magic of word music, in their love of scholarship and erudite lore as well as in their indolence and indecision, they were akin. In Coleridge we may find a hint of what Collins would have been had his genius fully flowered.

Southey, too, was a devotee of Collins. Had he written nothing else his enthusiastic appreciation in the *Life of Cowper* would reveal his admiration:

That he [Cowper] should never before have heard of Collins, shows how little Collins had been heard of in his life-time; and that Cowper in his knowledge of contemporary literature, was now awakening, as it were, from a sleep of twenty years. In the course of those years Collins's Odes, which were utterly negected on their first appearance, had obtained their due estimation. But it should also be remembered, that in the course of one generation these poems, without any adventitious aid to bring them into notice, were acknowledged to be the best of their kind in the language. Silently and imperceptibly they had risen by their own buoyancy, and their power was felt by every reader who had any true poetic feeling.[11]

In his *General Preface,* 10 May 1837, he pays another tribute to the poet:

Everyone who has an ear for metre and a heart for poetry must have felt how perfectly the metre of

Collins's *Ode to Evening* is in accordance with the imagery and the feeling.

His own admiration for the poet led him to attempt a number of unrhymed lyrics in the stanza form of the *Ode to Evening* or in variations on that form. *To Hymen* is in the form, and stanza six suggests the diction of Collins's ode in:

> And many a virtue come
>   To join thy happy train.

Other instances are: *Written on the First of January, To Recovery* (in which the epithet "nymph adored" suggests Collins), the *Death of Wallace, Ebb Tide,* and *Song of the Chikkashah Widow. To Horror* is a poor and melodramatic *Ode to Fear.* In *To Contemplation* the influence of the *Ode to Evening* is particularly strong, especially in the lines:

> Or LEAD ME WHERE, amid the TRANQUIL VALE,
> The broken streamlet flows in silver light;
>   And I will linger where the gale
>   O'er the banks of violets sighs,
> Listening to its SOFTENED SOUNDS arise,
> And hearken the DULL BEETLE'S DROWSY FLIGHT.

It is felt again in:

> Thee, meekest Power! I love to meet,
>   As oft with solitary pace,
> The ruined abbey's hallowed rounds I trace.

Stanza 2 of *Translation of a Greek Ode on Astronomy* bears a striking resemblance to a passage in the *Ode on the Poetical Character:*

> For then to the celestial palaces
> Urania leads,—Urania, she
>   The goddess who alone
>   Stands by the blazing throne,
> Effulgent with the light of Deity;
> Whom Wisdom, the creatrix, by his side
> Placed on the heights of yonder sky,
> And smiling with ambrosial love, unlocked
> The depths of Nature to her piercing eye,
> Angelic myriads struck their harps around;
>   And, with triumphant song,
>   The host of stars, a beauteous throng,
>   Around the ever-living Mind
> In jubilee their mystic dance begun;
>   When at thy leaping forth, O Sun!
>   The Morning started in affright,
> Astonished at thy birth, her child of Light!

And in *Vision of Judgment,* Canto I, the spell of the *Ode to Evening* is again felt:

> Derwent returning yet from eve a glassy
>   reflection,

> Where his expanded breast, then still and
>   smooth as a mirror
> Under the woods reposed . . .
> Pensive I stood, and alone; the hour and the
>   scene had subdued me . . .
> Then as I stood, the bell, which awhile from
>   its warning had rested,
> Sent forth its note again, toll, toll, through the
>   silence of evening.

Of the thirty-five thousand lines of verse which Southey estimated he had written by December, 1793, a generous share must have come from the inspiration of Collins.

Mr. Bronson[12] has said that Scott like Wordsworth found his inspiration elsewhere than in the pages of Collins. Yet Scott, too, robust in nature as he was, turned occasionally to the pages of the delicate and less fortunate poet with whom he felt a kinship. Scott's tribute to Collins in the *Bride of Triermain* is a commentary at once on the poet's genius and on his reputation:

> For Lucy loves (like Collins, ill-starred name,
> Whose lay's requital was that tardy fame,
> Who bound no laurel round his living head,
> Should hang it o'er his monument when dead)
> For Lucy loves to tread enchanted strand,
> And thread, like him, the maze of fairy land;
> Of golden battlements to view the gleam,
> And slumber soft by some Elysian stream.

The *Ode on the Popular Superstitions* naturally attracted Scott early, for here Collins had touched on a theme which Scott was to develop in the *Lady of the Lake* and the *Lord of the Isles.* In the *Minstrelsy of the Scottish Border* Scott included three supplemental stanzas to Collins's ode by his "valued friend," William Erskine, Esq., Advocate, which had already appeared in the *Edinburgh Magazine,* for April, 1788, the year in which the poem was found. Scott's comment that the stanzas are "worthy of the SUBLIME ORIGINAL" shows his own feeling for the poem. His motto to *Glenfinlas, or Lord Ronald's Coronach,* which originally appeared in Monk Lewis's *Tales of Wonder,* comes from the *Ode on the Popular Superstitions,* 65-9; in the poem itself Moy, the prophetic seer from Columb's isle, who has the power of second-sight, suggests the influence of Collins. Lines 33-6 embroider a superstition that Collins had neglected:

> For there [in Columb's isle] 'tis said, in
>   mystic mood,
> High converse with the dead they hold
>   And oft espy the fated shroud,
>   That shall the future corpse enfold.

Three times in the notes to the *Minstrelsy* Scott mentions Collins. In the *Introduction to the Tale of Tam-*

lane[13] Scott associates lines 58-9, 62-3 of the **Ode to Fear** (which he quotes inaccurately and apparently from memory) with St. John's Eve, in his mind the thrice-hallowed eve of Collins's poem. Again in his comment on Leyden's *Mermaid*[14] he refers to Collins's **Ode to Liberty,** 82, and the poet's note about the scorned mermaid who cast a mist over the Isle of Man. And in his notes on the *Gray Brother,* alluding to "classic Hawthornden" he quotes line 212 of the **Ode on the Popular Superstitions** as it appeared in the *Transactions of the Royal Society* copy: "The traveller now looks in vain for the leafy bower:

> Where Jonson sate in Drummond's social
>   shade."

There are also occasional suggestions in the historical romances that Scott remembered some of the other odes as well as the **Ode on the Popular Superstitions.** In the *Lay of the Last Minstrel,* I, xii, 4.

> Till to her bidding she could bow
> the viewless forms of air

echoes lines 65-6 of the **Ode on the Popular Superstitions,** a passage which Scott had already used as the motto to *Glenfinlas.* It is suggested again in *Lady of the Lake,* I, xxx:

> While viewless minstrels touch the string,
> 'Tis thus our charmed rhymes we sing.

And in *Soldier Rest* Scott must have remembered **Ode Written in the Beginning of the Year 1746** when he wrote:

> In our isle's enchanted hall,
> hands unseen thy couch are strewing,
>   fairy strains of music fall.

In the *Lord of the Isles* his allusion to the Seer of Skye and to "Iona's piles,"

> Where rest from mortal coil the Mighty of the
>   Isles,

suggests Collins as much as Martin Martin. And twice he echoes *The Passions.* In *Rokeby,* V, xvii, Rokeby's maid prays:

> Here to renew the strains she loved,
> at distance heard and well approved,

—a suggestion of *The Passions,* 60. In the *Vision of Don Roderick,* LXII:

> Or may I give adventurous fancy scope,
> And stretch a bold hand to the awful veil
> That hides futurity from anxious hope,
> bidding beyond it scenes of glory hail,

echoes "AND BAD THE LOVELY SCENES AT DISTANCE HAIL," line 32 of *The Passions.* In the Waverley novels Scott found very little occasion to remember Collins. He did, however, twice choose a motto at the head of a chapter from Collins's verse. The heading for Chapter IV of *The Monastery* comes from lines 58-9 and 61-2 of the *Ode to Fear,* rendered inaccurately. Chapter XI of *Peveril of the Peak* employs line 82 of the *Ode to Liberty* as its motto. In the introductory epistle to the *Fortunes of Nigel* he quotes two lines of the *Ode on the Popular Superstitions,* 68-9, as part of a discussion of the phenomenon of second sight or "deuteroscopy" as Scott calls it. In all three allusions it is evident that Collins's love of folk-lore most attracted Scott.

The evidence of Collins's direct influence on Scott is slight, but it reveals that Scott was familiar with a poet who had anticipated him in celebrating the glamor and fascination of the Highlands of Scotland.

Notes

[1] Knight, *Letters,* II, 358.

[2] *Ibid.,* III, 420.

[3] Knight, II, 419. Wordsworth was indirectly responsible for Crabb Robinson's expression of opinion about Collins. From Wordsworth's criticism of "brown hamlet" in Mrs. Barbauld's *Ode to Content* Crabb Robinson dissents: "for evening harmonizes with content, and the brown hamlet is the evening hamlet. Collins has with exquisite beauty described the coming on of evening: 'And hamlets brown and dim discovered spires'." (*Reminiscences,* ed. Sadler. I, 13).

[4] Cf. *Descriptive Sketches,* 115:

> That glimmer hoar in eve's last light descried
> Dim from the twilight water's shaggy side.

[5] *Biographia Literaria,* ed. Everyman, p. 10.

[6] *Table Talk,* April 21, 1811, ed. H. Ashe, p. 301.

[7] *Anima Poetae,* p. 4.

[8] *Letters,* ed. E. H. Coleridge, I, 196.

[9] Folio 21a, *Archiv,* XCVII, 1896, p. 352; fol. 25a, p. 354. To Coleridge, too, we owe a slight bit of evidence concerning Collins's influence on the continent, a problem upon which Mr. Woodhouse has touched (*TLS,* 1930, p. 838). Coleridge records of Klopstock (*Satyrane's Letters,* Ed. Everyman, p. 301): "An Englishman had presented him with the Odes of Collins, which he had read with pleasure." Herder, however, asserted "the infinite superiority of Klopstock's Odes

to all that Gray and Collins had ever written." (H. Crabb Robinson, *Diary and Reminiscences,* Ed. Sadler, I, 73.)

[10] See on this point J. L. Lowes, the *Road to Xanadu,* p. 399, p. 400, and E. Blunden, *TLS,* 1929, p. 592. Mr. Blunden also suggests that the scenery of the *Ode on the Poetical Character* (probably in the antistrophe) colors that of *Kubla Khan.*

[11] *Bohn Lib.,* I, 321.

[12] *Collins,* p. lvii.

[13] Ed. Crowell, p. 299.

[14] *Op. cit.,* p. 651.

Alan D. McKillop (essay date 1960)

SOURCE: "Collins's Ode to Evening—Background and Structure," in *Tennessee Studies in Literature,* Vol. V, 1960, pp. 73-84.

[*In the following essay, McKillop discusses the significance of the works of earlier poets and of Collins's own earlier work to his "Ode to Evening."*]

One of the earliest critical references to Collins's **Ode to Evening** is to be found in some "Observations on Poetry and Painting" in the *Universal Magazine* for January 1758:

> Few studious minds are unaffected with reading the representations of nature in a rural evening scene; especially if the artist has blended with the truth of imitation that undefineable delicacy of taste, to which even truth herself is often indebted for a more agreeable admittance into the heart. That succinct picture of the setting sun, in the 8th book of the Iliad.
>
> Now deep in ocean sunk the lamp of light, Drawing behind the cloudy veil of night;
>
> has very strong outlines, and commands the warmest approbation of our judgment; but, being unadorned by other circumstances, and wanting objects to enliven the landscape, the applause ends with the judgment, and never sinks deep into the heart. Whereas the following scene, in Mr. Collins's **Ode to the Evening,** being animated by proper allegorical personages, and coloured highly with incidental expressions, warms the breast with a sympathetic glow of retired thoughtfulness.[1]

The writer then quotes the sixth and seventh stanzas of Collins's poem, and continues: "The same may be observed in the following extract from that beautiful el-

egy written by Mr. Gray," quoting the first six stanzas. Without trying to read too much into these comments, we can see that they dwell on enlivened natural detail, the animating effect of "proper allegorical personages," and the sympathetic response of a meditative observer. Such a simple analysis would be almost too commonplace to repeat were it not that the relative priority of these elements and their relationship to one another are of some importance.

The third of the newly discovered **Drafts & Fragments** of Collins[2] gives us a glimpse of the prehistory of the **Ode to Evening**. I shall refer to this incomplete poem by the opening words of the first line, "**Ye Genii who in secret state**." The piece begins by addressing and rejecting the "Genii" or "powers" that rule crowded cities, and turns to praise of the retired life through the cycle of the seasons and amid wild nature; it takes the poet through the ideal day of *L'Allegro* and Thomson's *Summer,* and connects the dawn with "sweet Lorraine," the noontime retreat with the landscapes of "Rysdael," wild landscape with Salvator Rosa, and sunset colors with Lorrain again. Yet the poet continues, neither painting nor poetry can render the effect of moonlight, and he ends on a note of frustration. The **Ode to Evening** developed in part from the second part of this poem, beginning with the landscapes associated with Salvator:

> Then on some Heath all wild and bare
>   With more delight Ill stand
> Than He who sees with wondring air
>   The Works of Rosa's hand
>
> There where some Rocks deep Cavern gapes
>   Or in some tawny dell
> Ill seem to see the Wizzard Shapes
>   That from his Pencill fell
>
> But when soft Evening o'er the Plain
>   Her gleamy Mantle throws
> I'll mark the Clouds whence sweet Lorraine
>   His Colours chose
>
> Or from the Vale I'll lift my sight
>   To some
> Where e'er the Sun withdraws his light
>   The dying Lustre falls

With these stanzas we may compare Collins's two versions of the seventh stanza of the **Ode to Evening:**

> Then let me rove some wild and heathy Scene
> Or find some Ruin 'midst its dreary Dells,
>   Whose Walls more awful nod
>   By thy religious Gleams.
>
> Then lead, calm Vot'ress, where some sheety
>   lake

Cheers the lone heath, or some time-hallow'd
pile,
    Or up-land fallows grey
    Reflect its last cool gleam.

The first version has the wild landscape of Salvator from the early poem, and also something of the same light effect, especially if we conjecture the reading "walls" as the riming word in the second line of the fourth stanza quoted. The second version, however, with "its last cool gleam," is close to a following stanza in **"Ye Genii"** referring to the light of the moon:

What Art can paint the modest ray
    So sober chaste and cool
As round you Cliffs it seems to play
    Or skirts yon glimmring Pool?

The connection with Salvator Rosa and Claude Lorrain which critics have noted in the **Ode to Evening** is here confirmed. But, in place of a loose descriptive sequence, we have in the **Ode to Evening** the organization of nature description, allegorical figure, and meditative poet into a single scheme. Before considering the **Ode** in detail, we may note some of the various ways in which these aspects may appear together in the descriptive-allegorical mode. In **"Ye Genii"** itself personification is not pictorial, but Collins already has the idea of "Genii" who wield "secret powers" over the world of men, and of an opposing field in which "wild Nature" wields influence. We feel moreover that just below the surface is a power which we might call the spirit of "picture" or poetry. Somewhat similarly, in John Dyer's *Grongar Hill* we have a situation in which the persona invoked at the opening, "Silent Nymph, with curious eye," can be variously identified in the different versions as Fancy, or the muse of painting.[3] There is here a tendency, implicit in the tradition of Milton's minor poems, to identify the power invoked with the observer or poet, meditation with the meditative man. In both **"Ye Genii"** and *Grongar Hill* allegorical figures are secondary to the scene and the painter-poet.

Especially important for the **Ode to Evening** is Thomson's *Hymn on Solitude*. Here, though attention is fixed on the central personification, her qualities, haunts, attendants, and devotees, Solitude herself is not pictorially presented; a large part of the poem is given over to the varied manifestations of her spirit.

A thousand Shapes you wear with ease,
And still in every Shape you please.

She appears as a philosopher, a student of Nature, a recluse in the shade, a shepherd, a lover, or incarnated as the Countess of Hertford and her friend.[4] Besides this sequence of devotees, there is an attendant Miltonic train—Angels, Innocence, Contemplation, Religion, Urania. Solitude has a shrine, a "secret Cell" with "deep

Recesses"—a central place corresponding to the central person. In general, the *Hymn on Solitude* is an important link between the Miltonic imitation and the descriptive and allegorical ode. In particular, there is an important connection with the **Ode to Evening** in Thomson's use of the times of day:

Thine is th' unbounded Breath of Morn,
Just as the dew-bent Rose is born;
And while *Meridian* Fevers beat,
Thine is the Woodland dumb Retreat;
But chief, when Evening Scenes decay,
And the faint Landskip swims away,
Thine is the doubtful dear Decline,
And that best Hour of musing thine.

The last four lines give a slight sketch which Collins was later to elaborate and enrich.

The importance of the central allegorical persona in Thomson and Collins, with its background in Italian pictorial tradition as well as in earlier English poetry, has been fully and brilliantly demonstrated for the first time by Professor Jean Hagstrum.[5] His very close analysis shows a great range in degree of pictorial representation in Thomson, "from implicit, unvisualized figures, lurking suggestively behind his natural details, to those in the fully developed pictorial action" (p. 261). The fully developed pictorial action, with attention steadily fixed on the central persona, seems to me to be relatively rare in Thomson; but an excellent example is one given special attention by Hagstrum, the passage on the progress of the sun near the opening of *Summer:*

The vegetable World is also thine,
Parent of *Seasons!* who the Pomp precede
That waits thy Throne, as thro thy vast
    Domain,
Annual, along the bright Ecliptic-Road,
In World-rejoicing State, it moves sublime.
Mean-time th' expecting Nations, circled gay
With all the various Tribes of foodful Earth,
Implore thy Bounty, or send grateful up
A common Hymn: while, round thy beaming
    Car,
High-seen, the *Seasons* lead, in sprightly Dance
Harmonious knit, the rosy-finger'd *Hours,*
The *Zephyrs* floating loose, the timely *Rains,*
Of Bloom etherial the light-footed *Dews,*
And soften'd into Joy the surly *Storms.*
These, in successive Turn, with lavish, Hand
Shower every Beauty, every Fragrance shower,
Herbs, Flowers, and Fruits; till, kindling at thy
    Touch,
From Land to Land is flush'd the vernal Year.[6]

Hagstrum is no doubt correct in finding here the influence of Guido Reni's famous fresco "Aurora." Yet, unmistakable as this influence is, it seems to be virtually limited to the five lines or so describing the "beaming Car" and the attendants, indicated typographically by the sequence of italicized nouns from *Seasons* to *Storms*. And for these lines there is also a close Miltonic parallel:

> Universal *Pan*
> Knit with the *Graces* and the *Hours* in dance
> Led on the' Eternal Spring.
> (*Paradise Lost*, IV, 266-68.)

Milton's allegorical dance is included in a description of the beauties of Eden, full of action and motion, and is thus parallel to the natural processes described. What is most characteristic of Thomson in the lines quoted is the emphasis on pervasive and abundant vitality within the vast field of nature, and this is rendered only in part by fully pictorial personification; what had been a "Throne" easily becomes a "Car"; we see no occupant of the car dominating the scene, as in Guido, and the attendants blend easily with the forces of nature and the whole effect wrought in "the vernal Year." Our attention is not invited to dwell at length on a central allegorical figure, but to follow out the widely dispersive effects of a force which is personified for the nonce.

Though the Seasons and the various Powers of Nature appear in Thomson and are invoked as persons, the typical pattern includes the manifestation on a large scale in nature and the participation of the poet or observer. The scheme in a simple form appears, for example, at the opening of *Winter*:

> See, WINTER comes, to rule the vary'd Year,
> Sullen, and sad, with all his rising Train;
> *Vapours,* and *Clouds,* and *Storms.* Be these
>   my Theme,
> These, that exalt the Soul to solemn Thought,
> And heavenly Music. Welcome, kindred
>   Glooms!
> Cogenial Horrors, hail!

Each of the three aspects—the persona, the manifestations, the devotee—can be taken as a starting point. In the allegorical and descriptive ode the persona is naturally taken to be primary, but the poet at work may move subtly from one point of view to the other. The comparison between the persona in *The Seasons* and in the **Ode to Evening** has been stated with great care by Hagstrum: "Even in the **Ode to Evening,** in which the strategy of presentation is basically that of Thomson, natural detail has been subjected to greater imaginative modification than in any of Thomson's out-of-door descriptions. The personified figure of this lovely ode is more prominent, is attended by a greater number of subsidiary personifications, and is a more efficacious unifying force than are the figures in Thomson's verse" (p. 286). The critic's emphasis on the personified figure can be justified from the **Ode** itself. Evening is kept

before us as "pensive *Eve,"* "*Nymph* reserv'd," "*Maid* compos'd," "calm *Vot'ress,"* "meekest *Eve.*" She is invoked and viewed in adoration. She appears in a "shadowy Car," attended by *"Hours," "Elves,"* and "many a *Nymph* who wreaths her Brows with Sedge." Hagstrum's suggestion that we have here a "Vesper" corresponding to Guido's "Aurora" (p. 278) is illuminating, though the connection is more remote than in the passage already quoted from *Summer*. But again, we do not concentrate on a central figure. The personification of Evening is not a single picture but a series of manifestations, more subtle than but comparable to the series already noted in Thomson's *Hymn on Solitude*. As Blunden says, she is in succession "a country girl, a Fairy Queen, a priestess, a goddess, a ghost in the sky."[7] Perhaps it would be more accurate to say that these roles can be read into the poem. The figure of Evening is central but she is not in the spotlight, and the manifestations blend with the field of manifestation.

As in Thomson, the conception of the domain, realm, or sphere of influence marks out here a middle way between the fully pictorial persona and specific natural description. The traditional nature of this conception, which deserves more attention than we can give it here, may be seen by consulting the entries under, "Empire," "Kingdom," "Region," and "Reign" in John Arthos' study, *The Language of Natural Description in Eighteenth-Century Poetry* (Ann Arbor, 1949). The concept of the domain or realm offers easy transitions from the field of force to the field of vision, or *vice versa,* makes possible the rendering of a "felt influence" in objective or subjective form. Collins's Evening lives in her own realm; she at once dominates, pervades, and is immersed in a world whose extent can be variously defined as the theater of natural forces, the cycle of hours and seasons, the perspective of landscape painting, and the meditative poet's vision. The comparison with the coming of Evening in Thomson's *Summer* is inevitable:

> Confess'd from yonder slow-extinguish'd
>   Clouds,
> All Ether softening, sober *Evening* takes
> Her wonted Station in the middle Air;
> A thousand *Shadows* at her Beck, First *This*
> She sends on Earth; then *That* of deeper Dye
> Steals soft behind; and then a *Deeper* still,
> In Circle following Circle, gathers round,
> To close the Face of Things.[8]

Thomson's effect is more massive or cosmic than Collins's, and his suggestion of a dominant central figure, a pageant, and a train, is submerged in natural process. Both poets combine the personification of Evening with a descriptive sequence carefully graduated in time and space; both poets here deal with "imperfect vision," in which "the faint landskip swims away," in which night does not fall with "quenching gloom" but one shadow after another "steals soft behind."[9] Collins's details are more explicitly selected and arranged to form a continuum and stand in parallel with the progress of Evening. The run-on stanzas heighten this effect.

Since Collins begins with sound-effects, we may take them up first. The auditory counterpart of picturesque visualization may be illustrated from *The Passions,* where Melancholy

> from her wild sequester'd Seat,
> In Notes by Distance made more sweet,
> Pour'd thro' the mellow *Horn* her pensive
>   Soul:
>   And dashing soft from Rocks around,
>   Bubbling Runnels join'd the Sound;
> Thro' Glades and Glooms the mingled
>   Measure stole,
> Or o'er some haunted Stream with fond
>   Delay,
>   Round an holy Calm diffusing,
>   Love of Peace, and lonely Musing,
> In hollow Murmurs died away.

These are what Mrs. Radcliffe later called in so many words "*picturesque* sounds, if the expression may be allowed."[10] In the *Ode to Evening* Collins gets his sound effects less obtrusively: the ear of Eve is soothed by "solemn springs," revised from "brawling springs" in the first version. Many besides Wordsworth have commented on the improvement, the toning down of the sound, though it is hard to say how harsh a sound Collins may have meant by "brawling." The revision is clearly intended, however, to suggest a sound softened by distance and echo. Blunden notes the rendering of the murmurs and echoes of evening in the rimes and assonances of the poem, enhanced by the absence of end-rime, and his sensitive ear catches the echoing "now" in lines 5, 9, and 13.[11] Internal rime, assoanance, and the repetition of words make a sound-pattern at once intricate and relatively unobtrusive.

In the third and fourth stanzas we hear, magnified at close range and by the hush of evening, the "short shrill shriek" of the bat, the "small but sullen horn" and "heedless hum" of the beetle. The antecedents of the passage are *Faerie Queene,* II, xii, 36, *Macbeth,* III, ii, 40-43, *Lycidas,* line 28, and Gay, *Shepherd's Week,* III, 117, but the total effect is Collins's own. These close-up sounds and the more obviously picturesque sounds at a distance give an auditory range which is central for the first part of the poem. Léon Lemonnier finds ominous agitation here: "De temps à autre, passe un cri, un geste inexplicable, sans doute venu de l'au-delà. Il se peut que sous ce monde réel, d'étranges créatures se meuvent, qui s'efforcent de déchirer le voile, qui veulent nous observer."[12] Though this comment may heighten the effect overmuch into mysterious terror, it renders well the auditory depth of the verse and the suggestion of the occult power of Evening.

But there is yet another sound which the poet hopes may soothe the ear of Evening—the "oaten stop or pastoral song" which the poet himself essays. The phrases are from *Comus,* line 345, and blend the formula of the pastoral with the pattern of near and distant sounds; but the poet's singing is more than conventional. It is a pastoral version of a characteristic theme in Collins, the poet's quest. The new *Drafts & Fragments* seem to show that Collins began with the pastoral lyric, enriching it first with descriptive and then with allegorical elements. In some of his most characteristic work Collins frequently dwells on arrested inspiration, the recovery of the note of authentic passion, the exquisite and inaccessible quality of true simplicity; but these ideas are here attenuated into a gentle diffidence which pervades the long conditional sentence from line 1 to line 20. Can any song soothe the ear of Eve like the natural sounds congenial to the time?

The second stanza, however, does not fit into the scheme I have described.

> O *Nymph* reserv'd, while now the bright-hair'd
>   Sun
> Sits in yon western Tent, whose cloudy Skirts,
>   With Brede ethereal wove,
>   O'erhang his wavy Bed:

In presenting the after-glow of sunset, beyond and above the twilight, the poet alters the perspective and abandons the careful gradation of images. We may compare a passage in Milton's *Ode on the Morning of Christ's Nativity:*

> So when the Sun in bed,
> Curtain'd with cloudy red,
>   Pillows his chin upon an Orient wave—

The somewhat rare word "brede," associated with needlework, enhances the effect of the conceit. The image recurs in the "tented sky" of *The Poetical Character,* and more elaborately in the Second Epode of *Liberty:*

> Beyond yon braided Clouds that lie,
> Paving the light-embroider'd Sky:
> Amidst the bright pavilion'd Plains.

This passage is part of a cosmic progress, and extends the scene to an ideal other-world in which the shrine of Liberty stands eternally, but the general plan of the *Ode to Evening* might seem to exclude such an abrupt change of scale. Indeed, the scale is not really shifted here. Tillyard compares the *Nativity Ode* with Italian primitive painting,[13] and the comparison may help to illustrate the temporary abandonment of perspective in Collins's stanza. In relation to the rest of the poem it also illustrates the principle of the *morceau de fantaisie* which Wylie Sypher has applied to Collins's work, the principle of "discontinuity" or "dislocation of imagery."[14] But as a whole the ***Ode to Evening*** does not have the incoherence or disorder which Sypher's essay would make central for Collins.

There is no difficulty in accepting a division of the poem into three parts, lines 1-20, 21-40, and 41-52. The first is connected with the second by the progress of Evening and her attendants in lines 21-28. Just as the pastoral song of the first part blends with the actual sounds of evening, so the persona and the train merge with the scene. The shadowy figure of the poet then reappears, not as a pastoral singer but as a contemplative observer of what we have already described as a landscape in the manner of Salvator presented with Thomson's characteristic interest in imperfect vision. The two combine in the familiar passage:

> be mine the Hut,
> That from the Mountain's Side,
> Views Wilds, and swelling Floods,
>
> And Hamlets brown, and dim-discover'd Spires,
> And hears their simple Bell, and marks o'er all
> Thy Dewy Fingers draw
> The gradual dusky Veil.

Ainsworth's citations from Thomson are of great help here.[15] The elements of the view appear in part in many a picturesque prospect, such as *Spring,* lines 952-55, but the light effect is more closely related to the elaborate one in *Summer,* lines 1684-94:

> *Evening* yields
> The World to *Night;* not in her Winter-Robe
> Of massy Stygian Woof, but loose array'd
> In Mantle dun. A faint erroneous Ray,
> Glanc'd from th' imperfect Surfaces of Things,
> Flings half an Image on the straining Eye;
> While wavering Woods, and Villages, and
> Streams,
> And Rocks, and Mountain-tops that long
> retain'd
> Th' ascending Gleam, are all one swimming
> Scene,
> Uncertain if beheld.

Another link with Thomson is the famous epithet "dim-discover'd," which, as Quayle points out, comes from *Summer,* line 946.[16] The ordered prospect becomes more evanescent in Collins. It is appropriate that the same effect should reappear in Collins's ***Ode on the Death of Mr. Thomson:***

> And see, the fairy valleys fade,
> Dun *Night* has veil'd the solemn view!

As the vision fades in the "Hamlets brown" stanza, we are reminded of the earlier sound effects by the "simple Bell," which may be said to link the auditory effects of the first part with the visual effects of the second.

The "chill blust'ring Winds, or driving Rain," the change of weather that sends the poet to the mountain hut, anticipate the third and last part, where as in Thomson, the observer moves through the cycle of the seasons. But this extension of range weakens the poem. The succession of the seasons is mechanical, and Garrod's strictures on this "epilogue" must be admitted.[17] We have here an illustration of the tendency to incorporate in the form of the ode the ground-plan of a descriptive-didactic poem. Professor Norman Maclean, who has some important comments on the conclusion of this poem, notes that the poet here undertakes to introduce the sublime, wild, or awful aspects of his subject, as

> *Winter* yelling thro' the troublous Air,
> Affrights thy shrinking Train,
> And rudely rends thy Robes.[18]

Thus the spell of the quiet Evening is broken. And just as the subject is overextended by the cycle of the Seasons, so the train of Evening as evoked by Collins is broken by the troop of abstractions in the last stanza, be they "Fancy, Friendship, Science, smiling Peace," in 1746, or the same group with "rose-lipp'd Health" substituted for Peace in 1748. The group is assembled, as Maclean remarks, in the quest for an elevated and abstracted ending. This is not the true train of Collins's Evening; if we return to society, it is not to our profit. As Lemonnier rightly remarks, Collins's evening is essentially less social than Gray's. Collins is attempting to accommodate within his ode an abbreviated form of Thomson's rather relaxed blank-verse meditations. But the "sylvan shed" in which these figures gather, irritating though it may be to a modern reader, is not quite perfunctory; it is derived from the "hut" of line 34, which serves as a point of view for the second part, and it stands for the shrine, cell, temple, retreat, tomb, or bower which is to be found as a focal point in each of the odes. Collins always provides a building or lodging for his allegorical figures. It is hard for us to understand why he should feel the need for such a point of reference, but there is doubtless some connection with the pictorial tradition and the iconography of the period. The matter need not be fully discussed here, since the shrine in the ***Ode to Evening*** is a mere vestige. The real setting is the realm of the sights and sounds of Evening; the "sylvan shed" may be considered as an attempt to center the poem again after the over-extension that comes with the introduction of the sequence of the seasons. And the concluding line of the final version, "And hymn thy fav'rite name," is a last reminder of the poet himself as devotee, a last echo of the sounds that pervade the poem.

Notes

[1] *Universal Magazine,* XXII (1758), 1-4, especially p. 2. The couplet is inaccurately quoted from Pope's *Iliad,* VIII, 605-606.

[2] William Collins, *Drafts & Fragments of Verse,* ed. J. S. Cunningham, Oxford, 1956. Quotations from this edition are made by permission of the Clarendon Press.

[3] See John Dyer, *Grongar Hill,* ed. Richard Boys (Baltimore, 1941), pp. 68-69, 94-95.

[4] For the early history of the *Hymn on Solitude* see Helen S. Hughes, "Thomson and the Countess of Hertford," *Modern Philology,* XXV (1928), 447-449; *James Thomson: Letters and Documents,* ed. Alan D. McKillop (Lawrence, 1958), pp. 10-12. I have followed the text in Ralph's *Miscellany* (1729).

[5] Jean H. Hagstrum, *The Sister Arts: The Tradition of Literary Pictorialism and English Poetry from Dryden to Gray* (Chicago, 1958), especially chaps. IX and X.

[6] Summer, lines 112-31. All quotations from *The Seasons* follow the 1746 edition, with line-numbers as in Robertson's edition, Oxford Standard Authors.

[7] Edmund Blunden, *Nature in English Poetry* (New York, 1929), p. 43.

[8] *Summer,* lines 1647-54. Chester F. Chapin *(Personification in Eighteenth-Century English Poetry* [New York, 1955], p. 75), makes the comparison between this passage and Collins' *Ode,* with an interesting comment by the eighteenth-century critic John Scott, objecting to Thomson's blending of "natural description and personification."

[9] See Marjorie Nicolson, *Newton Demands the Muse* (Princeton, 1946), pp. 96-97, 115-116.

[10] Ann Radcliffe, *Mysteries of Udolpho,* I, vii.

[11] *Poems of William Collins,* ed. Edmund Blunden (London, 1929), p. 171; *Nature in English Literature,* pp. 39-40.

[12] Léon Lemonnier, *Les poètes anglais du xviii*ᵉ *siècle* (Paris, 1947), pp. 116-117.

[13] E. M. W. Tillyard, *Milton* (London, 1930), p. 37.

[14] Wylie Sypher, "The *Morceau de Fantaisie* in Verse: A New Approach to Collins," *University of Toronto Quarterly,* XV (1945), 65-69.

[15] E. G. Ainsworth, Jr., *Poor Collins* (Ithaca, 1937), pp. 192-193.

[16] Thomas Quayle, *Poetic Diction* (London, 1924), p. 116.

[17] H. W. Garrod, *Collins* (Oxford, 1928), p. 76.

[18] Norman Maclean, "From Action to Image: Theories of the Lyric in the Eighteenth Century," in *Critics and Criticism: Ancient and Modern* (Chicago, 1952), pp. 444-445.

Harold Bloom (essay date 1961)

SOURCE: "Collins's Ode on the Poetical Character," in *The Visonary Company: A Reading of English Poetry,* Doubleday & Company, Inc., 1961, pp. 3-10.

[*Below, Bloom analyzes Collins's "Ode on the Poetical Character" and places Collins's technique within the context of the works of Keats, William Blake, Wordsworth, Edmund Spenser, and John Milton.*]

> . . . if we say that the idea of God is merely a poetic idea, and that our notions of heaven and hell are merely poetry not so called, even if poetry that involves us vitally, the feeling of deliverance, of a release, of a perfection touched, of a vocation so that all men may know the truth and that the truth may set them free—if we say these things and if we are able to see the poet who achieved God and placed Him in His seat in heaven in all His glory, the poet himself, still in the ecstasy of the poem that completely accomplished his purpose, would have seemed, whether young or old, whether in rags or ceremonial robe, a man who needed what he had created, uttering the hymns of joy that followed his creation.
>
> —WALLACE STEVENS,
> *The Figure of the Youth as Virile Poet*[3]

To make a myth is to tell a story of your own invention, to speak a word that is your word alone, and yet the story is so told, the word so spoken, that they mean also the supernal things and transcend the glory of the ego able to explain itself to others. We say of Blake and Wordsworth that they are the greatest of the Romantic poets, and indeed the first poets fully to enter into the abyss of their own selves, and we mean that they perform for us the work of the ideal metaphysician or therapeutic idealist, which is the role our need has assigned to the modern poet.

William Collins is a poet of the Age of Sensibility and enthusiasm, of the conscious return to Spenser, Shakespeare, and Milton. We have progressed beyond studying Collins as a fitful prelude to Keats, or Blake as a freakish premanifestation of Romanticism. What does ally Collins and Keats, Blake and Wordsworth, is one of the great traditions of English poetry, the prophetic and Protestant line of Spenser and Milton, which reaches its radical limits in the generation after Wordsworth.

The characteristic concern of this line is with the double transformation of the individual and of nature; the apocalyptic ambition involved is to humanize nature, and to naturalize the imagination. The *Ode on the Poetical Character* shares this concern and, with great intensity, manifests this ambition.

The poem belongs to the class of the allegorical ode, which moves in the Romantic period from personification to mythopoeic confrontation, from subject-object experience to the organized or deliberate innocence of a confrontation of life by life, in which all natural objects come to be seen as animate with the one life within us and abroad.[4] The inherent values of eighteenth-century personification were undoubtedly very real, but the values of Collins' mythical confrontations are rather different from those of traditional personification. What distinguishes Collins from the Wartons, or Christopher Smart from Gray, is that Collins and Smart sometimes (as in the *Ode on the Poetical Character* and *Jubilate Agno*) attain a transfiguration of the matter of common perception. They do this, usually, by consciously simplifying, as Blake and Wordsworth do after them. They reduce the manifold of sensation to a number of objects that can actually be contemplated, which F. A. Pottle sets forth as *the* mark of the poetic imagination in Wordsworth.[5] Having created worlds with fewer and more animate objects, they proceed to dissolve the objects into one another, even as Blake will later view natural objects as "men seen afar" and as Wordsworth, in his supreme acts of imagination, will have "the edges of things begin to waver and fade out." The "fade-out" or fluid dissolving of the imagination is more familiar to us in Wordsworth and Keats and most radically evident in Shelley, but its presence in Collins is crucial, and constitutes much of the "confusion" of the *Ode on the Poetical Character*. The confusion of Collins' *Ode* is thematically deliberate, for in it Collins' soul, God, and nature are brought together in what Northrop Frye has called "a white-hot fusion of identity, an imaginative fiery furnace in which the reader may, if he chooses, make a fourth."[6] This fusion of identity, the highest imaginative moment in the poetry of Collins, establishes the *Ode on the Poetical Character* as one of the group of lyrics that Frye has usefully classified as "recognition poems," in which the usual associations of dream and waking are reversed, "So that it is experience that seems to be the nightmare and the vision that seems to be reality."[7] Within this larger group are the "poems of self-recognition, where the poet himself is involved in the awakening from experience into a visionary reality." Frye gives the *Ode on the Poetical Character, Kubla Khan,* and *Sailing to Byzantium* as examples, to which one can add the *Hymn to Intellectual Beauty* as a major Romantic representative of the type. Collins' *Ode,* like *Kubla Khan,* is on the borderline of another group of lyrics, the rhapsodic poems of iconic response, "where the poet feels taken possession of by some internal and quasi-personal force" as in the *Ode to the West Wind,* Robert Bridges' *Low Barometer,* or Hart Crane's Shelleyan masterpiece, *The Broken Tower.*

The fullest reading of the *Ode on the Poetical Character* is that of A. S. P. Woodhouse, who terms it "an allegory whose subject is the *creative imagination* and the poet's passionate desire for its power."[8] Woodhouse's reading is perhaps imaginatively less daring than Collins' poem, for the *Ode* goes beyond the poet's desire for the power, and suggests that a poet is born from a quasi-sexual union of God and Imagination. The celebrated bluestocking Mrs. Barbauld said of this allegory that it was "neither luminous nor decent," but Woodhouse calls it only a "repetition of the fact already simply stated: God imagined the world, and it sprang into being." But this central myth of the poem is both luminous and nonrepetitive, though as unorthodox as any myth-making is likely to be.

Collins begins the ode by repeating the central polemic of his literary generation. Spenser's school, the line of late Drayton, Milton, of Collins himself, is the one most blessed by the Faerie Queene, who by implication is the Muse herself. The polemic is not renewed until the close of the ode, when Collins will see himself "from Waller's myrtle shades retreating," in full flight from the school of Pope. The urbane "with light regard" in the first line of the ode is a probable indication that Collins is aware of his two "mistakes" in reading Book IV, Canto V, of *The Faerie Queene.* The magic girdle is Florimel's, but can be worn by whoever has "the vertue of chast love and wifehood true." At the solemn tourney it is Amoret who alone can wear it, as Florimel is not present, and the other ladies who are lack the prescribed "vertue." Collins is compounding Florimel and Amoret so as to get a creative contrary to his own idea of Fancy. Florimel and Amoret together represent the natural beauty of the world adorned by an inherent chastity. Fancy represents a beauty more enthusiastic than that of nature, and this more exuberant beauty is distinguished by an inherent sexuality. As Woodhouse says, to Collins "poetry is not primarily concerned with nature, but with a bright world of ideal forms."[9] But in Collins as in Blake this bright world is attained through an increase in sensual fulfillment. We have here almost a prelude to Wordsworth's myth of nature's marriage or Blake's myth of Beulah as the married land. The beauty of Florimel becomes transformed into the bright world of Fancy by a consummation analogous to sexual completion.

The girdle of Florimel is better not worn at all than applied to a "loath'd, dishonour'd side." The implication is that it is more horrible to assume unworthily "the cest of amplest pow'r" which is in young Fancy's gift. That gift is godlike; they who wear it, once they "gird their blest, prophetic loins," are able to "gaze her visions wild, and feel unmix'd her flame!" That the gift has a sexual element is made finely obvious by the diction.

The epode is a creation myth, and a startling rhapsody in the context of its literary age. Coleridge said of the epode that it had "inspired and whirled *me* along with greater agitations of enthusiasm than any but the most *'impassioned'* scene in Schiller or Shakespeare." Coleridge modified the value of his rapture by saying that the "impassioned" (he meant ordinary human passions) kind of poetry is more generally valuable, but *Kubla Khan,* with its echo of Collins' ode on the Passions and its youthful poet with flashing eyes and floating hair, indicates why the **Ode on the Poetical Character** had so strong an effect on Coleridge.

The concept of an all-creative and yet strictly male Deity has always been very satisfying to the moralizing temper of orthodox Judaism and Christianity, but it is imaginatively rather puzzling. The poem of creation can do very little with anything *ab nihilo,* for the imagination wishes to be indulged, as Wallace Stevens remarked, and opaque mysteries are not gratifying to it. Poets, even those as devout as Spenser and Wordsworth, have a tendency to parallel unorthodox speculations on the role of a female element in the creation. These speculations rise from the swamps of Neoplatonism, gnosticism, occultism, and that richest and dankest of morasses, the cabala. Collins' "lov'd enthusiast," young Fancy, who has long wooed the Creator, and who retires with Him behind a veiling cloud while seraphic wires sound His "sublimest triumph swelling," has her place in that long arcane tradition that stems from the cabalistic *Shekhina,* and that may include the Sapience of Spenser's *Hymne of Heavenly Beautie.*

There are no scholarly reasons for supposing that Collins was deep in the *esoterica* of theosophy, as we know Christopher Smart to have been. But while the passage from *Proverbs* VIII, 23-30, on Wisdom having been daily God's delight, rejoicing always before Him, when He appointed the foundations of the earth, is an adequate source for Milton, it is not for Collins' ode. Source study is not likely to help us here, any more than it has helped much in the comprehension of Spenser's *Hymnes.* Collins' Goddess Fancy is enigmatic enough in her function to make us probe further into the difficulty of the ode.

Collins saw himself as a poet separated by the school of Waller from a main tradition of the English Renaissance, the creation of a British mythology: the Faery Land of Spenser, the green world of Shakespeare's romances, the Biblical and prophetic self-identification of Milton. This reading of English poetic history, with Waller and Pope in the Satanic role, is itself of course a poetic myth, and a very productive one, in Blake and the Romantics as much as in Collins and the Wartons. We need not worry as to whether Collins is being fair or accurate in his reading of history; it is enough that he is telling us and himself a story, and that he at least believes the story to be true.

To emulate Spenser and Milton, Collins must first see man, nature, and poetry in their perspective, not that of Pope. Their perspective, at its limits, is that of the rugged sublime, in which the poet is an original, whose inventive capacity is divinely inspired. The poet is an "enthusiast" or possessed man, and what possesses him is Fancy, which itself is a "kindred power" to Heaven. So inspired, the enthusiast moves into nature to form out of it an imaged paradise of his heart's desires. His ambition is enormous, but is founded on his claim to potential divinity. This is the background of Blake's astonishing ambitions, and particularly of his myth of Orc, which I invoke now as a context in which to read Collins. Northrop Frye, in tracing the origins of Blake's Orc, considers the large claims of the poets of the Age of Sensibility and writes:

> It is in Collins' **Ode on the Poetical Character** that the most daring claim is made. There, not only does the poet in his creation imitate the creative power of God, but is himself a son of God and Fancy, a "rich-hair'd youth of morn" associated with the sun-god, like the Greek Apollo, a prophet and visionary of whom the last exemplar was Milton. This youth is the direct ancestor of Blake's Orc.[10]

Orc is the most complex and suggestive of Blake's symbolic figures. His name is based on his prime identity, which is that of the recurrent energy of human desire, frequently assigned by orthodox timidity to the realm of Orcus, or hell. Orc is the human imagination trying to burst out of the confines of nature, but this creative thrust in him is undifferentiated from merely organic energy. He is thus a very comprehensive myth, for he is Blake's Adonis and Blake's Prometheus, Blake's Apollo and Blake's Christ, and he is manifested in Blake's time by figures as diverse as Napoleon and Blake himself. This apparently bewildering range of identifications is possible because Orc is a cyclic figure; he is the babe of Blake's poem, *The Mental Traveller,* who goes around on the wheel of birth, youth, manhood, old age, and rebirth.

His relevant aspect here is that in which he resembles the Apollo of Keats's two *Hyperions,* the story of a poet's incarnation as a god of the sun. Blake's dialectic concerns man and nature, but is also a dialectic of poetry itself. Orc represents not only the sun in its dawn and spring but in their human analogies as well. He means new life and sexual renewal, which appear in the periodic overthrow of literary conventions as well as of restrictive social and religious forms. When we encounter a youth of the sun who incarnates a rebirth of poetry, and whose early existence is in an earthly paradise, then we encounter a myth of the birth of Orc, or rebirth of Apollo, whether we find him in Collins or Coleridge or Blake or Keats or Shelley.

What makes Collins' "rich-hair'd Youth of Morn" a direct ancestor of Blake's and Coleridge's youths is his attendant iconography, which is derived from the Bible and Spenser, the sources we should expect.

Blake's best and most famous portrait of Orc or the Romantic Apollo is his line engraving called traditionally "Glad Day" after the lines in *Romeo and Juliet:*

> Night's candles are burnt out, and jocund day
> Stands tiptoe on the misty mountain tops.

Blake's Orc dances on tiptoe, a superbly Renaissance figure, with both arms flung out and the light bursting from him. His eyes are flashing, and his floating hair is rich with light. He both reflects the sunlight and radiates light to it, and he treads underfoot the serpent and the bat as he dances. Blake's vision here may go back to the same source in Spenser that Collins' lines seem to echo:

> And Phoebus, fresh as brydegrome to his mate,
> Came dauncing forth, shaking his deawie
>   hayre,
> And hurld his glistring beams through gloomy
>   ayre.

Spenser echoes Solomon's Song, with its visions of a great marriage in nature, an appropriate resonance for the Red Crosse Knight's great epiphany as he stands fully armed in the sun, both reflecting and radiating light from his "sunbright armes."

If we take this myth of the Romantic Apollo to Collins' *Ode,* we can suddenly see the startling unity of vision that Collins has achieved in the second strophe of his poem. The band of Fancy, which only the true poet dare assume, is analogous to the girdle of Florimel only in being a danger to the unworthy. For Fancy's cest, or girdle, was woven on the "creating day" when God rested from his labors, but in the company of his spouse, Fancy, who long had wooed him. On this day, "in some diviner mood," God takes her. Amidst the triumphal music, Fancy breathes her magic notes aloud, and the poet as Orc, or Apollo, is born. We can trace in the features of Blake's Glad Day the self-portrait of the young Blake. Collins here, unlike Blake, or Coleridge at the climax of *Kubla Khan,* is not audacious enough to claim this full identification. Indeed, Collins' fear of such a claim dominates the last strophe of his poem. Yet Collins indicates the significance of this sudden incarnation for him by excitedly breaking into the second person invocatory address, which usually accompanies mythopoeic confrontation:

> And *thou,* thou rich-hair'd Youth of Morn,
> And all thy subject life, was born!

Everything in the ode before and after these lines is in the first or third person; Collins shows extraordinary artistry and a firm grasp of his subject by this moment of direct address, as in a supreme act of imagination he shares a meeting with a self he longs to become.

From this height of startled apprehension, in which the object world has dropped away, Collins as suddenly descends. If he were to entertain such "high presuming hopes" it would be "with rapture blind." For to incarnate the poet within oneself is to be a resident of that poet's paradise, inaccessible to Collins, which he pictures in the antistrophe.

An earthly paradise on an inaccessible mountain top suggests the structure of the *Purgatorio,* and introduces into Collins' poem another of the great archetypes of literature, which Frye has termed the point of epiphany, where a cyclical order of nature and a higher eternal order come together.[11] The Romantic form of this point is the natural tower of consciousness, as Wallace Stevens calls it, or the dread watchtower of man's absolute self, as Coleridge calls it in his poem *To William Wordsworth.*[12] Keats, in the *Ode to Psyche,* builds this point of epiphany within his own mind as a refuge for the love of Eros and Psyche. From the point of epiphany we look down benevolently to the natural world, free of its cyclic variation, and up to the eternal world, but we are still more involved in nature than the apocalyptic world need be. Blake calls this point the upper limit of Beulah. Wordsworth reaches it on top of Snowdon in the transfiguring climax of *The Prelude.* Keats's special accomplishment is to naturalize it, to locate it out of nature and within the poet's mind, as Stevens does after him. But Collins, like Smart or Cowper, is one of the doomed poets of an Age of Sensibility. His personal myth, which intimately allies his art and his life, is one of necessary historical defeat. The cliff on which Milton lay is "of rude access," and supernatural beings guard it. No manic seizure will bring Collins there, nor has he yet learned the Wordsworthian metaphysic of internalization that will be available to Keats. As the ode closes, Collins looks upward in vain:

> such bliss to one alone
> Of all the sons of soul was known,
> And Heav'n and Fancy, kindred pow'rs,
> Have now o'erturn'd th' inspiring bow'rs,
> Or curtain'd close such scene from ev'ry
>   future view.

The "inspiring bow'rs" are those of Spenser's Adonis and Milton's Eden, and are righted again in Blake and Wordsworth.

Notes

[3] *The Necessary Angel* (New York: Knopf, 1951).

[4] See M. H. Abrams, *The Mirror and the Lamp* (New York: 1953), pp. 55-56, 64-68, 288-89, 292-93.

[5] "The Eye and the Object in the Poetry of Wordsworth," in *Wordsworth,* ed. Dunklin (Princeton, 1951), pp. 23-42.

[6] "Towards Defining an Age of Sensibility," in *Eighteenth Century English Literature,* ed. Clifford (New York, 1959), p. 318.

[7] *Anatomy of Criticism* (Princeton, 1957), p. 301.

[8] "Collins and the Creative Imagination," in *Studies in English by Members of University College, Toronto,* ed. Wallace (Toronto, 1931), p. 60.

[9] *Ibid.,* p. 62.

[10] *Fearful Symmetry* (Princeton, 1947), pp. 169-70. My account of Orc is partly based on Frye's book.

[11] *Anatomy of Criticism,* pp. 203-06.

[12] See Wallace Stevens' *Credences of Summer,* III. or edition, 1953), p. 147.

Patricia Meyer Spacks (essay date 1983)

SOURCE: "The Eighteenth-Century Collins," in *Modern Language Quarterly,* Vol. 44, No. 1, March, 1983, pp. 3-22.

[*In the essay below, Spacks contends that critics are mistaken in classifying Collins as a Romantic poet; rather, she argues, he should be considered a second-rank eighteenth-century poet.*]

William Collins sounds different now from the Collins we used to know. For example, Paul S. Sherwin claims, "Collins feels, all right; but what he feels most urgently is his estrangement from the passionate integrity of unself-conscious or 'unmixed' feeling. Impatient and aching, he is a fever of himself, his intensity springing directly from baffled desire."[1] This feverish figure, "one of the doomed poets of an Age of Sensibility," to use Harold Bloom's words,[2] reveals, like Smart and "the great Romantics," a "struggle with his vocation," the fate of the post-Miltonic writer.[3] He explores problems of sexuality as well as of literary creativity;[4] he resembles Satan more than Milton (Sherwin, p. 32); his imagery partakes of the demonic.[5] Tormented, colorful writer of tormented, colorful verse, he does not much resemble an "eighteenth-century" poet.

Critical allegations of this sort imply a version of literary history (often a Freudified and personalized version) which blurs the century between Milton and Pope, a period that has long caused trouble for critics of poetry. Collins in his most conspicuous recent avatars gains stature mainly by his intimations of the future: a false teleology. The currently fashionable view privileges poetic sensibility, posits discernible relations between psyches and the texts they originate, appropriates Collins to the values of Romanticism. I shall argue that he belongs, rather, to the century of Pope and Johnson, the century in which he lived. (He died in 1759, only fifteen years after Pope.) If, as I believe, Collins inhabits the second rank of eighteenth-century, not nineteenth-century, poets, one must wonder why, unlike such indubitably second-rate contemporaries as Joseph Warton and far more even than Thomas Gray, he has captured the attention of thoughtful and perceptive late-twentieth-century critics who hint that he has the stature of an important Romantic poet or condescend to him because he fails to be sufficiently Romantic.

The new defenders of sublimity, anxiety, and the demonic have acquired their authority partly by sheer intelligence, partly by astute public relations, partly by their ability to perceive enduring human concerns implicit in even the most convention-dominated texts of the past. Their version of Collins sounds worthy of attention because the poet, as they present him, cares about what we care about. Close examination of the critical texts, however, may raise questions about whether the "caring" belongs to Collins or to his recent interpreters.

The most compelling Collins-critics share a Freudian orientation at times startling in its single-minded intensity. Thus Thomas Weiskel, writing about the poet's use of Oedipus in the **"Ode to Fear,"** comments, "It is exactly this ambivalent excitement and dread which the Freudians insist lie behind the mystery of the primal scene and its perceptional derivatives. Had Freud never lived, we would be driven to the hypothesis of the oedipal complex to make sense of these lines" (p. 116). Without Freud, in other words, Collins makes no sense. With Freud's help, critics discover in the poet a consistent substratum of torment. Consider Bloom, also on the **"Ode to Fear"**: "at how high a price Collins purchases this indefinite rapture, this cloudy Sublime! For his poem is one with his deepest repression of his own humanity, and accurately prophesies the terrible pathos of his fate, to make us remember him always, with all his gifts, as Dr. Johnson's 'Poor Collins.'"[6] Or Sherwin: "Occasionally, as in the **'Ode to Evening,'** [numinous or visionary possibilities] threaten to erupt, abandoning Collins to his anxieties, and while the temptation to range beyond even toward daemonic ground is scrupulously resisted, it is never completely subdued. For all its delicacy, Collins' Evening realm, like all of his art, is founded upon an unappeasable terror" (pp. 102-3).

Anxiety, the dominant emotion of the twentieth century, governs, in many of these perceptions, the eighteenth-century poet. We domesticate our forebears by discovering in them our own sufferings. Even Collins's most serene lyric, the **"Ode to Evening,"** testifies to his "terror"; his interest in fear as poetic subject proclaims his uncertainties. Instead of inquiring why the poet concerns himself with the literary dynamics of fear, these critics ask what Collins is afraid of. "Here is Collins, invoking Fear," Bloom writes, "yet what has he to fear except himself and John Milton?" (*Anxiety of Influence,* p. 110). According to Paul Fry, "Collins's Fear, fear of nothing but his own hobgoblinry, is really anxiety" (p. 132). Sherwin tells us, "Collins' fear is that he doesn't feel, or fear, enough" (p. 77). The line between poetic speaker and living person blurs when Bloom can link an ode's evocation of fear to its author's subsequent insanity or Sherwin make confident assertions about Collins's own fears. The interest of the poetry depends on the possibility of making provocative claims about its author.

These critics concentrate almost entirely on four poems by Collins, and mainly on three of them. Because of its announced subject, **"Ode to Fear"** lends itself particularly well to exegesis of anxiety; it also exemplifies the "daemonic" side of Collins, which links him most obviously with the Romantics.[7] **"Ode on the Poetical Character"** deals explicitly with questions of origins and makes the writing of poetry its poetic subject; critics who associate anxiety with problems of poetic genealogy therefore delight in it. **"Ode to Evening"** attracts attention by its innovative form and by its clear relations to the poetic past and the poetic future alike. And, for at least some critics, **"Ode on the Popular Superstitions of the Highlands of Scotland,"** which also demonstrates its author's awareness of the demonic and his concern with the sources of poetic power, merits close attention. The political odes, addressed to Peace or Liberty or mourning the death of a soldier in battle, are relatively neglected, as are the early eclogues and the odes on **"The Manners"** and **"The Passions."** On the whole these works perhaps lack the poetic merit of most of the widely discussed texts, but it is more relevant to point out that they seem less "interesting" than the others—which is to say, less immediately involved with issues that preoccupy twentieth-century readers. At any rate, the version of Collins that emerges from the most conspicuous current discussions depends on severe selectivity. A personification like "Observance" ("To me in Converse sweet impart, / To read in Man the native Heart")[8] does not lend itself readily to speculation about terror or the demonic.

The critics concern themselves, of course, with accomplishment as well as psychology. "What is at stake [for "Collins, Smart, and the great Romantics"]," Geoffrey Hartman writes, "is, in fact, the erection of a voice" (*Fate of Reading,* p. 167). The problem of "voice" in Collins has provoked considerable discussion. Fry, concerned with the development of the ode in English, links Collins and Gray as practitioners. "The occasion of the ode is vocative, presentational, yet what it repeats over and over is the dispersion of voice and presence from the text that stands in their place. This is true of all odes, but nowhere more clearly true than in Gray and Collins, who show unexampled daring, if I may, in their willing submission to the conventions of 'vocal' writing" (p. 126). Repetition rather than argument, Fry notes, provides the important "semaphores" of the ode (p. 125); Collins's style depends heavily on generic tradition. Weiskel speaks of the "radical uncertainty of tone which the sublime poem exhibits"; he continues, "The poor 'I,' or voice of these poems, is often thrown into affectation or attitudinizing of one kind or another in its effort to stay afloat on the turbulence of ideological change." The problem of tone that he locates is "how to be at once impassioned, high sounding, and sincere" (p. 109). Noting the "histrionic, sometimes hysterical, character" of Collins's odes, Hartman attributes this character to their evocation of "a power of vision they fear to use"—the problem of voice and tone thus leading back once more to that of fear and anxiety (*Beyond Formalism,* p. 326). And Sherwin sees Collins as involved in an "ordeal of soul making" which "consists largely of his efforts—under Milton's aegis—to discover a voice that expresses his own individual genius" (pp. 11-12).

Although only Weiskel mentions "uncertainty of tone" as an aspect of Collins's writing, all these critics imply the same thing. In effect they both reiterate and defend against the kind of charge Gray long ago leveled at Collins: "a fine Fancy, model'd upon the Antique, a bad Ear, great Variety of Words, & Images with no Choice at all."[9] Fine fancy and richness of diction with little control, bad ear, lack of choice in images: such poetic attributes, with their implied indiscriminacy, might generate tonal uncertainty with no need to allege "turbulence of ideological change" as a cause. Collins struggles to find a voice, he falls into hysterical modes, he submits to necessities which he appears not fully to understand. His critics interpret these facts as aspects of his interest for twentieth-century readers.

One possible explanation for the generosity of such interpretations emerges in Sherwin's book-length treatment. "Contra Johnson," Sherwin writes, "it can be argued that dread of the imagination's more-than-rational energy bespeaks too narrow a conception of reason and suggests that it is the rational in us which needs cleansing" (p. 80). The critic offers this as his own insight, not Collins's; indeed, he adds that "Collins . . . remains a stranger to this saving wisdom" (p. 80). The observation, and its characterization as "saving wisdom," betray the bias that once produced the description of Pope and Dryden as classics of our prose. The forces of "reason" and "imagination" square off once more; Hartman and Bloom and Fry and Weiskel, allying themselves with imagination, claim Collins for the irrational, the suprarational. His uncertainties, like his anxieties, associate him with those who go beyond reason.

The notion of the eighteenth century as an "Age of Prose and Reason" vanished long ago, one might suppose. But when Sherwin writes of "the contagion of the age" (p. 43), he means the century's alleged overvaluing of the rational. "How can the enlightened mind rid itself of itself?" he inquires (p. 43), posing this question as central to Collins's undertaking. Later, he characterizes the poet's techniques in the **"Ode to Fear"** as "a Dionysiac gesture aimed at abolishing the various Enlightenment constraints prohibiting intercourse between his actual self and the self of his desire" (p. 68). Up-to-date vocabulary, an old-fashioned view. Even Hartman and Bloom, with more apparently complicated understandings of the eighteenth century, sometimes hint at less blatant versions of a similar interpretation. When Hartman writes, of a poetic line extending from Collins to Coleridge by way of Smart, Chatterton, and Blake, "The genius of Poetry becomes a genie once more, a compelling psychic force that works its own salvation in a man, and often as an adversary to accepted values" (*Beyond Formalism,* p. 325), he implies the superiority of this salvationary poetic force to the "accepted values" it combats, the values of the age. Or when Bloom comments, with an air of large concession, "The inherent values of eighteenth-century personification were undoubtedly very real," one can hardly doubt that he finds "Collins' mythical confrontations" far superior to the "traditional personification" they supplant, because larger, more "imaginative," than such personification could ever be (*Visionary Company,* p. 8).

If Collins can be made to stand for good imagination as opposed to bad reason, his current critical resurgence becomes more comprehensible. In *The Visionary Company* Bloom summarizes the "myth" of literary history which Collins accepted; there is reason to believe that Bloom accepts it too:

> Collins saw himself as a poet separated by the school of Waller from a main tradition of the English Renaissance, the creation of a British mythology: the Faery Land of Spenser, the green world of Shakespeare's romances, the Biblical and prophetic self-identification of Milton. This reading of English poetic history, with Waller and Pope in the Satanic role, is itself of course a poetic myth, and a very productive one, in Blake and the Romantics as much as in Collins and the Wartons. (p. 11)

Collins's revival by neo-Romantic critics who share this vision of the fruitful poetic line depends on the perception that at least this one eighteenth-century poet participates in the ennobling tradition of Shakespeare and Spenser rather than the enervating one of Pope and Waller.

One recent study of Collins, Richard Wendorf's *William Collins and Eighteenth-Century English Poetry,* tries to put the poet back where he belongs, among his contemporaries.[10] Wendorf understands Collins as developing from a fairly orthodox eighteenth-century position to take gradual possession of an original idiom, technique, and subject. Finally, however, he sees Collins as a poet of limitation.

> Collins's is, for better and worse, a poetry of limitation. It would be difficult to think of another poet who has been so successful in emphasizing his own limitations, in suggesting poems that might be written and welcoming powers that might be felt. Collins's most impressive poems are often paradoxical or ambivalent, devoted either to the difficulties involved in achieving poetical success or to certain effects and materials that are considered to lie just beyond this poet's reach. But a poetry that celebrates its own limitations is ultimately constrained by them. I think we sense, especially in Collins's final poem, his own realization that there were certain boundaries beyond which his innovative approach could not be pushed. (p. 188)

This balanced assessment comes as a relief after so much overheated language about terror and the demonic, yet it too may confirm old stereotypes about the eighteenth century. Dr. Johnson made thrilling poetry of man's confrontation with his mortal limits, but Collins's version, in this summary, sounds less than thrilling. A poetry that backs away from its own sense of possibility, a poet aware of Romantic powers and of the unlikelihood of using them, a pervasive realization of boundaries: although Wendorf does not suggest that these aspects of Collins depends on his inhabiting a period in which reason and moderation were highly valued, such a conclusion might tempt any reader. Wendorf's summary reverses the interpretation that finds Collins interesting because he defies the standards of his age; now the poet no longer sounds interesting.

The problem of interpretation which Collins raises, in other words, involves his literary period as well as his literary accomplishment. Understood as a poet struggling to escape the constraints of inhibiting conventions and values, he earns attention by his promise of a glorious future: Wordsworth and Keats achieve the fruition which their predecessor intermittently foretells. This view depends on the critical myth that the Romantic movement defines the great moment of Anglo-Saxon literary history. Collins and Smart prophesy the coming of nineteenth-century poetic saviors; lyric poetry (including the lyric epic of Wordsworth) epitomizes what all poetry aspires to.

Without discounting the importance of recent critical illuminations of the great Romantics, one yet may observe that other myths can uncover other aspects of past poetry. For those writing in the eighteenth century, obviously, the early nineteenth century does not glimmer in the distance as the approaching era of poetic greatness. Despite their discomfort with aspects of available convention, poets like Collins and Smart write in and from their own time, not only against it. If Collins values Milton and Spenser and Shakespeare, so does Dr. Johnson (although, admittedly, for rather different reasons). Collins's themes in fact often duplicate those explored by contemporaries working in the tradition now understood as "classic" or "Augustan." Lack of clear commitment muffles his voice, but to read his confusions as daring and powerful inflates his reputation at the cost of obscuring the shape of his work. If we understand those confusions as marks of poetic insufficiency—thus returning to an old view of Collins—and see his utterance as analogous to that of quite un-Romantic contemporaries, we may discover different strengths.

First, however, it is worth thinking about why Collins has assumed his current aspect. His poetry provides an ideal text for "creative" criticism, the kind of criticism that inflates its own claims to literary power as well as the stature of its objects. Elements of the verse that fifty years ago provided grounds for critical reproach—dubious syntax, the poet's "mis-remembering" of earlier works, narrative confusion, abrupt shifts of tone, rhetorical vagueness—now increase the opportunities for interpretation; the poetry itself hardly restrains its readers. One can say almost anything about Collins while remaining within the limits of plausibility: a fact that may either unnerve or encourage the would-be critic. Verse that conspicuously fails to declare its own intent allows lavish exercise of critical power.

The poetic vagueness that generates critical freedom especially encourages antirational interpretations. Whatever Collins exemplifies, one could hardly claim him, in his poetic practice, as a proponent of reason. Imagination and originality have since Blake come to seem incontestable poetic virtues—indeed, virtues in life as well as literature. Collins's appeal for the critics and the attraction of their neo-Romantic elucidations depend partly on the seductiveness of such Romantic values. Readers encountering cloudy representations of personalized abstractions can forget the abstractions and discover a mythology by emphasizing the special ("imaginative") rather than the general ("conventional") aspects of such poetic figures. Critical empire-building has enlarged Romantic territory until Milton himself appears to inhabit it; such enlargement becomes possible only because imagination and originality have replaced reason and decorum and even moral energy as standards of accomplishment. To value the eighteenth century in its own terms risks the unexciting.

Donne and Herbert speak to the twentieth-century reader of familiar spiritual and emotional dilemmas; Wordsworth's suffering and exaltations prefigure other odysseys of the individual soul; but the idea of a struggle for reason and control no longer thrills many readers.

The "Romantic" Collins has obvious appeal for a twentieth-century audience. He resembles us not only in his emotions ("terror," "anxiety," "uncertainty") but in his preoccupations (the nature of the inner life, the nature and possibility of poetry). Neo-Romantic criticism manages often brilliantly to assimilate the past to the present. Nothing any longer seems distant, different; strangeness itself becomes an aspect of familiarity. Critics emphasize how Collins humanizes or demonizes fear or fancy; they thus suppress the problematic and alien aspect of the personified abstractions that may seem to twentieth-century readers even more peculiar than demons. If commentators acknowledge in passing this conventional aspect of Collins's personages, they hasten to emphasize his innovations, his using abstractions in new ways, for new purposes.

Much of Collins's manipulation of characters with names like *Fear* and *Vengeance* actually conforms to Johnson's conservative strictures:

> To exalt causes into agents, to invest abstract ideas with form, and animate them with activity has always been the right of poetry. But such airy beings are for the most part suffered only to do their natural office, and retire. Thus Fame tells a tale and Victory hovers over a general or perches on a standard; but Fame and Victory can do no more. To give them any real employment or ascribe to them any material agency is to make them allegorical no longer, but to shock the mind by ascribing effects to nonentity.[11]

Johnson goes on to complain about Milton's Sin and Death: they should not build a bridge, since immaterial agencies cannot cause material effects. Unlike Sin and Death, Collins's character Fear in **"The Passions,"** startled by the sound he himself has made, and the more complexly realized equivalent figure of the **"Ode to Fear,"** both causing and suffering terror, meet Johnson's standards: the actions of the character interpret the abstraction he represents. Collins's strongest personifications convey power beyond their functions of explanation and emphasis, but they do not pass the boundaries of those "traditional values" which Hartman opposes to Collins's.

The best personifications create their effects by evocative physical or emotional detail. Collins's odes, however, also contain beings whose nature receives virtually no specification: "Young *Fancy*," for example, from **"Ode on the Poetical Character,"** the subject of a good deal of recent discussion. She gives to chosen poets the magic girdle of poetic sanctity; she offers

"Visions wild" and a vaguely inspirational "Flame" (22); she retires with the presiding deity of the poem to his sapphire throne; and, along with "Heav'n" (18), she finally overturns the inspiring bowers of the poet's Eden. She has no physical reality, and her functions remain at least partially obscure. In 1797 Laetitia Barbauld said of this mysterious retirement with God that the allegory was "neither luminous nor decent."[12] Subsequent commentators have by and large pursued the question of decency but ignored that of luminosity, which, with its implication of revelatory force as well as of clarity, is in fact an important issue. Mrs. Barbauld presumably means that it is difficult to figure out what happens in the epode of Collins's ode. That difficulty—which in various forms pervades the entire poem—only encourages twentieth-century critical inventiveness. The critics declare their certainty ever more emphatically as they confront Collins's uncertainty. Thus Weiskel, on a single page about the epode (p. 128), uses the locutions "clearly," "of course," "surely," and "pretty clearly," and he concludes, in an impatient outburst, "If this doesn't suggest sexual union I don't know what does." He protests too much: almost nothing in Collins's text is clear or sure or a matter of course, and little seems even "pretty clear." Luminosity, however, no longer implies an accepted critical standard; its opposite, obscurity, attracts far more attention. Obscurity suggests "depth," "complexity"; on the grounds largely of his obscurity, it seems, Collins claims the epithet of "visionary."

Compared with the personifications of his eighteenth-century predecessors and contemporaries, Collins's imagined figures, despite their elaborative detail, rarely manifest the kind of energy one would expect to find associated with terms like "visionary" and "demonic." In the **"Ode to Fear,"** for instance, "Danger" inhabits an unusual setting and is "hideous":

> *Danger,* whose Limbs of Giant Mold
> What mortal Eye can fix'd behold?
> Who stalks his Round, an hideous Form,
> Howling amidst the Midnight Storm,
> Or throws him on the ridgy Steep
> Of some loose hanging Rock to sleep.
>
> (10-15)

I find him less scary than a more economically rendered group of personifications created by the young Pope in *Windsor-Forest:*

> Gigantick *Pride,* pale *Terror,* gloomy *Care,*
> And mad *Ambition,* shall attend her there:
> There purple *Vengeance* bath'd in Gore retires,
> Her Weapons blunted, and extinct her Fires:
> There hateful *Envy* her own Snakes shall feel,
> And *Persecution* mourn her broken Wheel:
> There *Faction* roar, *Rebellion* bite her Chain,
> And gasping Furies thirst for Blood in vain.
>
> (415-22)[13]

Drawing on an established iconographic tradition, Pope adapts it to his immediate poetic needs with brilliant selectivity: Envy stung by her own snakes, Rebellion biting her chain, Faction's roaring converted to an emblem of futility. In contrast, Collins's multiplication of actions sounds shrill, overinsistent. Unlike Pope, he sounds as though he does not quite know what he is doing.

Obscurity and confusion are not poetic virtues. A poet's insistence that his personifications are frightening does not make them so. Collins's determination to populate his odes with abstractions—some of them quite unrealized as poetic beings—does not constitute a triumph of poetic imagination, an escape from the constrictions of his age; on occasion these abstractions (Fancy, for instance) testify to imaginative failure or confusion. On the other hand, Collins has his own more modest virtues. The project he pursues links him with his non-Romantic contemporaries—not only Gray and Smart, concerned like him with the conundrum of what modern poetry can do, but Johnson and Reynolds and Young, concerned like him with the nature and implications of human limits.

The shape of Collins's preoccupations begins to emerge through a closer look at a personification mentioned earlier, Observance, from **"The Manners."** Collins's poem appeared in his collection of **Odes** in 1747. Two years later, Samuel Johnson published *The Vanity of Human Wishes,* which opens,

> Let observation with extensive view,
> Survey mankind, from China to Peru;
> Remark each anxious toil, each eager strife,
> And watch the busy scenes of crouded life;
> Then say. . . .
>
> (1-5)[14]

Collins invokes "Observance" in these terms:

> O Thou, who lov'st that ampler Range,
> Where Life's wide Prospects round thee
>   change, . . .
> To me in Converse sweet impart,
> To read in Man the native Heart,
> To learn, where Science sure is found,
> From Nature as she lives around. . . .
>
> (21-28)

Although Observance's view proves intensive as well as extensive, his first attributed quality emphasizes his "Range." He looks about as well as within; like Observation, he both *sees* and *says* ("Converse sweet"), and he too teaches his invoker, supplying skills rather than knowledge of human experience. Collins's shorter couplets lack the weight and tension of Johnson's, but his reliance on a personification devoid of pictorial reality to distance the speaker from his own concerns and to authorize a project of psychological and social investigation foretells the technique of Johnson's poem. A phrase like "Converse sweet"—utterly un-Johnsonian—reveals that Collins interests himself also in immediate feelings; but he embeds references to emotion in an insistently generalized context.

Unlike *The Vanity of Human Wishes,* **"The Manners"** imagines earthly possibilities beyond futility. It *imagines* rather than *discovers* them. Despite his invocation of Observance, the speaker (unlike Johnson's persona) observes nothing. He conjures up further personifications: the Manners, uncharacterized; Humour and Wit, evoked mainly through their apparel; finally Nature, the object of another elaborate invocation drawing on many literary references. Nature, whose personified form possesses not even specified gender, provides the alleged source of "Each forceful Thought, each prompted Deed" (72) and, apparently, the origins of feeling as well. The ode concludes with the speaker's expressed desire "To rove thy Scene-full World with Thee!" (78).

Before the end of the poem, in short, Collins moves far from Johnson in his articulated concerns. But only the preoccupation he shares with Johnson, the belief in the value of observation, emerges with clarity. The confusion of the rest, when compared with Johnson's certainty and authority, becomes vivid. The speaker in "The Manners" does not know what he wants most, or even whether he values primarily the human or the literary. His desire to rove a "Scene-full World" seems a pallid substitute for experience. The problem of "scene," which does not exist for Johnson, often preoccupies Collins. "Scene" is a problem, and "self," and the relation of the one to the other. Johnson, still convinced of poetry's didactic function, subordinates self and scene alike to moral purpose. Collins, unable to commit himself to either a didactic or an expressive theory of poetry, remains uncertain also about poetry's appropriate subject matter.

The word *Scene* occurs crucially in another Collins poem, the **"Ode on the Poetical Character,"** which concludes, after an evocation of Milton's Eden,

> And Heav'n, and *Fancy,* kindred Pow'rs,
> Have now o'erturn'd th' inspiring Bow'rs,
> Or curtain'd close such Scene from ev'ry
>   future View.
>
> (74-76)

Critics have pondered the role of Heaven and Fancy in this resolution. Sherwin, for instance: "The kindred powers of Heaven and Fancy—yet surely not Collins' kindred—have overturned the inspiring bower of Milton's mountain paradise, and he finds himself in a heaven-deserted age in which he must descend to the middle ground of the toiling moderns" (p. 88). Or Fry: "Why should Fancy wish to assist in her own disabling? . . . [Perhaps because] she is secretly a guard-

ian and not a pioneer of psychological borderlands, a timid sorceress of vocal presence who fears her own calling and finally refuses to invoke beings whose response she dreads. Even the creative imagination itself, Collins must finally admit, screens its own workings from consciousness" (p. 109).

The "heaven-deserted age," "the middle ground of the toiling moderns," even the idea of fancy's "disabling"— these comprise extrapolations from the text. The poem actually says, not that Heaven and Fancy have abandoned the poet, but that they have destroyed or concealed one particular "Scene," exemplified by Eden. Milton lolls beneath a tree in this particular Eden, but the final lines do not affirm that no one can live there now. No one can any longer be *inspired* by this setting, or no one can *view* it: the lines state only these equivalent possibilities.

One must ask why Heaven and Fancy have acted thus, and the answer, since the poem itself supplies none, will depend on individual predilection. The possibility of a relatively benign interpretation exists among others. Perhaps Heaven and Fancy have not unaccountably reversed their usual functions; perhaps they have only altered the available sources of poetic inspiration. If the poet can no longer see this particular scene, he must look elsewhere: not to religion (the metaphorical Eden) or to the external world (the literal garden, the "Scene-full World"); possibly to the life within?

The question mark belongs tonally to Collins himself. The **"Ode on the Poetical Character"** does not resolve its implicit question about the source of contemporary inspiration, nor did Collins ever find a satisfactory answer. Inspiration and subject matter are virtually identical, in the final lines of **"Ode on the Poetical Character,"** and Collins's problems about subject plague him to the end of his career. His apparent inability to commit himself to his intimations of possibility helps to account for the flabbiness of his weakest work. He backs away from what he has to say.

Perhaps poetic unsuccess only seems from outside like lack of courage. Collins may have suffered not failure of daring but failure of perception or of intellect as he explored the problem peculiar to his era, that of the extent and limits of the self's prerogatives. The boundaries of justifiable entitlement presented both a personal and a poetic dilemma. What am "I" allowed to do (roam the scene-full world, attend to my own feelings, concern myself with my country or my friends)? What can I write about? How do my public obligations as poet relate to my private impulses? Do my feelings impede or energize my verse? Wordsworth would write the poetry of the "egotistical sublime"; Collins, true to his moment in history, understood egotism as a difficulty: not something to be suppressed, necessarily, but something to be investigated. Just over half a century after his *Odes,* the literary world would fully discover the self as subject. We still live with that discovery and its consequences; Collins did not. His poetry asks questions which it provisionally and repetitiously answers; the answers amount to a late-Augustan compromise. The questioning itself generates much of the interest of Collins's poetry.

In the year of Collins's death, Edward Young, an old man, published *Conjectures on Original Composition.* A decade later, in a series of lectures delivered at the Royal Academy, Sir Joshua Reynolds insisted on the value of imitation and deprecated the notion of originality. Both men, unlike each other and unlike Collins in all obvious respects, dwell on versions of the question that preoccupies the poet: the rights of the creative self, the value of indulging it. The debate over originality only slightly disguises these issues. To go even farther afield, Fanny Burney's famous "shyness," her concern over what the role of author means to a female, transposes the same questions into a more modest mode; her character Evelina, silent in public, voluble on paper, struggles with similar issues. In another key, Dr. Johnson's musings in *The Rambler* and his agonized self-appraisals in his prayers and meditations also ponder the proper limits of the self's claims. "Dive deep into thy bosom," Young exhorts,

> learn the depth, extent, bias, and full fort of thy mind; contract full intimacy with the stranger within thee; excite and cherish every spark of intellectual light and heat, however smothered under former negligence, or scattered through the dull, dark mass of common thoughts; and collecting them into a body, let thy genius rise (if a genius thou hast) as the sun from chaos.[15]

Reynolds, Burney, and Johnson, conscious of dangers in such self-concentration, draw on external systems of authority to bound individual presumption. Artistic tradition, social decorum, and Christian faith provide standards and strategies for judging and controlling the self.

Collins, unwilling to trust the stranger within him, finds that faith, reason, and decorum offer slender support. Lacking the structure of established religious or secular mythologies, he generates his own pantheon, but his relation to actualities beyond himself remains uncomfortable. Much of his poetry consists of fantasy constructions which soothingly obscure literal facts of experience and perception. The "Scene-full World" contains possibilities more distressing than the gallery of florid figures like *"Vengeance"* (**"Ode to Fear,"** 20), the *"Fiend of Nature"* (**"Ode to Mercy,"** 15), or *"Britannia's Genius"* ("stain'd with Blood he strives to tear / Unseemly from his Sea-green Hair / The Wreaths of chearful *May*" [**"Ode, to a Lady on the Death of Colonel Ross,"** 2, 4-6]). From time to time, the poetry affords a glimpse of what it largely sup-

presses. Thus, Collins's fourth eclogue, after describing Circassian maids with "Their Eyes' blue languish, and their golden Hair" (56), announces with alarming specificity, "Those Hairs the *Tartar*'s cruel Hand shall rend" (58)—a detail inadequately contained by the eclogue's careful Popean couplets. Such a line suggests why Collins relies so heavily on vagueness.

In the background is the horror of death. Johnson suffered over the idea of being sent to hell and damned everlastingly; Collins returns insistently to death's physical realities. He indeed has something to fear besides Milton and himself. In **"Ode, to a Lady on the Death of Colonel Ross,"** where "ev'ry Sod . . . wraps the Dead" (41), the poet invokes a typical supporting cast: ghostly dead warriors, personified Freedom lying on the grass ("Her matted Tresses madly spread" [40]), "Imperial *Honor*'s awful Hand" (23), "Aërial Forms" (20). Then he acknowledges the possibility that "These pictur'd Glories" (50) may prove inadequate to soothe the survivor's grief for the dead man: "in Sorrow's distant Eye, / Expos'd and pale thou see'st him lie" (52-53). "Sorrow" sees an exposed corpse, not a set of fantasy figures. In **"Ode Occasion'd by the Death of Mr. Thomson,"** a dead poet inhabits an "Earthy Bed" (21); neither dirges nor the tears of Love and Pity will do him any good, hidden as he is beneath the "cold Turf" (32). In **"Ode on the Popular Superstitions of the Highlands of Scotland,"** a "luckless Swain" (104), drowned, becomes "a Pale and breathless Corse" (12), appearing to his sleeping wife with "blue swoln face" (131). (She shudders at the sight [130].) Collins confronts his own difficulty with such physical facts most directly in **"Ode, Written in the beginning of the Year 1746,"** one of his best poems, which juxtaposes the "Mold," "Sod," and "Clay" of the dead soldiers with another troop of fanciful personages (Spring, Honour, Freedom, "Fairy Hands," "Forms unseen") to declare the superiority of truth, even the truth of death, over fancy. When Spring returns to deck the graves, the poem alleges, "She there shall dress a sweeter Sod, / Than *Fancy*'s Feet have ever trod" (5-6). Yet the second stanza, a series of personifications, dramatizes the need for fancy as the only defense against death. Like many of Collins's poems, this one struggles with its own indeterminate subject, to declare both the value of truth and the poet's compulsion to decorate intolerable fact with created figures.

The implications of this short poem summarize important aspects of Collins's theme. The *feeling* self, facing the fact of death, can do nothing. The *poetic* self can invent, decorate, imagine, create; as a result, it distances painful reality. Dirges, like tears, do not help the dead, but they support survivors. Poems make pictures providing alternatives for fact. Poetry, in other words, does not imitate life, but neither does it openly express the feelings of the poet. It finds appropriate modes of disguise; its remoteness from external reality gives it value.

Read in the context of such a poetic program, the **"Ode to Fear"** assumes a rather different aspect. Full of "hobgoblinry," to appropriate Fry's term, it makes a point of its own factitiousness. As the opening lines insist, Fancy generates fear, which responds to "th' unreal Scene" (Collins's favorite kind of scene after all) only when Fancy lifts the veil obscuring it (3-4). The speaker's identification with his own personification ("Like Thee I start, like Thee disorder'd fly" [8]) consists mainly in his shared ability to create by fancy the unreal scene and then to respond to it. But Fancy also generates real emotional dangers: the threat of captivation by one's own fantasies ("Who, *Fear,* this ghastly Train can see, / And look not madly wild, like Thee?" [24-25]). The Greek tragic dramatists suggest a safe way of enjoying such emotion: through the role of reader, in which one can experience without penalty the "throbbing Heart" (42) of terror. The antistrophe, however, acknowledges that the world contains real causes for fear: rape, murder, the cries of drowning seamen—a sinister and disturbing set of evocations. With renewed ardency, therefore, an ardency of submission, the speaker returns to the position of reader, which alone protects him from an emotional reality he dreads. He will suspend disbelief in "each strange Tale" (57) he encounters, and he will avoid testing the authenticity of fearful legend. He begs Fear to teach him to "feel" like Shakespeare (69), able to imagine himself embracing at least this safely mediated form of terror, again the product of Fancy.

The "plot" of this poem resembles that of **"Ode, Written in the beginning of the Year 1746"** in its opposition between intolerable actuality—rape, murder, and the like—and necessary fancy. But fancy's necessity for Collins bears little relation to its urgency for Coleridge or Keats. Fancy implies a retreat from the "Scene-full World" which Collins desires but can neither inhabit nor interpret; "th' unreal Scene," more controllable, is thus safer.

"Ode on the Popular Superstitions of the Highlands of Scotland," Collins's last poem, which he did not complete, adumbrates a solution to the problem of self and scene: an Augustan reconciliation. Exploring what the speaker calls "Scenes that oer my soul prevail" (204), it uses imagination as a substitute for possibly threatening experience. The poet conjures up the landscape and legendry that engender excitement; he in effect "gives" the scene to his Scottish friend John Home, to whom it belongs by a right Collins cannot himself assert. He thus disclaims the imaginative possession that he demonstrates, adapting a strategy of disguise and defense comparable to that in the **"Ode to Fear."** The rhetorical framework of the later poem, however, conveys new assurance. **"Popular Superstitions"** begins and ends with discussions not of legend but of friendship. Home, returning to Scotland, is urged not to forget "that cordial Youth" (5) whom he and Collins have known, and not

to forget the "social Name" of the poet himself (10): "But think far-off how on the Southern coast / I met thy Friendship with an equal Flame!" (11-12). (The competitive note just hinted at here—"I'm as friendly as you are"—perhaps foretells the speaker's appropriation of his friend's subject.) The emotional bond between the two men justifies the Englishman in prescribing Home's itinerary and interests. More important, by the ode's end it has generated the speaker's authority. Some day he too may roam the glens and heaths of Scotland. "Mean time," he invokes the "Pow'rs" (215) of that realm to protect his friend: "To Him I lose, your kind protection lend / And *touch'd with Love, like Mine,* preserve my Absent Friend" (218-19; my italics). His own love has become the talisman, source and symbol of magic preservation; instead of yearning to participate in the energy of mysterious "Pow'rs," he invites them to partake of his own emotional vitality.

Like the group of conventional personifications (*"Fancy, Friendship, Science,* rose-lip'd *Health"*) that appear unexpectedly at the end of **"Ode to Evening"** (50), this allusion to the social context returns the poem to safe eighteenth-century ground. But it also returns the speaker to feelings he can boldly claim. Agreeable emotions of friendship, which sanctioned the poetic enterprise in the first place, promise stability of relationship. (Even in Home's absence, the friendship endures; indeed, it seems to strengthen in the course of the poet's musings on his friend's travels.) Providing a point of return from the more troubling feelings evoked by the thought of drowned countrymen or buried kings, the speaker's love for his friend, something within him that he can trust, authorizes his imaginative excursions through the scene-full world and guarantees his safe return. Pope ended his *Essay on Man* with the vision that "true SELF-LOVE and SOCIAL are the same" (396). Collins resolves his perplexity about what kind of freedom he can allow himself as poet by dissolving his solitary self into a social self—a social *name,* verbal equivalent for a self. His alliance with Home provides an organizing center, a point of view to clarify the purpose of imaginative wandering; it reduces the problem of subject and the problem of self by generating a focus that justifies the poet's fanciful exploring of the Highlands and alleviates the danger of self-absorption. He can at least imagine dealing with the *real*—the actual Highlands landscape—without dwelling only on death. Deprived of Eden, the poet can also look within, reveal his feelings about that landscape—as long as he assures himself of his continuing connection with another, his anchor in the world without. The presence of *Friendship* among the **"Ode to Evening"** personifications gives it equivalent importance to *Fancy;* the **"Popular Superstitions"** ode clarifies that importance. Friendship too is a generative force.

In comparison with the flamboyant distress of a soul grappling with the demonic, the resolution of poems and of problems through reliance on calm friendship sounds unexciting. But some of Collins's best poems, in my view, indeed achieve this sort of stasis: **"Ode, Written in the beginning of the Year 1746," "Ode to Evening," "Ode on the Popular Superstitions of the Highlands of Scotland."** This is the "eighteenth-century Collins": a quieter figure than the Romantic poet to whom we have become accustomed—and, on occasion, a better poet.

I read Collins's poems as a series of questions about the possibility of self-authorization. Aware that the poetic resources of both Milton and Shakespeare have vanished, and finding religious faith inaccessible (his dead inhabit the cold earth, not heaven), Collins discovers little outside himself to value securely. His contemporaries speculate about comparable problems, but locate solutions in various kinds of communal authority: religion (Johnson combating the horror of death and the dangers of the ego, Smart identifying himself with the heroes of his mythology) or social tradition (Churchill, Goldsmith). "Poor Collins" rarely succeeds in his search. Eden lost, the scene-full world posited but rarely discovered, he tries to convert his inner life to the kind of generalization that might substitute for external sanctions without making excessive claims for the self; he reveals the problematics of self as subject. His personifications of emotion (Pity, Fear, the Passions, Mercy, etc.) distance him from his own feeling by claiming its universality (not *my* pity, mankind's), although the poems in which he embeds these figures insistently, often confusedly, examine his own relation to such generalizations. His resort to social feeling at the end of the **"Superstitions"** ode involves another kind of externalization, possibly more successful because less desperate. The poetic self, Collins repeatedly concludes, dares do nothing alone. It must submit—to Shakespeare, to the subject matter belonging to a Scot, to the generalizations of the culture. Thus mediated, thus protected, it may generate poetry.

Like Johnson, Collins intermittently suspects that all predominance of imagination over reason is a degree of insanity. Many of his poems are more interesting to talk about than to read because of their uncontrolled imaginative explosions: in summary the poems sound visionary and exciting, but they do not compose any coherent poetic fabric. (The **"Ode on the Poetical Character"** is a conspicuous case in point.) The criticism that glorifies such writing for its intimations of a new sensibility—minimizing its incoherence and constantly deflected purpose, or attributing them to the bad influence of eighteenth-century rationality—ignores Collins's occasional true, modest achievement: a verse of quiet, faintly melancholy compromise.

Notes

[1] *Precious Bane: Collins and the Miltonic Legacy* (Austin: University of Texas Press, 1977), p. 51.

[2] *The Visionary Company: A Reading of English Romantic Poetry,* rev. ed. (Ithaca: Cornell University Press, 1971), p. 14.

[3] Geoffrey H. Hartman, *The Fate of Reading and Other Essays* (Chicago: University of Chicago Press, 1975), p. 167.

[4] Thomas Weiskel, *The Romantic Sublime: Studies in the Structure and Psychology of Transcendence* (Baltimore: Johns Hopkins University Press, 1976), e.g., pp. 116, 118, 132; Paul H. Fry, *The Poet's Calling in the English Ode* (New Haven: Yale University Press, 1980), p. 103.

[5] Geoffrey H. Hartman, *Beyond Formalism: Literary Essays, 1958-1970* (New Haven: Yale University Press, 1970), pp. 325, 331; Weiskel, p. 132; Sherwin, e.g., pp. 57, 67, 103; Fry, pp. 124-25.

[6] *The Anxiety of Influence: A Theory of Poetry* (New York: Oxford University Press, 1973), p. 111.

[7] Cf. Hartman: "For Wordsworth personification may be trivial, but it is not innocent. Collins had restored the psychological and ritual link between it and the demonic persona" (*Beyond Formalism,* p. 331).

[8] "The Manners. An Ode," lines 25-26, in *The Works of William Collins*, ed. Richard Wendorf and Charles Ryskamp (Oxford: Clarendon Press, 1979). Subsequent quotations from Collins are taken from this edition.

[9] Gray to Thomas Wharton, 27 December 1746, *Correspondence of Thomas Gray,* ed. Paget Toynbee and Leonard Whibley, 3 vols. (Oxford: Clarendon Press, 1935), I, 261.

[10] Minneapolis: University of Minnesota Press, 1981.

[11] *Lives of the English Poets,* ed. George Birkbeck Hill, 3 vols. (Oxford: Clarendon Press, 1905), I, 185.

[12] *The Poetical Works of William Collins,* with a prefatory essay by Mrs. Laetitia Barbauld (London, 1797), p. xxiii.

[13] *Pastoral Poetry and An Essay on Criticism,* ed. E. Audra and Aubrey Williams, Twickenham Edition of the Poems of Alexander Pope, I (New Haven: Yale University Press, 1961).

[14] *The Poems of Samuel Johnson,* ed. David Nichol Smith and Edward L. McAdam (Oxford: Clarendon Press, 1941).

[15] *Edward Young's Conjectures on Original Composition,* ed. Edith J. Morley (London: Longmans, Green, 1918), p. 24.

Blunden on the uniqueness of Collins's poetic style:

. . . Perhaps [Collins'] special mark is the intellectual command of his poetry, which never coldly shuts out the motion of his human simplicity. His topics include those for which it is insufficient to be autobiographical and immediate; for which great knowledge in perfect control, profound self-conquest is required. If Liberty is the subject, Collins is prepared with a rich history, in animated figures and dispositions, of Liberty through the ages. If the Poetic Character makes him vocal he instantly perceives the archetypal poetry of earth,

Yon tented sky, this laughing earth,

and the forces which beget and foster a work of imagination with critical insight and with glowing and harmonious allegory. It is not uncommon for English natures to be gracious or intimate in verse, but here is a poet whose vision extends delightedly over difficult distances, and who hears beyond the voices of the hour the "Music of the Grecian Theatre." In short he is creative, and for his purposes he dares employ the most remote and massive forms of civilization, or of myth. His longest and most carefully constructed Odes—of which he mentions "more perfect" copies—are of ample range, lofty aspiration, and bright and delicate ornament; while raising his cathedral or pleasure-house in dignity and sovereignty, he is skilful to supply each niche and window, each screen and mosaic. And his building is lyrical still. . . .

The Poems of William Collins,
ed. by Edmund Blunden. London: Frederick
Etchells & Hugh Macdonald, 1929.

Casey Finch (essay date 1987)

SOURCE: "Immediacy in the Odes of William Collins," in *Eighteenth-Century Studies,* Vol. 20, No. 3, Spring, 1987, pp. 275-95.

[*In the essay below, Finch argues that the sense of emptiness in Collins's odes stems from the poet's concept of immediacy and the inadequacy of language.*]

For poems that are often considered obscure, the 1746 *Odes* of William Collins have sparked surprisingly little debate in the criticism that has grown around them in the last two hundred years. Outside of a handful of minor controversies,[1] the critical literature overall is sadly homogeneous. Again and again, antecedents and models for the *Odes* are located in Milton, in Spenser, in Aristotle;[2] Collins is seen as a self-conscious "genius," a lonely singer of songs who, as such, prefigures the romantic poets;[3] and the poems themselves are described as visionary, pictorial, and sublime essays of the poetical imagination which combine within the odic form the tradition of the progress poem and the device

of personification.[4] In the midst of this fairly monotonous chorus of praise, a few critics have raised a single note of objection that should momentarily have caused a universal, reflective silence. Musgrove, for one, suggested that the very subjects of the *Odes* present a formidable and unsettling problem: "They do not seem to be *about* very much—or, at least, not about anything very interesting."[5] Another, Middleton Murry, argued that Collins' poetic "came near preventing him from having anything to express at all," that he sought "a perilous kind of purity that . . . hovers on the verge of emptiness."[6] For all their structural intricacy and verbal extravagance, the *Odes* seem, finally, to be without content.

By profession, most critics would take issue with such a disagreeable notion. Indeed, over the years, many have suggested various subjects for the poems. Currently there is more or less a consensus that all of the odes represent (sometimes remotely) variations or manifestations of the subject A. S. P. Woodhouse claimed for the **"Ode on the Poetical Character"**: "the *creative imagination* and the poet's passionate desire for its power,"[7] or, in Martha Collins' words, "the difficulty of writing poems or attaining the heights of former poets."[8] As Musgrove has it, "each Ode is descriptive of one of the qualities or circumstances essential to the attainment of the Poet's true stature."[9] But while true enough, these articulations are in themselves insufficient. Beside the poems about poetry of Stevens, say, or of Pope— full-bodied explorations of a very weighty subject matter—many of the 1746 *Odes* still seem to hover "on the verge of emptiness."

But if it is vain to search in them for conventional subject matter, how can we at once answer the objection and come to terms with these beautiful and elusive odes? Northrop Frye's distinction between product and process in literature is pertinent here. For Frye, the poetry of product is Aristotelian, esthetic, and objective; in it, the poet is present only as the voice of anonymous, authoritative communication. Like a weather report, the poetry of product is concerned with the external state of things, with subject matter. The poetry of process, by contrast, is Longinian and psychological; in *it,* "the qualities of subconscious association take the lead, and the poetry becomes hypnotically repetitive, incantatory, dreamlike and in the original sense of the word charming."[10] The poetry of process is oracular, ecstatic, trance-like, subjective. Now if we accept Paul Sherwin's suggestion that "Collins' poetry contains all the characteristics of a poetry of process delineated by Frye,"[11] this distinction enables us to accept Collins' seeming lack of subject matter, his "emptiness," more easily. Perhaps it is not subjects that Collins seeks at all, but rather a kind of visionary process. But precisely what kind of a process is at work, and to what end?

Critics have sought to describe the 1746 *Odes* with an exuberant but often foggy vocabulary. C. R. Stone has mentioned the "magic of the poems," Bloom their "apocalyptic ambition," McKillop their "primal rapture." Shuster has described the poems as "groping towards a visionary neo-Platonism," Sypher as "preconscious" and "bizarre" psychic representations which "may amount occasionally to surrealism." Barbauld sees in the *Odes* "the metaphysical," Frye a kind of "poetic primitivism," and Ainsworth an "evocation of a shadowy and visionary world." Hazlitt, for his part, says of Collins that he "catches rich glimpses of the bowers of Paradise," that a "rich distilled perfume emanates from the **'Ode on the Poetical Character'** like a breath of genius: a golden cloud envelops it, a honeyed paste of diction encrusts it, like a candied coat of auricula."[12] Each of these terms is unhelpful. Each is vague, esoteric, and, for those of us who do not believe in magic, unconvincing; I cite them only to suggest that too few of Collins' critics have extracted from his obvious concern with visionary experience its essence: immediacy in the literal sense, a fusion of subject and object.[13]

For Collins' *Odes* concern primarily the problem of immediacy, the process of attaining an unmediated experience in which votary becomes one with the invoked. This is, of course, the concern of much lyric poetry. But, as we shall see, in the 1746 *Odes* this process differs from most lyric modalities in at least one fundamental respect: immediacy for Collins is a radically linguistic phenomenon. Moreover, the very condition of Collins' project to broach immediate experience renders the enterprise impossible from the start. It is the consequence of this aporia that we must ultimately explore. First, however, it will be useful to articulate in some detail the poetic process by which unmediated experience is sought.

This process, I think, can be described with the terms that Ernst Cassirer, utilizing Usener's notion of the "momentary god," brought to his speculative but, for our purposes, extremely useful discussion of language and myth. For Cassirer, the geneses of language and myth are coincidental, simultaneous. The primal, immediate experience, the dramatic confrontation of pre-linguistic man with any form of intensity (leopard, precipice, thunder, or mountain spring bursting forth from the ground) provokes a kind of mythical awe in which thought "is captivated and enthralled by the intuition which suddenly confronts it."[14] Faced with such phenomena, all thought

> comes to rest in the immediate experience; the sensible present is so great that everything else dwindles before it. For a person whose apprehension is under the spell of this mythico-religious attitude, it is as though the whole world were simply annihilated; the immediate content, whatever it be, that commands his religious interest so completely fills his consciousness that nothing else can exist beside or apart from it. (pp. 32-33)

Confronted in this way with immediate experience, the self locates "all its energy on this single object, lives in it," indeed, dissolves (p. 33).

Immediacy, then, constitutes a profoundly reductive situation in which the self is overcome or "possessed" by the intense impression. For Cassirer, it is precisely at this moment that the deity originates. When immediate apprehension annihilates the sense of self, "when external reality is not merely viewed and contemplated, but overcomes a man in sheer immediacy, with emotions of fear or hope, terror or wish fulfillment," precisely then the "utmost tension between the subject and its object" arises. At that moment, "the spark jumps somehow across, the tension finds release, as the subjective excitement becomes objectified, and confronts the mind as a god or daemon." Leopard, shooting star, or field of dazzling yellow poppies—all can constitute Usener's mythico-religious protophenomena, all can evoke the momentary god in whose presence the wonderer, awestruck, loses all sense of self to the deity. "In absolute immediacy," as Usener has it, "the individual phenomenon is deified, without the intervention of even the most rudimentary class concept; that *one* thing you see before you, that and nothing else is the god" (p. 33).

Borrowing this set of notions, we can say that for Collins the process of evoking immediate, visionary experience involves what Cassirer would call a primeval confrontation with phenomena that become, from their force and intensity, momentary gods.[15] Now the direct confrontation of pre-linguistic man with a momentary god gives birth to language; it constitutes a "dynamic process which produces the verbal sound out of its own inner drive" (p. 34). The word or cry thus generated is ontologically inseparable from the confrontation that produced it.

> The word, like a god or a daemon, confronts man not as a creation of his own, but as something existent and significant in its own right, as an objective reality. As soon as the spark has jumped across, as soon as the tension and the emotion of the moment has found its discharge in the word or the mythical image, a sort of turning point has occurred in human mentality: the inner excitement which was a mere subjective state has vanished, and has been resolved into the objective form of myth or speech. (p. 36)

The word was God or, to cite Jacques Derrida's revision of St. John, "the sign and the divinity have the same place and time of birth."[16] The genesis of myth, then, is inscribed in the first utterance. And equally, the first utterance marks the origin of the deity, the inauguration of myth.

This first utterance is unlike any word in our language essentially in having a character that is purely expressive; intrinsically free from any symbolic or referential value, it denotes nothing. One way of articulating the precise nature of this utterance is to describe it, using Charles Peirce's terminology, as indexical. For Peirce, the relation of an indexical sign and its object is based on physical proximity, immediacy.[17] Peirce distinguishes symbolic signs, which bear a conventional or learned relation with their objects, from indexical signs, which bear with their objects purely a relation of proximity. Each and every word in our language is, in this sense, a symbolic sign; each can be used to refer to phenomena outside of immediate perception, each can be used to denote symbolically. By contrast, no word in our language can properly be called indexical. Indices are generated only in and by the physical presence of their objects; rather than denote objects or events either concretely present or perfectly abstract, indices express proximities, immediacies. Thus smoke is an indexical sign of fire because it can occur only proximate to fire. Or again, a pointing finger is an index of, say, a chalkboard: it "signifies its object solely by virtue of being really connected with it."[18]

Now, without wishing to overemphasize the applicability, I would argue that this vocabulary can help us to describe with some precision the visionary process at work in several at least of Collins' 1746 *Odes*. Collins seeks to re-create what we can call the experience of the momentary god, an experience that is coincidental with a mythical, indexical utterance. This process is necessarily invocatory; Collins is concerned with invoking a personification not as a means to an end, but as an end in itself; not as a mere rhetorical device, but in order to experience the personification as a momentary god.[19]

Invocation, it is true, is not in itself an extraordinary procedure in poetry. Indeed, it is commonplace, for many poets, a conventional and rather official device. It is useful to think of invocation as a particular kind of speech act which John L. Austin would call an "illocution," an attempt by the speaker to manipulate a hearer.[20] For Austin, every transaction of language is "locutionary" in the sense that it constitutes an act of verbal utterance, a linguistic event. Under this rubric, two kinds of specialized locutionary speech acts, "illocutions" and "perlocutions," can be differentiated. An illocution shares with all perlocutions the possibility of altering the condition of the hearer. It is unique, however, in being accomplished merely by communicating its intent to accomplish something.[21] Refining Austin's taxonomy, John Searle discerns twelve types of illocutionary verbs, one of which he calls a directive illocutionary verb: "ask, order, command, request, beg, plead, pray, entreat, and also invite, permit, advise," and, we might add, invoke.[22]

We can say, then, that many of Collins' *Odes* have the directive illocutionary force of invoking a personification. Of Simplicity, for instance, the speaker implores:

> O sister meek of Truth,
> To my admiring youth
> Thy sober aid and native charms infuse![23]

But of course all invocations are intended to have the illocutionary force of raising the specter of some deity, muse, personification, or power. What sets these particular utterances apart is that, for Collins, to invoke—literally to call, to give voice to—is precisely to enact an *indexical* illocution. The poet is concerned with generating an impossible process by which he experiences an unmediated state of being, an instant of concrete intensity, in short, the advent of a momentary god. Recalling Frye, we can say that Collins' is a poetry of process which attempts to bring subject and object "into a white-hot fusion of identity."[24] Collins calls on the various deities neither to carry him from the "dim-discovered tracts of mind,"[25] nor for mere poetic inspiration; rather, he invokes through indexical illocution a state of absolute immediacy and reciprocity with a momentary god.[26]

We might suggest, then, that the particularity of Collins' visionary poetic lies precisely in his efforts to enact an indexical modality. Thus the apostrophe, just cited, in the **"Ode to Simplicity"** functions inseparably from the deity it addresses; its prayer for Simplicity's charms is itself charming; *carmen* is invoked by *carmen*. Such, also, is the force in the **"Ode to Pity"** of the poet's words to the deity:

> Come, Pity, come, by Fancy's aid,
> Even now my thoughts, relenting maid,
> Thy temple's pride design.
>
> 　　　　　　　　　　　　(25-27)

This moment can be described as an illocutionary speech act that serves at once to invoke and to *constitute* the presence of the deity. Since *design* in the eighteenth century denoted—alongside its modern (often architectural) meaning—"nominate," "appoint," "designate," "signify," the word here carries at least two senses: to design(ate) is simultaneously to experience the momentary god; to signify is at once to provide fitting habitation for the deity. The invocation, then, functions just as the temple it portrays; it honors, signifies, and at the same time *houses* the deity. Collins' visionary language articulates an indexical epiphany; as in the **"Ode to Liberty,"** even as it speaks, it enacts, it consecrates a "place so fit" (10), a "shrine" (9) for the momentary god. Such, too, is the nature of the prayer with which the **"Ode to Simplicity"** concludes:

> Though taste, though genius bless
> To some divine excess,
> Faints the cold work till thou inspire the
> 　　whole;
> 　What each, what all supply
> 　May court, may charm our eye,
> Thou, only thou can'st raise the meeting soul!

> Of these let others ask
> To aid some mighty task:
> I only seek to find thy temperate vale,
> Where oft my reed might sound
> To maids and shepherds round,
> And all thy sons, O Nature, learn my tale.
>
> (43-54)

Here, rather than a fleeting fusion with the deity, a spirited but momentary "divine excess," the poet seeks a kind of prolonged cohabitation, a sustained reciprocity in which the "meeting soul" of the votary lifts itself to the uplifting deity. The indexical mode of this invocation gives rise to a striking reflexivity; just as the poetry that announces the privileging of simplicity over "divine excess" is itself simple and "temperate," like Simplicity's "vale," so the prayer for song is itself song, a sounding "reed."[27] In Richard Wendorf's words, Collins "calls for a fusion of his spirit that will lead, in turn, to an increased ability on his part to inspirit [the deity's] qualities in his own sweet and breathing lines."[28] We will discover, however, that such a reciprocity can be neither sustained nor, strictly speaking, even broached. Collins' richness and power lie, instead, in the rhetorical dexterity with which this unattainable condition of fusion is approached.

Despite the claims of the **"Ode to Simplicity,"** despite its avowed preference for mildness and decorum, the experience of the momentary god in Collins is sometimes approximated violently, through excess, without warning or preparation. In the **"Ode to Fear,"** the deity appears suddenly, abruptly:

> Ah Fear! Ah frantic Fear!
> I see, I see thee near.
>
> (5-6)

In *The Fate of Reading,* Geoffrey Hartman ascribes to this ode an epiphanic structure that "evokes the presence of a god, or vacillates sharply between imagined presence and absence. Its rhetoric is therefore a crisis-rhetoric" which "proceeds by dramatic turns of mood" with an ejaculative language.[29] The momentary god or, in Hartman's terms, the confrontational epiphany can erupt at any moment. A number of the 1746 *Odes*—one thinks, for instance, of **"The Passions. An Ode for Music"** and of the **"Ode on the Poetical Character"**—exhibit this sharp, confrontational sublimity. Indeed, even the relatively mild **"Ode to Liberty"** has its moments of "crisis":

> How may the poet now unfold
> What never tongue or numbers told?
> How learn delighted and amazed,
> What hands unknown that fabric raised?
> Even now before his favoured eyes,
> In Gothic pride it seems to rise!
>
> (113-118)

This Gothicism stands in sharp contrast with the classical restraint embodied by Simplicity, who

> Disdain'st the wealth of art,
> And gauds and pageant weeds and trailing
> pall:
> But com'st a decent maid
> In Attic robe arrayed.[30]

Too few critics have recognized the range in Collins' poetry from "Attic" simplicity to "Gothic" sublimity, from the modulated restraint of the Mediterranean South to the darker "excesses" of the North. For though the **"Ode to Liberty,"** for instance, embodies admirably the politeness and sobriety of eighteenth-century neoclassicism, though in it "Graecia's graceful orders join" (119) alike within the deity and the poem itself, the ode is nevertheless given to "dramatic turns of mood," to awful, Northern flashes of light:

> What new Alcaeus, Fancy-blest,
> Shall sing the sword in myrtles dressed . . .
> Till she her brightest lightnings round
> revealing,
> It leaped in glory forth and dealt her prompted
> wound!
>
> (7-12)

At other times, of course, the experience of the momentary god is less overtly, less frantically epiphanic. Sometimes it is broached only through an elaborate, incantatory language, as in the **"Ode to Evening,"** the first sentence of which is worth quoting here in full:

> If aught of oaten stop or pastoral song
> May hope, chaste Eve, to soothe thy modest ear,
> Like thy own solemn springs,
> Thy springs and dying gales,
> O nymph reserved, while now the bright-
> haired sun
> Sits in yon western tent, whose cloudy skirts,
> With brede ethereal wove,
> O'erhang his wavy bed;
> Now air is hushed, save where the weak-eyed
> bat
> With short shrill shriek flits by on leathern
> wing,
> Or where the beetle winds
> His small but sullen horn,
> As oft he rises midst the twilight path,
> Against the pilgrim borne in heedless hum:
> Now teach me, maid composed,
> To breathe some softened strain,
> Whose numbers stealing through thy
> darkening vale
> May not unseemly with its stillness suit;
> As musing slow, I hail
> Thy genial loved return!
>
> (1-20)

Hartman notes Collins' deployment, here, of "features characteristic of the sublime ode. . . . His extended apostrophe suggests the hieratic distance between votary and the invoked power, anticipates at the same time its presence, and leads into a narrative second half describing in greater detail the coming of the divinity and its effect on the poet." For Hartman, however, "the one feature conspicuously absent is the epiphany proper"; the poem is necessarily all anticipation without arrival because the poet addresses "in epiphanic terms a subject intrinsically nonepiphanic."[31] And, to be sure, the invocation is preparatory, unagitated, even elusive; it is given to digressions, to intricate embroidery. The language itself, so far from being ejaculative, is convoluted and indirect, the main clause in the deep structure—"Now teach me, maid composed, / To breathe some softened strain"—elaborately embedded in the twisting labyrinth the syntax coils around it.

Nevertheless, the **"Ode to Evening"** is only seemingly "nonepiphanic." The troublesomeness and opacity of this passage, the convoluted and interwoven syntax, are part of a rhetorical machinery calculated not only to prepare the poet for the deity, but indeed to *enact* an epiphanic modality. Meandering is for Collins a ritualistic strategy; it functions as a kind of incantation designed to invoke the experience of the momentary god with indexical language, a way of searching for a fleeting and elusive experience which can neither be reached by direct approach nor fixed by a formula. Thus, far from delaying, this "musing slow" *constitutes* the experience of the deity. When finally the deity is glimpsed, it is glimpsed because the barrier between the "epiphanic terms" and an "intrinsically nonepiphanic" subject has collapsed, because the hypnotic, ritualistic language has approximated, briefly, the very condition of indexicality: "I hail / Thy genial loved return!" The illocutionary force of hailing is merely to state the intention: I salute and invite, I welcome. In the indexical mode, however, the illocution, like a spell, gains the power to accomplish its intention: to hail is simultaneously to confront and fuse with the deity. Wendorf, citing Michael Fried's fine essay on absorption as a master theme in eighteenth-century painting and criticism, argues that at such moments votary and invoked exchange roles. "The speaker is completely absorbed by the spectacle he views (and creates), . . . is actually absorbed *into* the object of his contemplation."[32] But it would be slightly more accurate, I think, simply to say that in Collins' visionary poetic the barrier between poet and momentary god is dissolved, or, rather, that the rhetoric approximates such dissolution.

Càssirer's explanation is particularly applicable here. The word uttered at the advent of the momentary god is not a

> mere conventional symbol, but is merged with its object in an indissoluble unity. The conscious experience is not merely wedded to the word, but is

consumed by it. Whatever has been fixed by a name, henceforth is not only real, but is Reality.[33]

The barrier between symbol and meaning dissolves. Visionary reciprocity ensues, in Cassirer's words, "a relation of identity, of complete congruence between 'image' and 'object,' between the name and the thing" (58). At precisely those moments when an indexical modality is approximated, Collins attempts momentarily to suspend language as a medium solely for conveying separate content, in order to resurrect, alongside referential utterance, a kind of absolutely reflexive language inseparable from its origin and content. Like the "pilgrim," we are borne along, as it were, in "heedless hum."

In the **"Ode to Fear,"** this experience takes on an unusual ferocity. The poet, having invoked the deity—"Ah Fear! Ah frantic Fear! / I see, I see thee near" (5-6)—himself becomes fearful: "O Fear, I know thee by my throbbing heart" (42). But Fear, too, is fearful, looks "madly wild" (25). Poet and momentary god fuse into a volatile reflexivity:

> I know thy hurried step, thy haggard eye!
> Like thee I start, like thee disordered fly.
>
> (7-8)

Or again:

> Who, Fear, this ghastly train can see,
> And look not madly wild like thee?
>
> (24-25)

Fear, too, starts and flies from her hideous train, that is, from her attendant self. Hartman's comment here is illuminating: "We easily recognize this as a displaced or heightened mode of ritual identification. . . . Collins is not unwittingly adapting Horace's 'Si vis me flere.' If you want me to be terrified, you yourself must show terror." Indeed, a number of the odes "raise the ghosts they shudder at. Their histrionic, sometimes hysterical, character stems from the fact that they are indeed theatrical machines, evoking a power of vision they fear to use. Collins, like a sorcerer's apprentice, is close to being overpowered by the spirit he summons."[34] The presence of the momentary god is simultaneously desired and feared.

In **"The Passions. An Ode for Music,"** we discover how completely the deities themselves are given to the experience of reflexivity:

> First Fear his hand, its skill to try,
>   Amid the chords bewildered laid,
> And back recoiled, he knew not why,
>   Even at the sound himself had made.
>
> Next Anger rushed, his eyes on fire,
>   In lightnings owned his secret stings,

In one rude clash he struck the lyre,
　And swept with hurried hand the strings.

With woeful measures wan Despair
　Low sullen sounds his grief beguiled,
A solemn, strange and mingled air,
　'Twas sad by fits, by starts 'twas wild.

　　　　　　　　　　　　(17-28)

Wendorf has astutely described the reflexive nature of this relation between subject and object.[35] What he has not emphasized, however, is its volatility.

For if it can be said properly to occur at all, the experience of the momentary god occurs "but once" and lasts but "awhile." Fear's is a forceful but, after all, a "withering power." The Manners are "ever varying as they pass." And Peace wears a "transient smile."[36] This brevity, of course, is the very stuff of the progress poem. Pity, Fear, Simplicity, Liberty—all alight, as it were, upon the various Western cultures only briefly before flying off. The image of the veil—which, in one form or another, is central to Collins' mythmaking process—provides an apt visual manifestation of this volatility. This image occurs at significant and highly charged moments in the Odes. In the **"Ode on the Poetical Character,"** it is behind a "veiling cloud" (37) that God and Fancy give birth, through a "quasi-sexual" union, to the "rich-haired youth of morn" (39), whom Frye and Bloom associate with the sun-god, the Greek Apollo, and ultimately with the poet himself.[37] In the **"Ode to Evening,"** the goddess draws her "gradual dusky veil" (40) between herself and the poet.[38] And in the **"Ode to Fear,"** Jocasta is wrapped in the deity's "cloudy veil" (38), which, when lifted by Fancy, reveals the awful personification (4 ff.). For the veil hangs between poet and personification. When it is lifted, immediacy, the experience of the momentary god, ensues; when drawn down again, the moment passes and the condition of separation and exile resumes.

But the veil is language itself or, more properly, the linguistic medium, the very thing that can never simply be "lifted" away. As we have seen, the veil undergoes a double movement in Collins. For Fancy—the very force that in the **"Ode to Fear"** "lifts the veil" (4) and elsewhere gives birth to poetry itself—also curtains off the scene, presumably of her own inspiration. As we learn in the **"Ode on the Poetical Character"**:

　And Heaven and Fancy, kindred powers,
　Have now o'erturned the inspiring bowers,
Or curtained close such scene from every
　　future view.

　　　　　　　　　　　　(74-76)

What creates the poetical imagination, then, also destroys it; what opens, also closes the curtain. "Vision plots the end of vision." The will to immediacy is

infected from the beginning with the "destiny of its non-satisfaction."[39] Behind the dream of a non-referential, indexical language, of a field of discourse in which signifier and signified are inextricable, lies a profound contradiction. The project to create immediate experience through the linguistic medium, to use a thoroughly referential language in order to move beyond referentiality itself—this, of course, is deeply problematical. Paul Sherwin warns of the "danger, indeed the impossibility" even of

　pursuing such an ideal. To abandon oneself to the intensity of a continuous present ("to be an intensity without realizing it," as Gaston Bachelard writes) would be to live out existence in the manner of a Nietzschean Superman—an even more unlikely role for Collins than for Nietzsche himself.[40]

As Paul de Man points out, "unmediated expression is a philosophical impossibility." The belief that "in the language of poetry, sign and meaning can coincide, or at least be related to each other in the free and harmonious balance that we call beauty," is incoherent, as the structuralist critics never tire of insisting, a "specifically romantic delusion." "Immediacy," in Derrida's words, "is derived."[41]

What lies at the heart of this incoherency? It is, I think, the law of language itself. The perennial yearning *in* language that language be transparent. The dream of full presence: the white-hot fusion, the sheer reciprocity of subject and object; "the very place," in de Man's words, "where the contact with a superhuman origin of language has been preserved"[42]; a condition of transcendence, self-identity, radicality; in our terms, absolute indexical proximity of symbol and meaning; the experience of the momentary god; immediacy itself. Each of these, again, is delusory, incoherent, and carries within itself "the destiny of its non-satisfaction." At the same time, each echoes the impossible moment that inaugurates language itself: the desire to capture immediate experience in a system of mediation. This is the special burden of the poet's words, here worth repeating, in the **"Ode to Liberty"**:

　How may the poet now unfold
　What never tongue or numbers told?
　How learn delighted and amazed,
　What hands unknown that fabric raised?

　　　　　　　　　　　　(113-116)

Such is the desire for the "restitution of presence by language." Yet, however tenacious the will is for immediacy, however sincere or eloquent, "the presence that is thus delivered to us in the present is a chimera."[43]

What constitutes Collins' project, then, is an impossible dream. Language is irreducibly metaphorical and non-indexical. Each of its symbols is rent from its meaning as the very condition of its "iterability," that is, of its usefulness. There is no inaugurating moment—to speak of—when signifier and signified are one, when "the word, like a god or a daemon, confronts man not as a creation of his own, but as something existent and significant in its own right, as an objective reality." There is no momentary god, only the incoherent yearning of an encrusted language for immediacy, a golden age. **"The Passions. An Ode for Music,"** for instance, bears the burden of this knowledge:

> When Music, heavenly maid, was young,
> While yet in early Greece she sung,
> The Passions oft to hear her shell
> Thronged around her magic cell,
> Exulting, trembling, raging, fainting,
> Possessed beyond the muse's painting;
> By turns they felt the glowing mind,
> Disturbed, delighted, raised, refined.
>
> (1-8)

The relation here of Music and the Passions emblematizes the condition of indexicality, a kind of transparent and absolute reciprocity. But Collins insists on the gulf that separates us from any Edenic moment; as always, a fall has intervened and ruptured the unity:

> Till once, 'tis said, when all were fired,
> Filled with fury, rapt, inspired,
> From the supporting myrtles round
> They snatched her instruments of sound,
> And as they oft had heard apart
> Sweet lessons of her forceful art,
> Each, for madness ruled the hour,
> Would prove his own expressive power.
>
> (9-16)

Sherwin points out that each of the Passions—Fear, Anger, Despair, Hope, Revenge, and so forth—"reenacts Collins' vocational quest. Displaying 'his own expressive power,' each of the Passions corresponds to the performing self of Collins' various odes." When Fear, for instance, recoils "even at the sound himself ha[s] made" (20), we are reminded of Collins' tendency to recoil from the momentary gods his own lyre has conjured up. Nor is this tendency surprising. Since "the ecstatic aim of the individual Passions is immediate self-presence, the coincidence of cause and effect through the medium of sound,"[44] and since Collins, too, attempts to intermingle the mutually exclusive experiences of ecstacy and self-presence, to broach immediacy through media, his project is marked from the start by the condition of its own impossibility.

"The Passions," then, amounts to a mythic conceit for the fallen condition of language itself, communicative power violently separated both from its source and its telos. The archaeology that would unearth the site "where the contact with a superhuman origin of language has been preserved" in the end discovers only that the origin, "the point where the truth of things corresponded to a truthful discourse," lies at a "place of inevitable loss."[45] As Hartman, himself citing Cassirer, states, "standing in the midst of things, and specifically in the midst of the treachery of words, the artist bears the curse of mediacy."[46] *Immediacy* is the momentary god; and she, like the deity in Collins' **"Ode to Simplicity,"** has "turned [her] face, and fled her altered land." (36)

In Collins, as in Christopher Smart, "the very *medium* of representation—visionary language itself—has become questionable, or subject to a demand which it cannot meet except by being renewed." But for Collins this project of renewal itself functions as the condition of its own impossibility; again and again, it begins and culminates, not in renewal, but in the anxiety of lateness; not in immediacy, but in a poignant and empty longing, a profound fear "that our appetites—including that for presence—put a demand on the order of things which that order may not be able to satisfy; which, indeed, it may resent and reject." Far from a fusion with a momentary god, what Collins' poetic in the end enacts is a language of loss, a profound "anxiety for language-source, liturgy, and the entire process of representation."[47]

This loss, again, is thematically intrinsic to the progress poem. In the **"Ode to Liberty,"** for instance, we learn that only the scattered fragments of the deity remain, mere "remnants of her strength" (29):

> For sunny Florence, seat of art,
> Beneath her vines preserved a part,
> Till they, whom Science loved to name,
> (O who could fear it?) quenched her flame.
> And lo, an humbler relic laid
> In jealous Pisa's olive shade!
> See small Marino joins the theme,
> Though least, not last in thy esteem;
> Strike, louder strike the ennobling strings
> To those whose merchant sons were kings;
> To him who, decked with pearly pride,
> In Adria weds his green-haired bride;
> Hail, port of glory, wealth and pleasure,
> Ne'er let me change this Lydian measure:
> Nor e'er her former pride relate
> To sad Liguria's bleeding state.
>
> (34-49)

As she alights on Florence, Pisa, San Marino, and so forth, Liberty's power is strangely dispersed, enervated; Florence "preserved" but "a part" of the deity, Pisa a still "humbler relic." And today of Liberty's "former pride" only the "beauteous model still remains" (106). Collins is himself quite explicit about the futility of recovering the site of immediacy:

> Though now with hopeless toil we trace
> Time's backward rolls to find its place;

Whether the fiery-tressed Dane,
Or Roman's self o'erturned the fane,
Or in what heaven-left age it fell,
'Twere hard for modern song to tell

(95-100)

The fall of the Roman Empire is here rewritten as an allegory of the inevitable disruption of immediacy. To ask whether the "fane," the very temple of immediacy, has been "o'erturned" from within by "Roman's self" or from without by "the fiery-tressed Dane" is at once to ask whether language conditions or is conditioned by the inevitability of mediacy. But meanwhile the question itself *enacts* reflexively the very problematic it raises. Because "modern song" is by definition late, post-lapsarian, it functions inevitably *in* exile and *as* exile. These lines, then, encapsulate in miniature the dilemma, the condition of separation, at the heart of the 1746 **Odes**. This is precisely what it means to be exiled from the locus of immediacy: always searching—and always within language—for the "site of a fleeting articulation that discourse has obscured and finally lost."[48]

It is hardly surprising, then, that Collins is forever hesitating to commit himself to the endless quest for the site of immediacy. As one critic has noticed, Collins is indirect and taciturn; he is characteristically reticent.[49] Since language never "lifts the veil," but only twists and complicates it, Collins is naturally hesitant to speak and quick to silence. There is in the laconicism of the **Odes,** and in the thinness of Collins' entire oeuvre, the same archetypal silence that Frederic Jameson noted in Saussure, the "same legendary and august renunciation of speech of which the gesture of Rimbaud is emblematic."[50] The irony that the ambitions of a programmatically invocatory poet should lead in the end to a half-hidden but nevertheless august renunciation of speech is only apparent. For since the very possiblity of language marks a separation of subject and object, of votary and momentary god, the will to hymn and the will to silence are one and the same movement. Collins announces his project at the opening of **"The Manners. An Ode":**

Farewell, for clearer ken designed,
The dim-discovered tracts of mind:
Truths which, from action's paths retired,
My silent search in vain required!

(1-4)

Strangely, to abandon this "silent search," to throw aside the "prattling page" (24) and "oft-turned scrolls" (76) of scholarship or art, and to raise the voice in praise of the deity is, in the end, only to embrace another, still deeper silence. As Middleton Murry noticed in 1922, for Collins it is to erect a poetic that almost prevents him "from having anything to express at all," to seek "a perilous kind of purity that . . . hovers on the verge of emptiness." The dilemma of the Collinsean poetic is at once to speak this silence and

to silence this speech; the **Odes** enact their own elegy. So while it is strange, it is equally inevitable that the dream of immediacy should return finally to the praise of silence.

Notes

[1] Among the controversies, that which has continued longest and loudest is among the literary historians seeking to locate Collins within a particular school. Of those who have labeled him a pre-romantic, J. W. MacKail, "Collins, and the English Lyric," in *Essays by Diverse Hands,* ed. Henry Newbolt (London: Oxford University Press, 1921), pp. 1-23; Oswald Doughty, *English Lyric in the Age of Reason* (New York: Russell and Russell, 1922); Alan D. McKillop, "The Romanticism of William Collins," *Studies in Philology,* 20, No. 1 (1923), pp. 1-16; and Harold Bloom, *The Visionary Company* (Ithaca: Cornell University Press, 1971), pp. 1-15; are interesting. Other critics, among them E. M. W. Tillyard, "William Collins's 'Ode on the Death of Thomson,'" *A Review of English Literature,* 1, No. 3 (1960), pp. 30-38, insist that Collins is neo-classical. One critic, Wylie Sypher, "The *Morceau de Fantaisie* in Verse: A New Approach to Collins," *University of Toronto Quarterly,* 15 (1945-1946), pp. 65-69, even calls Collins rococo. For an old-fashioned, "evolutionary" literary history seeking to place Collins in a transitional period, see George N. Shuster, *The English Ode from Milton to Keats* (New York: Columbia University Press, 1940).

Another controversy involves a debate over the proper order and categorization of the odes more or less initiated by H. W. Garrod, *Collins* (Oxford: Oxford University Press, 1928); and addressed by S. Musgrove, "The Theme of Collins's Odes," *Notes and Queries,* 9 October 1943, pp. 214-17, and 23 October 1943, pp. 253-55; and Richard Quintana, "The Scheme of Collins's *Odes on Several Descriptive and Allegoric Subjects,"* in *Restoration and Eighteenth-Century Literature,* ed. Carrol Camden (Chicago: University of Chicago Press, 1963), pp. 371-80.

Still another controversy concerns the precise nature of Collins' personification. Criticism includes Bertrand H. Bronson, "Personification Reconsidered," *ELH,* 14, No. 3 (1947), pp. 163-80; Earl R. Wasserman, "The Inherent Values of Eighteenth-Century Personification," *PMLA,* 65 (1950), pp. 435-63; and Rachel Trickett, "The Augustan Pantheon: Mythology and Personification in Eighteenth-Century Poetry," in *Essays and Studies,* ed. Geoffrey Bullough (London: Wyman and Sons, 1953), pp. 71-86.

Finally, yet another controversy concerns Collins' pictorial relation to painting, criticism of which includes Jean H. Hagstrum, *The Sister Arts: The Tradition of Literary Pictorialism in English Poetry from Dryden to Gray* (Chicago: University of Chicago Press, 1958); Patricia Meyer Spacks, "Collins' Imagery," *Studies in Philology,* 62, No. 5 (1965), pp. 719-36; and Michael Fried, "Absorption: A Master Theme in Eighteenth-Century French Painting and Criticism," *Eighteenth-Century Studies,* 9, No. 2 (1975-1976), pp. 139-77.

[2] Worthwhile criticism in this tradition includes Norman Maclean, "From Action to Image: Theories of the Lyric in the Eighteenth Century," in *Critics and Criticism,* ed. R. S. Crane (Chicago: University of Chicago Press, 1952), pp. 404-60; Alan D. McKillop, "Collins's *Ode to Evening*—Background and Criticism," *Tennessee Studies in Literature,* 5 (1960), pp. 73-83; A. S. P. Woodhouse, "The Poetry of Collins Reconsidered," in *From Sensibility to Romanticism,* ed. Frederick W. Hilles and Harold Bloom (New York: Oxford University Press, 1965), pp. 93-137; and Paul Sherwin, *Precious Bane* (Austin: University of Texas Press, 1977).

[3] See note 1 above and also, for discussions of Collins' self-consciousness, Martha Collins, "The Self-Conscious Poet: The Case of William Collins," *ELH,* 42, No. 3 (1975), pp. 362-77; and Richard Wendorf, *William Collins and Eighteenth-Century English Poetry* (Minneapolis: University of Minnesota Press, 1981).

[4] See, for instance, the introduction to *The Poetical Works of Mr. William Collins,* ed. and introd. A. L. Barbauld (n.p.: n.p., 1797); and Edward Gay Ainsworth, *Poor Collins* (Ithaca: Cornell University Press, 1937).
[5] Musgrove, p. 215.

[6] John Middleton Murry, *Countries of the Mind* (New York: E. P. Dutton, 1922), pp. 86 and 94.

[7] A. S. P. Woodhouse, "Collins and the Creative Imagination: A Study in the Background of his *Odes,*" in *Studies in English by Members of the University College, Toronto,* ed. Wallace (Toronto: n.p., 1931), p. 60.

[8] Martha Collins, p. 365.

[9] Musgrove, p. 215.

[10] Northrop Frye, "Towards Defining an Age of Sensibility," *ELH,* 23, No. 2 (1956), pp. 144-52. Direct quotation from p. 148.

[11] Sherwin, p. 55.

[12] C. R. Stone, "A Literary Causerie: The Story of a Poem," *The Academy,* 8 December 1906, p. 587; Bloom, p. 8; McKillop, "Romanticism," p. 15; Shuster, p. 198; Sypher, p. 65; Barbauld, p. v; Northrop Frye, *Fearful Symmetry* (Boston: Beacon Press, 1947), p. 170; Ainsworth, p. 105; Hazlitt, quoted in Garrod, pp. 121 and 122.

[13] Critics who *have* discussed this aspect of Collins'

poetry include Earl R. Wasserman, "Collins' 'Ode on the Poetical Character,'" *ELH,* 34, No. 1 (1967); Fried; and Wendorf.

[14] Ernst Cassirer, *Language and Myth,* trans. Susanne K. Langer (New York: Dover, 1953), p. 32. Hereafter, references will be included parenthetically in the text.

[15] Sherwin first noticed this. See pp. 59 and 69.

[16] Jacques Derrida, *Of Grammatology,* trans. Gayatri Chakravorty Spivak (Baltimore: The Johns Hopkins University Press, 1974), p. 14.

[17] Charles Sanders Peirce, *Collected Papers of Charles Sanders Peirce,* ed. Charles Hartshorne and Paul Weill (Cambridge, Massachusetts: Harvard University Press, 1931-1958), III, p. 361.

[18] Peirce, III, p. 361.

[19] See John R. Crider, "Structure and Effect in Collins' Progress Poems," *Studies in Philology,* 60, No. 1 (1963), p. 60.

[20] John L. Austin, *How To Do Things with Words* (New York: Oxford University Press, 1965), passim.

[21] Jerrold M. Saddock, *Toward a Linguistic Theory of Speech Acts* (New York: Academic Press, 1974), p. 9. As well as the communication of intention, certain "appropriateness conditions" must be met.

[22] John R. Searle, "A Classification of Illocutionary Acts," *Language in Society,* 5 (1976), p. 11.

[23] William Collins, "Ode to Simplicity," 11. 25-27. All references to the poems are from Roger Lonsdale, ed., *The Poems of Thomas Gray, William Collins, and Oliver Goldsmith* (New York: W. W. Norton, 1969). Whenever convenient, line numbers will be included parenthetically in the text.

[24] Frye, "Age of Sensibility," p. 152.

[25] "The Manners, An Ode," 1. 2.

[26] I am indebted here to Paul H. Fry's discussion of invocation in *The Poet's Calling in the English Ode* (New Haven: Yale University Press, 1980).

[27] This ode, incidentally, exemplifies why it is insufficient to claim that Collins' poems are "about" poetry. The trouble with this assertion is not that it is untrue but, rather, that it is unspecific; for against such claims, we might argue, on the contrary, that they are specifically "about" *themselves,* that they raise quite overtly the problematic of their own status as utterances.

[28] Wendorf, p. 95.

[29] Geoffrey Hartman, *The Fate of Reading* (Chicago: University of Chicago Press, 1975), pp. 126-127.

[30] "Ode to Simplicity," 11. 8-11. See Wendorf, p. 94.

[31] Hartman, p. 138.

[32] Wendorf, p. 101.

[33] Cassirer, p. 58. It is interesting to recall, here, how in Collins the function of the name in consecration—"By Pella's bard, a magic name" ("Ode to Pity," 1.7 [see Wendorf, p. 98]); "By old Miletus" ("The Manners. An Ode," 1. 59)—is inseparable from its function in hymn. (Significantly, in the first example, "Pella's bard," Euripides, is not named but is associated with his death-place, and in the second Collins seems to have confused Aristides with the city where he lived. [Lonsdale, p. 475] Thus in both cases, for quite different reasons, we are dealing with toponyms of sorts.) One thinks, for instance, of the "Ode to Liberty"—

> The magic works, thou feel'st the strains,
> One holier name alone remains;
> The perfect spell shall then avail.
> Hail nymph, adored by Britain, hail!
>
> (60-64)

—or again, of the "Ode to Evening," which closes with a hymn to the deity:

> So long, sure-found beneath the sylvan shed,
> Shall Fancy, Friendship, Science, rose-lipped
>   Health,
>   Thy gentlest influence own,
>   And hymn thy favorite name!
>
> (49-52)

In a sense, then, absolute indexicality involves the uttering of a truly proper name.

[34] Geoffrey Hartman, *Beyond Formalism* (New Haven: Yale University Press, 1970), p. 326, and n. 29. The footnote continues: "His two odes on fear and pity treat of the 'tragic' emotions, those closest to sacred or ritualistic drama and hence closely concerned with *participation* [emphasis added]." I would substitute *reciprocity* for *participation*.

[35] Wendorf, see pp. 97-105.

[36] "Ode to Fear," 1. 69; "How Sleep the Brave," 1. 11; "Ode to Fear," 1. 43; "The Manners. An Ode," 1. 43; "Ode to Peace," 1. 19.

[37] Bloom, p. 9; Frye, *Fearful Symmetry*, p. 170. Lonsdale (who, incidentally, is not convinced of these associations) reminds us that "God has 'a cloud / Drawn round about [him] like a radiant Shrine' in *Par. Lost* iii 378-79 and is surrounded by a 'Golden Cloud' at vi 28."

[38] Dustin Griffin has an entirely different reading of this moment in the "Ode to Evening." He has suggested to me—quite persuasively—that here, when the veil is drawn down, the poet remains *behind* it and so has succeeded in a sustained fusing with the deity.

[39] Hartman *Beyond Formalism,* p. 329; Derrida, p. 143.

[40] Sherwin, p. 55.

[41] Paul de Man, *Blindness and Insight,* introd. Wlad Godzich, 2nd ed. rev. (Minneapolis: University of Minnesota Press, 1983), p. 9; p. 12; Derrida, p. 157.

[42] De Man, p. 189.

[43] Derrida, p. 153; p. 154.

[44] Sherwin, p. 58.

[45] Michel Foucault, "Nietzsche, Genealogy, History," in *Language, Counter-Memory, Practice: Selected Essays and Interviews,* ed. Donald F. Bouchard, trans. Bouchard and Sherry Simon (Ithaca: Cornell University Press, 1977), p. 143.

[46] Hartman, *Beyond Formalism,* p. 108.

[47] Hartman, *The Fate of Reading,* p. 78.

[48] Foucault, p. 143.

[49] Martha Collins, passim.

[50] Frederic Jameson, *The Prison-House of Language* (Princeton: Princeton University Press, 1972), p. 12.

Richard Feingold (essay date 1989)

SOURCE: An introduction to *Moralized Song: The Character of Augustan Lyricism*, Rutgers University Press, 1989, pp. 1-51.

[*In the following essay, Feingold examines some characteristics of Augustan poetry and compares the work of several poets, including Collins.*]

My subject here is the representation of inwardness in certain writings, usually poems, which, though they differ considerably from one another, still stand forth as easily recognizable documents of Augustan literary culture. My interest is in the writer's double effort to represent the experience of inwardness and at the same time speak to an audience imagined as present to him. This dual project is characteristic of Augustan literature and particularly of Augustan poetry: what it marks is the writer's insistent interest in the intersection of social and inward experience, an interest he reveals in his articulated and enacted wish to be seen as speaking with public authority even at the represented moment of self-absorption. To the effects produced by the rhetoric sufficient to that task I give the name Augustan lyricism.

The inwardness that the writer reveals may be his own, it may be another's—and that other may be either concretely imagined or universalized. As for the audience, it may be imagined as immediately, or as more distantly, present; it may be a figure in the text itself, explicitly addressed, or it may be constituted by the tacit yet clearly acknowledged presence of a reader. Whatever its form, an audience is always in some sense *there* as an object of address, and plainly or subtly the work enacts the writer's and the audience's contact with one another, a condition indispensable to the writer's assertion of his authority for speech. In the works discussed here, the representation of inwardness therefore, is always, in some sense a public occasion, a fact usually marked by the writer's didactic stance. Neoclassical poetry is unusually rich in writing whose explicit intention is didactic. Where this poetry is most accomplished, its didactic impulse is shaped to its representation of an inwardness that complicates the didactic material and, doing so, produces or enhances the effects I am calling Augustan lyricism.

An audience to speak to, a lesson to deliver, and a focus on inward experience—this complex blend of highly private subject matter and obviously public rhetoric is certainly a familiar feature of the most characteristic and significant poems of the eighteenth century. But the presence to the poet of his audience can seem to be a problematic—perhaps the most problematic—feature of Augustan representations of inwardness, especially to readers accustomed to romantic ways of representing the activity of the subjective consciousness. In recognizing the ubiquity of the imagined audience within Augustan poetry, we may easily recall John Stuart Mill's manifestly romantic insistence that in the specially charged species of writing he is willing to call "poetry," an audience can have neither place nor function. In Mill's scheme it is eloquence, but not poetry, which seeks an audience, for the purpose of eloquence is plainly to influence those to whom it is addressed, to convince them of notions, to induce in them feelings about notions.

These are social tasks above all, whereas for Mill it is solitude that marks the situation and the moment of poetry. In solitude, consciousness—determined and given shape by feeling—encounters itself only, and what it knows and says it knows and says for itself

alone. Poetry is "passion brooding over itself,"[1] and its expression, though written to be read, is not written to enact the poet's *contact* with the reader; it is written, indeed, to feign the impossibility of such contact (p. 349). Hence Mill's familiar insistence that poetry is the species of utterance which is *overheard*. Almost inevitably, Mill would come to identify this overhead utterance with lyric, and thus to identify lyric almost with poetry itself.

> Lyric poetry, as it was the earliest kind, is also, if the view we are now taking of poetry be correct, more eminently and peculiarly poetry than any other; it is the poetry most natural to a really poetic temperament, and least capable of being successfully imitated by one not so endowed by nature. [p. 359]

Mill's remarks about lyric, of course, hardly exhaust the subject; it is perfectly clear that he has no interest in what might be called the ceremonial or theatrical lyric popular in the seventeenth and eighteenth centuries, the greater and lesser odes of Dryden, of Gray, of Collins, of Smart, of Swift, and even, occasionally, of Pope. Nor is there in Mill's discussion of poetry any mention whatever of the writers of the two or three literary generations preceding William Wordsworth's, as if among them were none who found a rhetoric adequate to express "passion brooding over itself," and none who had recognized the possibility of such experience. And yet, whatever the limitations, and whatever the merits, of Mill's discussion, he seems to be implicitly responding to and providing a guide for inquiry into the poetic practice of those literary generations.[2]

What, after all, is signified by the scarcity in eighteenth-century poetry of the lyric writing that, pretending to be overheard, feigns the absence to each other of poet and reader or, more generally, of speaker and addressee? Nor is this a formal question only. For we are asking also about the experience that the formal situation is designed to represent: the experience of "passion brooding over itself."[3] What possibilities are there for representing this in a poetry whose commitment to public speech in public situations is marked by the insistent dominance of epistle, satire, and verse essay? In these forms, where so much that is said is meant to be *heard* (or read as if heard), how may the *overheard* component be recognized and listened for? And if in these public genres there is indeed a covertly present lyricism, what then of the *overtly* lyrical kinds—the elegies and the quiet odes, which even in their most intimate representations seem to seek a listener and perhaps a judge? These questions respond to the odd complexity of neoclassical poetry when the subject it engages is self-encounter, and when the experience it represents is primarily inward. They are questions that ask ultimately about the nature of lyric utterance within a rhetoric whose first task is to present the general experience of mankind as a knowable presence even in the moment of lyric solitude.[4]

. . . . .

My emphasis in this book is on the covertly lyrical rhetoric of the more obviously public genres: epistle, satire, verse essay, conversation. But, to begin, some consideration of the more familiarly, more overtly lyrical Augustan writing will be useful, because, as the questions I have been raising suggest, the strictly formal distinctions between the apparently personal and the apparently public kinds of poetry tend to mask the presence in both of similar rhetorical tensions. Moreover, these rhetorical tensions themselves can become a poem's central subject.

I shall illustrate with an ode of Horace, simply assuming his paradigmatic stature for the English poets of the eighteenth century, who found in his work a variety of models for writing about the intersection of private and public experience; in Horace's work, indeed, public and personal are virtually forms of thought and feeling.[5] Nor was it only about the intersection of the private and the public that Horace wrote, but also about those boundaries between the two orders of experience which were not to be violated.[6] Here is *Ode 1.24*, the elegy for Quintilius, which will illustrate the pressure contained within Augustan lyric utterance when it is given to the exploration of intensely powerful states of subjective consciousness:

Quis desiderio sit pudor aut modus
tam cari capitis? praecipe lugubres
cantus, Melpomene, cui liquidam pater
    vocem cum cithara dedit.

ergo Quinctilium perpetuus sopor
urget! cui Pudor et Iustitiae soror,
incorrupta Fides, nudaque Veritas
    quando ullum inveniet parem?

multis ille bonis flebilis occidit,
nulli flebilior quam tibi, Virgili.
tu frustra pius heu non ita creditum
    poscis Quinctilium deos.

quod si Threicio blandius Orpheo
auditam moderere arboribus fidem,
non vanae redeat sanguis imagini,
    quam virga semel horrida,

non lenis precibus fata recludere,
nigro compulerit Mercurius gregi.
durum: sed levius fit patientia,
    quidquid corrigere est nefas.[7]

[What restraint or measure should there be to grief for so dear a life? Teach me a song of mourning, O Melpomene, to whom the Father gave a liquid voice and with it the lyre. So now perpetual sleep presses itself upon Quintilius! When shall Honour, and unmoveable Loyalty, the sister of Justice, and plain Truth, ever find his peer? He dies mourned by many good men; by no one, Virgil, more than by you. In useless devotion you ask the gods for Quintilius, but, alas, he was not given to this life on such terms. Were you able more sweetly even than Thracian Orpheus to strike the strings the trees once heeded, still no blood would return to that empty shade, now that Mercury with his hideous rod has gathered it to the dark herd—Mercury, not easily persuaded to open the gates that Fate has shut. This is hard: but patience lightens the weight of those evils which it would be sinful to seek to set right.]

This poem, so obviously *about* an intense inward state, is nevertheless marked by language of an unmistakably public character. The poem's elegant and sometimes astonishing circumlocutions; the didactic charge of its concluding lines; the personified abstractions that suggest large attitudinal agreements, that is, Honor, Justice, Loyalty, Truth; and the poem's ceremonial manner—these register Horace's primary commitment to his hearers and thus to the decorums of a speech whose reticence must be the vehicle for its emotionally charged material. And that commitment is nowhere more plainly underlined than in the poem's opening. Here Horace's address to the muse acknowledges immediately that, between the powerful inwardness of grief and the act of speaking suitably about it, there must be some strain: "What restraint or limit should there be to grief for so dear a life? Teach me a song of mourning." In fact, the poem that follows is the very mourning song that gives answer to a question initially put as though no answer were possible or even desirable.

Such an answer must be complex enough not only to memorialize the dead Quintilius, but also to explore the problems inherent in such song as would meet that commitment. This task Horace accomplishes by his unexpected focus on the mourner, Virgil, whom Horace presents as both inconsolable and inarticulate. Once Horace has uttered his own memorial to the dead man, the accomplishment of his first two stanzas, he develops his poem as an address to Virgil. This address marks implicitly the contrast between what can be said and what *must not be said* ["nefas"], between Horace as artist and Virgil as mourner. It is Virgil, "frustra pius," who is represented as saying the "unspeakable"—beseeching the gods for the dead man's restoration. Perhaps most interesting and moving here is Horace's emphasis upon Virgil's fruitless speech, and upon the irony inherent in that supremely articulate man's incapacity for proper speech in this situation.

But Horace does not merely assert the fruitlessness of Virgil's speech; he emphasizes as well its *impiety*. In the beautiful moral lyricism of the two lines with which Horace ends his poem, the consolatory sympathy is obvious: "durum: sed levius fit patientia, / quidquid corrigere est nefas." But the final word surprises with its harshness. Heard in it is the deep connection between the idea of the unutterable and the idea of the impious, the unlawful, the unnatural. It is as if two kinds of speech are set in opposition to each other: the one, expressing Virgil's unutterable grief and *unspeakable* protest; the other, lawful, substantial, in accord with what is "right," what is "said," what "must be" (*fas— fari—fatum*)—in a word, with what is *authorized*. This is Horace's speech; it is the yield, finally, of his invocational request of the muse; indeed, his poem is bounded by that request, spoken in its opening lines, and by the final word of the final line—"nefas." And quite plainly, the muse gives, along with her lesson in the authorized sounds, a warning away from the sinful ones.

Now in aligning his own authorized song with what is pious, and Virgil's lament with what is unspeakable, Horace not only distinguishes between poem and outcry, but also between two kinds of poem. We see this in the question he sympathetically addresses to Virgil, the full force of which is not really clear until we have read to the end of the poem's last line.

> quod, si Threicio blandius Orpheo
> auditam moderere arboribus fidem,
> non vanae redeat sanguis imagini,
>   quam virga semel horrida,
>
> non lenis precibus fata recludere,
> nigro compulerit Mercurius gregi.

The sympathy so obvious here is accompanied still by a subtle disclaimer: we hear it in the complexity of "vanae . . . imagini," in which, as against Virgil's desperate and fantastical insistence upon the continuing substantiality of the dead man, Horace asserts, plainly, his bloodlessness, his shadowiness. Once again, Horace's assertion implies a distinction between two kinds of utterance: the kind associated with miraculous and enchanting and unnatural speech, the speech of Thracian Orpheus (which can figure to itself as though still possessing substance the mere image of the precious dead), and the pious, the sane, the *eloquent and reticent* speech Horace is composing here. In the context of this reticent speech, "imagini" works to associate two ideas—first, the bloodlessness of the dead man, and second, the trope, the metaphor, the *imago* (one feels strongly the suggestion that this is the "mere metaphor") of the mad speech of the Orphic poet, the phantasm only, *vana imago*. Each—the dead man, and the poet's useless trope—is unreal, insubstantial, without blood. For all the sympathy Horace feels, his speech brutally insists upon this point.

But in aligning his style of speech with "what is said" (and in taking "what is said" to be synonymous with "what is ordained"), Horace is not merely dismissing the orphic impulse and its way. He is also acknowledging its rootedness in rich desire, and acknowledging too the tragic implications of his own choice of style. If indeed Virgil's speech—and the outcome it seeks—is impious, "nefas," what are we to make of Horace's description of Virgil as "frustra pius": "tu frustra pius heu non ita creditum / poscis Quintilium deos"? It seems an astonishing oxymoron: "deceived in your devotion [to Quintilius]" would be the primary reading here, but "pius" obviously registers also the sense of "righteous before the gods", so that Virgil is seen to be not only self-deluded in his insane wish for the return of his friend, but also "deceived in his righteousness" with respect to the gods. The ironic possibility here accords with the strong but not unlikely resonance of "swindled" in "frustra." These are meanings that certainly complicate Horace's role as spokesman for the authorized vision. Obviously, he has burdened this expression, "frustra pius," in order to suggest how complex and strained are the choices faced by a human speaker who would align his speech with that of the gods: what can it be but an implied indictment of their ways to say of the mourner that he has been deceived or swindled in his piety? Or wanton in his secular *devotions?* Certainly, Horace's exclamation in this stanza, "heu," tells us how aware he is of Virgil's victimization. Moreover, Horace's representation of Mercury is in obviously ironic relationship with his larger effort to align his speech with that of the gods and to define this effort as an act of authorized piety. Unmistakable here is the relentlessness of the figure of Mercury and his hideousness:

> non vanae redeat sanguis imagini,
>   quam virga semel horrida,
>
> non lenis precibus fata recludere,
> nigro compulerit Mercurius gregi.

Here the rhetoric makes it impossible to accept simply Horace's effort to distinguish his speech from Virgil's on the grounds of piety. The hideous figure of Mercury works decisively to limit our affective commitment to "what is decreed" (here "fata") and to the style of human speech that seeks an accord with it. Moreover, the image of Mercury compelling the beloved friend (*caput carus,* the dear life) into the "dark herd" is a terrifying expression of dehumanization; it stimulates our sympathy for Virgil's desire to see "the blood return to the empty [perhaps even here the 'drained'] shade," and it underscores how problematic indeed is Horace's effort to associate his vision and style with the way things are—a notion here complicated by its articulation in the word "fata," whose deep connection to the words *fari* and *fas* (and "nefas") is played upon richly. The irony of "corrigere" most powerfully acknowledges the insufficiencies Horace himself perceives in his effort to speak substantially for "what is ordained": "it is hard, but patience eases the weight of those evils which it would be sinful [unspeakable] to set right." That is, what is spoken is not right. To change it is to set it right ("corrigere"). But to set it right is "nefas"—unspeakable, an abomination. The richness of the irony here requires no comment.

In its development, then, Horace's poem demonstrates that, to the question he initially addresses to the muse, there are two answers: Virgil's resists the limits that the decorums of substantial speech would impose upon speaking about grief (and perhaps upon imagining it), Horace's defines and enunciates them. The result is the reticent eloquence of the poem Horace gives us: a politeness that acknowledges and sympathizes with an experience that is, still, elusive and very threatening. Horace's reticence composes the poem, then, but it is Virgil's incapacity for restraint and for substantial speech which calls the poem into being and gives it shape.[8] In the play of Horace's way against Virgil's way, the poem's lyricism is made manifest, and what we *overhear* in this drama is Horace's coming to the recognition of the complexity of his stylistic and moral choices. Even in a poem so plainly marked by the gestures and conventions of social speech, much of what is meant is not finally *spoken out,* and though the poem's speaker is not situated in solitude, he is discovering the limits of the reach of his public voice.

. . . . .

Perhaps the most obvious characteristic of Horace's poem is its intricacy. This intricacy is a function of the poem's attention to the ironies inherent in Virgil's, that supremely articulate man's, incapacity in this situation for substantial speech, speech that accords with decree and with fate, speech, therefore, that *speaks out.* Such substantial speech cannot be adequate to Virgil's inner situation, and intricacy of the kind manifested in the Quintilius ode is perhaps inevitable in Augustan poetry when it is about intensely inward states of mind. Perhaps this happens because in Augustan poetry eloquence is regularly understood to have primarily public functions or to be an essentially social display. The intricacy Horace's poem displays, generated by its search for a decorous eloquence at the same time that it articulates its sympathy for what must not be said, enacts the poet's experience of strain in representing or in honoring powerfully subjective experience. And this experience of strain is itself a tacit subject of Augustan poems when they are about such experience. The meaning of speech and the meaning of inarticulateness are perceived as rich and complex matters, problematized, as we might now say, whenever the rhetoric of social display seeks to reveal the contours of inward experience.

In Horace's poem, Virgil is not represented as being without words, but he is seen as essentially inarticulate. This crucial point is enforced by Horace's decision to keep him from speaking for himself within the

rhetorical structure of the whole poem. That is, Horace attributes to Virgil a speech whose primary characteristic is its excess, but Horace does not *represent* that speech. Within *Horace's poem* Virgil himself has no voice of his own, and though the reader hears of Virgil's speech, he experiences it only as a silence. Now, especially interesting here is this enactment *within the poem* of the essential equivalence of verbal excess and silence, each a sign of a failure to reach substantial speech, each at the same time a sign of an inner experience of especial richness, in Virgil's case, his "unspeakable" desire for the "dear life."

In considering the association that Horace sees between Virgil's insubstantial speech, both excessive and unheard, and the intensity of his inner experience, we may call to mind those figures who belong to a later literary age but whose rhetorical situation is at least cognate with that of the Virgil we see in Horace's poem: figures such as Corporal Trim, Uncle Toby, Yorick, Harley. Excess and silence seem to mark their presence too, and the most eloquent moments of these heroes of sentimentalism are given out not by words, but by gestures; what we learn about them with most delight, we learn through feelings they enact rather than articulate, more accurately perhaps, through the fullness of feeling they point to. Indeed, the inarticulate eloquence of the hero of feeling, the sentimentalist, may well be a way of exploring concerns similar to those at the center of Horace's memorial ode. And more generally, in the overtly lyrical poetry of the eighteenth century, it is usual to discover the careful decorums of public speech shadowing forth and honoring certain rich states of mind of which speaking out is no necessary consequence. The complex ending of Thomas Gray's *Elegy,* for example, works to generate powerfully lyrical feeling without precisely defining it or describing its sources within the narrator. Indeed, the poem's concluding presentation of the speaker's own imagined monument, its reticent and unrevealing epitaph cut into it, clearly signals the way in which a public eloquence could be put to the task of honoring what it refuses to reveal, as if the refusal to reveal were itself an important constituent of valuable emotional experience. Here too, as in the Quintilius ode, intricate poetic activity will be generated by the poet's interest in the conditions of speech and speechlessness, but here the poet's refusal to commit himself entirely to his hearers even as he makes the sounds of public speech is more clearly brought forward than it is by Horace.[9] In the *Elegy* the poem's speaker is both Horace *and* Virgil: his is both the mastery of a reticent eloquence and the experience of a valued emotional excess.

Gray's gesturing at the presence of what he will not reveal I would define as a sentimental act; it marks the high value the writer places on inward experience, but also his somewhat contradictory suspicion that such experience can have no standing until it is translated into a heard language whose very good manners would give to the inward the grace and the status of the social. But then too, this uncertainty about the standing of the inward is accompanied also by the writer's hostility to the social, the speakable, the authorized. In Gray's poem, certainly, the public life is presented as knowable, as uninteresting, and as mean, and the poem's lyric effect is largely created by the speaker's incomplete effort at self-revelation played out against those assertions. What we are left with finally is the sense that having one's own story is all that counts, but publishing that story can only deface it. Gray's speaker wants, at one and the same time, the privileges of silence and of speech, to walk a stage where passion may brood over itself and still speak to a hearer. The special distinction of the *Elegy* is to have accorded moral dignity to this sentimental condition of mute articulateness.[10]

I want to turn now to a similarly revealing poem of William Collins in whose intricacies the rhetorical dynamics of Gray's *Elegy* can be seen to be played out in an even more complex fashion, all to demonstrate how an Augustan articulateness can be made to function in a situation in which, again, heard speech is situationally impossible. In *A Song from Shakespear's Cymbelyne* Collins has reimagined a dramatic action as a lyric poem, signaling in this his double effort to give standing to the experience of inwardness by linking it, if only allusively, to an originally public mode, the dramatic action, and *at the same time to resist the opportunities and obligations of public speech.* Collins's peculiar aim, like Gray's, is to honor silence and solitude, but also to authorize them—to be simultaneously inward and social, speechless and eloquent, sentimental and gentlemanly.

The intricacies of Collins's own *Song from Cymbelyne* result from its subtle use of the Shakespearean original, of course. But even the most cursory glance at the poem tells us that Collins had not only tuned his ear to "Fear no more the heat o' the sun"—the beautiful lyric that in the play ceremonializes the apparent death of Fidele, the real Imogen—but also drew together Shakespeare's "Song" *and* the dramatic movement immediately leading up to it. This he did, not merely to represent in his own terms the song of the two brothers at Fidele's burial, but to represent it by introducing into the situation a new line of sight altogether, one that would reveal the capacity of some distanced, indistinct, and generalized mourner for responding feelingly, *but without uttered words,* to that doubly fictional event. As in Horace's poem, it is the mourner and not the mourned who claims our central attention: but unlike Horace's dirge, and unlike Shake-speare's "Song," Collins's poem attenuates markedly its representation of the social dimension of the mourning situation.

Now in Horace's poem the social character of his response to Quintilius's death and Virgil's sorrow is per-

haps most clearly marked in the plain didacticism of the concluding thought, however complex the implications of that didacticism may be: "durum: sed levius fit patientia, / quidquid corrigere est nefas." In Shakespeare's "Song" a similar didactic charge is expressed in the recurring rhyme of "dust" and "must"—that is, in the utterly realistic insistence upon the plain inevitability, finality, and democracy of death:

> Golden lads and girls all must,
> As chimney-sweepers, come to dust . . .
> The sceptre, learning, physic, must
> All follow this, and come to dust . . .
> All lovers young, all lovers must
> Consign to thee and come to dust . . . [11]

But this is only one of several sounds we hear in the "Song": this plain realism is blended with a note of genuine pathos itself articulated as elegiac circumlocution—"Thou thy worldly task hast done, / Home art gone and ta'en thy wages . . ."—and elsewhere in the most direct of sayings—"Care no more to clothe and eat; / To thee the reed is as the oak." In this, the utterance of a distanced but sympathetic consciousness, we can hear yet another music too, that of the small couplets chanting the ceremonial imperatives in which the song is concluded and which ordain, as if it were a ritual action, the reverential silence which is, oddly, to *mark* Fidele's grave.[12]

> No exorciser harm thee.
> Nor no witchcraft charm thee.
> Ghost unlaid forbear thee.
> Nothing ill come hear thee.
> Quiet consummation have,
> And renowned by thy grave.

This blend of realism, pathos, and ceremonial dignity gives the song its character and is the final style of the lyric utterance of the two brothers who had *in the dialogue immediately preceding the song* argued gently over what constituted speech proper to the occasion. The song itself is produced as the resolution of their argument, which was about the suitability of such excessive, such *sentimental* language as this to the fact of death:

> With fairest flowers
> Whilst summer lasts and I live here, Fidele,
> I'll sweeten thy sad grave. Thou shalt not lack
> The flower that's like thy face, pale primrose, nor
> The azur'd harebell, like thy veins; no, nor
> The leaf of eglantine, whom not to slander,
> Outsweet'ned not thy breath.

This, Arviragus's speech, is interrupted in the impatience of grief by his brother, Guiderius: "Prithee have done, / And do not play in wench-like words with that / Which is so serious." Guiderius objects to the apparent excessiveness of his brother's rhetoric, its inadequacy to the fact of death, while Guiderius reveals what he himself would take to be a more appropriate style in the brusque phrase in which he summarizes his impatience with his brother's speech. He says simply: "To the grave." And yet Guiderius had a moment earlier uttered his own "wench-like words," entirely in response to the shock of Fidele's apparent death:

> Why, he but sleeps!
> If he be gone, I'll make his grave a bed.
> With female fairies will his tomb be haunted,
> And worms will not come to thee.

This expression of a rich fantasy—"Why, he but sleeps"—with its merely subjunctive acknowledgment of the "truth" ("If he be gone"), its indicative assertion of an impossibility ("And worms will not come to thee"), and its transformation of a grave to a bed—all this is hardly the blunt realism that the speaker is himself to insist upon in a moment. It is, like Virgil's unheard speech, an excessive, a *sentimental* expression of desire for the "dear life." And only in the wonderful song to come thirty lines later are the realism Guiderius insists upon and the desire he feels brought together and harmonized. But in creating that harmony, Shakespeare has eliminated in the "Song" all trace of the sentimentalist's excess. That is to say, in the dramatic action, the sentimentalist's emotional excess is—unlike Virgil's unheard lament and Gray's unrevealed sorrow—plain and outspoken. But then this very outspokenness permissible in the dialogue—indeed, it is the subject of the dramatic dialogue—is entirely suppressed in the lyric movement that resolves the stylistic disagreement the dramatic dialogue articulates. And the new music of this "Song"—the ceremonial, the pathetic, the elegiacal chant—is entirely denuded of the language of flower and fairy in which the brothers had expressed their excessive, sentimental, and fantasized desire to preserve Fidele from death and corruption.

But, and this is especially interesting, Collins's *Song from Cymbelyne* is grounded entirely in that sentimental language of the two brothers. In Collins's reworking of Shakespeare's "Song" there is no reference whatever to the sententious realism of their new "Song"; nor is there any enactment of the small dispute over proper speech which precedes that song. Nevertheless, Collins clearly signals his attention to that dispute. For, in his *Song from Cymbelyne,* Collins reproduces the earlier sentimental language of both brothers—the language they will give up—but does so in the same ceremonial cadences *that had marked their abandonment of the sentimental style.* And, in this union of ceremonial and sentimental speech, Collins has discovered a public voice for the inwardness of the sentimentalist. We hear the ceremonial music in "No wither'd Witch shall here be seen, / No goblins lead their nightly Crew . . ." and

in the following couplet, we hear the ceremonial and the sentimental: "The Female Fays shall haunt the Green, / And dress thy Grave with pearly Dew." The first two lines I have just cited plainly echo the ceremonial chant that concludes Shakespeare's song; equally clearly the second two lines pick up the excess of Guiderius's speech before it had been transformed into ceremonial song: "With female fairies will his tomb be haunted." Collins blends this, the language of Guiderius, to Arviragus's similarly expressed promise ("With fairest flowers . . . Fidele, I'll sweeten thy sad grave"), all in order to produce his new and now gentlemanly version of the speech of the young brothers: "The Female Fays shall haunt the Green, / And dress thy grave with pearly Dew."

What then has happened to the excessive, the sentimental utterance of the brothers' dramatic dialogue, which, as in Horace's memorial ode, represented a verbal fullness felt to be inappropriate both to the actuality of death and to the memorial song for the dead? Quite simply, Collins has pruned away that fullness. Arviragus's flowers—pale primrose, the azured harebell, the leaf of eglantine—each along with its analogue in some part of Fidele's anatomy, have been generalized to their simplest seasonal identity and ceremonial function:

> To fair Fidele's grassy Tomb
> 　Soft Maids, and Village Hinds shall bring
> Each op'ning Sweet, of earliest Bloom,
> 　And rifle all the breathing Spring.

Even more radical surgery is performed on Arviragus's robin, which Shakespeare gives us in this language:

> 　　　The raddock would,
> With charitable bill (O bill, sore shaming
> Those rich-left heirs that let their fathers lie
> Without a monument!), bring thee all this,
> Yea, and furr'd moss besides. When flow'rs
> 　are none,
> To winter-ground thy corse—

Here is Collins's version:

> The Redbreast oft at Ev'ning Hours
> 　Shall kindly lend his little Aid:
> With hoary Moss, and gather'd Flow'rs,
> 　To deck the Ground where thou art laid.

Obvious here is Collins's effort to do away with Arviragus's sententiousness and to tame his fervor; note the absence of exclamation, as well as the transformation of a desolate winter scene, spontaneously imagined, to an evening ceremony, regularly recurring. In this restraint Collins demonstrates that the reticence of ceremonial speech and the valued excess of the sentimentalist can, indeed, be harmonized, harmonized here in the generalizing decorums of Augustan eloquence, which has in Collins's version of the song become the sentimentalist's preferred style. Embodying these decorums, Collins's reworking of Shakespeare's scenario can give lyric articulation to the emotional and verbal excess which Shakespeare would dramatize in his dialogue but not allow in his "Song."

But the transformed sentimentalist who is the lyric speaker of Collins's poem and in whose Augustan decorums fullness of feeling has discovered its reticent eloquence—this lyric speaker has sought no occasion for speaking out. For, though he imagines the pastoral ceremony honoring Fidele, and even blesses it, he is by no means a participant in it. Indeed, he insists upon his separation from that ceremony and from its society, as his language makes clear: "soft Maids," "Village Hinds," "Shepherd Lads," and "melting Virgins"—it is for these that Fidele's tomb is a shrine. Not a member of this pastoral community (from which he excludes himself by the very act of naming it so conventionally and so elegantly), the speaker cannot appear in the poem as a presented figure at all. That is, he has taken from Shakespeare's play a dramatic action, and reimagined its cast of characters as a generalized and anonymous pastoral community; he then has excluded himself from participation in that community, but still asserted his own as the central consciousness of the scene he has thus re-created.

In this odd and intricate process, Collins creates a lyric poem out of a dramatic action and out of a set of actors, a single lyric speaker. Now this speaker, in his separation from a scene that is now not enacted but instead envisioned, can utter a speech that is not heard, but only *overheard*. But—and this is very important—the politeness and the ceremony of this overheard and entirely inward utterance are still the hallmarks of social speech. Were this a lyric constructed according to Mill's specifications, we would not expect to see written into it—at the moment, and at the site, of lyric speech—so clear, if tacit, a representation of the speaker's social self-awareness, here made plain in his insistence upon his separation from the very scene he broods over and claims emotional kinship with. But it is Collins's achievement to have represented the speaker's social self-awareness at the same time as he has made that representation the very condition of our entering into earshot of his *overheard address,* and thus into contact with his inwardness. Overheard address—this paradoxical, or at least odd, designation—best describes the character of Collins's lyric speech. It is the vehicle for the social display of inward experience.

Indeed, in transforming Shakespeare's dramatic action into a lyric poem, Collins seized the opportunity to create a new line of sight and with it a new register of feeling, the sight and feeling of the cultivated consciousness itself, socially and intellectually distinct from

the pastoral milieu of both play and poem, but emotionally involved in it, as the last two stanzas show:

> When howling Winds, and beating Rain,
>   In Tempests shake the sylvan Cell:
> Or midst the Chace on ev'ry Plain,
>   The tender Thought on thee shall dwell.
>
> Each lonely Scene shall thee restore,
>   For thee the Tear be duly shed:
> Belov'd, till Life could charm no more;
>   And mourn'd, till Pity's self be dead.

Note the primacy here of the "tender Thought": thinking it is not represented as an experience the speaker sympathetically shares, if only from a distance, with the pastoral characters, as are the ceremonies of the earlier stanzas at Fidele's shrine. Now instead, it is his alone, available to him either when pastoral society is unable to assemble for its pleasures ("In Tempests"), or when it is inappropriately engaged in them ("midst the Chace on ev'ry Plain"). So the shrine built in the previous four stanzas has all along been intended for this new speaker, not as a place at which he and the pastoral characters might "assemble," as in a dramatic action embodying the experience of an acknowledged community of feeling. The shrine is instead a stimulus to the speaker's own capacity to think the "tender Thought," to weep, to love, to mourn, and to pity. The initial representation of the speaker as in sympathy with the pastoral characters is somewhat inconsistent, then, with the poem's concluding emphasis on his social and psychological isolation from them, an inconsistency that reveals the poem's straining point. Nevertheless, what Collins has done seems an exquisite feat of language; he has fully articulated a scene of solitude in which eloquence has been associated not with public utterance or even with the participation in public ceremony, but rather with inwardness itself—the thinking of the "tender Thought," "each lonely Scene," the tear *"duly* shed" (note the insistence upon decorum in that adverb even as the action it describes is entirely private). These scenes of solitude and acts of silence are the home and deeds of the inward consciousness itself, for which the restoring of loss is equivalent to thinking about the lost object—"Each lonely Scene shall thee restore"—just as loving and mourning are equivalent states. It is finally that quality of consciousness, the sovereign inwardness of which is demonstrated in its extraordinary command of social speech and *simultaneously in its freedom from social declarativeness,* that Collins's poem is all about. That is, its subject is "Pity's self," and "Pity's self" is actually the poem's speaker—Pathos, the very muse of inwardness. The poem's *action,* moreover, is to represent Pathos or Feeling coming to consciousness of itself, or as Mill stipulated, "brooding over itself." But what Mill would have deemed generically impossible is the poem's remarkable accomplishment: the demonstration that only a social eloquence (the poem contains no more obvious a public locution than that final personification, "Pity's self") can fully honor and make intelligible what must be experienced only in solitude and can be known only inwardly.

. . . . .

Now, it is an oddity of Collins's **Song from Cymbelyne** that it is presented entirely without irony, because the opportunities for irony here are considerable. The most obvious is that, though Shakespeare's Fidele will almost immediately in the play awake from what has been only the appearance of death, as Collins's poem is given, Fidele's death is not to be undone. His (or her) life is now newly bounded by the poem, for the poem is complete in itself as the contemplation of Fidele's memorial, and in that, of Feeling's coming to the awareness of itself. The poem does not question, parody, nor ironize that experience, it just presents it. At the same time, then, that the poem calls our attention to its rather subtly elaborated system of allusions, it also insists that we willfully refuse to look beyond the single moment in the play to which they immediately refer. Were we to look beyond that moment and then to read the poem in the light of our better knowledge, it would be difficult to take its lyric speaker seriously. He would be read as a figure mourning a death that has not happened, he would become therefore vulnerable to irony, and the poem would be open to a more complex reading than our experience of it can verify. If we were, in a triumph of judgment, to see the speaker ironically, we would be undoing our own rich act of sympathetic reading, and the poem would become pointless. For the very purpose of its rhetoric is to cause the reader to become aware of himself resisting that interpretive temptation. In this he gains a power to resist the full claim of the sophistication which the poem's brief allusion to *Cymbeline* has itself called into play.

Collins's willingness to resist that full claim seems to me central to his lyric success in *A Song from Shakespear's Cymbelyne*. In fact, his insistence on calling attention to the bounds he is willing to impose on his literary sophistication is a quite explicit indication of the importance he attached to the freedom thus gained, a freedom he did not always command as a writer of lyric poetry. For, in fact, Collins's extraordinary literary sophistication is more usually the subject of his poetry than are the feelings and the visions that give names to his poems and that he pretends to invoke. In the very midst of his **Ode to Fear,** for example, at what might have been a moment of great intensity, are two footnotes he himself places within his text to cool it down by calling attention to his sources in Sophocles. If this is not a simple act of pedantry, it is certainly a complex one, central to his intention in the ode, which is not, after all, to represent his being overcome by Fear, but politely to represent a sophisticated literary consciousness toying with that possibility and en-

joying its distance from it. In his **Ode to Fear** Collins depends upon his reader's similarly sophisticated pleasure in catching the allusions, noting the discrepancies between source and poem, and deriving from this activity an affirmation, not of his power to feel Fear, but of the power his literacy gives him to make a game out of that possibility. The bond between poet and reader here is formed not by feeling, but by intelligence, by judgment, by sophistication.[13]

But the poise that characterizes Collins's **Song from Cymbelyne** seems to me a sign of sentimental expressiveness working its most interesting effects: such writing registers the author's awareness of the possibilities for ironizing his manner or parodying his material, but then his conscious resistance to doing so. To acknowledge those possibilities is to acknowledge the social claims of intelligence and judgment, to resist them is to embrace the pleasures of inwardness, and still to have one's intelligence and judgment endorsing that choice. Precisely this pointedly articulated, sentimental drama between intelligence and feeling produces the characteristic blend of lyricism and intellectual adroitness which is the special distinction of eighteenth-century poetry. Again, Gray's success in the *Elegy* in drawing the full evocative force from his rural material at the same time as he creates room and opportunity for the critical play of intelligence upon this rural material will stand as the primary example of the kind of pleasure a sentimental rhetoric can yield.

But when this kind of writing does not succeed—as, for example, in Gray's Eton College ode—the play of eloquence upon emotionally evocative material will seem intrusive. In such situations we can sense the poet reaching out too directly to his audience of readers, as if to assure them and himself that his lyrical material is not too much his own, not disruptive of the bond that social experience, intelligence, and literary sophistication have formed between them. The writer's fussiness rather than his intelligence is the most obvious message in the signals he sends out to assure the reader that despite the poem's personal charge it still is a record of shared public experience: it will pass judgment's muster. An example is Gray's use of the word "redolent" in the Eton College ode: it is not a bold straining beyond John Dryden's "honey redolent of Spring" to test the limits of our language (as Samuel Johnson disapprovingly thought),[14] but a fussy *reminder of* Dryden's usage. With that word Gray plays it safe, calling for support from Dryden's eloquent precedent to help establish his own authority for personal expression in his own poem. Gray's uncertainty in the personal and lyrical stance is evident also in the ode's shift into declamatory and pointed utterance, thoroughly inconsistent with the initially private and meditative situation the poem springs from: "Alas," "Yet see," "Ah, shew them," "Lo," and, of course, "No more: where ignorance is bliss, / 'Tis folly to be wise." The poem falls short in lyric power because it is not so much a record of what the poet felt and thought from his distant prospect of Eton College; it really registers instead his concern for his authority to speak about the experience.[15]

It is this concern for authority, this sense that poetic speech is warranted by a bond of intelligence, education, and sophistication between writer and reader, that often vitiates the portrayal of inwardness in the eighteenth-century lyric. The poet seems to think of his authority as a property of that bond, which he seeks to affirm, looking to it and not finally to his inner experience for the justification of his poem. When this happens, declamatory speech usually follows, since declamation more easily than the overheard speech of the lyric can stand as a demonstration of the intellectual and social bond the poet seeks with the reader. It is not surprising, therefore, to discover a mixture of lyricism and declamation pervading the period's lyric expression despite its formal variety, from Collins's visionary odes to William Cowper's unbroken conversation. Even so genuinely lyrical a talent as Robert Burns's, so late in the period, is disrupted and distorted by this mix, as in *The Cotter's Saturday Night,* where the charge of personal feeling so strongly binding the poet to his rural material dissipates itself in his search for a style to *distinguish* him from the peasantry. He tests no fewer than three languages in his effort to connect with his readers rather than with his subject: these languages are the dialect of the poor themselves, the "standard" English that sets the poet apart from the peasants, and then the borrowings from other poems that serve to link him in consciousness and sophistication with his readers and with high culture.

The most usual form of the poet's declamatory utterance in the lyric situation is didactic. In didactic address the eighteenth-century writer most regularly asserts his authority for speech; in didactic address he most often reveals himself in the role of writer, bonded to his audience by literary tradition, by intelligence, by judgment. Of course, the great variety of uses to which didactic address could be put, and of forms to which it could be shaped, itself speaks for the variousness of the conceptions of literary purpose and of literary *being* in the period. Jonathan Swift's pamphlets, for example, whether straight or satirical, all assume a writer in a position of some authority, with something *to say to* an audience, whatever the result of that saying may come to be. Alexander Pope's *Moral Essays* reveal by their very title their at least initially didactic intention, and his poetry throughout is rich in its presentation of serious and improving conversations in which the delivery of a lesson, as in Bethel's "sermon," is an important moment in a poem's thematic and emotional development. In the finest didactic literature, of course, an initially didactic stance will become richly complicated, and in this process the pos-

itive assumptions about the writer's bond with his audience which are implied in his didactic stance will be scrutinized; they may be rejected, or reaffirmed, or redefined.

In the obviously public poetry of the period—the poetry written for an audience, even if it be an audience of one, as in Swift's poems to Stella, even if it be a meditating reader, as in Johnson's *Vanity of Human Wishes,* or the recipient of an epistle, as in Pope's Horatian imitations—in this obviously public poetry, the representation of inwardness will usually be a function of the poet's scrutiny of his didactic stance. His rejection, or his reaffirmation, or his redefinition of it, will be seen as a humane complication of his lesson; and, in the process of complicating it, his poem will develop dramatically. The pleasure we derive from such writing comes from our sense that, shaping the lesson with which these poems direclty address us, there is in them a curve of feeling to which we become alert, and that in this curve of feeling we overhear something of the poet's inner experience as the lesson's teacher. Our responsiveness to the poem as such a record of the poet's inwardness gives us our sense of its lyric force, and in the dramatic accord the poet establishes between his didactic manner and his inwardness is to be discovered the largest lesson of his work, its yield of instructive pleasure.

What I am describing here I have earlier called covert lyricism—covert, because the poet's inwardness is not his ostensible, his first subject. Nor can we see from his rhetorical situation, his "speaking out," that it can *become* his subject. Thus, Oliver Goldsmith's *Deserted Village* begins with an explanatory letter about, of all things, a matter of historical fact, and proceeds as a discourse on social policy. But this covertly lyrical poem soon enough comes to reveal the remarkable resources for the representation of inwardness which were inherent in the forms of its public address, of which the didactic was Goldsmith's favorite. In their discovery of the resources of a covert lyricism, the poets I discuss in the following chapters were able to satisfy two demands that were soon to seem incompatible: that they speak out with authoritative eloquence, and that they still reveal their own rich inwardness. It was a project that the overt lyric approached with uncertainty, never commanded, and usually failed at.

Notes

The following abbreviations have been used in the notes:

ECS   Eighteenth-Century Studies

EIC   Essays in Criticism

ELH English Literary History

HLQ Huntington Library Quarterly

YR   Yale Review

¹ John Stuart Mill, "Thoughts on Poetry and Its Varieties," *Collected Works of John Stuart Mill,* ed. John M. Robson and Jack Stillinger, 25 vols. to date (Toronto and London: Univ. of Toronto Press and Routledge, Kegan and Paul, 1981), 1: 363.

² As these remarks indicate, M. H. Abrams's account of neoclassical and Romantic critical theories (especially his highlighting of Mill's presentation of the "expressive" position) has been of continuing usefulness to me; see *The Mirror and the Lamp* (New York: Norton, 1958), esp. pp. 21-26, 84-88, 103-114.

³ I ask these questions in the same spirit that S. L. Goldberg, writing about some manifestly romantic features of Pope's mind and art, comments: "To say all this, however, is not to claim that Pope was 'really' a Romantic, nor merely to repeat (what everyone knows) that 'Augustan' and 'Romantic' are very slippery terms. But it does suggest that the English Romantics differed from Pope less in *exhibiting* these characteristics, than in being philosophically conscious of them and of their fundamental importance, and so taking them as a conscious *program* for poetry." See his "Integrity and Life in Pope's Poetry" in *Studies in the Literature of the Eighteenth Century,* 2, ed. R. F. Brissenden (Canberra: Australia National Univ. Presses, 1973). My reference is to the reprint of this piece in *Pope: Recent Essays by Several Hands,* ed. Maynard Mack and James A. Winn (Hamden, Conn.: Archon, 1980, p. 41.)

⁴ Anne Williams in her important book, *Prophetic Strain* (Chicago: Univ. of Chicago Press, 1984), has sought to open up discussion of lyric impulse and lyric form in eighteenth-century poetry. Williams too is especially interested in poems not ostensibly lyric, but with strong lyric presence nonetheless, and she is willing to say that the most interesting of these in the eighteenth century, whether epistles or satires or elegies, are really all versions of what she calls the "greater lyric"—in period discussion usually called the "greater ode." In the poems she chooses for discussion, Williams emphasizes as a sign of their lyric character their presentation of a central consciousness, generally emerging as a prophetic voice, as it shapes and is shaped by its engagement with the "abiding issues about man, nature, and human life which have always occupied serious poets in their most ambitious work" (p. 2). A limitation of this valuable book, perhaps, is that in its emphasis on the prophetic voice of Augustan lyricism it misses the essentially social origins and commitments of that expression, and consequently the powerfully autobiographical cast, whether feigned or "actual," of its representations of inwardness. Lyricism for Williams is essentially a sign of consciousness coming to itself by transcending the social. In the poems I explore, the process usually involves a continuing negotiation between the inward and the social.

Donald Davie's succinct discussion of Augustan lyricism in his introduction to his collection of poems of that title has been very useful to me. Davie's interest, however, is not in the lyric of inwardness, but in the quite different "public" lyric, which in its various forms—the patriotic song, the hymn, the ballad—stood in essential contrast to the period's satire, and had its sources in attitudes toward public and religious experience more positive than those which gave rise to satire. Moreover, Davie focuses on the lyric that is "composed either to match an existing piece of music, or in the expectation and hope of a musical setting being contrived for it." See *The Augustan Lyric* (London: Heinemann, 1974), esp. pp. 2-6.

⁵ See Davie, pp. 7-8: "It is Horace above all who matters; the Horace of the *carmina.* For the pre-Augustan Catullus, the eighteenth century as a whole had less liking than the seventeenth century before it or the nineteenth century after. . . . It is the Horace of the *carmina* who stands for most of the eighteenth century as the type of the lyric poet." Davie emphasizes that aspect of Horace which Prior takes over and gives expression to in "A Better Answer to Cloe Jealous," for instance, that is, the "urbanity . . . which is neither more nor less than tact and sympathy and sureness in the handling of human relations within the decorous proprieties insisted on by a civilized society. . . . The more trivial the overt occasions [of these poems], the more the lesson goes home, for what is involved is precisely *nuance,* a nicety of human attention for which no occasion . . . is too trivial to be worth taking care about."

⁶ A point regularly made in Horace studies is that the autobiographical actuality of Horace's representations of his own personal experience is a difficult matter for his reader to be confident about. Horace is a poet of extraordinary elusiveness, yet one who nevertheless *seems* so often *to sound* as though *he might be* telling about *himself* (whatever *himself* might be taken to mean). Gordon Williams has explored this matter and has commented on the "immediacy that approximates to autobiography" to be found in some places in the *Satires,* and also on the markedly enhanced opportunities for self-presentation which Horace's originality in the verse epistle provided him. Entirely original to Horace's epistle was its accommodation to "any and every mood, any tone, and, being completely dependent upon the personality of the poet in relation to the particular addressee, it offered a form which was infinitely sensitive and responsive to autobiographical expression." But commenting in another place on Horace's self-representation in the love poetry, Williams writes: "There is much that is left unsaid in Horace's love-poetry. It is never sheer self-expression; always the poet's personality is away out of reach. . . . There is point and balance and objectivity of

statement, delight in contrasts and contradictions, mockery, often self-mockery, never self-revelation or confession without an ulterior motive." See *Tradition and Originality in Roman Poetry* (Oxford: Clarendon, 1968), pp. 438, 565.

[7] *Q. Horatii Flacci: Carminum Libri IV, Epodon Liber,* ed. T. E. Page (London: St. Martin's, 1977), pp. 23-24. The translation, with some changes of my own, is by C. E. Bennett, *Horace: Odes and Epodes* (Cambridge, Mass., and London: Harvard Univ. Press and Heinemann [Loeb Classical Library], 1978), p. 69.

[8] On the separation between Virgil and Horace in this ode, see Steele Commager, *The Odes of Horace: A Critical Study* (New Haven and London: Yale Univ. Press, 1962), pp. 287-290. Commager goes too far, I think, in saying that Horace's "cry of grief yields, by the poem's end, to an assertion of the order that grief defies." But Commager is certainly right to state that "Neither is absolute. Only the powerful balance is final: *frustra . . . heu.*"

[9] John Traugott's comment is pertinent here: "As sentimentalism is a cultural attitude, neither a philosophy nor a disease, it is futile to seek a definition that is more precise than such text-book cliches as 'delicacy of feeling and perception,' 'benevolism,' 'tender, romantic, or nostalgic feeling'; together with their pejorative analogues, 'preciousness,' 'bathos,' 'self-indulgent emotivity.' When we have repeated the cliches we have little more to say" ("Heart and Mask and Genre in Sentimental Comedy," *Eighteenth-Century Life,* 10, n.s. 3 [1986]: 140).

[10] Gray's solemn and agile masking of his inner life all the while he presents it as his central subject still seems a phenomenon cognate with the heartier playfulness of sentimental comedy. Here the triumphant fantasy is that the pure-hearted and transparent sincerity preferred by the sentimentalist, and the masking preferred by the worldly, can find an accord. Traugott writes: "In sentimental comedy, worldliness and sentiment, though opposites, seem to feed on one another. If the world is composed of nothing but masks the pretended desire of sentiment to penetrate the mask and spy out the naked heart is just another mask. The age did not choose between worldliness and sentiment; it chose both as paradoxical necessities. They could live together in the fantasy of triumph of the best comedy" (p. 143). On Gray's articulation of all that he needs to say about himself at the same time that he hides almost everything, see Bertrand Bronson, "On a Special Decorum in Gray's 'Elegy'" in *Facets of the Enlightenment* (Berkeley and Los Angeles: Univ. of California Press, 1968), pp. 157-158.

[11] Please see Appendix I for the scene from *Cymbeline,* Appendix II for A *Song from Cymbelyne* by William Collins.

[12] Note how the word "renowned" in the following citation suggests the possibility of something *public,* something known and noted emerging from all the silence and peace ordained by the prayer-like wishes, each of which describes not an event but the absence of one.

[13] "Even the striking depiction of the Furies as 'that rav'ning Brood of Fate / Who lap the Blood of Sorrow' is interrupted by an asterisk . . . which refers the reader to a scholarly note on the *Electra.* The passage in short announces its politeness in ways that seem designed to prevent the reader from confusing Collins' artificial vision with the naive enthusiasm of its Cibberian equivalent" (satirized by Pope in *Dunciad* III. 235-252). See Steven Knapp, *Personification and the Sublime: Milton to Coleridge,* (Cambridge, Mass., and London: Harvard Univ. Press, 1985), p. 94.

[14] "Gray thought his language more poetical as it was more remote from common use: finding in Dryden *honey redolent of Spring,* an expression that reaches the utmost limits of our language, Gray drove it a little more beyond common apprehension, by making *gales* to be *redolent of joy and youth*" (*Lives of the Poets,* ed. G. B. Hill, 3 vols. [Oxford: Clarendon, 1905], 3:435.)

[15] See M. H. Abrams, "Structure and Style in the Greater Romantic Lyric," in *From Sensibility to Romanticism,* ed. F. W. Hilles and H. Bloom (London, Oxford, New York: Oxford Univ. Press [Galaxy Books], 1965), p. 539: In the Eton College ode "Gray deliberately rendered both his observation and reflections in the hieratic style of a formal odic *oratio.* The poet's recollection of times past . . . is managed through an invocation to Father Thames . . . and the language throughout is heightened and stylized by the apostrophe, exclamation, rhetorical question and studied periphrasis. . . . Both reminiscence and reflection are depersonalized, and occur mainly as general propositions which are sometimes expressed as *sententiae* . . . and at other times as propositions . . . converted into the tableau and allegory form . . ."

Marshall Brown (essay date 1991)

SOURCE: "Collins's Evening Time," in *Preromanticism,* Stanford University Press, 1991, pp. 49-57.

[*In the excerpt below, Brown compares Thomas Gray's "Elegy Written in a Country Churchyard" with Collins's "Ode to Evening."*]

. . . As Gray's "Elegy" evokes the form of space, so Collins's **"Ode to Evening"** evokes that of time. And in the **"Ode"** as in the "Elegy" the evocation is not given from the start, but rather engendered through the poem's work. The "Elegy" begins with deficient modes of space—particular spaces, statuses, and stations—

that it succeeds in purging. Likewise, the **"Ode"** begins with deficient modes of time. Impure and unstable movement obscures the purified inner sense that the poem allows us finally to glimpse. No more than in the "Elegy" can the pure form of sensible intuition be attributed to an empirical consciousness, for it is precisely the discovery of what lies beyond empirical consciousness that is at issue. The "Elegy" progresses by means of a diffusion of consciousness, so that the concluding stanzas can speak for space in general in a voice that is beyond localization. That broadening may be inappropriate to the purification of the inner sense; in any case, it is not the method followed by the **"Ode."** Collins's speaker remains present, and baffled, throughout. The new sensibility emerges not at the end but, more mysteriously, from within the text of the poem. That makes the **"Ode"** a more difficult poem than the "Elegy" and perhaps explains the latter's markedly greater popularity, in its own day and since. The itinerary of the interpretation, however, will be very similar: an examination of the speaker's troubled temporality, followed eventually by a description of the poem's resolving breakthrough.

In many respects the **"Ode to Evening"** is opposed to the "Elegy." It is conventional in form and bold in diction. It approaches a natural universality in the middle, but then both of its versions retreat, in one text to a protected social position ("regardful of thy quiet Rule"), in the other to a protected location ("sure-found beneath the Sylvan Shed"). Collins protests too much that his goddess is cloistered, and he draws the veil, ever so gently, over the glimmering intuitions of roughness. Sexuality is denied and therefore neither comprehended nor controlled. In the imaginary progress of the seasons it is hard to say whether Spring courts or tends Eve, whether or not Summer's dalliance ("loves to sport") addresses her, whether "sallow *Autumn*" woos, protects, or denies her by covering her up with leaves. With Winter the repressed violence breaks out, turning Eve from the ground of being into an object. ("Robes," whose etymological association with robbery and rape is highlighted here, is the only one of Eve's attributes too specific to be associated with a diffused feature of the landscape.) Following these charged scenes the escape in the last stanza seems evasive and poetically awkward. A single bad pun present only in the final version is all that remains to remind us of the pacified sexuality of Gray's Epitaph: "and hymn [him] thy fav'rite Name!" Divinity is even less responsive here than in the Eton College ode and far less responsive than in the "Elegy." The speaker's conjectural refuge under the sylvan shed should not mislead us into believing that his anxieties have been quelled.

The "Elegy" manages to maintain an equilibrium between two orientations of desire: the social or artificial desire for power and the physical or natural desire for love. The natural noises of the swallow are poised against the gentry noises of cock and horn, housewifely labor against filial spontaneity, cultivation (harvest and furrow) against collection, ambition against grandeur, wealth against beauty, gem against flower, and so forth. Finally it reaches the null point where differences are abolished, a point "to Fortune and to Fame unknown," where it is impossible to say whether fortune means money and fame natural recognition, or fortune natural accomplishment and fame social repute. The **"Ode to Evening,"** by contrast, virtually excludes reference to social passions, creating an unbalance in which it rests uneasily. The speaker begins enfolded by evening, and where there is no distance, it is hard to understand what motivates the hesitant intensity of his appeal, or why he should need to discommode himself to follow a goddess who is everywhere. His feet are a little too eager and hint at a restless dissatisfaction that the text does little to explain. Only when the last stanza is so oddly imposed on the poem can we intuit why the transcendental or natural satisfactions of evening—"religious Gleams" or "last cool gleam," in the two versions of line 32—are so avidly sought and yet not enough. "Oaten Stop, or Pastoral Song" faintly evokes a tension in need of reconciliation (as if the reed were nature, the song culture), but tips the scales toward nature, as does the "Sylvan Shed," which confirms the unexpressed deficiency of civilized values. Even by Collins's usual standards the goddess is too powerfully mythic, the speaker too subconscious (he muses, but only his feet *will*). In this deprived state, what the poem enacts is a frustrated, lost, and inarticulate desire for stabilizing companionship.

It is essential to recognize how greatly the two versions of the final stanza diverge. The first version, "regardful of thy quiet Rule," emphatically moves into the social mode. *"Fancy, Friendship, Science,* smiling *Peace"* are an ascending series of qualities rising from the internal through the personal to the public and the communal. The revision, "sure-found beneath the Sylvan Shed," shies back into primitivism. Only one item is changed in the ensuing list, but that changes everything: *"Fancy, Friendship, Science,* rose-lip'd *Health"* now descends from the freedom of imagination and the generosity of friendship to the privacy of knowledge and the merely physical condition of the body. In the first version Fancy is irresponsible, Science productive, and "smiling" the sign of an attitude that encourages participation by all; in the second Fancy is liberating, Science is a private study (the "fair Science" of Gray's Epitaph), and "rose-lip'd" an unshared corporeal attribute, the object of admiration or even envy. The first series is too social for the poem, the second not social enough for the lonesome speaker. Both versions begin, "So long," with an awkward duration entirely disproportionate to the evanescence of evening. The last stanza, then, can be defended, if at all, only as a symptom of still unrequited placation. We need not believe the speaker's hypothetical "sure-found"; he persists in appealing to Evening because he does not possess her.

The speaker petitions Evening with the formula "*Maid compos'd.*" It is difficult to know whether the adjective is descriptive, desiderative, or propitiatory (an antiphrasis like "Eumenides"). Like almost everything else in the poem, composure is an issue rather than a possession. The formula calls the identity of Evening into question. She is a fleeting goddess who cannot be captured without surrendering her identity. In the "Elegy" the speaker's "me. / Now" evaporates into a universal perspective; in the **"Ode to Evening"** the loss of control functions similarly as an intuition of a reality beyond particularity. In what sense does Evening respond to the speaker's need for an Other? What kind of being is she, and where is she to be found?

Opposing Evening's real or desired composure is the speaker's distraction. His intricate syntax has difficulty keeping to the point. Consciousness for him is expansive and centrifugal: from folding star to circlet to attendants at the lamp to wreaths to the shedding of dew. Or it is diffusive, as in the gradually expanding phrases of lines 34-40, issuing in the all-encompassing veil. "Gradual dusky Veil" is itself a distracted phrase in its wandering from time to space via the double meaning of "dusky." It is curious that so muted a speaker asks to be taught "some softened strain"; evidently, there is a concealed strain on him that surfaces chiefly in his excessive sensitivity to the disturbing noises of the shrill bat and the sullen beetle and in his prickly reaction to the "heedless" hum. "Genial lov'd" suggests a desired if somewhat unequal reciprocity of affection. Beneath the petition to the "Maid compos'd" lies the desire to be made composed.[19]

In a poem that begins with song and ends with hymn, it is difficult to keep music out of the picture. As we shall see, this means ultimately that the Other who brings the promise of repose must be found as an inner voicing, not as an external, let alone a social, object of sight. The speaker wants to stay in step with Evening, to march to her tune: "Then lead, calm *Vot'ress.*" In this poem progress has the effect of subordinating visual impression to the rhythms of the day and the year. Even a "cool Gleam" can be too striking for the eye. The sublime epiphany of the first version ("Whose Walls more awful nod / By thy religious Gleams") gives pause for thought ("Or if . . ."); the natural epiphany of the revision provokes a softened, yet still anxious, temporal musing ("But when chill blustring Winds . . ."). At the end of the **"Ode to Simplicity"** Collins rejects the "divine Excess" of a "cold Work" that "may charm our Eye" in favor of "thy temp'rate Vale: / Where oft my Reed might sound . . . / And all thy Sons, O *Nature,* learn my Tale." "Evening" struggles more laboriously back from eye to ear: from what the hut views to the "simple Bell" that it hears, from the light of Summer and "sallow *Autumn*" to Winter's noise.

Collins, in general, is unwillingly a pictorial poet.[20] "The shad'wy Tribes of *Mind*" (**"Poetical Character,"** line 47) keep rising up in visions that never successfully materialize. They only "appear, / To hail the blooming Guest" (**"To a Lady on the Death of Colonel Ross,"** lines 29-30); and if they really come "And gaze with fix'd Delight" (**"Ross,"** line 33), they provoke an abrupt turn of thought to "deep Despair" and "joyless Eyes" (**"Ross,"** lines 37-42). Collins is savage about the temptation to visionary excess, calling it "Rapture blind" (**"Poetical Character,"** line 53). No rational consideration prompts the "But when" of **"Evening"** or the "But lo" of **"Ross"**; they can only be explained, I think, as a constitutional inability to be fulfilled by the satiety of the eye. Hence it is perhaps, that Collins's personifications remain parts and attributes rather than whole bodies. The eye is too singular in its perspective and in its framing of a scene; concord comes only from an ear that hears what all hear. Therefore even a "last cool Gleam" cannot calm Collins, whereas even Winter's yell can pave the way toward intimations of harmony. The curious movement to social virtues at the end of "Evening" and several other odes is one part of a complex of unprepared transitions that are motivated by a deep yearning for continuities such as only music can provide.

Natura non facit saltus is a maxim that the ode generically questions. With its "leaps" and "bounds" (Herder), its whooping and vaulting (Bloom), its form is predicated on discontinuities.[21] Music may sustain the ode's flow from underneath—the "melodies unheard" of the "Grecian Urn," the continuous but often unattended warbling of the nightingale, the twitterings of autumn's music—but the passion of sudden vision is its defining characteristic. In willingly moving from stop (especially in the stuttering phrase "If aught of oaten stop") toward song, the **"Ode to Evening"** is thus written consciously against the grain. Nevertheless, the poem cannot so easily escape its own destiny. However slowly Evening comes on, the pace picks up as it approaches the psychic plunge into Winter. At first the speaker steals after Eve, but the goddess who approaches almost unperceived departs first in the pomp of a royal procession and eventually, it seems, in fear and disarray. This is (perhaps following Thomson's 1726 *Winter,* lines 40-63) an ode of leave-taking that begins with the parousia of a repeated "now" and then strives throughout to delay a departure. Since the star of line 21 is already the evening star, the car that is then prepared must be destined not to bring Evening on the scene, but to carry her away. The natural background here is the light that flickers rapidly across the hills as the sun sets. This is, then, an increasingly if unsteadily animated pursuit poem. The eye leaps in a moment from star to flower or from lake to heath to upland fallows, following Evening's abrupt appearances.[22]

An acolyte of the hymnic ear who nevertheless foolishly entrusts his fate to the odic eye, the speaker loses the race for Evening.[23] He must always lose it because it is in Evening's nature never to abide her suitors. She is by nature "chaste"—another of the poem's conceptual puns that ruffle its wavy surface for those who read with the ear—because she is forever chased, never caught. "Shrinking Train" assures us that she will elude Winter too, whatever violence he may do to her regalia. In terms of the speaker's perceptions the poem ends in incoherence, with unfounded superlatives ("gentlest," "fav'rite") that single out undefined particulars of what should be a universal phenomenon (does she also have ungentle influences?) and thus miss the sought-after composure of the elusive goddess.

But in this ode the speaker is not the central figure, and his failure is the poem's success. As he loses his bearings, Evening grows on the poet. At first "reserved," hidden away in the dark corners of the landscape beneath the skirts of the setting sun and accompanied by minute, terrestrial phenomena, she gradually rises up through the landscape and into the sky. Eye and ear find her close up at the start, but spreading out into the distance later on. Attended at first by Hours but later by seasons, she begins small enough to be served by tiny elves and ends large enough for the leafy earth to be her lap. She begins subordinated to "the bright-hair'd Sun"; by the end her "Tresses" have replaced his, bathing in the atmosphere (spring's "Show'rs") while the sun's hair is bathed lower down, in the ocean. The speaker remains attached to fleeting earthly lights, whereas the celestial realities of the slowly setting sun and rising stars are larger and more continuous. The dusky veil covers the earth but opens the sky to view. Thus it is important that we take literally what is said of Winter, who attacks only the attributes of Evening. Her train shrinks; her robes are rent, too, but she has grown out from under them.[24] From this perspective—the poet's, as opposed to the speaker's—there is nothing abrupt about the ending or about the poem's other turns: the emergence and growth of Evening continue unabated.

Personification is here liberated from the constraints of visualization. Parousia fades away into a kind of manifestation that does not need to appear, or a personification without presence. Visual pallor (paly circlet, shadowy car, and the rest), allied with affective pallor (chaste, meekest, gentlest, together with *Fancy, Friendship, Science,* rose-lip'd *Health*") conjure up a notion of a substratum behind observable phenomena. To the speaker it verges on tragedy that Evening cannot be grasped, and he projects his frustrations onto a nature that breaks into violence in response to her retirement. But it is precisely in leaving that Evening shows forth her essence. The speaker anticipates an embodiment such as is characteristic of eighteenth-century personification (see Wasserman, "Inherent Values"); the poet finds instead a personification *in itself* that refuses to become a personification *for us*.

Evening becomes herself by outgrowing her fictive body. The corporeal form for which the speaker yearns is her spectral emanation, and it does indeed pass daily across the face of the earth. But the passage *beyond* is what makes her Evening. The speaker both fails and succeeds in his desire to join Evening by suiting his numbers to her stillness, a double outcome expressed by the otherwise baffling switch from violent Winter to rose-lipped Health. He fails because Evening has no body, no place, no home, and therefore cannot be found. But he succeeds because Evening is precisely what is always slipping away: hence, what steals through her vale may really suit it. To lose her as a phenomenon is to find her in thought.[25]

In its manifestations time is unsteady, sometimes abrupt, disruptive, or fragmented. Such it is when it calls us to conscious action:

> When Time his Northern Sons of Spoil
>   awoke,
>   And all the blended Work of Strength and
>   Grace,
>   With many a rude repeated Stroke
> And many a barb'rous Yell, to thousand
>   Fragments broke.
>
>   **("Ode to Liberty,"** lines 22-25)

But Evening is the steady, musical pulse beneath the manifestations of life. The various oedipal readings of the **"Ode to Evening"** are true to its surface, that is, to the tense imaginings of the speaker, but they miss the dark, unstated background that underwrites its poetic accomplishment. In continuation of my thesis that what matters most in this poem is what it keeps in the shadows, I suggest that its true name for Evening is the one that is never spoken, namely, Even-ing.[26]

The desire for desire is a common issue in this enfeebled period.[27] By the second version of the **"Ode to Evening"** the speaker manages to ask of Evening a slender boon: "Then lead . . . my willing Feet," replacing the first version's "Then let me rove." This falls far short of the "Teach me to feel" that, in one form or another, concludes most of the preceding odes in Collins's volume. Nor is his unstated longing for intensity of feeling requited. Instead, by joining with Evening, desire is transmuted. The "meeting Soul"—the phrase comes from the **"Ode to Simplicity,"** which forecasts "Evening" in many respects—finds no Other, but instead the generative inwardness of self. The quietism of the last lines sheds a new gleam on the moment of meeting. Epiphany and turn in one, "Thy genial lov'd Return" now suggests not so much reciprocity as reflexivity—return upon herself, rotation, not return to the speaker. It is in Evening's nature to produce nothing beyond glinting reflections, yet always to be coming around again, and her flow of spirits mingles with a flow of emotions. If Evening is a regent, her kingdom is a state of mind. She is not a supernatural being confronting us, but more like a supernature in which we find our Being, transcendental yet, in her humility, not in the least transcendent. By the time it reaches its safe and gentle—and by no means inappropriate—conclusion, the poem has drawn us into a movement that knows no outside. Desire is not re-aimed (to use Bloom's term), but refined away: it is no longer necessary where no impotent stasis threatens.

The poem calls into question the whole notion of the individual as an intentional being. As a cult form, the ode had always tended to submerge the one into the many (as in Keats's line "So let me be thy choir"), and to that extent there is no surprise when Collins's speakers lose themselves at the end in social virtues. But cult forms are primitive and chthonic, whereas the belatedness of **"Evening"** dissolves their earthy originality into atmospherics.[28] Roger Lonsdale's notes (Lonsdale, ed., *Poems*) inform us that "Springs," early in the first version, does not mean fountains or sources, but is rather a metalepsis for brooks—middles, rather than beginnings. The revision, "solemn Springs," avoids the solecism of "brawling Springs," but continues to question originality. The next line encourages a desynonymization: "Thy Springs, and dying Gales" urges "Springs" back toward living origins. The poem edges repeatedly in this way toward origins: in the pun on "born[e]," in the "Star *arising*," in the "*fresh'ning* Dew," in the preparation of the car. But as termination is tentative in the ode—a temporary refuge under a shed—so initiation is even more so. "While . . . while . . . while . . . or . . . so long": time marches on, with no beginning. Some things go to bed at night, others (bats, beetles, and stars) arise. In the eternal circulation of waters of feelings, of meanings, a relative renewal is possible, but no real initiation. Absolutes steal on us gradually—"last," "meekest," "gentlest"—as Evening is revealed to be, not the primitive, but the inside of being. Selfhood is not an oedipal confrontation with the Other, but a being-with-others in a progress without beginning or end, originality or imitation, desire or repletion.

These two poems, Gray's "Elegy" and Collins's **"Ode,"** took the urbane sublime style as far as it could go. Comparative thinking was always flexible, but also always entailed an element of competition in value or status. These two poems mute evaluation, eliminating the scale and universalizing relationship. The one comparative in Collins's ode is a mystery: if the "*Pleasures* sweet" are "lovelier still" than either the "fragrant *Hours*," the flowery elves, or the dewy nymphs, it can only be because they are more thoughtful—"pensive" and (at least by syntactic proximity) "shadowy." Pure mind takes over, effacing in the "Elegy" distinctions of higher and lower, leader and follower, or elder and younger, in the **"Ode"** distinctions of near and far, soft and loud, fast and slow. Hence we get in the former poem pure space without precedency, in the latter pure

sequence without domination. (This is a difficult argument about the **"Ode."** I remind the reader that it is predicated upon taking the storm in lines 33-34 and the later outburst of Winter as figments of the speaker's imagination that do not interrupt the real progress of Evening from "last cool Gleam" through "gradual dusky Veil" to the complete absorption of the "shrinking Train" into vast night.) The poems leave behind the urgent animism that calls forth spirits in all other significant poems of the period, such as I have illustrated from *Night Thoughts*.[29] Mind is left to its own devices, "musing slow," and finding its way to universals that are beyond time in the former poem, beyond space in the latter.

To go further was to provoke a crisis. For thought, however unpressured, is not spontaneous in either poem. It continues to depend on perceptions to trigger it. The thought is always about something, however vague or general. The Youth—any youth—Evening—any evening—space—time: these are still promptings from outside the mind. Though generalized and not evaluative, thought in these poems remains relational, and therefore also social. To rest thought in pure time and pure space together would mean eliminating any externality and, with it, any conventional measure of truth. Thought then becomes an auto-affection. Kant eventually learned how to give a philosophical content to this intersection of a transcendental ego with a thing in itself, an abstract subjectivity and a featureless objectivity, and various imaginative writers of the 1780s and beyond learned how to give it an empirical meaning. But for the moment that could only appear as the emptying out of all reality. The "Elegy" and the **"Ode"** thus stand conjointly on the brink of solipsism, which proceeded to become the biographical curse of so many poets of the next decades.[30] As poets, Gray and Collins could only retreat into Manners and Passions, or into primitivism. The end of "The Bard" directly conjures up the abyss of liberation, but via suicide, and dark shadows light in the mesode of the **"Ode on the Poetical Character"** (particularly in the figure of the tercel, who is blindfolded except when he hunts), but not to comforting effect. . . .

Notes

. . . [19] Evening must "compose the composer," as Wendorf says in *William Collins* 130. But he takes composition in a pictorial rather than a musical sense, arguing that there is little movement in the poem, "a poem-as-process that gradually evolves into a poem-as-product" (134). This is, as he accuses Collins of being in "How Sleep the Brave," unrealistically hopeful.

[20] In *The Figure in the Landscape* 165-71 Hunt likewise concludes that Collins is reluctantly pictorial—particularly significant from a critic who specializes in literature and the visual arts. Also instructive is McKillop's clear-sighted struggle to salvage the notion of Collins as a painterly poet in "Collins' *Ode to Evening*."

[21] Herder discusses *Würfe* and *Sprünge* in folksongs, but with the primitive passions of odes clearly in mind ("Auszug aus einem Briefwechsel über Ossian und die Lieder alter Völker," sect. 9, in *Sturm und Drang: Kritische Schriften* 534-39); Bloom's terms (*Figures* 7), while applied to a range of Coleridge's verse, likewise seem to me too apt to pass up.

[22] See Merle C. Brown, "On William Collins' 'Ode to Evening.'" Brown also comments well on energy and on balance in the poem, though I do not think, as he does, that these two qualities add up in this case to energetic balance.

[23] I adapt my sense of the relation of ode to hymn from Fry's groundbreaking study *The Poet's Calling* 4-10.

[24] I take "train" here to mean attendants, as it does in the similar context of the "Ode to Fear," lines 9 and 24. The train is shrinking because Evening has disrobed as she vanishes into the bare night sky, and most of her attendants have gone to bed with her. "Shrinking" could, of course, also mean cowering with fear. My contention is that to do Collins justice we must take all plausible readings into account, and that we get the most consistent picture if we attribute the emotive alternatives to the speaker and the literal ones to the controlling poet.

[25] Imagination had better use a footnote to run rampant. I have little hesitation in hearing an echo of "thy darkning Vale" in "the gradual dusky Veil": the place of Evening is really her attire in its changeableness. But is it legitimate, in "May not unseemly with its Stillness suit," to hear an allusion to the seamless vestment later torn by Winter's noise? The indirection of these lines ("May not un- . . . ," and the like) seems in any case an appropriate rhetorical dress for Evening, or, to put it in Collins's terms, fitting "Numbers" for his "willing Feet."

[26] Sherwin, *Precious Bane* 116, speaks of "Evening out of extremes," which is not quite the same. Sherwin's is the reading that most forcefully identifies Evening with speaker as his romantic self-image, and speaker with poem.

[27] See Weinsheimer, "Give Me Something to Desire," which also raises the issue of originality, to which I come in a moment.

[28] In *The Poet's Calling* 102-13, Fry has brilliantly related the belatedness of the "Ode on the Poetical Character" to the textualized solidity of the woven cest. I think that the "Brede *ethereal* wove" of "Evening," further dissolved by the partial echo of "*wavy* Bed," evaporates the problem. In "Poetical Character" scenes are "curtain'd close" behind a "veiling Cloud"; in "Evening" it is ambiguous whether the "gradual dusky Veil" is drawn open or shut. Other images that are freed from menace because they are duple, at least in affect, are "folding Star arising" ("folding" means shutting up or welcoming home) and the shadowy car that is prepared so late in the game. The "Ode to Evening" does not continue, but corrects the debilities of the poetical character.

[29] On animistic vividness see Jackson, *The Probable and the Marvelous* 39-88. Jackson overlooks the special character of the reticence in the "Elegy" and the **"Ode to Evening."** I would not, on the other hand, exclude as he does Johnson's *The Vanity of Human Wishes* from the period style. He distinguishes it as historical, but it is no more so than Collins's political odes or Gray's "Progress of Poesy," and no less animist (e.g., "And detestation rids th'indignant wall"), though it is more orthodox. In this connection see Sitter, "To *The Vanity of Human Wishes*."

[30] In pp. 284-86 of "Societal Models" Nemoianu argues that the "Elegy" negotiates this passage: "We witness the highly dramatic moment of the transubstantiation of an abstract epistemological subject into a living, breathing person." "Gray is . . . so extreme in his love of temperance that he becomes an extremist of non-expansion, and thus a Romantic." (This argument is not reproduced in the revised version of the essay printed in *A Theory of the Secondary*.) The difference between our readings is tonal; in particular, it depends on whether the Spenserian diction that describes the youth is felt to be conventional and generalizing or specific and individualizing. Perhaps it is best to call the "Elegy" a pivotal work that is amenable to being made romantic by a romantic reading.

FURTHER READING

Biography

Ainsworth, Edward Gay. *Poor Collins: His Life, His Art, and His Influence*. Ithaca, N.Y.: Cornell University Press, 1937, 340 p.

Comprehensive, general study of Collins's life, aesthetics, verse, influences, and literary reputation.

Carver, P. L. *The Life of a Poet: A Biography of William Collins*. New York: Horizon Press, 1967, 210 p.

Study of Collins's life which examines and draws extrapolations from the scarce primary material on the poet.

Criticism

Barry, Kevin. "William Collins." In *Language, Music and the Sign: A Study in Aesthetics, Poetics and Poetic Practice from Collins to Coleridge,* pp. 27-55. Cambridge, England: Cambridge University Press, 1987.

> Examines the interaction between poetry and music in Collins's poetry, focusing on the "Ode to Evening" as "a decisive instance of the use of ideas of language, music and poetry in the mid-eighteenth century."

Bloom, Harold. "From Topos to Trope, from Sensibility to Romanticism: Collins's 'Ode to Fear'." In *Studies in Eighteenth-Century British Art and Aesthetics,* edited by Ralph Cohen, pp. 182-203. Berkeley: University of California Press, 1985.

> Discusses the poetic modes sensibility and romanticism in Collins's poem "Ode to Fear."

Fry, Paul H. "The Tented Sky in the Odes of Collins." In *The Poet's Calling in the English Ode,* pp. 97-132. New Haven: Yale University Press, 1980.

> Detailed discussion of two problems in Collins's verse: the unification of private and public concerns, and the dramatic conflict between good and evil.

Hagstrum, Jean H. "William Collins." In *The Sister Arts: The Tradition of Literary Pictorialism and English Poetry from Dryden to Gray,* pp. 268-86. Chicago: University of Chicago Press, 1958.

> Study of pictorial elements in Collins's poetry, which Hagstrum relates to "his conception of the imagination, a power to which he was almost religiously dedicated and from which, it may be assumed, all the elements of his poems, but particularly the pictorial, were in some way derived."

Heller, Deborah. "Seeing But Not Believing: The Problem of Vision in Collins's Odes." *Texas Studies in Literature and Language* 35, No. 1 (Spring 1993): 103-23.

> Argues that Collins valued insightful discussion over visual description in his poetry.

Knapp, Steven. "The Practice of Sublime Personification: Collins' 'Ode to Fear'." In *Personification and the Sublime: Milton to Coleridge,* pp. 87-97. Cambridge: Harvard University Press, 1985.

> Argues that Collins promotes an ambivalent attitude toward fear in "Ode to Fear."

Maclean, Norman. "From Action to Image: Theories of the Lyric in the Eighteenth Century." In *Critics and Criticism: Ancient and Modern,* edited by R. S. Crane, pp. 408-60. Chicago: The University of Chicago Press, 1952.

Discusses the development of the ode and the way in which such poets as Collins and Thomas Gray pushed it in new directions.

Sherwin, Paul S. "A Poetry of the Evening Ear." In *Precious Bane: Collins and the Miltonic Legacy,* pp. 102-24. Austin: University of Texas Press, 1977.

> Considers Milton's influence on Collins's poetry, particularly Collins's "Ode to Evening."

Sigworth, Oliver F. "The Poetry and the Age." In *William Collins,* pp. 57-86. New York: Twayne Publishers, 1965.

> Describes how Collins's world and his poetry differs from contemporary experiences and how these differences may alienate the modern reader from Collins's work.

Sitter, John. "Ambition, Conversion, and Lyric Grace." In *Literary Loneliness in Mid-Eighteenth Century England,* pp. 104-56. Ithaca, N.Y.: Cornell University Press, 1982.

> Discusses the "Ode on the Poetical Character" and the Ode to Liberty" as conversion experiences.

Wasserman, Earl R. "Collins's 'Ode on the Poetical Character'." *ELH* 34, No. 1 (March 1967): 92-115.

> Studies the Platonic philosophy evident in Collins's "Ode on the Poetical Character."

Wendorf, Richard. "The *Odes* of 1746." In *William Collins and Eighteenth-Century English Poetry,* pp. 87-114. Minneapolis: University of Minnesota Press, 1981.

> Considers the *Odes on Several Descriptive and Allegoric Subjects* as a turning point in Collins's poetry.

Williamson, Paul. "William Collins and the Idea of Liberty." In *Tradition in Transition: Women Writers, Marginal Texts, and the Eighteenth-Century Canon,* edited by Alvaro Ribeiro and James G. Basker, pp. 257-74. Oxford: Clarendon Press, 1996.

> Examines Collins's role in the evolution of eighteenth-century poetry.

Woodhouse, A. S. P. "The Poetry of Collins Reconsidered." In *From Sensibility to Romanticism: Essays Presented to Frederick A. Pottle,* edited by Frederick W. Hilles and Harold Bloom, pp. 93-137. New York: Oxford University Press, 1965.

> Argues that Collins spanned two literary styles, taking elements from the earlier Neo-Classical school and developing aspects of the Romantic tradition.

Additional coverage of Collins's life and career is contained in the following source published by Gale Research: *Literature Criticism from 1400 to 1800*, Vol. 4.

Thomas Gray

1716-1771

English poet and essayist.

The following entry contains critical essays focusing on Gray's relationship to Preromanticism. For further information on Gray, see *LC*, Vol. 4.

INTRODUCTION

Gray is widely considered the most important English poet of the mid-eighteenth century. Evidencing in his poetry a studied, disciplined aestheticism, he was a major figure in the transition from the Neoclassical to the Romantic style in English letters. Although his poetic canon is small, it reveals a wide-ranging, sensitive, and scholarly mind, and confirms Gray's image as a craftsman obsessed with attaining a perfect blend of content and form. The author of such poems as "Ode on a Distant Prospect of Eton College" and "Ode on the Death of a Favourite Cat, Drowned in a Tub of Gold Fishes," among others, Gray is primarily remembered for his "Elegy Written in a Country Churchyard," one of the best known and most beloved poems in English literature. Perhaps the most famous and widely quoted appraisal of this poem, which is renowned as a sensitive, thoughtful soliloquy on death and the significance of being, was made by Gray's contemporary Samuel Johnson, who wrote, "'The Churchyard' abounds with images which find a mirrour in every mind, and with sentiments to which every bosom returns an echo." Gray is also esteemed for his prose, particularly his letters, which are said to rival those of his friend Horace Walpole in scope, elegance, and perspicuous observation of human life and the natural world.

Biographical Information

Born in London, Gray was the son of a milliner and her husband, a respected scrivener but a man of such abusive and, alternately, neglectful, moods that the couple separated when their son was quite young. Gray's mother raised the boy herself, making enough money at her trade to support the two of them and to send Gray to Eton in 1725. A shy, sensitive boy, Gray enjoyed the close company of only three other students: Thomas Ashton, Richard West, and Walpole, who, with Gray, styled themselves "the Quadruple Alliance" and were given to long walks together and precocious conversation about life and literature. West and Walpole later figured significantly in the develop-

ment of Gray's poetic career, which commenced during the four years Gray spent at Cambridge, to which he was admitted in 1734 and where he attracted notice as an accomplished writer of Latin verse. Leaving Cambridge without taking a degree, he joined Walpole shortly thereafter on an extended tour of Europe from 1739 to 1741, when the two quarreled and parted company.

Returning to England, Gray joined his mother at a house she had recently taken in rustic Stoke Poges, Buckinghamshire, and it was here that he wrote his earliest poems. In 1742, a key year in his life, he composed his first major poem, "Ode on the Spring," sending it to West—unknowingly—on the day of the latter's unexpected death at age twenty-six. Although West's death shocked and saddened Gray, it also apparently spurred him to poetic creativity; he immediately wrote his "Sonnet on the Death of Mr. West," "Ode to Adversity," and "Ode on a Distant Prospect of Eton College." Moved by contemplations of West's death and the peaceful setting of the parish church at Stoke Poges, Gray thereafter began composing the "Elegy," completing two separate versions by 1750. He submitted the revised version for comment to his by-now-reconciled friend, Walpole, who published it in 1751. In the meantime, Gray had recommended his studies at Cambridge, attaining a law degree in 1743. He lived at Cambridge for the rest of his life, leaving only for periods of study at the newly opened British Museum in London and for journeys to the Lake District and Scotland, travels movingly recorded in his commonplace book and letters. While Gray's early poems created little stir upon their publication in the 1740s, the "Elegy" brought him immediate critical and popular acclaim. The poem was widely reprinted and quoted, attaining during Gray's own lifetime the stature of a minor classic. In recognition of his prominent achievement, Gray was elected Regius Professor of Modern History at Cambridge in 1768, an office he held until his death, although he never once lectured. A melancholy, private man known for his erudition and wide range of interests, Gray was markedly cheered during the last years of his life through his friendship with a visiting Swiss student, Karl Viktor von Bonstetten, who figures significantly in the poet's correspondence.

Major Works

"Gray wrote at the very beginning of a certain literary epoch of which we, perhaps, stand at the very end," wrote G. K. Chesterton in 1932. "He represented that softening of the Classic which slowly turned it into the Romantic." From the start of his career, Gray's poetry displayed elements of the intuitive, the emotional, and the naturally metaphysical that departed from the established tenets of adherence to order, reason, and revealed wisdom characteristic of English Neoclassical literature. In addition, Gray introduced a disquieting element that later influenced the poetry of Romantics Samuel Taylor Coleridge and Percy Bysshe Shelley: the idea of terror as an adjunct of the sublime. While the subjects and themes of Gray's poetry anticipate the concerns of Romanticism, the formality of his language and his use of intricate and precise metrical patterns link him with the Neoclassical tradition. In fact, Gray's own remark to West that "the language of the age is never the language of poetry" helped to fuel a critical debate in the nineteenth century concerning Gray's originality and his sources of inspiration. Today, however, Gray is consistently viewed as an important transitional poet, not only for his innovations in subject matter but also for infusing new life into traditional forms through his exaltation of the imagination as the source of creativity. Aside from his influence on the development of English Romanticism, Gray is primarily remembered for the "Elegy," a work widely considered an exquisite meditation on mortality. As the "Elegy" opens, the poem's speaker reflects in the quiet darkness of the churchyard on the contrast between the lives of the rural poor and the lives of the wealthy and the ruling classes. The narrator goes on to consider his own repressed potential and the limited opportunities of the poor to achieve greatness. "For those who do not know the poem," wrote T. S. Eliot, "I will say briefly that it is, naturally, a meditation on mortality. The poet remarks that the graves are those of humble peasants who were once living and are now dead. In death we are all equal, and it does not matter whether we have an impressive monument or a plain stone. This leads to conjecture that one or two of the obscure people buried here may have had gifts which would have brought them to fame and power had circumstances favoured such success." When Gray made revisions to the "Elegy," he replaced the four concluding stanzas of the original version, which is known as the Eton MS, with fourteen new stanzas, which include Gray's thoughts on the nature and meaning of epitaphs.

The success of the "Elegy" focused critical attention on Gray for the rest of his career, leading to reappraisals of his earlier poetry and close scrutiny of his subsequent works. Of the early poems, the "Ode on a Distant Prospect of Eton College," a tribute by Gray to the setting of the happiest years of his life, became popular during Gray's lifetime and has since often been anthologized. Another popular early poem, "Ode on the Death of a Favourite Cat," humorously describes, in mock-tragic style, the fate of Walpole's cat, Selima, as she attempted one day to catch her master's goldfish. Among the poems Gray published after the "Elegy," "The Bard" and the "The Progress of Poesy" have been the subject of much critical discussion. Published together as *Odes* in 1757, "The Bard" and "The Progress of Poesy" reflect Gray's studies in Celtic mythology and English literary history.

Critical Reception

From the mid-eighteenth century to the present day, Gray's poetry has had many admirers and defenders, and a number of distinguished detractors as well. Scholars continue to puzzle over the antipathy held toward Gray by the first major hostile critic of his work, Samuel Johnson, who considered the "Elegy" Gray's only success. While no convincing answer has been put forward to explain Johnson's attitude, it has been noted that the two men, for some reason, simply disliked each other. Johnson's ascerbic *Life* (1781) of Gray stirred up a storm of critical debate on the merits of Gray's poetry that continued into the nineteenth century. In 1800 William Wordsworth attacked the poet in his "Preface" to *Lyrical Ballads*. Focusing on Gray's early "Sonnet on the Death of Mr. Richard West," Wordsworth derided Gray as a poet who "attempted to widen the space of separation betwixt prose and metrical composition, and was more than any other man curiously elaborate in the structure of his own poetic diction." A few years later, Wordsworth added: "Gray failed as a poet, not because he took too much pains, and so extinguished his animation, but because he had very little of that fiery quality to begin with, and his pains were of the wrong sort. He wrote English verses as his brother Eton schoolboys wrote Latin, filching a phrase now from one author and now from another." By the mid-nineteenth century, these issues were the subject of much critical discussion, with Coleridge, Edward Bulwer-Lytton, and Thomas Carlyle among those who typically described Gray's poetry as frigid, artificial, and overly elaborate. There have been no such major critical controversies during the twentieth century, but interest in Gray's work has continued unabated. The focus of modern critical attention has been the "Elegy," although scholars have recently begun examining Gray's correspondence for evidence of his emotional and physical attraction to other men, arguing that Gray's homosexuality strongly influenced his poetic achievement. Among the most frequently discussed aspects of the "Elegy" are its structure, narrative voice, and themes, including alienation, death, and the contrast between the poor and the great. Scholars have also assessed the relative merits of the two versions of the "Elegy" and examined the poem in relation to Gray's social sympathies and his so-called "private" and "public" voices.

PRINCIPAL WORKS

Ode on a Distant Prospect of Eton College (poetry) 1747

"Ode on the Death of a Favourite Cat, Drowned in a Tub of Gold Fishes" (poetry) 1748; published in *A Collection of Poems, by Several Hands*

"Ode [on the Spring]" (poetry) 1748; published in *A Collection of Poems, by Several Hands*

An Elegy Wrote in a Country Church Yard (poetry) 1751; also published as *Elegy Written in a Country Churchyard*, 1834

Designs by Mr. R. Bentley for Six Poems by Mr. T. Gray (poetry) 1753

*Odes (poetry) 1757

Ode Performed in the Senate-House at Cambridge July 1, 1769, at the Installation of His Grace Augustus Henry Fitzroy, Duke of Grafton, Chancellor of the University (poetry) 1769

On Lord Holland's Seat near Margate, Kent (poetry) 1769

The Poems of Mr. Gray (poetry) 1775

"Sonnet on the Death of Mr. Richard West" (poetry) 1775; published in the journal *Universal Magazine*

The Candidate (poetry) 1777; published in journal *London Evening Post*

The Works of Thomas Gray; Containing His Poems, and Correspondence with Several Eminent Literary Characters (poetry and letters) 1807

The Letters of Thomas Gray, Including the Correspondence of Gray and Mason. 3 vols. (letters) 1900-12

Essays and Criticisms (essays) 1911

Ode on the Pleasure Arising from Vicissitude, Left Unfinished by Mr. Gray, and since Completed. 2 vols. (poetry) 1933

The Selected Letters of Thomas Gray (letters) 1952

*This volume contains what are commonly called Gray's Pindaric odes: "The Bard" and "The Progress of Poesy."

CRITICISM

William Lyon Phelps (essay date 1895)

SOURCE: "The Romantic Movement Exemplified in Gray," in *The Beginnings of the Romantic Movement: A Study of Eighteenth-Century Literature*, Gordian Press, 1968, pp. 155-70.

[*In the following essay, originally published in 1895, Phelps traces the transition in Gray's works from Neoclassicism to Romanticism.*]

A chronological study of Gray's poetry and of the imagination and love of nature displayed in his prose remains, is not only deeply interesting in itself, but is highly important to the history of Romanticism. In him, the greatest literary man of the time, we find the best example of the steady growth of the Romantic movement. But before proceeding to the discussion of this, a word on Gray's sterility is necessary. The view given by Matthew Arnold in his famous essay[1] is entirely without foundation in fact. The reason why Gray wrote so little was not because he was chilled by the public taste of the age; he would probably have written no more had he lived a hundred years before or since. He was not the man to be depressed by an unfavorable environment; for his mind was ever open to new influences, and he welcomed with the utmost eagerness all genuine signs of promise. His correspondence shows how closely and intelligently he followed the course of contemporary literature; he had something to say about every new important book. The causes of his lack of production are simple enough to those who start with no pre-conceived theory, and who prefer a commonplace explanation built on facts to a fanciful one built on phrases. Gray was a scholar, devoted to solitary research, and severely critical, this kind of temperament is not primarily creative, and does not toss off immortal poems every few weeks. The time that Mason spent in production, Gray spent in acquisition, and when he did produce, the critical fastidiousness of the scholar appeared in every line. All his verses bear evidence of the most painstaking labor and rigorous self-criticism. Again, during his whole life he was handicapped by wretched health, which, although never souring him, made his temperament melancholy, and acted as a constant check on what creative activity he really possessed. And finally, he abhorred publicity and popularity. No one who reads his correspondence can doubt this fact. He hated to be dragged out from his scholarly seclusion, and evidently preferred complete obscurity to any noisy public reputation. This reserve was never affected; it was uniformly sincere, like everything else in Gray's character. His reticence was indeed extraordinary, keeping him not only from writing, but from publishing what he did write.[2] His own friends would have had no difficulty in explaining his scantiness of production. Horace Walpole, writing to George Montagu, Sept. 3, 1748, says: "I agree with you most absolutely in your opinion about Gray; he is the worst company in the world. From a melancholy turn, from living reclusely, and from a little too much dignity, he never converses easily; all his words are measured and chosen, and formed into sentences; his writings are admirable; he himself is not agreeable." Again, referring to Gray's slowness in composition, Walpole writes to Montagu, May 5, 1761. He is talking about Gray's proposed history of poetry, and he says: "If he rides Pegasus at his usual foot-pace, (he) will finish the first page two years hence." The adjective that perhaps best expresses Gray is *Fastidious*. He was as severe on the children of his own brain as he was on those of others; he never let them appear in public until he was sure everything was exactly as it should be. Even his greatest poem pleases more by its exquisite finish than by its depth of feeling. These three reasons, then, his scholarly temperament, his bad health, and his dignified reserve, account satisfactorily for his lack of fertility. If we wish to know why so deep and strong a nature produced so little poetry, we must look at the man, and not at his contemporaries. So much for Gray's sterility.[3]

Although Gray's biographers and critics have very seldom spoken of it, the most interesting thing in a study of his poetry—and the thing, of course, that exclusively concerns us here—is his steady progress in the direction of Romanticism. Beginning as a classicist and disciple of Dryden, he ended in thorough-going Romanticism.[4] His early poems contain nothing Romantic; his **"Elegy"** has something of the Romantic mood, but shows many conventional touches; in the Pindaric Odes the Romantic feeling asserts itself boldly; and he ends in enthusiastic study of Norse and Celtic poetry and mythology. Such a steady growth in the mind of the greatest poet of the time shows not only what he learned from the age, but what he taught it. Gray is a much more important factor in the Romantic movement than seems to be commonly supposed. This will appear from a brief examination of his poetry.

While at Florence in the summer of 1740, he began to write an epic poem in Latin, **"De Principiis Cogitan-**

di". Only two fragments were written,[5] but they made a piece of considerable length. This was an attempt to put in poetic form the philosophy of Locke. It shows how little he at that time understood his own future. The Gray of 1760 could no more have done a thing of this sort, than he could have written the *Essay on Man*. In these early years he was completely a Classicist. In 1748, when he was largely under Dryden's influence, he began a didactic poem in the heroic couplet, **"On the Alliance of Education and Government."** It is significant that he never finished either of these poems. Mathias said: "When Mr. Nichols once asked Mr. Gray, why he never finished that incomparable Fragment on 'The Alliance between good Government and good Education, in order to produce the happiness of mankind,' he said, *he could not;* and then explained himself in words of this kind, or to this effect: 'I have been used to write chiefly lyric poetry, in which, the poems being short, I have accustomed myself to polish every part of them with care; and as this has become a habit, I can scarcely write in any other manner; the labour of this in a *long* poem would hardly be tolerable.'"[6] Gray must have perceived early in this task that the game was not worth the candle.

In 1742 Gray wrote three Odes: **"On the Spring,"** **"On a Distant Prospect of Eton College,"** and **"To Adversity."** These well-known pieces contain little intimation of Gray's later work. They have nothing of the spirit of Romanticism, and might have been written by any Augustan of sufficient talent. The moralizing is wholly conventional, and the abundance of personified abstractions was in the height of fashion. The poems thus far mentioned represent Gray's first period. He was a disciple of Dryden, and a great admirer of Pope, for writing to Walpole in 1746, he calls Pope "the finest writer, one of them, we ever had."[7]

Gray's second period is represented by the **"Elegy,"** which he began in 1742 and finished in June, 1750.[8] He was in no haste to print it; the manuscript circulated among his friends, and was first printed anonymously, with a preface by Horace Walpole, February 16, 1751. How long Gray meant to keep the **"Elegy"** from the public is uncertain; circumstances compelled its publication. On February 10, 1751, the editor of the *Magazine of Magazines* requested permission to print it. This alarmed Gray; he flatly refused the editor's request, and wrote instantly to Walpole, asking him to get Dodsley to print it as soon as possible.[9]

The **"Elegy"** is not a Romantic poem; its moralizing is conventional, and pleased eighteenth century readers for that very reason. Scores of poems were written at that time in which the thought was neither above nor below that of the **"Elegy,"** and these poems have nearly all perished. What has kept Gray's contribution to the Church-yard school alive and popular through all changes in taste, is its absolute perfection of language. There are few poems in English literature that express the sentiment of the author with such felicity and beauty. This insures its immortality; and it is this fact that deservedly gives it the first place in Gray's literary productions.

But although the **"Elegy"** is not strictly Romantic, it is different from Gray's earlier work. It is Romantic in its *mood,* and stands as a transition between his period of Classicism and his more highly imaginative poetry. It was the culmination of the *Il Penseroso* school, and as I have shown, that school was in several ways intimately connected with the growth of the Romantic movement. There is one highly significant fact about the composition of the **"Elegy,"** which shows with perfect distinctness that its author was passing through a period of transition. One of its most famous stanzas Gray originally wrote as follows:—

> Some Village Cato with dauntless Breast
>   The little Tyrant of his Fields withstood;
> Some mute inglorious Tully here may rest;
>   Some Cæsar, guiltless of his Country's Blood.

The fact that Gray should originally have put down the Latin names, and afterwards inserted in their place the three names Hampden, Milton, Cromwell—taken from comparatively recent English history—is something certainly worth attention. It marks the transition from Classicism to Nationalism. In this stanza he shook off the shackles of pseudo-classicism; he made up his mind that English historical examples were equal in dignity to those taken from Latin literature. It was a long step forward, and although perhaps a small thing in itself, is an index to a profound change going on in Gray's mind.[10]

Gray's next work shows him well on the way toward Romanticism. In 1754 he wrote **"The Progress of Poesy,"** and in the same year began **"The Bard,"** which he finished in 1757. Both these Pindaric Odes were first printed in 1757, on Horace Walpole's press at Strawberry Hill—the first and the best things ever published there. These two odes, especially the latter, are the most imaginative poetry Gray ever produced, and were distinctly in advance of the age. They were above the popular conception of poetry, and their obscurity was increased by their allusiveness. The public did not take to them kindly; many people regarded them as we see Browning and Wagner regarded to-day. Their obscurity was ridiculed, and they were freely parodied.[11] Gray was a little hurt by all this, but he had foreseen their probable reception. He had written to Walpole, "I don't know but I may send him (Dodsley) very soon . . . an ode to his own tooth, a high Pindaric upon stilts, which one must be a better scholar than he is to understand a line of, and the very best scholars will understand but a little matter here and there."[12] Horace Walpole never forgave the age for its attitude toward Gray's odes. Again and again he refers to it in his correspondence, and it had much to do with his dislike for Dr. Johnson.[13] Walpole called the **Odes** "Shakspearian," "Pindaric," and "Sublime," and said they were "in the first rank of genius and poetry." But Walpole's opinions were largely influenced in this matter by personal pride, for his own taste was not at all reliable. He said Gray's **"Eton Ode"** was "far superior" to the **"Elegy."**[14]

In the Pindaric **Odes,** Gray ceased to follow the age; he struck out ahead of it, and helped to mould its literary taste. From this time people began to regard him as a Romanticist, and to look for wild and extravagant productions from his pen. When the *Castle of Otranto* appeared in 1764, Gray was by many believed to be the author. The **Odes** became much more popular after Gray's death—a sign of growth in public taste. This made Dr. Johnson angry, and had much to do with his satirical treatment of the **Odes** in his wretched *Life of Gray.* He did not like to think that Gray had really taught the people anything, and so he declared that the admiration for Gray was all hypocrisy, just as many honest people to-day make fun of those who admire Wagner's music. Johnson said that in Gray's **Odes** "many were content to be shewn beauties which they could not see." Undoubtedly Gray and Wagner have hypocrites among their admirers; but the fact that each helped to set a fashion is significant of a change in taste.

We now enter upon the last period of Gray's literary production. In 1755 Mallet's *Introduction a l' Histoire de Dannemarck* appeared. This had a powerful effect on Gray, and aroused his interest in Northern mythology, which he studied with the utmost enthusiasm. In 1761, Gray wrote **"The Fatal Sisters. From the Norse Tongue"**; also **"The Descent of Odin."** Evans's book on Welsh poetry, the *Specimens* (1764), stirred him up again, and he wrote **"The Triumphs of Owen."** These three poems were published in 1768, in the edition of his writings revised by himself. All this work, of course, is strictly Romantic.[15] In 1760, when the Ossianic *Fragments* appeared, Gray was wonderfully aroused. His friends knew he would be excited, for Walpole, writing to Dalrymple, April 4, 1760, said, "You originally pointed him out as a likely person to be charmed with the old Irish poetry you sent me." On receiving some specimens, Gray immediately wrote to Walpole as follows: "I am so charmed with the two specimens of Erse poetry, that I cannot help giving you the trouble to inquire a little farther about them and should wish to see a few lines of the original, that I may form some slight idea of the language, the measures, and the rhythm."[16] He then proceeds to make further comments. His own Romantic tastes come out strikingly in the following letter to Stonehewer, June, 1760. "I have received another Scotch packet with a third specimen, inferior in kind . . . but yet full of nature and noble wild feeling. . . . The idea, that struck and surprised me most, is the following. One of them (describing a storm of wind and rain) says:—

> Ghosts ride on the tempest to-night;
> Sweet is their voice between the gusts of wind;
> *Their songs are of other worlds!*

Did you never observe (*while rocking winds are piping loud*) that pause, as the gust is recollecting itself, and rising upon the ear in a shrill and plaintive note, like the swell of an Aeolian harp? I do assure you there is nothing in the world so like the voice of a spirit."[17] Gray continued to correspond with his friends about Ossian, saying that he had "gone mad" about it.[18]

The best way to show the growth toward Romanticism in Gray's poetry is to quote successively short passages from poems representative of all his periods of production. They will explain themselves.

From the **"Ode on the Spring,"** written 1742:—

> To Contemplation's sober eye
>   Such is the race of Man;
> And they that creep, and they that fly,
>   Shall end where they began.
> Alike the Busy and the Gay
> But flutter thro' life's little day,
>   In fortune's varying colours drest;
> Brush'd by the hand of rough Mischance,
> Or chill'd by Age, their airy dance
>   They leave, in dust to rest.

From **"The Alliance of Education and Government,"** written in 1748:—

> As sickly Plants betray a niggard earth,
> Whose barren bosom starves her gen'rous
>   birth,
> Nor genial warmth, nor genial juice retains
> Their roots to feed, and fill their verdant veins;
> And as in climes, where Winter holds his reign,
> The soil, tho' fertile, will not teem in vain,
> Forbids her gems to swell, her shades to rise,
> Nor trusts her blossoms to the churlish skies;
> So draw Mankind in vain the vital airs,
> Unform'd, unfriended, by those kindly cares,
> That health and vigour to the soul impart,
> Spread the young thought, and warm the
>   opening heart;
> So fond Instruction

etc. From the **"Elegy,"** 1742-50:—

> Now fades the glimmering landscape on the sight,
>   And all the air a solemn stillness holds,
> Save where the beetle wheels his droning flight,
>   And drowsy tinklings lull the distant folds;

> Save that from yonder ivy-mantled tow'r
>   The mopeing owl does to the moon complain
> Of such, as wandering near her secret bow'r,
>   Molest her ancient solitary reign.

From **"The Progress of Poesy,"** written 1754:—

> Woods, that wave o'er Delphi's steep,
> Isles, that crown th' Aegean deep,
> Fields, that cool Ilissus laves,
> Or where Maeander's amber waves
> In lingering Lab'rinths creep,
> How do your tuneful Echos languish,
> Mute, but to the voice of Anguish?
> Where each old poetic Mountain
>   Inspiration breath'd around;
> Ev'ry shade and hallow'd Fountain
>   Murmur'd deep a solemn sound;
> Till the sad Nine in Greece's evil hour
>   Left their Parnassus for the Latian plains.
> Alike they scorn the pomp of tyrant-Power,
>   And coward Vice, that revels in her chains.
> When Latium had her lofty spirit lost,
> They sought, oh Albion! next thy sea-encircled
>   coast.

From **"The Bard,"** written 1754-7:—

> On a rock, whose haughty brow,
>   Frowns o'er old Conway's foaming flood,
> Robed in the sable garb of woe,
>   With haggard eyes the Poet stood;
> (Loose his beard, and hoary hair
> Streamed, like a meteor, to the troubled air)
> And with a Master's hand, and Prophet's fire,
> Struck the deep sorrows of his lyre.
> Hark, how each giant-oak, and desert cave,
>   Sighs to the torrent's aweful voice beneath!
> O'er thee, oh King! their hundred arms they wave,
>   Revenge on thee in hoarser murmurs breath;
> Vocal no more, since Cambria's fatal day,
> To high-born Hoel's harp, or soft Llewellyn's lay.

From **"The Fatal Sisters,"** written 1761:—

> Now the storm begins to lower
>   (Haste, the loom of Hell prepare),
> Iron-sleet of arrowy shower
>   Hurtles in the darken'd air.

> See the griesly texture grow,
>   ('Tis of human entrails made,)
> And the weights, that play below,
>   Each a gasping Warriour's head.

> *Mista* black, terrific maid,
>   *Sangrida,* and *Hilda* see,
> Join the wayward work to aid;
>   'Tis the woof of victory.

Ere the ruddy sun be set,
  Pikes must shiver, javelins sing,
Blade with clattering buckler meet,
  Hauberk crash, and helmet ring.

From **"The Descent of Odin,"** written 1761:—

In the caverns of the west,
By *Odin's* fierce embrace comprest,
A wond'rous Boy shall *Rinda* bear,
Who ne'er shall comb his raven-hair,
Nor wash his visage in the stream,
Nor see the sun's departing beam;
Till he on *Hoder's* corse shall smile
Flaming on the fun'ral pile.
Now my weary lips I close:
Leave me, leave me to repose.

The significance of the above quotations is apparent at a glance. **"The Descent of Odin"** is about as different from the **"Ode on the Spring"** as can well be imagined.

As he advanced in life, Gray's ideas of poetry grew free in theory as well as in practise. His **"Observations on English Metre,"** written probably in 1760-61, and published in 1814, contains much interesting matter. Gray had planned to write a History of English poetry, but when he heard that Thomas Warton was engaged in that work, he gave up the idea, and handed over his material and general scheme to Warton. If Gray had completed a history of this kind, it would certainly have been more accurate than Warton's, and would probably have done as much service to Romanticism. A few words may be quoted from the **"Observations,"** to show how far Gray had advanced in his ideas since 1740. Speaking of Milton, he says, "The more we attend to the composition of Milton's harmony, the more we shall be sensible how he loved to vary his pauses, his measures and his feet, which gives that enchanting air of freedom and wildness to his versification, unconfined by any rules but those which his own feeling and the nature of his subject demands."[19]

Gray's prose remains are deeply interesting to the student of Romanticism. He was one of the first men in Europe who had any real appreciation of wild and Romantic scenery. It has now become so fashionable to be fond of mountains, and lakes, and picturesque landscapes, that it seems difficult to believe that all this is a modern taste. To-day the average summer traveler speaks enthusiastically of precipices, mountain cascades and shaded glens, and even to some extent interprets them by the imagination, but the average eighteenth century sojourner neither could nor would do anything of the sort. This appreciation of the picturesque in external nature has a close kinship with the Romantic movement in literature; for the same emotions are at the foundation of each.

The Classicists had no more love for wild nature than they had for Gothic architecture or Romantic poetry. Let us take Addison as a conspicuous example. "In one of his letters, dated December, 1701, he wrote that he had reached Geneva after 'a very troublesome journey over the Alps. My head is still giddy with mountains and precipices; and you can't imagine how much I am pleased with the sight of a plain!' This little phrase is a good illustration of the contempt for mountains, of the way they were regarded as wild, barbaric, useless excrescences. . . . The love of mountains is something really of modern, very modern, growth, the first traces of which we shall come across towards the middle of the last century. Before that time we find mountains spoken of in terms of the severest reprobation."[20]

Mountains and wild scenery were considered as objects not of beauty or grandeur, but of horror. But in Gray's letters we hear the modern tone.

In this respect he was even more in advance of his contemporaries than in his Romantic poetry. From first to last he was always a lover of wild nature; and, as this taste was so unfashionable, we may be sure of his sincerity. Toward the close of his life, this feeling in Gray becomes more and more noticeable. His Lake Journal is a marvel when we consider its date, for it is written in the true spirit of Wordsworth. But his *early* letters and journals show that he knew how to appreciate Romantic scenery. Take two extracts from his *Journal in France* (1739).[21] These words are interesting simply as showing what attracted Gray's attention: "Beautiful way, commonly on the side of a hill, cover'd with woods, the river Marne winding in the vale below, and Côteaux, cover'd with vines, riseing gently on the other side; fine prospect of the town of Joinville, with the castle on the top of the mountain, overlooking it. . . . Ruins of an old castle on the brow of a mountain, whose sides are cover'd with woods."[22] Again, describing the journey to Geneva: "The road runs over a Mountain, which gives you the first tast of the Alps, in it's magnificent rudeness, and steep precipices; set out from Echelles on horseback, to see the Grande Chartreuse, the way to it up a vast mountain, in many places the road not 2 yards broad; on one side the rock hanging over you, & on the other side a monstrous precipice. In the bottom runs a torrent . . . that works its way among the rocks with a mighty noise, and frequent Falls. You here meet with all the beauties so savage and horrid[23] a place can present you with; Rocks of various and uncouth figures, cascades pouring down from an immense height out of hanging Groves of Pine-Trees, & the solemn Sound of the Stream, that roars below, all concur to form one of the most poetical scenes imaginable."[24]

All this is remarkable language for the year 1739. Probably very few private journals of the eighteenth century can show anything similar to it; for Gray's feelings were, at that time, almost exclusively his own. One more remark of his on Alpine scenery may be quoted. He wrote to Richard West, November 16, 1739: "I own I have not, as yet, anywhere met with those grand and simple works of Art, that are to amaze one, and whose sight one is to be the better for; but those of Nature have astonished me beyond expression. In our little journey up to the Grande Chartreuse, I do not remember to have gone ten paces without an exclamation, that there was no restraining. Not a precipice, not a torrent, not a cliff, but is pregnant with religion and poetry. There are certain scenes that would awe an atheist into belief, without the help of other argument. One need not have a very fantastic imagination, to see spirits there at noonday; you have Death perpetually before your eyes, only so far removed, as to compose the mind without frightening it."[25]

Just thirty years later, Gray wrote another journal, which shows that he had progressed as rapidly in his appreciation of Nature as he had in his love of wild and passionate poetry. This is the *Journal in the Lakes,* written in 1769, and published in 1775. This document is of great value, as throwing light on the purely imaginative side of Gray's nature. He took this Lake trip alone, and wrote the Journal simply to amuse his friend, Dr. Wharton. Here we have a very different view of nature from that given by Dyer, Thomson and even by the Wartons. This remarkable Journal is written in the true Wordsworthian spirit. Gray not only observes but spiritually interprets nature. Two quotations will suffice to show how far Gray's taste had advanced since 1739: "Behind you are the magnificent heights of *Walla-crag;* opposite lie the thick hanging woods of Lord Egremont, and *Newland* valley, with green and smiling fields embosomed in the dark cliffs; to the left the jaws of *Borrodale,* with that turbulent chaos of mountain behind mountain, rolled in confusion; beneath you, and stretching far away to the right, the shining purity of the *Lake,* just ruffled by the breeze, enough to show it is alive, reflecting rocks, woods, fields, and inverted tops of mountains."[26]

The following passage is perhaps the most striking thing Gray ever wrote about nature: "In the evening walked alone down to the Lake by the side of *Crow-Park* after sun-set and saw the solemn colouring of night draw on, the last gleam of sunshine fading away on the hilltops, the deep serene of the waters, and the long shadows of the mountains thrown across them, till they nearly touched the hithermost shore. At distance heard the murmur of many water-falls not audible in the daytime. Wished for the Moon, but she was *dark to me and silent, hid in her vacant interlunar cave.*"

Mitford said: "No man was a greater admirer of nature than Mr. Gray, nor admired it with better taste." Perhaps Walpole had partly in mind Gray's superior appreciation of Alpine scenery when he wrote, in 1775:

"We rode over the Alps in the same chaise, but Pegasus drew on his side, and a cart-horse on mine."[28] There is something noble and truly beautiful in the way in which Walpole always insisted on his own inferiority to Gray. His attitude in this was never cringing; it was a pure tribute of admiration, and that, too, from a sensitive man who had been repeatedly snubbed by the very object of his praise.

It is interesting to notice the strange and strong contrast between the shy, reserved temperament of Gray, and the pronounced radicalism of his literary tastes. Had he been a demonstrative and gushing person like Mason, his utterances about mountains and Ossianic poetry would not seem so singular; but that this secluded scholar, who spent most of his hours over his books in Cambridge and the manuscripts in the British Museum, and who was always slow to speak, should have quietly cultivated tastes so distinctly Romantic—this is a noteworthy fact. It seems to show that the one-man power counts for something in literary developments. Gray influenced the age more than the age influenced him; he led rather than followed. In addition to all the various forces that we have observed as silently working in the Romantic movement, we must add the direct influence of the courage and genius of Gray.

Notes

[1] Ward's English Poets, Vol. III., p. 302. Both Mr. Perry and Mr. Gosse seem to support Arnold's view, but I am unable to see anything in it.

[2] He wrote, in English and Latin, more than 60 poems, but only 12 appeared in print during his lifetime; and his prose is all posthumous.

[3] After I had fully reached this conclusion, I read Mr. Tovey's recent book, Gray and His Friends. The Introduction to that book is the most judicious essay on Gray that I have ever seen in print, though Mr. Tovey does not discuss his connection with Romanticism. I was pleased to find that my view of Gray's sterility was very similar to Mr. Tovey's, who completely disposes of Arnold's theory.

[4] He never despised Dryden, however, though he went far beyond him. Oct. 2, 1765, he wrote to Beattie, "Remember Dryden, and be blind to all his faults." *Gray's Works*, Vol. III., p. 221.

[5] The second in 1742.

[6] *Mathias's Observations* (1815), page 52. This passage in itself goes a long way toward explaining Gray's sterility.

[7] *Gray's Works,* Vol. II., page 130.

[8] Gray's interesting letter to Walpole about the *Elegy,* June 12, 1750, may be found in his *Works,* Vol. II., page 209. He says: "You will, I hope, look upon it in the light of a thing with an end to it; a merit that most of my writings have wanted." He evidently felt the fragmentary nature of his previous work.

[9] This letter is in *Gray's Works,* Vol. II., page 210. It contains minute instructions about the printing of the poem, and says it must be published anonymously.

[10] This point is fully and suggestively treated in the *Saturday Review* for June 19, 1875, in an article called *A Lesson from Gray's Elegy.*

[11] Dr. Johnson said they were "two compositions at which the readers of poetry were at first content to gaze in mute amazement." In 1783, Dr. Johnson was violently attacked for this by the Rev. R. Potter, an enthusiastic admirer of Gray. Potter said that Gray's *Bard,* with its "wild and romantic scenery," etc., was "the finest ode in the world."

[12] *Works,* Vol. II., page 218.

[13] For Walpole's remarks on Gray's *Odes,* see his letters to Horace Mann, August 4, 1757, and to Lyttleton, August 25, 1757. See especially his letter to Mason, January 27, 1781, on Johnson's *Life of Gray.* Walpole afterward spoke of Johnson as a "babbling old woman." and a "wight on stilts."

[14] Letter to Lyttleton, August 25, 1757.

[15] Gosse says in his *Life of Gray,* page 163, that Gray not only takes precedence of English poets in the revival of Norse mythology, but even of the Scandinavian writers. But this is going too far. Mallet, in his *Histoire de Dannemarck,* Vol. II., page 309, speaks of a book on the "exploits des rois et des héros du Nord" published at Stockholm in 1737.

[16] *Works,* Vol. III., page 45.

[17] *Gray's Works,* Vol. III., page 47.

[18] Mr. Gosse has some interesting remarks on Gray and Ossian in his *Life of Gray,* page 149.

[19] *Works,* Vol. I., page 332.

[20] *Perry's Eighteenth Century Literature,* page 145. But much of our modern love for mountains and precipices is doubtless due to the circumstances in which we view them. Carried to the top of the Rigi in a comfortable car, we are in a condition to enjoy to the utmost the glorious view; but if the Rigi represented an obstacle, something that must be passed over with infinite discomfort and even peril, in order to reach a destination on the other side, I am sure we should not appreciate the view so keenly. This was the attitude in which Addison looked at the Alps.

[21] This was printed from the first time by Mr. Gosse in Vol. I. of his edition of *Gray's Works.*

[22] *Works,* Vol. I., page 240.

[23] The word sounds conventional, more like Augustan style; but what Gray goes on to say shows that it appealed to his own feelings in a very different way.

[24] *Works,* Vol. I., page 244.

[25] *Works,* Vol. II., page 44.

[26] *Works,* Vol. I., page 254.

[27] *Works,* Vol. I., page 258.

[28] Letter to Cole, December 10, 1775.

Stopford A. Brooke (essay date 1920)

SOURCE: "Collins and Gray," in *Naturalism in English Poetry*, E. P. Dutton & Company, 1920, pp. 42-65.

[*In the following excerpt, Brooke compares Gray's poetry with that of William Collins and delineates Gray's chief creative influences, assessing the impact of his works on the transition in English poetry from Neoclassicism to Romanticism.*]

. . . [William Collins and Thomas Gray are] connected with the school of Dryden and Pope by a certain artificial or conventional note in their diction, by a certain want of frank Naturalism; so that, even in their beautiful work, a note of commonplace is heard, a prosaic note. This is less in Collins than in Gray, but, in its occurrence in the poetry of both, they are together. The juxtaposition of their names, at this point, is not unfitting. At another point they are also together. They both went back in search of Nature and Beauty, not to Horace for an impulse to satirical poetry, or indeed to any of the Romans, not even to Vergil, but to the great nobility, simplicity and solid art of the Greek poets of the finer time—Gray more than Collins, but Collins with equal determination and an equal reverence for the Greek mastery and excellence. "Let us return," they said, "to the best masters, in order to know best how to shape our own work into beauty and dignity and exquisiteness." They did not reach the excellence they admired, but their aspiration had a profound effect on the career of the larger number of the English poets of the nineteenth century. Men rejected the artificial Classicism, with its limiting rules, of Pope, and pursued, not only after the noble, simple and passionate excellence of the Greek work, but also after the measured, temperate, selective, careful exquisiteness of the phrasing of a poet like Vergil. Moreover, they endeavoured to combine with this emulation of the classic excellence the love of the beautiful, as best disclosed in a close but ideal representation of Nature; both in the soul of man and in the images of the natural world. It was as yet only an endeavour, but it was begun.

Collins and Gray began this movement, but they lived in a prosaic age and in an age which imposed on them an artificial, not a natural, expression of their thoughts. And this prevented their work, under this new Greek impulse, from being as excellent as it might have been at another time in the history of literature. Had they been born after Wordsworth had restored the natural language of feeling to poetry, they would have been different poets indeed; and this is a point which, if I rightly remember, Matthew Arnold has made and laboured.

In these two ways—in a conventional diction which links them back to Pope and in a return to the spirit of the Greek classics—Collins and Gray may be considered as one. In other points, indeed, in their main poetic work and genius, they differed greatly from one another. The continual association of their names is a critical mistake. Collins had more natural art than Gray and desired it more. He saw and loved Simplicity, that gracious maid. She was taught by Nature to breathe her genuine thought, he said:

> In numbers warmly pure and sweetly strong.

He paints her, in Attic robe arrayed, the meek sister of Truth. It was she, he said, who alone could justly order and arrange the flowers of poetry that Beauty had collected. Even when divine excess filled the poet's soul, it was Simplicity who could give the frenzy the true warmth; for she alone can, by her spirit of soothing, sober, tender music, raise the soul of him who reads the verse into the true temper to enjoy the verse. "The passions in hall and bower own thy power no more," and he is thinking of the dead poetry of his time:

> Faint's the cold work till thou inspire the whole,

but give me Nature—simply Nature—the still, quiet, natural passion of the heart. There is my happiness; there my genius breathes with ease and loves its work:

> I only seek to find thy temperate vale,
>   Where oft my reed might sound
>   To maids and shepherds round,
> And all thy sons, O Nature! learn my tale.

These are the views concerning poetry he expresses in the "Ode to Simplicity." They are not the views of

Gray—they are the views of Wordsworth—and Collins first struck this high note of Naturalism. Rising through all the conventional phrasing of the time, through its allegorising and personifying way of representing thought and emotion, is this natural, simple note which Collins, wiser than his age, strove to attain. . . .

Thomas Gray, to whom we now turn, though not so true a poet as Collins, was more remarkable in the history of this poetic transition. He opened more new veins of poetry than Collins did, and he combined within himself a larger number of new tendencies of the time. Moreover, he was a man of greater knowledge than Collins; of wider sympathies; of a more conscious art; with a staid, moral, sententious philosophy of man, partly derived from Pope, of which philosophy Collins was, I imagine, a despiser; and with a pleasant humour of which Collins was incapable; a wider, more various man, but not a greater poet. At another point they also differed. Collins was feeble of character and many circumstances were against him. He fell at last into deep depression, almost bordering on madness, and his poetic vein dried up. Gray was strong and wise of character, his circumstances were happy and, though he suffered also from physical depression, this did not enfeeble his sane and steadfast mind. His powers remained undiminished to the end.

If we wish to know how this character of his bore upon, strengthened or enlarged his poetry, we cannot do better than read Matthew Arnold's essay upon him; which, though prefixed to extracts from his verse, says little or nothing concerning him as a poet, but very much concerning him as a man. Arnold's constant search in his later essays after the character, circumstances and society of the poets he discussed, in order to draw from these elements a critical estimate of their poetry, was useful work, provided it was kept within just limits. But he ran it into its extreme, and the extreme lowered his critical power. Finally it almost ruined it. Of course, the character of a poet has a great deal to do with his poetry, but it does not altogether make it. As far, however, as it does make it—as far as Gray's temper and life told on his poetry—we may let them alone. What Arnold has said of them could not be better said. But we must, in speaking of his poetry, mark especially the place he occupies in the growth of naturalist and romantic poetry, during this transition period.

First, an excellent scholar, he, far more than Collins, sought back to the great Classics, not as Pope did, to transfer them into modern dress, but to drench his soul with their spirit, to emulate their temperance, their high aims, their precision and clearness and, above all, their wide view of human nature. He studied them as models, but he used his study of them on his own subjects. No poet who cared for his art neglected, after him, the classic sources, however romantically he used the results of his study. Gray and Collins learned the high secrets and methods of their art from the Greeks; but the new freedom of their spirit not only prevented them from imitation, but also urged them into individual creation. They strove to assimilate the classic spirit but to use it in their own way.

Secondly, like Collins, and with greater industry, he studied the old poets of England. He felt how close and vital was the connexion between the ancient poets and the new poetry of his own day. He knew his Chaucer well. He wrote an essay on Lydgate. He loved the great Elizabethans—Spenser, Shakespeare and the rest. He read his Milton continuously. He projected a history of English poetry; and one regrets, near as he was to Dryden and Pope, that he did not trace their influence and fix their place in English poetry.

In doing this, he was continually in contact, not with artificial, but with high imaginative and passionate work, and also with a noble Naturalism, as far as Naturalism was concerned with human nature—a Naturalism freer, bolder, more universal, but less temperate than the Greek, a Naturalism which was always passing into Romanticism. And this continual contact with imagination and passion set him largely free from the power of the artificial school, and enabled him to push forward the new life in poetry. When we read his **"Ode on the Progress of Poesy"**—one of his fine things—we see how truly he tried to drink of these ancient springs, how fully he was conscious of the continuity of English Poetry.

Nevertheless, and this is a third matter, he was held back, by his nearness to the artificial and prosaic poetry of Dryden and Pope, from getting all out of these springs that he might otherwise have got. Neither imagination nor passion had its perfect work in him. His natural description, his criticism of life, his contemplative spirit, his melancholy, were, in his poetry, modified away from the natural expression of them, from imaginative simplicity, by the conventional school in which he had been educated. Again and again the commonplace and meaningless diction of the period spoils, or seems to spoil, the grace of his verse. Its sentiment is sometimes faded; its sentential phrasing too usual, too sententious; its expression too carefully, too academically wrought—and passion, save in his contemplative melancholy, and even in that too obviously elaborated, is altogether wanting. Nevertheless, he almost escaped from these prosaic elements. He made a great step forward. And, so far as his backward motion as a poet is concerned, I impute his nearness to full escape from mere conventions in poetry to the fact that the man he most admired, followed and studied was not Pope, but the more masculine and forceful Dryden. Gray, even though he was a somewhat sentimental moralist, a retired contemplator of man from the shades of a university, had force, when he pleased

to use it, in his poetry. Yet his plain connexion with a prosaic, non-natural age, even when he was chiefly connected with the enormous power of Dryden's giant genius, prevented him from using to their full strength the new poetic elements of his time and of his own nature.

Fourthly, he was not only a Naturalist in his study of man and the natural world, he was partly a Romantic, and pushed into a higher life the romantic elements in the transition. The first element of this Romanticism, first in point of time—its sentimental, personal melancholy—was his; and the thought-weighted, scholarly, careful representation of this element gave it, not only a stronger foundation in the spirit of the time than it had as yet possessed, but also a greater finish and art in its expression. It became more distinctly a subject for poetry; and it kept for a long time Gray's moral and philosophic touch. But this was not all he did for Romanticism. He recalled to English poetry the rude, ancient, history-crowded stories, the legends and wonders of the bardic tales of the early Britons of mediæval Wales, and of the Norse mythology. He opened out that new world of Romance, though only in short translations. He welcomed the Percy Reliques, the Celtic bric-à-brac of Macpherson's Ossian; and pitied, though he exposed, the romantic forgeries of Chatterton. Moreover, those rude romantic tales of Wales chimed in with his love of rude and savage scenery, in which he delighted to wander alone in picturesque thought. In all this he initiated a new romantic impulse, or at least gave the impulse a practical poetic form.

Fifthly, his work on Nature was not as unmixed as Thomson's nor as poetically felt as Collins'. Nature, in his poems, is always a background for humanity. It is the "most graceful ornament of poetry, but not its subject"—so he said. The youth who walks through the **"Elegy in the Country Churchyard"** loves the dewy morning, the rising sun, the beech at whose roots the babbling brook runs by, the glimmering stillness of the evening; but he loves them not wholly for their own sake. He loves them most because they echo the note of his imagination, contemplating the life of man. Nature, when it sympathises with his mood, is taken up into the art of Gray. In the **"Ode on a Distant Prospect of Eton College,"** the scenery recalls his youth. The fields and winds of Thames, and the hills that look on the river, bestow on him a momentary bliss and breathe into his tired manhood the gladness of his early spring. But he leaves them at once to mourn over the gloom which slowly gathers round manhood and age. The mourning is faded—so is the verse.

It is commonplace to say.

> Since sorrow never comes too late.
> And happiness too quickly flies.

And this commonplace note is one too frequently found in Gray.

At other times, he moralises Nature; as in the Ode **"On the Spring."** He paints the insect-youth at noontide; busy, eager, floating in the liquid light:

> Some lightly o'er the current skim,
> Some show their gaily-gilded trim
>   Quick-glancing in the sun. . . .
> To contemplation's sober eye
> Such is the race of man.

Yet he really loved Nature. She brought to him thought, feeling, poetry and religion. And he was one of the first who made her a constant study, who sought her in her wildness, who travelled far and wide to find her solitudes. His letters are full of careful and carefully composed descriptions, not so much of the cultivated and quiet landscape he loved in the **"Elegy"** and the "Odes," as of the mountains, moors, dells and gorges, torrents and streams of the Lake Country, of the Welsh solitudes, of the Scottish hills. In these, though he did not sing of them, he found an impulse of his song, and thence he took a deep impression into his quiet and sane religion. When he climbed the Gorge of the Grand Chartreuse, he felt the spirit of the place, "pregnant," he said, "with poetry and religion"; and it illustrates how far in front of France this English movement towards the sentiment of wild and solitary Nature was—that a modern French critic declares that the phrase could not have been written by any Frenchman of the time either in prose or verse. Here and there, in his poetry, this natural feeling for Nature (unhumanised, unmoralised) appears, but these instances are few and far between. Nor do they ever continue. They run up at once into some comparison with, some reflection on, human life. Moreover, they want that touch of simplicity, of natural joy, which Collins had. They are overwrought by art into a want of nature. The feeling in them is worn down by academic polishing. The art is more than the imagination; and as to the conception of a life, a spirit in Nature, on the edge of which he sometimes seems to tremble, and which would at once have uplifted his verse into a higher region, it is never really reached. The artificial age still stretched its dead hand over his work on Nature. It held him back from doing all he might have done in this way; from expressing all he felt. Nevertheless he set forward the poetry of Nature. He redeemed it from the mere cataloguing of Thomson. He brought into it careful composition. He harmonised it, up to a certain point, with man. It never could again be quite neglected in poetry. He opened the way to the addition to it of natural passion. That passion was at hand, and when it came, it was like the rising of the sun on the twilight landscape of Gray. He was a forerunner of it, but the true forerunner was Collins and not Gray.

There is one more thing to say of Gray as the poet of this transition time. I have dwelt on the rising tendency towards an interest in man as man, beyond the life of cities, beyond the cultivated cliques of society; interest in nations beyond England, interest in human life in the country, where it was close to Nature—in the farmer, the peasant and the poor. Gray, in spite of his wide knowledge, of his intellectual society, of his academic remoteness from the world, was touched by that growing tendency and expressed it in the poem by which he chiefly lives; which itself will always be dear to England and justly dear; the **"Elegy written in a Country Churchyard."** Dryden or Pope would have been for ever incapable of writing a line of it, not from want of genius, but from want of the spirit and feeling which inspires it, from want of sympathy with its subject, its view of Nature or of man. We cannot fancy Pope writing of the ploughman driving his weary oxen home, of the rude forefathers of the hamlet, of the labourer's wife and children,—of the harvesters and the woodmen in the joy of their toil, of their homely joys and destiny obscure, of the short and simple annals of the poor. And Gray writes of them, with careful art it is true, but with real sympathy. Even the somewhat exalted strain with which he treats the rustic dead, and fancies that

> Perhaps in this neglected spot is laid
> Some heart once pregnant with celestial fire—

some soul like Hampden, Milton or Cromwell, is redeemed from its fancifulness by the innate sincerity and grace of lines like these:

> Far from the madding crowd's ignoble strife,
>   Their sober wishes never learned to stray;
> Along the cool sequestered vale of life
>   They kept the noiseless tenor of their way.

Even the youth who is the personage of the poem, who mediates upon the country and the poor, has nought to do with the citied society of Dryden and Pope. He is one they would have passed by—one to fortune and to fame unknown, of wayward fancies, woeful, wan, forlorn, or crazed with care, or crossed with hopeless love—one of that wide class of solitary, sorrowful folk among the common classes of the earth, of whom the poetry of society took no notice, but whom Wordsworth chose as his friends, and the constant subject of his song.

For this advance in human sympathy—this more universal treatment of humanity—the world was now beginning to be ready. None of Gray's poems received so much acceptance from his contemporaries as this Elegy which praised the country and the poor with a poet's sympathy. And the tendency it recorded grew day by day in the heart of the public, till it built itself into the palace of Wordsworth's song. Gray did this for it. He laid its artistic foundation.

A. E. Dyson (essay date 1957)

SOURCE: "The Ambivalence of Gray's Elegy," in *Essays in Criticism*, Vol. VII, No. 3, July, 1957, pp. 257-61.

[*In the following essay, Dyson discusses Gray's conflicting attitudes toward rustic life as reflected in the "Elegy."*]

The prevailing impression we have on considering Gray's **'Elegy'** in retrospect is of its distinctive 'atmosphere', contemplative and Horatian. There is the stoic reflection on the transcience of earthly glory that we associate with this tradition, the same apparent preference for a Sabine Farm, 'far from the madding crowd's ignoble strife'. The gentle melancholy of the mood, as well as the syntax of stanzas 24 and 25, points to Gray himself as the subject of the Epitaph. It expresses a wish which, in this particular mood, he has for his whole future: to be 'marked out' by melancholy for her own, to live and die in peaceful rustic security.

But this is by no means all that the **'Elegy'** says, and it ignores some powerful emotional undercurrents. For Gray is seeing the 'rude Forefathers' of the hamlet in two rôles simultaneously, both as the happiest of men, and as victims. The plowman in stanza 1 is 'weary', the slumbering dead are rude and unlettered. The tombs 'with uncouth rhimes and shapeless sculptures deck'd' implore the passing tribute of a sigh as much for their uncouthness as for the death of their inmates. The obscurity of country life has restrained and killed the innate potentialities of the rustics, for good as well as for evil. Not only is the possible Cromwell comparatively guiltless, but the possible Milton is mute and inglorious, both forbidden by their lot any spectacular fulfilment. The obscurity, therefore, in which their happiness is supposed to consist is felt in terms of waste. The words 'mute' and 'inglorious' acquire an ambiguity from their context. They are words of deprivation and defeat, but they are here levelled up by juxtaposition with the 'guiltless' Cromwells almost to the status of happiness.

This basic ambivalence reveals conflicting emotional responses to the situation of the rustics, and these responses develop side by side as the poem progresses. From the Horatian viewpoint, the rude forefathers are more to be envied than pitied. Pomfret in his *Choice* asked little more from life (except, perhaps, the 'philosophic mind'), and Lady Chudworth in her *Resolve* wanted only

A soul, which cannot be depressed by grief,
Nor too much rais'd by the sublimest joy.

The Augustan quest for the golden mean excluded extremes of either emotion or achievement, and looked for happiness in detachment from the busy world of men. Pomfret and Lady Chudworth express an attitude to life which is typical of their age, and which survived sufficiently far into the eighteenth century to influence Gray. From this point of view, the lot of the 'forefathers' in the **'Elegy'** is little short of ideal.

Far from the madding crowd's ignoble strife,
Their sober wishes never learn'd to stray:
Along the cool sequester'd vale of life
They kept the noiseless tenor of their way.

In this and other stanzas Gray expresses a rational approval of the rustic life, and in the Epitaph he identifies himself, in wish-fulfilment, with it. The youth 'to fortune and to fame unknown' is not unlike Tennyson's Lady of Shalott before her choice—a legend to all men, but known to none. He represents, like Arnold's Scholar Gipsy after him, the ideal of a serene and untroubled existence—but an existence which is essentially an escape from life as we know it into a state less vulnerable to the 'thousand natural shocks that flesh is heir to'. The peace which he enjoys is nearer to death than to life, more like defeat than victory.

The contradiction inherent in this becomes clear as we notice that the rude forefathers, even while they are being offered to us as an ideal, are also being represented as victims, both of society and of the nature of things. The primary meanings of 'mute' and 'inglorious' suggest this, and there is a sense in which the extremism of the Miltons and Cromwells, whether good or bad ethically, is seen as good in so far as it is fulfilment, expression, achievement, 'life abundant'. The 'applause of listening Senates', the despising of dangers, the 'scattering of plenty o'er a smiling land' are positive and vital touchstones, beside which the rustic life is felt as a tragic waste. The rude forefathers were victims of a political system which forbade them their proper fulfilment. The 'genial current of their soul' was frozen by 'Chill Penury'. The hearts once 'pregnant with celestial fire' are now laid, unhonoured and unremembered, 'in some neglected spot'. The creative spirit was there, but it found no opportunity for expression. There is, in this reflection, a profound awareness of waste. Death is so cold and irrevocable (stanza 11), beauty so fleeting and futile (stanza 14). The rustic moralist may have been taught by his simple religion how to die, but ought he not rather to have been given a chance to live?

For who to dumb forgetfulness a prey,
This pleasing anxious being e'er resigned,
Left the warm precincts of the cheerful day,
Nor cast one longing, lingering look behind?

It is to be noted that the enemy to man's fulfilment is not only society, but Nature herself. The adjectives and verbs of the opening stanzas are narcotic and hostile: 'tolls', 'parting', 'lowing', 'plods', 'weary', 'fades', 'glimmering', 'droning', 'drowsy', 'lull', 'mop-ing', 'complain', 'secret', 'molest', 'ancient', 'solitary', 'heaves', 'mouldering', 'narrow cell', 'rude'. In stan-za 7, the harvesters are at war with Nature. In stan-za 14, beauty is the victim of a vast and mysterious universe; the gem lost in ocean's 'dark unfathomed caves', the flower wasted upon the 'desert air' which will destroy it. Finally, as the 'hoary-headed swain' indicates the grave of Gray (if it *is* Gray—the syntax is not clear, but the thought indicates that it is), the nearby wood smiles 'as in scorn'. (The phrase 'as in scorn' applies, in the first version of the poem, to the dead man, but in the final version it applies equally, by ambiguity, to the wood.) Nature, therefore, is a more primitive and dubious goddess here than in orthodox Augustan circles, and we might even discern that sense of the ruthless profusion and wastefulness of her works which has become a preoccupation with some post-Darwinian thinkers.

How far Gray was conscious of ambivalence in his '**Elegy**' we can probably not hope to decide. The 'graveyard mood' would have seemed to him, perhaps, as unified as the style in which he expresses it. He is unlikely to have shared our present-day awareness of complexity or a tension of opposites in such a mood. Even so, the two attitudes we have been considering exist quite explicitly, side by side, in the poem, and we can legitimately speculate on the subconscious respons-es to life which they reveal. These would seem to have included a shrinking from life, with its menaces and responsibilities (something very like the Freudian death-wish, in fact), and also a desire for life (the almost inevitable complementary pull). In a very personal way, the 'slumbering dead' must have seemed a reproach to Gray. He is aware, in the poem, of his social superi-ority to them. They were unlettered, he is a scholar; they had no opportunity of notable achievement, he, in his own academic sphere at least, has had it. But he has failed to take his own considerable opportunities; his vast learning was notoriously unproductive. He is very far from having the spirit of a Milton or a Cromwell. His letters often show him in a Hamlet-like strain of frustration and melancholia. He is like the Hamlet of Act V, assured of the impossibility of what he most desired, stoically resigned to life on these terms ('There's providence in the fall of a sparrow'), yet haunted by the futility of it all ('Alas, poor Yorrick'), and still balanc-ing in his mind the great alternative propositions ('To be or not to be'). All of these attitudes are present in the '**Elegy**,' though with less imaginative intensity, of course, than in *Hamlet*: and so the stanzas which ap-prove the lot of the forefathers spring not only from a reasoned Augustan belief in the rural life ('Let not ambition mock their useful toil' . . .), but also from a vicarious realisation of the death-wish. And Gray's frustration is apparent not only when he is pitying the rustics, but also when he is envying them; for it is their death, not their life, that he envies.

Gray often seems to be seeing his relationship to the 'great' as analogous to the rustics' relationship to himself. In the final stanzas he identifies himself with the rus-tics and dies to ambition and self-fulfilment with them, but here the ambivalence of emotional response is especially to be felt. 'A youth to fortune and to fame unknown' invites our pity; his simple contentment,

> He gained from Heaven ('twas all he wished)
> a friend calls for acquiescence.

So the emotional charge of the '**Elegy**' is far from simple, and that which is ostensibly offered as a good is *felt* in terms of waste. The reflections on the rustics' death in stanzas 4-7 become, by implication, a reflec-tion on their life. The 'lowly bed' from which they will not again be roused is the bed on which their life has been passed. The long silence and obscurity of the tomb is the same in kind as the condition in which life has drifted away. Their obscurity in death and their obscurity in life are equally symbolised by the buried gem and the wasted flower. And death, in its dual aspect as a longed-for rest and a dreaded waste, is present in a single image.

> Beneath those rugged elms, that yew-tree's shade,
>   Where heaves the turf in many a mould'ring
>   heap,
> Each in his narrow cell for ever laid,
>   The rude forefathers of the hamlet sleep . . .
>
> The breezy call of incense-breathing morn,
>   The swallow twitt'ring from the straw-built
>   shed,
> The cock's shrill clarion, or the echoing horn,
>   No more shall rouse them from their lowly bed.

Gray chooses sleep before action, like the lotus-eaters, and like Keats he is half in love with easeful death. But he also feels, with Milton's Belial, that any form of con-sciousness is to be preferred to oblivion, and, like Keats again, responds in some degree to a pull back to life—the 'incense-breathing morn' and the clarion cock-crow.

This complexity is by no means as rich as that in the *Ode To a Nightingale,* and the desire for life receives no expression comparable in power to Keats's nightin-gale-symbol of ideal and eternal beauty. But it is a complexity similar in kind, if not in poetic intensity, to that realised by Keats in the *Ode,* and this may well be one of the reasons why the '**Elegy**' has always found a 'mirror in every mind'.

Geoffrey Tillotson (essay date 1961)

SOURCE: "Gray's Ode on the Death of a Favourite Cat, Drowned in a Tub of Gold Fishes," in *Augustan Studies*, The Athlone Press, 1961, pp. 216-23.

[*In the following essay, Tillotson explains some of the literary allusions in Gray's "Ode on the Death of a Favourite Cat," at the same time remarking on Samuel Johnson's criticism of the poem.*]

Gray's ["**Ode on the Death of a Favourite Cat, Drowned in a Tub of Gold Fishes**"] is one of those poems that make allusions to other poems, and that expect the reader to catch them. We all know how the *Rape of the Lock* depends for the tone of its narrative and meaning on contrasts with the great epics, and the same is true in smaller compass of Gray's poem.

Nowadays, if a poet announced such a subject as the death of a cat, we should expect him to treat it seriously. But in 1742 the title allowed of comic treatment as an alternative, and Gray's choice was declared at once by the relationship of the title with the first line of the text:

'Twas on a lofty vase's side.

We now know that the receptacle in which the Strawberry Hill goldfish swam was a china bowl or vase.[1] Knowing this, we see that the word *tub* is Gray's deliberate alteration of the fact. There is a big difference between the two things, and was in 1742: Johnson's Dictionary, thirteen years later, defined the one as 'a large open vessel of wood', and the other as 'a vessel; generally a vessel rather for show than use'. Gray's *tub* is a deliberate lowering because he wants *vase* to be a heightening. When the poem was published in 1748 the reader, who knew nothing of the incident behind the poem except as the poem itself presented it—it was of course all he needed to know—noted the discrepancy and inferred the mock-heroic. That small stroke was an earnest of more of the same sort:

'Twas on a lofty vase's side,
Where China's gayest art had dy'd
  The azure flowers, that blow;
Demurest[2] of the tabby kind,[3]
The pensive Selima reclin'd,
  Gazed on the lake below.

Her conscious[4] tail her joy declar'd;
The fair round face, the snowy beard,
  The velvet of her paws,
Her coat, that with the tortoise vies,
Her ears of jet, and emerald eyes,
  She saw; and purr'd applause.

Still had she gaz'd; but 'midst the tide
Two angel forms were seen to glide,
  The Genii of the stream:
Their scaly armour's Tyrian hue
Thro' richest purple to the view
  Betray'd a golden gleam.

For the modern reader the clues are not perhaps obvious. *Tub* for *vase*, *armour* for *scales*—perhaps these are the only straws visible in the wind. But for the reader Gray had in mind, the cultivated reader of 1742, the wind was strong, and some of the straws, as we shall see, the size of forest-trees.

Almost as famous as Gray's poem is Johnson's comment on it in his Life of Gray, and the odd thing is that it shows him to have mistaken Gray's intentions—or at least to have ignored their point. And if so, with the wilfulness prompted by an imperfect sympathy. Johnson had little liking for Gray and for much of his work, the dislike of the writings being prompted in part at least by the dislike of the man.

The prickly relation of Gray and Johnson was much discussed during the half century following the inclusion of the Life of Gray in the *Lives of the Poets,* and all the more earnestly because at this time Gray was having so marked an effect on English poetry. For us, Johnson's Life of Gray is all the more unfortunate because it separates two men who by rights stand side by side. Johnson and Gray are men and writers remarkably alike, for, to put it sharply, if any other writer of 1751 could have written Gray's '**Elegy**' that writer was Johnson. They had both attained to the same estimate of human life, and had minds deeply learned, powerful, genial with ripe understanding, and impatient of cheapness. On the surface there were of course striking differences, and between any two actual living acquaintances surface is likely to count for more than inner worth. What they saw and heard of each other's externals gave them prickly grounds for dislike: Gray called Johnson 'ursa major, the great bear', and Johnson thought Gray a finicky exquisite. Left alive to write Gray's life, Johnson was too fair-minded not to salute Gray's solid greatness. Accordingly he praised the '**Elegy**' more highly than any other English poem: 'Had Gray written often thus it had been vain to blame, and useless to praise him';[5] and, having Mason's memoir of Gray before him with its ample quotations from the letters, he saw that Gray's 'mind had a large grasp'. But in the rest of his life his homage exists indirectly in the spiritedness of his writing—the Life of Gray is Johnson at his gayest. He is, however, spiritedly unfair. Even where we admit the justice in some of his strictures, we see them to cover too much. Gray's poetry, brief in quantity, is more various line by line than that of any other English poet, and to write, in Quintilian phrase, of his being 'tall by walking on tiptoe', or to discover 'glittering accumulations of ungraceful ornaments' is to ignore magnitude and jewels that are authentic, and to miss so much that is uniquely great.

His criticism of the ode on the cat has, one suspects, the brilliance of the wit who dazzles in order to get by. Johnson either does not recognize, or does not choose to, what is at the basis of the poem—what its kind is, in other words. To see its kind is to see its sense.

Johnson begins his account of the poem in this way:

> The poem on the Cat was doubtless by its author considered as a trifle, but it is not a happy trifle. In the first stanza 'the azure flowers that blow' shew resolutely a rhyme is sometimes made when it cannot easily be found.[6]

It almost seems that the *look* of the poem on the page, with its four- and three-foot lines, was enough to put him off, for he disliked ballads on principle, and so was disqualified for meeting any particular ballad, or ballad-like poem. If Gray's ode had, like the *Rape of the Lock,* been in heroic couplets, Johnson might have been fairer to it. He might then have read it closely enough to catch those references to epic that are the main-spring of the mock-epic method. It is because he disliked ballads that he did not see the point of the third line of the poem. What he disliked in that line cannot have been the actual word that rimed, for *blow* was then the ordinary prose word for a plant's act of flowering: it occurs in Gray's letters and in Johnson's Dictionary, and that the whole phrase has nothing would-be 'poetical' about it is shown by Wordsworth's having borrowed it for the quiet ending of one of his greatest poems:

> To me the meanest flower that blows can give
> Thoughts that do often lie too deep for tears.

What Johnson objected to was the redundancy of 'that blow', forgetting that redundancies of this cheerful jingling sort are part of the method of a true ballad, and so a grace in a mock-ballad. Looking for faults, he missed virtues. Blind to the pointed veering from *tub* to *vase,* he missed later on a more particular example of the mock-heroic method, an omission that explains the rest of what he objects to:

> Selima, the Cat, is called a nymph, with some violence both to language and sense; but there is good use made of it when it is done; for of the two lines,
>
> 'What female heart can gold despise?
>   What cat's averse to fish?'
>
> the first relates merely to the nymph, and the second only to the cat. The sixth stanza contains a melancholy truth, that 'a favourite has no friend,' but the last ends in a pointed sentence of no relation to the purpose; if what glistered had been 'gold' the cat would not have gone into the water; and, if she had, would not less have been drowned.[7]

'Selima, the Cat', writes Johnson, and had he been attentive he would have seen that that collocation is the key to the poem. The grand name that Walpole chose for his Persian was that of the heroine of Rowe's *Tamerlane,* a much acted play in the eighteenth century: she was the captive daughter of the Turk Bajazeth. (In a few years' time, as it happened, Walpole was to write an epilogue for the play.) Naming a cat after a princess, Walpole was himself inaugurating the mock-heroic. Gray crowned the proceeding first in little—by the heightening of *tub* to *vase*—and then grandly by referring the cat to the heroine of a famous play, and then to the heroine of the *Iliad* itself.

In the 'Argument' before the third Book in Pope's translation we read:

> The Armies being ready to engage, a single Combate is agreed upon between *Menelaus* and *Paris* (by the Intervention of *Hector*) for the Determination of the War. *Iris* is sent to call *Helena* to behold the Fight. She leads her to the Walls of *Troy,* where *Priam* sate with his Counsellors observing the *Græcian* Leaders on the Plain below, to whom *Helen* gives an Account of the chief of them.

And in the text itself:

> Within the Lines they[8] drew their Steeds around,
> And from their Chariots issu'd on the Ground:
> Next all unbuckling the rich Mail they wore,
> Lay'd their bright Arms along the sable Shore.

Helen is summoned by Iris to

> Approach, and view the wondrous Scene below.

In the description that follows she is accorded a 'fair Face',[9] over which she throws a 'snowy' veil, and in the conversation she holds with Priam about the Greek heroes, occur other words of Gray: she speaks of her 'conscious' shame, and he of the Sangaris that ran 'purple' with blood. We then hear of heralds who bring 'rich' wine and 'golden' goblets, and later on of 'Azure Armour' and 'purple' cuishes. More pointedly still we come on this:

> Meantime the brightest of the Female Kind,
> The matchless *Helen* o'er the Walls reclin'd.

The cat in her setting is so like Helen in hers that the poem at this point may be said to have a double subject. Of course the subject cannot be double throughout: Helen does not fall off the walls of Troy to be left to die. Nevertheless, having been given a strong sense of the woman in the cat, we take the cat story, *mutatis mutandis,* as also a story about woman, *in posse* if not *in esse,* and by analogy if not in fact. Nor as the poem proceeds does Gray let us forget the woman:

The hapless Nymph with wonder saw:
A whisker first and then a claw,
  With many an ardent wish,
She stretch'd in vain to reach the prize.
What female heart can gold despise?
  What Cat's averse to fish?

Presumptuous Maid! with looks intent
Again she stretch'd, again she bent,
  Nor knew the gulf between.
(Malignant Fate sat by, and smil'd)
The slipp'ry verge her feet beguil'd,
  She tumbled headlong in.

Eight times emerging from the flood
She mew'd to ev'ry watry God,
  Some speedy aid to send.
No Dolphin came, no Nereid stirr'd:
Nor cruel *Tom,* nor *Susan* heard.
  A Fav'rite has no friend!

The cat is called a 'Nymph', and when she stretches after the fish we get not only a rhetorical question about cats but one about cupidinous woman, which comes in with special neatness because, as it happens, the fish are 'Gold Fishes' (goldfish had only lately been brought to England,[10] and this added piquancy to the poem in 1748, justifying its long description of the fishes on the score of informativeness as well as art). Furthermore the cat is apostrophized in womanly terms as 'Presumptuous Maid!' and when the disaster is completing itself, the absence of help and the comment it prompts are applicable both to cats and human beings: 'No Dolphin came', as one did come to help Arion, 'no Nereid stirr'd', as they had stirred when Hylas fell into the stream, 'Nor cruel *Tom*', the footman, 'nor *Susan*', the maidservant, heard, for it is a universal truth that 'A fav'rite has no friend!'

Johnson's objection that no good use is made of the doubling of cat and woman (for his 'good use' is of course ironic) shows that he had missed the thoroughness with which the doubling proceeds. And his final thrust—'if what glistered had been "gold", the cat would not have gone into the water; and, if she had, would not less have been drowned', shows that he failed to see how the poem ends. Here is the last stanza that follows on the line just quoted:

From hence, ye Beauties, undeceiv'd,
Know, one false step is ne'er retriev'd,
  And be with caution bold.
Not all that tempts your wand'ring eyes
And heedless hearts, is lawful prize;
  Nor all, that glisters, gold.

At the end of his cat-poem Gray comes to his moral in accordance with the practice of all fablers.[11] 'From

hence' detaches what is now on the way from what went before, and 'ye Beauties' tells us that what is on the way is addressed to women. Johnson, missing this transition, criticizes the moral in vain: for the gold in the last line is as distinct from the golden colour of the fishes as 'ye Beauties' is from cats. The fable, in which a cat snatched fatally at some beautiful fish, is now over, and we are left with the human counsel it has suggested, and suggested all the more vividly because behind it lurked, and at times almost obtruded, the feminine in its human form. The moral is the better for the literary form, the mock-heroic, of what precedes it. We can detach the last stanza from the cat and attach it more readily to 'ye Beauties' just because Helen has stood behind the cat throughout the poem, Helen who did not control her wandering eyes, who did take a false step, and who did have too much boldness—a moral quality that Gray is not for disallowing to women completely![12] Homer, we recall, did not condemn Helen.

Johnson's treatment of Gray's poem has often been thought an act of elephantine ineptitude, but not always an unsuccessful one. I have heard it credited with having broken a butterfly upon a wheel. To liken Gray's ode to a butterfly is to insult its strength and pungency; to liken Johnson's method of criticism to a wheel is more felicitous, but the wheel, on the present occasion, rolls round without grazing the integrity of Gray's little masterpiece.

Notes

[1] It is now in the possession of Lord Derby, and appears as plate 71 of Mr Randolph Churchill's *Fifteen Famous Houses,* 1954.

[2] By Gray's time *demure* had become a sort of Homeric epithet for a cat, whether male or female but more usually the latter. Bacon's essay 'Of Nature in Men' had referred to one of the Æsopian fables in the following terms: 'Like as it was with *Æsopes Damosell,* turned from a Catt to a Woman; who sate very demurely, at the Boards End, till a Mouse ranne before her.' L'Estrange retained the term when translating another of the cat fables (*Fables, of Æsop,* 1669, third ed., p. 287): 'they spy'd a *Cat* upon a Shelf; that lay and look'd . . . Demurely.' Dryden used the epithet in his reference to one of these fables (I quote from Johnson's Dictionary, s.v. *demure*):

So cat, transform'd, sat gravely and demure,
'Till mouse appear'd, and thought himself
  secure.

(Greatly strengthened by Gray's use of it, the epithet recurs in nineteenth-century descriptions of cats: see *Blackwood's Magazine,* Nov. 1846, and the opening of *Through the Looking Glass*).

[3] See above, p. 54.

[4] See above, p. 77.

[5] *Lives of the Poets,* iii. 442.

[6] id., iii. 434.

[7] id., iii. 434.

[8] The Greeks and Trojans.

[9] The brilliant description of the cat's face comes from Pope: 'fair round Face' occurs in his version of 'The Wife of Bath, her Prologue' (and has no source in Chaucer). The description amusingly overlaps with the description of Helen's face. A contribution to the definition of 'fair' in these contexts comes from James's *Portrait of a Lady,* ch. I, where we read that Mr Touchet has a face 'with evenly-distributed features'.

[10] See A. R. Humphreys, 'Lords of Tartary', *Cambridge Journal,* III (1949), i.

[11] It is worth noting that one of Æsop's fables (no. 61 in L'Estrange's translation) recounts how Venus changed a beloved cat into a woman for the greater pleasure of a young man who admired her.

[12] One of the phrases of the 'moral' may be intended to refer pointedly to a couplet in the English translation of Ovid's *Ars Amandi,* where the common phrase 'lawful prize' is given an amorous sense: 'But that a Mistress may be lawful Prize, / None, but her Keeper, I am sure, denies.' (*Ovid's Art of Love . . . By Several Eminent Hands,* 1709, p. 223.)

Morris Golden (essay date 1964)

SOURCE: "Classical or Romantic?," in *Thomas Gray,* Grosset & Dunlap, 1964, pp. 127–46.

[*In the following essay, which forms the concluding chapter of Golden's full-length study of Gray, Golden briefly outlines some of the characteristics of Neoclassical and Romantic literature and then discusses Gray's poetry and his place in English literary history in relation to both traditions.*]

This study has been primarily concerned with Gray and with the nature and quality of his poems rather than with his and their place in English literature. Among many other things, poetry is a response to intellectual, particularly to literary, climates in effect at a given time and place. Furthermore, if it is significant poetry, as T. S. Eliot has pointed out, it changes the way one looks at what preceded it—as an outgrowth of tendencies one might not have been aware

of—and it evidently affects what follows by becoming a part of literary tradition.

The most famous attempt to relate Gray to his period—that of the English poet and critic Matthew Arnold—is also the most foolish. Arnold's argument, in effect, is that Gray might have been a very great poet but was thwarted by his time: "Gray, a born poet, fell upon an age of prose. He fell upon an age whose task was such as to call forth in general men's powers of understanding, wit and cleverness, rather than their deepest powers of mind and soul. . . . Poetry obeyed the bent of mind requisite for the due fulfilment of this task of the century. It was intellectual, argumentative, ingenious; not seeing things in their truth and beauty, not interpretative. Gray, with the qualities of mind and soul of a genuine poet, was isolated in his century."[1]

One wonders what this means and one is perplexed how to apply it to the author of **"The Bard"** and the **"Elegy,"** to say nothing of the earlier odes and the Norse translations. It is easier, perhaps, to see in it the sadness of a very similar poet justifying to himself his lack of absolute greatness. The point may be valid for some artists of the eighteenth century: in a period when probing into the poet's own most complex responses was not expected of him, tendencies in that direction would be stunted and much energy might be wasted in attempting a social approach. Perhaps Oliver Goldsmith might have poured himself out more freely if he had not felt obligated to discuss agrarian economics in his best poem; certainly Johnson's "Vanity of Human Wishes" would have been a different poem at another time, though it seems sufficiently to call forth men's deepest powers of mind and soul.

But what objective students are likely to miss in Gray is the very passion that Arnold assumes him to have started with, and they miss it in his life as well as his poetry. If the contemporary intellectual climate affected him so strongly as Arnold says, the influence was wholly beneficial: taking Arnold's criteria, one might say that it allowed Gray to develop most fully a poetic impetus which was mild to begin with and that his tools were often "intellectual, argumentative, ingenious." In any event, Arnold's might-have-been argument, while superficially attractive, cannot be settled. If looked at long enough, it has no meaning—it proposes essentially that Gray would have been another poet if he had been another poet, an enigmatic truth in which one can only rest uneasily.

Gray is often called a transitional poet, the transition being from "Neoclassicism" to "Romanticism." George Sherburn, for example, writes that "He typifies the transitional poet who loved tradition yet courted novelty. He excelled his contemporaries in meticulous workmanship and in ability to use new material—medieval Welsh or Scandinavian—with dramatic imaginative power. He sought sublime moods, *sensations fortes,* and elevated even primitive materials to noble Roman or heroic levels." H. J. C. Grierson implies a similar condition of tentativeness: "Gray's taste was not satisfied with the poetry of his own day . . . his poetic instinct led him to cast both behind and before, while yet he had not the strength of inspiration or courage of temperament to be a rebel in more than a very tentative fashion; and so Gray's poetry is at once the perfect flower of our Augustan age and carries within it the seeds of the romantic revival."

Oliver Elton sees Gray as a stylistic innovator who took "all that appealed to him in the manner of Milton, and all that appealed to him in the manner of Dryden and Dryden's followers, and . . . blend [ed] it into something of his own. . . ."; again, Elton speaks of Gray's classical "passion for structure and finish; for proportion, economy, and unity." To these connections with tradition Bertrand Bronson adds that Gray loved "tradition*s*": "In whatever direction [Pindaric, Miltonic, Scandinavian, Celtic], he probed for the quintessential, delighting to *report*—to bring home—the special virtues of each kind."[2]

Since *classical* and *romantic* seem to be inescapable in discussions of eighteenth-century literature, one should see what useful meanings can be attached to these words for the purpose of placing Gray both within the niche that he deserves in poetry at large and within the context of the changing temper of his time. The literature of the late seventeenth century and of the first half of the eighteenth in England is known as Neoclassical ("new" Classical); that beginning with the publication of the *Lyrical Ballads* (1798), the joint venture of Wordsworth and Coleridge, is usually called Romantic. The former is given its name because the most conspicuous writers consciously admired and imitated what they conceived to be the virtues of the Greek and Roman periods; the latter, for a variety of reasons, perhaps the most immediate of which was that some of the writers chose subjects remote in time or place from the normal concerns of Englishmen, subjects reminiscent of knightly romances. Mid-eighteenth-century critics like Johnson and novelists like Henry Fielding and Samuel Richardson used the word "Romantic" to designate fanciful escapist fiction of no moral use; Coleridge, in his "Kubla Khan," gives "Romantic" the most attractive connotations.

Many forests have been despoiled to provide paper for defining the differences between the terms, and almost as many in hazarding definitions of the period from the middle to the end of the eighteenth century, that in which Gray wrote. "Preromantic," long in fashion, has now been abandoned on logical grounds, for, as the writers were not anticipating a new mode, they evidently did not think of themselves as "pre" anything. "Post-Augustan" (the early eighteenth century is often called the Augustan Age, after the high point of classical Roman literature) is now, with more reason, more in vogue.

What must first be agreed upon is in which of two main senses we are to use the terms "classical" and "romantic." Shall we have them refer to distinct movements in literature, so that we may label as Romantics the early nineteenth-century writers? They do seem to have some characteristics in common, dissimilar as they are in ideas, techniques, and intentions. Or shall we use the terms as referring to recurring casts of temperament, of which the movements may be special manifestations? To arrive at the orientation of Gray, it seems most useful to examine the general distinctions in orientation through their manifestation in the writers of the two contrasting periods. We shall need to enter a great many exceptions, but we shall at least have something specific to deal with.

Before we proceed to this examination, it must be understood that neither of these contrasting attitudes is ever found in its pure form in any great writer or indeed, without risk of madness, in any human being. They are always complementary as well as contrasting parts of the human mind, in the unending contrast and equilibrium produced by the search for freedom and the search for order.

The basic distinction between the terms "classical" and "romantic" as applied to temperament, it seems to me, is that between the two most clearcut views of man's underlying nature—of what Freud and his followers call the *id.* In the course of history, one attitude has been more emphasized at one time and the other at another: from the standpoint of English literary history, the division has been most clearly apparent in the literatures of the early eighteenth century and the early nineteenth century, very possibly as a consequence of the social conditions of the times. This seat of the passions and the imagination, by whatever terms it has been called, has always been recognized as the source of both creativity and mortal danger. And the chief issue separating the two temperaments is the relative emphasis on the creativity or the danger: the Classical attitude tends to fear the free imagination as a sign of madness and as the parent of anarchy; but the Romantic slights the risks for the sake of the riches. At no time are all the writers dominated by the current emphasis, and very rarely does any one writer (Blake is one of the few examples) carry either view to its logical conclusion. But there undoubtedly may be, as there was at each of the times specified, a general climate of attitudes collected around the approach to man's underlying nature.

For reasons stretching back at least to the Renaissance and the Reformation, and achieving great prominence in the ferment of scientific, religious, and political changes in the seventeenth century, a complex of ideas surrounding the need for restraint, order, and limitation became dominant late in that century. Such a Classical complex shows itself in literature through increasing suspicion of "fancy" and of the "passions." This fear of madness, of chaos, if the imagination is allowed complete freedom, is connected, both explicitly and implicitly, with a traditional Christian suspicion of the evils of passion and its source in original sin: the Yahoos in Swift's *Gulliver's Travels* and the dangerously lunatic narrator of his *Tale of a Tub* are the embodiment of this view. The greatest writers, being then—as ever—sensitive to the complexity of life, did not exclude one side of this basic nature of man: Swift, in the same *Gulliver's Travels,* suggests that the exclusive worship of reason (in the land of the horses) is itself a form of mad excess. Pope, in the *Essay on Man,* tries to make a synthesis of reason and passion, has a sad respect for the power of what he calls the "ruling passion," and insists that reason without passion is sterile.

In contrast to the Classical insistence on restraint, Romanticism emanates from a complex of ideas involving freedom of the imagination and the passions; and it is perhaps most completely advocated in the tradition that includes Jean Jacques Rousseau, William Blake, Walt Whitman, and D. H. Lawrence. Though with many exceptions, Romanticism basically assumes that man's nature is good at bottom but has been corrupted by society and thwarted in its development by sterile reason. Again, most Romantics imply that this freedom is to be limited by a "natural" goodness and reason which will prevent, say, the shocking expression of the side of man's nature shown most recently in the Congo, in Algeria, and in Mississippi.

The Classical temper tends to be highly conservative and suspicious of innovations, which it regards as expressing a perverse self-importance that refuses to make the best of the world as it exists. For example, one may cite Swift's *Tale of a Tub* and, in a mass of writings tending toward the same end, his attacks on science and progress in Book III of *Gulliver's Travels.* Hence Neoclassicism in literature advocates a conservative adherence to traditional forms, styles, and subjects. But one may note, as the inevitable counterpoint in the works of individual writers on different subjects, Dryden's great interest in and respect for scientific progress; Pope's reverence for Newton; and Thomson's delight in both science and the spread of com-merce, a delight shared by the super-classical Addison. And Johnson, the last and in some ways the most doctrinaire of the great Neoclassicists, was fascinated by scientific experimentation, as was his similarly Neoclassical contemporary Benjamin Franklin. For most of these, however, the pleasure in science lies in its utility and not in its discovery of abstract knowledge.

The Romantic attitude, by contrast, delights in innovation since experimentation with new forms is necessary to suit new individual feelings. Blake, Wordsworth, Whitman, and Lawrence are most aware of themselves as explorers, though at times they may argue that they are merely rediscovering the past which their immediate predecessors have hidden. However, the social applications are again diverse and unpredictable: Shelley devoted himself to social and scientific experiment and innovation; Byron urged drastic social change; and Blake was an extreme revolutionary who sang democratic self-fulfillment. But Wordsworth and Coleridge, who began as social changers, ended as traditionalists; Keats, though a humanitarian and a democrat in his letters, offers no political or social doctrine in his poetry; and Carlyle and his host of followers into the present day seek the most determined sort of social regression.

The Neoclassicists of the eighteenth century almost unanimously insisted that literature must be morally instructive, an attitude which had for them the corollary that it must deal with the typical, the general, from which the most can be learned by the mass of mankind. Yet Johnson, who advised poets in his *Rasselas* not to count the stripes of the tulip but to deal with the general significance of tulipness—the condensed essence of this view—wanted Boswell to fill a biography with details, no matter how minor, since there is nothing too little for so little a being as man.

The Romantic attitude, as expressed by the writers of the nineteenth century, is likely to insist on the specific, the individual. This argument was also based on an ethical view, for the Romantics were convinced that truth lay in details; a generalization about all mankind is true of no one man, but an exact analysis of the state of one soul will tell us things that must be true of others. William Blake, reading the *Discourses* on art of the Classical Joshua Reynolds, wrote in the margin of a passage on the need for generalizing: "To Generalize is to be an Idiot. To Particularize is the Alone Distinction of Merit. General Knowledges are those Knowledges that Idiots possess."[3] In this statement, by the way, is the core of the difference in technique—localized in discussions of diction but also related to subject matter—which has caused most critics since Wordsworth to complain of the inferiority of eighteenth-century poetry. For example, it contributes to Arnold's analysis of the prosaic nature of the period. This basically Romantic theory is that, while prose is suitable for general statements, poetry must be specific to be true.

As a consequence of the concern for the typical and the general, the Neoclassical view leads to a legalistic humanitarianism, manifested most emphatically in the American Declaration of Independence. The bases for this view go back as far as the sources of all the major

Western religions, from the paganism of Greece and Rome through Judaism through Christianity, all of which insist that all men begin as equals before God. This tradition is reinforced in the eighteenth century by the dominance of the epistemology of John Locke, which is predicated on the equality at birth of all people who are born with their bodily organs and minds intact. It is further reinforced by a variety of ideas derived from the classics and was most effectively propagandized by the third Earl of Shaftesbury as a system of harmonies in which that person is best acclimated to the universe who is best attuned to the feelings of others. In this view, the fortunate, to be in harmony with the world's order, should reach out of themselves to see that the unfortunate have souls similar to their own and suffer as much as the fortunate would in the same circumstances. Perhaps the Man in Black in Goldsmith's *Citizen of the World* and Squire Allworthy in Fielding's *Tom Jones* most conspicuously embody this view of virtue. Since the necessary fellow-feeling must cause men to be pained by the pain of others, the theory goes, if they have their own interests at heart they will try to cure the pain of others.

As a result, England in the eighteenth century is notable for a widespread concern for charity of all sorts (including, for example, subscriptions to aid captured enemy soldiers in the Seven Years' War with France) and for improved treatment of beggars, "fallen women," prisoners, the very poor—in general, for all those who might have been the victims of society. At the same time, some of the most conspicuous Neoclassicists (such as Dryden, Pope, Swift, and Johnson) insisted on political subordination on the ground that only if everyone has his place can order be maintained—always a powerful rational response to the equally rational argument that all men were created equal.

The Romantic view, again to the contrary, tends to be that every man is unique and must be sensed and judged as an individual. Such a view inevitably leads to powerful emotional assertions both for and against liberty, equality, and fraternity. Blake is intuitively certain that every man—indeed, every bird—is a whole limitless world, and hence every man is sacred. Carlyle feels equally sure that greatness is an essence which bestows special privileges on its possessor, while no one need concern himself about inferior people.

Eighteenth-century Neoclassicism often relies for its theorizing on material existence, on "reality." As Ricardo Quintana has most concisely shown, both Swift's *Tale of a Tub* and his *Gulliver's Travels* aim to prove to the average deluded person that he continually invents something different from what is before him and calls his invention the world; the consequence is that he corrupts and ruins whatever he deals with.[4] Johnson, told that one cannot refute Bishop Berkeley's argument

that the world we seem to sense does not exist, kicks a stone so hard that he rebounds and says, "I refute it *thus*." At the same time, the Neoclassicists assume the existence of an ideal world, usually Christian. To the Romantic temperament—aware though it may be of the dirty socks of Swift's poem about college students—true reality is available in exalted states, transcendental experiences, which are summed up variously in the visions of Blake, or in the sensuous dream world of Keats, or in the ecstasies of love and revolution and damnation of Byron, or in Pater's insistence on burning through life with a hard, gemlike flame, or in Coleridge's parable about sin and redemption in the *Rime of the Ancient Mariner,* or in the exultation and destruction of Moby Dick's pursuer, Captain Ahab.

Neoclassical subject matter is likely to be social—man in relation to man—and to be concerned with practical ethics: Pope's *Essay on Man,* or Johnson's *Rambler* papers, or Addison and Steele's *Spectator,* or Defoe's *Moll Flanders,* or Samuel Richardson's *Clarissa.* The novel, which as Lionel Trilling has so brilliantly shown is the most inevitably social of all literary forms, reaches its first great peak in the eighteenth century. Such literature can be called "objective," in the sense that the writer is primarily concerned with standing off and examining the relations among men. While there may be an "I" in the novel or poem, this self is likely to be the public personality of the writer, usually revealing aspects of himself that are either neutral or creditable: Pope in his "Epistle to Dr. Arbuthnot," Gay in his *Town Eclogues,* Fielding in his novels. Though the finest works of the period, like *Gulliver's Travels* or "The Rape of the Lock" or *Tom Jones* or *Clarissa,* reveal a plentiful awareness by their authors that tendencies toward perversity exist everywhere, even in themselves, this revelation is usually by implication rather than direct statement. Romanticism, on the other hand, has frequently been called subjective. To Blake the world is how he imagines it; Wordsworth, in *The Prelude* particularly, painstakingly analyzes his own growth, omitting only what might be privately shameful; Rousseau, in his *Confessions,* tells all, perhaps even inventing shameful data. Romanticism is then often subjective in a double sense; it tends to use the author's experience as material and to see the world primarily in relation to the author's sensations.

Neoclassical subject matter is also likely to be adapted to a relatively stylized use of older literary patterns: nature poetry, for example, is often based on Virgil's *Georgics* or on a pastoral tradition stretching back to the Greek poet Theocritus. Appropriate subjects are developed in meters and forms that follow ancient elegies, epics, and odes. Satires are justified by and patterned on ancient examples; some of the most famous of the period are direct imitations—or allusions, since the author assumes the reader's familiarity with the originals and challenges comparison with them—

as for example Pope's direct use of Horace and Johnson's use of Juvenal. Satire is a particularly congenial form for the cast of temper most dominant in this period, since its rational approach most clearly and instructively shows the difference between what is and what should be. As a consequence, no greater satire exists in English than the works of Dryden, Swift, Pope, Johnson, and Fielding. On the whole, there is a strong feeling about what does and does not belong in certain kinds of poetry: the view prevails that there are genres which it is appropriate to use for the expression of the different emotions or for dealing with different subjects.

The Romantics respond, generally, that the subject matter of poetry is unlimited, that anything can legitimately be treated in any form. Of course, being practicing artists, the Romantics did not carry this view to extremes—anyone who deals with words is aware that he must fuse form and content, and that he therefore must vary form with content. However, the Romantic felt himself much freer to invent the form for the individual statement, or to let it evolve from the artistic conception. Coleridge, the greatest of English Romantic critics, most effectively developed this conception of organic form:

> No work of true genius dares want its appropriate form, neither indeed is there any danger of this. As it must not, so genius can not, be lawless; for it is even this that constitutes its genius—the power of acting creatively under laws of its own origination. . . . The form is mechanic, when on any given material we impress a predetermined form, not necessarily arising out of the properties of the material;—as when to a mass of wet clay we give whatever shape we wish it to retain when hardened. The organic form, on the other hand, is innate; it shapes, as it develops, itself from within, and the fullness of its development is one and the same with the perfection of its outward form. Such as the life is, such is the form.[5]

In developing this theory of literary form, Coleridge was responding to the philosophical view—recently seen as the very source of nineteenth-century Romanticism[6]—that the world itself was in a state of organic becoming; it was not the static machine that previous ages had thought it.

Among the interests usually said to distinguish the Romantics from their predecessors was the concentration by some poets on the special qualities of peasants, of commoners generally, and by others on imagined and distant places and things. The two authors of the *Lyrical Ballads* neatly divided these subjects between themselves: Wordsworth was to treat ordinary lives so as to show their extraordinary aspects and Coleridge was to bring extraordinary events into contact with our ordinary lives. A new interest in nature is also commonly ascribed to the Romantics. But while the in-

creased emphases are beyond question, the reader should be cautious in assuming that there was a sharp cleavage in subject matter. Swift, Gay, and Thomson, in the heart of Neoclassicism, dealt perhaps too exactly with the lives of ordinary men in poetry, and the novelists did so in prose, as did the playwrights. The eighteenth century also provides a good many examples of attempts to exploit the exotic: in the Celtic revival lurking through the century and appearing prominently from **"The Bard"** onward; in the cult of the Chinese and Oriental in general which derived from the mercantile contact with the East and from the translation of the *Arabian Nights;* and in the aesthetic of the sublime. The "Oriental Tale," for example, became a recognized genre, or rather a whole group of recognized genres. And there are quite a few fine nature poems, beginning with Denham's famous "Cooper's Hill" in the late seventeenth century and featuring Pope's "Windsor Forest" and his eclogues—to say nothing of the *Seasons* of Thomson (written in the 1720's, the height of the Neoclassical period, though often cited as "pre-Romantic" in its minute examination of nature).

Finally, Neoclassical writing, as a consequence of its insistence on the general and the morally useful, is likely to be more discursive than that of the Romantics and to use elaborate personifications rather than consciously developed and structurally dominant symbols. Again, this distinction cannot be absolute, since all art involves significance; and significance inevitably entails symbolism. One may cite, for example, Swift's "Modest Proposal," in which the inhuman exploitation of the Irish is symbolized in a plan for their rulers to eat Irish babies; or Pope's "Rape of the Lock," in which the lock itself becomes the symbol of a way of life. Such basically symbolic undercurrents as the subject—the childhood idyll as against adult evil—of the "Deserted Village"; or such conscious symbols as the pyramids of *Rasselas* or the girdle in William Collins's "Ode on the Poetical Character" are other examples.

The Romantics, on the whole, have a stronger—and poetically more appealing—tendency to represent a perception in a fresh symbol rather than to personify or discuss it, to avoid the prose linkages (to borrow T. S. Eliot's idea), and to concentrate on the poetic stuff of metaphor. They tend to a greater exploitation of both the conscious and unconscious symbols which reach into the human psyche and expand there, as in Blake's tiger or Shelley's west wind or the terrain of Coleridge's Xanadu. Coleridge's "Kubla Khan," for example, is a poem about the creative power of the imagination; but instead of using the word "imagination," he pictures its action as follows:

> A damsel with a dulcimer
> In a vision once I saw:
> It was an Abyssinian maid,
> And on her dulcimer she played,

Singing of Mount Abora.
Could I revive within me
Her symphony and song,
To such a deep delight 'twould win me,
That with music loud and long,
I would build that dome in air,
That sunny dome! those caves of ice!

Goldsmith, in "The Deserted Village," also sees the poetic imagination as a girl. But he is far more explicit and therefore, despite the tenderness and clarity of the diction, far more limited in the responses which he evokes:

And thou, sweet Poetry, thou loveliest maid,
Still first to fly where sensual joys invade;
Unfit, in these degenerate times of shame,
To catch the heart, or strike for honest fame;
Dear, charming nymph, neglected and decried,
My shame in crowds, my solitary pride;
Thou source of all my bliss, and all my woe,
That found'st me poor at first, and keep'st me so;
Thou guide by which the nobler arts excel,
Thou nurse of every virtue, fare thee well!

On the basis of these various criteria, we may try to see where Gray belongs by temperament and historical classification. Like everyone, he had tendencies in both directions; and, like the Victorian Matthew Arnold, he lived in a time that lay socially and intellectually between two worlds, one dying, the other struggling to be born. His advantage is often that he can set himself firmly in the traditions of the past and yet attempt to explore avenues for the future.

In respect to the first and basic division between complexes of ideas, for example, Gray seems to live in the best of both worlds. He is wedded to the ideas of order and regularity, as is evidenced by his extraordinary care as a craftsman, his elaborate and successful reliance on the most confining meters and metrical devices. At the same time he constantly strives, particularly in the two Pindaric Odes, to stretch the substance and appeal of his work beyond reason: he insists that the highest poetry, lyric poetry, demands a kind of demonic possession of the poet which communicates its transports to the reader, and he steadily exalts "fancy" or imagination at the expense of bare reason. He sees as a real misfortune his lack of the basic gusto—the deep involvement in human life—of those writers, like Shakespeare and Milton, whom he most admires. He yearns for the intensity and freedom with which to pour himself completely into living.

But this misfortune, which is also the underlying subject of much that he wrote, has its advantages. Arnold's pity for Gray as one whose poetic nature is limited and thwarted by the dullness of his time is completely misplaced (it might much better be said of Thomson, if it can be said at all). Gray, on the contrary, is immensely aided by his era's reliance on order; he better than anyone else was able to make use of it in stretching his relatively thin and sporadic inspiration to its utmost.

In the earlier works, through the **"Elegy,"** his achievement lay in infusing life into a number of traditional forms through an exquisite delicacy of ear, superb metrical craftsmanship, command over diction and picture, and an ability to feel in each conception something with a shape adaptable to his own deepest predilections. Each of his completed and published poems is in a form at least slightly different from every other one, for he persists in experimentation. In every attempt, he uses a form sanctioned by tradition—though his Scandinavian and Celtic experiments follow a tradition foreign and shocking to some of his Neoclassical readers; he sees what it can yield him; and then he tries another innovation.

Gray's genius is not in inventing the completely new (though one wonders which of the great poets, aside from Blake in his artistically monstrous prophetic books, invented where there was nothing in the past to work with). Rather, Gray brings some traditions to a perfection of concentration and purity, as in the Eton College ode and in the **"Elegy."** To other traditions, as in the Pindaric Odes, he restores a wholeness of life of which purely formal imitators had lost sight. By fusing wilder strains from the Gothic into the orderly Greek patterns, he brings a sense of the complementary elements of life to forms that had become petrified in mere rhetorical exercises. He is, therefore, at the summit of a development from the past in **"The Bard,"** not an innovator in form or subject. But, by his inclusion of material which had not previously been seen as appropriate to this development, he opened paths for further exploration.

On the question of the distinction between the general and the particular, Gray is solidly Classical in theory and practice. He is purely Classical in his belief that art should be concerned with what Plato called the ideal world of being and not with the material and shifting world of becoming. All of his work—including the change in the ending of the **"Elegy"**—aims to remove himself as a special case from the poem and to substitute a generalized personality, partaking of idealized qualities of his own, who can speak for one side of mankind. This intention is most apparent in the difference between his Latin passage on the death of West in his **"De Principiis Cogitandi"** and his English sonnet on the same subject, but it also appears in everything else that he wrote, notably in the **"Elegy"** and in the Pindaric Odes. In **"The Progress of Poesy,"** for example, Shakespeare, Milton, Dryden, and Gray are themselves and, more importantly, also types of imaginative poets. Anything which seems idiosyncratic is made a symptom of the general: Milton's blindness is not a personal misfortune but an illustration of the brilliance with which the light of truth and beauty, of God, strikes a mortal observer's eye. In **"The Bard"** the historical events prophesied are to be seen as the variegated horrors that attend the consequences of tyranny, not as the specific destinies of Edward I's posterity; and the symbolic suicide at the end is the disdain of the bard for the materialistic tyrant.

Gray's language, as has been pointed out, is designed to achieve the maximum of generalization combined with a maximum of musical and spectacular evocation—an aim which leads to a compression and novelty objectionable to such Neoclassical critics as Johnson and at the same time to a difference from ordinary speech objectionable to a Romantic critic like Wordsworth. The diction changes, as Gosse and others have observed, from the relatively standardized though precise and haunting personifications of Gray's youth—best shown in the Eton College ode and in the **"Elegy"**—to the more specific, fresh, and realistic phrasing of the Scandinavian translations. The Pindaric Odes, at a stage in between, offer the splendor of the earlier work with a minimum of its abstractness. In this respect, as in others, one can see a turning point in Gray's career separating the **"Elegy,"** which can fairly be called the highest expression of Gray as the traditionalist working only with elements sanctioned by the past, from the Pindaric Odes, in which he introduces added substance to the tradition.

Gray uses the ideal for moral reasons, or at least can justify it that way on the ground that it makes little useful difference to the world whether one young man is unsure how to spend his life (as for example in the **"Ode on the Spring"**) while the state of unsure, sensitive youthfulness is very much worth portraying. However, he is far less interested in the moral uses of poetry than are the theorists of his time. He once wrote to West that the phrase "didactic poetry" might well be a logical contradiction; and, though his writings are full of reflections on man's nature, they do not have didactic aims. The **"Ode on the Spring"** does not pretend to teach how man is to spend his life; rather it presents the dilemma of youth faced by life's apparent meaninglessness. The Eton ode offers no solution but that of the **"Hymn to Adversity"**—sympathy for others—again with the emphasis on picturing the state rather than on solving its problem with a moral imperative. The **"Elegy"** lays down no rules for facing death but instead reveals the narrator's response to modes of living and dying; and it ends with an epitaph to one who was overcome by contemplating the theme.

Paradoxically, the more "Romantic" Pindaric Odes seem to offer didactic statements. The first and more didactic has been condemned by the very advocates of didacticism; the second has been far more successful precisely because it presents the argument dramatically and spectacularly instead of asserting it directly. When one compares **"The Bard"** with Johnson's "Vanity of Human Wishes"—surely the best traditionally Neoclassical poem since Pope—one notes Johnson's vigorous insistence on the title theme at every point and on his detailed program at the end for achieving peace. Gray's concern is always for the picture, the visual symbol—as is the case with the Romantics. He is likely, however, particularly in the earlier poems, to reflect discursively in the older manner; or perhaps he can be said to conceive of poetry (before **"The Bard"**) as a representation of states of the soul through a mixture of image and thought.

Politically and socially, Gray shares the humanitarianism of his day, but it is complicated for him by two conflicting tendencies. On the one hand, his fastidiousness makes him feel set off from the world: he is either above it, as he says at times; or he is below it, as Roger Martin persuasively argues. More likely this fastidiousness is a result of an ambiguous compound of the two: he condemns the self that he cherishes for fearfulness and praises if for sensitivity. On the other hand, he is subject to a yearning for fellow-feeling which he manages to infuse into his best earlier work, notably in the Eton ode and in the **"Elegy."** The Pindaric Odes again exhibit a kind of Romantic apartness of the Bard as leader and savior of mankind that is anticipatory of Burns, Coleridge, and Shelley. In these later poems also, as well as in his translations, Gray shares the Romantic view (derived at least partly from the idea of the sublime, which is comprised in the Neoclassical aesthetic) that reality—that suitable for poetry—is to be seen in the highest transports of the imagination. Characteristically, Gray finds his justification in a poet of the past, Pindar, whom he strives in vain to emulate in this respect.

As has been suggested, Gray is fully settled in the poetic traditions; in fact, he outdoes his contemporaries in his concern for maintaining the proper genres. Along with the odes of William Collins, Gray's are the only important "regular" Pindarics, as against the laxer form popular before him. His satires and fragment of a didactic poem are in the obligatory heroic couplet; his fragment of a tragedy, in dutiful blank verse; his shorter odes, in forms clearly reminiscent of Horace and other ancients; and his **"Elegy,"** in the stanza agreed on as appropriate for melancholy reflections and in a meter sanctioned by the practice of Tibullus. At the same time that genres seem only reasonable to him (and to a certain extent, as has been said, they have seemed that way even to most Romantic poets—Shelley's elegy on Keats is not written in the ballad stanza, nor is Wordsworth's *Prelude*), Gray objects to rigidity in adherence to them, or indeed to any rules of criticism. While Gray does not go so far afield as the great Romantics in seeking variations in verse forms, his incorporation of Scandinavian and Welsh rhythms into the English tradition is as experimental as Byron's borrowing of Italian forms or as Coleridge's using the ballad stanza for serious purposes.

Gray's subject matter is largely limited in the earlier poems to literary sources, and the scenery is often borrowed from the classics rather than from his countryside. Even in **"The Bard"** the pictures are influenced by Italian Renaissance painting. At least in those works written and completed for the few whom he considered competent judges, he relies heavily on topics deriving from traditional practice. His imagination is tied to elevated, distinctively "poetic" pictures; though in the **"Elegy"** he achieves a distillation of ordinary life with sure touches, most of them have literary antecedents. He is not enough interested in other people generally to care about the details of their lives, as Wordsworth cares self-consciously and Byron naturally.

But Gray is fascinated by other modes of living, the more exotic the better. As W. Powell Jones has shown, Gray's reading interests were about evenly divided between history and travel books. When he finds a mode that means something in his search for a way out of the bounds of reason and gentility, a way to perceive and express the powerful and irrational urges that he shares with mankind, he seizes on it and incorporates it, no matter how violent: hence the gory primitive chants and tales that he translated so effectively. The test of poetic subject matter for Gray is always its degree of relevance to the pictures and music with which he wants to communicate the ideal.

Finally, though Gray does not explore the details of himself for poetic material, in the way that a Shelley, Rousseau, or Whitman can do, and though he insists that a screen between his unique self and the reader is necessary both for propriety and for the essential poetic idealization, in his work a recognizable human voice calls out to its brothers. If this decorous objectivity is the sign of the Classicist—and I am not at all sure that it is—then Gray combines with it an insistent assertion of his underlying emotional state. Such an assertion, in its combination of diffidence and pride, fear of life and bravery in seeking beyond the limits of the known, concern for the self stretching out to concern for the identical aspects of mankind, would seem, by contrast, Romantic.

Rather than say, with Arnold, that Gray was essentially a poet who was doomed to prose by a prosaic age, it seems evident that Gray is the perfect spokesman for a poetic age which is unclear in its position on the great and recurrent human problems—and notably about those dealing with the relations between the rational and the non-rational. Aware of this deficiency both in his time and in himself, Gray is better able than any one of his English contemporaries to work from a firm basis in the rational into an exploration of the irrational. From a peak of the Classical, he opens vistas for Romanticism.

Such a position inevitably entails an effect on his successors. Aside from his immense contemporary vogue, which filled magazines in the British Isles and America with elegies and Pindaric odes, his lasting influence on English literature and on our cultural heritage as readers of English has been pervasive. He inaugurated the Celtic revival, which in turn strongly reinforced the bardic ideal—the ideal of the poet as prophet and patriot—which is so important to Shelley, Byron, Keats, Whitman, and Yeats. His is an eloquent voice speaking for the freeing of the imagination; and though the Romantics decried his diction, they paid him the compliment, sometimes unconscious, of imitation. Wordsworth professedly wrote his "Ode to Duty" in the form of Gray's **"Hymn to Adversity."** Shelley's "To a Skylark" echoes Gray's unfinished (but posthumously printed) ode to vicissitude in its central image. One catches other indications of influence in casual lines and passages. Shelley's Prometheus is told, in a line borrowed from **"The Bard,"** that "Past ages crowd on thee" (*Prometheus Unbound,* I, 561); Byron's famous description of the gaiety in Brussels on the eve of Waterloo seems to expand the feeling of the passage on Richard II's reign in **"The Bard"**; in *Purple Dust* (1940) Sean O'Casey names a couple of tradition-bound Englishmen Stoke and Poges, alluding to the famous setting of the **"Elegy."** But the citation of specific examples of influence means little with a poet like Gray; his poetry has become part of all of us, readers and writers alike.

Gray's achievement was great, despite his obvious deficiencies—the lack of deeply passional involvement, of the emotional variety and intensity characteristic of the greatest masters. As compensation, he offers the most responsible sense of craftsmanship in English poetry—a sense which requires of him both perfection of finish and persistent experimentation. Though he wrote relatively little, that little included some of the most finished classical odes in the language; one of the finest reflective poems that we have, and surely the most beloved; Pindaric Odes of a unique splendor; and the first exploration, in beautifully polished work, of a rich vein of poetry which has yielded treasures to others as well. If this is all that can be said for masterly craftsmanship, it is a great deal.

Notes

[1] Matthew Arnold, *Essays in Criticism,* Second Series (London, 1889), pp. 91-92.

[2] George Sherburn, "The Restoration and Eighteenth Century," in Albert C. Baugh, *A Literary History of England* (New York, 1948), p. 1013; Grierson, *Background of English Literature,* p. 203; Elton, *Survey,*

II, 74; Bertrand H. Bronson, "The Pre-Romantic or Post-Augustan Mode," *ELH,* XX (1953), 22.

[3] Quoted in W. K. Wimsatt, Jr., *The Verbal Icon* (New York, 1958), p. 73.

[4] Ricardo Quintana, *The Mind and Art of Jonathan Swift* (London, 1936), *passim,* esp. p. 65.

[5] Quoted in F. O. Matthiesen, *American Renaissance* (New York, 1946), pp. 133-34.

[6] For an excellent discussion of this viewpoint and its proponents see Morse Peckham, "Toward a Theory of Romanticism," *Publications of the Modern Language Association,* LXVI (1951), 5-23.

Foerster on the modernity of Gray's "The Bard":

. . . **"The Bard"** must have seemed . . . perplexing in a time when such strange themes and such strange ways of handling those themes were the exception rather that the rule. For in the year of **"The Bard"** the primitivist movement was just beginning; only among a handful of Scotch historians and poets were there as yet any lively discussions about ancient poetry and its highly emotional character, about the rhapsodists and bards and the oral transmission of their verses. Nor had many poets attempted to reproduce the enthusiasm and wildness of primitive song. In fact the reading public and even the critics and scholars were still in the habit of regarding an early poet like Homer as one of their contemporaries. It was not until 1760 and after, with the appearance of the Ossianic poems and the many books on original genius, the history of man, and the rise and development of poetry, that the average person was able at all to see what Gray "would be at."

"The Bard" was therefore one of the first modern "primitive poems."

Donald M. Foerster, The Age of Johnson: Essays Presented to Chauncey Brewster Tinker, *Yale University Press, 1949.*

Patricia Meyer Spacks (essay date 1965)

SOURCE: "Statement and Artifice in Thomas Gray," in *Studies in English Literature: 1500-1900,* Vol. V, No. 3, Summer, 1965, pp. 519-32.

[*In the following essay, Spacks analyzes the language of "Ode on the Spring," "Sonnet on the Death of Mr. West," and "Ode on a Distant Prospect of Eton College," focusing on Gray's use of alternating rhetorical patterns.*]

The man of whom Adam Smith wrote, "[he] joins to the sublimity of Milton the elegance and harmony of Pope, and . . . nothing is wanting to render him, perhaps, the first poet in the English language, but to have written a little more," has been dismissed by Dr. Leavis, relegated by Donald Davie to the limbo reserved for those whose diction is impure, and attacked by A. R. Humphreys for embodying the worst poetic evils of his day. Time has not on the whole been kind to Thomas Gray.

One reason for modern dissatisfaction with the poet is the insistent artifice of his diction, its extremity suggested by his own famous pronouncement that "the language of the age is never the language of poetry." Wordsworth and Coleridge were among the first to disapprove. Although they disagreed about which details were farthest removed from true poetry, both used Gray's sonnet to exemplify all those eighteenth-century poems which consist merely of "translations of prose thoughts into poetic language."[1] Gray believed that "sense is nothing in poetry, but according to the dress she wears, & the scene she appears in."[2] Most modern commentators, following Wordsworth and Coleridge, have thought his muse rather overdressed, seeing in his poetry all the vices of eighteenth-century poetic diction without perceiving that he exemplifies the possibilities of that diction equally well. In 1963, however, F. Doherty provided a new approach. Examining Gray's language in some detail, he concluded that the poet's productions are of two kinds: those dominated by his "public," highly rhetorical "voice," and those in which his "real voice" is discernible.[3] The latter category includes most of the poems which seem relatively acceptable (in comparison with, for instance, Gray's long "Pindaric" odes) to the modern reader.

Mr. Doherty's analyses of individual passages are highly perceptive, but his examination of Gray raises further questions when one realizes how often the poems which he describes as manifesting the poet's "real voice" make use of a diction as contrived as that of the more formal pieces. Some of the poems written in 1742, usually taken as fairly direct expressions of personal emotion, demonstrate not only the artifice in technique in even Gray's most "sincere" poetic statement, but the way in which various sorts of artifice may be deliberately played off against one another. In the **"Ode on the Spring," "Ode on a Distant Prospect of Eton College,"** and **"Sonnet on the Death of Richard West,"** the poet has exploited structural patterns of alternation, passages of direct statement paired with those of highly artificial and indirect suggestion. The combination of a diction which deliberately conceals with a more personal mode of expression is largely responsible for the impact of these poems.

The **"Ode on the Spring"** is the most clearly "Augustan" of the 1742 group. Twenty-five years ago A. R. Humphreys summed up economically the objections that can be made to it: "It is impossible to accept, say, the **'Ode on the Spring'** seriously. It has a baroque charm; its warmth of colour, decorative personification, and playful solemnity give it individuality, though hardly perhaps of a different sort than if it were a scene painted on an opulent ceiling."[4] Its weaknesses, as defined by Professor Humphreys, are that it is imitative, pedantic, full of "classical pretence" and "anthropomorphic banality." It is clumsy, with "disconcerting hesitations of tone"; and it is totally lacking in personal observation.

Most of these objections are valid enough; yet the poem creates its highly individual effect through its *exploitation* of "classical pretence," its deliberate avoidance of personal observation, in conjunction with its ironic self-revelation. The poem's diction and its "pedantry" are alike most elaborate in the opening stanza, where conventional classical references jostle one another. We are offered Venus and the "rosy-bosom'd Hours," the "Attic warbler," "Cool Zephyrs": the classical paraphernalia of a sort of "nature poetry" which has little to do with nature. The effect of the stanza is to lead the reader's eye *away* from the object: "long-expecting flowers" insists on the flowers' role in the pattern of nature, removing stress from their appearance; "purple spring," as Geoffrey Tillotson has pointed out, refers not at all to the actual look of an English spring; even the lovely line, "The untaught harmony of spring," about the birds' songs, generalizes rather than describes. One may possibly extract from all this such a scene as is painted on ceilings, but only with effort. The stanza is not really pictorial. It evokes an atmosphere rather than a picture, a delicate, unrealistic, faintly mythological atmosphere, quite remote from actuality.

At the beginning of the second stanza, however, there is a shift in language: this sounds more convincingly like the poet's "real voice." The description now is visual as well as "atmospheric"; it sketches a scene with more specificity, more solidity, than that suggested by the poem's opening lines. The scene is, however, hardly less literary in its origins than the panorama which preceded it. The one specific allusion Gray's note here points out is to a native rather than a Latin source: Shakespeare now instead of Virgil. The specific allusion is to *A Midsummer Night's Dream,* but the scene of poet in rural landscape, as well as the reflections the setting immediately inspires, remind us readily too of Jacques in *As You Like It,* The description seems also to foretell that of the rural poet in the **"Elegy Written in a Country Churchyard"**:

> There at the foot of yonder nodding beech
> That wreathes its old fantastic roots so high,
> His listless length at noontide would he stretch,
> And pore upon the brook that babbles by.

Both portraits derive indirectly and generally from a more ancient tradition: that of the poet as a figure in pastoral, the swain as poetic orderer of his own experience, in harmony with the world of nature he inhabits.

The language of the second stanza is more concrete and direct than that of the first, its images more specific (the "broader, browner shade" of the oak versus "long-expecting flowers"; water with a "rushy brink" as opposed to the vague and evanescent "Cool Zephyrs"), its literary references less exclusively classical. Its tone also demonstrates a radical shift. Metaphorically as well as literally, the first stanza deals with "the clear blue sky." Its tone is elevated; the presentation implies by its concentration on aesthetic pleasure an optimistic view of the natural universe and of man's relation to it. The environment of the second stanza, on the other hand, is a "broader, browner shade." If the first stanza floats away into the heavens, the second remains very much tied to earth; the reflections of the poet who inhabits this landscape are accordingly melancholy:

> How vain the ardour of the Crowd,
> How low, how little are the Proud,
> How indigent the Great!

This is, however, a very easy sort of melancholy, as automatic a response as the optimism which the introductory mythologizing might produce. The reason for its automatic quality is immediately apparent in its source: Gray seems at pains to point out that these ideas about the world are the immediate product of poetic artifice.

> Beside some water's rushy brink
> With me the Muse shall sit, and think
> (At ease reclin'd in rustic state),
> How vain . . .

To stress the presence of the Muse in this setting is to emphasize the deliberate artificiality of the presentation as a whole; the description insists on the actual physical existence of the Muse as well as the poet in the landscape by dwelling on her posture ("At ease reclin'd") and hinting, through the oxymoron of "rustic state," the faintly humorous overtones implicit in the literal presence of this mythological figure in the concrete English setting. She reminds us that these particular lines about the futility of worldly endeavor have little to do with the *nature* of worldly endeavor. Their source is poetic convention; they represent an attitude rather than a perception.

The succeeding two stanzas continue the pattern of alternation between different modes of poetic artifice and the attitudes associated with them. In the third stanza the images, less emphatically classical (although there is a specific echo of Virgil here), remain conventionally "poetic" and once more stress physical elevation ("The insect youth are on the wing") and the emotional elevation associated with it. The fourth stanza, more closely connected with the preceding one than the second is with the first, shifts, like the second, to a melancholy perspective and an emphasis on earth rather than air ("their airy dance / They leave, in dust to rest"). Its subject matter and point of view, however, are clearly as contrived and as arbitrary as the earlier concern with the way "The busy murmur glows!"

The importance of the insistent artifice with which the poet presents his reflections, artifice emphasized by the alternations of mood, theme, reference, emerges fully only in the concluding stanza, where the speaker for the first time considers himself not as poet but as man. Until now, the ode has both presented and implied an image of its speaker as poetic contriver, and reminded us, by the nature of the language itself and by Gray's footnotes, how much the poem consists of contrivance. But at the end the artificial, decorative metaphor of insects which has been manipulated through two stanzas turns on itself and its creator, becoming suddenly strangely real. Artifice has controlled the poem, kept us from taking its insights very seriously; now that artifice reveals something extremely serious about the poet as human being. The conventional "poetic" assertion that insects are like people leads to the forcible realization that people may be like insects—and judging himself as an insect, the poet discovers his limitations as a man ("Poor moralist! and what art thou? / A solitary fly!"). He looks at the reality of his isolated life in terms of his own contrivance; the contrivance now produces fuller awareness of reality. The poignance of the speaker's self-discovery, however, is modified and enriched by the method which produces it. The poem's final effect is of a wry irony which both tempers and reveals the genuine pathos of Gray's sense of himself. If the poet's "voice" is less conspicuously "public" here than in his grander poems, it is still far from intimate: self-revelation emerges specifically through Gray's awareness of himself as poetic contriver. The poem may, as Lord David Cecil suggests, be one of the utterances of a sensitive spirit in a tragic world,[5] but it is more: in a sense its subject is the relation between artifice and reality. Artifice, perceived first as a device for shaping one's perception of reality in arbitrary ways (toward optimism or toward pessimism), ultimately helps to provide new insight into reality. The full logical and emotional movement of the poem is in a sense the direct opposite of that in the churchyard elegy, in which the problems of finding a personal role in the world are finally resolved in the figure of the poet. In the **"Ode on the Spring,"** on the other hand, the position of poet does not help the man to solve his private dilemma: it only reveals that dilemma to him.

In the **"Sonnet on the Death of Richard West"** the chief tension in the expression is not between two forms of artifice but between artifice and personal statement. Its importance has been recognized by Mr. Doherty

("we are being given an opposition between the 'poetic' presentation of morning and the personal, felt grief,") and by Geoffrey Tillotson. At the poem's opening, Professor Tillotson points out, Gray "means us to take the 'poetic diction' as dramatic—for though it is himself who is speaking, he speaks by means of quotations from others. . . . These things are stock-in-trade, and that is the point of Gray's rejection of them."[6] The sonnet's most conventional rhetoric, however, like that in the **"Ode on the Spring,"** serves a double purpose: it exists not simply to be rejected, but also to convey a complex structure of ideas.

Five years before his death, West included in a letter to Gray a long poem entitled *"Ad Amicos."* One section of it sheds light on Gray's later sonnet:

> I care not tho' this face be seen no more,
> The world will pass as chearful as before;
> Bright as before the Day-Star will appear
> The fields as verdant, and the skies as clear:
> Unknown and silent will depart my breath,
> Nor Nature e'er take notice of my death.
> Yet some there are (ere sunk in endless night)
> Within whose breasts my monument I'd write:
> Loved in my life, lamented in my end,
> Their praise would crown me, as their
> precepts mend.[7]

The conjunction between the attitude of "Nature" and that of the friend toward death is here crucial, as it was to be in Gray's sonnet, which supplies an ironic commentary on his friend's poem: for West's assurance that there is value in the lamentations of friendship, Gray substitutes the bitter conviction that his own isolation emblemizes the futility of mourning

> I fruitless mourn to him, that cannot hear,
> And weep the more because I weep in vain.

Like the **"Spring"** ode, the sonnet on West proceeds by alternations of technique and approach. Its opening quatrain is richest in conventional diction, which functions here, as so often in eighteenth-century poetry, to insist upon the essential tie between man and nature. Mornings, in the universe here invoked, are "smileing," the sun is animated as Phoebus, birds sing an "amorous Descant," fields, "chearful," "resume their green Attire." So emphatic is the insistence that even the inanimate universe partakes of the nature and values of man that it becomes almost painful—which is, of course, precisely the point.

In the second quatrain, one's attention is forced to the "lonely Anguish" of the poet. All is red, golden, green, in the opening lines; in the quatrain which follows them, all is bare and comparatively abstract. The hardly perceptible metaphors are embodied entirely in verbs: the poet's ears "repine" for other notes than those of the birds; his heart "melts"; joys "expire" in his breast. Nouns and adjectives have carried the weight of the figures in the opening picture of joyous nature; in the description of solitary grief, there is no picture at all.

The significance of the contrast is fully revealed in the third quatrain, which explains the vital fact—not explicitly recognized in West's poem—that all parts of nature function together, in a union which includes "happier Men," and all has a purpose. Appropriately, Gray here returns to that "poetic diction" so well-adapted to the presentation of optimistic views of the natural world. The lines are less colorful than the opening ones, but as highly figured; they convey also a new poignance (partly the result of the contrast that has been established), which is exemplified in the beautiful line, "To warm their little Loves the Birds complain."[8] Here is a fine emblem of the terrible difference Gray perceives between himself and the rest of the world: the "complaint" of the birds has a function and a value, it participates in the demonstration of love; his own quite different complaint reaches no hearer and produces no positive effect. West maintains that nature and friendship both provide compensations, of different sorts, for death; his point of view is that of the man conscious of his mortality, contemplating the prospect of his own dissolution. Gray, considering death from an equivalent viewpoint in the **"Elegy,"** was to manifest a similar attitude:

> For who to dumb Forgetfulness a prey,
> This pleasing anxious being e'er resign'd,
> Left the warm precincts of the chearful day,
>
> Nor cast one longing ling'ring look behind?
> On some fond breast the parting soul relies,
> Some pious drops the closing eye requires;
> Ev'n from the tomb the voice of Nature cries,
> Ev'n in our Ashes live their wonted Fires.

The prospective victim needs to believe in the existence of "some fond breasts," needs to feel that he will not be *entirely* prey to "dumb Forgetfulness." The "voice of Nature" cries from the tomb to the survivors who may preserve the "wonted Fires" of their departed friends perhaps by the power of their memory; more specifically, Gray's footnote reference to Petrarch and the context of the entire elegy suggest, by the power of poetry to preserve life. But the ultimate faith in the human significance of the poet which dominates the elegy is not so strong in the earlier sonnet, where the artifice of poetry, as in the **"Ode on the Spring,"** reveals its inadequacy to compensate for the ravages of feeling. Gray's viewpoint, in the West sonnet, is that of the survivor; he writes from direct knowledge rather than from observation. And, as the poet-survivor, he contradicts the more speculative conclusion of the passage from West's poem, insisting that nature, through its denial of grief, only intensifies one's sol-

itude in sorrow (solitude more intensely poignant than that perceived by the speaker in the end of the **"Ode on the Spring"**), and that the monument which West imagines within the breasts of his friends must be shaky indeed, when the natural universe refuses it any real foundation.

Wordsworth obviously perceived the deliberate alternation of rhetorical patterns in this sonnet. The five lines that he italicizes as "the only part of this Sonnet which is of any value" include all but one of the lines where Gray deals, in deliberately bare language, with his own isolation in suffering. (The sixth presumably fails to receive Wordsworth's accolade because it includes an "alas!".) Modern readers, however, may more readily see the extent to which Gray here—as often elsewhere—employs contrasting modes of poetry as a technique of cross-commentary. Certainly he does not reject the elaborate diction of his opening lines: he recognizes and exposes its value in conveying the beauty and unity of the natural world. But he recognizes also its limitations, as a mode of insight and of expression. It is not, after all, adequate to express the misery of solitary grief; the poet as artificer cannot merely through convention communicate the sorrow of the poet as man.

In the long **"Ode on a Distant Prospect of Eton College,"** rhetorical variations are more complex in technique and in function. Here too Gray's shifts of rhetoric deepen and complicate the meaning of his poem; the ode's form directly illuminates its content.

That content, simply stated, seems to be the glorification of boyhood at the expense of adulthood. Wordsworth praised the child for his supernal widom; Gray envies him his ignorance: "where ignorance is bliss, / 'Tis folly to be wise." But the ironies of this aphorism are so inclusive that they virtually transform the entire poem.

Sir Leslie Stephen complained about this ode that it "comes into conflict with one's common-sense. We know too well that an Eton boy is not always the happy and immaculate creature of Gray's fancy."[9] Certainly a more unrealistic picture of boyhood can seldom have been offered. The poem opens with a stanza so highly rhetorical that it might have been designed to provide examples of various figures and tropes. In ten lines we find repeated instances of apostrophe, metaphor, personification, alliteration, inversion, repetition, parallelism. The invocation to the towers of Eton has little reference to real experience, and the elaborate description it introduces of the joys of Eton's inhabitants is hardly more convincing. "Gray thought his language more poetical as it was more remote from common use," objected Dr. Johnson,[10] with particular reference to the phrase, "redolent of joy and youth," which Gray here uses to evoke the "gales" that blow from Eton; we may be tempted to agree. Perhaps even more "remote from common use" is the description of youthful sport:

> What idle progeny succeed
> To chase the rolling circle's speed,
> Or urge the flying ball?

The rhetorical tone is maintained, although the language is more immediately evocative, in the succeeding description of boyish enterprise:

> Some bold adventurers disdain
> The limits of their little reign,
> And unknown regions dare descry:
> Still as they run they look behind,
> They hear a voice in every wind,
> And snatch a fearful joy.

Finally, Gray presents a list of the students' attributes, including

> buxom health of rosy hue,
> Wild wit, invention ever-new,
> And lively chear of vigour born;
> The thoughtless day, the easy night . . .

In the three-stanza treatment of the denizens of Eton, the movement has been from particularity to generalization, from the concrete to the abstract. It may be hard to feel "particularity" in such a phrase as "the rolling circle's speed," but, elevated though it is, it, like all periphrases, refers to something specific (in this case, a hoop). The final stanza of the triad, on the other hand, deals solely with abstractions: "hope," "health," "wit," "fancy," "invention," "chear," "vigour." The poet's language now is less pretentious than that which he expends on swimming, bird-catching, and hoop-rolling; his nostalgic tone is more marked. But vague nostalgia and pretentious periphrasis have the same general effect: to make the reader acutely aware of the element of distance in this "distant prospect" of Eton. The past is perceived only through a haze; a light that never was on sea or land glows about the blissful young scholars. The persuasive artifice of the presentation, the unrelieved insistence of the rhetorical distancing, force the reader to be always conscious of the poet as manipulator of reality.

From the joys of youth the poem proceeds, after a transitional stanza, to the evils of maturity. The transition, intensely emotional, concludes, "Ah, tell them, they are men!" In its highly charged bareness, this line foretells the technique of the poem's final stanza; yet immediately after it Gray returns to his more elaborate style. He relies now almost entirely on heavy use of personification, a new form of artifice in this ode, and one which provides its own kind of "distancing" for the image of adulthood's horrors.

The personifications are very good of their kind. Like most such figures in their period, they are strongly traditional in conception, yet Gray individualizes them. The passions are, here as in so many other eighteenth-century poems, "the fury Passions." They are also, however, "The vulturs of the mind": an addition which removes their dignity, makes them more concretely destructive, may recall the tortures of Prometheus, sordid and endless. Despair is "grim-visag'd" and "comfortless": obvious epithets, but sharply evocative of despair's special qualities: its almost deliberate grimness, its inability either to offer comfort to its victim (like gentler forms of sorrow) or to receive comfort from any source. Infamy is "grinning," Madness, "moody"; Poverty "numbs the soul with icy hand." In each case, the relevant detail insists both upon the horror which these qualities have in common and on the special dreadfulness of each specific state.

Indeed, the descriptions of maturity—despite the fact that they are allegorical—are on the whole a good deal more concrete than those of youth. This parade of personifications comprises a metaphorical vision of adulthood to parallel the glamorized vision of youth that has preceded it. Gray seems to feel far more vividly (as is, of course, appropriate enough) the realities of manhood than those of youth, although certainly his nostalgia for childhood is as acute as his horror of the universal fate of the adult.

The allegorical presentation of phenomena, however vivid, is not "realistic"; the lack of realism in the description of man's fate is as striking as that in the evocation of childhood. The high rhetorical tone in both cases points to the fact that Gray's rhetoric is often associated with *imaginative* vision: his elaborations, decorations, heavy use of rhetorical tricks indicate his concern with something other than literal truth. In the sonnet on West, a vision of natural unity is placed in conjunction with the harsh reality of individual pain; in the **"Ode on the Spring,"** two "literary" visions ultimately reveal the actuality of the solitary poet. In the Eton ode, too, there are two visions: of childhood and of adulthood, both deliberately removed from actuality, both containing elements of truth.

The truth of the vision of manhood is immediately and forcibly apparent; the imaginative and emotional power of the personifications attest the conviction of the author, and one has no doubt of Gray's sincerity. The remoteness of personifications from actual experience, the "distancing" involved in the use of this device, are a way of emphasizing the horror of maturity in reality: one suspects that it is too dreadful to be discussed more directly; the poet must find metaphors to make his perceptions tolerable. This suspicion sheds light back on the earlier vision of childhood, and the way in which artifice makes this poem's intensely personal quality possible. If a man's perceptions about maturity are essentially insights into its horrors, it follows that he may find it necessary to glamorize his perceptions about childhood; if beauty cannot be located in the present, it must be asserted of the past or the future. Gray's clearly artificial presentation of childhood as "paradise" emphasizes the agony of his experience of adulthood. Mr. Doherty comments that in Gray's "more plangent poems" he reveals himself as "a man whose historical sensibility demands of him that the present be always seen as part of a movement of time." A sense of that movement is clearly present in this ode, but it is a movement relentlessly downward. Both visions emphasize this fact.

The final stanza of the Eton ode represents a return to the barer style which Gray used so effectively in the sonnet on West. In it there is only one strong metaphor, no striking inversions; the diction, with the exception of one rhetorical "ah!", is such as Wordsworth might approve. But the simpler style in no way denies the validity of the affirmations which the rhetorical sections have made; here emotion derives from vision without conflicting with it. Resignation is achieved as a result of perceptions which provide a more than "realistic" insight into the nature of reality.

That resignation, faintly bitter, is summed up in the final assertion of the folly of wisdom "where ignorance is bliss." Although the aphorism has the form of a general statement (and is frequently taken, out of context, to be one), its reference in the poem is particular, to the nature of youth and of manhood. Its fundamental ironies are twofold. First, the entire poem has demonstrated that the bliss of ignorance and the folly of wisdom are alike inevitable in human life. The concluding statement (like the earlier rhetorical question, "why should they know their fate?") appears to offer the possibility of choice, but in neither case does an alternative really exist. The nature of childhood, the nature of maturity, are foreordained: one may perhaps hope to be aware of them, but can do nothing to change them. It is the fate of mankind to move from blissful ignorance to foolish wisdom; it is perhaps the nature of men to coin aphorisms which justify both states.

Second, the poem as a whole has defined both "ignorance" and "wisdom" in ways involving built-in ironic overtones. "Ignorance" here is specifically ignorance of the horrors that lie in store for all human beings; "wisdom" consists in awareness of those horrors. A few years after Gray wrote his Eton ode, Dr. Johnson, in "The Vanity of Human Wishes," suggested his scorn of the suppliant for long life who

Hides from himself his state, and shuns to know,
That life protracted is protracted woe.

Scorn was possible for Johnson because he saw his characters in a religious context: it is shortsighted and

ridiculous to pray for length of life on earth if one is convinced that a better existence may be the aftermath of human suffering. In Gray's ode, on the other hand, the language of religious hope is reserved for references to departed childhood. That is the state of "bliss," that the "paradise" which thought can only destroy. The wisdom of adulthood is damning; failure to know that life protracted is protracted woe is the best that human existence can offer.

The sudden shift to relatively undecorated language in the final stanza emphasizes the despair which awareness of these ironies can produce. The stanza's first line echoes the earlier line which most clearly prepared for the ending. "Ah, tell them, they are men!" the poet cried before, of the schoolboys; now he reminds us, "To each his suff'rings: all are men." Children and adults alike participate inevitably in the miseries of being human. The straightforward language throws into sharp relief the earlier elaboration and reveals the intimate relation of form and content in the ode. For the artifice and formality which controlled the presentation of childhood's joy and maturity's misery reflect a further meaning of "wisdom." To this extent alone does the wisdom derived from experience have power: it can formulate its record of experience so as to make it artistically viable. The suffering of mankind is communicated no less intensely for being embodied in personifications, but the use of such figures suggests a kind of order and meaning in that suffering. The joys of boyhood are purged of imperfection by being rhetorically described; the conjunction of the two visions, of suffering and of joy, provides a perception of pattern in human life. But this function of wisdom, too, is merely folly. When rhetoric is virtually abandoned, as in the concluding stanza, and the poet speaks directly of his sense of the ultimate *disorder* of experience (suggested by the reversal of values in the final lines: the notion that wisdom is a high good is essential to most concepts of an ordered universe), his revelation is the more forceful for its contrast with what has gone before. Once more Gray has demonstrated his extraordinary skill at playing off highly controlled rhetoric against simple, direct statement.

The rhetorical oppositions manifested in these poems are, however, by no means characteristic of Gray's later work. They dramatize a sense of tension which was to remain important in his poetry, but in different forms. The poems I have selected for attention here are perhaps experimental in their playing with technique; their manipulation of artifice seems largely responsible for the conspicuous success of the experiments. In the relatively direct verse of the **"Elegy"** and the highly formalized patternings of the 1757 odes, however, Gray does not employ any clear alternations of technique, nor does he point to his own reliance on artifice. Instead, the conflicts of values which both interested and perplexed him as a poet are directly expressed as part of the subject. These later poems pose problems of a very complicated sort, problems best dealt with in terms of other formulations than those which provide perspective on the function of artifice in the poems of 1742.

Notes

[1] Samuel Taylor Coleridge, *Biographia Literaria,* 2 vols. (London, 1817), I, 20.

[2] Gray to Mason, 9 November 1758, *Correspondence of Thomas Gray,* ed. Paget Toynbee and Leonard Whibley, 3 vols. (Oxford, 1936), II, 593.

[3] The Two Voices of Gray," *Essays in Criticism,* XIII (1963), 222-230. 230.

[4] "A Classical Education and Eighteenth-Century Poetry," *Scrutiny,* VIII (1939), 204.

[5] "The Poetry of Thomas Gray," *Proceedings of the British Academy,* XXXI (1945), 51.

[6] "More About Poetic Diction," *Augustan Studies* (London, 1961), p. 88.

[7] Duncan C. Tovey, ed., *Gray and His Friends* (Cambridge, 1890), pp. 97-98. Another version of the text, with different, and less accurate, punctuation, is printed in William Mason's edition of *The Poems of Mr. Gray* (York, 1775). Both texts are taken from Gray's Commonplace Books.

[8] Mr. Doherty has an interesting discussion of the language of this line in "The Two Voices of Gray," p. 229.

[9] "Gray and His School," *Hours in a Library* (London, 1892), III, 118-119.

[10] *Lives of the English Poets,* ed. G. B. Hill, 3 vols. (Oxford, 1905), III, 435.

Stephen D. Cox (essay date 1980)

SOURCE: "Contexts of Significance: Thomas Gray," in *"The Stranger within Thee": Concepts of the Self in Late-Eighteenth-Century Literature*, University of Pittsburgh Press, 1980, pp. 82-98.

[*In the following chronological study of Gray's poetry, Cox considers the progression of Gray's ideas concerning humankind's limitations and the significance of the individual self.*]

The **"Elegy Written in a Country Churchyard"** expresses what Thomas Gray wished to believe—that the individual self is significant even when it lacks any visible signs of significance, such as power, wealth, or social recognition. Yet it was very difficult for Gray to find grounds for affirming the self. In some of his poems, he reduces human life to merely a lively consciousness of pain. In others, he finds reasons for portraying the self as significant, but his reasons are not always consistent with one another. In the **"Ode to Adversity,"** he bases man's significance on his capacity for sympathy and love, but in **"The Bard"** and **"The Triumphs of Owen,"** on his potential for a stern heroism; in the original version of the **"Elegy,"** Gray describes the self as acquiring dignity through resignation to fate, but in the final version he derives its significance from the tenacity of its desires. Although Gray wrote only a small number of poems, they display a remarkable variety—a variety that resulted not just from wandering interests and a kind of aimless versatility, but also from a lifelong hesitation about how to evaluate the significance of the self.

To understand Gray's particular difficulties, it is perhaps as useful to consider what his works do not, as what they actually do, express. Compare the **"Elegy,"** for instance, with some other eighteenth-century poems that take up the issue of man's significance: Pope's *Essay on Man,* Young's *Night Thoughts,* Johnson's *Vanity of Human Wishes,* Cowper's *Task.* Like the **"Elegy,"** all of these poems recognize the self's limitations, its inability to achieve fulfillment. But unlike the **"Elegy,"** all of them compensate for the weakness of the self by placing it in what could be called a larger context of significance—an order of reality that is greater than the individual experience, an order that incorporates the self and ensures its value. Some of these contexts originate in religious faith. Johnson describes the self as ultimately dependent on its relationship with God for a consciousness of its own dignity, for an assurance that it is not simply "helpless" and fated. Young, by celebrating the individual self as the most important object of God's creative and redemptive power, converts the immensity of the Newtonian universe, which might easily be seen as a threat to man's significance, into the best evidence of his dignity. Cowper suffered agonies of doubt concerning his own personal value, yet his evangelical religion enabled him to suggest a context in which the weak and obscure appear to possess the greatest importance: the humble, solitary Christian has a hidden significance in the divine plan, even though "the self-approving haughty world / . . . Deems him a cypher in the works of God."[1] But it is not necessary to propose an essentially Christian context in order to portray the self as significant: in the *Essay on Man,* Pope's consolation for the obscure sufferings of men is the argument that even human limitation is indispensable to the universe, because it enables man to fill a necessary place in the chain of being.

A context of significance provides a way, not merely of justifying the ways of God to man, but also of justifying the nature of man to himself. In addition, it furnishes a basis for discovering the moral identity of individual selves: a person can be considered good to the extent that he knows his place in the order of things. Also, and not least important, the belief that the individual's petty experience has a significant place in a greater and more rational existence is an invaluable aid to poetic rhetoric. The structure of the universe inspires the structure of poetry; no matter at what length a poet discourses on the frustrations of mundane existence, a hopeful climax, the revelation of an all-embracing order, is always available to him. For resolution he need not rely on private symbolism or purely personal emotions; he can employ the unequivocal logic of universal truth.

Gray, however, was unable to employ this positive rhetoric, because he could not affirm an external context of significance that could adequately compensate the self for its limitations. And this, I believe, could be one source of the "originality" that Samuel Johnson, writing his *Life* of Gray, discovered in the **"Elegy"**: "The four stanzas beginning *Yet even these bones,* are to me original: I have never seen the notions in any other place; yet he that reads them here, persuades himself that he has always felt them."[2] The passage from the **"Elegy,"** which describes the awkward eloquence of rustic tombstones, presents the poem's most universal statement about the nature of human life and aspiration. Having contrasted the wasted potential of the villagers with the marred achievement of the "Proud," Gray's speaker finds all people united in a common desire for their individual significance to be recognized:

> On some fond breast the parting soul relies,
> Some pious drops the closing eye requires;
> Ev'n from the tomb the voice of Nature cries,
> Ev'n in our Ashes live their wonted Fires.[3]

The four stanzas may be regarded as the climax of Gray's rhetoric, yet they are in no way consoling, at least in any conventional sense:

> Yet ev'n these bones from insult to protect
> Some frail memorial still erected nigh,
> With uncouth rhimes and shapeless sculpture
>   deck'd,
> Implores the passing tribute of a sigh.
>
> (ll. 77-80)

The last cry sounding from the gravestones does not compensate for the evanescence of life. As Gray reminds us, the memorials are as "frail" as the lives they commemorate. They are intended to elicit sympathy for the dead, but the most that Gray expects is "the passing tribute of a sigh." Instead of making an unequivocal declaration of the significance of human life, Gray derives comfort only from the irrepressible de-

mand for significance. Yet by reducing his positive rhetoric to a minimum, by refusing to rely on any context of significance exterior to the self, Gray succeeds in expressing the dignity of the self's most fundamental desires in the energy with which "the voice of Nature cries" from the imprisoning tomb.

As a professed Christian, Gray might be expected to refer to the self's relationship with God as the major source of its significance. But his belief was never strong enough to become a vital impulse in his poetry. Although one of his personal enemies, John Whalley, accused him of atheism,[4] Gray opposed "free-thinking" and considered Hume "refuted & vanquished" by his friend James Beattie's petulant attack in the *Essay on Truth*.[5] Yet in Gray's letters one looks in vain— among the weather reports, antiquarian speculations, and descriptions of landscapes—for an extended discussion of religion. It seems likely that Gray, who was himself a man of rather sceptical character, found little in what he regarded as the increasingly sceptical thought of his time that was capable of stimulating his interest in religion.[6] He sometimes used religion to console bereaved friends,[7] but any idea we may receive of his essential piety is not supported by the blank hopelessness of the epitaph he wrote for a child: "Few were the days allotted to his breath; / Here let him sleep in peace his night of death."[8]

Gray did, however, write a short essay, refuting the extreme scepticism of Lord Bolingbroke, that offers insight into his own views both of religion and of the self.[9] Bolingbroke's basic premise is well expressed in the familiar lines of his friend Pope: "Of God above, or Man below, / What can we reason, but from what we know?"[10] Bolingbroke's answer is that we have experiential evidence of God's "physical attributes" of power and wisdom, but no evidence sufficient to prove that his "moral attributes" are the same as what humans may call justice or benevolence. Gray finds Bolingbroke's philosophy offensive for two major reasons. First, by denying that there is any proof of an afterlife provided by a benevolent God, it deprives man of a comforting feeling of significance:

> He will tell you, that we, that is, the animals, vegetables, stones, and *other clods of earth,* are all connected in one immense design, that we are all Dramatis Personae, in different characters, and that we were not made for ourselves, but for the action. . . . Such is the consolation his philosophy gives us, and such the hope on which his tranquillity was founded.

Gray is shocked by Bolingbroke's ridicule of a passage in *The Religion of Nature Delineated* in which William Wollaston, in a "longing, lingering look behind," voices the fear of extinction at death; Gray believes that everyone who deserves to be called human would sympathize with Wollaston: "No thinking head, no heart, that has the least sensibility, but must have made the same reflection."[11] According to his friend Norton Nicholls, Gray took a similarly dim view of Hume's "irreligion," "because he said it was taking away the best consolation of man without substituting any thing of equal value in its place."[12]

Gray's other objection to Bolingbroke is again that of a man of sensibility whose feelings are the final arbiter of his beliefs. It is the idea that Bolingbroke's philosophy deprives religious emotions of their value. We could not worship God if we did not imagine that he is benevolent, and that he exercises his benevolence toward us individually: "If we are made only to bear our part in a system, without any regard to our own particular happiness, we can no longer worship him as our all-bounteous parent: There is no meaning in the term."

Now, it is interesting that although Gray disputes Bolingbroke's conclusions, he accepts his basic premise that experience is the only source of our knowledge of God. Gray therefore argues that none of God's attributes can be understood except by their resemblance to our own: "How can we form any notion of his unity, but from that unity of which we ourselves are conscious? How of his existence, but from our own consciousness of existing?" On this basis, Gray simply asserts his belief that God's moral attributes bear a general resemblance to what we perceive as human virtues. We may recall that Gray is the poet who, in **"De Principiis Cogitandi,"** wished to play Lucretius to Locke's Epicurus; he is clearly enough impressed by empirical philosophy to be convinced that all questions regarding the nature of God must ultimately be referred to immediate, individual experience.[13] But the "experience" on which Gray's religious hopes are primarily grounded is really a fear of the psychic alienation that may result from a lack of faith in God's benevolence: "The idea of his malevolence (an impiety I tremble to write) must succeed. We have nothing left but our fears, and those too vain; for whither can they lead but to despair and the sad desire of annihilation."

What evidence we have of Gray's somewhat desperate religious beliefs indicates that he was not disposed to reason very assiduously on this subject. He could find no basis for defending belief in God as anything but a projection of the self, an assertion of the self's desire for happiness and its fear of isolation. When he attempts, in his essay on Bolingbroke, to discover what may "connect" God "with us his creatures," he actually finds the "connection" only in human feelings. Perhaps he would have agreed with Emily Dickinson—another isolated self—that

> The abdication of Belief
> Makes the Behavior small—
> Better an ignis fatuus
> Than no illume at all.[14]

But it is not surprising that in his poetry Gray shows considerable reserve about presenting a religion centered in the self as the ground of the self's significance.

But religion does not provide the only context in which human life can be regarded as significant. The self can also derive its dignity from its social feelings and relations, from the sympathy it gives to others and receives from them in turn. The eighteenth century found the web of social sympathies such a useful context of significance that in many works of literature, self and sympathy became almost inseparable concepts. In Sterne's *Sentimental Journey,* Yorick's sympathy for the deranged Maria convinces him that he himself does, indeed, possess a soul. In *Tristram Shandy,* Uncle Toby and his friends are outwardly incompetent and insignificant figures; it is mainly their ability to sympathize with others that seems to give them personal dignity. As I have shown, even Richardson's Clarissa, who values herself so highly on her independence, still derives much of her self-esteem from other people's sympathy.

In the completed portion of his ambitious poem **"The Alliance of Education and Government,"** Gray defines man's basic characteristics as attraction to pleasure, aversion to pain, desire of self-protection—and sympathetic sensibility, the "social Smile & sympathetic Tear" (ll. 30-37). In this he shows his affinity to the empirical philosophers and aestheticians whom I have previously discussed. Yet he was seldom able to rely on sympathy as a context of significance.

This was partly because Gray's personal problems made him perpetually unsure of his own ability to gain sympathy from others. His frustrated and repressed homosexuality distanced him permanently from full intimacy with other people.[15] As if to confirm the assertions of contemporary philosophers that the self's better qualities are formed through sympathy with others, Gray—threatened by the outside world, lacking sympathy for its affairs, and suspecting, in turn, its lack of sympathy for him—looked within himself and discovered nothing.[16] Beneath his self-deprecating wit, Gray was in grim earnest when he told Horace Walpole, the idol of his youth, that philosophy had taught him that he only imagined he existed, but that "one lesson of thine, my dear Philosopher, will restore me to the use of my Senses, & make me think myself something."[17] Walpole's kindness had been "the only Idea of any social happiness that I have ever received almost"; Gray's self was "tiny" and "tiresome," but Walpole's was "large enough to serve for both of us."[18] But Walpole's kindness could never be sufficient to fulfill Gray's need for social happiness; Gray came to a full realization of that fact during their Continental tour. Years later, after the departure of Charles-Victor Bonstetten, the young Swiss student with whom he was infatuated, Gray wrote to him: "I did not conceive till now (I own) what it was to lose you, nor felt the solitude and insipidity of my own condition, before I possess'd the happiness of your friendship."[19]

But Gray had philosophical as well as personal difficulties in coming to terms with the concept of sympathy. In **"The Alliance of Education and Government,"** he is concerned, as one might expect from his admiration for Locke, with the issue of the self's dependence upon the outside world, but he shows that he wishes to believe that the self can attain significance regardless of the environment in which it is placed. The opposite opinion he denounces as an "Unmanly Thought!": "what Seasons can controul, / What fancied Zone can circumscribe the Soul?" (ll. 72-73). So much for the influence of literal climate, which so fascinated eighteenth-century thinkers; the poem's thesis, however, is that the self does indeed require at least an accommodating social environment in order to accomplish its full potential. And in notes that Gray apparently made for the poem's continuation, he emphasizes the necessity to the self of gaining social significance and recognition:

> One principal characteristic of vice in the present age is the contempt of fame.
>
> Many are the uses of good fame to a generous mind: it extends our existence and example into future ages . . . and prevents the prevalence of vice in a generation more corrupt even than our own. It is impossible to conquer that natural desire we have of being remembered.[20]

"Education and Government" was begun in 1748, about the same time that Gray was probably completing the **"Elegy"**; and he seems to have intended both works to express the self's desire for sympathy, even posthumous sympathy. However, in a letter also written about the time of the **"Elegy"**'s composition, he told Thomas Wharton exactly how consoling he thought "the passing tribute of a sigh" might be:

> I am not altogether of your Opinion, as to your Historical Consolation in time of Trouble, a calm Melancholy it may produce, a stiller Sort of Despair (& that only in some Circumstances & on some Constitutions) but I doubt no real Content or Comfort can ever arise in the human Mind, but from Hope. Old Balmerino [one of the Scotch Lords executed after the 1745 rebellion] when he had read his Paper to the People, pull'd off his Spectacles, spit upon his Handkerchief, & wiped them clean for the Use of his Posterity; & that is the last Page of his History.[21]

Gray's poems of 1742 reveal his inability to believe in the power of sympathy—or anything else—as an adequate compensation for the self's limitations. In the **"Ode to Adversity,"** written in August of that year, he attempts to use sympathy as a context of significance that can give purpose and dignity to individual suffering. He welcomes pain as a soul-maker; adversity alone can teach sympathy with others and, through it, self-knowledge:

> The gen'rous spark extinct revive,
> Teach me to love and to forgive,
> Exact my own defects to scan,
> What others are, to feel, and know myself a
> Man.
>
> (ll. 45-48)

But the **"Sonnet on the Death of Richard West,"** written in the same month, views adversity—and, indeed, the soul's sensibility to its feelings—as something that isolates the self, making it incapable of sharing sympathetically in the outside world. Gray's speaker cannot share the happiness of the world around him, and he regrets that the world does not share his grief: "My lonely Anguish melts no Heart, but mine."

Gray's other poems of 1742 also admit that the self is "circumscribed," and they examine the significance of human life from that standpoint. In the **"Ode on the Spring,"** the speaker, who contrasts his own reclusive life with the spontaneous hedonism of the "insect youth," establishes the ultimate significance of neither: the speaker's melancholy denies him immediate fulfillment, but age will soon destroy the pleasures of the "youth." In the inverted *carpe diem* of the **"Eton College"** ode, the aspect of the self that recognizes its own limitations once again delivers a somber—and this time a crushing—judgment on the faith of youthful spontaneity in its own ability to achieve happiness. As Ben Jones has said, Gray has a habit of making the self's limitations almost the definition of human life.[22] In the **"Eton"** ode, it is the consciousness of pain that is to inform the careless youths that "they are men." This is reminiscent of the **"Adversity"** ode, yet here sympathy fails to provide a context of significance. The final stanza suggests praise of those who can feel sympathy, but it does not imply that they can thereby escape the full burden of human wretchedness:

> To each his suff'rings: all are men,
> Condemn'd alike to groan,
> The tender for another's pain,
> Th' unfeeling for his own.
>
> (ll. 91-94)

It could certainly be said of Gray, as he himself said of Pope, that "no body ever took him for a Philosopher."[23] The speaker of the **"Eton"** ode is an image of everything that the eighteenth-century philosophers of sympathy feared—the isolated self, reflecting bitterly on its inability to accomplish anything of significance in either thought or action, incapacitated by its own consciousness from sharing the joys of others, yet regarding even its own wisdom as unprofitable "folly." In the **"Adversity"** ode, Gray's reliance on sympathy allows him to consider the self's interaction with its environment as something positive even when it produces pain; in the **"Eton"** ode, the self regards the outer world merely as something that will never respond to its own demands: "Ah happy hills, ah pleasing shade, / Ah fields belov'd in vain" (ll. 11-12).[24]

Gray's early poems, then, usually portray the self as isolated from any context in which it can achieve significance. While writing and revising the **"Elegy"** however, Gray struggled to find some way of expressing a less bitter view of the human situation. In his first attempt at concluding the poem, he suggested that a kind of moral significance can be attained by resigning oneself to fate:

> Hark how the sacred Calm, that broods around
> Bids ev'ry fierce tumultuous Passion cease
> In still small Accents whisp'ring from the Ground
> A grateful Earnest of eternal Peace[.]
>
> No more with Reason & thyself at strife;
> Give anxious Cares & endless Wishes room
> But thro' the cool sequester'd Vale of Life
> Pursue the silent Tenour of thy Doom.

Gray's critics have usually regarded these lines as a perfectly natural conclusion, one that is highly consistent with the rest of the poem.[25]

In fact, however, nothing in the **"Elegy"**'s earlier stanzas, except a general melancholy feeling, adequately prepares for this conclusion. Previously, Gray has discovered bitter images in the calm that he now chooses to call consoling: the landscape abandoned to darkness, the owl complaining of intruding footsteps, the ground heaving almost grotesquely above men imprisoned forever in their "narrow cells."[26] Nevertheless, the churchyard's "grateful Earnest of eternal Peace" is supposed to resolve the speaker's conflict with both "Reason" and himself; it convinces him not to try to fulfill himself by means of either magnificent virtues or illustrious crimes. Recognizing the grateful necessity of death, he will lead a life as idly silent as the grave. Other courses are possible, but they are too morally dangerous or emotionally troubling. Yet this sort of delicate pragmatism, despite the graceful language in which it is couched, transforms a poem that seemed to be working toward some vindication of the significance of human life into a safe and rather superficial homily.

Gray was not content with his original conclusion; and in revising it, as Ian Jack has aptly observed, he transformed "a poem of Christian Stoicism" into "a poem of Sensibility."[27] Of course, even in the original ending it is only the speaker's sensibility, his feeling of a "sacred Calm" in the village churchyard, that enables him to suggest that "eternal Peace" lies beyond the grave. As in his essay on Bolingbroke, Gray resorts to feeling as a basis for the idea that man may have significance in a religious context. But in the revised conclusion he relies far more heavily on pure emotion as the basis of the self's significance. Religion is no longer associated with resignation to one's "Doom," but with a fatherly God who responds to the speaker's emotional needs by giving him "('twas all he wish'd) a friend" (l. 124). And this God, in keeping with Gray's shaky religious convictions, is kept as vague and distant as he is undemanding. The focus remains firmly on what the speaker feels, rather than on what he ought to feel; it has shifted from the duty to repress one's desires to the dignity of indulging them, even if they are melancholy or frankly egoistic. Writing to Walpole in 1747, Gray said: "Nature and sorrow, and tenderness, are the true genius of [elegies] . . . poetical ornaments are foreign to the purpose; for they only show a man is not sorry;—and devotion worse; for it teaches him, that he ought not to be sorry, which is all the pleasure of the thing."[28] In his revision of the **"Elegy,"** therefore, Gray does not suggest that it is dishonorable in the speaker (who is obviously the subject of the poem's final section) that Melancholy should have "mark'd him for her own," that he should have behaved like one who was "craz'd with care, or cross'd in hopeless love" (ll. 120, 108). Just as the passionate cry from the tomb gives dignity to the dead villagers, so the speaker's passions are intended to give him significance as well.

In the **"Eton"** and **"Adversity"** odes, Gray had offered contradictory views of social sympathy's ability to provide a context of significance and a release from psychic isolation. Now, in the **"Elegy,"** he hesitates. Certainly his speaker is recommended as a sympathetic person—"He gave to Mis'ry all he had, a tear" (l. 123). He warmly sympathizes with the dead, and he wishes that other people—the Kindred Spirit and the Swain—may sympathize with him when he is dead. Yet except for one friend, who is referred to but does not appear, he has apparently isolated himself from other men. One of Gray's minor revisions occurred in the line, "Ev'n in our Ashes live their wonted Fires" (l. 92), which he originally wrote, "And buried Ashes glow with social Fires." The fiery need to have one's significance recognized is surely "social," since it produces appeals to other men for sympathy. By omitting the word, however, Gray was, perhaps, not merely repressing a bit of eighteenth-century poetic jargon; he was also emphasizing the individual nature of the need and the considerable possibility that it might never be fulfilled.

The Swain's description of the speaker contains conventional allusions to the melancholy Jaques of *As You Like It,* but it is still a portrait of Gray himself. My purpose is not to psychoanalyze the poet, but I think that a letter he wrote to Thomas Wharton in 1755 expresses his characteristic attitude toward other people: "as to Humanity you know my aversion to it; wch is barbarous & inhuman, but I can not help it. God forgive me."[29] His emotions varied from haughty contempt for other people to prostrate but unfulfilled need for them, and this is well expressed by the Swain's description of a man "now smiling as in scorn, / . . . Now drooping, woeful wan, like one forlorn, / Or craz'd with care, or cross'd in hopeless love" (ll. 105-08).[30] Throughout the **"Elegy"**'s conclusion, Gray emphasizes the self's isolation. Originally, he wrote that the Kindred Spirit who inquires the speaker's fate was delayed in the churchyard "by sympathetic Musings"; in the final version, he is led "by lonely contemplation" (l. 95). And, more important, Gray establishes the elaborate device of distancing the speaker into the second and then the third person and presenting fragmentary views of his character in a conversation between two other people and in the epitaph on his tomb. The visitor, though a "kindred Spirit," must be imagined as having little direct knowledge of the speaker, since he is forced to inquire of the Swain about him; and the Swain's own view of the speaker is purely external. Neither of them can be expected to have any particularly intimate sympathy for him. His virtues and frailties are best known to God—and, of course, to himself.[31] The epitaph, the Swain, and the Kindred Spirit are all projections of his own imagination, offering his own evaluation of his own significance.

In the **"Elegy,"** personal significance does not depend fundamentally on external relationships—with God, or with other people—or on external accomplishments, even the accomplishment of reciprocal sympathy. Gray's insecurities about the world, and about himself, did not allow him to trust such solutions. Significance depends instead—somewhat paradoxically, it is true—on "this pleasing anxious being," the individual self and the emotions it feels in facing its ultimately hopeless situation. Gray no longer views human limitations, as he did in the **"Eton"** ode, merely as threats to the self, but as a background against which the self can display its dignity of feeling.

This change in sentiment, or at least in rhetorical strategy, affords some insight into the reason why Gray, during the 1750s and 1760s, almost abandoned the poetry of reflection for the poetry of "sublimity" and gothic terrors represented in **"The Progress of Poesy," "The Bard,"** and the versions of Welsh and Norse poetry. Of course, one of Gray's purposes in some of these later poems was to dignify his own character as poet. This idea is supported by his conscious identification with the Bard,[32] his placement of himself in the great poetic tradition in **"The Progress of Poesy,"** and his choice, in **"The Death of Hoel,"** to translate a Welsh poem in which the narrator refers specifically to his own role as elegist of his people. Also, as Donald

Greene has written, Gray's interest in the gothic past provided him with "a means of escape from the real and present into a fantasy world."[33] Gray's threatened personality could be expected to enjoy compensatory wish-fulfillment, ego-involvement in glamorous situations impossible in his own unheroic life. Samuel Johnson might have been speaking of Gray's frustrated life when he wrote: "He who has nothing external that can divert him, must find pleasure in his own thoughts, and must conceive himself what he is not; for who is pleased with what he is?"[34]

But another motivation for Gray's later poetry can be discovered in his desire to represent the self as significant despite his almost morbid preoccupation with its limitations. It is important to recognize that his fantasies were usually of heroic virtue but not of heroic achievement. The world of Gray's "gothic" poems is ruled by a fate indifferent to illustrious personal qualities. In **"The Fatal Sisters,"** the Valkyries, pursuing their "weyward work," decide to kill or preserve without regard to personal value; they slay even men they admire:

> Low the dauntless Earl is laid,
> Gor'd with many a gaping wound;
> Fate demands a nobler head,
> Soon a King shall bite the ground.
>
>   (ll. 41-44)[35]

In the Latin text from which Gray translated **"The Descent of Odin,"** the mother of giants prophesies that "to the Twilight of the Gods / The Destroyers shall come."[36] In his version of these lines, Gray emphasizes and universalizes the prophecy: no inquirer will meet the prophetess again until

>   substantial Night
> Has reassum'd her ancient right;
> Till wrap'd in flames, in ruin hurl'd,
> Sinks the fabrick of the world.
>
>   (ll. 91-94)

In Gray's Latin text, the prophetess foretells the death of Balder in a simple statement of fact: "Surely the divine offspring / Will be affected by pain." Gray's translation is far more resonant: "Pain can reach the Sons of heav'n!" (l. 48). The prophecy becomes the shocking declaration of a universal truth: no one, not the gods themselves, is invulnerable to fate.

In translating **"The Triumphs of Owen,"** Gray describes a hero who is himself the agent of an indifferent fate that condemns men to "Despair, & honourable Death" (l. 36): a reflection of Gray's habitual attitude that personal virtue—"honour"—has no effect on man's destiny. **"The Death of Hoel"** is a more direct lesson in futility; it is in the greatest strength of their confidence and desire that Hoel and his friends are slaughtered:

Flush'd with mirth & hope they burn:
But none from Cattraeth's vale return,
Save Aeron brave, & Conan strong,
(Bursting thro' the bloody throng)
And I, the meanest of them all,
That live to weep, & sing their fall.

(ll. 19-24)

In some of his later poems, Gray apparently wished to suggest that poetry itself might in some way provide the self with a context of significance. Thus, in **"Co-nan"** he proclaims that memorial verse is "the Hero's sole reward"—a statement that has no precedent in the Latin text on which he based this poem.[37] And thus, in **"The Progress of Poesy,"** he asserts that poetry can compensate "Man's feeble race" for its limitations and thereby "justify the laws of Jove" (ll. 42-53). He apparently had a similar purpose in mind when he began **"The Bard."** An entry in his Commonplace Book shows that he originally intended the Bard to prophesy "that men shall never be wanting to celebrate true virtue and valour in immortal strains, to expose vice and infamous pleasure, and boldly censure tyranny and oppression." But as William Mason noted, "unhappily for his purpose, instances of English Poets were wanting"; they had not been immortal advocates of freedom, and Gray finally completed the poem without insisting on poetry's ability to dignify mankind.[38]

Irvin Ehrenpreis has suggested that "for all its splendor **"The Bard"** is an assertion of its author's impotence"; its hero's suicide reflects Gray's awareness that poetry, at least in his own time, could not be an active force in human life.[39] This may be true, but it was apparently not the effects of the Bard's actions that primarily interested Gray; his major purpose was to portray a man who maintains integrity in a hopeless situation in which any action would be ineffectual. The Bard tells Edward: "Be thine Despair, and scept'red Care, / To triumph, and to die, are mine" (ll. 141-42). His victory is one of character and emotion, not of action. The doom woven in his prophecy is to deprive Edward of his queen—"to sudden fate / . . . Half of thy heart we consecrate" (ll. 97-99)—but the Bard triumphs in the sympathy of the spirit comrades whom he sees before him. As in the **"Elegy,"** the isolated self relies on its imagination—its vision, in this case—to provide the sympathy it cannot otherwise attain. But even after his vision has passed, the Bard's solitary strength of character continues to distinguish him. His suicide is part of his triumph—a sign of practical impotence, surely, but also a sign of moral autonomy. Gray is careful to deny the Bard any external context of significance: "Deep in the roaring tide he plung'd to endless night" (l. 144). His dignity is measured not by any hope of effect or reward, but by strength of passion alone.

Most of the other protagonists of Gray's exotic poems are also placed in situations that emphasize their inde-pendent strength of character: Odin is fearless enough to descend to "Hela's drear abode" to learn the decisions of fate, Hoel's defeat in battle provides an occasion for a friend's praise of his exceptional magnanimity, and Owen's fortitude distinguishes him in the confusion of war:

Dauntless on his native sands
The Dragon-Son of Mona stands;
In glitt'ring arms & glory drest
High he rears his ruby crest.

(ll. 19-22)

The static, pictorial quality of Gray's descriptions, especially in **"The Bard,"** has often been noticed,[40] and this is a source of both strength and weakness in his later poems. The gothic poems are galleries of the ideal states in which Gray imagined that the self could attain its greatest significance. But the idealization is so complete, the selves represented so autonomous, so isolated from any but a purely fabulous environment, that the characters largely lack interest as personalities; they become merely heroic gestures. In order to create characters for whom one could feel an immediate emotional response, Gray chose to imitate poetry in which the self is placed in stark and desperate situations; as a result, most of his later poems lack intellectual and psychological complexity. Ironically, his characters depend for their interest largely on the extreme situations in which they are placed. He is perilously close to the practice of lesser poets of his century who relied on "sublime" stage settings to provide otherwise negligible characters with a context of significance, one that often, unfortunately, turned out to be merely rhetorical.

Anyone who attempts to analyze Gray's poetry must feel the ultimate inadequacy of any generalizations the critic may make about it. This is not only because Gray wrote a variety of different types of poetry with a corresponding variety of rhetorical strategies, or because his works are of uneven quality, or even because his finest poems can make criticism seem impertinence. It is also because his poetry lacks a central vision. His ideas are shifting, evanescent, his controlling attitude a vague *Angst*. He could seldom discern a vital relationship between the self and the outer world, yet he could not always find an effective way of portraying the self as the ground of its own significance. As a result, his view of life is narrow and fragmentary—at best, grandly pathetic; at worst, remote and sterile.

Notes

[1] *The Task,* VI, 940-43, in *Poetical Works,* ed. H. S. Milford, 4th ed., corrected by Norma Russell (London: Oxford University Press, 1971), pp. 239-40.

[2] *The Lives of the Most Eminent English Poets* (London, 1781), IV, 485.

[3] Lines 89-92. All quotations from Gray's poetry are from *The Complete Poems of Thomas Gray,* ed. H. W. Starr and J. R. Hendrickson (Oxford: Clarendon Press, 1966).

[4] Gray to Horace Walpole, Jan. or Feb. 1748, *Correspondence of Thomas Gray,* ed. Paget Toynbee and Leonard Whibley, corrections and additions by H. W. Starr (Oxford: Clarendon Press, 1971), I, 302.

[5] Norton Nicholls, "Reminiscences of Gray," in *Correspondence,* III, 1289. See also Gray to Beattie, July 2, 1770, ibid., p. 1141.

[6] On the decline of faith see Gray to Richard Stonhewer, Aug. 18, 1758, ibid., II, 583. The best survey of Gray's intellectual interests is William Powell Jones, *Thomas Gray, Scholar* (1937; rpt., New York: Russell and Russell, 1965).

[7] See, for example, Gray to Nicholls, Sept. 23, 1766, *Correspondence,* III, 935-36; Gray's lines for an epitaph on Mrs. William Mason, *Complete Poems,* p. 105.

[8] The epitaph seems to have been written for Robin Wharton; it appears in *Complete Poems,* p. 104.

[9] The essay is contained in William Mason's *Memoirs* of Gray, pp. 265-68, in *The Poems of Mr. Gray. To Which Are Prefixed Memoirs of His Life and Writings* (York, 1775).

[10] Alexander Pope, *An Essay on Man,* Twickenham Ed., ed. Maynard Mack (London: Methuen, 1950), I.17-18 (p. 14).

[11] See "Fragments or Minutes of Essays," in *The Works of the Late Right Honorable Henry St. John, Lord Viscount Bolingbroke* (London, 1754), V, 372-92, on Wollaston, *The Religion of Nature Delineated,* 4th ed. (London, 1726), p. 209. Bolingbroke's religious ideas are stated at large in the essays composing vol. V of his *Works.*

[12] "Reminiscences," in *Correspondence,* III, 1289.

[13] On the eighteenth-century Lockean approach to this issue, see Kenneth MacLean, *John Locke and English Literature of the Eighteenth Century* (1936; rpt., New York: Russell and Russell, 1962), pp. 146ff.

[14] "Those—Dying Then," in *The Poems of Emily Dickinson,* ed. Thomas H. Johnson (Cambridge, Mass.: Harvard University Press, 1955), III, 1069.

[15] Two interesting discussions of this issue are: G. S. Rousseau, "Gray's *Elegy* Reconsidered," *The Spectator,* Oct. 2, 1971, p. 490; and Jean H. Hagstrum, "Gray's Sensibility," in *Fearful Joy: Papers from the Thomas Gray Bicentenary Conference at Carleton University,* ed. James Downey and Ben Jones (Montreal: McGill-Queen's University Press, 1974), pp. 6-19.

[16] Roger Martin, Gray's perceptive biographer, examines his "impression de néant" and provides additional examples of it in his *Essai sur Thomas Gray* (Paris: Presses Universitaries de France, 1934), pp. 22-23.

[17] Jan. 14, 1735, *Correspondence,* I, 18.

[18] Mar. 28, 1738, and Dec., 1734, ibid., pp. 83-84, 12.

[19] April 12, 1770, ibid., III, 1118.

[20] Quoted in Mason, *Memoirs,* pp. 202-03.

[21] Sept. 11, 1746, *Correspondence,* I, 240.

[22] "Blake on Gray: Outlines of Recognition," in *Fearful Joy,* p. 129.

[23] To Walpole, Feb. 3, 1746, *Correspondence,* I, 230.

[24] I am in general agreement with Roger Lonsdale's conclusions, in his insightful discussion of the poems of 1742, about the sterility of isolated self-consciousness: see "The Poetry of Thomas Gray: Versions of the Self," *Proceedings of the British Academy,* 59 (1973), 114-18.

[25] Among the critics who have applauded Gray's original conclusion are: R. W. Ketton-Cremer, *Thomas Gray: A Biography* (Cambridge: Cambridge University Press, 1955), pp. 98-100; F. W. Bateson, *English Poetry: A Critical Introduction,* 2nd ed., rev. (New York: Barnes and Noble, 1966), pp. 128-31; and Clarence Tracy, "'Melancholy Mark'd Him for Her Own': Thomas Gray Two Hundred Years Afterwards," *Transactions of the Royal Society of Canada,* 4th ser., 9 (1971), 318.

[26] Lonsdale, "Poetry of Thomas Gray," pp. 107-08, furnishes additional reasons for regarding "the attempted calm of this conclusion to the poem" as "precarious." George T. Wright, in "Stillness and the Argument of Gray's *Elegy,*" *Modern Philology,* 74 (1977), 381-89, emphasizes the negative implications of the churchyard's stillness and accordingly finds the resignation of Gray's first conclusion inconsistent with the poem's argument. But although Wright may be correct in suggesting that "stillness and resistance to it compose [Gray's] argument," I cannot agree with his statement that the *Elegy*'s real "point" is "that we all need epitaphs" (p. 387); nor can I agree that, in the context of the poem, epitaphs and a reliance on God provide a real fulfillment of man's desire to resist death.

[27] Jack, "Gray's *Elegy* Reconsidered," in *From Sensibility to Romanticism: Essays Presented to Frederick A. Pottle,* ed. Frederick W. Hilles and Harold Bloom (New York: Oxford University Press, 1965), p. 146.

[28] Nov. 1747, *Correspondence,* I, 289.

[29] Mar. 9, 1755, ibid., p. 420.

[30] Most of the critics who have engaged in the long debate about whether the *Elegy's* description of the speaker refers personally to Gray or is purely impersonal or conventional would agree with Ketton-Cremer's judgment that the Swain offers a "strangely dramatised description of a poet in aspect and behaviour the complete antithesis of Gray" (*Thomas Gray,* p. 101). Such assertions seem rather surprising in view of what we know of Gray's character; they are well refuted by Hagstrum in "Gray's Sensibility," pp. 16-17.

[31] Frank Brady, "Structure and Meaning in Gray's *Elegy,*" in *From Sensibility to Romanticism,* pp. 185-87, gives more emphasis than I would to the speaker's partial fulfillment of himself through his one friendship, but he correctly emphasizes the speaker's isolation and the fact that the Epitaph shows that "only the individual can know to what extent he has fulfilled himself."

[32] Norton Nicholls wrote, "I asked him how he felt when he composed the *'Bard'.* 'Why I felt myself the bard.'" See "Reminiscences," *Correspondence,* III, 1290.

[33] "The Proper Language of Poetry: Gray, Johnson, and Others," in *Fearful Joy,* pp. 92-93.

[34] *The History of Rasselas Prince of Abissinia,* ed. Geoffrey Tillotson and Brian Jenkins (London: Oxford University Press, 1971), chap. XLIV (p. 114).

[35] Morris Golden, *Thomas Gray* (New York: Twayne, 1964), pp. 111, 113, comments on the way in which Gray "catches and amplifies . . . the sense of elemental amorality of the divinities" in *The Fatal Sisters.*

[36] Gray's text is translated in *Complete Poems,* pp. 216-18.

[37] As quoted in *Complete Poems,* p. 234.

[38] Mason quotes and discusses the Commonplace Book entry in *Poems of Mr. Gray,* pp. 91-92.

[39] "The Cistern and the Fountain: Art and Reality in Pope and Gray," in *Studies in Criticism and Aesthetics,* ed. Howard Anderson and John S. Shea (Minneapolis: University of Minnesota Press, 1967), pp. 174-75.

[40] See Jean Hagstrum, *The Sister Arts: The Tradition of Literary Pictorialism and English Poetry from Dryden to Gray* (Chicago: University of Chicago Press 1958), pp. 301-14; and Patricia Meyer Spacks, *The Poetry of Vision: Five Eighteenth-Century Poets* (Cambridge, Mass.: Harvard University Press, 1967), pp. 110-18.

Wallace Jackson (essay date 1987)

SOURCE: "Thomas Gray and the Dedicatory Muse," in *ELH,* Vol. 54, No. 2, Summer, 1987, pp. 277-98.

[*In the following essay, Jackson provides a detailed examination of Gray's treatment of the themes of desire and authority in his poetry.*]

I will be occupied here with one abiding question: what kingdom of the imagination does Thomas Gray wish to build? I do not think I can quite explain why he is the most disappointing poet of the English eighteenth century—disappointing, that is, in terms of what was expected of him—but I do hope to explore the nature of a failed enterprise that of its kind is unrivaled within the century. I attribute this failure to no cultural malaise, for it seems to me utterly and completely personal, nor do I propose that had Gray been born in the year he died (1771) he would have become another sort of poet, flourishing in and helping to create the poetic climate inhabited by Blake or Wordsworth or Coleridge. Rather, it appears, Gray could not fully serve the muse of his own dedication, the figure he deliberately wills into existence and to whom he devotes his powers.

Though I draw no analytical or interpretive conclusions bearing upon Gray's poetry from the facts of his life, I think them conspicuous and in need of restating at the beginning of this inquiry. Thomas Gray was the fifth of twelve children born to Dorothy and Philip Gray and the only one to survive infancy. His father, given to occasional and brutal fits of insanity, abused his wife physically during the several decades of their marriage. Though she separated from him, Philip threatened to "pursue her with all the vengeance possible," willing to "ruin himself to undo her, and his only son."[1] She returned to him. Thomas attended Eton and then Cambridge, where he was to live most of his quiet bachelor existence in Peterhouse and Pembroke Colleges. At Eton he met Richard West and Horace Walpole. With the exception of his mother, West was the most beloved person in Gray's life, and the early death of this promising young man was a distinct and grievous loss to Gray. He died in 1742, the year of Gray's greatest productivity, though some of the work of that year was inspired neither by West's death nor Gray's anticipation of it. After 1742 he wrote poetry sporadically and passed the larger part of his life in various historical, literary, and scientific activities. Toward the end he solicited and was given the Professorship of Modern History at Cambridge, though he never lectured nor published on the subject. The most impressive personal event of his last years was a brief and intense friendship with the young Swiss student, Charles-Victor de Bonstetten. Gray's attention to him was apparently complicated by physical desire, though no sexual relation is known or believed to have occurred between them. In his *Souvenirs* of 1831, Bonstetten reflected on his knowledge of the poet who had died more than half a century earlier: "Je crois que Gray n'avait jamais aimé, c'était le mot de l'énigme, il en était résulté une misère de coeur qui faisait contraste avec son imagination ardente et profond qui, au lieu de faire le bonheur de sa vie, n'en était que le tourment."[2] These are the very barest of surviving bones, yet they may lend some biographical anatomy to my argument, which, however, is in no way dependent upon a behavioral thesis.

West's death in the late spring of 1742 inspired the well-known elegiac sonnet, yet this is the shortest and least significant work of the year. The **"Ode on the Spring"** owes something to West's own ode sent to Gray on May 5, and the **"Eton College Ode"** may owe something also to West's recollective lines on Eton in his "Ode to Mary Magdelene." The **"Ode to Adversity"** and the **"Hymn to Ignorance"** (unfinished) complete the work of the year, which, together with 1741, may comprise the most emotionally critical period in Gray's life. He quarreled with Walpole during their European tour and travelled back to England alone in the summer. In November his father died; the extensive collection of extant letters is silent on this event. West's subsequent death did not interrupt the flow of poetry during the year, nor, most importantly, did it alter the essential character of what had been written previously.

The typical plot of the longer poems of 1742 takes the form of engagement with a figure of desire, sometimes repudiating it by way of ironic denigration, as in the **"Ode on the Spring,"** or by suggesting its futility, as in the **"Eton College Ode,"** or, more complexly, by transposing one figure into an opposite and alternative form, as in the **"Ode to Adversity."** In the **"Hymn to Ignorance,"** the mock-serious evocation of a quasi-Dunciadic goddess Ignorance is used to rebuke the "I" who longs for the maternal and daemonic presence. In various ways these four poems enact the imagination's quest for its tutelary spirit, its self-shaping identity, and the nature of that quest is played out within poems that have little ostensible relation to each other, but which in fact organize the imagination's desire for its own special muse. The **"Elegy Written in a Country Churchyard,"** which derives from these poems, is an outgrowth of the poet's search for the elegiac muse, and creates a peculiarly imaginative vision that leads into both **"The Progress of Poesy"** and **"The Bard,"**

the latter an effort by Gray to control the darkness that the **"Elegy"** summoned and to find in the night of his own muse the power of prophetic speaking. The large-scale issue in these poems is, then, the creation of the self's presiding muse and the poet's effort to explore the meaning of his dedication for his poetry.

The **"Ode on the Spring"** was written while West was yet alive and is to some extent a response to the ode he sent Gray on May 5, 1742. West's poem invokes spring ("the tardy May") within the familiar myth of reawakening and seasonal deity. As "fairest nymph" May is asked to resume her reign, to "Bring all the Graces in [her] train" (7-8), and be the beneficent goddess presiding over a reviving world.[3] She is in this context the obvious and unperplexed figure of desire. Gray's answer, his **"Ode to the Spring,"** was sent to West at just about the time of his death and returned unopened ("Sent to Fav: not knowing he was then Dead").[4] It takes the implicit form of elegy, a meditative displacement of spring from the context of renewal to that of death, and is not inconsistent with an earlier letter to West in which he explains himself as the frequent victim of "a white Melancholy, or rather Leucocholy," but also the occasional host to "another sort, black indeed, which I have now and then felt, that has somewhat in it like Tertullian's rule of faith, Credo quia impossibile est; for it believes, nay, is sure of every thing that is unlikely, so it be but frightful; and, on the other hand, excludes and shuts its eyes to the most possible hopes."[5]

The **"Ode on the Spring"** introduces "fair Venus" attended by "the rosy-bosomed Hours" (1-2) in order to repudiate her. The initial sexualized appeal is later transposed into the ironic diminishment of human desire likened to that of the "insect youth . . . / Eager to taste the honeyed spring" (25-26), and mediated through the "sober eye" of Contemplation. Already characteristic of Gray is the distant view advocated by a tutelary figure who endorses the terms of repudiation and isolation:

> Beside some water's rushy brink
> With me the Muse shall sit, and think
> (At ease reclined in rustic state)
> How vain the ardour of the crowd,
> How low, how little are the proud,
> How indigent the great!
>
>   (15-20)

The lines preview Gray's later and better known appreciation of rustic simplicity against the claims of the proud and great, but the more immediate issue turns on the inception of a poetic persona to be variously adapted and modified during the coming years. The companionable relation between poet and muse establishes a tutelary presence. Muse converts into the more formidable Contemplation, both figures of authority to be posed against the more directly sensual appeal of Love or Venus. (Contemplation will reappear in the **"Elegy"** as "lonely Contemplation" (95), where it will lead some kindred spirit to inquire into the poet's fate.)

The pleasure to which West's ode speaks so directly ("Come then, with Pleasure at they side" [25]) is figured in Gray's ode as "rosy-bosomed Hours," later transposed into the frivolous forms of insect youth in "gaily-gilded trim" (29), "dressed" in "Fortune's varying colours" (37), and finally subject to the indifferently directed indignities of "rough Mischance" (38). If indeed the effort is to chastise desire by debasing its appeal through various stages, from "rosy-bosomed" to "painted plumage" (47), the intention is equally to authorize repudiation through the controlling figures of "fortune" and "Mischance." West's injunction to "Create . . . / Peace, Plenty, Love, and Harmony" (27-28) is repositioned within the ambiguously asserted theme of *carpe diem* concluding Gray's ode, the reproof offered the speaker by the sportive kind: "We frolic, while 'tis May" (50), whereas the speaker is nothing other than a "solitary fly" (44).

If the poem admits rebuke of the speaker it does so by diminishing him within the reductive context he has himself fashioned for the "sportive kind." The strategy that reinvents the figure of love as "glittering female," passions as "hoarded sweets" and beauty as "painted plumage" (45-47) displaces the human onto an antithetical though analogous form of life. It is, in brief, designed to empty desire of its appeal, transmuting it by ironically extending and exploring the analogy between the ardent crowd ("the ardour of the crowd" [18]) and insect youth. The return of the figure of love as "glittering female" splits the object into two incompatible parts, and further defines the muse as a power endorsing withdrawal and repudiation. Contemplation is the figure created by thought ("With me the Muse shall sit, and think" [16]), the combined activity of poet and muse or the effect of the muse upon the poet. Contemplation as an instrument or agency of repression defeats the figure of desire. As an answer to West's frankly sensual image of an awakening May, a creative power, Gray depresses the figure of desire into proximity, or perhaps identification, with insect life, the implied relation between awakenings in spring common to each thereby carrying Gray's point. What awakens in the **"Ode on the Spring"** is a figure that cannot awaken desire and is also a subliminal image of desire as forbidden female ("glittering," "painted"). At the moment of closure, despite the ironic concession (and even because of it) the defeat of Venus is complete. Clearly, the ode specifies sexual withdrawal, announcing the uses to which the muse may be put and defining the very ground of vision that is the measure of the muse's authority. The poem may therefore offer a model for reading Gray's early poetry, which may continue to dramatize the various rejections of desire as the major

adventure of the resident ego within the poems. If so, we are given a poetry that is beginning to announce itself in the special sense of a clarified and dramatized relation between poet and muse, a drawing out of a particular imaginative province, a space within which, like Coleridge's honey-dew drunken visionary, the poet enacts his own magic. The visionary space is declared:

> Where'er the oak's thick branches stretch
> A broader browner shade;
> Where'er the rude and moss-grown beech
> O'er canopies the glade.
>
> (11-14)

The beech is the first of its sheltering kind; the "hoary-headed swain" will later locate the poet of the **"Elegy"** at "the foot of yonder nodding beech" (101).

In the **"Eton College Ode"** the iconography of desire is figured in the spectral presences of "grateful Science [who] still adores / Her Henry's holy shade" (3-4). The ode's opening implies the persistence of desire within the trope of loss and mourning, the landscape informed with elegiac sentiment. It is almost impossible to arbitrate the tonality implicit in "Henry's holy *shade*" in juxtaposition to the "expanse below" of "turf" and "*shade,* whose flowers among / Wanders the hoary Thames along," and those "happy hills" and "pleasing *shade*" of Eton's landscape (6-11; all my italics). The correspondence of spectral to natural facts (shade to shade) insists upon the interrelations of shade and shadow (*skot*: dark; shade, shadow). "Pleasing shade" anticipates the darkness of the **"Elegy"** ("And leaves the world to darkness and to me" [4]). Shade is thus both the unseen presence (Henry) *and* place darkly containing "hoary Thames" (9), the figure of authority invoked to "Say," to "show," and to "tell" the Etonians "they are men" (60). Shade is equally the place below ("And ye that from the stately brow / Of Windsor's heights the expanse below / Of grove, of lawn, of mead survey, / Whose turf, whose shade. . . ." [5-8]). As such it is the place from which phantoms arise: "Lo, in the vale of years beneath / A grisly troop are seen" (80-81).

Science and Henry are threshold figures, icons of desire and loss signifying the import of the speaker's return: the apprehension of yearning and loss. If "shade" is the determining ground of the real in the poem, what arises from the Etonian landscape are more shades, presences of future and further loss, "ministers of human fate" (56), the personifications Anger, Fear, Shame, et al., images of desire baffled and defeated: "Or pining Love shall waste their youth, / Or Jealousy with rankling tooth" (65-66). Such figures have the same imaginative status as Science and Henry, and the same strategy pertains as in the **"Ode on the Spring."** Desire and loss are unified within the elegiac consciousness; they exist as a single perception, the very ground of recognition inhabited by the speaker himself, the determining awareness of his return.

The antique presence of Father Thames tends to authorize the speaker's vision, acting as a silent confirmatory figure, another version of the tutelary Muse or Contemplation. The shade Henry is equivalent to various other dim figures in Gray's verse, those who have vanished and need to be recalled and recreated: the "busy housewife" and "village Hampden" of the **"Elegy."** Absence is elegiac presence, figures recovered from the vale of years beneath. An imagination disposed to engage with the world in this way is also likely to envision characters who have not yet existed, as in the Bard's evocation of an historical future: "'But oh! what solemn scenes on Snowden's height / 'Descending slow their glittering skirts unroll?'" (105-6).

Muse or Contemplation or Thames are agents of authority evoked precisely for the prophetic wisdom they possess, the judgments they render. One function of prophecy is thus to daemonize desire, transforming it into "pining Love" (as in Science's for Henry) or the "fury Passions" (61). The imagination's habit of prosopopoeia exposes the debased forms desire assumes ("Envy wan, and faded Care" [68]), even as the "race of man" in the **"Ode on the Spring"** is revealed as insect life to "Contemplation's sober eye" (31-32). Vision is always in the service of the revealed form, and in Gray the revelation takes the shape of a diminished, repudiated, or forbidden thing. The strategy of reductive acknowledgment in the **"Ode on the Spring"** coexists with the making of giant spectral forms in the **"Eton College Ode."** One strategy dismisses the dream of desire, the other encourages bad dreams, translating desire into the daemonic. Frye defines something very similar to this action in his discussion of quest-romance: "Translated into dream terms, the quest-romance is the search of the libido or desiring self for a fulfillment that will deliver it from the anxieties of reality but still contain that reality."[6] Fulfillment may require, as with Gray, that a protective maternal figure displace a threatening judicial figure of the same sex, and guilt is thereby dissipated in the approbation bestowed upon the obedient actor who has rejected desire. This summary describes another of the poems of 1742, the **"Ode to Adversity."**

The relation between Adversity and Virtue, both daughters of Jove, though the former is older and tutor to the latter, implies a correspondence within dissimilitude. Adversity, equipped with the icons of affliction ("iron scourge and torturing hour" [3]) has also an alternative "form benign," "a milder influence" (41,42). Virtue requires adversity to "form her infant mind" (12); the function of the tutelary spirit being to engender pity ("she learned to melt at others' woe" [16]), the instruction absorbed by Virtue, the "rigid lore / With patience many a year she bore" (13-14). This may be a proce-

dure that leaves Gray poised at the edge of the **"Elegy,"** even as it positions him securely within the mournful boundaries of elegiac sensibility. Virtue subdued by Adversity is tempered to the recognition of grief ("What sorrow was, thou bad'st her know" [15]) and preserved from the temptations of desire ("Scared at thy frown terrific, fly / Self-pleasing Folly's idle brood, / Wild Laughter, Noise, and thoughtless Joy, / And leave us leisure to be good" [17-20]). Adversity implored to "lay [her] chastening hand" on her "suppliant's head" and to appear "Not in thy Gorgon terrors clad, / Nor circled with the vengeful band / (As by the impious thou art seen)" (33-37) suggests an acute awareness of the sexualized daemonic, the threatening form of Adversity seen by those who are not "good." Desire converted into the antithetical form of horror is part of the paradoxical tutelage of Adversity, the latent power she is petitioned not to assume and which she exists to repudiate. The Medusan image clearly acts to dispel a sensuality happily diverted into the practice of virtue, but not before the ode has created within one identity both the figure of authority and the gothic figure of desire it exists to exorcise.

The chastened speaker who experiences Adversity's "milder influence," her "philosophic train" (42, 43) undergoes an orientation whereby feelings of guilt are translated into the generous emotions, "to love and to forgive" (46). Part of the purpose of the three poems is obviously to find a subject for Gray's muse, but also to make of the burden of anxiety the grounds of the humanistic imagination. Adversity takes place here with Muse, Contemplation, Thames, all figures authorizing the repudiation and rejection of desire. It is worth noting also that the relation between Virtue and Adversity previews the later relations between Shakespeare and his "mighty Mother," between Gray as infant and his muse, in **"The Progress of Poesy."** At the end of the **"Eton College Ode"** we are reminded that the suffering "all are men" (91). At the close of the **"Ode to Adversity"** the speaker, taught "to love and to forgive" is led to "know myself a man" (46-48).

No one would doubt, I think, that Gray's poems signal a radical sexual distress. In a literature that deals frequently with infants and infantile states it is hard to credit on the face of it Gray's "know myself a man." If the self assumes (a) virtue, it does so because Virtue is clearly the emergent figure of desire in the poem. She completes a circuit that begins with Venus in the **"Ode to the Spring"** and closes temporarily upon Virtue. Peter Sacks remarks that for the elegiac poet the "movement from loss to consolation . . . requires a deflection of desire," but in Gray the deflection precedes elegy or the elegiac occasion.[7] It is in fact the deflection of desire that creates the elegiac poet who will be neither the poet of romance (witness the fate of Venus) nor the bard of the sublime (notice the Gorgonian terrors of Adversity). The only sublime to be admitted is the prophetic vision, an early version of which is the **"Eton College Ode,"** the greater form that of **"The Bard."** The deflection of desire will lead inevitably but not immediately to thanatos, but before it arrives it has other stops to make. At the moment, however, we have arrived at the first clear castrative sacrifice in the progress of Gray's imagination (though I would want to suggest that the reduction to insect life in the earlier ode is a significant investment in sexual loss), the replacement of Virtue (both infant and female) by the poet. The substitution has had to pass through the horror of the Medusan figure. The more complex association in the poem is between the serpents and "Horror's funeral cry," (39), a relation that specifically indicates the immediate meaning of elegy for Gray. Because of the presence of Virtue that meaning is emptied of its horror, and the threat of castration is transposed into an acceptance of it. Gray therefore assumes the role of the figure of desire under the aegis of Adversity. This is what Freud calls an apotropaic act, one designed to ward off evil.

But I am arguing a more radical proposition: the warding off of evil can only be accomplished by the acceptance of an evil: castration and elegy are significantly related elements within the same imagination. At the same time, as Sacks makes clear, the "elegist's reward . . . often involve[s] inherited legacies and consoling identifications with symbolic, even immortal, figures of power."[8] These figures have been taking shape in Gray's poems. In the **"Ode on the Spring,"** Contemplation is so employed. The far more powerful and threatening figure of Adversity is pacified in a far more complex way but also requires a greater surrender of sexual identity. To some extent we may account on this basis for the curious representations of presence in Gray's later works, especially in the **"Elegy,"** wherein the scene of life is wholly imagined and where the "hoary-headed swain" and "kindred spirit" are figures in a future as yet unarrived. Absence then becomes the imaginative form of desire; what is desired is absence and absent, and the elimination of the "I" in favor of a "thee" is only another strategy of removal. Deflection is the desired mode of encounter, and evasion or incapacity is the satisfactory figure of fulfillment ("Some village Hampden," "Some Cromwell guiltless" [57, 60]).

Have we arrived at the moment when the elegiac poet has been created? The **"Hymn to Ignorance"** is a companion piece to the Eton ode because return is again the ostensible subject. Gray returns to Cambridge, invoking its "gothic fanes and antiquated towers" (2) much as he had Eton's "distant spires" and "antique towers" (1). However mockingly desire is proposed by the speaker of the poem, obviously written with the *Dunciad* in mind, Ignorance is that figure, the conflated Cibberian goddess and mighty mother. The Eton ode's recognition that "ignorance [small i] is bliss" (99) is reimagined so that Ignorance [large I] is a "soft salutary power" (9). The effort is to write Ignorance into Gray's ongoing history of abnegation, his return to Peterhouse as a Fellow-Commoner to read for a law degree on October 15, 1742. How should we understand this playful **"Hymn"** that is the only fragment of the 1742 poems? Ignorance is a maternal presence ("Prostrate with filial reverence I adore"), possessed of a "peaceful shade," whose "influence . . . / Augments the native darkness of the sky" (6-10). Ignorance is thus an early power of darkness ambivalently represented as undesirable within the terms of desire ("Thrice hath Hyperion rolled his annual race, / Since weeping I forsook thy fond embrace" [11-12]). Clearly, the oedipal actors include mother/muse (Ignorance), Hyperionic father, and the returning son/poet, Gray himself.

The departure from Cambridge—really from Ignorance—conceals and mocks an earlier and more radical separation. The return cannot be admitted by Gray within the oedipal formula, but it can be proposed both as symbolic substitute and as the negation of desire within the mock-epic manner. The figures of desire and authority are viewed within the perspective that comic repudiation permits. Though Gray *means* that his return is to night, and to an undeterminable extent a betrayal of the self, the complex of related elements further defines the goal of the journey—the recognition and creation of muse/mother. If, as Sacks indicates, the "primary desire" of the child is "for the extinction of desire itself," what better investment to make than in a *power* nominally grotesque?[9] The "I" of the **"Hymn"** is mocked effectively within the oedipal fantasy, though the fantasy contains the true form of desire.

Gray desires and desires not to desire, and ambivalence is sustained in somewhat the same way as in the **"Ode to Adversity."** The difference in the **"Hymn,"** however, is that the goddess is ostensibly repudiated, though of course she is not. The danger for the poet is possession, yet the contrary danger is not being able to write at all. Gray will work out these dramas of poetic identity within the later Pindaric odes. For the moment, however, of the four poems so far reviewed none is formally elegiac, though each in its way acknowledges death. The **"Hymn"** does so more than any of the others because it is directed to the recovery of what has suffered closure. Ignorance's function is to renew or recover (as was, in its way, that of the speaker of the Eton ode), to "bring the buried ages back to view" (35). This is almost identical to the task assumed by the poet in the **"Elegy,"** whose act is restorative in the sense that he makes present those who are in truth buried, and is inversely related to the bardic seer of the Pindaric poem, who makes present for Edward the as yet unborn.

Henceforth the generative ground of vision will be death itself. The repeated rejection and transformation of the figures of desire in the early poems now tends to turn into a coherence formed of desire and authority, as in the **"Ode to Adversity,"** or ironically approbated, as in the **"Hymn to Ignorance."** Some effort to heal a split between the two previously antithetical figures seems in progress in Gray's imagination, though the **"Hymn"** proposes a fusion of desire and authority too devastating to be countenanced except on its own terms. The *Dunciad* provided a model; the substitution of "I" for Cibberian fool is the necessary change for the self-satiric mode, the "I" intentionally and evasively self and not-self. As magna mater, Ignorance is now the complex entity made up of mother, muse, and death ("And all was Ignorance, and all was Night" [30]). The anti-sublime masks what Thomas Weiskel would call "transcendent self-justification," the daemonic identity that possession imposes.[10]

When Gray returns to writing poetry several years later, he composes two different poems that differently rebuke desire. Walpole's cat is not the Miltonic transgressor of **"The Progress of Poesy,"** "blasted with excess of light" for presuming to spy into the "secrets of the abyss" (101, 97). Yet she is another occasion of desire tempted beyond "lawful prize" into a watery grave. The **"Ode on the Death of a Favourite Cat"** (1747) is thus a cautionary tale, its purpose to deaden desire by revealing its effect upon the "Presumptuous maid!" Selima's investment in desire, her effort to apprehend "two angel forms," the "genii of the stream" (14, 15), is another investment in death, whether or not it is exactly as Blake's illustration would have it, an example of "a mutual love that she lacks and desires to experience."[11] Her fall, in any event, is another occasion of transgression, another drama of intended misappropriation. Implicit in the scene of desire is the unattainability of the object, and the abandonment of the supplicating figure to her fate: "Eight times emerging from the flood / She mewed to every watery god" (31-32). The fear of what lies beyond the self seems to govern Gray's perception of her ("Still had she gazed" [13] and no harm come to her). Selima's fate appears as if to Contemplation's sober eye in the concluding stanza, and elegy is now the mode for deriding desire. Selima's plunge is perhaps desire's dream to discover in its own depths the essential object, but the object is inseparable from death. The figure of desire is death.

In **"A Long Story"** (1750) the parodic form of the poet of the **"Elegy"** is created in the poem's weak trembling thing, also an outsider. The peeress whose judgment the poet fears, but who instead of rebuking him invites him to dinner, is the benign if not comic enactment of commanding females in the line of *magna mater,* and brought before her authority the poet disavows himself:

He once or twice had penned a sonnet;
Yet hoped that he might save his bacon:
Numbers would give their oaths upon it,
He ne'er was for a conjurer taken.

                                        (125-28)

The dramatization of **"A Long Story"** involves a flight from the figures of desire, the "heroines" who attempt to lure the poet into polite country pleasures, leaving a note ("a spell') upon the table; a dread of judgment, summed up in the imposing form of the Viscountess; and the representation and deflection of guilt within the formula of mock criminality: "When he the solemn hall had seen; / A sudden fit of ague shook him, / He stood as mute as poor Macleane" (118-20).

The self-presentation turns back upon the **"Elegy"**: the poet heard there by the swain, "'Muttering his wayward fancies'" (105), is here "something . . . heard to mutter, / 'How in the park beneath an old-tree / '(Without design to hurt the butter, / 'Or any malice to the poultry,) . . .'" (121-24). The old-tree is apparently the transplanted "nodding beech" of the **"Elegy,"** under which the poet "'His listless length at noontide would he stretch'" (103). What is concealed in **"A Long Story"** is the reality of an elegiac identity that cannot be communicated or received on its own terms within an alien context. Public recognition is evaded by parodic rebuke, and identity is imaged only as it would be perceived and understood by those outside the domain of elegiac vision. If **"The Favourite Cat"** images the fate of desire, **"A Long Story"** reflects the self-alienation imposed upon the poet by the necessities of his own vision; that is, the discrepancy between propria persona and poetic persona. The discontinuity of address, which everyone has noticed in the **"Elegy"**'s shift from "I" to "thee," is oddly present in the abrupt intrusiveness of another voice in **"A Long Story,"** whereby the speaker is rebuked for his tedium: "Your history whither you are spinning? / Can you do nothing but describe?" (19-20) Voice is both critical and unidentified—a function of what split within an identity that keeps eluding itself?—or is simply lost: "(Here 500 stanzas are lost)" (141). **"A Long Story"** is in fact a short one (145 lines) of identity mocked, or function abused ("whither are you spinning?"), and of voice lost. Yet the poem is also an occasion to contextualize and avow the yet to be announced "distant way" of **"The Progress of Poesy,"** as well as a pause on the path leading to that vigorous affirmation of elegiac identity, **"The Bard."**

For the moment what dominates Gray's imagination is an anxiety of office, of prophecy reduced to a lame absurdity, the dissolution of a calling into random mischief, in which the seer becomes merely a bothersome miscreant:

Who prowled the country far and near,
Bewitched the children of the peasants,

Dried up the cows and lamed the deer,
And sucked the eggs and killed the pheasants.

(45-48)

Village superstition is the debased version of poetic prophecy, and the poem itself is a concealed commentary on an identity that cannot cross boundaries.

The inception of **"The Progress of Poesy"** (1751) follows directly upon the publication of the **"Elegy."** Its motive is grounded in a further, yet concealed, rendering of the self-image present especially at the close of the **"Elegy."** In one sense, the poet of the **"Elegy"** remains unjustified; that is, without reference to the generative occasion that has made him what he is (though that occasion is frequently evident within the canon itself). **"The Progress"** addresses the issue by specifically associating the solitary poet with mother-muse, the female goddess to whom he owes the dedication of his powers. What he owes is the capacity to perceive "forms" illuminated by the "Muse's ray" (119), a substitute light that diminishes the Hyperionic presence in the ode and is "unborrowed of the sun" (120). Much of the ode, then, is directly leveled against any rising impulse to celebrate the poet of apocalyptic vision and to evoke instead the lonely bard of elegiac sentiment.

Ceres ("Ceres' golden reign" [9]) is originally an Italian deity embodying the generative power of nature. "Helicon's harmonious springs" (3) are obviously associated with generation ("The laughing flowers . . . / Drink life and fragrance as they flow" [5-6]). The lyre is the "Parent of sweet and solemn-breathing airs" (14). The three elements are brought into procreative proximity and dominate the opening of the poem. The first ternary closes upon Aphrodite ("Cytherea's day" [29]). The sea-born goddess is another figuring of generative force mingling in her progress the union of water and music ("brisk notes in cadence beating"; "arms sublime, that float upon the air" [34, 38]). She is the re-emergent Venus of the **"Ode on the Spring"** attended, as was Venus, by a train of celebrants ("the Graces homage pay" [37]). Here: "O'er her warm cheek and rising bosom move / The bloom of young desire and purple light of love" (40-41). There, in the **"Ode on the Spring,"** the "rosy-bosomed Hours, / . . . Disclose the long-expecting flowers, / And wake the purple year" (1-4).

However attractive the conflated figures of desire (Ceres, Lyre, Venus), there may yet be the faintest intimation that the demi-pastoral mode conceals its vipers ("In gliding state she [Venus] wins her easy way" [39]). I do not push the point beyond noticing that it is consistent with the various doubts the sexualized figure of desire has occasioned in the past. The more immediate challenge is the more conventional one, the familiar Etonian daemons: "Man's feeble race what ills await, / Labour, and penury, the racks of pain" (42-43). Such ills raise doubts about omnipotence, requiring that Gray's song "disprove" the "fond complaint," and "justify the laws of Jove" (46, 47). The Miltonic query waits upon the necessity: "Say, has he given in vain the heavenly Muse?" (48) Clearly, the recognition of loss rises in the second ternary against the figures of desire, disputing their power, and directly opposing them with their own negation, the elegiac presence of "Night and all her sickly dews" (49). Sickly dews are the alternative to Helicon's "thousand rills" (4), a reminder of the shrunken power of regenerative music within the context controlled by Night, a "mighty Mother" of sorts, who is licensed "Till down the eastern cliffs afar / Hyperion's march they spy and glittering shafts of war" (52-53). Hyperion is an idealized poetic figure, an emissary associated through eastern cliffs with Milton's Raphael, and more vaguely recollective of Christ's armory as he disposes half his might against Satan's legions. Yet the ode relegates his progress to an indefinite future, to an apocalyptic dawn that may be said to "justify the laws of Jove." The suspended presence of Hyperion (actually his departure from the poem) occurs almost at mid-point in its progress, at the close of the first strophe of the second ternary. By this means the defeat of the elegiac Night, the graveyard goddess whose "spectres wan and birds of boding cry" (50) are the antithesis to the "rosy-crowned Loves" (28) attendant upon Aphrodite, is deferred.

The "Muse" who now appears is a variation on the pastoral-maternal female, one who "designs to hear the savage youth repeat / In loose numbers wildly sweet / Their feather-cinctured chiefs and dusky loves" (60-62). She is thus a "soft salutary power" (**"Hymn to Ignorance"**), another "form benign" (**"Ode to Adversity"**). The muse (recall here the lyre as "Parent of sweet and solemn-breathing airs") pastoralizes the progress and the residual traces of generation are again imaged in

Woods that wave o'er Delphi's steep,
Isles that crown the Aegean deep,
Fields that cool Illissus laves,
Or where Maeander's amber waves
In lingering lab'rinths creep.

(66-70)

"Helicon's harmonious springs" redivivus.

Against Night the ode accumulates a formidable array of females and the oedipal fantasy is played out in pastoral embowerings: "In thy green lap was Nature's darling laid, / What time, where lucid Avon strayed, / To him the mighty Mother did unveil / Her awful face" (84-87). The anticipation of unveiling is what led the Miltonic voyeur to ride "sublime / Upon the seraph-wings of Ecstasy, / The secrets of the abyss to spy" (95-97). Yet, the laws of Jove are at least preserved in the regressive fantasy: the primal scene is never viewed. If anything, the promised Hyperionic march endowed with "glittering shafts of war" (53) is rendered irrelevant by "Such forms as glitter in the Muse's ray" (119), forms that tease Gray's own "infant eyes" (118) bringing him thereby into proximity to the Shakespearean "immortal boy" (91). Those "orient hues" that dazzled the child Gray were "unborrowed of the sun" (120); the ode begins to close upon the exclusion of the redemptive Hyperionic poet-emissary-god-father. An elaborate scene has been played out under the aegis of many mothers, one in which Gray, affiliated with the Shakespearean boy, is justified in his "distant way" (121). "Distant" echoes the context shared by Shakespeare and his mother: "Far from the sun and summer-gale" (83). The "dauntless child" (87), the "mighty Mother" and the benedictive waters all locate a pastoral paradise, another isolated place, another rejection of the male (Hyperionic) principle. Between the oedipal desire and the reflective passion of the elegiac poet there is no adequate ground. The "distant way" is necessitated by the inevitability with which desire is frustrated or proscribed, by the very nature of the unattainable figure, muse as mother, mother as muse. Given what we have learned of the scene of desire in the poem it is quite clear why Gray images himself as solitary voyager through the space of his own alienation and why desire must be absent at the moment of closure.

The Shakespearean child to whom the "golden keys" (91) are given is permissively granted oedipal play ("This can unlock the gates of joy" [92]) and access to elegiac sentiment ("horror . . . and thrilling fear, / . . . sympathetic tears" [93-94]). (The tears may have less to do with Shakespeare than with the poet of the **"Elegy"**: "He gave to misery all he had, a tear." [123]) If the poem's ostensible myth is a progress, it covertly licenses a regress and offers the needed apologia for the poet's own solitude. The laws of Jove cannot be justified by Thomas Gray (though they will not be violated by him) because they require a knowledge enormous, an Apollonian or Hyperionic arising, obviously precluded by oedipal desire. The derivation of the self at the end of the ode is predicated on the *meaning* of Poesy to Gray. That meaning has an obvious political and cultural dimension, but it has far more importantly the task of justifying an idealized (and suspect) self-image. The justifying forebear is Shakespeare (another poet of feeling), so that if Gray "inherit / Nor the pride nor ample pinion, / That the Theban eagle bear / . . . Yet oft before his infant eyes would run" (113-18).

The ideal self is situated somewhat like the melancholic outcast and village oddity, the "youth . . . unknown" (**"Elegy,"** 18). He is constellated in a poetic heaven, positioned "Beyond," "Beneath . . . but far above" (122-23), in any event, alone. Gray will not herald nor will he document the progress of the poet of "glittering

shafts" who will dispel "Disease and sorrow's weeping train, / And death, sad refuge from the storms of fate" (44-45). However wintry the elegiac climate, its waters ("storms") flow from the "sacred source of sympathetic tears" (94) and are ultimately traceable to the fountain of all song. "Helicon's harmonious springs."

"The Bard" has always been recognized as something of a companion-piece to **"The Progress."** It authorizes another elegiac identity, a solitary figure of prophetic power who, as elegiac seer eliciting the justice of redemptive history, more readily justifies the laws of Jove than any agent in the **"The Progress"** can. At the ode's opening he is "Robed in the sable garb of woe" (17), the very insignia of office. At its close he "plunge[s] to endless night" (144), another entrance into another darkness. The plunge into the abyss seems yet one more occasion of a wish-fulfillment fantasy. The poet in whom the authority of night is so invested ("Robed") returns to the authorizing ground of perception; the mighty mother is thus darkness itself, the unshaped figure of desire.

The poets of the **"Elegy"** and **"The Bard"** are antithetical voices. The former bespeaks a justice predicated on natural law ("Full many a flower is born to blush unseen") that requires the full engagement of the sympathetic imagination; the latter commands a justice that expunges the evil that has entered time and redeems the bardic visionaries. Such conceptions elicit two different if not wholly opposed responses to death and mourning. The "kindred spirit" is the self's similitude; the "'orb of day . . . [who] / 'Tomorrow . . . repairs the golden flood'" (136-37), has nothing to do with replications of the self, but everything to do with the Hyperionic renewal evaded in **"The Progress,"** or, more familiarly, with the rising soul and Christic redemption (a future nevertheless exclusive of the elegiac bard).

The poet who "Struck the deep sorrows of his lyre" (22) produces from that instrument not the "sweet and solemn-breathing airs" (14) of **"The Progress,"** but the harmonies of loss and consolation, the prophetic song that transforms elegy from its commemorative status to the designation of futurity (the temporality in which the law is justified). The ode thus locates "a target for a wrath that must be turned outward, the shifting of the burden of pain, the reversal from the passive suffering of hurt to the active causing of it, and above all, the assumption of the power to hurt."[12] Aggressively disposed, the elegiac ode is thereby conceivably motivated by the self-denying energies enlisted in the service of a poesy that cannot save its practitioners from Edward's brutality. The **"Elegy,"** on the other hand, repudiates power, the potency of act and voice; every approbated semblance of power is brought forth within diminished structures: village Hampdens, mute Miltons. **"The Bard"** grounds its authority differently, as the prophetic vision spins history out of itself, both seeing and creating: "'Weave the warp and weave the woof'" (49). "'(Weave we the woof. The thread is spun)'" (98).

Blake's sixth illustration to **"The Bard"** shows three poets who cling to the side of a cliff that "proves to be a mass of thick bloody ropes that are the clustered strings of a gigantic harp."[13] The harp strings are consistent with the threads of the prophetic loom, and the bloody ropes define the texture of which futurity is to be composed. The loom is the poetic instrument; object and function are identical. The rising soul, the "form divine" (115), is Renaissance Elizabeth, the figure of justice (a mighty mother?) concealed in time. Renewal in the **"Elegy"** via the kindred spirit is sublimed in the greater historical pageant of **"The Bard,"** in the energy that makes of succession something both more and other than the duplication of a previous sensibility. Time itself holds the emergent mystery of its regeneration, and elegy is the medium in which it is mirrored. For Gray to have come this far almost mandates the work of his last years, the translations and adaptations of Norse and Welsh poetry. But his arrival there also marks the place beyond which his vision does not go. I will come to these poems in a moment, but something first need be said about his last long fragment, the **"Ode on the Pleasure Arising from Vicissitude"** (1754-55).

The **"Eton College Ode"** identifies the progress of human life in terms of disjunction, absolute separation between youth and age. The **"Ode on Vicissitude"** recreates through the language of kindredness the law of succession and cycle: "Still, where rosy Pleasure leads, / See a kindred grief pursue" (33-34). "Rosy Pleasure" is conjoined here to an opposite that does not dispel it but follows it in an inevitable cyclical progress (yet another progress), a rationalized vision of endless alternation. The "blended form" (39) composed by the two figures arbitrates the previous displacements of the figure of desire by that of authority, and unifies the one with the other in what is apparently Gray's version of the marriage of heaven and hell. "Kindred" brings into focus the pattern of mourning and consolation, completing the elegiac design by filling-in the sequence of grief and recovery: "Behind the steps that Misery treads, / Approaching Comfort view" (35-36). The reversal following the succession of Pleasure by Grief (Comfort after Misery) presents time as a medium invulnerable to the lamentations of the returning Etonian visitor. The earlier calamity is averted by opposing continuity to discontinuity, by finding the principle of authority (and desire) in the figure of Vicissitude itself, a figure who imposes an Adversity-like "chastening":

> The hues of bliss more brightly glow,
> Chastised by sabler tints of woe.
>
> (37-38)

Once more the ode negates its initial figure of desire, "the golden Morn aloft" who

> wooes the tardy spring,
> Till April starts, and calls around
> The sleeping fragrance from the ground;
> And lightly o'er the living scene
> Scatters his freshest, tenderest green.
>
> (4-8)

Morn and April are two figures of commencement, each gradually replaced in the poem by the superior vision that sees with "foreward and reverted eyes" (24). The companionable pastoral presences give way to tableaux in which the kindred activities of mourning and consolation are enacted, "Soft Reflection" tracing with her hand "Smiles on past Misfortune's brow," or "o'er the cheek of Sorrow throw[ing] / A melancholy grace" (25-28). The initial act of wooing becomes, then, another sort of engagement, Grief pursuing rosy Pleasure, Comfort approaching Misery. In this context the "blended form" is a substitutional form, a sublimation of the frankly sexual ardor governing the relation between Morn and April, now transformed into a depersonalized aesthetic, in which "artful strife" and "strength and harmony" (39, 40), displace the seductive Morn who "With vermeil cheek and whispers soft / . . . wooes the tardy spring" (3-4). The ode is dominated by the metamorphosis of courtship into consolation, and the elegiac presence of Vicissitude is another figure companionable to Contemplation or Adversity, those personifications under whose earlier aegis desire was eliminated from the field of vision.

The force of the poem is to celebrate April ("The birds his presence greet; / But chief the sky-lark warbles high / His trembling thrilling ecstasy" [12-14]) and then to drive him into the category of things succeeded by other things, while gradually replacing him and Morn with the graveyard statuary that derives from the **"Elegy."** The figures of consolation, acting as they do to displace and dominate, urge fulfillment of the elegiac consciousness, tend to pictorialize the law of Vicissitude, and offer their own enactments of desexualized love. Vicissitude distantly responds to the mockery visited upon the alienated moralist of the **"Ode on the Spring"**; it corrects the isolation of the "solitary fly" within the structure of loss and gain, absence and presence, and in this way further explores the domain of elegy and the remedies for death and denial elegy provides. Vicissitude is itself (unlike Adversity) the neutralized figure of no gender, representing thereby no threatening image of the sexual horrific, but a power of the law realized in and through "blended form" and "artful strife."

The specific elegiac context is recalled and localized in those "deepest shades, that dimly lower / And blacken round our weary way" (30-31). The ode merely revisits another place, much like the revisiting of Eton by the disillusioned speaker or the return of Gray to Cambridge in the **"Hymn to Ignorance."** Here the return is to the opening of the **"Elegy,"** to "darkness" (again) and to the landscape over which the "ploughman . . . plods his weary way." The movement from weary way to weary way defines the condition of progress, the pilgrimage that is daily farther from the figures of desire and closer to the uncertain fruition implicit sometimes in forms of kinship, and sometimes, as in **"The Progress of Poesy,"** in a "distant way." The *way* is thus a progress ultimately joined; it is the dim measure of hope tacitly evident in Gray's vision ("Hope . . . / Gilds with a gleam of distant day" [29-32]), but way is also the path leading to that to which all paths lead. For Gray elegy is invested with the meaning of way, so that all of Gray's poems are poems of progress, journeys in which the peculiarity of imaginative challenge resides in discovering on the way something other than the circularity of ends that are constituted of beginnings ("And they that creep, and they that fly, / Shall end where they began" [**"Ode on the Spring,"** 33-34]). Like all fragments **"Vicissitude"** is bemused in its own progress, but it bespeaks a law that is one of the few principles of elegiac consolation. A symbolic order seems predicated on the trope of kindred, on the relation that incorporates muse-mother and poet-child or embraces the inquiring successor, that extends to include "some fond breast" on which "the parting soul relies" (**"Elegy,"** 89), or reaches into the community of bards.

What, finally, is the appeal of the Norse and Welsh poetry to Gray's imagination in the last decade of his life? **"The Fatal Sisters"** and **"The Descent of Odin"** are poems of prophecy, the first dominated by "twelve gigantic figures resembling women" ("Preface") whose purpose is to weave the web of futurity, and whose way leads to and through another field of the dead ("As the paths of fate we tread, / Wading through the ensanguined field" [29-30]). **"The Fatal Sisters"** is an effort to mythologize the elegiac muse within the dim Scandinavian twilight, and presumably a counter vision to Macpherson's Celtic ghosts, about which Gray was *"extasié."*[14] The translations, however, are not sponsored by a rivalry of picturesque lore, but coexist with the determining impulses of Gray's imagination from the beginning of his career, which now culminate in the urge to find in myth and legend the authorization that has so far evaded him. These poems resume where **"The Bard"** leaves off; they are attempts to make a poetry of prophetic speaking and arise from the intimate association between prophecy and death.

The easily identifiable figure of desire evident in the early verse is now banished, her place taken by terrifying images of vast forms, by "Mista black, terrific maid, / Sangria and Hilda" (17-18), by "Gondula and Geira" (31). Such women Gray has seen over and again; they appear first as Contemplation or Adversity, now

as mythic presences. They possess a primitive size and durability, representing in themselves the combined identities of muse-mother-death, the final unified form of desire and authority toward which his own imagination has been traveling. As they move through the fields of war, the "Clouds of carnage" (50) finally and effectively "blot the sun," the last vestige of Hyperionic presence in Gray's poetry.

"The Descent of Odin" concerns Odin's visit to the underworld, prior to Balder's death, to discover his son's fate; he learns from the prophetess that Hoder will murder Balder and that Vali, the son of Odin and Rinda, will avenge the crime. The journey to the kingdom of Hela, Goddess of Death, is based on the traditional quest-drama, here involving a journey to the place of death to waken the source of voice, the "prophetic maid" (20) who not only discloses the future to Odin but is revealed by him as the "mother of the giant-brood" (86). Odin wakes her with "runic rhyme; / Thrice pronounced in accents dread" (22-23). Though self-described as "a Warrior's son," and the chief of the gods in Norse mythology, Odin is also a speaker of the mysteries to which the maid-mother responds. Quest ends in Hela's underworld with the maid denying prophetic knowledge to any future "enquirer . . . / . . . till substantial Night / Has reassumed her ancient right" (88-92). The world left to darkness and to Gray is now, in the maid's last oracular utterance, a vision of ultimate closure, when "wrapped in flames, in ruin hurled, / Sinks the fabric of the world" (93-94). The rest—for Gray—was almost silence. "Substantial Night" is the final invocation, the figure beyond which there are no further figures.

Notes

[1] Cited by R. W. Ketton-Cremer, *Thomas Gray: A Biography* (Cambridge: Cambridge Univ. Press, 1955), 17.

[2] Ketton-Cremer, 253.

[3] *The Correspondence of Thomas Gray*, ed. Toynbee, Paget, and Leonard Whibley (Oxford: Clarendon Press, 1935), 1:201 (West to Gray, May 5, 1742).

[4] *The Poems of Gray, Collins, and Goldsmith*, ed. Roger Lonsdale (London: Longmans, 1969), 47. All quotations from Gray's poetry follow this edition; line numbers are cited parenthetically in the text.

[5] *Correspondence*, 1:209 (Gray to West, May 27, 1742).

[6] Northrop Frye, *Anatomy of Criticism* (Princeton: Princeton Univ. Press, 1957), 193.

[7] Peter Sacks, *The English Elegy: Studies in the Genre from Spenser to Yeats* (Baltimore: Johns Hopkins Univ. Press, 1985), 7.

[8] Sacks, 8.

[9] Sacks, 16.

[10] See Thomas Weiskel, "The Ethos of Alienation: Two Versions of Transcendence," in *The Romantic Sublime: Studies in the Structure and Psychology of Transcendence* (Baltimore: Johns Hopkins Univ. Press, 1976), 34-62.

[11] Irene Tayler, *Blake's Illustrations to the Poems of Gray* (Princeton: Princeton Univ. Press, 1971), 66.

[12] Sacks, 110.

[13] Tayler, 99.

[14] *Correspondence,* 2:680 (Gray to Wharton, c. June 20, 1760).

Henry Weinfeld (essay date 1991)

SOURCE: "Gray's Elegy and the Dissolution of the Pastoral," in *The Poet without a Name: Gray's "Elegy" and the Problem of History*, Southern Illinois University Press, 1991, pp. 150-63.

[*In the following essay on the "Elegy," Weinfeld defines Gray's place within the history of the pastoral genre.*]

Like all poems that are central to their time, and hence to the historical matrix, the **"Elegy"** is embedded in a tradition (or series of traditions) that it simultaneously subverts. In chapter 3 we saw this to be the case with respect to the heroic, elegiac, and pastoral traditions (although these overlapping categories should not be construed as being more than heuristic devices for the organization of diverse historical particulars). In the case of the pastoral, however, because of its intimate connection to the "problem of history," we are confronted with a series of issues that require fuller theoretical elaboration than could be offered in the context of the sequential reading of chapter 3. For if the problem of history (in the sense of task or telos) is to overcome the problem of history (in the sense of deprivation), then the pastoral is that form which, at a certain stage of historical development, is entrusted with this crucial theme.

In the Introduction to this study, I suggested that the pastoral is primarily constituted by the problem of history and only secondarily, or contingently, by the figure of the shepherd. Even if we concede that there was something "natural" in the choice of the shepherd, if Theocritus had made some other figure the focal point of his *Idylls* and if his imitators had followed suit, then, although the genre would have adopted a

different name, nothing essential would have been changed. And even if we choose to adopt Pope's minimal definition of the pastoral, as a form involving the "imitation of the action of a shepherd, or one considered under that character,"[1] still, this leaves us with the problem of penetrating beneath the surface of the form to understand the nature of the representation involved, since clearly the lives of shepherds in and of themselves are not what is really at issue but only a pretext for getting at something else.[2]

What is salient to the pastoral, in any event, is not merely the figure of the shepherd per se but the figure of the *poet-as-shepherd,* a figure that involves a synthesis, under the aegis of poetry itself (since it is in and through poetry that this synthesis is effected), of the upper and lower classes (the aristocracy and the peasantry). The figure of the poet-as-shepherd is informed, in the first place, by the myth of the Golden Age, according to which the original condition of mankind was characterized by harmony and natural sufficiency, without the necessity of either labor or law. Here, for instance, is Ovid's account of the Golden Age myth in the *Metamorphoses* (in Arthur Golding's Elizabethan translation):

> Then sprang up first the golden Age, which of
>   itself maintainde,
> The truth and right of every thing unforst and
>   unconstrainde.
> There was no fear of punishment, there was
>   no threatning lawe
> In brazen tables nayled up, to keep the folke
>   in awe.
> There was no man would crouch or creepe to
>   Judge with cap in hand,
> They lived safe without a Judge in every
>   Realme and Lande
> The loftie Pyntree was not hewen from
>   mountaines where it stood,
> In seeking straunge and forren landes to rove
>   upon the flood.
> Men knew none other countries yet, than were
>   themselves did keepe:
> There was no towne enclosed yet, with walles
>   and ditches deepe.
> No horne nor trumpet was in use, no sword
>   nor helmet worne.
> The worlde was suche as souldiers helpe
>   might easly be forsworne.
> The fertile earth as yet was free, untoucht of
>   spade or plough,
> And yet it yeelded of itselfe of every things
>   inough.[3]

At the heart of the pastoral, then, is nostalgia—nostalgia not so much for the past as for a mode of life that never existed but that the poet locates in the dim confines of the past.[4] For this reason, however, as W. W.

Greg pointed out in his landmark study of the pastoral early in the century, there has often been a good deal of confusion as to the origins of the form:

> We are often, for instance, told that it is the earliest of all forms of poetry, that it characterizes primitive people and permeates ancient literature. Song is, indeed, as old as human language, and in a sense no doubt the poetry of the pastoral age may be said to have been pastoral. It does not, however, follow that it bears any essential resemblance to that which subsequent ages have designated by the name.[5]

The distinction between the pastoral and the poetry of the "pastoral age" is crucial because, as Greg observes, "a constant element in the pastoral is the recognition of a contrast, implicit or expressed, between pastoral life and some more complex type of civilization."[6] Other writers have emphasized the same point. Frank Kermode, for example, notes that "the first condition of pastoral is that it is an urban product,"[7] and Renato Poggioli, that the pastoral originated not in Hellenic but in Hellenistic times, "with the decline of the ancient *polis* and . . . the appearance of a quasi-modern metropolis."[8] To this one must add, however, that as an urban product, the pastoral is obliged to camouflage its origins, and that this is intrinsic to the transcendental or utopian basis of the form. Here we arrive at the essence of the pastoral: by superimposing the values of a civilized upper class onto a fictional agrarian landscape, the pastoral projects the vision of a reconciliation between Nature and History, such that civilization appears as an *unmediated* extension of Nature itself.

As Greg remarks, the importance of the pastoral as a form lies in the fact that it is "the expression of instincts and impulses deep-rooted in the nature of humanity."[9] But from a Marxist perspective, it might be observed that these instincts and impulses are conditioned by the division of labor and the attendant alienation resulting from the formation of social classes—in short, by the problem of history, which is at once a product and the origin of cultural development. From this point of view, the pastoral is a utopian form insofar as it projects a vision in which the highest attainments of civilization—including poetry itself—are possessed *without the necessity of history.*[10] The utopian synthesis implicit in the pastoral involves a kind of telescoping of the problem of history, with the result that the actual process of history is submerged and circumscribed, as it were. Yet at the same time, the pastoral points to the final mastery of man over Nature—to the *end* of history, both in the sense of its practical conclusion and also of its telos.

The pastoral is thus insulated from history and hence from the problem of history in its negative aspect. As Poggioli beautifully remarks, the desire on the part of the pastoral to *forget history,* which is what links it to the Golden Age myth (whether or not the latter is explicitly foregrounded), is, in a sense, true of poetry as a whole—and this is perhaps why there are so many different "versions" of pastoral:

> In a certain sense, and in its purest form, the pastoral represents ideally the Golden Age of poetry. Poetry, however, is not only the child of fancy, but also the daughter of memory; and this makes her the sister of history. It is when she tries to forget her sister, and yearns after a dreamland outside of time, that poetry becomes idyllic, if not in form at least in content.[11]

This yearning for a dreamland outside of time must, however, be concretized in temporal terms; thus, since the future is a mere abstraction and since the poverty of the present is what has occasioned the yearning in the first place, the pastoral turns for its images to the past—or rather to a past of its own devising.

The attempt on the part of the pastoral to "forget history" has often been regarded as mere escapism, especially by the Marxist tradition, but this is inaccurate or at least insufficiently nuanced. Under certain circumstances, the pastoral can become mere escapism; but in itself, and insofar as it is capable of producing great works of art, the pastoral impulse is a utopian response to the same problem of history that will later emerge explicitly in the **"Elegy."** In the pastoral, however, the problem of history is represented only from the standpoint of a kind of abstract idealism, as if the *problem* posed by history had been factored out from the outset and the Earthly Paradise already attained. In the world of historical relationships, the art of poetry, requiring leisure and knowledge in the highest degree, is the product of a social surplus and thus the province not of shepherds but of a privileged upper class; yet what the poet-as-shepherd motif concretizes is precisely a situation in which the aristocrat and the shepherd are not isolated by social differences but, under the transcendental aegis of poetry, can exist as one.

The pastoral thus involves a negation of social differences, but there are two perspectives from which this can be interpreted. On the one hand, following the tendency of at least one strain of Marxism, we can reduce the pastoral to a mere ideological formation: we can say that the "organic" society posited by the pastoral is nothing more than an attempt on the part of a ruling elite (whether aristocratic or bourgeois) to deny the existence of social inequality and to present the illusion of social harmony.[12] On the other hand, accepting the idealism of the pastoral as sincere, we can maintain that its utopian dream is a "necessary fiction" that, in presenting us with the vision of *un*alienated man, serves to create the conditions in which that vision can eventually be realized. From this point of view, the very idealism of the pastoral (as of art in general) is itself a kind of social praxis and not merely the distorted reflection of prevailing social norms.

The two perspectives taken together represent opposing sides of an aesthetic debate that has its roots in the argument between Plato and Plotinus.[13] But both are overly schematic in that they fail to take account of how the aesthetic possibilities afforded by the pastoral are mediated by actual historical circumstances. Whatever our attitude to the pastoral may be in theory, it is clear, in any event, that the pastoral vision of an Earthly Paradise, from its reemergence in the Renaissance to its demise in the eighteenth century, is absolutely central to European art. That is why the form undergoes so many permutations during the period and why its generic possibilities seem virtually endless. In Shakespeare's romantic comedies, for example, not only the stage but the entire theater becomes a vehicle for the creation of an enchanted space in which the upper and lower classes can, if not merge, at least mingle on equal terms. The pastoral ethos of noblesse oblige, binding up all classes into an organic whole, is intended to have a humanizing impact particularly on those in the uppermost ranks of society—so that when Duke Senior and his retinue leave the Forest of Arden, or when Prospero bids farewell to his island and returns to Milan, it is not, presumably, to be guided solely by the Machiavellian pursuit of power.

Such, at any rate, is the social myth perpetuated by the pastoral. But how, then, explain the demise of the transcendental pastoral, a demise which, most commentators would agree, occurred in the eighteenth century? Perhaps we can say that if the negation of social differences inherent in the pastoral is a "necessary fiction" because it presents the vision of *un*alienated man, it ceases to be so at the point at which man becomes capable of eliminating the forms of alienation in practice. When this point is reached—or at least, when it is glimpsed as a real possibility by the intellectual center (as it seems to have been during the Enlightenment)—then the transcendental pastoral forfeits its utopian function and takes on instead the reactionary lineaments of an ideological weapon that is wielded in the narrow interests of those in power rather than in the universal interests of humanity as a whole. At this point, the pastoral becomes a mere husk of itself, denuded of its authentic utopian content, and the utopian impulse passes to a tendency which, having emerged from the pastoral, is realistic and antipastoral in its orientation. Amid the "puerile conceits of the Petit Trianon," in Greg's phrase,[14] where we find Marie Antoinette playing at being a milkmaid, the final image cast by the pastoral is shadowed by the Revolution.

"The modern world," writes Poggioli, "destroyed the conventional and traditional pastoral through four cultural trends that arose together and partly coincided. These were the humanitarian outlook, the idea of mate-rial progress, the scientific spirit, and artistic realism."[15] Ironically, it is precisely the point at which the belief in material progress takes hold that we see the demise of the transcendental pastoral, for at that point the old dream of an Earthly Paradise comes to seem an actual obstacle to the task at hand. "Till we have built Jerusalem, / In Englands green & pleasant Land," writes Blake at the close of the eighteenth century,[16] but here the emphasis is no longer on dreaming but on building and transforming. In *The Communist Manifesto,* that document in which the spirit of "scientific" socialism emerges from its utopian variant, Marx offers the bourgeoisie what is in effect a backhanded compliment for having "put an end to all patriarchal, idyllic relations." "For exploitation, veiled by religious and political illusions," he remarks, "it has substituted naked, shameless, direct, brutal exploitation."[17] From a certain point of view, "there is no document of civilization which is not at the same time a document of barbarism," as Walter Benjamin observes in one of his "Theses on the Philosophy of History."[18] However that may be, by the middle of the eighteenth century, the long period in which the old pastoral conventions had furnished the artist with an enabling fiction, through which he could represent his deepest hopes and ideals, has come to an end. To make use of the poet-as-shepherd motif and the other props of the genre in the old, naive way now comes to seem an insincere denial of the actual impoverishment of the rural working class.

If the **"Elegy"** represents the symbolic dissolution of the pastoral, this is because it is in the **"Elegy"** that the problem of history—which, in its sublimated form, had given rise to the pastoral in the first place—is fully comprehended for the first time. However, the demise of the old pastoral in English poetry can be traced to an earlier point in the eighteenth century, when the transcendental synthesis implicit in the form has begun to break down but before the *meaning* of this crisis has been fully grasped.

In Pope's "Discourse on Pastoral Poetry" (1717), for example, we can already sense a certain amount of repressed disquietude resulting from the cleavage between the pastoral idealization and actual social conditions. "We must," writes Pope, "use some illusion to render a Pastoral delightful; and this consists in exposing the best only of a shepherd's life, and in concealing its miseries."[19] The point, once again, is not that poets were previously naive in regard to the illusion underlying pastoral but rather that they had felt no need to justify it. The fact that Pope now begins to speak in terms of the pastoral *illusion* indicates that he is already treading on rather shaky ground.

In light of Pope's "Discourse," it is interesting that the first frontal attack on the transcendental pastoral was mounted three years earlier, in 1714, by his friend John Gay, in a series of six eclogues entitled *The Shep-*

herd's Week. Gay's attitude in this work warrants close attention, not only because it reflects the collapse of the transcendental pastoral but also because it indicates the degree to which the "antipastoral" tendency that emerges in the wake of the collapse can allow for the venting of a social snobbism that may always have been latent in the older form but that was generally repressed. The negation of social differences that we have seen to be intrinsic to the pastoral is a fundamentally ambiguous phenomenon: it can either express the desire for an Earthly Paradise or it can reflect the camouflaging of social inequities. There are, however, possibly as many versions of antipastoral as there are of pastoral.

Written as a burlesque imitation of Spenser's *Shepherd's Calendar,* Gay's poem remains a pastoral in the minimal sense of Pope's definition; but, as the "Proem" to the work makes clear, *The Shepherd's Week* undermines the metaphysical basis of the pastoral by denuding it of its Golden Age myth:

> Other Poet travailing in this plain High-way of Pastoral know I none. Yet, certes, such it behoveth a Pastoral to be, as Nature in the Country affordeth; and the Manners also meetly copied from the rustical Folk therein. In this also my Love to my native Country *Britain* much pricketh me forward, to describe aright the Manners of our own honest and laborious Plough-men, in no wise sure more unworthy a *British* Poet's imitation, than those of *Sicily* or *Arcadie;* albeit, not ignorant I am, what a Rout and Rabblement of Critical Gallimawfy hath been made of late Days by certain young Men of insipid Delicacy, concerning, I wist not what, *Golden Age,* and other outrageous Conceits, to which they would confine Pastoral. Whereof, I avow, I account not at all, knowing no Age so justly to be stiled *Golden,* as this of *our Soveraign Lady Queen* ANNE.

> This idle trumpery (only fit for Schools and School-boys) unto that ancient *Dorick* Shepherd *Theocritus,* or his Mates, was never known; he rightly, throughout his fifth *Idyll,* maketh his Louts give foul Language and behold their Goats at Rut in all Simplicity.[20]

The Shepherd's Week is superficially an attempt to demystify the pastoral, but the argument could be made that in actuality it is more mystified than the transcendental pastoral itself because it has simply lost touch with the historical problematic that is submerged in the older form. Gay's shepherds are mere country bumpkins, and thus the idealistic vision of the transcendental pastoral is reduced to farce in his work. Gay's attitude betrays a fundamental ambivalence: on the one hand, by attacking the Golden Age myth he places himself on the side of the Moderns (in the still raging Battle of the Ancient and Moderns), and this, of course, allows him to engage in patriotic flattery of a rather fulsome kind; but on the other hand, affecting an an-

tique "pastoral" style, he claims that he is returning to "the true ancient guise of Theocritus." The utopian pastoral had made use of archaism as a way of distancing itself from the present, but in Gay's contradictory gestures we can see that the old tropes and conventions have been reduced to the status of a mere entertainment.

In the eclogues themselves, Gay's archaism is the vehicle of bathos and serves to heighten the discrepancy between the eclogue form and the coarseness of rural manners. Dr. Johnson, we know, hated pastoral; but it is difficult to credit his comment, that "the effect of reality and truth became conspicuous, even when the intention was to shew [Gay's shepherds] groveling and degraded. These Pastorals became popular and were read with delight, as just representations of rural manners and occupations."[21] On the contrary, the net effect of Gay's satire is not realism but, as the following passage indicates (in which the voice of Ambition and Grandeur is heard behind that of the Maid), one long, drawn-out Augustan sneer (carefully modulated, it is true) at the old-fashioned literary form it espouses and at the "quaintness" of country life in general:

> Ah! didst thou know what Proffers I withstood,
> When late I met the *Squire* in yonder Wood!
> To me he sped, regardless of his Game,
> While all my Cheek was glowing red with Shame;
> My Lip he kiss'd, and prais'd my healthful Look,
> Then from his Purse of Silk a *Guinea* took,
> Into my Hand he forc'd the tempting Gold,
> While I with modest struggling broke his Hold.
> He swore that *Dick* in Liv'ry strip'd with Lace,
> Should wed me soon to keep me from Disgrace;
> But I no Footman priz'd nor golden Fee,
> For what is Lace or Gold compar'd to thee?[22]

The demise of the old pastoral coincides with a number of new forms or tendencies that are all in their own ways dominated by the spirit of realism (or pseudo-realism) that emerges in the eighteenth century. The relationship of these newly emergent forms, both to actual social conditions, on the one hand, and to the vision of *communitas* stemming from the Golden Age myth, on the other, is quite different from that of the old pastoral. Although they are sometimes grouped together under the "antipastoral" rubric, if the latter is seen in monolithic terms it can be as distorting as the "pastoral" label itself. For instance, *The Shepherd's Week* is clearly antipastoral in the sense that Gay is attacking the transcendental vision embodied in the old pastoral; but on the other hand, Gay maintains the props of the old pastoral, which thus becomes the husk of itself in his hands. From a social standpoint, there is no difference essentially between the Tory spirit motivating Gay's and Pope's pastorals, even though Pope remains formally within the context of the old pastoral while Gay does not. Although the breakdown of the old pastoral occurs under the aegis of the new realism,

Gay's rustics have no more intrinsic reality than Spenser's (but Spenser, we must remember, was not striving for realism), and it is clear that they are merely grist for his satiric, but not very serious, mill.

The case is very different with George Crabbe's poem *The Village* (1783), a poem of the utmost seriousness, which comes in the wake both of the Industrial Revolution and, we immediately feel, of Gray's **"Elegy"**. *The Village* opens with a series of chastened and chastening "Remarks upon Pastoral Poetry" (as the poet himself refers to them), in which the conventions of the old pastoral are explicitly viewed as an ideological subterfuge:

> Fled are those times, when, in harmonious strains,
> The rustic poet praised his native plains:
> No shepherds now, in smooth alternate verse,
> Their country's beauty or their nymphs' rehearse;
> Yet still for these we frame the tender strain,
> Still in our lays fond Corydons complain,
> And shepherds' boys their amorous pains reveal,
> The only pains, alas! they never feel.
> On Mincio's banks, in Caesar's bounteous reign,
> If Tityrus found the Golden Age again,
> Must sleepy bards the flattering dream prolong,
> Mechanic echoes of the Mantuan song?
> From Truth and Nature shall we widely stray,
> Where Virgil, not where Fancy, leads the way?
> Yes, thus the Muses sing of happy swains,
> Because the Muses never knew their pains:
> They boast their peasants' pipes; but peasants now
> Resign their pipes and plod behind the plough;
> And few, amid the rural-tribe, have time
> To number syllables, and play with rhyme;
> Save honest Duck, what son of verse could share
> The poet's rapture and the peasant's care?[23]

Oddly enough, although Crabbe polemicizes against the pastoral fiction, he does not wholly dispense with it, as his suggestion that in former times "the rustic poet praised his native plains" indicates. To us it goes without saying that shepherds have always been poor and that those privileged enough to become poets have never been shepherds; apparently, however, the pastoral myth could still be maintained even after the pastoral conventions had been abandoned. Crabbe writes as one who regards those conventions as being now in bad taste because they contrast so markedly with existing social conditions; at the same time, he implicitly invokes a past in which the pastoral mirrored reality.

In *The Village*, which was published in 1783, the anti-pastoral tendency is fully manifest, but in *The Deserted Village*, which appeared thirteen years earlier, what is lamented is precisely the loss of the "pastoral" way of life. The social changes lamented by Goldsmith are clearly connected to the demise of the transcendental pastoral (and for the reasons that Crabbe enunciates); but,

interestingly, as the two poems taken together indicate, the demise of the transcendental pastoral is synonymous with the advent of a new form, one that might be termed the demotic pastoral. Where the transcendental or utopian pastoral superimposed the values of the aristocracy upon an imaginary rural landscape, synthesizing the nobleman and the shepherd in the poet-as-shepherd motif (because it was under the aegis of poetry that this transcendental synthesis was effected), the demotic pastoral involves at least the attempt (though one that is sometimes distorted and insincere) at realism in its depiction of the peasantry. Similarly, where the transcendental pastoral had insulated itself from history, the demotic pastoral involves an engagement with precisely those historical factors that led to the loss of the "pastoral" way of life and the loss of the transcendental pastoral itself—though often this engagement with history is so fraught with bourgeois sentimentalism as to be entirely unhistorical in its net effect.

Both tendencies are very much in evidence in *The Deserted Village*. On the one hand, Goldsmith is as realistic as Marx himself in his understanding of how the Enclosure Acts and the incursions of capitalism have changed the face of the countryside:

> Ye friends to truth, ye statesmen who survey
> The rich man's joys increase, the poor's decay,
> 'Tis yours to judge, how wide the limits stand
> Between a splendid and a happy land.
> Proud swells the tide with loads of freighted ore,
> And shouting Folly hails them from her shore;
> Hoards, even beyond the miser's wish abound,
> And rich men flock from all the world around.
> Yet count our gains. This wealth is but a name
> That leaves our useful products still the same.
> Not so the loss. The man of wealth and pride,
> Takes up a space that many poor supplied;
> Space for his lake, his park's extended bounds,
> Space for his horses, equipage, and hounds;
> The robe that wraps his limbs in silken sloth,
> Has robbed the neighbouring field of half their
>   growth;
> His seat, where solitary sports are seen,
> Indignant spurns the cottage from the green;
> Around the world each needful product flies,
> For all the luxuries the world supplies.
> While thus the land adorned for pleasure all
> In barren splendour feebly waits the fall.[24]

On the other hand, where Marx is unsparing in his analysis of how the bourgeoisie has "rescued a considerable part of the population from the idiocy of rural life,"[25] Goldsmith depicts the life of the vanished peasantry essentially as an idyll in which "health and plenty cheered the labouring swain" (2).

Gray's hypothetical description of the lives of the Forefathers, in stanzas 5-7 of the **"Elegy,"** is similarly idyllic; moreover, as we noted in chapter 3, the sense of loss evoked by these stanzas is not merely in relation to individuals who are "no more" but, as in *The Deserted Village,* to a way of life and an entire class. However, where in Goldsmith's poem this is the sole perspective that is adumbrated, in the **"Elegy"** it is countered by the development of a thematic strain that is at odds *both* with the transcendental pastoral and with the as yet unarticulated demotic pastoral: the theme of unfulfilled potential (or "death-in-life")—which is to say, the "problem of history."

In relation to the pastoral, then, Gray can be seen as coming both at the end of a long tradition and at the beginning of a new one—and here we should remember that the poem was published almost at the exact midpoint of the century, at the point historians have traditionally marked as the onset of the Industrial Revolution and, with it, the Modern era. Gray's reinterpretation of the idealistic pastoral tendency from the standpoint of the realistic georgic tendency allows for a balancing of thematic and generic possibilities that gives the poem an extraordinary resonance and richness of scope. The **"Elegy"** thus stands at the center of a confluence of forces that will lead to the emergence of several new forms, including the antipastoral tendency of Crabbe and the demotic pastoral tendency that will later culminate in Wordsworth.[26] The emergence of the problem of history in the **"Elegy,"** together with the contrast between the rich and the poor that is a consequence of this thematic development, is thus connected to the dissolution of the transcendental pastoral; but it is also connected to a new vision that, though only implicit, makes itself felt in the poem as a kind of "trembling hope" for the future. As we saw in chapter 3, the *principle of universality* is latent from the very outset in the figure of the passing bell, which, in resonating throughout the poem, connects us to Donne's "No man is an island" meditation. In the **"Elegy,"** however, the principle of universality cannot explicitly emerge until the socioeconomic aspect of Gray's dialectic has been fully developed—lest the poem succumb to what for its own time would have been mere devotional cliché. And yet, the suspension of the principle of universality is ultimately what allows the evocation of the universal to be felt with so much force when it finally does emerge. Similarly, although the explicit emergence of the "problem of history" in the **"Elegy"** is tantamount to the dissolution of the transcendental pastoral, the utopian impulse that had been dominant in the old pastoral is burdened by a deepening melancholia but is not lost.

Notes

[1] See Introduction, n. 1.

[2] The conclusion arrived at by Paul Alpers, in a recent attempt to define pastoral, replicates Pope's minimal definition. Alpers sees the lives of shepherds as what he calls the "representative anecdote" of pastoral: "To say that shepherds' lives is the representative anecdote of pastoral means that pastoral works are representations of shepherds who are felt to be representative of some other or of all other men" ("What Is Pastoral?" *Critical Inquiry,* 8:3 [Spring 1982], 456). However, Alpers makes no effort to explain the nature of the representation involved, or even why a central literary genre should have focused on the figure of the shepherd in the first place; consequently, since the generic marker itself means "pertaining to shepherds," his attempt at definition is merely tautological.

[3] Ovid, *Metamorphoses,* trans. Arthur Golding (1567; New York: Macmillan, 1965), 1:103-16.

[4] My discussion of the relationship between pastoral poetry and nostalgia overlaps at a number of points with Laurence Lerner's discussion in *The Uses of Nostalgia: Studies in Pastoral Poetry* (New York: Schocken, 1972).

[5] W. W. Greg, *Pastoral Poetry and Pastoral Drama* (1906; New York: Russell and Russell, 1959), 4.

[6] Ibid.

[7] Frank Kermode, *English Pastoral Poetry* (London: George G. Harrap, 1952), 14.

[8] Renato Poggioli, *The Oaten Flute: Essays on Pastoral Poetry and the Pastoral Ideal* (Cambridge, Mass.: Harvard University Press, 1975), 3.

[9] Greg, 2.

[10] It will be noted that I am using the term "utopian" in a very general sense, as pertaining to the notion of an Earthly Paradise. To the extent that the term connotes an explicit recognition of and struggle against prevailing conditions, it cannot, of course, be applied to the pastoral.

[11] Poggioli, 41.

[12] The concept of *ideology* and its relationship to art is an extremely vexed issue in Marxist thought and has resulted in a great deal of confusion. When Marx uses the term "ideology" (as in his references to "bourgeois ideology"), he almost always uses it to mean a species of systemic falsehood whose ultimate purpose is to uphold the prevailing social system. Marx's use of the term is thus, emphatically, nonrelativistic: he writes from a "privileged" standpoint as one in possession of truth. Furthermore, on those occasions in which Marx writes about art or literature, he generally refrains even from broaching the concept of ideology, and certainly the tendency of so-called vulgar Marxism to reduce art

to ideology is foreign to his own impulse to privilege the work of art. Later Marxists, however, particularly those of the Althusserian school, tend to see all thought as bound by ideological constructs. From this point of view, however (which is certainly foreign to Marx's explicit voluntarism, although perhaps implicit in certain structuralist aspects of his system), the concept of ideology becomes a distinction without a difference.

[13] Plato, it will be recalled, sees art essentially as a representation (mimesis) of physical appearances that stands as a representation of the true forms—and thus as one step further removed from Truth than the phenomena themselves. Plotinus, however, while accepting Plato's Doctrine of Ideas, argues (against Plato) that the work of art transcends the phenomenal world by establishing a direct relationship to the forms.

[14] Greg, 2.

[15] Poggioli, 31.

[16] "Preface to *Milton,*" *The Poetry and Prose of William Blake,* ed. David V. Erdman (New York: Doubleday, 1970), 15-16.

[17] Karl Marx and Friedrich Engels, "Manifesto of the Communist Party," trans. Samuel Moore, in *Marx and Engels: Basic Writings on Politics and Philosophy,* ed. Lewis S. Feuer (New York: Doubleday, 1959), 9.

[18] Walter Benjamin, *Illuminations,* ed. Hannah Arendt (New York: Schocken, 1969), 256.

[19] Pope, *Pastoral Poetry and An Essay on Criticism,* 27.

[20] *Poetry and Prose of John Gay,* ed. Vinton A. Dearing and Charles E. Beckwith. 2 vols. (Oxford: The Clarendon Press, 1974), 1:90.

[21] *Lives of the English Poets,* 2:269; cited by Stuart Curran, *Poetic Form and British Romanticism* (New York: Oxford University Press, 1986), 92.

[22] *Poetry and Prose of John Gay,* 1:107.

[23] George Crabbe, *Poems,* ed. Adolphus William Ward (Cambridge: Cambridge University Press, 1905), 1:1-28.

[24] "The Deserted Village," *Collected Works of Oliver Goldsmith,* ed. Arthur Friedman (London: Oxford University Press, 1966), 4:265-86. Further references to the poem will be given by line number in the text.

[25] Marx, "The Communist Manifesto," 11.

[26] This is the reason that two such eminent theorists of the pastoral as Poggioli and Erwin Panofsky can speak of the *Elegy* in terms that are precisely antithetical. In his analysis of the *Et in Arcadia ego* motif, Panofsky observes that Virgil was the first poet to align the pastoral with elegiac nostalgia, "opening up the dimension of the past and thus inaugurating the long line of poetry that was to culminate in Thomas Gray" (*Meaning in the Visual Arts* [Garden City, N.Y.: Doubleday, 1955], 301). Conversely, in a discussion of *The Village* Poggioli associates the antipastoral tendency of Crabbe with Gray: "Instead of describing fictitious beings and an imaginary way of life, Crabbe chooses to depict 'the poor laborious natives of the place,' and to sing, like Gray in his *"Elegy,"* the short and simple annals of the poor'" (p. 31).

Marshall Brown (essay date 1991)

SOURCE: "Gray's Churchyard Space," in *Preromanticism,* Stanford University Press, 1991, pp. 42-8.

[*In the following excerpt, Brown illustrates how Gray generalizes from the particular in the "Elegy" to create a sense of universal experience.*]

. . . Space has always been recognized as a problem in Gray's **Elegy.**" The speculation concerning the location of Gray's churchyard is as idle as that concerning Goldsmith's Aurora, yet also as natural. For it reflects the tension that runs through the poem between particular place and universal space. In the early stanzas the repeated possessives drive toward local dominions, and so indeed do the definite articles.[6] At twilight the private consciousness faces dormancy unless it is rescued by positioned singularities ("Save where," "Save that from yonder ivy-mantled tow'r"). Dominion is ubiquitous: in the owl's "solitary reign," the children's envied sire, the war to subdue nature to cultivation. It is not by chance that the three model figures named in the fifteenth stanza were all politically involved in bloody tyranny, nor that the body politic provides the standard for judging the village's emulation or privation. In the "precincts of the . . . day" presence always commands, however limited its terrain, and funeral monuments compete to prolong the paternal domination of the forefathers. If they cannot demand homage, they can at least implore "the passing tribute of a sigh." If nothing else survives, the heaving turf of line 14 remains a literally posthumous assertion of territoriality. In country and city alike, action stratifies mankind into levels of domination, and, discomfortingly, identity remains conceived as place in the scale of being. Hence the promptings from the poem itself toward finding the churchyard. It has no power if it has no location, and no reality or truth if it has no power.

On so imperious a mentality Gray casts a light too cool to be called irony. Its ideal is a repose that the noises of the place disturb. Thus, the erotically charged gem and flower retain their purity only so long as their unnatural locations protect them. ("Ray serene" is properly a sky phrase—"serene" means "of evening"—doubly displaced, in a cave and under water.) Though Ambition errs in mocking "useful toil," Gray's own tone becomes condescending when he reaches "homely joys, and destiny obscure"; though Grandeur shouldn't smile at annals so "short and simple" that they are heard rather than read, Gray himself seems to discredit the poor when he calls them "noiseless," not audible at all. This is, one notes, a poem of the day, not of the year: properly speaking, these poor can have no annals, but only an "artless tale."[7] Gray hovers constantly, as in this phrase, on the brink of oxymoron (fires living in ashes, "mindful of th' unhonour'd"), which it is easy to interpret as rejection, as if for Gray *any* mode of 'life' is finally unacceptable."[8] No doubt about it, the poem expresses reservations about rich Cromwells and poor, mute Miltons alike.

Still, reserve is to be carefully distinguished from criticism.[9] Gray had previously appeared in public representing three versions of minimalism: the insects of the **"Ode on the Spring,"** the children's games of the Eton College ode, and the bath-os of the **"Ode on the Death of a Favourite Cat."** The **"Elegy"** keeps a more even tenor than any of these, striving for a sublimity of the subliminal variety that Gianni Scalia has called "the sublime of depth."[10] It wants to take a stand without asserting any pride of place. Its fundamental principle is a return to the ground: a combination of regression and leveling most clearly seen in the seventh stanza, which retreats from harvest through plowing to setting out, and then concludes, in less conflictual language, with the hewing of wood. Negations are as plentiful as possessives, yet they are typically oblique or postponed so as not to cancel out the strong diction and heroic images. The poem works as hard to compare rich and poor as to contrast them. They share life as well as illusions. Death destroys the illusions: "The boast of heraldry, the pomp of pow'r, / And all that beauty, all that wealth e'er gave." But it does not put out the flame of life, which survives, perhaps only in epitaphs and in "trembling hope," but which is assuredly there: "Ev'n from the tomb the voice of Nature cries, / Ev'n in our Ashes live their wonted Fires."

The animals, the muttering poet, the lisping children, and the "still small Accents whisp'ring from the Ground" (Eton College manuscript, line 83) are all forms of the voice of nature that is forever speaking. For as heartlessly as the poem criticizes social existence—all forms of social existence—even as firmly is it attached to natural life. It is not a poem written in blackness like the **"Ode on the Spring"** ("Thy sun is set," line 49) or confirming blackness like the Eton College ode, where the speaker faces "shade" (the rhyme word in line 4 and again in line 11), only imagines the children whom Father Thames is supposed actually to "ha[ve] seen," and eventually views "black Misfortune's bale-

ful train" and "The painful family of Death." Rather the **"Elegy"** is situated at twilight and with its eye on "the warm precincts of the chearful day." Death is mute and deaf (lines 43-44); the Epitaph is the text of life.

But it is life in its most general form, reinterpreted so as to speak to mankind generally. Where all men are comparable, consciousness seeks a universal voice. The poem's one "me" (line 4) adjoins its one "now" (line 5), but immediately gives way under the impulse of Gray's conception to "all" (line 6, changed from "now" in the Eton College manuscript). As there is no place, no individual who is the subject of the Epitaph, and no year, so there is also no day in the poem, but rather an eternal, timeless moment. Gray's resignation purges the dross of anxiousness out of our pleasing being, leaving the intimacy of a heavenly "friend" and the passivity of a "trembling hope." It is a successful quietism that transmutes the restless, heaving turf of the beginning into the concluding "lap of Earth." At eve-ning, as contours dissolve, the universal eye looks beyond individual destinies—why should we know their fate?—toward the enveloping space of earth and heaven. Man leaves the turbulence of (urban) society and (rural) family in order to reenter his general home in the friendship of spirits and the protection of Mother Nature and Father God. In itself death is privation, but for Gray relationship persists and enlarges at the end of life.[11]

In diction, imagery, and argument, then, Gray presses in this poem toward a universal consciousness.[12] Beginning in a compound of obscurity and contradiction, the poem veers stanza by stanza from silence to noise, high to low, dark evening to bright morn, field to home, peace to conflict, poor to rich. These are gestures toward comprehensiveness in a world whose totality is composed of parts. The poetical youth is an outsider to this entire psychosocial economy. "His wayward fancies" (line 106) are constitutionally placeless, and the antique language that describes him belongs nowhere. A youth in a world of hoary-headed swains and aged thorns, a figure of morning (and noon) in a poem for which morning exists "No more" (line 20), a being born, it seems, only to die,[13] he negates all the earlier contradictions and classifications: "nor yet beside the rill [nature], / Nor up the lawn [gentry], nor at the wood [laboring peasantry]." In pointing out the lines summarizing the youth's "fate," the "hoary-headed Swain" takes a step beyond the silent, "hoary Thames" at Windsor, yet without achieving prophetic authority, since he is illiterate, enjoys a merely conjectured existence, and discerns only part of the youth's fate. Perplexity better describes the tone of the swain's speech, with its grave puns ("pore," "lay"); in it the youth escapes capture, a figure alien yet ubiquitous. The Epitaph shifts abruptly yet again; after the vivid personifications in the body of the elegy and the exotic Spenserianism of the swain's speech, the poem ends in grayly looming abstractions. It has the pallor of a language for which differences no longer exist.

After so many appeals to voice and so many failures of merely metaphorical reading (Knowledge's "ample page" ne'er unrolled, history not "read . . . in a nation's eyes," the babbling brook listlessly pored over), after the bookish language of the swain's speech and his curious designation of the Epitaph itself as a "lay," this arrival at a plain-style written text functions as a release. The reader's muted voice neither can nor needs to say much, but his brevity is accompanied by a settled clarity, completion (a large bounty as largely recompensed), and universality ("all") that subsume all the foregoing partitions and contradictions. For once the eighteenth century gives us the image of something known fully and in itself, rather than partially and relationally. The knowledge is purchased with the loss of power and position: the contents are impoverished, the knower undefined. One could hardly say, finally, who the youth is, since neither his merits nor his frailty are disclosed. Only metaphysicals remain definite here ("the lap of Earth," "the Bosom of his Father and his God"), and the four indefinite articles stand in striking contrast to all the abstract definite articles of the main text. Thus, it is not that someone comes in the end to know someone or something. Yet the poem still evokes the possibility of a language and a consciousness beyond station, beyond definition, and beyond identity.[14]

It is far from obvious to take the **"Elegy"** as a poem about the mind.[15] One's primary impression is, perhaps, that it is a remarkably physical poem. Movement is everywhere, in the plowman's way, the paths of glory, the genial current of the soul, the noiseless tenor of the villagers' way, the passing tribute of a sigh, the parting soul, the roving youth. For so traditional a society, it is a remarkably restless existence. The villagers' ardor is more than tinged with sexuality—"Some heart once pregnant with celestial fire"—and so is that of city dwellers:

> But Knowledge to their eyes her ample page
> Rich with the spoils of time did ne'er unroll;
> Chill Penury repress'd their noble rage,
> And froze the genial current of the soul.

This stanza, which praises the city indirectly by describing how impoverished rural life is, proves on reflection to be obliquely sarcastic about urban culture as well. For it is followed immediately by the famous gem and flower stanza. With its "spoils of time," we may infer in retrospect, the city ravages the sweetness of desert flowers, and its warm "current," while "genial," may not protect the serene purity of pearls so well as the "unfathom'd caves of ocean." Passions lurk in both environments, and they are distinctly not those of the mind alone.

Yet they act on the mind. What George Wright calls the poem's Berkeleyanism lies in the fact that passions seek less an object than a receptor, whether it be the owl's moon, the politician's listening senates, or the sigh that responds to the frail memorial. The poem may recognize a sexual dynamism to knowledge—despoiling time, unrolling her ample page—but its vector is antiphysical. Owl and moon preside over the churchyard in an alliance of wisdom and chastity aiming to protect a bower from molestation. While the verbs are active, inversions and syntactic ambiguities damp their noble rage. Of the three exemplary villagers, it is the mute, inglorious Milton who is specifically said to "rest" (as Hutchings points out, "Syntax of Death" [in *Studies in Philology* 81 (1984): 505]), allying him with another poet, the youth of the artless lines. At the end, death mysteriously consumes passion: one day the youth is lovelorn, the next he has vanished. Gray clear-sightedly concedes the omnipresence of bodily impulses, yet his message is that the only fruition and repose are of the mind.

Critics have written of the instability of Gray's poetry, its constant self-criticism and inability to ground the self.[16] This is true to a point, but it is to condemn Gray to the "narrow cell" of the forefathers and to deny him the "large . . . bounty" of the poetic youth. In the main body of the **"Elegy,"** to be sure, the quasi-sexual violence of fathers and forefathers is omnipresent—molesting owls, felling trees, ogling the spoils of Knowledge, secreting "The struggling pangs of conscious truth," and quenching "the blushes of ingenuous shame"—yet the Epitaph imagines as a surrogate a family romance of purest ray serene. Merits and frailties rest hand in hand in the androgynous lap-bosom of Nature-God, in a utopia purged of sexual desire (since the youth wished only "a friend") and of the turbulence of "fame and fortune." *"Fair Science"* retains the merest tinge of a purified eroticism, as does the single tear, while the youth as unknown knower becomes a figure of objectless, apathic cognition. The **"Elegy"** gives a voice that can be perceived without being uttered and an abode that needs neither a local habitation nor a name. "Common place" is the perfect term for the churchyard in whose grave lines all may rest.[17]

For a poem often thought to be a paean to rural laborers, the **"Elegy"** has a startlingly impoverished notion of work. Rather than conceiving it as a cooperative and constructive process—of which Adam Smith was to give so powerful an account in *The Wealth of Nations*—Gray's partitive consciousness divides work into periods ("evening care," line 22), repetitive events ("Oft," line 25), impersonal encounters ("Their furrow oft the stubborn glebe has broke," line 26), and synecdochic reductions ("How bow'd the woods beneath their sturdy stroke!" line 28). None of the associated adjectives—"busy," "jocund," "sturdy"—implies comprehension, and "toil" (line 29) is, precisely, thoughtless, primitive effort. Gray eliminated in revision a stanza containing the phrase "our Labours done," for rural labor knows no finality. Urban life, by contrast, is imaged as finality without effort: "the pomp of pow'r" without the struggle, "The paths of glory" without the conquest, "the rod of empire" that sways without earning the right, "the spoils of time" without the battle, "Th' applause of list'ning senates" without the victory, distribution ("To scatter plenty o'er a smiling land") without production. The widely separated smiles of disdainful grandeur (line 31) and of the people (line 63) suggest the city's detachment from the producing substratum, while the competition among the farmer's children for "the envied kiss" (line 24) signals that the rural struggle has no end. Such partitioning of the spheres of life both ironizes and idealizes: ironizes because all spheres are incomplete segments of a whole present only in the mind of the poet, idealizes because each element is absolutized as a changeless essence. What is systematically excluded is the order of appropriation—work that, by making something, makes it one's own.[18]

That is how Gray manages to convey a spatial imagination—with a full complement of divisions, locations, and affinities—that nevertheless remains universal. It is a world of possession without property. Possessives designate actions ("plods his weary way," "wheels his droning flight," "ply her evening care," "their sturdy stroke"), commonalities ("Their furrow," "their team"), parts of living beings ("their eyes," "Their name," "its old fantastic roots"), usurpation ("her secret bow'r," "The little Tyrant of his fields"), death's domain ("his narrow cell," "their lowly bed"). Only once—before the Epitaph, where all the conditions are changed—does the poem single out an object of possession, and then only in an affective relationship: "his fav'rite tree" (line 110). Nothing is owned, and hence nothing concrete can be imparted: "And all that beauty, all that wealth e'er gave," "He gave to Mis'ry all he had, a tear." Everything and nothing is shared with all and none in a world that is everywhere and nowhere. Life is emptied of its contents in order to make of the universe one vast container.

Critics often write as if the **"Elegy"** stays put and meditates on a particular, though unidentifiable, place. We do it more justice if we assume that the poem—like every work of art, I believe—acts to transform its initial conditions. The indefinite articles of the Epitaph should teach us at last how precise is the indefinite article of the title. We must learn not to seek knowledge of a particular place, as if to possess it mentally, but instead to accept a settled consciousness without a founding gesture or explicit starting "point." Rather than defining a social ideal, the poem turns away from social aspirations in order to evoke the transcendental basis of all experience. . . .

Notes

. . .[6] The definite article implies, first, belonging to an already known world (*the* curfew, vs. *a* curfew, which would anticipate subsequent clarification) yet, second, general rather than particular (*the* vs. *this*). On the kinetics of the definite article see Weinrich, *Sprache in Texten* 163-76 and 186-98, and Guillaume, *Langage* 143-66.

[7] Cleanth Brooks points out the impropriety of the word "annals" in *The Well Wrought Urn* III. The proper, altogether unpretentious term is "journals." Cf. *Spectator,* no. 317 (3: 156): "One may become wiser and better by several Methods of Employing ones self in Secrecy and Silence, and do what is laudable without Noise or Ostentation. I would, however, recommend to every one of my Readers, the keeping a Journal of their Lives for one Week." The poem gives us, of course, only one, unwritten and truncated journal, in the swain's account of the youth.

[8] Edwards, *Imagination and Power* 128-29. I follow, rather, Hutchings, "Syntax of Death."

[9] In his *Criticism on the Elegy* 40, John Young nicely holds Gray's "whiggish prejudices" responsible for the "fairy land" aura of poetic vagueness in the political stanzas.

[10] Scalia developed the notion of the "sublime in basso" in unpublished remarks at the conference "Il Sublime: "Creazione e catastrofe," Univ. of Bologna, May, 1984. See the related discussion by Franci in the published proceedings ("Sulla soglia").

[11] Cf. the interesting Freudian account of Gray in Jackson, "Thomas Gray and the Dedicatory Muse." Jackson argues persuasively that "the generative ground of vision [is] death" (287), but he imposes too dialectically negative a sense of death on Gray, for whom "death is a shaper" that "provides a dynamic impetus," with no "suggestion of a misanthropic or 'misbiotic' attitude" (Nemoianu, *A Theory of the Secondary* 121). There has to be a self—in the full romantic sense—before there can be, as Jackson says in his essay, a "betrayal of the self" (286). Cf. also Peter Brooks, *Reading for the Plot* 34, apropos of Rousseau's *Confessions*: "To imagine one's self-composed obituary read at the Judgment Day constitutes the farthest reach in the anticipation of retrospective narrative understanding. It is one that all narratives no doubt would wish to make." With the greater generality of the lyric, the "Elegy" satisfies this yearning, but in the form of a narrative of no one in particular in an unbounded space that is liberated from "the geometrical sense of plotting" (Brooks 24). Gray's spatializing can be highlighted by contrasting the "Elegy" to the time-saturated imitation by J. Cunningham, "An Elegy on a Pile of

Ruins," in Chalmers, *English Poets* 14: 443-45, esp. lines 133-36: "Vain then are pyramids, and motto'd stones, / And monumental trophies rais'd on high! / For Time confounds them with the crumbling bones, / That mix'd in hasty graves unnotic'd lie."

[12] See Wright's Berkeleyan reading ("Stillness and the Argument of Gray's Elegy"), which finds an ironic reversal in death, weakly overruled by the Epitaph—another suggestive account that goes astray by treating (eighteenth-century) continuity and flux as (romantic) dialectical contradiction.

[13] I owe to Steve Dillon the observation that "born[e]" in the funeral procession, line 114, is an ironic echo that undermines the positive associations of birth in the gem and flower stanza, lines 54-55.

[14] Cleanth Brooks's reading, "Gray's Storied Urn," in *The Well Wrought Urn* 105-23, attempts to salvage his notion of a poem as a self-contained organism by using the first 116 lines to contextualize the Epitaph. He is perceptive enough to concede that "I am not altogether convinced" (121), for, indeed, the Epitaph breaks free of all such bounds. He is answered by Bateson ("Gray's 'Elegy' Reconsidered," in *English Poetry* 127-35). Bateson gives the best compact account of the poem's inconsistencies in structure and ideology, concluding that the familiar, revised ending betrays Gray's genuine position "in the central social tradition of his time" (56). My analysis of flux in the poem is intended to show how it can seem both organic and inorganic, romantic and Augustan, strong and weak: its conclusion transforms the conditions of thought, but not yet the contents of thought. In a thought-provoking though sketchy essay ("Gray's 'Elegy'"), Bygrave calls this "a kind of repressed dialectic of self and society" (173) whose "displaced name . . . is not death but 'Romanticism'" (174).

[15] Rzepka, however, takes the "Elegy" as the founding text of his study, *The Self as Mind* 2-9, in a section called "The Body Vanishes: Solipsism and Vision in Gray's 'Elegy.'" Rzepka discusses well the persons in the poem as personifications of the speaker's psychic state. But though he sees the poem's task as "to reunite inner and outer" (8), he sees inwardness and "visionary solipsism" (9) as its sole subject. He overlooks the tradition—from Berkeley to both Kant and Coleridge—for which outness is as much a mental construct as inwardness.

[16] On Gray's instability see Cox, *Stranger* 82-98, and (in passing, about Gray as a typical figure of the period) Blom, "Eighteenth-Century Reflexive Process Poetry."

[17] Observing the poem's prevailingly negative rhetoric, the disappearance of the "I," and the persistent sense of passing, Anne Williams (*Prophetic Strain* 93-110) reads its mood as resignation to "passing on," i.e., to mortality. Yet she sees a movement at the start through fadings and endings toward "a kind of resurrection" in stanza 4 (100). I take that movement of release to be general and fundamental in the poem. Sacks, in his brief and reluctant treatment of the "Elegy" (*The English Elegy* 133-37), berates it as a "poem about the dying of a voice" (136) that leaves the poet "enshrined in a highly literary, even divine obscurity" (137). My discussion may help to clarify why Gray's masterpiece is refractory to the experiential, individual psychology that forms the basis of Sacks's book. Sacks begins, it may be further noted, by questioning Gray's relevance to his topic, since the title "Elegy" (rather than the original "Stanzas") was due to Gray's friend William Mason. Why mention this, since "elegy" appears in the title of no other poem that Sacks interprets? Perhaps Gray's impersonality, so forcefully acknowledged by Sacks's resistance, should be understood in terms of generic self-reference—an elegy on the elegy, and specifically on indulgence in grief and mourning, whose travails are one of the labors that Gray's ease ("haply," "one morn I missed him") conspicuously spares us.

[18] This exclusion is the unrecognized reason why, as Empson says in his commentary on the poem, "one could not estimate the amount of bourgeois ideology 'really in' the verse of Gray" (*Some Versions of Pastoral* 5). . . .

Andrew Dillon (essay date 1992)

SOURCE: "Depression and Release," in *North Dakota Quarterly*, Vol. 60, No. 4, Fall, 1992, pp. 128-34.

[*In the following essay on the "Elegy," Dillon comments on Gray's identification with the deceased farmers of the poem.*]

The **"Elegy Written in a Country Churchyard"** can be read as a journey of recognition conceived in dusk and worked out—not in a miasma of depression—but in the light of a symbolic self-destruction. The poem contains a drama of identification with the buried farmers of the village of Stoke Poges; however, this identification yields the poet a brief delivery from his rather narrow life. Moreover, the development of the poem has a quasi-heroic quality, for it grows out of a shorter early version that is a more emotionally distanced study of man's final destiny. When Thomas Gray returned to the Eton manuscript of the **"Elegy,"** he filled the new ending with far more intimate feelings.

The poem opens with the speaker's evocation of the world immediately around the graveyard; it then focuses on a plowman, who "homeward plods his weary way" (3). As if at home in the oncoming darkness, Gray clearly includes himself in the poem in stanzas that are full of a mournful music; suddenly, the verbs take on an almost independent energy: the turf "heaves" as the poet observes the graves as "many a mould'ring heap" (14). As will be later developed, this heaving of the earth suggests a kind of life within.

A series of vital images follows as if the quiet, celibate scholar perceived the farmers' lives in moments of dreamy wistfulness. In spite of the need to point out that the cheerful aspects of the laborers' mornings exist for them no more, the speaker describes elements of dawn: "breezy," "twitt'ring" (17, 18)—"the cock's shrill clarion" (19). There follows a series of pictures of a very different end of day than Thomas Gray could know: the "blazing hearth," the "busy houswife," children, and their climbing of the farmer's knees (21-24). Finally, stanza seven depicts the farmer's daily life:

> Oft did the harvest to their sickle yield,
> Their furrow oft the stubborn glebe has broke;
> How jocund did they drive their team afield!
> How bow'd the woods beneath their sturdy
>   stroke!
>
> (25-28)

These verbs evidence virile strength; they portray a celebration of physical power in that stroke that bows the woods. This may have been merely an idealization of everyday life, but it does touch on what could have been a psychological problem for Gray; it evokes the pride that rises from earning one's own way.

Gray's fellowship at Cambridge gave him a life-long tenure for a somewhat elegant—if narrow—scholarly existence. He was never required to teach and never delivered a lecture. Clarence Tracy asserts that Gray "lived for years on public patronage" and goes on to say that "his friend, Mason, made it a virtue in him that he never dirtied his mind with any intention of earning his living" ["Melancholy Marked Him for Her Own," in *Fearful Joy: Papers from the Thomas Gray Bicentenary Conference at Carlton University*]. Tracy also quotes Mason as saying his "life was spent in that kind of learned leisure, which has only self-improvement and self-gratification for its object" (38).[1]

Gray's biographer, Ketton-Cremer, suggests, "the man of reading and reflection often feels an envious admiration for the man of physical skill" [*Thomas Gray: A Biography*]. However, Gray modulates any such response into an identification—as well as a defense of the farmers against the putative disdain of the upper classes. When he honors the simple graves of the poor, he points out that the "storied urn" and "animated bust" (41) of the aristocrat cannot bring back the dead, as if in an urgent exhortation of the prosperous—or that side of Thomas Gray that has enjoyed a life of leisure.

Gray goes on to suggest the possibility that here may lie "some heart once pregnant with celestial fire" (46), but "chill Penury repress'd their noble rage" (51) because they lacked the good fortune of having an education (49-50).[2] The farmers, then, were left in pastoral innocence like the famous flower "born to blush unseen" (55). The poem is now near its first ending, which is preserved only in the Eton manuscript of Gray's **"Elegy."** Here, perhaps somewhat self-consciously, Gray implies that learning, worldly power, and leisure could do little but corrupt:

> The thoughtless World to Majesty may bow
> Exalt the brave, & idolize Success
> But more to Innocence their Safety owe
> Than Power & Genius e'er conspired to bless
>
> And thou, who mindful of the unhonour'd Dead
> Dost in these Notes their artless Tale relate
> By Night & lonely Contemplation led
> To linger in the gloomy Walks of Fate
>
> Hark how the sacred Calm, that broods around
> Bids ev'ry fierce tumultuous Passion cease
> In still small Accents whisp'ring from the Ground
> A grateful Earnest of eternal Peace
>
> No more with Reason & thyself at Strife;
> Give anxious Cares & endless Wishes room
> But thro' the cool sequester'd Vale of Life
> Pursue the silent Tenour of thy Doom.
>
> (Gray 40)

A close look at Starr and Hendrickson's rendition of the sixth line of the Eton manuscript excerpt [in their edition of *The Complete Poems of Thomas Gray*] shows an alteration to the word "their" from the original "thy." Of course, this "thy" might have been meant only to refer to the narrator of the poem as he possessed the poem—but it may very well have indicated a deeper involvement as if Gray were briefly identifying with the dead in a melancholic assessment of what his life had become.

The moment of ambiguity between whether "thy" referred only to the tale or to the life of the narrator is resolved when Gray struck out "thy" and rewrote "their," for the line now seems to concern no one except the dead farmers. However, the brief scratchings remain to suggest that the **"Elegy"** was for his own existence and that he had briefly included himself among the dead.

When he was much younger, Gray had written a four-line Latin fragment, "O lachrymarum Fons—O fountain of tears" (140). Starr and Hendrickson's translation is: "O fountain of tears which have their sacred sources in the sensitive soul! Four times blessed he who has felt thee, holy Nymph, bubbling up from depths of his heart" (141). This is a moving evocation of the ability to feel as if reaching out to the self's own source of tears; moreover, it suggests an earlier psychological breakthrough in response to depression. While Ian Jack asserts that Gray dropped the original four-stanza ending of his **"Elegy"** because "it preached a Stoic attitude to life that he could not accept" ["Gray's *Elegy* Reconsidered" in *From Sensibility to Romanticism,* edited by Frederick W. Hilles and Harold Bloom] it is as likely a conjecture that the new ending was yet another breakthrough in understanding for Gray, since it formed an escape from the depressing aspects of merely pursuing what he called "the silent Tenour of thy Doom" (Eton ms. 88).

R. W. Ketton-Cremer has demonstrated Gray's depression; it seems likely to infer an etiology of that condition in "his father's brutality to his mother" and in Gray's subsequent dependence on his mother. David Cecil points out "by the easy-going University regulations of those days he could go on residing in the college free, for as long as he wanted" [*Two Quiet Lives*]. Cecil also quotes one early letter to a friend saying, "When you have seen one of my days, you have seen a whole year of my life. They go round and round like a blind horse in the mill, only he has the satisfaction of fancying he makes progress, and gets some ground: my eyes are open enough to see the same dull prospect, and having made four and twenty steps more, I shall now be just where I was."

When Gray took up the Eton manuscript to write the ending with which readers are familiar, the farmers are the ones who keep to the "sequester'd vale of life"—and keep "the noiseless tenor of their way" (75-76). This last word, "way," is, of course, a significant change from Gray's term for himself in the earlier version: "of thy doom" (Eton ms. 88). Moreover, his new understanding is accompanied by a second major surge of energy:

> Far from the madding crowd's ignoble strife,
> Their sober wishes never learn'd to stray;
> Along the cool sequester'd vale of life
> They kept the noiseless tenor of their way.
>
> (73-76)

Later, Gray united himself with the farmers and all mankind in tremendously original lines:

> For who to dumb Forgetfulness a prey,
> This pleasing anxious being e'er resign'd,
> Left the warm precincts of the chearful day,
> Nor cast one longing ling'ring look behind?
>
> On some fond breast the parting soul relies,
> Some pious drops the closing eye requires;
> Ev'n from the tomb the voice of Nature cries,
> Ev'n in our Ashes live their wonted Fires.
>
> (85-92)

Dr. Johnson said of the two stanzas that contain the ashes line, "I have never seen the notions in any other place; yet he that reads them here, persuades himself that he has always felt them" (Ketton-Cremer). The poet means to suggest that life is still speaking from the buried ashes—yet whose ashes are these? They are those of the safe dead, yet they also form a melancholic, personal estimation of the poet—alive but in the ashes of an entombed self.

When Gray asserts, "Ev'n from the tomb the voice of Nature cries" (91), he must feel the strength of a tremendous moment of human projection; his living soul is speaking for the abstraction, Nature. Then, the idea is reinforced with, "Ev'n in our Ashes live their wonted Fires" (92). In the "our" of this line, Gray achieves a kind of emotional closure and becomes more nearly one with the ironically vital dead.[3]

Perhaps it is at this exact moment of desperate recognition that he becomes "the central figure of the poem and occupies that place until the end" (Ketton-Cremer). At any rate, in the next line, Gray speaks of "thee," who relates these lines (93). Of course, the "me" of the beginning of the poem (4) and the "thee" here are the same being, for Gray suddenly distances his spirit from his everyday self. Moreover, this objectification of the soul is Gray's chance to take the whole journey of imagination—and the poem becomes his elegy, "*his* storied urn" as Cleanth Brooks suggests [in *The Well Wrought Urn*].

Gray then invokes a "hoary-headed Swain" (97) who would by chance ("haply") describe the poem's speaker, now depicted as a rather romantic youth, who is seen as pale and wandering, possibly "craz'd with care, or cross'd in hopeless love" (108). Frank Brady suggests [in "Structure and meaning in Gray's *Elegy,*" in *From Sensibility to Romanticism,* edited by Hilles and Bloom] that "the swain's description of the narrator" shows that the narrator's "life is apparently unproductive and unfulfilled" (184). Then, the Swain is to tell the reader, who is suddenly referred to as a "kindred Spirit" (96), that the narrator is dead! He then invites the reader to read the narrator's epitaph, where an offering of the soul to God is recorded. We must understand that Gray—as narrator—has imaginatively entered the local society and has been long known to the swain, who is the second living farmer in the poem. In fact, he is the older parallel of the earlier rustic who "homeward plods his weary way" (3). That previous figure may have given Gray the first intimation of the farmer's warm reception at home as this imaginary swain yields Gray his escape from mere static contemplation.

The poet has now managed to stage a symbolic death so that his epitaph can be read in the churchyard. It is an unusual conception that allows Gray to break through the natural terror of dying in order to forge a relationship between a fear of death and an acceptance of that death. As the swain describes it, Gray's Romantic crisis becomes a self-immolation, a brief escape from his life, for he has moved on to a fearful insight: it is as if Gray and the deceased farmers share a complex species of mortality where the vital dead are more alive than the living speaker feels he is. Their very ashes contain a fire of life that the speaker senses he is missing, and, thus, they are the object of his sympathetic projection.

Perhaps Gray's personal sense of a buried life can be best approached from the end of the epitaph in which we are earlier told that "Melancholy mark'd him for her own" (120):

> No farther seek his merits to disclose,
> Or draw his frailties from their dread abode,
> (There they alike in trembling hope repose)
> The bosom of his Father and his God.
>
> (125-28)

His frailties are undefined, but they are seen as existing along with his merits in a trembling condition lodged in "the bosom of his Father and his God." It is a strange view of eternal love that reposes the deceased one's attributes only in trembling hope—forever. Indeed, it is depressing, for it pictures God as a stern, judgmental father who holds this split youth (merits and frailties) in eternal abeyance like a bird in winter.

Gray's **"Elegy,"** then, is as much about depression as it is about other species of entombments. Moreover, three years before his death in 1771, in the **"Ode for Music,"** Gray once again referred to melancholy:

> Oft at the blush of dawn
> I trod your level lawn,
> Oft woo'd the gleam of *Cynthia* silver-bright
> In cloisters dim, far from the haunts of Folly,
> With Freedom by my Side, and soft-ey'd
>   Melancholy.
>
> (30-34)

Ketton-Cremer suggests that the lines reflect Gray's life at Cambridge "remotely but unmistakably" (237).

However, the **"Elegy"** works because of the exquisite beauty of its language and the psychic complicity of the minds of readers with that of Thomas Gray. Our guide has disappeared; however, that is not an idiosyncratic moment of desertion but a great release of the imagination. Nevertheless, the vitality we project to the farmers and the buried speaker, is, of course, our own. Moreover, the poem serves as Gray's self-wrought

myth, where life's verve is celebrated, a descent into the earth is recorded, yet a resurrection is shown. In fact, the **"Elegy"** presents the reader with the "moment of awareness, the essential substance of myth" [P. J. Aldus, *Mousetrap: Structure and Meaning in "Hamlet"*]. Therefore, readers return to the poem to take a journey underground while still in "this pleasing anxious being" (86). However, the **"Elegy"**'s exchange for our energy is a delight which turns us back to the world as we depart the poem's mimetic twilight with our own "wonted fires."

Notes

[1] David Cecil points out that Gray was appointed Regius Professor of History in 1768—three years before his death. A wave of academic reform was in the air that same year, and "Gray was asked, in his new official capacity, to give his opinion" on what the Professor of History should actually do. He decided to prepare a lecture, but that never got "further than the first sketch." Cecil goes on to say that Gray suffered great guilt about this situation (231-34).

[2] In 1768, Gray wrote a letter to Horace Walpole in which he suggested that he might understand in more than one way how a "heart once pregnant with celestial fire" could be stymied. He said, "However, I will be candid (for you seem to be so with me) and avow to you, that till fourscore-and-ten, whenever the humour takes me, I will write, because I like it; and because I like myself better when I do so. If I do not write much, it is because I cannot" (Ketton-Cremer 226). As to education, which was Gray's good fortune, the poet does seem to express a concern about that fortune at least four times in the "Elegy." He speaks of the unlettered farmers, that is, "rude forefathers" (16), and he again emphasizes their lack of knowledge (49-50). Later, the "hoary-headed Swain" (97) seems to be unable to read and suggests that the reader of the "Elegy"—the "kindred Spirit" (96)—approach and read the narrator's own gravestone. Finally, "Fair Science"—that is, knowledge—is said to have been favorable to the narrator. Thus, we may assume Gray was keenly aware of his privileged position and that he may have suffered some guilt about it.

[3] Furthermore, a study of the ashes line's compositional history shows the version in the Eton ms.—"And buried Ashes glow with social Fires." Starr and Hendrickson also give the version (in the same footnote) of the first edition (1751): "Awake, and faithful to her wonted Fires" (41). The line's last change arrives only in 1753 in the eighth edition (Ketton-Cremer 289). Here Gray fashions that useful ambiguity that includes the rustics, Gray, and all humankind: "Ev'n in our Ashes live their wonted Fires." It was his final touch to the **"Elegy."**

FURTHER READING

Biography

Ketton-Cremer, R. W. *Thomas Gray: A Biography.* Cambridge: Cambridge University Press, 1955, 310 p.

A detailed and insightful biography, replete with apt quotations from Gray's correspondence and several portraits of Gray and his contemporaries.

Mason, W[illiam]. "Memoirs & c." In *The Works of Thomas Gray*, 3d ed., by Thomas Gray, pp. 127ff. London: Vernor, Hood, and Sharpe, 1807.

Highly favorable impressions of Gray's life and work by the poet's editor and longtime friend.

Mitford, John. "The Life of Thomas Gray." In *The Poetical Works of Thomas Gray*, by Thomas Gray, pp. i-cxxiv. London: William Pickering, 1836.

An eloquent and predominantly accurate biography that corrects several faulty assumptions propounded by William Mason in his memoirs of Gray.

Criticism

Bentman, Raymond. "Thomas Gray and the Poetry of 'Hopeless Love'." *Journal of the History of Sexuality* 3, No. 2 (October 1992): 203-22.

Discusses Gray's emotional and sexual attraction to other men as evidenced in his letters and poems and comments on attitudes toward sodomy in early-eighteenth-century England.

Brady, Frank. "Structure and Meaning in Gray's 'Elegy'." In *From Sensibility to Romanticism: Essays Presented to Frederick A. Pottle*, edited by Frederick W. Hilles and Harold Bloom, pp. 177-89. New York: Oxford University Pres, 1965.

Details the structural transformation of the "Elegy" effected by Gray's revision of the poem.

Bygrave, Stephen. "Gray's 'Elegy': Inscribing the Twilight." In *Post-Structuralist Readings of English Poetry*, edited by Richard Machin and Christopher Norris, pp. 162-75. Cambridge: Cambridge University Press, 1987.

Explores the relationship between the "'private' syntax" and "'public' diction" of the "Elegy." Bygrave uses a number of other critical interpretations of the poem to buttress his argument.

Carper, Thomas R. "Gray's Personal Elegy." *Studies in English Literature, 1500-1900* XVII, No. 3 (Summer 1977): 451-62.

Questions the critical theory that the later version of the "Elegy" is impersonal and objective in comparison with the earlier version. Carper maintains that both versions are intimately personal, noting that the primary themes of the "Elegy"—family, nature, and social rank—had been important concerns of Gray's since his college days.

Downey, James, and Ben Jones, eds. *Fearful Joy: Papers from the Thomas Gray Bicentenary Conference at Carleton University.* Montreal: McGill-Queens University Press, 1974, 266 p.

A collection of sixteen essays on Gray that, according to the editors, address "almost every important feature of his life and work." Among the subjects discussed are Gray's writings, including his correspondence; his scholarship; and his relationship to a number of other poets, including William Blake, Samuel Taylor Cole-ridge, William Wordsworth, and John Keats.

Edgecombe, R. S. "Diction and Allusion in Two Early Odes by Gray." *The Durham University Journal* n.s. XLVIII, No. 1 (December 1986): 31-6.

Examines the language of "Ode on the Spring" and "Ode on a Distant Prospect of Eton College," arguing that "the diction of these odes . . . is far from being the insensitively pompous and over-massive thing it is sometimes made out to be."

Edwards, Thomas R. "From Satire to Solitude." In *Imagination and Power: A Study of Poetry on Public Themes*, pp. 83-139. London: Chatto & Windus, 1971.

Comments on the themes of isolation and identity in the "Elegy" and examines Gray's attitudes toward rural and city life.

Ellis, R. J. "Plodding Plowmen: Issues of Labour and Literacy in Gray's 'Elegy'." In *The Independent Spirit: John Clare and the Self-Taught Tradition*, pp. 27-43. Helpston, England: The John Clare Society and The Margaret Grainger Memorial Trust, 1994.

An essay on the "Elegy" in which Ellis discusses the "stonecutter debate"—the question of the identity of "thee" in line ninety-three of the poem—in terms of the disparity between conventional pastoral discourse and actual rural conditions in mid-eighteenth-century England.

Foerster, Donald M. "Thomas Gray." In *The Age of Johnson: Essays Presented to Chauncey Brewster Tinker*, edited by Frederick W. Hilles, pp. 217-26. New Haven: Yale University Press, 1949.

Examines Gray's reasons for writing and his attitude toward poetry, focusing on "The Bard."

Fry, Paul H. "The Tented Sky in the Odes of Collins." In *The Poet's Calling in the English Ode*, pp. 97-132. New Haven: Yale University Press, 1980.

Analyzes Gray's odes as self-conscious experiments in the art of writing poetry, focusing on Gray's "human" and "public" poetic voices, his sense of alienation, and his theme of "distance as absence."

Gleckner, Robert F. *Gray Agonistes: Thomas Gray and Masculine Friendship.* Baltimore: The Johns Hopkins University Press, 1997, 231 p.

Studies Gray's "borrowings" from the poet John Milton and charts Gray's relationship with Richard West through an examination of both Gray's poetry and letters.

Golden, Morris. *Thomas Gray.* Rev. ed. Boston: Twayne Publishers, 1988, 156 p.

A revised version of Golden's 1964 study of Gray. While Golden is "primarily concerned with Gray and with the nature and quality of his poems rather than with his and their place in English literature," he includes chapters entitled "Gray, the Man" and "Classical or Romantic?"

Hagstrum, Jean H. "Thomas Gray." In *The Sister Arts: The Tradition of Literary Pictorialism and English Poetry from Dryden to Gray,* pp. 287-314. Chicago: University of Chicago Press, 1958.

Studies the pictorial elements in Gray's verse, focusing on the "Elegy," "The Progress of Poesy," and "The Bard."

Hutchings, W. "Conversations with a Shadow: Thomas Gray's Latin Poems to Richard West." *Studies in Philology* XCII, No. 1 (Winter 1995): 118-39.

Examines the Latin poems Gray wrote for Richard West, noting that, for Gray, the Latin language afforded the most intimate form of communication with his most intimate friend.

Hutchings, W. B., and William Ruddick, eds. *Thomas Gray: Contemporary Essays.* Liverpool: Liverpool University Press, 1993, 279 p.

Twelve recent essays on Gray covering a range of topics, including the critical history of Gray's works, Gray's relationship to Lord Byron and William Wordsworth, Gray's poetic style, and Gray's travel writings.

Jack, Ian. "Gray's 'Elegy' Reconsidered." In *From Sensibility to Romanticism: Essays Presented to Frederick A. Pottle,* edited by Frederick W. Hilles and Harold Bloom, pp. 139-69. New York: Oxford University Press, 1965.

A close study of the "Elegy" focusing on the technical aspects of Gray's diction and on the various poetic influences evident in the work.

Kaul, Suvir. *Thomas Gray and Literary Authority: A Study in Ideology and Poetics.* Stanford: Stanford University Press, 1992, 269 p.

A reading of Gray's poems in terms of eighteenth-century cultural politics. Kaul studies the formal features, representational methods, thematic concerns, and ideological priorites of Gray's verse within the context of the literary and social practices of his day.

Lonsdale, Roger. "The Poetry of Thomas Gray: Versions of the Self." In *Proceedings of the British Academy,* Vol. LIX, pp. 105-23. London: Oxford University Press, 1975.

Uses the differences between the two versions of the "Elegy" as a starting point for a discussion of Gray's exploration of his poetic self.

Maclean, Kenneth. "The Distant Way: Imagination and Image in Gray's Poetry." In *Fearful Joy: Papers from the Thomas Gray Bicentenary Conference at Carlton University,* edited by James Downey and Ben Jones, pp. 136-45. McGill-Queen's University Press, 1974.

Identifies the major themes and images in Gray's poetry, and concludes that "nature and art move evenly across his page, as do feeling and learning."

Pettersson, Torsten. *Literary Interpretation: Current Models and a New Departure.* Abo: Abo Akademis Forlag - Abo Academy Press, 1988, 132 p.

Defines the nature and characteristics of literary criticism in the twentieth century using four different critical interpretations of the "Elegy" as a point of departure.

Redford, Bruce. "The Allusiveness of Thomas Gray." In *The Converse of the Pen: Acts of Intimacy in the Eighteenth-Century Letter,* pp. 95-132. Chicago: University of Chicago Press, 1986.

Examines Gray's use of "elusion, allusion, and illusion" in his letters to friends, linking the obliquity of Gray's correspondence to his need for privacy.

Sha, Richard C. "Gray's Political 'Elegy': Poetry as the Burial of History." *Philological Quarterly* 69, No. 3 (Summer 1990): 337-57.

Seeks to understand the "Elegy" in terms of the historical particulars surrounding the poem, focusing on Gray's treatment of the rural poor.

Starr, Herbert W., ed. *Twentieth Century Interpretations of Gray's Elegy: A Collection of Critical Essays.* Englewood Cliffs, N. J.: Prentice-Hall, 1968, 120 p.

A collection of twelve important modern essays on the "Elegy." Critics represented include Ian Jack, A. E. Dyson, and Cleanth Brooks.

Summers, Claude J., ed. *Homosexuality in Renaissance and Enlightenment England: Literary Reresentations in Historical Context.* New York: Haworth Press, 1992, 222 p.

Argues that the features of the "Elegy" commonly attributed to Gray's melancholy were actually shaped by Gray's own awareness of his homosexuality.

Watson, George. "The Voice of Gray." *Critical Quarterly* 19, No. 4 (Winter 1977): 51-7.

Explores the nature and purpose of Gray's use of grammatical indeterminacies in the "Elegy."

Weinbrot, Howard D. "Gray's 'Elegy': A Poem of Moral Choice and Resolution." *Studies in English Literature, 1500-1900* XVIII, No. 3 (Summer 1978): 537-51.

Argues that the "Elegy" is about eternal life, rather than death, because the speaker of the poem surrenders himself to God's will by learning to accept his humble station in life.

Wright, George T. "Stillness and the Argument of Gray's 'Elegy'." *Modern Philology* 74, No. 4 (May 1977): 381-89.

Contends that the principal subject of the "Elegy" is the nature and meaning of epitaphs.

Zionkowski, Linda. "Bridging the Gulf between: The Poet and the Audience in the Work of Gray." *ELH* 58, No. 2 (Summer 1991): 331-50.

Discusses Gray's views on his role as an author, his relationship with his audience, and his attitude toward the contemporary system of literature.

Additional coverage of Gray's life and career is contained in the following sources published by Gale Research: *Literature Criticism from 1400 to 1800,* **Vol. 4 and** *Poetry Criticism,* **Vol. 2.**

James Thomson

1700-1748

Scottish poet and dramatist.

The following entry contains critical essays on Thomson's relationship to Preromanticism. For further information on Thomson's career, see *LC,* vols. 16 and 29.

INTRODUCTION

Regarded as one of the leading poets in eighteenth-century European literature, Thomson is primarily known for *The Seasons* (1726-30), a four-part poetic work about nature and its cyclical transformations. Considered Thomson's masterpiece, *The Seasons* had a significant influence on eighteenth-century English and continental literature, both reflecting the period's fascination with nature and establishing a model for pastoral poetry throughout Europe. This poem constitutes the basis for claims that Thomson anticipated the rise of Romanticism in British poetry. Thomson is also known for other major and minor works, including *The Castle of Indolence* (1748) and his patriotic poem "Rule Britannia," from the masque *Alfred* (1740), written with David Mallet and set to music by Thomas Augustine Arne. Since the poem debuted in 1740, Great Britain has used "Rule Britannia" as a musical declaration of national power and pride.

Biographical Information

Born the son of a clergyman in southern Scotland, Thomson grew up in the kind of picturesque rural environment he often depicted in his poetry. After following a course of study at Edinburgh University that prepared him for a career in the ministry, Thomson decided instead to pursue a literary career, for which he moved to London in 1725. There, he was able to write while employed as a tutor. He worked on *The Seasons* for the next several years, publishing "Winter" in 1726, "Summer" the following year, "Spring" in 1728, and "Autumn" in 1730. Even after publishing the cycle as a whole that same year, Thomson continued reworking his masterpiece, eventually publishing a revised edition in 1744. At its first printing, the poem was received enthusiastically and lifted its author to literary fame. In a period when poets lived on patronage rather than sales, Thomson's success procured him an attractive position as the travelling companion and tutor to Charles Talbot, son of the future Lord Chancellor. Thomson held this post, which provided him with the opportunity of visiting France and Italy, until 1733, when he became Secretary of Briefs in the Court

of Chancery. He lost this appointment in 1737 due to the death of the Lord Chancellor. The following year, upon the intervention of his friend George Lyttelton, the poet received an annual pension from the Prince of Wales. His financial situation became quite comfortable in 1744, when he was named Surveyor-General of the Leeward Islands. Highly esteemed by literary London, surrounded by loyal friends, and the recipient of sinecures, royalties, and a royal pension, Thomson spent his last years quietly, in a fine house in Kew Lane, Richmond, not far from his friend Alexander Pope.

Major Works

Described by many critics as a precursor of Romanticism, Thomson is nevertheless firmly rooted in the Classicism and Rationalism prevalent in his own era. Like other Neoclassical poets, he understood the world through the paramount significance he accorded science. Thomson venerated the scientist and philosopher Sir Isaac Newton, whose philosophy of nature defined the intellectual paradigms of the period. Newton's influence reveals itself extensively in *The Seasons*, where the Newtonian concept of God as architect and guardian of a highly-ordered and hierarchical universe clearly shaped Thomson's descriptions of nature. Thomson also turned to Newton for accurate poetic description, as did many other poets; the seminal scientific work from which Thomson benefited was Newton's *Opticks* (1740), a treatise explaining the nature of color and light. Thomson's poetic forbearers include John Milton, author of the epic *Paradise Lost*, and Edmund Spenser, whose best known work is *The Faerie Queene*. Milton's influence appears in the stately blank verse and latinate vocabulary of *The Seasons*.

Despite a foundation in the conventions of his own past and present, Thomson created poetry with innovations that many critics have hailed as significantly forward-looking. These experiments appear especially in the non-narrative, wholly descriptive verses of *The Seasons*. While emulating Milton, Thomson superimposed his own idiosyncratic diction onto the archaic poetic form, thus creating unprecedented images and harmonies. The pictorial emphasis of his descriptions drew on and later influenced landscape painters; for example, he inspired the English painter J. M. W. Turner, who honored Thomson in his 1811 work entitled *Thomson's Aeolian Harp*. The most dramatically historic impact of *The Seasons* appears, however, in the works of English Romantic poets, including William Cowper, William Wordsworth, and John Keats. Thomson's reputation as a Preromantic arises from his descriptions of nature, which incorporated both the observer and, especially, the centrality of the emotions elicited by the contemplation of nature's majesty.

As Patricia Meyer Spacks has noted, however, Thomson's emotive depictions of nature constitute only a limited portion of his entire corpus. Much of the rest of his writing, both poetic and dramatic, stresses instead social and even moral issues. In *Liberty* (1735-36), a five-part poetical panorama of various countries and their governments and mores, Thomson drew from the optimistic moralism of Anthony Ashley Cooper, Lord Shaftesbury, to extol the unrivalled virtues of Britain's political system. *The Castle of Indolence*, a verse allegory based explicitly on Spenser's *The Faerie Queene*, expounds on the ills of indolence and the blessings of industry. Thomson's other writings include incidental poems, exemplified by love lyrics, and five dramas; the latter, according to critics, seldom rise above rhetorical bombast.

Critical Reception

For a century following its publication, *The Seasons* guaranteed Thomson's literary fame and popularity. Embraced both by critics and a general population characterized by a growing literacy rate, the poem made Thomson a prominent figure whose influence spread broadly over time and geography. In the German-speaking world, Thomson's admirers included Albrecht von Haller, author of the poem *Die Alpen* (*The Alps*), Ewald von Kleist, who wrote *Frühling* (*Spring*), the lyric poet Johann Peter Uz, and Gotthold Ephraim Lessing. In an adaptation by Gottfried von Swieten, the poem served Franz Joseph Haydn as a text for his celebrated oratorio *Die Jahreszeiten*. In France, Thomson was praised by Voltaire and emulated by various poets. His influence can also be seen in the pastoral poetry of the Spaniard Juan Melendez Valdés.

Hilbert H. Campbell, in his 1979 *James Thomson*, has argued that the classification of Thomson as a "Preromantic poet" stems from the biases of critics themselves: Romanticism has long been a more favored period in literary history than has the Augustan, or Neoclassical, period during which Thomson lived. "In this persistent and one-sided critical tradition," Campbell contends, "Thomson's accomplishments, virtues, and faults were all measured by the yardstick of how well or how poorly he managed to foreshadow Wordsworth." The critics in this tradition have emphasized those qualities in Thomson's poetry that looked forward to some of the primary values of the Romantics, particularly originality and celebration of nature. William Hazlitt, an influential essayist writing in the Romantic era, thought highly of Thomson, naming him the foremost descriptive poet of the time.

By and large, Thomson's critics have praised his subject matter and originality while expressing reservations about his technical skills. For example, such eminent contemporaries as Pope and Samuel Johnson, who recognized *The Seasons* as a remarkable literary accomplishment, noted its compositional weakness. Wordsworth acknowledged Thomson's talent but complained about his "vicious style." By the late nineteenth-century, commentators including George Saintsbury and Edmund Gosse focused on the formal structure of Thomson's poetry, identifying faults in his style and diction. Twentieth-century critics have offered a more balanced assessment of Thomson's poetry, noting that imperfections and dissonances hardly diminish his poetic voice. They have questioned earlier evalutions of Thomson's diction and style, arguing that some of his cadences may sound awkward because they are heard outside the context of Scottish speech. Finally, critics including Campbell and Spacks have suggested that Thomson needs to be studied more in the context of his own literary period, rather than compared extensively with the conventions of Romanticism.

PRINCIPAL WORKS

Winter. A Poem (poetry) 1726

CRITICISM

J. More (essay date 1777)

SOURCE: "On the Originality of *The Seasons*," in
*Strictures, Critical and Sentimental, on Thomson's
"Seasons,"* Garland Publishing, Inc., 1970, pp. 167-87.

[*In the following chapter from his book-length study of*
The Seasons, *first published in 1777, More praises
Thomson's originality in both the objects he describes
and his language. More contends that human nature,
in a love of novelty, seeks originality; therefore, according to More, Thomson's poetry is greatly in syn-
chrony with the desires of human nature.*]

> *To such the bounteous Providence of Heav'n,*
> *In every breast implanting this desire*
> *Of objects new and strange, to urge us on*
> *With unremitted labour to pursue*
> *Those sacred stores that wait the rip'ning foul*
> *In Truth's exhaustless bosom.——*

[Previously] we have attempted. . . an imperfect sketch
of the leading object to which the **Seasons** of Thomson are chiefly directed. The great and only general
effect, which he seems most solicitous to produce in
the minds of his readers, is a full acquiescence in the
economy, and a filial confidence in the Author of
Nature. And he paints every part of the year, and every

genial form that wakes, to the plastic energy of poetical enthusiasm, in colours peculiarly adapted to his
purpose. He does not satisfy himself, however, with
simply arraying the conceptions of others in a dress of
his own. This contemptible species of plagiarism, was
not more beneath his genius than repugnant to his taste.
He had immediate recourse to nature for all his materials, and she intrusted with confidence her secrets to
his care. For however in other respects he should offend against the established dogmas of criticism, his
poetry every where discovers the strongest traits of
originality. All his ideas, sentiments and versification
seem peculiarly his own. There is a beautiful wildness
in his numbers, unpolished as they sometimes are; a
manliness and majesty in his language, a decorum and
spirit in his images, and a likeness in most of his descriptions, singularly new, inimitable and striking. And
what of all others is perhaps the most decisive mark of
a poetical mind, the objects he describes, though frequently common and familiar, strike us some how in a
new light.

The human system, like every other work of nature, is
progressive, and arrives at perfection by imperceptible
degrees. We are never thoroughly satisfied in our best
acquisitions, the largest prospects stint not our views,
the whole range of the senses bound not our desires.
Some distant object in every possible position, breaks
in upon our rest, fires the heart with new ardour, and
pushes onward to new attainments. Wherever we direct our sight or attention, novelty in a thousand forms
tempts our wishes and solicits our acquaintance. Thus
impelled by a restless and in-satiable curiosity, we
are still making new experiments on every thing
around us, indulging new feelings from every change
that affects us, and accumulating new ideas from
whatever comes within the sphere of observation.

How happily does our poet adapt his descriptions to
this strange peculiarity in the human system. He never
overlooks our love of variety, nor fatigues the attention with a tedious and minute display of one object.
He knew in what a constant and curious alternation
our best sensations succeed each other, and generally
suits them all with delicacy and precision. And his
felicity in blending a certain spicery of novelty with
nature and truth, through all their various windings
and gradations, is extremely uncommon. "*Thomson,*
says a writer already quoted, *in that beautiful descriptive poem, the **Seasons**, pleases by the justness of his
painting, but his greatest merit consists in impressing
the mind with numberless beauties of nature in her
various and successive forms, which formerly passed
unheeded——*"

Inattention, though the worst is perhaps one of the
most prevalent habits in the human temper. That suggests insensibility to circumstances and things which
tinctures the disposition and manners of most men, not

only plunges them into many inconveniences which they might otherwise have escaped, but deprives them of many pleasures which they might otherwise enjoy. The whole aspect of nature is so full of meaning, teems with so many beauties, and exhibits such a vast profusion of unexpected varieties, that every sensation she awakens contributes some how to human happiness. In heaven above, and the earth beneath, still some new object catches the wandering eye, and fills the contemplative mind with a fresh accession of delight. Not a brook that murmurs as it runs, not a breeze that rustles among the branches, not a cow that lows on the plain, not a lamb that bleats and browzes on the hill, not a bird that nestles and sings among the bushes, not a sight we see, nor a sound we hear, which addresses not every faculty of the soul and every feeling of the heart, in the simplest, sweetest, most persuasive accents, and which discovers not some new quality, or creates some new sensation.

To Thomson we are greatly indebted for thus employing his descriptive talents in rousing imagination and the heart to that charming glass of novelty which sparkles around us in the sweetest lustre, and sheds a fragrance sufficiently delicious to every sense. His muse in catering for her own pleasure administers to ours. He obviously despises every art, and even poetry itself, but in so far as it contributes to the embellishment, convenience, or comfort of life, and has either an immediate or oblique direction to make men wiser, better and happier. He wished them possessed of all the ease, tranquillity, and delight which their present condition affords, and to share the bounties of Providence with liberality and gratitude. His constitutional temper, notwithstanding the strongest sensibility, was originally cheerful, he had been long under the tuition of that philosophy that gives its disciples the mastery of themselves, and his poem is every where enriched with the natural ebullitions of a glad heart. To awaken in others a series of sentiments so grateful to his own mind, was no doubt one reason that set him about writing the *Seasons*. And they will last as long as the language, a beautiful monument of benevolence as well as of genius.

There is no dissipating the unthinking languor of stupidity, without producing certain emotions of surprise. And this can only be done in description, by a delicate selection of such circumstances as are best calculated to startle the fancy or strike the heart. All new objects occasion new feelings, and the effect uniformly corresponds with the cause. Whatever regards us with an inimical aspect, awakens painful sensations, but things of a more friendly and generous appearance are accompanied with those of a pleasing and congenial nature. This in all the fine arts is a source of inexhaustible beauty, and feeds imagination with an endless series of the purest and most exquisite delicacies. And the only difference between vulgar and elegant or enlarged

minds is, that the latter have what the former want, a quick instinctive, habitual discernment, not only of every thing that affects them, but of every affection to which they are subject. To this fine principle original writers owe all their distinction. They perceive every object through a medium peculiar to themselves, and are often blamed for their conceptions, with a partiality as barbarous and absurd as that which should instigate us to censure, or rather insult the strong for vanquishing the weak, or the swift for outrunning the slow. Indeed, they have seldom very little merit or demerit, either in the ideas which occupy their minds, or the feelings that agitate their hearts. Fancy is seldom a voluntary agent, but always and every where, as obsequious to the influence of novelty as an orb to the attraction of its sphere. In this light Thomson moves in a circle, and with a dignity and propriety wholly his own. His attachment to rural simplicity and romantic solitude, was early and singular. Scenes, where nature wantons in the wildest irregularity, were homogeneous to his mind. While yet a child he has been known to steal away from his little companions, who sometimes found him strolling all alone among brakes, thickets, the banks of streams, and the sides of hills; which even then seemed possessed of some secret enchantment, which corresponded to the soft inexplicable movements of his rising genius. From this sauntering and pensive habit he acquired an aukwardness of manner which never forsook him, but secured an intercourse with the essence and arrangement of things, which sufficiently supplied his want of the graces with an uncommon stock of sensibility and science. Hence almost every passage in the *Seasons*, however faulty in other respects, is equally replete with novelty and truth. It is well known that he was accustomed, even after he came to England, engrossed as he then was, by the best company, and familiar with the most shining characters of the age, to disengage himself from them all, and frequent the most sequestered and celebrated spots in the neighbourhood. There, if he felt no new emanations, or imbibed no new conceptions, he could recollect the old at his leisure, wait the happy returns of genius, and catch the delightful afflatus of inspiration. Then he mused and philosophised by turns on every proximate object and circumstance, and seldom left the place till he had reduced the various thoughts and sentiments it suggested to a regular consistency, if not to complete versification. His mornings and evenings, especially in composing the *Seasons*, were generally spent in this manner. And to the resolute and manly preference of such innocent and rational amusements he owes most of his fame. For this first and best of all his poems derives its chief popularity, not so much from the justness, of which few are competent judges, as from the beautiful novelty of his painting, of which all are sensible.

One would imagine the subject of the *Seasons*, at first view, not the most susceptible of invention. But what is it a truly original genius will not improve. Every thing is prolific of novelty in the hand of a Master. His ideas are not the crude conceptions of dulness, nor his sentiments either the vapid yawning of a listless, or the insignificant prattle of an empty heart. He generally plans intirely for himself, and always executes in a manner preceded by nothing similar. The light he strikes out is so singular, and withal so true, that we are equally pleased with what we never saw before, and surprised that we now only see it for the first time. Who, for example, till Virgil appeared, expected to find the fable of the Iliad capable of being thus beautifully diversified with new elegance and truth. In like manner the metamorphoses of Nature, through all the different stages of excellence, takes place—one animal assumes the form of another; the acorn starts up into a full grown tree, and the inanimate creation, though apparently perfect, is in a state of perpetual revolution and vicissitude.—

In descriptive poetry, as in landscape-painting, fancy has the fullest scope. Here, however, fiction does not consist in feigning objects unknown to the senses, but in embellishing them with colours, endowing them with qualities, connecting them by relations, and disposing them in attitudes and groupes of which we have little or no acquaintance. In truth, ideal arrangements are endless. While our affections retain their usual aversion to uniformity, the multifarious objects of our respective senses and faculties must unavoidably admit of new combinations. This, like every other art, improves by practice. For the more a fertile imagination creates or fabricates, the exercise becomes the easier, new veins of verisimilitude are disclosed, and we may give over for want of patience or strength, but not of materials. The human genius is so versatile, and the original sources of beauty so inexhaustible, that every new inspection of the most common and familiar phenomena of nature, discover a thousand new variations, distinctions and resemblances, at the same time that it opens up a multiplicity of avenues, where novelty wantons in all her charms, where science displays her happiest attractions, where fancy is feasted, and the heart in transport. Such is the situation in which Thomson shines, and sheds a lustre around him, which few imitators of the same simple and genuine original have hitherto surpassed. And it has been affirmed in my hearing, by some in whose judgment I have the fullest confidence, and whose profession and science give them a right to speak decisively, that the pieces of *Poussin* are not more uncommon, exotic, and classical, the sketches of *Lorenese* more daring and sublime, or the descriptions of *Titian* more happy, natural, graceful, varied and charming, than his. So that to a reader of taste, who can relish nature in her rudest as well as in her most polished and splendid shapes, it is hardly possible to mention a poem of the same extent that will furnish him with as much novelty, or better reward a perusal.—

It is not easy to conceive for what reason, but our critics in general, with all their drowsy and laborious commentaries, have been very sparing in their attentions to Thomson. The neglect, it may be thought, is the less injurious, that those they have buried amidst the greatest piles of literature, are commonly the least read. One however, and not the least eminent of his cotemporaries, mentions the Author of the *Seasons* in terms so proper and polite, that I know not how to illustrate this part of the subject better than by transcribing what he says—

"Thomson was blessed with a strong and copious fancy; he hath enriched poetry with a variety of new and original images, which he painted from nature itself, and from his own actual observations: his descriptions have therefore a distinctness and truth, which are utterly wanting to those, of poets who have only copied from each other, and have never looked abroad on the objects themselves. Thomson was accustomed to wander away into the country for days and for weeks, attentive to, "each rural sight, each rural found," while many a poet who has dwelt for years in the Strand, has attempted to describe fields and rivers, and generally succeeded accordingly. Hence that nauseous repetition of the same circumstances; hence that disgusting impropriety of introducing what may be called a set of hereditary images, without proper regard to the age, or climate, or occasion in which they were formerly used. Though the diction of the *Seasons* is sometimes harsh and inharmonious, and sometimes turgid and obscure, and though in many instances, the numbers are not sufficiently diversified by different pauses, yet is this poem on the whole, from the numberless strokes of nature in which it abounds, one of the most captivating and amusing in our language, and which, as its beauties are not of a transitory kind, as depending on particular customs and manners, will ever be perused with delight. The scenes of Thomson are frequently as wild and romantic as those of Salvator Rosa, varied with precipices and torrents, and "castled cliffs," and deep vallies, with piny mountains, and the gloomiest caverns. Innumerable are the little circumstances in his descriptions, totally unobserved by all his predecessors. What poet hath ever taken notice of the leaf, that towards the end of autumn.

> Incessant rustles from the mournful grove,
> Oft startling such as, studious, walk below,
> And slowly circles through the waving air?

Or who, in speaking of a summer evening, hath ever mentioned,

> The quail that clamours for his running
>   mate?

Or the following natural image at the same time of the year?

Wide o'er the thistly lawn, as swells the breeze,
A whitening shower of vegetable down
Amusive floats.———

In what other poet, do we find the silence and expectation that procedes an April shower insisted on.

The stealing shower is scarce to patter heard,
By such as wander through the forest walks,
Beneath th' umbrageous multitude of leaves.

How full, particular and picturesque is this assemblage of circumstances that attend a very keen frost in a night of winter!

Loud rings the frozen earth, and hard
    reflects
A double noise; while at his evening watch
The village dog deters the nightly thief;
The heifer lows; the distant water-fall
Swells in the breeze; and with the hasty tread
Of traveller, the hollow-sounding plain
Shakes from afar.———

In no one subject are common writers more confused and unmeaning, than in their descriptions of rivers, which are generally said only to wind and to murmur, while their qualities and courses are seldom accurately marked. Examine the exactness of the ensuing description, and consider what a perfect idea it communicates to the mind.

Around th' adjoining brook, that purls along
The vocal grove, now fretting o'er a rock,
Now scarcely moving through a reedy pool,
Now starting to a sudden stream, and now
Gently diffus'd into a limpid plain;
A various groupe the herds and flocks compose,
Rural confusion!———

A groupe worthy the pencil of Giacomo da Bassano, and so minutely delineated, that he might have worked from this sketch;

———On the grassy bank
Some ruminating lie; while others stand
Half in the flood, and often bending sip
The circling surface.———

He adds, that the ox in the middle of them,

———From his sides
The troublous insects lashes, to his sides
Returning still.———

A natural circumstance, that to the best of my remembrance hath escaped even the natural Theocritus. Nor do I recollect that any poet hath been struck with the murmurs of the numberless insects, that swarm abroad at the noon of summer's day; as attendants of the evening indeed, they have been mentioned;

Resounds the living surface of the ground:
Nor undelightful is the ceaseless hum
To him who muses through the woods at noon;
Or drowsy shepherd, as he lies reclin'd
With half-shut eyes.———

But the novelty and nature we admire in the descriptions of Thomson are by no means his only excellencies; he is equally to be praised, for impressing on our minds the effects, which the scene delineated would have on the present spectator or hearer. Thus having spoken of the roaring of the savages in a wilderness of Africa, he introduces a captive, who, though just escaped from prison and slavery under the tyrant of Morocco, is so terrified and astonished at the dreadful uproar, that

The wretch half wishes for his bonds again.

Thus also having described a caravan lost and overwhelmed in one of those whirlwinds that so frequently agitate and lift up the whole sands of the desert, he finishes his picture by adding that,

———In Cairo's crouded streets,
Th' impatient merchant, wondering waits in vain,
And Mecca saddens at the long delay.

And thus, lastly, in describing the pestilence that destroyed the British troops at the siege of Carthagena, he has used a circumstance inimitably lively, picturesque, and striking to the imagination; for he says that the Admiral not only heard the groans of the sick that echoed from ship to ship, but that he also pensively stood, and listened at midnight to the dashing of the waters, occasioned by throwing the dead bodies into the sea;

Heard, nightly, plung'd into the sullen waves,
The frequent corse.———

A minute and particular enumeration of circumstances judiciously selected, is what chiefly discriminates poetry from history, and renders the former, for that reason, a more close and faithful representation of nature than the latter. And if our poets would accustom themselves to contemplate fully every object, before they attempted to describe it, they would not fail of giving their readers more new and more complete images than they generally do.

These observations on Thomson, which however would not have been so large, *if there had been already any considerable criticism on his character,* might be still augmented by an examination and developement of the beauties in the loves of the birds in Spring,—a

view of the torrid zone in Summer,—the rise of fountains and rivers in Autumn,—a man perishing in the
snows in Winter,—the wolves descending from the
Alps,—and a view of winter within the polar circle,
which are all of them highly-finished originals."

William Bayne (essay date 1898)

SOURCE: "The Castle of Indolence," in *James Thomson*, Oliphant Anderson, 1922, pp. 129-43.

[*In the following study, originally published in 1898,
of* The Castle of Indolence, *Bayne places the poem
between the tradition of Edmund Spenser, whose* Faery
Queen *Thomson deliberately imitated, and poetic innovations that looked forward to Romanticism in general and John Keats in particular. Bayne examines
both Thomson's aesthetic method and the strength of
his poem as an allegorical narrative.*]

Spenser was a long-established favourite of Thomson's,
and he therefore took up a very congenial piece of
work when he began his *Castle of Indolence,* avowed-
ly based upon the great epic narrative of the 'poet's
poet.' The poem was begun, according to his own
words, as early as 1733, and engaged his attention at
intervals of more or less duration till its publication in
1748. It formed another 'departure' in his poetry. The
intention of the writer obviously was that the work
should be a reflection of his ideas and capabilities as
an artist—as an artist especially of the effects of poetical cadence, and of the literary grace of language. The
result fully justified his aim. No imitation of a similar
kind ever made has attained so near a rank of excellence to the original as do certain passages of *The
Castle of Indolence* to *The Faery Queen.* Although
Thomson's poem was the principal achievement of the
sort in his day, Spenser awakened an active spirit of
enthusiasm among English writers in the first half of
the eighteenth century. In 1736 Gilbert West published
his *Education,* written 'in imitation of the style and
manners of Spenser's *Faery Queen,*' which was rewarded with considerable popular favour. This was
followed by Akenside's *Virtuoso* in 1737, and by Shenstone's *Schoolmistress* in 1742. But none of these productions takes any serious place as a faithful replica of
Spenser's style. The stanza is correctly and fluently
written; but so bereft is it in every case of its engaging
beauty that the manner of its use approaches perilously
near to travesty. These imitations in general fully merit
the criticism passed in the *Lives of the Poets* upon
those of West. 'Works of this kind may deserve praise
as proofs of great industry, and great nicety of observation; but the highest praise, the praise of genius,
they do not claim. The noblest beauties of art are those
of which the effect is co-extended with rational nature,
or at least with the whole circle of polished life; what
is less than this can be only pretty, the plaything of a

fashion, and the amusement of a day.' But *The Castle
of Indolence* baffles the dire condemnation of this
category. A professed and successful imitation of Spenser, it is also much more: a quite spontaneous and
living poem.

The comparison in method between *The Seasons* and
The Castle of Indolence is fraught with suggestive
interest. In *The Seasons* we have the poet, in his most
representative character, dealing with the intrinsic imaginative elements of his art, with the conception, vividness, and lively comprehension of his ideas; in *The
Castle of Indolence* he seeks to emphasise the power
of expression of his thought, the aptness and felicity of
his language, the beauty and tunefulness of phrase and
rhythm. In *The Seasons* we recognise chiefly the hand
of the poet; in *The Castle of Indolence* the hand of the
artist. In the one he achieves distinction beside those
whose special office it has been to grasp and vivify
some poetic truth; in the other he enters the select
ranks of the formal stylists of our literature. Here he
belongs of right to the school of Coleridge and Keats.
In deft and curious arrangement of topic, and in the
exercise of subtle peculiarities of form and diction, *The
Castle of Indolence* bears adequate consideration beside the masterpieces of the great romanticists of our
own century. Nor does this excellence in point of outward form remain its simple recommendation. The poet's
imagination asserts its capacity to answer to the particular demands made upon it by the conditions of the
form upon which he works; and the result is something
of that ethereal temper which characterises alone the
best products in rare and delicate romance. Realistic,
in a sense, in *The Seasons,* Thomson now becomes
the exponent of an idealism in poetry. The region of
The Castle of Indolence has no locality or name. It is
a region of dream, of entrancing vision and enticing
sound, of sun-flushed skies and radiant air, of bright
sward and purple hill, of murmurous forest and melodious river, but where there lurks, moreover, depth of
horror, and where landscape not far removed shines
fair beneath a temperate day. It is a region consecrated
indeed by the 'light that never was on sea or land.'

No work of poetry between the time of Spenser and
Thomson is so marked by this absolutely delicate ide-
alising tendency; nothing like it appears again till the
time of Keats. We do not hear much about the significance of Thomson's part in setting forth anew the
'sweet-slipping movement' and charm of the Spenserian manner as a model for the poets of the nineteenth
century literary renaissance; but there can be no doubt
about the validity of his right in this matter. In the
romantic method, so excellently represented by Thomson, Keats may be taken as the most direct successor
who understood the extraordinary richness of the note
that was struck in *The Castle of Indolence;* for though
there is its mystic glamour in the poetry of Coleridge,
Keats, in his work, combines in a more general way,

the main aims in the literary design of Thomson. The supreme greatness of Coleridge and of Keats has tended to dim the less splendid glory of their distinguished predecessor; but the claim of his accomplishment in this direction demands acknowledgment. The matter is valuable if only as an item in the historical development of our literature. Mr Theodore Watts-Dunton, in an admirable essay on *Chatterton,* contributed to Ward's *English Poets,* points out with conclusive force that the gracefully light and flexible octosyllabic rhythms, which became so great a power in the hands of Coleridge and Scott, had already received efficient illustration from the bright genius of Chatterton. The brilliancy of conception, the wealth of imagery, the ample command of the musical resources of language displayed in *The Castle of Indolence,* certainly seem to constrain the like recognition of a strong claim on the part of its author as a master of style in which worked some of the greatest who came after him.

The Faery Queen was not only the model upon which Thomson based his *Castle of Indolence,* but it supplied him with a definite hint as to the very scene in which he should set his narrative. This was the House of Sleep, whence the wizard Archimago sent for a dream by which to cast a spell over the Red Cross Knight:

> And more to tell him in his slumber soft,
> A trickling stream from high rock tumbling
> down,
> And ever-drizzling rain upon the loft,
> Mix'd with a murmuring wind, much like the
> sound
> Of swarming bees, did cast him in a swound.
> No other noise, no people's troublous cries,
> That still are wont t'annoy the walled town,
> Might there be heard; but careless Quiet lies
> Wrapt in eternal silence, far from enemies.

But this hint given him, Thomson owed nothing more with respect to the actual evolution of his story. With the playful picture of the little society at North Haw as a nucleus, he wove his own fascinating romance, original, picturesque, and stored with new and strange allusions. The figures who act in the drama, if not altogether novel, are freshly and decisively drawn; while the circumstances by which they are surrounded, and the light in which their activity is made clear and captivating, take their origin from no source but that of the moulding imagination of the poet himself. The difference in the matter of allusiveness between Spenser and Thomson is emphatic enough. The bounteous fields from which Spenser chiefly garnered his imposing array of literary allusions were medieval legend and classical mythology. In *The Faery Queen* no surprise attends the reader should he now and again even meet the co-existence of persons and events from these sources so widely separated by time and space; when per-haps Venus and the Graces are introduced side by side with historic personages of a new era,

> Knights of Logres and of Lyonesse,
> Tristrem, and Pelleas, and Pellenore.

In *The Castle of Indolence,* a totally different fund of illustration is utilised. Now it is Oriental story that lends its personages and its incidents as enriching factors; the literary treasures of Chaldea and Arabia and their neighbouring kingdoms, and these almost solely, afford the material wherewith the poet of *The Castle of Indolence* adorns his story.

Although the art, rather than the subject-matter, of the allegory may be fairly premised—indubitably so from the superiority of the art to the story with which it deals—to have given the poet most concern, the theme which he strove to elaborate is important enough. This designates the old and perennial story of the conflict between Pleasure and Duty. The poetical literature of the eighteenth century evinced a special leaning to this subject. This bias, ultimately borrowed from the supremely ethical tone which pervaded the religious discussion of the day, affected alike all and sundry in the busy class of poetical writers. No doubt Thomson's choice was also considerably guided by the precise nature associated with allegory in the pages of Spenser. But the didactic spirit was abroad in the eighteenth century with a power of exceeding energy. It did not, however, enter into poetical art with very satisfactory result. The doctrine that poetry is a criticism of life has much to commend it; but, as far as it is pertinent, there must be the admission that the poetical outcome should be conditioned by laws of beauty as well as of truth. The heroic measure of the eighteenth century writers with its inflexible and unvaried rhythmical arrangement, approximating in a hazardous degree to the bald usage of prose, did not offer a medium at all attractive for the unreserved enunciation of moral and philosophical truth. Not that it is utterly inimical to the statement of such solid truth. Wordsworth's *Happy Warrior,* though not so successful a poem as his *Ode to Duty,* is, nevertheless, far from an unsuccessful poem. Yet the professedly didactic poets of the early part of the eighteenth century, with their love of paradox, of hazy abstraction, and the mere gratification, as it sometimes seems, of a forcible iteration of words, produced no great didactic poem. It has been said with a good deal of justice even of Pope's *Essay on Man* that he 'spins the thread of his verbosity finer than the staple of his argument.' Young, in the main merely a follower of Pope, succeeded in placing the didactic poem in a still less agreeable light. With an occasional evanescent gleam of poetry in his *Night Thoughts,* Young, as a rule, simply forges his way through the extensive and unrelieved course of his ascetic message with a solemnity at once depressing and amusing. With Young, morality is not only a serious but a sombre affair. Little wonder is it that Madam de Staël ingenuously associated him with Ossian and the Northern Scalds as the prime cause of our national melancholy. The poetical transition made in passing from the perusal of a writer like Young, to the allegorical method of Thomson, is of the most significant character. Both works alike inculcate momentous truth; both works are alike sound and decisive in what they aim to enforce. But in the entire legitimate appeal of the argument of each, how far does the one outvie the other! Inasmuch as both are to be judged as poetry, the predominant merit of the one stands out with singular clearness. The morality of the one cannot be dissevered from that of the formal tractate; that of the other partakes in a very great degree of the transforming and heightening power of imagination.

The two parts of *The Castle of Indolence* have a kind of antithetical relation. The first canto, describing the abode and circumstances of the wizard Indolence, teems with rich and resplendent imagery; the vein in which the narrative is conveyed is of the most delicately-wrought sweetness. The more restrained gift of the poet is revealed in the second canto. Now, the pictures are less finely-drawn and less gorgeous; the music of the verse is touched with less aerial tone; the diction has not so much subtlety and skilful refinement of workmanship. The allegory, in short, assumes conditions that do not so readily kindle in the glow of the poet's imagination. The story of the triumph of Industry brings him back to the concrete affairs of the everyday world, and to the necessity of emphasising the value and character of its normal activities. The didactic element more decidedly prevails, and though to Thomson as well as to Spenser it was vouchsafed to inspire brightness into the didactic note of poetry, it was scarcely given to either to form it, 'musical as is Apollo's lute.'

Interesting alike from their biographical interest and their nice elaboration is the group of portraits that are introduced in the first canto, and that formed the first suggestive draft of the whole poem. The least distinct is the first, which may be a composite presentment. Were it not that the author speaks of Paterson, to whose personality it answers with considerable faithfulness, the resemblance might be as aptly referred to Collins. Perhaps the original idea was taken from the character of Paterson, to be afterwards developed and coloured with various hints from that of Collins, who was no infrequent dweller in the society of Thomson in his last years. The second portrait also bears some slight divergence from the original of Armstrong, to whom tradition has generally applied it. Thomson, indeed, averred that Armstrong was the victim of a 'certain kind of spleen that is both humane and agreeable, like Jacques in the play;' but another report speaks of Armstrong's ready share in London social affairs, and makes it plain that 'pensiveness' was certainly not a

prominent feature of his character. Welby, who is said to have been the third of the group, did not belong to the choice literary coterie at Richmond. He must have gained admittance to this poetical distinction from sheer merit of his personal characteristics, which receive such pointed and humorous setting in the poem. The fourth portrait was in all likelihood that of young Forbes of Culloden, but this, like the first two, is a somewhat generalised drawing. Any young man of sprightly and masculine character would answer equally well. The friendship of Thomson with Forbes, however, gives much reliableness to the conjecture that the description is one from life. Lyttelton's portrait is faithfully and gracefully done. The poet does not err, as he was so prone to do, on the side of exaggeration; but presents a clear and natural picture of the estimable friend of his later life. The last three portraits—those of Quin, the poet himself, and Murdoch—have the most piquant character, and are perhaps most felicitous of all. Quin is drawn with sympathetic firmness. Lyttelton has generally received the credit of writing the inimitable account of Thomson himself. If so, he accomplished a portraiture of rare spirit and exactness. Familiar enough in some of its particulars, the whole stanza may be cited as reflecting with quaintly humorous precision and effect the character of the poet.

> A bard here dwelt, more fat than bard beseems;
> Who void of envy, guile, and lust of gain,
> On virtue still, and Nature's pleasing themes,
> Poured forth his unpremeditated strain:
> The world forsaking with a calm disdain,
> Here laughed he careless in his easy seat;
> Here quaffed, encircled with his joyous train;
> Oft-moralizing sage! his ditty sweet
> He loathed much to write, he cared to repeat.

The contrast between the artistic method of *The Seasons* and that of *The Castle of Indolence* is most definitely brought out in the first canto of the second poem. No approach is made in *The Seasons,* vivid and striking as are so many of its descriptive passages, to the superb imagery of the introductory part of *The Castle of Indolence;* and of the marvellously fine rhythmical cadences of the Spenserian imitation there may, indeed, be said to be no trace at all in the earlier poem. No better summary of this salient factor of *The Castle of Indolence* could be desired than that expressed in these words of Mr Logie Robertson:—"Now the style is serious, grave, and solemn; now it is cheerful, lively, and gay. It sometimes borders on burlesque, mostly of a brisk and airy character. There are, however, numerous descriptive passages of clear ringing and exalted melody, sufficient in themselves to rank Thomson as a genuine singer of commanding rank." As a typical instance of these passages, where it may be added, the poet proves that he possessed the gift of harmonious movement, which is so lacking in the blank verse of *The Seasons,* there is here given the stanza which describes the music of the harp of Æolus. *Christabel* contains nothing better.

> Ah me! what hand can touch the string so
>   fine?
> Who up the lofty diapason roll
> Such sweet, such sad, such solemn airs divine,
> Then let them down again into the soul:
> Now rising love they fanned; now pleasing
>   dole
> They breathed, in tender musings, thro' the
>   heart;
> And now a graver sacred strain they stole,
> As when seraphic hands a hymn impart:
> Wild warbling nature all; above the reach of
>   art.

Nothing of this bewitching music is to be heard in the second canto, where the Knight of Industry and his energetic train are depicted. The solemnity of his position lends to the poet's verse something of its soberness. The epithets lack the brightness and lucidity of the first canto; the rhythm is more moderated and exact. But one or two passages, especially that in which appears the hortatory song of the bard, are written in well-compounded verse of great excellence—nervous, fluent, and graceful. This is, perhaps, best noticeable in the comparison made between the vigour belonging to Nature and its reflection in man.

> Is not the field, with living culture green,
> A sight more joyous than the dead morass?
> Do not the skies, with active ether clean,
> And fanned by sprightly zephyrs, far surpass
> The foul November fogs, and slumbrous mass
> With which sad Nature veils her drooping face?
> Does not the mountain stream, as clear as glass,
> Gay-dancing on, the putrid pool disgrace?
> The same in all holds true, but chief in human
>   race.

> It was not by vile loitering in ease
> That Greece obtained the brighter palm of art;
> That soft yet ardent Athens learned to please,
> To keen the wit, and to sublime the heart:
> In all supreme! complete in every part!
> It was not thence majestic Rome arose,
> And o'er the nations shook her conquering dart:
> For sluggard's brow the laurel never grows;
> Renown is not the child of indolent repose.

> Had unambitious mortals minded nought,
> But in loose joy their time to wear away;
> Had they alone the lap of dalliance sought,
> Pleased on her pillow their dull heads to lay,
> Rude Nature's state had been our state to-day;
> No cities e'er their towery fronts had raised,
> No arts had made us opulent and gay;
> With brother brutes the human race had grazed;

> None e'er had soared to fame, none honoured
>   been, none praised.

> Great Homer's song had never fired the breast
> To thirst of glory and heroic deeds;
> Sweet Maro's muse, sunk in inglorious rest,
> Had silent slept amid the Mincian reeds:
> The wits of modern time had told their beads,
> The monkish legends been their only strains;
> Our Milton's Eden had lain wrapt in weeds,
> Our Shakespeare strolled and laughed with
>   Warwick swains,
> Nor had my master Spenser charmed his
>   Mulla's plains.

The realistic scene of horror with which the poem concludes, though terminating somewhat abruptly, is drawn with intense and masterly force. Slight as it is, and thrown into denser obscurity by the magnificence and extent of the scenes in which it is enclosed, it takes a noteworthy place in its own line of poetical art. It may not have suggested, but certainly deserves a place beside, the description of the final terrors that beset the path of Browning's 'Childe Roland.'

The apparent value of *The Castle of Indolence* as an example of the application of careful æsthetic conditions in poetry makes it less needful to dwell upon the character of the work as an allegory. Thomson himself, although he published the poem as an avowed effort in allegorical reflection, probably did not feel that this feature of the story was of paramount note. His preface, in truth, declares as much. It runs as follows:— 'This poem being writ in the manner of Spenser, the obsolete words, and a simplicity of diction in some of the lines which borders on the ludicrous, were necessary to make the imitation more perfect. And the style of that admirable poet, as well as the measure in which he wrote, are, as it were, appropriated by custom to all allegorical poems writ in our language; just as in French the style of Marot, who lived under Francis the First, has been used in tales and familiar epistles of the age of Louis the Fourteenth.' Clearly, the material and strain of the allegory do not bulk very largely in the consideration of the author. But in the matter of just evolution of the allegorical materials of the story, Thomson reached a requisite amount of success. The scene is perfectly realised; the characters are drawn with distinctiveness and breadth; the moral to be derived from the story does not thrust itself unpleasantly upon the attention. In respect of structural arrangement, indeed, the allegory of *The Castle of Indolence* is sufficiently praiseworthy. Especially has this to be said of the balance preserved throughout the development of the allegorical narrative. Though it were scarcely justifiable to bring an allegorical effort so much less ambitious into any sort of comparison with the great allegories of Spenser and Bunyan, yet the merit of adequate discrimination as to the respective places of allegory and romance in a narrative of the kind seems, at least, to be carried out with signal faithfulness by the author of **The Castle of Indolence**. The clear outlines of Bunyan's landscapes and the actuality of his personages save his work from the overpowering depression incidental to the general arrangement of his didactic narrative; while Spenser's gorgeous scenes and moving episodes fulfil a like virtue for his great epic. Both of these allegories are weighed down by unvitalised material, by ethical or theological doctrine, and other matters, that hardly come with perfect right into the natural progress of the story. There is good reason to think even from the slighter performance which Thomson achieved, that had he extended the plan of his work, built turret and pinnacle on the pleasing edifice which he raised, the result would have been a great and very convincing testimony to the genius of the designer and builder.

Tennyson, in the recent biography of the late laureate by his son, is reported to have declared that Thomson was his earliest model. The appreciation thus begun was not abandoned, we may infer, in the critical conclusions of his later years. He has, at any rate, signified his sincere approval of **The Castle of Indolence** in the imaginative beauty, rich colouring, and finished literary form of *The Lotos Eaters*. The imitation, though individual enough, plainly intimates the closeness and fulness with which the earlier artistic masterpiece had enlisted his regard. The sun-tinted sky, the soothing streams, the sombre pine, the 'joy of calm,' all point to one undoubted source. Tennyson's power of limpid and magical expression was all his own; and so too was his gift of intricate and delicious harmony; but it may be said with every truth that in this poem, at least, he was not forgetful of the unique picturesqueness and winning music of the art of **The Castle of Indolence**.

G. C. Macauley (essay date 1908)

SOURCE: "Conclusion," in *James Thomson*, Macmillan and Co., Limited, 1908, pp. 234-42.

[*In the excerpt below, Macauley examines Thomson's influence on later poets, especially as the decades led into Romanticism. He asserts that the primary distinction between Thomson and the Romantics is their differing concepts of nature.*]

Hardly any English eighteenth-century poet, who wrote after Thomson, was quite uninfluenced by him. The use of blank verse in narrative and descriptive poetry became a fashion. Mallet's *Excursion,* in 1728, Somerville's *Chase,* 1734, Glover's *Leonidas,* 1737, Young's *Night Thoughts,* 1742, Akenside's *Pleasures of the Imagination,* and Armstrong's *Art of Preserving Health,* both in 1744, all in a certain sense owe their form of verse to Thomson's bold initiative. So great was the

vogue, that Goldsmith, in 1765, sets down blank verse, in company with party spirit, as one of the almost indispensable conditions of popularity: "What reception a poem may find which has neither abuse, party, nor blank verse to support it, I cannot tell, nor am I solicitous to know."

If we wish to appreciate the poetic quality of **The Seasons,** we cannot do better than to compare Thomson's work with that of his friend Mallet, a man of considerable literary talent, who was dealing with nearly the same themes at the same time. The style, diction, and verse are very similar, a fact to be accounted for partly by their constant communication with one another, and partly by direct imitation on Mallet's part of the poems which Thomson had already published. Mallet declares that description of "some of the most remarkable appearances of Nature" is the only intention of his work, but its inferiority in natural description to **The Seasons** is obvious on every page. The author is always aiming at sensational effects, either by representation of the abnormal occurrences of the physical world, earthquakes and volcanic eruptions, for example, or by the agency of ghosts and churchyard horrors, which he had successfully employed in his ballad of *William and Margaret*. His supernaturalism is very crude compared with Thomson's; and when he describes a natural scene of a common kind, he does not produce the same effect of artistic harmony. The following is a favourable example:—

> On this hoar Hill, that climbs above the Plain
> Half-way up Heaven ambitious, pleas'd we stand,
> Respiring purer Air, whose Gale ascends
> Full-fraught with Health, from Herbs and Flowers exhal'd.
> Above, the Round of Ether without Cloud,
> Boundless Expansion, all unruffled shines.
> Beneath, the far-stretch'd Landscape, Hill and Dale;
> The Precipice abrupt; the distant Main;
> The nearer Forest in wide circuit spread,
> Solemn Recess and still! whose mazy Walks
> Fair Truth and Wisdom love; the bordering Lawn,
> With Flocks and Herds enrich'd; the daisied Vale;
> The River's Azure and the Meadow's Green,
> Grateful Diversity! allure the Eye
> Abroad to rove amidst unnumber'd Charms.

This is pretty enough in detail, but it is not very well combined, and the same is true of most of Mallet's other descriptions.

Savage's *Wanderer,* published in 1729, though much less like Thomson's work, and not written in blank verse, affords at least as remarkable an instance of the influence of Thomson; for Savage, though, as Johnson tells us, he lived for some time in close personal relation with Thomson, did not, properly speaking, belong to his school, but rather to that of Pope. Such a description as the following was unmistakably written under the influence of Thomson, to whom the author had already paid a tribute in his poem:—

> South-west behind you hill the sloping sun
> To Ocean's verge his fluent course has run;
> His parting eyes a watery radiance shed,
> Glance through the vale and tip the mountain's
>   head;
> To which oppos'd the shadowy gulfs below
> Beauteous reflect the parti-colour'd snow.

The influence which was exerted by Thomson on the later poetry of the century was more indirect, but none the less real. Thomson's view of Nature was mainly objective, while that of the romantic school is personal. This is the really essential distinction, and it is analogous to the distinction between epic and lyric in other fields of poetry. Thomson presents the natural scene for its own sake, the romantic poet cares less for the scene than for the emotions with which the scene is harmonised. Thomson has something of the romantic spirit, but this is not the dominant note of his poetry, and where the external influence most strongly moves his soul, the lyric expression to which it gives rise more often has for its subject the power and wisdom of God, than a purely self-centred emotion.

> By swift degrees the love of Nature works,
> And warms the bosom; till at last, sublim'd
> To rapture and enthusiastic heat,
> We feel the present Deity, and taste
> The joy of God to see a happy world.
>   (*Spring*, 899 ff.)

Passages may, no doubt, be quoted, in which the spirit is attuned to its surroundings in the romantic sense of the expression; *e.g.* **Summer**, 516 ff.:—

> Still let me pierce into the midnight depth
> Of yonder grove, of wildest, largest growth;
> That forming high in air a woodland quire,
> Nods o'er the mount beneath. At every step,
> Solemn and slow, the shadows blacker fall,
> And all is awful, listening gloom around.
>   These are the haunts of Meditation, etc.

So also the influences of Autumn, as represented by the luxuriance of the harvest, are addressed in the prayer,—

> Breathe your still song into the reaper's heart,
> As home he goes beneath the joyous moon.

Or under another aspect they are personified for the poet himself as the Power of Philosophic Melancholy

(*Autumn*, 988 ff.). Yet the principle upon which these varying moods depend is not so much the imaginative faculty of the individual, as a certain divinely appointed harmony in the universe; and this is very clearly expressed in a passage which originally followed that which has been quoted above from **Spring**, but was afterwards displaced to make more convenient room for the tribute to Lyttelton:—

> 'Tis Harmony, that world-attuning power,
> By which all beings are adjusted, each
> To all around, impelling and impell'd
> In endless circulation, that inspires
> This universal smile. Thus the glad skies,
> The wide-rejoicing earth, the woods, the streams,
> With every life they hold, down to the flower
> That paints the lovely vale, or insect-wing
> Wav'd o'er the shepherd's slumber, touch the
>   mind
> To nature tun'd, with a light-flying hand
> Invisible; quick-urging thro' the nerves
> The glittering spirits in a flood of day.

Mr. Robertson is quite right in saying that this anticipates the teaching of Wordsworth, but it is not by virtue of this teaching that Wordsworth is "romantic."

Thomson has no preference for the strange and wild in scenery, though he does not altogether exclude it, and he seems to have felt to some extent the fascination of remoteness, as is shown in some of his accounts of tropical rivers and forests, and in his references to the Hebrides and St. Kilda. Perhaps, however, the nearest approach which he makes to the "romantic" spirit is in his suggestions of the supernatural in connection with the intercourse of the living with the spirits of the dead, as in **Summer**, 538 ff.:—

> Shook sudden from the bosom of the sky,
> A thousand shapes or glide athwart the dusk,
> Or stalk majestic on. . . .
> Here frequent at the visionary hour,
> When musing midnight reigns, or silent noon,
> Angelic harps are in full concert heard,
> And voices chanting from the wood-crown'd hill,
> The deepening dale, or inmost sylvan glade.

Or again, **Autumn**, 1033 ff.,

> Where angel forms athwart the solemn dusk,
> Tremendous sweep, or seem to sweep along;
> And voices more than human, thro' the void
> Deep-sounding, seize th' enthusiastic ear.
>   (*Autumn*, 1033 ff.)

Collins, no doubt, would willingly have acknowledged a large debt to Thomson, to whom he was also personally attached; and Gray owed him more perhaps than he was aware of. There are several phrases in Gray's poems which testify to his familiarity with *The Seasons:* he has borrowed the "listening senates" of the *Elegy* from *Autumn,* 15, the epithet "many-twinkling," in the *Progress of Poesy,* from *Spring,* 158, "The secrets of the abyss," from *Autumn,* 778; while the line "Deep majestic, smooth and strong," seems to have been suggested by *Autumn,* 122. The thoughts expressed in *Spring,* 51 ff.,—

> Nor ye who live
> In luxury and ease, in pomp and pride,
> Think these lost themes unworthy of your
>   ear,

and in *Winter,* 597-603, have been reproduced in the *Elegy.* The lines of *Winter,* 311 ff.,—

> In vain for him th' officious wife prepares
> The fire fair blazing and the vestment warm;
> In vain his little children, peeping out
> Into the mingling storm, demand their sire,

must have been consciously or unconsciously in his mind when he wrote the stanza:—

> For them no more the blazing hearth shall burn,
>   Or busy housewife ply her evening care:
> No children run to lisp their sire's return,
>   Or climb his knees the envied kiss to share.

But it must be remembered that the treatment of landscape by Gray and Collins is essentially different from that which we find in Thomson. For him it is primarily an object of æsthetic appreciation, with them it is subordinate to the lyrical emotion. The same is true of Burns, who nevertheless was a great admirer of "Thomson's landscape glow," and who refers to him frequently in his letters. Meanwhile we find in Cowper something of a return to Thomson's manner; but the difference is noteworthy. Whatever may be the outward form of Cowper's poetry, it is essentially personal. His view of Nature is not universal, like Thomson's, but confined to the particular scenes and localities with which he himself was familiar. His portrait-painting of Nature is wonderfully delicate and true, but is hardly the result of an enthusiastic devotion to the object of his art. His religion was no natural Deism, like Thomson's, and depended not upon his view of Nature, but upon Christian revelation. He feels that it is only the man whom truth has already made free, who can dare to exult in the glories of Creation. Nature serves chiefly to divert his thoughts from morbid introspection, and so to rescue him from despair. Everything, therefore, has a personal note, though in some passages this is more or less concealed, and something like Thomson's objectivity seems to be attained. There are, however, always some important differences between their methods. Cowper's descriptions have much more the character of set pictures:—

> Here Ouse, slow winding through a level plain
> Of spacious meads, with cattle sprinkled o'er,
> Conducts the eye along his sinuous course
> Delighted. There, fast rooted in their bank,
> Stand, never overlook'd, our favourite elms,
> That screen the herdsman's solitary hut;
> While far beyond, and overthwart the stream,
> That, as with molten glass, inlays the vale,
> The sloping land recedes into the clouds.
>   (*The Task,* i. 163 ff.)

On this or some similar scene Sainte-Beuve justly remarks, "On copierait ce paysage avec le pinceau," and again, "Les Flamands ont trouvé leur égal en poésie." His observation, in fact, is more minute and particular than Thomson's: he deals in details rather than broad general effects: in a woodland scene each separate tree is characterised. And the details are of objects endeared by familiarity, "which daily view'd please daily,"—"our favourite elms," the often-visited cottage, the tower from which comes the accustomed music of the bells, and the well-known Ouse winding through its meadows.

In many respects, nevertheless, these two poets, so different in temperament, resembled one another in feeling. For both, the interest of the scenes which they describe is deeply connected with human life and human labour, and the beauty which they appreciate is that which is connected closely with the supply of human wants. Scenes are not admired by either of them because they are desolate, or because they suggest images of danger or death, though both are capable of feeling the awe which is inspired by the manifestations of elemental power in nature. For both the family and the home are peculiarly sacred. Both are true lovers of their country, Thomson with the proud and unquestioning patriotism which might have been expected in the author of **"Rule Britannia,"** Cowper with a more wistful, but not less genuine affection,—"England, with all thy faults, I love thee still." Both express strongly their sympathy with the sufferings of the lower animals, and both are enthusiasts for liberty. Finally, both Thomson and Cowper have strong religious feelings, though in the former of the two the religion is not distinctively Christian. For both the delight in the beauty of external nature is deeply connected with a sense of the divine power and goodness which is therein displayed.

On the relation of Thomson to Wordsworth something has been said generally in an earlier chapter. Here it is sufficient to observe that Wordsworth's early descriptive poems, and especially that entitled *An Evening Walk,* show distinct traces of familiarity with *The Seasons,* and that *The Castle of Indolence* was his pocket-companion.

The influence of Thomson upon the Continent was an important one. Certainly no English poet before his time had obtained so much currency in France or

Germany, or produced so marked an effect upon foreign literature. *The Seasons* was translated in 1759 by Mme. Bontemps into French prose, and found a number of imitators, Saint-Lambert, Léonard, whose poem *Les Saisons,* said to be "imitated from Thomson," is in fact to a great extent a translation, and finally Delille; but here again the less direct and obvious influence is the more important. Rousseau, who in *La Nouvelle Héloïse* set the example of a "romantic" treatment of scenery, undoubtedly owed something appreciable to the fashion set by Thomson.

In Germany *The Seasons* met with a still more enthusiastic reception. The metrical translation of Brockes, who was himself a poet of the picturesque school, appeared in 1744, and was followed by several prose versions. Brockes was nearly akin to Thomson in feeling, and caught the spirit of his original admirably, but adopted an almost intolerable metre for his translation. The school of descriptive poetry in Germany was profoundly influenced by Thomson, and his poetical work was enthusiastically praised by Lessing, Wieland, and Gessner. Kleist, in his *Frühling,* is mainly a follower of Thomson, though he does not seem to have known the original English text of *The Seasons*. He abandons in this poem the minute description of details, and succeeds in attaining to something of the epic breadth of the English poet. The enthusiasm for Nature, inspired to a great extent by Thomson, was a strong element here also in the transition to the emotional symbolism which we find in the later poetry of the century.

Myra Reynolds (essay date 1909)

SOURCE: "Indications of a New Attitude toward Nature in the Poetry of the Eighteenth Century," in *The Treatment of Nature in English Poetry: Between Pope and Wordsworth,* The University of Chicago Press, 1909, pp. 58-202.

[In the excerpt that follows, Reynolds portrays Thomson as an early Romantic poet, a claim she substantiates with a list of the traits that qualify him, including his apeal to the senses and the "freedom" that characterizes the natural world portrayed in The Seasons.*]*

. . . James Thomson (1700-1748) is confessedly the most important figure in the early history of Romanticism. He foreshadowed the new spirit in various ways, as in his strong love of liberty, his constant plea for the poor as against the rich, his preference for blank verse, his imitation of older models, especially Spenser, and in his tendency toward comprehensive schemes; but his chief importance is in his attitude toward external Nature. If, however, we take into consideration all his work, we shall find in more than three-fourths of it the utmost apparent indifference to Nature. In the five trag-

edies written between 1738 and 1748 there is no hint that their author knew more of the world about him than the veriest classicist of them all. In "Alfred" (1740), written by Thomson and Mallet, there are occasional descriptive touches, but these are almost too slight to mention when we think what effects might have been produced in a play the action of which occurs on a beautiful wooded island inhabited only by a few peasants. In the other tragedies Nature is drawn upon merely for conventional similitudes, as in "Edward and Elenora" (1739), where five of the eleven similitudes are the comparison of rage or fierce passions to tempests; or in "Sophonisba," an earlier play (1728), where there is not a fresher or more forceful comparison than that of an army to a torrent, passion to a whirlwind, the hero to a lion, and the heroine to a blooming morn. In the 3,300 lines of the tedious poem, "Liberty" (1734-36), not more than fifty refer to external Nature, and of these the only passages that suggest, even remotely, the author of "The Seasons" are the descriptions of the sullen land of Sarmatia and the shaggy mountain charms of the Swiss Alps. "The Castle of Indolence," written in 1733, is the only one of the poems written after 1730 that indicates any genuine love of Nature. The charm of this poem for modern readers is perhaps largely due to its use of external Nature, for, though there is little of the rich, elaborate description characteristic of "The Seasons," what there is, is so exquisitely appropriate that all the listless, luxurious life of this land of soft delights is seen through a romantic and picturesque setting of waving, shadowy woods, sunny glades, and silver streams. Yet a closer study of the descriptive stanzas shows little more than a musically felicitous combination of the attributes conventionally recognized as belonging to a pleasing landscape. The only lines really indicative of a love of Nature such as the classicists had not known are the following from the second canto:

> I care not, Fortune, what you me deny:
> You can not rob me of free Nature's grace;
> You can not shut the windows of the sky,
> Through which Aurora shows her brightening face;
> You can not bar my constant feet to trace
> The woods and lawns, by living stream, at eve.

It is to "The Seasons" (1726-30) that we must go if we wish to understand Thomson's work as a poet of Nature. A brief analysis of the study of external Nature in these poems will serve to show both in what respects Thomson's work was the outcome of a new spirit, and in what respects its affiliations are with the old.

An important part of Thomson's poetical endowment was his quick sensitiveness to the sights and sounds and odors of the world about him. He looked on Nature with the eye of an artist, but not of an artist in black and white. It was not form but color that attracted him. There are occasional descriptions, as of the garden in **"Spring"** and of the precious stones in **"Summer,"** where the lines glow like a painter's palette, and throughout **"The Seasons"** there is a general impression of rich and varied coloring. That this impression is stronger than a list of the color terms used would seem to justify is due to two facts, both characteristic of Thomson's work in general. In the first place he did not care for nicely discriminated shades or delicate tints. He loved broad masses of strong, clear color. He dwells with ever new delight on blue as seen in the sky or reflected in water, and on green, "smiling Nature's universal robe." In the second place he is especially rich in such words as indicate color in general without specification as to the kind. "The flushing year," "every-coloured glory," "the boundless blush of spring," "the innumerous-coloured scene of things," "unnumbered dyes," "hues on hues," are typical phrases. Motion also caught his eye more quickly than form. The dancing light and shade in a forest pathway, the waving of branches, the flow of water, the rapid flight or slow march of clouds, the golden, shadowy sweep of wind over ripened grain, count for much in the pleasurable impression made upon his mind by different scenes.

It is evident that Thomson received more through his eye than through his ear, but he was very far from being indifferent to the sounds of Nature. The hum of bees, the low of cattle, the bleating of sheep are frequently noted. The songs of birds, while often represented by some general phase, as "the music of the woods," or "woodland hymns," are now and then more minutely specified, as in the fine description of the "symphony of spring." There is also effective representation of the sounds heard in storms, as in the summer thunderstorm. The most frequent sounds are, as is inevitable in an English poet whose facts come from actual observation, those made by water, as the plaint of purling rills, the thunder of impetuous torrents, or the growling of frost-imprisoned rivers.

While Thomson was not the first poet to speak of the odor of the bean-flower, his words show a keen appreciation of that perfume, and certainly the "smell of dairy" was a country odor first poetically noticed by him. His sensitiveness to odors is not especially marked, yet it is safe to say that he was in this respect more observant than his immediate predecessors or contemporaries.

In reading the poetry of Nature after Dryden in historical sequence, there is, in coming to **"The Seasons,"** a sudden sense of freedom and elation, a sense of having at last come upon a poet who writes freely and spontaneously from a large personal experience, whose facts press in upon him even too abundantly. He knows many kinds of Nature and under varying aspects. His garden picture, though somewhat too much in the floral catalogue style, shows how well he knew the cultivated flowers he described, and he speaks with no less loving minuteness of furze, the thorny brake, the purple heather, dewy cowslips, white hawthorn, and lilies of the vale. It is a pleasure to see how much he knew about birds. He describes their habits with remarkable accuracy and minuteness. He shows their tender arts in courtship, their skill in nest-building, and the "pious frauds" whereby they lure away the would-be trespasser. In no poetry between Marvell and Thomson do we find birds so fully described, and Marvell has nothing so charming and sympathetic as Thomson's winter red-breast. Thomson's scope is also wider in that he knew the birds of the seashore as well as those of wood and meadow. Equally close attention is given to the various domestic fowl. The peacock had flaunted his painted tail through poetry for a hundred years, and is now for the first time outranked as an object of interested observation by the hen, the duck, and the turkey. The frequent descriptions of domestic animals. especially the sheep, the horse, and the ox, also show minute knowledge such as could not have been gained from books. It is, moreover, a significant fact that through these numerous and varied studies there runs a genuine love for animals. Thomson was, at least in poetic theory, a vegetarian, and he vigorously denounced the killing of animals for food as conduct worthy only of wild beasts. His poetical invectives against hunting are as vigorous as Cowper's. He objects to caging birds, and his indignation waxes high over the bees "robb'd and murder'd" by man's tyranny. The only unoffending animal that escapes Thomson's wide sympathy is the fish. The skill with which the monarch of the brook is lured from his dark haunt and at last "gaily" dragged to land is described with a gusto in curious contrast to the pity lavished on the tortured worm that may have served for bait.

As we have just seen, the animals that Thomson described were those that any country lad might know rather than those that had been canonically set apart for poetical service. The same independent judgment is evident in his study of other neglected realms in the world of Nature. He gloried in storms and winter. Though he now and then falls into the conventional phraseology, and speaks of winter as drear and awful, he yet in the same breath exclaims that he finds its horrors congenial. The contrast of a first winter in London turns his mind with full emphasis to the days of his youth when he wandered with unceasing joy through virgin snows, and listened to the roar of the winds and the bursting torrent, and watched the deep tempest brewing in the grim sky. Such experiences he remembers with joy for they "exalt the soul to solemn thought." Through all the descriptive portions of the **"Winter"** there is a vigorous, manly enthusiasm as tonic and bracing as the bright, frosty days themselves. Thomson's pleasure in the sterner phenomena of Nature is further shown by his evident delight in tracing the progress of any storm, whether the thunder storm of summer, the devastating wind and rain of autumn, or the black gloom of a winter tempest. These fierce tempests certainly are of more comparative importance in **"The Seasons"** than they are in Nature. Their frequent choice may be in part due to their dramatic qualities of rapidity and force. The crashing and hurtling of the elements was a subject not unsuited to Thomson's splendid but ponderous and swelling style. But in the main it is only fair to suppose that he wrote of storms well because he had many times watched them with an interest that had made him remember them.

With many other aspects of Nature was Thomson familiar. He knew much of the sky both by day and by night. His few short descriptions of the starry heavens are worth more than all Young's far-sought epithets. One phrase concerning the radiant orbs

> That more than deck, that animate the sky,

seems a conscious turning away from the old artificial conception. One of the finest moon-light passages is reminiscent of Milton in two lines,

> Now through the passing cloud she seems to
>   stoop,
> Now up the pure cerulean rides sublime,

but the close,

> The whole air whitens with a boundless tide
> Of silver radiance, trembling round the world,

is Thomson's own, and is a good example of the full sweet harmony that marks his verse at its best. There are many passages and apparently casual phrases indicative of the closeness with which he watched clouds. The doubling fogs that roll around the hills and wrap the world in a "formless gray confusion" through which the shepherd stalks gigantic is described with a Wordsworthian felicity and precision.

The descriptions referred to below of early morning, of sunset, of evening, and of night may be perhaps taken as among the best examples of their sort in **"The Seasons."** As a whole they show conclusively from what long intimacy with Nature Thomson wrote. The very freshness of morning breathes from the sunrise picture in **"Summer"** and the little picture in **"Autumn"** is more delicately suggestive than many a more pretentious description of the dawning day. The sunset after the rain in **"Spring"** is one of the best examples of Thomson's power to paint word pictures. It would be difficult for any canvas to present a scene at once so mellow and radiant, and so transfused with the joy of a renovated earth. As exquisite in their way are the descriptions of the slow approach of "Sober Evening" with her circling shadows and the softly swelling breeze

that stirs the stream and wood; and the later description of the strange uncertain mingling of light and darkness in a summer night in England. These passages and others that might be quoted show to what fine issues Thomson's pen was sometimes touched, but it cannot be denied that his really intimate and exact knowledge of Nature and her ways could not hold all his descriptions subject to the charm of simplicity and truth.

As further illustrative of Thomson's knowledge of all that pertained to the country we have his admirably vivid and detailed accounts of the homely labors of a farmer's life, as plowing, sowing, reaping, hay making, and sheep shearing. Of these the sheep shearing is the most simply charming and natural. It is also the most noteworthy, because sheep and shepherds had long been the very substance out of which pastorals were woven so that in such descriptions the contrast between the new and the old way of looking at country life is sharply defined. Thomson's pastoral queen and shepherd king are at the opposite pole from the sentimental, affected, useless nymphs and swains who had before posed as the guardians of English sheep. His shepherds are sturdy fellows, doing honest work and plenty of it, and as such they had no predecessors in English classical poetry. The sheep, too, are real animals. They have to be watched with a vigilance of which no flower-crowned swain playing on an oaten pipe would be capable. And they must be washed and sheared and branded. In winter they must be housed and fed, no matter what the dangers on the dark, stormy hills. It is this strong, refreshing air of reality in Thomson's poetry, and his unfeigned respect and admiration for the actual country life in England that completed the work begun by the ugly satire of Swift and the mock pastorals of Gay, and made the old, conventional, pseudo-classic pastoral from that time on an impossibility in English poetry.

The phrase, "dislike of boundaries," is perhaps not very apt, but it may serve to describe what is certainly a pervasive quality of Thomson's work, and a significant quality, for if there was one thing more pleasing than another to an orthodox classicist it was a well-defined limit. Thomson preferred the blank verse to the couplet because the unrhymed, flowing lines gave a certain freedom. There is an air of abundance, of even undue exuberance about much of his work. Even his diction presents this idea of lavishness. There is a surprisingly large number of such words as "effulgent," "refulgent," "effusion," "diffusion," "suffusion," "profusion," from the roots "fundo" and "fulgeo" with their idea of a liberal pouring out. "Luxuriant," "ample," "prodigal," "boundless," "unending," "ceaseless," "immense," "interminable," "immeasurable," "vast," "infinite," are typical words.

> Profusely poured around,
> Materials infinite,

Infinite splendor wide investing all,

To the far horizon wide-diffused,
A boundless deep immensity of shade,

Night, a shade immense, magnificent and vast,

are typical phrases. In one short description the birds
are "innumerous;" they are "prodigal" of harmony; their
joy overflows in music "unconfined;" the song of the
linnets is "poured out profusely." In another short
passage the stores of the vale are "lavish," the lily is
"luxuriant" and grows in fair "profusion," the flowers
are "unnumbered," beauty is "unbounded," and bees
fly in "swarming millions." When images come into
his mind it is by the ten thousand. In spring the country is "one boundless blush," "far diffused around." He
loves the "liberal air," "lavish fragrance," "full luxuriance," "extensive harvests," "immeasurable," or "exhaustless" stores, "copious exhalations." All is superlative, exaggerated, scornful of limits. It was "the unbounded scheme of things" that most appealed to him.

The same point receives illustration in his sense for
landscape. He rejoiced in a wide view. He loved to seek
out some proud eminence and there let his eye wander
"far excursive," and dwell on "boundless prospects."
Such scenes not only gave him a chance for picturesque enumerations without any especial demand for
minute discrimination, but they satisfied his preference
for grand, general effects.

Closely connected with the sense for landscape is the
use of geographical romance, or the heightening of
poetic effect by the accumulation of sounding geographical names. The finest example of this device is
in the lines descriptive of the thunder re-echoed among
the mountains. In this passage the impression of sublimity is due to the suggestions of mysterious elemental forces subtly associated with such names as
Carnarvon, Penmaenmawr, Snowdon, Thule, and Chev-
iot. This mental following of the thunder from peak
to distant peak, this endeavor to strengthen the impression by the use of the remote and the unknown,
show a mind set toward romantic rather than classical
ideals.

A further indication of Thomson's defiance of limits is
his curiosity. His mind goes back of the present fact
and restlessly strives after causes and origins. In imagination he seeks to penetrate to the vast eternal springs
from which Nature refreshes the earth. The most poetic example of this questioning spirit is in his address
to the winds that blow with boisterous sweep to swell
the terrors of the storm.

In what far-distant region of the sky,
Hush'd in deep silence, sleep you when 'tis
　　calm?

The classical spirit held itself to useful questions that
could have some rational answer. It is the romantic
spirit that pushes its inquiries into the realms of the
unknowable.

Throughout this study of Thomson's work there has
been an implicit recognition of his strong love for Nature. This fact receives further definite confirmation from
his letters. It is interesting to note that his early life was
almost as fortunate in its environment as Wordsworth's.
When he was a year old his father moved to Southdean,
a small hamlet near Jedborough. Here the lad remained
till he entered the university at Edinburgh at fifteen, and
here he apparently passed most of his vacations till he
went to London at twenty-five. One of his especial
friends was Dr. Cranston of Ancrum whose love of
Nature was equal to his own. Thomson's letters to Dr.
Cranston, though somewhat stilted and high-flown, show
clearly the eagerness with which they had together explored the picturesque country along the Tiviot and its
tributary streams, the Ale and the Jed. In the first letter
from London, under the date April 3, 1725, was written,
"I wish you joy of the spring." In September of the
same year Thomson wrote from Barnet:

> Now I imagine you seized with a fine romantic kind
> of melancholy on the fading of the year; now I
> figure you wandering, philosophical and pensive,
> 'midst the brown, wither'd groves, while the leaves
> rustle under your feet, the sun gives a farewell
> parting gleam, and the birds

Stir the faint note and but attempt to sing.

> Then again when the heavens wear a more gloomy
> aspect, the winds whistle, and the waters spout, I
> see you in the well-known clough, beneath the
> solemn arch of tall, thick embowering trees, listening
> to the amusing lull of the many steep, moss-grown
> cascades, while deep, divine contemplation, the
> genius of the place, prompts each swelling awful
> thought. I am sure you would not resign your place
> in that scene at any easy rate. None ever enjoyed it
> to the height you do, and you are worthy of it.
> There I walk in spirit and disport in its beloved
> gloom. This country I am in is not very entertaining;
> no variety but that of woods, and them we have in
> abundance; but where is the living stream? the airy
> mountain? or the hanging rock? with twenty other
> things that elegantly please the lover of nature.
> Nature delights me in every form.

Later in life Thomson was "more fat than bard be-
seems," and correspondingly indolent, and his biographers give the impression that no beauty of the world
about him could compete with the charms of an easy
chair. But his letters still bear witness to a love of
Nature as real if not as active as that of his youth. In
July, 1743, he wrote to Mr. Lyttleton promising to
spend some weeks with him at Hagley:

As this will fall in Autumn, I shall like it the better, for I think that season of the year the most pleasing and the most poetical. The spirits are not then dissipated with the gaiety of spring, and the glaring light of summer, but composed into a serious and tempered joy. The year is perfect. . . . . The muses, whom you obligingly say I shall bring with me, I shall find with you—the muses of the great, simple country, not the little, fine-lady muses of Richmond Hill.

Again four or five years later, he wrote to Paterson, "Retirement and nature are more and more my passion every day."

This passion for Nature finds frequent expression in the poems, but no citation of specific instances can be so convincing as the general impression of unforced personal enthusiasm made upon the reader of "**The Seasons.**" Moreover, Thomson's conception of the effect of Nature on man, the next topic, may be fairly counted as but a transcript from his own experience, and therefore as further illustrative of his love for Nature.

In **"The Seasons"** as in preceding poetry both man and Nature have a place, but there is a great transfer of emphasis. Nature had been ignored or counted as the servant, the background, the accompaniment of man. Now the human incidents are few and unimportant and are used chiefly to lay additional stress by their tone on the spirit characteristic of each season. Nature is loved and studied and described purely for her own sake. There is very little use of natural facts as similes for human qualities, and there is, practically, no use of pathetic fallacy. The effect of Nature on the man sensitive to her high ministration is represented as twofold. In the first place and chiefly, she storms his senses with her ravishing delights. She gives him pleasures of the most rich and varied sort. She enchants him with color and harmony and perfume. These pleasures are, however, of the eye and ear. They do not touch the deeper joys of the heart. Of the appeal of Nature to the soul of man, in the true Wordsworthian sense, Thomson knew little. Yet occasional passages indicate that he had received from Nature gifts higher than that of mere external, sensuous enjoyment. He attributes to Nature in at least a partially Wordsworthian sense, the power of soothing, elevating, and instructing. He sings the "infusive force" of spring on man,

> When heaven and earth as if contending vie
> To raise his being, and serene his soul.

It is his delight to "meditate the book of Nature" for thence he hopes to "learn the moral song." At the soft evening hour, he

> lonely loves
> To seek the distant hills, and there converse
> With nature, there to harmonize his heart.

Not only does he attend to Nature's voice from month to month, and watch with admiration her every shape, but he

> Feels all her sweet emotions at his heart.

While these and a few other similar passages would hardly be remarked in the poetry of Nature after Wordsworth, they are of great historical importance because they show the early beginning of that spirit which received its final and perfect expression seventy years later in "The Lyrical Ballads."

Thomson's two dominant conceptions in his thought of God in Nature were as the almighty Creator and the ever-active Ruler. The whole tenor of his poems goes to show that he saw in Nature not God himself but God's hand. Even his invocations to Nature, animate and inanimate, to praise God in one general song of adoration, are but highly emotional and figurative statements of the conception that God is not all, but Lord of all. Now and then, however, in the midst of the old ideas there comes the breath of a new thought. In one line we find the cold, conventional idea; in the next, an intimation of divine immanence. God's beauty walks forth in the spring. His spirit breathes in the gales. The seasons "are but the varied God." God is the Universal Soul of Heaven and earth. He is the Essential Presence in all Nature. Such sentences as these, whether uttered consciously, or half unconsciously under the influence of poetic excitement, clearly prefigure the modern conception of the union and inter-penetration of the physical and spiritual worlds.

Of the two general points to be kept in view in the study of Thomson as a poet of Nature the second was a consideration of his affiliations with the classical spirit. It is surprising to observe in how few respects such affiliations can be justly predicated. There are occasional references to his Doric reed, and frequent invocations to his muse. As preliminary justification of his choice of themes are quotations from Virgil and Horace. The authority of the "Rural Maro" and the example of Cincinnatus lend added dignity to the English plow. Personifications of the conventional type often appear. There is one purely didactic description of the cure for a pest of insects, and another description of the method by which bees are robbed of their honey, that are evidently framed on Latin models. Nor do we miss the ever-recurring advice to read the page of the Mantuan swain beneath a spreading tree on a warm noon.

We also find that toward mountains and the sea Thomson held almost the traditional attitude. His nearness to the coast and his knowledge of shore birds show that he could not have been entirely ignorant of the ocean, but it apparently made little impression on him, for he seldom mentions it even casually, and but once with any emphasis. It is then one of the elements of a wild, fierce storm that sweeps the coast. A few of his epithets for mountains, as "keen-air'd" and "forest-rustling," are new though not especially felicitous, and he often mentions mountains by name, or as bounding some distant prospect. But in general his conception and his phraseology are those of his contemporaries. He speaks of the Alps as "dreadful," as "horrid, vast, sublime," and again as "horrid mountains." There is nowhere any evidence of the modern feeling toward mountains, though there are frequent expressions of appreciative love for green hills.

The point in which Thomson shows strongest traces of the old influence is his diction. He often has the new thought before he has found the appropriate dress for it. Birds are still the "plumy" or "feathery people," and fish are the "finny race." "Shaggy" and "nodding" are used of mountains and rocks and forests, and "deformed" and "inverted" of winter, in true classical fashion. "Maze" is one of his most frequent words. "Horrid" still holds a useful place. "Amusing" is five times applied to the charms of some landscape. Leaves are the "honours" of trees, paths are "erroneous," caverns "sweat," and all sorts of things are "innumerous." He also makes large use of Latinized words such as "turgent," "bibulous," "relucent," "luculent," "irriguous," "gelid," "ovarious," "incult," "concactive," "hyperborean." These words can hardly be said to belong to any received poetic diction. They are rather a mannerism of Thomson's style, and an outgrowth of his delight in swelling, sounding phrases.

From this summary we at once perceive how few and comparatively unimportant were the characteristics held in common by Thomson and the classicists in their treatment of external Nature.

This study of **"The Seasons"** shows that so far as intrinsic worth is concerned the poems are marked by a strange mingling of merits and defects, but that, considered in their historical place in the development of the poetry of Nature, their importance and striking originality can hardly be overstated. Though Thomson talked the language of his day, his thought was a new one. He taught clearly, though without emphasis, the power of Nature to quiet the passions and elevate the mind of man, and he intimated a deeper thought of divine immanence in the phenomena of Nature. But his great service to the men of his day was that he shut up their books, led them out of their parks, and taught them to look on Nature with enthusiasm. This service is of the greater historical value because it was so well adapted to the times. To begin with, it was a necessary first step. People cannot love what they do not know. Lead them to Nature, teach them to observe with amazement and delight, and the other steps follow in due course in accordance with the power of each soul to receive the deeper influences of Nature. In the sec-

ond place, men were just ready to take this first decisive step away from the artificial to the natural. The work of the poets who immediately preceded Thomson had been too slight and fragmentary to count for much in the way of influence, yet they were most clear indications of a tendency, a silent preparation of the general poetic mind, for such work as Thomson's. He was at once and easily understood because, while his poems in their spontaneous freshness and charm, their rich, easy fulness of description, their minute observation, their sweep of view, their unforced enthusiasm, must have come as a revelation, it was a revelation in no sense defiant or iconoclastic. In the main it was a revelation of new delights, not of disturbing theories, or vexing problems. A touch more of subtley, of vision, of mystery, of the faculty divine, and Thomson might have waited for recognition as Wordsworth did. . . .

Patricia Meyer Spacks (essay date 1959)

SOURCE: "The Poet as Teacher: Morality in *The Seasons*," in *The Varied God: A Critical Study of Thomson's "The Seasons,"* University of California Press, 1959, pp. 143-75.

[*In the excerpt that follows, Spacks concentrates on a trait that separates Thomson from Romanticism: a tendency to make nature a vehicle for and secondary to moral messages regarding human behavior. In general, she stresses a prevailing inconsistency in Thomson's images of nature.*]

> And hark how blithe the throstle sings;
> He, too, is no mean preacher.
> Come forth into the light of things,
> Let nature be your teacher.

So Wordsworth was to write in *Lyrical Ballads,* with a perception of the possibilities of nature as teacher far different from anything ever hinted by Thomson. Wordsworth's "nature" taught by working on the emotions; Thomson's did nothing so undignified. The eighteenth-century poet, in his concern with morality, falls in many ways into the typical pattern of his time, defined by Lovejoy more than a quarter of a century ago.[1] He looked to the "pure light of nature" for authority; gradually, as nature became less and less important to him, he turned to presenting the rules of morality without feeling the need for any explicit authority behind them.

I

An effective method of justifying his interest in nature, to himself and to his public, was, Thomson discovered, to insist on the relation between nature and human morality. Shaftesbury had long since exploited this relationship when Thomson began writing *The*

Seasons; in this area especially it is easy to see his influence on the poet.[2]

Shaftesbury's basic principle of the divine perfection of "Nature," the whole order of creation, led him easily into consideration of human nature, which must, like the rest of creation, be essentially good. It was for his moral teachings that Thomson specifically praised him, in lines first added in 1730 to the catalogue of the great in "**Summer**."

> The generous Ashley thine, the friend of man,
> Who scan'd his nature with a brother's eye,
> His weakness prompt to shade, to raise his aim,
> To touch the finer movements of the mind,
> And with the moral beauty charm the heart.
>   ("**Summer**" B, ll. 611-615)

The physical and moral worlds, affirmed Shaftesbury in his revelation of moral beauty, are two expressions of the same cosmic order; both should be guides and objects of study for man. And both are quite sufficient guides. The physical universe, naturally harmonious and good in every detail, offers adequate evidence for the existence of a Deity. Its evils can never be real, only apparent. The nature of man is likewise good and harmonious; man is naturally virtuous and naturally social, Hobbes to the contrary notwithstanding. This is not to say that the Golden Age must be past. The natural condition of man is not necessarily his original one; it is rather the state in which he realizes most fully his inner intention or individuating principle. In "Advice to an Author," Shaftesbury explains, somewhat confusingly, that the person taught by Nature alone is generally less "natural" than those who have progressed "by reflection and the assistance of art."[3] He admits, patronizingly, that in some instances the person formed by Nature may be so fortunate as to possess some of the valuable "natural" virtues, but this sort of person can only be an exception. Natural good is not, after all, necessarily related to Nature. The inconsistency is disturbing.

It does not, however, appear to disturb Shaftesbury. He proceeds to advocate that human beings follow nature, in an effort to reproduce within themselves the harmony of the external world. Beauty and goodness are essentially the same: beauty, external; goodness, internal. The virtuous man recognizes what is good by its beauty. Man has a natural "moral sense," but this must be improved by training, and it may be injured by various sources of error, including orthodox religion. Belief in future rewards and punishments robs our actions of moral value. The truest incentive to virtue is actually self-love, for self-love and social love are essentially the same. The greatest pleasure for the individual is to be obtained by the exercise of virtue in the form of benevolence to others. "To possess the social affections full and entire . . . is 'to live according to Nature, and the Dictates and Rules of supreme

Wisdom. This is Morality, Justice, Piety, and natural Religion.'"[4] Shaftesbury feels, finally, that one can arrive at a scheme of moral arithmetic, by which happiness can be shown in detail to be directly proportionate to virtue.[5]

Such a satisfactorily ordered scheme of things could not but appeal to Thomson: the Shaftesburian influence shows itself more or less blatantly throughout his work. In the early stages of *The Seasons,* especially, there is no apparent conflict between the Shaftesburian moralizing and the poet's basic theme of nature. Yet the direction of emphasis necessarily changes with the introduction of material implicitly concerned with the human rather than with the universal, and Thomson's use of nature undergoes some interesting modifications as a result.

The tendency, in the Shaftesburian sections, is for nature to lose importance as self-existent reality and to become symbolically or allegorically significant—as material for analogy, for example. Thus, in the 1727 version of "**Summer**" appears a passage on the joys of benevolence as opposed to the horrors of wickedness ("**Summer**" A, ll. 949-963). The setting of the sun provides the pretext for this digression, and also forms the basis for the analogy which justifies it: the rapid disappearance of the day, "illusive, and perplext" (l. 949), is like the review of the day's events for "The Hard, the Lewd, the Cruel, and the False" (l. 955). The possessor of Shaftesbury's "harmonious Mind" (l. 958), on the other hand, who diffuses beneficence "Boastless, as now descends the silent Dew" (l. 961), finds in the review of the day's events or of his life's, only "inward Rapture" (l. 963). There is considerable skill in the interweaving of natural metaphor with direct moralistic statement, although the passage is weakened by the poet's failure to exploit fully the value of his images, and by overstatement—the wicked men, for example, are described (ll. 957-958) as having spent the day snatching the morsel from the orphan's mouth to give their dogs.

More unqualifiedly successful in the use of natural analogy is the 1730 revision of the conclusion to "**Winter**," which also involves a disquisition on the superiority of virtue to vice. In its original form, this passage, which begins with consideration of the obvious analogy between the course of the seasons and the course of human life, weakens seriously toward the end because the analogy, never developed, is abandoned in favor of strictly human emphasis. The second birth of heaven and earth is to bring with it full understanding of "th' Eternal Scheme" ("**Winter**" A, l. 380). But that scheme has nothing to do, apparently, with the cosmos—only with the seeming ills of humanity. And despite the fact that similar statements of the same theme are common in the eighteenth century, appearing in the works of thinkers as diverse as John Locke and the Reverend Samuel Clarke, poets from Pope to Akenside—or perhaps because of that fact—it is disturbing to find such a passage standing as conclusion to a poem profoundly concerned with nature.

In 1730, the single change which makes the greatest difference in the effect of the concluding passage is the introduction of another simple natural analogy, a logical extension of the original one. Thomson's consideration of eternity (which, incidentally, contains more explicit emphasis on the theme of natural order than before) now concludes—and **"Winter"** likewise—with

> The storms of Wintry time will quickly pass,
> And one unbounded Spring encircle all.
> > (**"Winter"** C, ll. 780-781)

The idea is common enough—it occurs, for example, in John Armstrong's **"Winter,"** published soon after Thomson's first version—but this particular metaphorical use of it is brilliant indeed. By providing a symbolic link between the disparate themes of nature and human morality, it unifies two topics that were beginning to conflict in Thomson's work, and provides for **"Winter"** a conclusion of great connotative force.

All too often, however, reflection on Shaftesbury's themes seems to lead Thomson into using nature merely as a minor pretext for digression, or even into neglecting it altogether, as in the passage on the noble work of the 1729 Jail Committee (**"Winter"** C, ll. 334-364). The famous description of the country man dying in the snow, for example, loses impact by being used simply as an excuse to urge careless city-dwellers to think of all the suffering in the world:

> Ah little think they, while they dance along,
> How many feel this very moment, death
> And all the sad variety of pain.
> > (**"Winter"** C, ll. 300-302)

A detailed exposition of possible varieties of human suffering leads to the highly predictable moral:

> Thought but fond man
> Of these, and all the thousand nameless ills . . .
> The conscious heart of Charity would warm,
> And his wide wish Benevolence dilate;
> The social tear would rise, the social sigh;
> And into clear perfection, gradual bliss,
> Refining still, the social passions work.
> > (**"Winter"** C, ll. 323-324, 329-333)

Such lines might have been written by any number of eighteenth-century poets. Although in the moralistic sections, as in the ones on nature, Thomson's diction is adjusted to its purpose, such passages have retained little force. In the sections on nature, the poet, trying to say something specific and often fresh, uses con-

ventional diction to add to his newer purpose the weight of tradition. In the more extraneous lines on benevolence, however, he is saying something as conventional as his diction. Far lesser poets said precisely the same thing in almost the same way. Take, for example, the long-forgotten James Harris:

> For to man
> What dearer is than man? Say you, who prove
> The kindly call, the social sympathy,
> What but this call, this social sympathy,
> Tempers to standard due the vain exult
> Of prosperous fortune? What but this refines
> Soft pity's pain, and sweetens every care,
> Each friendly care we feel for human kind?[6]

Thomson's verse is more expert, but not essentially a great deal better.

Two of his three narrative additions, dominated by the Shaftesburian principle that virtue equals happiness and incorporating many of Shaftesbury's precepts, also use na-ture simply as pretext, implicitly rejecting its importance. The tale of Palaemon and Lavinia, which first appeared in the 1730 **"Autumn,"** begins with exhortations to benevolence:

> Be not too narrow, husband-men! but fling
> From the full sheaf, with charitable stealth,
> The liberal handful. Think, oh grateful think!
> How good the God of harvest is to you . . .
> > The various turns
> Of fortune ponder; that your sons may want
> What now, with hard reluctance, faint, ye give.
> > (**"Autumn"** A, ll. 174-177, 181-183)

As usual, looseness of logic is paralleled by looseness of diction: the precise function of "faint" in the last line would be difficult to define. The real explanation of this passage lies in the moral story to which it is an appropriate introduction.

The plot of this episode is a sentimental perversion of the Biblical tale of Ruth and Boaz. Lovely young Lavinia and her widowed mother, reduced to poverty, live in a poor cottage. Lavinia goes to glean the fields of rich young Palaemon, who succumbs immediately to her charms, but will not own his love because the world would laugh at him for choosing a poor gleaner. He is not, however, punished for snobbish scruples. When he discovers that Lavinia is actually the daughter of his former patron, Acasto, all is well: love combines with benevolence, and he acquires a sense of virtue by proposing to the woman he wanted all along. So, of course, they

> flourish'd long in mutual bliss, and rear'd
> A numerous offspring, lovely like themselves,
> And good, the grace of all the country round.
> > (**"Autumn"** A, ll. 305-307)

The facile sentimentality of all this suggests Tennyson at his worst—describing, for example, in "The Lord of Burleigh," the lady who

> Shaped her heart with woman's meekness
> To all duties of her rank;
> And a gentle consort made he,
> And her gentle mind was such
> That she grew a noble lady,
> And the people loved her much.

The sentimentality of this poem, indeed, exceeds that of the Lavinia tale. Tennyson's country girl who marries a nobleman sickens and dies in her newly exalted rank; Lavinia gets along quite well. Thomson is like the Victorian poet, however, in his serene assurance that wealth and rank may be equivalent to virtue. Like Tennyson, too, he seems sometimes convinced that the expression of fine sentiments relieves him of the obligation to think.

The edition of 1730 also contained, in the second version of "Summer" (ll. 980-1037), the new story of Damon and Musidora. With its slightly prurient atmosphere and fervid description, this is probably to modern readers the most offensive of Thomson's narratives. That its salacious aspects did not decrease its attraction for nineteenth-century readers, however, is suggested by Wordsworth's remark that all well-thumbed copies of *The Seasons* opened at this tale.[7] In its original form, the version of 1730, the story describes Damon as a young man devoted to false philosophy and scornful of the force of beauty. While he was sitting in the woods one day, he spied three young ladies, Sacharissa, Amoret, and Musidora. Despite all the classical allusions invoked to elevate the succeeding scene, the point of the thirty-nine lines of adolescently salacious description is that the girls undressed and swam, while Damon watched, enthralled. The moral?

> the latent Damon drew
> Such draughts of love and beauty to the soul,
> As put his harsh philosophy to flight,
> The joyless search of long-deluded years;
> And Musidora fixing in his heart,
> Inform'd, and humaniz'd him into man.
> ("**Summer**" B, ll. 1032-1037)

The intellectual content of this story offers a dramatic contrast to Thomson's earlier views. "**Summer**," which presents the long, impassioned praise of philosophy, now contains, also, an episode the point of which is that it is better to devote one's attention to man—or woman—than to philosophy. To be sure, Damon is described as a devotee of *false* philosophy. But the ardent search for the secrets of true philosophy, the efforts of a Locke or a Newton, would be equally incompatible with sitting in the woods watching naked women. The tale suggests once again that Thomson's

sense of values had changed, and with it his convictions about the proper study of mankind. Even more clearly, it indicates his concern with popular appeal: this story would surely attract many whose interest in nature was slight. It is significant that in the frontispiece to "**Summer**" in the subscription quarto of 1730, William Kent chose to direct his efforts to illustration of this tale: indeed, he added a fourth naked lady for good measure.

The story was successful enough to make Thomson want to expand it for the third edition of "**Summer**" in 1744. In the new version, its theme is altogether changed. No longer is there the slightest attempt to relate the episode to nature or even philosophy. Now it is simply a story in itself, its salacious aspects emphasized, although the virtue-equals-happiness theme remains. Damon, it seems, is already in love with Musidora. He is sitting in the woods musing on his love when she comes, alone, to swim. As she undresses, he watches, panting ("not Paris on the shady Top / Of Ida panted stronger"; ll. 1296-1297), despite the fact that a delicate refinement known to few urges him to retire. Finally he retreats, leaving a note explaining to the young lady that he is guarding her so that no one else can peek. Feeling shame void of guilt, admiration of her lover's flame, and a sense of self-approving beauty, she leaves Damon a note saying that the time may come when he need not fly. The relation of this episode to the theme of man is far more apparent than its relevance to the poet's original concern with nature.

Both the tale of Lavinia and that of Damon originate in material vaguely related to nature. Lavinia and her mother are simple country folk, in close contact with the natural world; Damon wanders in the woods and his realization takes place in the surroundings of nature. But the major changes in the account of Damon and the minor ones of 1744 in the story of Lavinia alike stress the human, providing evidence of how complete Thomson's essential disregard for the theme of nature could be—even when nature was his pretext.

II

It was not Shaftesbury's influence alone, naturally, that drew Thomson away from his original concerns. The moralistic passages which seem attributable to no single influence show a similar chronological development from early attempts to combine the themes of nature and of man to later concentration almost entirely on the human.

Some of Thomson's early moralistic passages seem direct outgrowths of his original preoccupation, with natural order and harmony. Beginning with "**Summer**," in 1727, the poet introduced various discussions of possible ways in which nature might influence man. "**Summer**," for example, expresses the poet's desire to repair to a dark grove, the haunt of meditation. There, he maintains, people of ancient times have been inspired toward virtue and poetry by "Angels, and immortal Forms, / On heavenly Errands bent" (**"Summer"** A, ll. 412-413), which perform the "Offices of Love" (l. 423) for virtuous men of all sorts. When they speak to him, however, they deal with subjects more clearly related to nature. First they announce their participation in the universal pattern; then they admonish the poet to retire to the dim recesses they haunt and "Of Nature sing with Us, and Nature's God" (ll. 439-442). The idea of nature as escape from the evils of the world thus emerges again, this time combined with a variation on the theme of man as leader of the universal chorus of praise for the natural order.

The mysterious "forms" of this passage appear also in Mallet; again, the difference between **"Summer"** and *The Excursion* is illuminating. In Mallet's poem, the angels lend their good influence through whispers which

> Inspire new vigour, purer light supply,
> And kindle every virtue into flame.

This is apparently the extent of their mission, and the poet's reflection upon their inspiration is interesting:

> Thus ever fix'd
> In solitude, may I, obscurely safe,
> Deceive mankind, and steal through life along,
> As slides the foot of Time, unmark'd, unknown.[8]

For Thomson, the mysterious forms may provide inspiration and release in their reminder of the great pattern of nature; for Mallet, with his more conventional pose, they represent a means of avoiding altogether the tumult of the world. Mallet thus allies himself with the most common attitude toward nature in his time, an attitude which led men to seek and praise nature for the most classical of reasons: as a source of tranquility for meditation. As George Williams put it, "Nature is a place where a good Augustan may learn to know himself and may cultivate his soul."[9]

Examples of glorification of nature for this sort of reason were abundant in Thomson's time, and they offer a partial explanation for the statement that "romanticism is not a reaction away from neo-classicism, but is a growth out of it."[10] Thomson's vision of nature, however, with its more broadly philosophic implications, carries far more emotional weight. When he is true to it, he seems perhaps more essentially a forerunner of the nineteenth-century nature poets than any of his contemporaries.

We see this attitude toward the cosmos implicit in the description of the "immortal Forms"; the lines are redeemed by the clear attempt to relate them to the primary concept of natural order, whereas in *The Excursion,* since they have no really integral function, they are merely one more fragment in a poem of fragments. Although the two works belong to the same verse tradition, Thomson's is the more successful mainly because of the essential unity of conception behind it.

In Thomson's later years, however, his discussions of the effects of nature on man tended to place more emphasis on man, less on nature. In his own explanation of the organization of **"Spring,"** the poet states, "This Season is described as it affects the various parts of Nature, ascending from the lower to the higher; . . . Its influence on inanimate Matter, on Vegetables, on brute Animals, and last on Man."[11] The poet also mentions his "concluding with a Dissuasive from the wild and irregular passion of love." His increasing emphasis on human morality is here apparent; the poem makes it even clearer.

For the long section dealing with the influence of spring on human love is completely dominated by the view that nature is important because it is meaningful to man. There is the account of how spring makes the virgin's bosom heave, the adjuration to watch out for "betraying Man" (**"Spring"** A, ll. 877-895). More important, however, is the passage (ll. 896-1024) dealing with the effects of love on young men.

For the man, too, should beware of love. Once it strikes, an image is fixed in his mind which drives out all else. From this image he attempts in vain to flee: nature is now first significantly introduced.

> 'Tis nought but Gloom around. The darken'd Sun
> Loses his Light. The rosy-bosom'd Spring
> To weeping Fancy pines; and yon bright Arch
> Of Heaven low-bends into a dusky Vault.
> All Nature fades extinct.
>
> ("Spring" A, ll. 912-916)

Man, in other words, can influence the very forms of nature. Thomson had previously (ll. 426-440) rejected the imagination as unequal to imitating nature; now he seems to imply that the imagination—at least when stimulated by lovesickness—modifies human perceptions of nature to the extent that nature itself seems actually changed.

This is not the only possibility which Thomson explores. The presence of sympathy in the natural world is next suggested, as the lover

> restless runs
> To glimmering Shades, and sympathetic Glooms,
> Where the dun Umbrage o'er the falling Stream
> Romantic hangs; there thro' the pensive Dusk
> Strays, in Heart-thrilling Meditation lost,
> Indulging all to Love: or on the Bank

> Thrown, amid drooping Lillies, swells the Breeze
> With Sighs unceasing, and the Brook with Tears.
>   (ll. 928-935)

In the lover's dreams, the most skillfully handled part of the passage (and a part which seems to owe an obvious debt to Pope's "Eloisa to Abelard"), natural scenes become symbols for mental and emotional states. The lover wanders "Thro' Forests huge, and long un-travel'd Heaths / With Desolation brown" (ll. 973-974); he wades a turbid stream, trying in vain to reach his loved one on the far shore, and is borne away by the flood or sunk beneath the water. Beds of roses are symbols of joy (l. 993); a storm represents the chaos of the lover's mind (ll. 1015-1017); he is led by love in-to thorny wilds "Thro' flowery-tempting Paths" (l. 1021).

All of this represents what must have been a conscious and careful effort to relate to the primary theme of *The Seasons* a passage dangerously close to irrelevance. Yet nature is, after all, simply an embellishment in these sections: man is the primary subject, his difficul-ties and values the true object of emphasis.

It is an easy step from passages in which nature is a decorative object to those in which it disappears alto-gether; the two sorts exist side by side in "**Spring**."

>   Ten thousand Fears,
> Invented wild, ten thousand frantic Views
> Of horrid Rivals, hanging on the Charms
> For which he melts in Fondness, eat him up
> With fervent Anguish, and consuming Pine.
> In vain Reproaches lend their idle Aid,
> Deceitful Pride, and Resolution frail,
> Giving a Moment's Ease. Reflection pours,
> Afresh, her Beauties on his busy Thought,
> Her first Endearments, twining round the Soul
> With all the Witchcraft of ensnaring Love.
>   (**"Spring"** A, ll. 1004-1014)

This may be a universal lover, deliberately nonindivid-ualized, but the generalized abstractions seem so de-void of conviction as to lack even emblematic force. There is an atmosphere of exaggeration, or turgidity, about this; the lines represent a total rejection of the valuable discipline implicit in the acceptance of nature as theme, the discipline which, as we have seen, so often produces a fruitful tension between diction and content in Thomson's best work.

It comes as no surprise that the conclusion of **"Spring"** also concentrates on the human, but the contrast be-tween the use of the seasons in symbolic relation to man here and in the conclusion of **"Winter"** is significant. After more elaborate consideration of love's evils, Thom-son finally contemplates the ideally happy couple, pos-sessed of "Truth, Goodness, Honour, Harmony and Love" (l. 1055), and their ideal offspring. He concludes:

> And thus their Moments fly; the Seasons thus,
> As ceaseless round a jarring World they roll,
> Still find Them happy; and consenting Spring
> Sheds her own rosy Garland on their Head:
> Till Evening comes at last, cool, gentle, calm;
> When after the long vernal Day of Life,
> Enamour'd more, as Soul approaches Soul,
> Together, down They sink in social Sleep.
>   (**"Spring"** A, ll. 1075-1082)

Instead of making any effort to work out an analogy between the seasons and human life, Thomson is here content to describe the course of life—with amazing superficiality—as one long *vernal* day. Nature is re-duced to a trivial image. The seasons are significant because they find the lovers happy; spring is useful in shedding garlands to reward them. How different from the view at the end of **"Winter,"** when winter becomes an image of time to contrast with spring-eternity! There is a serious loosening of intellectual fiber here, a ten-dency to relax the diction as the content becomes more conventional—the proper study of mankind.

III

Examples of Thomson's gradual turning away from nature to man could be multiplied in many directions. One area in which the resultant confusion appears clear-ly, however, is in his passages of explicit moral injunc-tion and teaching, some of which have already been discussed in relation to Shaftesbury. Such moralistic passages may use nature as starting point; they frequently involve the poet in tangled intellectual positions.

Sometimes, when the moralistic sections come in close conjunction with lines of brilliant description, the con-trast points up vividly the difference in poetic quality between Thomson the nature lover and Thomson the moralist. In **"Summer,"** for example, a diatribe against late sleeping grows directly from some delicately love-ly natural description:

> Blue, thro' the Dusk, the smoking Currents
>   shine;
> And, from the bladed Field, th'unhunted Hare
> Limps aukward: while along the Forest-Glade,
> The wild Deer trip, and, often turning, gaze
> At early Passenger.
>   (**"Summer"** A, ll. 43-47)

The description may encourage early rising; the mor-alizing certainly does the reverse:

> Falsely luxurious, will not Man awake,
> And starting from the Bed of Sloth, enjoy
> The cool, the fragrant, and the silent Hour, . . .
> And is there ought in Sleep can charm the
>   Wise?
> To lie in dead Oblivion . . .

Or else to feaverish Vanity alive,
Wilder'd, and tossing thro' distemper'd Dreams.
("**Summer**" A, ll. 54-56, 57-58, 62-63)

A sense of artifice dominates this, in contrast to the profound originality and sincerity of the description.

The same sort of pattern appears in the other moralistic sections: in all of them, the poet seems self-conscious; in many, ridiculous. Swimming is justified because it is "the purest Exercise of Health" ("**Summer**" A, l. 927); because it is a good thing to know how to swim in case a life needs saving; because Caesar learned to "subdue the Wave" (l. 936) when he was very young; finally, because the mind, closely allied to the body, receives a secret aid from the body's purity. Vegetarianism is justified because man is formed by nature "of milder Clay" ("**Spring**" A, l. 394) than wild animals, which are stung to carnivorousness by hunger and necessity, and incapable of pity. But the discussion of vegetarianism incorporates its own denial:

> Thus the feeling Heart
> Would tenderly suggest. But 'tis enough,
> In this late Age, adventurous to have touch'd
> Light on the Numbers of the Samian Sage.
> High Heaven beside forbids the daring Strain,
> Whose wisest Will has fix'd us in a State,
> Which must not yet to pure Perfection rise.
> ("**Spring**" A, ll. 419-425)

As in his treatment of the Golden Age, Thomson would have us believe finally that he is merely versifying the views of another: we sense that the poem is being padded. There seems no intellectual or poetic content in this discussion, for which the poet explicitly disclaims responsibility. Moreover, he destroys the argument he has advanced without appearing to recognize that he is doing anything of the sort. The principal objection to the carnivorous habits of man throughout the discussion has been that it lowers man to the status of beasts; yet at the end Thomson implies, with his reference to the Great Chain of Being, that it is, after all, in the nature of the human animal to be carnivorous. This basic inconsistency emphasizes the sense of inconsequence which a modern reader is likely to derive from the moralizing of *The Seasons*.

In his treatments of hunting and fishing we may see the clearest examples of Thomson's moralizing. The denunciation of hunting also demonstrates a certain wavering of position. At the beginning of the long passage on hunting (which, including the description of the after-hunt feast, occupies "**Autumn**" A, ll. 357-558), we see a hint of the sportsman's zest as Thomson confesses that he is tempted to deal with the scenes of the hunt. He recovers after twenty lines, however, with the affirmation that "These are not subjects for the peaceful muse" (l. 376), which prefers everything to

be alive and happy. To support his advocacy of animal harmony, the poet then describes the hunt from the point of view of the hare and of the fleeing stag, who sobs as he runs through the woods and finally stands at bay with "the big round tears" (l. 451) running down his face. (Yet in "**Spring**," previously, Thomson had pointed out—line 396—that man is the only animal enabled by nature to weep.)

But Thomson cannot give up hunting quite so easily. He decides next to find some rationalization for it: hunting is all right, he maintains, as long as its object is bloodthirsty and destructive animals—the lion, the wolf, and the boar. These, to be sure, do not exist in England; but Britons may be permitted to hunt the fox.

In its morality, this position is fairly typical of eighteenth-century poetizing on hunting. William Somerville, for example, says approximately the same thing, although with different emphasis:

> Ye proud oppressors, whose vain hearts exult
> In wantonness of power, 'gainst the brute race,
> Fierce robbers like yourselves, a guiltless war
> Wage uncontrol'd: here quench your thirst of
>   blood;
> But learn from Aurengzebe to spare mankind.[12]

It was possible thus to have it both ways: to indulge oneself in the joys of hunting without pangs of conscience, while still demonstrating a proper softness of heart by objecting to the pursuit of gentle animals, who are not "fierce robbers." Thomson feels himself on safer ground, obviously, and presents his position more enthusiastically, when he denounces hunting of any kind as a pursuit for women: he does so at some length.

Such passages of direct moralizing are interspersed, in this lengthy treatment of hunting, with enthusiastic descriptions of the hunt itself and of the later festivities—descriptions sometimes impenetrable in syntax, though not lacking in vigor.

> But first the fuel'd chimney blazes wide;
> The tankards foam; and the strong table groans
> Beneath the smoking sirloin, stretch'd immense
> From side to side; on which, with fell intent,
> They deep incision make, and talk the while
> Of England's glory, ne'er to be defac'd,
> While hence they borrow vigour: or amain
> Into the pasty plung'd, at intervals,
> If stomach keen can intervals allow,
> Relating how it ran, and how it fell.
> Then sated Hunger bids his brother Thirst
> Produce the mighty bowl; the mighty bowl,
> Swell'd high with fiery juice, steams liberal
>   round
> A potent gale.
> ("**Autumn**" A, ll. 498-511)

Exactly what was plunged into the pasty, and, for that matter, what was the "it" which ran and fell, remains obscure until later revisions. Moreover, Thomson's approval of meat eating, including the consumption of a pasty (traditionally made with venison from innocent animals) is somewhat surprising in view of his condemnation of hunting the gentle beasts and his support of vegetarianism. Neither the grammatical nor the logical haziness of these lines destroys the sense of gusto which animates them, but both weaknesses are likely to contribute to a reader's feeling that the poet is not thoroughly at home in this particular mode of expression. In its excursions into the mock-heroic, its personifications, its combination of the comparatively trivial ("the smoking sirloin") with the important ("England's glory, ne'er to be defac'd"), the passage is characteristic of much eighteenth-century poetry—but certainly not of Thomson's early work. Its method, like its material, stresses the human. The fact that Thomson could include, so early as 1730, a single section of more than two hundred lines dealing entirely with the affairs of men, is itself significant; the sense of unsureness combined with conventionality that the passage conveys makes it even more glaring.

Our poet's reflections on trout fishing also project a certain atmosphere of confusion. Added to the 1744 version of **"Spring,"** the lines exemplify both the poet's pleasure in the spectacle of man in action and his delight in extracting sentimental reflections from the most unlikely material.

> But let not on thy Hook the tortur'd Worm,
> Convulsive, twist in agonizing Folds,
> Which by rapacious Hunger swallow'd deep
> Gives, as you tear it from the bleeding Breast
> Of the weak, helpless, uncomplaining Wretch,
> Harsh Pain and Horror to the tender Hand.
>
> (**"Spring"** C, ll. 386-391)

First, it seems, one is to pity the worm. Then, somehow, the same worm is to cause pain and horror to the hand when that hand tears it from the bleeding breast of an uncomplaining wretch who can only be the trout. Yet the poet proceeds to a detailed and enthusiastic description of the technique and joys of fly-fishing, with not the slightest evidence of any more pity for the weak, helpless, uncomplaining wretch who is no less hooked because hooked with a fly. Having given a sop to his humanitarian instincts, the poet is free to enjoy the sport; the process is essentially the same as the one he goes through before the description of the fox hunt. His unsureness and lack of authority in dealing with narrow and sentimental moralizing have been communicated once again.

IV

A more significant, because more extensive, area of intellectual confusion produced by Thomson's shifts of em-

phasis has been touched upon by many commentators. This is the dilemma about primitivism and progress, which caused the poet many shifts in point of view, many reversals of emphasis.

Lovejoy pointed out some time ago that the basic principles of the Enlightenment, which shaped deism and the neoclassic theory of literature, included rationalistic primitivism—a belief that the earliest men, uncorrupted by tradition, were in the best position to understand universal truths—and a negative philosophy of history which maintained that all apparent progress is really change for the worse.[13] Such primitivism, such an attitude toward history, appear in Thomson's presentation of the Golden Age in the 1728 **"Spring."** Emphasis here, in accordance with the poet's early philosophy, is on the benefice of nature, combined with man's acceptance of this beneficence and his harmonious participation in the natural order.

Many of the details of the description are derived from Dryden's version of Virgil's fourth "Eclogue," in which the Golden Age is in the future; but Thomson's is emphatically in the past. Indeed, when he turns to the present he labels it "these Iron Times, / These Dregs of Life" (**"Spring"** A, ll. 326-327), in which the human mind "Has lost that Harmony ineffable, / Which forms the Soul of Happiness" (ll. 328-329). He follows Bishop Burnet in the subsequent presentation of the idea that nature is fallen with fallen man, and that only after the deluge which punished man's sins did seasons develop.

So it seems that the natural man, whose untrained grapes burst automatically "into Floods of Wine" (l. 304) and whose sheep came already dyed (ll. 313-317), was a more virtuous specimen than his civilized successor, dweller in a fallen world, and in less intimate communication with nature. Thomson uses secondhand material expertly here—perhaps because he remains conscious of its relevance to the whole problem of the relation between man and nature. The discussion of the Golden Age, however, might well have embarrassed the poet later. Indeed, in 1744 he eliminated the section (**"Spring"** A, ll. 296-323) which implied the glories of being without commerce or industry, and increased his emphasis on modern times by the addition of fourteen new lines and the changing of several others.

Two years after the publication of the passage on the Golden Age (in **"Spring"** A, 1728), in the first edition of **"Autumn"** Thomson returned to the theme of the natural man in a different way: the poet's primitivism was no longer simply chronological. This time his subject was the good life: the passage (**"Autumn"** A, ll. 1131-1247) defines and praises it, and contrasts it with the evil alternative modes of conduct. The ideal state of existence, it seems, is that of the retired man, who dwells deep in the vale and "Drinks the pure pleasures of the rural Life" (l. 1134). He lacks the crowd of flatterers, the glittering robes, the rare foods and wines, the sleepless nights, and the hollow moments which attend a more civilized way of life. Instead, he is rich in nature's bounty: the aesthetic pleasures of nature, the nourishment of natural food, the truth and innocence which nature encourages, and nature's ever-blooming health, unambitious toil, calm contemplation, and poetic ease. Others may choose to roam the seas, sack cities, explore, use legal methods to perpetrate various undefined evils, lead political uprisings, enjoy the intrigue of courts, or "tread the weary labyrinth of state" (l. 1194). The country man is unmoved by political upheavals. He attends only to Nature's voice, feels her fine emotions, takes what she gives and wants no more. He enjoys reading what the muse has sung of the progress of the seasons (an ingenious bit of self-encouragement, this) or, perhaps, even writing of such subjects. He is happy in all the seasons; he possesses imaginative power and heroic virtue, and enjoys the blessings of love and parenthood. Nor does he scorn amusement, for happiness and true philosophy "Still are, and have been of the smiling kind" (l. 1243). His life is that

> Led by primaeval ages, incorrupt,
> When God himself, and Angels dwelt with men!
> ("**Autumn**" A, ll. 1246-1247)

For this sort of thing, too, Thomson had classical precedent, nor was he alone in his own time. An expressed desire to cultivate rural virtue was not uncommon in eighteenth-century poetry. John Langhorne, to take a minor example, produced a charming poem on the good life in the country:

> Virtue dwells in Arden's vale;
> There her hallow'd temples rise,
> There her incense greets the skies,
> Grateful as the morning gale. . . .
> There the fountains clearer flow,
> Flowers in brighter beauty blow;
> For, with Peace and Virtue, there
> Lives the happy villager.
> Distant still from Arden's vale
> Are the woes the bad bewail. . . .[14]

And Virgil had done almost the same thing; in, for example, *Georgics* II. 458-474.

But the very fact that Thomson could depend so closely on a Virgilian model seems to have led him into a presentation marked by dictional and logical ambiguities.

> What tho' his wine
> Flows not from brighter gems; nor sunk in beds,
> Oft of gay care, he tosses out the night;
> Or, thoughtless, sleeps at best in idle state.
> What tho' depriv'd of these fantastic joys,

> That still amuse the wanton, still deceive;
> A face of pleasure, but a heart of pain;
> Their hollow moments undelighted all.
> ("**Autumn**" A, ll. 1145-1152)

The "brighter gems" at the beginning of these lines are somewhat obscure; it is difficult to decide what the gems are and what they are brighter than. The verb "depriv'd," in connection with the status of the retired man, implies that there is something to be desired in the joys of the rich, even though they are only "fantastic." Even more disturbing is the structure of the last two lines, in which the possessor of the face of pleasure and the heart of pain is obscure and the reference of "their" seems cloudy: it is presumably to the "wanton," but there seems to be only one of him.

Thomson himself came to recognize some of the difficulties in the passage. His 1744 revision (**"Autumn"** B) eliminates the "brighter gems" and clarifies both the opening lines and some of the later ones. The fact remains, however, that this section, with its stress on human values, lacks the tightness and power of many of the passages more closely concerned with nature.

Its difficulties, however, come not from the fact that its governing concept is weak or faulty. The central idea of the passage is the precise sort of harmony between man and nature that is envisioned in most of "**Autumn**." Man is the master, nature exists mainly for his sake. There are emotional possibilities in this concept; if it is not so moving or so imaginatively presented as the earlier idea that man is a part of nature; it is none the less pleasant. It is agreeable, though not altogether convincing to a generation that has read *Tobacco Road,* to think of the farmer enjoying "still retreats, and flowery solitudes" (l. 1201), as it is agreeable to contemplate Langhorne's happy villager who dwells far from all the woes the bad bewail. The real weakness of the passage comes from its suggestion of a sense of unsureness in the author. We do not really believe that Thomson believes it. There can be no doubt about the poet's sincerity in the passages on natural harmony in "**Winter**" and "**Summer**," but one can easi-ly doubt his sincerity in the later passages on the joys of the natural man. The fact that most of the material in these passages is secondhand is itself significant. Thomson is versifying views which at the moment appear to him respectable or convenient, not necessarily those which move him most deeply. The results, inevitably, are wavering of diction, weakness of emotion.

In 1744, returning to the theme of the virtuous natural man in the present, Thomson introduced into "**Winter**" more secondhand material: an account of the residents of Lapland, who provide a sharp contrast to civilized man. They

Despise th'insensate barbarous Trade of War;
They ask no more than simple Nature gives,
They love their Mountains and enjoy their Storms.
No false Desires, no Pride-created Wants,
Disturb the peaceful Current of their Days.

     (**"Winter"** E, ll. 844-848)

Their wives are kind and unblemished; they themselves seem ideal:

> Thrice happy Race! By Poverty secur'd
> From legal Plunder and rapacious Power:
> In whom fell Interest never yet has sown
> The Seeds of Vice; whose spotless Swains
> ne'er knew
> Injurious Deed, nor, blasted by the Breath
> Of faithless Love, their blooming Daughters
> Woe.
>
>   (**"Winter"** E, ll. 881-886)

The simple fact that Thomson looked on the Laplanders' state as rosy is not itself so significant as the fact that their specific virtues all appear to be conceived as the opposites of civilized vices. The implication is that the dweller in Lapland is far more to be envied than the resident of London, who might have to cope with legal plunder or faithless love. The poet has already placed his Golden Age in the past, describing the present as the dregs of life. Now he emphasizes his aversion to war, pride-created wants (those admirable fosterers of commerce), and civilized vice in general.

It comes as something of a shock, after this, to discover Thomson uncritically absorbing more travel-book material, this time explaining that it is also in the northern regions that "the last of mankind live" (**"Winter"** C, l. 688) in an environment where "Human Nature just begins to dawn" (l. 691)—or, to follow a later edition, where human nature "wears it's rudest Form" (**"Winter"** E, l. 940). The grossness of this race, who dwell by "the wild Oby" (**"Winter"** E, l. 937) of Russia, may be accounted for by the fact that the sun scarcely penetrates to this area and Winter reigns alone. Of course, precisely the same might be said of Lapland—but in his discussion of Lapland Thomson has only praise for the wonders of moon and stars. It seems strange to find the idea of the disastrous effects of eternal winter in a poem that explicitly remarks on the renovating force of Winter, commenting (**"Winter"** C, ll. 561-563) that desolation is visible only to the thoughtless eye.

These Russians are not the only primitive people who turn out to be the reverse of virtuous. The revisions of 1744 introduce a new passage on African savages, described as an "Ill-fated Race" because

> the softening Arts of Peace,
> Whate'er the humanizing Muses teach;

The Godlike Wisdom of the temper'd Breast; . . .
Kind equal Rule, the Government of Laws,
And all-protecting Freedom, which alone
Sustains the Name and Dignity of Man:
These are not theirs. The Parent-Sun himself
Seems o'er this World of Slaves to tyrannize.

   (**"Summer"** C, ll. 867-869, 873-877)

The passage goes on to point out that all gentle virtues seek milder climates, where there are fewer ruthless deeds, less mad jealousy and blind rage. Like Tennyson, Thomson, even when lured into temporary enchantment with the wonders of the tropics (in the same edition he refers to tropic isles as the seat of blameless Pan, "yet undisturb'd / By christian Crimes and Europe's cruel Sons"; **"Summer"** C, ll. 846-847), feels obliged to insist that he counts the gray barbarian lower than the Christian child.

His attitude toward natural man, in short, is by no means constant. Nor is his attitude toward modern civilization, which, as we have seen, he explicitly rejects in connection with his excursions into primitivism. Often, on the other hand, he seems totally convinced of its glories. In the first edition of **"Summer,"** for example, occurs a lengthy passage of praise for modern Britain. The attitudes represented by it also occur rather frequently in eighteenth-century poetry; Oliver Goldsmith, for example, is, like Thomson, capable of lumping together a variety of attributes under the general classification of British virtue, in "The Traveler."

>   my genius spreads her wing,
> And flies where Britain courts the western
> spring; . . .
> There all around the gentlest breezes stray,
> There gentle music melts on every spray;
> Creation's mildest charms are there combined,
> Extremes are only in the master's mind!
> Stern o'er each bosom Reason holds her state,
> With daring aims irregularly great,
> Pride in their port, defiance in their eye,
> I see the lords of human kind pass by,
> Intent on high designs, a thoughtful band,
> By forms unfashion'd, fresh from Nature's hand;
> Fierce in their native hardiness of soul,
> True to imagin'd right, above control,
> While ev'n the peasant boasts these rights to scan,
> And learns to venerate himself as man.

Compare Thomson:

> Happy Britannia! where the Queen of Arts,
> Inspiring Vigour, Liberty, abroad,
> Walks thro' the Land of Heroes, unconfin'd,
> And scatters Plenty with unsparing Hand.
> Rich is thy Soil, and merciful thy Skies; . . .
> Thy Country teems with Wealth;
> And Property assures it to the Swain,

Pleas'd, and unweary'd, in his certain Toil. . . .
    thy thoughtful Sires preside;
In Genius, and substantial Learning high;
For every Vertue, every Worth renown'd,
Sincere, plain-hearted, hospitable, kind,
Yet like the mustering Thunder when provok'd;
The Scourge of Tyrants, and the sole Resource
Of such as under grim Oppression groan.
(**"Summer"** A, ll. 498-502, 510-512, 528-534)

In tone, in atmosphere, the two passages are almost identical. It is an atmosphere compounded of emotional catchwords, a tone which demands nothing of the reader except complacency. Completely appropriate to Goldsmith's purposes, it is less easily acceptable in Thomson—and the poet feels obliged to apologize:

Thus far, transported by my Country's Love,
Nobly digressive from my Theme, I've aim'd
To sing her Praises, in ambitious Verse;
While, slightly to recount, I simply meant,
The various Summer-Horrors, which infest
Kingdoms that scorch below severer Suns.
        (**"Summer"** A, ll. 610-615)

The fact that the digression was "noble," and that it was undoubtedly agreeable to Thomson's contemporaries, in no way lessens its digressiveness or the sense of inappropriateness with which one plods through it. The scheme of values upon which the passage is based has virtually no relation to the scheme underlying most of the rest of the poem. It is a conventional set of moral standards, and the conventional language the poet uses in dealing with it suggests that he was writing off the surface of his mind, confident of acceptance because his sentiments were so correct, feeling no obligation to precision of diction because this was a sort of poetry in which content was far more important than style.

Indeed, lack of dictional control is characteristic of the sections of **The Seasons** which place their emphasis on such concerns. Let us examine in more detail a few lines of the digression on England's glories:

Full are thy Cities with the Sons of Art;
And Trade, and Joy, in every busy Street,
Mingling, are heard: even Drudgery, Himself,
As at the Car He sweats, or, dusty, hews
The Palace-Stone, looks gay. Thy crowded Ports,
Where rising Masts an endless Prospect yield,
With Labour burn, and eccho to the Shouts
Of hurry'd Sailour.
        (**"Summer"** A, ll. 513-520)

In sentiment, this is irreproachable by eighteenth-century standards. It is, as a matter of fact, an excellent example of a certain sort of manifestation of Augustan optimism. The enthusiasm for Britain's industrial progress, the feeling that commercial activity of any sort is admirable per se, the simple equation of trade with joy: these are characteristic of the time.

But the terms in which Thomson chooses to communicate this vision of progress are actually extremely ambiguous. An audience of his own time, sharing his convictions, might accept the import intended without recognizing a contradictory substratum, but the twentieth-century reader is not so automatically on the poet's side. Perusing an account of Drudgery, sweating and dusty, laboring on the stones of others' palaces, we do not necessarily accept the simple assertion that he "looks gay" as adequate counterbalance to the negative aspects of his situation already introduced. The whole section, positive in intent, is full of negative implications, the result of poorly disciplined diction. Britain's ports *burn* with labor. Burning implies energy and heat; energy, at least, is a desirable connotation in the circumstances, and heat not a particularly undesirable one. But burning also implies destruction. The result of a fire is ashes; men burn themselves out: the verb suggests the unpleasant aspects of the scene more strongly than the pleasant ones. The ports are *crowded*—a disagreeable state of affairs, if a commercially promising one; the sailor is *hurried*—we sense the tremendous pressure behind the façade of success. The ambiguities of the poet's diction work against him rather than for him, because the idea he attempts to present is simple, not complex, and words of complex import destroy, not strengthen it. The same sort of weakness may be found in most of the long praise of Britain, emphasizing the debilitating effect that too close attention to man can have in such a poem as **The Seasons**. Conventional diction in conjunction with conventional ideas unredeemed by the sense of deep personal participation by the author: the result is a flabby sort of poetry, interesting only historically.

Another passage founded on the same sort of assumptions as the long one on England, although apparently far more closely related to nature, is the glorification of plowing in the **"Spring"** of 1728. Again, the digression originates in contemplation of a natural scene. It attempts, however, to justify a human pursuit closely related to nature by reference to standards divorced from nature: allusions to famous historical figures. We are told, by way of reassurance, that Virgil sang about plowing; that great men in the past devoted themselves to the "sacred Plow" (**"Spring"** A, l. 57); that classical heroes, after performing their heroic feats, were willing to seize the plow and live "greatly independent" (l. 64). In the second section of the passage, Britons are urged to cultivate the plow as a means of increasing the dominance of man over nature and of Britain over the world. England is already the mistress of the seas, Thomson points out; why should she not control the land as thoroughly? If Britons will only plow, their country may be "th'exhaustless Granary of the World"

(l. 75) and clothe less fortunate naked nations. Thomson's expressed reason for cultivating the ground, in other words, has to do only with the affairs of men: man is to exercise control over nature for the sake of other men. John Dyer said the same thing. Britain's delight, he observed, is

> To fold the world with harmony, and spread
> Among the habitations of mankind,
> The various wealth of toil, and what her fleece,
> To clothe the naked, and her skilful looms,
> Peculiar give.[15]

Or there is Robert Dodsley, who shares Thomson's enthusiasm for the plow:

> Of these, the honour'd plough claims chief regard,
> Hence bread to man, who heretofore on mast
> Fed with his fellow-brute, in woods and wilds,
> Himself uncultur'd as the soil he trod.[16]

Dodsley's praise of the plow, however, also suggests a problem latent in all this glorification of agriculture, commerce, naval supremacy. Implicit in the high regard for civilized human accomplishment is condemnation of man in his natural state. Dodsley makes it explicit enough, in the lines just quoted. Thomson does the same, but not until 1730, in the first edition of **"Autumn."** Here occur more than a hundred lines on the glories of industry in the standard mode of eighteenth-century panegyric verse.[17] Thomson's patriotism betrayed him here, as it did often, into a discussion based on assumptions far different from those which underlay the earlier parts of **The Seasons.**

For now Thomson allies himself with the poets of his century whose concerns were entirely with the affairs of men, not at all with nature or metaphysics. Consider, for example, Richard Glover's poem, "London: Or, the Progress of Commerce." In it we find this glorification of personified Commerce:

> Thou, gracious Commerce, from his cheerless
>   caves
> In horrid rocks and solitary woods,
> The helpless wand'rer, man, forlorn and
>   wild,
> Didst charm to sweet society; didst cast
> The deep foundations, where the future
>   pride
> Of mightiest cities rose. . . .
>   last to crown
> Thy bounties, goddess, thy unrival'd toils
> For man, still urging thy inventive mind,
> Thou gavst him letters.[18]

Other gifts of Commerce listed by Glover include law, learning, wisdom, the revelation of nature's works, music, virtue, and poetry.

In Glover, whose title reveals his theme, this is the sort of thing we expect. But should we find the same sentiments in James Thomson, praiser of a Golden Age in which the original state of man was a beneficiary of the benevolence of nature? In the **"Autumn"** section on Industry (version A, ll. 43-157), the resemblance to Glover's ideas is startling—the sole difference is that Industry instead of Commerce is glorified. The passage has already been discussed in chapter iii, as an example of the weakness of certain parts of **The Seasons** in the final version of the poem. The praise of industry took exactly the same form, however, in the first edition of **"Autumn,"** insisting that the great achievement of man is the control of nature, not harmonious participation in the natural pattern, making clear Thomson's new attitude toward the position of man, and asserting serenely, in language much like Glover's, that

> All is the gift of Industry; whate'er
> Exalts, embellishes, and renders life
> Delightful.
>
>   (**"Autumn"** A, ll. 148-150)

Similar in implication and method is the long passage on sheepshearing and the glories of England derived therefrom added to the third edition of **"Summer"** ("Summer" C, ll. 371-431), which can hardly fail to recall Dr. Johnson's comment on Dyer's "Fleece": "The woolcomber and the poet appear to me such discordant natures, that an attempt to bring them together is to *couple the serpent with the fowl.*"[19]

The accomplishments of Peter the Great become an important theme in the 1744 **"Winter"** (E, ll. 950-987), in a section in praise of government, which lifts men from savage stupor. This follows immediately the lines on the woes and evils of the last of mankind who dwell beside the Oby; its sentiments are a logical consequence of condemnation of man in a state of nature.

But these lines occur in the same part of **The Seasons** as those praising the noble residents of Lapland. Primitive stoicism and love were there the criteria of virtue; navies and cities have now become the standards of accomplishment. And **"Autumn,"** which contains the lengthy section praising industry, has also the passage (version A, ll. 1131-1247; some of these lines were quoted earlier) fervently glorifying the rural life. In the former passage, cities are held up as the proud achievement of industry in contrast with the original brutish state of man. The glorification of the rural life, however, assumes that cities are "guilty" per se (**"Autumn"** A, l. 1245); the picture of city life in the third edition of **"Winter"** (ll. 528-542) suggests that cities are primarily the haunts of vanity and vice, to be contrasted with the sincerity of simple villages and their pleasures (ll. 515-527). The merchant's achievements, the ships that sail the oceans and assure Britain's dominion of the seas, are praised when industry is praised. But toward the end of **"Autumn"** (A, ll. 1174-1179) Thomson places those who brave the flood in the same class as those who exult in the widow's wail and the virgin's shriek when cities are sacked.

The inconsistencies in Thomson's attitude toward progress and civilization, then, correspond exactly to the inconsistencies in his attitude toward the state of natural man. They are, of course, connected with his difficulty in deciding whether primitivism or the idea of progress appealed to him more. R. D. Havens, recognizing this dichotomy in Thomson's thought, suggests that it "sprang from a cleavage in his life" which "led to one in his work, in his taste, and in his sense of values."[20] The cleavage in the poet's life, Havens feels, was between his boyhood love of nature and the country and his more mature conviction of the glories of progress, trade, and patriotism, fostered by his association with the rich and powerful. The same conflict by which Havens attempts to account for the poet's wavering between adherence to primitivism and to progress might also help to explain his apparent difficulty in deciding whether he was really more interested in nature or in men.

It might be possible to reconcile glorification of cities or trade with denunciation of them, and Thomson probably went through thought processes intended to achieve such a reconciliation. He does not, however, indicate them to his reader. Thought has no apparent place in the catalogues of fine feelings into which the poet falls so easily. He seems to be led by the mood of the moment, and by a sense of the fitness of things dictated increasingly by consciousness of tradition rather than by his own perceptions. The model of the *Georgics,* of course, was enough to inspire such digressions as those on patriotism, and patriotism in the eighteenth century implied a conviction of progress. In the second edition of **"Winter,"** Thomson had given evidence of his devotion to Virgil and the *Georgics* by including in his preface his own translation of a passage from that poem. In the early years of *The Seasons,* the georgic inspiration seemed to mean mainly devotion to the wonders of nature and their implications. The lines Thomson chose to translate indicate the primary area of his youthful interest: they are concerned with the wonders of the universe, and an appeal to the muses to reveal these wonders to the poet. As the years went on, however, one suspects that the *Georgics* began more consistently to mean to Thomson what they meant to his contemporaries. Christopher Smart could give instructions on the growing of hops, John Philips on the production of cider; Thomson turned to the plow and the glories of industry, and became more and more the child of his century.

. . . . .

The course of Thomson's gradual shift in emphasis from nature to man, in short, was marked by the development of emotional and intellectual confusion. The revisions of *The Seasons* reflect, as we have seen, widely diverse and contradictory attitudes about the significance of nature to man: nature might influence man; man might influence nature; nature might be important simply in providing analogies, metaphors, poetic decoration. The revisions indicate the poet's wavering about various moral questions—the joy of trout fishing versus its cruelty, for example. And they suggest a complete ambiguity in his position about the relative virtue of natural and civilized man.

Such confusion in the poet made for weakness in the poetry. Although it is far too simple to say that Thomson was always good when writing about nature, always bad when writing about man, the fact remains that the general trend was for his poetry dominated by a unified view of nature to be superior . . .

Notes

[1] A. O. Lovejoy, "The Parallel of Deism and Classicism," *Modern Philology,* 29 (1931), 281-299.

[2] For an extreme statement of the theory that Shaftesbury was the primary influence on Thomson's philosophy, see C. A. Moore, "Shaftesbury and the Ethical Poets in England, 1700-1760," *PMLA,* 21 (1916), 264-325; and "The Return to Nature in English Poetry," *Studies in Philology,* 14 (1917), 243-291.

[3] Shaftesbury, *Characteristics,* "Advice to an Author," I, 125.

[4] Basil Willey, *The Eighteenth-Century Background* (London, 1949), p. 73.

[5] For a fuller discussion of Shaftesbury's views, see: J. M. Robertson's introduction to his edition of Shaftesbury (Shaftesbury, *Characteristics,* I, ix-xlv); Moore's article in *PMLA* (cited in n. 2, above); and Willey, *op. cit.,* chap. iv, "Natural Morality—Shaftesbury," pp. 57-75.

[6] James Harris, "Concord" (1751). Quoted in Moore's *PMLA* article (see n. 2, above), p. 295.

[7] See Douglas Grant, *James Thomson* (London, 1951), p. 103.

[8] David Mallet, *The Excursion,* Chalmers, XIV, 18. The preceding quotation from Mallet is from the same source.

[9] George G. Williams, "The Beginnings of Nature Poetry in the Eighteenth Century," *Studies in Philology,* 27, (1930), p. 596.

[10] *Ibid.,* p. 584.

[11] "The Argument," prefaced first to the version of "Spring" in the 1730 quarto.

[12] William Somerville, "The Chase," Chalmers, XI, 162.

[13] Lovejoy, *op.cit.* (in n. 1, above), pp. 288-290.

[14] John Langhorne, "The Happy Villager," Chalmers, XVI, 460-461.

[15] John Dyer, "The Fleece," Chalmers, XIII, 249.

[16] Robert Dodsley, "Agriculture," Chalmers, XV, 352.

[17] The passage occupies "Autumn" A, ll. 43-157. For a discussion of other practitioners in this genre see C. A. Moore, "Whig Panegyric Verse, 1700-1760," *PMLA,* 41 (1926), 362-401.

[18] Richard Glover, "London: Or, the Progress of Commerce," Chalmers, XVII, 19.

[19] Samuel Johnson, *Lives of the English Poets,* ed. G. B. Hill (Oxford, 1905), II, 387.

[20] R. D. Havens, "Primitivism and the Idea of Progress in Thomson," *Studies in Philology,* 29 (1932), p. 41.

Ralph Cohen (essay date 1962)

SOURCE: "Literary Criticism and Artistic Interpretation: Eighteenth-Century English Illustrations of *The Seasons,*" in *Reason and Imagination: Studies in the History of Ideas 1600-1800*, edited by J. A. Mazzeo, Columbia University Press, 1962, pp. 279-306.

[*In the following essay, Cohen uses illustrations for different editions of* The Seasons *as the basis for an argument about changing standards for interpretion. In the process, he suggests that Thomson's poem was broad enough to encompass the range of meanings captured by the illustrators.*]

Art historians have made clear that paintings not only can be, but need to be interpreted to be understood. Such works are assumed to be nonverbal communications, and they belong to a significant realm of human behaviour. Psychologists have pointed out that 'art both codifies and interprets. . . . Symbolic representation in art is more than merely a code; it also contains a comment, an interpretation, and a suggestion of how to understand its symbols.'[1] When illustrations or paintings are exemplifications of specific passages or parts of a poem, they are governed by principles of interpretation, and they constitute nonverbal criticisms. It is possible for an interpretation—whether verbal or non-

verbal—to be irrelevant to the poem, but such irrelevance is discoverable only upon analysis.

The fact that poetry or painting or sculpture could serve as interpretation or explanation of each other was recognized in the eighteenth century; Addison declared that 'poetry being in some respects an art of designing as well as painting or sculpture, they may serve as comments upon each other.'[2] Lord Roscommon had earlier noted that looking at painting and looking at drama involved common visual terms. Charles Lamotte wrote that art gives subjects to poetry as poetry gives subjects to art.[3] Joseph Spence in *Polymetis* used poetry to explain the iconography of ancient sculpture;[4] the development of the very word 'illustration' is an example of this interpretive function.

The original meaning of 'illustration' was 'explanation' or 'spiritual enlightenment.' Bullokar in 1676 defined 'to illustrate' as 'to make famous, or noble, to unfold or explain.' 'Illustration,' 'illustrious,' 'lustre' continued to be applied in 1713 by Henry Felton to spiritual illumination in literature or life. By the end of the eighteenth century, however, the term had come to be identified with engravings, and the meaning was extended to 'embellishment' as well as 'explanation.'[5] The reason for this was that illustrations or nonverbal explanations had become, as a result of increased production and lowering of artistic standards, merely decoration. Solomon Gessner wrote that the 'warmth of imagination, without which there can be no invention, is either enfeebled or totally lost,' by constantly engraving works of others.[6] The explanatory basis of illustration, therefore, tended to be minimized and its decorative function exploited; the defenders of book illustration at the beginning of the nineteenth century sought to win it status as an independent art or brought in 'explanation' as a subsidiary function. In 1824, for example, Richard Plowman defined 'illustration' as 'nothing more than the exemplification of works of literature by works of art,'[7] but he urged that it could also be an incentive to topographical and biographical (portrait) study as well as an incentive to interpretation by causing the reader to reflect on the words and the seen (scene).

Illustration plays an extremely important part in the criticism of *The Seasons* because for more than one hundred and fifty years it was the most illustrated poem in the English language. By examining the verbal criticism in the light of nonverbal criticism, the range of literary inquiry can be determined. For there were subjects, tones, insights which this inquiry could have undertaken, but neglected or resisted. And it is equally possible to specify the range of the illustrations. Literary criticism, for example, neglected the emotive unity of each season which William Kent illustrated in 1730, and did not develop explanations for it until John Aikin in 1777. Moreover the critics neglected until the nineteenth century the mythological and natural interrelations so that the processes of nature were not seen as recurrent forces which man had in all seasons to accept. Even Thomson's concern with diverse social and economic classes was neglected by critics until John Wilson stressed it in 1831.

The literary critics, however, recognized the independence of Thomson's nature descriptions, and in 1756 Joseph Warton even singled out a number of scenes for painting, but landscape illustrations in which the figures were insignificant began at the very end of the eighteenth century and only became characteristic in the mid-nineteenth century. Literary critics obviously dealt with a great many subjects, such as diction, imagery, comparisons between different works which illustrations could not depict, but even within the range of eighteenth-century illustration there was a frequent disregard for the moving passages such as the walk in *Spring* or the falling of the snow in *Winter*.

The resistance of literary critics to Thomson's burlesque passages—Lord Lyttelton removed the fox-hunt from the 1751 edition of Thomson's works—is revealed by their offence at such passages; illustrations, however, present caricature as an element of the poem. Wordsworth's comment (1815) that in 'any well-used copy of **the Seasons** the book generally opens of itself with the rhapsody on love, or with one of the stories (perhaps Damon and Musidora)'[8] reflected the prudish critical fears, whereas the tradition of the nude led artists to illustrate the passage, some even recognizing the ironic tone of the description.

If illustration can function as nonverbal criticism, it can also function as an independent work of art, but it cannot function as both simultaneously. Thomas Pennant praised Thomson as a naturalist and sprigs of flowers serve as end pieces in some editions. This function of decorative illustration began as early as 1730 in B. Picart's engravings of the statues of the seasons at Versailles, which had no relevance to Thomson's mythology. Illustrations sometimes show no actual knowledge of the poem, as Raymond Picart has remarked of Racine's eighteenth-century illustrators: 'engravers who think out for themselves the problem of illustrating, by re-reading the text they have to illustrate are very few.'[9] But most of Thomson's eighteenth-century illustrators did read the text, and William Kent, for example, revised his depiction of Musidora in the *Summer* illustration (1744) to accord with Thomson's revision of the Musidora passage.

Thomson's *Seasons* provided the text and perhaps even the incentive for many of Turner's and Constable's paintings. 'How I pity the unfeeling landscape painter, whom the sublime pictures of Tomson [*sic*] cannot inspire,' wrote Solomon Gessner.[10] But the inspiration of one art by another must not be confused with the interpretation of one art by another. This confusion of

function has steered discussions of two arts, especially in *The Seasons,* into blind alleys. Thomas Twining remarked in 1789 that Greek poetry 'had no Thomsons because, they had no Claudes'; Sir Harris Nicolas wrote in 1830 that 'his pictures of scenery and of rural life are the productions of a master, and render him the Claude of Poets,' and the 1855 editor of Thomson remarked that 'no other poet combined to an equal extent the glow of Claude and the gloom of Salvator.'[11] Such remarks are statements about the causes of poetry or the similarity (or identity) of subject matter or effects in two arts. Neither Elizabeth Manwaring nor any other critic has provided information demonstrating that Thomson was familiar with Claude or Rosa in 1730, the publication date of the first edition of the poem. Ralph Williams has argued that *Summer* (1727) included many more 'prospect' scenes than *Winter* (1726) because Thomson was close to the poet-painter John Dyer during this period. But *Spring,* published the following year (1728), indicates no continuity of this approach and underlines the unlikeliness of Williams's explanation.[12] Although 'nature' could serve poet and painter as subject, the examination of 'effects' requires, at the least, specific works which can be examined. Passages have been compared with paintings which Thomson may or may not have seen, and 'effects' derived from similarities in subject matter rather than from an analysis of artistic qualities. Such approaches overlook the fact that the poets themselves were aware of classical and renaissance traditions governing 'poetical pictures.' John Hughes, for example, traced descriptions of morning in poets from Homer to Otway, indicating the consistency of pictorial imagery:

> In some of these Poetical Pictures which I have here set before the Reader, the Heavens only are shewn, and the first Springing of Light there. In others the Earth is taken into the Prospect, with her Flowers wet with Dew, and her rising Vapours. And sometimes the Occupations of living Creatures, proper to the Season, are represented and afford a yet greater Diversity of amusing Images.[13]

What this essay does, therefore, to avoid the vagueness of such discussions, is to locate specific interrelations of the arts; these occur in the illustrations to specific passages in the poem and in the interpretation of these passages. The illustrations need to be 'read' with the text, and in this respect they partake of Hogarth's concept of narrative painting. Early eighteenth-century definitions of 'read' meant not only 'to read a book' (peruse) but (Bailey) 'to guess, divine or foretell,' and Johnson included 'to discover by character or marks; to learn by observation.' To consider illustrations as needing to be read is not inconsistent with these definitions, and the illustrations from 1730 to 1800 are governed by diverse reading premises.

The significance of illustrations for theory of criticism is irrefutable: they supported, supplemented, or contradicted verbal criticisms, but above all they tested the-ories of assumed relations between descriptive poetry and painting. This test concept was clearly and force-fully expressed in 1807:

> I have often thought that there is no better way to prove the defects or excellences of a poet, in respect to his descriptive powers or knowledge of nature, than by making a composition for a picture from the images which he raises, and from his own description of his characters and their actions. You by these means put him on trial; you will detect every deviation from nature; and when his performance is brought to this strict examination, it will sometimes happen, that what in words might seem like a true represen-tation of nature to the poet, to the painter may appear much like a false witness in the court of justice, and he will soon be convinced that the admired work is no more than an ingenious falsehood.[14]

One critical theory that was 'put on trial' by the illus-trations was that 'words . . . are but Pictures of the Thought.'[15] The illustrations constituted a refutation of this doctrine by making explicit that pictures always involved more than the words, or a selection of the words; that the same words created different pictures; that some words led not to specific pictures but to imaginative associations expressed in pictures. John Landseer, in 1807, even though he admitted that the arts could not always achieve similar effects, explained that an image such as 'the breezy call of incense-breath-ing morn' could be engraved—was indeed in the *Au-rora* of Count Goudt—but that those 'who have not enjoyed this early freshness, in a romantic country, cannot forcibly enjoy this print, because it operates—like all the higher efforts in art, by stimulating the imagination to more than is exhibited.'[16]

Illustrations also tested the critics' use of painting vocabulary by actual illustrations, supposedly exam-ples of this vocabulary. Robert Shiels wrote of Thom-son that 'the object he paints stands full before the eye, we admire it in all its lustre.'[17] But the English illustrations to *The Seasons* up to 1753 did not display close views of objects, so that the kind of 'painting' Shiels described was independent of the available ex-amples to the poem and prescriptive of other types. And in 1852 James R. Boyd pointed out that eigh-teenth-century literary critics tended to use 'picturesque' in contexts quite different from artists.[18]

Another kind of criticism directly tested by illustra-tions was the naming of passages that were excellent 'paintings.' Joseph Warton, for example, referred to a summer scene (11. 485-489) as 'worthy the pencil of Giocomo da Bassano, and so minutely delineated, that he might have worked from this sketch.'[19] The 'vari-ous groups' of herds and flocks had been included in Kent's design for summer and were a small part of the plenitude of the summer landscape, not a minutely

delineated painting. When in 1793 Thomas Stothard drew the 'group' as a single illustration, the illustrative concept had changed from a picture of the unity of the season to a fragmented detail of the emotive coherence of man and animal, as seen in the shape of the shep-herd and the sheep. The two designs revealed quite different interpretations despite the fact that they used the same scene as subject.

The very first illustration (1730) implied that poetic as well as artistic vision was selective and emotive, but although the art critic Jonathan Richardson recognized this, literary critics developed a theory of imagined use of reality only in the second half of the century. Kent's emotive or associative view of unity rather than the dramatic view described by some literary critics came to be taken for granted, although not as a result of his illustrations. Percival Stockdale, for example, wrote in 1793: 'To excite that eager and anxious curiosity, sus-pense and expectation, which it is incumbent on the writer of a novel or of a drama to raise, did not enter into the plan of the Seasons.'[20] By the last decade of the century, some literary criticism stressed the need for heightened selectivity or perspectives as a basis for criticizing the poem, and the illustrations which abound-ed in the presentation of a variety of specific scenes supported this view. They also attacked theories of literal accuracy, for each illustration served to refute the literalness of the poem.

In the pathetic of *The Seasons,* the illustrators of the 1790's supplemented criticism by interpreting benevo-lence and 'goodness' in terms of the human family; with regard to the sublime of *The Seasons*—what Robert Shiels had in 1753 called Thomson's finest quality—they presented sufficiently varied instances to question the concept for criticism. The illustrations seized upon certain characteristics of the poem, and these were reshuffled in importance, depending upon the interpretation. The choice among the total possibil-ities within the four seasons tended to be restricted, but even within these limits certain scenes—such as fishing (*Spring,* 11. 379-442), Musidora, Celadon and Amelia (*Summer,* 11. 1171-1222), the man dying in the snow (*Winter,* 11. 275-321), boys skating (*Winter,* 11. 760-771)—were frequently redone, whereas the lone-ly mariner (*Summer,* 11. 939-950), Stothard's bare winter scene, or the drowning sailor (*Summer,* 11. 992-1000) were undertaken only once in the eighteenth century. Such repetition not only served to clarify individual interpretations, but provided examples of the robust-ness, vigour and broad social range of *The Seasons* (in 'Haying,' *Summer,* 11. 352-360, and in 'Sheep-shear-ing,' *Summer,* 11. 394-411) deliberately rejected by literary critics for moral or social reasons.[21]

The illustrations, moreover, provided an iconography which suggested the interchangeability of certain im-ages and actions in the poem, such as the lonely wayfaring stranger (*Winter,* 11. 179-180) and the shepherd who himself becomes a lonely stranger in the storm (*Winter,* 11. 277-283). And especially in illustrations which were reworked and reinterpreted, such as the education of the young or the meeting of Palemon and Lavinia, it was possible to recognize the legitimate range of interpretation, that is, the provision of foreground, background, and expressive behaviour which the poet omitted and the illustrator required. The difference, therefore, between William Hamilton's parents teaching the young at the table (1797) and Henry Singleton's parents observing the children at their prayers, the books still lying open, specified an increased morality and sentimentality of interpretation.

The interpretative shifts from the Kent illustrations to those of the last two decades of the eighteenth century revealed, in the multiple scene illustrations, a considerable reduction in detail and scenes; unity became more representative and less encyclopædic. The variations of detail applied to one activity rather than a multiplicity of activities—ploughing and planting, for example, became representative of spring. The narrowed selection supported the verbal arguments of critics like Patrick Murdoch and James Beattie who sought to identify in the poem what the former called Thomson's 'distinguishing qualities of *mind* and *heart.*'[22] These illustrations sought to capture the characteristic elements of the seasons with reference to their expressiveness, whereas Kent sought the characteristic elements with reference to conventions of a genre.

Simultaneous with continued interpretations of unity were single scenes of representative moments. These scenes fragmented the poem far more than Kent's illustrations but, by their selection, they insisted that some passages were more typical than others. Single scenes rather than multiple scenes predominated, but within these there existed a diversity of interpretative comments far more related to current literary criticism than to the earlier comments of Thomson or his contemporaries.

There was an obvious increase in the number of scenes depicted so that the concept of 'typical' was called into question by the varied attempt to picture typicality. But despite the increase, the areas of the typical were limited to the sublime, the pathetic, and the picturesque. The high frequency of domestic scenes supported verbal statements by critics like John Aikin, Percival Stockdale, and James Beattie, who found Thomson's benevolence and piety throughout the poem. 'The rural character,' wrote Aikin, 'as delineated in his feelings, contains all the softness, purity and simplicity that are feigned of the golden age.'[23]

This view was not, however, unanimous among the illustrators. Thomas Stothard selected scenes depicting the gentleness and piety of man and nature, but Charles Ansell (*Spring,* 11. 690-694) and Charles Catton (the terrified sailor) and Richard Corbould (the lonely mariner, *Summer,* 11. *939-950*) selected highly expressive scenes of human nastiness, terror, and loneliness. These direct expressive statements sought to capture a view of nature different from that of Kent or Stothard. They sought the immense, uncontrollable processes of nature overcoming man, or the archetypal moments of human experience. The individual and the family, the contrasting views of isolation and sociability were seen resolved in the varied powers of nature, and such resolutions supplanted the contrasts of status fused in the great chain of being.

II

In 1730 two sets of engravings were published, one for the octavo edition and another for the quarto. The octavo edition, issued twice in 1730, contained engravings for each season (B. Picart, designer; J. Clark, engraver), based on 'marble statues in the Garden of Versailles 7 foot high.' There were also tailpieces which had no relation to the poem (*Summer* and *Autumn* both showed a knight on horseback slaying a dragon), but the headpiece to *Summer* showed one man assisting another in sowing, and *Autumn* displayed a man in an attitude of contemplation with a book in his hand, sitting near a tree, a scene that at the end of the century became a clue to the lonely poet.

In the quarto edition of 1730 were published the Kent-Tardieu engravings, containing a frontispiece for each season. The Picart-Clark illustrations were reprinted only once again, in 1735, but the Kent designs were twice reengraved for smaller editions by Pierre Fourdrinier during Thomson's lifetime, and by Neist, Ridge, Donaldson and others after his death. There exist no comments by Thomson on these engravings, but it appears likely that the continuation of this set and the discontinuance of Picart's was in itself an expression of preference, perhaps also a judgment. Moreover, Thomson's respect for Kent as a landscaper was written into *The Seasons* in his praise of Esher Park (*Summer,* 11. 1431-1432): 'Enchanting vale! beyond whate'er the Muse / Has of Achaia or Hesperia sung!'[24]

Jean Hagstrum has suggested that the Kent illustrations suffered from badly drawn allegorical figures, and Edgar Breitenbach has objected to the allegorical figures because they are 'hollow, worn-out metaphorical imagery.'[25] But it should be stated that there exist different criteria for the illustration as interpretation and the illustration as an independent work of art, for a 'bad' engraving may be a valuable commentary upon artistic tradition or the text.

The engravings to *The Seasons* were marked, from the very beginning, by conflicting allegorical and naturalistic tendencies. Just as the poem addressed 'gentle

Spring' and personified it (*Spring,* 1. 1), so, too, the illustrations in 1730 sought to convey this allegorical and naturalistic view of spring. In his designs Kent attempted to create a representative picture of the unity of each season, governed by the great chain of being leading in a series of inclined planes from natural to allegorical figures, and including earth, water, clouds, and animals, man and heavenly figures. However, the analogical unity suggested by the engravings was not that of the subject matter of each season, but the relation between the distant past and the immediate present—the movement from rural immediacy to the vague mountains in the background.

Margaret Jourdain has written that Kent's designs for *The Seasons* show Italian influences, and Bertrand Bronson has called the lower halves of the engravings 'faintly Claudian,'[26] but a comparison between Claude's *An Autumnal Evening* and Kent's *Autumn* reveals that only the use of trees as a framing device and the faint mountains in the background suggest a similarity, for the management of movement and the handling of planes are considerably different. Kent's designs were representations of types of unity in *The Seasons,* designed with a close knowledge of the particular poem, and they differed from the single-scene designs he created for *The Faerie Queene* and Gay's *Fables.* The artistic landscape tradition was absorbed and altered by the literary text.

Early illustrations for *The Seasons* show the concentration on unity rather than particularity of each season that Warton was to recommend in 1756. At least for the designer in 1730, the unity of the poem did not represent an issue, just as the letter to the London *Journal* in 1726 praised Thomson for the manner in which he connected reflections with descriptions.[27] Swift objected to the lack of unity of action in *The Seasons,* declaring (1732) that the seasons 'are all description, and nothing is doing; whereas Milton engages me in actions of the highest importance,'[28] but Kent's illustrations implied a unity of feeling and moral value.

The unity which Kent created involved a spatial view of the supernatural and natural worlds. The upper half of each design represented the personified allegorical introduction to the season, and the bottom half several naturalistic scenes from the poem. Each of the four plates was seen from a direct and central point of view from which the countryside ascended, either to the right or the left. In the central background each plate had a mountain, faintly drawn. The engraving moved to the background in a series of inclined planes, each of which grew fainter as one looked out on the mountain. Clouds separated these planes from the allegorical figures which presided over the entire scene.

Since each season included men, women, animals, and supernatural beings, Kent was able to convey a rela-

tion between the orders of nature, beast, man, and the heavens that Thomson himself accepted. In *Spring* (11. 860-866) Thomson wrote:

> The informing Author in his works appears:
> Chief, lovely Spring, in thee and thy soft
>   scenes
> The smiling God is seen—while water, earth,
> And air attest his bounty, which exalts
> The brute-creation to this finer thought
> And annual melts their undesigning hearts
> Profusely thus in tenderness and joy.

This attempt to convey in design the relation between heaven and earth which Thomson's *Spring* included, involved, for Kent, a careful selection of scenes. The whole top half of the design was devoted to the first allegorical lines of the poem, and those dealing with surly winter and the 'bright bull' of the zodiac, although these passages occupied a very small part of the season.

> Come, gentle Spring, etherial mildness, come,
> And from the bosom of yon dropping cloud,
> While music wakes around, veiled in a shower
> Of shadowing roses, on our plains descend.
>   (11. 1-4)

In addition to the area occupied, it was connected to the earth by the rainbow, a description indicated in the poem (lines 203-212). As for the naturalistic scenes, the engraving included the poet as a swain playing to the Countess of Hertford (11. 5-10), the shepherd pointing to the rainbow (11. 212-217), the ducks and swans in the pond (11. 776-782), the cooing dove in amorous chase (11. 786-788), the shepherd on the mountain brow with his sportive lambs (11. 832-838), a hall (the home of one of the lovers?), a lover and his beloved (11. 962-979). Kent omitted all scenes involving violence or sorrow—the robbing of the nightingale's nest, the violent love-making of the bulls (11. 792-808), the lover's dream of death (11. 1052-1073); what he included were specific scenes representing the benevolent variety of the universe.

The interpretation, therefore, was not based upon mere subject matter, because the order and manner of treatment were different. It conveyed the activity of the allegorical figures who were in motion, and while the heavens were moving and acting the natural universe received their benefits. In visual terms Kent interpreted Thomson's argument to *Spring:* 'This Season is described as it affects the various parts of Nature, ascending from the lower to the higher; and mixed with digressions arising from the Subject.'[29] Spring and her train were sportively in motion, matched only by the earthly gambolling lambs. Thus the significance of the introduction to spring was the expression of those forces attributed to God:

But chief
Chief, lovely Spring, in thee and in thy soft
  scenes,
The smiling God is seen.

The function of the rainbow, too, was central to this interpretation of spring as a smiling season; the beauty of the heavens was reflected in the pond, and, like a smile, it was engaging and ephemeral. Thomson had the boy chasing the rainbow in the field, and it was an example of Kent's presentation of heavenly effects to create heaven's reflection in the pond. Not only did Kent analogize the relation between heaven and man, but he also created a structural relation between earth and the heavens. When, in 1744, Thomson added a poetic prospect from Hagley Hall, it was a possibility that the poetic passage was placed next to the lovers in the text not only because of the ideal love of Lyttelton and his wife, but also because of the 'hall' that already existed in the illustration (despite the fact that it was not a prospect view). For Thomson's description summarized the dusky landscape and the mountains 'like far clouds.'

> your eye excursive roams—
> Wide-stretching from the Hall, in whose kind
>   haunt
> The hospitable Genius lingers still,
> To where the broken landscape, by degrees
> Ascending, roughens into rigid hills
> O'er which the Cambrian mountains, like far
>   clouds
> That skirt the blue horizon, dusky rise.
> (***Spring,*** 11. 956-962)

The mountains, compared to 'far clouds,' were marked by the arc-like quality of the clouds supporting and surrounding spring. Thus the rising hills were the earthly counterparts of the beclouded heaven; by establishing a relation between foreground and background (mountains) which was analogous to that between earth and heaven (top and bottom of the design) Kent created a visual unity between the hill and dales, reflective of that benevolence to be found in the allegorical heavens.

The use of inclined planes conveyed a series of incidents in the poem. But, despite the fact that Shaftesbury and later Lessing argued that a painting revealed instantaneous time, it was not possible to see all the incidents simultaneously. Moreover, the diverse scenes implied a succession of some type, whether circular or random, all appropriate to spring, and in that sense implied a period—a season—of time rather than simultaneous occurrences. Kent's illustration could be properly understood only if read within the context of specific passages. Perception was not a matter of mere instantaneous response; Dryden earlier had noted this, despite the assumption that the action, passions, and manners in a picture were theoretically to be discerned

'in the twinkling of an eye.' For, as he remarked in the discussion of Poussin's painting of 'the *Institution of the Blessed Sacrament,*' there was 'but one indivisible point of time observed; but one action performed by so many persons, in one room, and at the same table; yet the eye cannot comprehend at once the whole object, nor the mind follow it so fast; 'tis considered at leisure and seen by intervals.'[30]

The variety of incident in the poem, involving shifts in place and time, was incorporated in the engraving through artistic concepts of place and time. By the use of heavy and light shading, the mountain in the distance appeared faint and the immediate foreground very dark. But the relation between them was such that the different actions—the swain playing to the lady and the faint shepherd on the brow of the mountain—which had been seen precisely and closely in the poem were seen at receding distances in the engraving. Yet, although the shepherd grew fainter, he also grew closer to heaven. And the manner in which simultaneous and similar actions in the foreground and on the mountain could be both vivid and faint gave to the illustration a meaning independent of distance.

The poem and the illustration expressed common views of nature and man, Kent's interpretation of the poem being the smiling reflection on earth of the heavenly benevolence in **Spring,** of the astonishing power and ferocity of nature in **Winter**. This was, of course, a highly selective view of Thomson's **Spring,** but it was one view that Thomson developed. There were, too, other methods by which Kent interpreted the poem: he developed a series of correspondences between physical shapes on earth and heaven, just as Thomson compared the Cambrian mountains to 'far clouds'—

> To where the broken landscape, by degrees
> Ascending, roughens into rigid hills
> O'er which the Cambrian mountains, like far
>   clouds
> That skirt the blue horizon, dusky rise.
> (***Spring,*** 11. 959-962)

—and the mountains of snow to 'an atmosphere of clouds':

> And icy mountains high on mountains piled
> Seem to the shivering sailor from afar
> Shapeless and white, an atmosphere of clouds.
> (***Winter,*** 11. 906-908)

Kent used particular scenes from the poem in his design, but the significance of these incidents was not identical with that in the poem. Neither the order nor the emphasis was the same. He used the introduction to **Spring,** the rainbow, the passion of the groves, and others, but the subjects and their role in the poem became materials to be converted into a different kind of entity in the engraving. The incidents served to establish an identification for the illustration, but the basis for the comparison was in the attitude which the artist had toward his materials, the manner in which he joined the incidents together. Thus, the introduction to *Spring,* which functioned in the poem as a formal device to create aesthetic distance, became in the illustration the central allegorical force presiding over all the events and, because of its role in the design, formed a basis for correspondence between the heavens and earth. The framing or formal device was accomplished by the marginal trees within which the whole scene was viewed.

Kent's illustration supported the proposition voiced by Addison and others that in the arts the same effects could be achieved by different means. But the second interpretative implication was that 'unity' involved selective elements and that 'wholeness' in the poem was not synonymous with wholeness of interpretation. The illustration depended upon a variety of detail both of incident and nature, so that the lambs in the foreground and on the mountain's brow, the shepherd piping to his lady and the man making love to the woman, the classical structure and the cluster of farm houses, served to convey the contrasting views of simplicity and refinement. But the illustration lacked the sensuousness, the awareness of natural processes characteristic of Thomson's description, for example, of spring flowers:

> And in yon mingled wilderness of flowers,
> Fair-handed Spring unbosoms every grace—
> Throws out the snow-drop and the crocus first,
> The daisy, primrose, violet darkly blue,
> And polyanthus of unnumbered dyes.
>
> (11. 528-532)

III

For approximately fifty years (1730-80) the illustrations which dominated *The Seasons* were those by William Kent. These illustrations or reengravings of them appeared in English editions of 1736, 1738, 1744, 1746, 1750, 1752, 1756, 1757, 1758, 1761, 1762, 1763, 1764, 1766, 1767, 1768, 1773, 1774, 1778, 1782. In the 1770's, however, there appeared two sets of illustrations—those by George Wright engraved by E. Malpas, (1770?) and those by David Allan, and William Hamilton engraved by [James?] Caldwell, 1778—which, while continuing some aspects of Kent's work, moved in different directions. It was not, however, until 1793, when reworkings of the Kent plates were reprinted for the last time—Daniel Dodd, designer, Thomas Cook, engraver—that Kent's direct influence disappeared from illustrations of *The Seasons.* In 1770 George Wright, while still presenting several scenes from the poem in a single plate, was nevertheless intent upon a purely naturalistic unity, and the 1778 Hamilton-Caldwell illustrations separated the allegorical sculptures for each season from plates presenting single, naturalistic scenes from the poem. Both sets of illustrations, however, were at one in moralizing the poem by eliminating or isolating the classical personifications. The poem was studded with reworkings of the *Georgics,* and Kent's illustration had conveyed the relation between classical and Christian concepts by means of artistic conventions. But Wright's and subsequent illustrations began to disengage the classical from the Christian view.

Wright's designs, inept as they were, had significance because they were the first which completely naturalized the poem, creating a complete separation between rural and other natural environments that was unsupported by Thomson's own words.

The notes Wright appended to the illustrated edition are directed to a new audience, and they mark the beginning of his self-imposed task of moral anthologist. In 1782, his anthology *Dear Variety, Suited to all Ages and Conditions of Life* contained the following advertisement: 'The ensuing compilation may be justly stiled *Variety,* as it consists of a *Variety* of extracts from *various* authors, upon *various* subjects; a *variety* of sentiments from *various* publications, collected at *various* times, and will doubtless be perused by *various* readers.'[31] And in *Gentleman's Miscellany* (1797) he quoted in the preface a *Monthly* Reviewer of 1788 on a previous collection, *Pleasing Reflections on Life and Manners:* 'Miscellaneous collections of this kind are become very numerous; but as they generally consist of *moral* pieces, they are, to say the least of them, innocent as well as entertaining. The multiplication, therefore, of such compliments, is of no disservice to society.[32]

Wright's illustrations, therefore, were directed to the same class which purchased the anthologies, and his badly designed frontpiece was based on the poet who retreated into the 'midwood shade.'

> Hence let me haste into the mid-wood shade,
> Where scarce a sunbeam wanders through the
>   gloom,
> And on the dark-green grass, beside the brink
> Of haunted stream, that by the roots of oak
> Rolls o'er the rocky channel, lie at large
> And sing the glories of the circling year.
>
> (*Summer,* 11. 9-14)

The subject he chose to illustrate was one which, after 1790, became a commonplace in Thomson illustration: the isolated poet. The poet was aware of the conflicts between critics and creators and of his own increasing isolation; Wordsworth even pointed out the need for the poet to create his own audience. But the literary critics of *The Seasons* did not consider the wandering poet-narrator a significant figure in the work, except as he framed the point of view; however, in the illustrations of Stothard, Cranner, or Roberts, he possessed the contemplative, dreamy qualities which were to become characteristic traits.

In criticism the disengagement of classical personification from moralized nature was argued by John Aikin (1778), who identified the unity of the poem with the seasonal laws of natural science and rejected the urban passages. Aikin sought not only to limit the poem to naturalistic subjects, with religious digressions, but he was the first to declare that the poem was the beginning of a new genre—description.

The David Allan-William Hamilton illustrations to the very edition for which Aikin wrote his 'Essay on the Plan and Character of Thomson's *Seasons*' still contained pseudo-classical allegorical figures representing each of the seasons. Thus the illustrations presented two views of the poem, one of which insisted upon the applicability of the classical heritage as represented in sculpture. Not only did these illustrations (reprinted 1779, 1792, 1796) continue a double focus on the poem, but the removal of the allegorical figures to the title page as vignettes or ornaments was further indication of the artistic reduction of their importance from the central place given them by Kent. In 1792 Charles Ansell designed and A. Birrell engraved a title-page which contained a globe surrounded in a circle by the signs of the zodiac, but the illustrations to the text were naturalistic. In 1794 Thomas Stothard engraved a title-page to *The Seasons* in which four allegorized female figures in a ring were tied to the lines from the *Hymn:*

> Mysterious round! What skill, what force divine,
> Deep felt, in these appear! a simple train,
> Yet so delightful mix'd with such kind art,
> Such beauty and beneficence combine,
>
> (11. 21-24)

The allegorized seasons had become four maidens, and the personifications in *The Seasons* who were masculine and feminine were supplanted by a naturalistic and prettified view. Even William Hamilton's attempt to recombine the allegorical and the naturalistic in 1797 failed. The headpiece to *Spring* was a combination of a single allegorical balloon-like figure of Spring floating on clouds with a garland of roses in the background of which appeared the sign of the zodiac and in the foreground two farming scenes: ploughing and planting. The naturalistic scenes were separate frames quite unrelated to allegorical spring. In the 1802 (also 1805) edition edited by the Reverend Mr. J. Evans, the allegorized female figures of the seasons were relegated to the ends of each season and placed as tailpieces, in emblematic poses, although Summer and Autumn were the same figures. And in the title piece to the 1818 edition from the Chiswick Press, engraved by Thomp-

son, the four seasons were naturalistic figures, walking with representative burdens, Spring being, as Thomson created her, the only woman among the seasons. But in addition to the reduction of importance of the allegorical figures, usually females, and their incorporation into the females of the naturalistic scenes, a similar process was apparent in the transfer of emblematic attributes from cherubs—as indicative of the seasons—to children. In the Ansell-Birrell (1792) illustrations, a cherub introduced each season, but the cherub was not clearly distinguishable from an infant, and in Hamilton's *Winter* the cherub had become a child skating.

According to Edgar Breitenbach, Kent's personifications of Spring and her train belong to a tradition of the late Middle Ages: 'The scheme of composition is astonishingly similar to the ones of the "planet children" representations in the fifteenth century, which likewise show, under the reign of the astral rules of providence, a survey of human occupations.[33] But whether 'planet children' or *putti,* Kent's figures were moved from an allegorical tradition to a more literal personification by Hamilton, and to naturalistic poses by Stothard and others. Of the roles of children, there existed three types: the child as representative of the season as a whole (Ansell-Birrell's *Winter*), the child within the family related to the past through adults, home, books—involving idealized relationships within the group (Hamilton's *Paternal Instruction*), and one example (Ansell-Birrell) of children as mean—nest-snatching.

The domestication of *The Seasons,* a process apparent in the illustrations of this decade, involved simultaneously its praise as a poem expressing sentiments and feelings. Regardless of the obvious attempt to sell editions by sentiment, the absence of nature as an entity, that is, without people, was especially notable. The engravings, by disengaging themselves from a single point of view, also left behind a significant artistic tradition: the allegorical imagery which had been part of a long tradition in painting.

The Kent illustrations contained no naturalistic children, not even the swain chasing the rainbow. But beginning in 1792, the illustrations for an entire decade celebrated and sentimentalized the role of the child. The passage from the poem on paternal instruction—*Spring,* 11. 1152-1156—was illustrated by Stothard (1794) as were the passages on sheep-shearing, skating, and story-telling (*Winter,* 11. 617-620). Thomson had in *Autumn* referred to the love of kindred among many values of rural life: 'The little strong embrace / Of prattling children, twin'd around his neck' (11. 1339-1344). But in the Cruikshank-Laurie illustrations, scenes from the poem which did not contain children suddenly accumulated them; thus the fisherman urged 'to thy sport repair' (*Spring,* 11. 396-442) brought his family, and instead of the lover (Stothard, 1793) gathering nuts for his beloved (*Autumn,* 11. 610-619), a child shook the tree and another held the basket. Children swam and children skated, and in the 1797 illustrations by Hamilton, five out of seventeen illustrations to the four seasons included children, a far greater proportion than the space devoted to them even in the last draft of the poem.

The domestication of *The Seasons* had its complementary development in literary criticism with John More's argument (1777) of the moral value of the poem and the attention to narratives and moralizing in Aikin's essay. Such comments were, however, beginning to be seriously questioned by the end of the century, though still repeated. John Aikin himself pointed out that in this respect Thomson was most easily imitated: 'excellent as the moral and sentimental part of his work must appear to every congenial mind, it is, perhaps, that in which he may the most easily be rivalled.'[34] 'Moral sentiment,' wrote John Scott (1785), quoting an 'ingenious critic,' 'is the cheapest product of the human mind.'[35] But another aspect of the importance of childhood in Thomsonian criticism was the Earl of Buchan's assumption—obviously dependent upon Rousseau—that Thomson's infancy and early years were spent in the 'pastoral country of Teviotdale in Scotland, which is full of the elements of natural beauty, wood, water, eminence and rock, with intermixture of rich and beautiful meadow,' and there a child will receive impressions most conducive to genius 'more readily than in towns or villages.'[36]

The frequent editions during this period—there were thirty-two publications, exclusive of American and foreign, from 1790 to 1799—indicated the widened appeal of *The Seasons*. There was a widened audience for the poem, to which the illustrations could cater, and both Thomas Campbell and Tennyson referred to *The Seasons* as the poem which early led them to look feelingly on nature. This view was clearly put by John Landseer (1807): 'Every artist that is worthy of his appellation, desires and endeavours by his works, that the average or general feeling of the Society to which those works address themselves, shall sympathize or accord with his own.'[37]

The social illustrations presented idealized views of the family, but in so far as these views were single scenes, they served as fragmentary insights which could be representative or particular but could not be indicative of the poem's diversity. Nevertheless this fragmentation by moving social behaviour—or its opposite—to the foreground, concentrated on expressiveness, acuteness of detail, and the contrast between sharpness of human form and the encompassing vagueness of nature.

Scenes of death in *Winter* were sometimes included with scenes of domestic bliss even in the same season. The illustrations conveyed the poem's unevenness of

attitude, though Stockdale and Beattie insisted on its benevolence or purity. A good example of this procedure was the 1793 edition, which contained the fishing scene populated with children uncreated by Thomson and an illustration of the terrified sailor. In the illustration, the very mouth of the fish can be seen caught on the hook, and in Catton's design of the terrified sailor the scene is pictured as though the spectator were directly in front of the open-eyed, open-mouthed mariner and his sinking ship. Thus a sense of immediacy was created by closeness, and expressiveness of the scene made possible direct sympathy from the viewer.

This view of expression provided an interpretation similar to that developed by Robert Heron in an essay on *The Seasons* in the same volume. Heron defined poetry as the operation of sentiments and images (in this order) on the imagination and feelings, and then proceeded to compare the imagery of *The Seasons* with that of other works.[38] Thomson's passage was as follows:

> A faint deceitful calm,
> A fluttering gale, the demon sends before,
> To tempt the spreading sail. Then down at
>   once,
> Precipitant, descends a mingled mass
> Of roaring winds and flame and rushing floods.
> In wild amazement fixed the sailor stands.
> Art is too slow: By rapid rate oppressed,
> His broad-winged vessel drinks the whelming
>   tide,
> Hid in the bosom of the black abyss.
>   (*Summer,* 11. 992-1000)

The passage described the contrast between the 'deceitful calm' and the precipitant onslaught of the waves, the manner in which the forces of nature suddenly surrounded and 'hid' the sinking ship. The insignificance of the sailor and his fright before the powers of nature is noted by the single line 'In wild amazement fix'd the sailor stands.' But the illustrator, Catton, made the expression of the sailor central, and he interpreted the passage as the terror of man in the face of the violent forces of nature. The sailor, standing with eyes popping, mouth open, jacket unbuttoned, legs set apart—in the position of terrified amazement, of immovable uncontrol—is surrounded by a cave of waves, a 'black abyss.' The open-mouthed man is about to be swallowed by the huge mouth of waves, one sailor having already been sucked from the vessel, others clutching supports of the sinking ship. Thus man and nature are seen as two forces, the expressiveness of man helplessly overcome by the dark surrounding power, the circular tide and hollow wave indicating continuous time as well as continuous action. The interpretation of the illustration, therefore, conveyed the poem's development of clashing forces, despite the fact that it did so by altering the action of conflict. The critic, however, who would have examined Thomson's imagery, would have discovered that the vessel was personified—'drinks the whelming tide, / Hid in the bosom of the black abyss' and would have discovered that the ship is seen in a suicidal image of comfort or love ('hid in the bosom of the black abyss').

The artistic interpretation was expressed through associations, and indeed, the centrality of the mariner was the result of a painting tradition. For this reason, the 'reading' of these illustrations demanded a language of gesture that was often associative rather than directly responsive to the poem. The 'reading' or 'interpretation' required for single scenes, containing frequently the pertinent passage at the foot of the illustration, was different from that applied to Kent's designs. The mariner involved a considerable alteration of emphasis as well as fact, for Thomson had made reference to 'the sailor,' not to a crew. Such changes of fact occurred in many illustrations: for example, G. Wright annotated 'steers' as 'oxen' (*Spring,* 11. 35-36) and then drew horses or donkeys as plough animals. But the difference between factual changes and interpretative changes was considerable. Expressive illustrations of the seventeen-nineties attempted to interpret not facts or literal statements, but the associative or emotive qualities of the poem. They sought to interpret language through gesture and feeling by direct proximity. The reduction of scenes, therefore, was an attempt to create immediacy rather than an artistic procedure which presupposed instantaneous response. And the amorphous shape of the background—as in William Hamilton's illustration of Caledon and Amelia—became the deliberately undefined nature in which man lived and died.

Thomson's use of nature as background can be studied in these illustrations with respect to a concept such as the 'sublime.' Illustrations of 'sublime' passages in *The Seasons* revealed that Thomson's 'sublime' language and his situations were used in diverse contexts. The poetic terms used by Thomson for the sublime included 'astonish,' 'astound,' 'admire,' 'daunt,' 'dreadful' ('dreadful motion'), 'howling' ('howling waste'), 'stiffened' ('stiffened corpse'), 'froze,' 'polished,' 'marbled.' The terms were related to death, to the final absence of mobility, to dread of death, to awe, moral and physical, though they could be used to suggest the pleasurable sublime in such a phrase as 'pleasing dread.'

The poem contained varied uses of the sublime: the cattle killed by lightning—'and stretched below / A lifeless group the blasted cattle lie' (*Summer,* 11. 452)—the sailor in 'wild amazement fixed' (*Summer,* 1. 997), the amazed swain who 'runs / To catch the falling glory' (*Spring,* 11. 214-215), the Eastern tyrants who know not love but only 'bosom-slaves, meanly possessed / Of a mere lifeless, violated form' (*Spring,* 11. 1133-1134). Caledon staring at the dead Amelia,

Pierced by severe amazement, hating life
Speechless, and fixed in all the death of woe.
So, faint resemblance! on the marble tomb,
The well-dissembled mourner stooping stands,
For ever silent and for ever sad.
                    (*Summer,* 11. 1218-1222)

The nude Musidora returning from her swim and discovering the note from Damon,

   With wild surprize,
As if to marble struck, devoid of sense,
A stupid moment motionless she stood.
                    (*Summer,* 11. 1344-1346)

The illustrations of the sailor, the swain, Caledon, and Musidora made clear that the conceptions of the sublime involved not only situations and places, but applied to good or bad situations, to serious or sentimental ones. Johnson's definition of 'amazement'—'astonishment or perplexity, caused by an unexpected object, whether good or bad—in the former case it is mixed with admiration, in the latter with fear'—summarized only some of the uses of the term in *The Seasons*. The critical value of illustrations of passages identified as 'sublime' was that they interpreted a variety of specific instances. These illustrations and John Scott's and Robert Heron's examination of specific passages were all the consequence of a view insisting on the critical descent to particulars. But the illustrations also drew attention to concepts assumed to be clear in one art, but not equally clear or traditional in another. Thus the illustrations supported the diversity of meaning of 'sublime' by indicating the variety of contextural characteristics.

The criticism implicit in the illustrations, governed by artistic traditions, were not identical with literary criticisms, even when both were interpretative. For it was self-evident that artistic interpretation, keyed to specific passages, dealt with the range of the poet, his attitude toward his material, his organization or unity, and his attitude to the audience. The Kent illustrations, for example, dealt with unity in a formalized rural or landscape view. But Stothard's illustrations (1793) domesticating the poem were directed at an audience with sentimental attitudes toward the family and nature. That *The Seasons* contained both these elements could be certified by an analysis of specific passages. The illustrations of Stothard and other designers who did individual scenes seemed to encourage interpreting *The Seasons* as a series of poems, what Robert Shiels in 1753 had called an 'assemblage of ideas.'[39] But the random quality of the illustrations seemed sufficient warranty against such procedure. Interpretation, in other words, had to be analysed with respect to specific concepts such as unity, the sublime, or the pathetic.

There were many critical areas to which illustrations were not relevant. Even within analysis they could not handle versification, and they could handle imagery only if language was assumed to be pictured. The tests of poetic value could be treated only if they were based on vividness, visual or imaged, and illustration could only eliminate such inadequate theories, not provide better ones. But the study of illustrations reveal that they implied solutions to literary problems (emotive unity) often before such unity was articulated, and that they pointed to a range of illustration which criticism often deliberately or for literary reasons ignored—like the nude and Thomson's burlesque. Such illustrations also demonstrated, in the last decade of the eighteenth century, that valuable interpretative practices often resulted from pressures external to the poem. In the 1790's twelve new sets of illustrations were published, exclusive of the reprints of earlier illustrations. (This flurry of interpretation continued for two more decades—seven from 1800 to 1810, five from 1810 to 1820.) Such variety of interpretation did not always do justice either to the art or the poem. But in themes of the isolated poet, or the lover's dream, the illustrations called attention to subjects completely ignored in the literary comments on the poem.

The illustrations in the eighteenth century conveyed the interpretative transitions from the hierarchical views of landscape to the expressive interrelation between man and nature. From the fusion of convention and diversity seen as inclined planes in a great chain, it moved to man as an object of nature surrounded and often engulfed by it. From illustrations of 'unified' views it moved to single fragments, representative either of 'wholes' or of significant actions. In moving from the significance of background as hierarchical to the foreground as detailed and particularized, it moved from a view of eternity governed by status to eternity as connected with past and future (nature or family). And it moved finally from an interrelation of personified nature and naturalistic activity to man's representative role, both of forces which surrounded him and those which shaped him. Only Charles Catton and Henry Fuseli among the illustrators at the turn of the century saw the forces of nature, as Thomson did, in process; among the critics, such insight had to wait for William Hazlitt.

Notes

[1] Jurgen Ruesch, *Nonverbal Communication* (Berkeley and Los Angeles, 1956), pp. 30-31.

[2] Joseph Addison, *Dialogues upon the Usefulness of Ancient Medals, in Works,* ed. by Thomas Tickell (London, 1804), V, 20-21; Robert Wolseley, 'Preface to Rochester's *Valentinian* (1685),' *Critical Essays of the Seventeenth Century,* ed. by J. E. Spingarn (Bloomington, Ind., 1957), III, 16-17; John Dryden, *Essays,* ed. by W. P. Ker (Oxford, 1900), II, 130-131; Richard Blackmore, *The Lay Monastery,* 31 (Jan. 25,

1713), quoted in Nathan Drake, *The Gleaner* (London, 1811), I, 33-35.

[3] Lord Roscommon, 'Notes to Horace of the Art of Poetry,' *Poems* (London, 1717), p. 278. For a discussion of the interpretative significance of stage setting, paintings, and book illustration upon Shakespeare criticism, see W. Moelywyn Merchant, *Shakespeare and the Artist* (London, Oxford, 1959). For an extensive review of classical and later writers who accepted this interchange, see Charles Lamotte, *An Essay upon Poetry and Painting* (Dublin, 1745), pp. 41-49.

[4] Joseph Spence, *Polymetis* (London, 1755), 2d ed., p. 291. See also, John Scott, *Critical Essays* (London, 1785), p. 205n, who proposed an interpretative illustration for 11. 49-52 of Gray's 'Elegy.' For study of interrelation of the arts in emblem literature see Henri Stegemeier, 'Problems of Emblem Literature,' *JEGP,* XLV (1946), 26-37; for bibliography see Robert J. Clements, 'Iconography on the Nature and Inspiration of Poetry in Renaissance Emblem Literature,' *PMLA,* LXX (1955), 781-804.

[5] [John Bullokar] *An English Expositour* (Cambridge, 1676). Henry Felton, *A Dissertation on Reading the Classics* (London, 1713), pp. 7, 225, 'lustre'; p. 7, 'illustrious'; pp. 95, 120, 'illustrations.' For a study of the term 'ornament' see Ruth Wallerstein, *Studies in Seventeenth-Century Poetry* (Wisconsin, 1950), pp. 13-15, and John Bray, *A History of English Critical Terms* (Boston, 1898), pp. 212-214.

[6] Solomon Gessner, 'Letter on Landscape Painting,' *New Idylles,* trans. by W. Hooper (London, 1776), p. 99; *Eighteenth-Century Book Illustration,* ed. by Philip Hofer (Los Angeles, 1956), p. iii.

[7] Richard Plowman, *An Essay on the Illustration of Books* (London, 1824), p. 9; William Gilpin, *An Essay on Prints* (1768; London, 1802), 5th ed., pp. 1-30; Carl P. Moritz, *Travels of Carl Phillipp Moritz in England in 1782* (reprint of English trans. of 1795), intro. by P. E. Matheson, (London, 1924), p. 9; 'Address,' *The Poetical Works of James Thomson* (London, C. Cooke, 1800), pp. v-vi.

[8] William Wordsworth, *Works* (London, 1909), p. 871.

[9] 'Racine and Chauveau,' *Journal of the Warburg and Courtauld Institutes,* XIV (1951), 260.

[10] Gessner, p. 102.

[11] Thomas Twining, *Aristotle's Treatise on Poetry* (London, 1789), p. 35; *The Poetical Works of James Thomson,* ed. by Sir Harris Nicolas, p. lxxxi; *The Poetical Works of Thomson, Goldsmith, and Gray* (London, 1855), p. xxvi.

[12] For discussions of poetry and painting in *The Seasons* see Elizabeth Manwaring, *Italian Landscape in Eighteenth Century England* (New York, 1925), pp. 100-108; Jean Hagstrum, *The Sister Arts* (Chicago, 1958), pp. 243-267; Alan D. McKillop, *The Background of Thomson's Seasons* (Minnesota, 1942), p. 71.

[13] *Poems on Several Occasions* (London, 1735), II, 334.

[14] *The Artist,* IX (May 9, 1807), 3-4.

[15] Abraham Cowley, 'To the Royal Society' (1667), 1. 69.

[16] *Lectures on the Art of Engraving* (London, 1807), p. 174.

[17] 'The Life of James Thomson,' in *The Lives of the Poets,* ed. by T. Cibber (London, 1753); V, 202.

[18] *The Seasons,* ed. by James R. Boyd (New York, 1852), p. 156.

[19] *An Essay on the Genius and Writings of Pope* (1756; London, 1782), I, 46.

[20] Quoted in Stockdale's own *Lectures on the Truly Eminent English Poets* (London, 1807), II, 114.

[21] See John Scott, *Critical Essays* (London, 1785), pp. 322-325.

[22] Patrick Murdoch, 'An Account of the Life and Writings of Mr. James Thomson,' in *The Works of James Thomson* (London, 1762), I, xix.

[23] 'An Essay on the Plan and Character of Thomson's Seasons' (1778), reprinted in *The Seasons* (London, 1802), p. lxii.

[24] *The Poetical Works of James Thomson,* ed. by J. Logie Robertson (London, 1951). All quotations from *The Seasons* are taken from this edition. The critical edition of *The Seasons,* including all revisions, is Otto Zippel, ed., *Thomson's Seasons, Palaestra,* LXVI (Berlin, 1908).

[25] Hagstrum, p. 263. Edgar Breitenbach, 'The Bibliography of Illustrated books,' *The Library Association Record* (May, 1935), II, 179.

[26] Jourdain, *The Work of William Kent* (London, 1948), p. 73; Bronson, *Printing as an Index of Taste in Eighteenth Century England* (New York, The New York Public Library, 1958), p. 35.

[27] London *Journal* (1726), as quoted in McKillop, p. 175.

[28] Jonathan Swift, Letter to Charles Wogan (August 2, 1732), in *The Correspondence of Jonathan Swift,* ed. by F. Elrington Ball (London, 1913), IV, 330.

[29] Thomson, 'Argument to Spring' (1728).

[30] Dryden, *Essays,* II, 132.

[31] George Wright, *Dear Variety,* 1782.

[32] George Wright, *Gentlemen's Miscellany,* 1797.

[33] Breitenbach, p. 197.

[34] John More, *Strictures Critical and Sentimental on Thomson's Seasons* (London, 1777), p. 166; Aikin, pp. lxii-lxiii.

[35] Scott, p. 143.

[36] Earl of Buchan (David Stuart), *Essays on the Life and Writings of Fletcher of Saltoun and the Poet Thomson* (London, 1792), p. 183.

[37] Landseer, p. 219.

[38] Robert Heron, 'A Critical Essay on the Seasons,' in *The Seasons* (Perth, 1793), p. 4.

[39] Shiels, p. 202.

Percy G. Adams (essay date 1977)

SOURCE: "James Thomson's Luxuriant Language," in *Graces of Harmony: Alliteration, Assonance, and Consonance in Eighteenth-Century British Poetry*, The University of Georgia Press, 1977, pp. 118-35.

[*In the essay reprinted below, Adams provides a detailed reading of the sounds in Thomson's blank verse. Looking at Thomson in the context of other Neoclassical poets, Adams concludes that Thomson strove for a "fitting of sound to sense."*]

Few poems have been so often reprinted or so often condemned and admired as James Thomson's **The Seasons,**[1] and one of the most controversial of that once popular poem's characteristics is its diction. Although Dr. Johnson admired Thomson, he spoke for a large group of readers, including Wordsworth and Hazlitt, when in *The Lives of the English Poets* he said of one aspect of Thomson's diction, it "is in the highest degree florid and luxuriant. . . . It is too exuberant and sometimes can be charged with filling the ear more than the mind."[2] But an even greater number of readers, if not always such honored ones, have liked Thomson's language, from John More's (1777) praise of the "luxuriant images," to Robert Bell's (1860) admiration for the "richness and luxuriance of phrase," to the twentieth century's scholarly defense.[3] In spite, however, of the perennially strong protest against Dr. Johnson's charges about the ear-filling qualities of Thomson's poetry, nowhere in the long and still lingering debate has anyone spoken of the nature of the sounds in that luxuriant language.

The neglect is all the more perplexing when we remember, first, that the poet himself insisted that he chose blank verse for *The Seasons* because it is "far more harmonious than rhyme" and, second, because he once listed "music" ahead of image, sentiment, and thought as one of the four chief characteristics of poetry.[4] Furthermore, it has been shown that repetition is perhaps "the most important structural principle" in *The Seasons*,[5] and repetition is perhaps the most important characteristic of music, whether by that term we mean pure music or the pleasing sounds that words can produce. Now Thomson made less use of rhyme, anaphora, and incremental repetition than did most other eighteenth-century poets, and his metrical stresses are not so regular as those in the heroic couplet, but he did employ alliteration, assonance, and consonance with as much variety and subtlety, as frequently and consciously, as any other important writer of his day. Nowhere in Ralph Cohen's thorough tracing of Thomson criticism, however, is any one of these three terms mentioned, and yet a study of Thomson's use of such acoustic devices will reveal much about the nature of his luxuriant language.

Like Dryden and Pope he went against conservative critical theory and employed phonic echoes in abundance. Their concentration in *The Seasons* is, in fact, far greater than for a relatively unornamental poet such as Wordsworth. The first 200 lines of *Winter,* for example, have at least 100 alliterations and 110 assonances, a proportion in each case of about one to two lines, while the opening 200 lines of Wordsworth's *Prelude* have, by a generous count, only 1 assonance to 5 lines and even fewer alliterations. The contrast becomes still more significant if one notes that over 20 of Thomson's echoes, and only 5 of Wordsworth's, are polysyllabic.[6] As with other poets of his day and just before, Thomson's auditory appeal is heaviest in the purple passages, especially those describing the sights and sounds of nature, and less heavy in narrative or argumentative sections. In this image from *Spring,* for example, there are perhaps 16 stressed syllables every one of which is involved in at least one echo:[7]

> Th'expansive Atmosphere is cramp'd with Cold;
> But full of Life, and vivifying Soul,
> Lifts the light Clouds sublime, and spreads
>   them thin.
>
> (28-30)

In the 3 lines there are 4 assonances—2 of 3 syllables, 1 of 4, and the end echo in "cold" and "soul"—to go

with the alliterations, two polysyllabic, of [f], [k], and [l] and the consonance of [l], [t], and [dz]. Although he does have sections with relatively few such echoes, as in the long account of the pleasures of evening reading in *Winter,* Thomson employed ornaments of sound as much as his chief models Lucretius, Virgil, Dryden, and Pope.

In order to show that these acoustic aids are typical of Thomson and at the same time more profuse than for poets with whom he is sometimes associated, we can compare a well-known passage in the poetry of John Keats with a similar one in *The Seasons*. Keats's lush *Autumn* opens,

> Season of mists and mellow fruitfulness,
>   Close bosom-friend of the maturing sun;
> Conspiring with him how to load and bless
>   With fruit the vines that roun[d] the thatch-
>   eaves run;
> To bend with apples the moss'd cottage trees,
>   And fill all fruit with ripeness to the core;
>   To swell the gourd, and plump the hazel
>   shells
> With a sweet kernel; to set budding more,
>   And still more, later flowers for the bees,
>   Until they think warm days will never cease,
>   For Summer has o'er-brimm[ed] their
>   clammy cells.

Thomson's *Autumn* has many such sensuous descriptions, including one so like that in the later poem:

> In chearful error, let us tread the maze
> Of Autumn, unconfin'd and taste, reviv'd,
> The breath of orchard big with bending fruit.
> Obedient to the breeze, and beating ray,
> From the deep-loaded bough a mellow shower,
> Incessant melts away. The juicy pear
> Lies, in a soft profusion, scatter'd round.
> A various sweetness swells the gentle race.
>
> (626-33)

The question now is not which of the two groups of images is more attractive, either lexically or acoustically, but, rather, which poet depended more on internal echoes for his effects, for his appeal to the reader's ear. Keats is to be considered a more decorative poet than, say, Wordsworth, and while this opening section of "To Autumn" is indeed ripe with language that appeals to the sight and the touch—*mists, mellow, core, moss'd, gourd, kernel, clammy*—it obviously has far fewer phonic echoes than the passage from Thomson. Of perhaps fifty-three stressed syllables in Keats's lines, only twenty-two are involved in any kind of internal alliteration, assonance, or consonance, and only three of them twice. On the other hand, of Thomson's thirty-eight stressed syllables, twenty-seven participate in such internal echoes, thirteen of them at least twice, a strikingly greater proportion. Nor is the proportion noticeably altered if one counts the end repetitions in both passages. The chief difference is not in the consonant echoes; Keats has at most five assonances, each of two syllables, while Thomson, in a shorter passage, has eleven—one of four syllables, one of three—that, in spite of the seven initial [b]'s in three lines, dominate his description.[8] Thomson's ornaments of language are indeed more luxuriant than those of Keats or Wordsworth or, for that matter, perhaps any important early nineteenth-century poet. Furthermore, we can now show that they were often conscious on his part, as conscious as they were with his friend Pope.

Because Thomson worked for twenty years at improving, altering, and expanding his major poem, we can study not only the growth of the poet's mind but also the development of his art and technique. Such a study is made easier by Otto Zippel's 1908 volume[9] containing all the many editions of *The Seasons* from the first appearance of *Winter* in 1726 to the final authorized version of the four *Seasons* in 1746, two years before Thomson's death. *Winter* alone was expanded to four times its original length.

There are many kinds of changes that the poem underwent, and Thomson had many reasons for making them.[10] He altered the structure: a short passage on Scotland and a description of the aurora borealis, for example, both in the first edition of *Summer,* he moved to the 1730 *Autumn,* which was further lengthened by the transference of almost 100 lines from *Winter.* He inserted narratives to make the whole more lively and dramatic, one of them being the tale of the cottager lost in a snow storm. Like Coleridge after him he read travel books in order to find more colorful and appropriate images, among them the northern ice formations described in Martens's *Voyage into Spitzbergen and Greenland* of 1711. He added primitivistic passages about the Laplanders and the English country life and a humanitarian appeal for improved conditions in English jails. And through the years he added to or altered his consonant and vowel repetitions, even though from the beginning he emphasized what he called the "music" of language. By comparing the various editions of *The Seasons* one can find many examples of Thomson's desire to fill the ear.

Very often the changes in sound accompany changes in imagery. In *Summer* when "bounteous Power" (1728.433) became "Parent-Power" (1744.540), the poet discarded a weak image for a better one and at the same time gave up an assonance for an alliteration. Nearby, the phrase "I stand aghast" (1728.455) was changed to "I check my steps" (1744.589). In modifying what he decided was an overly strong image, Thomson lost his assonance but was able to find another to take its place. One of the best improvements in the imagery of *Summer* has to do with

the description of a waterfall. In 1728 the short passage ended with "tormented" water falling

> From Steep to Steep, with wild, infracted C*o*urse,
> And, re*s*[t]less, r*o*aring to the humble Vale.
> (465-66)

By 1746 the image was extended to sharpen the contrast between the turbulent fall at the beginning and the quiet vale at the end:

> And falling *f*ast from gr*a*dual Sl*o*pe to Sl*o*pe,
> With wild infr*a*cted C*o*urse, and l*e*ssen'd R*o*ar,
> It g*a*ins a s*a*fer B*e*d, and steals, at l*a*st,
> Along the M*a*zes of the quiet V*a*le. (603-6)

But while Thomson was improving the image, he managed to add numerous ornaments of sound—the [f] and [l] alliterations, the three [a]'s, two more [o]'s, two [ɛ]'s, and two pairs of [e]'s—all in stressed syllables.

One of the most interesting alterations in *Summer* occurs in the tale of Damon, who in 1727 secretly watched three naked girls bathing in a cool stream. By 1744 the three girls had become only the beautiful Musidora, for whom the now gallant Damon left a note before turning his head and stealing away. The much longer account in the final version ends with four of the most echo-laden lines in *The Seasons,* those describing Musidora's feelings on finding the note:

> With w*i*ld Surpr*i*ze,
> As if to Marble str*u*ck, dev*o*id of Sense,
> A st*u*pid Moment motionless she st*oo*d:
> So st*a*nds the St*a*tue that ench*a*nts the World.
> (1336-39)

Although the five-syllable alliteration of the [st] phonestheme—carefully prepared for—stands out, Thomson also employed an [m] alliteration and three assonances involving at least eight vowels. One of the unique facts about this luxuriant language, however, is that in earlier editions the last line is found in an entirely different context (1730.1019). Thomson liked it so much that in 1744 he picked it up intact, moved it, made it fit the new story, and tied it to the other lines with the echo that stressed the girl's stunned inability to move.

That Thomson apparently worked hardest with assonance can be shown with certain examples from *Spring*. In 1728 he wrote,

> Wh*i*le in the rosy V*a*le
> Love breath'd his *I*nfant Sighs, from Anguish
>   fr*ee*,
> Fragrant with Bl*i*ss, and only wept for Joy.
> (276-78)

In 1730 he gave up *Fragrant* for *Replete,* thereby losing the [fr] alliteration but adding a third stressed [i]. Then in 1744 and 1746 the final version read,

> While in the rosy Va*le*
> Love breath'd his *I*nfant Sighs from Anguish f*ree,*
> And full repl*ete* with Bl*iss;* save the sw*eet*
> Pain. (276-78)

Thomson had brought back the [f] alliteration, added four other echoes, and ended with a four-syllable assonance of [i]. Elsewhere in *Spring* a phrase without any echo, "to deck the flowing Hair" (1728.447), was almost entirely rewritten to provide an assonance,

> to gr*a*ce thy br*ai*ded Hair. (1744.447)

In the 1728 *Summer* Thomson wrote,

> Of younder Gr*o*ve, of w*i*ldest, largest Gr*o*wth;
> That, h*i*gh embowering in the middle Air . . .
> (404-5)

These lines, already heavy with echoes, became in 1744,

> Of yonder Gr*o*ve, of w*i*ldest largest Gr*o*wth;
> That, f*o*rming h*i*gh in A*i*r a woodland qu*i*re . . .
> (517-18)

By moving "Air" back and changing other words in the second line, Thomson was able not only to make use of what Dryden had called the beauties of *r* but to run the vowel of *wildest* through three syllables. The same care for vowel echoes can be found in the texts of any *Season*.[11]

Sometimes, of course, Thomson was willing to part with a good sound in order to achieve a more important end, as he did once when he lost two assonances and a consonance in one line of *Winter* (1730.8) so he could borrow the word *ocean* from that line, move it to a nearby passage, and avoid repetition. But his revisions were much more liable to improve the echoes, or add entirely new ones. The 1744 *Summer,* for example, reworks a 1727 scene of unusual lurid darkness that slowly covers a grove of trees and then mantles the whole sky just before a crushing storm of hail descends. The earlier passage describes the cloud in four and one-half lines:

> *Thence Niter, Sulphur,* Vitriol, *on the Day*
> Stream, and *fermenting in yon baleful Cloud,*
> Extensive o'er the World, *a reddening Gloom!*
> In dreadful promptitude to spring, await
> The high Command. . . . (741-45)

The later description, which kept the words italicized in the passage just quoted, was expanded to these eight and one-half lines:

> Thence N*i*ter, Sulphur, and the f*ie*ry Sp*ume*
> Of fat Bit*umen,* stea*m*ing on the D*ay,*
> With v*a*rious-tinctur'd Tr*a*ins of l*a*tent Flame,
> Pollu*te* the Sky, and in yon b*a*leful Clou*d,*
> A re*d*dening Gloom, a Magazine of F*ate,*
> Fermen*t;* till, by the Touch etherial r*ou*s'd,
> The dash of Cl*o*uds, or *i*rritating Wa*r*
> Of fighting W*i*nds, while all is calm below,
> They furious spring. (1100-1108)

This final picture is no doubt far superior in both visual and tactual imagery—*Spume, Bitumen, tinctur'd, Pollute*—but it is infinitely more ear appealing. That ear appeal is, of course, the result of a variety of effects, but outstanding among them are the thick phonic repetitions. While in the original there are perhaps one effective consonance and three assonances, one polysyllabic, in the final version there are four excellent final consonant echoes—("Spu*me,*" "Bitumen," "Stea*m*ing"), ("la*t*ent," "Pollu*te*"; "Fa*te,*" "Fermen*t*"), and ("*i*rritating Wa*r*"); there are seven alliterations, and there are five vowel echoes, including the five [e]'s in six successive stressed syllables beginning with "Day." It is one of Thomson's most attractive passages and was possible only because through the years he concentrated so hard on improving his work and, perhaps as much as anything else, on increasing its acoustic appeal.

It is now known that Lord Lyttelton gave Thomson some small help in improving *The Seasons,* and it was long thought that Pope's handwriting could be found in the margins of Thomson's manuscripts. But while by the middle of the nineteenth century Thomson was shown to have been independent of Pope's direct help,[12] there is no doubt that Pope's influence was exerted indirectly on his friend's major poem. The 1744 *Seasons* has more changes than can be found in any other edition; some of them echo lines written by Pope, who died that year. And the similar passages are among the most ear appealing by two of the most ear-conscious poets who wrote in English. Just as in *Windsor Forest* Pope paraphrased more than one line from Denham's *Cooper's Hill* or borrowed Dryden's "well-breath'd Beagles," Thomson was willing to take phrases from *Windsor Forest.* In 1713 Pope had rewritten an old line of the manuscript version of that poem and ended with

> Nor P*o* so swells the f*a*bling P*o*et's Lays. (227)

In 1746, also completely reworking an old line, Thomson wrote,

> The f*a*bling P*o*ets took their g*o*lden *A*ge.
> (*Spring* 325)

Not only did he borrow Pope's "fabling Poets"; he managed to work in the same [e] and [o] assonances.

Even better as an example of sound similarity in the two poets is Thomson's mind- and ear-filling description of shooting stars in *Winter* (127-28):

> The Stars obtuse em*it* a sh*i*vering Ray;
> Or frequent *seem* to sh*oot* athwar*t* the Gl*oom*.

The second of these lines is remarkably like one from Pope's *Rape of the Lock* (2.82);

> Purs*ue* the St*ars* that sh*oot* athw*art* the
> Nigh*t*.

In each of the two lines every stressed syllable starts or continues an echo of at least one phone. Pope has two assonances and one three-syllable consonance of [t] to reproduce the shooting. Thomson also has two assonances, and while he toned down the shooting by omitting one final [t], he emphasized the image of winter gloom by echoing the vowel of that word and, especially, by adding the consonance of [m].

Although Thomson seems to have learned something about sound effects from his friend Pope, there is one chief difference between the way echoes are employed in *The Seasons* and the way they are employed in Pope's poems: Thomson was less able to emphasize rhetorical or structural balance by balancing sounds. The difference, of course, stems primarily from the fact that Thomson's run-on blank verse—without the rhyme, without such a regular cadence, without any rule regarding the caesura—did not lend itself to such neat cognitive effects as did the Popeian couplet, and even his rhyming Spenserian stanzas in *The Castle of Indolence* have relatively few of them. He was, nevertheless, too much a product of the eighteenth century to avoid structural balance completely, and when he did employ it he was as prone as Dryden and Pope to let sounds emphasize the balance. About two-thirds of the lines in *The Seasons* are end-stopped and can, therefore, more easily fit the patterns developed by the couplet. In *Autumn,* for example, Thomson wrote,

> Presents the dow*n*y peach; the shi*n*ing plumb,
>   (664)

> The tankards *f*oam; and the strong table g*r*oans.
>   (499)

In one line the parallel adjectives consonate while their nouns alliterate; in the other, the parallel subjects alliterate and their verbs assonate. Also in *Autumn* the parallel verbs alone can alliterate:

> Sudden, the ditches swell; the meadows swim,
>   (333)

> To swim along, and swell the mazy dance;
>   (586)

or they can assonate:

> To j*oy* at anguish, and del*igh*t in blood, (396)

> To r*ai*se the Virtues, anim*a*te the Bliss. (596)

Perhaps Thomson's best balanced consonance is in a zeugma found in *The Castle of Indolence,*

> Sere*n*e yet war*m*, huma*n*e yet fir*m* his mind,
>   (1.65)

where the primary adjectives end in [n] and the secondary adjectives in [m].[13]

The caesural sound balance favored so much by writers of the heroic couplet is found surprisingly often in Thomson's blank verse. Here two lines in a row in *Winter* emphasize the medial caesura, one with assonance, the other with assonance and alliteration:

> Frosty, succ*ee*d; and thro' the bl*ue* Ser*e*ne,
> For S*igh*t too *f*ine, th'etherial N*i*ter *fl*ies.
>   (693-94)

Close by, the first of two lines has a caesural consonance of [l] while the second has a double assonance in a chiasmus that Pope or Dryden might have written:

> Where sits the Sou*l*, intense, co*ll*ected, coo*l*,[14]
> Br*igh*t as the Sk*ies*, and as the S*ea*son K*ee*n.
>   (702-3)

Although anaphora was even more a favourite rhetorical weapon with eighteenth-century poets than with their successors—except perhaps Walt Whitman—many of them[15] were aware that the device could be made more subtle by reducing the number of repeated words and combining them with consonant or vowel echoes. Here Thomson contrived a kind of anaphoric alliteration:

> How dead the Vegetable Kingdom lies!
> How dumb the tuneful! (*Winter* 1027-28)

And in *Winter* he can be discovered creating an assonance that has something of the effect of anaphora. In 1726 he wrote,

> To lay their Passions in a gentle Calm,
> And woo lone Qu*i*et, in her s*i*lent Walks,
>   (38-39)

which in 1730 was transferred to *Autumn* thus:

> To s*oo*th the throbbing Passions into Peace
> And w*oo* lone Qu*i*et in her s*i*lent Walks.
>   (908-9)

His final version had retained the sounding second line entire, but the first line added not only the [p] alliteration but the word *soothe* so that the two initial stressed syllables would have the same vowel.

Since there are a number of run-on lines in **The Seasons,** Thomson did not in that poem so often as Pope or Dryden emphasize line endings with a vowel or consonant repetition in the final stressed syllables, even though his blank verse will be found to have more such terminal echoes than any blank verse written outside the eighteenth century. Three times in **Winter,** for example, there are successive terminal alliterations, among them "bitter Bread," "wintry Winds" (335-36); and three times there are successive terminal assonances, among them "double Sons," "brightest Skies" (591-92). The end rhymes of **The Castle of Indolence** attract far more phonic repetitions at the ends of lines, perhaps as many as are to be found in the heroic couplet. There are seven of them, in fact, in two stanzas of that poem (1.72, 77).

Blank verse may not be so suitable for sound parallelism as the heroic couplet, but Thomson's blank verse was eminently suited for other kinds of emphasis and for the fitting of sound to sense. Just as much as any poet from Chaucer to Pope, for example, he tied adjective to noun with a vowel or consonant echo. Often one can catch him in the act of altering a word in order to achieve this kind of binding. In 1728 he wrote "homely Fowls"; in 1744 he wrote "household fowls." In the same way "hilly Wave" became "inflated Wave," and "employless Greyhound" was changed to "vacant Greyhound." "Mighty Pride" already had the assonance, but Thomson improved the image by exchanging *Mighty* for *Tyrant* even though he carefully kept the vowel echo.[16]

Because of the nature of its content Thomson's blank verse may have more attempts at extended onomatopoeia than Pope's heroic couplets, as many perhaps as Dryden's *Georgics.* In an early Lucretian attack on luxury, he wrote,

> A Season's Glitter! In soft-circling Robes.
>   (**Summer** 1727.300)

Then seeing an opportunity not only to add a more scathing image but to tie sound to sense by means of phonic echoes, in particular a consonance, he revised the line to read,

> A Season's Glitter! Thus they flutter on.
>   (1744.348)

In "shiver every feather" he repeated the final [v] of the onomatopoeic *shiver.* With a nearby word *restless* he echoed in Popeian fashion the initial [r], the final [s] phonesthemes, even the initial weak [l], of the even

more onomatopoeic *rustling,* and he extended the sound of the same word by placing it close to *incessant.*[17]

One of Thomson's great teachers in the poetry of nature and reflection was Lucretius. But the author of *De Rerum Natura* was also a master of the sense-echoing phrase,[18] attempting to convey with language the crackling of fire, the running of water, the movements of humans and animals. And he tried musical instruments in such lines as "tympana tenta tonant palmis et cymbala circum" (2.618). Although Thomson had no occasion to give us the instruments of an orchestra, he often hoped to suggest the sounds of nature. With the phonesthemes [s] and [l] and the diphthong [aU], he believed he was capturing the owl's sad sound:

> Assiduous, in his Bower, the wailing Owl
> Plies his sad Song. (**Winter** 142-43)

With the same [l] and [s] to go with other appropriate sounds—some of them phonesthemes—final [d], [n], and [nd], initial [w] and [st], he tried the equally sad wail of the nightingale, at the same time making the passage more acoustically attractive with at least five assonances in five lines:

>   she sings
> Her Sorrows thro' the Night; and, on the Bough
> Sad-sitting, still at every dying Fall
> Takes up again her lamentable Strain
> Of winding Woe, till wide around the Wood[s]
> Sigh at her Song, and with her Wail resound.
>   (**Spring** 720-25)

The consonants [l] and [n], as well as [s], are favorites for imitating in language the softer sights and sounds of nature. In *Spring* when

>   the Lily drinks
> The latent Rill, scarce oozing thro' the Grass,
> Of Growth luxuriant, (495-97)

Thomson not only repeated the vowel of the sound-sense *ooze;* he alliterated and consonated the [l]'s of *Lily,* echoed the [s] of *grass,* and provided three [I]'s, one of the front vowels Dryden also liked for such scenes. And as with Dryden, another front vowel, [i], was a favorite with Thomson if his nature scene was more or less calm. In *Spring,* for example, he made a plea for walking

> Where the Breeze blows from yon extended
> Field
> Of blossom'd Beans, (502-3)

and in an *Autumn* paean to his friend Dodington's country seat, the poet ran nine stressed front vowels—all close to [i]—through four lines, beginning the passage thus,

In this glad season, while his last, best beams
The sun sheds equal o'er the meeken'd day,
                                          (641ff.)

and in 1744 adding another such vowel to the first line in this fashion,

In this glad Season, while his sweetest
    beams, . . . (654)

The same vowel, combined with a medley of other phonic recurrences, was—again with Thomson as well as with other poets—apparently best for sleepy scenes, as in this primitivistic account of a happy, carefree, but lazy, awakening in an early spring:

The first fresh Dawn then wak'd the
    gladden'd Race
Of uncorrupted Men, nor blush'd to see
The Sluggard sleep beneath her sacred
    Beam.

                              (*Spring* 242-44)

Although Thomson was less idealistic about the backward Eskimos described by travelers, he was even more onomatopoeic with their cold, lifeless sleeping, his seven-word image, with five heavy syllables, thick and slow with [s] and [z] consonance and two assonances:

Immers'd in Furs,
Doze the gross Race. (*Winter* 943-44)

Just as yellow was perhaps Thomson's favorite color, light was one of his favorite images, and following a well-established tradition he was liable to let the sound of [əI, aI] control such images. In *Summer* the sun suffuses the "lively Diamond" with "Collected Light" (142-43), and unheeding men "pass / An idle Summer-Life in Fortune's Shine" till time comes "Behind, and strikes them from the Book of Life" (346-47, 351). Thomson's other works make constant use of this phonestheme, for example, **"A Poem Sacred to the Memory of Sir Isaac Newton,"** which recounts the great scientist's many interests in the physical world, including his experiments with light and the refracting of light. Here, in three passages of six, seven, and eight lines that tell of those experiments, Thomson subdued his other sound echoes in order to let the diphthong [aI, əI] dominate.[20] And his last important poem, *Liberty,* because of the nature of its subject, echoes the phonestheme in dozens of passages, whether Thomson was speaking of physical brightness or of the light of virtue or knowledge.[21]

As with all his auditory effects, one can often discover Thomson working for improvement in his fitting of sound to sense. In attempting to imitate the sound of winter winds, he wrote in 1730,

Muttering, the winds at eve, with hoarser
    voice
Blow blustering from the south. (*Winter* 701-2)

This version he altered slightly in 1744 to read thus:

Muttering, the Winds at Eve, with Blunted
    Point,
Blow hollow-blustering from the South. (988-89)

The first pair of lines is rich in echoes, but the final pair has more and may be even better as a representation of the winds Thomson had in mind. While he gave up the [s] consonance of the onomatopoeic "hoarser voice," its replacement, "blunted point," produced all sorts of effects. First, it kept the vowel that was needed to assonate with *Winds*. Second, it repeated the final, stressed [t] of *Muttering* not once but twice. Third, since the words *Muttering* and *Blustering* were a bit far apart for the assonance to be heard best, *blunted,* inserted half way between, caused the three-syllable vowel echo to be most effective. And fourth, *blunted* added a third [bl] to the initial echoes in the very onomatopoeic *Blow* and *blustering*. Throughout his career Thomson worked in this fashion at such sound-sense patterns.

There is no doubt, then, that the popular modern defense of Thomson's so-called neoclassical diction and luxuriant language needs to note how much the consonant and vowel echoes affect the quality of that language. Bernard Fehr,[22] for example, talks of sentence syntax, versification, and descriptive epithets when he analyzes "a lavish display of rococo" in seven lines of *Autumn,* but he does not notice that in the seven lines there are five assonances—one of three syllables—and three alliterations—also one of three syllables. Geoffrey Tillotson defends the image in *Winter* (261-62) of "The bleating Kind" that "*Eye* the bleak heaven" without regard for the two assonances and the alliteration that must have helped determine Thomson's choice of words. The Thomson line that has perhaps evoked the most divergent opinions is one in *Spring* (361),

A shoreless ocean tumbled round the globe,"

from an eighteenth-century comment that the image is inappropriate to Bonamy Dobrée's belief that the line is "miraculous." It may be that the words were selected here for sound as much as for sense. At least, the image strikes the eye no more than the three [o]'s resound in the ear. It may be too that Thomson's poems do not "fill the ear more than the mind" but that, at their best, the oral appeal is related to the intellectual and emotional involvement. But whether any reader condemns or admires those poems, their "luxuriant language" depends very much on the phonic echoes that were as important to the eighteenth century's blank verse as to its heroic couplet.

Notes

[1] See Ralph Cohen, *The Art of Discrimination: Thomson's "The Seasons" and the Language of Criticism* (Berkeley: Univ. of California Press, 1964).

[2] Scott, Wordsworth, and Hazlitt also praised Thomson but found fault with his language. See Cohen, pp. 326-39 especially.

[3] See Cohen, pp. 331, 342, 361-62.

[4] In Thomson's letter to Sir John Clerk, January 18, 1728, in *James Thomson (1700-1748): Letters and Documents,* ed. Alan Dugald McKillop (Lawrence: Univ. of Kansas Press, 1958), p. 59; and again in *Summer,* line 1747 (see n. 7 below).

[5] By Bailey McBride, "The Poetry of James Thomson (1700-1748)," (Diss. Univ. of Tennessee, 1966). Repetition is also an important structural technique in the poetry of Lucretius, one of Thomson's masters. See especially Rosamund E. Deutsch ["The Pattern of Sound in Lucretius" (Diss. Bryn Mawr, 1939).]

[6] At times, of course, Wordsworth—writing language hardly that of common men—did employ phonic echoes, as in these lines from the *Prelude* quoted for other reasons by Spacks, p. 110 (see n. 10):

> Angling I went, or trod the trackless hills
> By mists bewildered, suddenly mine eyes
> Have glanced upon him distant a few steps,
> In size a giant, stalking through thick fog,
> His sheep like Greenland bears.

[7] All quotations from *The Seasons* are taken from Otto Zippel, *Thomson's "Seasons": Critical Edition* (Berlin: Mayer and Müller, 1908). If no edition is indicated with the line number, the edition is that of 1746. All quotations from other poems by Thomson will be from J. Logie Robertson, ed., *The Complete Poetical Works of James Thomson* (London: Oxford Univ. Press, 1908).

[8] There are other passages in these two poets which are similar. On the Grecian Urn is that "bold lover" to whom Keats addressed some of his greatest lines:

> never canst thou kiss,
> Though winning near the goal—yet, do not
>   grieve;
> She cannot fade, though thou hast not thy
>   bliss,
> For ever wilt thou love, and she be fair.

Thomson also had a frustrated lover (*Summer* 1212ff.), whose dejection he compared to that depicted in a piece of statuary:

> on the Marble-Tom[b]
> The well-dissembled Mourner stooping stands,
> For ever silent, and for ever sad.

Here, even if we include Keats's one end rhyme with his two alliterations and two assonances of [I], Thomson has more phonal repetition in his much shorter passage—three alliterations, including the [st] phones-theme and the neatly balanced [s] in "silent" and "sad," the consonance of [m], and three assonances.

[9] See n. 7 above.

[10] The best studies of Thomson's revisions are to be found in Zippel, Robertson, and Dugald McKillop, *The Background of Thomson's "Seasons"* (Hamden, Connecticut: Archon Books, 1961). No one of these, however, is concerned with any revision that involves altering the sounds of words. Nor is Patricia Mayer Spacks, in her fine *The Varied God: A Critical Study of Thomson's The Seasons* (Berkeley/Los Angeles: Univ. of California Press, 1959). See, for example, her chapter 6, "Description in *The Seasons.*"

[11] For example, in the 1730 *Autumn* he wrote,

> where astride
> The lubber Power himself triumphant sits,
> (555-56)

which became in 1744,

> where astride
> The lubber Power, in filthy Triumph sits.
> (560-61)

By exchanging two words for one and shifting the accent in *triumphant* to that in *triumph,* Thomson lost one assonance but gained two.

[12] Cohen, p. 341.

[13] It was possible, of course, for Thomson to employ balanced sounds without restricting them to a single line as the heroic couplet nearly always did. In *Winter* he assonated the verb of one end-stopped line with the parallel verb found in the next (other echoes are not marked):

> enough to light the Chace,
> Or guide their daring Steps to Finland-Fairs.
> (864-65)

Even in run-on lines he could alliterate the balancing nouns and consonate the balancing verbs:

> I solitary court
> Th'inspiring breeze; and meditate the book
> Of Nature. (*Autumn* 669-71)

[14] In Kenneth Burke's system "collected, cool" would provide both an example of "alliteration" of *c-c,* even though the first *c* is weak, and an example of consonantal chiasmus in the *l-c* (/l/-/k/) of *collected* and the *c-l* (/k/-/l/) of *cool.* ["On Musicality in Verse," The Philosophy of Literary form (1941; rpt. New York: Vintage Books, 1957).]

[15] See, for example, the section on Dr. Johnson in chapter 5.

[16] For these alterations see *Summer* (1727) 212, 214; (1744) 230, 232; *Winter* (1730) 145; (1744) 166; and *Autumn* (1730) 965; (1744) 1035.

[17] For these examples see *Spring* (1744) 584; and *Winter* (1744) 150-51.

[18] See chapter I.

[19] One of his most obvious attempts at rendering the nightingale's song is in *Summer,* where initial [s] occurs five times:

Thro' the soft *S*ilence of the *l*istening *N*ight,
The sober-suited *S*ongstress tr*i*lls her *L*ay.
                                                (745-46)

[20] As in these lines:

Even Light itself, which every thing displays
Shone undiscover'd, till his br*i*ghter m*i*nd
Untwisted all the sh*i*ning robe of day;
And, from the wh*i*tening undistinguish'd
    blaze,
Collecting every ray into his k*i*nd,
To the charm'd *eye* educ'd the gorgeous train
Of Parent-Colours. (96-102)

See also lines 5-11 and 125-31.

[21] Physical brightness:

To where the deep adorning C*y*clad *I*sles
In sh*i*ning Prospect r*i*se, (2.105-6)

Fair sh*i*ne the slippery Days, ent*i*cing Sk*i*es
Of Favour sm*i*le; (5.532-33)

the light of virtue or knowledge:

This H*i*ve of Sc*i*ence, shedding Sweets div*i*ne,
                                                (2.143)

Virtues that sh*i*ne the L*i*ght of Humankind,
                                                (3.114)

Br*i*ght r*i*sing Eras instant rushed to L*i*ght.
                                                (5.564)

[22] For Fehr, Tillotson, and the comments on the "shore-less Ocean" line, all in this paragraph, see Cohen, pp. 241-42, 361-63.

R. R. Agrawal (essay date 1981)

SOURCE: "The Poet of Transition," in *Tradition and Experiment in the Poetry of James Thomson,* Institut für Anglistik und Amerikanistik, 1981, pp. 196-214.

[*In the essay that follows, Agrawal contends that Thomson anticipated Romantic poetry not in his rejection of or relationship to the Neoclassicism of his own age, but rather by reviving the romanticism of Elizabethan poetry.*]

Thomson bridges two distinct epochs in literary history. He played the epilogue to the school of classicism and prologue to the school of Romanticism. While retaining his allegiance to the school of Pope, he heralded the dawn of romanticism in more than one way. The general tone and style of all his work link him to the neo-classical school of poetry, while his subject and forms of poetic expression point to the poetry of the new age.[1] But Thomson is not quite a transitional poet in the conventional sense of the term. He is rather a link, maintaining the continuity of the romantic tradition between the Elizabethans and the great Romantics of the nineteenth century. He brings certain Elizabethan literary values down to his own age and forestalls the Romantic age to come. His *Castle of Indolence,* written in the manner of Spenser, and *The Seasons,* written in the manner of Milton, not only revive the old romantic mood of the Elizabethans, but also strike the dawn of modern Romanticism by introducing some new romantic elements unknown even to the Elizabethans. All these mixed traits of Thomson's poetry have already been discussed in detail earlier at appropriate places. Yet for the purpose of finally evaluating Thomson as a poet of transition, it is necessary to recapitulate them briefly here.

Thomson, to begin with, shares some of the broad characteristics of the Augustan school of poetry. The most important trait of his poetry, which connects him with the Augustan tradition, is its didactic spirit. The didactic element in his poetry is the outcome of two factors—the poet's intense love of Spenser and his adherence to the vogue of didacticism in the eighteenth-century poetry. Thomson was deeply influenced by the moral earnestness and allegory of Spenser's *Faerie Queene.*[2] Further, the Augustan conception that all poetry is "a course of moral medicine", and that "the end of poetry is to instruct by pleasing", also encouraged him to be didactic. Consequently, in practically all his poems—right from the *Juvenilia* to *The Castle of Indolence*—there is a touch of moral preaching. Sometimes, as in the early poems, he discourses upon the futility and mutability of life,[3] and sometimes, as in *The Seasons,* he lectures on a variety of moral subjects.[4] In *Liberty* he dwells upon the importance of personal and public virtues,[5] whereas in *The Castle of Indolence* he builds up a kind of Spenserian moral allegory.[6] Besides, there is a lot of commonplace moralizing in almost all of his poems. Even his dramas are not free from this didactic spirit.[7]

Thomson's Nature poetry is largely encumbered with this didactic zeal. Though he excels in pure descriptions of natural scenes, for which he has been deservedly praised, he does not succeed in entirely divesting himself of his preaching vein. He generally moralizes on the scenes of Nature, and "describes the sea and sky and mountains with the more or less intention of preaching a sermon upon them."[8] Even his 'prospect' passages in *The Seasons* are either followed or preceded by a moral bearing upon them.[9] All this shows the impact of the didactic approach to Nature which was so characteristic of the school of Pope.[10] Thus he is largely didactic both by promise and by performance. And to say that Thomson is didactic is simply to say that he was an eighteenth-century poet, for every poet of that century thought it his duty to be didactic.[11]

Thomson further links himself to the classical school by occasionally subordinating Nature to man.[12] This is seen in two ways. First, he paints Nature as a background for portraying human character. In these situations he regards Man as superior to Nature:

> Man superior walks
> Amid the glad creation.[13]

The human tales in *The Seasons* are especially illustrative of this kind of treatment of Nature.[14] Secondly, Thomson also subordinates Nature to man in the typical eighteenth-century fashion. Many of his individual natural scenes and landscapes have been painted, for example, not so much for their own beauty as for the association of the poet's patrons and benefactors with them.[15] In such cases, Nature occupies a place secondary to man.

In his philosophy of Nature also Thomson was more with the age in which he lived than with the age which was to come. His faith in the Physico-theological and deistical philosophies of his day definitely coloured and influenced his attitude to Nature. Therefore Thomson often subordinates Nature to an all-pervading higher Power that resembles either the Newtonian Deity or the benevolent God of the deists.[16] Thomson's pantheistic effusions, rare and occasional as they are, are sufficiently conditioned by these two lines of faith of his time. Thus in his treatment of Nature Thomson is not wholly a pre-romantic poet. "Though in his feeling for the sights and sounds of the countryside and the affectionate detail with which he could describe them,

he displays a sensibility rather different from that which we readily associate with the spirit of the age, in his moralizing, his using natural description as a jumping-off place for generalizations about man, and his deistic view of order, he spoke with the view of his age and pleased his contemporaries."[17]

Thomson's frequent resort to satire further connects him with the Augustans. Satire was the hallmark of Augustan poetry, and Thomson, in interspersing satirical touches in his poems, was only following the bent of the age.[18] But as a satirist he is markedly different from such monarchs of satire as Dryden, Pope, Swift and Young. The satirical vein in Thomson is characterized by his innate generosity and sympathy for mankind. His satire, therefore, is never pungent or offensive like that of Swift. Nor is it personal or vindictive like that of Dryden or Pope.[19] It is essentially motivated by the spirit of moral and social reform. Thomson directs his poetic lash against the social follies and evils of his day, aiming at moral improvement and not at the gratification of spite. He mocks at human frailty not to appease his misanthropic malice like Swift but to tickle man into the consciousness of his follies and thereby to effect a purging process towards enlightenment. Thus in *The Seasons* he satirises man's excessive greed for wealth and opulence, as it breeds great many moral and social evils.[20] The satirical passages in *Liberty* are directed against the political, economic, social and moral evils prevailing in Italy, Greece, Rome and Great Britain.[21] In *The Castle of Indolence* the poet attacks man's savage thirst of gain—the root cause of his unending toil and tribulation.[22] Here he comes very near to the author of *The Vanity of Human Wishes.* The satire in his dramas, chiefly inspired by his patriotic sentiment, is directed against party-spirit vis-à-vis national interests.[23] Thus the satirical element in Thomson's works is directed chiefly against the materialistic, malevolent and sectarian conceptions and practices of the eighteenth-century English society. This makes Thomson a typical eighteenth-century poet.

The classicists believed in order, discipline and moderation in emotional and imaginative fervour. They did not allow themselves to be swayed by sentiments. Thomson usually succeeds in maintaining this emotional discipline and moderation, sometimes even in the most tempting situations. He refrained from describing a heart assailed with immodest or uncontrollable passions. This consciousness of maintaining classical decency and discipline seems to weigh heavy upon his natural poetic enthusiasm. No man was animated, for example, by a stronger or more disinterested love of public service and freedom than Thomson. Yet his *Liberty,* though not without some poetic touches, is, on the whole, a cold and frigid work. It lacks that vivacity of heart and imaginative glow which characterize Byron's *Childe Harold.* Similarly, his philanthropic and humanitarian outbursts in *The Seasons,* though inspired by genuine benevolent sentiments, are devoid of that intensity of feeling which distinguishes Wordsworth's or Shelley's studies of suffering humanity. His tragedies, though not without merit as dramatic compositions, are cold and vapid. His heroes and heroines relate their woes in good verse, but the reader remains unmoved, and follows them to their fate with stoic indifference. In a word, generally speaking, we do not find in Thomson those surging passions of the heart which give life and animation to the poetry of the Romantics.[24]

But the most remarkable neo-classical characteristic of Thomson's poetry is his adherence to the conventional poetic diction and style. He remained faithful to the conventions and mannerisms of the eighteenth-century poetic diction and style. Even when his ideas and sentiments belong to the nineteenth century, his vocabulary and construction of sentences are thoroughly Augustan. In this connection his deliberate imitation of some of the stock linguistic and stylistic devices of Milton, Virgil and the early Scottish poets is noteworthy. His enthusiastic imitation of the Miltonic style and diction resulted in most of that pompous artificiality and unpleasant mannerisms which so largely characterize his language and style.[25] His love of bombast and rhetoric, and his consequent use of the gorgeous and tumid diction are largely due to the Virgilian influence on him.[26] In the like manner, the prolixity and diffuseness of his 'rococo' style may essentially be attributed to his imitation of the poetic style of his early Scottish predecessors. His abundant use of such linguistic and literary artifices as stereotyped and grandiloquent words and phrases, compound epithets, frigid periphrases and stilted personifications, shows his susceptibility to the standard demands of the day.[27] "The chief fault of Thomson's poetry in general", remarks William Bayne, "is its infelicity of style, linguistic and poetical. It was, of course, impossible that Thomson could altogether avoid the peculiar diction of his age, though it may be wished that he had occasionally less emphasized its verbosity."[28]

These characteristics of Thomson's poetry not only exhibit his allegiance to his age but also lead some of his critics, such as Macaulay, to regard him as "essentially a representative of his own age".[29]

But this is less than half the truth. Thomson's classicism forms but one thread in the generally romantic pattern of his poetry. Thomson's romanticism has two phases. In the first phase he revives the romantic spirit of the great Elizabethans, and in the second he forestalls the major tendencies of the 'new' Romantics. The second phase marks Thomson's reaction against the conventional rigidities of the Neo-classical school. It consists of some entirely new and bold experiments in aesthetic and literary values which, though largely inspired by his love of the Elizabethans, were however

unknown even to them.[30] It is these experiments that heralded the dawn of modern romanticism. But these two phases are so intermixed and overlapping each other that they cannot be distinctly demarcated. Therefore they will have to be considered together.

The revival and restoration of the genuine love of Nature is the most romantic feature of Thomson's poetry.[31] The Augustans attached so much importance to the treatment of human nature—men and manners—that the love of Nature for itself had been quite forgotten. This does not, of course, mean that there was absolutely no Nature poetry written in that age. Poets like Parnell, Lady Winchilsea, John Gay, Philips and even Pope himself wrote Nature poetry, and even gave some beautiful descriptions of external Nature. But natural description with them, as Stopford A. Brooke points out, "was an artificial trick, not a passionate record of feeling."[32] They were not without some power of observation but they were conspicuously wanting in enthusiasm for Nature. The chief merit of Thomson, therefore, lies not only in the fact that in that age of 'town poetry' he made Nature the central theme of his principal poem, but also in that he painted Nature directly from reality and with great enthusiasm.[33] It is important to note that at a time when poets usually placed reason above all other faculties, Thomson revived the springs of spontaneous emotion and feeling in his approach to Nature.[34] As Nature was to him not only a living entity but also an emblem of divine power and goodness,[35] it aroused in him noble and holy emotions. As such his descriptions of natural phenomena are not always purely descriptive, they mostly embody a deeper meaning. Even in some of his most descriptive passages there is, as Patricia Meyer Spacks points out, meaning more than vision, "insight more than sight",[36] and this is a romantic quality.[37] In this spiritualization of Nature, Thomson clearly anticipates Wordsworth.[38]

Besides, in the accurate and vivid description of the benignant aspects of Nature in different seasons Thomson has no rival in the entire range of English poetry.[39] In the pictorial quality of his landscapes he stands comparison with the greatest painters of Nature like Wordsworth, Keats, Tennyson and Arnold.[40] Thus the notable feature of Thomson's Nature poetry, in which he makes a remarkable advance over the 'methodized' painting of Nature by his contemporaries, is that his landscape has the meticulous accuracy of a scientist, the detailed minuteness of a photographer, the picturesqueness of an Italian painter, and the vividness and enthusiasm of a poet. It is in this sense that Thomson should be regarded as the pioneer of that great movement, the Return to Nature.[41]

Another equally remarkable feature of Thomson's treatment of Nature, in which also he breaks with his age, is his picturesque rendering of external Nature for its own sake. None of his predecessors or contemporaries, who had occasionally painted external Nature, regarded the phenomena of Nature as objects of poetry in and for themselves. They treated Nature only as a background to human life. Natural description with them was usually decorative. Thomson was the first modern poet to paint Nature for its own sake.[42] He either conceives of man and Nature as co-existent and co-equals, or he presents them as two separate entities. This direct description of Nature for its own sake is the most romantic characteristic of Thomson's treatment of Nature. It is a commendable improvement upon the eighteenth-century manner of subordinating Nature to man and a definite advancement towards Keats's objective approach to Nature. In thus recognising the independent identity of Nature and in arousing love, admiration and veneration for her, Thomson initiated one of the most important trends of the Romantic Movement.[43]

Yet another remarkable feature of Thomson's delineation of Nature, in which, again, he is ahead of his time, is his scientific truth and curiosity. Thomson, the Nature poet, is, at heart, a Newtonian physicist. He is, in fact, a scientist in the garb of a poet. He enters into partnership with the scientist and is not only accurate in his natural descriptions but also satisfies the scientific curiosity of his readers by giving a scientific analysis and explanation of many a natural phenomenon.[44] He was, thus, the first notable poet to derive poetic inspiration from natural sciences. In this respect he anticipated Shelley—the most scientific of the Romantic poets.

And lastly, Thomson's occasional touches of the wild and the savage, the awful and the mysterious, the remote and the unfamiliar in Nature mark the typically romantic temper in his otherwise quiet, naturalistic poetry. His depiction of Nature in its wild aspects and violent moods, and his description of such stupendous and mysterious works of Nature as arouse 'rapturous terror',[45] gave the cue to poets like Coleridge, Byron and Scott for their typically romantic nature poetry.[46] Thomson also anticipated the Romantic poets like Wordsworth, Coleridge and Keats in his skilful use of travel literature, through which he imparted to his landscape the magic of distance, in terms of both time and place.[47] Besides, the distinct touches of pensive melancholy[48] and romantic solitude,[49] which Victor Hugo considers a distinguishing quality of the romantic art, and which gained more and more hold upon English poetry as the century advanced, are also seen in certain passages in *The Seasons*.

Another major romantic trend in Thomson's poetry is to be seen in his democratic spirit and humanitarianism. Thomson was the first great poet in the neo-classical age, who democratized poetry, liberating it from the hothouse atmosphere of courts and palaces and setting it into hamlets and cottages. Instead of patronizing the upper strata of society in the metropolis, which formed the main theme of Augustan poetry, Thomson selected for the theme of his poetry the rustic world—the simple and natural life of men living in rural background. Man, who had especially fascinated Pope and Dryden in his cultivated state,[50] grew more and more romantically fascinating to Thomson in his natural or primitive state. Thomson, thus, put into vogue a new democratic type of poetry dealing with the peasantry, shepherds, workfolk and farm-hands. The life of haughty aristocrats, sly politicians, insolent industrialists and all-powerful kings and monarchs had lost all fascination for him.[51] His muse delighted to sing of the "short and simple annals of the poor". His sympathetic portrayal of the unsophisticated and unlettered countryfolk, with all their penury, misery and suffering,[52] initiated a tradition which continued unabated in Gray, Goldsmith, Cowper, Crabbe and Burns, and ultimately culminated in Wordsworth, whose poetry championed the cause of the suffering humanity.[53]

Nor was Thomson's love and compassion confined to suffering humanity alone. Animals, birds and insects also came within his compass.[54] Thus Thomson, perhaps unconsciously, started a cult that found favour not only with a large number of Romantic and Victorian poets and authors but also with the philanthropists of the present century. He may almost be hailed as the grand patriarch of the *Society for the Prevention of Cruelty to Animals*. Referring to Thomson's unbounded sympathy for our dumb brethren Douglas Grant says, "Thomson was far in advance of his time. . . . Had Shelley wished to illustrate his dictum, that poets are the unacknowledged legislators of mankind, he could not have chosen a better example than Thomson's crusade against cruelty. His appeal on behalf of the timid hare (for example), expressed as it was in fine and moving verse, was irresistible."[55]

There is yet another notable aspect of Thomson's humanitarianism. His love of mankind was not confined to his own countrymen. The Augustan poets, no doubt, made 'mankind' the 'proper study' of their poetry, but this 'mankind' was confined to the sophisticated world of London only. It had nothing to do with the vast range of humanity beyond London, or at any rate beyond England. But Thomson, for the first time in that age, took a wider view. He carried his sympathies beyond the bounds of England and embraced the whole world. He takes us from the Tropics[56] to the polar circles.[57] He sings of Italy, Rome and Greece, taking a deep interest in the social life of the people there.[58] Thus his universal love and compassion for the poor and his hatred of oppression and injustice in every form and shape made him the poet of the whole human race.[59] This cosmopolitan interest—the love for human fraternity—which Thomson introduced into English poetry, was carried on by poets like Goldsmith and Cowper until it touched its climax in Coleridge, Wordsworth, Byron, Shelley and Browning.[60]

Thomson's cosmopolitanism is, however, more than matched with his high sense of patriotism and national pride. But they are not contradictory or in opposition to each other. It is indeed a wrong logic to hold, especially in the case of Thomson, that one who loves one's own country must hate or be hostile towards other lands. In Thomson patriotism and cosmopolitanism are perfectly compatible with each other. In this healthy and broad-based enlightened sense, patriotism is as romantic a poetic sentiment as humanitarianism or cosmopolitanism. Thomson's patriotic outbursts are markedly fervid and poetic in character and tone. They are interspersed in all his works. The patriotic sentiments as expressed in *Liberty, Britannia* and *Rule Britannia,* and in some of the passages in *The Seasons* and *The Castle of Indolence,* are worthy of all praise and admiration.[61] Even his dramas are deeply marked with this patriotic note. In these patriotic effusions and in this high sense of national pride Thomson is the forerunner of Burns, Byron, Campbell, Scott, Tennyson and Kipling.[62]

Thomson's next major contribution to the growth of English Romanticism was his revival of the Gothic and Medieval interests. The terms 'Gothic' and 'Medieval' were held in contempt by the Augustans. Their successors, however, sought to revivify and brighten this forgotten period of antiquity. "In the Middle Ages lay", says Phelps, "just the material for which the romantic spirit yearned."[63] Horace Walpole, Thomas Warton, Richard Hurd, Percy and Macpherson not only revived and implanted a taste for medieval life in literature but also created a passion for it in the new generation. But Thomson, earlier than any of these, first revived this taste in English poetry. In *The Castle of Indolence* he recreates not only the adventure and chivalry but also the colour and glamour of the Middle Ages.[64] The atmosphere of supernatural magic and enchantment, wonder and mystery, makes it a typically medieval poem. The lurid surroundings, the awe-inspiring sounds of the fell ghosts and fiends, the heart-appalling scenes and situations lend a Gothic colour to it. In the revival of these effects Thomson showed the way not only to the Romantic poets like Coleridge, Keats and Scott but also to the writers of the Gothic novel.[65] In this sense also Thomson is the morning star of Romanticism.

Another important contribution of Thomson to the rise of Romanticism is his lyricism or subjectivity. Classical poetry, in the main, is objective or narrative, while Romantic poetry is subjective or lyrical. Thomson's love lyrics and songs are intensely subjective. To the sober temper and rational outlook of the Augustans, love was taboo. Thomson violated this cynical code of morality by writing highly emotional and poignant love lyrics and songs. Some of his songs, especially those dedicated to Amanda, his real object of love and admiration, embody not only the rapture and ecstasy of love and beauty but also the romantic agony and despondency caused by frustration in love.[66] There is a depth and poignancy in his treatment of love which is rarely found in the conventional love songs of any poet of the period. His songs are, in fact, a study in the emotional autobiography of the poet and in that they anticipate the love lyrics of Shelley, Keats and Byron.

In the 'literature of melancholy', again, Thomson strikes a romantic note.[67] His memorial and elegiac verses, though in the tradition of the eighteenth century funeral elegies, are remarkable for their sincerity of feeling and romantic melancholy.[68] The poet's sincere remembrance of the departed souls and his melancholy reflections on the inevitability of death are intensely touching. These elegiac verses are forerunners of the Churchyard School of poetry, which made a deep impression on the romantic temper of the rising generation.[69] Thomson made an appreciable contribution to this trend by striking the 'note of romantic despair' in eighteenth-century poetry.

No less significant are Thomson's bold experiments in metre, stanza-form and versification. His revival of blank verse and the Spenserian stanza—two important Elizabethan metres—at a time when the Heroic couplet reigned supreme, heralded a new era in eighteenth-century versification. Thomson not only used these forms of verse effectively in his principal works but also made them popular by achieving a large variety of effects through them. He thus prepared the background for the more effective handling of these Elizabethan metres by the Romantic and Victorian poets.

Take, for example, Thomson's use of blank verse. He employed this form of verse effectively in some of his most important poems such as *The Seasons, Liberty, Britannia,* and also in his dramas. He, thus, showed not only its spaciousness, its much needed freedom and easy adaptability to a large variety of subjects but also its great musical power by achieving through it the musical sweetness of Milton's verse.[70] Consequently, he inspired a large number of poets—both his contemporaries and successors who had grown weary of the monotony and rigidity of the closed Heroic couplet—to take to blank verse. He, thus, paved the way for the more effective use of blank verse by the great Romantics.[71]

Similarly, Thomson's revival of the Spenserian stanza proved equally refreshing in that age of the Heroic couplet.[72] His highly effective use of this stanza-form in *The Castle of Indolence*[73] went a long way in subverting the closed couplet and in popularizing the Spenserian stanza which was later used more effectively by the Romantics like Byron, Keats, Scott, Shelley and Tennyson.[74] This was also his remarkable contribution to the rise of modern Romanticism.

And lastly, even in his diction and style, where he could not quite get clear of Pope and his followers,

Thomson showed some new tendencies. In that age of artificiality when English literature had been corrupted by the continental, especially French spirit and style, Thomson was the first important poet to revive the indigenous Elizabethan style and implant it in the soil of the country.[75] His imitation of Spenser's archaism and other linguistic effects enabled him largely to liberate himself from the rigid Augustan pomp and turgidity of diction. Thus he enriched the contemporary poetic diction with a rare grace and sweetness which showed the poet's genius in a new direction. The new elements of colour, imagination, strangeness, mystery, suggestion and picturesqueness which were associated with Thomson's archaic words and expressions imparted a certain distinct glamour and charm to his diction,[76] which anticipated the warm imaginative diction of the Romantic poets like Shelley, Byron and Scott. His creation of original and graceful forms of expression[77] led towards Coleridge's diction, while his refreshing use of compound words and epithets[78] pointed the way to Keats and Tennyson.

Thus Thomson's poetry is an amalgam of three elements—the old romantic spirit of the Elizabethans, the classical excellences of his own day, and the new anticipatory tendencies of the nineteenth-century Romanticism. These three elements are so interfused with one another in his poetry that it is well-nigh impossible to separate them or to assess the relative predominance of the one over the other. All that can be said with a certain amount of certainty is that with the advance of his poetic career the romantic values progressively took more and more hold over the classical, until they touched the high watermark in his last important poem, **The Castle of Indolence**. It is quite probable, therefore, as Phelps remarks, that "Thomson might have done still more work in the same field had his life not been so suddenly cut short."[79] Thomson, therefore, is not only a neo-classicist and a belated Elizabethan, but also the earliest precursor of the Modern Romanticism.

To conclude, then, Thomson was an important figure in the process of transition between Pope and Wordsworth. As a matter of fact, he initiated that transition.[80] And in the transition initiated by him, his love of the Elizabethans played a significant role. It would not be wrong to say that the new romantic element in Thomson was due not so much to his reaction against neo-classicism as to his revival of some of the prominent romantic tendencies of Elizabethan poetry. In his attempt to revive the Elizabethan Romanticism, Thomson unwittingly introduced some new elements which later proved to be his decisive experiments in theme, versification and style. These bold experiments of his were enthusiastically taken up by Gray, Collins and several others, and through them they were ultimately passed on to the great Romantics who, generally speaking, accepted them as the creed of their poetic career.[81] In fact, what was tested and experimented by Thom-

son unconsciously was later proclaimed and accepted by the Romantics with conviction. In this way Thomson occupies a very important position as a transitional poet in the history of English poetry. While he holds out one hand to the great classical age, he advances the other to the old romantic school of Elizabethans, and thus he makes his own contribution both in matter and in manner to the rise of the nineteenth-century Romanticism. Thomson, therefore, is not quite a poet of transition, as he is commonly believed to be, but one who keeps the torch of the great Elizabethans burning, howsoever dimly, to light the age to come.

Notes

[1] George Saintsbury remarks,

> Thomson stood apart from the Augustan school in his subjects of interest, and in his selection of metres. But he shared, and rather went beyond, the predilection of that school for a peculiar stilted 'poetic diction', partly founded on the classicism of Milton, but largely tempered from less genuine sources.
> —*A Short History of English Literature*, p. 569.

[2] Vide Chapter V.

[3] Vide Chapter II.

[4] Vide Chapter III.

[5] Vide Chapter VI.

[6] Vide Chapter V.

[7] Vide Chapter VI.

[8] Leslie Stephen: *English Literature and Society in the Eighteenth Century*, p. 131.

[9] Vide Chapter III.

[10] L. Stephen writes:

> Thomson had studied Milton and Spenser without being forced to look through Pope's spectacles. Still he cannot quite trust himself. He is still afraid, and not without reason, that pure description will fall into flat prose.
> —*English Literature and Society in the Eighteenth Century*, p. 131.

[11] Cf.

> A true Augustan, he (Thomson) is alive to the poet's responsibility to teach, to exhort, to be actively a man of his time. Thus he loads his Muse with luggage so heavy and so awkward that movement is difficult and soaring impossible.
> A. M. Oliver: "The Scottish Augustans" in *Scottish Poetry: A Critical Survey*, ed. James Kinsley, p. 128.

[12] This is not, however, the general tendency of Thomson's Nature poetry. More often he presents Nature as a phenomenon independent and complete in itself. . . .

[13] *Spring,* ll. 170-71.

[14] Vide Chapter III.

[15] Ditto.

[16] Ditto.

[17] David Daiches: *A Critical History of English Literature,* Vol. II (London, 1961), p. 655.

[18]   A large portion of all the Queen Anne and early Georgian literature is composed of work wholly or in part satirical. . . . The cold, hard worldliness of Augustan life found its natural expression in polished wit and satire.
     Phelps: *The Beginnings of the English Romantic Movement,* p. 14.

[19] The only exception is Thomson's personal attack on Jeremy Collier and Cibber in the poem *To the Memory of Mr. Congreve.* . . .

[20] Vide Chapter III.

[21] Vide Chapter VI.

[22] Vide Chapter V.

[23] Vide Chapter VI.

[24] While comparing Thomson's *Hymn On The Seasons* with Coleridge's *Hymn Before Sunrise,* D. C. Tovey remarks, "But in Thomson's verse there is less both of the poet's eye and of the poet's heart; there is rhetoric rather than true enthusiasm." "Memoir of Thomson", prefixed to *Works,* Vol. I, p. XCVI. This remark strikes the keynote of Thomson's poetry at large.

[25] Vide Chapters IV and V.

[26] Vide Chapter IV.

[27] Vide Chapters IV, V and VI.

Referring to the neo-classical traits of Thomson's 'composite style', John C. Shairp writes,

   It is heavy, cumbrous, oratorical, overloaded with epithets, full of artificial invocations, 'personified abstractions', and insipid classicalities.
     —*On Poetic Interpretation of Nature,* pp. 186-87.

[28] Ed., *Poems by James Thomson,* p. XXVIII.

Sir George Douglas relates Thomson's stylistic 'artificiality' to his age:

Blame the age in which he lived, if so you are minded. It was an age of reason, of mild enlightenment; comfortable, prosperous, picturesque; the golden mediocrity of Anne and of the first two Georges: but it was an age of prose rather than of poetry. So by all means blame the age, if such be your pleasure, for Thomson's stiffness and his artificiality.
     —*Scottish Poetry,* p. 71.

[29] Macaulay: *James Thomson,* p. 93.

In this connection the views of Rayner Unwin also deserve notice: He observes:

Although he (Thomson) was writing on a subject and in a manner different from the contemporary practice, he did not disturb old-established theories, but rather added to them by revealing new delights and broadening an existing vision. Thomson was not even an incipient romantic. In literature as in life he was a neighbour and friend of Pope, but whereas Pope turned to the city for his pleasure and his prey, Thomson was most happy under the beech-trees in Hagley Park.
     —*The Rural Muse,* pp. 37-38.

[30] Referring to the influence of Spenser, which led Thomson to forestall the new age, Dr. Maar remarks:

An interest in Spenser does not ipso facto imply the definite influx of Modern Romanticism. In some cases it meant only a survival of Elizabethan Romance; for a new romantic element unknown to Spenser we have to wait till the appearance of *The Castle of Indolence.*
     —*A History of Modern English Romanticism,* Vol. I, p. 226.

[31] A word by way of an explanation seems necessary here. Stopford A. Brooke, distinguishing Naturalism from Romanticism, holds Thomson to be a Naturalist rather than a romantic poet (See *Naturalism in English Poetry,* p. 44). But such an intricate terminological distinction does not seem to be relevant for our purpose. Both of these terms denote a kind of love of a larger and freer life in literature. Both of them are opposed alike to neoclassical conventions and ideals of poetry. In fact, they have, as Henry Beers points out, "a common root: the desire, namely, to escape into the fresh air and into freer conditions, from a literature which dealt, in a strictly regulated way, with the indoor life of a highly artificial society" (*A History of English Romanticism in the Eighteenth Century,* p. 102).

[32] *Naturalism in English Poetry,* p. 28.

[33] Vide Chapter III.

Referring to Thomson's great and sustained enthusiasm for Nature, George Gilfillan remarks:

His great power lay in his deep, glowing, childlike enthusiasm for nature, and in the fullness with which

he retained this on to mature manhood; so that, while in understanding he was thirty, in freshness of feeling he was only thirteen.
        Ed., *Thomson's Poetical Works* (Edinburgh, 1853), p. xvi.

[34] With reference to Thomson's emotional appreciation of Nature, Douglas Grant observes,

His theme was Nature, but he could not rest content to describe it objectively. Its beauty prompted his imagination to contemplate it philosophically and to appreciate it emotionally. . . . He moved the emphasis from reason to emotion, and when Keats cried, 'Oh! for a life of sensations rather than of thoughts', he was saying loudly what Thomson had whispered in the autumn fields.
        —*James Thomson: Poet of 'The Seasons'*, pp. 106, 107.

(The 'autumn fields' refer to a passage in *Autumn*, ll. 950-69.)

Referring to Thomson's pre-romantic enthusiasm and emotionalism exhibited in his poetry, C. G. Osgood remarks,

He (Thomson) instinctively saw Nature and life as a poet sees them. . . . . . Furthermore without intention or flaming zeal, he was a harbinger of the profound emotional awakening of men which was not far off—the so-called Romantic Movement.
        —*The Voice of England*, p. 318.

[35] Vide Chapter III.

[36] *The Poetry of Vision*, p. 22.

[37] Defining the true romantic nature imagery W. K. Wimsatt writes:

The common feat of the romantic nature poets was to read meanings into the landscape . . . characteristically . . . concerning the spirit or soul of things. . . . And that meaning especially was summoned out of the very surface of nature itself. It was embodied imaginatively and without the explicit religious or philosophic statement which one will find in classical or Christian instances.
        —"The Structure of Romantic Nature Imagery" in *The Age of Johnson: Essays Presented to Chauncey Brewster Tinker* (New Haven, 1949), p. 298.

[38] Oliver Elton writes:

Thomson is penetrated with the feeling that there is an omnipresent life and mind behind phenomena. It is often nobly expressed, though it is not exactly mystical; he is, more than once, visibly prophetic of Wordsworth.
        —*The English Muse*, p. 286.

[39] Vide Chapter III.

[40] John C. Shairp remarks,

Thomson has been called the Claude of poets. And his way of handling Nature stands to that of Wordsworth or Tennyson much as Claude's landscapes do to those of Turner or some of the modern painters.
        On Poetic Interpretation of Nature, pp. 189-90.

Thomson's picturesque rendering of Nature has already been discussed in detail in Chapter III.

[41] Cf.

He (Thomson), and none else, was the pioneer—and a great pioneer—of the eighteenth century romantic movement, especially, of course, in its thorough concern in the interpretation of outward Nature. . . . As far as the romantic idea of Nature is concerned, Thomson is quite unrivalled by any poet of his generation.
        William Bayne, ed., *Poems by James Thomson*, p. xii.

[42] Vide Chapter III.

[43] Stopford A. Brooke observes:

The point at which he (Thomson) is quite new, which started a new poetry, which gives him his crowning place in English song, where he was most the Naturalist, not the Romantic, though the Romantics took up his work into theirs—was his natural description; his love of Nature for her own sake. He not only restored natural description to poetry—it had existed before him—but he made a new kind of it—direct description of the doings and appearance of Nature; without any reference to man—for her own sake. . . . Thomson paints her as she is, and as she acts, and while he does so, man is secondary. . . . This was unknown before. This is original—the beginning of a new subject, of a new world of verse.
        —*Naturalism in English Poetry*, p. 47.

[44] Thomson's scientific explanations of the theory of rainbow and that of thunder are typical examples of this kind. See Chapter III.

[45] Vide Chapter III.

[46] For Thomson's influence on these poets, see Ch. VIII.

[47] Vide Chapters III and V.

[48] E.g.,

                        Sudden he starts,
Shook from his tender trance, and restless runs
To glimmering shades and sympathetic glooms,
Where the dun umbrage o'er the falling stream
Romantic hangs.
                        —*Spring*, ll. 1024-28.

[49] E.g.

Thrice happy he, who on the sunless side
Of a romantic mountain, forest-crowned,
Beneath the whole collected shades reclines;
Or in the gelid caverns, woodbine-wrought
And fresh bedewed with ever-spouting streams,
Sits coolly calm; while all the world without,
Unsatisfied and sick, tosses in noon.
　　　　　　　　　—Summer, ll. 458-64.

Here Thomson anticipates Wordsworth's contemplative awareness of solitude.

[50] Referring to the aristocratic complex of the Augustan poet, Sutherland remarks that

his standards, his values, his emotions and intellectual interests, his mode of expressing himself, are often characteristic of the upper class.
　　　　—A Preface to Eighteenth Century Poetry, p. 50.

[51] While describing the pleasures of rural life, Thomson writes:

The fall of kings,
The rage of nations, and the crush of states
Move not the man who, from the world
　　escaped,
In still retreats and flowery solitudes

To Nature's voice attends from month to month,
And day to day, through the revolving year.
　　　　　　　　　—Autumn, ll. 1302-07.

[52] Vide Chapter III.

[53] Thomson's influence on these poets has been discussed in Chapter VIII.

Referring to Thomson's humanitarianism, Stopford A. Brooke observes:

What Rousseau did for France with more energy and more reality, Thomson did for England; and Thomson was the forerunner of Rousseau in this work.
　　　　—Naturalism in English Poetry, p. 46.

[54] Vide Chapter III.

[55] *James Thomson: Poet of 'The Seasons'*, p. 105.

(Thomson's 'appeal on behalf of the timid hare' refers to a passage in *Autumn*, ll. 401-25.)

[56] *Summer*, ll. 629ff.

[57] *Winter*, ll. 794ff.

[58] The reference is to *Liberty*.

[59] Appreciating and commending Thomson's philosophy of mankind, Voltaire wrote:

I discovered in him (Thomson) a great genius, and a great simplicity, I liked in him the poet and the true philosopher, I mean the lover of mankind. I think that without a good stock of such a philosophy a poet is just above a fiddler, who amuses our ears and cannot go to our soul.
　　　—A letter from Voltaire to Mr. Lyttelton on receiving a copy of Thomson's Works, dated "Paris, 17th May, 1790. N.St."

[60] Cf.

The spirit of Cosmopolitanism, the consideration of universal man all over the world, and the sympathy with the whole race, is one of the elements which Thomson reintroduced into English poetry. It has never ceased to influence that poetry from then till now.
　　　Stopford A. Brooke: *Naturalism in English Poetry*, p. 53.

[61] Mark, for example, his patriotic address to Great Britain in *The Seasons*:

Island of bliss! amid the subject seas
That thunder round thy rocky coasts, set up,
At once the wonder, terror, and delight,
Of distant nations, whose remotest shore
Can soon be shaken by thy naval arm;
Not to be shook thyself, but all assaults
Baffling, like thy hoar cliffs the loud sea-wave.
　　　　　　　　　—Summer, ll. 1595-1601.

[62] Cf.

Thomson's patriotism took its particular form from the nature of the theme which so greatly engrossed him. Not the historical, so much as the geographical or scenic associations of his country stirred his poetical zeal. In this, indeed, he joins with the select poetical brotherhood of his native land. The impassioned fondness of the Scot for the "land of brown heath", that pulsed like a heart-beat through the ballads and the work of the "Makers", down to the poetry of Burns and Scott, thrills with lively expression in the verse of Thomson. . . . Born at a later date, he would undoubtedly have rejoiced in the increased stability of the British constitution; and the stirring notes of poetical celebration of British prowess and daring expressed by Campbell and Tennyson would not have failed to secure in him an eager and competent supporter.
　　　—William Bayne, ed., *Poems By James Thomson*, pp. xxx-xxxi.

[63] *The Beginnings of the English Romantic Movement*, p. 5.

[64] Vide Chapter V.

[65] Thomson's influence on these poets and novelists has been discussed in Chapter VIII.

[66] Vide Chapter VI.

[67] Phelps says,

> The literature of melancholy must certainly be con-sidered an important factor in the beginnings of Romanticism.
> —*The Beginnings of the English Romantic Move-ment,* p. 101.

[68] Vide Chapter VI.

[69] Referring to the impact of the Churchyard School of poetry on the rise of the Romantic Movement, Phelps says that

> the tones of despair, the odor of the charnel-house, the world-old meditation on the shortness of life and the certainty of death—the new emphasis laid on all this evidently contained seeds of the Romantic Movement.
> —*The Beginnings of the English Romantic Move-ment,* pp. 99-100.

[70] Vide Chapter IV.

[71] The influence of Thomsonian blank verse on the succeeding poets has been discussed in Chapter VIII.

[72] Henry A. Beers remarks:

> To ears that had heard from childhood the tinkle of the couplet, with its monotonously recurring rhyme, its inevitable caesura, its narrow imprisonment of the sense, it must have been a relief to turn to the amplitude of Spenser's stanza, 'the full strong sail of his great verse'.
> —*A History of English Romanticism in the Eighteenth Century,* p. 77.

[73] Vide Chapter V.

[74] The impact of Thomson's *Castle of Indolence* on the versification of these poets has been discussed in Chapter VIII.

[75] Cf.

> Thomson was the first poet of eminence who rebelled against the artificial importations from the continent, and strove, we believe in part unconsciously, to bring literature back to a purer style, and to imbue it with a spirit closer to nature.
> —J. M. Whirter and G. Hay, eds., *The Poetical Works of James Thomson,* p. xxxiii.

[76] Vide Chapter V.

[77] Ditto.

[78] Vide Chapter IV.

[79] *The Beginnings of the English Romantic Movement,* p. 76.
This view is supported by one of the stanzas in *The Castle of Indolence* itself. The poet here proposes to sing of some more romantic themes:

> Come on, my muse, nor stoop to low despair,
> Thou imp of Jove, touched by celestial fire!
> Thou yet shalt sing of war, and actions fair,
> Which the bold sons of Britain will inspire;
> Of ancient bards thou yet shalt sweep the lyre;
>
> Thou yet shalt tread in tragic pall the stage,
> Paint love's enchanting woes, the hero's ire.
> —Canto I, st. 32, ll. 1-7.

It is quite probable that Thomson might have written on these romantic themes if he had lived longer.

[80] While describing Thomson and Young as important figures in the transition between Pope and Wordsworth, Stopford A. Brooke remarks,

> They initiated that transition; and both of them brought into it elements which have continued, under diverse forms, and diverse atmospheres of thought, to exist in poetry up to the present day.
> —*Naturalism in English Poetry,* p. 52.

[81] While assessing the historical importance of Thomson's work in the eighteenth century, A. H. Thompson says:

> It (Thomson's work) called attention to a field of verse which his contemporaries, absorbed in the study of man, in ethical reflection and moral satire, had ceased to cultivate; it looked back with admira-tion to models which were almost forgotten, and, through its influence on the poetry of Collins and Gray, it lent impulse to the progress which was to culminate in the romantic movement.
> "Thomson and Natural Description in Poetry" in *The Cambridge History of English Literature,* Vol. X, p. 93.

Marshall Brown (essay date 1991)

SOURCE: "Formal Balance in Thomson and Collins," in *Preromanticism,* Stanford University Press, 1991, pp. 24-8.

[*In the following excerpt, Brown looks at Thomson—and especially at his alleged inconsistencies—as part of the poetry of the "urbane sublime." At the base of the apparent "wanderings" in this poetry, Brown finds a notion of the social that creates coherence.*]

. . . Because of its inherent discretion the urbane sublime is able to tolerate many apparent paradoxes. It is both high and light, sophisticated and primitive, liberal and aristocratic, elevated and capable of describing the most mundane phenomena, innovative and doggedly conventional.[17] It is perhaps the presence of these contradictory impulses, rather than its unnatural inflation, that often makes modern readers ill at ease with eighteenth-century poetry, and it is certainly the persistence of contradictory impulses that makes the history of eighteenth-century poetry so baffling to write. Having used the Eton College ode to illustrate the style, I should like to turn to Thomson's *Seasons* in order to demonstrate the intellectual coherence underneath the superficial inconsistencies and seemingly ill-defined ideology of this poetry.

The issue is the way form constrains style. Poetic diction, in particular, has generally been studied in historical perspective, at the expense of its contextual function.[18] Often, in serious as in satiric verse, a principle of com-pensation applies. Thus the Eton College ode spends its most rotund Latinity on the children's games and falls back on monosyllabic Anglo-Saxon adjectives for its more sublime and visionary moments. The passage on birds' nests in Thomson's **"Spring,"** lines 631-86, offers an even more obvious example of this reverse decorum. On the one hand, there is a clear vertical hierarchy, with "humble" nests on the ground and the various other types sorted by altitude; the sense of propriety is strengthened by the repetition "kind Concealment," "kind Duty," "kindly Care," where "kind" has the connotation "appropriate to the species." Yet on the other hand, the tree birds build simple "Nests"; the somewhat less dignified, thievish swallow erects a somewhat more pretentious "Habitation," while the ground-nesting species are granted the noblest oratory: "humble Texture," "artful Fabrick," and even, surprisingly, "Domes" (Latin *domus*). Similarly, while the idle male bird, who "takes his Stand / High," is described in generally simple diction, his menial better half "assiduous sits," a bad etymological pun that elevates even as it ridicules.[19]

One of Thomson's hesitations illuminates the impulse behind this reverse decorum. The first version of **"Win-ter"** describes how cattle, when they return at evening, "ask, with meaning Low, their wonted Stalls" (line 124).[20] The revision, made a few months later, reveals the concealed lexical and grammatical ambiguities so typical of the urbane sublime: it changes the capitalization to "with Meaning low," thus inverting the hierarchy of adjective and noun. By means of this metamorphosis the animal noise is shown to be a meaningful speech act. The transformation is paradigmatic of the style as a whole. The urbane sublime cannot condescend to an object without elevating it. Yet neither can it express sympathy without taking cognizance of difference: the Low may have a meaning, but it is a "Meaning *low*." No matter how egalitarian the gestures, the sense of hierarchy is inescapable. Indeed, both leveling and gradation are implicit in the adjective-noun structure that forms the backbone of the style. Whether the adjective and noun are related as species to genus, abstract to concrete, or figurative to literal, the pairing of words almost always implies a divided perspective and yet also works to moderate the rigid stratifications of "classical" decorum.[21]

The pacing and structure of *The Seasons* exhibit a comparable differentiated moderation, or "art of discrimination" as Ralph Cohen has called it.[22] The poem was most carefully composed and the contribution of each word duly weighed. Yet as methodically as Thom-son went to work, the constant effect is one of wandering and of choices still to be made; the tone remains deliberative rather than decisive. The poet sustains his slow progress through the year by nourishing a permanent sense of anticipation, and he typically resists temptations toward culmination.

Just as the rejection of prophecy characterizes Gray's poetry from the early "Latin Verses at Eton" ("Fata obstant; metam Parcae posuere sciendi," line 79) to the late "Descent of Odin" (where the prophetess herself commands in lines 88-89, "That never shall enquirer come / To break my iron sleep again"), so too *The Seasons* regularly retreats from transcendence. Thus after finding himself "in airy Vision rapt," Thomson's "every Sense / Wakes from the Charm of Thought: swift-shrinking back, / I check my Steps" (**"Summer,"** lines 585-89; this version has been toned down from the earlier, "I stand aghast"). After a passing enthusiasm for "visionary Vales," he draws back with the line, "Or is this Gloom too much?" (**"Autumn,"** lines 1030-37). After hymning nature's stunning impact on his "ravish'd Eye," he concedes, "But if to that unequal" (lines 1365, 1367). Most notably, the end of the whole poem subsides from present epiphany (**"Winter,"** lines 1041-43: "And see! / 'Tis come, the glorious Morn! the second Birth / Of Heaven, and Earth") to merely predicted epiphany (1068-69: "The Storms of WINTRY TIME will quickly pass, / And one unbounded SPRING encircle All"). To the eighteenth-century rhymester, even "ecstasies" arrive "by degrees."[23] We are faced with a great intensity of verbal energy at every point, but with a diffuse and enervating whole.

Concomitantly, the forms preferred by the age are the georgic, the progress, and the loco-descriptive poem. Each of these combines steady movement with an affectionate dwelling on particulars, and in consequence a rhetoric develops in which the compactness of the classical period is compromised by excessive itemization. The many diffuse catalogues in *The Seasons* are obviously deficient in rhetorical unity and focus, but even in the Eton College ode the strict triadic cadences of the opening stanzas succumb as the excitement grows:

> *This* racks the joints, *this* fires the veins,
> *That* every labouring sinew strains,
> *Those* in the deeper vitals rage:
> Lo, *Poverty* to fill the band,
> That numbs the soul with icy hand,
> And slow-consuming *Age*.[24]

In *The Seasons* this technique of discrimination by means of superfluous enumeration is related to an emphasis on gradual, deliberate order, presided over by a host of mild, intermediate divinities, each with its own realm, and with no universal controlling power in evidence. In lieu of the fixed, sculptural "stationing" that Keats praised in Milton, there is a flexible positioning; the mind tries to assign each spirit "to his Rank," but the perceptions are indistinct and changing, "ever rising with the rising Mind" (**"Summer,"** lines 1793, 1805). Evening, that mild spirit that so entranced men's minds later in the century (see Hartman, "Evening Star"), best represents Thomson's moderation as well:

> Confess'd from yonder slow-extinguish'd Clouds,
> All Ether softening, sober *Evening* takes
> Her wonted Station in the middle Air;
> A thousand *Shadows* at her Beck. First *This*
> She sends on Earth; then *That* of deeper Dye
> Steals soft behind; and then a *Deeper* still,
> In Circle following Circle, gathers round,
> To close the Face of Things. A fresher Gale
> Begins to wave the Wood, and stir the Stream,
> Sweeping with shadowy Gust the Fields of Corn;
> While the Quail clamours for his running Mate.
> Wide o'er the thistly Lawn, as swells the Breeze,
> A whitening Shower of vegetable Down
> Amusive floats. The kind impartial Care
> Of Nature nought disdains: thoughtful to feed
> Her lowest Sons, and clothe the coming Year,
> From Field to Field the feather'd Seeds she wings.
>   (**"Summer,"** lines 1647-63)

In so gentle a matriarchy as that of nature, how could life help but be pleasant? Little in Thomson's world is firm and earthbound or surging and fiery; instead, when summer's heat is not simply "Exuberant Spring," then it is almost always a liquid, "dazling Deluge" that (punningly?) "reigns" (**"Summer,"** lines 697, 435). Indeed, Thomson is fascinated, as in the lines on Evening, with air and water, the ambient elements that allow suspended substances to move easily up and down through the many levels of existence. Above all, as the multiple puns of the lines on the mock snowfall show, air and water are "amusive," intrinsically poetical because they imitate the "musing," deliberate course of thought itself. Thomson's early Preface to **"Winter"** harps on this theme as it describes the temperate pleasures of his poem's "calm, wide, Survey" of nature. Poetry, he says, is associated with "the most charming Power of Imagination, the most exalting Force of Thought, the most affecting Touch of Sentiment"; it displays "a finer, and more amusing, Scene of Things"; it can "amuse the Fancy, enlighten the Head, and warm the Heart."[25]

What passes for artifice and inconsistency is thus more adequately understood, at least in the better poetry of the century, as the easy, "musing" acceptance of shifting orders and fluid hierarchies.[26] This applies to politics as well as to poetic forms. Thomson, like Gray, Akenside, and the Wartons, can startle the present-day reader by simultaneously praising modern liberty and ancient privilege without any sense of strain:

> Oh, QUEEN of Men!
> Beneath whose Sceptre in essential Rights
> Equal they live, tho' plac'd for common Good,
> Various, or in Subjection or Command;
> And that by common choice.
>   (Thomson, *Liberty* 3.328-32)

Yet there is no inconsistency to such a political vision; its viability is demonstrated equally by the examples of ancient Rome and of modern Britain with her "BOUNDED KINGS" (4.1146).[27] Nor is there any greater inconsistency to the century's flexible conception of formal structure and poetic style. These, like the politics, reflect the poets' view of the nature of society. For if we ask what determines both the tone and the organizational sense of the urbane sublime, the answer is its social basis.

"Social" is the word that resolves the apparent paradoxes of the urbane sublime: "I believe there was never so reserved a solitary, but felt some degree of pleasure at the first glimpse of an human figure. The soul, however, unconscious of its social bias in a crowd, will in solitude feel some attraction towards the first person that we meet" (Shenstone, *Men and Manners,* entry 75, p. 150). The Muse, as Thomson says, is "most delighted, when she social sees / The whole mix'd Animal-Creation round / Alive, and happy" (**"Autumn,"** lines 381-83). In the best of all possible worlds even the vegetable kingdom would be social: "Great Spring, before, / Green'd all the Year; and Fruits and Blossoms blush'd, / In social Sweetness, on the self-same Bough" (**"Spring,"** lines 320-22). In these lines the very alliterations are sociably sorted, as often in Thomson, into neighboring pairs.[28] The word's range—from the nobly societal to the collegially sociable—reflects the range of the style itself, yet all the variations are reducible to a single concept, the continuous give-and-take of social intercourse. . . .

Notes

[17] . . . Cf. Pope's letter to Walsh, July 2, 1706: "To bestow heightening on every part is monstrous: Some parts ought to be lower than the rest," etc. (*Correspondence* 1:19). Similarly, in commenting on the proper way to translate Homer, Pope states in the Postscript to his translation of the *Odyssey:* "To read thro' a whole work in this strain is like traveling all along on the ridge of a hill; which is not half so agreeable as sometimes gradually to rise, and sometimes gently to descend, as the way leads, and as the end of the journey directs" (*Poems* 10: 388).

[18] Perhaps this deficient attention to immediate context may excuse the insensitive attack on Thomson in Sherbo, *English Poetic Diction* 158-80.

[19] There has still not been enough attention paid to the "deeply buried and always reticent" puns in Pope's nonsatiric verse. (The phrase is Mack's, "Wit and Poetry and Pope" 32.) Like one of Thomson's inverse decorums, for instance, the sublime, neoplatonizing treatment of nature in the *Essay on Criticism* is prepared by a rarefied pun that suggests the mutuality of high and low: "Would all but *stoop* to what they *under-stand*" (line 67, hyphen added). This principle of compensation is ubiquitous in the verse of the period; see, for one instance, the humble graves that "heave the crumbled Ground" in Parnell's "A Night-Piece on Death" (line 30), while the monuments of the rich are undermined by hollowness and irony; for another, see the theology of Smart's Seatonian Prize hymns, where, as Donald Marshall has written, "The style is sublimely obscure, but courteously explicates itself" ("The Development of Blank-Verse Poetry" 222).

[20] This line is misleadingly emended in Sambrook's text but correctly reported in his Appendix D.

[21] "One of the more permanent functions of the word [honest] . . . was to soften the assertion of class, or contrariwise to maintain the assertion in a softened form" (Empson, *Structure* 200).

[22] Cohen, *The Art of Discrimination.* More useful in application to literary works is Cohen's essay "On the Interrelations of Eighteenth-Century Literary Forms."

[23] Thomas Warton, "Ode on the Approach of Summer," in Chalmers, *English Poets* 18: 106.

[24] For some additional remarks on the historical significance of Gray's enumerations see Tillotson, "Methods of Description." Siskin's *Historicity* 94-124 is a nice discussion of the way that eighteenth-century additive organization turns into romantic temporal flow and development, which he aptly calls a "positing of growth as continuous revision" (103). Where, how-ever, he sees "epistemological and ultimately spiritual limitations" in eighteenth-century "fragments whose sum approaches but cannot equal the whole" (102), I see a "middle state" that is not impelled toward totalizations.

[25] Thomson, *Seasons,* pp. 303-5. See Cohen's valuable discussions of Thomson's punning, which he calls "illusive allusion," in *The Unfolding of "The Seasons"* 39-40 and passim (consult index). I will not detail here all my points of agreement and disagreement with Cohen's commentary, but I would like to call attention to the excellent pages on sociability (252-92) and to what seems a misleading treatment of summer as a fiery season.

[26] Typical of the poets' conscious preference for loose over rigid forms is Gray's criticism of Buffon's "Love of System, . . . the most contrary Thing in the World to a Science, entirely grounded upon experiments, & that has nothing to do with Vivacity of Imagination" (letter to Wharton, Aug. 9, 1750, *Correspondence* 1: 329). For more documentation see Greene's witty essay "Logical Structure."

[27] Cf. also Goldsmith's *The Citizen of the World,* letter 50 (*Collected Works* 2: 212), which praises the "ductility of the laws" in England. Goldsmith argues that there can be more liberty and looser enforcement of the laws in aristocratic England than in a democracy because the state is stronger by nature. Barrell, in *English Literature in History,* gives a fine account of the flexible comprehensiveness of politics, society, and language in the period and of the unsettling dynamic that eventually bequeathed to the romantics a "crisis of social knowledge" (209); chap. 2 (51-109) concerns Thomson and John Dyer.

[28] In *Graces of Harmony* (118-36) Percy G. Adams comments copiously on Thomson's "attractive," "ear appealing," "pleasing" sound effects. . . .

FURTHER READING

Biography

Grant, Douglas. *James Thomson, Poet of The Seasons.* London: Cresset Press, 1951, 308 p.

Considered the standard biography of Thomson;

includes lengthy commentaries on *The Seasons* and *The Castle of Indolence*.

Sambrook, James. *James Thomson, 1700-1748: A Life.* Oxford: Clarendon Press, 1991, 332 p.

    A biographical study of the author's life and works with an emphasis on his social and political context.

Scott, Mary Jane W. *James Thomson, Anglo-Scot.* Athens, Ga., and London: The University of Georgia Press, 1988, 373 p.

    A biography that attempts to account for "the distinctive influences which the poet's Scottish background had upon is work."

Criticism

Bush, Douglas. "Newtonianism, Rationalism, and Sentimentalism." In his *Science and English Poetry: A Historical Sketch, 1590-1950,* pp. 51-78. New York: Oxford University Press, 1950.

    Includes comments on the Newtonian inspiration of Thomson's poetry of nature. Contends that Thomson, like Newton, viewed God as immanent in all creation.

Campbell, Hilbert H. *James Thomson.* Boston: Twayne Publishers, 1979, 175 p.

    An introductory biographical and critical study. Campbell traces the life and major works of Thomson, and examines his reputation and influence.

Cohen, Ralph. *The Art of Discrimination: Thomson's* The Seasons *and the Language of Criticism.* Berkeley and Los Angeles: University of California Press, 1964, 529 p.

    An examination of the literary criticism generated in response to *The Seasons* over two centuries.

——. *The Unfolding of* The Seasons. Baltimore: The Johns Hopkins Press, 1970, 338 p.

    An important study that systematically examines the poetry of *The Seasons,* focusing on Thomson's unified vision of man's place in an ever-changing environment.

Courthope, W. J. "Philosophical English Poetry in the Eighteenth Century: Influence of Deism, Nature-Worship, Liberty, and the Arts." In his *A History of English Poetry,* Vol. V, pp. 272-326. London: Macmillan, 1905.

    Includes a concise overview of Thomson's life and works, with critical commentary on *The Seasons* and *The Castle of Indolence.*

Gosse, Edmund. "The Dawn of Naturalism in Poetry." In his *A History of Eighteenth-Century Literature,* pp. 207-41. New York: Macmillan Co.

    Contains a succinct biographical and critical survey of Thomson's life and career.

Irlam, Shaun. "Gerrymandered Geographies: Exoticism in Thomson and Chateaubriand." *MLN* 108, No. 4 (September 1993): 891-912.

    A postcolonial analysis of *The Seasons* which uses Thomson's poem to consider eighteenth-century, European notions of nationhood and imperialism.

Kenshur, Oscar. *Open Form and the Shape of Ideas: Literary Structures as Representations of Philosophical Concepts in the Seventeenth and Eighteenth Centuries.* Lewisburg: Bucknell University Press, 1986, 140 p.

    A theoretical analysis that relates Thomson's form in *The Seasons* to specific philosophies of knowledge and divinity.

McKillop, Alan Dugald. *The Background of Thomson's "Seasons."* Minneapolis: University of Minnesota Press, 1942, 191 p.

    Discusses the philosophical, literary, scientific, and geographical underpinnings of *The Seasons.*

Nicolson, Marjorie Hope. "Aesthetic Implications of the *Opticks.*" In her *Newton Demands the Muse: Newton's "Opticks" and the Eighteenth Century Poets,* pp. 107-17. Hamden, Conn., and London: Archon Books, 1963.

    Places Thomson at the forefront of new aesthetic approaches to the depiction of color and light in poetry.

Spacks, Patricia Meyer. "James Thomson: The Retreat from Vision." In *The Poetry of Vision: Five Eighteenth-Century Poets,* pp. 46-65. Cambridge: Harvard University Press, 1967.

    Detailed analysis of the role of emotion in *The Castle of Indolence.* According to Spacks, Thomson demonstrates both the appeal of his sensual verse and its ultimate danger.

Spencer, Jeffry B. "James Thomson and Ideal Landscape: The Triumph of Pictorialism." In his *Heroic Nature: Ideal Landscape in English Poetry from Marvell to Thomson,* pp. 253-95. Evanston, Ill.: Northwestern University Press, 1973.

    Examines the ways in which the descriptive technique of *The Seasons* and *The Castle of Indolence* stems from Thomson's considerable appreciation of the visual arts.

Stephen, Sir Leslie. "Thomson." In his *History of the English Thought in the Eighteenth Century,* Vol. II, pp. 360-62. New York: G. P. Putnam's Sons, 1876.

    Includes a discussion of the intellectual background of Thomson's poetry; posits that Thomson, despite his emotional response to nature, assumed an intellectual attitude, viewing it as the ultimate argument against atheism.

Stormer, Phillip Ronald. "Holding 'High Converse with the Mighty Dead': Morality and Politics in James Thomson's *Winter.*" *English Language Notes* XXIX, No. 3 (March 1992): 27-40.

Closely examines Thomson's revisions in one passage of "Winter" and concludes that "each version becomes a more cohesive whole, thematically stronger."

Thompson, Francis. "James Thomson." *The Academy* n.s. 51, No. 1302 (April 17, 1897): 417.

Denigrates Thomson as a poet whose name "stands for little or nothing" and is preserved only because of its frequent association with John Milton and William Wordsworth.

Walker, Imogene B. *James Thomson (B.V.): A Critical Study.* Ithaca: Cornell University Press, 1950, 212 p.

One of the standard biocritical studies.

Additional coverage of Thomson's life and career is contained in the following sources published by Gale Research: *Literature Criticism from 1400 to 1800,* **Vols. 16 and 29; and** *Dictionary of Literary Biography,* **Vol. 95.**

Edward Young

1683-1765

English poet, essayist, and dramatist.

The following entry contains critical essays focusing on Young's relationship to Preromanticism. For further information on Young, see *LC*, Vol. 3.

INTRODUCTION

Young's reputation and influence as a poet rest largely on his long poem *The Complaint; or, Night Thoughts* (1742) and his essay *Conjectures on Original Composition* (1759). Both were quite popular in the eighteenth century and tended to evoke or anticipate many themes—melancholy, subjective expression, an interest in the sublime, a rejection of classical forms, and the celebration of individual genius—which were to become central concerns of the Romantic movement. For these reasons, Young is seen as an important bridge between Neoclassicism and Romanticism, and even by some, as a very early Romantic.

Biographical Information

Young was born in Hampshire to the rector of Upham and his wife. He attended New College and Corpus Christi at Oxford University and subsequently was awarded a law fellowship at All Souls College. In 1719 Young earned a doctorate in Civil Laws, but apparently had little interest in pursuing a career in his field of study. Meanwhile he had begun his literary career, publishing his first poem, "An Epistle to the Rt. Hon. George Lord Lansdowne," in 1713. A man of high ambition and many interests outside literature and law, Young was plagued by career disappointments throughout his life. He failed in his bid for a seat in Parliament and was similarly frustrated in the clerical career he embarked upon after taking Holy Orders in 1728; although he was soon appointed a royal chaplain, he never felt that the recognition he achieved equaled his true merits. Young's ambition was particularly evident in his literary career and most of his early poems are dedicated to people of wealth and influence. He did enjoy sporadic patronage and encouragement, most notably from Philip, Duke of Wharton, but never to the extent he felt was his due, and even his popular successes, especially his long poem *Night Thoughts,* did not alleviate his sense of disappointment. Some commentators have contended that these failures and frustrations contribute to the melancholy tone of most of his writing. In 1731 Young married Lady Elizabeth Lee, the widowed daughter of the Earl of Lichfield, and they had one son. But Young suffered losses in

his personal life as well: within a five-year span in the 1740s, his wife, his step-daughter, and her husband all died. This succession of deaths was one of the motivating factors that prompted him to write *Night Thoughts.* Critics have disagreed about the extent to which the gloomy and depressed persona of *Night Thoughts* represents Young himself. Some find elements of hope in his last poem, *Resignation,* but most contend that Young's last years were lonely and bitter and that he died a profoundly disappointed man.

Major Works

Like many eighteenth-century authors, Young wrote in a sometimes surprising variety of genres. *Night Thoughts,* a 10,000 line poem which some critics take to be a response to Pope's *Essay on Man,* is a soliloquy addressed to Lorenzo, a young profligate whom the narrator seeks to impress with the sorrow of the world and the majesty of God. It is divided into nine parts, each signifying a particular night. In general terms, the first five nights comprise a subjective description of grief, while the remaining four are largely an exercise in Christian apologetics. The work received high acclaim when it was first published, admired as much for its religious and moral principles as for its poetic achievement. The public imagination was captivated by both the poem's implicit autobiographical aspect and the melancholy brooding that inspired and informed *Night Thoughts*; the poem set the tone of fascination with the macabre employed by subsequent writers of the so-called Graveyard school, including Robert Blair, author of *The Grave* (1743) and Thomas Gray, author of *Elegy Written in a Country Churchyard* (1751). The fame of *Night Thoughts* spread quickly to Europe and the poem was translated into numerous languages. Critics from Young's time to the present day have complained that Young's sometimes irregular meters, as well as his rhymes, phrasing, and grammar, are often graceless and awkward. But they have likewise noted his occasional rich use of imagery, and his bent for epigrammatic expression, even if he seemed unable to sustain these talents throughout any given work. The minor objections made to the poem echoed those leveled against Young's work as a whole—redundancy and the occasional awkwardness of expression—but these reservations did not dim the poem's popularity or influence, especially among the Romantics. Young's philosophical and emotional connection to Romanticism is most clear in his essay *Conjectures on Original Composition,* written in the form of letters to his friend Samuel Richardson. Many consider it an early Romantic manifesto shaped by a mid-century revival of interest in Longinus's *On the Sublime*. In this essay Young declares his personal tenets of literary criticism, arguing strongly for a reduced reliance on classical formalism and for the freedom of original creativity and individual genius. Arguing against "easy imitation," Young called for the poetic imagination to encompass all of the world, including and especially nature and the supra-natural, and to value the subjective aspect of poetic creation. He also insisted upon the use of blank verse over rhymed couplets. Many of these themes would later be championed by William Wordsworth in his *Lyrical Ballads*. Although the *Conjectures* received a share of popularity in the eighteenth century, particularly in Germany, it is largely in retrospect that the essay's full value as a link between Neoclassicism and Romanticism has been appreciated.

Most of Young's other work has received comparatively little critical attention, and significantly less approbation. Of his early work, little has been deemed of lasting interest. In general, his early poems were damned with faint praise in the eighteenth century; their reception has been even more cool in recent times. More well-received was Young's series of satires. Although pointed and witty, they are generally good-natured and display little of the biting sarcasm and caustic ill-humor that characterize other satires of the eighteenth century. The satires were quite popular when published and despite some adverse criticism, some modern critics believe their merit approaches that of *Night Thoughts* or *Conjectures*. Revealing as they do a humorous side of Young rarely seen in his poetry, they are considered by many commentators to be the most accessible of all Young's work to twentieth-century readers. Young also wrote several dramas, all tragedies, which were fairly popular in their day. His plays, *The Revenge* (1721), *Busiris, King of Egypt* (1719), and *The Brothers* (1753), all share themes of revenge, hatred, and violence. The plays' high melodrama suited the theatrical taste of the day, but as dramatic standards and expectations have changed, the interest of the tragedies has declined and many critics have found Young's themes disturbing. *The Centaur Not Fabulous* (1755), a diatribe written in the form of letters to a hypothetical friend, is an attack on what Young deemed the loose morals of his day. Though his contemporaries approved the piece, today it is generally derided for its overt moralizing. Young's final poem, *Resignation* (1761), has been seen by many critics as the poet's last attempt to come to terms with the disappointments in his life and with his fear of death. How far he succeeded in these efforts is debatable; while some believe the poem is the work of a man at last reconciled to fate, others contend that Young's attempt at resignation was a failure and that he remained fundamentally unconvinced by his own arguments.

Critical Reception

After a somewhat tepid response to his early literary work, Young achieved considerable popular and even financial success for his poems, satires and dramas. But this high regard did not generally last into the nineteenth and twentieth centuries. Part of the change in critical perception of Young's work seems to hinge largely on changing critical and cultural tastes. This is especially true of the satires and dramas. In the case of *Night Thoughts,* while it helped to build Young's reputation as a major poet in his day, the poem's reputation began to falter with changing critical perceptions in the early nineteenth century. Critics began to find the extreme melancholy of *Night Thoughts* verging on the morbid, and the emotional outpouring of despair, which accounted for so much of the poem's appeal in the eighteenth century, came to be viewed as excessive and affected. The overt didacticism of the poem also came under attack, as did the spiritual validity of its message of hopelessness. Still, *Night Thoughts* retained its adherents; even those who deplored what was termed its gloomy bad taste and poetic irregularities acknowledged that the poem was original and showed flashes of genius. Twentieth-century critics have had similar complaints about the poem's heavy-handed religious didacticism, affected emotionalism, and morbid preoccupation with death. But modern critics have found the poem to be interesting and valuable, sometimes more for what it aspires to than what it achieves. Ultimately, Young is regarded as a minor poet, though not an unimportant one, since his work anticipated and influenced Romanticism in England and Germany, and his *Conjectures* remains a valued contribution to the history of literary criticism.

PRINCIPAL WORKS

An Epistle to the Rt. Hon. George Lord Lansdowne (poetry) 1713
A Poem on the Last Day (poetry) 1713
The Force of Religion; or, Vanquished Love (poetry) 1714
Busiris, King of Egypt (drama) 1719
A Paraphrase of the Book of Job (poetry) 1719
The Revenge (drama) 1721
*Satire I (satire) 1725
*Satire II (satire) 1725
*Satire III (satire) 1725
*Satire IV (satire) 1725
*Satire the Last (satire) 1726; also published as *Satire VII, 1726
*Satire V (satire) 1727
*Satire VI (satire) 1728
***The Complaint; or Night Thoughts: Night the First: On Life, Death, and Immortality* (poetry) 1742
***Night the Second: On Time, Death, and Friendship* (poetry) 1742
***Night the Third: Narcissa* (poetry) 1742
***Night the Fourth: The Christian Triumph* (poetry) 1743
***Night the Fifth: The Relapse* (poetry) 1743
***Night the Sixth: The Infidel Reclaimed, Part I* (poetry) 1744
***Night the Seventh: The Infidel Reclaimed, Part II* (poetry) 1744
***Night the Eighth: Virtue's Apology; or, the Man of the World Answered* (poetry) 1745
***Night the Ninth: The Consolation* (poetry) 1746
The Brothers (drama) 1753
****The Centaur Not Fabulous* (prose) 1755
Conjectures on Original Composition in a Letter to the Author of Sir Charles Grandison (prose) 1759
Resignation (poetry) 1761
The Complete Works, Poetry and Prose, of the Rev. Edward Young, LL.D (poetry, drama, and prose) 1854

*These works were collected, revised, and published as *Love of Fame; or, The Universal Passion in Seven Characteristical Satires* in 1728.

**These works were published as *The Complaint; or Night Thoughts* in 1750.
***This work was also published as *The Centaur Not Fabulous, in Six Letters to a Friend, on the Life in Vogue* in 1755.

CRITICISM

Courtney Melmoth (essay date 1776)

SOURCE: *Observatons on "The Night Thoughts" of Dr. Young with Occasional Remarks on The Beauties of Poetical Composition*, Richardson and Urquhart, 1776, 211 p.

[*In the following excerpt from his commentary on Young's* Night Thoughts, *Melmoth discusses the style, imagery, and language of the "Ninth Night"—writing in the form of a letter to his friend Archibald.*]

. . . **Night the Ninth,** as it is the last, so is it by much the longest of the work, and considered together, not inferior to the former parts. It is chiefly argumentative, and it is not very easy to unite argument and poetry. Poetry certainly has a fairer chance to delight in works of fancy, and argument in matters of fact. The spirit of poetry is imagination and fable; the spirit of argument is *Truth,* simple, single Truth. Poetry is the product of genius. Argument is the department of judgement. Not but poetical images, like elegant dresses, are often an advantage to the native beauty; and some of our best compositions, I mean our most sacred ones likewise, the Scriptures for instance, owe half their influence, perhaps more, to those sublimities, of language, and poetic simplicity in which the greatest and noblest truths are conveyed. But still, imagination is more immediately natural to the genius of poetry; and in support of this I might quote Shakespear, Milton, and every successful poet ancient and modern, in our language and in every other. Imagination may be allowed to decorate truth, and therefore Truth and Poetry are often friends. But yet, argument allows very circumscribed decorations, in comparison of those airy and animated effusions, which flow warm and wild from the true poetical heart.

A poet who stands at the very top of Parnassus, is not only in himself an *instance* of the truth of this opinion, but even expresses it in words:

> The poet's eye, in a fine phrenzy rowling,
> Doth glance from earth to Heaven, from Heav'n to earth;
> And as *imagination* bodies forth
> The forms of things unknown, the poet's pen
> Turns them to shape, and gives to airy *nothing*
> A local habitation, and a name.

Perhaps it is not possible to unite the argumentative with the poetical in any composition, the Scriptures excepted; they are always an exception, in a greater degree, than we find them in the *Essay on Man.* Bolingbroke's philosophy is embellished with Pope's poetry; and it must be confest, that virtue always rises in her charms, and seems indeed to assume new and more resistless attractions, when she comes innocently arrayed in the robes of poesy; when her language is more lofty, and her voice more melodious. Prophet and poet were you know once the same thing; yet still I must insist, that Fancy is is the field for poetry to expatiate in. If she delights in the friendship of Truth, she is enchanted and inspired by the endearments of Fancy: It may not be unuseful to you, to illustrate this:

As I have had occasion to mention the *Essay on Man* and Mr. Pope, let our first examples be derived from his writings. We begin with a quotation of *argument*.

> What wou'd this man? now upward wou'd he
>   soar,
> And little less than angel, wou'd be more;
> Now looking downwards just as griev'd
>   *appears,*
> To want the strength of bulls, the fur of *bears;*
> Made for his use all creatures if he call,
> Say what their use had he the powers of all?
>
>   · · · · ·
>
> Each beast, each insect, happy in its own,
> Is Heav'n unkind to man, and man alone?
> Shall he alone, whom rational we call,
> Be pleased with nothing, if not blest with all?

In this, as in fifty other passages, there is a beautiful share of morality and poetry. But pray attend to the voice of the latter in her own province, viz. in a work of imagination—the *Rape of the Lock.* You are intimate with the poem, and therefore I may spare myself the trouble of references: Select what I will, you will know where about I am.

> Belinda smil'd, and all the world was gay,
> All but the Sylph;—with careful thoughts
>   opprest,
> Th' impending woe sat heavy on his breast.
> He summons strait his denizens of air,
> The lucid squadrons round the sails repair;
> Soft o'er the shrouds aërial whispers breathe,
> That seem'd but Zephyrs to the train beneath;
> Some to the fun their insect wings unfold,
> Waft on the breeze, or sink in clouds of gold;
> Transparent forms, too fine for mortal sight,
> Their slurid bodies half dissolv'd in light.
> &c. &c.

Next their business and pleasures.

> Some in the fields of purest æther play,
> And bask, and whiten in the blaze of day;
> Some guide the course of wand'ring orbs on
>   high,
> Or roll the planets thro' the boundless sky;
> Some, less refin'd, beneath the moon's pale
>   light,

> Pursue the stars that shoot athwart the night;
> Or search the mists in grosser air below,
> Or dip their pinions in the painted bow;
> Or brew, &c. &c.

Then the department of others, whose province it is to attend the ladies.

> To save the powder from too rude a gale,
> Nor let the imprison'd essences exhale;
> To draw fresh colours from the vernal flowers,
> To steal from rainbows e'er they drop in
>   showers
> A brighter wash, &c.

Our *ideas* of angelic and infernal natures must be *imaginary.* What in the world of *argumentative* poetry can equal the imagery of the following descriptions of Raphael and Satan, by Milton.

> At once, on th' Eastern cliff of Paradise
> He lights, and to his proper shape returns
> A seraph wing'd; fix wings he wore, to shade
> His lineaments divine; the pair that clad
> Each shoulder broad, came mantling o'er his
>   breast
> With regal ornament; the middle pair,
> Girt like a starry zone his waste, and round
> Skirted his loins and thighs with downy gold
> And colours dipt in heav'n; the third his feet
> Shadow'd from either heel with feathered mail
> Sky-tinctur'd grain. Like Maia's son he stood
> And shook his plumes, that heavenly fragrance
>   fill'd
> The circuit wide.

The *contrast,* in the person of the Devil, not only promotes and corroborates our present purpose, but is an evidence of Milton's amazing imagination, which could, in colours so lively, and in imagery so bold and glowing, represent, as best suited his design, either an evil Spirit, or a Seraph; an Angel of Light, or a Demon of Darkness.

> Thus Satan talking to his nearest mate,
> With head uplift above the wave, and eyes
> That sparkling blaz'd his other parts besides
> Prone on the flood, extended long and large,
> Lay floating many a rood.————
>
>   · · · · ·
>
> Forthwith, upright he rears from off the pool
> His mighty stature: On each hand the flames
> Driv'n backward, slope their pointing spires
>   and roll'd
> In billows, leave i'th' midst a horrid vale.
> Then with expanded wings he steers his
>   flight
> Aloft, incumbent on the dusky air
> That felt unusual weight.————

Well might Mr. Addison remark, that Milton triumphs over all the poets both modern and ancient, in the *greatness of his sentiment;* but truly Homer needs not have been excepted. If in point of sublimity, Homer is his *equal,* methinks the compliment is sufficient.

Although I confine these letters, as above hinted, totally to *English* compositions, yet here I cannot resist referring you to an enchanting description of the descent of "Maia's son" in Homer. It is in the 24th Book of his *Iliad,* ver. 339. Dr. Newton, the editor of *Paradise Lost,* has quoted a literal imitation of it from Virgil. Vide *Æn.* 4. ver. 238.

> Dixerat: Ille patris magni parere parabat
> Imperio, &c. &c.

The admirable Shakespear, "Fancy's Child," gives us the last instance—one instance out of a thousand Archibald. I fix upon Prospero's abjuration of his art.

> Ye elves of hills, brooks, standing lakes, and
>   groves,
> And ye, that on the sands with printless foot
> Do chase the ebbing Neptune; and do fly him
> When he comes back; you demy-puppets, that
> By moonshine do the green four ringlets make
> Whereof the ewe not bites; and you, whose
>   pastime
> Is to make midnight mushrooms, that rejoice
> To hear the solemn curfew; by whose aid
> (Weak masters tho' you be) I have bedimm'd
> The noon-tide sun, call'd forth the mutinous
>   winds,
> And 'twixt the green sea and the azur'd vault
> Set roaring war; to the dread, rattling thunder
> Have I given fire, and rifted Jove's stout oak
> With his own bolt: The strong-bas'd promontory
> Have I made shake, and by the spurs pluckt up
> The pine, and cedar; but this rough magic I here
>   abjure.
>
>   THE TEMPEST.

In close of this part of our subject, let me recommend Spencer to your attention: A poet whose fancy and genius will, in spite of certain *obsoletenesses,* be coëval with language and the world.

I have said thus much on the heads of poetry and argument, partly for your sake and partly for our Author's. A large proportion of the **Night Thoughts,** is employed in such a train of argument as renders poetry almost incompatible: for which reason perhaps, such contemplations should for the most part be contented with prose. Some contend, that blank verse *is* nearly prose; an assertion, which, were it true, robs the best and greatest writers the world has produced of their poetic character: On this principle, Milton, Shakespear, Young, Thomson, &c. &c are not eminent poets—nay, not po-

ets at all: As if the mere ding-dong of rhime, or echo of sounds, were the only characteristics of poetry. At this rate also Shakespear is prosaic, and Sternhold is poetical! Preposterous! Of this enough. . . .

                    . . . . .

The Consolation opens in an interesting manner.

> As when a traveller, &c.

In the middle of the reflections, our Author recites, generally, what has been already sung, and introduces this recitation with an apt allusion: As it will give you a recapitulatory satisfaction, and refresh in your memory the various subjects which have been contemplated, I will insert the verses here.

> As when o'erlaboured, and inclin'd to breathe,
> A panting traveller, some rising ground,
> Some small ascent, has gain'd, he turns him round,
> And measures with his eye the various vale,
> The fields, woods, meads, and rivers he has past;
> And, satiate of his journey, thinks of home,
> Endear'd by distance, nor affects more toil;
> Thus I, though small, indeed, is that ascent
> The muse has gain'd, review the paths she trod;
> Various, extensive, beaten but by few;
> And, conscious of her prudence in repose,
> Pause; and with pleasure meditate an end,
> &c.
> Thro' many a field of *moral* and *divine,*
> The muse has stray'd; and much of *sorrow*
>   seen
> In human ways; and much of *false* and *vain;*
> Which none, who travel this bad road, can miss.
> O'er *friends deceas'd* full heartily she wept;
> Of *love divine,* the wonders she display'd;
> Prov'd man *immortal;* shew'd the source of joy;
> The *grand tribunal* rais'd; assign'd the bounds
> Of *human grief:* In *few,* to close the whole,
> The moral muse has shadow'd out a sketch,
> Tho' not in form, nor with a Raphael stroke:
> Of *most* our weakness needs *believe,* or *do,*
> In this our land of travel, and of hope,
> For peace on *earth,* or prospect of the *skies.*

We must now look a little back. The poet enters into a description of the *last day,* in this Night's Contemplation: In his works also you will find another poem on the same subject. In both places the sentiments are devout and noble; but I believe this important theme has been more *poetically* managed by an Author, who, if I mistake not, is still living—Dr. Oglevie,—vide,— *Day of Judgement.* There is much grandeur in these *conjectures* of our poet.

> At *midnight,* when mankind is wrapt in peace,
> And worldly fancy feeds on golden dreams;

To give more dread to man's most dreadful hour,
At midnight, 'tis presum'd, this pomp will burst
From tenfold darkness; sudden, as the spark
From smitten steel; from nit'rous grain the blaze.
Man, starting from his couch, shall sleep no
    more!
The day is broke, which never more shall close!
Above, around, beneath, amazement all!
Terror and glory join'd in their extremes!
Our *God* in grandeur, and our *world* on fire!
All nature struggling in the pangs of death!

The description is here aweful, but there is an error in the poetry. I have more than once taken notice of Young's want of skill in arrangement of his images: Another instance is in these lines.

1. Terror

2. Terror and glory, join'd in their extremes.

3. Our God in grandeur, and our world on fire.

1. All nature struggling in the pangs of death.

The effect which might have been produced by these verses is ruin'd; for the last line should, without all question, be first, I mean before the middle one, as I have markt them. The reason is obvious: "Our God in grandeur", annihilates every other glory; even "Nature struggling in the pangs of death," and "our world on fire," are nothing to it: So that in strict poetical propriety, our God in grandeur ought to close the whole passage: All that can come *after,* even the burning universe, is weak and impotent.

A moral, I might also say an astronomical and philosophical survey, of the Nocturnal Heavens, is likewise a part of this Night's subject; but the sentiments are chiefly repetitions of what was said in the former books, where Cynthia is so often mention'd, and all her "starry train." The address to Night at the opening of the survey, is finely poetical.

          —————O majestic night!
Nature's great ancestor, day's elder born!
And fated to survive the transient fun!
By mortals, and immortals, seen with awe!
A starry crown thy raven brow adorns,
An azure zone thy waist; clouds, in heav'ns
    loom,
Wrought through varieties of shape and shade,
In ample folds of drapery divine,
Thy flowing mantle form; and, heav'n
    throughout,
Voluminously pour thy pompous train.

As the Doctor in a former book described, and even in this, describes the Nights as favourable to virtue and

wisdom, let us now see what he says on considering that, it is also favourable to vice and folly.

          —————The trembling stars
See, crimes gigantic, stalking through the
    gloom
With front erect, that hide their head by day,
And making night still darker by their deeds.
Slumb'ring in covert, till the shades descend,
Rapine and *murder,* link't, now prowl for
    prey.
The miser earths his treasure; and the thief,
Watching the mole, half-beggars him e'er morn.
Now plots, and foul *conspiracies,* awake;
And, muffling up their horrors from the moon,
Havock and devastation they prepare;
Now sons of riot in mid-revel, rage.
And now the rank adulterer;
Ascends secure; and laughs at Gods, and men.

This description confesses a master: If I compare it with what follows it ought *indeed* to be the work of a master.

          —————Now o'er one half the world
Nature seems dead, and wicked dreams abuse
The curtain'd sleep; now witchcraft celebrates
Pale heart's offerings; and wither'd murder,
Alarm'd by his centinel, the wolf,
Whose howl's his watch, thus with his stealthy
    pace,
With Tarquin's ravishing strides, towards his
    design
Moves like a ghost.

                           SHAKESPEAR.

You will be pleased with the *questions* that succeed on the God of Night.

Who turns his eye on nature's midnight face,
But must enquire—"What hand behind the scene
What arm almighty, put these wheeling globes
In motion, and wound up, the vast machine?
Who rounded in his palm these spacious orbs?
Who bowl'd them flaming thro' the dark
    profound,
Numerous as glittering gems of morning dew,
       . . . . .
And set the bosom of *old night* on fire."
                        NIGHT THOUGHTS.

The *answer* is a strain equally lofty.

          —————He, whose potent word,
Like the loud trumpet, levy'd first their powers
In night's in glorious empire, where they slept
In beds of darkness: arm'd them with fierce
    flames,
Arrang'd, and disciplin'd, and cloath'd in gold.

But sufficient of extract; the remainder of this, my last Epistle, shall be engaged in shewing you some *slips* in the *Consolation;* slips, which are however never excus'd by the world, to a man of Dr. Young's genius.... I shall be obliged now to write miscellaneously; reviewing the book, and marking an error, where I find it without length of quotation. I once more mark our Author's hackneying a word. . .

> ————Deputed conscience scales
> The dread tribunal, and *forestalls* our doom;
> *Forestalls,* and by *forstalling* proves it sure.

Recounting the wonders of the last day, he says,

> All nature, like an earthquake trembling round,
> All deities, like *summer's swarms* on wing;
> All *basking* in the full meridan blaze.

This simile of the summer swarm being bad, is among the great errors of composition: The Author means, I suppose, as *thick* as summer swarms; but that meaning is so faintly *implied,* not *exprest,* that it admits a bald interpretation. Deities, like summer swarms. How insignificant! *all basking* too; worse and worse! Can we carry with us the idea of Angels, and yet imagine that on *such* a day they would, like wanton summer swarms, be *basking* in the blaze, by which the world is to be destroyed. Basking is even a word of *luxurious idleness.*

Young is often defective in harmony, as here,

> Earth's actors change earth's transitory scenes;

Or here,

> The sweet, the clement, mediatorial hour.

Once more,

> Laborious. 'Tis impracticable quite,

Cutting and clipping words is not well:

> Angels *can't* tell me, angels *cannot* guess.

This is to accommodate the measure, but sense and elegance suffer by it.

Coining words, or even risquing infrequent ones, is as bad.

> Monarchs of all elaps'd, or *unarriv'd.*

Again,

> *Eliminate* my spirit, give it range.

> *Elance* thy thought.

An *unadept* in mysteries.

> Affords an emblem of *millennial* love,
> That *horologe* machinery divine;
> Breeds all that *un-celestial* discord.

> ————Shall mysteries descend
> From *un-mysterious?*————
> Than this *call'd un-miraculous* survey;
> Of subterranean, *excavated* grots.

> Mark how the *labyrinthian* turns they take.

> Push out its *corrugate,* expansive make.

It is not elegant to use the same word, (particularly if it be of remarkable kind) too frequently,

> And ne'er *unlock* her resolution more,
> And fly through infinite and all *unlock.*

Though I have abjur'd further extract, yet I cannot avoid finding room for our Author's fine description of the sun. He speaks of it as an *evidence* of omnipotence.

> Full ample the dominions of the sun!
> Full glorious to behold! how far, how wide,
> The matchless monarch, from his flaming throne,
> Lavish of lustre, throws his beams about him,
> Farther, and faster, than a thought can fly,
> And feeds his planets, with eternal fires! . . .

J. Mitford (essay date 1864)

SOURCE: "Life of Young," in *The Poetical Works of Edward Young,* Little, Brown and Company, 1864, pp. vii-li.

[*Here, Mitford comments on Young's satires,* Original Composition, *and several other works, noting that the* Night Thoughts *show "fertility of thought and luxuriance of imagination."*]

. . . The Satires of Young were published separately, in folio, under the title of ***The Universal Passion***. The first appeared, in folio, in the year 1725, and the last was finished in the beginning of 1726. The fifth Satire on Woman was not published till 1727, and the sixth not till 1728, when they were all collected and introduced with a preface, in which the author hints that poetry is not favourable to preferment or honors. He acquired, however, the sum of three thousand pounds by these poems; of which Spence, on the authority of Rawlinson, says two thousand was bestowed by the Duke of Grafton, and that when one of his friends exclaimed, "Two thousand pounds for a poem," he said, it was the best bargain he ever made in his life, for the poem was worth four thousand. The satires are inscribed by Young to illustrious names, the Duke of Dorset, Mr. Dodington, Mr. Spencer Compton, and Sir Robert Walpole. His panegyricks did not go unrewarded; for in his poem of Instalment, addressed to the minister, he acknowledges with gratitude that he has received the bounty of the crown.

> My breast, O Walpole, glows with grateful fire,
> The streams of royal bounty turned by thee
> Refresh the dry domains of poetry.

It is said that Swift pronounced of these satires that they should be either more angry or more merry, an observation not made without justice, but which seems to have arisen from some passages in Young's preface.

These Satires are the production of a mind rendered acute by observation, enriched by reflection, and polished with wit. They abound in ingenious and humorous allusions. They show much knowledge of life, experience of society, and acquaintance with that learning that is drawn from books. Their defects appear to me to consist in their being too epigrammatic, by which single couplets sparkle with a brilliancy and point, that concentrates the allusion or image within their narrow bounds, and separates it from the rest of the poem. Many passages read like a continued string of epigrams; whereas the good execution of a poem, as of a painting, looks to each particular part only as it bears upon the whole; the finish of one is regulated by another; the colouring of one object, if necessary, is lowered to bring it in harmony with the rest; and nothing is admitted, which, heightening the brilliancy of particular passages, tends to cast over the rest a flat and unnatural hue. If we were allowed to bring to poetry the language of a sister art, if might be complained that there is a *spottiness* in the execution of these satires disagreeable to a pure and correct taste. Unfortunately joined to this careful and elaborate polish of some more sparkling passages, we find an occasional versification careless and unfinished; some rhymes are defective in exactness and some are wanting. But the great defect is in the perpetual exaggeration of the sentiment, which mars the delicacy of the wit, destroys the justice of the satire, and forfeits the confidence of the reader. There is no gradation of censure or of praise, no middle tint bringing the lights and shadows into harmony, no diminishing perspective in the moral view. All objects are equally bright, and equally near, and all represented in a distorted and disproportionate size. In the following passage, touching on the distempered taste of those who prefer the gaiety of cities, to rural charms and the society of nature, the poet passes on through different illustrations, all exaggerated, till he ends with a fiction unnatural and absurd.

> Such Fulvia's passion for the town—fresh air,
> An odd effect, gives vapour to the fair.

> Green fields, and shady groves, and crystal
>   springs,
> And larks, and nightingales are *odious* things.
> But smoke, and dust, and noise, and crowds
>   delight;
> And to be press'd to death transports her quite:
> When silver rivulets play thro' flowery meads,
> And woodbines give their sweets and limes their
>   shades,
> *Black kennels' absent odours she regrets,*
> *And stops her nose at beds of violets.*

It may be proper to observe, that these satires were published before those of Pope. Goldsmith says "that they were in higher reputation when published, than they stand at present. That Young seems fonder of dazzling than of pleasing, of raising our admiration for his wit than our dislike of the follies he ridicules." They were followed by the Instalment, addressed to Sir Robert Walpole, which was, with great propriety, afterwards suppressed; for Burleigh and Godolphin are made to descend from heaven "with purple wings," and stars, and garters, to instal the minister.

The reign of the new king was ushered in by Young with an *Ode to Ocean:* the hint of it was taken from a passage in the royal speech, which recommended the encouragement of seamen, and the abolition of the forcible means of impressment. Its execution is sufficient to show that Young's strength did not lie in lyric poetry. It often swells into bombast, and as often falls into flatness; the choice of the versification was injudicious, though the author says he borrowed it from Dryden, as his subject was great, to express majesty. Prefixed to the original publication was an *Ode to the King Pater Patriæ,* and an *Essay on Lyric Poetry;* neither of those are preserved. The ode, which originally consisted of seventy-three stanzas, Young reduced in his own edition to forty-nine. Among the passages omitted is a *wish* that concluded the poem, and which was contained in thirteen stanzas. The essay is a performance of no merit, written with a constant endeavour to be smart and witty; in the style of those who profess to consider learning and dulness as inseparable; who wish to unite the fine gentleman to the scholar, and who can find nothing more to say of the ancient lyric poets, than that the muse of Pindar is like Sacharissa, and that Sappho is passionately tender, like Lady————. . . .

Of the *Night Thoughts,* which were published from 1742 to 1744, Young's favourite and most finished poem, it may be said, that they show a mind stored with reading and reflexion, purified by virtuous feelings, and supported by religious hope. There is in them fertility of thought and luxurance of imagination, an originality in the style, an expansion of sentiment, and an accumulation of argument and illustration, which seems almost boundless. With little or no narrative, and but few touches of personal character, the interest is endeavoured to be maintained by the greatness of the subject, the deep and important reflections, and the copious stores of observation. The poem is filled with wise maxims of moral conduct and religious faith: and the poetical language is well chosen without being very select, or elaborately formed. But there is a want of a clear connection in the subject; every image is amplified to the utmost; every argument expanded and varied, as much as the greatest fertility of the fancy could effect. The subject is pursued through every gradation of feeling, and every channel of thought. There is no selection, no discreet and graceful reservation; no mark of that experienced taste that knows exactly when the purpose has been effected, and which leaves the rest to be supplied by the imagination of the reader. Reflection follows on reflection, and thought on thought, in such close succession, that, as in books of maxims, one truth obstructs and obliterates another; an expression, otherwise permanent, is destroyed as soon as formed; and we feel, I am afraid, in reading this poem of Young, as we do in the perusal of Seneca, that no progress, no advancement is made: we seem to move in a perpetually dazzling circle of argument and reflection, and analogy, and metaphor, and illustration, without the power of passing beyond it; and it is on this account that the perusal of both these writers, however delightful for a season, soon fatigues and dissatisfies the mind. Any one who will compare the moral writings of Cicero and Seneca in this respect, will soon mark the distinction to which I allude. Besides, the copiousness of expression outruns the extent of the matter. The words overload the subject; and the magnificence of language is not always supported by a corresponding grandeur of thought. There is too great a uniformity of subject for the length of the poem, to keep the attention enlivened, the fancy amused, or even the feelings awake; especially when not adorned by any peculiar harmony of numbers, or connected with the progress of a narrative. In the conclusion of the *Centaur not Fabulous,* Young acknowledges his not being able to quit his subject. "My busy mind (he says) perpetually suggests new hints; my heart knows not how to refrain from pursuing them. The volume grows upon my hands, till its bulk would defeat its end; new rays of thought dart in upon me, which, like cross lights, confound and perplex each other." The flow of his versification was with Young of secondary importance, and made subservient to the vigorous enforcement of the subject. Nothing can be well more inartificial, or inharmonious; it is cut up into short sentences, and terminates with the pause at the end of the line. Very seldom can it boast of that flowing harmony and those modulated cadences which other poets have produced; and which in Milton, and among those of later times, have arisen to the highest excellence, and afforded the most exquisite delight. The high strain of religious feeling, and elevated language, is often debased by vulgar or satirical expressions, as "the same old slabbered tale,"—"peruse the parson'd page," or when he says,

> Walk thoughtful on the silent solemn shore
> Of that vast ocean it must sail too soon,
> *And put good works aboard.*

When he calls God "the great Philanthropist," it surely is in a taste that cannot be approved; and such lines as the following—

> When later there's less time to play the fool—

are out of harmony with the grave and sacred character of the poem. I remember once (said Warburton) reading a poem called the *Night Thoughts* to Mr. Pope, where the poet was always on the strain and labouring for expression: "This is a strange man," said he, "he seems to think with the apothecaries that *Album Græcum* is better than an ordinary stool."

In 1745, Young wrote *Reflexions on the Public Situation of the Kingdom* addressed to the Duke of Newcastle; it was originally printed as the conclusion of the *Night Thoughts,* though very properly he did not include it in the collection of his other works; the mediocrity of its execution has consigned it to a deserved oblivion.

In 1753, the tragedy of the *Brothers,* which had lain by him above thirty years, appeared on the stage. Young had intended to apply the profits of this play to the Society for the Propagation of the Gospel, but as they fell much short of his expectations, he made up the sum of a thousand pounds from his own pocket

His next performance was the *Centaur not Fabulous,* in six letters to a friend, on the life in vogue; the conclusion is dated November 29th, 1754; the character of Altamont has been given, whether justly or not, to the notorious Lord Euston, a man whose name has only reached posterity, from the unusual load of infamy with which it is covered. This work is written with vigour, animation, and eloquence; expounding the doc-trines of moral truth, with elegance of illustration and power of argument. It is full of imagery, yet abounds too much in poetical allusions, and those decorations which the fertility of Young's imagination so easily supplied. There is also the same want of harmony in this, as in Young's poetical works. Parts read like the *Night Thoughts* before they were modelled into verse, and parts have the wit and epigrammatic point which seem the rude materials of his lively and pungent satires. . . .

The letter in prose, on *Original Composition,* addressed to Richardson, the author of *Clarissa,* appeared in 1759. There is in it much sound criticism, many valuable observations, and a spirit and eloquence which betrayed none of the infirmities of age. In 1762, a short time before his death, and when he was upwards of four-score, he printed his poem of **Resignation**; here for the first time, a decay of his powers is manifested.—"Ætas extrema multum etiam eloquentiæ demsit, dum fessa mente retinet silentii impatientiam." He says that it was not intended for publication, but that imperfect copies having got abroad, he was obliged to publish something, lest a copy still more imperfect should fall into the press. It is in fact little else than the subject of the **Night Thoughts** again worked up, but with a flatness of expression, and a feebleness of execution, which may be expected and pardoned in a bard of four score. . . .

Marjorie Hope Nicolson (essay date 1959)

SOURCE: *Mountain Gloom and Mountain Glory: The Development of the Aesthetics of the Infinite*, Cornell, 1959, 403 p.

[*In the following excerpt from her full-length study of the "aesthetics of the infinite" Nicolson discusses eighteenth-century concepts of the sublime and identifies Young as a perfect example of a poet of the sublime.*]

. . . "When you are criticising the philosophy of an epoch," wrote Alfred North Whitehead, "do not chiefly direct your attention to those intellectual positions which its exponents feel it necessary explicity to defend. There will be some fundamental assumptions which adherents of all the variant systems within the epoch unconsciously presuppose. Such assumptions appear so obvious that people do not know what they are assuming because no other way of putting things has ever occurred to them."[37] We shall remember Whitehead's words as we seek the causes of the change in mountain attitudes that began to take place sometime in the late seventeenth century in England. Various fundamental assumptions, accepted for generations, had to be broken down before new attitudes appeared. In 1611 John Donne, lamenting the corruption of microcosm, geocosm, and macrocosm, wrote:

> But keeps the earth her round proportion still?
> Doth not a Tenarif, or higher Hill
> Rise so high like a Rocke, that one might thinke
> The floating Moone would shipwrack there, and
>   sinke? . . .
> Are these but warts, and pock-holes in the face
> Of th' earth? Thinke so: but yet confesse, in this
> The worlds proportion disfigured is.[38]

Involved in this passage are various "unconscious presuppositions" strange to us but familiar to Donne's contemporaries. The language of Donne's passage echoes literary conventions inherited from the classics and the Bible. The idea that mountains are a blemish to the earth goes back to theological positions long argued by Christian and Jewish Fathers. The basic conception of the "round proportion" of the earth, now disfigured by Teneriffe and other hills, implies an aesthetic accepted by classical and medieval philosophers. In addition to these literary, theological, and philosophical conventions and traditions—all of which must disappear before the attitudes we take for granted can emerge—there are scientific problems which did not occur to Donne, problems which we call geological. Even after we have gone back to the classics and the Fathers to determine "unconscious presuppositions" that led Donne and others to think and speak of mountains as they did, we shall be at less than mid-point of our search, "as one who on his journey baits at noon."

While one group of fundamental assumptions and unconscious presuppositions die, others are born, as in a redwood forest young trees rise, perhaps to guard, perhaps to supplant the dying giant of a thousand years. At the moment men find themselves between the two worlds, one dead, one struggling to be born, we shall find a clash and conflict between various "intellectual positions which its exponents feel it necessary explicitly to defend"—one of the important battles in the long warfare of science versus religion, another Titanomachy with mountains becoming missiles hurled by either side. As the battle subsided, the mountains we see today began to appear to men who looked at them with new eyes, seeing them no longer as "warts, and pock-holes in the face Of th' earth," but as the grandest, most majestic objects on the terrestrial globe, discovering in them the "Sublime."

Historians and critics have done little justice to English genius and originality, so far as the Sublime is concerned. Almost unanimously they have insisted that the conception of sublimity as it developed in the eighteenth century had its origin in a rhetorical treatise, that it was the result of ideas expressed in the *Peri Hupsous* of the pseudo-Longinus, as translated and interpreted by Boileau in 1674. Here again we find the tendency to attribute changes in one art to development in another. When the critics who have considered the problem distinguish between two "Sublimes," they give priority, chronologically and qualitatively, to a rhetorical Sublime, which, as Ronald Crane has said, "is that quality, difficult to determine, but easily detectable to sensitive minds . . . which gives distinction to works of literature and plastic art."[39] If they consider the natural Sublime (the Sublime in external Nature), they tend to classify it as "a degraded form of Longinianism," following upon the rhetorical theory, but debasing it, "showing itself in an excessive emotion for natural objects in the external world." Insofar as they find a Longinian source for this, they discover it in one passing remark in the *Peri Hupsous,* in which Longinus said that men do not admire "the little streams, transparent though they be, and useful too, but Nile, or Tiber, or Rhine, and far more than all, Ocean."

Let us consider the evidence offered by scholars for the effect in England of the rhetorical Sublime. The fragmentary work of Longinus had been available in England throughout the seventeenth century, both in the original and in translation. Between the first edition of 1554 and John Hall's English translation of 1652, at least five editions appeared. Yet Samuel Monk, who has most exhaustively traced the Longinian tradition in England, can find no real interest in Longinus before 1674. He says:

> One might reasonably hope to find a noticeable increase in references to Longinus from this time on [1652]. Ninety-eight years had passed since the *editio princeps* had been printed, and both a Latin and an English translation were in existence. But the time had not yet come for Longinus to gain the ear of the critical world, and we find his name mentioned seldom. Milton himself, with all of his interest in the ancients, seems not to have felt Longinus's charm. In his essay "Of Education," he mentions Longinus as one of the teachers of "a graceful and ornate rhetoric," but that is all. It is a strange paradox that the most sublime of English poets should not have caught from Longinus the suggestion of the sublime as the expression of ultimate values in art, beyond the reach of rhetoric and her handmaidens, the rules. He did not; and it was left to the propounders of an adolescent aesthetic in the next century to find in John Milton's poems, not a "graceful and ornate rhetoric," but the supreme illustration of whatever particular type of the sublime they advocated.[40]

"The time had not come for Longinus to gain the ear of the critical world." Before 1674, when in a single year Boileau published his *L'Art Poétique* and his *Traité du Sublime ou du Merveilleux traduit du grec du Longin,* there seems no evidence that any important English writer was interested in the Greek rhetorical treatise. When the influence of the Longinian rhetoric began to appear, it was less that of Longinus himself than of Longinus-according-to-Boileau, who had somewhat clipped the wings of Pegasus. Radical in its science, more responsive than the continent to the "new philosophy," neoclassical England tended to remain conservative and derivative in its literary criticism. But if the rhetorical Sublime, its roots set down in France, was largely a transplantation, the natural Sublime was flowering in England well before the turn of the century, and travelers to the Alps were "ravished" and "rapt" by greatness, appalled and enthralled by the vast, the grand, the Sublime in external Nature.

In this study I am speaking only of what happened in England. The same phenomenon did not occur in France, where adulation of grand Nature appears later than in England and is possibly as derivative from England as the rhetorical Sublime in England was derivative from France. There are important differences in cultural outlook here, implied in "A Dissertation upon the Word Vast" which Saint-Evremond read to the French Academy, warning his countrymen:

> *Great* is a perfection of Minds; Vast always a *Defect*. A just and regulated Extent makes the Great; an immoderate Greatness the *Vast. Vast* signifies an excessive Greatness. Vast Things differ mightily from those which make an agreeable Impression upon us. *Vasta Solitudo . . .* 'tis a wild Solitude, where we are frighted with being alone. . . . Vast Forest put us into a Fright; the Sight loses it self in looking over Vast Plains. . . . Rivers too large, Overflowings and Inundations displease us by the Noise and Violence of their Billows, and our Eyes cannot with any Pleasure behold their Vast Extent.[41]

Boileau was thinking of rhetorical style rather than of natural scenery, when he wrote in *L'Art Poétique:*

> J'aime mieux un ruisseau qui sur la molle arène
> Dans un pré plein de fleurs lentement se
>   promène,
> Qu'un torrent débordé qui, d'un cours orageux,
> Roule, plein de gravier, sur un terrain fangeux.[42]

Yet the implication is the same. In the mid-century Montesquieu lamented what he called "the destruction of the Sublime" among his countrymen, attributing it to the effect of the "new philosophy," by which he meant the Cartesian philosophy with its emphasis upon clear and distinct laws.[43] But England had caught other implications from a "new philosophy," as we shall see, and even the vastness that seemed excessive to Saint-Evremond was not vast enough for English taste, rivers never too large, inundations—even volcanoes and earthquakes—never too mighty for their imaginations.

Sometime during the eighteenth century the English discovered a new world. In a way, they were like the imaginary cosmic voyagers who, from Lucian to writers of modern science-fiction, have traveled to the moon or planets to find worlds that puzzle, amaze, astound, enthrall by their very differences from our world. Perhaps the experience of eighteenth-century Englishmen was in some ways like that of C. S. Lewis' Ransom in *Out of the Silent Planet*[44] who after a voyage through space reached the new world of Malacandra. His foreboding imagination had peopled the new world with monsters, had led him to expect either rocky desolation or a network of nightmare machines. "But something he learned. Before anything else he learned that Malacandra was beautiful; and he even reflected how odd it was that this possibility had never entered into his speculations about it." For a time he could not analyze or define that beauty; he could indeed only feel rather than comprehend what made it beautiful:

> A mass of something purple, so huge that he took it for a heather-covered mountain, was his first impression; on the other side, beyond the larger

water, there was something of the same kind. But there, he could see over top of it. Beyond were strange upright shapes of whitish green: too jagged and irregular for buildings, too thin and steep for mountains. Beyond and above these again was the rose-coloured cloud-like mass.

"He gazed about him, and the very intensity of his desire to take in the new world at a glance defeated him." He could not describe what he was seeing. Indeed he did not know what he saw, for there was no parallel in his terrestrial experience. As Mr. Lewis says, "Moreover, he knew nothing yet well enough to see it: you cannot see things till you know roughly what they are."

Such—to a great extent—was the experience of many eighteenth-century Englishmen who discovered the Sublime in the external world. Perhaps they may be forgiven for their exaggerations, for their insistence that "the bigger, the better," for the fact that they spoke a language of extravagant hyperbole. To express their experience, new in the history of the human race, there was neither speech nor language.

. . . . .

. . . The climax of the conception of the "vast Sublime" is found in the *"Ninth Night"* of the *Night Thoughts.* No poet was ever more "space intoxicated" than Edward Young, nor did any other eighteenth-century poet or aesthetician equal him in his obsession with the "psychology of infinity"—the effect of vastness and the vast upon the soul of man. He is par excellence the poet of the Sublime. There is no Beauty in the *"Ninth Night,"* no landscape, no color, only passing feeling for the small and exquisite, though, to be sure, he acknowledged the minute in Nature as evidence of God's power:

> True; all things speak a God; but in the small,
> Men trace out him; in great, he seizes Man;
> Seizes, and elevates, and raps, and fills.[64]

As I have said elsewhere: "There is no color in the world of the *Night Thoughts;* there is only light, the 'confluence of ethereal fires From urns unnumber'd,' streaming from the steep of heaven. Young's external nature is dark and void of color. His was, indeed, the kind of world which the telescope had shown the moon to be, a world shining only by reflected light, white and dead."[65] Young had no desire to emulate the "excursion" poets in describing Nature on this earth. His song "shot, ambitious of unbounded scenes, Beyond the flaming limits of the world." His canvas is interstellar space, his technique that of the cosmic voyagers, the "soaring souls that sail among the spheres." Like Shaftesbury's Philocles, Young's Lorenzo, who had remained obstinately unconvinced throughout eight long, tedious books of the *Night Thoughts,* was converted by the "mathematic glories of the skies," after

his mentor led him on a series of cosmic voyages, to approach, as closely as human imagination can ever approach, the Source of Vastness, the true Infinite:

> Loose me from earth's inclosure, from the sun's
> Contracted circle set my heart at large;
> Eliminate my spirit, give it range
> Through provinces of thought yet unexplor'd. . . .
> Thy travels dost thou boast o'er foreign realms:
> Thou stranger to the world! thy tour begin.[66]

"The soul of man was made to walk the skies." From prison released, imagination, spirit, and soul rise to freedom in an infinity native to them, as finite earth had never been. Here for the first time

> she can rove at large;
> There, freely can respire, dilate, extend,
> In full proportion let loose all her pow'rs;
> And, undeluded, grasp at something great.[67]

In space, "the noble pasture of the mind," the soul "expatiates, strengthens, and exults," realizing to the full potentialities which had long lain dormant:

> How great,
> How glorious, then, appears the mind of man,
> When in it all the stars, and planets, roll!
> And what it seems, it is; Great objects make
> Great minds, enlarging as their views enlarge;
> Those still more godlike, as these more divine.[68]

Greatness and vastness are the keynotes of the *"Ninth Night,"* as they were the basis of Young's belief. His is the Romantic insatiability that refuses to be content with the present or with the finite in any form. It is the mood of Henry Power's "elastical souls of the universe," who recognized no "Non Plus Ultra," of Henry More and of Thomas Traherne, whose souls would not be satisfied with less than the all they could never attain. There is no frustration here—only an exultant awareness that there are worlds beyond, that the more man knows, the more there is to know, that the true greatness of man lies in his ability to aspire far beyond his potentialities. Happiness lies in aspiration, in discontent with limitations:

> The mind that would be happy, must be great,
> Great in its wishes; great in its surveys.
> Extended views a narrow mind extend;
> Push out its corrugate, expansive make.[69]

The discontent is "divine," implanted by God in man, who has a "previous sense of objects great." This is God's way of leading man on from limitation to infinite perfection:

> Nature delights in progress; in advance
> From worse to better: But when minds ascend,
> Progress, in part, depends upon themselves.[70]

Here for the first time Young uses the word "progress" in the sense in which it has been understood down to our own time. If "progress" is not yet as inevitable in Nature as it became in the Darwinian period, nevertheless Young has gone far beyond the simple idea of "progress" of the Baconian generation. Man can, if he will, proceed farther and farther in perfectibility through the full range of powers native to him, by refusing to be content with the limitations which the finite would impose upon him, by giving free rein to that "soul," which is not finite but infinite:

> The soul of man, His face design'd to see,
> Who gave these wonders to be seen by Man,
> Has here a previous sense of objects great,
> On which to dwell; to stretch to that expanse
> Of thought, to rise to that exalted height
> Of admiration, to contract that awe,
> And give her whole capacities that strength,
> Which best may qualify for final joy.
> The more our spirits are enlarg'd on earth,
> The deeper draughts shall they receive of
>   Heav'n.[71]

Whether Infinite Space or Infinite God—in Young's vocabulary they seem to be much the same, though his emphasis is even more upon Space than upon God—

> Nothing can satisfy, but what confounds;
> Nothing, but what astonishes, is true.[72]

In spite of Young's obsession with infinite space, he did not forget that other concept which had dawned upon his generation—infinite time. "Eternity," he said, "is written in the stars." As he led his pupil on the journeys through the universe of stars and planets, he mused:

> The boundless space, through which these rovers
>   take
> Their restless roam, suggests the sister thought
> Of boundless time.[73]

The old limitations of time and space are gone. The long-winged hawk of human imagination has not only world enough, but cosmic universe beyond cosmic universe, stretching perhaps to infinity. Time, which had long been limited by the Six Days' works—even by six millennia—has become Eternity. The dread of the end of the world that had hovered so possessively over the earlier seventeenth century has vanished before a sense of space and time more intoxicating than it has ever been since the mid-eighteenth century. The Millennium has come—and has come on earth.

In a single passage in the ***"Ninth Night,"*** Young indicated the basic shift in taste that makes the new aesthetics of the eighteenth and nineteenth centuries different from all that went before. For centuries aestheticians had been more interested in Art than in external Nature. The "great," the "amazing," the "marvellous" had been found in the Seven Wonders of the World—the pyramids, the hanging gardens of Babylon, the Temple of Diana at Ephesus, the Colossus, the Olympian Zeus of Phidias, the Pharos. All these were the works of man, the works of Art. With one exception Young dismissed such "childish toys":

> Thy watery columns squirted to the clouds!
> Thy bason'd rivers and imprison'd seas!
> Thy mountains moulded into forms of men!
> Thy hundred-gated capitals . . .
> Arches triumphal, theatres immense
> Or nodding gardens pendent in mid-air!

These are the work of "Vain Art! thou pigmy pow'r," that seems to swell and strut with pride, only to show its own littleness. In one work of Art alone he found greatness. Like Addison before him, Byron later, and his own contemporary Dyer, he said: "Enter a temple. It will strike an awe." Even the pagan temples might be "proud to meet their gods halfway"; in Christian cathedrals men felt the shadow of divinity.

Far greater than the works of man were the works of Nature in the geocosm, reflecting as they did the vastness of Space and Deity:

> Seas, rivers, mountains, forests, deserts, rocks,
> The promontory's height, the depth profound
> Of subterranean, excavated grots,
> Black-brow'd, and vaulted high, and yawning
>   wide,
> From Nature's structure, or the scoop of Time:
> If ample of dimension, vast of size,
> Ev'n these an aggrandizing impulse give;
> Of solemn thought enthusiastic heights
> Ev'n these infuse.

"But what of vast in these?" Young asks. He replies, "Nothing:—or we must own the skies forgot." Yet great objects make great minds, and even the lesser majesties of earth discovered by Young's contemporaries had enlarged their thoughts and led them to greater awe for the true Vast from whom their own potentialities were drawn.

From Art—far less important now than it had been for centuries—through grand Nature in this world, through cosmic Space, eighteenth-century imagination rose to the true Vast, the Infinite. From that Infinite, through the reaches of space discovered by the new astronomy, sublimity descended to exalt and ennoble "the wide Sea and the Mountains of the Earth." Such was the process of "The Aesthetics of the Infinite.". . .

Notes

. . .[37] Whitehead, *Science and the Modern World*, p. 71.

[38] John Donne, "An Anatomy of the World: The First Anniversary," in *Complete Poetry and Selected Prose*, ed. by John Hayward (Bloomsbury, 1929), pp. 204-205, ll. 284-301.

[39] I quote from a review of Samuel Monk's *The Sublime* written by Ronald Crane in *Philological Quarterly*, XV (1936), 165-167. I am willing to agree with Mr. Crane that many of the exponents of the "natural Sublime" were "psychologists inquiring about the emotions, not critics investigating the sources of high excellence in art," and more than willing to grant that there was debasement of the Sublime among third-rate eighteenth-century poets. But I feel that Professors Crane and Monk and various others have their cart before their horse. In England, as I shall attempt to show, the "natural Sublime" was earlier than the "rhetorical Sublime" and, far from being merely a "debased" Longinianism, was deeply sincere and religious in origin. Longinus did little else for the "natural Sublime" than to offer some assistance in vocabulary.

[40] Samuel Monk, *The Sublime: A Study of Critical Theories in XVIII-Century England* (New York, 1935), p. 20.

[41] *The Works of Mr. de St. Evermont* (London, 1700), I, 364-389.

[42] *L'Art Poétique*, I, 165-170, in Nicolas Boileau-Despréaux, *Œuvres Complètes* (Paris, 1873), II, 304.

[43] C. de S. Montesquieu, *Pensées et Fragmentes inédits* (Bordeaux, 1899-1901), I, 221-222.

[44] C. S. Lewis, *Out of the Silent Planet* (New York, 1946), pp. 40-42.

. . . . .

[64] Young, *Night Thoughts*, IX, 772-774.

[65] *Newton Demands the Muse*, p. 150.

[66] *Night Thoughts*, IX, 586-606.

[67] *Ibid.*, IX, 1016-1023.

[68] *Ibid.*, IX, 1059-1064.

[69] *Ibid.*, IX, 1379-1382.

[70] *Ibid.*, IX, 1957-1959.

[71] *Ibid.*, IX, 568-577.

[72] *Ibid.*, IX, 836-837.

[73] *Ibid.*, IX, 1172-1174.

[74] *Ibid.*, IX, 905-931. I have purposely reversed Young's order. . . .

Isabel St. John Bliss (essay date 1969)

SOURCE: *Edward Young*, Twayne Publishers, Inc., 1969, pp. 111-48.

[*In the following excerpt from her full-length study of Young, Bliss summarizes and analyzes Young's* Night Thoughts, *and* Conjectures on Original Composition.]

The ***Night Thoughts*** constitutes Young's greatest achievement; and widely read in England, on the Continent, and in America, it exerted a good deal of influence, was highly admired, and much quoted. While the initial popular reception came in some measure from the familiarity of much of the subject matter and the widespread interest in it, the main interest came from the sense of freshness, newness, and originality and from the feeling of personal immediacy. On the whole, Young's achievement was not in enunciating new doctrines: he was not an original theologian nor philosopher. Well versed in contemporary ideas, he was a poet; and he gave expression to those ideas in a language striking in effective figures and imagery, with a feeling of warmth and ardor.

Unfortunately, the extreme length of the series of nine poems as a whole—a drawback even in its own day—presents a formidable barrier today when "a long poem" is considered "a contradiction in terms." Furthermore, the whole series is not readily accessible, selections in anthologies being almost invariably confined to **Night I**. But there is no reason to condemn it offhand because it is not of this generation. Written in the 1740's, it is obviously not in the fashion of the mid-twentieth century: "It needs no ghost come from the tomb to tell us this." But many misleading generalizations, based on failure to read the poem (or poems) and on a blind acceptance of some of the misconceptions that gained currency in the late eighteenth century, and others contributed also by ignorance and prejudice in the nineteenth century, and repeated in reference to Young in the twentieth century, are formidable deterrents to the uninformed modern reader. Consideration of the actual poem in relation to its background dispels such misconceptions and indicates something of its real nature.

The nine poems were evidently not planned ahead as a series to constitute a whole: one idea suggested another, one *Night* led to the next, and the poet's pleasure in ramification of details and in developing one idea in a variety of ways led to increasing length. Along with a good deal of repetition there is a difference in emphasis and purpose: the first five *Nights* (of 459, 694, 556, 842, and 1068 lines, respectively) are chiefly concerned with moral reflections on life, death, and human nature; and the last four (of 819, 1480, 1417, and 2434 lines, respectively) are almost wholly devoted to Christian apologetics. Even in the first group there is a difference, the so-called elegiac note being more stressed in the second and third *Nights* than in the other two.

Yet the general organization in each is adequate for such a discursive poem, and the discernible connections and cross references contribute to a certain unity of the whole. Each *Night* has a separate title; and, in the characteristic eighteenth-century custom, a descriptive subtitle indicates the major topics. The theme of immortality as an essential in Christianity runs through and unites the whole. Each poem is written in the first person, as a man meditating in the quiet of night on universal themes not necessarily gloomy but serious, reflecting on ideas which had concerned Young in his own experience, reading, observation of life, and thinking, and had found expression to a large extent in his earlier writings, his letters, and his conversation as recorded by his letter-writing friends. The poems are not literal autobiography, and the "persona" does not represent all of Young.

The method of dialogue, used throughout the series, was that of many argumentative prose treatises to clarify points in discussion by presenting conversation between A and B, or their largely uncharacterized equivalents. Young adapts the dialogue form to secure a feeling of personal participation, immediacy, and emotional involvement by having the speaker address arguments and exhortations to the practically silent member of the dialogue, Lorenzo. Slightly characterized as a young man for whom the speaker is much concerned, and who is somewhat chameleon-like in nature, Lorenzo is in the *Nights I-IV* for the most part the "man of pleasure," the "man of the world," the libertine; and in *Nights VI-IX* he is mostly the "atheist" who must be led to realize the existence of God, but sometimes he is inconsistently the "Deist" who accepts natural religion but rejects revealed Christianity. Elements of all of these different characterizations may be found to some extent in most of the *Nights*. To give a more personal effect, Young uses the "characteristical" method he had used so effectively in his *Satires,* and which he uses in Lorenzo, and in several other instances of named characters as well as many unnamed ones designated as "a man I knew" or some such formula. To consider them actual identifiable people is a serious error.

In the *Night Thoughts* Young uses blank verse, at the time a form which seemed new, as heroic couplet had so long dominated the poetic fashion, though the revival of blank verse had been in progress for some years. Many of the rhetorical characteristics of his earlier poetry are apparent here also. Because of the general unfamiliarity with the content of the *Night Thoughts,* a brief summary of each of the separate poems is of value. The title of the first of the series, *"The Complaint,"* became the general title for *Nights I-VIII,* and the final *Night* was entitled *"The Consolation,"* indicating an answer or completion.

I *Summary of Each* Night

In **Night I, "On Life, Death, and Immortality,"** the poet, sleepless from grief, is reminded of death by the quiet sleep of the world around. His prayer of invocation for divine aid "to lighten and to cheer" and to "strike wisdom from my soul" suggests the purpose and nature of the poem:

> O lead my mind
> (A mind that fain would wander from its woe),
> Lead it through various scenes of life and death;
> And from each scene, the noblest truths inspire.

The striking of the clock suggests thought of the passing of time and man's waste of it. This thought leads to reflection on the contrasting elements of man's nature as mortal man and immortal soul, with thoughts on the consoling idea that those mourned as dead are living in a larger life, and on the folly of pinning all desires on transitory earthly things. The poet's joy in life had been blasted by the triple loss of friends in a short time: ". . . and thrice my peace was slain; / And thrice, ere thrice yon moon had fill'd her horn" (I, 212-13). But, realizing that he is not alone in such grief and that death is universal, he says that he must not indulge in personal grief; but, aware of troubles of mankind, and deploring the lack of benevolence in the world, he must help others. Addressing Lorenzo, a young man of pleasure, he says that warnings of the impermanence of earthly joys are not unkind; and, referring to the unexpected death of their good friend Philander, who had been unaware of his fatal disease, he warns Lorenzo not to count on the future but to live so as to be always in a state of preparedness for death. The folly of man is that he is always about to live, always about to reform: "He resolves; and re-resolves; then dies the same." The lark's song announces dawn. The poet, striving to "cheer the sullen gloom" of grief, wishes for the genius of Homer, Milton, and Pope; and he says he seeks to supplement Pope's omission of the theme of immortality: "Immortal man I sing."

Night II, "Of Time, Death, and Friendship," begins also with midnight sleeplessness and grief; and, with his fortitude and realization of the universality of human woes, he is determined not to dwell on his personal troubles. The poet, turning to Lorenzo, considers themes suggested by the death of Philander—time, death, friendship, and Philander's "final scene." The theme of time—its value, the folly of wasting time, and the irrevocability of past time—is discussed (from line 25 to line 354) with many effective illustrations. Next, for about one hundred lines, the poet is concerned with "death the leveller"—universal and inevitable—and with the value of reminders of it for man, who is prone to give it little thought and to ignore the way life slips by. Then the poet turns to thoughts of Philander and the theme of friendship, the joy and value of conversation with a friend, the basis of wisdom and happiness in friendship—all shared with Philander, a friend for twenty years. In conclusion he describes Philander's death, "the temple of my theme," which showed his friend, though suddenly faced with death, "undamp'd by doubt, undarken'd by despair," but marked by peace and hope.

Night III, **"Narcissa,"** opens also with nocturnal sleeplessness and grief, and then turns again to the thought of death, here introduced with a specific characteristical illustration (whereas in *Night II* the illustration had been developed at the end). The death of Narcissa, which had occurred shortly after that of Philander and was indeed hastened by his death, differed from his in that she was a young, beautiful, innocent girl, whose death had not been entirely unexpected. Stricken with disease, she had been hurried "with parental haste" to the South, had died there, had been denied a grave because of religious bigotry, and had been buried secretly. An emotion-charged denunciation of such bigotry—not only this Roman Catholic manifestation of the "cursed ungodliness of zeal," but of mankind's general and all-too-common lack of benevolence—indicates that the poet is here dealing with more than one specific situation. The focus on Narcissa's death, on what he calls "my touching tale," comprises only 125 lines of the 536 lines of the whole *Night,* and consequently furnishes a specific illustration of general topics which are considered in *Night III.* The repetitions of life, the staleness of most of the pleasures of the sensual man are contrasted with the more abiding satisfactions of a virtuous man who finds increasing richness pointing to its culmination in the next life. With such thoughts, death loses its dreadfulness, becomes "the great counseller," "the deliverer," "the rewarder," "the crown of life"—not an end but a beginning.

Night IV, **"The Christian Triumph; Containing our only Cure for the Fear of Death; and Proper Sentiments of Heart on that Inestimable Blessing,"** develops more fully—as its greater length permits—some of the same ideas found in the first three *Nights.* Repudiating fears which "black-boding man" may have of physical death, the poet argues that the aged man has no reason to fear death, for it is the deliverer from a life which holds less and less for him, with death of friends and the few remaining pleasures at best "a

thrice-told tale." Familiar with the disappointments and reverses of life, sickened by the folly of those aged people who continue to grasp for earthly triumphs, the poet, free from worldly ambition, finds pleasure in retirement. It is guilt alone that makes men fear death. Then, addressing Lorenzo again, he develops the thought that hope comes only through Christ and describes ecstatically the triumph of Christ and the revelation of the Divine in the beauty of the night sky. This leads to the point that the greatest sign of God is seen in his creature, Man, and this to the consideration of the immortal nature of man, whose passions as well as his reason are God-given, and whose soul will be admitted to celestial circles through death. To Lorenzo he points out the supreme value of religion, the sole hope through Christ, the proof of immortality seen in nature, and the necessary proofs from reason to supplement faith.

Night V, **"The Relapse,"** repeats much of the material of the preceding *Nights* but in different words and at greater length. Addressing Lorenzo, the poet agrees that much poetry has been written on unworthy subjects and celebrating vain joys, but he says that his poems are to propound truths of the first importance. He invokes divine aid, finds inspiration in the stars and the quiet of night, feels again his grief from bereavements, but also therein finds wisdom. The themes of this poem are to include man's attitude to death, "the various kinds of grief; the faults of age"; and the nature of death. He will "range the plenteous intellectual field" to gather thoughts to oppose the "moral maladies of man" through reason.

For Lorenzo's benefit he considers the lessons to be learned from Narcissa's early death: the realization of the transitory and uncertain nature of life, the futility of much that is valued in it. Her youth is a reminder to the old of swiftly passing time. Her gaiety stresses the uncertainty of death's approach. This point is further developed by an illustrative allegorical little story of Death as a masquerader, stealing upon people in the midst of their enjoyments. Narcissa's wealth is a reminder that Death the leveler is no respecter of the "fortunate." Additional illustration is given in a series of examples of types of men sacrificing virtue and happiness in the pursuit of wealth. The sad story of Lysander and Aspasia—both blessed in "youth, form, fortune, fame," but dying tragically on the eve of their marriage—adds a further illustration of life's uncertainty and of death's frequent unexpectedness.

Night VI, **"The Infidel Reclaimed,"** has a descriptive subtitle: "Containing the Nature, Proof, and Importance of Immortality. Part I.—Where, among other things, Glory and Riches are particularly considered." It is also provided with a preface indicating the great amount of contemporary dispute about religion and a belief that it may all be reduced to one question: "Is man immortal, or is he not?" Arguments supporting immortality are to be presented, ones "from principles which infidels admit in common with believers."

The poet again begins his poem in midnight meditation by recalling the loss of a loved one, later referred to as Lucia. He describes the agony of watching her years of illness and the slow approach of death, the eventual "death the deliverer." Then he states his theme: immortality—its nature, proof, importance. As he considers its nature, he describes in enthusiastic, figurative terms the various possibilities of the joys of the immortal soul where there will be no limit to intellectual development, where the whole unlimited field of knowledge will unfold, and where the marvels of creation as a whole will be seen. Proofs of immortality are based on the analogy of nature, the symbolic parallel in the continuous succession of night and day and in the cycle of the seasons. Matter is immortal; can the spirit die? Another "proof" is seen in the marvelous achievements of man in the physical world, in remaking the world for his use—lands reclaimed from the sea, fine arts and noble temples, rivers turned to new courses, dry plains irrigated, canals connecting seas, great navies, and Britain's navy "that awes the world to peace": "Whose footsteps these?—Immortals have been here." Additional proofs are promised in the next *Night*.

Night VII, "**Being the Second Part of the Infidel Reclaimed. Containing the Nature, Proof, and Importance of Immortality,**" has a longer preface, as befits a longer poem, in which the belief in immortality is again seen as the fundamental support of virtue; and doubt of such belief is the basis of the infidel's error. "Some arguments for immortality, new at least to me," are to be developed in the poem in the hope "that an unprejudiced infidel must necessarily receive some advantageous impressions from them."

Beginning the poem with a reference to the recent death of Pope and to the probability of his own death soon, the poet asserts the truth of immortality and promises proofs from the nature of man, from his feelings. Man's discontent in this world and his hopes suggest a future life, for otherwise he is worse off than the lower animals; for they know nothing of the doubts, fears, fruitless hopes, regrets, despairs, which embitter man's life. "Admit immortal life," and virtue becomes reasonable and hope is sustained. "New, unexpected witnesses" of immortality against the infidel may be found even in man's natural "ambition, pleasure, love of gain," all of which suggest a seeking for the unattainable here and, if rightly directed, are indications of the great potentialities of his nature: "I feel a grandeur in the passions too." Without immortality man's search for happiness would be in vain.

In over three hundred lines the poet pictures the horrors of life if man were denied immortality, the mean-

inglessness of it, and the impossibility of thinking that such a world could be the creation of a God. But, "If man's immortal, there's a God in Heaven." So, from the nature of man, his passions and powers, his gradually developing reason, his fear of death; from the nature of hope and of virtue; from knowledge and love; and from the difficulty of understanding the complexities of man otherwise, the necessity of immortality is demonstrated. Realizing that his discussion is becoming rather lengthy and repetitious, the poet sums up his main points by reference to Philander's death: without immortality, his life—so admirable and virtuous, so full of pain—would be without meaning. Immortality is essential for man's happiness; and in this need is seen an argument in its defense.

Nights VI and *VII,* forming a two-part whole, have almost nothing of the personal elegiac note (the last reference to Philander being little more than a device to link these poems to the preceding *Nights*); and both are devoted to one aspect of Christian apologetics. The "arguments" of the former are largely from the outward indications of man's nature, and those of the latter from his inner nature, his feelings, ambitions, passions. *Night VII* recalls Young's most outstanding sermon, "**The True Estimate.**"

Night VIII, "**Virtue's Apology; or, The Man of the World Answered. In which are considered, the Love of this Life; the Ambition and Pleasure, with the Wit and Wisdom of the World,**" continues in 1417 lines the discussion of *Night VII* with an effort to convince Lorenzo, here a "man of the world," of the vanity of human life without immortality. The whole poem consists largely of a wealth of striking metaphors illustrating ideas frequently discussed in the earlier *Nights*. A few illustrative examples will suffice: The glory of eternity will

> . . . swallow time's ambitions, as the vast
> Leviathan the bubbles vain that ride
> High on the foaming billow.
>
> (VIII,35-39)

Here life becomes a "Fantastic chase of shadows hunting shades" (VIII,73). Stunned with noise and choked with dust, men compete "on life's stage, one inch above the grave" (VIII,85-88). The poet bids Lorenzo consider the future for his little son Florello when he is ready to enter "the world," to be received into public life by "men of the world," engrossed in "the fatal stratagems of peace," who behind the mask of politeness conceal their ruthless selfishness. What then will be Florello's education "Through serpentine obliquities of life, / And the dark labyrinth of human hearts?"

Many examples of men of the world are given: "A man I knew, who lived upon a smile. . . ." Two men of the court, trying to outwit each other, are pictured as

> . . . two state rooks,
> Studious their nests to feather in a trice,
> With all the necromantics of their art,
> Playing the game of faces on each other,
> Making court sweetmeats of their latest gall . . .
> (VIII,343-51)

The other parts of the triple theme, ambition and pleasure, are shown paradoxically to be the root of vice or virtue, depending on one's conception of life. "Bliss has no being, virtue has no strength, / But from the prospect of immortal life" (VIII,1189-90). Wit is good in its place, but "Sense is our helmet, wit is but the plume." He warns Lorenzo not to let the "cooings of the world allure" him.

Night IX and Last, "The Consolation: containing among things, I. A Moral Survey of the Nocturnal Heavens. II. A Night Address to the Deity,"

written as a unit in itself but also as the last of the series, is by far the longest, with 2434 lines; and, in many ways, it is by far the most interesting, in spite of some repetition of the earlier material. It opens with an extended epic simile: As when a traveller, weary, rests at evening in a cottage, thinks over his search of what he cannot find, and "cheers himself with song," so the poet, "long-travelled in the ways of men" and "waiting the sweet hour of rest," soothes the pains of age with "a serious song."

The first 539 lines are akin to the earlier *Nights*: the poet invokes the inspiration of Night for "one labour more"; addresses Lorenzo as a man of the world; and, starting with the *ubi sunt* theme, develops many examples of the transiency of life from the "actors of the last year's scene" and from the relics of the past and reminders of past generations. Thought of the future ending of the world leads to the picture of the Last Day, reminiscent of Young's early poem on the then-popular theme, with the imagery of a mighty drama in a mighty theater. Time itself will end, and eternity begin. Again, as in the other *Nights,* the poet maintains the value of troubles, pains, and evils in the disciplining of man for the immortal life. At this point he announces a change in theme and style: "The consolation cancels the complaint." A second epic simile, akin to that opening the poem, pictures the tired traveller resting on a hilltop, looking back over the country passed through, and thinking of his wished-for home; just so, the poet will pause, look back, and "meditate an end," though that end is "still remote; so fruitfull is my theme." His résumé sums up the preceding *Nights*.

Now comes the change. The theme? "Night's grandeurs," the beauty of the starry heavens, the contemplation of which can expand thought, exalt admiration, arouse awe, and fit "capacities" for "final joy." The poet's invocation for divine inspiration in his "daring song" recalls Milton:

> Thou, who did'st touch the lip of Jesse's son,
> Rapt in sweet contemplation of these fires,
> . . . Teach me by this stupendous scaffolding,
> Creation's golden steps, to climb to thee.
> (IX,582-92)

He then invites Lorenzo to accompany him on a "tour" of the heavens to "kindle our devotion at the stars."

This "Moral Survey of the Nocturnal Heavens," perhaps the best part of the whole **Night Thoughts,** is primarily devoted to demonstrating proofs of the existence of God from the evidence of nature in order to combat the disbelief of the atheist, represented by Lorenzo. "This prospect vast" is, if rightly considered,

> . . . nature's system of divinity,
> And every student of the night inspires.
> 'Tis elder scripture, writ by God's own hand;
> Scripture authentic, uncorrupt by man.
> (IX,644-46)

> Devotion! daughter of astronomy!
> An undevout astronomer is mad.
> True; all things speak a God, but in the small,
> Men trace him out; in great, he seizes man—
> Seizes and elevates, and wraps, and fills
> With new inquiries.
> (IX,771-76)

The immensities of the universe revealed by the new astronomy of Newton suggest mysteries beyond man's comprehension. All the wonders of this world and of human achievements are dwarfed by the wonders of the night's stars. Yet, deplorable to think of, the night, which so plainly evidences the being and powers of God, is used by corrupt men, blind to the divine evidence above them, as a time for vice and crime, as they make "the night still darker by their deeds."

The Greek philosophers had read the truths of natural religion in the stars; Christians, with revealed religion as well, have a double light. In a series of metaphors, he exults in the wonders of the starry firmament, calling it "the noble pasture of the mind"; "the garden of the Deity, / Blossom'd with stars"; "the breastplate of the true High Priest, / Ardent with gems oracular" (IX,1038-45). By contemplation of such great objects, man's mind is made greater and his views enlarged. As he meditates on the "mathematic glories of the skies," he rises to ecstatic wonder and amazement: "Orb above orb ascending without end! . . . What, then, the wondrous space through which they roll? . . . 'Tis comprehension's absolute defeat" (IX,1095-1106). The idea of infinity—infinite space, infinite time—finds enraptured expression:

> How distant some of these nocturnal suns!
> So distant (says the sage) 'twere not absurd

To doubt, if beams, set out at nature's birth,
Are yet arrived at this so foreign world,
Though nothing half so rapid as their flight.
(IX,1225-29)

Realizing that many of man's preconceived and treasured ideas may be destroyed by new scientific evidence, he prays for clarity of vision and for an open mind to face reality as revealed by astronomy, to see "Things as they are, unalter'd through the glass of worldly wishes" (IX,1327-30). The great vistas opened to the mind by the development of the telescope fire his imagination: "A thousand worlds? There's room for millions more." At the other extreme, the microscope has revealed the wonders "of fine-spun nature exquisitely small," wonders "though demonstrated, still ill-conceived." Contemplation's nocturnal tour, though visiting other solar systems where "larger suns inhabit higher spheres," and suggesting the possibilities of other inhabited planets, does not reveal the abode of the Deity. God is everywhere. Young, with a grasp of the modern science of his day, expresses his conception of gradual progress in the development of the universe: "Nature delights in progress—in advance / From worse to better" (IX,1959-60). He suggests also a progress of the soul, going through various stages of development in its immortal life.

Perhaps, lest his great emphasis on natural religion should lead the reader to confuse his position with that of the Deists, the poet, combining the religious ecstasy of this vision of the infinite universe of worlds on worlds, of a God far beyond man's comprehension, with the Christian revelation, concludes with an apostrophe to the Trinity (IX,2194-2362). Now he approaches the end of his long poem, *The Consolation,* "for all who read": "Then farewell Night! Of darkness now no more! / Joy breaks, shines, triumphs; 'tis eternal day" (IX,2376-77).

II *Some Misconceptions about the* **Night Thoughts**

Dangers in interpretating the characteristical illustrations, particularly in the earlier *Nights,* as actual individuals in Young's life have already been indicated. This is what was done by some literal-minded readers in the last half of the eighteenth century. A valuable piece of modern scholarship has thrown light on what seems to have stimulated the identification complex.[1] *Night IV* on its first appearance as a separate poem had been provided with a little preface apparently designed as a kind of apology for, or justification of, its somewhat meandering nature by saying that, "As the occasion of this poem was real, not fictitious, so the method pursued in it was rather imposed by what spontaneously arose in the author's mind on that occasion, than meditated or designed. . . . The reason of it is, that the facts mentioned did naturally pour these moral reflections on the thought of the writer."

The "facts" in *Night IV* are primarily the transitory nature of life and the promise of Christianity (with no development of the elegiac examples of *Nights I-III*). Reference to Young's recovery from serious illness and to his disillusionment with court promises may be considered "real, not fictitious"; and that such facts did "pour" these moral reflections cannot be denied. The main point is to explain the spontaneous and unpremediated method of organization. It is to be remembered that a somewhat similar expression is found in the Preface to **"The True Estimate"** that the observations are "by no means drawn from books but the life. . . ." The observations made in the *Night Thoughts* were similarly drawn from Young's life and thought.

In 1750 when Richardson was printing his collected edition of the nine poems, he felt that there should be an introductory preface; and, unable to persuade Young to write one, he suggested that part of the Preface to *Night IV* should be used henceforth as a preface to the whole. Young apparently felt no preface was necessary; but, not much concerned about it, he consented to let Richardson do what he thought advisable. Unfortunately, therefore, when printed as an introductory preface, it was interpreted as applying to the whole; and the conception that all was to be taken as "real and not fictitious" led the literal-minded to attempts at identification of the named characters. Who was Lorenzo? Who was Philander? Who was Narcissa? What three deaths within three months?

With a zest akin to that of the would-be identifiers of Shakespeare's Dark Lady of the Sonnets, attempts were made to fit various actual persons into what seemed given details and, for the most part, with small concern for chronology or common sense—or even lines of the poem. It was really with Narcissa that such identifiers had a field day. The death of Narcissa, with some resemblances to that of Elizabeth Lee to be sure, was taken as a literal account, although there were some difficulties in detail. There grew up a legend of Young as an old man, burying his daughter by stealth, and later mourning among the tombs a triple loss of daughter, friend, and wife, and retiring altogether from social contacts to give himself up to grief and elegiac lamentation. In France the legend of Narcissa flourished especially, mostly with romantic disregard of known facts.[2]

But it was, perhaps, in the identification of Lorenzo that the most extreme limit of absurdity was reached. Though Young had ample opportunity to see and know many a young man who could suggest characteristics for Lorenzo, many identifiers preferred to consider him the poet's son—despite the fact that Frederick was about ten years old when the first *Nights* were written and that it seems a bit hard on him to identify him with the libertine Lorenzo, a widower with a motherless little boy. What price chronology? While there always seem to be people to whom the desire to identify characters is greater than the enjoyment of a creative poem, such an approach is, to say the least, a mistaken and unavailing one in understanding and enjoying the *Night Thoughts*. Fortunately, it has been largely abandoned. Other misconceptions, however, grew out of it and contributed to continuing prejudice.

Insinuations, based on ignorance and prejudice, were made that the contrast between the wholly fictitious pictures of Young as a lachrymose, doddering recluse, bewailing his private griefs, or as a place-seeking man, ambitious of wealth and position, on the one hand, and his themes of eternal values, on the other, indicate a basic insincerity in the poet. And these insinuations were responsible for conceptions which warped some nineteenth-century and even twentieth-century estimates of him.

Unfortunately too, a general misconception that the whole series of the nine poems is "gloomy" has prejudiced many against reading it. Actually, the "melancholy" is on the whole more akin to Milton's "divinest melancholy" or contemplation. The invocation early in *Night I* for divine inspiration makes it evident that the poet is not seeking paths of gloom: "O lead my mind / (A mind that fain would wander *from* its woe). . . ." The poet's optimistic belief in the potentialities of human nature contrasts sharply with the dark scenes of actual life he portrays, scenes no darker than reality, introduced to show the abuse of God-given possibilities. Above all, Young's religious faith is optimistic, with the promise of immortality. Nor indeed does he picture this life as necessarily all unhappy. He warns against expecting unalloyed happiness, and against seeking it in abandonment to the passions and in mere materialism. But, in opposition to gloom, he says, "'Tis impious in a good man to be sad" (IV,675).

III *Relation of the* **Night Thoughts** *to Prose and Poetry on Death*[3]

Though Young's personal bereavements doubtless stimulated to a large extent the writing of the *Night Thoughts,* the whole experience of his life and the great interests of the time must also be taken into account. *Nights I-V* are directly in line with a vast number of prose treatises and poems connected with death. There was an astonishing number of books whose descriptive titles indicate such topics as "consolations against the fear of death," "the four last things," and moral benefits to be learned from bereavements. While a reading of a number of the most outstanding treatises shows a difference in plan and to some extent in specific doctrines, they are all much alike in aim and general scope of material. They are all designed to provide a philosophy wherewith to face death without fear; and, as a basis of such philosophy they emphasize the truth of immortality, which they endeavor to prove by analogy.

This doctrine accepted, the conception of this life as preparation for the next and of death as a transition, as an entrance to, rather than an end of, life is inevitable. Contemplation of death in such a light is hence not a morbid preoccupation but a sensible and practical procedure, leading to a correct evaluation of temporal and eternal things and to a realization of the necessity for constant preparation for entrance to the future life. Consideration of the means of everlasting salvation involves discussion of human nature, the need for regeneration and repentance, and the relation between faith and good works. The troubles and trials of life; the transitory nature of earthly happiness; and the loss of friends, regarded as reminders of death, become really blessings in that they turn men's minds from worldly interests to thoughts of eternity and may therefore be instrumental in securing eternal happiness. The obvious resemblance to the aims and material of these popular treatises readily explains something of the immediate popularity of the earlier *Night Thoughts*.

While, of course, death had been a theme in poetry for centuries, the vast quantity of eighteenth-century poetry concerning death needs to be taken into account. The poems may be divided roughly into two groups: first, those akin to the prose treatises; and, second, those concerned with the physical death of the body. Those in the first group consist of meditations on death, regarded as the leveler, the deliverer, the door to a future life; on the transitory nature of life, the need to be prepared for death, and the value of the wise use of time; and, depending on the length of the poem, of theological reflection on the course of life—all with the idea of dispelling fear of death through Christian faith. It is obviously to this group that the *Night Thoughts* belongs.

Those of the second group, not an entirely new type indeed but numbering many outstanding examples, seem to have been designed to please by horrifying (a type of appeal not new then and not extinct today!), dwelling with macabre details on physical death and the fate of the body in the grave. The most outstanding is probably Robert Blair's *The Grave*. This type of poem came to be accurately enough called "graveyard poetry." An analysis of the elements in a great number of such poems shows the essential characteristics present in greater or less degree: The time should be night; the setting, a place of burial, which, in a poem of any length, should be described. If it is in a building, such as Westminister Abbey, the gloomy deserted interior, with any sound echoing fearfully through the vaults, should be pictured. If in a churchyard, there should be a ruined church nearby with an owl or other bird crying out; yew trees or osiers near the graves; and, apart from the mouldering tombstones, a few skulls or other bones lying around have a good effect. Other details may be added to bring home to the reader the horrors of death. Other less morbid aspects of the theme of death may be included; but, to be classified as "graveyard poetry," a poem should include all or some of these characteristics. To consider the *Night Thoughts* as belonging in this group is one of the most serious misconceptions of Young's masterpiece and indicates a failure to read the poem. None of the characteristic elements are developed; indeed, the poet dismisses them as the "bugbears of a winter's eve" (IV, 10-12). Contrary to what some illustrators later chose to depict, the setting is not that of a cemetery.

There is indeed a good deal of significance in the title itself, *Night Thoughts;* that is, thoughts at night. A number of similarly named poems—"Midnight and Daily Thoughts," "A Night Thought," "Midnight Thought (On the Death of Mrs. E. H.),"" which consists of reflections on moral preparation for death, "A Thought for Eternity," "Meditations on Death"—use night as the background, free from distractions of the day, and as suitable for serious thought on life and death. These seem to constitute one genre of poems on death; "night piece," the other. A "piece" early in the seventeenth century indicated a painting or picture of a scene, and in literary use a "night piece" came to suggest a funereal landscape, as in Thomas Parnell's *A Night Piece on Death,* one of the most outstanding of the "graveyard" poems. Young himself had used the term in his sermon, *A True Estimate:* ". . . a mind haunted with fear is a hideous *night piece* of storm, precipice, ruins, tombs, and apparitions." But, in his greatest poem, Young was writing not a "night piece" but "night *thoughts.*"

IV *Theological and Apologetic Background of* Night Thoughts

The religious fervor in the poem—because warmth in religion in this period has frequently been attributed only to the Methodist movement, and because the poem was praised by both John Wesley and his brother Charles—has led to a suggestion that Young may have been influenced by Methodism. Cited in this theory are such passages insisting on the necessity for emotional intensity in religion as this example:

> Think you my song too turbulent? too warm?
> . . . O for warmer still!
> Shall Heaven, which gave us ardour, and has shown
> Her own for men so strongly, not disdain
> . . . That prose of piety, a lukewarm praise?
> (IV, 628-45)

Warmth in religion, however, was not peculiar to Methodism. Lukewarmness had been deplored by Tillotson and others in the late seventeenth century. Dean Edward Young, the father of the poet, had regarded it as both unworthy and dangerous: "There grows more scandal to Religion from Lukewarmness, than from open Profaneness. . . . There grows more hazard to

souls from Lukewarmness than there does from open Profaneness."[4] Evidences from chronology argue against Wesleyan influence on Young, for Methodism did not assume its characteristic traits until 1738; and not until field-preaching was started in 1739 did it attract widespread attention. Young's religious views were formulated long before then, and indeed the *Night Thoughts* show no clear reflection of any ideas peculiarly Methodist. The background of his religious thought belongs to the current of rationalism of outstanding significance in the Anglican Church in the late seventeenth and eighteenth century.

The developments in rationalism made it inevitable that the rationalistic strain in the Church should become of increasing significance. The Roman Catholic questioning of the position of Protestantism, as lacking the basis of an infallible church, spurred Anglican demonstrations of the reasonableness of Christianity and the stressing of the basic substructure of natural religion. By natural religion was meant the knowledge of the existence and attributes of God, the laws of morality, and the truth of immortality which was innate in the human mind or readily learned from nature through reason without any supernatural revelation, and which was as much taught by God as the truths usually considered revealed. The extremes of "enthusiasm" of the numerous fanatical sects of the Commonwealth period and their extravagant claims of personal revelations caused skepticism of any revelation unless checked by reason.

Of the great divines who preached a rational religion in the late seventeenth century none was more popular and influential than John Tillotson. His sermons went through many editions and were widely read in the eighteenth century—and are still very readable today. He considered that the most satisfactory method of establishing the truths of religion was to begin by demonstrating the principles of natural religion and "from that to advance to the proof of Christianity and of the Scriptures, which being once solidly done would soon settle all other things." The term "reason," so frequently used by the rationalistic clergy, did not always mean exactly the same thing; but, for the most part, it seems to mean a faculty, innate but requiring education and development. It differs from the similar divine faculty in degree rather than in kind, serving as an infallible means of judging between good and evil, and is designed to be the guide of the senses and passions; it is a faculty distinguishing men from the lower animals, and serving as the one means of judging the truth.

The salient features of rational orthodoxy include: reason as the basis of faith and the test of revelation; natural religion as the basis of revealed religion; emphasis on good works and morality as essential elements in religion; theories of human nature as not entirely depraved and the passions as intrinsically good;

happiness as the motivation of human actions; sociability and benevolence as natural to mankind. The great degree to which reflections of these ideas are readily found throughout *Night Thoughts* indicates that their background is in the current of rational orthodoxy.

Defenses of Christianity were by no means new, but they were particularly numerous at the time. The Boyle lectures on the evidences of Christianity, an annual series of eight sermons established by the will of Robert Boyle, a great scientist himself, were of great interest and influence from 1692 on. In Newton, scientist and theologian, Christianity found an invaluable champion; his great astronomical discoveries afforded new sources for teleological arguments for the apologists, and his statement that more light would be shed on religious truths as more of the secrets of nature were learned gave great promise of continued aid from science. Young was evidently very familiar with much of the apologetic writing of the period.[5] In *Nights VI-VIII* he followed very closely the ideas and expression of purposes of Bishop Gastrell's *Moral Proofs of the Certainty of a Future State* (1725), a book which Young reborrowed from the Duchess of Portland about the time he was writing *Night VI* (*Bath MSS*, p. 156).

But it was chiefly in Newtonian astronomy that Young found inspiration for his defenses of religion. Through it he found new vistas of thought and reality which fascinated him and kindled his imagination. His prayer for release from the limitations of "earth's enclosure" so that his mind might be free to explore the new realms of thought and climb "creation's golden steps" to God indicates the purpose of this "tour through nature's universal orb," the much used "tour" by which apologists for religion sought to prove the existence of God through astronomical details furnished by Newton. The "mathematick glories of the skies" with the myriads of stars moving harmoniously—"Orb above orb ascending without end! / Circle in circle, without end, enclosed!"—provided evidence of God.

Young's knowledge of Newtonian astronomy was definitely up to date in details which he used in giving the old teleological arguments a new life from the new evidences of design afforded in the night skies: In "What order, beauty, motion, distance, size! / Concertion of design! how exquisite!" (IX,1422-23), Young shows a grasp not only of the implications of Newton's discoveries but also of infinity of time and space. From contemplating such ideas he had a feeling of intellectual enlargement and an insatiable desire to know more and more, even if old cherished ideas might be thereby shattered; and he prays for clarity of mind to find and face truth. The great glory of immortality is its promise of ever continuing intellectual development and limitless knowledge, in keeping with the conceptions of infinity afforded by astronomy. In the apologetics of *Night IX* Young gave exultant poetic

expression to ideas and theories considered vital in the religious beliefs of his time, and he used those aspects of astronomy which appealed to his imagination and offered possibilities of poetic development. His own intellectual pleasure in such contemplation was something he wished to share also:

> Nor is the profit greater than the joy,
> If human hearts at glorious objects glow,
> And admiration can inspire delight.
>
> (IX,733-35)

V *Poetics of* **Night Thoughts**

In a period when long, discursive poems were in vogue, the **Night Thoughts,** individually and collectively, found ready acceptance. Young's first use of blank verse seemed somewhat new at the time. The chief effect of newness came from the sense of great personal involvement, of emotional intensity; and this effect was achieved not only from discussion in dialogue of great themes of universal concern, illustrated from current life and thought and designed for immediate individual application, but also through the rhetorical style. A variety of devices secures the effect of a speaker tremendously involved in efforts to influence a man for whom he is concerned, through his rapturous contemplation of the beauty and significance of the night skies, his religious optimism, and his realistic appraisal of the evil and shortcomings of mankind. The effect is cumulative—from the piling up of images, of metaphor on metaphor, detail on detail. Often the effect is that of breathless enthusiasm, of an effort to express in words truths which transcend human expression.

It would be virtually impossible to find many pages without examples of such rhetorical devices as apostrophe, exclamation, questions, elaborate repetition. Thus a feeling of urgency is suggested in the transition to a new theme: "What yet remains? Much! much! a mighty debt / To be discharged: these thoughts, O Night! are thine . . ." (IX,539-40). Young is fond of paradox and contradiction: "How poor, how rich, how abject, how august, / How complicate, how wonderful, is man!" (I,67-68). And of the motions of the stars he exclaims:

> Confusion unconfused! nor less admire
> The tumult untumultuous; all on the wing!
> In motion all, yet what profound repose!
>
> (IX,1116-18)

He enjoys such interlocking repetitions as:

> Sweet harmonist! and beautiful as sweet!
> And young as beautiful! and soft as young!
> And gay as soft! and innocent as gay!
> And happy (if aught happy here), as good!
>
> (III,81-84)

But in the variety, originality, and abundance of his metaphors one sees Young's most characteristic expression. Abstractions gain concreteness. That natural religion may be learned from the night stars leads to their designation as "the manuscript of heaven," "elder scripture," "material picture of benevolence," "Heaven's golden alphabet," "a radiant choir," all turning the universe to a "temple." A variety of metaphors comments on the unperceived speed of time's passing: ". . . time steals on with downy feet" (V,407); "Folly sings six, while nature points at twelve" (V,635). The striking of the clock is "the knell of my departed hours."

> Time, in advance, behind him hides his wings,
> And seems to creep, decrepit with his age.
> Behold him, when pass'd by; what then is seen,
> But his broad pinions swifter than the winds?
> And all mankind, in contradiction strong,
> Rueful, aghast, cry out on his career.
>
> (II,139-44)

A series of metaphors may be introduced in one passage: life in this world is

> . . . the bud of being, the dim dawn,
> The twilight of our day,
> the vestibule . . .
>
> (I,122-24)

Much of the imagery of his metaphors reflects the interests and experience of Young's life: his acquaintance with law and assizes; his familiarity with theater and drama; his observations of the court; his abiding interest in ships and the sea.

Above all, Young's style indicates his pleasure in the ramifications of his ideas, of following one suggested by another, and then another and another, expressed this way and then that. His strength is the cumulative effect; but his weakness is prolixity, undue length, and repetition. No poem of the length of the *Night Thoughts* can be without poetic lapses and less inspired moments. But it is not solely from the least good parts that Young's success should be evaluated. Its positive virtues are those that led Johnson to praise it for its "copiousness" and "magnificence of vast extent and endless diversity," and to consider it one of the few poems that gained from being in blank verse.

. . . . .

. . ."Conjectures on Original Composition"

Conjectures on Original Composition in a Letter to the Author of Sir Charles Grandison, published in May, 1759, is an astonishing production for a man of seventy-six. Its exuberant, forward-looking attitude, its repudiation of dependence on the past, its stress on originality and individual self-confidence, its indignation at pettiness and servility to rules, its ranking Shakespeare with the greatest of the Greek dramatists, its hope for future writers equalling or surpassing the great writers of the past—all suggest a youthful vigor of mind and imagination unusual at his age. It would be an incredible production if it indicated entirely new convictions on his part. While it shows the final development of his views, it does not contradict his past writings. It was no impromptu production, but the result of long deliberation and careful revision.

A glance back over his whole literary career recalls his interest in questions of literary criticism—his awareness and evaluation of theories and practice of the drama, qualities and characteristics of the ode, the nature of satire. His letters, especially those to Tickell, show a lively interest in contemporary literature. But most significant, as pointing forward to the ***Conjectures,*** is the value he always put on originality; and his characteristic tendency to point out that, whatever he is doing, is "new," or "new at least to me." As far back as 1728 in his ***Discourse on Ode,*** he had maintained the superiority of "originals" over "imitations." He evidently mulled over such ideas for many years. What then led him to the ***Conjectures*** so late in life?

When in 1756 Young was honored by Joseph Warton's dedication to him of the first part of his *Essay on Pope,* he seems to have been so struck with some comments in that dedication that he was led to attempt to crystallize his own views by writing. Warton's ideas that seem to have started him concerned the distinction between a man of wit, a man of sense, and a true poet; his point that one essential of a true poet is "a creative and glowing imagination"; and the comment that the sublime and the pathetic are the "two chief nerves of all genuine poetry." The ***Conjectures*** as finally published owes much of its zest, not only to the championing of individual independence, but also to the vigor and the metaphoric imagery of his expression.

As the second part of the title indicates, Young uses the device of a letter to a friend to secure a personal quality lacking in a formal essay or treatise, and to permit a freer organization. His opening paragraph, disarmingly apologizing for occupying his old age with "the pastime here sent you," not only suggests that the work is "miscellaneous in its nature" and free from usual rules in its development, but also shows evidence of careful organization in the provision for the last part of the letter: "I have endeavoured to make some amends, by digressing into subjects more important, and more suitable to my season of life. A serious thought standing single among many of lighter nature, will sometimes strike the careless wanderer after amusement only, with useful awe: as monumental marbles scattered in a wide pleasure garden. . . . To such a monument I may conduct you. . . ." He reminds the friend whom he is addressing that another "friend" had asked for "our sentiments on *Original* and *Moral* Composition," and he states that he will begin with original composition and later will consider serious drama and moral composition.

Before turning to his main theme, which appeals to him as "an original subject to me, who have seen nothing hitherto written on it," he considers the value in general of composition. Though some have said that too much is being written, he affirms that, provided it is based on "sound Understanding and the Public Good," "the more composition the better." It provides a recreation, a refuge, and a source of delight: "It opens a back-door out of the bustle of this busy, and idle world, into a delicious garden of moral and intellectual fruits and flowers; the key of which is denied the rest of mankind. When stung with idle anxieties, or teased with fruitless impertinence, or yawning over insipid diversions, then we perceive the blessings of a letter'd recess. . . ." Composition can afford a refuge from the rush of the city and a protection from the "sloth and sensuality" of the country. Above all, it can relieve "the languors of old age," and give honorable occupation to him "whose unsteady pen vibrates to the last in the cause of religion, of virtue, or learning."

Young then turns to the main theme and, in a metaphor of gardens, plants, and growing things, which is a dominant metaphor throughout, he introduces his major terms: "The mind of a man of genius is a fertile and pleasant field . . . it enjoys a perpetual spring. Of that spring, *Originals* are the fairest flowers: *Imitations* are of quicker growth, but fainter bloom." He indicates that he will use the term "Originals" for those who imitate nature, and "Imitations" for those who imitate authors. The first is always superior to the second: "An *Original* may be said to be of a vegetable nature; it rises spontaneously from the root of genius; it *grows,* it is not made." Since thoughts, as well as words, get worn with use, writers should think for themselves: "We may as well grow good by another's virtue, or fat by another's food, as famous by another's thought."

Why is it, he asks, that there are so few originals? It is largely because the writings of the past overawe writers of the present: "They *engross* our attention, . . .; they *prejudice* our judgment in favour of their abilities . . .; and they *intimidate* us with the splendor of their renown." Although writers of the past are of great importance to those of the present, they should be admired, not copied. This distinction between copying and imitating other writers leads him to a differentiation between the relative value of genius and learning. Learning is "a great lover of rules"; genius, with less interest in rules, "has ever been supposed to partake of something divine," and surpasses learning, great though its worth is.

A supreme example of a modern genius is Shakespeare. There are two kinds of genius: first, the "adult," which "comes out of nature's hand" fully grown; and second, the "infantine," which must be nursed and educated by learning, and which is sometimes in danger of being misled or smothered. Genius, Young feels, is less rare than is usually believed; and the great danger to genius comes from imitation. In the first place, imitation prevents progress in "the liberal and politer arts." Next, it encourages conformity: "Born Originals, how comes it to pass that we die Copies? That meddling ape Imitation . . . destroys all mental individuality." Furthermore, imitation "makes us think little"; and it leads to the production of big books with little value.

Questioning why the moderns, equal in ability to the ancients, should fall short in achievement, Young suggests that the ancients had a more favorable intellectual climate: they had great patrons who provided "the marvelous sunshine" which encouraged the "crop" of the "fruits of genius." The trouble with the moderns is that they do not realize the potential dimensions of the human mind. To encourage original composition, Young gives two rules: (1) *Know thyself;* and (2) *Reverence thyself:* "Therefore . . . learn the depth, extent, bias, and full fort of thy mind; . . . excite and cherish every spark of intellectual light and heat . . . let not great examples, or authorities, browbeat thy reason into too great a diffidence of thyself." This enthusiastic counsel, developed at greater length, distinguishes Young from many critics of the past who had endeavored to restrain the would-be writer, bidding him keep in mind his limitations.

Young continues with a discussion of the difference between "the well-accomplished scholar, and the divinely-inspired enthusiast." Hence comes the inferiority of translations. More significant than his consideration of the limitations of Pope and Swift is his enthusiastic and optimistic idea of the progress of poetry: ". . . the day may come, when the moderns may proudly look back . . . reputing *Homer* and *Demosthenes,* as the dawn of divine genius. . . ." Parallels in other fields of knowledge suggest such progress: ". . . and these are new food to the genius of a polite writer; these are as the root, and composition, as the flower, and as the root spreads, and thrives, shall the flower fail?" There is hope for new developments in original writing, especially in England, which has already had great Originals—Bacon, Boyle, Newton, Shakespeare, Milton. The moral obligation of writers is to follow their example as Originals. The "gift of talents implies an injunction of their use." He alludes to the original composition of the novels of Richardson, who converted fiction to moral ends.

As he celebrates the supreme achievement of Shakespeare, an Original and the equal of the Greek dramatists, he embarks on the topic of serious drama; and, in the course of his discussion, he indicates the flaw in several of the outstanding English dramatists: Ben Jonson was an imitator, weighed down by learning; Dryden's tragedies lacked pathos, and were further ruined by rhyme; Addison's *Cato* suffered from the same lack of pathos: "His beauties sparkle, but do not warm. . . ." In coming to Addison's prose, to which Young rightly feels his lasting reputation will be due, he touches on moral composition, and goes quickly on to the serious digression mentioned at the beginning—the story about Addison's calling his stepson to his deathbed and saying, "See in what peace a Christian can die." All Addison's "compositions are but the noble preface; the grand work is his death." Evidently aware of the degree to which this final part is unrelated to the main topic, Young comments: "This you will think a long digression" (a comment none will gainsay). This is the "monumental marble" designed to promote serious thought.

With definite allusion to an idea expressed by Addison in the *Spectator* (No. 349) that "the end of a man's life is often compared to the winding up of a well written play," Young, now referring to Addison's death, bids us "regard the person departing as an actor of a part. . . . This was a Roscius on the stage of life; his exit how great? Ye lovers of virtue! *plaudite.*" Young adds in a postscript that further discussion of Addison as an Original will be given "in my next."

Modern scholarship has shed interesting light on the postscript and on how Young came to include the unrelated last part concerning Addison's death.[8] Young had apparently planned to write two essays, one on original and one on moral composition; and the story of Addison's death was to be the high spot of the second story. Richardson, enthusiastic about the hitherto unknown anecdote, persuaded him to move it to the first paper and made some suggestions about telescoping it into its new setting. Though Young struggled with the second paper, he did not complete it; and the reference in the postscript was left dangling. Young had great doubt about the advisability of the changed position of the anecdote, and after publication Richardson too felt it a mistake—as did many others (Richardson, *Correspondence,* II, 54).

The immediate reception of the **Conjectures** was good.[9] Richardson wrote to Young that such people as Onslow, Johnson, Warburton, and Allen of Bath had expressed pleasure in it. Unfortunately, the papers giving Johnson's more detailed opinions, which Richardson said he had sent, never reached Young. Various favorable comments appeared in periodicals. The *Monthly Review,* though disliking the style, praised Young as having the "qualities of a genius of the first rank" and considered his observations as "new, striking, and just." Many of the readers were struck with the amazing youthfulness shown in the writing of a man of Young's advanced years. His friend Mrs. Delany declared it "is

written with the spirit of twenty-five rather than four score years of age."

The meeting of Young and Johnson at Richardson's house which Johnson spoke of to Boswell many years later is unfortunately not discussed in extant letters of the time it took place, somewhere between January and May, 1759. Boswell recorded that Johnson said he was surprised that Young considered as novelties what he thought very common thoughts.[10] Just which points Johnson had in mind is not clear. Certainly Young had himself much earlier expressed many of the same ideas, and there was a vast amount of discussion of related points during the century.

Though both Young and Richardson seemed somewhat interested in further revisions, there were only a few minor verbal changes in the second edition, later in the same year, 1759. No other editions appeared during Young's life. The **Conjectures** had a much greater reception and exerted a much greater influence in Germany: within two years of its publication, two translations into German appeared; and these have been credited with playing a large part in the development of the "storm and stress" movement. Though the **Conjectures** was included in the various *Complete Works* from 1773 on, no separate, new edition was published in England until the end of the second decade of the twentieth century. The edition by Edith Morley of 1918 did a good deal to revive interest in it, and it has come to be considered an influence in the Romantic movement. It is now included in various anthologies of literary criticism, as a whole or in part; and **Conjectures** is therefore more accessible than most of his other writings.

Notes

[1] PETTIT, *Bibliography* . . . , p. 27, pp. 39-41.

[2] H. W. O'CONNOR, "The Narcissa Episode in Young's *Night Thoughts,"* *Publications of the Modern Language Association of America,* XXXIV (1919), 130-49.

[3] I. ST. J. BLISS, "Thought Background of Young's *Night Thoughts."* (Unpublished Doctoral Dissertation, The University of Chicago, 1931).

[4] DEAN EDWARD YOUNG, *Sermons on Several Occasions* (London, 1720), II, 331.

[5] I. ST. J. BLISS, "Young's *Night Thoughts* in Relation to Contemporary Christian Apologetics," *Publications of the Modern Language Association of America,* XLIX (1934), 37-70.

. . . . .

[8] ALAN MCKILLOP, "Richardson, Young, and the **Conjectures,"** *Modern Philology,* XXII (1925), 391-404.

[9] EDITH MORLEY, ed., EDWARD YOUNG, *Conjectures on Original Composition* (London, 1918), pp. 50-53.

[10] JAMES BOSWELL, *Journal of a Tour to the Hebrides,* ed. F. A. POTTLE and C. H. BENNETT (New York, 1936), p. 234.

Saintsbury on the qualities of Young's satire:

. . . Not many people, perhaps, have read *The Universal Passion*, which is a pity. For it is not only, as Johnson said, "a very great performance," but what he notices as a charge against it is "a series of epigrams," ought to commend it to the present day which prides itself on its own epigrammaticity. Only, Young's epigrams do not depend upon cheap, and sometimes quite empty paradox. Nor does the stoutest Johnsonian, even though he go with his master in deciding that Young "plays only on the surface of life; he never penetrates the recesses of the mind," go on with him to hold that "the whole power of his poetry is exhausted by a single perusal." Young might have retorted that it was the surface of life that he here *meant* to deal; and that, later, in the *Night Thoughts*, he has by no means shunned the depths. But the fault of Johnson's judgment—a characteristic one—lies in the last sentence. It by no means follows—it is a false analogy and a real paralogism—that a superficial treatment must itself be of only passing interest. Pope is much more superficial than Young; yet some of those who hold Pope's poetry cheapest as poetry, would confess that they never tire of the special pleasure which, as literature, it is fitted to give and does give to them. It is true that Young's is a much less artistically wrought and polished super-ficies than Pope's, and so it may please less. But John-son's error, like others of his, arose from confining attention to the *matter* instead of extending it, if not devoting it principally, to the treatment. . . .

George Saintsbury, The Peace of the Augustans, G. Bell and Sons, Ltd., 1916.

Daniel W. Odell (essay date 1971)

SOURCE: "Young's *Night Thoughts* and the Tradition of Divine Poetry," in *Ball State University Forum*, Vol. XII, No. 2, Spring, 1971, pp. 3-13.

[*Below, Odell explores the ways in which "Young fully adopts the theory of divine poetry inherited from the preceding centuries and modified for the eighteenth century."*]

Such prominent characteristics of Young's *Night Thoughts* as the urge to edify, the constant display of emotion, and the use of a personal, confessional tone are usually discussed in the context of Young's life or of the romantic poetry to come or of both. H. H. Clark, for example, attributes the subjective, personal note to the life and character of Young and to his concept of original genius. He explains Young's emotionalism in terms of a "romantic" aspiration, which is "indefinite and expansive" and leads to "ennui and restless melancholy": Young lacks "true Christian aspiration," which is "focused . . . on the imitation of Christ as he appears revealed in the Scriptures." Other critics also find the "personal" element in the poem more significant than Young's avowed purpose of answering the optimism of Pope, and their approaches are based on the biography of Young. Thus C. V. Wicker discovers in Young a "new treatment of melancholy . . . cast in a mold neither traditional nor conventional, but shaped by his own inner broodings," primarily the fear of death. Amy Reed says that unlike Thomson in the *Seasons*, "Young, a sick soul . . . invariably proceeds from reflections on his own wretchedness." John W. Draper finds the poem a didactic lamentation in which Young sentimentally celebrates deaths in his own family: "the atmosphere of gloom, as in the Puritan elegists . . . is largely personal to the author: he is more sorry for his own sorrows than for any ill that may betide either the deceased or the dissolute youth to whom he addresses his moral apothegms."[1]

Without denying that Young's urge to edify, his tone and display of emotion are in some sense explicable in biographical terms, I would like to suggest that such characteristics are perhaps better understood by reference to what Lily B. Campbell has called the Renaissance-Christian tradition of divine poetry.

In commenting on the origins of the tradition as it was first exemplified in such poems as Saluste du Bartas' *La Muse Chretiene* (1574), Campbell remarks that when Urania, the muse of astronomy, became the muse of Christian poetry, "she became the center of a whole doctrine and defense of Christian poetry which had been gradually growing up in Christian Europe and in England." Du Bartas' poem contained an apologia which "gave unity to the movement's tenets, many of which are but Christianized interpretations of precepts familiar as classical heritages. . . ."[2] Campbell lists the tenets of the theory as follows:

(1) Poetry must be reclaimed from the base uses to which it has been put.

(2) Poetry must be recognized as a heavenly gift, not the result of study and learning.

(3) The first poetry was divine poetry, the poetry of the Bible, but later writers used poetry for profane purposes.

(4) The high subject will bring about a worthy style.

(5) Biblical story must be substituted for pagan mythology: the dove of the Holy Ghost for Pegasus, Noah's flood for Deucalion's, etc.

(6) Better material for poetry lies in the history of faith's effects than in old classical stories.

(7) Poetry should give profit with its pleasure.

(8) Eternal fame can come only to the poet who writes of eternal things.

Within the first two decades of the eighteenth century the essential elements of the doctrine of divine poetry were adopted and modified for Augustan literature by John Dennis, Sir Richard Blackmore, and Isaac Watts. In common, (1) they criticized the degraded state of contemporary poetry and defended its proper use; (2) they called for the use of Christian themes and subject matter under the inspiration of the Christian muse, Urania; (3) they defended the passions and poetic "enthusiasm," and stressed the Sublime as brought about by exalted religious ideas; and (4) they emphasized the idea that genius is more a matter of nature than of art.[3] That Young was aware of the tradition of divine poetry, if not Augustan use of it, is apparent in his early poems **"The Last Day"** (1714) and **"A Paraphrase of Part of the Book of Job"** (1719). Although the latter is a paraphrase, Young uses the authority of Longinus for sublime touches that he freely adds. The former is essentially a traditional Christian treatment of the four last things but shows explicit signs of adherence to the requirements of divine poetry.

In the opening lines of **"The Last Day,"** Young distinguishes his aim from that of secular poets, especially contemporary eulogists of Marlborough, and asserts that he will "draw a deeper scene": the end of the world and God's final judgment of mankind.[4] He rejects the "vain-glorious Muse" of those who devote themselves to worldly "Fame." His muse is a "melancholy maid" whom "dismal scenes delight, / Frequent at tombs, and in the realms of Night" (I. 143-45). Led by his muse at night out under the starry skies, the great temple of the universe, he casts his heart before the eternal throne and asks inspiration so that his mind may be raised to heaven as he writes of his "great subject": "O! permit the gloom of solemn night / To sacred thought may forcibly invite" (II. 361-62). Against idle pastorals and secular panegyrics he proclaims the primacy and universality of "sacred song": "The Muse is wont in narrow bounds to sing, / To teach the swain, or celebrate the king. . . . I sing to men and angels; angels join / While such the theme, their sacred songs with mine" (II. 7-12). He refuses to use false mythology and to enslave art to servile ends:

Expect not here the known successful arts
To win attention, and command our hearts:

Fiction, be far away; let no machine
Descending here, no fabled God, be seen:
Behold the GOD of gods indeed descend,
And worlds unnumber'd His approach attend!

[II. 155-60]

"The Last Day" brought Young high repute in those circles interested in the reform of poetry. Thomas Warton the Elder, for example, praised Young's religious purpose and the "wondrous theme" of the poem. And the anonymous poet of "Some Thought on Reading Mr. Young's Poem on the Last Day" (1718) eulogized Young as one whom "Urania did indeed inspire, / Here the bless'd maid did generously impart / The strength of genius and the blaze of art." The same author praised the "mournful numbers" of Watt's poem on the Last Day and Mrs. Rowe's ability to set "the unbelieving world on fire" and to provide "more exalted themes / Than sporting lambs, or pretty purling streams;" and he called upon Addison to contribute to the genre.[5]

In the *Night Thoughts* (1742-45) Young fully adopts the theory of divine poetry inherited from the preceding centuries and modified for the eighteenth century by Dennis, Blackmore, and Watts:

(1) Young repeatedly attacks the abuse of poetry and asserts the rightness and seriousness of his own purpose in singing the Christian truths about death and immortality. He dismisses the muse of frivolous and sensual poetry which lacks the guidance of reason: "Take PHOEBUS to yourselves, ye basking bards! / Inebriate at fair Fortune's fountain-head . . . / Where Sense runs savage, broke from Reason's chain" (III. 19-22). Imagination which is not controlled by reason corrupts art: such "Imagination is the Paphian shop" where are forged "foul Ideas . . . Which murder all thy time, health, wealth, and fame" (VIII. 994-99).

Young refuses to pervert the passions and to use "fiction." In Young's poem, not "sirens only" but "angels sing." Do you think, Young asks his adversary Lorenzo,

to find pastimes here?
No guilty passion blown into a flame,
No foible flatter'd, dignity disgraced,
No fairy field of fiction, all on flower,
No rainbow colours here, or silken tale;
But solemn counsels, images of awe,
Truths which Eternity lets fall on man.

[V. 67-73]

Young's apparent rejection of the "fairy field of fiction" has led one critic to say of his poem that "in the light of his enthusiasm for the freedom of the human soul, and in light of his later *Conjectures* Young's distrust of lawless genius comes as something of a surprise."[6] In the *Night Thoughts* as well as the *Conjectures,* however, genius is autonomous within its own sphere, but is always subject to the higher truth of Christian revelation.[7] In poetry, "but what is moral, nought is great." The muse blushes at her degenerate sons who "raise the low, to magnify the mean, / And subtilize the gross into refined: / . . . Wit, a true Pagan, deifies the brute, / And lifts our swine-enjoyments from the mire" (V. 8-9, 13-14). Such art is "cursed," and no "powers of genius" can "consecrate enormities with song."

The abuse of poetry, nevertheless, is no argument against its proper use, which is to please by teaching divine truths. Let not "inexpiable strains / Condemn the Muse that knows her dignity," Young says, for it is the purpose of the divine muse to "run the round of universal space, / To visit being universal there, / And Being's Source, that utmost flight of mind!" (V. 53-54, 58-60). Those who would reject poetry forget that in inspired Scripture, poetry is the handmaid of religion: "foes to song" may be "well-meaning men" but they have "quite forgotten half" their "Bible's praise." The poet who is guided by divine truth "Dispels the mists our sultry passions raise, / From objects low, terrestrial, and obscene; / And shows the real estimate of things" (V. 330-32). And in conveying truth, such a poet cannot but bring pleasure:

> Patron of pleasure, doter on delight!
> I am thy rival; pleasure I profess;
> Pleasure the purpose of my gloomy song.
> Pleasure is nought but Virtu's gayer
>   name. . . .
> Virtue the root, and Pleasure is the flower;
> And honest EPICURCUS' foes were fools.
>
> [VIII. 570-76]

As a singer of divine poetry, Young rejects the classical laurel in favor of the Christian palm. After expressing the wish that his poem like his soul become immortal, he turns on himself and exclaims: "No!—the soul disdains / A mark so mean; far nobler hope inflames; / If endless ages can outweigh an hour, / Let not the laurel, but the palm, inspire" (VI. 71-75). Young prefers to interpret the desire for eternal fame as a sign of man's natural desire for immortality of the soul (VII. 359-66).

(2) Young uses Christian themes and subject matter under the aegis of the Christian muse. Like Milton, who was perhaps the primary influence on the *Night Thoughts,*[8] Young invokes Urania as a symbol of the Holy Spirit, who inspires him at night. His theme may be "common" but not so his song if she

> My song invokes, URANIA, deigns to smile.
> The charm that chains us to the World, her
>   foe,
> If she dissolves, the man of earth, at once,

> Starts from his trance, and sighs for other
>   scenes;
> Scenes, where these sparks of night, these stars,
>   shall shine
> Unnumber'd suns; (for all things as they are
> The bless'd behold;) and, in one glory, pour
> Their blended blaze on man's astonish'd sight;
> A blaze,—the least illustrious object there.
>
> [VIII. 24-33]

Young drinks with "sacred thirst" from the Christian stream of the Holy Spirit, which is a "purer stream / And fuller of the God, than that which burst / From famed Castalia. . . ." (V. 107-10; cf. IV. 301-303).

The subject matter of the *Night Thoughts* may be regarded as a fulfillment of the requests of Dennis, Blackmore, and Watts for a serious poetry concerned with Christian themes. Watts, for example, expresses the demand clearly when he contrasts the truths of Christian doctrine with the legends of classical myth, saying that "if we survey the one as themes divinely true, and the other as a medley of fooleries which we can never believe; the advantages for touching the springs of passion will fall infinitely on the side of the Christian poet." Moreover, Watts' exhortation to poets to adapt Christian themes to the contemporary scene and to dramatize the struggle of the Christian toward salvation reads like a prescription for Young's focus on the meaning to the speaker of the death of three loved ones, the stated occasion of the poem. Watts sees no reason to borrow either plan or history from the ancient Jews or early martyrs, for the "affairs of this life, with their reference to a life to come, would shine bright in a dramatic description; . . . modern scenes would be better understood by most readers, and the application would be much more easy."[9] Further evidence of Young's concern to bring Christianity into the hearts and lives of his readers is the fact that the speaker in the *Night Thoughts* makes use of traditional forms of religious meditation.[10]

(3) In general, Young uses the stated occasion of the poem, the deaths of loved ones, to support the doctrine of immortality. In so doing, he concerns himself with the truths of both natural and revealed religion, both with manifestations of God's love and wisdom in the terrestrial and celestial worlds and with such traditional doctrines of Christian revelation as the Redemption and the Last Day. His handling of such themes follows from his conception of man's nature, and involves a defense of the passions and of "enthusiasm," and a major stress on the Sublime.

Young believes that man, though fallen in Adam, still possesses the capacity to rise if he repents his sins and chooses "Virtue, which Christian motives best inspire! / And bliss, which Christian schemes alone insure!" (III. 394-95). With John Dennis,[11] Young holds that the happiness of man depends upon his "naked will," for by his choices "Each man makes his own stature," and his nature is such that "ill choice insures ill fate." For man, "though sullied and dishonour'd" by the Fall, is, by means of the Redemption, "still divine" and the "heir of glory." By the Redemption, man has become potentially "a glorious partner with the Deity." Furthermore, the Resurrection provided man with the "proof supreme" of the doctrine of immortality, and the prospect of "evolutions of surprising fate," a concept of indefinite material, moral, and intellectual progress, was opened to him. From these Christian views of Young flow his emphases on the passions and the Sublime, and his defense of "enthusiasm."

For Young, the Christian dispensation places value on all of man's faculties: "Our heads, our hearts, our passions, and our powers, / Speak the same language; call us to the skies" (VII. 63-64). Man's faculties are divine, and properly used they work harmoniously to bring him happiness. Man's reason is a "heaven-lighted lamp" which illuminates truth, for Christ, "To give lost Reason life, . . . pour'd His own." Reason is "that god in man," the voice of conscience: "What Reason bids, GOD bids." Reason is the "sovereign power"

> Which Sense and Fancy summons to the bar;
> Interrogates, approves, or reprehends;
> And from the mass those underling import,
> From their materials sifted, and refined . . .
> Strikes out, with master-hand, a copy fair
> Of His idea, whose indulgent thought
> Long, long ere Chaos teem'd, plann'd human
>   bliss!
>
> [VI. 449-53, 459-61]

There may be conflict between reason and the passions. At times, reason may be "Passion's foe," for the affections may "err in human hearts; / Mistake their objects, or transgress their bounds" (VIII. 547-48). But the proper objects of the passions are ordained in heaven: "Meet objects for our passions Heaven ordain'd, / Objects that challenge all their fire, and leave / No fault but in defect. . . ." (VII. 70-72). Young goes so far as to say that "Reason the means, Affections choose our end; / Means have no merit, if our end amiss. / If wrong our hearts, our heads are right in vain" (VI. 279-81).

In contrast to those theologians (presumably Christian Stoics) who believe reason and the passions incompatible, Young feels that the passions may and should be legitimately exercised now as they were in Eden before the Fall. He tells "gentle theologues of calmer kind," that man's passions did not spring from "Corruption":

> I feel a grandeur in the Passions . . .
> Which speaks their high descent, and glorious
>   end;
> Which speaks them rays of an eternal fire.

In Paradise itself they burnt as strong,
Ere ADAM fell, though wiser in their aim.
> [VII. 528-32]

Though now our passions may run mad, we know how they may be reclaimed: when "appetite wears Reason's golden chain," the passions are "taught to fly at nought but infinite." Then "nought ministers delight" to man but "what his glowing passions can engage."

Even when reason is silent, the passions proclaim their true end: "Were Reason silent, boundless Passion speaks / A future scene of boundless objects too, / And brings glad tidings of eternal day" (VII. 548-50). Thus man's insatiable desire to know and to love shows "boundless appetite, and boundless power," and "these demonstrate boundless objects too." Even such worldly passions as ambition, pleasure, and love of gain, properly directed, may lead man to heaven.

Like reason and the passions, "Our senses . . . are Divine." Contrary to the Stoics, the senses may and must be trusted. "Austerity" may knit "her cloudy brow" at "the praise / Of Pleasure," Young concedes, but he responds: "Ye modern Stoics! hear my soft reply:— / Their senses men will trust;" for "Pleasure came from Heaven" not "to turn human *brutal,* but to build / *Divine* on human. . . ." (VIII. 579-83, 641-42).

An appropriate enthusiasm, then, is justifiable. The passions are not the "Pagans of the soul," but like man's reason and senses, they are "baptized," "ordain'd / To touch things sacred." Young scorns "Quietists," the "cold-hearted, frozen formalists," who are unmoved by great religious ideas that ought to rouse the affective faculties and raise man to the Sublime: "Heaven, which gave us ardour" disdains "What smooth emollients in theology, / Recumbent Virtue's downy doctors preach" (IV. 641-44).

The "Sublime" in the ***Night Thoughts*** has been discussed recently by Marjorie Nicolson in relation to the development of the "Aesthetics of the Infinite." Nicolson finds in Night IX "the climax of the conception of the 'vast Sublime'." Under the influence of the concepts of infinite space and time revealed by the new astronomy, Young discloses an obsession with the "effect of vastness and the vast upon the soul of man," and a preference for external nature to art.[12] For example, Young finds in the night skies "Nature's most august, / Inspiring aspect!" (IX. 561-62). There his soul discovers

> . . . a previous scene of objects great
> On which to dwell; to stretch to that expanse
> Of thought, to rise to that exalted height
> Of admiration, to contract that awe,
> And give her whole capacities that strength,
> Which best may qualify for final joy.
>
> [IX. 572-77]

Viewing interstellar space, the soul can "every power unfold, / And rise into sublimities of thought" (IX. 634-35).

While it is true that Young finds the "vast" Sublime in viewing the heavens, he continues the emphasis of Dennis, Blackmore, and Watts on the superiority of Christian revelation as a source of ideas which evoke the Sublime. Dennis, for example, holds that Milton's depiction of the creation of the world is superior to Vergil's, not because Milton possessed the greater genius, but because Vergil used the false Epicurean hypothesis to explain the creation.[13] Furthermore, Dennis argues that enthusiastic terror, hence Sublimity, may be produced by the ideas of "Gods, Daemons, Hell, Spirits and Souls of Men, Miracles, Prodiges, Enchantments, Witchcrafts, Thunder, Tempests, raging Seas, Inundations, Torrents, Earthquakes, Volcanoes, Monsters, Serpents, Lions, Tygers, Fire, War, Pestilence, Famine, Etc." But nothing is so terrible, Dennis says, as the wrath and vengeance of an angry God, for "nothing is so unavoidable as the Vengeance design'd by it."[14]

In the light of Christian revelation, Young finds that one immortal soul is more mysterious and important than the celestial heavens. Thus was Young led to what has been called the "Christian sublime,"[15] as distinguished from the "natural" Sublime. Young admits that the "vastness" of the night skies seems to belittle man: "Turn up thine eye, survey this midnight scene; / What are Earth's kingdoms to yon boundless orbs, / Of human souls, one day the destined range?" (VII. 1244-46). But he immediately adds that even the whole material creation cannot fill the mind of man:

> And what you boundless orbs to godlike man?
> Those numerous worlds that throng the firmament,
> And ask more space in heaven, can roll at large
> In man's capacious thought, and still leave room
> For ampler orbs, for new creations, there.
>   [VII. 1247-51]

Man is great and godlike because he is immortal and therefore capable of endless material, intellectual, and moral progress:

> IMMORTAL! Ages past, yet nothing gone!
> Morn without eve! a race without a goal,
> Unshorten'd by progression infinite!
> Futurity for ever future! Life
> Beginning still where computation ends!
> 'Tis the description of a Deity!
>   [VI. 542-47]

The idea of man's immortal soul as the "genuine cause of every deed Divine" (VII. 1015), the prize over which

the divine and infernal powers fought in heaven, is a "vast" idea which leads Young to exhort his adversary Lorenzo to "wake, / Rise to the thought: exert, expand thy soul / To take the vast idea: it denies / All else the name of great" (VII. 1050-53). Such an idea "thunders to the thought; / Reason amazes; gratitude o'erwhelms. . . . / Quick kindles all that is Divine within us; / Nor leaves one loitering thought beneath the stars" (VI. 557-58, 563-64). Every man can be raised by such a great thought:

> Enthusiastic this? then all are weak,
> But rank enthusiasts. To this godlike height
> Some souls have soar'd, or martyrs ne'er had bled;
> And all may do, what has by man been done.
> Who, beaten by these sublunary storms,
> Boundless, interminable joys can weigh,
> Unraptured, unexalted, uninflamed?
>   [VI. 603-609]

The doctrines associated with immortality such as the Redemption and the Last Day also exalt man. In the light of the Redemption, for example, the material creation with its unnumbered worlds which night reveals is a "beam," a "mere effluvium" of God's majesty. The very stars see on earth "a bounty not indulged on high," compared to which their sublimity is "humble." The morning stars sang at the creation, but man is "*Creation's* great superior" because he has been redeemed: "Redemption! 'Twas creation more sublime. . . ." (IV. 450, 455).

The idea of the Redemption is so great as to be incomprehensible to creatures: "Its value vast, ungrasp'd by minds create" (IV. 241). But even a "heart of stone . . . glows at thoughts like these," and is enraptured, elevated, inflamed. It is "impious to be calm" about such a subject, concerning which "Passion is reason, transport, temper." Meditation on the transformation effected in man by the Redemption carries Young away to

> . . . boundless walks of raptured thought! where gods
> Encounter and embrace me! What new births
> Of strange adventure, foreign to the sun;
> Where now what charms, perhaps whate'er exists,
> Old Time and fair Creation, are forgot!
>   [IV. 512-16]

Such contemplations raise thought so high that one can never "glance on man / Unraptured, uninflamed."

Young's emphasis on the Last Day as a source of the Sublime derives from his insistence that "virtues grow on immortality" and that "Rewards and punishments made GOD adored; / And hopes and fears give Conscience all her power" (VII. 1172, 1175-6). Such an attitude is akin to that of Dennis. Young treats the Last Day at length in Night IX, first as prefigured by Noah's flood. In a vision unlocked by midnight thought, Young sees the form of the first deluge, an idea of "ghastly nature and enormous size" which "assaults" his "sight," "chills" his "blood," and "shakes" his "frame." He next envisions the final conflagration, an "Amazing period" in which the earth trembles, mountains burn up, and rivers pour fire, while from the heavens the Judge descends in "grandeur terrible." The Judge pronounces sentence, and the guilty drop into everlasting fire. What strikes the reader here as elsewhere about Young's emotionalism is not the revelation of his inner life but the conventionality of such a set piece intended to evoke the Christian Sublime in a rather typical adherence to the tenets of the tradition of divine poetry.

Young also finds a source of the Sublime in what Dennis called man's "divine qualities," that is, his virtues.[16] Thus the Christian virtues exhibited by the death of the good man, Philander, provide Young with a "theme most affecting, most sublime, / Momentous most to man," a theme hitherto "by genius unawaked" (II. 610-12). Recalling the suddenness of Philander's death, Young is moved by terror and pity, but he is amazed and overjoyed at the memory of the Christian fortitude with which Philander transcends the limitations of man by comforting his comforters. Here is the majesty of virtue assisted by grace; and here also perhaps is an anticipation of Young's treatment of the death of Addison in the *Conjectures* about a decade later.

(4) The *Night Thoughts* reveals a theoretical preference for considering genius more a matter of nature than of art, "nature" meaning, in A. O. Lovejoy's definition, "those expressions of human nature which are most spontaneous, unpremeditated, untouched by reflection or design, and free from the bondage of social convention."[17]

The preface to the *Night Thoughts* was originally the preface to only Night IV,[18] but I see no reason it cannot characterize the entire poem, for in one sense it represents what by Young's time was more or less a convention in the tradition of divine poetry. In his preface, Young says that "As the occasion of this poem was real, not fictitious; so the method pursued in it was rather imposed by what spontaneously arose in the author's mind on that occasion, than meditated or designed." The "common mode of poetry," he continues, is "from long narrations to draw short morals," but here "the narrative is short, and the morality arising from it makes the bulk of the poem. The reason of it is, that the facts mentioned did naturally pour these moral reflections on the thought of the writer" (Nichols edition, I. 46). He adds that he is uncertain whether "Providence, or inclination, will permit him to go any farther" than Night IV, for "this thing was entered on purely as a refuge under uneasiness, when more proper

studies wanted sufficient relish to detain the writer's attention to them." Young, of course, went on to write five more "Nights," totaling thousands of additional lines, and in general he adheres to the tradition of divine poetry throughout the entire poem.

There is precedent for Young's emphasis on spontaneity. An earlier exponent of divine poetry, Henry Lok, makes a similar claim in his dedication to the "Christian reader," which prefaced his *Sundry Christian Passions* (1593), a sonnet sequence using Bible story as a frame of reference. Lok asserts that he had "rather followed the force of mine owne inward feeling, then [sic] outward ornaments of Poeticall fictions or amplifications, as best beseeming the naked clothing of simple truth, & true Analogie of the Histories whereto they alude, and harmonie of scriptures whence they are borrowed."[19]

Furthermore, Young's contemporary Isaac Watts reveals the same kind of emphasis in the preface to his elegy "A Funeral Poem on the Death of Thomas Gunston, Esq." (1702). Although the poem itself does not depart from the basic conventions of the funeral elegy, it uses the invocation to Urania familiar in divine poetry, and Watts claims that his natural, spontaneous feelings rendered unnecessary the methods of art. He declares that he needed no art "to supply the defect of nature, and to feign a sorrow," for "the vast and tender sense I have of the loss" makes "all methods of art needless, whilst natural grief supplies more than all." Thus he says he pursued "no other topics of elegy than what my passion and my senses led" to. And he exploits fully the pathetic personal details suggested by his subject. Watts nevertheless shows awareness of the neoclassic distinction between private and public feelings when he says that he did not intend to design a complete elegy for public view, but wrote for himself "as a friend of the dead, and to ease my full soul by breathing out my own complaints."[20] That Watts did publish the poem may be an indication that as a divine poet he would make public his "personal" feelings. Lacking Watts' statement that he wrote for himself and not for public view, Young's avowal, however, is perhaps a sign of the changing relationship between public and poet, although Young remained self-consciously aware that "the man who shows his heart" might be "hooted for his nudities and scorned."

The emphasis in Young's preface is developed and sharpened in several significant passages in his poem. In general Young believes that the powers of his soul endow man with great potentialities for moral, intellectual, especially artistic, progress. Thus the great soul with an "energy Divine" is able to transcend time and space, and to reach the "vast Unseen, the Future fathomless!" (VI. 248-50). The man who "lives to Nature," that is, who exploits the possibilities of his own human nature, "rarely can be poor," for there is true wealth and creativity in souls that can command

Creations new in Fancy's field to rise!
Souls, that can grasp whate'er th' Almighty
    made,
And wander wild through things impossible!
What wealth, in faculties of endless growth,
In quenchless passions violent to crave,
In liberty to choose, in power to reach,
And in duration, (how thy riches rise!)
Duration to perpetuate-boundless bliss!

[VI. 469-76]

Since "Each man makes his own stature," each man
should rely on his own native powers and experience,
rather than on borrowed knowledge: the "forager on
others' wisdom, leaves / Her native farm, near reason,
quite untill'd" (V. 258-59). Man should see that "Genius needs not go to school," for the learned, who
immerse themselves in "volumes deep," neglect what lies
before them "in the page / Of Nature, and Experience."
But the man who knows himself will recognize and
ought to develop his true nature and genius:

Objects are but th' occasion; ours th' exploit;
Ours is the cloth, the pencil, and the paint,
Which Nature's admirable picture draws;
And beautifies Creation's ample dome.
Like Milton's Eve, when gazing on the lake,
Man makes the matchless image man admires.
Say then, shall man, his thoughts all sent
    abroad,
(Superior wonders in himself forgot,)
His admiration waste on objects round,
When Heaven makes him the soul of all he
    sees?[21]

[VI. 431-40]

By such emphasis on genius and individuality, then,
together with his belief in the high purpose of poetry
raised to the Sublime by Christian themes, Young allied himself with Augustan exponents of the tradition
of divine poetry. And it is in light of Young's promul-
gation of this tradition that we may assess such views
of the *Night Thoughts* as the one which calls it "the
antithesis of almost all that neo-classical poetry stands
for."[22] Young's poem reflects more the adaptation of a
traditional conception of poetry than the sudden appearance of a radically innovative critical theory or
practice.

Notes

[1] H. H. Clark, "The Romanticism of Edward Young,"
*Transactions of the Wisconsin Academy of Science,
Arts, and Letters,* 24 (1929), 7, 12-13; C. V. Wicker,
"Edward Young and the Fear of Death: A Study in
Romantic Melancholy," *The University of New Mex-
ico Publications in Language and Literature,* No. 10
(1952), p. 31; Amy Reed, *The Background of Gray's
Elegy* (New York: Columbia Univ. Press, 1924), p.

192; John W. Draper, *The Funeral Elegy and the Rise
of English Romanticism* (New York: N. Y. Univ.
Press, 1929), p. 307.

[2] Lily B. Campbell, "The Christian Muse," *The Huntington Library Bulletin,* No. 8 (1935), pp. 44-45.
Campbell incorporates the substance of this article in
*Divine Poetry and Drama in Sixteenth-Century En-
gland* (Berkeley: Univ. of Calif. Press, 1959) from
which I quote (p. 80) the tenets of the movement.

[3] See Floyd Chester Medford, Jr., "Two Augustans and
the Sacred Muse: The Theory of Divine Poetry in Sir
Richard Blackmore and John Dennis," Diss. Texas
1957.

[4] "The Last Day," I. 1-10. This poem as well as the
Night Thoughts will be cited from Edward Young, *The
Complete Works,* ed. James Nichols, 2 vols. (London,
1854; rpt. Hildesheim, G. Olms, 1968), and subsequent
references will appear in the text.

[5] See I. 286-87, 293-95, 297 in the Nichols edition,
which reprints the two eulogies.

[6] Margaret M. Fitzgerald, *First Follow Nature: Primitivism in English Poetry 1725-1750* (New York: King's
Crown Press, 1947), p. 207.

[7] In the *Conjectures on Original Composition,* ed. E. J.
Morley (New York: Longmans, 1918), Young says that
with "regard to the moral world, *conscience,* with regard to the intellectual, *genius,* is that god within"
(p. 15). And he warns "self-taught philosophers of our
age" against the "most fatal of errors," valuing genius
above divine truth.

[8] R. D. Havens, *The Influence of Milton on English
Poetry* (Cambridge, Mass.: Harvard Univ. Press, 1922),
pp. 590-94; Marjorie Nicholson, *Mountain Gloom and
Mountain Glory: The Development of the Aesthetics of
the Infinite* (Ithaca, N. Y.: Cornell Univ. Press, 1959),
p. 232.

[9] The quotations from Watts are from the preface to
the seventh edition of *Horae Lyricae* (1936) in *The
Works of the English Poets,* ed. A. Chalmers (London:
J. Johnson, 1810), XIII, 17.

[10] *Eighteenth Century Poetry and Prose,* ed. Louis I.
Bredvold, et al., 2nd ed. (New York: Ronald Press,
1956), p. 511.

[11] "Do but earnestly desire of God to incline your
Affections to Him their primitive Object; Do but desire it, and he will incline them, and the great Business
of Religion is done, the Harmony of the Human Faculties restor'd, and the Felicity of the first Man, in
some measure at least, renew'd. . . ." See John Dennis,

"The Advancement and Reformation of Modern Poetry," *Critical Works,* ed. E. N. Hooker (Baltimore: Johns Hopkins Press, 1939), I, 260. Subsequent references to Dennis will be to the Hooker edition.

[12] Nicholson, *Mountain Gloom and Mountain Glory,* p. 362.

[13] Dennis, I, 276.

[14] Dennis, I, 361-62.

[15] Alan D. McKillop, *English Literature From Dryden to Burns* (New York: Appleton-Century-Crofts, 1948), p. 186.

[16] Dennis, I, 354.

[17] A. O. Lovejoy, "On the Discrimination of Romanticisms," *Essays in the History of Ideas* (New York: Putnam, 1960), p. 238.

[18] Isabel St. John Bliss, *Edward Young* (New York: Twayne, 1969), p. 123.

[19] Lok is quoted by Lily B. Campbell, *Divine Poetry and Drama in Sixteenth-Century England* (Cambridge, Cambridge Univ. Press, 1959), p. 131.

[20] Chalmers, *English Poets,* XIII, 77.

[21] The epistemological basis of the creative process and the relationship of the faculties described in this and similar passages quoted is Neoplatonic and anticipates Young's emphasis in the *Conjectures* on genius, originality, and freedom from rules: see D. W. Odell, "Locke, Cudworth and Young's *Night Thoughts,*" *En-glish Language Notes,* 4 (1967), 188-93.

[22] James A. Sutherland, *A Preface to Eighteenth Century Poetry* (Oxford: Clarendon Press, 1948), p. 160.

C. C. Barfoot (essay date 1987)

SOURCE: "'Paradise Unlost': Edward Young among the Stars," in *Between Dream and Nature: Essays on Utopia and Dystopia,* edited by Dominic Baker-Smith and C. C. Barfoot, Rodopi, 1987, pp. 139-71.

[*In the following essay Barfoot examines utopian themes and images in Young's* Night Thoughts.]

> Moreover, so boundless are the bold excursions of the human mind, that in the vast void beyond real existence, it can call forth shadowy beings, and unknown worlds, as numerous, as bright, and, per-

haps, as lasting, as the stars; such quite-original beauties we may call Paradisaical,

> *Natos sine semine flores.*   OVID.[1]

Can one legitimately smuggle Edward Young into a conference (or a book) on Utopia? Well, in one of the more easily available nineteenth-century editions of *Young's Night Thoughts* (by 1853 the inclusion of the author's name in the abbreviated title seems to have been already traditional), we find the editor, the Rev. George Gilfillan, a friend of De Quincey and Carlyle, proclaiming enthusiastically that "Young deserves praise for the following things":

> 1*st,* He has nobly sung the magnitude and unutterable glory of the starry hosts. His soul kindles, triumphs, exults under the midnight canopy .... in the last part of the poem. Escaped from dark and mournful contemplations on Man, Death, Infidelity, and Earth's "melancholy map," he sees the stars like bright milestones on the way to heaven, and his spirit is glad within him, and tumultuous is the grandeur, and fierce and rapid the torrent, of his song.

> 2*dly,* He has brought out, better than any other poet, the religion of the stars. . . . Young, we need scarcely say, finds in the nocturnal heavens lessons neither of Atheism nor of Superstition, but of Religion, and reads in the face of Old Night her divine origin, the witness she bears to the existence of God, her dependence upon her Author, and her subordination to His purposes. He had magnified, as Newton himself could not so eloquently have done, the extent of the universe; and yet his loyalty to Scripture compels him to intimate that this system, so far from being God, or infinite, or, strictly speaking, Divine, is to perish and pass away.[2]

It is important to record that this extreme, and undoubtedly at the time already old-fashioned, view was expressed only four years before the appearance, in January 1857, of the essay which is said to have finally exploded Young's reputation—George Eliot's aptly titled examination of his all too evident "Worldliness" which, in the wake of worldly failure, his rhetorically effusive "Other-Worldliness" sought to disguise or to distract attention from.[3]

But it is as a (possibly *the*) poet of the stars,[4] as a poet of genuine "other worldliness" that, even allowing for the persuasive force of George Eliot's charges, one feels justified in linking Young and his "night thoughts", in particular those of **"Night the Ninth and Last",** the lengthy and apt culmination of the work, to the utopian theme. Even the blank verse form of *The Complaint: Or, Night-Thoughts on Life, Death, and Immortality* (to give Young's poem its full, proper title[5]) is not without its other-worldly implications. The greater part of Young's other poetry is in rhyme, a great deal of it, as one might expect, in rhyming couplets: for instance, his very first published poem, **The Last Day** (1713)—a significant early choice considering his later achievement in *Night Thoughts*—and his first real success, *Love of Fame, The Universal Passion* in **"Seven Characteristical Satires"** (1725-8). Critics com-menting upon Young's choice of blank verse in *Night Thoughts* have commonly pointed to the success of Thomson's *The Seasons* (1730), which so impressed the older poet. But at least after his own success with *Night Thoughts,* Young could afford to directly imply another reason for his choice of blank verse, "a term of diminution" which he objected to, since "what we mean by blank verse, is verse unfallen, uncurst; verse reclaim'd, reinthron'd in the true *language of the Gods;* who never thunder'd, nor suffer'd their *Homer* to thunder, in Rhime"[6]—in fact, the verse form of "Paradise unlost", of which the culminating section of **Night Thoughts** attempts, with some accomplishment, to give us a glimpse.

Paradise, lost or unlost, has evident associations with the Golden Age, and with its traditions before Saturn fell, which led to the fall of man more irrevocable than the fall of Adam and Eve, which was itself a consequence of Satan's fall. In popular imagining at least, and even in common academic use (as books and conferences reveal), "Utopia", "Paradise", the "Golden Age" tend to bear comparable resonances and similar connotations: "Aurea prima sata est aetas, quae vindice nullo, / sponte sua, sine lege fidem rectumque colebat" ("Golden was that first age, which, with no one to compel, without a law, of its own will, kept faith and did the right").[7] This is not really Utopia, of course—at least, not More's Utopia, nor the Paradise of either the Bible or Milton. However, there are resemblances between the three places of a perfected, if vulnerable, style of living, both in their physical and moral geography and in their literary provenance and uses. "Utopia", "Paradise", the "Golden Age" all indicate places that are insular or isolated (for obvious mythical, fictional and moral advantages). The men of the Golden Age knew only their own shores and had dipped no pine tree "into the watery plain to visit other lands" (*Met* I 95-6). More's Utopia is a crescent shaped island (although it had not always been "compassed about with the sea"—a state which had been achieved by King Utopus' engineering work[8]). According to Milton "this mount / Of Paradise" only became "an island" ("salt and bare, / The haunt of seals and orcs, and sea-mews' clang"—in Alastair Fowler's brisk summary "a bare island in the Persian Gulf"[9]) after the Flood. But before that, of course, it had had its "verdurous wall" (*PL* IV 143), which failed to keep Satan out, but which later, after the expulsion of Adam and Eve, was strengthened with extra angelic guards to prevent anybody ever getting in again. It is notable that when Britain has been extolled patriotically, its island status has been exploited as a means to forge a link between the Golden Age, Utopia and Paradise, as

in John of Gaunt's famous speech in *Richard II* (II i 39-50) or the Queen's speech in *Cymbeline* (III i 17-23).[10]

Edward Young's starry night is clearly no simple island nor even a walled retreat; but self-evidently it is remote, and physically it is out of the reach of man or any other earthly creature whose soul has not been parted from the flesh. Although partly visible through a telescope, it can only be "read" in a style analogous to the way that More's *Utopia* can be literally read, by someone fired with the appropriate imaginative propulsion. Young offers support to our more particular analogy by calling the firmament or the skies "the Garden of the DEITY, / Blossom'd with Stars, redundant in the Growth / Of Fruit ambrosial" (IX 1042-4) and by attributing to the furthest reach of God's "mighty Building" and "The Suburbs of Creation" a "Wall / Whose Battlements look o'er into the Vale / Of Non-Existence" (IX 1510-22). Moreover Young is carried away at one moment of speculation to wonder if the "One Universe" is "too small":

> in the Map
> Of universal *Nature,* as a Speck,
> Like fair BRITANNIA in our little Ball;
> Exceeding fair, and glorious, for its Size,
> But, elsewhere, far out-measur'd, far outshone?
> In *Fancy* (for the *Fact* beyond us lies)
> Canst thou not figure it, an *Isle,* almost
> Too small for Notice, in the *Vast* of Being;
> Sever'd by mighty Seas of *unbuilt* Space,
> From other *Realms;* from ample *Continents*
> Of higher Life, where nobler Natives dwell;
> Less *Northern,* less remote from DEITY,
> Glowing beneath the *Line* of the SUPREME;
> Where Souls in Excellence make Haste, put forth
> Luxuriant Growths; nor the late Autumn wait
> Of *Human* Worth, but ripen soon to Gods?
> (IX 1594-1612)

In such a passage as this Young's fantasy anticipates some of the gawdy of science-fiction, as well as echoing Renaissance arguments about the plurality of worlds, and justifies the use as an epigraph to this paper that passage from his **Conjectures on Original Composition** which associates such flights of fancy with the ability to contemplate Paradise. That particular quotation from **Conjectures** ends with a quotation from Ovid, "Natos sine semine flores" ("the flowers that sprang unplanted"), from that same paragraph of the first book of the *Metamorphoses* describing the Golden Age from which we have already quoted the opening lines.[11]

The writers, the poets, who describe the Golden Age, or Paradise, or Utopia, share more than a willingness to indulge in what Young calls "the bold excursions of the human mind". They also usually share a desire to teach by a description of their little state or garden or landscape how things really ought to be. The Golden Age, or Paradise, or Utopia is a measure of how far man has fallen, of the extent of his decline, of the distance from the origin which he so disturbingly fails to live up to. The didactic or even the satiric frame and basis of More's _Utopia_ is self-evident and is made particularly clear in the opening conversation of Raphael Hythloday and his account of his experiences at Cardinal Morton's table. Equally clear is the reforming context and purpose of Young's "_Moral_ Survey of the _Nocturnal_ Heavens", as he announces the section on the title page of "NIGHT the NINTH and LAST": "THE / CONSOLATION. / Containing, among other Things, / I. A _Moral_ Survey of the _Nocturnal_ Heavens. / II. A _Night_-ADDRESS to the DEITY." ("among other Things" referring to an effective account of the Apocalypse and the Last Judgement in some 200 lines preceding the "_Moral Survey_" of the heavens).

Edward Young's first great success had been a set of satires (published before those of Pope), and in **_Night Thoughts_** he follows the precedent of Milton in "Lycidas" and in _Paradise Lost_ of mixing with the elevated lyrical or epic vein an amount of abusive satirical writing: for instance, in "NIGHT the EIGHTH" ("VIRTUE'S APOLOGY; / OR, / The Man _of the_ WORLD _Answered_"):

> In foreign Realms (for thou hast travell'd far)
> How curious to contemplate two State-Rooks,
> Studious their Nests to feather in a Trice,
> With all the _Necromantics_ of their Art,
> Playing the Game of _Faces_ on each other,
> Making Court Sweet-meats of their latent Gall,
> In foolish Hope, to steal each other's Trust;
> Both cheating, both exulting, both deceiv'd;
> And, sometimes, both (let Earth rejoice) undone!
>
> (VIII 343-51)

There is less of this kind of vituperation in the last book, but such a passage as the following (in which Young addresses the "Bord'rers on the Coast of Bliss", the inhabitants "Of this so foreign, unterrestrial Sphere, / Where Mortal, _untranslated,_ never stray'd") may well be compared in content and tone with the outrage expressed by Hythloday or More himself in _Utopia:_

> "With War, This fatal Hour,
> EUROPA groans (so call we a small Field,
> Where Kings run mad). In _Our_ World, DEATH deputes
> _Intemperance_ to do the Work of _Age!_
> And, hanging up the Quiver _Nature_ gave him,
> As slow of Execution, for Dispatch
> Sends forth _Imperial_ Butchers; bids they slay
> Their Sheep (the silly Sheep they fleec'd before),
> And toss him twice Ten thousand at a Meal.
> Sit all _your_ Executioners on Thrones?
> With _you,_ can Rage for Plunder make a _God?_

> And _Bloodshed_ wash out ev'ry other Stain?—
> But You, perhaps, can't bleed: From Matter gross
> Your _Spirits_ clean, are delicately clad
> In fine-spun Æther, privileg'd to soar,
> Unloaded, uninfected; How unlike
> The Lot of Man! How few of human Race
> By their own _Mud_ unmurder'd! . . ."
>
> (IX 1782-97)

The abuse of political, social and spiritual evils, which are not at all to be distinguished, is part of the didactic purpose that More's and Young's work share: both are sermons presented in the guise of imaginative excursions. In a significant sense **Night Thoughts,** the last Night especially, like _Utopia_ is also a traveller's tale of a purely imaginative kind: "Loose me from _Earth's_ Inclosure, from the _Sun's_ / _Contracted_ Circle set my Heart at large", Young proclaims, "Eliminate my Spirit, give it Range / Thro' Provinces of Thought yet unexplor'd" (IX 589-92); "Above our Atmosphere's intestine Wars, / . . . / Above the Northern Nests of feather'd Snows, / . . . / Above misconstru'd Omens of the Sky, / . . . /Elance thy Thought" (launch thy thought, rather like a rocket: IX 620-30). "In Mid-way Flight Imagination tires; / Yet soon re-prunes her Wing to soar again" (1220-1): true, by the middle of the eighteenth century this kind of inspirational imagery and ecstatic rhetoric was a convention, even a cliché, of "the sublime poem"; but in Young's case, in its thematic and dramatic placing in the context of scanning the skies, the language sustains a conviction and its rhythms an energetic buoyancy that carry the reader:

> In ardent _Contemplation's_ rapid Car,
> From _Earth,_ as from my Barrier, I set out.
> How swift I mount! Diminish'd _Earth_ recedes;
> I pass the _Moon;_ and, from her farther Side,
> Pierce Heav'n's blue Curtain; strike into _Remote;_
> Where, with his lifted Tube, the subtil Sage
> His artificial, airy Journey takes,
> And to _Celestial_ lengthens _Human_ Sight.
> I pause at ev'ry _Planet_ on my Road,
> And ask for HIM who gives their Orbs to roll,
> Their Foreheads fair to shine. From SATURN's Ring,
> In which, of _Earth's_ an Army might be lost,
> With the bold _Comet,_ take my bolder Flight,
> Amid those _sov'reign_ Glories of the Skies,
> Of independent, native Lustre, proud;
> The Souls of Systems! and the Lords of Life,
> Thro' their wide Empires!—What behold I _now_?
> A Wilderness of Wonders burning round;
> Where _larger_ Suns inhabit _higher_ Spheres;
> Perhaps the _Villas_ of descending Gods!
> Nor halt I here; my Toil is but begun;
> 'Tis but the Threshold of the DEITY;
> Or, far beneath it, I am grovelling still.
>
> (IX 1715-37)

The reminder that this is but an imaginary journey through space is neatly conveyed in the reference to "the subtil Sage"'s "lifted Tube"—which has the double effect of indicating how distances in the universe are normally perceived and taken in and, at the same time, of suggesting (for a moment at least through the perspective that we are given of the telescope) that we are experiencing an unusual and superior voyage of discovery which passes and surpasses the usual method of the astronomer. This passage, like many in the **"Ninth Night"** reminds us that this poem is indeed inspired by the achievements of Sir Isaac Newton, but there is also an element of fantasy and the fantastic in such a description which aligns it with many another traveller's tale, including those of Raphael Hythloday, and nearer at hand, in time at least, of Lemuel Gulliver. The element of futuristic science fiction even extends to the imagining of lost empires and hidden realms. References to "the *Villas* of descending Gods" risks, and probably does not avoid, bathos; but at the same time it may equally well be regarded as a credibilizing detail that persuades the reader of the verisimilitude of the mental flight and indicates even to an unsympathetic critic how firmly the actual experience is lodged in Young's imagination: the very banality of imaginative detail helps to secure the excitable rhetoric.

But like Utopia itself this is a place to learn from: "This Prospect vast, what is it?—Weigh'd aright, / 'Tis Nature's System of Divinity, / . . . . / 'Tis *elder* Scripture, writ by GOD's own Hand; / Scripture authentic! Uncorrupt by Man" (IX 643-7). Young claims that his "Mind, op'ning at this Scene, imbibes / The moral Emanations of the Skies" (IX 847-8), since man has been given the build ("A Make to Man directive of his Thought; / A Make set upright, pointing to the Stars" (IX 870-1) "to read this Manuscript of Heaven" (IX 873), to "read the Stars" (IX 1304): a metaphor extended with, perhaps, over-expansive enthusiasm some 300 lines later:

> DIVINE INSTRUCTOR! Thy *first* Volume, *This,*
> For *Man's* Perusal; All in CAPITALS!
> In *Moon* and *Stars* (Heav'n's golden Alphabet!)
> Emblaz'd to seize the Sight; who *runs,* may *read;*
> Who *reads,* can *understand.* 'Tis Unconfin'd
> To *Christian* Land, or *Jewry;* fairly writ,
> In Language universal, to MANKIND:
> A Language, Lofty to the Learn'd; yet Plain
> To Those that feed the Flock, or guide the
>   Plough,
> Or, from its Husk, strike out the bounding
>   Grain.
> A Language, worthy the GREAT MIND, that speaks!
> *Preface,* and *Comment,* to the *Sacred Page!*
> Which oft refers its Reader to the Skies,
> As pre-supposing his First Lesson *there,*
> And Scripture self a *Fragment, That* unread.

> Stupendous Book of Wisdom, to the Wise!
> Stupendous Book! and open'd, NIGHT! by thee.
>   (IX 1659-75)

(And later Young claims that he has "half read o'er the Volume of the Skies"—IX 2020).

What we find in Young's **Night Thoughts,** especially in this last Night ("The Consolation") are three strands. In the first place, Young is an old-fashioned, although to his contemporaries a still fashionable and familiar, theologian, of no great originality. Young is seeking to convert the Deists, the Atheists, the current Infidels— rakes, wastrels, libertine gamblers and whoremongers, the commonplace list of enemies to respectable society and conventional belief in eighteenth-century sermons and moral essays—who are represented in this poem by Lorenzo. This much debated figure, who could not be Edward Young's son, may well be considered the poet's own *alter* (alternative, evil) *ego* whom he seeks to convert by the evidence of the universe and the planetary systems. This is "Physico" or "Astro-Theology" of the kind that the Boyle lectures established in 1692 tended to promote.[12] Newton himself had corresponded with the first Boyle lecturer, Richard Bentley, supporting his teleological arguments.[13] And as Isabel Bliss demonstrates such astro-Christian apologetics abound, usually with the overt support of Newton and other scientists, so that in his own day Edward Young's popularity "may be found in the fact that he was giving poetical expression to the theories that were felt to be vital in the religious life of the time":[14]

> But, Miracles apart, who sees HIM not,
> *Nature's* CONTROULER, AUTHOR, GUIDE, and END?
> Who turns his eye on *Nature's* Midnight Face,
> But must inquire—"What Hand behind the Scene,
> "What Arm Almighty, put these wheeling Globes
> "In Motion, and wound up the vast Machine?
> "Who rounded in his Palm these spacious Orbs?
> "Who bowl'd them flaming thro' the dark
>   Profound,
> "Num'rous as glitt'ring Gems of Morning-Dew,
> "Or Sparks from populous Cities in a Blaze,
> "And set the Bosom of *Old Night* on Fire?
> "Peopled her Desert, and made Horror *smile?*"
>   (IX 1272-84)

But besides being a preacher, Young was also clearly one of those genuinely interested in and inspired by Newtonian astronomy—for instance, he was a subscriber to Henry Pemberton's *A View of Sir Isaac Newton's Philosophy* (1728) and was apparently abreast of contemporary knowledge of the subject.[15] He not only sees in the universe evidences of God, but also implies that Sir Isaac Newton and his discoveries were part of the Divine plan, which, he suggests in his ironical interrogatives, has been revealed by a special scientific Providence:

"Then whence these glorious Forms
And boundless Flights, from *Shapeless,* and
  Repos'd?
Has Matter *more* than Motion? Has it Thought,
Judgement, and Genius? Is it deeply learn'd
In *Mathematics?* Has it fram'd *such* Laws.
Which but to *guess,* a NEWTON made immortal?—
If so, how each *sage* Atom laughs at me,
Who think a *Clod* inferior to a *Man!"*
                                    (IX 1475-82)

And at one point he exclaims:

O for a Telescope His Throne to reach!
Tell me, ye Learn'd on *Earth!* or Blest *Above!*
Ye searching, ye *Newtonian* Angels! tell,
Where, your Great MASTER's Orb? His Planets,
  where?
Those *conscious* Satellites, those *Morning-Stars,*
First-born of DEITY!
                                    (IX 1834-9)

On a number of occasions he successfully combines an admiring sense of Newtonian order with spiritual and religious elevation:

Then mark
The *Mathematic* Glories of the Skies,
In Number, Weight, and Measure, all ordain'd.
. . . . .
Orb above Orb ascending without End!
Circle in Circle, without End, inclos'd!
Wheel within Wheel; EZEKIAL! like to Thine!
Like Thine, it seems a Vision, or a Dream;
Tho' *seen,* we labour to believe it *true!*
                                    (IX 1079-1101)

This last passage with its stress on observation, on the act and wonders of seeing is characteristic of the poets living at the time when Newton's *Opticks* (1714) made its first impact.[16] As Young says, "Who sees, but is confounded, or convinc'd? / . . . / Mankind was sent into the World to *see*" (IX 861-3); and the verb "to see" in its various forms and synonyms of seeing occurs regularly throughout the poem, as some of the passages already quoted demonstrate. But more significant is the extent to which the two visions meet: optical vision, the mysteries and mechanics of which much exercised the speculations of Newton and his contemporaries, and spiritual and mystical vision. One cannot miss the real millenarian, or millennial fervour—the second of the two terms being used by Young himself:

The Planets of each System represent
Kind Neighbours; mutual Amity prevails;
Sweet Interchange of Rays, receiv'd, return'd;
Enlight'ning, and enlighten'd! All, at once,
Attracking, and attracted! Patriot-like,
None sins against the Welfare of the Whole;

But their reciprocal, unselfish Aid,
Affords an Emblem of *Millennial* Love.
                                    (IX 698-705)

And this is a vision that expands in scale and exultation so that Young has no doubt that man's mortal aspirations are to be fulfilled among the stars:

How Great,
How Glorious, *then,* appears the *Mind* of Man,
When in it All the Stars, and Planets, roll!
And what it *seems,* it *is: Great* Objects make
Great Minds, enlarging as their Views enlarge;
Those still more Godlike, as *These* more Divine.
  And *more* divine than *These,* thou canst not
  see.
Dazled, o'erpow'r'd, with the delicious Draught
Of miscellaneous Splendors, how I reel
From Thought to Thought, inebriate, without
  End!
An *Eden,* This! a PARADISE *unlost!*
I meet the DEITY in ev'ry View,
And tremble at my Nakedness before Him!
O that I could but reach the *Tree of Life!*
For *Here* it grows, unguarded from our Taste;
No *Flaming Sword* denies our Entrance *Here;*
Would Man but gather, he might *live for ever.*
                                    (IX 1061-77)

Throughout most of **"Night the Ninth and Last"** all three aspects of Young—the Christian apologist, the student of Newtonian science and the millenarian—are combined in a heady mixture of exhortation and rapture. Convincingly he persuades one that he is truly consumed by his imaginative experience and that he himself is in the condition of that spiritual being ("With Aspect mild, and elevated Eye / . . . seated on a Mount serene") whom he describes with such admiration in **"Night the Eighth";** a figure who "longs, in Infinite, to lose all Bound" (VIII 1083-1140).[17] So I would want to argue that although, as many scholars have already shown, Young is not particularly original in his material, and might be said to be entirely derivative, nevertheless he transforms, one might even appropriately say, transfigures his sources perhaps through the very recklessness of his rhetoric and the risk he runs in attracting ridicule.[18]

2.

In *The Story of Utopias,* Lewis Mumford claims that "there is a gap in the Utopian tradition between the seventeenth century and the nineteenth", and adds: "Utopia, the place that must be built, faded into no-man's land, the spot to which one might escape."[19] Following our own experiences in encounters with Young's **Night Thoughts,** especially the last Night, perhaps one should broaden Mumford's proposition to suggest that the vision of Utopia in the eighteenth century went not only with Robinson Crusoe to his tropical island (which is what Mumford argues) but into the Newtonian skies as well. The excitement generated by Newton's work created an intoxicating brew of science and theology which stimulated a fervent though rational and consequently passive millenarianism, which preferred to wait for the inevitable transformations of progressive enlightenment rather than become involved in active campaigning. Therefore, to a large extent the millennium was to be regarded as an aesthetic experience, just as progress itself had become an artistic idea.

In those passages which have been quoted as representing Young's millennial fervour, there is a sense of both having your pie in the sky, and still being able to consume it down on earth. The "PARADISE *unlost*" is clearly in the heavens, but at the same time the vision sustains one now—"the Firmament" is "The noble Pasture of the *Mind*" (IX 1036-9) and "Affords an Emblem of *Millennial* Love" (IX 705): an emblem of what might be realized on earth should the mind continue to feed on this vision of heavens that has become so universal that its moral effects are felt throughout civilized society. That Newtonian astronomy supports a notion of improvement in the spiritual condition of mankind might be one of the implications of Pope's famous couplet: "Nature, and Nature's Laws lay hid in Night. / God said, *Let Newton Be!* and All was *Light*." (1730) and indicates an ameliorative attitude to the human condition that displaced earlier kinds of Utopianism. Science, and a belief in scientific progress, the development of an historical outlook which began to measure present gains against the literal and cultural "backwardness" of the past, all contribute to the suggestion that Utopia or the millennium would eventually arrive as a destination determined by history.

As Norman Cohn reminds us in the Introduction to *The Pursuit of the Millennium,* "Millenarian sects or movements always picture salvation as (a) collective, in the sense that it is to be enjoyed by the faithful as a collectivity; (b) terrestrial, in the sense that it is to be realized on this earth and not in some other-worldly heaven; (c) imminent . . . ; (d) total . . . ; (e) miraculous . . ."[20] And in *Millennium and Utopia: A Study in the Background of the Idea of Progress,* Ernest Lee Tuveson has demonstrated the transformation of ideas about the Apocalypse, an interest which revived in the Renaissance, particularly among reformers, into a confidence in a progressive view of religion and the world. This resulted in the eighteenth century in a number of important and influential works which were assured that the scientific, philosophical and theological progress of recent years would before very long issue in a perfected state of life on earth and the beginning of God's promised millennium.[21] It is unlikely that Edward Young was not familiar with Thomas Burnet's *Theory of the Earth* (1684-1690) and later books it provoked and inspired.

Indeed, in a striking paragraph in his ***Conjectures on Original Composition,*** Young reveals millenarium sympathies couched in terms very like some of those one finds among Tuveson's witnesses:

> *since* an impartial Providence scatters talents indifferently, as thro' all orders of persons, so thro' all periods of time; *since* a marvelous light, unenjoy'd of old, is pour'd on us by revelation, with larger prospects extending our Understanding, with brighter objects enriching our Imagination, with an inestimable prize setting our Passions on fire, thus strengthening every power that enables composition to shine; *since,* there has been no fall in man on this side *Adam,* who left no works, and the works of all other antients are our auxiliars against themselves, as being perpetual spurs to our ambition, and shining lamps in our path to fame; *since,* this world is a school, as well for intellectual, as moral, advance; and the longer human nature is at school, the better scholar it should be; *since,* as the moral world expects its glorious Milennium, the world intellectual may hope, by the rules of analogy for some superior degrees of excellence to crown her latter scenes. . . . All these particulars, I say, consider'd, why should it seem altogether impossible, that heaven's latest editions of the human mind may be the most correct, and fair; that the day may come, when the moderns may proudly look back on the comparative darkness of for-mer ages, on the children of antiquity; reputing *Homer,* and *Demosthenes,* as the dawn of divine Genius; and on *Athens* as the cradle of infant Fame. . . .[22]

Although George Eliot mocked Edward Young's curious combination of "worldliness and other-worldliness", this combination is, perhaps, just what creates the millennial tone in his poem. Young's heavens can be seen as representing the "vertical Utopia"[23] that transcends Utopia—the presence in the **Ninth Night** of the vision of the Apocalypse would tend to support this, as would the final paragraph of the poem in which Young addresses both God and Night, welcoming a future "When TIME . . . / . . . . / In NATURE's ample Ruins lies intomb'd; / And MIDNIGHT, *Universal* Midnight! reigns" (IX 2431-4). Equally one can see in his work an example of Utopia being replaced by the City of God.[24] But, however vertical Young's vision of the millennium may be; however it may resemble the City of God, it is achieved essentially by bringing closer the vision of the stars, the celestial panorama visible to man and compassed within the scope of his imagination by virtue of Newtonian physics and teleological speculation inspired by the New Philosophy. This displaced Utopia, this eighteenth-century version of the millennium, is to be established by the power of the telescope and faith in mathematical demonstration.[25]

The last lines of ***Night Thoughts*** just quoted seem also to be a rejoinder to Pope's pessimistically apocalyptic conclusion to *The Dunciad:*

Lo! thy dread Empire, CHAOS! is restor'd;
Light dies before thy uncreating word:
Thy hand, great Anarch! lets the Curtain fall;
And Universal Darkness buries All.

Daniel W. Odell has already written about "Young's *Night Thoughts* as an Answer to Pope's *Essay on Man*",[26] but Young could be implying at the end of his poem that Pope's City of Dreadful Night, his Dystopia of *The Dunciad,* will be redeemed by the approaching night that is not a chaos but an orderly transfiguration of planets and stars indicating God's order and control; a "verklärte" rather than an "aufgeklärte Nacht"—"a *new* Creation . . . / The World's great Picture soften'd to the Sight" (IX 1679-80)—representing the power of the Deity who at various times is addressed as "glorious Architect" (IX 766), "mighty BUILDER" (IX 817), "Great OECONOMIST" (IX 1089), "Great ARTIST" (IX 1322), "DIVINE INSTRUCTOR" (IX 1659) and "Great PROPRIETOR" (IX 1887):

Devotion! Daughter of Astronomy!
An *undevout* Astronomer is *mad.*
True; All Things speak a GOD; but in the Small,
Man traces out *Him;* in Great, *He* seizes Man;
Seizes, and elevates, and raps, and fills
With new Inquiries, 'mid Associates new.
Tell me, ye Stars! ye Planets! tell me, all
Ye Starr'd, and Planeted, Inhabitants! What is it?
What are these Sons of Wonder? Say, proud
    Arch!
(Within whose azure Palaces they dwell)
Built with Divine Ambition! in Disdain
Of Limit built! built in the Taste of Heaven!
Vast Concave! Ample Dome! Wast thou design'd
A meet Apartment for the DEITY?
                                        (IX 772-85)

3.

If one detects in Young a critical response to Pope, equally one can see why Blake would have responded to *Night Thoughts*. Undoubtedly Blake would hardly have shared Young's particular theological outlook, and would have disapproved fiercely of his admiration for Newton, whom Blake repudiated as the arch apostle of Urizenic materialism. But they would have joined faith in the transformation of Albion. The millenarianism we detect in *Night Thoughts* touches the visionary transformations of Blake's *Jerusalem,* which records an abysm in the history of mankind when "the Starry Heavens are fled from the mighty limbs of Albion" (Plate 75:27), but ends:

All Human Forms identified, even Tree, Metal,
    Earth & Stone:
                                        all
Human Forms identified, living, going forth &
    returning

                            wearied
Into the Planetary lives of Years, Months, Days
    & Hours;

                            reposing,
And then Awakening into his Bosom in the Life
    of Immortality.

And I heard the Name of their Emanations: they
    are named

                            Jerusalem.
                            (Plate 99)

But it is not only "The moral Emanations of the Skies" (IX 848), which in one form or another, Blake and Young have in common; one recalls that one of the illustrations that Blake did for **"Night the Second"** illustrated the following lines:

Measuring his Motions by revolving Spheres;
That Horologe Machinery Divine.
Hours, Days, and Months, and Years, his
    Children, play,
Like num'rous Wings, around him, as he flies:
Or, rather, as unequal Plumes they shape
His ample Pinions, swift as darted Flame,
To gain his Goal, to reach his antient Rest,
And join anew *Eternity* his Sire;
In his *Immutability* to nest,
When Worlds, that count his Circles *now,*
    unhing'd,
(Fate the loud Signal sounding) headlong rush
To *timeless* Night and Chaos, whence they rose.
                                        (II 211-22)[27]

A curious combination this of Pope and Young: both to be redeemed by Blake as earlier he had attempted to save Milton from his errors. In this way, millenniums and Utopias touch, and the nineteenth century, having lost faith in the redemptive values and power of Newtonian physics, strives to salvage what it can from the eighteenth. In literature such eschatological dramas may be necessary to rescue the imagination: chiliasm exploding the conventions and errors of outdated structures of feeling, thought and form.

Perhaps one way of describing the essentially passive Millenium of the eighteenth century is as the dissolution of the earthly in the heavenly or as the permeation of the celestial in the material. One of the arguments that emerges from this consideration of Edward Young, and the last Night of *Night Thoughts* especially, is that the Rector of Welwyn is an essential figure in the transformation of Milton's physically hard-edged universe created in *Paradise Lost,* where despite the poet's (and Raphael's) refusal to confirm the Copernican system, one experiences a material cosmography of solid bodies and precise locations and distances, into the spacially obliterated and temporally compressed world of Blake's Prophetic works. This may have been achieved by a switch, in the words of Josephine Miles's description of "The Sublime Poem", to the "vocabulary of cosmic passion and sense impression".[28] Milton, despite his doubts as to whether the sun or the earth is in the centre, takes the universe for granted as a stage for his epic narrative. Despite the gratitude and wonder which Raphael seeks to stir in Adam and Milton in the reader at the glories of God's creation, the tone of even the most exalted parts of *Paradise Lost* conveys a steady sense of this is how it was at the time of creation and, allowing for the deleterious consequences of the Fall, this is how on the whole it continues to be. In no way could one call the description of the creation of the sun and moon and the stars in Book VII (339ff.) matter of fact, but the poet's command of syntax and metre and the confidence of diction ensure a stability for the action that firmly locates it in space and time, as the Lord with "the golden compasses, prepared / In God's eternal store, to circumscribe / This universe and all created things . . ." (VII 255-7). Whether one believes that Milton gives an adequate visual account or not, the cosmos is evidently there, capacious but ruggedly furnished. This derives not so much from the visual description as such as from the confidence with which everyone from God the Father downwards assumes the existence of the material world which they have to negotiate and survive in.[29]

When we come to Blake and the other Romantics, this confidence in the physical has evaporated. Blake's work throughout represents an epic lament for the binding of man in a space and time from which only his threatened and endangered imagination can free him. Space and time are manifestations of the usurping power of Urizenic mathematics;[30] and with space and time go the chains and manacles, which are as inevitable as the transferring of God's golden compasses to Urizen and Newton.[31] To Blake imprisonment and freedom are internal states of being; political repression is the outward sign of such "mind-forg'd manacles" ("London" in *Songs of Experience*). Eternity is also within; and Paradise is both lost and regained within the individual. Each man restores Albion for himself; were all men able to restore the Albion within him then Britain too, and the world, would be restored to Eternity.

Young, possibly with other eighteenth-century practitioners of the Sublime, represents a halfway stage between Milton and Blake. With him, we are not made aware so much of the cosmos itself as of the poet's exclamatory feelings being projected into boundless space: the universe with its celestial cycles and machinery of nicely calculated motions is rather like a cosmic gymnasium for the exercise of emotional muscles. Although the universe has not yet been interiorized, it is presented as an extension of Young's sensibility, an enlarged ego-chamber; one could equally say that it possesses him or he possesses it. In any event the universe "out there" does not seem to have an independent existence, as it still does have in Milton (despite attempts to show that *Paradise Lost,* too, is mainly designed to dramatize psychological space). Young's feelings about the universe that Newton has constructed for him are those of a colonist. Whereas Blake is constantly seeking to demonstrate how the fourfold vision of redeemed man is available within us if only we will cleanse "the doors of perception" (*The Marriage of Heaven and Hell,* Plate 14) and keep our Zoas in their places; Young is the first to imply that if a "PARADISE *unlost*" is in the heavens, at the end of a telescope, it is also ours to be gathered through the eye into the bosom of our feelings.[32] He is equally drawn to a millennium out of time or at the end of time and a perfected state of being within time, which may amount to the same thing, since "boundless *Space* . . . / . . . suggests the Sister-Thought / Of boundless *Time*" (IX 1174-6).

With the general assumption of the merging of the subjective and the objective, in Romanticism it is difficult to judge to what extent we are to believe that the re-attainment of Paradise or the creation of Utopia has been achieved or is within sight of achievement in what we like to term "the real world", or is to be celebrated as a state of mind, symbolically, within. Wordsworth emphasizes how we should look to Nature to cultivate a "spontaneous wisdom" within us, to teach us "more of man, / Of moral evil and of good, / Than all the sages can" ("The Tables Turned" in *Lyrical Ballads*). The implication of Wordsworth's work is that each of us, through an attentive and receptive heart should cultivate an inner security able to withstand the loss of hope and eventually remove from society the tensions that promote revolution. This belief that the world will improve in accordance with the enlarged vision and hearts of individuals need not be seen only as an evasion of demands for social change, but also as an inevitable outcome of the Romantic poet's aspirations and his essential trust in the pre-eminence of the individual's sensibility, which so potently blends his perception of the external world with his empathic response.[33]

Even in the case of such a "poet of perfectibility" as Shelley,[34] it is difficult to see how his vision of the transformed universe in the last act of *Prometheus Unbound* could be conceived of as actually being effected in reality (one is drawn to say, "for real"). The ethereal lyricism is stirring enough to colour the mind and imagination of the reader, but how the love which Earth declares "interpenetrates my granite mass" (IV 370) might actually shift the balance of power in the world or help to reshape institutions could never be demonstrated. However, one should add, that it is Shelley, the acknowledged heir of Godwin, and the unconscious successor of Blake, who became the Romantic poet who actually inspired at least one utopian community in the nineteenth century.[35]

The other Romantic who had direct political influence was, of course, Coleridge. It is not clear whether the concept of Pantisocracy or its failure tells one most about the nature of Romantic utopianism. But it is not this early failure which is most significant in considering Coleridge's political influence, whatever its consequence might have been for his poetic career as the laureate who celebrated a "stately pleasure dome" that he himself could not build and voyages that ended disastrously. It is in his later prose writings that he expressed his faith in the progress which he identified with the hope that was one of the "positive ends" of the state.[36] Indeed Coleridge's later vision of the efficacious role of the clerisy suggests the possible translation of Utopia into every village of the land:

> That to every parish throughout the kingdom there is transplanted a germ of civilization; that in the remotest villages there is a nucleus, round which the capabilities of the place may crystallise and brighten; a model sufficiently superior to excite, yet sufficiently near to encourage and facilitate, imitation; *this* unobtrusive, continuous agency of a Protestant Church Establishment, *this* it is, which the patriot, and the philanthropist, who would fain unite the love of peace with the faith in the progressive amelioration of mankind, cannot estimate at too high a price . . .[37]

"The progressive amelioration of mankind" gives us the clue to the essential balanced attitude of the Romantics and their immediate successors to utopian notions. The eighteenth century had so effectively established, in theory and practice, a belief in progress and destroyed the "illusion of Finality",[38] that no imaginative man, let alone any poet, would wish to commit himself to some scheme of things that would actually seek to achieve a conclusive end. Romantic assumptions of organicism and vitalism involved the creed that life was continually renewing itself, remaking itself, even evolving. Constant change, perpetual improvement, evolution replaced utopianism as an image of a once-for-all perfected society. The dynamic model of change taken for granted in Romantic writing was later to be impersonalized as process, dialectical and determined, in later nineteenth-century thought. The Romantics interiorize Paradise (as Milton's Michael had predicted: *PL* XII 587); their successors (including Karl Marx) on occasions spoke of Utopia as an extremely distant end of historical process: a projection into historical space of the unlost Paradise within. Modern industrial society was not achieved without destructive and painful side effects which spawned all those many later nineteenth-century utopian communities and fictions that attempted to capture the benefits of technology without the traumas, leaving its citizens free to cultivate the sensibilities that poets like Edward Young had first begun to exercise.[39]

Notes

[1] Edward Young, *Conjectures on Original Composition* (1759), Scolar Press facsimile of the 1st edn, Leeds, 1966, p. 70.

[2] *Young's Night Thoughts,* with Life, Critical Dissertation, and Explanatory Notes, by the Rev. George Gilfillan, Edinburgh, 1853, xxi-xxii.

[3] "Worldliness and Other-Worldliness: The Poet Young" in *Essays of George Eliot,* ed. Thomas Pinney, London, 1963, pp. 335-85.

[4] As distinct from Dante or Milton, who might be more truly considered poets of Heaven and Hell, and the regions between.

[5] Young's *Complaint: Or, Night-Thoughts* was published for the first time in its complete form in 1750, although individual "Nights" had been appearing since 1742 (I, II & III in 1742, IV & V in 1743, VI & VII in 1744, VIII in 1745, and IX in 1746). All the quotations in this article are taken from a copy of 1768, which apart from minor details on the title page conforms to the issue of 1755, described as "A NEW EDITION, Corrected by the Author" (see Henry Pettit, *A Bibliography of Young's Night Thoughts,* Boulder, Colorado, 1954, p. 41). All capitals and italics in the quotations are as in this edition. However all line numbers are from Gilfillan's edition.

[6] *Conjectures,* p. 60. Since later in this article a comparison is to be made with Blake, it is perhaps worth reminding ourselves of his comments on the freedom of verse in what amounts to his "Preface" to *Jerusalem* (Plate 3: "To the Public"): "When this Verse was first dictated to me, I consider'd a Monotonous Cadence, like that used by Milton & Shakespeare & all writers of English Blank Verse, derived from the modern bondage of Rhyming, to be a necessary and indispensible part of Verse. But I soon found that in the mouth of a true Orator such monotony was not only awkward, but as much a bondage as rhyme itself. I therefore have produced a variety in every line, both of cadences & number of syllables. . . . Poetry Fetter'd Fetters the Human Race" (Blake, *Complete Writings,* ed. Geoffrey Keynes, Oxford, 1969, p. 621).

[7] Ovid, *Metamorphosis,* I, 89-90, Loeb Classical Library edn and trans., 1977.

[8] *Sir Thomas More's Utopia* (in Robynson's translation), ed. J. Churton Collins, Oxford, 1904, p. 49 (cf. Penguin Classics edn, pp. 69-70).

[9] Milton, *Paradise Lost,* XI 834-5, and n. 829-38 in Longman Annotated English Poets edition, ed. Alastair Fowler, London, 1971.

[10] For the traditions of patriotic praise that associated Britain with various forms of paradise, see commentary on John of Gaunt's speech in the New Arden edition of *Richard II,* ed. Peter Ure, London, 5th edn, 1961, esp. on II i 42; and note the passage from Sylvester's Du Bartas given in Appendix IV of that edition (p. 207) and the article by Josephine Waters Bennett, "Britain among the Fortunate Isles", *SP,* LIII (1956), 114-40, cited and summarized on p. 208.

[11] In "Night 9" there is one reference to the Golden Age: "Enjoy your happy Realms their golden Age? / And had your EDEN an abstemious Eve" (1773-4). . . .

[12] "According to the terms of [his] will . . . a lecturer was to be chosen annually to preach eight sermons on the evidences of Christianity" (see Isabel St John Bliss, "Young's *Night Thoughts* in Relation to Contemporary Christian Apologetics", *PMLA* XLIV (1934), 38). As a young man of 20, Robert Boyle had been a friend of Samuel Hartlib, who planned the utopian Christian kingdoms of "Antilia" and, later, "Macaria" (1641)—see W. H. G. Armytage, *Heavens Below: Utopian Experiments in England 1560-1960,* London, 1961, pp. 8-9.

[13] See Bliss, 48-50. For the pervasive influence of Newton on Anglican theologians and in particular his association with the Boyle lectures, see Margaret C. Jacob, *The Newtonians and the English Revolution 1689-1720,* New York, 1976, esp. chs 4 & 5.

[14] Bliss, 55.

[15] Bliss, 58.

[16] The response of eighteenth-century poets to the *Opticks* is well documented in Marjorie Hope Nicolson's *Newton Demands the Muse,* Princeton, 1946. However, despite his interest in the astronomical evidences of God, Young on occasions sounds the traditional Christian warning against overestimating the value of learning: "Humble *Love* / And not proud *Reason,* keeps the Door of Heav'n; / *Love* finds Admission, where proud *Science* fails. / Man's Science is the Culture of his Heart; / And not to lose his Plumbet in the Depths / Of *Nature,* or the more Profound of GOD. / Either to know, is an Attempt that sets / The Wisest on a Level with the Fool. / To fathom *Nature* (ill-attempted *Here!*) / Past Doubt is deep Philosophy *Above;* / Higher Degrees in Bliss Archangels take, / As deeper learn'd; the Deepest, learning still. / For, what a *Thunder* of Omnipotence / (So might I dare to speak!) is *seen* in All! / In *Man!* in *Earth!* In more amazing *Skies!* / Teaching this Lesson, *Pride* is loth to learn— / 'Not *deeply* to Discern, not *much* to *Know,* / Mankind was born to WONDER, and ADORE'" (IX 1858-75).

[17] It is hardly surprising in view of the *élan* and expansive measures of the poem that "boundless" and "unbound-ed" are favourite words throughout *Night Thoughts,* and, as we have seen, the first of these words has even found an appropriate place in the prose of *Conjectures.* Conceptually the notion of "boundlessness", as I will attempt to show on another occasion, accounts for the attraction and the fascination of Newtonian cosmology for so many eighteenth-century poets, since it is both limitless in its implications and orderly in its account of the unbounded universe. See Marjorie Hope Nicolson's comment on Edward Young and the "aesthetics of the infinite" in her *Mountain Gloom and Mountain Glory,* Ithaca/New York, 1959 (a book which touches at several places many of the themes of this essay): "No poet was ever more 'space intoxicated' than Edward Young, nor did any other eighteenth-century poet or aesthetician equal him in his obsession with the 'psychology of infinity'—the effect of vastness and the vast upon the soul of man. . . . His canvas is interstellar space, his technique that of the cosmic voyagers, the 'soaring souls that sail among the spheres'" (pp. 362-3). The phrase from Young at the end of that quotation comes from the following passage: "Thou *Stranger* to the *World!* thy Tour *begin;* / Thy Tour thro' *Nature's* universal Orb. / *Nature* delineates her whole Chart at large, / On soaring Souls, that sail among the Spheres" (IX 608-611).

[18] Such sources, for instance, as Addison's *Spectator* 565 (Friday, July 9, 1714 in Everyman Library edn, reset 1945, 4, pp. 279-83) which allows us to identify "the Sage" of Young's "So distant (says the Sage), 'twere not absurd / To doubt, if Beams, set out at *Nature's* Birth, / Are yet arrived at this so foreign World" (IX 1227-9) as *"Huygenius"* who "carries this thought so far, that he does not think it impossible there may be Stars whose Light is not yet travelled down to us, since their first Creation" (280). In view of n. 17, the following sentence of Addison's is particularly interesting: "There is no Question but the Universe has certain Bounds set to it; but when we consider that is the Work of infinite Power, prompted by infinite Goodness, with an infinite Space to exert it self in, how can our Imagination set any Bounds to it?" Since both writers are to some extent dealing with period commonplaces and reveal enthusiasms and responses that were widespread, drawing their knowledge from the same popularizing accounts, it is difficult to prove the direct influence of one writer upon the other. However, it is also unnecessary, since what the comparison mainly reveals is shared knowledge and interests, and the similarities and differences in tone and rhetorical effect. The last *Spectator* of all (635: Monday, December 30, 1714, Everyman edn, pp. 463-7) by Henry Grove may have been of equal relevance to Young's concerns and touches upon several of the themes of "Night 9", and shares something of the same rapture.

[19] Lewis Mumford, *The Story of Utopias,* New York, 1922; Viking Press paperback, 1969, p. 113, although Mumford's statement must be to some extent qualified by Armytage's account of eighteenth-century Utopian ambitions in *Heavens Below,* chs 5-7. Frank E. and Fritzie P. Manuel in *Utopian Thought in the Western World,* Cambridge, Mass., 1979, confirm the conclusions that one derives from other studies of the period (e.g. Peter Gay's *The Enlightenment,* New York & London, 1966 & 1970 and Paul Hazard, *European Thought in the Eighteenth Century,* Penguin edn, 1965) that the issue of Utopianism in the eighteenth century is mainly confined to discussions of progress and perfectibility (see notes 34, 36 & 38 below).

[20] Norman Cohn, *The Pursuit of the Millennium,* London, 1957; paperback rpt, 1970, p. 13. As far as "(e) miraculous" is concerned Young acknowledges that miracles have been necessary—"When Mankind falls asleep, / A *Miracle* is sent, as an Alarm" (IX 1248-9)—but he implies that in an Age taught by Newton miracles are superfluous, since they "do not, *can* not, more amaze the Mind, / Than This, *call'd* un-miraculous Survey, / If *duly* weigh'd, if *rationally* seen, / If seen with *human* Eyes" (IX 1263-6).

[21] Ernest Lee Tuveson, *Millennium and Utopia: A Study in the Background of the Idea of Progress,* Berkeley, 1949; paperback rpt, New York, 1964, pp. 104-12 and ch. IV: "Nature's Simple Plot: the Credo of Progress". See ch. 3 of the study by Margaret C. Jacob cited in n. 13 above which develops Tuveson and qualifies his interpretation, since she believes that "Ideas of progress in Anglican circles during the eighteenth century owe their origin more to smugness than to a rethinking of the meaning of the millennium" and "millenarianism died with the older generation of latitudinarians whose religious sensibility had been forged by the seventeenth-century revolution": however, "if [the Newtonians] imagined any sort of utopia it would have been a state where stability and order predominated, where the principles of Newton ruled nature and presented a model for the ordering of society" (*op. cit.,* 139-40). The peculiar fervour of Young's work, especially of "Night 9", seems to suggest that in the mid-eighteenth century it was still possible to combine something close to millennial rapture with an excited faith in science as a means of progressive revelation—science working with nature to ensure an increasing spiritual ascent: "*Nature* delights in Progress; in Advance / From Worse to Better: But, when *Minds* ascend, / Progress, in Part, depends upon *Themselves.* / Heav'n aids Exertion; Greater makes the Great; / The *voluntary* Little lessens more: / O be a *Man!* and thou shalt be a *God!* / And *Half Self-made!*—Ambition how Divine" (IX 1960-66).

[22] *Conjectures,* 72-4.

[23] On apocalyptic transcendence to the "vertical Utopia" see Paul Tillich, "Critique and Justification of Utopia" in *Utopias and Utopian Thought,* ed. Frank E. Manuel, Beacon paperback, Boston, 1967, pp. 296-309.

[24] This particular displacement is discussed by Northrop Frye in "Varieties of Literary Utopias" (*Utopias and Utopian Thought,* p. 34ff.).

[25] In view of what he claims about blank verse . . . , the lack of fluency in Young's own unrhymed iambic pentameter, which tends to fall into couplets or even single lines, suggests that same mixture of worldliness and other-worldliness. If "blank verse, is verse unfallen, uncurst; verse reclaim'd, reinthron'd in the true *language of the Gods*", then Young's verse is not entirely reclaimed from the rhyming couplet, and still shows signs of its fallen, curst origins. As we have already seen (n. 6) it was left to Blake to attempt to achieve the final liberation and redemption from the tyranny of the line.

[26] *SEL* XII (1972), 481-501.

[27] The first four Nights of *Night Thoughts* as published by Richard Edwards with Blake's illustrations in 1797 is available in a facsimile edition ("reproduced at 65% of the original size") from Dover Publications, New York, 1975. The illustration in question is p. 26; however, the text there has been normalized, and the one quoted here is from the 1768 issue of *Night Thoughts.*

[28] Josephine Miles, *Eras and Modes in English Poetry,* Berkeley and Los Angeles, 1957, p. 57. This is her second distinguishing characteristic of the sublime poem. The first helps to account for the manner by which Edward Young hopes to escape the curse of fallen verse even though he is neither fluent in the blank verse styles of Shakespeare and Milton before him, nor able to anticipate the ease of Cowper and Wordsworth at their best. Professor Miles describes the "cumulative phrasal structure" of the sublime poem, "its piling up of nouns and epithets, participles and compounds, with a very minimum of clausal subordination and active verbs". The third characteristic she notes is an "internal rather than external patterning of sound, the interior tonal shadings and onomatopoeias of its unrhymed verse". Together with the strong visual reinforcement of Young's verse—the italics and capitals and exclamation marks which one finds in the eighteenth-century texts—one may agree that "these major traits make for an exceptionally panoramic and panegyric verse, emotional, pictorial, noble, universal, and tonal, rising to the height of heaven and of feeling in the style traditionally known as grand or sublime".

[29] It is the very materiality of the War in Heaven in *Paradise Lost* VI which causes Milton and his readers particular problems: if spiritual beings cannot be irrep-

arably damaged by material assault they cannot, in fact, be defeated either physically or morally. Therefore the battles are charades demonstrating a moral disposition, but otherwise inconsequential.

[30] See Donald Ault, *Visionary Physics: Blake's Response to Newton,* Chicago and London, 1974. Ault suggests that it was the very imaginative appeal of Newton's system that inspired Blake to attempt to create "a new Imaginative countervision" . . . . Indeed what needs to be investigated is the role that mathematics played in dissolving the physical universe that we find in Milton into the fluid world of Blake's prophetic poetry. Already one senses with Pope's depiction of "Mad *Mathesis*" who "alone was unconfin'd, / Too mad for mere material chains to bind, / Now to pure Space lifts her extatic stare, / Now running round the Circle, finds it square" (*The Dunciad* IV 31-4) the recognition of a world coming into existence in which abstraction and theory through the imagination threatened a man's faith in the secure nature of matter. In such a state it is no surprise that *"Mystery"* should "to *Mathematics* fly!" (IV 647).

[31] In two of Blake's most famous designs, the print usually known as "The Ancient of Days" (also used as the frontispiece to *Europe,* 1794) and the large colour print of "Newton" (1795), the compasses that Milton derived for his account of the Creation from Proverbs (8:27), have been put into the hands of a Urizenic figure in the one print and of Newton at the bottom of the Sea of Time and Space in the other. Martin Butlin notes that "the composition of 'The Ancient of Days' is based on the frontispiece to the de luxe 1729 edition of Motte's translation of Newton's *Principia*" (*William Blake,* Tate Gallery Catalogue, 1978, pp. 52-53). So in both designs Newton is implicated.

[32] On Blake's use of Young's *Night Thoughts* as a parodic source for *The Four Zoas,* see John Howard, *Infernal Poetics: Poetic Structure in Blake's Lambeth Prophecies,* London and Toronto, 1984, pp. 217-19. Howard notes especially Blake's attack on Young's concern with "futurity" by identifying it as an obsession of Urizen's.

[33] Evidence for the merging of the objective and subjective is to be found throughout Wordsworth's *Prelude,* but one of the most directly graphic instances is to be found in "Tintern Abbey": "Once again / Do I behold these steep and lofty cliffs, / Which on a wild secluded scene impress / Thoughts of more deep seclusion" (4-7), where we find "cliffs" impressing "thoughts" on a "scene". It is in the same poem (105-6) that Wordsworth acknowledges "a close resemblance to an admirable line of Young, the exact expression of which I cannot recollect". It is particularly relevant in the present context that Wordsworth's lines—"of all the mighty world / Of eye and ear, both what they half create, / And what perceive" (the note is appended to the line ending with "create")—echo Young's lines from "NIGHT the SIXTH" of *Night Thoughts,* in which he describes "Our *Senses,* as our *Reason* . . . divine" taking in "the landscape [*sic*] of the World, / At a small Inlet, which a Grain might close, / [to] half create the wond'rous World they see" (VI 425-7). It is not surprising that this phrase should lodge in the memory of a Romantic poet only too conscious of the collaboration of vision, consciousness, and the external object in creating our sense of material reality.

[34] The description is from J. B. Bury, *The Idea of Progress,* London, 1932; paperback rpt, Dover Publications, New York, 1955, p. 233. William Godwin as an intermediary between eighteenth-century French ideas of perfectibility and Shelley is implied in Bury's discussion of "The Theory of Progress in England" (ch. XII). For a recent discussion of Rousseau's "concept of perfectibility" as coming "as close as possible to supplying a purely formal . . . definition of man", and its ambiguous relationship to Romanticism and Romantic creation myths, see Paul A. Cantor, *Creature and Creator: Myth-making and English Romanticism,* Cambridge, 1984, pp. 4-25. In the Introduction to his translation of the *Discours sur l'origine de l'inégalité* (1754), Maurice Cranston reminds us that Rousseau's "'perfectibilité' . . . means not at all a potentiality for perfection, but simply a capacity for self-betterment" (A *Discourse on Inequality,* Penguin, 1984, p. 33).

[35] See *Heavens Below,* p. 199. Art as a substitute for active Utopianism . . . is reflected in Cantor's consideration of the third stage of Romantic myth-making: "the stage portrayed in the apocalyptic phase of Romantic myth, symbolizing some form of revolution, originally conceived as coming about through political means, but later thought of as a more purely spiritual liberation, accomplished through art itself" (p. 22).

[36] See *The Collected Works of Samuel Taylor Coleridge,* 6, *Lay Sermons,* ed. R. J. White, London, 1972, p. 216. Cf. n. 6 on p. 63 of the same volume, where one of Coleridge's annotations is quoted: ". . . for man is destined to be guided by higher principles, by universal views, which can never be fulfilled in this state of existence,—by a spirit of progressiveness which can never be accomplished, for then it would cease to be." The two works in this volume, *The Statesman's Manual* and *A Lay Sermon,* date respectively from 1816 and 1817.

[37] *The Collected Works of Samuel Taylor Coleridge,* 10, *On the Constitution of the Church and State,* ed. John Colmer, London, 1976, p. 75. The work was first published in 1830. For Coleridge's earlier poetic feelings about Utopian schemes see his sonnet on "Pantisocracy" (1794), where in 11. 7-9 he sounds a note not so very

different from the final paragraph of "Kubla Khan", which suggests a possible association between the underlying sentiments of the two texts. A second sonnet "On the Prospect of establishing a Pantisocracy in America" is only uncertainly attributed to Coleridge (Coleridge, *Poetical Works,* ed. Ernest Hartley Coleridge, Oxford Standard Authors edn, 1967 rpt, pp. 68-9).

[38] Bury, p. 351. For another account of eighteenth-century considerations of perfectibility and the movement of the nineteenth century to social Darwinism, see Sidney Pollard, *The Idea of Progress,* London, 1968, chs II & III. Pollard notes that "Godwin has been called a Utopian rather than a believer in progress, but his state of perfection was a long way off, and required a slow process of evolution and amelioration"; and goes on to quote Godwin to demonstrate that it was he who "translated the French idea of 'perfectibility' most correctly in terms of evolution rather than Utopia" (pp. 70-71).

[39] And later writers such as James Joyce continued to emulate in the first half at least of the twentieth century. Towards the end of Bloomsday (16th June 1904) Leopold Bloom and Stephen Dedalus emerging "from obscurity by a passage from the rere of the house into the penumbra of the garden" were confronted by the spectacle of "The heaventree of stars hung with humid nightblue fruit". Further contemplation and self-interrogation leads Bloom logically to conclude "That it was not a heaventree, not a heavengrot, not a heavenbeast, not a heavenman. That it was a Utopia, there being no known method from the known to the unknown: an infinity, renderable equally finite by the suppositious probable apposition of one or more bodies equally of the same and of different magnitudes: a mobility of illusory forms immobilised in space, remobilised in air: a past which possibly had ceased to exist as the present before its future spectators had entered actual present existence" (*Ulysses,* Penguin edn, 1969, pp. 619-22). Cf. n. 18 above: does the spirit of Edward Young live on in Leopold Bloom and in Joyce, his creator?

Stephen Cornford (essay date 1989)

SOURCE: An introducton to *Night Thoughts,* by Edward Young, edited by Stephen Cornford, Cambridge University Press, 1989, pp. 1-32.

[*In the following excerpt Cornford analyzes several themes in, and contexts for, Young's* Night Thoughts.]

The Grandeur of my Subject

Where *is* God my maker, who giveth songs in the night?

(Job 35.10)

The invocation to '*Night,* sable Goddess' at the outset of *The Complaint* (1.18) is the sign of Young's sublime search for the secret place of God. Darkness, paradoxically 'aiding Intellectual Light' (IX.2411), will facilitate religious and poetic revelation. Biblically and mystically, Young exchanges Pope's '*clear, unchang'd* and *Universal* Light' for Vaughan's 'deep, but dazling darkness' (*An Essay on Criticism,* 71; 'The Night', 49). He rejects the lucidity and precision of daylight in favour of night's 'mitigated Lustre' (IX.724). Darkness has 'more divinity' than sunlight, because it 'strikes Thought inward' (V.128-9), it encourages virtue (V.138), and it promotes Christian belief: 'By Night an Atheist half-believes a God' (V.176). The poet chants his poem 'beneath the Glimpses of the Moon' (IX.2087), which 'through every distant Age, / Has held a Lamp to *Wisdom*' (V.178). It is in the moonlight that Socrates—Young's model of the sublime enquirer—has 'private Audience' (V.188) with the source of all wisdom. Undisturbed by the sun which 'gives him to the Tumult of the World' (V.193), Socrates is 'intimate with GOD' (IX.988). Just as for Burke obscurity was a precondition of artistic sublimity—the Bible's force and power, for instance, deriving from its *lack* of clarity—so for Young the sense of mystery induced by darkness was the precondition of religious revelation:

> Attend—The sacred Mysteries begin—
> My solemn *Night-born* Adjuration hear.
>
> (IX.209-2)

Young's summary of the teaching of Socrates (IX.998-1016) reads like a checklist of the eighteenth-century sublime, defined by a modern critic as 'a name for those experiences whose power seemed incommensurate with a human scale or with formal elegance . . . an experience of transcendence, a surpassing of conventions or reasonable limits, an attempt to come to terms with the unimaginable' (M. Price, 'The Sublime Poem', p. 194). Young attempts no less than 'To lay hold / By more than feeble *Faith* on the *Supreme*' (VI.90-1), 'to see / Things as they are, unalter'd thro' the Glass / Of worldly Wishes' (IX.1329-31). Many of Young's contemporaries felt he had succeeded. In *An Essay on the Genius and Writings of Pope* (dedicated to Young), Joseph Warton praised Young as 'a sublime and original genius' (II, p. 144) for choosing a religious subject which had enabled him to reach the sublime heights which had eluded Pope, whose didactic subjects were essentially unpoetic (*ibid.,* I, pp. ii-iii). Richardson also contrasted Young with Pope, associating sublimity—the criterion of true poetry—with Young's Christian subject:

> Pope's . . . was not the genius *to lift our souls to Heaven,* had it soared ever so freely, since it soared not in the Christian beam; but there is an eagle, whose eyes pierce through the shades of midnight,

that does indeed *transport* us, and the apotheosis is your's.

(Young, *Correspondence,* p. 448)

Warton and Richardson were suggesting that *Night Thoughts* was a return in an age of secular poetry to religious, and therefore imaginative, themes. In the seventeenth century, Milton, Cowley and Prior had argued against the imitation of classical precedents by urging that poetry could and should have an explicitly Christian content, and many eighteenth-century writers felt the contrast with their own age's secular verse. John Dennis, for example, thought that

By divesting it self of Religion [modern poetry] is fallen from its Dignity, and its original Nature and Excellence; and from the greatest Production of the Mind of Man, is dwindled to an extravagant and vain Amusement.

(*Critical Works,* I, p. 365)

Milton provided Dennis with the most recent example of an outstanding religious writer, and echoes of *Paradise Lost* can be found in a great deal of eighteenth-century poetry, not least in *Night Thoughts.* More distant in time, but no less influential, were the Old Testament writings, which, in the course of Young's lifetime, came to be appreciated in aesthetic and imaginative, as well as in theological, terms—as great literature as well as scripture, as potent examples of the oriental spirit which had also inspired the classical authors:

If *not* inspir'd, that pregnant Page had stood,
Time's Treasure! and the Wonder of the Wise!

(VIII.775-6)

Many poets, hoping to inject some of the Bible's literary qualities into their verse, paraphrased well-known passages of scripture. In 1719 Young had written a paraphrase on part of what he called 'the noblest, and most antient Poem in the World', claiming that for 'Spirit in Thought, and Energy in Style . . . *Eastern* Poetry', like the book of Job, outshone the epics of Homer and Virgil (*A Paraphrase on Job,* notes to page I; *The Guardian,* II, p. 14). Young experienced in the apparent spontaneity of Old Testament literature the same exhilarating sensation of freedom that Cowley had felt on observing that the prophets 'pass from one thing to another with almost *Invisible connexions*' (*Poems,* p. 214n), and that Robert Lowth would analyse in his *Lectures on the Sacred Poetry of the Hebrews,* delivered in Oxford in the 1740s:

Naturally free, and of too ardent a spirit to be confined by rule, [poetry of the prophetic kind] is usually guided by the nature of the subject only, and the impulse of divine inspiration. (II, p. 69)

. . . the nature of the prophetic impulse . . . bears away the mind with irresistible violence, and frequently in rapid transitions from near to remote objects, from human to divine.

(II, pp. 85-6)

In *Night Thoughts,* Young overtly aspired to the free and limitless style of the Hebrew prophet-poets. '*The Method pursued in it*'—he wrote in his Preface— '*was rather* imposed, *by what spontaneously arose in the Author's Mind, on that Occasion, than* meditated, *or* designed.' Young's method reflects the influence of Locke, who had observed 'what passes in our Minds, how our *Ideas* there in train constantly some vanish, and others begin to appear' (*Essay,* p. 195). It also reflects the popularity of the 'Pindaric' ode in the seventeenth and eighteenth centuries. 'Rapturous, somewhat abrupt, and immethodical to a vulgar Eye' (Young, *Ocean. An Ode,* p. 19), these odes epitomised greatness and freedom, 'unconstricted versing, formless form' (M. A. Doody, *The Daring Muse,* p. 250). In the interests of poetic freedom, *Night Thoughts* casts off what Young had come to feel was the 'shackle', or 'manacle', or 'fetter', of rhyme.[1] Young's *Conjectures on Original Composition* propagates the ideal by explicitly associating the poet's sublime aspirations with blank verse: 'verse unfallen, uncurst; verse reclaim'd, reinthron'd in the true *language of the gods;* who never thunder'd, nor suffer'd their *Homer* to thunder, in rhime' (*Conjectures,* p. 60).

With hindsight, it is clear that English poets (such as Smart and Blake) were able to take on the mantle of the biblical writers only after they had absorbed Lowth's discovery of such Hebrew prosodic techniques as 'parallelism'. Young's metrics now sound traditional: the couplet dominates in *Night Thoughts* even in its absence, and the poem's diction is often just as constrained as that of the rhyming *Paraphrase on Job.* Many of Young's contemporaries, however, thought his blank verse integral to the formless, inspirational style, which in turn seemed particularly appropriate to the Christian rememberer meditating on the tombs:

Life glides away, *Lorenzo!,* like a Brook;
For ever changing, unperceiv'd the Change.

(V. 401-2)

The formlessness, the freedom and the blank verse appealed equally to the secular, associative poet. In *The Prelude,* the river recurs as an image of the progress of the human mind, and of the poem; and the style of *Night Thoughts* must have seemed highly congenial to a poet who thought his task was to awake the

feeling of life endless, the one thought
By which we live, infinity and God.

(*The Prelude,* 1805, XIII.183-4)

In essence, this was also Young's ambition in *Night Thoughts*. Evoking the religious excitement of the Old Testament writers, Young intended to show what could still be done in poetry to speak in an heroic strain of the sublime theme of Christian salvation. Moving from complaint to consolation, from atheism to a hope of immortality, the poem is an apology for Christian dogma. At one level it is therefore a moral dissertation which marshals arguments and evidences for the proof of doctrines which eighteenth-century Christians thought could be proved or disproved. Young made no attempt to disguise the hortatory nature of his poem. He is just as severe as Dennis on those who write or read poetry for fashionable but fruitless ends (II.456-60). He extols sacred wisdom over mere wit (VIII.1237-49), asking 'Who wants Amusement in the Flame of Battle?' (II.62). He wants 'no trivial, or inglorious *Theme*' (VII.1474). But Christian morality also inspires the soul to 'soar':

> I find my Inspiration in my Theme;
> The Grandeur of my Subject is my Muse.
>
> (IX.195-6)

The life of virtue recommended by the Christian priest culminates in the Christian poet's encounter with God (IX.580). Young and his Christian reader would not have consciously separated the poem's pedagogy from its sublimity. Temporal piety was conditioned by a transcendent hope, and true religion was the starting point for the sublime imaginer.

The passing of time (IX.298), the transience of fame (VIII.500-10), and the decline of empire (VII.1033) prompted sublime thoughts in Young, but most of his illustrations of 'a Sublimity, that frightens, astonishes, and ravishes the Mind of a Reader' (Aaron Hill, *The Creation*, p. 7), he found in the Bible. Mount Sinai, the Red Sea, the sons of Korah, the fiery furnace of Shadrach, Meshach and Abednego (VII.1108-16), Leviathan (VIII.36), Samson (IX.2431), the crucifixion (IV.166-83, 575-95) and the last judgement are all deployed as affective examples of the sublime. Young, like many eighteenth-century poets, wrote *A Poem on the Last Day* (1713), finding in the last judgement a theme ideal for transcending the every-day world. It is especially imminent throughout the final Night, but Young's theology sees in 'Eruptions, Earthquakes, Comets, Lightnings' (IX.160) and the movement of the planets, ever-present signs of the end, signals of attack which hang over 'This poor terrestrial Citadel of Man' (IX.163). The day of judgement speaks of reasonable, appropriate rewards and final justice; but it also involves 'Comprehension's absolute Defeat' (IX.1107), and the suprarational vision of heaven's king with 'Face unveil'd' (IX.580). This blend of reason and revelation is reflected in the texture of the verse, where theological argument is fused with, and punctuated by, sublime exclamations. Thought and sentiment coincide: 'I think of nothing else; I see! I feel it!' (IX.264).

For the poet of *Night Thoughts,* 'Nature is Christian' (IV.704), 'Nature . . . to man Speaks Wisdom' (VI.671-3). The poet's 'Song but echoes what Great *Nature* speaks' (IX.2022). Occasionally, therefore, the poetic self is dramatically situated amid 'Seas, Rivers, Mountains, Forests, Desarts, Rocks' (IX.908). Storms (IX.620-30) and the ocean provoke Addisonian thoughts on the 'melancholy Face of human Life' (VIII.175), inspiring the soul to 'rise into Sublimities of Thought' (IX.635) and 'think of *more* than *Man*' (IX.630). More than anything else, though, the firmament inspired eighteenth-century poets to feel 'Rapture, involv'd in raptures' (Hill, 'The Transport', *Works,* III, p. 232). Like Hill, Richard Blackmore (*The Creation*), James Ralph (*Night*) and Thomson (*The Seasons,* 'Summer' and 'Winter'), Young embarks on a literary tour of the universe, as he had also done in *Poem on the Last Day*. He pours his 'flowing Numbers o'er the flaming Skies', he cannot see 'what more / Invites the Muse' (IX.1902-5), and *Night Thoughts* shares the prevalent contemporary fascination with the ideas of 'boundless', unlimited space (IV.427, 512) and an infinity of worlds. Man kindles his devotion at the stars (IX.1943), which 'were made to fashion the Sublime / Of human Hearts, and *wiser* make the *Wise*' (IX.966-7). The Cambridge Platonist Henry More had 'equated the vast distances revealed by the telescope . . . with the omnipresence of God as the ground of the universe' (E. Tuveson, 'Space, Deity and the "Natural Sublime,"' p. 24); and *Night Thoughts* encourages the belief that in the reaches of space man can find the being of God. The physical universe is endowed with significance, and demonstrates God's incomprehensibility, providence, infinity, omnipresence, power, goodness and mercy (IX.835-2027);[2] and astronomical contemplation inevitably prompts a rational commitment to Christian belief (VII.1226-39). More significantly, if space, like God extended but not corporeal, can be seen as God's 'Sensory' (Newton's term), then in some sense the mind of man is also an attribute of God, for the firmament is:

> The noble Pasture of the *Mind,*
> Which there expatiates, strengthens, and exults,
> And riots thro' the Luxuries of Thought.
>
> (IX.1039-41. Cf. IX.847-8, 1061-6)

For eighteenth-century writers, the ever-expanding reaches of the universe spoke metaphorically of the imaginative progress and growth of the human mind. The telescope revealed a world

> where the Mind,
> In endless Growth and infinite Ascent,
> Rises from State to State, and World to World.
>
> (Thomson, 'Winter', 606-8)

The prospects of space demanded of poets an active imaginative and devotional response. The poet of *Night Thoughts* finds 'some superior Point' (VI.174) in space from where his 'due-distanc'd eye' (VI.595) will gain a 'stupendous view' (VI.600). It is a personal, individual viewpoint, the poet has an 'illumin'd Eye' (VI.176), and

> The World . . .
> Its ample Sphere, its universal Frame,
> In full Dimensions, swells to the Survey;
> And enters, at one Glance, the ravisht Sight.
>
> (VI.167-73)

The preacher argues that such self-involving, all-encompassing perspectives prefigure the views which will be granted to man in eternity (IX.1171-84). For the imaginative poet, however, the perceptions of eternity, 'Unbroken . . . illustrious, and entire' (VI.170), are already available, the imagination mediating a feeling of divine presence. By exercising sensibility and feeling, man can make the grandeur of the external material world a property of the self:

> How Glorious, then, appears the *Mind* of Man,
> When in it All the Stars, and Planets, roll?
> And what it *seems* it *is; Great* Objects make
> *Great* Minds.
>
> (IX.1062-5)

Thus, sublimity, though it might be a property of the object, is more importantly a faculty of the observer (IX.1012). By the end of the eighteenth century both object and response were in a more integrated fashion to be the concern of poets, but already in *Night Thoughts* the sublime is dependent on the response that nature or the firmament evokes in the observer (IX.904-16). This sublime amounts to a state of awareness. While Gray and Collins are concerned with secular creativity and self-fulfilment, Young is concerned with Christian awareness, and the complex processes of eternal self-realisation and salvation. Behind the simple morality of 'virtuous YOUNG' (Thomson, *The Seasons,* 'Autumn', 667)—'teach us to be kind' (I.297), 'Man wants but Little; nor that Little, long' (IV.118)—there is a prophetic urging to awake, to be aware: 'Hear, O ye Nations! hear it, O ye dead' (IV.272). In imaginative and Christian terms 'all Men are about to live. / For ever on the Brink of being born' (I.399-400). The poet's task, like the preacher's, is to show that men cannot wait at this point forever. They must live up to their potential dignity as sublime souls (IX.1018-27).

To a certain extent *Night Thoughts* was obviously intended to be what it has often been criticised for being: a collection of biblical and astronomical images and motifs deployed by a prophet-figure searching after sublime models in an attempt to touch his readers' hearts. It was by design that *Night Thoughts* lacks the irony, comedy, self-deprecation and satirical exposure of a great deal of eighteenth-century literature; and Young's repeated transcendent motifs should be seen, not as marks of bathos (the occupational hazard of sublimity), but as vital signs to a predominantly Christian readership well-endowed to receive, interpret and appreciate them in imaginative terms.

Contemplating our Distant Selves

> O FOR the Voice—of What? of Whom?—What Voice
> Can answer to my Wants, in *such* Ascent.
>
> (IX.1592-3)

Night Thoughts asks what subject the sublime Christian poet might find, and what voice he might adopt. The speaker often claims an evangelical authority for his productions. He is preaching 'the Word'. The poem is therefore sustained by unquestioned doctrines of Christian revelation. But all this is not enough. Like Gray, Collins and Goldsmith, Young sets as much store by the simple authority of the individual perceiver. As in much mid-eighteenth-century poetry, this individual makes his unique presence felt by self-consciously describing the progress of his own poem (II.284, IV.124, V.294, IX.513), and by introducing personal anecdotes. The poem itself is held together to a large extent only by the poet's thoughts and sentiments. All the while, however, he is defining the characteristics of a type—whose sensibility is distinctly poetic. This type is separated from urban society, the court, and the political scene, or at least he repents of his past involvement (IV.80-96). He is uncorrupted by learning and civilisation (VII.1138). He is shy, 'ill at Ease, / In this, not *his own* Place, this foreign Field' (VII.40-1). His goal is a close, solitary walk with God (III.6). He is the archetypal Christian voyager or wanderer (IX.1-16), journeying alone 'In this our Land of Travel' (IX.538). The poem's astronomical and night-time perspectives are focused on this solitary poetic type (IX.750), and theologically too, the creation and continuance of the universe is justified by the redemption of the individual as sinner (IV.498).

In *Conjectures* Young wrote: 'contract full intimacy with the stranger within thee' (p. 53), and in *Night Thoughts* there is much of the self-questioning and introspection characteristic of religious conversions. Ostensibly, the poet is converting a character called Lorenzo—who moves from various rationalistic and Deistic positions to the knowledge of God and the hope of immortality. But Lorenzo's voice is at times so eloquent, and the poet knows so intimately the thoughts of Lorenzo, that it often seems as if the poet and Lorenzo are two sides of one personality, tormented by the feeling that 'that which I do, I allow not; for what I would, that do I not; but what I hate, that do I' (Romans 7.15). When the poet peeps into Lorenzo's covered heart (IX.2073) he is obeying the imperative of self-scrutiny. He knows himself to be diseased (IX.38). His 'Change of *Heart*' and 'The CONSOLATION [which] cancels the COMPLAINT' occur only when Lorenzo's arguments have been hushed (IX.510-11).

Night Thoughts was one of the first long meditative poems to speak of 'men as they are men within themselves' (Wordsworth, *The Prelude,* 1850, XIII.226), existing within a universe perceived as personal vision. The image of the backward-looking traveller in *The Prelude* (1850, IX.9-16) is Wordsworth's acknowledgement of Young's poetic individualism, for it echoes an image in ***Night Thoughts*** (IX.513-39). Wordsworth must have recognised that Young had defined his figure of the solitary poet against a contemporary suspicion of too much individuality. The hermit might be a stock figure in much eighteenth-century verse (see John Cunningham's *The Contemplatist,* the younger Thomas Warton's *The Pleasures of Melancholy,* and Thomas Parnell's 'The Hermit'), but more often than not he has a socially-derived notion of being alone. Solitude, so often, is 'the Nurse of Woe' (Parnell, 'A Hymn to Contentment', *Poems,* p. 159). Pope's garden at Twickenham may have provided opportunities for retirement, but it was close enough to the city for him closely to observe, and participate in, the London scene. Even Thomson's rural retirement is essentially a shared moral experience (*The Seasons,* 'Autumn', 1235-8). Johnson equated individuality with solitariness as a deprivation: 'Here sit poor I, with nothing but my own solitary individuality' (Johnson, *Letters,* II, p. 75). He links solitariness with madness and immorality: 'If I escape the example of bad men, I want likewise the counsel and conversation of the good' (*Rasselas,* p. 57). So Johnson claims his audience's attention because his 'opinions are the result, not of solitary conjectures, but of practise and experience' (Johnson, *The Rambler,* IV, p. 28).

Young tends not to see any contradiction, even though he read and appreciated *The Rambler* (see Boswell, *Life of Johnson,* I, pp. 214-15). Like Akenside in *The Pleasures of Imagination* (I.554-8), Young equates poetic inspiration with solitude. His vision of Socrates associates insight with being alone: 'Sacred *Silence* whispering Truths Divine' (IX.2412). From the beginning of Night I Young creates an alienated, solitary, but Christian frame of mind: 'I tremble at myself, / And in myself am lost! At home a Stranger' (I.80-1. Cf. VII.41). And as for Johnson's concern for moral example, Young thinks that innocence and virtue can only be safeguarded in solitude:

> We see, we hear with Peril; *Safety* dwells
> Remote from *Multitude.*
>   (V.163-4)

The emphasis on individuality was of course sanctioned by the Old Testament and Christian concept of divine inspiration. Milton had stressed the authority of the inspired prophetic individual, and his poetry reaffirmed the idea that God speaks through the suffering and faith of individuals. Many of the seventeenth-century lyric writers also compared themselves with the Hebrew prophets, visionaries with a unique message from God. Milton and these poets were not afraid that it might be impossible to distinguish between true inspiration and mere enthusiasm—between (in Shaftesbury's terms) '*a real* feeling of the Divine Presence . . . and *a false one*' (*Characteristicks,* I, p. 53). These were the fears of writers such as Swift, Hartley and Johnson. By contrast, James Hervey and the Wesley brothers approved of ***Night Thoughts*** precisely because it stresses beliefs such as the depravity of man and the reality of the supernatural which were highly congenial to enthusiastic Christianity, combining them with, and justifying them by, a belief in personal feeling as an authoritative guide to truth.[3] Young's reliance on subjective individualism has much in common with the experimental faith of the Methodists; and if the doctrines of Methodism 'are a commentary on the worth and possibilities of the individual soul' (M. L. Edwards, *After Wesley,* p. 37—quoted in H. N. Fairchild, *Religious Trends in English Poetry,* II, p. 86), Young shares many Methodist principles. At one point in ***Night Thoughts*** Young is not afraid to accept the name of enthusiast (VI.603).

In ***Conjectures,*** the poet's original genius, the ability to make a powerful emotional impact on the reader, 'has ever been supposed to partake of something divine' (p. 27), and is 'from heaven' (p. 37). Like Akenside, Savage and Wordsworth, Young knows that the flame of his genius descends from heaven itself (V.97-109). Young consequently criticises the aesthetics and theology of Pope. Respect for authority and imitation of the ancients are Roman Catholic principles unworthy of a Protestant who should elevate the authority of the individual. Pope's

> taste partook the error of his religion; it denied not worship to saints and angels; that is, to writers, who, canonized for ages, have received their apotheosis from established and universal fame. True Poesy, like true religion, abhors idolatory; and though it honours the memory of the exemplary, and takes them willingly (yet cautiously) as guides in the way to glory; real, though unexampled, excellence is its only aim; nor looks it for any inspiration less than divine.
>   (*Conjectures,* pp. 67-8)

In religion and in poetics the message is clear: man must discover for himself what it is like to walk with God. Young grafts the Protestant obsessions with personal status, salvation and election on to his poetry. As a justified Protestant his status depends on particular election; and his role as an inspired poet is similarly verified.

Singular and separate, the poet cannot speak on behalf of the mass of men. Rather, he preaches or prophesies, the figure of Lorenzo making possible direct address to the reader as sinner. The sublime exhortation forestalls any argument. The seer's message is true because of the status of the messenger. **Night Thoughts** might be a poem about Christian doctrine, an attempt, therefore, to speak of the propositional coherence of Christianity. But while never denying reasoned propositional truth, **Night Thoughts** also represents the most extended and ambitious attempt in the first half of the eighteenth century to revitalise locutionary truth. With Gray, Thomson, Collins, Chatterton and Macpherson, Young has his place in the development of the bardic persona. Gray's bard 'triumphs' because of strength of character and individual emotion. With a much more clearly Christian perspective Young also celebrates the creative and redemptive power of the individual prophetic imaginer, claiming as his own the prophetic, oriental force inspiring the Old Testament writers (II.405). . . .

Notes

[1] See Young, *Ocean, An Ode*, p. 26; William Thompson, Preface, *Paraphrase on . . . Job;* Thomson, *The Seasons*, 'Autumn', 646. Regarding *Night Thoughts*, Johnson wrote that 'The wild diffusion of the sentiments and the digressive sallies of the imagination would have been compressed and restrained by confinement to rhyme' (*Lives*, III, p. 395).

[2] See I. St J. Bliss, 'Night Thoughts in Relation to Contemporary Christian Apologetics', p. 60.

[3] In *Meditations and Contemplations*, Hervey quotes extensively from *Night Thoughts* (I, pp. 86-7; II, pp. 203-4). See Charles Wesley, *Journal*, II, p. 106; T. W. Herbert, *John Wesley as Editor and Author*, pp. 79-82.

Works Cited

Primary works

Biblical citations refer to the Authorišed Version, in particular to an edition published in London in 1702, which also contains the 1662 *Book of Common Prayer* referred to above.

Addison, Joseph, *Works*, edited by Thomas Tickell, 4 vols. (London, 1721)

Akenside, Mark, *The Pleasures of Imagination* (London, 1744) . . .

Biographia Britannica, 6 vols. and Supplement (London, 1747-66)

Blackmore, Richard, *The Creation: A Philosophical Poem* (London, 1712) . . .

Blair, Robert, *The Grave* (London, 1743)

Blake, William, *Complete Writings*, edited by G. Keynes (Oxford, 1966)

————, *Designs for Edward Young's 'Night Thoughts': A Complete Edition*, edited by D. V. Erdman, J. E. Grant, E. J. Rose and M. J. Tolley, 2 vols. (Oxford, 1980) . . .

Boswell, James, *Life of Johnson*, edited by G. B. Hill, revised by L. F. Powell, 6 vols. (Oxford, 1934-64) . . .

Butler, Joseph, *The Analogy of Religion Natural and Revealed, to the Constitution and Course of Nature* (London, 1736) . . .

Cecil, Richard, *Works*, 3 vols. (London, 1816) . . .

Coleridge, Samuel Taylor, *Collected Letters*, edited by E. L. Griggs, 6 vols. (Oxford, 1956-71) . . .

Cowper, William, *Letters and Prose Writings*, edited by J. King and C. Ryskamp, 5 vols. (Oxford, 1979-86)

————, *Poems, 1742-82*, edited by J. D. Baird and C. Ryskamp (Oxford, 1980)

————, *Poetical Works*, edited by H. S. Milford, fourth edition (London, 1967)

Crabbe, George, *Poetical Works and Life*, edited by his son, 8 vols. (London, 1834) . . .

Cudworth, Ralph, *A Treatise Concerning Eternal and Immutable Morality* (London, 1731) . . .

Dennis, John, *Critical Works*, edited by E. N. Hooker, 2 vols. (Baltimore, Ohio, 1939-43) . . .

Eliot, George, 'Worldliness and Other-Worldliness: The Poet Young', *The Essays of George Eliot*, edited by T. Pinney (London, 1963), 335-85 . . .

Forbes, William, *An Account of the Life and Writings of James Beattie*, 2 vols. (Edinburgh, 1806) . . .

Gastrell, Francis, *A Moral Proof of the Certainty of a Future State* (London, 1725) . . .

Goldsmith, Oliver, *Collected Works*, edited by A. Friedman, 5 vols. (Oxford, 1966) . . .

Gray, Thomas, *Poetical Works*, edited by R. Lonsdale (Oxford, 1977)

Guardian, The, fourth edition, 2 vols. (London, 1726) . . .

Herbert, George, *Works*, edited by F. E. Hutchinson (Oxford, 1941)

Hervey, James, *Meditations and Contemplations,* seventh edition, 2 vols. (London, 1750)

Hill, Aaron, *The Creation . . . With a Preface to Mr. Pope concerning the Sublimity of the Ancient Hebrew Poetry, and a material and obvious Defect in the English* (London, 1720; edited by G. G. Pahl, Augustan Reprint Society, Los Angeles, 1949)

———, *Works,* 4 vols. (London, 1753) . . .

Hume, David, *Dialogues concerning Natural Religion,* edited by N. K. Smith (Oxford, 1935)

Johnson, Samuel, *The History of Rasselas, Prince of Abissinia,* edited by G. Tillotson and B. Jenkins (Oxford, 1971)

———, *Letters,* edited by R. W. Chapman, 3 vols. (Oxford, 1952)

———, *Lives of the English Poets,* edited by G. B. Hill, 3 vols. (Oxford, 1905)

———, *The Rambler* (vols. III-V of the Yale Edition), 3 vols., edited by W. J. Bate and A. B. Straus (New Haven, Connecticut and London, 1969) . . .

Keats, John, *Letters, 1814-1821,* edited by H. E. Rollins, 2 vols. (Cambridge, Mass., 1958) . . .

Law, William, *Works,* 9 vols. (London, 1762) . . .

Locke, John, *An Essay Concerning Human Understanding,* edited by P. H. Nidditch (Oxford, 1971)

Lowth, Robert, *Lectures on the Sacred Poetry of the Hebrews,* translated by G. Gregory, 2 vols. (London, 1787)

Milton, John, *Poems,* edited by J. Carey and A. Fowler (London, 1968)

Montagu, Henry, First Earl of Manchester, *Manchester al Mondo: Contemplatio Mortis Et Immortalitatis,* ninth impression (London, 1667) . . .

Parnell, Thomas, *Poems on Several Occasions* (London, 1722) . . .

Pope, Alexander, *The Iliad of Homer,* edited by M. Mack *et al.,* 2 vols. (London, 1967)

———, *The Odyssey of Homer,* edited by M. Mack *et al.,* 2 vols. (London, 1967)

———, *Poems,* edited by J. Butt (London, 1963)

———, *Works,* edited by Joseph Warton, 9 vols. (London, 1797) . . .

Richardson, Samuel, *Aesop's Fables. With Instructive Morals and Reflections . . . design'd to promote Religion, Morality, and Universal Benevolence* (London, no date)

———, *Correspondence,* edited by Anna Laetitia Barbauld, 6 vols. (London, 1804)

Russell, W. C., *The Book of Authors* (London, 1871)

Savage, Richard, *Poetical Works,* edited by C. Tracy (Cambridge, 1962) . . .

Shaftesbury, Anthony Ashley Cooper, Third Earl of, *Characteristicks,* 3 vols. (London, 1714) . . .

Taylor, Jeremy, *The Worthy Communicant, or A Discourse of the Nature, Effects, and Blessings Consequent to the Worthy Receiving of the Lord's Supper* (London, 1660)

Thompson, William, *A Poetical Paraphrase on Part of the Book of Job* (London, 1726)

Thomson, James, *Complete Poetical Works,* edited by J. L. Robertson (London, 1908) *The Seasons,* edited by J. Sambrook (Oxford, 1981)

———, *Thraliana: The Diary of Mrs. Hester Lynch Thrale 1776-1809,* edited by K. C. Balderstone, 2 vols. (Oxford, 1942)

Tillotson, John, *Works,* 2 vols. (London, 1712) . . .

Vaughan, Henry, *Works,* edited by L. C. Martin (Oxford, 1957)

Virgil, with a translation by H. R. Fairclough, 2 vols. (London, 1968)

Wake, William, *Preparation for Death. Being a Letter Sent to a Young Gentlewoman in France, in a Dangerous Distemper, of which She Died,* fifth edition (London, 1719) . . .

Warton, Joseph, *An Essay on the Genius and Writings of Pope,* fifth edition, 2 vols. (London, 1806)

Warton, Thomas, Thomas, and Joseph, *The Three Wartons: A Choice of their Verse,* edited by E. Partridge (London, 1927) . . .

Wesley, Charles, *Hymns and Sacred Poems,* 2 vols. (Bristol, 1755) *Journal,* edited by T. Jackson, 2 vols. (London, 1849) . . .

Wordsworth, William, *Poetical Works,* edited by E. de Selincourt and H. Darbishire, 5 vols. (Oxford, 1940-9)

————, *The Prelude, 1799, 1805, 1850,* edited by J. Wordsworth *et al.* (New York and London, 1979)

Young, Edward, *Busiris, King of Egypt, A Tragedy,* second edition (London, 1722)

————, *Conjectures on Original Composition. In a Letter to the Author of Sir Charles Grandison,* second edition (London, 1759)

————, *Correspondence, 1683-1765,* edited by H. Pettit (Oxford, 1971)

————, *Love of Fame, the Universal Passion. In Seven Characteristical Satires,* second edition (London, 1728)

————, *Ocean. An Ode. Occasion'd by His Majesty's late Royal Encouragement of the Sea-Service. To which is prefix'd, An Ode to the King: And a Discourse on Ode. By the Author of the Universal Passion* (London, 1728)

————, *A Paraphrase on Part of the Book of Job* (London, 1719)

————, *A Poem on the Last Day* (Oxford, 1713)

————, *The Revenge, A Tragedy* (London, 1721)

Secondary works

Bliss, I. St J., '*Night Thoughts* in Relation to Contemporary Christian Apologetics', *PMLA,* 49 (1934), 37-40 . . .

Doody, M. A., *The Daring Muse: Augustan Poetry Reconsidered* (Cambridge, 1985)

Edwards, M. L., *After Wesley* (London, 1935) . . .

Fairchild, H. N. *Religious Trends in English Poetry,* 6 vols. (New York, 1939-68) . . .

Herbert, T. W., *John Wesley as Editor and Author* (Princeton, N. J., 1940)

O'Connor, H. W., 'The Narcissa Episode in Young's *Night Thoughts*', *PMLA,* 34 (1919), 130-49 . . .

Pettit, H., 'A Bibliography of Young's *Night Thoughts*', *University of Colorado Studies,* Series in Language and Literature, 5 (1954), 1-52

Price, M., 'The Sublime Poem: Pictures and Powers', *Yale Review,* 58 (1968-9), 194-213 . . .

Tuveson, E., 'Space, Deity and the "Natural Sublime,"' *Modern Language Quarterly,* 12 (1951), 20-38

Wicker, C. V., *Edward Young and the Fear of Death: A Study in Romantic Melancholy* (Albuquerque, 1952) . . .

Cheryl Wanko (essay date 1991)

SOURCE: "The Making of a Minor Poet: Edward Young and Literary Taxonomy," in *English Studies,* Netherlands, Vol. 72, No. 4, August, 1991, pp. 355-67.

[*In the following essay Wanko describes critical reception of Young's works and argues that his critical reputation has suffered because of the development of a literary taxonomy into which he does not neatly fit.*]

All literary historians recognize the extraordinary success of Edward Young's *Night Thoughts* (1742-6) and the poem's influence both in England and on the Continent. George Saintsbury, Oliver Elton, George Sherburn, and John Butt each devote several pages of their histories to describing Young's immense popularity during the eighteenth and early nineteenth centuries. Yet the space Young occupies in these volumes is often grudgingly allotted. While admitting the poem's importance. Sherburn declares *Night Thoughts* to be now unreadable. Others deprecate Young more overtly: William Bowman Piper labels Young a 'fallible, a minor poet'; Eric Rothstein indulges his wit at Young's expense; Paul Fussell blames the insincerity of eighteenth-century graveyard poetry on 'performers like Edward Young'.[1] From the eighteenth century to the twentieth, Young's reputation has suffered a precipitous decline.

Why did this decline occur? Scholars and critics have not yet adequately addressed this question or the broader questions behind it. Both Henry Pettit and Harold Forster, Young's latest biographer, have chronicled in detail the waning of Young's reputation in the late eighteenth and early nineteenth centuries.[2] Their efforts, however, isolate criticism of *Night Thoughts* from larger currents of critical evaluation of poetry; we need to see Young's reputation in its context to understand its decline. Yet change in evaluation is not the sole cause of Young's reduced reputation. Perhaps Young is also a victim of the shrinking eighteenth-century canon that J. Paul Hunter recently described, but Young had lost much of his reputation as a poet worthy of serious study long before the development of the economic problems Hunter notes.[3] Other explanations must exist for Young's relegation to the status of a minor poet.

In this article I will argue that, in addition to changing critical standards, Young's reputation has also suffered because of the development of our system of literary taxonomy. The artificially imposed periodization of 'Augustan' (or 'neo-classical') and 'Romantic' eras has caused critics to distort eighteenth and nineteenth-century evaluations of poets like Young.[4] Revisionary efforts of late twentieth-century scholars such as B. H. Bronson, Howard Weinbrot, and Marilyn Butler have not dispelled completely the potency of these labels nor provided restitution to the eighteenth-century writers victimized by them.[5] However, we can usefully extend and apply their revisionary arguments by showing the historical *effects* of such labels on literary reputations. For even if such categories as 'Romantic' and 'Augustan' are breaking down, the damage to poets such as Young has already occurred. Our taxonomy has forced writers of poetry which has not corresponded wholly to either the 'Augustan' or 'Romantic' model—that of Collins, Thomson, and others, but, most dramatically, Young—into obscurity and disrepute.

To understand how Young lost his status as a major poet, we will first examine the criteria by which eighteenth and nineteenth-century commentators evaluated Young, then still a major figure. We must realize, however, as recent reception theorists and New Historicists would remind us, that our perception of the past is already mediated by our present historical horizon. Within our historical limitations, we must try to determine which criteria have later been designated as 'Augustan' or 'Romantic', noticing those that remain unaccounted for in this two-period system. Looking at these two terms' separate claims on Young's poetry will allow us to see how the terms distort the history they try to preserve. Our desire to explain historical change in terms of reaction or rebellion against previous aesthetic standards, a desire that generates a list of antithetical qualities of Augustanism or Neoclassicism and Romanticism as Abrams describes them in his *A Glossary of Literary Terms,* relegates poets like Young, who fit neatly into neither category, to minor poethood. The apparently non-judgmental status of not belonging to either category becomes decisively judgmental: if poets do not fit, they are not as important (i.e., not as *good*) as others who fit better. Thus, our taxonomy does not merely *describe; it evaluates.* By using Young as a test case we can better understand the mechanisms by which the canon, through its 'descriptive' taxonomy, selects its constituents and suppresses others.

I. *Eighteenth-Century Evaluations of* Night Thoughts

Let us begin with eighteenth-century criticisms of Young's work and then determine how later critics have appropriated eighteenth-century evaluative criteria into the schema of 'Augustan' and 'Romantic'. We will notice that the two sets of criteria do not coincide: the qualities that Young's contemporaries valued or deprecated in *Night Thoughts* have been divided into two uneasy categories by later writers, thereby distorting our view of mid-eighteenth-century poetry.

In 1742, Young published the first three of his *Night Thoughts;* he completed all nine by 1746. Although Young had enjoyed some success with his satires in the 1720s, the publication of *Night Thoughts* brought him literary fame and established him as a major poetic genius of the day. Reception of the poem has been amply documented by W. Thomas and, more recently, Forster.[6] One critique of the poem, however, Samuel Jackson Pratt's *Observations on the Night Thoughts of Dr. Young* (1776), has been surprisingly neglected.[7] Forster mentions it only in passing; Thomas's important study and Henry Pettit's 'The English Rejection of Young's *Night Thoughts'* both ignore it. As the only extended eighteenth-century study of *Night Thoughts,* Pratt's *Observations* is crucial to the following discussion of eighteenth-century views of the poem.

While Pratt's study is generally favorable to *Night Thoughts,* we can cite many other enthusiastic contemporary responses to the poem. Boswell called it 'a mass of the grandest and richest poetry that human genius has ever produced'. Goldsmith used it as an authoritative measure of literary merit, and Pratt tells us that Goldsmith thought the first *Night* the best of the nine. Herbert Croft, author of 'Johnson's' *Life of Young,* calls the *Night Thoughts* 'extraordinary poems'.[8] Most opinions, however, give us little sense of the grounds for the writer's praise. Johnson's critical remarks at the end of Croft's *Life* and Pratt's book give us the best view of the specific criteria by which Young was judged.

Eighteenth-century critics judged *Night Thoughts* on four principal criteria: morality, poetic sincerity, versification, and 'excess' in length and language. Pratt claims that *Night Thoughts* emphasizes morality instead of narrative: he affirms it as a fact, neither deploring nor applauding. *Night Thoughts* is 'a Poem of *Morality,* containing no great variety of character, or chain of heroic events'. He praises Young's piety and pathos, and notes the 'resemblance, betwixt Dr. Young's Poetry, and Dr. Johnson's Prose . . . the same solid, serious, and forcible manner of expressing, reflections, equally pious and poetical . . . distinguish both'.[9] Most eighteenth-century readers admired Young's didacticism: Boswell says that 'No book whatever can be recommended to young persons, with better hopes of seasoning their minds with *vital religion,* than Young's *"Night Thoughts"'*.[10] Samuel Richardson, Young's friend at the end of his life, especially esteemed this aspect of Young's work.

Although the didactic morality of poems like *Night Thoughts* was important to eighteenth-century readers, these same readers also insisted that the moral sentiments be unfeigned. Both Pratt and Croft stress Young's reasons for composing *Night Thoughts,* his loss of three family members within three months (a false conclusion both writers derive from Young's statements in *Night Thoughts* itself). Pratt explains that although Young's morbid melancholy might have been unhealthy, it was sincere. He relates the story of Young's pleasure in sitting through winter nights in the parish churchyard, and, by the emphasis he gives the story, he implies that a poet's verse should reflect the poet's life.[11] Young receives approval from the writer of the satirical 'The Motives for Writing. A Dream' (1761) for the same reason: the writer does not attribute Young's poetry to vanity or ambition but to 'exalted genius and universal philanthropy'.[12] Croft, however, worries about the dangers of such comparisons: 'Still, is it altogether fair to dress up the poet for the man, and to bring the gloominess of the *Night Thoughts* to prove the gloominess of Young, and to shew that his genius, like the genius of Swift, was in some measure the sullen inspiration of discontent?'[13] Although Croft implies a negative answer, his question indicates that the issue was significant to his audience.

Eighteenth-century critics also considered the versification of *Night Thoughts* an important issue. Pratt calls attention to the beauties and blemishes of Young's versification, complaining about Young's love of alliteration and arguing that Young did not adequately comprehend the judicious use of the full stop.[14] While Johnson does not discuss Young's verse in such detail, he notes Young's originality with approbation: Young's 'versification is his own, neither his blank nor his rhyming lines have any resemblance to those of former writers'. He praises Young's choice of blank verse in *Night Thoughts:* 'The wild diffusion of the sentiments and the digressive sallies of imagination would have been compressed and restrained by confinement to rhyme'.[15] Jean Hagstrum has argued that although Johnson usually insisted on 'variety in uniformity' in versification, for *Night Thoughts* he makes exceptions.[16]

Comments on the versification of *Night Thoughts* often relate to eighteenth-century writers' most frequent complaint against Young: 'excess', both in length and language. Critics applied this criterion to many aspects of *Night Thoughts:* Young did not know when to stop; he repeated the same sentiments and lingered too long on the same subjects (especially death); he overused metaphors; his uncontrolled emotion led him into bombast. Pratt charges *Night Thoughts* with all of these faults. He tells us that the excessive length is caused in part by repetition: in analyzing one image he states, '[t]hus you see the image is the *same,* and by changing the mode of expressing it, *five* lines are given, where *two* might have done better'. Although Pratt admires Young's verse, he also must admit '[t]here is no end of transcribing this writer's *iterations*'. Johnson maintains that '[t]he excellence of this work is not exactness, but copiousness', but he seems to have held a minority opinion. Forster notes how Young's extending his poem past *Night Five* disgusted William Shenstone, an acquaintance of Elizabeth Carter, and others. Commenting on Young's language, Pratt also criticizes its overdramatic qualities and compares its 'fustian' with that of the Restoration playwright Nathaniel Lee. He de-plored Young's inability to control his metaphorical language and his tendency to affectation, in part because they lead *Night Thoughts* into murky obscurity; thus Pratt admonishes his reader to 'study *perspicuity*'. Joseph Warton remarks on the stylistic effusiveness which Pratt criticizes: 'So little sensible are we of our own imperfections, that the very last time I saw Dr. Young, he was severely censuring and ridiculing the false pomp of fustian writers, and the nauseousness of *bombast*'.[17] Charges of 'excess' constitute the bulk of the eighteenth-century criticisms of *Night Thoughts*.

Although we could certainly cite other remarks on *Night Thoughts,* the four types discussed above dominate and encompass most others. Twentieth-century criticism, however, does not merely identify these particular evaluative criteria but also classifies them according to the Augustan/Romantic dichotomy. For instance, twentieth-century critics usually attribute didactic morality more to an Augustan than a Romantic sensibility. Most agree with Shelley, who considered didactic poetry to be his 'abhorrance'.[18] Bonamy Dobrée, who identifies moralizing poetry as 'common drugget stuff', has admitted to its popularity in the first half of the eighteenth century; Sherburn notes that there was 'much moralizing' in mid-century verse. John Butt tells us that mid-century poets turned to the ode, the Romantic form *par excellence,* as an 'attractive escape from didactic poetry and essays on moral subjects'.[19] Yet in the 1815 Preface to his *Poetical Works,* Wordsworth approvingly cites *Night Thoughts* and Cowper's *The Task* as 'excellent examples' of 'a composite order' of poetry that combines descriptive, didactic, and philosophically satirical elements.[20] Abrams explains that the Romantic idea of didacticism (as opposed to the Augustan) directly *makes* us better people instead of merely *telling* us to be better, but Abrams seems to redefine didacticism rather than differentiate two types.[21] Twentieth-century critics almost unanimously describe overt didacticism as an eighteenth-century quality.

'Poetic sincerity', on the other hand, is aligned with our conception of Romanticism. Although Leon Guilhamet defends Young's poetic sincerity in *Night Thoughts,* he eventually concludes that Wordsworth writes the 'first truly "sincere"' poetry.[22] Abrams tells us that the Romantics believed sincerity 'the primary criterion, if not the *sine qua non,* of excellence in poetry'.[23] Influenced by such critics as Abrams, our present view of Romanticism maintains that poetry results from the expression of honest emotion. We encounter problems, however, if we use sincerity to distinguish Romanticism from Augustanism. Pratt values Young's sincerity, and Croft feels he must defend Young from critics who insist on continuity between life and art—both evaluated *Night Thoughts* for an eighteenth-century audience. Our current concepts of periodization encourage us to see this criterion as indicative of 'preromanticism'.

When we consider Pratt's concern with Young's versification, we return to traditional Augustan territory. Twentieth-century critics explain that eighteenth-century poets and critics were much more strictly bound by classical genres and their rules and that the nineteenth century is a welcome release from these rules.[24] Norman Maclean differentiates the two periods by saying that 'the principles which had long served to divide poetry into kinds and to arrange them in a hierarchy . . . were not first principles to the Romantics. By the principles fundamental to the Romantics, poetry in the highest sense was one as the soul is'.[25] Saintsbury describes the rules presented in Edward Bysshe's *Art of English Poetry* (1702) as 'base and mechanical', yet tells us that the book 'expressed the actual poetic practice of serious poets from Pope to Goldsmith: and it expressed the deliberate theoretic creed of such a critic as Johnson'.[26] Saintsbury's characterization of what he called '18th century orthodoxy' and the definitions of 'Augustan' and 'Romantic' reinforced by such an influential scholar's comments on versification do not allow for such inconsistencies as Johnson's approval of a poet's occasional 'wild diffusion' and 'digressive sallies'. Yet Stuart Curran has recently felt obliged to argue that, for Romanticism, 'form, rather than being generally dismissed in the period, is a significant key to its character'.[27] Twentieth-century critics have underestimated the Romantic poets' passionate interest in the line and the shape of verse.

More perplexing are the criteria associated with Young's 'excess'. Is this, in our twentieth-century view, a typically Augustan or Romantic basis for judgment? We many want to claim economy as a universal criterion of poetic excellence—until we remember such poets as Whitman and realize that each era defines its own idea of excess. The criticisms on the excesses of *Night Thoughts* hint at another recognized Augustan/Romantic distinction, that between control and spontaneity. Yet Young's excesses often occur in qualities that the eighteenth century supposedly valued: antithesis, point, wit.[28] As we will see in the next section, nineteenth-century writers appreciated Young's excesses as little as their eighteenth-century counterparts had.

When we attribute certain criteria to particular periods, we face three possibilities: our choices may coincide with contemporary evaluations (as we see in the didacticism criterion); our choices may introduce a distorted sense of history (such as the criteria of authorial sincerity and versification); or our choices may have few or no correspondences to the actual strengths and weaknesses of the poets writing during that time (as in the case of Young's 'excess'). Although we could think of Young's 'excess' as merely the major fault of a minor poet and that therefore the criteria used to judge him are unimportant, I would argue instead that the consideration of his 'excess' does not follow his twentieth-century status as a minor poet but precedes it: 'excess'

is not a criterion crucial to our Augustan/Romantic differentiation, and thus scholars cannot comfortably situate Young in either category. Eric Rothstein has suggested that 'the most serious flaws in eighteenth-century poetry are likely to lie precisely where the generality of critics have been least inclined to look for them: in too little craftmanship and logic, in too much sublime ambition and free-flapping imagination'.[29] Any poet whose main limitation or strength lies in an area that does not correspond to the criteria used for evaluation will probably be ejected from serious consideration as a 'major' poet. This is the fate of any poet who has been relegated to the status of 'popular', from Young to Walter Scott to Felicia Hemans.

Whether these differentiations actually exist is irrelevant once the taxonomy begins to enforce them, conferring value on those poets whose work conforms to all of the current nexuses of aesthetic evaluation and denying value to those poets, like Young, whose work does not match up. Other variables also enter the equation: the late twentieth century's opinions of 'excess' may have more to do with New Critical standards than with the Augustan / Romantic split. New Criticism simply does not value the repetitiveness and effusion of poetry like Young's; 'unity' is difficult to find in such a long serialized poem; and Young's verse strongly resists close reading. New Critics can study Pope's work because it displays the requisite qualities for their type of examination.[30] Young, however, has all the mechanisms of literary history and evaluation working against him.

II Nineteenth-Century Evaluations of Eighteenth-Century Poetry

Misrepresentation of evaluation through literary taxonomy occurs for the nineteenth century as well as the eighteenth. Although often cited as 'preromantic', Young's poetry fits as uncomfortably with the evaluative schemes of the nineteenth century as it did with those of the previous century, not because of the evaluations themselves, but because of the ways later readers have chosen to interpret those evaluations. I am not arguing that standards of poetic value did not change: undoubtedly they did. But as Upali Amarasinghe reminds us, the nineteenth-century 'revolution' against earlier poets was much more complex, much more gradual, and much less widespread than most critics have assumed.[31] To explain how twentieth-century taxonomy misconstrues nineteenth-century views, I first must sketch the major criteria by which other eighteenth-century poets were judged in the nineteenth century and then compare them to the criteria used to judge Young.

The famous 'Pope controversy' reveals the criteria by which some writers chose to distance themselves from the aesthetic values of the previous century. The most frequent charge against Pope's poetics was that of

French influence; James Chandler has argued that this fundamental criticism resulted from early nineteenth-century British nationalism.[32] Pope's nineteenth-century detractors claimed that the French influence of strict versification and rhyme encouraged artificiality in English poetry. Wordsworth, for example, expresses his displeasure with the epitaphs collected in *Elegant Extracts:* 'there is scarcely one [epitaph] which is not thoroughly tainted by the artifices which have overrun our writings in metre since the days of Dryden and Pope'.[33] Less irritably, Coleridge described the poets of the previous century as primarily a 'school of French poetry, condensed and invigorated by English understanding'.[34] This 'French influence' of artificiality caused poets to write only of the surface of life, indulging in decorative 'wit' instead of true poetical feeling. Editors and critics of eighteenth-century poets, such as Joseph Warton (editor of Pope's works in 1797), deplored the poets' love of 'wit' instead of the 'pathetic' or the 'sublime'.[35]

Warton's comments emphasize the importance of appropriate subject matter to some nineteenth-century writers. Satire and irony were too harsh for 'pure' poetry; Pope's satires displayed too much wit at the expense of feeling. Urban and political subjects were denigrated to make room for poems on nature—the former subjects often, again, attributed to French influence. W. L. Bowles's edition of Pope in 1806 extended Warton's critique in *Essay on the Genius and Writings of Pope* (1756, 1782), condemning Pope's work to a secondary order of poetry mainly because of its subject matter: fashionable, 'artificial' life. Speculations on subject matter often led to judgments of the poet's moral character, as indeed happened with Pope in the nineteenth century. Bowles was particularly scandalized by Pope's attachments to Martha and Teresa Blount and called their correspondence 'indecent, and sometimes *profane*'.[36]

This brief survey of Pope's nineteenth-century reputation thus presents one array of criteria by which eighteenth-century poets were judged. But choosing Pope as our sole representative distorts the dynamics of literary change: nineteenth-century writers did not judge all poets by the same standards. Looking at evaluations of Young's poetry during the same period gives us a different version of how this period distinguished itself from its past. Criticisms of Young's satires yield a set of evaluative criteria similar to what we have seen with Pope. But to the degree that Young's *Night Thoughts* differed from his satires (and therefore Pope's verse), the criteria shift. Some of the terms by which Young was judged are familiar; for instance, Coleridge thought that 'Young . . . was not a poet to be read through at once. His love of point and wit had often put an end to his pathos and sublimity; but there were parts in him which must be immortal'.[37] Coleridge regrets the lack of 'pathos and sublimity' and indul-

gence in wit—both points used to condemn Pope—but he finds other parts of Young's poem 'immortal'. Since Coleridge also describes taking long walks pondering Young's verse, we may deduce that he found depths in Young that most 'Romantics' did not find in other eighteenth-century poets.

The blank verse of *Night Thoughts* exempted Young from the charges of French versification. Yet his lines came under attack for different reasons. Nathan Drake, in *Essays, Biographical, Critical, and Historical, Illustrative of the Tatler, Spectator, and Guardian* (1805), complained

> [t]he versification is, with few exceptions, totally devoid of that variety of pause, that richness and continuity of melody, which give to blank verse its characteristic charms, its depth, its energy and force. For pages together, there is frequently more monotony in the construction of the lines of Young, than in any specimens of the rhymed couplet. Yet his verses are, it cannot be denied, for the most part, sparkling and sententious, but at the same time insufferably loaded with antithesis and point.[38]

Young's blank verse is thus even *worse* than the French-influenced couplet. However, Drake's demands for variety of line and rhythm arise from the same dissatisfaction other nineteenth-century critics found in the repetitive couplet.

Drake's comments on antithesis and point amplify Coleridge's criticism of Young's wit. In his 1819 *Specimens of the British Poets*, Thomas Campbell repeats Drake's judgment: the beauty of *Night Thoughts* 'is thickly marred by false wit and overlaboured antithesis: indeed his whole ideas seem to have been in a state of antithesis while he composed the poem'.[39] These criticisms overlap with criticisms of Pope by their emphasis on wit, an extension of French artificiality (French influence, however, is never mentioned in reference to Young). Yet Young's critics complain not that Young included or used wit—although some late eighteenth-century critics disapproved of it—but that he *overused* it: once again, we return to the criterion of 'excess', but this time shifted to a different aspect of his poetry.[40] Percival Stockdale believed that Young 'is apt to prolong a forcible, and shining thought, to its debility, and its death; by an Ovidian redundance, and puerility' and bemoaned Young's fustian.[41] In 1830, the Rev. John Mitford praises in *Night Thoughts* a 'fertility of thought and luxuriance of imagination, an originality in the style, an expansion of sentiment, and an accumulation of argument and illustration, which seems almost boundless', but at the same time cites this effusiveness as a fault: 'every image is amplified to the utmost; every argument expanded and varied, as much as the greatest fertility of the fancy could effect . . . There is no selection, no discreet and graceful reservation'.[42] Judging by the frequency with which this complaint arises, we may deduce that Young's extravagance contributed much to the demise of his reputation.

Another familiar criterion appears in criticism of Young that does not appear in contemporary discussions of Pope, the question of poetic sincerity. Drake and Campbell charge Young with false wit; Campbell accuses him of false sublimity. These critiques differ from accusations of Augustan 'artificiality' in that Young's critics attribute to Young an active willingness to deceive, a charge that proved fatal in 1857 when George Eliot condemned him for 'radical insincerity' as a poet. She asserted that Young contemplated his own ego in place of external beauty or eternal truth. Like other nineteenth-century critics, Eliot disapproved of the poetic license by which Young compressed deaths occurring over three years to the period of three months for the purposes of his poem. Her disgust was further exacerbated by his constant attempts to attain preferment at court—behavior at odds with the pious resignation counseled in *Night Thoughts*.[43]

Eliot's diatribe was the last in a series of skeptical readings. Even the sincerity of the melancholy expressed in *Night Thoughts* had received cautious scrutiny: Drake states that '[t]he general tenor of the Night Thoughts is so dark and querulous, so evidently the result of morbid melancholy, that I much question whether any person has been benefited by their perusal'.[44] While Drake does not doubt Young's melancholy, Campbell complains that 'the melancholy and wit of Young do not make up to us the idea of a conceivable or natural being'.[45] In 1837, S. C. Hall writes in his collection of verse, *The Book of Gems,* that:

> [i]n also admitting that in his Night Thoughts are to be found numerous passages of lofty and sustained reflection, it should be added that that work, neither in plan nor in execution, deserves the reputation it has acquired. It was not worthy of Young, after the life he had lived, to sit down near its close in a fit of resentful melancholy, and strive to terrify the world with the bugbears of religious horror. This is surely not what a true poet would have done, whose duty and whose pride it is to make poetry shed light and life upon man, not darkness and death . . . [46]

Hall's critique also responds to the didactic elements of Young's poem, belittling Young's teaching as needlessly terrifying people with 'bugbears'.

Early nineteenth-century criticism of Young both differed from and resembled concurrent criticism of Pope. Young's status in the twentieth century, to which we now turn, primarily results from how later readers extended and consolidated these two overlapping sets of criteria.

III. *Taxonomic Pressure and Young's Twentieth-Century Status*

While changing tastes in poetry contributed to the decline in Young's reputation, how we have *interpreted* those changes through our taxonomy has had much more impact. Because Pope was the greatest of eighteenth-century poets (so recognized by most nineteenth-century critics), he became the representative of all poetry of the previous century—poetry against which the nineteenth century reacted. By seeing him as the poet most different from themselves, nineteenth-century writers defined themselves against him. Later critics then saw this definition as indicative of the qualities which separate Augustan from Romantic. Since nineteenth-century critics approached Young's poetry differently than they did Pope's, this system of definition affects evaluation of Young's work differently.

As we have seen, the poetry of Young and Pope is criticized for inappropriate wit and problematic versification, but only Young is blamed for emotional effusion and excess and a lack of sincerity in his sublimity and his melancholy. Twentieth-century critics often identify the presence of those qualities as peculiar to Romanticism: the poet overcome and transported by his verse, the indulgence in melancholic musings. Not surprisingly, critics cite these qualities when describing the 'preromanticism' of Young's work.[47] Paul Van Tieghem, for instance, comments on Young's 'accents mélancholiques': 'C'est surtout par cet aspect que Young est préromantique'. He also claims that Young 'marche en tête du long cortège des poètes romantiques, amants de la Nuit et de la Lune'.[48] The focus on the self, condemned by Eliot as insensitive egotism, is for Van Tieghem also evidence of Young's Romanticism.[49]

Although more recent critics such as John Sitter, Howard Weinbrot, and Morse Peckham have discredited the term 'preromanticism', the desire to see Young and other eighteenth-century poets as aspiring to the particular genius of Wordsworth dies hard.[50] Even Forster champions the Romantic qualities of *Night Thoughts:* 'These were not the calm reflections of a philosophical Augustan but the agonized search for comfort of a suffering soul . . . It is the essence of romanticism to look inward and expose one's heart—and preferably a bleeding heart'. For Forster, Young is 'a precursor of the Romantic revolution'.[51] We can see the same urge to classify in recent critical dialogue on Gray, Collins, and Crabbe in the 1970s and 1980s as scholars debate whether these poets are Augustan or Romantic, both or neither. Patricia Meyer Spacks has helpfully called our attention to the historical distortions caused by scholars' efforts to claim Collins for Romanticism: 'The criticism that glorifies such writing for its intimations of a new sensibility—minimizing its incoherence and constantly deflected purpose, or attributing them to the bad influence of eighteenth-century rationality—ignores

Collins's occasional true, modest achievement'.[52] The same literary history machine operates on Young with one difference: Young is not so easily squeezed into the Romantic mold; therefore he has been more easily excluded from the critical canon. Of all the later eighteenth-century poets, Young is actually probably the least 'preromantic', if we judge by the more heated arguments continuing in the studies of other poets. This relative lack of 'preromanticism' hinders rather than helps his reputation: since his poetry does not lead toward Romanticism as directly as others' poetry, we have less reason to value him and more reason to ignore him.[53]

Why the appeal of taxonomic labels such as 'Augustan' and 'Romantic'? For one thing, they make literary history more manageable by reducing complex changes to mere oppositions. As Frank Kermode has explained, 'The naming of a period . . . always entails the construction of such a myth, which simplifies history and makes valuation of the work of one period easier by devaluing another period (usually the one that comes immediately before)'.[54] By focussing on differences between two small 'representative' groups of poets, as we do with Pope and the Romantics, we automatically demote those poets like Young who have similarities with both groups. Categories that emphasize sameness, such as preromantic (and, less harmfully, post-Augustan), introduce historical distortion of their own, as Sitter and others have noted.[55] 'Transitional' does not depend on the names of these major periods, yet it still stresses poets' distance from the two main groups; these poets are merely ports of call on the way to the final destination. Using with caution or even eliminating terms such as 'Augustan', as revisionists suggest, may help us in future work; however, the exclusion encouraged by our labels has already occurred.

Young's case is especially interesting because he slips into obscurity through two different matrixes. The first is the changing criteria of poetic evaluation, from the eighteenth to the nineteenth century: he simply went out of style. Yet neither Pope nor Swift met the same fate, although their poetry also became unfashionable. As nineteenth-century writers distanced themselves from earlier poetry, their views in turn engendered the familiar Augustan/Romantic labels that have since undergone considerable change in definition but have lost none of their taxonomic force. The second matrix, then, is our modern notion of the Augustan/Romantic split. Born from real historical forces, these labels have changed from descriptive to prescriptive nomenclature. Instead of merely locating what Jurij Tynjanov and then Roman Jakobson called the 'dominant' of each period's aesthetic value, they instead *confer* aesthetic value. Young is neither an Augustan nor a Romantic because neither the eighteenth nor the nineteenth-century evaluations of *Night Thoughts* correspond to what we now identify as Augustan or Romantic. Our view of

the nineteenth-century's reluctance to consider Young's work as similar to Pope's testifies to their critical acumen and yet makes ambiguous Young's stance in relation to these two periods.

In sum, if we do not have a label for a poet's work, the poet is immediately liable to suspicion and dismissal from the canon. The ways in which modern scholars try to re-fashion Young and others into Romantics reveal the importance of these labels to a poet's reputation. We attempt to link his poetry to that which we do appreciate, Romanticism. In some cases this strategy is successful: by enforcing Blake's similarities with other Romantics, modern scholars have helped make him a 'major' Romantic poet. But since we do not have an aesthetic code now that can appreciate *Night Thoughts* as it is, we can only see his poetry as what it is not. Through the pressure of periodization on literary evaluations of the past, Young thus remains a minor poet.

Notes

[1] Sherburn, *The Restoration and Eighteenth Century (1660-1789)*, vol. 3 of *A Literary History of England*, ed. Albert C. Baugh (New York, 1948), 945; Piper, *The Heroic Couplet* (Cleveland, 1969), 368; Rothstein, *Restoration and Eighteenth-Century Poetry 1660-1780* (Boston, 1981), 144; Fussell, *The Rhetorical World of Augustan Humanism* (Oxford, 1965), 285.

[2] Pettit, 'The English Rejection of Young's *Night Thoughts*', *University of Colorado Studies, Series in Language and Literature* 6 (1957): 23-38; Forster, *Edward Young, The Poet of the Night Thoughts, 1683-1765* (Alburgh, 1986).

[3] 'Canon of Generations, Generation of Canons', *Modern Language Studies* 18 (1988): 38-46.

[4] The terms 'Augustan' and 'neo-classic' are sometimes differentiated, sometimes used interchangeably. James William Johnson in *The Formation of English Neo-Classical Thought* (Princeton, 1967) provides a useful discussion of both. M. H. Abrams's definition of 'Augustan Age' in his *A Glossary of Literary Terms* (5th ed.; New York, 1988) quickly directs the reader to an extended discussion between 'Neoclassic and Romantic', implying an equivalence between the two eighteenth-century labels. I choose to conduct my discussion in terms of 'Augustanism' because, chronologically, this label seems to correspond better to Young's lifespan. However, I hope that my argument points out the difficulty of using any period label innocently.

[5] For alternatives to the period definitions perpetuated by Ralph Cohen, M. H. Abrams, and others, see Bronson's 'When Was Neoclassicism?' in *Studies in Criticism and Aesthetics, 1660-1800*, ed. Howard Anderson and John S. Shea (Minneapolis, 1967): 13-35;

Weinbrot's *Augustus Caesar in 'Augustan' England* (Princeton, 1978); and Butler's *Romantics, Rebels, and Reactionaries: English Literature and its Background, 1760-1830* (New York, 1981).

[6] W. Thomas, *Le Poète Edward Young* (Paris, 1901).

[7] (London, 1776; repr., New York, 1970). This work (and others by Pratt) was published under the pseudonym 'Courtney Melmoth'.

[8] Boswell, *Boswell's Life of Johnson,* ed. George Birkbeck Hill; rev. ed. L. F. Powell, 6 vols. (Oxford, 1934-1950), 4: 60, Goldsmith, 'Memoirs of M. de Voltaire', *Collected Works of Oliver Goldsmith,* ed. Arthur Friedman, 5 vols. (Oxford, 1966), 3: 253. Pratt, 50. Croft, 'Life of Young', *Lives of the English Poets,* Samuel Johnson, ed. George Birkbeck Hill, 3 vols. (1905; repr. New York, 1967), 3: 384.

[9] Pratt, 7, 4-5.

[10] Boswell, 4: 61.

[11] Pratt, 131.

[12] *The Court Magazine* (December 1761): 168.

[13] 'Life of Young', 379.

[14] Pratt, 80, 22.

[15] 'Life of Young', 399, 395.

[16] Hagstrum, *Samuel Johnson's Literary Criticism* (1952; repr. Chicago, 1967), 103, 193. Hagstrum is very sensitive to the problems of taxonomy in relation to Johnson: 'to attempt to determine the ingredients in the Johnsonian mixture of the classical and the romantic is, it seems to me, an impossible task, chiefly because the terms have not been and perhaps can never be satisfactorily defined and because no great writer of the Age of Reason can be pressed into those molds' (xvi).

[17] Pratt, 10, 46. 'Life of Young', 396. Forster, 200. Pratt, 37-8, 25. Warton, *An Essay on the Genius and Writings of Pope,* vol. 2 (1782; repr., New York, 1970), 149.

[18] From the preface to *Prometheus Unbound,* in *The Complete Poetical Works of Shelley,* ed. Thomas Hutchinson (London, 1967), 207.

[19] Dobrée, *English Literature in the Early Eighteenth Century, 1700-1740* (Oxford, 1959), 146; Sherburn, 1006; Butt, *The Mid-Eighteenth Century,* ed. Geoffrey Carnall (Oxford, 1979), 65.

[20] *The Prose Works of William Wordsworth,* ed. W. J. B. Owen and Jane Worthington Smyser, 3 vols. (Oxford, 1974), 3: 28.

[21] Abrams, *The Mirror and the Lamp* (New York, 1953), 329-30.

[22] *The Sincere Ideal: Studies on Sincerity in Eighteenth-Century English Literature* (Montreal and London, 1974), 187, 277.

[23] Abrams, *Mirror and Lamp,* 318.

[24] For a more detailed scholarly analysis of the differences in versification between the two periods, see Paul Fussell's *Theory of Prosody in Eighteenth-Century England* (New London, 1954).

[25] 'From Action to Image: Theories of the Lyric in the Eighteenth Century', *Critics and Criticism,* ed. R. S. Crane (Chicago, 1952), 459.

[26] *A History of Criticism and Literary Taste in Europe,* 3 vols. (1900-04; repr. London, 1949), 2: 428, 429.

[27] *Poetic Form and British Romanticism* (New York, 1986), vii.

[28] Allan Rodway is tempted to classify excess as a Romantic characteristic, yet must admit that 'there are different degrees of excess in different periods, and different kinds of excess in different places and peoples'. *The Romantic Conflict* (London, 1963), 6.

[29] *Restoration and Eighteenth-Century Poetry,* 144.

[30] Cleanth Brooks uses *The Rape of the Lock* as one of his seminal close readings in *The Well-Wrought Urn* (New York, 1947), 80-104.

[31] The information in the following section on the Pope controversy depends heavily on Amarasinghe's helpful book, *Dryden and Pope in the Early Nineteenth Century* (Cambridge, 1962). See also James Chandler's 'The Pope Controversy: Romantic Poetics and the English Canon', *Critical Inquiry* 10 (1984): 481-509.

[32] Chandler, 486-87.

[33] 'Essay upon Epitaphs III', *Prose Works,* 2: 84.

[34] *Biographia Literaria,* ed. James Engell and Walter Jackson Bate (Princeton, 1983), 1: 18.

[35] Amarasinghe, 42-3.

[36] *The Works of Alexander Pope, Esq.* 10 vols. (London, 1806), 1: cxxix.

[37] *The Table Talk and Omniana of Samuel Taylor Coleridge,* ed. T. Ashe (London, 1903), 297.

[38] 3 vols. (London, 1805), 3: 257-58.

[39] 7 vols. (London, 1819) 6: 44.

[40] For an example of eighteenth-century disapproval of Young's wit see the *Annual Register* for 1765 (London, 1766), 35.

[41] *Lectures on the Truly Eminent English Poets,* 2 vols. (London, 1807), 1: 545-6.

[42] *The Poetical Works of Edward Young,* ed. Rev. J. Mitford (London, [1830]), xxxvii, xxxvi-viii.

[43] 'Worldliness and Otherworldliness: The Poet Young', *Westminster Review* 67 (January 1857): 1-23.

[44] Drake, 3: 257.

[45] Campbell, 7: 352.

[46] 3 vols. (London, 1837), II: 42.

[47] Other scholars, most prominently Thomas McFarland (*Originality and Imagination,* Baltimore, 1985, page 5) and Abrams (*The Mirror and the Lamp*) consider Young's *Conjectures on Original Composition* as a milestone of preromanticism. Abrams states that 'In England the high-water mark of the worship of uniqueness and originality had come and passed with Young's *Conjectures'* (114). However, this essay had little admitted influence on later poets: in my reading of the poetry and prose of the early nineteenth century, I have encountered no mention of *Conjectures.* Sherburn also states that the essay does not mark the 'revolution in criticism' often attributed to it (945). Therefore, I will not deal with the 'preromanticism' of Young's essay in my argument.

[48] Van Tieghem, *Le Préromantisme,* vol. 2 (Paris, 1929), 36, 36, 29. Other scholars who classify Young as a preromantic include H. H. Clark in 'The Romanticism of Young', *Transcripts of the Wisconsin Academy* 24 (1929): 45-63; C. V. Wicker in *Edward Young and the Fear of Death: A Study in Romantic Melancholy* (Albuquerque, 1952); and Anne Williams, *Prophetic Strain* (Chicago, 1984).

[49] Eleanor M. Sickels in *The Gloomy Egoist: Moods and Themes of Melancholy form Gray to Keats* (New York, 1932) also recognizes Young's egotism as a 'harbinger of romanticism' although she qualifies her statement by also attributing it to Christianity's emphasis on individual salvation (30).

[50] See Sitter, *Literary Loneliness in Mid-Eighteenth-Century England* (Ithaca, 1982), 79; Weinbrot, 241.

[Peckham] states bluntly, 'I would recommend the total abandonment of the term "preromantic"' in 'Toward a Theory of Romanticism', *PMLA* 66 (1951): 21.

[51] Forster, 180, 386.

[52] 'The Eighteenth-Century Collins', *Modern Language Quarterly* 44 (1983): 22.

[53] Significantly, of the traditionally 'preromantic' poets, Gray, Cowper, Thomson, Collins, Smart, and Crabbe all have Oxford standard editions, but Young and Shenstone do not.

[54] *History and Value* (Oxford, 1988), 143.

[55] See also Margaret Anne Doody's *The Daring Muse* (Cambridge, 1985), 2-3; Rothstein's *Restoration and Eighteenth-Century Poetry,* xi.

Marshall Brown (essay date 1991)

SOURCE: "The Direction of Young's Thoughts," in *Preromanticism,* Stanford University Press, 1991, pp. 34-9.

[*In the following excerpt from his study of Preromanticism, Brown gives an overview of Young, focusing on his* Night Thoughts *and locating him in the literary tradition.*]

. . . Nowhere is the musing character of eighteenth-century consciousness more apparent than in Young's **Night Thoughts.** Young gives us, consequently, the best occasion for considering the direction and purpose of an apparently aimless meander. Though few today would dare to call this poem "captivating," as Percival Stockdale did early in the nineteenth century (*Lectures* 1: 587), and though Young's writing is relatively free from conventional poetic diction, it would be a mistake to overlook his urbanity. The poem is not a silent meditation, but rather a long monologue addressed to a reprobate named Lorenzo, and Young is careful to vary the pacing, to lighten the tone with ironic sallies, and to intersperse frequent parenthetical asides and self-references, all so as to preserve a conversational feeling. While the poem's theme is the correction of the individual, its standards are social, and its very discursiveness is seen as the best weapon against false pride:

> In *Contemplation* is his proud Resource?
> 'Tis poor, as proud, by *Converse* unsustain'd;
> Rude Thought runs wild in *Contemplation*'s Field;
> *Converse,* the Menage, breaks it to the Bit
> Of due Restraint; and *Emulation*'s Spur
> Gives graceful Energy, by Rivals aw'd
> 'Tis Converse qualifies for Solitude.
>
> (2.488-94)

The rhetoric is informal and completely nonperiodic; the current of thought never stops, but only ebbs and flows as each sentence funnels into a successor of greater or lesser intensity. The view of life is Heraclitean—"Life glides away, *Lorenzo!* Like a Brook; / For ever changing, unperceiv'd the Change" (5.401-2)—and the poem's utter formlessness mirrors this view of life. Wherever it is opened—and some early editions are indexed to facilitate browsing—the reader enters into the middle of an elevated, consoling conversation.

This very formlessness, so hard to appreciate today, was one source of the poem's charm in its own day. The great enemy, the great divide, as Young often says, was death, and by avoiding any divisions or articulations the final reckoning could be postponed indefinitely. It is fitting that the longest night by far is called "The Consolation," for length, expansiveness, and infinite repetition constitute the best anodyne against the fear of death:

> Dost ask *Lorenzo,* why so warmly prest,
> By Repetition hammer'd on thine Ear,
> The Thought of Death? . . .
> . . . That Thought ply'd Home,
> Will soon reduce the ghastly *Precipice*
> O'er hanging Hell, will soften the Descent,
> And gently slope our Passage to the Grave.
>
> (5.682-89)

Everything described in the poem turns out to be gentle, nothing abrupt; everything is intermediate, nothing absolute; everything is in flux, nothing fixed. "The World's no Neuter," says Young (8.376), and he means that there is no impartial, unchanging standard of reference. All things are value-laden, and all values are relative and variable. The poem's theodicy is based not on rational persuasion, but rather on making the reader conscious of the eternal variability of life. Young's most common strategy is easy to paraphrase: things may look bad, but they might be worse, and worse, and worse, and so they come to seem, by contrast, better, and better, and better. The only absolute is that the value of things must be determined by our consciousness of them:

> WORTH, conscious Worth! should *absolutely*
>   reign;
> And other Joys ask Leave for their Approach;
> Nor, unexamin'd, ever Leave obtain.
>
> (8.978-80)

The aim of *Night Thoughts* is to examine our feelings and to make us conscious of the variability and relativity of values. But to the eighteenth-century mind this is a tautology: all consciousness is consciousness of relative value. Thus Young writes, "So grieve, as conscious, Grief may rise to Joy; / So joy, as conscious, Joy to Grief may fall" (8.763-64). One might therefore just as well say the aim of *Night Thoughts* is, simply and absolutely, to make us conscious. This is what I meant when I said that the urbane sublime imitated the musing course of thought. In its deliberate ebb and flow, in its indeterminacy, in its hierarchic tendency, in its heightening of experience, the urbane sublime expresses the very form of eighteenth-century consciousness.[31]

In his *Augustan Poetic Diction,* Geoffrey Tillotson points out that the word "conscious" was never ethically neutral in eighteenth-century usage, but always positively or negatively charged (77). One spoke of "conscious pride," "conscious shame," "conscious sin," "conscious virtue." Thus Steele writes, "every Thought is attended with Consciousness and Representativeness; the Mind has nothing presented to it, but what is immediately followed by a Reflection or Conscience, which tells you whether that which was so presented is graceful or unbecoming" (*Spectator,* no. 38; I: 160). For Steele, it must be added, there is also the possibility of excess self-consciousness, which he terms "Affectation." For the sublime poets, on the other hand, consciousness is all: "Is *Conscience,* then, / No Part of Nature? Is she not *Supreme?*" (*Night Thoughts* 8.841-42). The urbane sublime style is intended to interest and affect the reader, to heighten his moral sensibilities, in sum, to correct and educate his "brute unconscious gaze" (Thomson, "A Hymn on the Seasons," line 28).

In the eighteenth century consciousness is hardly to be distinguished from intuition, knowledge from faith; even Hume, though he exposed this state of affairs to view, despaired of changing it. We do not find the grand oppositions of romantic dialectic—spirit against matter, general against particular, eternal against temporal—and the poetry can only seem incoherent if we look for them. Instead there is nuanced gradation, slow accumulation, and constant flux. At times, *Night Thoughts* can seem almost Wordsworthian (it is even quoted in "Tintern Abbey"), but it lacks Wordsworth's stoppings and reversals, his overflowings, submergings of consciousness and restorations, in short the dialectical intensity of the Wordsworthian sublime. Indeed, Young's poem, though less discreet and therefore less intriguing than Gray's Eton College ode, is a particularly valuable witness because it so clearly reveals the presuppositions of the age. Death, for instance, is not the annihilation of life, but its culminating stage: "Our Birth is nothing but our Death begun" (5.719). Immortality is not the opposite of mortal life, nor even simply its perpetuation; it is an intensification, "the Crown of Life" (3.526): "It is but Life / In stronger Thread of brighter Colour spun, / And spun for ever" (6.77-79). Death does not terminate our consciousness but elevates it:

> In Life embark'd, we smoothly down the Tide
> On *Time* descend, but not on *Time* intent;

Amus'd, unconscious of the gliding Wave;
Till on a sudden we perceive a Shock;
We start, awake, look out; what see we there?
Our brittle Bark is burst on *Charon's* Shore.

(5.411-16)

This last quotation, to be sure, forces a distinction, but it is a distinction that the poem has already clarified. Death is a shock. But it is only a shock to the "brute unconscious gaze" of the natural savage. It is not a shock to those who have been educated in their lifetime to a conscious, rational faith:

Faith builds a Bridge across the Gulph of Death,
To break the Shock blind *Nature* cannot shun,
And lands Thought smoothly on the farther
  Shore.

(4.721-23)[32]

Though Young does give in cursory fashion the customary proofs of religion, he does not view reason primarily as dialectics, but rather as the ground of belief:

My Heart became the Convert of my Head;
And made that Choice, which once was but my
  Fate.
"On Argument alone my Faith is built:"
Reason pursu'd is *Faith*; and unpursu'd
Where Proof invites, 'tis Reason, then, no more.

(4.740-44)

This last theme is sounded again and again: the head and the heart are allied; thought consciously prolonged is feeling:[33]

Think you my Song, too turbulent? too warm?
Are *Passions,* then, the Pagans of the Soul?
Reason alone baptiz'd? alone *ordain'd*
To touch Things sacred? Oh for warmer still!

. . .

Passion is Reason, Transport Temper *here.*

(4.628-31, 640)

The cool and the warm, reason and passion, urbanity and sublimity are mutually self-sustaining.[34] The apparent inconsistencies of eighteenth-century poetry are not contingent facts of an unsuccessful style, but constitutive structures of a particular form of experience. Where consciousness is understood as the elevation of sensation, all things become manifest, not in themselves and not by contrast with their opposites, but by comparison with higher or lower degrees on a scale of intensities. "Nothing is great or little otherwise than by Comparison," says Swift's Gulliver (2.1; p. 87); "all judgment is comparative," says Johnson's Imlac (*Rasselas,* chap. 30, p. 80). The serious exists only in relation to the more comic, elevation of style only with reference to its potential degradation, the liberal or new only as a relaxed modality of the aristocratic or old; order and formal perfection are inseparable from freedom and formal flexibility; nature and organism are hardly distinguishable from art and mechanism; poetry and prose differ only in degree of intensity. Indeed, even dissolute scheming and divine wisdom are related "as the waining, and the waxing Moon" (*Night Thoughts* 5.352). The very lines most ridiculed by George Eliot—"More generous Sorrow while it sinks, exalts, / And conscious Virtue mitigates the Pang" (I.300-301)—find their explanation as yet another expression of this creed. Constant rising and sinking are a part of man's middle state, and consciousnessness is the force that both recognizes our instability and reconciles us to it.[35]

From this point of view even the fascination with ghosts and Muses becomes comprehensible. They are figures of conscious, that is, of heightened, perception. Young says as much, using an image that, however much it may seem to anticipate the "Ode to the West Wind," speaks for a vastly different sensibility:

Truth bids me look on Men, as *Autumn* Leaves,
And all they bleed for, as the Summer's Dust,
Driv'n by the Whirlwind, lighted by her Beams,
I widen my Horizon, gain new Powers,
See Things invisible, feel Things remote,
Am present with Futurities.

(5.336-41)

Young, like Shelley, speaks of being haunted, but it is a happy haunting that emphasizes the copresence of the spirits and declines to be "the trumpet of a prophecy":

Pale *worldly Wisdom* loses all her Charms;
In pompous Promise from her Schemes profound,
If future Fate she plans, 'tis all in Leaves
Like *Sibyl,* unsubstantial, fleeting Bliss!
At the first Blast it vanishes in Air.

(5.345-49)

The personified "Things invisible" that abound in the poetry of the century thus body forth the expanded horizon and broader perspective of the enlightened mind, as opposed to the "heedless," earthbound superstitions of Collins's hermit.[36] The spirits are the reminders of the social bond, the universal intercourse, and the comparability of all things.

Notes

. . .[31] Pope is again comparable. His form too is social even when the content is at its most personal. Neither he nor Collins could rest content with the pilgrim's heedless hum, and repeated statements in his letters show that even the retreats to the isolation of his garden had a quasi-social function, to "converse with myself." As Patey has well said, "Art and life, the public and the private, the corporate and the personal are continuous for the Popean self" ("Art and Integrity" 369). Like Young, who was taken for the author of the anonymous *Essay on Man,* Pope aimed to promote man's self-knowledge as a creature of a "middle state," in his varying relation to higher and lower spheres. Indeed, in his gloomier moods Pope could sound much like a more gifted Young, conceding that human reason is nothing more than heightened imagination and that optimism is a corollary of despair, as in the following letter to Caryll, July 13, 1714 (*Correspondence* 1: 236): "Half the things that employ our heads deserve not the name of thoughts, for they are only stronger dreams or impressions upon the imagination; our schemes of government, our systems of philosophy, our golden words of poetry, are all but so many shadow images and airy prospects, which arise to us but so much the livelier and more frequent as we are more overcast with darkness, wrapt in the night, and disturbed with the fumes of human vanity." Patey contrasts Pope with Young (as does Price, *To the Palace of Wisdom* 345-51), though conceding at one point that the difference is a matter of "degree" (377). Jackson's "Thomas Gray: "Drowning in Human Voices" criticizes dichotomized readings on the way to an interesting discussion of Gray as wayfarer: "The distinction between public and private is voided in the very fact that voice is equally and simultaneously one and the other" (371). Barrell, "The Public Figure and the Private Eye," is a sensitive probing of the diction of Collins's "Ode to Evening" in the same spirit.

³² Likewise James Hervey writes in "Meditations Among the Tombs": "How *short* the transition, from time to eternity! The partition, nothing more than the breath in our nostrils; and the transition may be made, in the twinkling of an eye" (*Meditations* 18). On the transition past death see McKillop, *Background* 22-25, and Chipka, "Stranger" 541-66.

³³ The continuity of thought and feeling is well discussed in Brissenden, *Virtue in Distress* 22-55.

³⁴ The strains on the eighteenth-century synthesis can be observed in Lowth's *Lectures* (delivered in Latin in 1741-50, published in 1753). In lecture 14, "The Sublime," Lowth says, in pointed contrast to the lines of Young just quoted, "In a word, Reason speaks literally, the Passions practically" (1: 308). Much in the *Lectures* points toward this kind of dissociated sensibility, which is linked to what Lowth calls the "sublime of language." Yet he begins by saying that Hebrew, lacking vowels, "has remained altogether silent" (lecture 3; 2: 66). There is also much in the *Lectures* that continues the "sublime of sentiment" deriving from Boileau and the more fluid sensibility of the earlier part of the century, such as the account of mixed style in lecture 26 and the flexibly classicizing formal analyses, in lectures 30-34, of the *Song of Solomon* as an epithalamium and of *Job* as an imperfect tragedy.

³⁵ This essential fluidity of eighteenth-century thought has of course not gone unnoticed—see, for instance, the parallels cited by Carnochan in *Lemuel Gulliver's Mirror for Man* 128-29—but the full consequences are rarely drawn. Thus, Brower's "Form and Defect of Form" intelligently yet, in my view, mistakenly dichotomizes eighteenth-century poetic procedures; he can be corrected by Cohen's "Association of Ideas." For a recognition of eighteenth-century relativism leading to a large-scale and penetrating attack on its numerous forms, see Bachelard, *Formation.* On the relation of art and nature see Battestin's excellent essays on eighteenth-century pastoral, in *The Providence of Wit,* chaps. 2 and 4; one might also cite lines like Parnell's "And all the Nature, all the Art, of Love" ("Hesiod: Or the Rise of Woman," line 56), as well as the same poem's reference to "native Tropes" (line 62), a characteristically fluid notion that would only involve a problematical dialectic if found in an author later than Rousseau. On the admittedly vexed question of the "poetry of statement," Hume's opinion in "Of the Standard of Taste" needs to be considered: "Every kind of composition, even the most poetical, is nothing but a chain of propositions and reasonings; not always, indeed, the justest and most exact, but still plausible and specious, however disguised by the colouring of the imagination" (*Essays* 240).

³⁶ Siskin, *Historicity* 68-77, is an excellent discussion of how personification in eighteenth-century poetry "helps to figure both the sense of a universal human community, whose uniformity is the basis for all communication, and the sense of a select literary community that is grafted upon it" (71). The ensuing account of Wordsworth's attack on personification (77-84) is one-sided; see my discussion of the topic in Chap. 12 below, "Wordsworth's Old Gray Stone." Maclean, "Personification but Not Poetry," argues that personification fails in its aim of evoking pure imagination and that in eighteenth-century poems horizontal description often stands in for imaginative elevation. The diagnosis is true for the most part, but the essay does not address the question of what effect the personifications then do have in practice. It should be juxtaposed to Davie's claim in "Personification" for an innate tendency of language to tap natural energies.

FURTHER READING

Biography

Forster, Harold. *Edward Young: The Poet of the Night Thoughts 1683-1765.* Alburgh, England: The Erskine Press, 1986, 434 p.

Recent biographical study of Young, drawing on the extensive correspondence of Young first published in 1971.

Criticism

Abrams, M. H. *The Mirror and the Lamp: Romantic Theory and the Critical Tradition.* New York: Oxford University Press, 1953, 406 p.

A classic overview study of the Romantic critical tradition in the nineteenth century. It includes a discussion of natural genius and Young's *Conjectures on Original Composition.*

Bliss, Isabel St. John. "Young's *Night Thoughts* in Relation to Contemporary Christian Apologetics." *PMLA* XLIX, No. 1 (March 1934): 37-70.

Analysis of Young's major work in the context of eighteenth-century discussions of Christian apologetics.

Clark, Harry Hayden. "The Romanticism of Edward Young." *Transactions of the Wisconsin Academy of Sciences, Arts, and Letters* XXIV (1929): 1-46.

Describes and analyzes Young's relationship to the Romantic movement and argues that Young can be considered an early Romantic poet.

McKillop, Alan D. "Richardson, Young, and the *Conjectures.*" *Modern Philology* XXII, No. 4 (May 1925): 391-404.

Discussion of the correspondence between Young and Samuel Richardson during Young's writing of *Conjectures on Original Composition.* McKillop chronicles the exchange and finds evidence that Richardson had a significant influence on the shape of the work.

Nussbaum, Felicity A. "Enemies and Enviers: Minor Eigh-teenth-Century Satires." In *The Brink of All We Hate: English Satires on Women, 1660-1750,* pp. 117-36. Lexington: University Press of Kentucky, 1984.

Discusses Young's satires on women in *Love of Fame; or The Universal Passion,* placing them in relation to other satires in the literary tradition.

Odell, Daniel W. "Young's *Night Thoughts* as an Answer to Pope's *Essay on Man.*" *Studies in English Literature 1500-1900* XII, No. 3 (Summer 1972): 481-501.

Contrasts Young's conception of man's place in the divine plan with that of Alexander Pope in his *Essay on Man.*

Parker, Gerald D. "The Moor's Progress: A Study of Edward Young's Tragedy, *The Revenge.*" *Theatre Research International* VI, No. 3 (Autumn 1981): 172-95.

Traces the theatrical history of the character of Zanga and of the basic plot of *The Revenge,* then compares Young's treatment of plot and character with that of several other playwrights, including William Shakespeare.

Phillips, Patricia. "Richardson, Young, and the *Conjectures*; Another Interpretation." *Studia Neophilologica* LIII, No. 1 (1981): 107-12.

Recent refutation of Alan McKillop's claims about Richardson's influence on Young's *Conjectures on Original Composition* (see above). Drawing on Young's complete correspondence, Phillips reveals a more complex genesis of the essay.

Roberts, J. Graeme. "Political Satire in Young's *The Brothers.*" *English Studies* 58, No. 4 (August 1977): 319-23.

Theorizes that Young's drama *The Brothers* contains pointed political satire aimed at Robert Walpole.

Additional coverage of Young's life and career is contained in the following source published by Gale Research: *Literature Criticism from 1400 to 1800,* Vol. 3.

Literature
Criticism from
1400 to 1800

Cumulative Indexes

How to Use This Index

The main references

Calvino, Italo
1923-1985.....CLC 5, 8, 11, 22, 33, 39,
73; SSC 3

list all author entries in the following Gale Literary Criticism series:

BLC = *Black Literature Criticism*
CLC = *Contemporary Literary Criticism*
CLR = *Children's Literature Review*
CMLC = *Classical and Medieval Literature Criticism*
DA = *DISCovering Authors*
DC = *Drama Criticism*
HLC = *Hispanic Literature Criticism*
LC = *Literature Criticism from 1400 to 1800*
NCLC = *Nineteenth-Century Literature Criticism*
PC = *Poetry Criticism*
SSC = *Short Story Criticism*
TCLC = *Twentieth-Century Literary Criticism*
WLC = *World Literature Criticism, 1500 to the Present*

The cross-references

See also CANR 23; CA 85-88;
obituary CA 116

list all author entries in the following Gale biographical and literary sources:

AAYA = *Authors & Artists for Young Adults*
AITN = *Authors in the News*
BEST = *Bestsellers* -
BW = *Black Writers*
CA = *Contemporary Authors*
CAAS = *Contemporary Authors Autobiography Series*
CABS = *Contemporary Authors Bibliographical Series*
CANR = *Contemporary Authors New Revision Series*
CAP = *Contemporary Authors Permanent Series*
CDALB = *Concise Dictionary of American Literary Biography*
CDBLB = *Concise Dictionary of British Literary Biography*
DLB = *Dictionary of Literary Biography*
DLBD = *Dictionary of Literary Biography Documentary Series*
DLBY = *Dictionary of Literary Biography Yearbook*
HW = *Hispanic Writers*
JRDA = *Junior DISCovering Authors*
MAICYA = *Major Authors and Illustrators for Children and Young Adults*
MTCW = *Major 20th-Century Writers*
NNAL = *Native North American Literature*
SAAS = *Something about the Author Autobiography Series*
SATA = *Something about the Author*
YABC = *Yesterday's Authors of Books for Children*

Literary Criticism Series
Cumulative Author Index

Abasiyanik, Sait Faik 1906-1954
See Sait Faik
See also CA 123

Abbey, Edward 1927-1989 ...... **CLC 36, 59**
See also CA 45-48; 128; CANR 2, 41

Abbott, Lee K(ittredge) 1947- ...... **CLC 48**
See also CA 124; CANR 51; DLB 130

Abe, Kobo
1924-1993 .... **CLC 8, 22, 53, 81;**
DAM NOV
See also CA 65-68; 140; CANR 24, 60;
DLB 182; MTCW

Abelard, Peter c. 1079-c. 1142 ... **CMLC 11**
See also DLB 115

Abell, Kjeld 1901-1961............ **CLC 15**
See also CA 111

Abish, Walter 1931-.............. **CLC 22**
See also CA 101; CANR 37; DLB 130

Abrahams, Peter (Henry) 1919- ..... **CLC 4**
See also BW 1; CA 57-60; CANR 26;
DLB 117; MTCW

Abrams, M(eyer) H(oward) 1912-... **CLC 24**
See also CA 57-60; CANR 13, 33; DLB 67

Abse, Dannie
1923-... **CLC 7, 29; DAB; DAM POET**
See also CA 53-56; CAAS 1; CANR 4, 46;
DLB 27

Achebe, (Albert) Chinua(lumogu)
1930- ..... **CLC 1, 3, 5, 7, 11, 26, 51, 75;**
BLC; DA; DAB; DAC; DAM MST,
MULT, NOV; WLC
See also AAYA 15; BW 2; CA 1-4R;
CANR 6, 26, 47; CLR 20; DLB 117;
MAICYA; MTCW; SATA 40;
SATA-Brief 38

Acker, Kathy 1948- .... **CLC 45**
See also CA 117; 122; CANR 55

Ackroyd, Peter 1949-.......... **CLC 34, 52**
See also CA 123; 127; CANR 51; DLB 155;
INT 127

Acorn, Milton 1923-........ **CLC 15; DAC**
See also CA 103; DLB 53; INT 103

Adamov, Arthur
1908-1970 .... **CLC 4, 25; DAM DRAM**
See also CA 17-18; 25-28R; CAP 2; MTCW

Adams, Alice (Boyd)
1926- .... **CLC 6, 13, 46; SSC 24**
See also CA 81-84; CANR 26, 53;
DLBY 86; INT CANR-26; MTCW

Adams, Andy 1859-1935.......... **TCLC 56**
See also YABC 1

Adams, Douglas (Noel)
1952- .... **CLC 27, 60; DAM POP**
See also AAYA 4; BEST 89:3; CA 106;
CANR 34; DLBY 83; JRDA

Adams, Francis 1862-1893....... **NCLC 33**

Adams, Henry (Brooks)
1838-1918 ...... **TCLC 4, 52; DA; DAB;**
DAC; DAM MST
See also CA 104; 133; DLB 12, 47

Adams, Richard (George)
1920- .... **CLC 4, 5, 18; DAM NOV**
See also AAYA 16; AITN 1, 2; CA 49-52;
CANR 3, 35; CLR 20; JRDA; MAICYA;
MTCW; SATA 7, 69

Adamson, Joy(-Friederike Victoria)
1910-1980 .... **CLC 17**
See also CA 69-72; 93-96; CANR 22;
MTCW; SATA 11; SATA-Obit 22

Adcock, Fleur 1934-.............. **CLC 41**
See also CA 25-28R; CAAS 23; CANR 11,
34; DLB 40

Addams, Charles (Samuel)
1912-1988 .... **CLC 30**
See also CA 61-64; 126; CANR 12

Addison, Joseph 1672-1719 .... **LC 18**
See also CDBLB 1660-1789; DLB 101

Adler, Alfred (F.) 1870-1937 ...... **TCLC 61**
See also CA 119; 159

Adler, C(arole) S(chwerdtfeger)
1932-...................... **CLC 35**
See also AAYA 4; CA 89-92; CANR 19,
40; JRDA; MAICYA; SAAS 15;
SATA 26, 63

Adler, Renata 1938-............ **CLC 8, 31**
See also CA 49-52; CANR 5, 22, 52;
MTCW

Ady, Endre 1877-1919 .... **TCLC 11**
See also CA 107

Aeschylus
525B.C.-456B.C........ **CMLC 11; DA;**
DAB; DAC; DAM DRAM, MST; WLCS
See also DLB 176

Africa, Ben
See Bosman, Herman Charles

Afton, Effie
See Harper, Frances Ellen Watkins

Agapida, Fray Antonio
See Irving, Washington

Agee, James (Rufus)
1909-1955 .... **TCLC 1, 19; DAM NOV**
See also AITN 1; CA 108; 148;
CDALB 1941-1968; DLB 2, 26, 152

Aghill, Gordon
See Silverberg, Robert

Agnon, S(hmuel) Y(osef Halevi)
1888-1970 .... **CLC 4, 8, 14; SSC 29**
See also CA 17-18; 25-28R; CANR 60;
CAP 2; MTCW

Agrippa von Nettesheim, Henry Cornelius
1486-1535 .... **LC 27**

Aherne, Owen
See Cassill, R(onald) V(erlin)

Ai 1947-.................. **CLC 4, 14, 69**
See also CA 85-88; CAAS 13; DLB 120

Aickman, Robert (Fordyce)
1914-1981 .... **CLC 57**
See also CA 5-8R; CANR 3

Aiken, Conrad (Potter)
1889-1973 .... **CLC 1, 3, 5, 10, 52;**
DAM NOV, POET; SSC 9
See also CA 5-8R; 45-48; CANR 4, 60;
CDALB 1929-1941; DLB 9, 45, 102;
MTCW; SATA 3, 30

Aiken, Joan (Delano) 1924-........ **CLC 35**
See also AAYA 1; CA 9-12R; CANR 4, 23,
34; CLR 1, 19; DLB 161; JRDA;
MAICYA; MTCW; SAAS 1; SATA 2,
30, 73

Ainsworth, William Harrison
1805-1882 .... **NCLC 13**
See also DLB 21; SATA 24

Aitmatov, Chingiz (Torekulovich)
1928- .... **CLC 71**
See also CA 103; CANR 38; MTCW;
SATA 56

Akers, Floyd
See Baum, L(yman) Frank

Akhmadulina, Bella Akhatovna
1937- .... **CLC 53; DAM POET**
See also CA 65-68

Akhmatova, Anna
1888-1966 .... **CLC 11, 25, 64;**
DAM POET; PC 2
See also CA 19-20; 25-28R; CANR 35;
CAP 1; MTCW

Aksakov, Sergei Timofeyvich
1791-1859 .... **NCLC 2**

Aksenov, Vassily
See Aksyonov, Vassily (Pavlovich)

Aksyonov, Vassily (Pavlovich)
1932- .... **CLC 22, 37, 101**
See also CA 53-56; CANR 12, 48

Akutagawa, Ryunosuke
1892-1927 .... **TCLC 16**
See also CA 117; 154

Alain 1868-1951 .... **TCLC 41**

Alain-Fournier.................... TCLC 6
See also Fournier, Henri Alban
See also DLB 65

Alarcon, Pedro Antonio de
1833-1891 .... **NCLC 1**

Alas (y Urena), Leopoldo (Enrique Garcia)
1852-1901 .... **TCLC 29**
See also CA 113; 131; HW

Anderson, C. Farley
See Mencken, H(enry) L(ouis); Nathan, George Jean

Anderson, Jessica (Margaret) Queale
1916- .... **CLC 37**
See also CA 9-12R; CANR 4, 62

Anderson, Jon (Victor)
1940- .... **CLC 9; DAM POET**
See also CA 25-28R; CANR 20

Anderson, Lindsay (Gordon)
1923-1994 .... **CLC 20**
See also CA 125; 128; 146

Anderson, Maxwell
1888-1959 ..... **TCLC 2; DAM DRAM**
See also CA 105; 152; DLB 7

Anderson, Poul (William) 1926- .... **CLC 15**
See also AAYA 5; CA 1-4R; CAAS 2;
CANR 2, 15, 34; DLB 8; INT CANR-15;
MTCW; SATA 90; SATA-Brief 39

Anderson, Robert (Woodruff)
1917- .... **CLC 23; DAM DRAM**
See also AITN 1; CA 21-24R; CANR 32;
DLB 7

Anderson, Sherwood
1876-1941 .... **TCLC 1, 10, 24; DA;
DAB; DAC; DAM MST, NOV; SSC 1;
WLC**

See also CA 104; 121; CANR 61;
CDALB 1917-1929; DLB 4, 9, 86;
DLBD 1; MTCW

Andier, Pierre
See Desnos, Robert

Andouard
See Giraudoux, (Hippolyte) Jean

Andrade, Carlos Drummond de ...... **CLC 18**
See also Drummond de Andrade, Carlos

Andrade, Mario de 1893-1945 ..... **TCLC 43**

Andreae, Johann V(alentin)
1586-1654 .... **LC 32**
See also DLB 164

Andreas-Salome, Lou 1861-1937 ... **TCLC 56**
See also DLB 66

Andress, Lesley
See Sanders, Lawrence

Andrewes, Lancelot 1555-1626 .... **LC 5**
See also DLB 151, 172

Andrews, Cicily Fairfield
See West, Rebecca

Andrews, Elton V.
See Pohl, Frederik

Andreyev, Leonid (Nikolaevich)
1871-1919 .... **TCLC 3**
See also CA 104

Andric, Ivo 1892-1975 .... **CLC 8**
See also CA 81-84; 57-60; CANR 43, 60;
DLB 147; MTCW

Androvar
See Prado (Calvo), Pedro

Angelique, Pierre
See Bataille, Georges

Angell, Roger 1920- .... **CLC 26**
See also CA 57-60; CANR 13, 44; DLB 171

Angelou, Maya
1928- .... **CLC 12, 35, 64, 77; BLC; DA;
DAB; DAC; DAM MST, MULT, POET,
POP; WLCS**
See also AAYA 7, 20; BW 2; CA 65-68;
CANR 19, 42; DLB 38; MTCW;
SATA 49

Anna Comnena 1083-1153 ...... **CMLC 25**

Annensky, Innokenty (Fyodorovich)
1856-1909 .... **TCLC 14**
See also CA 110; 155

Annunzio, Gabriele d'
See D'Annunzio, Gabriele

Anodos
See Coleridge, Mary E(lizabeth)

Anon, Charles Robert
See Pessoa, Fernando (Antonio Nogueira)

Anouilh, Jean (Marie Lucien Pierre)
1910-1987 ...... **CLC 1, 3, 8, 13, 40, 50;
DAM DRAM**
See also CA 17-20R; 123; CANR 32;
MTCW

Anthony, Florence
See Ai

Anthony, John
See Ciardi, John (Anthony)

Anthony, Peter
See Shaffer, Anthony (Joshua); Shaffer,
Peter (Levin)

Anthony, Piers 1934- .. **CLC 35; DAM POP**
See also AAYA 11; CA 21-24R; CANR 28,
56; DLB 8; MTCW; SAAS 22; SATA 84

Antoine, Marc
See Proust, (Valentin-Louis-George-Eugene-)
Marcel

Antoninus, Brother
See Everson, William (Oliver)

Antonioni, Michelangelo 1912- ..... **CLC 20**
See also CA 73-76; CANR 45

Antschel, Paul 1920-1970
See Celan, Paul
See also CA 85-88; CANR 33, 61; MTCW

Anwar, Chairil 1922-1949 .... **TCLC 22**
See also CA 121

Apollinaire, Guillaume
1880-1918 .... **TCLC 3, 8, 51;
DAM POET; PC 7**
See also Kostrowitzki, Wilhelm Apollinaris
de
See also CA 152

Appelfeld, Aharon 1932- .... **CLC 23, 47**
See also CA 112; 133

Apple, Max (Isaac) 1941- .... **CLC 9, 33**
See also CA 81-84; CANR 19, 54; DLB 130

Appleman, Philip (Dean) 1926- ..... **CLC 51**
See also CA 13-16R; CAAS 18; CANR 6,
29, 56

Appleton, Lawrence
See Lovecraft, H(oward) P(hillips)

Apteryx
See Eliot, T(homas) S(tearns)

Apuleius, (Lucius Madaurensis)
125(?)-175(?) .... **CMLC 1**

Aquin, Hubert 1929-1977 .... **CLC 15**
See also CA 105; DLB 53

Aragon, Louis
1897-1982 ..... **CLC 3, 22; DAM NOV,
POET**
See also CA 69-72; 108; CANR 28;
DLB 72; MTCW

Arany, Janos 1817-1882 .... **NCLC 34**

Arbuthnot, John 1667-1735 .... **LC 1**
See also DLB 101

Archer, Herbert Winslow
See Mencken, H(enry) L(ouis)

Archer, Jeffrey (Howard)
1940- .... **CLC 28; DAM POP**
See also AAYA 16; BEST 89:3; CA 77-80;
CANR 22, 52; INT CANR-22

Archer, Jules 1915- .... **CLC 12**
See also CA 9-12R; CANR 6; SAAS 5;
SATA 4, 85

Archer, Lee
See Ellison, Harlan (Jay)

Arden, John
1930- ..... **CLC 6, 13, 15; DAM DRAM**
See also CA 13-16R; CAAS 4; CANR 31;
DLB 13; MTCW

Arenas, Reinaldo
1943-1990 ...... **CLC 41; DAM MULT;
HLC**
See also CA 124; 128; 133; DLB 145; HW

Arendt, Hannah 1906-1975 ..... **CLC 66, 98**
See also CA 17-20R; 61-64; CANR 26, 60;
MTCW

Aretino, Pietro 1492-1556 .... **LC 12**

Arghezi, Tudor .... **CLC 80**
See also Theodorescu, Ion N.

Arguedas, Jose Maria
1911-1969 .... **CLC 10, 18**
See also CA 89-92; DLB 113; HW

Argueta, Manlio 1936- .... **CLC 31**
See also CA 131; DLB 145; HW

Ariosto, Ludovico 1474-1533 .... **LC 6**

Aristides
See Epstein, Joseph

Aristophanes
450B.C.-385B.C. .... **CMLC 4; DA;
DAB; DAC; DAM DRAM, MST; DC 2;
WLCS**
See also DLB 176

Arlt, Roberto (Godofredo Christophersen)
1900-1942 ..... **TCLC 29; DAM MULT;
HLC**
See also CA 123; 131; HW

Armah, Ayi Kwei
1939- .... **CLC 5, 33; BLC;
DAM MULT, POET**
See also BW 1; CA 61-64; CANR 21;
DLB 117; MTCW

Armatrading, Joan 1950- .... **CLC 17**
See also CA 114

Arnette, Robert
See Silverberg, Robert

**Arnim, Achim von (Ludwig Joachim von
Arnim)** 1781-1831 ... **NCLC 5; SSC 29**
See also DLB 90

Arnim, Bettina von 1785-1859 .... **NCLC 38**
See also DLB 90

Arnold, Matthew
1822-1888 ..... NCLC 6, 29; DA; DAB;
DAC; DAM MST, POET; PC 5; WLC
See also CDBLB 1832-1890; DLB 32, 57

Arnold, Thomas 1795-1842 ...... NCLC 18
See also DLB 55

Arnow, Harriette (Louisa) Simpson
1908-1986 .... CLC 2, 7, 18
See also CA 9-12R; 118; CANR 14; DLB 6;
MTCW; SATA 42; SATA-Obit 47

Arp, Hans
See Arp, Jean

Arp, Jean 1887-1966............... CLC 5
See also CA 81-84; 25-28R; CANR 42

Arrabal
See Arrabal, Fernando

Arrabal, Fernando 1932- ... CLC 2, 9, 18, 58
See also CA 9-12R; CANR 15

Arrick, Fran...................... CLC 30
See also Gaberman, Judie Angell

Artaud, Antonin (Marie Joseph)
1896-1948 ... TCLC 3, 36; DAM DRAM
See also CA 104; 149

Arthur, Ruth M(abel) 1905-1979.... CLC 12
See also CA 9-12R; 85-88; CANR 4;
SATA 7, 26

Artsybashev, Mikhail (Petrovich)
1878-1927 .... TCLC 31

Arundel, Honor (Morfydd)
1919-1973 .... CLC 17
See also CA 21-22; 41-44R; CAP 2;
CLR 35; SATA 4; SATA-Obit 24

Arzner, Dorothy 1897-1979........ CLC 98

Asch, Sholem 1880-1957 .... TCLC 3
See also CA 105

Ash, Shalom
See Asch, Sholem

Ashbery, John (Lawrence)
1927- ...... CLC 2, 3, 4, 6, 9, 13, 15, 25,
41, 77; DAM POET
See also CA 5-8R; CANR 9, 37; DLB 5,
165; DLBY 81; INT CANR-9; MTCW

Ashdown, Clifford
See Freeman, R(ichard) Austin

Ashe, Gordon
See Creasey, John

Ashton-Warner, Sylvia (Constance)
1908-1984 .... CLC 19
See also CA 69-72; 112; CANR 29; MTCW

Asimov, Isaac
1920-1992 ...... CLC 1, 3, 9, 19, 26, 76,
92; DAM POP
See also AAYA 13; BEST 90:2; CA 1-4R;
137; CANR 2, 19, 36, 60; CLR 12;
DLB 8; DLBY 92; INT CANR-19;
JRDA; MAICYA; MTCW; SATA 1, 26,
74

Assis, Joaquim Maria Machado de
See Machado de Assis, Joaquim Maria

Astley, Thea (Beatrice May)
1925- .... CLC 41
See also CA 65-68; CANR 11, 43

Aston, James
See White, T(erence) H(anbury)

Asturias, Miguel Angel
1899-1974 .... CLC 3, 8, 13;
DAM MULT, NOV; HLC
See also CA 25-28; 49-52; CANR 32;
CAP 2; DLB 113; HW; MTCW

Atares, Carlos Saura
See Saura (Atares), Carlos

Atheling, William
See Pound, Ezra (Weston Loomis)

Atheling, William, Jr.
See Blish, James (Benjamin)

Atherton, Gertrude (Franklin Horn)
1857-1948 .... TCLC 2
See also CA 104; 155; DLB 9, 78

Atherton, Lucius
See Masters, Edgar Lee

Atkins, Jack
See Harris, Mark

Atkinson, Kate.................... CLC 99

Attaway, William (Alexander)
1911-1986 .... CLC 92; BLC;
DAM MULT
See also BW 2; CA 143; DLB 76

Atticus
See Fleming, Ian (Lancaster)

Atwood, Margaret (Eleanor)
1939- ..... CLC 2, 3, 4, 8, 13, 15, 25, 44,
84; DA; DAB; DAC; DAM MST, NOV,
POET; PC 8; SSC 2; WLC
See also AAYA 12; BEST 89:2; CA 49-52;
CANR 3, 24, 33, 59; DLB 53;
INT CANR-24; MTCW; SATA 50

Aubigny, Pierre d'
See Mencken, H(enry) L(ouis)

Aubin, Penelope 1685-1731(?)........ LC 9
See also DLB 39

Auchincloss, Louis (Stanton)
1917- .... CLC 4, 6, 9, 18, 45;
DAM NOV; SSC 22
See also CA 1-4R; CANR 6, 29, 55; DLB 2;
DLBY 80; INT CANR-29; MTCW

Auden, W(ystan) H(ugh)
1907-1973 ...... CLC 1, 2, 3, 4, 6, 9, 11,
14, 43; DA; DAB; DAC; DAM DRAM,
MST, POET; PC 1; WLC
See also AAYA 18; CA 9-12R; 45-48;
CANR 5, 61; CDBLB 1914-1945;
DLB 10, 20; MTCW

Audiberti, Jacques
1900-1965 ...... CLC 38; DAM DRAM
See also CA 25-28R

Audubon, John James
1785-1851 .... NCLC 47

Auel, Jean M(arie)
1936- .... CLC 31; DAM POP
See also AAYA 7; BEST 90:4; CA 103;
CANR 21; INT CANR-21; SATA 91

Auerbach, Erich 1892-1957 ...... TCLC 43
See also CA 118; 155

Augier, Emile 1820-1889 .... NCLC 31

August, John
See De Voto, Bernard (Augustine)

Augustine, St. 354-430 ...... CMLC 6; DAB

Aurelius
See Bourne, Randolph S(illiman)

Aurobindo, Sri 1872-1950 .... TCLC 63

Austen, Jane
1775-1817 ..... NCLC 1, 13, 19, 33, 51;
DA; DAB; DAC; DAM MST, NOV;
WLC
See also AAYA 19; CDBLB 1789-1832;
DLB 116

Auster, Paul 1947-................ CLC 47
See also CA 69-72; CANR 23, 52

Austin, Frank
See Faust, Frederick (Schiller)

Austin, Mary (Hunter)
1868-1934 .... TCLC 25
See also CA 109; DLB 9, 78

Autran Dourado, Waldomiro
See Dourado, (Waldomiro Freitas) Autran

Averroes 1126-1198 .... CMLC 7
See also DLB 115

Avicenna 980-1037 .... CMLC 16
See also DLB 115

Avison, Margaret
1918- .... CLC 2, 4, 97; DAC;
DAM POET
See also CA 17-20R; DLB 53; MTCW

Axton, David
See Koontz, Dean R(ay)

Ayckbourn, Alan
1939- ...... CLC 5, 8, 18, 33, 74; DAB;
DAM DRAM
See also CA 21-24R; CANR 31, 59;
DLB 13; MTCW

Aydy, Catherine
See Tennant, Emma (Christina)

Ayme, Marcel (Andre) 1902-1967... CLC 11
See also CA 89-92; CLR 25; DLB 72;
SATA 91

Ayrton, Michael 1921-1975........ CLC 7
See also CA 5-8R; 61-64; CANR 9, 21

Azorin....................... CLC 11
See also Martinez Ruiz, Jose

Azuela, Mariano
1873-1952 ..... TCLC 3; DAM MULT;
HLC
See also CA 104; 131; HW; MTCW

Baastad, Babbis Friis
See Friis-Baastad, Babbis Ellinor

Bab
See Gilbert, W(illiam) S(chwenck)

Babbis, Eleanor
See Friis-Baastad, Babbis Ellinor

Babel, Isaac
See Babel, Isaak (Emmanuilovich)

Babel, Isaak (Emmanuilovich)
1894-1941(?) ...... TCLC 2, 13; SSC 16
See also CA 104; 155

Babits, Mihaly 1883-1941 .... TCLC 14
See also CA 114

Babur 1483-1530................. LC 18

Bacchelli, Riccardo 1891-1985 ..... CLC 19
See also CA 29-32R; 117

Bach, Richard (David)
1936- ...... CLC 14; DAM NOV, POP
See also AITN 1; BEST 89:2; CA 9-12R;
CANR 18; MTCW; SATA 13

Bachman, Richard
See King, Stephen (Edwin)

Bachmann, Ingeborg 1926-1973..... **CLC 69**
See also CA 93-96; 45-48; DLB 85

Bacon, Francis 1561-1626 ...... **LC 18, 32**
See also CDBLB Before 1660; DLB 151

Bacon, Roger 1214(?)-1292 ...... **CMLC 14**
See also DLB 115

Bacovia, George................. **TCLC 24**
See also Vasiliu, Gheorghe

Badanes, Jerome 1937-........... **CLC 59**

Bagehot, Walter 1826-1877 ...... **NCLC 10**
See also DLB 55

Bagnold, Enid
1889-1981 ...... **CLC 25; DAM DRAM**
See also CA 5-8R; 103; CANR 5, 40;
DLB 13, 160; MAICYA; SATA 1, 25

Bagritsky, Eduard 1895-1934 ..... **TCLC 60**

Bagrjana, Elisaveta
See Belcheva, Elisaveta

Bagryana, Elisaveta............... **CLC 10**
See also Belcheva, Elisaveta
See also DLB 147

Bailey, Paul 1937-............... **CLC 45**
See also CA 21-24R; CANR 16, 62;
DLB 14

Baillie, Joanna 1762-1851 .... **NCLC 2**
See also DLB 93

Bainbridge, Beryl (Margaret)
1933-.... **CLC 4, 5, 8, 10, 14, 18, 22, 62;**
DAM NOV
See also CA 21-24R; CANR 24, 55;
DLB 14; MTCW

Baker, Elliott 1922-............... **CLC 8**
See also CA 45-48; CANR 2

Baker, Jean H.................. **TCLC 3, 10**
See also Russell, George William

Baker, Nicholson
1957-............ **CLC 61; DAM POP**
See also CA 135

Baker, Ray Stannard 1870-1946... **TCLC 47**
See also CA 118

Baker, Russell (Wayne) 1925-...... **CLC 31**
See also BEST 89:4; CA 57-60; CANR 11,
41, 59; MTCW

Bakhtin, M.
See Bakhtin, Mikhail Mikhailovich

Bakhtin, M. M.
See Bakhtin, Mikhail Mikhailovich

Bakhtin, Mikhail
See Bakhtin, Mikhail Mikhailovich

Bakhtin, Mikhail Mikhailovich
1895-1975 .... **CLC 83**
See also CA 128; 113

Bakshi, Ralph 1938(?)-............ **CLC 26**
See also CA 112; 138

Bakunin, Mikhail (Alexandrovich)
1814-1876 .... **NCLC 25, 58**

Baldwin, James (Arthur)
1924-1987 ...... **CLC 1, 2, 3, 4, 5, 8, 13,**
15, 17, 42, 50, 67, 90; BLC; DA; DAB;
DAC; DAM MST, MULT, NOV, POP;
DC 1; SSC 10; WLC
See also AAYA 4; BW 1; CA 1-4R; 124;
CABS 1; CANR 3, 24;
CDALB 1941-1968; DLB 2, 7, 33;
DLBY 87; MTCW; SATA 9;
SATA-Obit 54

Ballard, J(ames) G(raham)
1930- .... **CLC 3, 6, 14, 36; DAM NOV,**
POP; SSC 1
See also AAYA 3; CA 5-8R; CANR 15, 39;
DLB 14; MTCW; SATA 93

Balmont, Konstantin (Dmitriyevich)
1867-1943 .... **TCLC 11**
See also CA 109; 155

Balzac, Honore de
1799-1850 .... **NCLC 5, 35, 53; DA;**
DAB; DAC; DAM MST, NOV; SSC 5;
WLC
See also DLB 119

Bambara, Toni Cade
1939-1995 ...... **CLC 19, 88; BLC; DA;**
DAC; DAM MST, MULT; WLCS
See also AAYA 5; BW 2; CA 29-32R; 150;
CANR 24, 49; DLB 38; MTCW

Bamdad, A.
See Shamlu, Ahmad

Banat, D. R.
See Bradbury, Ray (Douglas)

Bancroft, Laura
See Baum, L(yman) Frank

Banim, John 1798-1842 .... **NCLC 13**
See also DLB 116, 158, 159

Banim, Michael 1796-1874 ...... **NCLC 13**
See also DLB 158, 159

Banjo, The
See Paterson, A(ndrew) B(arton)

Banks, Iain
See Banks, Iain M(enzies)

Banks, Iain M(enzies) 1954-....... **CLC 34**
See also CA 123; 128; CANR 61; INT 128

Banks, Lynne Reid .... **CLC 23**
See also Reid Banks, Lynne
See also AAYA 6

Banks, Russell 1940-........... **CLC 37, 72**
See also CA 65-68; CAAS 15; CANR 19,
52; DLB 130

Banville, John 1945-.............. **CLC 46**
See also CA 117; 128; DLB 14; INT 128

Banville, Theodore (Faullain) de
1832-1891 .... **NCLC 9**

Baraka, Amiri
1934- .... **CLC 1, 2, 3, 5, 10, 14, 33;**
BLC; DA; DAC; DAM MST, MULT,
POET, POP; DC 6; PC 4; WLCS
See also Jones, LeRoi
See also BW 2; CA 21-24R; CABS 3;
CANR 27, 38, 61; CDALB 1941-1968;
DLB 5, 7, 16, 38; DLBD 8; MTCW

Barbauld, Anna Laetitia
1743-1825 .... **NCLC 50**
See also DLB 107, 109, 142, 158

Barbellion, W. N. P.............. **TCLC 24**
See also Cummings, Bruce F(rederick)

Barbera, Jack (Vincent) 1945-...... **CLC 44**
See also CA 110; CANR 45

Barbey d'Aurevilly, Jules Amedee
1808-1889 .... **NCLC 1; SSC 17**
See also DLB 119

Barbusse, Henri 1873-1935 .... **TCLC 5**
See also CA 105; 154; DLB 65

Barclay, Bill
See Moorcock, Michael (John)

Barclay, William Ewert
See Moorcock, Michael (John)

Barea, Arturo 1897-1957 .... **TCLC 14**
See also CA 111

Barfoot, Joan 1946-.............. **CLC 18**
See also CA 105

Baring, Maurice 1874-1945 .... **TCLC 8**
See also CA 105; DLB 34

Barker, Clive 1952- ... **CLC 52; DAM POP**
See also AAYA 10; BEST 90:3; CA 121;
129; INT 129; MTCW

Barker, George Granville
1913-1991 ..... **CLC 8, 48; DAM POET**
See also CA 9-12R; 135; CANR 7, 38;
DLB 20; MTCW

Barker, Harley Granville
See Granville-Barker, Harley
See also DLB 10

Barker, Howard 1946-............ **CLC 37**
See also CA 102; DLB 13

Barker, Pat(ricia) 1943-........ **CLC 32, 94**
See also CA 117; 122; CANR 50; INT 122

Barlow, Joel 1754-1812 .... **NCLC 23**
See also DLB 37

Barnard, Mary (Ethel) 1909-....... **CLC 48**
See also CA 21-22; CAP 2

Barnes, Djuna
1892-1982 ... **CLC 3, 4, 8, 11, 29; SSC 3**
See also CA 9-12R; 107; CANR 16, 55;
DLB 4, 9, 45; MTCW

Barnes, Julian (Patrick)
1946-................... **CLC 42; DAB**
See also CA 102; CANR 19, 54; DLBY 93

Barnes, Peter 1931-............. **CLC 5, 56**
See also CA 65-68; CAAS 12; CANR 33,
34; DLB 13; MTCW

Baroja (y Nessi), Pio
1872-1956 .... **TCLC 8; HLC**
See also CA 104

Baron, David
See Pinter, Harold

Baron Corvo
See Rolfe, Frederick (William Serafino
Austin Lewis Mary)

Barondess, Sue K(aufman)
1926-1977 .... **CLC 8**
See also Kaufman, Sue
See also CA 1-4R; 69-72; CANR 1

Baron de Teive
See Pessoa, Fernando (Antonio Nogueira)

Barres, Maurice 1862-1923 .... **TCLC 47**
See also DLB 123

Belitt, Ben 1911-............... **CLC 22**
See also CA 13-16R; CAAS 4; CANR 7;
DLB 5

Bell, Gertrude 1868-1926........ **TCLC 67**
See also DLB 174

Bell, James Madison
1826-1902 .... **TCLC 43; BLC;**
DAM MULT
See also BW 1; CA 122; 124; DLB 50

Bell, Madison Smartt 1957-.... **CLC 41, 102**
See also CA 111; CANR 28, 54

Bell, Marvin (Hartley)
1937- .... **CLC 8, 31; DAM POET**
See also CA 21-24R; CAAS 14; CANR 59;
DLB 5; MTCW

Bell, W. L. D.
See Mencken, H(enry) L(ouis)

Bellamy, Atwood C.
See Mencken, H(enry) L(ouis)

Bellamy, Edward 1850-1898 ...... **NCLC 4**
See also DLB 12

Bellin, Edward J.
See Kuttner, Henry

Belloc, (Joseph) Hilaire (Pierre Sebastien
Rene Swanton)
1870-1953 ... **TCLC 7, 18; DAM POET**
See also CA 106; 152; DLB 19, 100, 141,
174; YABC 1

Belloc, Joseph Peter Rene Hilaire
See Belloc, (Joseph) Hilaire (Pierre Sebastien
Rene Swanton)

Belloc, Joseph Pierre Hilaire
See Belloc, (Joseph) Hilaire (Pierre Sebastien
Rene Swanton)

Belloc, M. A.
See Lowndes, Marie Adelaide (Belloc)

Bellow, Saul
1915- ...... **CLC 1, 2, 3, 6, 8, 10, 13, 15,**
25, 33, 34, 63, 79; DA; DAB; DAC;
DAM MST, NOV, POP; SSC 14; WLC
See also AITN 2; BEST 89:3; CA 5-8R;
CABS 1; CANR 29, 53;
CDALB 1941-1968; DLB 2, 28; DLBD 3;
DLBY 82; MTCW

Belser, Reimond Karel Maria de 1929-
See Ruyslinck, Ward
See also CA 152

Bely, Andrey .... **TCLC 7; PC 11**
See also Bugayev, Boris Nikolayevich

Benary, Margot
See Benary-Isbert, Margot

Benary-Isbert, Margot 1889-1979... **CLC 12**
See also CA 5-8R; 89-92; CANR 4;
CLR 12; MAICYA; SATA 2;
SATA-Obit 21

Benavente (y Martinez), Jacinto
1866-1954 ..... **TCLC 3; DAM DRAM,**
MULT
See also CA 106; 131; HW; MTCW

Benchley, Peter (Bradford)
1940- ..... **CLC 4, 8; DAM NOV, POP**
See also AAYA 14; AITN 2; CA 17-20R;
CANR 12, 35; MTCW; SATA 3, 89

Benchley, Robert (Charles)
1889-1945 .... **TCLC 1, 55**
See also CA 105; 153; DLB 11

Benda, Julien 1867-1956 .... **TCLC 60**
See also CA 120; 154

Benedict, Ruth (Fulton)
1887-1948 .... **TCLC 60**
See also CA 158

Benedict of Nursia, Saint
c. 480-c. 543 .... **CMLC 25**

Benedikt, Michael 1935- .... **CLC 4, 14**
See also CA 13-16R; CANR 7; DLB 5

Benet, Juan 1927-................. **CLC 28**
See also CA 143

Benet, Stephen Vincent
1898-1943 ...... **TCLC 7; DAM POET;**
SSC 10
See also CA 104; 152; DLB 4, 48, 102;
YABC 1

Benet, William Rose
1886-1950 ...... **TCLC 28; DAM POET**
See also CA 118; 152; DLB 45

Benford, Gregory (Albert) 1941-.... **CLC 52**
See also CA 69-72; CAAS 27; CANR 12,
24, 49; DLBY 82

Bengtsson, Frans (Gunnar)
1894-1954 .... **TCLC 48**

Benjamin, David
See Slavitt, David R(ytman)

Benjamin, Lois
See Gould, Lois

Benjamin, Walter 1892-1940..... **TCLC 39**

Benn, Gottfried 1886-1956........ **TCLC 3**
See also CA 106; 153; DLB 56

Bennett, Alan
1934- ... **CLC 45, 77; DAB; DAM MST**
See also CA 103; CANR 35, 55; MTCW

Bennett, (Enoch) Arnold
1867-1931 .... **TCLC 5, 20**
See also CA 106; 155; CDBLB 1890-1914;
DLB 10, 34, 98, 135

Bennett, Elizabeth
See Mitchell, Margaret (Munnerlyn)

Bennett, George Harold 1930-
See Bennett, Hal
See also BW 1; CA 97-100

Bennett, Hal .... **CLC 5**
See also Bennett, George Harold
See also DLB 33

Bennett, Jay 1912-............... **CLC 35**
See also AAYA 10; CA 69-72; CANR 11,
42; JRDA; SAAS 4; SATA 41, 87;
SATA-Brief 27

Bennett, Louise (Simone)
1919- ..... **CLC 28; BLC; DAM MULT**
See also BW 2; CA 151; DLB 117

Benson, E(dward) F(rederic)
1867-1940 .... **TCLC 27**
See also CA 114; 157; DLB 135, 153

Benson, Jackson J. 1930-.......... **CLC 34**
See also CA 25-28R; DLB 111

Benson, Sally 1900-1972 .... **CLC 17**
See also CA 19-20; 37-40R; CAP 1;
SATA 1, 35; SATA-Obit 27

Benson, Stella 1892-1933........ **TCLC 17**
See also CA 117; 155; DLB 36, 162

Bentham, Jeremy 1748-1832 ..... **NCLC 38**
See also DLB 107, 158

Bentley, E(dmund) C(lerihew)
1875-1956 .... **TCLC 12**
See also CA 108; DLB 70

Bentley, Eric (Russell) 1916-...... **CLC 24**
See also CA 5-8R; CANR 6; INT CANR-6

Beranger, Pierre Jean de
1780-1857 .... **NCLC 34**

Berdyaev, Nicolas
See Berdyaev, Nikolai (Aleksandrovich)

Berdyaev, Nikolai (Aleksandrovich)
1874-1948 .... **TCLC 67**
See also CA 120; 157

Berdyayev, Nikolai (Aleksandrovich)
See Berdyaev, Nikolai (Aleksandrovich)

Berendt, John (Lawrence) 1939-.... **CLC 86**
See also CA 146

Berger, Colonel
See Malraux, (Georges-)Andre

Berger, John (Peter) 1926- ...... **CLC 2, 19**
See also CA 81-84; CANR 51; DLB 14

Berger, Melvin H. 1927-.......... **CLC 12**
See also CA 5-8R; CANR 4; CLR 32;
SAAS 2; SATA 5, 88

Berger, Thomas (Louis)
1924- .... **CLC 3, 5, 8, 11, 18, 38;**
DAM NOV
See also CA 1-4R; CANR 5, 28, 51; DLB 2;
DLBY 80; INT CANR-28; MTCW

Bergman, (Ernst) Ingmar
1918- .... **CLC 16, 72**
See also CA 81-84; CANR 33

Bergson, Henri 1859-1941....... **TCLC 32**

Bergstein, Eleanor 1938-.......... **CLC 4**
See also CA 53-56; CANR 5

Berkoff, Steven 1937-............ **CLC 56**
See also CA 104

Bermant, Chaim (Icyk) 1929- ...... **CLC 40**
See also CA 57-60; CANR 6, 31, 57

Bern, Victoria
See Fisher, M(ary) F(rances) K(ennedy)

Bernanos, (Paul Louis) Georges
1888-1948 .... **TCLC 3**
See also CA 104; 130; DLB 72

Bernard, April 1956- .... **CLC 59**
See also CA 131

Berne, Victoria
See Fisher, M(ary) F(rances) K(ennedy)

Bernhard, Thomas
1931-1989 .... **CLC 3, 32, 61**
See also CA 85-88; 127; CANR 32, 57;
DLB 85, 124; MTCW

Bernhardt, Sarah (Henriette Rosine)
1844-1923 .... **TCLC 75**
See also CA 157

Berriault, Gina 1926-............. **CLC 54**
See also CA 116; 129; DLB 130

Berrigan, Daniel 1921-............ **CLC 4**
See also CA 33-36R; CAAS 1; CANR 11,
43; DLB 5

Berrigan, Edmund Joseph Michael, Jr.
1934-1983
See Berrigan, Ted
See also CA 61-64; 110; CANR 14

Berrigan, Ted..................... **CLC 37**
See also Berrigan, Edmund Joseph Michael,
Jr.
See also DLB 5, 169

Berry, Charles Edward Anderson 1931-
See Berry, Chuck
See also CA 115

Berry, Chuck.................... **CLC 17**
See also Berry, Charles Edward Anderson

Berry, Jonas
See Ashbery, John (Lawrence)

Berry, Wendell (Erdman)
1934-............. **CLC 4, 6, 8, 27, 46;**
DAM POET
See also AITN 1; CA 73-76; CANR 50;
DLB 5, 6

Berryman, John
1914-1972 ...... **CLC 1, 2, 3, 4, 6, 8, 10,**
13, 25, 62; DAM POET
See also CA 13-16; 33-36R; CABS 2;
CANR 35; CAP 1; CDALB 1941-1968;
DLB 48; MTCW

Bertolucci, Bernardo 1940- .... **CLC 16**
See also CA 106

Berton, Pierre (Francis De Marigny)
1920-........................ **CLC 104**
See also CA 1-4R; CANR 2, 56; DLB 68

Bertrand, Aloysius 1807-1841 .... **NCLC 31**

Bertran de Born c. 1140-1215 ..... **CMLC 5**

Besant, Annie (Wood) 1847-1933 ... **TCLC 9**
See also CA 105

Bessie, Alvah 1904-1985.......... **CLC 23**
See also CA 5-8R; 116; CANR 2; DLB 26

Bethlen, T. D.
See Silverberg, Robert

Beti, Mongo.... **CLC 27; BLC; DAM MULT**
See also Biyidi, Alexandre

Betjeman, John
1906-1984 .... **CLC 2, 6, 10, 34, 43;**
DAB; DAM MST, POET
See also CA 9-12R; 112; CANR 33, 56;
CDBLB 1945-1960; DLB 20; DLBY 84;
MTCW

Bettelheim, Bruno 1903-1990 ...... **CLC 79**
See also CA 81-84; 131; CANR 23, 61;
MTCW

Betti, Ugo 1892-1953 .... **TCLC 5**
See also CA 104; 155

Betts, Doris (Waugh) 1932-.... **CLC 3, 6, 28**
See also CA 13-16R; CANR 9; DLBY 82;
INT CANR-9

Bevan, Alistair
See Roberts, Keith (John Kingston)

Bialik, Chaim Nachman
1873-1934 .... **TCLC 25**

Bickerstaff, Isaac
See Swift, Jonathan

Bidart, Frank 1939- .... **CLC 33**
See also CA 140

Bienek, Horst 1930-........... **CLC 7, 11**
See also CA 73-76; DLB 75

Bierce, Ambrose (Gwinett)
1842-1914(?) .... **TCLC 1, 7, 44; DA;**
DAC; DAM MST; SSC 9; WLC
See also CA 104; 139; CDALB 1865-1917;
DLB 11, 12, 23, 71, 74

Biggers, Earl Derr 1884-1933 ..... **TCLC 65**
See also CA 108; 153

Billings, Josh
See Shaw, Henry Wheeler

Billington, (Lady) Rachel (Mary)
1942-...................... **CLC 43**
See also AITN 2; CA 33-36R; CANR 44

Binyon, T(imothy) J(ohn) 1936- .... **CLC 34**
See also CA 111; CANR 28

Bioy Casares, Adolfo
1914-.............. **CLC 4, 8, 13, 88;**
DAM MULT; HLC; SSC 17
See also CA 29-32R; CANR 19, 43;
DLB 113; HW; MTCW

Bird, Cordwainer
See Ellison, Harlan (Jay)

Bird, Robert Montgomery
1806-1854 .... **NCLC 1**

Birney, (Alfred) Earle
1904-.......... **CLC 1, 4, 6, 11; DAC;**
DAM MST, POET
See also CA 1-4R; CANR 5, 20; DLB 88;
MTCW

Bishop, Elizabeth
1911-1979 ...... **CLC 1, 4, 9, 13, 15, 32;**
DA; DAC; DAM MST, POET; PC 3
See also CA 5-8R; 89-92; CABS 2;
CANR 26, 61; CDALB 1968-1988;
DLB 5, 169; MTCW; SATA-Obit 24

Bishop, John 1935-............... **CLC 10**
See also CA 105

Bissett, Bill 1939-.......... **CLC 18; PC 14**
See also CA 69-72; CAAS 19; CANR 15;
DLB 53; MTCW

Bitov, Andrei (Georgievich) 1937-.... **CLC 57**
See also CA 142

Biyidi, Alexandre 1932-
See Beti, Mongo
See also BW 1; CA 114; 124; MTCW

Bjarme, Brynjolf
See Ibsen, Henrik (Johan)

Bjornson, Bjornstjerne (Martinius)
1832-1910 .... **TCLC 7, 37**
See also CA 104

Black, Robert
See Holdstock, Robert P.

Blackburn, Paul 1926-1971 ...... **CLC 9, 43**
See also CA 81-84; 33-36R; CANR 34;
DLB 16; DLBY 81

Black Elk
1863-1950 ..... **TCLC 33; DAM MULT**
See also CA 144; NNAL

Black Hobart
See Sanders, (James) Ed(ward)

Blacklin, Malcolm
See Chambers, Aidan

Blackmore, R(ichard) D(oddridge)
1825-1900 .... **TCLC 27**
See also CA 120; DLB 18

Blackmur, R(ichard) P(almer)
1904-1965 .... **CLC 2, 24**
See also CA 11-12; 25-28R; CAP 1; DLB 63

Black Tarantula
See Acker, Kathy

Blackwood, Algernon (Henry)
1869-1951 .... **TCLC 5**
See also CA 105; 150; DLB 153, 156, 178

Blackwood, Caroline
1931-1996 .... **CLC 6, 9, 100**
See also CA 85-88; 151; CANR 32, 61;
DLB 14; MTCW

Blade, Alexander
See Hamilton, Edmond; Silverberg, Robert

Blaga, Lucian 1895-1961 .... **CLC 75**

Blair, Eric (Arthur) 1903-1950
See Orwell, George
See also CA 104; 132; DA; DAB; DAC;
DAM MST, NOV; MTCW; SATA 29

Blais, Marie-Claire
1939-....... **CLC 2, 4, 6, 13, 22; DAC;**
DAM MST
See also CA 21-24R; CAAS 4; CANR 38;
DLB 53; MTCW

Blaise, Clark 1940-............... **CLC 29**
See also AITN 2; CA 53-56; CAAS 3;
CANR 5; DLB 53

Blake, Fairley
See De Voto, Bernard (Augustine)

Blake, Nicholas
See Day Lewis, C(ecil)
See also DLB 77

Blake, William
1757-1827 .... **NCLC 13, 37, 57; DA;**
DAB; DAC; DAM MST, POET; PC 12;
WLC
See also CDBLB 1789-1832; DLB 93, 163;
MAICYA; SATA 30

Blake, William J(ames) 1894-1969 ... **PC 12**
See also CA 5-8R; 25-28R

Blasco Ibanez, Vicente
1867-1928 .... **TCLC 12; DAM NOV**
See also CA 110; 131; HW; MTCW

Blatty, William Peter
1928- .... **CLC 2; DAM POP**
See also CA 5-8R; CANR 9

Bleeck, Oliver
See Thomas, Ross (Elmore)

Blessing, Lee 1949-............... **CLC 54**

Blish, James (Benjamin)
1921-1975 .... **CLC 14**
See also CA 1-4R; 57-60; CANR 3; DLB 8;
MTCW; SATA 66

Bliss, Reginald
See Wells, H(erbert) G(eorge)

Blixen, Karen (Christentze Dinesen)
1885-1962
See Dinesen, Isak
See also CA 25-28; CANR 22, 50; CAP 2;
MTCW; SATA 44

Bloch, Robert (Albert) 1917-1994... **CLC 33**
See also CA 5-8R; 146; CAAS 20; CANR 5;
DLB 44; INT CANR-5; SATA 12;
SATA-Obit 82

Blok, Alexander (Alexandrovich)
1880-1921 . . . . **TCLC 5**
See also CA 104

Blom, Jan
See Breytenbach, Breyten

Bloom, Harold 1930- . . . . **CLC 24, 103**
See also CA 13-16R; CANR 39; DLB 67

Bloomfield, Aurelius
See Bourne, Randolph S(illiman)

Blount, Roy (Alton), Jr. 1941- . . . . . **CLC 38**
See also CA 53-56; CANR 10, 28, 61;
INT CANR-28; MTCW

Bloy, Leon 1846-1917 . . . . **TCLC 22**
See also CA 121; DLB 123

Blume, Judy (Sussman)
1938- . . . **CLC 12, 30; DAM NOV, POP**
See also AAYA 3; CA 29-32R; CANR 13,
37; CLR 2, 15; DLB 52; JRDA;
MAICYA; MTCW; SATA 2, 31, 79

Blunden, Edmund (Charles)
1896-1974 . . . . **CLC 2, 56**
See also CA 17-18; 45-48; CANR 54;
CAP 2; DLB 20, 100, 155; MTCW

Bly, Robert (Elwood)
1926- . . . . **CLC 1, 2, 5, 10, 15, 38;**
DAM POET
See also CA 5-8R; CANR 41; DLB 5;
MTCW

Boas, Franz 1858-1942 . . . . **TCLC 56**
See also CA 115

Bobette
See Simenon, Georges (Jacques Christian)

Boccaccio, Giovanni
1313-1375 . . . . **CMLC 13; SSC 10**

Bochco, Steven 1943- . . . . **CLC 35**
See also AAYA 11; CA 124; 138

Bodenheim, Maxwell 1892-1954 . . . **TCLC 44**
See also CA 110; DLB 9, 45

Bodker, Cecil 1927- . . . . **CLC 21**
See also CA 73-76; CANR 13, 44; CLR 23;
MAICYA; SATA 14

Boell, Heinrich (Theodor)
1917-1985 . . . . **CLC 2, 3, 6, 9, 11, 15, 27,**
32, 72; DA; DAB; DAC; DAM MST,
NOV; SSC 23; WLC
See also CA 21-24R; 116; CANR 24;
DLB 69; DLBY 85; MTCW

Boerne, Alfred
See Doeblin, Alfred

Boethius 480(?)-524(?) . . . . **CMLC 15**
See also DLB 115

Bogan, Louise
1897-1970 . . . . **CLC 4, 39, 46, 93;**
DAM POET; PC 12
See also CA 73-76; 25-28R; CANR 33;
DLB 45, 169; MTCW

Bogarde, Dirk . . . . **CLC 19**
See also Van Den Bogarde, Derek Jules
Gaspard Ulric Niven
See also DLB 14

Bogosian, Eric 1953- . . . . **CLC 45**
See also CA 138

Bograd, Larry 1953- . . . . **CLC 35**
See also CA 93-96; CANR 57; SAAS 21;
SATA 33, 89

Boiardo, Matteo Maria 1441-1494 . . . . **LC 6**

Boileau-Despreaux, Nicolas
1636-1711 . . . . **LC 3**

Bojer, Johan 1872-1959 . . . . **TCLC 64**

Boland, Eavan (Aisling)
1944- . . . . **CLC 40, 67; DAM POET**
See also CA 143; CANR 61; DLB 40

Bolt, Lee
See Faust, Frederick (Schiller)

Bolt, Robert (Oxton)
1924-1995 . . . . . . **CLC 14; DAM DRAM**
See also CA 17-20R; 147; CANR 35;
DLB 13; MTCW

Bombet, Louis-Alexandre-Cesar
See Stendhal

Bomkauf
See Kaufman, Bob (Garnell)

Bonaventura . . . . **NCLC 35**
See also DLB 90

Bond, Edward
1934- . . . **CLC 4, 6, 13, 23; DAM DRAM**
See also CA 25-28R; CANR 38; DLB 13;
MTCW

Bonham, Frank 1914-1989 . . . . **CLC 12**
See also AAYA 1; CA 9-12R; CANR 4, 36;
JRDA; MAICYA; SAAS 3; SATA 1, 49;
SATA-Obit 62

Bonnefoy, Yves
1923- . . . . . . **CLC 9, 15, 58; DAM MST,**
POET
See also CA 85-88; CANR 33; MTCW

Bontemps, Arna(ud Wendell)
1902-1973 . . . . **CLC 1, 18; BLC;**
DAM MULT, NOV, POET
See also BW 1; CA 1-4R; 41-44R; CANR 4,
35; CLR 6; DLB 48, 51; JRDA;
MAICYA; MTCW; SATA 2, 44;
SATA-Obit 24

Booth, Martin 1944- . . . . **CLC 13**
See also CA 93-96; CAAS 2

Booth, Philip 1925- . . . . **CLC 23**
See also CA 5-8R; CANR 5; DLBY 82

Booth, Wayne C(layson) 1921- . . . . . . **CLC 24**
See also CA 1-4R; CAAS 5; CANR 3, 43;
DLB 67

Borchert, Wolfgang 1921-1947 . . . . . **TCLC 5**
See also CA 104; DLB 69, 124

Borel, Petrus 1809-1859 . . . . **NCLC 41**

Borges, Jorge Luis
1899-1986 . . . **CLC 1, 2, 3, 4, 6, 8, 9, 10,**
13, 19, 44, 48, 83; DA; DAB; DAC;
DAM MST, MULT; HLC; SSC 4; WLC
See also AAYA 19; CA 21-24R; CANR 19,
33; DLB 113; DLBY 86; HW; MTCW

Borowski, Tadeusz 1922-1951 . . . . . . **TCLC 9**
See also CA 106; 154

Borrow, George (Henry)
1803-1881 . . . . **NCLC 9**
See also DLB 21, 55, 166

Bosman, Herman Charles
1905-1951 . . . . **TCLC 49**
See also Malan, Herman
See also CA 160

Bosschere, Jean de 1878(?)-1953 . . . **TCLC 19**
See also CA 115

Boswell, James
1740-1795 . . . . . . **LC 4; DA; DAB; DAC;**
DAM MST; WLC
See also CDBLB 1660-1789; DLB 104, 142

Bottoms, David 1949- . . . . **CLC 53**
See also CA 105; CANR 22; DLB 120;
DLBY 83

Boucicault, Dion 1820-1890 . . . . . . **NCLC 41**

Boucolon, Maryse 1937(?)-
See Conde, Maryse
See also CA 110; CANR 30, 53

Bourget, Paul (Charles Joseph)
1852-1935 . . . . **TCLC 12**
See also CA 107; DLB 123

Bourjaily, Vance (Nye) 1922- . . . . **CLC 8, 62**
See also CA 1-4R; CAAS 1; CANR 2;
DLB 2, 143

Bourne, Randolph S(illiman)
1886-1918 . . . . **TCLC 16**
See also CA 117; 155; DLB 63

Bova, Ben(jamin William) 1932- . . . . **CLC 45**
See also AAYA 16; CA 5-8R; CAAS 18;
CANR 11, 56; CLR 3; DLBY 81;
INT CANR-11; MAICYA; MTCW;
SATA 6, 68

Bowen, Elizabeth (Dorothea Cole)
1899-1973 . . . . . . **CLC 1, 3, 6, 11, 15, 22;**
DAM NOV; SSC 3, 28
See also CA 17-18; 41-44R; CANR 35;
CAP 2; CDBLB 1945-1960; DLB 15, 162;
MTCW

Bowering, George 1935- . . . . **CLC 15, 47**
See also CA 21-24R; CAAS 16; CANR 10;
DLB 53

Bowering, Marilyn R(uthe) 1949- . . . **CLC 32**
See also CA 101; CANR 49

Bowers, Edgar 1924- . . . . **CLC 9**
See also CA 5-8R; CANR 24; DLB 5

Bowie, David . . . . **CLC 17**
See also Jones, David Robert

Bowles, Jane (Sydney)
1917-1973 . . . . **CLC 3, 68**
See also CA 19-20; 41-44R; CAP 2

Bowles, Paul (Frederick)
1910- . . . . **CLC 1, 2, 19, 53; SSC 3**
See also CA 1-4R; CAAS 1; CANR 1, 19,
50; DLB 5, 6; MTCW

Box, Edgar
See Vidal, Gore

Boyd, Nancy
See Millay, Edna St. Vincent

Boyd, William 1952- . . . . **CLC 28, 53, 70**
See also CA 114; 120; CANR 51

Boyle, Kay
1902-1992 . . . . . **CLC 1, 5, 19, 58; SSC 5**
See also CA 13-16R; 140; CAAS 1;
CANR 29, 61; DLB 4, 9, 48, 86;
DLBY 93; MTCW

Boyle, Mark
See Kienzle, William X(avier)

Boyle, Patrick 1905-1982 . . . . **CLC 19**
See also CA 127

Boyle, T. C. 1948-
See Boyle, T(homas) Coraghessan

Boyle, T(homas) Coraghessan
1948- ..... **CLC 36, 55, 90; DAM POP;**
SSC 16
See also BEST 90:4; CA 120; CANR 44;
DLBY 86

Boz
See Dickens, Charles (John Huffam)

Brackenridge, Hugh Henry
1748-1816 .... **NCLC 7**
See also DLB 11, 37

Bradbury, Edward P.
See Moorcock, Michael (John)

Bradbury, Malcolm (Stanley)
1932- .... **CLC 32, 61; DAM NOV**
See also CA 1-4R; CANR 1, 33; DLB 14;
MTCW

Bradbury, Ray (Douglas)
1920- .... **CLC 1, 3, 10, 15, 42, 98; DA;**
DAB; DAC; DAM MST, NOV, POP;
SSC 29; WLC
See also AAYA 15; AITN 1, 2; CA 1-4R;
CANR 2, 30; CDALB 1968-1988; DLB 2,
8; MTCW; SATA 11, 64

Bradford, Gamaliel 1863-1932..... **TCLC 36**
See also CA 160; DLB 17

Bradley, David (Henry, Jr.)
1950- ..... **CLC 23; BLC; DAM MULT**
See also BW 1; CA 104; CANR 26; DLB 33

Bradley, John Ed(mund, Jr.)
1958- .... **CLC 55**
See also CA 139

Bradley, Marion Zimmer
1930- .... **CLC 30; DAM POP**
See also AAYA 9; CA 57-60; CAAS 10;
CANR 7, 31, 51; DLB 8; MTCW;
SATA 90

Bradstreet, Anne
1612(?)-1672 ...... **LC 4, 30; DA; DAC;**
DAM MST, POET; PC 10
See also CDALB 1640-1865; DLB 24

Brady, Joan 1939- .... **CLC 86**
See also CA 141

Bragg, Melvyn 1939- .... **CLC 10**
See also BEST 89:3; CA 57-60; CANR 10,
48; DLB 14

Braine, John (Gerard)
1922-1986 .... **CLC 1, 3, 41**
See also CA 1-4R; 120; CANR 1, 33;
CDBLB 1945-1960; DLB 15; DLBY 86;
MTCW

Bramah, Ernest 1868-1942....... **TCLC 72**
See also CA 156; DLB 70

Brammer, William 1930(?)-1978 .... **CLC 31**
See also CA 77-80

Brancati, Vitaliano 1907-1954..... **TCLC 12**
See also CA 109

Brancato, Robin F(idler) 1936- ..... **CLC 35**
See also AAYA 9; CA 69-72; CANR 11,
45; CLR 32; JRDA; SAAS 9; SATA 23

Brand, Max
See Faust, Frederick (Schiller)

Brand, Millen 1906-1980.......... **CLC 7**
See also CA 21-24R; 97-100

Branden, Barbara .... **CLC 44**
See also CA 148

Brandes, Georg (Morris Cohen)
1842-1927 .... **TCLC 10**
See also CA 105

Brandys, Kazimierz 1916- .... **CLC 62**

Branley, Franklyn M(ansfield)
1915- .... **CLC 21**
See also CA 33-36R; CANR 14, 39;
CLR 13; MAICYA; SAAS 16; SATA 4,
68

Brathwaite, Edward Kamau
1930- .... **CLC 11; DAM POET**
See also BW 2; CA 25-28R; CANR 11, 26,
47; DLB 125

Brautigan, Richard (Gary)
1935-1984 .... **CLC 1, 3, 5, 9, 12, 34, 42;**
DAM NOV
See also CA 53-56; 113; CANR 34; DLB 2,
5; DLBY 80, 84; MTCW; SATA 56

Brave Bird, Mary 1953-
See Crow Dog, Mary (Ellen)
See also NNAL

Braverman, Kate 1950- .... **CLC 67**
See also CA 89-92

Brecht, (Eugen) Bertolt (Friedrich)
1898-1956 ...... **TCLC 1, 6, 13, 35; DA;**
DAB; DAC; DAM DRAM, MST; DC 3;
WLC
See also CA 104; 133; CANR 62; DLB 56,
124; MTCW

Brecht, Eugen Berthold Friedrich
See Brecht, (Eugen) Bertolt (Friedrich)

Bremer, Fredrika 1801-1865 ..... **NCLC 11**

Brennan, Christopher John
1870-1932 .... **TCLC 17**
See also CA 117

Brennan, Maeve 1917- .... **CLC 5**
See also CA 81-84

Brentano, Clemens (Maria)
1778-1842 .... **NCLC 1**
See also DLB 90

Brent of Bin Bin
See Franklin, (Stella Maraia Sarah) Miles

Brenton, Howard 1942- .... **CLC 31**
See also CA 69-72; CANR 33; DLB 13;
MTCW

Breslin, James 1930-
See Breslin, Jimmy
See also CA 73-76; CANR 31; DAM NOV;
MTCW

Breslin, Jimmy .... **CLC 4, 43**
See also Breslin, James
See also AITN 1

Bresson, Robert 1901- .... **CLC 16**
See also CA 110; CANR 49

Breton, Andre
1896-1966 ..... **CLC 2, 9, 15, 54; PC 15**
See also CA 19-20; 25-28R; CANR 40, 60;
CAP 2; DLB 65; MTCW

Breytenbach, Breyten
1939(?)- ...... **CLC 23, 37; DAM POET**
See also CA 113; 129; CANR 61

Bridgers, Sue Ellen 1942- .... **CLC 26**
See also AAYA 8; CA 65-68; CANR 11,
36; CLR 18; DLB 52; JRDA; MAICYA;
SAAS 1; SATA 22, 90

Bridges, Robert (Seymour)
1844-1930 .... **TCLC 1; DAM POET**
See also CA 104; 152; CDBLB 1890-1914;
DLB 19, 98

Bridie, James .... **TCLC 3**
See also Mavor, Osborne Henry
See also DLB 10

Brin, David 1950- .... **CLC 34**
See also AAYA 21; CA 102; CANR 24;
INT CANR-24; SATA 65

Brink, Andre (Philippus)
1935- .... **CLC 18, 36**
See also CA 104; CANR 39, 62; INT 103;
MTCW

Brinsmead, H(esba) F(ay) 1922- .... **CLC 21**
See also CA 21-24R; CANR 10; CLR 47;
MAICYA; SAAS 5; SATA 18, 78

Brittain, Vera (Mary)
1893(?)-1970 .... **CLC 23**
See also CA 13-16; 25-28R; CANR 58;
CAP 1; MTCW

Broch, Hermann 1886-1951....... **TCLC 20**
See also CA 117; DLB 85, 124

Brock, Rose
See Hansen, Joseph

Brodkey, Harold (Roy) 1930-1996 .. **CLC 56**
See also CA 111; 151; DLB 130

Brodsky, Iosif Alexandrovich 1940-1996
See Brodsky, Joseph
See also AITN 1; CA 41-44R; 151;
CANR 37; DAM POET; MTCW

Brodsky, Joseph
1940-1996 .. **CLC 4, 6, 13, 36, 100; PC 9**
See also Brodsky, Iosif Alexandrovich

Brodsky, Michael (Mark) 1948- .... **CLC 19**
See also CA 102; CANR 18, 41, 58

Bromell, Henry 1947-............. **CLC 5**
See also CA 53-56; CANR 9

Bromfield, Louis (Brucker)
1896-1956 .... **TCLC 11**
See also CA 107; 155; DLB 4, 9, 86

Broner, E(sther) M(asserman)
1930- .... **CLC 19**
See also CA 17-20R; CANR 8, 25; DLB 28

Bronk, William 1918-............. **CLC 10**
See also CA 89-92; CANR 23; DLB 165

Bronstein, Lev Davidovich
See Trotsky, Leon

Bronte, Anne 1820-1849.......... **NCLC 4**
See also DLB 21

Bronte, Charlotte
1816-1855 ..... **NCLC 3, 8, 33, 58; DA;**
DAB; DAC; DAM MST, NOV; WLC
See also AAYA 17; CDBLB 1832-1890;
DLB 21, 159

Bronte, Emily (Jane)
1818-1848 .... **NCLC 16, 35; DA; DAB;**
DAC; DAM MST, NOV, POET; PC 8;
WLC
See also AAYA 17; CDBLB 1832-1890;
DLB 21, 32

Brooke, Frances 1724-1789 .... **LC 6**
See also DLB 39, 99

Brooke, Henry 1703(?)-1783 .... **LC 1**
See also DLB 39

Brooke, Rupert (Chawner)
1887-1915 ...... **TCLC 2, 7; DA; DAB;
DAC; DAM MST, POET; WLC**
See also CA 104; 132; CANR 61;
CDBLB 1914-1945; DLB 19; MTCW

Brooke-Haven, P.
See Wodehouse, P(elham) G(renville)

Brooke-Rose, Christine 1926(?)- .... **CLC 40**
See also CA 13-16R; CANR 58; DLB 14

Brookner, Anita
1928- .... **CLC 32, 34, 51; DAB;
DAM POP**
See also CA 114; 120; CANR 37, 56;
DLBY 87; MTCW

Brooks, Cleanth 1906-1994 ..... **CLC 24, 86**
See also CA 17-20R; 145; CANR 33, 35;
DLB 63; DLBY 94; INT CANR-35;
MTCW

Brooks, George
See Baum, L(yman) Frank

Brooks, Gwendolyn
1917- ...... **CLC 1, 2, 4, 5, 15, 49; BLC;
DA; DAC; DAM MST, MULT, POET;
PC 7; WLC**
See also AAYA 20; AITN 1; BW 2;
CA 1-4R; CANR 1, 27, 52;
CDALB 1941-1968; CLR 27; DLB 5, 76,
165; MTCW; SATA 6

Brooks, Mel...................... **CLC 12**
See also Kaminsky, Melvin
See also AAYA 13; DLB 26

Brooks, Peter 1938-.............. **CLC 34**
See also CA 45-48; CANR 1

Brooks, Van Wyck 1886-1963...... **CLC 29**
See also CA 1-4R; CANR 6; DLB 45, 63,
103

Brophy, Brigid (Antonia)
1929-1995 .... **CLC 6, 11, 29**
See also CA 5-8R; 149; CAAS 4; CANR 25,
53; DLB 14; MTCW

Brosman, Catharine Savage 1934-.... **CLC 9**
See also CA 61-64; CANR 21, 46

Brother Antoninus
See Everson, William (Oliver)

Broughton, T(homas) Alan 1936- ... **CLC 19**
See also CA 45-48; CANR 2, 23, 48

Broumas, Olga 1949-.......... **CLC 10, 73**
See also CA 85-88; CANR 20

Brown, Alan 1951-.............. **CLC 99**

Brown, Charles Brockden
1771-1810 .... **NCLC 22**
See also CDALB 1640-1865; DLB 37, 59,
73

Brown, Christy 1932-1981........ **CLC 63**
See also CA 105; 104; DLB 14

Brown, Claude
1937- ..... **CLC 30; BLC; DAM MULT**
See also AAYA 7; BW 1; CA 73-76

Brown, Dee (Alexander)
1908- .... **CLC 18, 47; DAM POP**
See also CA 13-16R; CAAS 6; CANR 11,
45, 60; DLBY 80; MTCW; SATA 5

Brown, George
See Wertmueller, Lina

Brown, George Douglas
1869-1902 .... **TCLC 28**

Brown, George Mackay
1921-1996 .... **CLC 5, 48, 100**
See also CA 21-24R; 151; CAAS 6;
CANR 12, 37, 62; DLB 14, 27, 139;
MTCW; SATA 35

Brown, (William) Larry 1951-...... **CLC 73**
See also CA 130; 134; INT 133

Brown, Moses
See Barrett, William (Christopher)

Brown, Rita Mae
1944- ..... **CLC 18, 43, 79; DAM NOV,
POP**
See also CA 45-48; CANR 2, 11, 35, 62;
INT CANR-11; MTCW

Brown, Roderick (Langmere) Haig-
See Haig-Brown, Roderick (Langmere)

Brown, Rosellen 1939-........... **CLC 32**
See also CA 77-80; CAAS 10; CANR 14, 44

Brown, Sterling Allen
1901-1989 .... **CLC 1, 23, 59; BLC;
DAM MULT, POET**
See also BW 1; CA 85-88; 127; CANR 26;
DLB 48, 51, 63; MTCW

Brown, Will
See Ainsworth, William Harrison

Brown, William Wells
1813-1884 .... **NCLC 2; BLC;
DAM MULT; DC 1**
See also DLB 3, 50

Browne, (Clyde) Jackson 1948(?)-... **CLC 21**
See also CA 120

Browning, Elizabeth Barrett
1806-1861 .... **NCLC 1, 16, 61; DA;
DAB; DAC; DAM MST, POET; PC 6;
WLC**
See also CDBLB 1832-1890; DLB 32

Browning, Robert
1812-1889 .... **NCLC 19; DA; DAB;
DAC; DAM MST, POET; PC 2; WLCS**
See also CDBLB 1832-1890; DLB 32, 163;
YABC 1

Browning, Tod 1882-1962 .... **CLC 16**
See also CA 141; 117

Brownson, Orestes (Augustus)
1803-1876 .... **NCLC 50**

Bruccoli, Matthew J(oseph) 1931-.. **CLC 34**
See also CA 9-12R; CANR 7; DLB 103

Bruce, Lenny.................... **CLC 21**
See also Schneider, Leonard Alfred

Bruin, John
See Brutus, Dennis

Brulard, Henri
See Stendhal

Brulls, Christian
See Simenon, Georges (Jacques Christian)

Brunner, John (Kilian Houston)
1934-1995 ...... **CLC 8, 10; DAM POP**
See also CA 1-4R; 149; CAAS 8; CANR 2,
37; MTCW

Bruno, Giordano 1548-1600........ **LC 27**

Brutus, Dennis
1924- ..... **CLC 43; BLC; DAM MULT,
POET**
See also BW 2; CA 49-52; CAAS 14;
CANR 2, 27, 42; DLB 117

Bryan, C(ourtlandt) D(ixon) B(arnes)
1936- .... **CLC 29**
See also CA 73-76; CANR 13;
INT CANR-13

Bryan, Michael
See Moore, Brian

Bryant, William Cullen
1794-1878 ..... **NCLC 6, 46; DA; DAB;
DAC; DAM MST, POET**
See also CDALB 1640-1865; DLB 3, 43, 59

Bryusov, Valery Yakovlevich
1873-1924 .... **TCLC 10**
See also CA 107; 155

Buchan, John
1875-1940 .... **TCLC 41; DAB;
DAM POP**
See also CA 108; 145; DLB 34, 70, 156;
YABC 2

Buchanan, George 1506-1582 .... **LC 4**

Buchheim, Lothar-Guenther 1918-... **CLC 6**
See also CA 85-88

Buchner, (Karl) Georg
1813-1837 .... **NCLC 26**

Buchwald, Art(hur) 1925-.......... **CLC 33**
See also AITN 1; CA 5-8R; CANR 21;
MTCW; SATA 10

Buck, Pearl S(ydenstricker)
1892-1973 .... **CLC 7, 11, 18; DA; DAB;
DAC; DAM MST, NOV**
See also AITN 1; CA 1-4R; 41-44R;
CANR 1, 34; DLB 9, 102; MTCW;
SATA 1, 25

Buckler, Ernest
1908-1984 .. **CLC 13; DAC; DAM MST**
See also CA 11-12; 114; CAP 1; DLB 68;
SATA 47

Buckley, Vincent (Thomas)
1925-1988 .... **CLC 57**
See also CA 101

Buckley, William F(rank), Jr.
1925- .... **CLC 7, 18, 37; DAM POP**
See also AITN 1; CA 1-4R; CANR 1, 24,
53; DLB 137; DLBY 80; INT CANR-24;
MTCW

Buechner, (Carl) Frederick
1926- ...... **CLC 2, 4, 6, 9; DAM NOV**
See also CA 13-16R; CANR 11, 39;
DLBY 80; INT CANR-11; MTCW

Buell, John (Edward) 1927-........ **CLC 10**
See also CA 1-4R; DLB 53

Buero Vallejo, Antonio 1916-... **CLC 15, 46**
See also CA 106; CANR 24, 49; HW;
MTCW

Bufalino, Gesualdo 1920(?)-........ **CLC 74**

Bugayev, Boris Nikolayevich 1880-1934
See Bely, Andrey
See also CA 104

Bukowski, Charles
1920-1994 . . . . **CLC 2, 5, 9, 41, 82;**
DAM NOV, POET; PC 18
See also CA 17-20R; 144; CANR 40, 62;
DLB 5, 130, 169; MTCW

Bulgakov, Mikhail (Afanas'evich)
1891-1940 . . . . **TCLC 2, 16;**
DAM DRAM, NOV; SSC 18
See also CA 105; 152

Bulgya, Alexander Alexandrovich
1901-1956 . . . . **TCLC 53**
See also Fadeyev, Alexander
See also CA 117

Bullins, Ed
1935- . . . . **CLC 1, 5, 7; BLC;**
DAM DRAM, MULT; DC 6
See also BW 2; CA 49-52; CAAS 16;
CANR 24, 46; DLB 7, 38; MTCW

Bulwer-Lytton, Edward (George Earle Lytton)
1803-1873 . . . . **NCLC 1, 45**
See also DLB 21

Bunin, Ivan Alexeyevich
1870-1953 . . . . **TCLC 6; SSC 5**
See also CA 104

Bunting, Basil
1900-1985 . . . . **CLC 10, 39, 47;**
DAM POET
See also CA 53-56; 115; CANR 7; DLB 20

Bunuel, Luis
1900-1983 . . . . **CLC 16, 80;**
DAM MULT; HLC
See also CA 101; 110; CANR 32; HW

Bunyan, John
1628-1688 . . . . . . **LC 4; DA; DAB; DAC;**
DAM MST; WLC
See also CDBLB 1660-1789; DLB 39

Burckhardt, Jacob (Christoph)
1818-1897 . . . . **NCLC 49**

Burford, Eleanor
See Hibbert, Eleanor Alice Burford

Burgess, Anthony
CLC 1, 2, 4, 5, 8, 10, 13, 15, 22, 40, 62,
81, 94; DAB
See also Wilson, John (Anthony) Burgess
See also AITN 1; CDBLB 1960 to Present;
DLB 14

Burke, Edmund
1729(?)-1797 . . . . . . **LC 7, 36; DA; DAB;**
DAC; DAM MST; WLC
See also DLB 104

Burke, Kenneth (Duva)
1897-1993 . . . . **CLC 2, 24**
See also CA 5-8R; 143; CANR 39; DLB 45,
63; MTCW

Burke, Leda
See Garnett, David

Burke, Ralph
See Silverberg, Robert

Burke, Thomas 1886-1945 . . . . **TCLC 63**
See also CA 113; 155

Burney, Fanny 1752-1840 . . . . **NCLC 12, 54**
See also DLB 39

Burns, Robert 1759-1796 . . . . **PC 6**
See also CDBLB 1789-1832; DA; DAB;
DAC; DAM MST, POET; DLB 109;
WLC

Burns, Tex
See L'Amour, Louis (Dearborn)

Burnshaw, Stanley 1906- . . . . . **CLC 3, 13, 44**
See also CA 9-12R; DLB 48

Burr, Anne 1937- . . . . **CLC 6**
See also CA 25-28R

Burroughs, Edgar Rice
1875-1950 . . . . **TCLC 2, 32; DAM NOV**
See also AAYA 11; CA 104; 132; DLB 8;
MTCW; SATA 41

Burroughs, William S(eward)
1914-1997 . . . . . . **CLC 1, 2, 5, 15, 22, 42,**
75; DA; DAB; DAC; DAM MST, NOV,
POP; WLC
See also AITN 2; CA 9-12R; 160;
CANR 20, 52; DLB 2, 8, 16, 152;
DLBY 81; MTCW

Burton, Richard F. 1821-1890 . . . . **NCLC 42**
See also DLB 55, 184

Busch, Frederick 1941- . . . **CLC 7, 10, 18, 47**
See also CA 33-36R; CAAS 1; CANR 45;
DLB 6

Bush, Ronald 1946- . . . . **CLC 34**
See also CA 136

Bustos, F(rancisco)
See Borges, Jorge Luis

Bustos Domecq, H(onorio)
See Bioy Casares, Adolfo; Borges, Jorge
Luis

Butler, Octavia E(stelle)
1947- . . . . . **CLC 38; DAM MULT, POP**
See also AAYA 18; BW 2; CA 73-76;
CANR 12, 24, 38; DLB 33; MTCW;
SATA 84

Butler, Robert Olen (Jr.)
1945- . . . . **CLC 81; DAM POP**
See also CA 112; DLB 173; INT 112

Butler, Samuel 1612-1680 . . . . **LC 16**
See also DLB 101, 126

Butler, Samuel
1835-1902 . . . . . . **TCLC 1, 33; DA; DAB;**
DAC; DAM MST, NOV; WLC
See also CA 143; CDBLB 1890-1914;
DLB 18, 57, 174

Butler, Walter C.
See Faust, Frederick (Schiller)

Butor, Michel (Marie Francois)
1926- . . . . **CLC 1, 3, 8, 11, 15**
See also CA 9-12R; CANR 33; DLB 83;
MTCW

Buzo, Alexander (John) 1944- . . . . . . **CLC 61**
See also CA 97-100; CANR 17, 39

Buzzati, Dino 1906-1972 . . . . **CLC 36**
See also CA 160; 33-36R; DLB 177

Byars, Betsy (Cromer) 1928- . . . . **CLC 35**
See also AAYA 19; CA 33-36R; CANR 18,
36, 57; CLR 1, 16; DLB 52;
INT CANR-18; JRDA; MAICYA;
MTCW; SAAS 1; SATA 4, 46, 80

Byatt, A(ntonia) S(usan Drabble)
1936- . . . **CLC 19, 65; DAM NOV, POP**
See also CA 13-16R; CANR 13, 33, 50;
DLB 14; MTCW

Byrne, David 1952- . . . . **CLC 26**
See also CA 127

Byrne, John Keyes 1926-
See Leonard, Hugh
See also CA 102; INT 102

Byron, George Gordon (Noel)
1788-1824 . . . . . **NCLC 2, 12; DA; DAB;**
DAC; DAM MST, POET; PC 16; WLC
See also CDBLB 1789-1832; DLB 96, 110

Byron, Robert 1905-1941 . . . . **TCLC 67**
See also CA 160

C. 3. 3.
See Wilde, Oscar (Fingal O'Flahertie Wills)

Caballero, Fernan 1796-1877 . . . . . **NCLC 10**

Cabell, Branch
See Cabell, James Branch

Cabell, James Branch 1879-1958 . . . **TCLC 6**
See also CA 105; 152; DLB 9, 78

Cable, George Washington
1844-1925 . . . . **TCLC 4; SSC 4**
See also CA 104; 155; DLB 12, 74;
DLBD 13

Cabral de Melo Neto, Joao
1920- . . . . **CLC 76; DAM MULT**
See also CA 151

Cabrera Infante, G(uillermo)
1929- . . . . . **CLC 5, 25, 45; DAM MULT;**
HLC
See also CA 85-88; CANR 29; DLB 113;
HW; MTCW

Cade, Toni
See Bambara, Toni Cade

Cadmus and Harmonia
See Buchan, John

Caedmon fl. 658-680 . . . . **CMLC 7**
See also DLB 146

Caeiro, Alberto
See Pessoa, Fernando (Antonio Nogueira)

Cage, John (Milton, Jr.) 1912- . . . . . **CLC 41**
See also CA 13-16R; CANR 9;
INT CANR-9

Cahan, Abraham 1860-1951 . . . . **TCLC 71**
See also CA 108; 154; DLB 9, 25, 28

Cain, G.
See Cabrera Infante, G(uillermo)

Cain, Guillermo
See Cabrera Infante, G(uillermo)

Cain, James M(allahan)
1892-1977 . . . . **CLC 3, 11, 28**
See also AITN 1; CA 17-20R; 73-76;
CANR 8, 34, 61; MTCW

Caine, Mark
See Raphael, Frederic (Michael)

Calasso, Roberto 1941- . . . . **CLC 81**
See also CA 143

Calderon de la Barca, Pedro
1600-1681 . . . . **LC 23; DC 3**

Caldwell, Erskine (Preston)
1903-1987 . . . . **CLC 1, 8, 14, 50, 60;**
DAM NOV; SSC 19
See also AITN 1; CA 1-4R; 121; CAAS 1;
CANR 2, 33; DLB 9, 86; MTCW

Caldwell, (Janet Miriam) Taylor (Holland)
1900-1985 . . . . **CLC 2, 28, 39;**
DAM NOV, POP
See also CA 5-8R; 116; CANR 5

Calhoun, John Caldwell
1782-1850 . . . . **NCLC 15**
See also DLB 3

Calisher, Hortense
1911- . . . . . **CLC 2, 4, 8, 38; DAM NOV;
SSC 15**
See also CA 1-4R; CANR 1, 22; DLB 2;
INT CANR-22; MTCW

Callaghan, Morley Edward
1903-1990 . . . . . **CLC 3, 14, 41, 65; DAC;
DAM MST**
See also CA 9-12R; 132; CANR 33;
DLB 68; MTCW

Callimachus
c. 305B.C.-c. 240B.C. . . . . **CMLC 18**
See also DLB 176

Calvin, John 1509-1564 . . . . **LC 37**

Calvino, Italo
1923-1985 . . . . . **CLC 5, 8, 11, 22, 33, 39,
73; DAM NOV; SSC 3**
See also CA 85-88; 116; CANR 23, 61;
MTCW

Cameron, Carey 1952- . . . . **CLC 59**
See also CA 135

Cameron, Peter 1959- . . . . **CLC 44**
See also CA 125; CANR 50

Campana, Dino 1885-1932 . . . . **TCLC 20**
See also CA 117; DLB 114

Campanella, Tommaso 1568-1639 . . . . **LC 32**

Campbell, John W(ood, Jr.)
1910-1971 . . . . **CLC 32**
See also CA 21-22; 29-32R; CANR 34;
CAP 2; DLB 8; MTCW

Campbell, Joseph 1904-1987 . . . . **CLC 69**
See also AAYA 3; BEST 89:2; CA 1-4R;
124; CANR 3, 28, 61; MTCW

Campbell, Maria 1940- . . . . **CLC 85; DAC**
See also CA 102; CANR 54; NNAL

Campbell, (John) Ramsey
1946- . . . . **CLC 42; SSC 19**
See also CA 57-60; CANR 7; INT CANR-7

Campbell, (Ignatius) Roy (Dunnachie)
1901-1957 . . . . **TCLC 5**
See also CA 104; 155; DLB 20

Campbell, Thomas 1777-1844 . . . . **NCLC 19**
See also DLB 93; 144

Campbell, Wilfred . . . . **TCLC 9**
See also Campbell, William

Campbell, William 1858(?)-1918
See Campbell, Wilfred
See also CA 106; DLB 92

Campion, Jane . . . . **CLC 95**
See also CA 138

Campos, Alvaro de
See Pessoa, Fernando (Antonio Nogueira)

Camus, Albert
1913-1960 . . . . **CLC 1, 2, 4, 9, 11, 14, 32,
63, 69; DA; DAB; DAC; DAM DRAM,
MST, NOV; DC 2; SSC 9; WLC**
See also CA 89-92; DLB 72; MTCW

Canby, Vincent 1924- . . . . **CLC 13**
See also CA 81-84

Cancale
See Desnos, Robert

Canetti, Elias
1905-1994 . . . . . . **CLC 3, 14, 25, 75, 86**
See also CA 21-24R; 146; CANR 23, 61;
DLB 85, 124; MTCW

Canin, Ethan 1960- . . . . **CLC 55**
See also CA 131; 135

Cannon, Curt
See Hunter, Evan

Cape, Judith
See Page, P(atricia) K(athleen)

Capek, Karel
1890-1938 . . . . . . **TCLC 6, 37; DA; DAB;
DAC; DAM DRAM, MST, NOV; DC 1;
WLC**
See also CA 104; 140

Capote, Truman
1924-1984 . . . . . . **CLC 1, 3, 8, 13, 19, 34,
38, 58; DA; DAB; DAC; DAM MST,
NOV, POP; SSC 2; WLC**
See also CA 5-8R; 113; CANR 18, 62;
CDALB 1941-1968; DLB 2; DLBY 80,
84; MTCW; SATA 91

Capra, Frank 1897-1991 . . . . **CLC 16**
See also CA 61-64; 135

Caputo, Philip 1941- . . . . **CLC 32**
See also CA 73-76; CANR 40

Card, Orson Scott
1951- . . . . . **CLC 44, 47, 50; DAM POP**
See also AAYA 11; CA 102; CANR 27, 47;
INT CANR-27; MTCW; SATA 83

Cardenal, Ernesto
1925- . . . . **CLC 31; DAM MULT,
POET; HLC**
See also CA 49-52; CANR 2, 32; HW;
MTCW

Cardozo, Benjamin N(athan)
1870-1938 . . . . **TCLC 65**
See also CA 117

Carducci, Giosue 1835-1907 . . . . . . **TCLC 32**

Carew, Thomas 1595(?)-1640 . . . . **LC 13**
See also DLB 126

Carey, Ernestine Gilbreth 1908- . . . . **CLC 17**
See also CA 5-8R; SATA 2

Carey, Peter 1943- . . . . **CLC 40, 55, 96**
See also CA 123; 127; CANR 53; INT 127;
MTCW; SATA 94

Carleton, William 1794-1869 . . . . . . **NCLC 3**
See also DLB 159

Carlisle, Henry (Coffin) 1926- . . . . . . **CLC 33**
See also CA 13-16R; CANR 15

Carlsen, Chris
See Holdstock, Robert P.

Carlson, Ron(ald F.) 1947- . . . . **CLC 54**
See also CA 105; CANR 27

Carlyle, Thomas
1795-1881 . . . . **NCLC 22; DA; DAB;
DAC; DAM MST**
See also CDBLB 1789-1832; DLB 55; 144

Carman, (William) Bliss
1861-1929 . . . . **TCLC 7; DAC**
See also CA 104; 152; DLB 92

Carnegie, Dale 1888-1955 . . . . **TCLC 53**

Carossa, Hans 1878-1956 . . . . **TCLC 48**
See also DLB 66

Carpenter, Don(ald Richard)
1931-1995 . . . . **CLC 41**
See also CA 45-48; 149; CANR 1

Carpentier (y Valmont), Alejo
1904-1980 . . . . **CLC 8, 11, 38;
DAM MULT; HLC**
See also CA 65-68; 97-100; CANR 11;
DLB 113; HW

Carr, Caleb 1955(?)- . . . . **CLC 86**
See also CA 147

Carr, Emily 1871-1945 . . . . **TCLC 32**
See also CA 159; DLB 68

Carr, John Dickson 1906-1977 . . . . . . **CLC 3**
See also Fairbairn, Roger
See also CA 49-52; 69-72; CANR 3, 33, 60;
MTCW

Carr, Philippa
See Hibbert, Eleanor Alice Burford

Carr, Virginia Spencer 1929- . . . . . . **CLC 34**
See also CA 61-64; DLB 111

Carrere, Emmanuel 1957- . . . . **CLC 89**

Carrier, Roch
1937- . . . **CLC 13, 78; DAC; DAM MST**
See also CA 130; CANR 61; DLB 53

Carroll, James P. 1943(?)- . . . . **CLC 38**
See also CA 81-84

Carroll, Jim 1951- . . . . **CLC 35**
See also AAYA 17; CA 45-48; CANR 42

Carroll, Lewis . . . . . **NCLC 2, 53; PC 18; WLC**
See also Dodgson, Charles Lutwidge
See also CDBLB 1832-1890; CLR 2, 18;
DLB 18, 163, 178; JRDA

Carroll, Paul Vincent 1900-1968 . . . . **CLC 10**
See also CA 9-12R; 25-28R; DLB 10

Carruth, Hayden
1921- . . . . . . **CLC 4, 7, 10, 18, 84; PC 10**
See also CA 9-12R; CANR 4, 38, 59;
DLB 5, 165; INT CANR-4; MTCW;
SATA 47

Carson, Rachel Louise
1907-1964 . . . . **CLC 71; DAM POP**
See also CA 77-80; CANR 35; MTCW;
SATA 23

Carter, Angela (Olive)
1940-1992 . . . . . **CLC 5, 41, 76; SSC 13**
See also CA 53-56; 136; CANR 12, 36, 61;
DLB 14; MTCW; SATA 66;
SATA-Obit 70

Carter, Nick
See Smith, Martin Cruz

Carver, Raymond
1938-1988 . . . . **CLC 22, 36, 53, 55;
DAM NOV; SSC 8**
See also CA 33-36R; 126; CANR 17, 34, 61;
DLB 130; DLBY 84, 88; MTCW

Cary, Elizabeth, Lady Falkland
1585-1639 . . . . **LC 30**

Cary, (Arthur) Joyce (Lunel)
1888-1957 . . . . **TCLC 1, 29**
See also CA 104; CDBLB 1914-1945;
DLB 15, 100

Casanova de Seingalt, Giovanni Jacopo
1725-1798 . . . . **LC 13**

Casares, Adolfo Bioy
See Bioy Casares, Adolfo

Chatterje, Sarat Chandra　1876-1936(?)
See Chatterji, Saratchandra
See also CA 109

Chatterji, Bankim Chandra
1838-1894 . . . . **NCLC 19**

Chatterji, Saratchandra . . . . **TCLC 13**
See also Chatterje, Sarat Chandra

Chatterton, Thomas
1752-1770 . . . . **LC 3; DAM POET**
See also DLB 109

Chatwin, (Charles) Bruce
1940-1989 . . **CLC 28, 57, 59; DAM POP**
See also AAYA 4; BEST 90:1; CA 85-88;
127

Chaucer, Daniel
See Ford, Ford Madox

Chaucer, Geoffrey
1340(?)-1400 . . . . **LC 17; DA; DAB;
DAC; DAM MST, POET; PC 19; WLCS**
See also CDBLB Before 1660; DLB 146

Chaviaras, Strates　1935-
See Haviaras, Stratis
See also CA 105

Chayefsky, Paddy . . . . **CLC 23**
See also Chayefsky, Sidney
See also DLB 7, 44; DLBY 81

Chayefsky, Sidney　1923-1981
See Chayefsky, Paddy
See also CA 9-12R; 104; CANR 18;
DAM DRAM

Chedid, Andree　1920- . . . . **CLC 47**
See also CA 145

Cheever, John
1912-1982 . . . . . . **CLC 3, 7, 8, 11, 15, 25,
64; DA; DAB; DAC; DAM MST, NOV,
POP; SSC 1; WLC**
See also CA 5-8R; 106; CABS 1; CANR 5,
27; CDALB 1941-1968; DLB 2, 102;
DLBY 80, 82; INT CANR-5; MTCW

Cheever, Susan　1943- . . . . **CLC 18, 48**
See also CA 103; CANR 27, 51; DLBY 82;
INT CANR-27

Chekhonte, Antosha
See Chekhov, Anton (Pavlovich)

Chekhov, Anton (Pavlovich)
1860-1904 . . . . . **TCLC 3, 10, 31, 55; DA;
DAB; DAC; DAM DRAM, MST; SSC 2,
28; WLC**
See also CA 104; 124; SATA 90

Chernyshevsky, Nikolay Gavrilovich
1828-1889 . . . . **NCLC 1**

Cherry, Carolyn Janice　1942-
See Cherryh, C. J.
See also CA 65-68; CANR 10

Cherryh, C. J. . . . . **CLC 35**
See also Cherry, Carolyn Janice
See also DLBY 80; SATA 93

Chesnutt, Charles W(addell)
1858-1932 . . . . **TCLC 5, 39; BLC;
DAM MULT; SSC 7**
See also BW 1; CA 106; 125; DLB 12, 50,
78; MTCW

Chester, Alfred　1929(?)-1971 . . . . **CLC 49**
See also CA 33-36R; DLB 130

Chesterton, G(ilbert) K(eith)
1874-1936 . . . . **TCLC 1, 6, 64;
DAM NOV, POET; SSC 1**
See also CA 104; 132; CDBLB 1914-1945;
DLB 10, 19, 34, 70, 98, 149, 178; MTCW;
SATA 27

Chiang Pin-chin　1904-1986
See Ding Ling
See also CA 118

Ch'ien Chung-shu　1910- . . . . **CLC 22**
See also CA 130; MTCW

Child, L. Maria
See Child, Lydia Maria

Child, Lydia Maria　1802-1880 . . . . **NCLC 6**
See also DLB 1, 74; SATA 67

Child, Mrs.
See Child, Lydia Maria

Child, Philip　1898-1978 . . . . **CLC 19, 68**
See also CA 13-14; CAP 1; SATA 47

Childers, (Robert) Erskine
1870-1922 . . . . **TCLC 65**
See also CA 113; 153; DLB 70

Childress, Alice
1920-1994 . . . . **CLC 12, 15, 86, 96; BLC;
DAM DRAM, MULT, NOV; DC 4**
See also AAYA 8; BW 2; CA 45-48; 146;
CANR 3, 27, 50; CLR 14; DLB 7, 38;
JRDA; MAICYA; MTCW; SATA 7, 48,
81

Chin, Frank (Chew, Jr.)　1940- . . . . **DC 7**
See also CA 33-36R; DAM MULT

Chislett, (Margaret) Anne　1943- . . . . **CLC 34**
See also CA 151

Chitty, Thomas Willes　1926- . . . . **CLC 11**
See also Hinde, Thomas
See also CA 5-8R

Chivers, Thomas Holley
1809-1858 . . . . **NCLC 49**
See also DLB 3

Chomette, Rene Lucien　1898-1981
See Clair, Rene
See also CA 103

Chopin, Kate
. . **TCLC 5, 14; DA; DAB; SSC 8; WLCS**
See also Chopin, Katherine
See also CDALB 1865-1917; DLB 12, 78

Chopin, Katherine　1851-1904
See Chopin, Kate
See also CA 104; 122; DAC; DAM MST,
NOV

Chretien de Troyes
c. 12th cent. - . . . . **CMLC 10**

Christie
See Ichikawa, Kon

Christie, Agatha (Mary Clarissa)
1890-1976 . . . . . . **CLC 1, 6, 8, 12, 39, 48;
DAB; DAC; DAM NOV**
See also AAYA 9; AITN 1, 2; CA 17-20R;
61-64; CANR 10, 37; CDBLB 1914-1945;
DLB 13, 77; MTCW; SATA 36

Christie, (Ann) Philippa
See Pearce, Philippa
See also CA 5-8R; CANR 4

Christine de Pizan　1365(?)-1431(?) . . . . **LC 9**

Chubb, Elmer
See Masters, Edgar Lee

Chulkov, Mikhail Dmitrievich
1743-1792 . . . . **LC 2**
See also DLB 150

Churchill, Caryl　1938- . . . **CLC 31, 55; DC 5**
See also CA 102; CANR 22, 46; DLB 13;
MTCW

Churchill, Charles　1731-1764 . . . . **LC 3**
See also DLB 109

Chute, Carolyn　1947- . . . . **CLC 39**
See also CA 123

Ciardi, John (Anthony)
1916-1986 . . . . **CLC 10, 40, 44;
DAM POET**
See also CA 5-8R; 118; CAAS 2; CANR 5,
33; CLR 19; DLB 5; DLBY 86;
INT CANR-5; MAICYA; MTCW;
SATA 1, 65; SATA-Obit 46

Cicero, Marcus Tullius
106B.C.-43B.C. . . . . **CMLC 3**

Cimino, Michael　1943- . . . . **CLC 16**
See also CA 105

Cioran, E(mil) M.　1911-1995 . . . . . . **CLC 64**
See also CA 25-28R; 149

Cisneros, Sandra
1954- . . . . . **CLC 69; DAM MULT; HLC**
See also AAYA 9; CA 131; DLB 122, 152;
HW

Cixous, Helene　1937- . . . . **CLC 92**
See also CA 126; CANR 55; DLB 83;
MTCW

Clair, Rene . . . . **CLC 20**
See also Chomette, Rene Lucien

Clampitt, Amy　1920-1994 . . . **CLC 32; PC 19**
See also CA 110; 146; CANR 29; DLB 105

Clancy, Thomas L., Jr.　1947-
See Clancy, Tom
See also CA 125; 131; CANR 62; INT 131;
MTCW

Clancy, Tom . . . . . **CLC 45; DAM NOV, POP**
See also Clancy, Thomas L., Jr.
See also AAYA 9; BEST 89:1, 90:1

Clare, John
1793-1864 . . . . **NCLC 9; DAB;
DAM POET**
See also DLB 55, 96

Clarin
See Alas (y Urena), Leopoldo (Enrique
Garcia)

Clark, Al C.
See Goines, Donald

Clark, (Robert) Brian　1932- . . . . **CLC 29**
See also CA 41-44R

Clark, Curt
See Westlake, Donald E(dwin)

Clark, Eleanor　1913-1996 . . . . **CLC 5, 19**
See also CA 9-12R; 151; CANR 41; DLB 6

Clark, J. P.
See Clark, John Pepper
See also DLB 117

Clark, John Pepper
1935- .... **CLC 38; BLC; DAM DRAM, MULT; DC 5**
See also Clark, J. P.
See also BW 1; CA 65-68; CANR 16

Clark, M. R.
See Clark, Mavis Thorpe

Clark, Mavis Thorpe 1909- .... **CLC 12**
See also CA 57-60; CANR 8, 37; CLR 30;
MAICYA; SAAS 5; SATA 8, 74

Clark, Walter Van Tilburg
1909-1971 .... **CLC 28**
See also CA 9-12R; 33-36R; DLB 9;
SATA 8

Clarke, Arthur C(harles)
1917- .... **CLC 1, 4, 13, 18, 35; DAM POP; SSC 3**
See also AAYA 4; CA 1-4R; CANR 2, 28,
55; JRDA; MAICYA; MTCW; SATA 13,
70

Clarke, Austin
1896-1974 ...... **CLC 6, 9; DAM POET**
See also CA 29-32; 49-52; CAP 2; DLB 10,
20

Clarke, Austin C(hesterfield)
1934- .... **CLC 8, 53; BLC; DAC; DAM MULT**
See also BW 1; CA 25-28R; CAAS 16;
CANR 14, 32; DLB 53, 125

Clarke, Gillian 1937- .... **CLC 61**
See also CA 106; DLB 40

Clarke, Marcus (Andrew Hislop)
1846-1881 .... **NCLC 19**

Clarke, Shirley 1925- .... **CLC 16**

Clash, The
See Headon, (Nicky) Topper; Jones, Mick;
Simonon, Paul; Strummer, Joe

Claudel, Paul (Louis Charles Marie)
1868-1955 .... **TCLC 2, 10**
See also CA 104

Clavell, James (duMaresq)
1925-1994 .... **CLC 6, 25, 87; DAM NOV, POP**
See also CA 25-28R; 146; CANR 26, 48;
MTCW

Cleaver, (Leroy) Eldridge
1935- ..... **CLC 30; BLC; DAM MULT**
See also BW 1; CA 21-24R; CANR 16

Cleese, John (Marwood) 1939- ..... **CLC 21**
See also Monty Python
See also CA 112; 116; CANR 35; MTCW

Cleishbotham, Jebediah
See Scott, Walter

Cleland, John 1710-1789 .... **LC 2**
See also DLB 39

Clemens, Samuel Langhorne 1835-1910
See Twain, Mark
See also CA 104; 135; CDALB 1865-1917;
DA; DAB; DAC; DAM MST, NOV;
DLB 11, 12, 23, 64, 74; JRDA;
MAICYA; YABC 2

Cleophil
See Congreve, William

Clerihew, E.
See Bentley, E(dmund) C(lerihew)

Clerk, N. W.
See Lewis, C(live) S(taples)

Cliff, Jimmy .... **CLC 21**
See also Chambers, James

Clifton, (Thelma) Lucille
1936- .... **CLC 19, 66; BLC; DAM MULT, POET; PC 17**
See also BW 2; CA 49-52; CANR 2, 24, 42;
CLR 5; DLB 5, 41; MAICYA; MTCW;
SATA 20, 69

Clinton, Dirk
See Silverberg, Robert

Clough, Arthur Hugh 1819-1861 .. **NCLC 27**
See also DLB 32

Clutha, Janet Paterson Frame 1924-
See Frame, Janet
See also CA 1-4R; CANR 2, 36; MTCW

Clyne, Terence
See Blatty, William Peter

Cobalt, Martin
See Mayne, William (James Carter)

Cobbett, William 1763-1835 ..... **NCLC 49**
See also DLB 43, 107, 158

Coburn, D(onald) L(ee) 1938- ...... **CLC 10**
See also CA 89-92

Cocteau, Jean (Maurice Eugene Clement)
1889-1963 .... **CLC 1, 8, 15, 16, 43; DA; DAB; DAC; DAM DRAM, MST, NOV; WLC**
See also CA 25-28; CANR 40; CAP 2;
DLB 65; MTCW

Codrescu, Andrei
1946- .... **CLC 46; DAM POET**
See also CA 33-36R; CAAS 19; CANR 13,
34, 53

Coe, Max
See Bourne, Randolph S(illiman)

Coe, Tucker
See Westlake, Donald E(dwin)

Coetzee, J(ohn) M(ichael)
1940- ...... **CLC 23, 33, 66; DAM NOV**
See also CA 77-80; CANR 41, 54; MTCW

Coffey, Brian
See Koontz, Dean R(ay)

Cohan, George M(ichael)
1878-1942 .... **TCLC 60**
See also CA 157

Cohen, Arthur A(llen)
1928-1986 .... **CLC 7, 31**
See also CA 1-4R; 120; CANR 1, 17, 42;
DLB 28

Cohen, Leonard (Norman)
1934- .... **CLC 3, 38; DAC; DAM MST**
See also CA 21-24R; CANR 14; DLB 53;
MTCW

Cohen, Matt 1942- .... **CLC 19; DAC**
See also CA 61-64; CAAS 18; CANR 40;
DLB 53

Cohen-Solal, Annie 19(?)- .... **CLC 50**

Colegate, Isabel 1931- .... **CLC 36**
See also CA 17-20R; CANR 8, 22; DLB 14;
INT CANR-22; MTCW

Coleman, Emmett
See Reed, Ishmael

Coleridge, M. E.
See Coleridge, Mary E(lizabeth)

Coleridge, Mary E(lizabeth)
1861-1907 .... **TCLC 73**
See also CA 116; DLB 19, 98

Coleridge, Samuel Taylor
1772-1834 ..... **NCLC 9, 54; DA; DAB; DAC; DAM MST, POET; PC 11; WLC**
See also CDBLB 1789-1832; DLB 93, 107

Coleridge, Sara 1802-1852 ...... **NCLC 31**

Coles, Don 1928- .... **CLC 46**
See also CA 115; CANR 38

Colette, (Sidonie-Gabrielle)
1873-1954 .... **TCLC 1, 5, 16; DAM NOV; SSC 10**
See also CA 104; 131; DLB 65; MTCW

Collett, (Jacobine) Camilla (Wergeland)
1813-1895 .... **NCLC 22**

Collier, Christopher 1930- .... **CLC 30**
See also AAYA 13; CA 33-36R; CANR 13,
33; JRDA; MAICYA; SATA 16, 70

Collier, James L(incoln)
1928- .... **CLC 30; DAM POP**
See also AAYA 13; CA 9-12R; CANR 4,
33, 60; CLR 3; JRDA; MAICYA;
SAAS 21; SATA 8, 70

Collier, Jeremy 1650-1726 .... **LC 6**

Collier, John 1901-1980 .... **SSC 19**
See also CA 65-68; 97-100; CANR 10;
DLB 77

Collingwood, R(obin) G(eorge)
1889(?)-1943 .... **TCLC 67**
See also CA 117; 155

Collins, Hunt
See Hunter, Evan

Collins, Linda 1931- .... **CLC 44**
See also CA 125

Collins, (William) Wilkie
1824-1889 .... **NCLC 1, 18**
See also CDBLB 1832-1890; DLB 18, 70,
159

Collins, William
1721-1759 ...... **LC 4, 40; DAM POET**
See also DLB 109

Collodi, Carlo 1826-1890 .... **NCLC 54**
See also Lorenzini, Carlo
See also CLR 5

Colman, George
See Glassco, John

Colt, Winchester Remington
See Hubbard, L(afayette) Ron(ald)

Colter, Cyrus 1910- .... **CLC 58**
See also BW 1; CA 65-68; CANR 10;
DLB 33

Colton, James
See Hansen, Joseph

Colum, Padraic 1881-1972 .... **CLC 28**
See also CA 73-76; 33-36R; CANR 35;
CLR 36; MAICYA; MTCW; SATA 15

Colvin, James
See Moorcock, Michael (John)

Colwin, Laurie (E.)
1944-1992 .... **CLC 5, 13, 23, 84**
See also CA 89-92; 139; CANR 20, 46;
DLBY 80; MTCW

Comfort, Alex(ander)
1920- . . . . **CLC 7; DAM POP**
See also CA 1-4R; CANR 1, 45

Comfort, Montgomery
See Campbell, (John) Ramsey

Compton-Burnett, I(vy)
1884(?)-1969 . . . . . **CLC 1, 3, 10, 15, 34;**
DAM NOV
See also CA 1-4R; 25-28R; CANR 4;
DLB 36; MTCW

Comstock, Anthony 1844-1915 . . . . **TCLC 13**
See also CA 110

Comte, Auguste 1798-1857. . . . . . **NCLC 54**

Conan Doyle, Arthur
See Doyle, Arthur Conan

Conde, Maryse
1937- . . . . **CLC 52, 92; DAM MULT**
See also Boucolon, Maryse
See also BW 2

Condillac, Etienne Bonnot de
1714-1780 . . . . **LC 26**

Condon, Richard (Thomas)
1915-1996 . . . . . **CLC 4, 6, 8, 10, 45, 100;**
DAM NOV
See also BEST 90:3; CA 1-4R; 151;
CAAS 1; CANR 2, 23; INT CANR-23;
MTCW

Confucius
551B.C.-479B.C. . . . . **CMLC 19; DA;**
DAB; DAC; DAM MST; WLCS

Congreve, William
1670-1729 . . . . **LC 5, 21; DA; DAB;**
DAC; DAM DRAM, MST, POET;
DC 2; WLC
See also CDBLB 1660-1789; DLB 39, 84

Connell, Evan S(helby), Jr.
1924- . . . . **CLC 4, 6, 45; DAM NOV**
See also AAYA 7; CA 1-4R; CAAS 2;
CANR 2, 39; DLB 2; DLBY 81; MTCW

Connelly, Marc(us Cook)
1890-1980 . . . . **CLC 7**
See also CA 85-88; 102; CANR 30; DLB 7;
DLBY 80; SATA-Obit 25

Connor, Ralph . . . . **TCLC 31**
See also Gordon, Charles William
See also DLB 92

Conrad, Joseph
1857-1924 . . . . **TCLC 1, 6, 13, 25, 43, 57;**
DA; DAB; DAC; DAM MST, NOV;
SSC 9; WLC
See also CA 104; 131; CANR 60;
CDBLB 1890-1914; DLB 10, 34, 98, 156;
MTCW; SATA 27

Conrad, Robert Arnold
See Hart, Moss

Conroy, Donald Pat(rick)
1945- . . . **CLC 30, 74; DAM NOV, POP**
See also AAYA 8; AITN 1; CA 85-88;
CANR 24, 53; DLB 6; MTCW

Constant (de Rebecque), (Henri) Benjamin
1767-1830 . . . . **NCLC 6**
See also DLB 119

Conybeare, Charles Augustus
See Eliot, T(homas) S(tearns)

Cook, Michael 1933- . . . . **CLC 58**
See also CA 93-96; DLB 53

Cook, Robin 1940- . . . . **CLC 14; DAM POP**
See also BEST 90:2; CA 108; 111;
CANR 41; INT 111

Cook, Roy
See Silverberg, Robert

Cooke, Elizabeth 1948- . . . . **CLC 55**
See also CA 129

Cooke, John Esten 1830-1886. . . . . **NCLC 5**
See also DLB 3

Cooke, John Estes
See Baum, L(yman) Frank

Cooke, M. E.
See Creasey, John

Cooke, Margaret
See Creasey, John

Cook-Lynn, Elizabeth
1930- . . . . **CLC 93; DAM MULT**
See also CA 133; DLB 175; NNAL

Cooney, Ray . . . . **CLC 62**

Cooper, Douglas 1960- . . . . **CLC 86**

Cooper, Henry St. John
See Creasey, John

Cooper, J(oan) California
. . . . **CLC 56; DAM MULT**
See also AAYA 12; BW 1; CA 125;
CANR 55

Cooper, James Fenimore
1789-1851 . . . . **NCLC 1, 27, 54**
See also AAYA 22; CDALB 1640-1865;
DLB 3; SATA 19

Coover, Robert (Lowell)
1932- . . . . **CLC 3, 7, 15, 32, 46, 87;**
DAM NOV; SSC 15
See also CA 45-48; CANR 3, 37, 58;
DLB 2; DLBY 81; MTCW

Copeland, Stewart (Armstrong)
1952- . . . . **CLC 26**

Coppard, A(lfred) E(dgar)
1878-1957 . . . . **TCLC 5; SSC 21**
See also CA 114; DLB 162; YABC 1

Coppee, Francois 1842-1908 . . . . . . **TCLC 25**

Coppola, Francis Ford 1939- . . . . **CLC 16**
See also CA 77-80; CANR 40; DLB 44

Corbiere, Tristan 1845-1875 . . . . . **NCLC 43**

Corcoran, Barbara 1911- . . . . **CLC 17**
See also AAYA 14; CA 21-24R; CAAS 2;
CANR 11, 28, 48; DLB 52; JRDA;
SAAS 20; SATA 3, 77

Cordelier, Maurice
See Giraudoux, (Hippolyte) Jean

Corelli, Marie 1855-1924. . . . . **TCLC 51**
See also Mackay, Mary
See also DLB 34, 156

Corman, Cid. . . . . **CLC 9**
See also Corman, Sidney
See also CAAS 2; DLB 5

Corman, Sidney 1924-
See Corman, Cid
See also CA 85-88; CANR 44; DAM POET

Cormier, Robert (Edmund)
1925- . . . . **CLC 12, 30; DA; DAB; DAC;**
DAM MST, NOV
See also AAYA 3, 19; CA 1-4R; CANR 5,
23; CDALB 1968-1988; CLR 12; DLB 52;
INT CANR-23; JRDA; MAICYA;
MTCW; SATA 10, 45, 83

Corn, Alfred (DeWitt III) 1943- . . . . **CLC 33**
See also CA 104; CAAS 25; CANR 44;
DLB 120; DLBY 80

Corneille, Pierre
1606-1684 . . . . **LC 28; DAB; DAM MST**

Cornwell, David (John Moore)
1931- . . . . **CLC 9, 15; DAM POP**
See also le Carre, John
See also CA 5-8R; CANR 13, 33, 59;
MTCW

Corso, (Nunzio) Gregory 1930- . . . **CLC 1, 11**
See also CA 5-8R; CANR 41; DLB 5, 16;
MTCW

Cortazar, Julio
1914-1984 . . . . . . **CLC 2, 3, 5, 10, 13, 15,**
33, 34, 92; DAM MULT, NOV; HLC;
SSC 7
See also CA 21-24R; CANR 12, 32;
DLB 113; HW; MTCW

CORTES, HERNAN 1484-1547. . . . . **LC 31**

Corwin, Cecil
See Kornbluth, C(yril) M.

Cosic, Dobrica 1921- . . . . **CLC 14**
See also CA 122; 138; DLB 181

Costain, Thomas B(ertram)
1885-1965 . . . . **CLC 30**
See also CA 5-8R; 25-28R; DLB 9

Costantini, Humberto
1924(?)-1987 . . . . **CLC 49**
See also CA 131; 122; HW

Costello, Elvis 1955- . . . . **CLC 21**

Cotes, Cecil V.
See Duncan, Sara Jeannette

Cotter, Joseph Seamon Sr.
1861-1949 . . . . **TCLC 28; BLC;**
DAM MULT
See also BW 1; CA 124; DLB 50

Couch, Arthur Thomas Quiller
See Quiller-Couch, Arthur Thomas

Coulton, James
See Hansen, Joseph

Couperus, Louis (Marie Anne)
1863-1923 . . . . **TCLC 15**
See also CA 115

Coupland, Douglas
1961- . . . . **CLC 85; DAC; DAM POP**
See also CA 142; CANR 57

Court, Wesli
See Turco, Lewis (Putnam)

Courtenay, Bryce 1933- . . . . **CLC 59**
See also CA 138

Courtney, Robert
See Ellison, Harlan (Jay)

Cousteau, Jacques-Yves
1910-1997 . . . . **CLC 30**
See also CA 65-68; 159; CANR 15; MTCW;
SATA 38

Defoe, Daniel
1660(?)-1731 .... **LC 1; DA; DAB; DAC;**
DAM MST, NOV; WLC
See also CDBLB 1660-1789; DLB 39, 95,
101; JRDA; MAICYA; SATA 22

de Gourmont, Remy(-Marie-Charles)
See Gourmont, Remy (-Marie-Charles) de

de Hartog, Jan 1914- .... **CLC 19**
See also CA 1-4R; CANR 1

de Hostos, E. M.
See Hostos (y Bonilla), Eugenio Maria de

de Hostos, Eugenio M.
See Hostos (y Bonilla), Eugenio Maria de

Deighton, Len .... **CLC 4, 7, 22, 46**
See also Deighton, Leonard Cyril
See also AAYA 6; BEST 89:2;
CDBLB 1960 to Present; DLB 87

Deighton, Leonard Cyril 1929-
See Deighton, Len
See also CA 9-12R; CANR 19, 33;
DAM NOV, POP; MTCW

Dekker, Thomas
1572(?)-1632 ..... **LC 22; DAM DRAM**
See also CDBLB Before 1660; DLB 62, 172

Delafield, E. M. 1890-1943 ...... **TCLC 61**
See also Dashwood, Edmee Elizabeth
Monica de la Pasture
See also DLB 34

de la Mare, Walter (John)
1873-1956 .... **TCLC 4, 53; DAB; DAC;**
DAM MST, POET; SSC 14; WLC
See also CDBLB 1914-1945; CLR 23;
DLB 162; SATA 16

Delaney, Franey
See O'Hara, John (Henry)

Delaney, Shelagh
1939- .... **CLC 29; DAM DRAM**
See also CA 17-20R; CANR 30;
CDBLB 1960 to Present; DLB 13;
MTCW

Delany, Mary (Granville Pendarves)
1700-1788 .... **LC 12**

Delany, Samuel R(ay, Jr.)
1942- .... **CLC 8, 14, 38; BLC;**
DAM MULT
See also BW 2; CA 81-84; CANR 27, 43;
DLB 8, 33; MTCW

De La Ramee, (Marie) Louise 1839-1908
See Ouida
See also SATA 20

de la Roche, Mazo 1879-1961 ...... **CLC 14**
See also CA 85-88; CANR 30; DLB 68;
SATA 64

De La Salle, Innocent
See Hartmann, Sadakichi

Delbanco, Nicholas (Franklin)
1942- .... **CLC 6, 13**
See also CA 17-20R; CAAS 2; CANR 29,
55; DLB 6

del Castillo, Michel 1933- .... **CLC 38**
See also CA 109

Deledda, Grazia (Cosima)
1875(?)-1936 .... **TCLC 23**
See also CA 123

Delibes, Miguel .... **CLC 8, 18**
See also Delibes Setien, Miguel

Delibes Setien, Miguel 1920-
See Delibes, Miguel
See also CA 45-48; CANR 1, 32; HW;
MTCW

DeLillo, Don
1936- ..... **CLC 8, 10, 13, 27, 39, 54, 76;**
DAM NOV, POP
See also BEST 89:1; CA 81-84; CANR 21;
DLB 6, 173; MTCW

de Lisser, H. G.
See De Lisser, H(erbert) G(eorge)
See also DLB 117

De Lisser, H(erbert) G(eorge)
1878-1944 .... **TCLC 12**
See also de Lisser, H. G.
See also BW 2; CA 109; 152

Deloria, Vine (Victor), Jr.
1933- .... **CLC 21; DAM MULT**
See also CA 53-56; CANR 5, 20, 48;
DLB 175; MTCW; NNAL; SATA 21

Del Vecchio, John M(ichael)
1947- .... **CLC 29**
See also CA 110; DLBD 9

de Man, Paul (Adolph Michel)
1919-1983 .... **CLC 55**
See also CA 128; 111; CANR 61; DLB 67;
MTCW

De Marinis, Rick 1934- .... **CLC 54**
See also CA 57-60; CAAS 24; CANR 9, 25,
50

Dembry, R. Emmet
See Murfree, Mary Noailles

Demby, William
1922- ..... **CLC 53; BLC; DAM MULT**
See also BW 1; CA 81-84; DLB 33

de Menton, Francisco
See Chin, Frank (Chew, Jr.)

Demijohn, Thom
See Disch, Thomas M(ichael)

de Montherlant, Henry (Milon)
See Montherlant, Henry (Milon) de

Demosthenes 384B.C.-322B.C. .... **CMLC 13**
See also DLB 176

de Natale, Francine
See Malzberg, Barry N(athaniel)

Denby, Edwin (Orr) 1903-1983 ..... **CLC 48**
See also CA 138; 110

Denis, Julio
See Cortazar, Julio

Denmark, Harrison
See Zelazny, Roger (Joseph)

Dennis, John 1658-1734 .... **LC 11**
See also DLB 101

Dennis, Nigel (Forbes) 1912-1989 .... **CLC 8**
See also CA 25-28R; 129; DLB 13, 15;
MTCW

Dent, Lester 1904(?)-1959 .... **TCLC 72**
See also CA 112

De Palma, Brian (Russell) 1940-.... **CLC 20**
See also CA 109

De Quincey, Thomas 1785-1859 ... **NCLC 4**
See also CDBLB 1789-1832; DLB 110; 144

Deren, Eleanora 1908(?)-1961
See Deren, Maya
See also CA 111

Deren, Maya 1917-1961...... **CLC 16, 102**
See also Deren, Eleanora

Derleth, August (William)
1909-1971 .... **CLC 31**
See also CA 1-4R; 29-32R; CANR 4;
DLB 9; SATA 5

Der Nister 1884-1950 .... **TCLC 56**

de Routisie, Albert
See Aragon, Louis

Derrida, Jacques 1930-........ **CLC 24, 87**
See also CA 124; 127

Derry Down Derry
See Lear, Edward

Dersonnes, Jacques
See Simenon, Georges (Jacques Christian)

Desai, Anita
1937- .... **CLC 19, 37, 97; DAB;**
DAM NOV
See also CA 81-84; CANR 33, 53; MTCW;
SATA 63

de Saint-Luc, Jean
See Glassco, John

de Saint Roman, Arnaud
See Aragon, Louis

Descartes, Rene 1596-1650 ..... **LC 20, 35**

De Sica, Vittorio 1901(?)-1974 ..... **CLC 20**
See also CA 117

Desnos, Robert 1900-1945........ **TCLC 22**
See also CA 121; 151

Destouches, Louis-Ferdinand
1894-1961 .... **CLC 9, 15**
See also Celine, Louis-Ferdinand
See also CA 85-88; CANR 28; MTCW

de Tolignac, Gaston
See Griffith, D(avid Lewelyn) W(ark)

Deutsch, Babette 1895-1982 .... **CLC 18**
See also CA 1-4R; 108; CANR 4; DLB 45;
SATA 1; SATA-Obit 33

Devenant, William 1606-1649 .... **LC 13**

Devkota, Laxmiprasad
1909-1959 .... **TCLC 23**
See also CA 123

De Voto, Bernard (Augustine)
1897-1955 .... **TCLC 29**
See also CA 113; 160; DLB 9

De Vries, Peter
1910-1993 .... **CLC 1, 2, 3, 7, 10, 28, 46;**
DAM NOV
See also CA 17-20R; 142; CANR 41;
DLB 6; DLBY 82; MTCW

Dexter, John
See Bradley, Marion Zimmer

Dexter, Martin
See Faust, Frederick (Schiller)

Dexter, Pete
1943- .... **CLC 34, 55; DAM POP**
See also BEST 89:2; CA 127; 131; INT 131;
MTCW

Diamano, Silmang
See Senghor, Leopold Sedar

Diamond, Neil 1941- .... **CLC 30**
See also CA 108

Diaz del Castillo, Bernal 1496-1584 .. **LC 31**

di Bassetto, Corno
   See Shaw, George Bernard

Dick, Philip K(indred)
   1928-1982 . . . . **CLC 10, 30, 72;**
                          DAM NOV, POP
   See also CA 49-52; 106; CANR 2, 16;
      DLB 8; MTCW

Dickens, Charles (John Huffam)
   1812-1870 . . . . . . **NCLC 3, 8, 18, 26, 37,**
      50; DA; DAB; DAC; DAM MST, NOV;
                          SSC 17; WLC
   See also CDBLB 1832-1890; DLB 21, 55,
      70, 159, 166; JRDA; MAICYA; SATA 15

Dickey, James (Lafayette)
   1923-1997 . . . . **CLC 1, 2, 4, 7, 10, 15, 47;**
                    DAM NOV, POET, POP
   See also AITN 1, 2; CA 9-12R; 156;
      CABS 2; CANR 10, 48, 61;
      CDALB 1968-1988; DLB 5; DLBD 7;
      DLBY 82, 93, 96; INT CANR-10;
      MTCW

Dickey, William 1928-1994 . . . . . . **CLC 3, 28**
   See also CA 9-12R; 145; CANR 24; DLB 5

Dickinson, Charles 1951- . . . . **CLC 49**
   See also CA 128

Dickinson, Emily (Elizabeth)
   1830-1886 . . . . **NCLC 21; DA; DAB;**
      DAC; DAM MST, POET; PC 1; WLC
   See also AAYA 22; CDALB 1865-1917;
      DLB 1; SATA 29

Dickinson, Peter (Malcolm)
   1927- . . . . **CLC 12, 35**
   See also AAYA 9; CA 41-44R; CANR 31,
      58; CLR 29; DLB 87, 161; JRDA;
      MAICYA; SATA 5, 62, 95

Dickson, Carr
   See Carr, John Dickson

Dickson, Carter
   See Carr, John Dickson

Diderot, Denis 1713-1784 . . . . **LC 26**

Didion, Joan
   1934- . . **CLC 1, 3, 8, 14, 32; DAM NOV**
   See also AITN 1; CA 5-8R; CANR 14, 52;
      CDALB 1968-1988; DLB 2, 173;
      DLBY 81, 86; MTCW

Dietrich, Robert
   See Hunt, E(verette) Howard, (Jr.)

Dillard, Annie
   1945- . . . . **CLC 9, 60; DAM NOV**
   See also AAYA 6; CA 49-52; CANR 3, 43,
      62; DLBY 80; MTCW; SATA 10

Dillard, R(ichard) H(enry) W(ilde)
   1937- . . . . **CLC 5**
   See also CA 21-24R; CAAS 7; CANR 10;
      DLB 5

Dillon, Eilis 1920-1994 . . . . **CLC 17**
   See also CA 9-12R; 147; CAAS 3; CANR 4,
      38; CLR 26; MAICYA; SATA 2, 74;
      SATA-Obit 83

Dimont, Penelope
   See Mortimer, Penelope (Ruth)

Dinesen, Isak . . . . **CLC 10, 29, 95; SSC 7**
   See also Blixen, Karen (Christentze
      Dinesen)

Ding Ling . . . . **CLC 68**
   See also Chiang Pin-chin

Disch, Thomas M(ichael) 1940- . . . **CLC 7, 36**
   See also AAYA 17; CA 21-24R; CAAS 4;
      CANR 17, 36, 54; CLR 18; DLB 8;
      MAICYA; MTCW; SAAS 15; SATA 92

Disch, Tom
   See Disch, Thomas M(ichael)

d'Isly, Georges
   See Simenon, Georges (Jacques Christian)

Disraeli, Benjamin 1804-1881 . . **NCLC 2, 39**
   See also DLB 21, 55

Ditcum, Steve
   See Crumb, R(obert)

Dixon, Paige
   See Corcoran, Barbara

Dixon, Stephen 1936- . . . . . **CLC 52; SSC 16**
   See also CA 89-92; CANR 17, 40, 54;
      DLB 130

Doak, Annie
   See Dillard, Annie

Dobell, Sydney Thompson
   1824-1874 . . . . **NCLC 43**
   See also DLB 32

Doblin, Alfred . . . . **TCLC 13**
   See also Doeblin, Alfred

Dobrolyubov, Nikolai Alexandrovich
   1836-1861 . . . . **NCLC 5**

Dobyns, Stephen 1941- . . . . **CLC 37**
   See also CA 45-48; CANR 2, 18

Doctorow, E(dgar) L(aurence)
   1931- . . . . . **CLC 6, 11, 15, 18, 37, 44, 65;**
                      DAM NOV, POP
   See also AAYA 22; AITN 2; BEST 89:3;
      CA 45-48; CANR 2, 33, 51;
      CDALB 1968-1988; DLB 2, 28, 173;
      DLBY 80; MTCW

Dodgson, Charles Lutwidge 1832-1898
   See Carroll, Lewis
   See also CLR 2; DA; DAB; DAC;
      DAM MST, NOV, POET; MAICYA;
      YABC 2

Dodson, Owen (Vincent)
   1914-1983 . . . . **CLC 79; BLC;**
                          DAM MULT
   See also BW 1; CA 65-68; 110; CANR 24;
      DLB 76

Doeblin, Alfred 1878-1957 . . . . **TCLC 13**
   See also Doblin, Alfred
   See also CA 110; 141; DLB 66

Doerr, Harriet 1910- . . . . **CLC 34**
   See also CA 117; 122; CANR 47; INT 122

Domecq, H(onorio) Bustos
   See Bioy Casares, Adolfo; Borges, Jorge
      Luis

Domini, Rey
   See Lorde, Audre (Geraldine)

Dominique
   See Proust, (Valentin-Louis-George-Eugene-)
      Marcel

Don, A
   See Stephen, Leslie

Donaldson, Stephen R.
   1947- . . . . **CLC 46; DAM POP**
   See also CA 89-92; CANR 13, 55;
      INT CANR-13

Donleavy, J(ames) P(atrick)
   1926- . . . . **CLC 1, 4, 6, 10, 45**
   See also AITN 2; CA 9-12R; CANR 24, 49,
      62; DLB 6, 173; INT CANR-24; MTCW

Donne, John
   1572-1631 . . . . **LC 10, 24; DA; DAB;**
      DAC; DAM MST, POET; PC 1
   See also CDBLB Before 1660; DLB 121,
      151

Donnell, David 1939(?)- . . . . **CLC 34**

Donoghue, P. S.
   See Hunt, E(verette) Howard, (Jr.)

Donoso (Yanez), Jose
   1924-1996 . . . . **CLC 4, 8, 11, 32, 99;**
                         DAM MULT; HLC
   See also CA 81-84; 155; CANR 32;
      DLB 113; HW; MTCW

Donovan, John 1928-1992 . . . . **CLC 35**
   See also AAYA 20; CA 97-100; 137;
      CLR 3; MAICYA; SATA 72;
      SATA-Brief 29

Don Roberto
   See Cunninghame Graham, R(obert)
      B(ontine)

Doolittle, Hilda
   1886-1961 . . . . . **CLC 3, 8, 14, 31, 34, 73;**
      DA; DAC; DAM MST, POET; PC 5;
                            WLC
   See also H. D.
   See also CA 97-100; CANR 35; DLB 4, 45;
      MTCW

Dorfman, Ariel
   1942- . . . . **CLC 48, 77; DAM MULT;**
                           HLC
   See also CA 124; 130; HW; INT 130

Dorn, Edward (Merton) 1929- . . . **CLC 10, 18**
   See also CA 93-96; CANR 42; DLB 5;
      INT 93-96

Dorsan, Luc
   See Simenon, Georges (Jacques Christian)

Dorsange, Jean
   See Simenon, Georges (Jacques Christian)

Dos Passos, John (Roderigo)
   1896-1970 . . . . . . **CLC 1, 4, 8, 11, 15, 25,**
      34, 82; DA; DAB; DAC; DAM MST,
                      NOV; WLC
   See also CA 1-4R; 29-32R; CANR 3;
      CDALB 1929-1941; DLB 4, 9; DLBD 1,
      15; DLBY 96; MTCW

Dossage, Jean
   See Simenon, Georges (Jacques Christian)

Dostoevsky, Fedor Mikhailovich
   1821-1881 . . . . . . **NCLC 2, 7, 21, 33, 43;**
      DA; DAB; DAC; DAM MST, NOV;
                       SSC 2; WLC

Doughty, Charles M(ontagu)
   1843-1926 . . . . **TCLC 27**
   See also CA 115; DLB 19, 57, 174

Douglas, Ellen . . . . **CLC 73**
   See also Haxton, Josephine Ayres;
      Williamson, Ellen Douglas

Douglas, Gavin 1475(?)-1522 . . . . **LC 20**

Douglas, Keith (Castellain)
   1920-1944 . . . . **TCLC 40**
   See also CA 160; DLB 27

Douglas, Leonard
See Bradbury, Ray (Douglas)

Douglas, Michael
See Crichton, (John) Michael

Douglas, Norman 1868-1952 ...... TCLC 68

Douglass, Frederick
1817(?)-1895 .... NCLC 7, 55; BLC; DA;
DAC; DAM MST, MULT; WLC
See also CDALB 1640-1865; DLB 1, 43, 50,
79; SATA 29

Dourado, (Waldomiro Freitas) Autran
1926- .... CLC 23, 60
See also CA 25-28R; CANR 34

Dourado, Waldomiro Autran
See Dourado, (Waldomiro Freitas) Autran

Dove, Rita (Frances)
1952- .... CLC 50, 81; DAM MULT,
POET; PC 6
See also BW 2; CA 109; CAAS 19;
CANR 27, 42; DLB 120

Dowell, Coleman 1925-1985........ CLC 60
See also CA 25-28R; 117; CANR 10;
DLB 130

Dowson, Ernest (Christopher)
1867-1900 .... TCLC 4
See also CA 105; 150; DLB 19, 135

Doyle, A. Conan
See Doyle, Arthur Conan

Doyle, Arthur Conan
1859-1930 .... TCLC 7; DA; DAB;
DAC; DAM MST, NOV; SSC 12; WLC
See also AAYA 14; CA 104; 122;
CDBLB 1890-1914; DLB 18, 70, 156, 178;
MTCW; SATA 24

Doyle, Conan
See Doyle, Arthur Conan

Doyle, John
See Graves, Robert (von Ranke)

Doyle, Roddy 1958(?)- .... CLC 81
See also AAYA 14; CA 143

Doyle, Sir A. Conan
See Doyle, Arthur Conan

Doyle, Sir Arthur Conan
See Doyle, Arthur Conan

Dr. A
See Asimov, Isaac; Silverstein, Alvin

Drabble, Margaret
1939- .... CLC 2, 3, 5, 8, 10, 22, 53;
DAB; DAC; DAM MST, NOV, POP
See also CA 13-16R; CANR 18, 35;
CDBLB 1960 to Present; DLB 14, 155;
MTCW; SATA 48

Drapier, M. B.
See Swift, Jonathan

Drayham, James
See Mencken, H(enry) L(ouis)

Drayton, Michael 1563-1631........ LC 8

Dreadstone, Carl
See Campbell, (John) Ramsey

Dreiser, Theodore (Herman Albert)
1871-1945 .... TCLC 10, 18, 35; DA;
DAC; DAM MST, NOV; WLC
See also CA 106; 132; CDALB 1865-1917;
DLB 9, 12, 102, 137; DLBD 1; MTCW

Drexler, Rosalyn 1926- .... CLC 2, 6
See also CA 81-84

Dreyer, Carl Theodor 1889-1968.... CLC 16
See also CA 116

Drieu la Rochelle, Pierre(-Eugene)
1893-1945 .... TCLC 21
See also CA 117; DLB 72

Drinkwater, John 1882-1937 ...... TCLC 57
See also CA 109; 149; DLB 10, 19, 149

Drop Shot
See Cable, George Washington

Droste-Hulshoff, Annette Freiin von
1797-1848 .... NCLC 3
See also DLB 133

Drummond, Walter
See Silverberg, Robert

Drummond, William Henry
1854-1907 .... TCLC 25
See also CA 160; DLB 92

Drummond de Andrade, Carlos
1902-1987 .... CLC 18
See also Andrade, Carlos Drummond de
See also CA 132; 123

Drury, Allen (Stuart) 1918-........ CLC 37
See also CA 57-60; CANR 18, 52;
INT CANR-18

Dryden, John
1631-1700 .... LC 3, 21; DA; DAB;
DAC; DAM DRAM, MST, POET;
DC 3; WLC
See also CDBLB 1660-1789; DLB 80, 101,
131

Duberman, Martin 1930- .... CLC 8
See also CA 1-4R; CANR 2

Dubie, Norman (Evans) 1945-...... CLC 36
See also CA 69-72; CANR 12; DLB 120

Du Bois, W(illiam) E(dward) B(urghardt)
1868-1963 .... CLC 1, 2, 13, 64, 96;
BLC; DA; DAC; DAM MST,
NOV; WLC
See also BW 1; CA 85-88; CANR 34;
CDALB 1865-1917; DLB 47, 50, 91;
MTCW; SATA 42

Dubus, Andre
1936- .... CLC 13, 36, 97; SSC 15
See also CA 21-24R; CANR 17; DLB 130;
INT CANR-17

Duca Minimo
See D'Annunzio, Gabriele

Ducharme, Rejean 1941- .... CLC 74
See also DLB 60

Duclos, Charles Pinot 1704-1772 ..... LC 1

Dudek, Louis 1918- .... CLC 11, 19
See also CA 45-48; CAAS 14; CANR 1;
DLB 88

Duerrenmatt, Friedrich
1921-1990 ...... CLC 1, 4, 8, 11, 15, 43,
102; DAM DRAM
See also CA 17-20R; CANR 33; DLB 69,
124; MTCW

Duffy, Bruce (?)-................. CLC 50

Duffy, Maureen 1933- .... CLC 37
See also CA 25-28R; CANR 33; DLB 14;
MTCW

Dugan, Alan 1923- .... CLC 2, 6
See also CA 81-84; DLB 5

du Gard, Roger Martin
See Martin du Gard, Roger

Duhamel, Georges 1884-1966 .... CLC 8
See also CA 81-84; 25-28R; CANR 35;
DLB 65; MTCW

Dujardin, Edouard (Emile Louis)
1861-1949 .... TCLC 13
See also CA 109; DLB 123

Dulles, John Foster 1888-1959 .... TCLC 72
See also CA 115; 149

Dumas, Alexandre (Davy de la Pailleterie)
1802-1870 .... NCLC 11; DA; DAB;
DAC; DAM MST, NOV; WLC
See also DLB 119; SATA 18

Dumas, Alexandre
1824-1895 .... NCLC 9; DC 1
See also AAYA 22

Dumas, Claudine
See Malzberg, Barry N(athaniel)

Dumas, Henry L. 1934-1968 ..... CLC 6, 62
See also BW 1; CA 85-88; DLB 41

du Maurier, Daphne
1907-1989 .... CLC 6, 11, 59; DAB;
DAC; DAM MST, POP; SSC 18
See also CA 5-8R; 128; CANR 6, 55;
MTCW; SATA 27; SATA-Obit 60

Dunbar, Paul Laurence
1872-1906 ...... TCLC 2, 12; BLC; DA;
DAC; DAM MST, MULT, POET; PC 5;
SSC 8; WLC
See also BW 1; CA 104; 124;
CDALB 1865-1917; DLB 50, 54, 78;
SATA 34

Dunbar, William 1460(?)-1530(?) .... LC 20
See also DLB 132, 146

Duncan, Dora Angela
See Duncan, Isadora

Duncan, Isadora 1877(?)-1927..... TCLC 68
See also CA 118; 149

Duncan, Lois 1934-.............. CLC 26
See also AAYA 4; CA 1-4R; CANR 2, 23,
36; CLR 29; JRDA; MAICYA; SAAS 2;
SATA 1, 36, 75

Duncan, Robert (Edward)
1919-1988 .... CLC 1, 2, 4, 7, 15, 41, 55;
DAM POET; PC 2
See also CA 9-12R; 124; CANR 28, 62;
DLB 5, 16; MTCW

Duncan, Sara Jeannette
1861-1922 .... TCLC 60
See also CA 157; DLB 92

Dunlap, William 1766-1839 .... NCLC 2
See also DLB 30, 37, 59

Dunn, Douglas (Eaglesham)
1942- .... CLC 6, 40
See also CA 45-48; CANR 2, 33; DLB 40;
MTCW

Dunn, Katherine (Karen) 1945-..... CLC 71
See also CA 33-36R

Dunn, Stephen 1939- .... CLC 36
See also CA 33-36R; CANR 12, 48, 53;
DLB 105

Dunne, Finley Peter 1867-1936.... **TCLC 28**
See also CA 108; DLB 11, 23

Dunne, John Gregory 1932-........ **CLC 28**
See also CA 25-28R; CANR 14, 50;
DLBY 80

Dunsany, Edward John Moreton Drax
Plunkett 1878-1957
See Dunsany, Lord
See also CA 104; 148; DLB 10

Dunsany, Lord................ **TCLC 2, 59**
See also Dunsany, Edward John Moreton
Drax Plunkett
See also DLB 77, 153, 156

du Perry, Jean
See Simenon, Georges (Jacques Christian)

Durang, Christopher (Ferdinand)
1949- .... **CLC 27, 38**
See also CA 105; CANR 50

Duras, Marguerite
1914-1996 ..... **CLC 3, 6, 11, 20, 34, 40,**
68, 100
See also CA 25-28R; 151; CANR 50;
DLB 83; MTCW

Durban, (Rosa) Pam 1947-........ **CLC 39**
See also CA 123

Durcan, Paul
1944- .... **CLC 43, 70; DAM POET**
See also CA 134

Durkheim, Emile 1858-1917 ...... **TCLC 55**

Durrell, Lawrence (George)
1912-1990 .... **CLC 1, 4, 6, 8, 13, 27, 41;**
DAM NOV
See also CA 9-12R; 132; CANR 40;
CDBLB 1945-1960; DLB 15, 27;
DLBY 90; MTCW

Durrenmatt, Friedrich
See Duerrenmatt, Friedrich

Dutt, Toru 1856-1877.......... **NCLC 29**

Dwight, Timothy 1752-1817...... **NCLC 13**
See also DLB 37

Dworkin, Andrea 1946- .... **CLC 43**
See also CA 77-80; CAAS 21; CANR 16,
39; INT CANR-16; MTCW

Dwyer, Deanna
See Koontz, Dean R(ay)

Dwyer, K. R.
See Koontz, Dean R(ay)

Dye, Richard
See De Voto, Bernard (Augustine)

Dylan, Bob 1941- ...... **CLC 3, 4, 6, 12, 77**
See also CA 41-44R; DLB 16

Eagleton, Terence (Francis) 1943-
See Eagleton, Terry
See also CA 57-60; CANR 7, 23; MTCW

Eagleton, Terry .... **CLC 63**
See also Eagleton, Terence (Francis)

Early, Jack
See Scoppettone, Sandra

East, Michael
See West, Morris L(anglo)

Eastaway, Edward
See Thomas, (Philip) Edward

Eastlake, William (Derry)
1917-1997 .... **CLC 8**
See also CA 5-8R; 158; CAAS 1; CANR 5;
DLB 6; INT CANR-5

Eastman, Charles A(lexander)
1858-1939 ..... **TCLC 55; DAM MULT**
See also DLB 175; NNAL; YABC 1

Eberhart, Richard (Ghormley)
1904- .. **CLC 3, 11, 19, 56; DAM POET**
See also CA 1-4R; CANR 2;
CDALB 1941-1968; DLB 48; MTCW

Eberstadt, Fernanda 1960-........ **CLC 39**
See also CA 136

Echegaray (y Eizaguirre), Jose (Maria Waldo)
1832-1916 .... **TCLC 4**
See also CA 104; CANR 32; HW; MTCW

Echeverria, (Jose) Esteban (Antonino)
1805-1851 .... **NCLC 18**

Echo
See Proust, (Valentin-Louis-George-Eugene-)
Marcel

Eckert, Allan W. 1931- .... **CLC 17**
See also AAYA 18; CA 13-16R; CANR 14,
45; INT CANR-14; SAAS 21; SATA 29,
91; SATA-Brief 27

Eckhart, Meister 1260(?)-1328(?) .. **CMLC 9**
See also DLB 115

Eckmar, F. R.
See de Hartog, Jan

Eco, Umberto
1932- ... **CLC 28, 60; DAM NOV, POP**
See also BEST 90:1; CA 77-80; CANR 12,
33, 55; MTCW

Eddison, E(ric) R(ucker)
1882-1945 .... **TCLC 15**
See also CA 109; 156

Eddy, Mary (Morse) Baker
1821-1910 .... **TCLC 71**
See also CA 113

Edel, (Joseph) Leon 1907-...... **CLC 29, 34**
See also CA 1-4R; CANR 1, 22; DLB 103;
INT CANR-22

Eden, Emily 1797-1869 .... **NCLC 10**

Edgar, David
1948- .... **CLC 42; DAM DRAM**
See also CA 57-60; CANR 12, 61; DLB 13;
MTCW

Edgerton, Clyde (Carlyle) 1944- .... **CLC 39**
See also AAYA 17; CA 118; 134; INT 134

Edgeworth, Maria 1768-1849... **NCLC 1, 51**
See also DLB 116, 159, 163; SATA 21

Edmonds, Paul
See Kuttner, Henry

Edmonds, Walter D(umaux) 1903- .. **CLC 35**
See also CA 5-8R; CANR 2; DLB 9;
MAICYA; SAAS 4; SATA 1, 27

Edmondson, Wallace
See Ellison, Harlan (Jay)

Edson, Russell .... **CLC 13**
See also CA 33-36R

Edwards, Bronwen Elizabeth
See Rose, Wendy

Edwards, G(erald) B(asil)
1899-1976 .... **CLC 25**
See also CA 110

Edwards, Gus 1939-.............. **CLC 43**
See also CA 108; INT 108

Edwards, Jonathan
1703-1758 .... **LC 7; DA; DAC;**
DAM MST
See also DLB 24

Efron, Marina Ivanovna Tsvetaeva
See Tsvetaeva (Efron), Marina (Ivanovna)

Ehle, John (Marsden, Jr.) 1925-.... **CLC 27**
See also CA 9-12R

Ehrenbourg, Ilya (Grigoryevich)
See Ehrenburg, Ilya (Grigoryevich)

Ehrenburg, Ilya (Grigoryevich)
1891-1967 .... **CLC 18, 34, 62**
See also CA 102; 25-28R

Ehrenburg, Ilyo (Grigoryevich)
See Ehrenburg, Ilya (Grigoryevich)

Eich, Guenter 1907-1972 .... **CLC 15**
See also CA 111; 93-96; DLB 69, 124

Eichendorff, Joseph Freiherr von
1788-1857 .... **NCLC 8**
See also DLB 90

Eigner, Larry...................... **CLC 9**
See also Eigner, Laurence (Joel)
See also CAAS 23; DLB 5

Eigner, Laurence (Joel) 1927-1996
See Eigner, Larry
See also CA 9-12R; 151; CANR 6

Einstein, Albert 1879-1955 .... **TCLC 65**
See also CA 121; 133; MTCW

Eiseley, Loren Corey 1907-1977..... **CLC 7**
See also AAYA 5; CA 1-4R; 73-76;
CANR 6

Eisenstadt, Jill 1963-............. **CLC 50**
See also CA 140

Eisenstein, Sergei (Mikhailovich)
1898-1948 .... **TCLC 57**
See also CA 114; 149

Eisner, Simon
See Kornbluth, C(yril) M.

Ekeloef, (Bengt) Gunnar
1907-1968 .... **CLC 27; DAM POET**
See also CA 123; 25-28R

Ekelof, (Bengt) Gunnar
See Ekeloef, (Bengt) Gunnar

Ekelund, Vilhelm 1880-1949 ...... **TCLC 75**

Ekwensi, C. O. D.
See Ekwensi, Cyprian (Odiatu Duaka)

Ekwensi, Cyprian (Odiatu Duaka)
1921- ...... **CLC 4; BLC; DAM MULT**
See also BW 2; CA 29-32R; CANR 18, 42;
DLB 117; MTCW; SATA 66

Elaine .... **TCLC 18**
See also Leverson, Ada

El Crummo
See Crumb, R(obert)

Elia
See Lamb, Charles

Eliade, Mircea 1907-1986 .... **CLC 19**
See also CA 65-68; 119; CANR 30, 62;
MTCW

Eliot, A. D.
See Jewett, (Theodora) Sarah Orne

Eliot, Alice
See Jewett, (Theodora) Sarah Orne

Eliot, Dan
See Silverberg, Robert

Eliot, George
1819-1880 . . . . . **NCLC 4, 13, 23, 41, 49;**
DA; DAB; DAC; DAM MST, NOV;
WLC
See also CDBLB 1832-1890; DLB 21, 35, 55

Eliot, John 1604-1690 . . . . **LC 5**
See also DLB 24

Eliot, T(homas) S(tearns)
1888-1965 . . . . . **CLC 1, 2, 3, 6, 9, 10, 13,**
15, 24, 34, 41, 55, 57; DA; DAB; DAC;
DAM DRAM, MST, POET; PC 5;
WLC 2
See also CA 5-8R; 25-28R; CANR 41;
CDALB 1929-1941; DLB 7, 10, 45, 63;
DLBY 88; MTCW

Elizabeth 1866-1941 . . . . **TCLC 41**

Elkin, Stanley L(awrence)
1930-1995 . . . . . . **CLC 4, 6, 9, 14, 27, 51,**
91; DAM NOV, POP; SSC 12
See also CA 9-12R; 148; CANR 8, 46;
DLB 2, 28; DLBY 80; INT CANR-8;
MTCW

Elledge, Scott . . . . **CLC 34**

Elliot, Don
See Silverberg, Robert

Elliott, Don
See Silverberg, Robert

Elliott, George P(aul) 1918-1980 . . . . . **CLC 2**
See also CA 1-4R; 97-100; CANR 2

Elliott, Janice 1931- . . . . **CLC 47**
See also CA 13-16R; CANR 8, 29; DLB 14

Elliott, Sumner Locke 1917-1991 . . . **CLC 38**
See also CA 5-8R; 134; CANR 2, 21

Elliott, William
See Bradbury, Ray (Douglas)

Ellis, A. E. . . . . **CLC 7**

Ellis, Alice Thomas . . . . **CLC 40**
See also Haycraft, Anna

Ellis, Bret Easton
1964- . . . . **CLC 39, 71; DAM POP**
See also AAYA 2; CA 118; 123; CANR 51;
INT 123

Ellis, (Henry) Havelock
1859-1939 . . . . **TCLC 14**
See also CA 109

Ellis, Landon
See Ellison, Harlan (Jay)

Ellis, Trey 1962- . . . . **CLC 55**
See also CA 146

Ellison, Harlan (Jay)
1934- . . . . . . **CLC 1, 13, 42; DAM POP;**
SSC 14
See also CA 5-8R; CANR 5, 46; DLB 8;
INT CANR-5; MTCW

Ellison, Ralph (Waldo)
1914-1994 . . . . **CLC 1, 3, 11, 54, 86;**
BLC; DA; DAB; DAC; DAM MST,
MULT, NOV; SSC 26; WLC
See also AAYA 19; BW 1; CA 9-12R; 145;
CANR 24, 53; CDALB 1941-1968;
DLB 2, 76; DLBY 94; MTCW

Ellmann, Lucy (Elizabeth) 1956- . . . . **CLC 61**
See also CA 128

Ellmann, Richard (David)
1918-1987 . . . . **CLC 50**
See also BEST 89:2; CA 1-4R; 122;
CANR 2, 28, 61; DLB 103; DLBY 87;
MTCW

Elman, Richard 1934- . . . . **CLC 19**
See also CA 17-20R; CAAS 3; CANR 47

Elron
See Hubbard, L(afayette) Ron(ald)

Eluard, Paul . . . . **TCLC 7, 41**
See also Grindel, Eugene

Elyot, Sir Thomas 1490(?)-1546 . . . . . **LC 11**

Elytis, Odysseus
1911-1996 . . . . **CLC 15, 49, 100;**
DAM POET
See also CA 102; 151; MTCW

Emecheta, (Florence Onye) Buchi
1944- . . **CLC 14, 48; BLC; DAM MULT**
See also BW 2; CA 81-84; CANR 27;
DLB 117; MTCW; SATA 66

Emerson, Ralph Waldo
1803-1882 . . . . . **NCLC 1, 38; DA; DAB;**
DAC; DAM MST, POET; PC 18; WLC
See also CDALB 1640-1865; DLB 1, 59, 73

Eminescu, Mihail 1850-1889 . . . . . **NCLC 33**

Empson, William
1906-1984 . . . . **CLC 3, 8, 19, 33, 34**
See also CA 17-20R; 112; CANR 31, 61;
DLB 20; MTCW

Enchi Fumiko (Ueda) 1905-1986 . . . . **CLC 31**
See also CA 129; 121

Ende, Michael (Andreas Helmuth)
1929-1995 . . . . **CLC 31**
See also CA 118; 124; 149; CANR 36;
CLR 14; DLB 75; MAICYA; SATA 61;
SATA-Brief 42; SATA-Obit 86

Endo, Shusaku
1923-1996 . . . . **CLC 7, 14, 19, 54, 99;**
DAM NOV
See also CA 29-32R; 153; CANR 21, 54;
DLB 182; MTCW

Engel, Marian 1933-1985 . . . . **CLC 36**
See also CA 25-28R; CANR 12; DLB 53;
INT CANR-12

Engelhardt, Frederick
See Hubbard, L(afayette) Ron(ald)

Enright, D(ennis) J(oseph)
1920- . . . . **CLC 4, 8, 31**
See also CA 1-4R; CANR 1, 42; DLB 27;
SATA 25

Enzensberger, Hans Magnus
1929- . . . . **CLC 43**
See also CA 116; 119

Ephron, Nora 1941- . . . . **CLC 17, 31**
See also AITN 2; CA 65-68; CANR 12, 39

Epicurus 341B.C.-270B.C. . . . . **CMLC 21**
See also DLB 176

Epsilon
See Betjeman, John

Epstein, Daniel Mark 1948- . . . . **CLC 7**
See also CA 49-52; CANR 2, 53

Epstein, Jacob 1956- . . . . **CLC 19**
See also CA 114

Epstein, Joseph 1937- . . . . **CLC 39**
See also CA 112; 119; CANR 50

Epstein, Leslie 1938- . . . . **CLC 27**
See also CA 73-76; CAAS 12; CANR 23

Equiano, Olaudah
1745(?)-1797 . . . . **LC 16; BLC;**
DAM MULT
See also DLB 37, 50

ER . . . . **TCLC 33**
See also CA 160; DLB 85

Erasmus, Desiderius 1469(?)-1536 . . . . **LC 16**

Erdman, Paul E(mil) 1932- . . . . **CLC 25**
See also AITN 1; CA 61-64; CANR 13, 43

Erdrich, Louise
1954- . . . . **CLC 39, 54; DAM MULT,**
NOV, POP
See also AAYA 10; BEST 89:1; CA 114;
CANR 41, 62; DLB 152, 175; MTCW;
NNAL; SATA 94

Erenburg, Ilya (Grigoryevich)
See Ehrenburg, Ilya (Grigoryevich)

Erickson, Stephen Michael 1950-
See Erickson, Steve
See also CA 129

Erickson, Steve 1950- . . . . **CLC 64**
See also Erickson, Stephen Michael
See also CANR 60

Ericson, Walter
See Fast, Howard (Melvin)

Eriksson, Buntel
See Bergman, (Ernst) Ingmar

Ernaux, Annie 1940- . . . . **CLC 88**
See also CA 147

Eschenbach, Wolfram von
See Wolfram von Eschenbach

Eseki, Bruno
See Mphahlele, Ezekiel

Esenin, Sergei (Alexandrovich)
1895-1925 . . . . **TCLC 4**
See also CA 104

Eshleman, Clayton 1935- . . . . **CLC 7**
See also CA 33-36R; CAAS 6; DLB 5

Espriella, Don Manuel Alvarez
See Southey, Robert

Espriu, Salvador 1913-1985 . . . . **CLC 9**
See also CA 154; 115; DLB 134

Espronceda, Jose de 1808-1842 . . . **NCLC 39**

Esse, James
See Stephens, James

Esterbrook, Tom
See Hubbard, L(afayette) Ron(ald)

Estleman, Loren D.
1952- . . . . . . **CLC 48; DAM NOV, POP**
See also CA 85-88; CANR 27;
INT CANR-27; MTCW

Euclid 306B.C.-283B.C. . . . . **CMLC 25**

Eugenides, Jeffrey 1960(?)- . . . . **CLC 81**
See also CA 144

Euripides
c. 485B.C.-406B.C. . . . . . **CMLC 23; DA;**
DAB; DAC; DAM DRAM, MST; DC 4;
WLCS
See also DLB 176

Ferrer, Gabriel (Francisco Victor) Miro
  See Miro (Ferrer), Gabriel (Francisco Victor)

Ferrier, Susan (Edmonstone)
  1782-1854 .... NCLC 8
  See also DLB 116

Ferrigno, Robert 1948(?)-.......... CLC 65
  See also CA 140

Ferron, Jacques 1921-1985 ... CLC 94; DAC
  See also CA 117; 129; DLB 60

Feuchtwanger, Lion 1884-1958 ..... TCLC 3
  See also CA 104; DLB 66

Feuillet, Octave 1821-1890 ...... NCLC 45

Feydeau, Georges (Leon Jules Marie)
  1862-1921 ..... TCLC 22; DAM DRAM
  See also CA 113; 152

Fichte, Johann Gottlieb
  1762-1814 .... NCLC 62
  See also DLB 90

Ficino, Marsilio 1433-1499 .... LC 12

Fiedeler, Hans
  See Doeblin, Alfred

Fiedler, Leslie A(aron)
  1917- .... CLC 4, 13, 24
  See also CA 9-12R; CANR 7; DLB 28, 67;
  MTCW

Field, Andrew 1938-.............. CLC 44
  See also CA 97-100; CANR 25

Field, Eugene 1850-1895 .... NCLC 3
  See also DLB 23, 42, 140; DLBD 13;
  MAICYA; SATA 16

Field, Gans T.
  See Wellman, Manly Wade

Field, Michael .... TCLC 43

Field, Peter
  See Hobson, Laura Z(ametkin)

Fielding, Henry
  1707-1754 ...... LC 1; DA; DAB; DAC;
  DAM DRAM, MST, NOV; WLC
  See also CDBLB 1660-1789; DLB 39, 84,
  101

Fielding, Sarah 1710-1768 .... LC 1
  See also DLB 39

Fierstein, Harvey (Forbes)
  1954- ..... CLC 33; DAM DRAM, POP
  See also CA 123; 129

Figes, Eva 1932-................ CLC 31
  See also CA 53-56; CANR 4, 44; DLB 14

Finch, Robert (Duer Claydon)
  1900- .... CLC 18
  See also CA 57-60; CANR 9, 24, 49;
  DLB 88

Findley, Timothy
  1930- .. CLC 27, 102; DAC; DAM MST
  See also CA 25-28R; CANR 12, 42;
  DLB 53

Fink, William
  See Mencken, H(enry) L(ouis)

Firbank, Louis 1942-
  See Reed, Lou
  See also CA 117

Firbank, (Arthur Annesley) Ronald
  1886-1926 .... TCLC 1
  See also CA 104; DLB 36

Fisher, M(ary) F(rances) K(ennedy)
  1908-1992 .... CLC 76, 87
  See also CA 77-80; 138; CANR 44

Fisher, Roy 1930-................ CLC 25
  See also CA 81-84; CAAS 10; CANR 16;
  DLB 40

Fisher, Rudolph
  1897-1934 .... TCLC 11; BLC;
  DAM MULT; SSC 25
  See also BW 1; CA 107; 124; DLB 51, 102

Fisher, Vardis (Alvero) 1895-1968.... CLC 7
  See also CA 5-8R; 25-28R; DLB 9

Fiske, Tarleton
  See Bloch, Robert (Albert)

Fitch, Clarke
  See Sinclair, Upton (Beall)

Fitch, John IV
  See Cormier, Robert (Edmund)

Fitzgerald, Captain Hugh
  See Baum, L(yman) Frank

FitzGerald, Edward 1809-1883 .... NCLC 9
  See also DLB 32

Fitzgerald, F(rancis) Scott (Key)
  1896-1940 .... TCLC 1, 6, 14, 28, 55;
  DA; DAB; DAC; DAM MST, NOV;
  SSC 6; WLC
  See also AITN 1; CA 110; 123;
  CDALB 1917-1929; DLB 4, 9, 86;
  DLBD 1, 15, 16; DLBY 81, 96; MTCW

Fitzgerald, Penelope 1916-... CLC 19, 51, 61
  See also CA 85-88; CAAS 10; CANR 56;
  DLB 14

Fitzgerald, Robert (Stuart)
  1910-1985 .... CLC 39
  See also CA 1-4R; 114; CANR 1; DLBY 80

FitzGerald, Robert D(avid)
  1902-1987 .... CLC 19
  See also CA 17-20R

Fitzgerald, Zelda (Sayre)
  1900-1948 .... TCLC 52
  See also CA 117; 126; DLBY 84

Flanagan, Thomas (James Bonner)
  1923- .... CLC 25, 52
  See also CA 108; CANR 55; DLBY 80;
  INT 108; MTCW

Flaubert, Gustave
  1821-1880 .... NCLC 2, 10, 19, 62; DA;
  DAB; DAC; DAM MST, NOV; SSC 11;
  WLC
  See also DLB 119

Flecker, Herman Elroy
  See Flecker, (Herman) James Elroy

Flecker, (Herman) James Elroy
  1884-1915 .... TCLC 43
  See also CA 109; 150; DLB 10, 19

Fleming, Ian (Lancaster)
  1908-1964 ...... CLC 3, 30; DAM POP
  See also CA 5-8R; CANR 59;
  CDBLB 1945-1960; DLB 87; MTCW;
  SATA 9

Fleming, Thomas (James) 1927- .... CLC 37
  See also CA 5-8R; CANR 10;
  INT CANR-10; SATA 8

Fletcher, John 1579-1625..... LC 33; DC 6
  See also CDBLB Before 1660; DLB 58

Fletcher, John Gould 1886-1950... TCLC 35
  See also CA 107; DLB 4, 45

Fleur, Paul
  See Pohl, Frederik

Flooglebuckle, Al
  See Spiegelman, Art

Flying Officer X
  See Bates, H(erbert) E(rnest)

Fo, Dario 1926-..... CLC 32; DAM DRAM
  See also CA 116; 128; MTCW

Fogarty, Jonathan Titulescu Esq.
  See Farrell, James T(homas)

Folke, Will
  See Bloch, Robert (Albert)

Follett, Ken(neth Martin)
  1949- ...... CLC 18; DAM NOV, POP
  See also AAYA 6; BEST 89:4; CA 81-84;
  CANR 13, 33, 54; DLB 87; DLBY 81;
  INT CANR-33; MTCW

Fontane, Theodor 1819-1898..... NCLC 26
  See also DLB 129

Foote, Horton
  1916- ...... CLC 51, 91; DAM DRAM
  See also CA 73-76; CANR 34, 51; DLB 26;
  INT CANR-34

Foote, Shelby
  1916- ...... CLC 75; DAM NOV, POP
  See also CA 5-8R; CANR 3, 45; DLB 2, 17

Forbes, Esther 1891-1967.......... CLC 12
  See also AAYA 17; CA 13-14; 25-28R;
  CAP 1; CLR 27; DLB 22; JRDA;
  MAICYA; SATA 2

Forche, Carolyn (Louise)
  1950- .... CLC 25, 83, 86; DAM POET;
  PC 10
  See also CA 109; 117; CANR 50; DLB 5;
  INT 117

Ford, Elbur
  See Hibbert, Eleanor Alice Burford

Ford, Ford Madox
  1873-1939 .... TCLC 1, 15, 39, 57;
  DAM NOV
  See also CA 104; 132; CDBLB 1914-1945;
  DLB 162; MTCW

Ford, Henry 1863-1947 .... TCLC 73
  See also CA 115; 148

Ford, John 1895-1973............. CLC 16
  See also CA 45-48

Ford, Richard .... CLC 99

Ford, Richard 1944-.............. CLC 46
  See also CA 69-72; CANR 11, 47

Ford, Webster
  See Masters, Edgar Lee

Foreman, Richard 1937-.......... CLC 50
  See also CA 65-68; CANR 32

Forester, C(ecil) S(cott)
  1899-1966 .... CLC 35
  See also CA 73-76; 25-28R; SATA 13

Forez
  See Mauriac, Francois (Charles)

Forman, James Douglas 1932-...... CLC 21
  See also AAYA 17; CA 9-12R; CANR 4,
  19, 42; JRDA; MAICYA; SATA 8, 70

Fornes, Maria Irene 1930-..... **CLC 39, 61**
See also CA 25-28R; CANR 28; DLB 7;
HW; INT CANR-28; MTCW

Forrest, Leon 1937- .... **CLC 4**
See also BW 2; CA 89-92; CAAS 7;
CANR 25, 52; DLB 33

Forster, E(dward) M(organ)
1879-1970 ..... **CLC 1, 2, 3, 4, 9, 10, 13,
15, 22, 45, 77; DA; DAB; DAC;
DAM MST, NOV; SSC 27; WLC**
See also AAYA 2; CA 13-14; 25-28R;
CANR 45; CAP 1; CDBLB 1914-1945;
DLB 34, 98, 162, 178; DLBD 10; MTCW;
SATA 57

Forster, John 1812-1876 .... **NCLC 11**
See also DLB 144, 184

Forsyth, Frederick
1938- .. **CLC 2, 5, 36; DAM NOV, POP**
See also BEST 89:4; CA 85-88; CANR 38,
62; DLB 87; MTCW

Forten, Charlotte L. .... **TCLC 16; BLC**
See also Grimke, Charlotte L(ottie) Forten
See also DLB 50

Foscolo, Ugo 1778-1827......... **NCLC 8**

Fosse, Bob .... **CLC 20**
See also Fosse, Robert Louis

Fosse, Robert Louis 1927-1987
See Fosse, Bob
See also CA 110; 123

Foster, Stephen Collins
1826-1864 .... **NCLC 26**

Foucault, Michel
1926-1984 .... **CLC 31, 34, 69**
See also CA 105; 113; CANR 34; MTCW

Fouque, Friedrich (Heinrich Karl) de la Motte
1777-1843 .... **NCLC 2**
See also DLB 90

Fourier, Charles 1772-1837 ...... **NCLC 51**

Fournier, Henri Alban 1886-1914
See Alain-Fournier
See also CA 104

Fournier, Pierre 1916-........... **CLC 11**
See also Gascar, Pierre
See also CA 89-92; CANR 16, 40

Fowles, John
1926- ...... **CLC 1, 2, 3, 4, 6, 9, 10, 15,
33, 87; DAB; DAC; DAM MST**
See also CA 5-8R; CANR 25; CDBLB 1960
to Present; DLB 14, 139; MTCW;
SATA 22

Fox, Paula 1923-................ **CLC 2, 8**
See also AAYA 3; CA 73-76; CANR 20,
36, 62; CLR 1, 44; DLB 52; JRDA;
MAICYA; MTCW; SATA 17, 60

Fox, William Price (Jr.) 1926- ..... **CLC 22**
See also CA 17-20R; CAAS 19; CANR 11;
DLB 2; DLBY 81

Foxe, John 1516(?)-1587 .... **LC 14**

Frame, Janet
1924-... **CLC 2, 3, 6, 22, 66, 96; SSC 29**
See also Clutha, Janet Paterson Frame

France, Anatole .... **TCLC 9**
See also Thibault, Jacques Anatole Francois
See also DLB 123

Francis, Claude 19(?)- .... **CLC 50**

Francis, Dick
1920- ... **CLC 2, 22, 42, 102; DAM POP**
See also AAYA 5, 21; BEST 89:3; CA 5-8R;
CANR 9, 42; CDBLB 1960 to Present;
DLB 87; INT CANR-9; MTCW

Francis, Robert (Churchill)
1901-1987 .... **CLC 15**
See also CA 1-4R; 123; CANR 1

Frank, Anne(lies Marie)
1929-1945 .... **TCLC 17; DA; DAB;
DAC; DAM MST; WLC**
See also AAYA 12; CA 113; 133; MTCW;
SATA 87; SATA-Brief 42

Frank, Elizabeth 1945-........... **CLC 39**
See also CA 121; 126; INT 126

Frankl, Viktor E(mil) 1905-........ **CLC 93**
See also CA 65-68

Franklin, Benjamin
See Hasek, Jaroslav (Matej Frantisek)

Franklin, Benjamin
1706-1790 ..... **LC 25; DA; DAB; DAC;
DAM MST; WLCS**
See also CDALB 1640-1865; DLB 24, 43,
73

Franklin, (Stella Maraia Sarah) Miles
1879-1954 .... **TCLC 7**
See also CA 104

Fraser, (Lady) Antonia (Pakenham)
1932- .... **CLC 32**
See also CA 85-88; CANR 44; MTCW;
SATA-Brief 32

Fraser, George MacDonald 1925-.... **CLC 7**
See also CA 45-48; CANR 2, 48

Fraser, Sylvia 1935-.............. **CLC 64**
See also CA 45-48; CANR 1, 16, 60

Frayn, Michael
1933- .... **CLC 3, 7, 31, 47;
DAM DRAM, NOV**
See also CA 5-8R; CANR 30; DLB 13, 14;
MTCW

Fraze, Candida (Merrill) 1945-..... **CLC 50**
See also CA 126

Frazer, J(ames) G(eorge)
1854-1941 .... **TCLC 32**
See also CA 118

Frazer, Robert Caine
See Creasey, John

Frazer, Sir James George
See Frazer, J(ames) G(eorge)

Frazier, Ian 1951-................ **CLC 46**
See also CA 130; CANR 54

Frederic, Harold 1856-1898...... **NCLC 10**
See also DLB 12, 23; DLBD 13

Frederick, John
See Faust, Frederick (Schiller)

Frederick the Great 1712-1786 ...... **LC 14**

Fredro, Aleksander 1793-1876..... **NCLC 8**

Freeling, Nicolas 1927- .... **CLC 38**
See also CA 49-52; CAAS 12; CANR 1, 17,
50; DLB 87

Freeman, Douglas Southall
1886-1953 .... **TCLC 11**
See also CA 109; DLB 17

Freeman, Judith 1946-............ **CLC 55**
See also CA 148

Freeman, Mary Eleanor Wilkins
1852-1930 .... **TCLC 9; SSC 1**
See also CA 106; DLB 12, 78

Freeman, R(ichard) Austin
1862-1943 .... **TCLC 21**
See also CA 113; DLB 70

French, Albert 1943- .... **CLC 86**

French, Marilyn
1929- .... **CLC 10, 18, 60;
DAM DRAM, NOV, POP**
See also CA 69-72; CANR 3, 31;
INT CANR-31; MTCW

French, Paul
See Asimov, Isaac

Freneau, Philip Morin 1752-1832 .. **NCLC 1**
See also DLB 37, 43

Freud, Sigmund 1856-1939 .... **TCLC 52**
See also CA 115; 133; MTCW

Friedan, Betty (Naomi) 1921-...... **CLC 74**
See also CA 65-68; CANR 18, 45; MTCW

Friedlander, Saul 1932-........... **CLC 90**
See also CA 117; 130

Friedman, B(ernard) H(arper)
1926-..................... **CLC 7**
See also CA 1-4R; CANR 3, 48

Friedman, Bruce Jay 1930-.... **CLC 3, 5, 56**
See also CA 9-12R; CANR 25, 52; DLB 2,
28; INT CANR-25

Friel, Brian 1929-.......... **CLC 5, 42, 59**
See also CA 21-24R; CANR 33; DLB 13;
MTCW

Friis-Baastad, Babbis Ellinor
1921-1970 .... **CLC 12**
See also CA 17-20R; 134; SATA 7

Frisch, Max (Rudolf)
1911-1991 ..... **CLC 3, 9, 14, 18, 32, 44;
DAM DRAM, NOV**
See also CA 85-88; 134; CANR 32;
DLB 69, 124; MTCW

Fromentin, Eugene (Samuel Auguste)
1820-1876 .... **NCLC 10**
See also DLB 123

Frost, Frederick
See Faust, Frederick (Schiller)

Frost, Robert (Lee)
1874-1963 ..... **CLC 1, 3, 4, 9, 10, 13, 15,
26, 34, 44; DA; DAB; DAC; DAM MST,
POET; PC 1; WLC**
See also AAYA 21; CA 89-92; CANR 33;
CDALB 1917-1929; DLB 54; DLBD 7;
MTCW; SATA 14

Froude, James Anthony
1818-1894 .... **NCLC 43**
See also DLB 18, 57, 144

Froy, Herald
See Waterhouse, Keith (Spencer)

Fry, Christopher
1907- ..... **CLC 2, 10, 14; DAM DRAM**
See also CA 17-20R; CAAS 23; CANR 9,
30; DLB 13; MTCW; SATA 66

Frye, (Herman) Northrop
1912-1991 .... **CLC 24, 70**
See also CA 5-8R; 133; CANR 8, 37;
DLB 67, 68; MTCW

Gary, Romain . . . . CLC 25
See also Kacew, Romain
See also DLB 83

Gascar, Pierre . . . . CLC 11
See also Fournier, Pierre

Gascoyne, David (Emery) 1916- . . . . CLC 45
See also CA 65-68; CANR 10, 28, 54;
DLB 20; MTCW

Gaskell, Elizabeth Cleghorn
1810-1865 . . . . NCLC 5; DAB;
DAM MST; SSC 25
See also CDBLB 1832-1890; DLB 21, 144,
159

Gass, William H(oward)
1924- . . . CLC 1, 2, 8, 11, 15, 39; SSC 12
See also CA 17-20R; CANR 30; DLB 2;
MTCW

Gasset, Jose Ortega y
See Ortega y Gasset, Jose

Gates, Henry Louis, Jr.
1950- . . . . CLC 65; DAM MULT
See also BW 2; CA 109; CANR 25, 53;
DLB 67

Gautier, Theophile
1811-1872 . . . . NCLC 1, 59;
DAM POET; PC 18; SSC 20
See also DLB 119

Gawsworth, John
See Bates, H(erbert) E(rnest)

Gay, Oliver
See Gogarty, Oliver St. John

Gaye, Marvin (Penze) 1939-1984 . . . CLC 26
See also CA 112

Gebler, Carlo (Ernest) 1954- . . . . CLC 39
See also CA 119; 133

Gee, Maggie (Mary) 1948- . . . . CLC 57
See also CA 130

Gee, Maurice (Gough) 1931- . . . . . . CLC 29
See also CA 97-100; SATA 46

Gelbart, Larry (Simon) 1923- . . . CLC 21, 61
See also CA 73-76; CANR 45

Gelber, Jack 1932- . . . . CLC 1, 6, 14, 79
See also CA 1-4R; CANR 2; DLB 7

Gellhorn, Martha (Ellis) 1908- . . CLC 14, 60
See also CA 77-80; CANR 44; DLBY 82

Genet, Jean
1910-1986 . . . . . . CLC 1, 2, 5, 10, 14, 44,
46; DAM DRAM
See also CA 13-16R; CANR 18; DLB 72;
DLBY 86; MTCW

Gent, Peter 1942- . . . . CLC 29
See also AITN 1; CA 89-92; DLBY 82

Gentlewoman in New England, A
See Bradstreet, Anne

Gentlewoman in Those Parts, A
See Bradstreet, Anne

George, Jean Craighead 1919- . . . . . . CLC 35
See also AAYA 8; CA 5-8R; CANR 25;
CLR 1; DLB 52; JRDA; MAICYA;
SATA 2, 68

George, Stefan (Anton)
1868-1933 . . . . TCLC 2, 14
See also CA 104

Georges, Georges Martin
See Simenon, Georges (Jacques Christian)

Gerhardi, William Alexander
See Gerhardie, William Alexander

Gerhardie, William Alexander
1895-1977 . . . . CLC 5
See also CA 25-28R; 73-76; CANR 18;
DLB 36

Gerstler, Amy 1956- . . . . CLC 70
See also CA 146

Gertler, T. . . . . CLC 34
See also CA 116; 121; INT 121

Ghalib . . . . NCLC 39
See also Ghalib, Hsadullah Khan

Ghalib, Hsadullah Khan 1797-1869
See Ghalib
See also DAM POET

Ghelderode, Michel de
1898-1962 . . . . CLC 6, 11; DAM DRAM
See also CA 85-88; CANR 40

Ghiselin, Brewster 1903- . . . . CLC 23
See also CA 13-16R; CAAS 10; CANR 13

Ghose, Zulfikar 1935- . . . . CLC 42
See also CA 65-68

Ghosh, Amitav 1956- . . . . CLC 44
See also CA 147

Giacosa, Giuseppe 1847-1906 . . . . . . TCLC 7
See also CA 104

Gibb, Lee
See Waterhouse, Keith (Spencer)

Gibbon, Lewis Grassic . . . . TCLC 4
See also Mitchell, James Leslie

Gibbons, Kaye
1960- . . . . CLC 50, 88; DAM POP
See also CA 151

Gibran, Kahlil
1883-1931 . . . . TCLC 1, 9; DAM POET,
POP; PC 9
See also CA 104; 150

Gibran, Khalil
See Gibran, Kahlil

Gibson, William
1914- . . . . CLC 23; DA; DAB; DAC;
DAM DRAM, MST
See also CA 9-12R; CANR 9, 42; DLB 7;
SATA 66

Gibson, William (Ford)
1948- . . . . CLC 39, 63; DAM POP
See also AAYA 12; CA 126; 133; CANR 52

Gide, Andre (Paul Guillaume)
1869-1951 . . . . TCLC 5, 12, 36; DA;
DAB; DAC; DAM MST, NOV; SSC 13;
WLC
See also CA 104; 124; DLB 65; MTCW

Gifford, Barry (Colby) 1946- . . . . CLC 34
See also CA 65-68; CANR 9, 30, 40

Gilbert, Frank
See De Voto, Bernard (Augustine)

Gilbert, W(illiam) S(chwenck)
1836-1911 . . . . . CLC 3; DAM DRAM,
POET
See also CA 104; SATA 36

Gilbreth, Frank B., Jr. 1911- . . . . CLC 17
See also CA 9-12R; SATA 2

Gilchrist, Ellen
1935- . . . . CLC 34, 48; DAM POP;
SSC 14
See also CA 113; 116; CANR 41, 61;
DLB 130; MTCW

Giles, Molly 1942- . . . . CLC 39
See also CA 126

Gill, Patrick
See Creasey, John

Gilliam, Terry (Vance) 1940- . . . . . . CLC 21
See also Monty Python
See also AAYA 19; CA 108; 113;
CANR 35; INT 113

Gillian, Jerry
See Gilliam, Terry (Vance)

Gilliatt, Penelope (Ann Douglass)
1932-1993 . . . . CLC 2, 10, 13, 53
See also AITN 2; CA 13-16R; 141;
CANR 49; DLB 14

Gilman, Charlotte (Anna) Perkins (Stetson)
1860-1935 . . . . TCLC 9, 37; SSC 13
See also CA 106; 150

Gilmour, David 1949- . . . . CLC 35
See also CA 138; 147

Gilpin, William 1724-1804 . . . . NCLC 30

Gilray, J. D.
See Mencken, H(enry) L(ouis)

Gilroy, Frank D(aniel) 1925- . . . . CLC 2
See also CA 81-84; CANR 32; DLB 7

Gilstrap, John 1957(?)- . . . . CLC 99
See also CA 160

Ginsberg, Allen
1926-1997 . . . . . CLC 1, 2, 3, 4, 6, 13, 36,
69; DA; DAB; DAC; DAM MST, POET;
PC 4; WLC 3
See also AITN 1; CA 1-4R; 157; CANR 2,
41; CDALB 1941-1968; DLB 5, 16, 169;
MTCW

Ginzburg, Natalia
1916-1991 . . . . CLC 5, 11, 54, 70
See also CA 85-88; 135; CANR 33;
DLB 177; MTCW

Giono, Jean 1895-1970 . . . . CLC 4, 11
See also CA 45-48; 29-32R; CANR 2, 35;
DLB 72; MTCW

Giovanni, Nikki
1943- . . . . . . CLC 2, 4, 19, 64; BLC; DA;
DAB; DAC; DAM MST, MULT, POET;
PC 19; WLCS
See also AAYA 22; AITN 1; BW 2;
CA 29-32R; CAAS 6; CANR 18, 41, 60;
CLR 6; DLB 5, 41; INT CANR-18;
MAICYA; MTCW; SATA 24

Giovene, Andrea 1904- . . . . CLC 7
See also CA 85-88

Gippius, Zinaida (Nikolayevna) 1869-1945
See Hippius, Zinaida
See also CA 106

Giraudoux, (Hippolyte) Jean
1882-1944 . . . . TCLC 2, 7; DAM DRAM
See also CA 104; DLB 65

Gironella, Jose Maria 1917- . . . . CLC 11
See also CA 101

Gissing, George (Robert)
1857-1903 . . . . TCLC 3, 24, 47
See also CA 105; DLB 18, 135, 184

Goyen, (Charles) William
1915-1983 . . . . **CLC 5, 8, 14, 40**
See also AITN 2; CA 5-8R; 110; CANR 6;
DLB 2; DLBY 83; INT CANR-6

Goytisolo, Juan
1931- . . . . . **CLC 5, 10, 23; DAM MULT;**
HLC
See also CA 85-88; CANR 32, 61; HW;
MTCW

Gozzano, Guido 1883-1916 . . . . **PC 10**
See also CA 154; DLB 114

Gozzi, (Conte) Carlo 1720-1806 . . **NCLC 23**

Grabbe, Christian Dietrich
1801-1836 . . . . **NCLC 2**
See also DLB 133

Grace, Patricia 1937- . . . . **CLC 56**

Gracian y Morales, Baltasar
1601-1658 . . . . **LC 15**

Gracq, Julien . . . . **CLC 11, 48**
See also Poirier, Louis
See also DLB 83

Grade, Chaim 1910-1982 . . . . **CLC 10**
See also CA 93-96; 107

Graduate of Oxford, A
See Ruskin, John

Grafton, Garth
See Duncan, Sara Jeannette

Graham, John
See Phillips, David Graham

Graham, Jorie 1951- . . . . **CLC 48**
See also CA 111; DLB 120

Graham, R(obert) B(ontine) Cunninghame
See Cunninghame Graham, R(obert)
B(ontine)
See also DLB 98, 135, 174

Graham, Robert
See Haldeman, Joe (William)

Graham, Tom
See Lewis, (Harry) Sinclair

Graham, W(illiam) S(ydney)
1918-1986 . . . . **CLC 29**
See also CA 73-76; 118; DLB 20

Graham, Winston (Mawdsley)
1910- . . . . **CLC 23**
See also CA 49-52; CANR 2, 22, 45;
DLB 77

Grahame, Kenneth
1859-1932 . . . . **TCLC 64; DAB**
See also CA 108; 136; CLR 5; DLB 34, 141,
178; MAICYA; YABC 1

Grant, Skeeter
See Spiegelman, Art

Granville-Barker, Harley
1877-1946 . . . . . . **TCLC 2; DAM DRAM**
See also Barker, Harley Granville
See also CA 104

Grass, Guenter (Wilhelm)
1927- . . . . . **CLC 1, 2, 4, 6, 11, 15, 22, 32,**
49, 88; DA; DAB; DAC; DAM MST,
NOV; WLC
See also CA 13-16R; CANR 20; DLB 75,
124; MTCW

Gratton, Thomas
See Hulme, T(homas) E(rnest)

Grau, Shirley Ann
1929- . . . . **CLC 4, 9; SSC 15**
See also CA 89-92; CANR 22; DLB 2;
INT CANR-22; MTCW

Gravel, Fern
See Hall, James Norman

Graver, Elizabeth 1964- . . . . **CLC 70**
See also CA 135

Graves, Richard Perceval 1945- . . . . **CLC 44**
See also CA 65-68; CANR 9, 26, 51

Graves, Robert (von Ranke)
1895-1985 . . . . . . **CLC 1, 2, 6, 11, 39, 44,**
45; DAB; DAC; DAM MST, POET;
PC 6
See also CA 5-8R; 117; CANR 5, 36;
CDBLB 1914-1945; DLB 20, 100;
DLBY 85; MTCW; SATA 45

Graves, Valerie
See Bradley, Marion Zimmer

Gray, Alasdair (James) 1934- . . . . . . **CLC 41**
See also CA 126; CANR 47; INT 126;
MTCW

Gray, Amlin 1946- . . . . **CLC 29**
See also CA 138

Gray, Francine du Plessix
1930- . . . . **CLC 22; DAM NOV**
See also BEST 90:3; CA 61-64; CAAS 2;
CANR 11, 33; INT CANR-11; MTCW

Gray, John (Henry) 1866-1934 . . . . **TCLC 19**
See also CA 119

Gray, Simon (James Holliday)
1936- . . . . **CLC 9, 14, 36**
See also AITN 1; CA 21-24R; CAAS 3;
CANR 32; DLB 13; MTCW

Gray, Spalding
1941- . . . . . . **CLC 49; DAM POP; DC 7**
See also CA 128

Gray, Thomas
1716-1771 . . . . **LC 4, 40; DA; DAB;**
DAC; DAM MST; PC 2; WLC
See also CDBLB 1660-1789; DLB 109

Grayson, David
See Baker, Ray Stannard

Grayson, Richard (A.) 1951- . . . . **CLC 38**
See also CA 85-88; CANR 14, 31, 57

Greeley, Andrew M(oran)
1928- . . . . **CLC 28; DAM POP**
See also CA 5-8R; CAAS 7; CANR 7, 43;
MTCW

Green, Anna Katharine
1846-1935 . . . . **TCLC 63**
See also CA 112; 159

Green, Brian
See Card, Orson Scott

Green, Hannah
See Greenberg, Joanne (Goldenberg)

Green, Hannah 1927(?)-1996 . . . . **CLC 3**
See also CA 73-76; CANR 59

Green, Henry 1905-1973 . . . . . **CLC 2, 13, 97**
See also Yorke, Henry Vincent
See also DLB 15

Green, Julian (Hartridge) 1900-
See Green, Julien
See also CA 21-24R; CANR 33; DLB 4, 72;
MTCW

Green, Julien . . . . **CLC 3, 11, 77**
See also Green, Julian (Hartridge)

Green, Paul (Eliot)
1894-1981 . . . . . . **CLC 25; DAM DRAM**
See also AITN 1; CA 5-8R; 103; CANR 3;
DLB 7, 9; DLBY 81

Greenberg, Ivan 1908-1973
See Rahv, Philip
See also CA 85-88

Greenberg, Joanne (Goldenberg)
1932- . . . . **CLC 7, 30**
See also AAYA 12; CA 5-8R; CANR 14,
32; SATA 25

Greenberg, Richard 1959(?)- . . . . **CLC 57**
See also CA 138

Greene, Bette 1934- . . . . **CLC 30**
See also AAYA 7; CA 53-56; CANR 4;
CLR 2; JRDA; MAICYA; SAAS 16;
SATA 8

Greene, Gael . . . . **CLC 8**
See also CA 13-16R; CANR 10

Greene, Graham (Henry)
1904-1991 . . . . **CLC 1, 3, 6, 9, 14, 18, 27,**
37, 70, 72; DA; DAB; DAC; DAM MST,
NOV; SSC 29; WLC
See also AITN 2; CA 13-16R; 133;
CANR 35, 61; CDBLB 1945-1960;
DLB 13, 15, 77, 100, 162; DLBY 91;
MTCW; SATA 20

Greer, Richard
See Silverberg, Robert

Gregor, Arthur 1923- . . . . **CLC 9**
See also CA 25-28R; CAAS 10; CANR 11;
SATA 36

Gregor, Lee
See Pohl, Frederik

Gregory, Isabella Augusta (Persse)
1852-1932 . . . . **TCLC 1**
See also CA 104; DLB 10

Gregory, J. Dennis
See Williams, John A(lfred)

Grendon, Stephen
See Derleth, August (William)

Grenville, Kate 1950- . . . . **CLC 61**
See also CA 118; CANR 53

Grenville, Pelham
See Wodehouse, P(elham) G(renville)

Greve, Felix Paul (Berthold Friedrich)
1879-1948
See Grove, Frederick Philip
See also CA 104; 141; DAC; DAM MST

Grey, Zane
1872-1939 . . . . **TCLC 6; DAM POP**
See also CA 104; 132; DLB 9; MTCW

Grieg, (Johan) Nordahl (Brun)
1902-1943 . . . . **TCLC 10**
See also CA 107

Grieve, C(hristopher) M(urray)
1892-1978 . . . . **CLC 11, 19; DAM POET**
See also MacDiarmid, Hugh; Pteleon
See also CA 5-8R; 85-88; CANR 33;
MTCW

Griffin, Gerald 1803-1840 . . . . **NCLC 7**
See also DLB 159

Griffin, John Howard   1920-1980.... **CLC 68**
See also AITN 1; CA 1-4R; 101; CANR 2

Griffin, Peter   1942- .... **CLC 39**
See also CA 136

Griffith, D(avid Lewelyn) W(ark)
1875(?)-1948 .... **TCLC 68**
See also CA 119; 150

Griffith, Lawrence
See Griffith, D(avid Lewelyn) W(ark)

Griffiths, Trevor   1935- .... **CLC 13, 52**
See also CA 97-100; CANR 45; DLB 13

Grigson, Geoffrey (Edward Harvey)
1905-1985 .... **CLC 7, 39**
See also CA 25-28R; 118; CANR 20, 33;
DLB 27; MTCW

Grillparzer, Franz   1791-1872...... **NCLC 1**
See also DLB 133

Grimble, Reverend Charles James
See Eliot, T(homas) S(tearns)

Grimke, Charlotte L(ottie) Forten
1837(?)-1914
See Forten, Charlotte L.
See also BW 1; CA 117; 124; DAM MULT,
POET

Grimm, Jacob Ludwig Karl
1785-1863 .... **NCLC 3**
See also DLB 90; MAICYA; SATA 22

Grimm, Wilhelm Karl   1786-1859 .. **NCLC 3**
See also DLB 90; MAICYA; SATA 22

Grimmelshausen, Johann Jakob Christoffel
von   1621-1676 .... **LC 6**
See also DLB 168

Grindel, Eugene   1895-1952
See Eluard, Paul
See also CA 104

Grisham, John   1955- .. **CLC 84; DAM POP**
See also AAYA 14; CA 138; CANR 47

Grossman, David   1954- .... **CLC 67**
See also CA 138

Grossman, Vasily (Semenovich)
1905-1964 .... **CLC 41**
See also CA 124; 130; MTCW

Grove, Frederick Philip .... **TCLC 4**
See also Greve, Felix Paul (Berthold
Friedrich)
See also DLB 92

Grubb
See Crumb, R(obert)

Grumbach, Doris (Isaac)
1918- .... **CLC 13, 22, 64**
See also CA 5-8R; CAAS 2; CANR 9, 42;
INT CANR-9

Grundtvig, Nicolai Frederik Severin
1783-1872 .... **NCLC 1**

Grunge
See Crumb, R(obert)

Grunwald, Lisa   1959- .... **CLC 44**
See also CA 120

Guare, John
1938- .... **CLC 8, 14, 29, 67;**
DAM DRAM
See also CA 73-76; CANR 21; DLB 7;
MTCW

Gudjonsson, Halldor Kiljan   1902-
See Laxness, Halldor
See also CA 103

Guenter, Erich
See Eich, Guenter

Guest, Barbara   1920- .... **CLC 34**
See also CA 25-28R; CANR 11, 44; DLB 5

Guest, Judith (Ann)
1936- .... **CLC 8, 30; DAM NOV, POP**
See also AAYA 7; CA 77-80; CANR 15;
INT CANR-15; MTCW

Guevara, Che .... **CLC 87; HLC**
See also Guevara (Serna), Ernesto

Guevara (Serna), Ernesto   1928-1967
See Guevara, Che
See also CA 127; 111; CANR 56;
DAM MULT; HW

Guild, Nicholas M.   1944- .... **CLC 33**
See also CA 93-96

Guillemin, Jacques
See Sartre, Jean-Paul

Guillen, Jorge
1893-1984 ...... **CLC 11; DAM MULT,**
POET
See also CA 89-92; 112; DLB 108; HW

Guillen, Nicolas (Cristobal)
1902-1989 .... **CLC 48, 79; BLC;**
DAM MST, MULT, POET; HLC
See also BW 2; CA 116; 125; 129; HW

Guillevic, (Eugene)   1907- .... **CLC 33**
See also CA 93-96

Guillois
See Desnos, Robert

Guillois, Valentin
See Desnos, Robert

Guiney, Louise Imogen
1861-1920 .... **TCLC 41**
See also CA 160; DLB 54

Guiraldes, Ricardo (Guillermo)
1886-1927 .... **TCLC 39**
See also CA 131; HW; MTCW

Gumilev, Nikolai Stephanovich
1886-1921 .... **TCLC 60**

Gunesekera, Romesh   1954- .... **CLC 91**
See also CA 159

Gunn, Bill .... **CLC 5**
See also Gunn, William Harrison
See also DLB 38

Gunn, Thom(son William)
1929- .... **CLC 3, 6, 18, 32, 81;**
DAM POET
See also CA 17-20R; CANR 9, 33;
CDBLB 1960 to Present; DLB 27;
INT CANR-33; MTCW

Gunn, William Harrison   1934(?)-1989
See Gunn, Bill
See also AITN 1; BW 1; CA 13-16R; 128;
CANR 12, 25

Gunnars, Kristjana   1948- .... **CLC 69**
See also CA 113; DLB 60

Gurdjieff, G(eorgei) I(vanovich)
1877(?)-1949 .... **TCLC 71**
See also CA 157

Gurganus, Allan
1947- .... **CLC 70; DAM POP**
See also BEST 90:1; CA 135

Gurney, A(lbert) R(amsdell), Jr.
1930- .... **CLC 32, 50, 54; DAM DRAM**
See also CA 77-80; CANR 32

Gurney, Ivor (Bertie)   1890-1937 ... **TCLC 33**

Gurney, Peter
See Gurney, A(lbert) R(amsdell), Jr.

Guro, Elena   1877-1913.......... **TCLC 56**

Gustafson, James M(oody)   1925- .. **CLC 100**
See also CA 25-28R; CANR 37

Gustafson, Ralph (Barker)   1909-.... **CLC 36**
See also CA 21-24R; CANR 8, 45; DLB 88

Gut, Gom
See Simenon, Georges (Jacques Christian)

Guterson, David   1956- .... **CLC 91**
See also CA 132

Guthrie, A(lfred) B(ertram), Jr.
1901-1991 .... **CLC 23**
See also CA 57-60; 134; CANR 24; DLB 6;
SATA 62; SATA-Obit 67

Guthrie, Isobel
See Grieve, C(hristopher) M(urray)

Guthrie, Woodrow Wilson   1912-1967
See Guthrie, Woody
See also CA 113; 93-96

Guthrie, Woody .... **CLC 35**
See also Guthrie, Woodrow Wilson

Guy, Rosa (Cuthbert)   1928- .... **CLC 26**
See also AAYA 4; BW 2; CA 17-20R;
CANR 14, 34; CLR 13; DLB 33; JRDA;
MAICYA; SATA 14, 62

Gwendolyn
See Bennett, (Enoch) Arnold

H. D. .... **CLC 3, 8, 14, 31, 34, 73; PC 5**
See also Doolittle, Hilda

H. de V.
See Buchan, John

Haavikko, Paavo Juhani
1931- .... **CLC 18, 34**
See also CA 106

Habbema, Koos
See Heijermans, Herman

Habermas, Juergen   1929- .... **CLC 104**
See also CA 109

Habermas, Jurgen
See Habermas, Juergen

Hacker, Marilyn
1942- .... **CLC 5, 9, 23, 72, 91;**
DAM POET
See also CA 77-80; DLB 120

Haggard, H(enry) Rider
1856-1925 .... **TCLC 11**
See also CA 108; 148; DLB 70, 156, 174,
178; SATA 16

Hagiosy, L.
See Larbaud, Valery (Nicolas)

Hagiwara Sakutaro
1886-1942 .... **TCLC 60; PC 18**

Haig, Fenil
See Ford, Ford Madox

Haig-Brown, Roderick (Langmere)
  1908-1976 .... **CLC 21**
  See also CA 5-8R; 69-72; CANR 4, 38;
  CLR 31; DLB 88; MAICYA; SATA 12

Hailey, Arthur
  1920- .... **CLC 5; DAM NOV, POP**
  See also AITN 2; BEST 90:3; CA 1-4R;
  CANR 2, 36; DLB 88; DLBY 82; MTCW

Hailey, Elizabeth Forsythe 1938-... **CLC 40**
  See also CA 93-96; CAAS 1; CANR 15, 48;
  INT CANR-15

Haines, John (Meade) 1924-....... **CLC 58**
  See also CA 17-20R; CANR 13, 34; DLB 5

Hakluyt, Richard 1552-1616 .... **LC 31**

Haldeman, Joe (William) 1943-..... **CLC 61**
  See also CA 53-56; CAAS 25; CANR 6;
  DLB 8; INT CANR-6

Haley, Alex(ander Murray Palmer)
  1921-1992 .... **CLC 8, 12, 76; BLC; DA;**
    DAB; DAC; DAM MST, MULT, POP
  See also BW 2; CA 77-80; 136; CANR 61;
  DLB 38; MTCW

Haliburton, Thomas Chandler
  1796-1865 .... **NCLC 15**
  See also DLB 11, 99

Hall, Donald (Andrew, Jr.)
  1928- .. **CLC 1, 13, 37, 59; DAM POET**
  See also CA 5-8R; CAAS 7; CANR 2, 44;
  DLB 5; SATA 23

Hall, Frederic Sauser
  See Sauser-Hall, Frederic

Hall, James
  See Kuttner, Henry

Hall, James Norman 1887-1951 ... **TCLC 23**
  See also CA 123; SATA 21

Hall, (Marguerite) Radclyffe
  1886-1943 .... **TCLC 12**
  See also CA 110; 150

Hall, Rodney 1935- .... **CLC 51**
  See also CA 109

Halleck, Fitz-Greene 1790-1867 .. **NCLC 47**
  See also DLB 3

Halliday, Michael
  See Creasey, John

Halpern, Daniel 1945- .... **CLC 14**
  See also CA 33-36R

Hamburger, Michael (Peter Leopold)
  1924- .... **CLC 5, 14**
  See also CA 5-8R; CAAS 4; CANR 2, 47;
  DLB 27

Hamill, Pete 1935- .... **CLC 10**
  See also CA 25-28R; CANR 18

Hamilton, Alexander
  1755(?)-1804 .... **NCLC 49**
  See also DLB 37

Hamilton, Clive
  See Lewis, C(live) S(taples)

Hamilton, Edmond 1904-1977 .... **CLC 1**
  See also CA 1-4R; CANR 3; DLB 8

Hamilton, Eugene (Jacob) Lee
  See Lee-Hamilton, Eugene (Jacob)

Hamilton, Franklin
  See Silverberg, Robert

Hamilton, Gail
  See Corcoran, Barbara

Hamilton, Mollie
  See Kaye, M(ary) M(argaret)

Hamilton, (Anthony Walter) Patrick
  1904-1962 .... **CLC 51**
  See also CA 113; DLB 10

Hamilton, Virginia
  1936- .... **CLC 26; DAM MULT**
  See also AAYA 2, 21; BW 2; CA 25-28R;
  CANR 20, 37; CLR 1, 11, 40; DLB 33,
  52; INT CANR-20; JRDA; MAICYA;
  MTCW; SATA 4, 56, 79

Hammett, (Samuel) Dashiell
  1894-1961 .... **CLC 3, 5, 10, 19, 47;**
    SSC 17
  See also AITN 1; CA 81-84; CANR 42;
  CDALB 1929-1941; DLBD 6; DLBY 96;
  MTCW

Hammon, Jupiter
  1711(?)-1800(?) .... **NCLC 5; BLC;**
    DAM MULT, POET; PC 16
  See also DLB 31, 50

Hammond, Keith
  See Kuttner, Henry

Hamner, Earl (Henry), Jr. 1923- ... **CLC 12**
  See also AITN 2; CA 73-76; DLB 6

Hampton, Christopher (James)
  1946- .... **CLC 4**
  See also CA 25-28R; DLB 13; MTCW

Hamsun, Knut .... **TCLC 2, 14, 49**
  See also Pedersen, Knut

Handke, Peter
  1942- .... **CLC 5, 8, 10, 15, 38;**
    DAM DRAM, NOV
  See also CA 77-80; CANR 33; DLB 85,
  124; MTCW

Hanley, James 1901-1985 ... **CLC 3, 5, 8, 13**
  See also CA 73-76; 117; CANR 36; MTCW

Hannah, Barry 1942-....... **CLC 23, 38, 90**
  See also CA 108; 110; CANR 43; DLB 6;
  INT 110; MTCW

Hannon, Ezra
  See Hunter, Evan

Hansberry, Lorraine (Vivian)
  1930-1965 ...... **CLC 17, 62; BLC; DA;**
    DAB; DAC; DAM DRAM, MST,
    MULT; DC 2
  See also BW 1; CA 109; 25-28R; CABS 3;
  CANR 58; CDALB 1941-1968; DLB 7,
  38; MTCW

Hansen, Joseph 1923-............ **CLC 38**
  See also CA 29-32R; CAAS 17; CANR 16,
  44; INT CANR-16

Hansen, Martin A. 1909-1955..... **TCLC 32**

Hanson, Kenneth O(stlin) 1922-.... **CLC 13**
  See also CA 53-56; CANR 7

Hardwick, Elizabeth
  1916-........... **CLC 13; DAM NOV**
  See also CA 5-8R; CANR 3, 32; DLB 6;
  MTCW

Hardy, Thomas
  1840-1928 ...... **TCLC 4, 10, 18, 32, 48,**
    53, 72; DA; DAB; DAC; DAM MST,
    NOV, POET; PC 8; SSC 2; WLC
  See also CA 104; 123; CDBLB 1890-1914;
  DLB 18, 19, 135; MTCW

Hare, David 1947- .... **CLC 29, 58**
  See also CA 97-100; CANR 39; DLB 13;
  MTCW

Harford, Henry
  See Hudson, W(illiam) H(enry)

Hargrave, Leonie
  See Disch, Thomas M(ichael)

Harjo, Joy 1951- ... **CLC 83; DAM MULT**
  See also CA 114; CANR 35; DLB 120, 175;
  NNAL

Harlan, Louis R(udolph) 1922-..... **CLC 34**
  See also CA 21-24R; CANR 25, 55

Harling, Robert 1951(?)- .... **CLC 53**
  See also CA 147

Harmon, William (Ruth) 1938-..... **CLC 38**
  See also CA 33-36R; CANR 14, 32, 35;
  SATA 65

Harper, F. E. W.
  See Harper, Frances Ellen Watkins

Harper, Frances E. W.
  See Harper, Frances Ellen Watkins

Harper, Frances E. Watkins
  See Harper, Frances Ellen Watkins

Harper, Frances Ellen
  See Harper, Frances Ellen Watkins

Harper, Frances Ellen Watkins
  1825-1911 .... **TCLC 14; BLC;**
    DAM MULT, POET
  See also BW 1; CA 111; 125; DLB 50

Harper, Michael S(teven) 1938- .. **CLC 7, 22**
  See also BW 1; CA 33-36R; CANR 24;
  DLB 41

Harper, Mrs. F. E. W.
  See Harper, Frances Ellen Watkins

Harris, Christie (Lucy) Irwin
  1907-..................... **CLC 12**
  See also CA 5-8R; CANR 6; CLR 47;
  DLB 88; JRDA; MAICYA; SAAS 10;
  SATA 6, 74

Harris, Frank 1856-1931 .... **TCLC 24**
  See also CA 109; 150; DLB 156

Harris, George Washington
  1814-1869 .... **NCLC 23**
  See also DLB 3, 11

Harris, Joel Chandler
  1848-1908 .... **TCLC 2; SSC 19**
  See also CA 104; 137; DLB 11, 23, 42, 78,
  91; MAICYA; YABC 1

Harris, John (Wyndham Parkes Lucas)
  Beynon 1903-1969
  See Wyndham, John
  See also CA 102; 89-92

Harris, MacDonald................ **CLC 9**
  See also Heiney, Donald (William)

Harris, Mark 1922- .... **CLC 19**
  See also CA 5-8R; CAAS 3; CANR 2, 55;
  DLB 2; DLBY 80

Harris, (Theodore) Wilson 1921-.... **CLC 25**
See also BW 2; CA 65-68; CAAS 16;
CANR 11, 27; DLB 117; MTCW

Harrison, Elizabeth Cavanna 1909-
See Cavanna, Betty
See also CA 9-12R; CANR 6, 27

Harrison, Harry (Max) 1925-...... **CLC 42**
See also CA 1-4R; CANR 5, 21; DLB 8;
SATA 4

Harrison, James (Thomas)
1937-...... **CLC 6, 14, 33, 66; SSC 19**
See also CA 13-16R; CANR 8, 51;
DLBY 82; INT CANR-8

Harrison, Jim
See Harrison, James (Thomas)

Harrison, Kathryn 1961-......... **CLC 70**
See also CA 144

Harrison, Tony 1937-............. **CLC 43**
See also CA 65-68; CANR 44; DLB 40;
MTCW

Harriss, Will(ard Irvin) 1922-...... **CLC 34**
See also CA 111

Harson, Sley
See Ellison, Harlan (Jay)

Hart, Ellis
See Ellison, Harlan (Jay)

Hart, Josephine
1942(?)-.......... **CLC 70; DAM POP**
See also CA 138

Hart, Moss
1904-1961 ...... **CLC 66; DAM DRAM**
See also CA 109; 89-92; DLB 7

Harte, (Francis) Bret(t)
1836(?)-1902 .... **TCLC 1, 25; DA; DAC;**
DAM MST; SSC 8; WLC
See also CA 104; 140; CDALB 1865-1917;
DLB 12, 64, 74, 79; SATA 26

Hartley, L(eslie) P(oles)
1895-1972 .... **CLC 2, 22**
See also CA 45-48; 37-40R; CANR 33;
DLB 15, 139; MTCW

Hartman, Geoffrey H. 1929-....... **CLC 27**
See also CA 117; 125; DLB 67

Hartmann, Sadakichi 1867-1944... **TCLC 73**
See also CA 157; DLB 54

Hartmann von Aue
c. 1160-c. 1205 .... **CMLC 15**
See also DLB 138

Hartmann von Aue 1170-1210.... **CMLC 15**

Haruf, Kent 1943- .... **CLC 34**
See also CA 149

Harwood, Ronald
1934-.... **CLC 32; DAM DRAM, MST**
See also CA 1-4R; CANR 4, 55; DLB 13

Hasek, Jaroslav (Matej Frantisek)
1883-1923 .... **TCLC 4**
See also CA 104; 129; MTCW

Hass, Robert
1941-.......... **CLC 18, 39, 99; PC 16**
See also CA 111; CANR 30, 50; DLB 105;
SATA 94

Hastings, Hudson
See Kuttner, Henry

Hastings, Selina.................. **CLC 44**

Hathorne, John 1641-1717......... **LC 38**

Hatteras, Amelia
See Mencken, H(enry) L(ouis)

Hatteras, Owen.................. **TCLC 18**
See also Mencken, H(enry) L(ouis); Nathan,
George Jean

Hauptmann, Gerhart (Johann Robert)
1862-1946 ...... **TCLC 4; DAM DRAM**
See also CA 104; 153; DLB 66, 118

Havel, Vaclav
1936-................. **CLC 25, 58, 65;**
DAM DRAM; DC 6
See also CA 104; CANR 36; MTCW

Haviaras, Stratis.................. **CLC 33**
See also Chaviaras, Strates

Hawes, Stephen 1475(?)-1523(?) ..... **LC 17**

Hawkes, John (Clendennin Burne, Jr.)
1925-...... **CLC 1, 2, 3, 4, 7, 9, 14, 15,**
27, 49
See also CA 1-4R; CANR 2, 47; DLB 2, 7;
DLBY 80; MTCW

Hawking, S. W.
See Hawking, Stephen W(illiam)

Hawking, Stephen W(illiam)
1942-...................... **CLC 63**
See also AAYA 13; BEST 89:1; CA 126;
129; CANR 48

Hawthorne, Julian 1846-1934 ..... **TCLC 25**

Hawthorne, Nathaniel
1804-1864 .... **NCLC 39; DA; DAB;**
DAC; DAM MST, NOV; SSC 29; WLC
See also AAYA 18; CDALB 1640-1865;
DLB 1, 74; YABC 2

Haxton, Josephine Ayres 1921-
See Douglas, Ellen
See also CA 115; CANR 41

Hayaseca y Eizaguirre, Jorge
See Echegaray (y Eizaguirre), Jose (Maria
Waldo)

Hayashi Fumiko 1904-1951....... **TCLC 27**
See also DLB 180

Haycraft, Anna
See Ellis, Alice Thomas
See also CA 122

Hayden, Robert E(arl)
1913-1980 ...... **CLC 5, 9, 14, 37; BLC;**
DA; DAC; DAM MST, MULT, POET;
PC 6
See also BW 1; CA 69-72; 97-100; CABS 2;
CANR 24; CDALB 1941-1968; DLB 5,
76; MTCW; SATA 19; SATA-Obit 26

Hayford, J(oseph) E(phraim) Casely
See Casely-Hayford, J(oseph) E(phraim)

Hayman, Ronald 1932-........... **CLC 44**
See also CA 25-28R; CANR 18, 50;
DLB 155

Haywood, Eliza (Fowler)
1693(?)-1756 .... **LC 1**

Hazlitt, William 1778-1830...... **NCLC 29**
See also DLB 110, 158

Hazzard, Shirley 1931- .... **CLC 18**
See also CA 9-12R; CANR 4; DLBY 82;
MTCW

Head, Bessie
1937-1986 .... **CLC 25, 67; BL**
DAM MUL
See also BW 2; CA 29-32R; 119; CANR 2
DLB 117; MTCW

Headon, (Nicky) Topper 1956(?)- ... **CLC 3**

Heaney, Seamus (Justin)
1939- ...... **CLC 5, 7, 14, 25, 37, 74, 9**
DAB; DAM POET; PC 18; WLC
See also CA 85-88; CANR 25, 48;
CDBLB 1960 to Present; DLB 40;
DLBY 95; MTCW

Hearn, (Patricio) Lafcadio (Tessima Carlos)
1850-1904 .... **TCLC**
See also CA 105; DLB 12, 78

Hearne, Vicki 1946-.............. **CLC 5**
See also CA 139

Hearon, Shelby 1931-............. **CLC 6**
See also AITN 2; CA 25-28R; CANR 18,
48

Heat-Moon, William Least.......... **CLC 2**
See also Trogdon, William (Lewis)
See also AAYA 9

Hebbel, Friedrich
1813-1863 .... **NCLC 43; DAM DRAM**
See also DLB 129

Hebert, Anne
1916- .... **CLC 4, 13, 29; DAC**
DAM MST, POE
See also CA 85-88; DLB 68; MTCW

Hecht, Anthony (Evan)
1923- ...... **CLC 8, 13, 19; DAM POE**
See also CA 9-12R; CANR 6; DLB 5, 169

Hecht, Ben 1894-1964 .... **CLC**
See also CA 85-88; DLB 7, 9, 25, 26, 28, 86

Hedayat, Sadeq 1903-1951........ **TCLC 2**
See also CA 120

Hegel, Georg Wilhelm Friedrich
1770-1831 .... **NCLC 4**
See also DLB 90

Heidegger, Martin 1889-1976 ...... **CLC 2**
See also CA 81-84; 65-68; CANR 34;
MTCW

Heidenstam, (Carl Gustaf) Verner von
1859-1940 .... **TCLC**
See also CA 104

Heifner, Jack 1946-.............. **CLC 1**
See also CA 105; CANR 47

Heijermans, Herman 1864-1924 ... **TCLC 2**
See also CA 123

Heilbrun, Carolyn G(old) 1926-..... **CLC 2**
See also CA 45-48; CANR 1, 28, 58

Heine, Heinrich 1797-1856 .... **NCLC 4, 5**
See also DLB 90

Heinemann, Larry (Curtiss) 1944- .. **CLC 5**
See also CA 110; CAAS 21; CANR 31;
DLBD 9; INT CANR-31

Heiney, Donald (William) 1921-1993
See Harris, MacDonald
See also CA 1-4R; 142; CANR 3, 58

Hijuelos, Oscar
1951- .... **CLC 65; DAM MULT, POP;**
HLC
See also BEST 90:1; CA 123; CANR 50;
DLB 145; HW

Hikmet, Nazim 1902(?)-1963....... **CLC 40**
See also CA 141; 93-96

Hildegard von Bingen
1098-1179 .... **CMLC 20**
See also DLB 148

Hildesheimer, Wolfgang
1916-1991 .... **CLC 49**
See also CA 101; 135; DLB 69, 124

Hill, Geoffrey (William)
1932- ... **CLC 5, 8, 18, 45; DAM POET**
See also CA 81-84; CANR 21;
CDBLB 1960 to Present; DLB 40;
MTCW

Hill, George Roy 1921- .... **CLC 26**
See also CA 110; 122

Hill, John
See Koontz, Dean R(ay)

Hill, Susan (Elizabeth)
1942- .. **CLC 4; DAB; DAM MST, NOV**
See also CA 33-36R; CANR 29; DLB 14,
139; MTCW

Hillerman, Tony
1925- .... **CLC 62; DAM POP**
See also AAYA 6; BEST 89:1; CA 29-32R;
CANR 21, 42; SATA 6

Hillesum, Etty 1914-1943 .... **TCLC 49**
See also CA 137

Hilliard, Noel (Harvey) 1929-...... **CLC 15**
See also CA 9-12R; CANR 7

Hillis, Rick 1956-................. **CLC 66**
See also CA 134

Hilton, James 1900-1954........ **TCLC 21**
See also CA 108; DLB 34, 77; SATA 34

Himes, Chester (Bomar)
1909-1984 .... **CLC 2, 4, 7, 18, 58; BLC;**
DAM MULT
See also BW 2; CA 25-28R; 114; CANR 22;
DLB 2, 76, 143; MTCW

Hinde, Thomas .... **CLC 6, 11**
See also Chitty, Thomas Willes

Hindin, Nathan
See Bloch, Robert (Albert)

Hine, (William) Daryl 1936-....... **CLC 15**
See also CA 1-4R; CAAS 15; CANR 1, 20;
DLB 60

Hinkson, Katharine Tynan
See Tynan, Katharine

Hinton, S(usan) E(loise)
1950- .... **CLC 30; DA; DAB; DAC;**
DAM MST, NOV
See also AAYA 2; CA 81-84; CANR 32,
62; CLR 3, 23; JRDA; MAICYA;
MTCW; SATA 19, 58

Hippius, Zinaida .... **TCLC 9**
See also Gippius, Zinaida (Nikolayevna)

Hiraoka, Kimitake 1925-1970
See Mishima, Yukio
See also CA 97-100; 29-32R; DAM DRAM;
MTCW

Hirsch, E(ric) D(onald), Jr. 1928-... **CLC 79**
See also CA 25-28R; CANR 27, 51;
DLB 67; INT CANR-27; MTCW

Hirsch, Edward 1950- .... **CLC 31, 50**
See also CA 104; CANR 20, 42; DLB 120

Hitchcock, Alfred (Joseph)
1899-1980 .... **CLC 16**
See also AAYA 22; CA 159; 97-100;
SATA 27; SATA-Obit 24

Hitler, Adolf 1889-1945 .... **TCLC 53**
See also CA 117; 147

Hoagland, Edward 1932-......... **CLC 28**
See also CA 1-4R; CANR 2, 31, 57; DLB 6;
SATA 51

Hoban, Russell (Conwell)
1925- .... **CLC 7, 25; DAM NOV**
See also CA 5-8R; CANR 23, 37; CLR 3;
DLB 52; MAICYA; MTCW; SATA 1,
40, 78

Hobbes, Thomas 1588-1679........ **LC 36**
See also DLB 151

Hobbs, Perry
See Blackmur, R(ichard) P(almer)

Hobson, Laura Z(ametkin)
1900-1986 .... **CLC 7, 25**
See also CA 17-20R; 118; CANR 55;
DLB 28; SATA 52

Hochhuth, Rolf
1931- ..... **CLC 4, 11, 18; DAM DRAM**
See also CA 5-8R; CANR 33; DLB 124;
MTCW

Hochman, Sandra 1936-......... **CLC 3, 8**
See also CA 5-8R; DLB 5

Hochwaelder, Fritz
1911-1986 ...... **CLC 36; DAM DRAM**
See also CA 29-32R; 120; CANR 42;
MTCW

Hochwalder, Fritz
See Hochwaelder, Fritz

Hocking, Mary (Eunice) 1921- ..... **CLC 13**
See also CA 101; CANR 18, 40

Hodgins, Jack 1938-.............. **CLC 23**
See also CA 93-96; DLB 60

Hodgson, William Hope
1877(?)-1918 .... **TCLC 13**
See also CA 111; DLB 70, 153, 156, 178

Hoeg, Peter 1957-................ **CLC 95**
See also CA 151

Hoffman, Alice
1952- .... **CLC 51; DAM NOV**
See also CA 77-80; CANR 34; MTCW

Hoffman, Daniel (Gerard)
1923-................. **CLC 6, 13, 23**
See also CA 1-4R; CANR 4; DLB 5

Hoffman, Stanley 1944-............ **CLC 5**
See also CA 77-80

Hoffman, William M(oses) 1939-... **CLC 40**
See also CA 57-60; CANR 11

Hoffmann, E(rnst) T(heodor) A(madeus)
1776-1822 .... **NCLC 2; SSC 13**
See also DLB 90; SATA 27

Hofmann, Gert 1931-............. **CLC 54**
See also CA 128

Hofmannsthal, Hugo von
1874-1929 .... **TCLC 11; DAM DRAM;**
DC 4
See also CA 106; 153; DLB 81, 118

Hogan, Linda
1947- .... **CLC 73; DAM MULT**
See also CA 120; CANR 45; DLB 175;
NNAL

Hogarth, Charles
See Creasey, John

Hogarth, Emmett
See Polonsky, Abraham (Lincoln)

Hogg, James 1770-1835.......... **NCLC 4**
See also DLB 93, 116, 159

Holbach, Paul Henri Thiry Baron
1723-1789 .... **LC 14**

Holberg, Ludvig 1684-1754 .... **LC 6**

Holden, Ursula 1921-............ **CLC 18**
See also CA 101; CAAS 8; CANR 22

Holderlin, (Johann Christian) Friedrich
1770-1843 .... **NCLC 16; PC 4**

Holdstock, Robert
See Holdstock, Robert P.

Holdstock, Robert P. 1948-........ **CLC 39**
See also CA 131

Holland, Isabelle 1920- .... **CLC 21**
See also AAYA 11; CA 21-24R; CANR 10,
25, 47; JRDA; MAICYA; SATA 8, 70

Holland, Marcus
See Caldwell, (Janet Miriam) Taylor
(Holland)

Hollander, John 1929-...... **CLC 2, 5, 8, 14**
See also CA 1-4R; CANR 1, 52; DLB 5;
SATA 13

Hollander, Paul
See Silverberg, Robert

Holleran, Andrew 1943(?)-......... **CLC 38**
See also CA 144

Hollinghurst, Alan 1954-....... **CLC 55, 91**
See also CA 114

Hollis, Jim
See Summers, Hollis (Spurgeon, Jr.)

Holly, Buddy 1936-1959 .... **TCLC 65**

Holmes, Gordon
See Shiel, M(atthew) P(hipps)

Holmes, John
See Souster, (Holmes) Raymond

Holmes, John Clellon 1926-1988.... **CLC 56**
See also CA 9-12R; 125; CANR 4; DLB 16

Holmes, Oliver Wendell
1809-1894 .... **NCLC 14**
See also CDALB 1640-1865; DLB 1;
SATA 34

Holmes, Raymond
See Souster, (Holmes) Raymond

Holt, Victoria
See Hibbert, Eleanor Alice Burford

Holub, Miroslav 1923-............. **CLC 4**
See also CA 21-24R; CANR 10

Homer
c. 8th cent. B.C.-..... **CMLC 1, 16; DA;**
DAB; DAC; DAM MST, POET; WLCS
See also DLB 176

Hulme, T(homas) E(rnest)
1883-1917 .... TCLC 21
See also CA 117; DLB 19

Hume, David 1711-1776............. LC 7
See also DLB 104

Humphrey, William 1924-1997 ..... CLC 45
See also CA 77-80; 160; DLB 6

Humphreys, Emyr Owen 1919-..... CLC 47
See also CA 5-8R; CANR 3, 24; DLB 15

Humphreys, Josephine 1945-.... CLC 34, 57
See also CA 121; 127; INT 127

Huneker, James Gibbons
1857-1921 .... TCLC 65
See also DLB 71

Hungerford, Pixie
See Brinsmead, H(esba) F(ay)

Hunt, E(verette) Howard, (Jr.)
1918- .... CLC 3
See also AITN 1; CA 45-48; CANR 2, 47

Hunt, Kyle
See Creasey, John

Hunt, (James Henry) Leigh
1784-1859 ...... NCLC 1; DAM POET

Hunt, Marsha 1946-............... CLC 70
See also BW 2; CA 143

Hunt, Violet 1866-1942 .... TCLC 53
See also DLB 162

Hunter, E. Waldo
See Sturgeon, Theodore (Hamilton)

Hunter, Evan
1926- .... CLC 11, 31; DAM POP
See also CA 5-8R; CANR 5, 38, 62;
DLBY 82; INT CANR-5; MTCW;
SATA 25

Hunter, Kristin (Eggleston) 1931-... CLC 35
See also AITN 1; BW 1; CA 13-16R;
CANR 13; CLR 3; DLB 33;
INT CANR-13; MAICYA; SAAS 10;
SATA 12

Hunter, Mollie 1922-............. CLC 21
See also McIlwraith, Maureen Mollie
Hunter
See also AAYA 13; CANR 37; CLR 25;
DLB 161; JRDA; MAICYA; SAAS 7;
SATA 54

Hunter, Robert (?)-1734............. LC 7

Hurston, Zora Neale
1903-1960 .... CLC 7, 30, 61; BLC; DA;
DAC; DAM MST, MULT, NOV; SSC 4;
WLCS
See also AAYA 15; BW 1; CA 85-88;
CANR 61; DLB 51, 86; MTCW

Huston, John (Marcellus)
1906-1987 .... CLC 20
See also CA 73-76; 123; CANR 34; DLB 26

Hustvedt, Siri 1955-.............. CLC 76
See also CA 137

Hutten, Ulrich von 1488-1523....... LC 16
See also DLB 179

Huxley, Aldous (Leonard)
1894-1963 ..... CLC 1, 3, 4, 5, 8, 11, 18,
35, 79; DA; DAB; DAC; DAM MST,
NOV; WLC
See also AAYA 11; CA 85-88; CANR 44;
CDBLB 1914-1945; DLB 36, 100, 162;
MTCW; SATA 63

Huysmans, Charles Marie Georges
1848-1907
See Huysmans, Joris-Karl
See also CA 104

Huysmans, Joris-Karl........... TCLC 7, 69
See also Huysmans, Charles Marie Georges
See also DLB 123

Hwang, David Henry
1957- .... CLC 55; DAM DRAM; DC 4
See also CA 127; 132; INT 132

Hyde, Anthony 1946-............. CLC 42
See also CA 136

Hyde, Margaret O(ldroyd) 1917- ... CLC 21
See also CA 1-4R; CANR 1, 36; CLR 23;
JRDA; MAICYA; SAAS 8; SATA 1, 42,
76

Hynes, James 1956(?)-............ CLC 65

Ian, Janis 1951- .... CLC 21
See also CA 105

Ibanez, Vicente Blasco
See Blasco Ibanez, Vicente

Ibarguengoitia, Jorge 1928-1983.... CLC 37
See also CA 124; 113; HW

Ibsen, Henrik (Johan)
1828-1906 .... TCLC 2, 8, 16, 37, 52;
DA; DAB; DAC; DAM DRAM, MST;
DC 2; WLC
See also CA 104; 141

Ibuse Masuji 1898-1993........... CLC 22
See also CA 127; 141; DLB 180

Ichikawa, Kon 1915-.............. CLC 20
See also CA 121

Idle, Eric 1943-.................. CLC 21
See also Monty Python
See also CA 116; CANR 35

Ignatow, David 1914-...... CLC 4, 7, 14, 40
See also CA 9-12R; CAAS 3; CANR 31, 57;
DLB 5

Ihimaera, Witi 1944- .... CLC 46
See also CA 77-80

Ilf, Ilya........................ TCLC 21
See also Fainzilberg, Ilya Arnoldovich

Illyes, Gyula 1902-1983 .... PC 16
See also CA 114; 109

Immermann, Karl (Lebrecht)
1796-1840 .... NCLC 4, 49
See also DLB 133

Inchbald, Elizabeth 1753-1821 ... NCLC 62
See also DLB 39, 89

Inclan, Ramon (Maria) del Valle
See Valle-Inclan, Ramon (Maria) del

Infante, G(uillermo) Cabrera
See Cabrera Infante, G(uillermo)

Ingalls, Rachel (Holmes) 1940-..... CLC 42
See also CA 123; 127

Ingamells, Rex 1913-1955 .... TCLC 35

Inge, William (Motter)
1913-1973 .. CLC 1, 8, 19; DAM DRAM
See also CA 9-12R; CDALB 1941-1968;
DLB 7; MTCW

Ingelow, Jean 1820-1897 .... NCLC 39
See also DLB 35, 163; SATA 33

Ingram, Willis J.
See Harris, Mark

Innaurato, Albert (F.) 1948(?)- .. CLC 21, 60
See also CA 115; 122; INT 122

Innes, Michael
See Stewart, J(ohn) I(nnes) M(ackintosh)

Ionesco, Eugene
1909-1994 .... CLC 1, 4, 6, 9, 11, 15, 41,
86; DA; DAB; DAC; DAM DRAM,
MST; WLC
See also CA 9-12R; 144; CANR 55;
MTCW; SATA 7; SATA-Obit 79

Iqbal, Muhammad 1873-1938 ..... TCLC 28

Ireland, Patrick
See O'Doherty, Brian

Iron, Ralph
See Schreiner, Olive (Emilie Albertina)

Irving, John (Winslow)
1942- ..... CLC 13, 23, 38; DAM NOV,
POP
See also AAYA 8; BEST 89:3; CA 25-28R;
CANR 28; DLB 6; DLBY 82; MTCW

Irving, Washington
1783-1859 ..... NCLC 2, 19; DA; DAB;
DAM MST; SSC 2; WLC
See also CDALB 1640-1865; DLB 3, 11, 30,
59, 73, 74; YABC 2

Irwin, P. K.
See Page, P(atricia) K(athleen)

Isaacs, Susan 1943- ... CLC 32; DAM POP
See also BEST 89:1; CA 89-92; CANR 20,
41; INT CANR-20; MTCW

Isherwood, Christopher (William Bradshaw)
1904-1986 .... CLC 1, 9, 11, 14, 44;
DAM DRAM, NOV
See also CA 13-16R; 117; CANR 35;
DLB 15; DLBY 86; MTCW

Ishiguro, Kazuo
1954- ...... CLC 27, 56, 59; DAM NOV
See also BEST 90:2; CA 120; CANR 49;
MTCW

Ishikawa, Hakuhin
See Ishikawa, Takuboku

Ishikawa, Takuboku
1886(?)-1912 .... TCLC 15;
DAM POET; PC 10
See also CA 113; 153

Iskander, Fazil 1929-............. CLC 47
See also CA 102

Isler, Alan (David) 1934-.......... CLC 91
See also CA 156

Ivan IV 1530-1584 .... LC 17

Ivanov, Vyacheslav Ivanovich
1866-1949 .... TCLC 33
See also CA 122

Ivask, Ivar Vidrik 1927-1992....... CLC 14
See also CA 37-40R; 139; CANR 24

Ives, Morgan
See Bradley, Marion Zimmer

J. R. S.
See Gogarty, Oliver St. John

Jabran, Kahlil
See Gibran, Kahlil

Jabran, Khalil
See Gibran, Kahlil

Jackson, Daniel
See Wingrove, David (John)

Jackson, Jesse 1908-1983 .... **CLC 12**
See also BW 1; CA 25-28R; 109; CANR 27;
CLR 28; MAICYA; SATA 2, 29;
SATA-Obit 48

Jackson, Laura (Riding) 1901-1991
See Riding, Laura
See also CA 65-68; 135; CANR 28; DLB 48

Jackson, Sam
See Trumbo, Dalton

Jackson, Sara
See Wingrove, David (John)

Jackson, Shirley
1919-1965 .... **CLC 11, 60, 87; DA;
DAC; DAM MST; SSC 9; WLC**
See also AAYA 9; CA 1-4R; 25-28R;
CANR 4, 52; CDALB 1941-1968; DLB 6;
SATA 2

Jacob, (Cyprien-)Max 1876-1944 ... **TCLC 6**
See also CA 104

Jacobs, Jim 1942- .... **CLC 12**
See also CA 97-100; INT 97-100

Jacobs, W(illiam) W(ymark)
1863-1943 .... **TCLC 22**
See also CA 121; DLB 135

Jacobsen, Jens Peter 1847-1885 .. **NCLC 34**

Jacobsen, Josephine 1908- ..... **CLC 48, 102**
See also CA 33-36R; CAAS 18; CANR 23,
48

Jacobson, Dan 1929- .... **CLC 4, 14**
See also CA 1-4R; CANR 2, 25; DLB 14;
MTCW

Jacqueline
See Carpentier (y Valmont), Alejo

Jagger, Mick 1944- .... **CLC 17**

Jakes, John (William)
1932- ...... **CLC 29; DAM NOV, POP**
See also BEST 89:4; CA 57-60; CANR 10,
43; DLBY 83; INT CANR-10; MTCW;
SATA 62

James, Andrew
See Kirkup, James

James, C(yril) L(ionel) R(obert)
1901-1989 .... **CLC 33**
See also BW 2; CA 117; 125; 128;
CANR 62; DLB 125; MTCW

James, Daniel (Lewis) 1911-1988
See Santiago, Danny
See also CA 125

James, Dynely
See Mayne, William (James Carter)

James, Henry Sr. 1811-1882 ..... **NCLC 53**

James, Henry
1843-1916 ..... **TCLC 2, 11, 24, 40, 47,
64; DA; DAB; DAC; DAM MST, NOV;
SSC 8; WLC**
See also CA 104; 132; CDALB 1865-1917;
DLB 12, 71, 74; DLBD 13; MTCW

James, M. R.
See James, Montague (Rhodes)
See also DLB 156

James, Montague (Rhodes)
1862-1936 .... **TCLC 6; SSC 16**
See also CA 104

James, P. D. .... **CLC 18, 46**
See also White, Phyllis Dorothy James
See also BEST 90:2; CDBLB 1960 to
Present; DLB 87

James, Philip
See Moorcock, Michael (John)

James, William 1842-1910 ..... **TCLC 15, 32**
See also CA 109

James I 1394-1437 .... **LC 20**

Jameson, Anna 1794-1860 .... **NCLC 43**
See also DLB 99, 166

Jami, Nur al-Din 'Abd al-Rahman
1414-1492 .... **LC 9**

Jammes, Francis 1868-1938 .... **TCLC 75**

Jandl, Ernst 1925- .... **CLC 34**

Janowitz, Tama
1957- .... **CLC 43; DAM POP**
See also CA 106; CANR 52

Japrisot, Sebastien 1931- .... **CLC 90**

Jarrell, Randall
1914-1965 ...... **CLC 1, 2, 6, 9, 13, 49;
DAM POET**
See also CA 5-8R; 25-28R; CABS 2;
CANR 6, 34; CDALB 1941-1968; CLR 6;
DLB 48, 52; MAICYA; MTCW; SATA 7

Jarry, Alfred
1873-1907 .... **TCLC 2, 14;
DAM DRAM; SSC 20**
See also CA 104; 153

Jarvis, E. K.
See Bloch, Robert (Albert); Ellison, Harlan
(Jay); Silverberg, Robert

Jeake, Samuel, Jr.
See Aiken, Conrad (Potter)

Jean Paul 1763-1825 .... **NCLC 7**

Jefferies, (John) Richard
1848-1887 .... **NCLC 47**
See also DLB 98, 141; SATA 16

Jeffers, (John) Robinson
1887-1962 .... **CLC 2, 3, 11, 15, 54; DA;
DAC; DAM MST, POET; PC 17; WLC**
See also CA 85-88; CANR 35;
CDALB 1917-1929; DLB 45; MTCW

Jefferson, Janet
See Mencken, H(enry) L(ouis)

Jefferson, Thomas 1743-1826 .... **NCLC 11**
See also CDALB 1640-1865; DLB 31

Jeffrey, Francis 1773-1850....... **NCLC 33**
See also DLB 107

Jelakowitch, Ivan
See Heijermans, Herman

Jellicoe, (Patricia) Ann 1927- ...... **CLC 27**
See also CA 85-88; DLB 13

Jen, Gish .... **CLC 70**
See also Jen, Lillian

Jen, Lillian 1956(?)-
See Jen, Gish
See also CA 135

Jenkins, (John) Robin 1912- ...... **CLC 52**
See also CA 1-4R; CANR 1; DLB 14

Jennings, Elizabeth (Joan)
1926- .... **CLC 5, 14**
See also CA 61-64; CAAS 5; CANR 8, 39;
DLB 27; MTCW; SATA 66

Jennings, Waylon 1937- .... **CLC 21**

Jensen, Johannes V. 1873-1950.... **TCLC 41**

Jensen, Laura (Linnea) 1948- ...... **CLC 37**
See also CA 103

Jerome, Jerome K(lapka)
1859-1927 .... **TCLC 23**
See also CA 119; DLB 10, 34, 135

Jerrold, Douglas William
1803-1857 .... **NCLC 2**
See also DLB 158, 159

Jewett, (Theodora) Sarah Orne
1849-1909 .... **TCLC 1, 22; SSC 6**
See also CA 108; 127; DLB 12, 74;
SATA 15

Jewsbury, Geraldine (Endsor)
1812-1880 .... **NCLC 22**
See also DLB 21

Jhabvala, Ruth Prawer
1927- .... **CLC 4, 8, 29, 94; DAB;
DAM NOV**
See also CA 1-4R; CANR 2, 29, 51;
DLB 139; INT CANR-29; MTCW

Jibran, Kahlil
See Gibran, Kahlil

Jibran, Khalil
See Gibran, Kahlil

Jiles, Paulette 1943- .... **CLC 13, 58**
See also CA 101

Jimenez (Mantecon), Juan Ramon
1881-1958 ..... **TCLC 4; DAM MULT,
POET; HLC; PC 7**
See also CA 104; 131; DLB 134; HW;
MTCW

Jimenez, Ramon
See Jimenez (Mantecon), Juan Ramon

Jimenez Mantecon, Juan
See Jimenez (Mantecon), Juan Ramon

Joel, Billy .... **CLC 26**
See also Joel, William Martin

Joel, William Martin 1949-
See Joel, Billy
See also CA 108

John of the Cross, St. 1542-1591 .... **LC 18**

Johnson, B(ryan) S(tanley William)
1933-1973 .... **CLC 6, 9**
See also CA 9-12R; 53-56; CANR 9;
DLB 14, 40

Johnson, Benj. F. of Boo
See Riley, James Whitcomb

Johnson, Benjamin F. of Boo
See Riley, James Whitcomb

Johnson, Charles (Richard)
1948- .... **CLC 7, 51, 65; BLC;
DAM MULT**
See also BW 2; CA 116; CAAS 18;
CANR 42; DLB 33

Johnson, Denis 1949-............. **CLC 52**
See also CA 117; 121; DLB 120

Johnson, Diane 1934-....... **CLC 5, 13, 48**
See also CA 41-44R; CANR 17, 40, 62;
DLBY 80; INT CANR-17; MTCW

Johnson, Eyvind (Olof Verner)
1900-1976 .... **CLC 14**
See also CA 73-76; 69-72; CANR 34

Johnson, J. R.
See James, C(yril) L(ionel) R(obert)

Johnson, James Weldon
1871-1938 .... **TCLC 3, 19; BLC;**
DAM MULT, POET
See also BW 1; CA 104; 125;
CDALB 1917-1929; CLR 32; DLB 51;
MTCW; SATA 31

Johnson, Joyce 1935-............ **CLC 58**
See also CA 125; 129

Johnson, Lionel (Pigot)
1867-1902 .... **TCLC 19**
See also CA 117; DLB 19

Johnson, Mel
See Malzberg, Barry N(athaniel)

Johnson, Pamela Hansford
1912-1981 .... **CLC 1, 7, 27**
See also CA 1-4R; 104; CANR 2, 28;
DLB 15; MTCW

Johnson, Robert 1911(?)-1938..... **TCLC 69**

Johnson, Samuel
1709-1784 ..... **LC 15; DA; DAB; DAC;**
DAM MST; WLC
See also CDBLB 1660-1789; DLB 39, 95,
104, 142

Johnson, Uwe
1934-1984 .... **CLC 5, 10, 15, 40**
See also CA 1-4R; 112; CANR 1, 39;
DLB 75; MTCW

Johnston, George (Benson) 1913-... **CLC 51**
See also CA 1-4R; CANR 5, 20; DLB 88

Johnston, Jennifer 1930-.......... **CLC 7**
See also CA 85-88; DLB 14

Jolley, (Monica) Elizabeth
1923- .... **CLC 46; SSC 19**
See also CA 127; CAAS 13; CANR 59

Jones, Arthur Llewellyn 1863-1947
See Machen, Arthur
See also CA 104

Jones, D(ouglas) G(ordon) 1929-.... **CLC 10**
See also CA 29-32R; CANR 13; DLB 53

Jones, David (Michael)
1895-1974 .... **CLC 2, 4, 7, 13, 42**
See also CA 9-12R; 53-56; CANR 28;
CDBLB 1945-1960; DLB 20, 100; MTCW

Jones, David Robert 1947-
See Bowie, David
See also CA 103

Jones, Diana Wynne 1934- .... **CLC 26**
See also AAYA 12; CA 49-52; CANR 4,
26, 56; CLR 23; DLB 161; JRDA;
MAICYA; SAAS 7; SATA 9, 70

Jones, Edward P. 1950-.......... **CLC 76**
See also BW 2; CA 142

Jones, Gayl
1949- .... **CLC 6, 9; BLC; DAM MULT**
See also BW 2; CA 77-80; CANR 27;
DLB 33; MTCW

Jones, James 1921-1977.... **CLC 1, 3, 10, 39**
See also AITN 1, 2; CA 1-4R; 69-72;
CANR 6; DLB 2, 143; MTCW

Jones, John J.
See Lovecraft, H(oward) P(hillips)

Jones, LeRoi .... **CLC 1, 2, 3, 5, 10, 14**
See also Baraka, Amiri

Jones, Louis B. .... **CLC 65**
See also CA 141

Jones, Madison (Percy, Jr.) 1925-... **CLC 4**
See also CA 13-16R; CAAS 11; CANR 7,
54; DLB 152

Jones, Mervyn 1922-............ **CLC 10, 52**
See also CA 45-48; CAAS 5; CANR 1;
MTCW

Jones, Mick 1956(?)-............ **CLC 30**

Jones, Nettie (Pearl) 1941-........ **CLC 34**
See also BW 2; CA 137; CAAS 20

Jones, Preston 1936-1979 .... **CLC 10**
See also CA 73-76; 89-92; DLB 7

Jones, Robert F(rancis) 1934-....... **CLC 7**
See also CA 49-52; CANR 2, 61

Jones, Rod 1953- .... **CLC 50**
See also CA 128

Jones, Terence Graham Parry
1942-....................... **CLC 21**
See also Jones, Terry; Monty Python
See also CA 112; 116; CANR 35; INT 116

Jones, Terry
See Jones, Terence Graham Parry
See also SATA 67; SATA-Brief 51

Jones, Thom 1945(?)-............. **CLC 81**
See also CA 157

Jong, Erica
1942-............. **CLC 4, 6, 8, 18, 83;**
DAM NOV, POP
See also AITN 1; BEST 90:2; CA 73-76;
CANR 26, 52; DLB 2, 5, 28, 152;
INT CANR-26; MTCW

Jonson, Ben(jamin)
1572(?)-1637 ...... **LC 6, 33; DA; DAB;**
DAC; DAM DRAM, MST, POET;
DC 4; PC 17; WLC
See also CDBLB Before 1660; DLB 62, 121

Jordan, June
1936- ..... **CLC 5, 11, 23; DAM MULT,**
POET
See also AAYA 2; BW 2; CA 33-36R;
CANR 25; CLR 10; DLB 38; MAICYA;
MTCW; SATA 4

Jordan, Pat(rick M.) 1941-........ **CLC 37**
See also CA 33-36R

Jorgensen, Ivar
See Ellison, Harlan (Jay)

Jorgenson, Ivar
See Silverberg, Robert

Josephus, Flavius c. 37-100...... **CMLC 13**

Josipovici, Gabriel 1940-........ **CLC 6, 43**
See also CA 37-40R; CAAS 8; CANR 47;
DLB 14

Joubert, Joseph 1754-1824 .... **NCLC 9**

Jouve, Pierre Jean 1887-1976...... **CLC 47**
See also CA 65-68

Joyce, James (Augustine Aloysius)
1882-1941 .... **TCLC 3, 8, 16, 35, 52;**
DA; DAB; DAC; DAM MST, NOV,
POET; SSC 26; WLC
See also CA 104; 126; CDBLB 1914-1945;
DLB 10, 19, 36, 162; MTCW

Jozsef, Attila 1905-1937......... **TCLC 22**
See also CA 116

Juana Ines de la Cruz 1651(?)-1695 ... **LC 5**

Judd, Cyril
See Kornbluth, C(yril) M.; Pohl, Frederik

Julian of Norwich 1342(?)-1416(?) .... **LC 6**
See also DLB 146

Juniper, Alex
See Hospital, Janette Turner

Junius
See Luxemburg, Rosa

Just, Ward (Swift) 1935-........ **CLC 4, 27**
See also CA 25-28R; CANR 32;
INT CANR-32

Justice, Donald (Rodney)
1925- ..... **CLC 6, 19, 102; DAM POET**
See also CA 5-8R; CANR 26, 54;
DLBY 83; INT CANR-26

Juvenal c. 55-c. 127 .... **CMLC 8**

Juvenis
See Bourne, Randolph S(illiman)

Kacew, Romain 1914-1980
See Gary, Romain
See also CA 108; 102

Kadare, Ismail 1936- .... **CLC 52**

Kadohata, Cynthia................. **CLC 59**
See also CA 140

Kafka, Franz
1883-1924 .... **TCLC 2, 6, 13, 29, 47, 53;**
DA; DAB; DAC; DAM MST, NOV;
SSC 29; WLC
See also CA 105; 126; DLB 81; MTCW

Kahanovitsch, Pinkhes
See Der Nister

Kahn, Roger 1927-............... **CLC 30**
See also CA 25-28R; CANR 44; DLB 171;
SATA 37

Kain, Saul
See Sassoon, Siegfried (Lorraine)

Kaiser, Georg 1878-1945 .... **TCLC 9**
See also CA 106; DLB 124

Kaletski, Alexander 1946-......... **CLC 39**
See also CA 118; 143

Kalidasa fl. c. 400-.............. **CMLC 9**

Kallman, Chester (Simon)
1921-1975 .... **CLC 2**
See also CA 45-48; 53-56; CANR 3

Kaminsky, Melvin 1926-
See Brooks, Mel
See also CA 65-68; CANR 16

Kaminsky, Stuart M(elvin) 1934-... **CLC 59**
See also CA 73-76; CANR 29, 53

Kane, Francis
See Robbins, Harold

Kane, Paul
See Simon, Paul (Frederick)

Kane, Wilson
See Bloch, Robert (Albert)

Kanin, Garson 1912-............ **CLC 22**
See also AITN 1; CA 5-8R; CANR 7;
DLB 7

Kaniuk, Yoram 1930-............ **CLC 19**
See also CA 134

Kant, Immanuel 1724-1804 ...... **NCLC 27**
See also DLB 94

Kantor, MacKinlay 1904-1977 ...... **CLC 7**
See also CA 61-64; 73-76; CANR 60;
DLB 9, 102

Kaplan, David Michael 1946- ...... **CLC 50**

Kaplan, James 1951- .... **CLC 59**
See also CA 135

Karageorge, Michael
See Anderson, Poul (William)

Karamzin, Nikolai Mikhailovich
1766-1826 .... **NCLC 3**
See also DLB 150

Karapanou, Margarita 1946-....... **CLC 13**
See also CA 101

Karinthy, Frigyes 1887-1938...... **TCLC 47**

Karl, Frederick R(obert) 1927-..... **CLC 34**
See also CA 5-8R; CANR 3, 44

Kastel, Warren
See Silverberg, Robert

Kataev, Evgeny Petrovich 1903-1942
See Petrov, Evgeny
See also CA 120

Kataphusin
See Ruskin, John

Katz, Steve 1935-................ **CLC 47**
See also CA 25-28R; CAAS 14; CANR 12;
DLBY 83

Kauffman, Janet 1945-............ **CLC 42**
See also CA 117; CANR 43; DLBY 86

Kaufman, Bob (Garnell)
1925-1986 .... **CLC 49**
See also BW 1; CA 41-44R; 118; CANR 22;
DLB 16, 41

Kaufman, George S.
1889-1961 ...... **CLC 38; DAM DRAM**
See also CA 108; 93-96; DLB 7; INT 108

Kaufman, Sue .... **CLC 3, 8**
See also Barondess, Sue K(aufman)

Kavafis, Konstantinos Petrou 1863-1933
See Cavafy, C(onstantine) P(eter)
See also CA 104

Kavan, Anna 1901-1968...... **CLC 5, 13, 82**
See also CA 5-8R; CANR 6, 57; MTCW

Kavanagh, Dan
See Barnes, Julian (Patrick)

Kavanagh, Patrick (Joseph)
1904-1967 .... **CLC 22**
See also CA 123; 25-28R; DLB 15, 20;
MTCW

Kawabata, Yasunari
1899-1972 .... **CLC 2, 5, 9, 18;**
DAM MULT; SSC 17
See also CA 93-96; 33-36R; DLB 180

Kaye, M(ary) M(argaret) 1909-..... **CLC 28**
See also CA 89-92; CANR 24, 60; MTCW;
SATA 62

Kaye, Mollie
See Kaye, M(ary) M(argaret)

Kaye-Smith, Sheila 1887-1956..... **TCLC 20**
See also CA 118; DLB 36

Kaymor, Patrice Maguilene
See Senghor, Leopold Sedar

Kazan, Elia 1909-............ **CLC 6, 16, 63**
See also CA 21-24R; CANR 32

Kazantzakis, Nikos
1883(?)-1957 .... **TCLC 2, 5, 33**
See also CA 105; 132; MTCW

Kazin, Alfred 1915- .... **CLC 34, 38**
See also CA 1-4R; CAAS 7; CANR 1, 45;
DLB 67

Keane, Mary Nesta (Skrine) 1904-1996
See Keane, Molly
See also CA 108; 114; 151

Keane, Molly.................. **CLC 31**
See also Keane, Mary Nesta (Skrine)
See also INT 114

Keates, Jonathan 19(?)-........... **CLC 34**

Keaton, Buster 1895-1966 .... **CLC 20**

Keats, John
1795-1821 .... **NCLC 8; DA; DAB;**
DAC; DAM MST, POET; PC 1; WLC
See also CDBLB 1789-1832; DLB 96, 110

Keene, Donald 1922- .... **CLC 34**
See also CA 1-4R; CANR 5

Keillor, Garrison.................. **CLC 40**
See also Keillor, Gary (Edward)
See also AAYA 2; BEST 89:3; DLBY 87;
SATA 58

Keillor, Gary (Edward) 1942-
See Keillor, Garrison
See also CA 111; 117; CANR 36, 59;
DAM POP; MTCW

Keith, Michael
See Hubbard, L(afayette) Ron(ald)

Keller, Gottfried
1819-1890 .... **NCLC 2; SSC 26**
See also DLB 129

Kellerman, Jonathan
1949- .... **CLC 44; DAM POP**
See also BEST 90:1; CA 106; CANR 29, 51;
INT CANR-29

Kelley, William Melvin 1937-...... **CLC 22**
See also BW 1; CA 77-80; CANR 27;
DLB 33

Kellogg, Marjorie 1922-............ **CLC 2**
See also CA 81-84

Kellow, Kathleen
See Hibbert, Eleanor Alice Burford

Kelly, M(ilton) T(erry) 1947-....... **CLC 55**
See also CA 97-100; CAAS 22; CANR 19,
43

Kelman, James 1946-.......... **CLC 58, 86**
See also CA 148

Kemal, Yashar 1923- .... **CLC 14, 29**
See also CA 89-92; CANR 44

Kemble, Fanny 1809-1893 .... **NCLC 18**
See also DLB 32

Kemelman, Harry 1908-1996........ **CLC 2**
See also AITN 1; CA 9-12R; 155; CANR 6;
DLB 28

Kempe, Margery 1373(?)-1440(?) ..... **LC 6**
See also DLB 146

Kempis, Thomas a 1380-1471 .... **LC 11**

Kendall, Henry 1839-1882....... **NCLC 12**

Keneally, Thomas (Michael)
1935- ..... **CLC 5, 8, 10, 14, 19, 27, 43;**
DAM NOV
See also CA 85-88; CANR 10, 50; MTCW

Kennedy, Adrienne (Lita)
1931- ..... **CLC 66; BLC; DAM MULT;**
DC 5
See also BW 2; CA 103; CAAS 20; CABS 3;
CANR 26, 53; DLB 38

Kennedy, John Pendleton
1795-1870 .... **NCLC 2**
See also DLB 3

Kennedy, Joseph Charles 1929-
See Kennedy, X. J.
See also CA 1-4R; CANR 4, 30, 40;
SATA 14, 86

Kennedy, William
1928- ... **CLC 6, 28, 34, 53; DAM NOV**
See also AAYA 1; CA 85-88; CANR 14,
31; DLB 143; DLBY 85; INT CANR-31;
MTCW; SATA 57

Kennedy, X. J................. **CLC 8, 42**
See also Kennedy, Joseph Charles
See also CAAS 9; CLR 27; DLB 5;
SAAS 22

Kenny, Maurice (Francis)
1929- .... **CLC 87; DAM MULT**
See also CA 144; CAAS 22; DLB 175;
NNAL

Kent, Kelvin
See Kuttner, Henry

Kenton, Maxwell
See Southern, Terry

Kenyon, Robert O.
See Kuttner, Henry

Kerouac, Jack ..... **CLC 1, 2, 3, 5, 14, 29, 61**
See also Kerouac, Jean-Louis Lebris de
See also CDALB 1941-1968; DLB 2, 16;
DLBD 3; DLBY 95

Kerouac, Jean-Louis Lebris de 1922-1969
See Kerouac, Jack
See also AITN 1; CA 5-8R; 25-28R;
CANR 26, 54; DA; DAB; DAC;
DAM MST, NOV, POET, POP; MTCW;
WLC

Kerr, Jean 1923-................ **CLC 22**
See also CA 5-8R; CANR 7; INT CANR-7

Kerr, M. E. .... **CLC 12, 35**
See also Meaker, Marijane (Agnes)
See also AAYA 2; CLR 29; SAAS 1

Kerr, Robert .... **CLC 55**

Kerrigan, (Thomas) Anthony
1918- .... **CLC 4, 6**
See also CA 49-52; CAAS 11; CANR 4

Kerry, Lois
See Duncan, Lois

Kesey, Ken (Elton)
1935- ..... **CLC 1, 3, 6, 11, 46, 64; DA;**
DAB; DAC; DAM MST, NOV, POP;
WLC
See also CA 1-4R; CANR 22, 38;
CDALB 1968-1988; DLB 2, 16; MTCW;
SATA 66

Koch, C(hristopher) J(ohn)   1932- . . .   **CLC 42**
     See also CA 127

Koch, Christopher
     See Koch, C(hristopher) J(ohn)

Koch, Kenneth
     1925- . . . . **CLC 5, 8, 44; DAM POET**
     See also CA 1-4R; CANR 6, 36, 57; DLB 5;
     INT CANR-36; SATA 65

Kochanowski, Jan   1530-1584 . . . .   **LC 10**

Kock, Charles Paul de
     1794-1871 . . . .   **NCLC 16**

Koda Shigeyuki   1867-1947
     See Rohan, Koda
     See also CA 121

Koestler, Arthur
     1905-1983 . . . .   **CLC 1, 3, 6, 8, 15, 33**
     See also CA 1-4R; 109; CANR 1, 33;
     CDBLB 1945-1960; DLBY 83; MTCW

Kogawa, Joy Nozomi
     1935- . . . . . .   **CLC 78; DAC; DAM MST,**
                                                          MULT
     See also CA 101; CANR 19, 62

Kohout, Pavel   1928- . . . .   **CLC 13**
     See also CA 45-48; CANR 3

Koizumi, Yakumo
     See Hearn, (Patricio) Lafcadio (Tessima
     Carlos)

Kolmar, Gertrud   1894-1943 . . . . . .   **TCLC 40**

Komunyakaa, Yusef   1947- . . . . . .   **CLC 86, 94**
     See also CA 147; DLB 120

Konrad, George
     See Konrad, Gyoergy

Konrad, Gyoergy   1933- . . . . . .   **CLC 4, 10, 73**
     See also CA 85-88

Konwicki, Tadeusz   1926- . . . . .   **CLC 8, 28, 54**
     See also CA 101; CAAS 9; CANR 39, 59;
     MTCW

Koontz, Dean R(ay)
     1945- . . . . . .   **CLC 78; DAM NOV, POP**
     See also AAYA 9; BEST 89:3, 90:2;
     CA 108; CANR 19, 36, 52; MTCW;
     SATA 92

Kopit, Arthur (Lee)
     1937- . . . . .   **CLC 1, 18, 33; DAM DRAM**
     See also AITN 1; CA 81-84; CABS 3;
     DLB 7; MTCW

Kops, Bernard   1926- . . . .   **CLC 4**
     See also CA 5-8R; DLB 13

Kornbluth, C(yril) M.   1923-1958 . . . .   **TCLC 8**
     See also CA 105; 160; DLB 8

Korolenko, V. G.
     See Korolenko, Vladimir Galaktionovich

Korolenko, Vladimir
     See Korolenko, Vladimir Galaktionovich

Korolenko, Vladimir G.
     See Korolenko, Vladimir Galaktionovich

Korolenko, Vladimir Galaktionovich
     1853-1921 . . . .   **TCLC 22**
     See also CA 121

Korzybski, Alfred (Habdank Skarbek)
     1879-1950 . . . .   **TCLC 61**
     See also CA 123; 160

Kosinski, Jerzy (Nikodem)
     1933-1991 . . . .   **CLC 1, 2, 3, 6, 10, 15, 53,**
                                                    70; DAM NOV
     See also CA 17-20R; 134; CANR 9, 46;
     DLB 2; DLBY 82; MTCW

Kostelanetz, Richard (Cory)   1940- . .   **CLC 28**
     See also CA 13-16R; CAAS 8; CANR 38

Kostrowitzki, Wilhelm Apollinaris de
     1880-1918
     See Apollinaire, Guillaume
     See also CA 104

Kotlowitz, Robert   1924- . . . .   **CLC 4**
     See also CA 33-36R; CANR 36

Kotzebue, August (Friedrich Ferdinand) von
     1761-1819 . . . .   **NCLC 25**
     See also DLB 94

Kotzwinkle, William   1938- . . .   **CLC 5, 14, 35**
     See also CA 45-48; CANR 3, 44; CLR 6;
     DLB 173; MAICYA; SATA 24, 70

Kowna, Stancy
     See Szymborska, Wislawa

Kozol, Jonathan   1936- . . . .   **CLC 17**
     See also CA 61-64; CANR 16, 45

Kozoll, Michael   1940(?)- . . . .   **CLC 35**

Kramer, Kathryn   19(?)- . . . .   **CLC 34**

Kramer, Larry   1935- . .   **CLC 42; DAM POP**
     See also CA 124; 126; CANR 60

Krasicki, Ignacy   1735-1801 . . . .   **NCLC 8**

Krasinski, Zygmunt   1812-1859 . . . .   **NCLC 4**

Kraus, Karl   1874-1936 . . . .   **TCLC 5**
     See also CA 104; DLB 118

Kreve (Mickevicius), Vincas
     1882-1954 . . . .   **TCLC 27**

Kristeva, Julia   1941- . . . .   **CLC 77**
     See also CA 154

Kristofferson, Kris   1936- . . . .   **CLC 26**
     See also CA 104

Krizanc, John   1956- . . . .   **CLC 57**

Krleza, Miroslav   1893-1981 . . . .   **CLC 8**
     See also CA 97-100; 105; CANR 50;
     DLB 147

Kroetsch, Robert
     1927- . . . .   **CLC 5, 23, 57; DAC;**
                                                      DAM POET
     See also CA 17-20R; CANR 8, 38; DLB 53;
     MTCW

Kroetz, Franz
     See Kroetz, Franz Xaver

Kroetz, Franz Xaver   1946- . . . .   **CLC 41**
     See also CA 130

Kroker, Arthur   1945- . . . .   **CLC 77**

Kropotkin, Peter (Aleksieevich)
     1842-1921 . . . .   **TCLC 36**
     See also CA 119

Krotkov, Yuri   1917- . . . .   **CLC 19**
     See also CA 102

Krumb
     See Crumb, R(obert)

Krumgold, Joseph (Quincy)
     1908-1980 . . . .   **CLC 12**
     See also CA 9-12R; 101; CANR 7;
     MAICYA; SATA 1, 48; SATA-Obit 23

Krumwitz
     See Crumb, R(obert)

Krutch, Joseph Wood   1893-1970 . . . .   **CLC 24**
     See also CA 1-4R; 25-28R; CANR 4;
     DLB 63

Krutzch, Gus
     See Eliot, T(homas) S(tearns)

Krylov, Ivan Andreevich
     1768(?)-1844 . . . .   **NCLC 1**
     See also DLB 150

Kubin, Alfred (Leopold Isidor)
     1877-1959 . . . .   **TCLC 23**
     See also CA 112; 149; DLB 81

Kubrick, Stanley   1928- . . . .   **CLC 16**
     See also CA 81-84; CANR 33; DLB 26

Kumin, Maxine (Winokur)
     1925- . . . . .   **CLC 5, 13, 28; DAM POET;**
                                                          PC 15
     See also AITN 2; CA 1-4R; CAAS 8;
     CANR 1, 21; DLB 5; MTCW; SATA 12

Kundera, Milan
     1929- . . . .   **CLC 4, 9, 19, 32, 68;**
                                                DAM NOV; SSC 24
     See also AAYA 2; CA 85-88; CANR 19,
     52; MTCW

Kunene, Mazisi (Raymond)   1930- . . .   **CLC 85**
     See also BW 1; CA 125; DLB 117

Kunitz, Stanley (Jasspon)
     1905- . . . .   **CLC 6, 11, 14; PC 19**
     See also CA 41-44R; CANR 26, 57;
     DLB 48; INT CANR-26; MTCW

Kunze, Reiner   1933- . . . .   **CLC 10**
     See also CA 93-96; DLB 75

Kuprin, Aleksandr Ivanovich
     1870-1938 . . . .   **TCLC 5**
     See also CA 104

Kureishi, Hanif   1954(?)- . . . .   **CLC 64**
     See also CA 139

Kurosawa, Akira
     1910- . . . .   **CLC 16; DAM MULT**
     See also AAYA 11; CA 101; CANR 46

Kushner, Tony
     1957(?)- . . . .   **CLC 81; DAM DRAM**
     See also CA 144

Kuttner, Henry   1915-1958 . . . .   **TCLC 10**
     See also Vance, Jack
     See also CA 107; 157; DLB 8

Kuzma, Greg   1944- . . . .   **CLC 7**
     See also CA 33-36R

Kuzmin, Mikhail   1872(?)-1936 . . . .   **TCLC 40**

Kyd, Thomas
     1558-1594 . . . .   **LC 22; DAM DRAM;**
                                                                DC 3
     See also DLB 62

Kyprianos, Iossif
     See Samarakis, Antonis

La Bruyere, Jean de   1645-1696 . . . . .   **LC 17**

Lacan, Jacques (Marie Emile)
     1901-1981 . . . .   **CLC 75**
     See also CA 121; 104

Laclos, Pierre Ambroise Francois Choderlos
     de   1741-1803 . . . .   **NCLC 4**

La Colere, Francois
     See Aragon, Louis

Lacolere, Francois
See Aragon, Louis

La Deshabilleuse
See Simenon, Georges (Jacques Christian)

Lady Gregory
See Gregory, Isabella Augusta (Persse)

Lady of Quality, A
See Bagnold, Enid

La Fayette, Marie (Madelaine Pioche de la Vergne Comtes   1634-1693 . . . . . . LC 2

Lafayette, Rene
See Hubbard, L(afayette) Ron(ald)

Laforgue, Jules
1860-1887 . . . . NCLC 5, 53; PC 14;
SSC 20

Lagerkvist, Paer (Fabian)
1891-1974 . . . . CLC 7, 10, 13, 54;
DAM DRAM, NOV
See also Lagerkvist, Par
See also CA 85-88; 49-52; MTCW

Lagerkvist, Par . . . . SSC 12
See also Lagerkvist, Paer (Fabian)

Lagerloef, Selma (Ottiliana Lovisa)
1858-1940 . . . . TCLC 4, 36
See also Lagerlof, Selma (Ottiliana Lovisa)
See also CA 108; SATA 15

Lagerlof, Selma (Ottiliana Lovisa)
See Lagerloef, Selma (Ottiliana Lovisa)
See also CLR 7; SATA 15

La Guma, (Justin) Alex(ander)
1925-1985 . . . . CLC 19; DAM NOV
See also BW 1; CA 49-52; 118; CANR 25;
DLB 117; MTCW

Laidlaw, A. K.
See Grieve, C(hristopher) M(urray)

Lainez, Manuel Mujica
See Mujica Lainez, Manuel
See also HW

Laing, R(onald) D(avid)
1927-1989 . . . . CLC 95
See also CA 107; 129; CANR 34; MTCW

Lamartine, Alphonse (Marie Louis Prat) de
1790-1869 . . . . . NCLC 11; DAM POET;
PC 16

Lamb, Charles
1775-1834 . . . . NCLC 10; DA; DAB;
DAC; DAM MST; WLC
See also CDBLB 1789-1832; DLB 93, 107,
163; SATA 17

Lamb, Lady Caroline   1785-1828 . . NCLC 38
See also DLB 116

Lamming, George (William)
1927- . . . . CLC 2, 4, 66; BLC;
DAM MULT
See also BW 2; CA 85-88; CANR 26;
DLB 125; MTCW

L'Amour, Louis (Dearborn)
1908-1988 . . . . CLC 25, 55; DAM NOV,
POP
See also AAYA 16; AITN 2; BEST 89:2;
CA 1-4R; 125; CANR 3, 25, 40;
DLBY 80; MTCW

Lampedusa, Giuseppe (Tomasi) di
1896-1957 . . . . TCLC 13
See also Tomasi di Lampedusa, Giuseppe
See also DLB 177

Lampman, Archibald   1861-1899 . . NCLC 25
See also DLB 92

Lancaster, Bruce   1896-1963 . . . . CLC 36
See also CA 9-10; CAP 1; SATA 9

Lanchester, John . . . . CLC 99

Landau, Mark Alexandrovich
See Aldanov, Mark (Alexandrovich)

Landau-Aldanov, Mark Alexandrovich
See Aldanov, Mark (Alexandrovich)

Landis, Jerry
See Simon, Paul (Frederick)

Landis, John   1950- . . . . CLC 26
See also CA 112; 122

Landolfi, Tommaso   1908-1979 . . . CLC 11, 49
See also CA 127; 117; DLB 177

Landon, Letitia Elizabeth
1802-1838 . . . . NCLC 15
See also DLB 96

Landor, Walter Savage
1775-1864 . . . . NCLC 14
See also DLB 93, 107

Landwirth, Heinz   1927-
See Lind, Jakov
See also CA 9-12R; CANR 7

Lane, Patrick
1939- . . . . CLC 25; DAM POET
See also CA 97-100; CANR 54; DLB 53;
INT 97-100

Lang, Andrew   1844-1912 . . . . TCLC 16
See also CA 114; 137; DLB 98, 141, 184;
MAICYA; SATA 16

Lang, Fritz   1890-1976 . . . . CLC 20, 103
See also CA 77-80; 69-72; CANR 30

Lange, John
See Crichton, (John) Michael

Langer, Elinor   1939- . . . . CLC 34
See also CA 121

Langland, William
1330(?)-1400(?) . . . . . . LC 19; DA; DAB;
DAC; DAM MST, POET
See also DLB 146

Langstaff, Launcelot
See Irving, Washington

Lanier, Sidney
1842-1881 . . . . . . NCLC 6; DAM POET
See also DLB 64; DLBD 13; MAICYA;
SATA 18

Lanyer, Aemilia   1569-1645 . . . . . . LC 10, 30
See also DLB 121

Lao Tzu . . . . CMLC 7

Lapine, James (Elliot)   1949- . . . . CLC 39
See also CA 123; 130; CANR 54; INT 130

Larbaud, Valery (Nicolas)
1881-1957 . . . . TCLC 9
See also CA 106; 152

Lardner, Ring
See Lardner, Ring(gold) W(ilmer)

Lardner, Ring W., Jr.
See Lardner, Ring(gold) W(ilmer)

Lardner, Ring(gold) W(ilmer)
1885-1933 . . . . TCLC 2, 14
See also CA 104; 131; CDALB 1917-1929;
DLB 11, 25, 86; DLBD 16; MTCW

Laredo, Betty
See Codrescu, Andrei

Larkin, Maia
See Wojciechowska, Maia (Teresa)

Larkin, Philip (Arthur)
1922-1985 . . . . CLC 3, 5, 8, 9, 13, 18, 33,
39, 64; DAB; DAM MST, POET
See also CA 5-8R; 117; CANR 24, 62;
CDBLB 1960 to Present; DLB 27;
MTCW

Larra (y Sanchez de Castro), Mariano Jose de
1809-1837 . . . . NCLC 17

Larsen, Eric   1941- . . . . CLC 55
See also CA 132

Larsen, Nella
1891-1964 . . . . CLC 37; BLC;
DAM MULT
See also BW 1; CA 125; DLB 51

Larson, Charles R(aymond)   1938- . . . CLC 31
See also CA 53-56; CANR 4

Larson, Jonathan   1961(?)-1996 . . . . . CLC 99

Las Casas, Bartolome de   1474-1566 . . LC 31

Lasch, Christopher   1932-1994 . . . . . CLC 102
See also CA 73-76; 144; CANR 25; MTCW

Lasker-Schueler, Else   1869-1945 . . TCLC 57
See also DLB 66, 124

Latham, Jean Lee   1902- . . . . CLC 12
See also AITN 1; CA 5-8R; CANR 7;
MAICYA; SATA 2, 68

Latham, Mavis
See Clark, Mavis Thorpe

Lathen, Emma . . . . CLC 2
See also Hennissart, Martha; Latsis, Mary
J(ane)

Lathrop, Francis
See Leiber, Fritz (Reuter, Jr.)

Latsis, Mary J(ane)
See Lathen, Emma
See also CA 85-88

Lattimore, Richmond (Alexander)
1906-1984 . . . . CLC 3
See also CA 1-4R; 112; CANR 1

Laughlin, James   1914- . . . . CLC 49
See also CA 21-24R; CAAS 22; CANR 9,
47; DLB 48; DLBY 96

Laurence, (Jean) Margaret (Wemyss)
1926-1987 . . . . CLC 3, 6, 13, 50, 62;
DAC; DAM MST; SSC 7
See also CA 5-8R; 121; CANR 33; DLB 53;
MTCW; SATA-Obit 50

Laurent, Antoine   1952- . . . . CLC 50

Lauscher, Hermann
See Hesse, Hermann

Lautreamont, Comte de
1846-1870 . . . . NCLC 12; SSC 14

Laverty, Donald
See Blish, James (Benjamin)

Lavin, Mary
1912-1996 . . . . CLC 4, 18, 99; SSC 4
See also CA 9-12R; 151; CANR 33;
DLB 15; MTCW

Lavond, Paul Dennis
See Kornbluth, C(yril) M.; Pohl, Frederik

Lindbergh, Anne (Spencer) Morrow
1906- .... **CLC 82; DAM NOV**
See also CA 17-20R; CANR 16; MTCW;
SATA 33

Lindsay, David 1878-1945 .... **TCLC 15**
See also CA 113

Lindsay, (Nicholas) Vachel
1879-1931 .... **TCLC 17; DA; DAC;
DAM MST, POET; WLC**
See also CA 114; 135; CDALB 1865-1917;
DLB 54; SATA 40

Linke-Poot
See Doeblin, Alfred

Linney, Romulus 1930- .... **CLC 51**
See also CA 1-4R; CANR 40, 44

Linton, Eliza Lynn 1822-1898.... **NCLC 41**
See also DLB 18

Li Po 701-763 .... **CMLC 2**

Lipsius, Justus 1547-1606 .... **LC 16**

Lipsyte, Robert (Michael)
1938- .... **CLC 21; DA; DAC;
DAM MST, NOV**
See also AAYA 7; CA 17-20R; CANR 8,
57; CLR 23; JRDA; MAICYA; SATA 5,
68

Lish, Gordon (Jay) 1934-.. **CLC 45; SSC 18**
See also CA 113; 117; DLB 130; INT 117

Lispector, Clarice 1925-1977....... **CLC 43**
See also CA 139; 116; DLB 113

Littell, Robert 1935(?)- .... **CLC 42**
See also CA 109; 112

Little, Malcolm 1925-1965
See Malcolm X
See also BW 1; CA 125; 111; DA; DAB;
DAC; DAM MST, MULT; MTCW

Littlewit, Humphrey Gent.
See Lovecraft, H(oward) P(hillips)

Litwos
See Sienkiewicz, Henryk (Adam Alexander
Pius)

Liu E 1857-1909............... **TCLC 15**
See also CA 115

Lively, Penelope (Margaret)
1933- .... **CLC 32, 50; DAM NOV**
See also CA 41-44R; CANR 29; CLR 7;
DLB 14, 161; JRDA; MAICYA; MTCW;
SATA 7, 60

Livesay, Dorothy (Kathleen)
1909- .... **CLC 4, 15, 79; DAC;
DAM MST, POET**
See also AITN 2; CA 25-28R; CAAS 8;
CANR 36; DLB 68; MTCW

Livy c. 59B.C.-c. 17 .... **CMLC 11**

Lizardi, Jose Joaquin Fernandez de
1776-1827 .... **NCLC 30**

Llewellyn, Richard
See Llewellyn Lloyd, Richard Dafydd
Vivian
See also DLB 15

Llewellyn Lloyd, Richard Dafydd Vivian
1906-1983 .... **CLC 7, 80**
See Llewellyn, Richard
See also CA 53-56; 111; CANR 7;
SATA 11; SATA-Obit 37

Llosa, (Jorge) Mario (Pedro) Vargas
See Vargas Llosa, (Jorge) Mario (Pedro)

Lloyd Webber, Andrew 1948-
See Webber, Andrew Lloyd
See also AAYA 1; CA 116; 149;
DAM DRAM; SATA 56

Llull, Ramon c. 1235-c. 1316..... **CMLC 12**

Locke, Alain (Le Roy)
1886-1954 .... **TCLC 43**
See also BW 1; CA 106; 124; DLB 51

Locke, John 1632-1704 .... **LC 7, 35**
See also DLB 101

Locke-Elliott, Sumner
See Elliott, Sumner Locke

Lockhart, John Gibson
1794-1854 .... **NCLC 6**
See also DLB 110, 116, 144

Lodge, David (John)
1935- .... **CLC 36; DAM POP**
See also BEST 90:1; CA 17-20R; CANR 19,
53; DLB 14; INT CANR-19; MTCW

Loennbohm, Armas Eino Leopold 1878-1926
See Leino, Eino
See also CA 123

Loewinsohn, Ron(ald William)
1937- .... **CLC 52**
See also CA 25-28R

Logan, Jake
See Smith, Martin Cruz

Logan, John (Burton) 1923-1987..... **CLC 5**
See also CA 77-80; 124; CANR 45; DLB 5

Lo Kuan-chung 1330(?)-1400(?)..... **LC 12**

Lombard, Nap
See Johnson, Pamela Hansford

London, Jack.. **TCLC 9, 15, 39; SSC 4; WLC**
See also London, John Griffith
See also AAYA 13; AITN 2;
CDALB 1865-1917; DLB 8, 12, 78;
SATA 18

London, John Griffith 1876-1916
See London, Jack
See also CA 110; 119; DA; DAB; DAC;
DAM MST, NOV; JRDA; MAICYA;
MTCW

Long, Emmett
See Leonard, Elmore (John, Jr.)

Longbaugh, Harry
See Goldman, William (W.)

Longfellow, Henry Wadsworth
1807-1882 .... **NCLC 2, 45; DA; DAB;
DAC; DAM MST, POET; WLCS**
See also CDALB 1640-1865; DLB 1, 59;
SATA 19

Longley, Michael 1939-.......... **CLC 29**
See also CA 102; DLB 40

Longus fl. c. 2nd cent. -.......... **CMLC 7**

Longway, A. Hugh
See Lang, Andrew

Lonnrot, Elias 1802-1884........ **NCLC 53**

Lopate, Phillip 1943-............ **CLC 29**
See also CA 97-100; DLBY 80; INT 97-100

Lopez Portillo (y Pacheco), Jose
1920- .... **CLC 46**
See also CA 129; HW

Lopez y Fuentes, Gregorio
1897(?)-1966 .... **CLC 32**
See also CA 131; HW

Lorca, Federico Garcia
See Garcia Lorca, Federico

Lord, Bette Bao 1938-............ **CLC 23**
See also BEST 90:3; CA 107; CANR 41;
INT 107; SATA 58

Lord Auch
See Bataille, Georges

Lord Byron
See Byron, George Gordon (Noel)

Lorde, Audre (Geraldine)
1934-1992 .... **CLC 18, 71; BLC;
DAM MULT, POET; PC 12**
See also BW 1; CA 25-28R; 142; CANR 16,
26, 46; DLB 41; MTCW

Lord Houghton
See Milnes, Richard Monckton

Lord Jeffrey
See Jeffrey, Francis

Lorenzini, Carlo 1826-1890
See Collodi, Carlo
See also MAICYA; SATA 29

Lorenzo, Heberto Padilla
See Padilla (Lorenzo), Heberto

Loris
See Hofmannsthal, Hugo von

Loti, Pierre .... **TCLC 11**
See also Viaud, (Louis Marie) Julien
See also DLB 123

Louie, David Wong 1954-......... **CLC 70**
See also CA 139

Louis, Father M.
See Merton, Thomas

Lovecraft, H(oward) P(hillips)
1890-1937 .... **TCLC 4, 22; DAM POP;
SSC 3**
See also AAYA 14; CA 104; 133; MTCW

Lovelace, Earl 1935-.............. **CLC 51**
See also BW 2; CA 77-80; CANR 41;
DLB 125; MTCW

Lovelace, Richard 1618-1657........ **LC 24**
See also DLB 131

Lowell, Amy
1874-1925 .... **TCLC 1, 8; DAM POET;
PC 13**
See also CA 104; 151; DLB 54, 140

Lowell, James Russell 1819-1891 .. **NCLC 2**
See also CDALB 1640-1865; DLB 1, 11, 64,
79

Lowell, Robert (Traill Spence, Jr.)
1917-1977 .... **CLC 1, 2, 3, 4, 5, 8, 9, 11,
15, 37; DA; DAB; DAC; DAM MST,
NOV; PC 3; WLC**
See also CA 9-12R; 73-76; CABS 2;
CANR 26, 60; DLB 5, 169; MTCW

Lowndes, Marie Adelaide (Belloc)
1868-1947 .... **TCLC 12**
See also CA 107; DLB 70

Lowry, (Clarence) Malcolm
1909-1957 .... **TCLC 6, 40**
See also CA 105; 131; CANR 62;
CDBLB 1945-1960; DLB 15; MTCW

MacNeice, (Frederick) Louis
1907-1963 ...... **CLC 1, 4, 10, 53; DAB;**
DAM POET
See also CA 85-88; CANR 61; DLB 10, 20;
MTCW

MacNeill, Dand
See Fraser, George MacDonald

Macpherson, James 1736-1796 ...... **LC 29**
See also DLB 109

Macpherson, (Jean) Jay 1931- ...... **CLC 14**
See also CA 5-8R; DLB 53

MacShane, Frank 1927- .... **CLC 39**
See also CA 9-12R; CANR 3, 33; DLB 111

Macumber, Mari
See Sandoz, Mari(e Susette)

Madach, Imre 1823-1864 .... **NCLC 19**

Madden, (Jerry) David 1933- .... **CLC 5, 15**
See also CA 1-4R; CAAS 3; CANR 4, 45;
DLB 6; MTCW

Maddern, Al(an)
See Ellison, Harlan (Jay)

Madhubuti, Haki R.
1942- .... **CLC 6, 73; BLC;**
DAM MULT, POET; PC 5
See also Lee, Don L.
See also BW 2; CA 73-76; CANR 24, 51;
DLB 5, 41; DLBD 8

Maepenn, Hugh
See Kuttner, Henry

Maepenn, K. H.
See Kuttner, Henry

Maeterlinck, Maurice
1862-1949 ...... **TCLC 3; DAM DRAM**
See also CA 104; 136; SATA 66

Maginn, William 1794-1842 ...... **NCLC 8**
See also DLB 110, 159

Mahapatra, Jayanta
1928- .... **CLC 33; DAM MULT**
See also CA 73-76; CAAS 9; CANR 15, 33

Mahfouz, Naguib (Abdel Aziz Al-Sabilgi)
1911(?)-
See Mahfuz, Najib
See also BEST 89:2; CA 128; CANR 55;
DAM NOV; MTCW

Mahfuz, Najib .... **CLC 52, 55**
See also Mahfouz, Naguib (Abdel Aziz
Al-Sabilgi)
See also DLBY 88

Mahon, Derek 1941- .... **CLC 27**
See also CA 113; 128; DLB 40

Mailer, Norman
1923- ...... **CLC 1, 2, 3, 4, 5, 8, 11, 14,**
28, 39, 74; DA; DAB; DAC; DAM MST,
NOV, POP
See also AITN 2; CA 9-12R; CABS 1;
CANR 28; CDALB 1968-1988; DLB 2,
16, 28; DLBD 3; DLBY 80, 83; MTCW

Maillet, Antonine 1929- ...... **CLC 54; DAC**
See also CA 115; 120; CANR 46; DLB 60;
INT 120

Mais, Roger 1905-1955 .... **TCLC 8**
See also BW 1; CA 105; 124; DLB 125;
MTCW

Maistre, Joseph de 1753-1821 .... **NCLC 37**

Maitland, Frederic 1850-1906 ..... **TCLC 65**

Maitland, Sara (Louise) 1950- ...... **CLC 49**
See also CA 69-72; CANR 13, 59

Major, Clarence
1936- .... **CLC 3, 19, 48; BLC;**
DAM MULT
See also BW 2; CA 21-24R; CAAS 6;
CANR 13, 25, 53; DLB 33

Major, Kevin (Gerald)
1949- .... **CLC 26; DAC**
See also AAYA 16; CA 97-100; CANR 21,
38; CLR 11; DLB 60; INT CANR-21;
JRDA; MAICYA; SATA 32, 82

Maki, James
See Ozu, Yasujiro

Malabaila, Damiano
See Levi, Primo

Malamud, Bernard
1914-1986 ...... **CLC 1, 2, 3, 5, 8, 9, 11,**
18, 27, 44, 78, 85; DA; DAB; DAC;
DAM MST, NOV, POP; SSC 15; WLC
See also AAYA 16; CA 5-8R; 118; CABS 1;
CANR 28, 62; CDALB 1941-1968;
DLB 2, 28, 152; DLBY 80, 86; MTCW

Malan, Herman
See Bosman, Herman Charles; Bosman,
Herman Charles

Malaparte, Curzio 1898-1957 ..... **TCLC 52**

Malcolm, Dan
See Silverberg, Robert

Malcolm X .... **CLC 82; BLC; WLCS**
See also Little, Malcolm

Malherbe, Francois de 1555-1628 ..... **LC 5**

Mallarme, Stephane
1842-1898 .... **NCLC 4, 41;**
DAM POET; PC 4

Mallet-Joris, Francoise 1930- ...... **CLC 11**
See also CA 65-68; CANR 17; DLB 83

Malley, Ern
See McAuley, James Phillip

Mallowan, Agatha Christie
See Christie, Agatha (Mary Clarissa)

Maloff, Saul 1922- .... **CLC 5**
See also CA 33-36R

Malone, Louis
See MacNeice, (Frederick) Louis

Malone, Michael (Christopher)
1942- .... **CLC 43**
See also CA 77-80; CANR 14, 32, 57

Malory, (Sir) Thomas
1410(?)-1471(?) ...... **LC 11; DA; DAB;**
DAC; DAM MST; WLCS
See also CDBLB Before 1660; DLB 146;
SATA 59; SATA-Brief 33

Malouf, (George Joseph) David
1934- .... **CLC 28, 86**
See also CA 124; CANR 50

Malraux, (Georges-)Andre
1901-1976 ...... **CLC 1, 4, 9, 13, 15, 57;**
DAM NOV
See also CA 21-22; 69-72; CANR 34, 58;
CAP 2; DLB 72; MTCW

Malzberg, Barry N(athaniel) 1939- ... **CLC 7**
See also CA 61-64; CAAS 4; CANR 16;
DLB 8

Mamet, David (Alan)
1947- .... **CLC 9, 15, 34, 46, 91;**
DAM DRAM; DC 4
See also AAYA 3; CA 81-84; CABS 3;
CANR 15, 41; DLB 7; MTCW

Mamoulian, Rouben (Zachary)
1897-1987 .... **CLC 16**
See also CA 25-28R; 124

Mandelstam, Osip (Emilievich)
1891(?)-1938(?) ...... **TCLC 2, 6; PC 14**
See also CA 104; 150

Mander, (Mary) Jane 1877-1949 ... **TCLC 31**

Mandeville, John fl. 1350- .... **CMLC 19**
See also DLB 146

Mandiargues, Andre Pieyre de .... **CLC 41**
See also Pieyre de Mandiargues, Andre
See also DLB 83

Mandrake, Ethel Belle
See Thurman, Wallace (Henry)

Mangan, James Clarence
1803-1849 .... **NCLC 27**

Maniere, J.-E.
See Giraudoux, (Hippolyte) Jean

Manley, (Mary) Delariviere
1672(?)-1724 .... **LC 1**
See also DLB 39, 80

Mann, Abel
See Creasey, John

Mann, Emily 1952- .... **DC 7**
See also CA 130; CANR 55

Mann, (Luiz) Heinrich 1871-1950 ... **TCLC 9**
See also CA 106; DLB 66

Mann, (Paul) Thomas
1875-1955 .... **TCLC 2, 8, 14, 21, 35, 44,**
60; DA; DAB; DAC; DAM MST, NOV;
SSC 5; WLC
See also CA 104; 128; DLB 66; MTCW

Mannheim, Karl 1893-1947 ...... **TCLC 65**

Manning, David
See Faust, Frederick (Schiller)

Manning, Frederic 1887(?)-1935 ... **TCLC 25**
See also CA 124

Manning, Olivia 1915-1980 ...... **CLC 5, 19**
See also CA 5-8R; 101; CANR 29; MTCW

Mano, D. Keith 1942- .... **CLC 2, 10**
See also CA 25-28R; CAAS 6; CANR 26,
57; DLB 6

Mansfield, Katherine
.. **TCLC 2, 8, 39; DAB; SSC 9, 23; WLC**
See also Beauchamp, Kathleen Mansfield
See also DLB 162

Manso, Peter 1940- .... **CLC 39**
See also CA 29-32R; CANR 44

Mantecon, Juan Jimenez
See Jimenez (Mantecon), Juan Ramon

Manton, Peter
See Creasey, John

Man Without a Spleen, A
See Chekhov, Anton (Pavlovich)

Manzoni, Alessandro 1785-1873 .. **NCLC 29**

Mapu, Abraham (ben Jekutiel)
1808-1867 .... **NCLC 18**

Mara, Sally
See Queneau, Raymond

Marat, Jean Paul 1743-1793 . . . . **LC 10**

Marcel, Gabriel Honore
    1889-1973 . . . . **CLC 15**
    See also CA 102; 45-48; MTCW

Marchbanks, Samuel
    See Davies, (William) Robertson

Marchi, Giacomo
    See Bassani, Giorgio

Margulies, Donald . . . . **CLC 76**

Marie de France c. 12th cent. - . . . . **CMLC 8**

Marie de l'Incarnation 1599-1672 . . . . **LC 10**

Marier, Captain Victor
    See Griffith, D(avid Lewelyn) W(ark)

Mariner, Scott
    See Pohl, Frederik

Marinetti, Filippo Tommaso
    1876-1944 . . . . **TCLC 10**
    See also CA 107; DLB 114

Marivaux, Pierre Carlet de Chamblain de
    1688-1763 . . . . **LC 4; DC 7**

Markandaya, Kamala . . . . **CLC 8, 38**
    See also Taylor, Kamala (Purnaiya)

Markfield, Wallace 1926- . . . . **CLC 8**
    See also CA 69-72; CAAS 3; DLB 2, 28

Markham, Edwin 1852-1940 . . . . . . **TCLC 47**
    See also CA 160; DLB 54

Markham, Robert
    See Amis, Kingsley (William)

Marks, J
    See Highwater, Jamake (Mamake)

Marks-Highwater, J
    See Highwater, Jamake (Mamake)

Markson, David M(errill) 1927- . . . . **CLC 67**
    See also CA 49-52; CANR 1

Marley, Bob . . . . **CLC 17**
    See also Marley, Robert Nesta

Marley, Robert Nesta 1945-1981
    See Marley, Bob
    See also CA 107; 103

Marlowe, Christopher
    1564-1593 . . . . . **LC 22; DA; DAB; DAC;**
        DAM DRAM, MST; DC 1; WLC
    See also CDBLB Before 1660; DLB 62

Marlowe, Stephen 1928-
    See Queen, Ellery
    See also CA 13-16R; CANR 6, 55

Marmontel, Jean-Francois
    1723-1799 . . . . **LC 2**

Marquand, John P(hillips)
    1893-1960 . . . . **CLC 2, 10**
    See also CA 85-88; DLB 9, 102

Marques, Rene
    1919-1979 . . . . . . **CLC 96; DAM MULT;**
        HLC
    See also CA 97-100; 85-88; DLB 113; HW

Marquez, Gabriel (Jose) Garcia
    See Garcia Marquez, Gabriel (Jose)

Marquis, Don(ald Robert Perry)
    1878-1937 . . . . **TCLC 7**
    See also CA 104; DLB 11, 25

Marric, J. J.
    See Creasey, John

Marrow, Bernard
    See Moore, Brian

Marryat, Frederick 1792-1848 . . . . **NCLC 3**
    See also DLB 21, 163

Marsden, James
    See Creasey, John

Marsh, (Edith) Ngaio
    1899-1982 . . . . . . **CLC 7, 53; DAM POP**
    See also CA 9-12R; CANR 6, 58; DLB 77;
        MTCW

Marshall, Garry 1934- . . . . **CLC 17**
    See also AAYA 3; CA 111; SATA 60

Marshall, Paule
    1929- . . . . **CLC 27, 72; BLC;**
        DAM MULT; SSC 3
    See also BW 2; CA 77-80; CANR 25;
        DLB 157; MTCW

Marsten, Richard
    See Hunter, Evan

Marston, John
    1576-1634 . . . . **LC 33; DAM DRAM**
    See also DLB 58, 172

Martha, Henry
    See Harris, Mark

Marti, Jose
    1853-1895 . . . . **NCLC 63; DAM MULT;**
        HLC

Martial c. 40-c. 104 . . . . **PC 10**

Martin, Ken
    See Hubbard, L(afayette) Ron(ald)

Martin, Richard
    See Creasey, John

Martin, Steve 1945- . . . . **CLC 30**
    See also CA 97-100; CANR 30; MTCW

Martin, Valerie 1948- . . . . **CLC 89**
    See also BEST 90:2; CA 85-88; CANR 49

Martin, Violet Florence
    1862-1915 . . . . **TCLC 51**

Martin, Webber
    See Silverberg, Robert

Martindale, Patrick Victor
    See White, Patrick (Victor Martindale)

Martin du Gard, Roger
    1881-1958 . . . . **TCLC 24**
    See also CA 118; DLB 65

Martineau, Harriet 1802-1876 . . . . **NCLC 26**
    See also DLB 21, 55, 159, 163, 166;
        YABC 2

Martines, Julia
    See O'Faolain, Julia

Martinez, Enrique Gonzalez
    See Gonzalez Martinez, Enrique

Martinez, Jacinto Benavente y
    See Benavente (y Martinez), Jacinto

Martinez Ruiz, Jose 1873-1967
    See Azorin; Ruiz, Jose Martinez
    See also CA 93-96; HW

Martinez Sierra, Gregorio
    1881-1947 . . . . **TCLC 6**
    See also CA 115

Martinez Sierra, Maria (de la O'LeJarraga)
    1874-1974 . . . . **TCLC 6**
    See also CA 115

Martinsen, Martin
    See Follett, Ken(neth Martin)

Martinson, Harry (Edmund)
    1904-1978 . . . . **CLC 14**
    See also CA 77-80; CANR 34

Marut, Ret
    See Traven, B.

Marut, Robert
    See Traven, B.

Marvell, Andrew
    1621-1678 . . . . . . **LC 4; DA; DAB; DAC;**
        DAM MST, POET; PC 10; WLC
    See also CDBLB 1660-1789; DLB 131

Marx, Karl (Heinrich)
    1818-1883 . . . . **NCLC 17**
    See also DLB 129

Masaoka Shiki . . . . **TCLC 18**
    See also Masaoka Tsunenori

Masaoka Tsunenori 1867-1902
    See Masaoka Shiki
    See also CA 117

Masefield, John (Edward)
    1878-1967 . . . . **CLC 11, 47; DAM POET**
    See also CA 19-20; 25-28R; CANR 33;
        CAP 2; CDBLB 1890-1914; DLB 10, 19,
        153, 160; MTCW; SATA 19

Maso, Carole 19(?)- . . . . **CLC 44**

Mason, Bobbie Ann
    1940- . . . . **CLC 28, 43, 82; SSC 4**
    See also AAYA 5; CA 53-56; CANR 11,
        31, 58; DLB 173; DLBY 87;
        INT CANR-31; MTCW

Mason, Ernst
    See Pohl, Frederik

Mason, Lee W.
    See Malzberg, Barry N(athaniel)

Mason, Nick 1945- . . . . **CLC 35**

Mason, Tally
    See Derleth, August (William)

Mass, William
    See Gibson, William

Masters, Edgar Lee
    1868-1950 . . . . . . **TCLC 2, 25; DA; DAC;**
        DAM MST, POET; PC 1; WLCS
    See also CA 104; 133; CDALB 1865-1917;
        DLB 54; MTCW

Masters, Hilary 1928- . . . . **CLC 48**
    See also CA 25-28R; CANR 13, 47

Mastrosimone, William 19(?)- . . . . . . **CLC 36**

Mathe, Albert
    See Camus, Albert

Mather, Cotton 1663-1728 . . . . **LC 38**
    See also CDALB 1640-1865; DLB 24, 30,
        140

Mather, Increase 1639-1723 . . . . **LC 38**
    See also DLB 24

Matheson, Richard Burton 1926- . . . **CLC 37**
    See also CA 97-100; DLB 8, 44; INT 97-100

Mathews, Harry 1930- . . . . **CLC 6, 52**
    See also CA 21-24R; CAAS 6; CANR 18,
        40

Mathews, John Joseph
    1894-1979 . . . . . **CLC 84; DAM MULT**
    See also CA 19-20; 142; CANR 45; CAP 2;
    DLB 175; NNAL

Mathias, Roland (Glyn) 1915- . . . . . . **CLC 45**
    See also CA 97-100; CANR 19, 41; DLB 27

Matsuo Basho 1644-1694. . . . . **PC 3**
    See also DAM POET

Mattheson, Rodney
    See Creasey, John

Matthews, Greg 1949- . . . . **CLC 45**
    See also CA 135

Matthews, William 1942- . . . . **CLC 40**
    See also CA 29-32R; CAAS 18; CANR 12,
    57; DLB 5

Matthias, John (Edward) 1941- . . . . . . **CLC 9**
    See also CA 33-36R; CANR 56

Matthiessen, Peter
    1927- . . . . **CLC 5, 7, 11, 32, 64;**
    DAM NOV
    See also AAYA 6; BEST 90:4; CA 9-12R;
    CANR 21, 50; DLB 6, 173; MTCW;
    SATA 27

Maturin, Charles Robert
    1780(?)-1824 . . . . **NCLC 6**
    See also DLB 178

Matute (Ausejo), Ana Maria
    1925- . . . . **CLC 11**
    See also CA 89-92; MTCW

Maugham, W. S.
    See Maugham, W(illiam) Somerset

Maugham, W(illiam) Somerset
    1874-1965 . . . . **CLC 1, 11, 15, 67, 93;**
    DA; DAB; DAC; DAM DRAM, MST,
    NOV; SSC 8; WLC
    See also CA 5-8R; 25-28R; CANR 40;
    CDBLB 1914-1945; DLB 10, 36, 77, 100,
    162; MTCW; SATA 54

Maugham, William Somerset
    See Maugham, W(illiam) Somerset

Maupassant, (Henri Rene Albert) Guy de
    1850-1893 . . . . . **NCLC 1, 42; DA; DAB;**
    DAC; DAM MST; SSC 1; WLC
    See also DLB 123

Maupin, Armistead
    1944- . . . . **CLC 95; DAM POP**
    See also CA 125; 130; CANR 58; INT 130

Maurhut, Richard
    See Traven, B.

Mauriac, Claude 1914-1996. . . . . **CLC 9**
    See also CA 89-92; 152; DLB 83

Mauriac, Francois (Charles)
    1885-1970 . . . . **CLC 4, 9, 56; SSC 24**
    See also CA 25-28; CAP 2; DLB 65;
    MTCW

Mavor, Osborne Henry 1888-1951
    See Bridie, James
    See also CA 104

Maxwell, William (Keepers, Jr.)
    1908- . . . . **CLC 19**
    See also CA 93-96; CANR 54; DLBY 80;
    INT 93-96

May, Elaine 1932- . . . . **CLC 16**
    See also CA 124; 142; DLB 44

Mayakovski, Vladimir (Vladimirovich)
    1893-1930 . . . . **TCLC 4, 18**
    See also CA 104; 158

Mayhew, Henry 1812-1887 . . . . . . **NCLC 31**
    See also DLB 18, 55

Mayle, Peter 1939(?)- . . . . **CLC 89**
    See also CA 139

Maynard, Joyce 1953- . . . . **CLC 23**
    See also CA 111; 129

Mayne, William (James Carter)
    1928- . . . . **CLC 12**
    See also AAYA 20; CA 9-12R; CANR 37;
    CLR 25; JRDA; MAICYA; SAAS 11;
    SATA 6, 68

Mayo, Jim
    See L'Amour, Louis (Dearborn)

Maysles, Albert 1926- . . . . **CLC 16**
    See also CA 29-32R

Maysles, David 1932- . . . . **CLC 16**

Mazer, Norma Fox 1931- . . . . **CLC 26**
    See also AAYA 5; CA 69-72; CANR 12,
    32; CLR 23; JRDA; MAICYA; SAAS 1;
    SATA 24, 67

Mazzini, Guiseppe 1805-1872 . . . . **NCLC 34**

McAuley, James Phillip
    1917-1976 . . . . **CLC 45**
    See also CA 97-100

McBain, Ed
    See Hunter, Evan

McBrien, William Augustine
    1930- . . . . **CLC 44**
    See also CA 107

McCaffrey, Anne (Inez)
    1926- . . . . . . **CLC 17; DAM NOV, POP**
    See also AAYA 6; AITN 2; BEST 89:2;
    CA 25-28R; CANR 15, 35, 55; DLB 8;
    JRDA; MAICYA; MTCW; SAAS 11;
    SATA 8, 70

McCall, Nathan 1955(?)- . . . . **CLC 86**
    See also CA 146

McCann, Arthur
    See Campbell, John W(ood, Jr.)

McCann, Edson
    See Pohl, Frederik

McCarthy, Charles, Jr. 1933-
    See McCarthy, Cormac
    See also CANR 42; DAM POP

McCarthy, Cormac
    1933- . . . . **CLC 4, 57, 59, 101**
    See also McCarthy, Charles, Jr.
    See also DLB 6, 143

McCarthy, Mary (Therese)
    1912-1989 . . . . . . **CLC 1, 3, 5, 14, 24, 39,**
    59; SSC 24
    See also CA 5-8R; 129; CANR 16, 50;
    DLB 2; DLBY 81; INT CANR-16;
    MTCW

McCartney, (James) Paul
    1942- . . . . **CLC 12, 35**
    See also CA 146

McCauley, Stephen (D.) 1955- . . . . . **CLC 50**
    See also CA 141

McClure, Michael (Thomas)
    1932- . . . . **CLC 6, 10**
    See also CA 21-24R; CANR 17, 46;
    DLB 16

McCorkle, Jill (Collins) 1958- . . . . . . **CLC 51**
    See also CA 121; DLBY 87

McCourt, James 1941- . . . . **CLC 5**
    See also CA 57-60

McCoy, Horace (Stanley)
    1897-1955 . . . . **TCLC 28**
    See also CA 108; 155; DLB 9

McCrae, John 1872-1918 . . . . **TCLC 12**
    See also CA 109; DLB 92

McCreigh, James
    See Pohl, Frederik

McCullers, (Lula) Carson (Smith)
    1917-1967 . . . . **CLC 1, 4, 10, 12, 48, 100;**
    DA; DAB; DAC; DAM MST, NOV;
    SSC 9, 24; WLC
    See also AAYA 21; CA 5-8R; 25-28R;
    CABS 1, 3; CANR 18;
    CDALB 1941-1968; DLB 2, 7, 173;
    MTCW; SATA 27

McCulloch, John Tyler
    See Burroughs, Edgar Rice

McCullough, Colleen
    1938(?)- . . . . **CLC 27; DAM NOV, POP**
    See also CA 81-84; CANR 17, 46; MTCW

McDermott, Alice 1953- . . . . **CLC 90**
    See also CA 109; CANR 40

McElroy, Joseph 1930- . . . . **CLC 5, 47**
    See also CA 17-20R

McEwan, Ian (Russell)
    1948- . . . . **CLC 13, 66; DAM NOV**
    See also BEST 90:4; CA 61-64; CANR 14,
    41; DLB 14; MTCW

McFadden, David 1940- . . . . **CLC 48**
    See also CA 104; DLB 60; INT 104

McFarland, Dennis 1950- . . . . **CLC 65**

McGahern, John
    1934- . . . . **CLC 5, 9, 48; SSC 17**
    See also CA 17-20R; CANR 29; DLB 14;
    MTCW

McGinley, Patrick (Anthony)
    1937- . . . . **CLC 41**
    See also CA 120; 127; CANR 56; INT 127

McGinley, Phyllis 1905-1978 . . . . . . **CLC 14**
    See also CA 9-12R; 77-80; CANR 19;
    DLB 11, 48; SATA 2, 44; SATA-Obit 24

McGinniss, Joe 1942- . . . . **CLC 32**
    See also AITN 2; BEST 89:2; CA 25-28R;
    CANR 26; INT CANR-26

McGivern, Maureen Daly
    See Daly, Maureen

McGrath, Patrick 1950- . . . . **CLC 55**
    See also CA 136

McGrath, Thomas (Matthew)
    1916-1990 . . . . **CLC 28, 59; DAM POET**
    See also CA 9-12R; 132; CANR 6, 33;
    MTCW; SATA 41; SATA-Obit 66

McGuane, Thomas (Francis III)
    1939- . . . . **CLC 3, 7, 18, 45**
    See also AITN 2; CA 49-52; CANR 5, 24,
    49; DLB 2; DLBY 80; INT CANR-24;
    MTCW

Mickiewicz, Adam 1798-1855 . . . . . **NCLC 3**

Middleton, Christopher 1926- . . . . . . **CLC 13**
See also CA 13-16R; CANR 29, 54;
DLB 40

Middleton, Richard (Barham)
1882-1911 . . . . **TCLC 56**
See also DLB 156

Middleton, Stanley 1919- . . . . **CLC 7, 38**
See also CA 25-28R; CAAS 23; CANR 21,
46; DLB 14

Middleton, Thomas
1580-1627 . . . . . . **LC 33; DAM DRAM,
MST; DC 5**
See also DLB 58

Migueis, Jose Rodrigues 1901- . . . . . **CLC 10**

Mikszath, Kalman 1847-1910 . . . . . **TCLC 31**

Miles, Jack . . . . **CLC 100**

Miles, Josephine (Louise)
1911-1985 . . . . **CLC 1, 2, 14, 34, 39;
DAM POET**
See also CA 1-4R; 116; CANR 2, 55;
DLB 48

Militant
See Sandburg, Carl (August)

Mill, John Stuart 1806-1873 . . **NCLC 11, 58**
See also CDBLB 1832-1890; DLB 55

Millar, Kenneth
1915-1983 . . . . **CLC 14; DAM POP**
See Macdonald, Ross
See also CA 9-12R; 110; CANR 16; DLB 2;
DLBD 6; DLBY 83; MTCW

Millay, E. Vincent
See Millay, Edna St. Vincent

Millay, Edna St. Vincent
1892-1950 . . . . . . **TCLC 4, 49; DA; DAB;
DAC; DAM MST, POET; PC 6; WLCS**
See also CA 104; 130; CDALB 1917-1929;
DLB 45; MTCW

Miller, Arthur
1915- . . . . **CLC 1, 2, 6, 10, 15, 26, 47, 78;
DA; DAB; DAC; DAM DRAM, MST;
DC 1; WLC**
See also AAYA 15; AITN 1; CA 1-4R;
CABS 3; CANR 2, 30, 54;
CDALB 1941-1968; DLB 7; MTCW

Miller, Henry (Valentine)
1891-1980 . . . . **CLC 1, 2, 4, 9, 14, 43, 84;
DA; DAB; DAC; DAM MST, NOV;
WLC**
See also CA 9-12R; 97-100; CANR 33;
CDALB 1929-1941; DLB 4, 9; DLBY 80;
MTCW

Miller, Jason 1939(?)- . . . . **CLC 2**
See also AITN 1; CA 73-76; DLB 7

Miller, Sue 1943- . . . . . **CLC 44; DAM POP**
See also BEST 90:3; CA 139; CANR 59;
DLB 143

Miller, Walter M(ichael, Jr.)
1923- . . . . **CLC 4, 30**
See also CA 85-88; DLB 8

Millett, Kate 1934- . . . . **CLC 67**
See also AITN 1; CA 73-76; CANR 32, 53;
MTCW

Millhauser, Steven 1943- . . . . **CLC 21, 54**
See also CA 110; 111; DLB 2; INT 111

Millin, Sarah Gertrude 1889-1968 . . **CLC 49**
See also CA 102; 93-96

Milne, A(lan) A(lexander)
1882-1956 . . . . **TCLC 6; DAB; DAC;
DAM MST**
See also CA 104; 133; CLR 1, 26; DLB 10,
77, 100, 160; MAICYA; MTCW;
YABC 1

Milner, Ron(ald)
1938- . . . . **CLC 56; BLC; DAM MULT**
See also AITN 1; BW 1; CA 73-76;
CANR 24; DLB 38; MTCW

Milnes, Richard Monckton
1809-1885 . . . . **NCLC 61**
See also DLB 32, 184

Milosz, Czeslaw
1911- . . . . **CLC 5, 11, 22, 31, 56, 82;
DAM MST, POET; PC 8; WLCS**
See also CA 81-84; CANR 23, 51; MTCW

Milton, John
1608-1674 . . . . . . **LC 9; DA; DAB; DAC;
DAM MST, POET; PC 19; WLC**
See also CDBLB 1660-1789; DLB 131, 151

Min, Anchee 1957- . . . . **CLC 86**
See also CA 146

Minehaha, Cornelius
See Wedekind, (Benjamin) Frank(lin)

Miner, Valerie 1947- . . . . **CLC 40**
See also CA 97-100; CANR 59

Minimo, Duca
See D'Annunzio, Gabriele

Minot, Susan 1956- . . . . **CLC 44**
See also CA 134

Minus, Ed 1938- . . . . **CLC 39**

Miranda, Javier
See Bioy Casares, Adolfo

Mirbeau, Octave 1848-1917 . . . . . . **TCLC 55**
See also DLB 123

Miro (Ferrer), Gabriel (Francisco Victor)
1879-1930 . . . . **TCLC 5**
See also CA 104

Mishima, Yukio
1925-1970 . . . . **CLC 2, 4, 6, 9, 27; DC 1;
SSC 4**
See also Hiraoka, Kimitake
See also DLB 182

Mistral, Frederic 1830-1914 . . . . . . **TCLC 51**
See also CA 122

Mistral, Gabriela . . . . **TCLC 2; HLC**
See also Godoy Alcayaga, Lucila

Mistry, Rohinton 1952- . . . . . . **CLC 71; DAC**
See also CA 141

Mitchell, Clyde
See Ellison, Harlan (Jay); Silverberg, Robert

Mitchell, James Leslie 1901-1935
See Gibbon, Lewis Grassic
See also CA 104; DLB 15

Mitchell, Joni 1943- . . . . **CLC 12**
See also CA 112

Mitchell, Joseph (Quincy)
1908-1996 . . . . **CLC 98**
See also CA 77-80; 152; DLBY 96

Mitchell, Margaret (Munnerlyn)
1900-1949 . . . . . . **TCLC 11; DAM NOV,
POP**
See also CA 109; 125; CANR 55; DLB 9;
MTCW

Mitchell, Peggy
See Mitchell, Margaret (Munnerlyn)

Mitchell, S(ilas) Weir 1829-1914 . . **TCLC 36**

Mitchell, W(illiam) O(rmond)
1914- . . . . . . **CLC 25; DAC; DAM MST**
See also CA 77-80; CANR 15, 43; DLB 88

Mitford, Mary Russell 1787-1855 . . **NCLC 4**
See also DLB 110, 116

Mitford, Nancy 1904-1973 . . . . **CLC 44**
See also CA 9-12R

Miyamoto, Yuriko 1899-1951 . . . . . **TCLC 37**
See also DLB 180

Mizoguchi, Kenji 1898-1956 . . . . . . **TCLC 72**

Mo, Timothy (Peter) 1950(?)- . . . . . . **CLC 46**
See also CA 117; MTCW

Modarressi, Taghi (M.) 1931- . . . . . . **CLC 44**
See also CA 121; 134; INT 134

Modiano, Patrick (Jean) 1945- . . . . . **CLC 18**
See also CA 85-88; CANR 17, 40; DLB 83

Moerck, Paal
See Roelvaag, O(le) E(dvart)

Mofolo, Thomas (Mokopu)
1875(?)-1948 . . . . **TCLC 22; BLC;
DAM MULT**
See also CA 121; 153

Mohr, Nicholasa
1935- . . . . . **CLC 12; DAM MULT; HLC**
See also AAYA 8; CA 49-52; CANR 1, 32;
CLR 22; DLB 145; HW; JRDA; SAAS 8;
SATA 8

Mojtabai, A(nn) G(race)
1938- . . . . **CLC 5, 9, 15, 29**
See also CA 85-88

Moliere
1622-1673 . . . . . **LC 28; DA; DAB; DAC;
DAM DRAM, MST; WLC**

Molin, Charles
See Mayne, William (James Carter)

Molnar, Ferenc
1878-1952 . . . . . **TCLC 20; DAM DRAM**
See also CA 109; 153

Momaday, N(avarre) Scott
1934- . . . . . **CLC 2, 19, 85, 95; DA; DAB;
DAC; DAM MST, MULT, NOV, POP;
WLCS**
See also AAYA 11; CA 25-28R; CANR 14,
34; DLB 143, 175; INT CANR-14;
MTCW; NNAL; SATA 48;
SATA-Brief 30

Monette, Paul 1945-1995 . . . . **CLC 82**
See also CA 139; 147

Monroe, Harriet 1860-1936 . . . . **TCLC 12**
See also CA 109; DLB 54, 91

Monroe, Lyle
See Heinlein, Robert A(nson)

Montagu, Elizabeth 1917- . . . . **NCLC 7**
See also CA 9-12R

Montagu, Mary (Pierrepont) Wortley
1689-1762 . . . . **LC 9; PC 16**
See also DLB 95, 101

Mossgiel, Rab
See Burns, Robert

Motion, Andrew (Peter) 1952-...... **CLC 47**
See also CA 146; DLB 40

Motley, Willard (Francis)
1909-1965 .... **CLC 18**
See also BW 1; CA 117; 106; DLB 76, 143

Motoori, Norinaga 1730-1801 .... **NCLC 45**

Mott, Michael (Charles Alston)
1930-.................... **CLC 15, 34**
See also CA 5-8R; CAAS 7; CANR 7, 29

Mountain Wolf Woman
1884-1960 .... **CLC 92**
See also CA 144; NNAL

Moure, Erin 1955- .... **CLC 88**
See also CA 113; DLB 60

Mowat, Farley (McGill)
1921- ...... **CLC 26; DAC; DAM MST**
See also AAYA 1; CA 1-4R; CANR 4, 24,
42; CLR 20; DLB 68; INT CANAR-24;
JRDA; MAICYA; MTCW; SATA 3, 55

Moyers, Bill 1934- .... **CLC 74**
See also AITN 2; CA 61-64; CANR 31, 52

Mphahlele, Es'kia
See Mphahlele, Ezekiel
See also DLB 125

Mphahlele, Ezekiel
1919- ..... **CLC 25; BLC; DAM MULT**
See also Mphahlele, Es'kia
See also BW 2; CA 81-84; CANR 26

Mqhayi, S(amuel) E(dward) K(rune Loliwe)
1875-1945 .... **TCLC 25; BLC;
DAM MULT**
See also CA 153

Mrozek, Slawomir 1930-....... **CLC 3, 13**
See also CA 13-16R; CAAS 10; CANR 29;
MTCW

Mrs. Belloc-Lowndes
See Lowndes, Marie Adelaide (Belloc)

Mtwa, Percy (?)-................. **CLC 47**

Mueller, Lisel 1924-.......... **CLC 13, 51**
See also CA 93-96; DLB 105

Muir, Edwin 1887-1959 .... **TCLC 2**
See also CA 104; DLB 20, 100

Muir, John 1838-1914 .... **TCLC 28**

Mujica Lainez, Manuel
1910-1984 .... **CLC 31**
See also Lainez, Manuel Mujica
See also CA 81-84; 112; CANR 32; HW

Mukherjee, Bharati
1940- .... **CLC 53; DAM NOV**
See also BEST 89:2; CA 107; CANR 45;
DLB 60; MTCW

Muldoon, Paul
1951- .... **CLC 32, 72; DAM POET**
See also CA 113; 129; CANR 52; DLB 40;
INT 129

Mulisch, Harry 1927-............ **CLC 42**
See also CA 9-12R; CANR 6, 26, 56

Mull, Martin 1943-.............. **CLC 17**
See also CA 105

Mulock, Dinah Maria
See Craik, Dinah Maria (Mulock)

Munford, Robert 1737(?)-1783 ...... **LC 5**
See also DLB 31

Mungo, Raymond 1946-.......... **CLC 72**
See also CA 49-52; CANR 2

Munro, Alice
1931- ...... **CLC 6, 10, 19, 50, 95; DAC;
DAM MST, NOV; SSC 3; WLCS**
See also AITN 2; CA 33-36R; CANR 33,
53; DLB 53; MTCW; SATA 29

Munro, H(ector) H(ugh) 1870-1916
See Saki
See also CA 104; 130; CDBLB 1890-1914;
DA; DAB; DAC; DAM MST, NOV;
DLB 34, 162; MTCW; WLC

Murasaki, Lady................. **CMLC 1**

Murdoch, (Jean) Iris
1919- ...... **CLC 1, 2, 3, 4, 6, 8, 11, 15,
22, 31, 51; DAB; DAC; DAM MST,
NOV**
See also CA 13-16R; CANR 8, 43;
CDBLB 1960 to Present; DLB 14;
INT CANR-8; MTCW

Murfree, Mary Noailles
1850-1922 .... **SSC 22**
See also CA 122; DLB 12, 74

Murnau, Friedrich Wilhelm
See Plumpe, Friedrich Wilhelm

Murphy, Richard 1927-.......... **CLC 41**
See also CA 29-32R; DLB 40

Murphy, Sylvia 1937-............. **CLC 34**
See also CA 121

Murphy, Thomas (Bernard) 1935-... **CLC 51**
See also CA 101

Murray, Albert L. 1916- .... **CLC 73**
See also BW 2; CA 49-52; CANR 26, 52;
DLB 38

Murray, Judith Sargent
1751-1820 .... **NCLC 63**
See also DLB 37

Murray, Les(lie) A(llan)
1938- .... **CLC 40; DAM POET**
See also CA 21-24R; CANR 11, 27, 56

Murry, J. Middleton
See Murry, John Middleton

Murry, John Middleton
1889-1957 .... **TCLC 16**
See also CA 118; DLB 149

Musgrave, Susan 1951- .... **CLC 13, 54**
See also CA 69-72; CANR 45

Musil, Robert (Edler von)
1880-1942 .... **TCLC 12, 68; SSC 18**
See also CA 109; CANR 55; DLB 81, 124

Muske, Carol 1945- .... **CLC 90**
See also Muske-Dukes, Carol (Anne)

Muske-Dukes, Carol (Anne) 1945-
See Muske, Carol
See also CA 65-68; CANR 32

Musset, (Louis Charles) Alfred de
1810-1857 .... **NCLC 7**

My Brother's Brother
See Chekhov, Anton (Pavlovich)

Myers, L(eopold) H(amilton)
1881-1944 .... **TCLC 59**
See also CA 157; DLB 15

Myers, Walter Dean
1937- ..... **CLC 35; BLC; DAM MULT,
NOV**
See also AAYA 4; BW 2; CA 33-36R;
CANR 20, 42; CLR 4, 16, 35; DLB 33;
INT CANR-20; JRDA; MAICYA;
SAAS 2; SATA 41, 71; SATA-Brief 27

Myers, Walter M.
See Myers, Walter Dean

Myles, Symon
See Follett, Ken(neth Martin)

Nabokov, Vladimir (Vladimirovich)
1899-1977 ..... **CLC 1, 2, 3, 6, 8, 11, 15,
23, 44, 46, 64; DA; DAB; DAC;
DAM MST, NOV; SSC 11; WLC**
See also CA 5-8R; 69-72; CANR 20;
CDALB 1941-1968; DLB 2; DLBD 3;
DLBY 80, 91; MTCW

Nagai Kafu 1879-1959 .... **TCLC 51**
See also Nagai Sokichi
See also DLB 180

Nagai Sokichi 1879-1959
See Nagai Kafu
See also CA 117

Nagy, Laszlo 1925-1978........... **CLC 7**
See also CA 129; 112

Naipaul, Shiva(dhar Srinivasa)
1945-1985 ..... **CLC 32, 39; DAM NOV**
See also CA 110; 112; 116; CANR 33;
DLB 157; DLBY 85; MTCW

Naipaul, V(idiadhar) S(urajprasad)
1932- .... **CLC 4, 7, 9, 13, 18, 37; DAB;
DAC; DAM MST, NOV**
See also CA 1-4R; CANR 1, 33, 51;
CDBLB 1960 to Present; DLB 125;
DLBY 85; MTCW

Nakos, Lilika 1899(?)-........... **CLC 29**

Narayan, R(asipuram) K(rishnaswami)
1906- ...... **CLC 7, 28, 47; DAM NOV;
SSC 25**
See also CA 81-84; CANR 33, 61; MTCW;
SATA 62

Nash, (Frediric) Ogden
1902-1971 .... **CLC 23; DAM POET**
See also CA 13-14; 29-32R; CANR 34, 61;
CAP 1; DLB 11; MAICYA; MTCW;
SATA 2, 46

Nathan, Daniel
See Dannay, Frederic

Nathan, George Jean 1882-1958 ... **TCLC 18**
See also Hatteras, Owen
See also CA 114; DLB 137

Natsume, Kinnosuke 1867-1916
See Natsume, Soseki
See also CA 104

Natsume, Soseki 1867-1916..... **TCLC 2, 10**
See also Natsume, Kinnosuke
See also DLB 180

Natti, (Mary) Lee 1919-
See Kingman, Lee
See also CA 5-8R; CANR 2

Naylor, Gloria
1950- ..... **CLC 28, 52; BLC; DA; DAC;
DAM MST, MULT, NOV, POP; WLCS**
See also AAYA 6; BW 2; CA 107;
CANR 27, 51; DLB 173; MTCW

Neihardt, John Gneisenau
1881-1973 . . . . **CLC 32**
See also CA 13-14; CAP 1; DLB 9, 54

Nekrasov, Nikolai Alekseevich
1821-1878 . . . . **NCLC 11**

Nelligan, Emile 1879-1941 . . . . **TCLC 14**
See also CA 114; DLB 92

Nelson, Willie 1933- . . . . **CLC 17**
See also CA 107

Nemerov, Howard (Stanley)
1920-1991 . . . . **CLC 2, 6, 9, 36;**
DAM POET
See also CA 1-4R; 134; CABS 2; CANR 1,
27, 53; DLB 5, 6; DLBY 83;
INT CANR-27; MTCW

Neruda, Pablo
1904-1973 . . . . . **CLC 1, 2, 5, 7, 9, 28, 62;**
DA; DAB; DAC; DAM MST, MULT,
POET; HLC; PC 4; WLC
See also CA 19-20; 45-48; CAP 2; HW;
MTCW

Nerval, Gerard de
1808-1855 . . . . . **NCLC 1; PC 13; SSC 18**

Nervo, (Jose) Amado (Ruiz de)
1870-1919 . . . . **TCLC 11**
See also CA 109; 131; HW

Nessi, Pio Baroja y
See Baroja (y Nessi), Pio

Nestroy, Johann 1801-1862 . . . . . . **NCLC 42**
See also DLB 133

Netterville, Luke
See O'Grady, Standish (James)

Neufeld, John (Arthur) 1938- . . . . . . **CLC 17**
See also AAYA 11; CA 25-28R; CANR 11,
37, 56; MAICYA; SAAS 3; SATA 6, 81

Neville, Emily Cheney 1919- . . . . **CLC 12**
See also CA 5-8R; CANR 3, 37; JRDA;
MAICYA; SAAS 2; SATA 1

Newbound, Bernard Slade 1930-
See Slade, Bernard
See also CA 81-84; CANR 49;
DAM DRAM

Newby, P(ercy) H(oward)
1918- . . . . **CLC 2, 13; DAM NOV**
See also CA 5-8R; CANR 32; DLB 15;
MTCW

Newlove, Donald 1928- . . . . **CLC 6**
See also CA 29-32R; CANR 25

Newlove, John (Herbert) 1938- . . . . . **CLC 14**
See also CA 21-24R; CANR 9, 25

Newman, Charles 1938- . . . . **CLC 2, 8**
See also CA 21-24R

Newman, Edwin (Harold) 1919- . . . . **CLC 14**
See also AITN 1; CA 69-72; CANR 5

Newman, John Henry
1801-1890 . . . . **NCLC 38**
See also DLB 18, 32, 55

Newton, Suzanne 1936- . . . . **CLC 35**
See also CA 41-44R; CANR 14; JRDA;
SATA 5, 77

Nexo, Martin Andersen
1869-1954 . . . . **TCLC 43**

Nezval, Vitezslav 1900-1958 . . . . . . **TCLC 44**
See also CA 123

Ng, Fae Myenne 1957(?)- . . . . **CLC 81**
See also CA 146

Ngema, Mbongeni 1955- . . . . **CLC 57**
See also BW 2; CA 143

Ngugi, James T(hiong'o) . . . . **CLC 3, 7, 13**
See also Ngugi wa Thiong'o

Ngugi wa Thiong'o
1938- . . . . . **CLC 36; BLC; DAM MULT,**
NOV
See also Ngugi, James T(hiong'o)
See also BW 2; CA 81-84; CANR 27, 58;
DLB 125; MTCW

Nichol, B(arrie) P(hillip)
1944-1988 . . . . **CLC 18**
See also CA 53-56; DLB 53; SATA 66

Nichols, John (Treadwell) 1940- . . . . **CLC 38**
See also CA 9-12R; CAAS 2; CANR 6;
DLBY 82

Nichols, Leigh
See Koontz, Dean R(ay)

Nichols, Peter (Richard)
1927- . . . . **CLC 5, 36, 65**
See also CA 104; CANR 33; DLB 13;
MTCW

Nicolas, F. R. E.
See Freeling, Nicolas

Niedecker, Lorine
1903-1970 . . . . **CLC 10, 42; DAM POET**
See also CA 25-28; CAP 2; DLB 48

Nietzsche, Friedrich (Wilhelm)
1844-1900 . . . . **TCLC 10, 18, 55**
See also CA 107; 121; DLB 129

Nievo, Ippolito 1831-1861 . . . . **NCLC 22**

Nightingale, Anne Redmon 1943-
See Redmon, Anne
See also CA 103

Nik. T. O.
See Annensky, Innokenty (Fyodorovich)

Nin, Anais
1903-1977 . . . . . . **CLC 1, 4, 8, 11, 14, 60;**
DAM NOV, POP; SSC 10
See also AITN 2; CA 13-16R; 69-72;
CANR 22, 53; DLB 2, 4, 152; MTCW

Nishiwaki, Junzaburo 1894-1982 . . . . **PC 15**
See also CA 107

Nissenson, Hugh 1933- . . . . **CLC 4, 9**
See also CA 17-20R; CANR 27; DLB 28

Niven, Larry . . . . **CLC 8**
See also Niven, Laurence Van Cott
See also DLB 8

Niven, Laurence Van Cott 1938-
See Niven, Larry
See also CA 21-24R; CAAS 12; CANR 14,
44; DAM POP; MTCW; SATA 95

Nixon, Agnes Eckhardt 1927- . . . . . . **CLC 21**
See also CA 110

Nizan, Paul 1905-1940 . . . . **TCLC 40**
See also DLB 72

Nkosi, Lewis
1936- . . . . . **CLC 45; BLC; DAM MULT**
See also BW 1; CA 65-68; CANR 27;
DLB 157

Nodier, (Jean) Charles (Emmanuel)
1780-1844 . . . . **NCLC 19**
See also DLB 119

Nolan, Christopher 1965- . . . . **CLC 58**
See also CA 111

Noon, Jeff 1957- . . . . **CLC 91**
See also CA 148

Norden, Charles
See Durrell, Lawrence (George)

Nordhoff, Charles (Bernard)
1887-1947 . . . . **TCLC 23**
See also CA 108; DLB 9; SATA 23

Norfolk, Lawrence 1963- . . . . **CLC 76**
See also CA 144

Norman, Marsha
1947- . . . . **CLC 28; DAM DRAM**
See also CA 105; CABS 3; CANR 41;
DLBY 84

Norris, Frank 1870-1902 . . . . **SSC 28**
See also Norris, (Benjamin) Frank(lin, Jr.)
See also CDALB 1865-1917; DLB 12, 71

Norris, (Benjamin) Frank(lin, Jr.)
1870-1902 . . . . **TCLC 24**
See also Norris, Frank
See also CA 110; 160

Norris, Leslie 1921- . . . . **CLC 14**
See also CA 11-12; CANR 14; CAP 1;
DLB 27

North, Andrew
See Norton, Andre

North, Anthony
See Koontz, Dean R(ay)

North, Captain George
See Stevenson, Robert Louis (Balfour)

North, Milou
See Erdrich, Louise

Northrup, B. A.
See Hubbard, L(afayette) Ron(ald)

North Staffs
See Hulme, T(homas) E(rnest)

Norton, Alice Mary
See Norton, Andre
See also MAICYA; SATA 1, 43

Norton, Andre 1912- . . . . **CLC 12**
See also Norton, Alice Mary
See also AAYA 14; CA 1-4R; CANR 2, 31;
DLB 8, 52; JRDA; MTCW; SATA 91

Norton, Caroline 1808-1877 . . . . . . **NCLC 47**
See also DLB 21, 159

Norway, Nevil Shute 1899-1960
See Shute, Nevil
See also CA 102; 93-96

Norwid, Cyprian Kamil
1821-1883 . . . . **NCLC 17**

Nosille, Nabrah
See Ellison, Harlan (Jay)

Nossack, Hans Erich 1901-1978 . . . . . **CLC 6**
See also CA 93-96; 85-88; DLB 69

Nostradamus 1503-1566 . . . . **LC 27**

Nosu, Chuji
See Ozu, Yasujiro

Notenburg, Eleanora (Genrikhovna) von
See Guro, Elena

Nova, Craig 1945- . . . . **CLC 7, 31**
See also CA 45-48; CANR 2, 53

Novak, Joseph
See Kosinski, Jerzy (Nikodem)

Novalis 1772-1801 .... NCLC 13
See also DLB 90

Novis, Emile
See Weil, Simone (Adolphine)

Nowlan, Alden (Albert)
1933-1983 .. **CLC 15; DAC; DAM MST**
See also CA 9-12R; CANR 5; DLB 53

Noyes, Alfred 1880-1958 .... TCLC 7
See also CA 104; DLB 20

Nunn, Kem .... CLC 34
See also CA 159

Nye, Robert
1939- .... **CLC 13, 42; DAM NOV**
See also CA 33-36R; CANR 29; DLB 14;
MTCW; SATA 6

Nyro, Laura 1947- .... CLC 17

Oates, Joyce Carol
1938- ...... **CLC 1, 2, 3, 6, 9, 11, 15, 19,
33, 52; DA; DAB; DAC; DAM MST,
NOV, POP; SSC 6; WLC**
See also AAYA 15; AITN 1; BEST 89:2;
CA 5-8R; CANR 25, 45;
CDALB 1968-1988; DLB 2, 5, 130;
DLBY 81; INT CANR-25; MTCW

O'Brien, Darcy 1939- .... CLC 11
See also CA 21-24R; CANR 8, 59

O'Brien, E. G.
See Clarke, Arthur C(harles)

O'Brien, Edna
1936- .... **CLC 3, 5, 8, 13, 36, 65;
DAM NOV; SSC 10**
See also CA 1-4R; CANR 6, 41;
CDBLB 1960 to Present; DLB 14;
MTCW

O'Brien, Fitz-James 1828-1862... NCLC 21
See also DLB 74

O'Brien, Flann .... CLC 1, 4, 5, 7, 10, 47
See also O Nuallain, Brian

O'Brien, Richard 1942- .... CLC 17
See also CA 124

O'Brien, (William) Tim(othy)
1946- ... CLC 7, 19, 40, 103; DAM POP
See also AAYA 16; CA 85-88; CANR 40,
58; DLB 152; DLBD 9; DLBY 80

Obstfelder, Sigbjoern 1866-1900... TCLC 23
See also CA 123

O'Casey, Sean
1880-1964 ...... **CLC 1, 5, 9, 11, 15, 88;
DAB; DAC; DAM DRAM, MST; WLCS**
See also CA 89-92; CANR 62;
CDBLB 1914-1945; DLB 10; MTCW

O'Cathasaigh, Sean
See O'Casey, Sean

Ochs, Phil 1940-1976 .... CLC 17
See also CA 65-68

O'Connor, Edwin (Greene)
1918-1968 .... CLC 14
See also CA 93-96; 25-28R

O'Connor, (Mary) Flannery
1925-1964 .... **CLC 1, 2, 3, 6, 10, 13, 15,
21, 66, 104; DA; DAB; DAC;
DAM MST, NOV; SSC 1; WLC**
See also AAYA 7; CA 1-4R; CANR 3, 41;
CDALB 1941-1968; DLB 2, 152;
DLBD 12; DLBY 80; MTCW

O'Connor, Frank .... **CLC 23; SSC 5**
See also O'Donovan, Michael John
See also DLB 162

O'Dell, Scott 1898-1989 .... CLC 30
See also AAYA 3; CA 61-64; 129;
CANR 12, 30; CLR 1, 16; DLB 52;
JRDA; MAICYA; SATA 12, 60

Odets, Clifford
1906-1963 .... **CLC 2, 28, 98;
DAM DRAM; DC 6**
See also CA 85-88; CANR 62; DLB 7, 26;
MTCW

O'Doherty, Brian 1934- .... CLC 76
See also CA 105

O'Donnell, K. M.
See Malzberg, Barry N(athaniel)

O'Donnell, Lawrence
See Kuttner, Henry

O'Donovan, Michael John
1903-1966 .... CLC 14
See also O'Connor, Frank
See also CA 93-96

Oe, Kenzaburo
1935- ..... **CLC 10, 36, 86; DAM NOV;
SSC 20**
See also CA 97-100; CANR 36, 50;
DLB 182; DLBY 94; MTCW

O'Faolain, Julia 1932- .... CLC 6, 19, 47
See also CA 81-84; CAAS 2; CANR 12, 61;
DLB 14; MTCW

O'Faolain, Sean
1900-1991 .... **CLC 1, 7, 14, 32, 70;
SSC 13**
See also CA 61-64; 134; CANR 12;
DLB 15, 162; MTCW

O'Flaherty, Liam
1896-1984 .... **CLC 5, 34; SSC 6**
See also CA 101; 113; CANR 35; DLB 36,
162; DLBY 84; MTCW

Ogilvy, Gavin
See Barrie, J(ames) M(atthew)

O'Grady, Standish (James)
1846-1928 .... TCLC 5
See also CA 104; 157

O'Grady, Timothy 1951- .... CLC 59
See also CA 138

O'Hara, Frank
1926-1966 .... **CLC 2, 5, 13, 78;
DAM POET**
See also CA 9-12R; 25-28R; CANR 33;
DLB 5, 16; MTCW

O'Hara, John (Henry)
1905-1970 ...... **CLC 1, 2, 3, 6, 11, 42;
DAM NOV; SSC 15**
See also CA 5-8R; 25-28R; CANR 31, 60;
CDALB 1929-1941; DLB 9, 86; DLBD 2;
MTCW

O Hehir, Diana 1922- .... CLC 41
See also CA 93-96

Okigbo, Christopher (Ifenayichukwu)
1932-1967 .... **CLC 25, 84; BLC;
DAM MULT, POET; PC 7**
See also BW 1; CA 77-80; DLB 125;
MTCW

Okri, Ben 1959- .... CLC 87
See also BW 2; CA 130; 138; DLB 157;
INT 138

Olds, Sharon
1942- ..... **CLC 32, 39, 85; DAM POET**
See also CA 101; CANR 18, 41; DLB 120

Oldstyle, Jonathan
See Irving, Washington

Olesha, Yuri (Karlovich)
1899-1960 .... CLC 8
See also CA 85-88

Oliphant, Laurence
1829(?)-1888 .... NCLC 47
See also DLB 18, 166

Oliphant, Margaret (Oliphant Wilson)
1828-1897 .... **NCLC 11, 61; SSC 25**
See also DLB 18, 159

Oliver, Mary 1935- .... CLC 19, 34, 98
See also CA 21-24R; CANR 9, 43; DLB 5

Olivier, Laurence (Kerr)
1907-1989 .... CLC 20
See also CA 111; 150; 129

Olsen, Tillie
1913- ..... **CLC 4, 13; DA; DAB; DAC;
DAM MST; SSC 11**
See also CA 1-4R; CANR 1, 43; DLB 28;
DLBY 80; MTCW

Olson, Charles (John)
1910-1970 ..... **CLC 1, 2, 5, 6, 9, 11, 29;
DAM POET; PC 19**
See also CA 13-16; 25-28R; CABS 2;
CANR 35, 61; CAP 1; DLB 5, 16;
MTCW

Olson, Toby 1937- .... CLC 28
See also CA 65-68; CANR 9, 31

Olyesha, Yuri
See Olesha, Yuri (Karlovich)

Ondaatje, (Philip) Michael
1943- .... **CLC 14, 29, 51, 76; DAB;
DAC; DAM MST**
See also CA 77-80; CANR 42; DLB 60

Oneal, Elizabeth 1934-
See Oneal, Zibby
See also CA 106; CANR 28; MAICYA;
SATA 30, 82

Oneal, Zibby .... CLC 30
See also Oneal, Elizabeth
See also AAYA 5; CLR 13; JRDA

O'Neill, Eugene (Gladstone)
1888-1953 ...... **TCLC 1, 6, 27, 49; DA;
DAB; DAC; DAM DRAM, MST; WLC**
See also AITN 1; CA 110; 132;
CDALB 1929-1941; DLB 7; MTCW

Onetti, Juan Carlos
1909-1994 .... **CLC 7, 10; DAM MULT,
NOV; SSC 23**
See also CA 85-88; 145; CANR 32;
DLB 113; HW; MTCW

O Nuallain, Brian 1911-1966
See O'Brien, Flann
See also CA 21-22; 25-28R; CAP 2

Oppen, George 1908-1984 .... CLC 7, 13, 34
See also CA 13-16R; 113; CANR 8; DLB 5,
165

Oppenheim, E(dward) Phillips
1866-1946 .... **TCLC 45**
See also CA 111; DLB 70

Origen c. 185-c. 254 .... **CMLC 19**

Orlovitz, Gil 1918-1973 .... **CLC 22**
See also CA 77-80; 45-48; DLB 2, 5

Orris
See Ingelow, Jean

Ortega y Gasset, Jose
1883-1955 ..... **TCLC 9; DAM MULT;**
HLC
See also CA 106; 130; HW; MTCW

Ortese, Anna Maria 1914- .... **CLC 89**
See also DLB 177

Ortiz, Simon J(oseph)
1941- .... **CLC 45; DAM MULT,**
POET; PC 17
See also CA 134; DLB 120, 175; NNAL

Orton, Joe .... **CLC 4, 13, 43; DC 3**
See also Orton, John Kingsley
See also CDBLB 1960 to Present; DLB 13

Orton, John Kingsley 1933-1967
See Orton, Joe
See also CA 85-88; CANR 35;
DAM DRAM; MTCW

Orwell, George
..... **TCLC 2, 6, 15, 31, 51; DAB; WLC**
See also Blair, Eric (Arthur)
See also CDBLB 1945-1960; DLB 15, 98

Osborne, David
See Silverberg, Robert

Osborne, George
See Silverberg, Robert

Osborne, John (James)
1929-1994 ..... **CLC 1, 2, 5, 11, 45; DA;**
DAB; DAC; DAM DRAM, MST; WLC
See also CA 13-16R; 147; CANR 21, 56;
CDBLB 1945-1960; DLB 13; MTCW

Osborne, Lawrence 1958- .... **CLC 50**

Oshima, Nagisa 1932- .... **CLC 20**
See also CA 116; 121

Oskison, John Milton
1874-1947 ..... **TCLC 35; DAM MULT**
See also CA 144; DLB 175; NNAL

Ossoli, Sarah Margaret (Fuller marchesa d')
1810-1850
See Fuller, Margaret
See also SATA 25

Ostrovsky, Alexander
1823-1886 .... **NCLC 30, 57**

Otero, Blas de 1916-1979 .... **CLC 11**
See also CA 89-92; DLB 134

Otto, Whitney 1955- .... **CLC 70**
See also CA 140

Ouida .... **TCLC 43**
See also De La Ramee, (Marie) Louise
See also DLB 18, 156

Ousmane, Sembene 1923- .... **CLC 66; BLC**
See also BW 1; CA 117; 125; MTCW

Ovid
43B.C.-18(?) ... **CMLC 7; DAM POET;**
PC 2

Owen, Hugh
See Faust, Frederick (Schiller)

Owen, Wilfred (Edward Salter)
1893-1918 ...... **TCLC 5, 27; DA; DAB;**
DAC; DAM MST, POET; PC 19; WLC
See also CA 104; 141; CDBLB 1914-1945;
DLB 20

Owens, Rochelle 1936- .... **CLC 8**
See also CA 17-20R; CAAS 2; CANR 39

Oz, Amos
1939- .... **CLC 5, 8, 11, 27, 33, 54;**
DAM NOV
See also CA 53-56; CANR 27, 47; MTCW

Ozick, Cynthia
1928- .... **CLC 3, 7, 28, 62; DAM NOV,**
POP; SSC 15
See also BEST 90:1; CA 17-20R; CANR 23,
58; DLB 28, 152; DLBY 82;
INT CANR-23; MTCW

Ozu, Yasujiro 1903-1963 .... **CLC 16**
See also CA 112

Pacheco, C.
See Pessoa, Fernando (Antonio Nogueira)

Pa Chin .... **CLC 18**
See also Li Fei-kan

Pack, Robert 1929- .... **CLC 13**
See also CA 1-4R; CANR 3, 44; DLB 5

Padgett, Lewis
See Kuttner, Henry

Padilla (Lorenzo), Heberto 1932- ... **CLC 38**
See also AITN 1; CA 123; 131; HW

Page, Jimmy 1944- .... **CLC 12**

Page, Louise 1955- .... **CLC 40**
See also CA 140

Page, P(atricia) K(athleen)
1916- .... **CLC 7, 18; DAC; DAM MST;**
PC 12
See also CA 53-56; CANR 4, 22; DLB 68;
MTCW

Page, Thomas Nelson 1853-1922 .... **SSC 23**
See also CA 118; DLB 12, 78; DLBD 13

Pagels, Elaine Hiesey 1943- ...... **CLC 104**
See also CA 45-48; CANR 2, 24, 51

Paget, Violet 1856-1935
See Lee, Vernon
See also CA 104

Paget-Lowe, Henry
See Lovecraft, H(oward) P(hillips)

Paglia, Camille (Anna) 1947- .... **CLC 68**
See also CA 140

Paige, Richard
See Koontz, Dean R(ay)

Paine, Thomas 1737-1809 .... **NCLC 62**
See also CDALB 1640-1865; DLB 31, 43,
73, 158

Pakenham, Antonia
See Fraser, (Lady) Antonia (Pakenham)

Palamas, Kostes 1859-1943 .... **TCLC 5**
See also CA 105

Palazzeschi, Aldo 1885-1974 ...... **CLC 11**
See also CA 89-92; 53-56; DLB 114

Paley, Grace
1922- .... **CLC 4, 6, 37; DAM POP;**
SSC 8
See also CA 25-28R; CANR 13, 46;
DLB 28; INT CANR-13; MTCW

Palin, Michael (Edward) 1943- ..... **CLC 21**
See also Monty Python
See also CA 107; CANR 35; SATA 67

Palliser, Charles 1947- .... **CLC 65**
See also CA 136

Palma, Ricardo 1833-1919 .... **TCLC 29**

Pancake, Breece Dexter 1952-1979
See Pancake, Breece D'J
See also CA 123; 109

Pancake, Breece D'J .... **CLC 29**
See also Pancake, Breece Dexter
See also DLB 130

Panko, Rudy
See Gogol, Nikolai (Vasilyevich)

Papadiamantis, Alexandros
1851-1911 .... **TCLC 29**

Papadiamantopoulos, Johannes 1856-1910
See Moreas, Jean
See also CA 117

Papini, Giovanni 1881-1956 ...... **TCLC 22**
See also CA 121

Paracelsus 1493-1541 .... **LC 14**
See also DLB 179

Parasol, Peter
See Stevens, Wallace

Pareto, Vilfredo 1848-1923 ...... **TCLC 69**

Parfenie, Maria
See Codrescu, Andrei

Parini, Jay (Lee) 1948- .... **CLC 54**
See also CA 97-100; CAAS 16; CANR 32

Park, Jordan
See Kornbluth, C(yril) M.; Pohl, Frederik

Park, Robert E(zra) 1864-1944 .... **TCLC 73**
See also CA 122

Parker, Bert
See Ellison, Harlan (Jay)

Parker, Dorothy (Rothschild)
1893-1967 .... **CLC 15, 68;**
DAM POET; SSC 2
See also CA 19-20; 25-28R; CAP 2;
DLB 11, 45, 86; MTCW

Parker, Robert B(rown)
1932- ...... **CLC 27; DAM NOV, POP**
See also BEST 89:4; CA 49-52; CANR 1,
26, 52; INT CANR-26; MTCW

Parkin, Frank 1940- .... **CLC 43**
See also CA 147

Parkman, Francis, Jr.
1823-1893 .... **NCLC 12**
See also DLB 1, 30

Parks, Gordon (Alexander Buchanan)
1912- ... **CLC 1, 16; BLC; DAM MULT**
See also AITN 2; BW 2; CA 41-44R;
CANR 26; DLB 33; SATA 8

Parmenides
c. 515B.C.-c. 450B.C. .... **CMLC 22**
See also DLB 176

Parnell, Thomas 1679-1718 .... **LC 3**
See also DLB 94

Parra, Nicanor
1914- .... **CLC 2, 102; DAM MULT;**
HLC
See also CA 85-88; CANR 32; HW; MTCW

Parrish, Mary Frances
See Fisher, M(ary) F(rances) K(ennedy)

Parson
See Coleridge, Samuel Taylor

Parson Lot
See Kingsley, Charles

Partridge, Anthony
See Oppenheim, E(dward) Phillips

Pascal, Blaise 1623-1662 . . . . **LC 35**

Pascoli, Giovanni 1855-1912 . . . . . . **TCLC 45**

Pasolini, Pier Paolo
1922-1975 . . . . **CLC 20, 37; PC 17**
See also CA 93-96; 61-64; DLB 128, 177;
MTCW

Pasquini
See Silone, Ignazio

Pastan, Linda (Olenik)
1932- . . . . **CLC 27; DAM POET**
See also CA 61-64; CANR 18, 40, 61;
DLB 5

Pasternak, Boris (Leonidovich)
1890-1960 . . . . . . **CLC 7, 10, 18, 63; DA;**
DAB; DAC; DAM MST, NOV, POET;
PC 6; WLC
See also CA 127; 116; MTCW

Patchen, Kenneth
1911-1972 . . . **CLC 1, 2, 18; DAM POET**
See also CA 1-4R; 33-36R; CANR 3, 35;
DLB 16, 48; MTCW

Pater, Walter (Horatio)
1839-1894 . . . . **NCLC 7**
See also CDBLB 1832-1890; DLB 57, 156

Paterson, A(ndrew) B(arton)
1864-1941 . . . . **TCLC 32**
See also CA 155

Paterson, Katherine (Womeldorf)
1932- . . . . **CLC 12, 30**
See also AAYA 1; CA 21-24R; CANR 28,
59; CLR 7; DLB 52; JRDA; MAICYA;
MTCW; SATA 13, 53, 92

Patmore, Coventry Kersey Dighton
1823-1896 . . . . **NCLC 9**
See also DLB 35, 98

Paton, Alan (Stewart)
1903-1988 . . . . . . **CLC 4, 10, 25, 55; DA;**
DAB; DAC; DAM MST, NOV; WLC
See also CA 13-16; 125; CANR 22; CAP 1;
MTCW; SATA 11; SATA-Obit 56

Paton Walsh, Gillian 1937-
See Walsh, Jill Paton
See also CANR 38; JRDA; MAICYA;
SAAS 3; SATA 4, 72

Paulding, James Kirke 1778-1860 . . **NCLC 2**
See also DLB 3, 59, 74

Paulin, Thomas Neilson 1949-
See Paulin, Tom
See also CA 123; 128

Paulin, Tom . . . . **CLC 37**
See also Paulin, Thomas Neilson
See also DLB 40

Paustovsky, Konstantin (Georgievich)
1892-1968 . . . . **CLC 40**
See also CA 93-96; 25-28R

Pavese, Cesare
1908-1950 . . . . . **TCLC 3; PC 13; SSC 19**
See also CA 104; DLB 128, 177

Pavic, Milorad 1929- . . . . **CLC 60**
See also CA 136; DLB 181

Payne, Alan
See Jakes, John (William)

Paz, Gil
See Lugones, Leopoldo

Paz, Octavio
1914- . . . . **CLC 3, 4, 6, 10, 19, 51, 65;**
DA; DAB; DAC; DAM MST, MULT,
POET; HLC; PC 1; WLC
See also CA 73-96; CANR 32; DLBY 90;
HW; MTCW

p'Bitek, Okot
1931-1982 . . . . **CLC 96; BLC;**
DAM MULT
See also BW 2; CA 124; 107; DLB 125;
MTCW

Peacock, Molly 1947- . . . . **CLC 60**
See also CA 103; CAAS 21; CANR 52;
DLB 120

Peacock, Thomas Love
1785-1866 . . . . **NCLC 22**
See also DLB 96, 116

Peake, Mervyn 1911-1968 . . . . **CLC 7, 54**
See also CA 5-8R; 25-28R; CANR 3;
DLB 15, 160; MTCW; SATA 23

Pearce, Philippa . . . . **CLC 21**
See also Christie, (Ann) Philippa
See also CLR 9; DLB 161; MAICYA;
SATA 1, 67

Pearl, Eric
See Elman, Richard

Pearson, T(homas) R(eid) 1956- . . . . **CLC 39**
See also CA 120; 130; INT 130

Peck, Dale 1967- . . . . **CLC 81**
See also CA 146

Peck, John 1941- . . . . **CLC 3**
See also CA 49-52; CANR 3

Peck, Richard (Wayne) 1934- . . . . . . **CLC 21**
See also AAYA 1; CA 85-88; CANR 19,
38; CLR 15; INT CANR-19; JRDA;
MAICYA; SAAS 2; SATA 18, 55

Peck, Robert Newton
1928- . . **CLC 17; DA; DAC; DAM MST**
See also AAYA 3; CA 81-84; CANR 31;
CLR 45; JRDA; MAICYA; SAAS 1;
SATA 21, 62

Peckinpah, (David) Sam(uel)
1925-1984 . . . . **CLC 20**
See also CA 109; 114

Pedersen, Knut 1859-1952
See Hamsun, Knut
See also CA 104; 119; MTCW

Peeslake, Gaffer
See Durrell, Lawrence (George)

Peguy, Charles Pierre
1873-1914 . . . . **TCLC 10**
See also CA 107

Pena, Ramon del Valle y
See Valle-Inclan, Ramon (Maria) del

Pendennis, Arthur Esquir
See Thackeray, William Makepeace

Penn, William 1644-1718 . . . . **LC 25**
See also DLB 24

PEPECE
See Prado (Calvo), Pedro

Pepys, Samuel
1633-1703 . . . . . **LC 11; DA; DAB; DAC;**
DAM MST; WLC
See also CDBLB 1660-1789; DLB 101

Percy, Walker
1916-1990 . . . . **CLC 2, 3, 6, 8, 14, 18, 47,**
65; DAM NOV, POP
See also CA 1-4R; 131; CANR 1, 23;
DLB 2; DLBY 80, 90; MTCW

Perec, Georges 1936-1982 . . . . **CLC 56**
See also CA 141; DLB 83

Pereda (y Sanchez de Porrua), Jose Maria de
1833-1906 . . . . **TCLC 16**
See also CA 117

Pereda y Porrua, Jose Maria de
See Pereda (y Sanchez de Porrua), Jose
Maria de

Peregoy, George Weems
See Mencken, H(enry) L(ouis)

Perelman, S(idney) J(oseph)
1904-1979 . . . . . . **CLC 3, 5, 9, 15, 23, 44,**
49; DAM DRAM
See also AITN 1, 2; CA 73-76; 89-92;
CANR 18; DLB 11, 44; MTCW

Peret, Benjamin 1899-1959 . . . . **TCLC 20**
See also CA 117

Peretz, Isaac Loeb
1851(?)-1915 . . . . **TCLC 16; SSC 26**
See also CA 109

Peretz, Yitzkhok Leibush
See Peretz, Isaac Loeb

Perez Galdos, Benito 1843-1920 . . . **TCLC 27**
See also CA 125; 153; HW

Perrault, Charles 1628-1703 . . . . **LC 2**
See also MAICYA; SATA 25

Perry, Brighton
See Sherwood, Robert E(mmet)

Perse, St.-John . . . . **CLC 4, 11, 46**
See also Leger, (Marie-Rene Auguste) Alexis
Saint-Leger

Perutz, Leo 1882-1957 . . . . **TCLC 60**
See also DLB 81

Peseenz, Tulio F.
See Lopez y Fuentes, Gregorio

Pesetsky, Bette 1932- . . . . **CLC 28**
See also CA 133; DLB 130

Peshkov, Alexei Maximovich 1868-1936
See Gorky, Maxim
See also CA 105; 141; DA; DAC;
DAM DRAM, MST, NOV

Pessoa, Fernando (Antonio Nogueira)
1888-1935 . . . . **TCLC 27; HLC**
See also CA 125

Peterkin, Julia Mood 1880-1961 . . . . **CLC 31**
See also CA 102; DLB 9

Peters, Joan K(aren) 1945- . . . . **CLC 39**
See also CA 158

Peters, Robert L(ouis) 1924- . . . . **CLC 7**
See also CA 13-16R; CAAS 8; DLB 105

Petofi, Sandor 1823-1849 . . . . **NCLC 21**

Petrakis, Harry Mark   1923-........ CLC 3
See also CA 9-12R; CANR 4, 30

Petrarch
1304-1374 .... CMLC 20; DAM POET;
PC 8

Petrov, Evgeny .... TCLC 21
See also Kataev, Evgeny Petrovich

Petry, Ann (Lane) 1908-1997... CLC 1, 7, 18
See also BW 1; CA 5-8R; 157; CAAS 6;
CANR 4, 46; CLR 12; DLB 76; JRDA;
MAICYA; MTCW; SATA 5;
SATA-Obit 94

Petursson, Halligrimur 1614-1674 .... LC 8

Philips, Katherine 1632-1664........ LC 30
See also DLB 131

Philipson, Morris H. 1926-........ CLC 53
See also CA 1-4R; CANR 4

Phillips, Caryl
1958- .... CLC 96; DAM MULT
See also BW 2; CA 141; DLB 157

Phillips, David Graham
1867-1911 .... TCLC 44
See also CA 108; DLB 9, 12

Phillips, Jack
See Sandburg, Carl (August)

Phillips, Jayne Anne
1952- .... CLC 15, 33; SSC 16
See also CA 101; CANR 24, 50; DLBY 80;
INT CANR-24; MTCW

Phillips, Richard
See Dick, Philip K(indred)

Phillips, Robert (Schaeffer) 1938-... CLC 28
See also CA 17-20R; CAAS 13; CANR 8;
DLB 105

Phillips, Ward
See Lovecraft, H(oward) P(hillips)

Piccolo, Lucio 1901-1969......... CLC 13
See also CA 97-100; DLB 114

Pickthall, Marjorie L(owry) C(hristie)
1883-1922 .... TCLC 21
See also CA 107; DLB 92

Pico della Mirandola, Giovanni
1463-1494 .... LC 15

Piercy, Marge
1936- .... CLC 3, 6, 14, 18, 27, 62
See also CA 21-24R; CAAS 1; CANR 13,
43; DLB 120; MTCW

Piers, Robert
See Anthony, Piers

Pieyre de Mandiargues, Andre 1909-1991
See Mandiargues, Andre Pieyre de
See also CA 103; 136; CANR 22

Pilnyak, Boris .... TCLC 23
See also Vogau, Boris Andreyevich

Pincherle, Alberto
1907-1990 ..... CLC 11, 18; DAM NOV
See also Moravia, Alberto
See also CA 25-28R; 132; CANR 33;
MTCW

Pinckney, Darryl 1953-........... CLC 76
See also BW 2; CA 143

Pindar   518B.C.-446B.C.... CMLC 12; PC 19
See also DLB 176

Pineda, Cecile 1942-............. CLC 39
See also CA 118

Pinero, Arthur Wing
1855-1934 ..... TCLC 32; DAM DRAM
See also CA 110; 153; DLB 10

Pinero, Miguel (Antonio Gomez)
1946-1988 .... CLC 4, 55
See also CA 61-64; 125; CANR 29; HW

Pinget, Robert 1919-1997 .... CLC 7, 13, 37
See also CA 85-88; 160; DLB 83

Pink Floyd
See Barrett, (Roger) Syd; Gilmour, David;
Mason, Nick; Waters, Roger; Wright,
Rick

Pinkney, Edward 1802-1828 ..... NCLC 31

Pinkwater, Daniel Manus 1941-.... CLC 35
See also Pinkwater, Manus
See also AAYA 1; CA 29-32R; CANR 12,
38; CLR 4; JRDA; MAICYA; SAAS 3;
SATA 46, 76

Pinkwater, Manus
See Pinkwater, Daniel Manus
See also SATA 8

Pinsky, Robert
1940- .. CLC 9, 19, 38, 94; DAM POET
See also CA 29-32R; CAAS 4; CANR 58;
DLBY 82

Pinta, Harold
See Pinter, Harold

Pinter, Harold
1930- ..... CLC 1, 3, 6, 9, 11, 15, 27, 58,
73; DA; DAB; DAC; DAM DRAM,
MST; WLC
See also CA 5-8R; CANR 33; CDBLB 1960
to Present; DLB 13; MTCW

Piozzi, Hester Lynch (Thrale)
1741-1821 .... NCLC 57
See also DLB 104, 142

Pirandello, Luigi
1867-1936 ...... TCLC 4, 29; DA; DAB;
DAC; DAM DRAM, MST; DC 5;
SSC 22; WLC
See also CA 104; 153

Pirsig, Robert M(aynard)
1928- .... CLC 4, 6, 73; DAM POP
See also CA 53-56; CANR 42; MTCW;
SATA 39

Pisarev, Dmitry Ivanovich
1840-1868 .... NCLC 25

Pix, Mary (Griffith) 1666-1709....... LC 8
See also DLB 80

Pixerecourt, Guilbert de
1773-1844 .... NCLC 39

Plaatje, Sol(omon) T(shekisho)
1876-1932 .... TCLC 73
See also BW 2; CA 141

Plaidy, Jean
See Hibbert, Eleanor Alice Burford

Planche, James Robinson
1796-1880 .... NCLC 42

Plant, Robert 1948- .... CLC 12

Plante, David (Robert)
1940- .... CLC 7, 23, 38; DAM NOV
See also CA 37-40R; CANR 12, 36, 58;
DLBY 83; INT CANR-12; MTCW

Plath, Sylvia
1932-1963 ..... CLC 1, 2, 3, 5, 9, 11, 14,
17, 50, 51, 62; DA; DAB; DAC;
DAM MST, POET; PC 1; WLC
See also AAYA 13; CA 19-20; CANR 34;
CAP 2; CDALB 1941-1968; DLB 5, 6,
152; MTCW

Plato
428(?)B.C.-348(?)B.C..... CMLC 8; DA;
DAB; DAC; DAM MST; WLCS
See also DLB 176

Platonov, Andrei .... TCLC 14
See also Klimentov, Andrei Platonovich

Platt, Kin 1911- .... CLC 26
See also AAYA 11; CA 17-20R; CANR 11;
JRDA; SAAS 17; SATA 21, 86

Plautus   c. 251B.C.-184B.C........... DC 6

Plick et Plock
See Simenon, Georges (Jacques Christian)

Plimpton, George (Ames) 1927-..... CLC 36
See also AITN 1; CA 21-24R; CANR 32;
MTCW; SATA 10

Pliny the Elder   c. 23-79........ CMLC 23

Plomer, William Charles Franklin
1903-1973 .... CLC 4, 8
See also CA 21-22; CANR 34; CAP 2;
DLB 20, 162; MTCW; SATA 24

Plowman, Piers
See Kavanagh, Patrick (Joseph)

Plum, J.
See Wodehouse, P(elham) G(renville)

Plumly, Stanley (Ross) 1939- ...... CLC 33
See also CA 108; 110; DLB 5; INT 110

Plumpe, Friedrich Wilhelm
1888-1931 .... TCLC 53
See also CA 112

Poe, Edgar Allan
1809-1849 .... NCLC 1, 16, 55; DA;
DAB; DAC; DAM MST, POET; PC 1;
SSC 1, 22; WLC
See also AAYA 14; CDALB 1640-1865;
DLB 3, 59, 73, 74; SATA 23

Poet of Titchfield Street, The
See Pound, Ezra (Weston Loomis)

Pohl, Frederik 1919- ..... CLC 18; SSC 25
See also CA 61-64; CAAS 1; CANR 11, 37;
DLB 8; INT CANR-11; MTCW;
SATA 24

Poirier, Louis 1910-
See Gracq, Julien
See also CA 122; 126

Poitier, Sidney 1927-............. CLC 26
See also BW 1; CA 117

Polanski, Roman 1933- .... CLC 16
See also CA 77-80

Poliakoff, Stephen 1952- .... CLC 38
See also CA 106; DLB 13

Police, The
See Copeland, Stewart (Armstrong);
Summers, Andrew James; Sumner,
Gordon Matthew

Polidori, John William
1795-1821 .... NCLC 51
See also DLB 116

Pollitt, Katha 1949- .... **CLC 28**
See also CA 120; 122; MTCW

Pollock, (Mary) Sharon
1936- .... **CLC 50; DAC; DAM DRAM,
MST**
See also CA 141; DLB 60

Polo, Marco 1254-1324 .... **CMLC 15**

Polonsky, Abraham (Lincoln)
1910- .... **CLC 92**
See also CA 104; DLB 26; INT 104

Polybius c. 200B.C.-c. 118B.C. .... **CMLC 17**
See also DLB 176

Pomerance, Bernard
1940- .... **CLC 13; DAM DRAM**
See also CA 101; CANR 49

Ponge, Francis (Jean Gaston Alfred)
1899-1988 ..... **CLC 6, 18; DAM POET**
See also CA 85-88; 126; CANR 40

Pontoppidan, Henrik 1857-1943 ... **TCLC 29**

Poole, Josephine .... **CLC 17**
See also Helyar, Jane Penelope Josephine
See also SAAS 2; SATA 5

Popa, Vasko 1922-1991 .... **CLC 19**
See also CA 112; 148; DLB 181

Pope, Alexander
1688-1744 ...... **LC 3; DA; DAB; DAC;
DAM MST, POET; WLC**
See also CDBLB 1660-1789; DLB 95, 101

Porter, Connie (Rose) 1959(?)- ..... **CLC 70**
See also BW 2; CA 142; SATA 81

Porter, Gene(va Grace) Stratton
1863(?)-1924 .... **TCLC 21**
See also CA 112

Porter, Katherine Anne
1890-1980 ...... **CLC 1, 3, 7, 10, 13, 15,
27, 101; DA; DAB; DAC; DAM MST,
NOV; SSC 4**
See also AITN 2; CA 1-4R; 101; CANR 1;
DLB 4, 9, 102; DLBD 12; DLBY 80;
MTCW; SATA 39; SATA-Obit 23

Porter, Peter (Neville Frederick)
1929- .... **CLC 5, 13, 33**
See also CA 85-88; DLB 40

Porter, William Sydney 1862-1910
See Henry, O.
See also CA 104; 131; CDALB 1865-1917;
DA; DAB; DAC; DAM MST; DLB 12,
78, 79; MTCW; YABC 2

Portillo (y Pacheco), Jose Lopez
See Lopez Portillo (y Pacheco), Jose

Post, Melville Davisson
1869-1930 .... **TCLC 39**
See also CA 110

Potok, Chaim
1929- .... **CLC 2, 7, 14, 26; DAM NOV**
See also AAYA 15; AITN 1, 2; CA 17-20R;
CANR 19, 35; DLB 28, 152;
INT CANR-19; MTCW; SATA 33

Potter, (Helen) Beatrix 1866-1943
See Webb, (Martha) Beatrice (Potter)
See also MAICYA

Potter, Dennis (Christopher George)
1935-1994 .... **CLC 58, 86**
See also CA 107; 145; CANR 33, 61;
MTCW

Pound, Ezra (Weston Loomis)
1885-1972 ...... **CLC 1, 2, 3, 4, 5, 7, 10,
13, 18, 34, 48, 50; DA; DAB; DAC;
DAM MST, POET; PC 4; WLC**
See also CA 5-8R; 37-40R; CANR 40;
CDALB 1917-1929; DLB 4, 45, 63;
DLBD 15; MTCW

Povod, Reinaldo 1959-1994 .... **CLC 44**
See also CA 136; 146

Powell, Adam Clayton, Jr.
1908-1972 .... **CLC 89; BLC;
DAM MULT**
See also BW 1; CA 102; 33-36R

Powell, Anthony (Dymoke)
1905- .... **CLC 1, 3, 7, 9, 10, 31**
See also CA 1-4R; CANR 1, 32, 62;
CDBLB 1945-1960; DLB 15; MTCW

Powell, Dawn 1897-1965 .... **CLC 66**
See also CA 5-8R

Powell, Padgett 1952- .... **CLC 34**
See also CA 126

Power, Susan 1961- .... **CLC 91**

Powers, J(ames) F(arl)
1917- .... **CLC 1, 4, 8, 57; SSC 4**
See also CA 1-4R; CANR 2, 61; DLB 130;
MTCW

Powers, John J(ames) 1945-
See Powers, John R.
See also CA 69-72

Powers, John R. .... **CLC 66**
See also Powers, John J(ames)

Powers, Richard (S.) 1957- .... **CLC 93**
See also CA 148

Pownall, David 1938- .... **CLC 10**
See also CA 89-92; CAAS 18; CANR 49;
DLB 14

Powys, John Cowper
1872-1963 .... **CLC 7, 9, 15, 46**
See also CA 85-88; DLB 15; MTCW

Powys, T(heodore) F(rancis)
1875-1953 .... **TCLC 9**
See also CA 106; DLB 36, 162

Prado (Calvo), Pedro 1886-1952 ... **TCLC 75**
See also CA 131; HW

Prager, Emily 1952- .... **CLC 56**

Pratt, E(dwin) J(ohn)
1883(?)-1964 .... **CLC 19; DAC;
DAM POET**
See also CA 141; 93-96; DLB 92

Premchand .... **TCLC 21**
See also Srivastava, Dhanpat Rai

Preussler, Otfried 1923- .... **CLC 17**
See also CA 77-80; SATA 24

Prevert, Jacques (Henri Marie)
1900-1977 .... **CLC 15**
See also CA 77-80; 69-72; CANR 29, 61;
MTCW; SATA-Obit 30

Prevost, Abbe (Antoine Francois)
1697-1763 .... **LC 1**

Price, (Edward) Reynolds
1933- .... **CLC 3, 6, 13, 43, 50, 63;
DAM NOV; SSC 22**
See also CA 1-4R; CANR 1, 37, 57; DLB 2;
INT CANR-37

Price, Richard 1949- .... **CLC 6, 12**
See also CA 49-52; CANR 3; DLBY 81

Prichard, Katharine Susannah
1883-1969 .... **CLC 46**
See also CA 11-12; CANR 33; CAP 1;
MTCW; SATA 66

Priestley, J(ohn) B(oynton)
1894-1984 .... **CLC 2, 5, 9, 34;
DAM DRAM, NOV**
See also CA 9-12R; 113; CANR 33;
CDBLB 1914-1945; DLB 10, 34, 77, 100,
139; DLBY 84; MTCW

Prince 1958(?)- .... **CLC 35**

Prince, F(rank) T(empleton) 1912- .. **CLC 22**
See also CA 101; CANR 43; DLB 20

Prince Kropotkin
See Kropotkin, Peter (Aleksieevich)

Prior, Matthew 1664-1721 .... **LC 4**
See also DLB 95

Prishvin, Mikhail 1873-1954 ...... **TCLC 75**

Pritchard, William H(arrison)
1932- .... **CLC 34**
See also CA 65-68; CANR 23; DLB 111

Pritchett, V(ictor) S(awdon)
1900-1997 .... **CLC 5, 13, 15, 41;
DAM NOV; SSC 14**
See also CA 61-64; 157; CANR 31;
DLB 15, 139; MTCW

Private 19022
See Manning, Frederic

Probst, Mark 1925- .... **CLC 59**
See also CA 130

Prokosch, Frederic 1908-1989 .... **CLC 4, 48**
See also CA 73-76; 128; DLB 48

Prophet, The
See Dreiser, Theodore (Herman Albert)

Prose, Francine 1947- .... **CLC 45**
See also CA 109; 112; CANR 46

Proudhon
See Cunha, Euclides (Rodrigues Pimenta) da

Proulx, E. Annie 1935- .... **CLC 81**

Proust, (Valentin-Louis-George-Eugene-)
Marcel
1871-1922 .... **TCLC 7, 13, 33; DA;
DAB; DAC; DAM MST, NOV; WLC**
See also CA 104; 120; DLB 65; MTCW

Prowler, Harley
See Masters, Edgar Lee

Prus, Boleslaw 1845-1912 .... **TCLC 48**

Pryor, Richard (Franklin Lenox Thomas)
1940- .... **CLC 26**
See also CA 122

Przybyszewski, Stanislaw
1868-1927 .... **TCLC 36**
See also CA 160; DLB 66

Pteleon
See Grieve, C(hristopher) M(urray)
See also DAM POET

Puckett, Lute
See Masters, Edgar Lee

Puig, Manuel
1932-1990 . . . . CLC **3, 5, 10, 28, 65;**
DAM MULT; HLC
See also CA 45-48; CANR 2, 32; DLB 113;
HW; MTCW

Purdy, Al(fred Wellington)
1918- . . . . CLC **3, 6, 14, 50; DAC;**
DAM MST, POET
See also CA 81-84; CAAS 17; CANR 42;
DLB 88

Purdy, James (Amos)
1923- . . . . CLC **2, 4, 10, 28, 52**
See also CA 33-36R; CAAS 1; CANR 19,
51; DLB 2; INT CANR-19; MTCW

Pure, Simon
See Swinnerton, Frank Arthur

Pushkin, Alexander (Sergeyevich)
1799-1837 . . . . . NCLC **3, 27; DA; DAB;**
DAC; DAM DRAM, MST, POET;
PC 10; SSC 27; WLC
See also SATA 61

P'u Sung-ling 1640-1715 . . . . LC **3**

Putnam, Arthur Lee
See Alger, Horatio, Jr.

Puzo, Mario
1920- . . . . . CLC **1, 2, 6, 36; DAM NOV,**
POP
See also CA 65-68; CANR 4, 42; DLB 6;
MTCW

Pygge, Edward
See Barnes, Julian (Patrick)

Pyle, Ernest Taylor 1900-1945
See Pyle, Ernie
See also CA 115; 160

Pyle, Ernie 1900-1945 . . . . TCLC **75**
See also Pyle, Ernest Taylor
See also DLB 29

Pym, Barbara (Mary Crampton)
1913-1980 . . . . CLC **13, 19, 37**
See also CA 13-14; 97-100; CANR 13, 34;
CAP 1; DLB 14; DLBY 87; MTCW

Pynchon, Thomas (Ruggles, Jr.)
1937- . . . . . CLC **2, 3, 6, 9, 11, 18, 33, 62,**
72; DA; DAB; DAC; DAM MST, NOV,
POP; SSC 14; WLC
See also BEST 90:2; CA 17-20R; CANR 22,
46; DLB 2, 173; MTCW

Pythagoras
c. 570B.C.-c. 500B.C. . . . . CMLC **22**
See also DLB 176

Qian Zhongshu
See Ch'ien Chung-shu

Qroll
See Dagerman, Stig (Halvard)

Quarrington, Paul (Lewis) 1953- . . . . CLC **65**
See also CA 129; CANR 62

Quasimodo, Salvatore 1901-1968 . . . CLC **10**
See also CA 13-16; 25-28R; CAP 1;
DLB 114; MTCW

Quay, Stephen 1947- . . . . CLC **95**

Quay, The Brothers
See Quay, Stephen; Quay, Timothy

Quay, Timothy 1947- . . . . CLC **95**

Queen, Ellery . . . . CLC **3, 11**
See also Dannay, Frederic; Davidson,
Avram; Lee, Manfred B(ennington);
Marlowe, Stephen; Sturgeon, Theodore
(Hamilton); Vance, John Holbrook

Queen, Ellery, Jr.
See Dannay, Frederic; Lee, Manfred
B(ennington)

Queneau, Raymond
1903-1976 . . . . CLC **2, 5, 10, 42**
See also CA 77-80; 69-72; CANR 32;
DLB 72; MTCW

Quevedo, Francisco de 1580-1645 . . . . LC **23**

Quiller-Couch, Arthur Thomas
1863-1944 . . . . TCLC **53**
See also CA 118; DLB 135, 153

Quin, Ann (Marie) 1936-1973 . . . . CLC **6**
See also CA 9-12R; 45-48; DLB 14

Quinn, Martin
See Smith, Martin Cruz

Quinn, Peter 1947- . . . . CLC **91**

Quinn, Simon
See Smith, Martin Cruz

Quiroga, Horacio (Sylvestre)
1878-1937 . . . . . TCLC **20; DAM MULT;**
HLC
See also CA 117; 131; HW; MTCW

Quoirez, Francoise 1935- . . . . CLC **9**
See also Sagan, Francoise
See also CA 49-52; CANR 6, 39; MTCW

Raabe, Wilhelm 1831-1910 . . . . TCLC **45**
See also DLB 129

Rabe, David (William)
1940- . . . . . . CLC **4, 8, 33; DAM DRAM**
See also CA 85-88; CABS 3; CANR 59;
DLB 7

Rabelais, Francois
1483-1553 . . . . . . LC **5; DA; DAB; DAC;**
DAM MST; WLC

Rabinovitch, Sholem 1859-1916
See Aleichem, Sholom
See also CA 104

Rachilde 1860-1953 . . . . TCLC **67**
See also DLB 123

Racine, Jean
1639-1699 . . . . LC **28; DAB; DAM MST**

Radcliffe, Ann (Ward)
1764-1823 . . . . NCLC **6, 55**
See also DLB 39, 178

Radiguet, Raymond 1903-1923 . . . . TCLC **29**
See also DLB 65

Radnoti, Miklos 1909-1944 . . . . TCLC **16**
See also CA 118

Rado, James 1939- . . . . CLC **17**
See also CA 105

Radvanyi, Netty 1900-1983
See Seghers, Anna
See also CA 85-88; 110

Rae, Ben
See Griffiths, Trevor

Raeburn, John (Hay) 1941- . . . . CLC **34**
See also CA 57-60

Ragni, Gerome 1942-1991 . . . . CLC **17**
See also CA 105; 134

Rahv, Philip 1908-1973 . . . . CLC **24**
See also Greenberg, Ivan
See also DLB 137

Raine, Craig 1944- . . . . CLC **32, 103**
See also CA 108; CANR 29, 51; DLB 40

Raine, Kathleen (Jessie) 1908- . . . CLC **7, 45**
See also CA 85-88; CANR 46; DLB 20;
MTCW

Rainis, Janis 1865-1929 . . . . TCLC **29**

Rakosi, Carl . . . . CLC **47**
See also Rawley, Callman
See also CAAS 5

Raleigh, Richard
See Lovecraft, H(oward) P(hillips)

Raleigh, Sir Walter
1554(?)-1618 . . . . LC **31, 39**
See also CDBLB Before 1660; DLB 172

Rallentando, H. P.
See Sayers, Dorothy L(eigh)

Ramal, Walter
See de la Mare, Walter (John)

Ramon, Juan
See Jimenez (Mantecon), Juan Ramon

Ramos, Graciliano 1892-1953 . . . . . TCLC **32**

Rampersad, Arnold 1941- . . . . CLC **44**
See also BW 2; CA 127; 133; DLB 111;
INT 133

Rampling, Anne
See Rice, Anne

Ramsay, Allan 1684(?)-1758 . . . . LC **29**
See also DLB 95

Ramuz, Charles-Ferdinand
1878-1947 . . . . TCLC **33**

Rand, Ayn
1905-1982 . . . . . . CLC **3, 30, 44, 79; DA;**
DAC; DAM MST, NOV, POP; WLC
See also AAYA 10; CA 13-16R; 105;
CANR 27; MTCW

Randall, Dudley (Felker)
1914- . . . . . . CLC **1; BLC; DAM MULT**
See also BW 1; CA 25-28R; CANR 23;
DLB 41

Randall, Robert
See Silverberg, Robert

Ranger, Ken
See Creasey, John

Ransom, John Crowe
1888-1974 . . . . CLC **2, 4, 5, 11, 24;**
DAM POET
See also CA 5-8R; 49-52; CANR 6, 34;
DLB 45, 63; MTCW

Rao, Raja 1909- . . . CLC **25, 56; DAM NOV**
See also CA 73-76; CANR 51; MTCW

Raphael, Frederic (Michael)
1931- . . . . CLC **2, 14**
See also CA 1-4R; CANR 1; DLB 14

Ratcliffe, James P.
See Mencken, H(enry) L(ouis)

Rathbone, Julian 1935- . . . . CLC **41**
See also CA 101; CANR 34

Rattigan, Terence (Mervyn)
1911-1977 . . . . CLC **7; DAM DRAM**
See also CA 85-88; 73-76;
CDBLB 1945-1960; DLB 13; MTCW

Ratushinskaya, Irina 1954- . . . . **CLC 54**
See also CA 129

Raven, Simon (Arthur Noel)
1927- . . . . **CLC 14**
See also CA 81-84

Rawley, Callman 1903-
See Rakosi, Carl
See also CA 21-24R; CANR 12, 32

Rawlings, Marjorie Kinnan
1896-1953 . . . . **TCLC 4**
See also AAYA 20; CA 104; 137; DLB 9,
22, 102; JRDA; MAICYA; YABC 1

Ray, Satyajit
1921-1992 . . . **CLC 16, 76; DAM MULT**
See also CA 114; 137

Read, Herbert Edward 1893-1968. . . . **CLC 4**
See also CA 85-88; 25-28R; DLB 20, 149

Read, Piers Paul 1941- . . . . . . **CLC 4, 10, 25**
See also CA 21-24R; CANR 38; DLB 14;
SATA 21

Reade, Charles 1814-1884 . . . . **NCLC 2**
See also DLB 21

Reade, Hamish
See Gray, Simon (James Holliday)

Reading, Peter 1946- . . . . **CLC 47**
See also CA 103; CANR 46; DLB 40

Reaney, James
1926- . . . . . . **CLC 13; DAC; DAM MST**
See also CA 41-44R; CAAS 15; CANR 42;
DLB 68; SATA 43

Rebreanu, Liviu 1885-1944 . . . . . . **TCLC 28**

Rechy, John (Francisco)
1934- . . . . **CLC 1, 7, 14, 18;**
DAM MULT; HLC
See also CA 5-8R; CAAS 4; CANR 6, 32;
DLB 122; DLBY 82; HW; INT CANR-6

Redcam, Tom 1870-1933 . . . . **TCLC 25**

Reddin, Keith. . . . . **CLC 67**

Redgrove, Peter (William)
1932- . . . . **CLC 6, 41**
See also CA 1-4R; CANR 3, 39; DLB 40

Redmon, Anne. . . . . **CLC 22**
See also Nightingale, Anne Redmon
See also DLBY 86

Reed, Eliot
See Ambler, Eric

Reed, Ishmael
1938- . . . . **CLC 2, 3, 5, 6, 13, 32, 60;**
BLC; DAM MULT
See also BW 2; CA 21-24R; CANR 25, 48;
DLB 2, 5, 33, 169; DLBD 8; MTCW

Reed, John (Silas) 1887-1920 . . . . . . **TCLC 9**
See also CA 106

Reed, Lou. . . . . **CLC 21**
See also Firbank, Louis

Reeve, Clara 1729-1807 . . . . **NCLC 19**
See also DLB 39

Reich, Wilhelm 1897-1957. . . . . . . **TCLC 57**

Reid, Christopher (John) 1949-. . . . . **CLC 33**
See also CA 140; DLB 40

Reid, Desmond
See Moorcock, Michael (John)

Reid Banks, Lynne 1929-
See Banks, Lynne Reid
See also CA 1-4R; CANR 6, 22, 38;
CLR 24; JRDA; MAICYA; SATA 22, 75

Reilly, William K.
See Creasey, John

Reiner, Max
See Caldwell, (Janet Miriam) Taylor
(Holland)

Reis, Ricardo
See Pessoa, Fernando (Antonio Nogueira)

Remarque, Erich Maria
1898-1970 . . . . **CLC 21; DA; DAB; DAC;**
DAM MST, NOV
See also CA 77-80; 29-32R; DLB 56;
MTCW

Remizov, A.
See Remizov, Aleksei (Mikhailovich)

Remizov, A. M.
See Remizov, Aleksei (Mikhailovich)

Remizov, Aleksei (Mikhailovich)
1877-1957 . . . . **TCLC 27**
See also CA 125; 133

Renan, Joseph Ernest
1823-1892 . . . . **NCLC 26**

Renard, Jules 1864-1910 . . . . **TCLC 17**
See also CA 117

Renault, Mary. . . . . **CLC 3, 11, 17**
See also Challans, Mary
See also DLBY 83

Rendell, Ruth (Barbara)
1930- . . . . **CLC 28, 48; DAM POP**
See also Vine, Barbara
See also CA 109; CANR 32, 52; DLB 87;
INT CANR-32; MTCW

Renoir, Jean 1894-1979 . . . . **CLC 20**
See also CA 129; 85-88

Resnais, Alain 1922-. . . . . **CLC 16**

Reverdy, Pierre 1889-1960 . . . . **CLC 53**
See also CA 97-100; 89-92

Rexroth, Kenneth
1905-1982 . . . . . . **CLC 1, 2, 6, 11, 22, 49;**
DAM POET
See also CA 5-8R; 107; CANR 14, 34;
CDALB 1941-1968; DLB 16, 48, 165;
DLBY 82; INT CANR-14; MTCW

Reyes, Alfonso 1889-1959 . . . . **TCLC 33**
See also CA 131; HW

Reyes y Basoalto, Ricardo Eliecer Neftali
See Neruda, Pablo

Reymont, Wladyslaw (Stanislaw)
1868(?)-1925 . . . . **TCLC 5**
See also CA 104

Reynolds, Jonathan 1942- . . . . **CLC 6, 38**
See also CA 65-68; CANR 28

Reynolds, Joshua 1723-1792 . . . . **LC 15**
See also DLB 104

Reynolds, Michael Shane 1937- . . . . **CLC 44**
See also CA 65-68; CANR 9

Reznikoff, Charles 1894-1976 . . . . **CLC 9**
See also CA 33-36; 61-64; CAP 2; DLB 28,
45

Rezzori (d'Arezzo), Gregor von
1914- . . . . **CLC 25**
See also CA 122; 136

Rhine, Richard
See Silverstein, Alvin

Rhodes, Eugene Manlove
1869-1934 . . . . **TCLC 53**

R'hoone
See Balzac, Honore de

Rhys, Jean
1890(?)-1979 . . . . **CLC 2, 4, 6, 14, 19, 51;**
DAM NOV; SSC 21
See also CA 25-28R; 85-88; CANR 35, 62;
CDBLB 1945-1960; DLB 36, 117, 162;
MTCW

Ribeiro, Darcy 1922-1997 . . . . **CLC 34**
See also CA 33-36R; 156

Ribeiro, Joao Ubaldo (Osorio Pimentel)
1941- . . . . **CLC 10, 67**
See also CA 81-84

Ribman, Ronald (Burt) 1932- . . . . **CLC 7**
See also CA 21-24R; CANR 46

Ricci, Nino 1959-. . . . . **CLC 70**
See also CA 137

Rice, Anne 1941- . . . . . **CLC 41; DAM POP**
See also AAYA 9; BEST 89:2; CA 65-68;
CANR 12, 36, 53

Rice, Elmer (Leopold)
1892-1967 . . . . **CLC 7, 49; DAM DRAM**
See also CA 21-22; 25-28R; CAP 2; DLB 4,
7; MTCW

Rice, Tim(othy Miles Bindon)
1944- . . . . **CLC 21**
See also CA 103; CANR 46

Rich, Adrienne (Cecile)
1929- . . . . **CLC 3, 6, 7, 11, 18, 36, 73, 76;**
DAM POET; PC 5
See also CA 9-12R; CANR 20, 53; DLB 5,
67; MTCW

Rich, Barbara
See Graves, Robert (von Ranke)

Rich, Robert
See Trumbo, Dalton

Richard, Keith. . . . . **CLC 17**
See also Richards, Keith

Richards, David Adams
1950- . . . . **CLC 59; DAC**
See also CA 93-96; CANR 60; DLB 53

Richards, I(vor) A(rmstrong)
1893-1979 . . . . **CLC 14, 24**
See also CA 41-44R; 89-92; CANR 34;
DLB 27

Richards, Keith 1943-
See Richard, Keith
See also CA 107

Richardson, Anne
See Roiphe, Anne (Richardson)

Richardson, Dorothy Miller
1873-1957 . . . . **TCLC 3**
See also CA 104; DLB 36

Richardson, Ethel Florence (Lindesay)
1870-1946
See Richardson, Henry Handel
See also CA 105

Richardson, Henry Handel. . . . . **TCLC 4**
See also Richardson, Ethel Florence
(Lindesay)

Richardson, John
1796-1852 . . . . **NCLC 55; DAC**
See also DLB 99

Richardson, Samuel
1689-1761 . . . . . . **LC 1; DA; DAB; DAC;**
DAM MST, NOV; WLC
See also CDBLB 1660-1789; DLB 39

Richler, Mordecai
1931- . . . . **CLC 3, 5, 9, 13, 18, 46, 70;**
DAC; DAM MST, NOV
See also AITN 1; CA 65-68; CANR 31, 62;
CLR 17; DLB 53; MAICYA; MTCW;
SATA 44; SATA-Brief 27

Richter, Conrad (Michael)
1890-1968 . . . . **CLC 30**
See also AAYA 21; CA 5-8R; 25-28R;
CANR 23; DLB 9; MTCW; SATA 3

Ricostranza, Tom
See Ellis, Trey

Riddell, J. H. 1832-1906 . . . . **TCLC 40**

Riding, Laura . . . . **CLC 3, 7**
See also Jackson, Laura (Riding)

Riefenstahl, Berta Helene Amalia 1902-
See Riefenstahl, Leni
See also CA 108

Riefenstahl, Leni . . . . **CLC 16**
See also Riefenstahl, Berta Helene Amalia

Riffe, Ernest
See Bergman, (Ernst) Ingmar

Riggs, (Rolla) Lynn
1899-1954 . . . . . **TCLC 56; DAM MULT**
See also CA 144; DLB 175; NNAL

Riley, James Whitcomb
1849-1916 . . . . . . **TCLC 51; DAM POET**
See also CA 118; 137; MAICYA; SATA 17

Riley, Tex
See Creasey, John

Rilke, Rainer Maria
1875-1926 . . . . **TCLC 1, 6, 19;**
DAM POET; PC 2
See also CA 104; 132; CANR 62; DLB 81;
MTCW

Rimbaud, (Jean Nicolas) Arthur
1854-1891 . . . . . **NCLC 4, 35; DA; DAB;**
DAC; DAM MST, POET; PC 3; WLC

Rinehart, Mary Roberts
1876-1958 . . . . **TCLC 52**
See also CA 108

Ringmaster, The
See Mencken, H(enry) L(ouis)

Ringwood, Gwen(dolyn Margaret) Pharis
1910-1984 . . . . **CLC 48**
See also CA 148; 112; DLB 88

Rio, Michel 19(?)- . . . . **CLC 43**

Ritsos, Giannes
See Ritsos, Yannis

Ritsos, Yannis 1909-1990 . . . . . **CLC 6, 13, 31**
See also CA 77-80; 133; CANR 39, 61;
MTCW

Ritter, Erika 1948(?)- . . . . **CLC 52**

Rivera, Jose Eustasio 1889-1928 . . . **TCLC 35**
See also HW

Rivers, Conrad Kent 1933-1968 . . . . . . **CLC 1**
See also BW 1; CA 85-88; DLB 41

Rivers, Elfrida
See Bradley, Marion Zimmer

Riverside, John
See Heinlein, Robert A(nson)

Rizal, Jose 1861-1896 . . . . **NCLC 27**

Roa Bastos, Augusto (Antonio)
1917- . . . . . **CLC 45; DAM MULT; HLC**
See also CA 131; DLB 113; HW

Robbe-Grillet, Alain
1922- . . . . . . **CLC 1, 2, 4, 6, 8, 10, 14, 43**
See also CA 9-12R; CANR 33; DLB 83;
MTCW

Robbins, Harold
1916- . . . . **CLC 5; DAM NOV**
See also CA 73-76; CANR 26, 54; MTCW

Robbins, Thomas Eugene 1936-
See Robbins, Tom
See also CA 81-84; CANR 29, 59;
DAM NOV, POP; MTCW

Robbins, Tom . . . . **CLC 9, 32, 64**
See also Robbins, Thomas Eugene
See also BEST 90:3; DLBY 80

Robbins, Trina 1938- . . . . **CLC 21**
See also CA 128

Roberts, Charles G(eorge) D(ouglas)
1860-1943 . . . . **TCLC 8**
See also CA 105; CLR 33; DLB 92;
SATA 88; SATA-Brief 29

Roberts, Elizabeth Madox
1886-1941 . . . . **TCLC 68**
See also CA 111; DLB 9, 54, 102;
SATA 33; SATA-Brief 27

Roberts, Kate 1891-1985 . . . . **CLC 15**
See also CA 107; 116

Roberts, Keith (John Kingston)
1935- . . . . **CLC 14**
See also CA 25-28R; CANR 46

Roberts, Kenneth (Lewis)
1885-1957 . . . . **TCLC 23**
See also CA 109; DLB 9

Roberts, Michele (B.) 1949- . . . . **CLC 48**
See also CA 115; CANR 58

Robertson, Ellis
See Ellison, Harlan (Jay); Silverberg, Robert

Robertson, Thomas William
1829-1871 . . . . **NCLC 35; DAM DRAM**

Robeson, Kenneth
See Dent, Lester

Robinson, Edwin Arlington
1869-1935 . . . . **TCLC 5; DA; DAC;**
DAM MST, POET; PC 1
See also CA 104; 133; CDALB 1865-1917;
DLB 54; MTCW

Robinson, Henry Crabb
1775-1867 . . . . **NCLC 15**
See also DLB 107

Robinson, Jill 1936- . . . . **CLC 10**
See also CA 102; INT 102

Robinson, Kim Stanley 1952- . . . . . . **CLC 34**
See also CA 126

Robinson, Lloyd
See Silverberg, Robert

Robinson, Marilynne 1944- . . . . **CLC 25**
See also CA 116

Robinson, Smokey . . . . **CLC 21**
See also Robinson, William, Jr.

Robinson, William, Jr. 1940-
See Robinson, Smokey
See also CA 116

Robison, Mary 1949- . . . . **CLC 42, 98**
See also CA 113; 116; DLB 130; INT 116

Rod, Edouard 1857-1910 . . . . **TCLC 52**

Roddenberry, Eugene Wesley 1921-1991
See Roddenberry, Gene
See also CA 110; 135; CANR 37; SATA 45;
SATA-Obit 69

Roddenberry, Gene . . . . **CLC 17**
See also Roddenberry, Eugene Wesley
See also AAYA 5; SATA-Obit 69

Rodgers, Mary 1931- . . . . **CLC 12**
See also CA 49-52; CANR 8, 55; CLR 20;
INT CANR-8; JRDA; MAICYA;
SATA 8

Rodgers, W(illiam) R(obert)
1909-1969 . . . . **CLC 7**
See also CA 85-88; DLB 20

Rodman, Eric
See Silverberg, Robert

Rodman, Howard 1920(?)-1985 . . . . . **CLC 65**
See also CA 118

Rodman, Maia
See Wojciechowska, Maia (Teresa)

Rodriguez, Claudio 1934- . . . . **CLC 10**
See also DLB 134

Roelvaag, O(le) E(dvart)
1876-1931 . . . . **TCLC 17**
See also CA 117; DLB 9

Roethke, Theodore (Huebner)
1908-1963 . . . . . . **CLC 1, 3, 8, 11, 19, 46,**
101; DAM POET; PC 15
See also CA 81-84; CABS 2;
CDALB 1941-1968; DLB 5; MTCW

Rogers, Thomas Hunton 1927- . . . . . **CLC 57**
See also CA 89-92; INT 89-92

Rogers, Will(iam Penn Adair)
1879-1935 . . . **TCLC 8, 71; DAM MULT**
See also CA 105; 144; DLB 11; NNAL

Rogin, Gilbert 1929- . . . . **CLC 18**
See also CA 65-68; CANR 15

Rohan, Koda . . . . **TCLC 22**
See also Koda Shigeyuki

Rohlfs, Anna Katharine Green
See Green, Anna Katharine

Rohmer, Eric . . . . **CLC 16**
See also Scherer, Jean-Marie Maurice

Rohmer, Sax . . . . **TCLC 28**
See also Ward, Arthur Henry Sarsfield
See also DLB 70

Roiphe, Anne (Richardson)
1935- . . . . **CLC 3, 9**
See also CA 89-92; CANR 45; DLBY 80;
INT 89-92

Rojas, Fernando de 1465-1541 . . . . . . **LC 23**

Rolfe, Frederick (William Serafino Austin
Lewis Mary) 1860-1913 . . . . . . **TCLC 12**
See also CA 107; DLB 34, 156

Rolland, Romain 1866-1944 . . . . **TCLC 23**
See also CA 118; DLB 65

Rolle, Richard c. 1300-c. 1349 . . . **CMLC 21**
See also DLB 146

Rolvaag, O(le) E(dvart)
See Roelvaag, O(le) E(dvart)

Romain Arnaud, Saint
See Aragon, Louis

Romains, Jules 1885-1972 . . . . **CLC 7**
See also CA 85-88; CANR 34; DLB 65;
MTCW

Romero, Jose Ruben 1890-1952 . . . **TCLC 14**
See also CA 114; 131; HW

Ronsard, Pierre de
1524-1585 . . . . **LC 6; PC 11**

Rooke, Leon
1934- . . . . **CLC 25, 34; DAM POP**
See also CA 25-28R; CANR 23, 53

Roosevelt, Theodore 1858-1919 . . . . **TCLC 69**
See also CA 115; DLB 47

Roper, William 1498-1578 . . . . **LC 10**

Roquelaure, A. N.
See Rice, Anne

Rosa, Joao Guimaraes 1908-1967 . . . **CLC 23**
See also CA 89-92; DLB 113

Rose, Wendy
1948- . . . . **CLC 85; DAM MULT; PC 13**
See also CA 53-56; CANR 5, 51; DLB 175;
NNAL; SATA 12

Rosen, R. D.
See Rosen, Richard (Dean)

Rosen, Richard (Dean) 1949- . . . . **CLC 39**
See also CA 77-80; CANR 62;
INT CANR-30

Rosenberg, Isaac 1890-1918 . . . . . . **TCLC 12**
See also CA 107; DLB 20

Rosenblatt, Joe . . . . **CLC 15**
See also Rosenblatt, Joseph

Rosenblatt, Joseph 1933-
See Rosenblatt, Joe
See also CA 89-92; INT 89-92

Rosenfeld, Samuel 1896-1963
See Tzara, Tristan
See also CA 89-92

Rosenstock, Sami
See Tzara, Tristan

Rosenstock, Samuel
See Tzara, Tristan

Rosenthal, M(acha) L(ouis)
1917-1996 . . . . **CLC 28**
See also CA 1-4R; 152; CAAS 6; CANR 4,
51; DLB 5; SATA 59

Ross, Barnaby
See Dannay, Frederic

Ross, Bernard L.
See Follett, Ken(neth Martin)

Ross, J. H.
See Lawrence, T(homas) E(dward)

Ross, Martin
See Martin, Violet Florence
See also DLB 135

Ross, (James) Sinclair
1908- . . . . . . **CLC 13; DAC; DAM MST;
SSC 24**
See also CA 73-76; DLB 88

Rossetti, Christina (Georgina)
1830-1894 . . . . . **NCLC 2, 50; DA; DAB;
DAC; DAM MST, POET; PC 7; WLC**
See also DLB 35, 163; MAICYA; SATA 20

Rossetti, Dante Gabriel
1828-1882 . . . . **NCLC 4; DA; DAB;
DAC; DAM MST, POET; WLC**
See also CDBLB 1832-1890; DLB 35

Rossner, Judith (Perelman)
1935- . . . . **CLC 6, 9, 29**
See also AITN 2; BEST 90:3; CA 17-20R;
CANR 18, 51; DLB 6; INT CANR-18;
MTCW

Rostand, Edmond (Eugene Alexis)
1868-1918 . . . . . . **TCLC 6, 37; DA; DAB;
DAC; DAM DRAM, MST**
See also CA 104; 126; MTCW

Roth, Henry 1906-1995 . . . **CLC 2, 6, 11, 104**
See also CA 11-12; 149; CANR 38; CAP 1;
DLB 28; MTCW

Roth, Philip (Milton)
1933- . . . . . . **CLC 1, 2, 3, 4, 6, 9, 15, 22,
31, 47, 66, 86; DA; DAB; DAC;
DAM MST, NOV, POP; SSC 26; WLC**
See also BEST 90:3; CA 1-4R; CANR 1, 22,
36, 55; CDALB 1968-1988; DLB 2, 28,
173; DLBY 82; MTCW

Rothenberg, Jerome 1931- . . . . **CLC 6, 57**
See also CA 45-48; CANR 1; DLB 5

Roumain, Jacques (Jean Baptiste)
1907-1944 . . . . **TCLC 19; BLC;
DAM MULT**
See also BW 1; CA 117; 125

Rourke, Constance (Mayfield)
1885-1941 . . . . **TCLC 12**
See also CA 107; YABC 1

Rousseau, Jean-Baptiste 1671-1741 . . . **LC 9**

Rousseau, Jean-Jacques
1712-1778 . . . . **LC 14, 36; DA; DAB;
DAC; DAM MST; WLC**

Roussel, Raymond 1877-1933 . . . . . **TCLC 20**
See also CA 117

Rovit, Earl (Herbert) 1927- . . . . **CLC 7**
See also CA 5-8R; CANR 12

Rowe, Nicholas 1674-1718 . . . . **LC 8**
See also DLB 84

Rowley, Ames Dorrance
See Lovecraft, H(oward) P(hillips)

Rowson, Susanna Haswell
1762(?)-1824 . . . . **NCLC 5**
See also DLB 37

Roy, Gabrielle
1909-1983 . . . . **CLC 10, 14; DAB; DAC;
DAM MST**
See also CA 53-56; 110; CANR 5, 61;
DLB 68; MTCW

Rozewicz, Tadeusz
1921- . . . . **CLC 9, 23; DAM POET**
See also CA 108; CANR 36; MTCW

Ruark, Gibbons 1941- . . . . **CLC 3**
See also CA 33-36R; CAAS 23; CANR 14,
31, 57; DLB 120

Rubens, Bernice (Ruth) 1923- . . . **CLC 19, 31**
See also CA 25-28R; CANR 33; DLB 14;
MTCW

Rubin, Harold
See Robbins, Harold

Rudkin, (James) David 1936- . . . . . . **CLC 14**
See also CA 89-92; DLB 13

Rudnik, Raphael 1933- . . . . **CLC 7**
See also CA 29-32R

Ruffian, M.
See Hasek, Jaroslav (Matej Frantisek)

Ruiz, Jose Martinez . . . . **CLC 11**
See also Martinez Ruiz, Jose

Rukeyser, Muriel
1913-1980 . . . . **CLC 6, 10, 15, 27;
DAM POET; PC 12**
See also CA 5-8R; 93-96; CANR 26, 60;
DLB 48; MTCW; SATA-Obit 22

Rule, Jane (Vance) 1931- . . . . **CLC 27**
See also CA 25-28R; CAAS 18; CANR 12;
DLB 60

Rulfo, Juan
1918-1986 . . . . **CLC 8, 80; DAM MULT;
HLC; SSC 25**
See also CA 85-88; 118; CANR 26;
DLB 113; HW; MTCW

Rumi, Jalal al-Din 1297-1373 . . . . **CMLC 20**

Runeberg, Johan 1804-1877 . . . . . . **NCLC 41**

Runyon, (Alfred) Damon
1884(?)-1946 . . . . **TCLC 10**
See also CA 107; DLB 11, 86, 171

Rush, Norman 1933- . . . . **CLC 44**
See also CA 121; 126; INT 126

Rushdie, (Ahmed) Salman
1947- . . . . **CLC 23, 31, 55, 100; DAB;
DAC; DAM MST, NOV, POP; WLCS**
See also BEST 89:3; CA 108; 111;
CANR 33, 56; INT 111; MTCW

Rushforth, Peter (Scott) 1945- . . . . . **CLC 19**
See also CA 101

Ruskin, John 1819-1900 . . . . **TCLC 63**
See also CA 114; 129; CDBLB 1832-1890;
DLB 55, 163; SATA 24

Russ, Joanna 1937- . . . . **CLC 15**
See also CA 25-28R; CANR 11, 31; DLB 8;
MTCW

Russell, George William 1867-1935
See Baker, Jean H.
See also CA 104; 153; CDBLB 1890-1914;
DAM POET

Russell, (Henry) Ken(neth Alfred)
1927- . . . . **CLC 16**
See also CA 105

Russell, Willy 1947- . . . . **CLC 60**

Rutherford, Mark . . . . **TCLC 25**
See also White, William Hale
See also DLB 18

Ruyslinck, Ward 1929- . . . . **CLC 14**
See also Belser, Reimond Karel Maria de

Ryan, Cornelius (John) 1920-1974 . . . **CLC 7**
See also CA 69-72; 53-56; CANR 38

Ryan, Michael 1946- . . . . **CLC 65**
See also CA 49-52; DLBY 82

Ryan, Tim
See Dent, Lester

Rybakov, Anatoli (Naumovich)
1911- . . . . **CLC 23, 53**
See also CA 126; 135; SATA 79

Ryder, Jonathan
See Ludlum, Robert

Ryga, George
1932-1987 . . **CLC 14; DAC; DAM MST**
See also CA 101; 124; CANR 43; DLB 60

S. H.
See Hartmann, Sadakichi

S. S.
See Sassoon, Siegfried (Lorraine)

Saba, Umberto 1883-1957 . . . . **TCLC 33**
See also CA 144; DLB 114

Sabatini, Rafael 1875-1950 . . . . **TCLC 47**

Sabato, Ernesto (R.)
1911- . . . . . . **CLC 10, 23; DAM MULT;**
HLC
See also CA 97-100; CANR 32; DLB 145;
HW; MTCW

Sacastru, Martin
See Bioy Casares, Adolfo

Sacher-Masoch, Leopold von
1836(?)-1895 . . . . **NCLC 31**

Sachs, Marilyn (Stickle) 1927- . . . . . **CLC 35**
See also AAYA 2; CA 17-20R; CANR 13,
47; CLR 2; JRDA; MAICYA; SAAS 2;
SATA 3, 68

Sachs, Nelly 1891-1970 . . . . **CLC 14, 98**
See also CA 17-18; 25-28R; CAP 2

Sackler, Howard (Oliver)
1929-1982 . . . . **CLC 14**
See also CA 61-64; 108; CANR 30; DLB 7

Sacks, Oliver (Wolf) 1933- . . . . **CLC 67**
See also CA 53-56; CANR 28, 50;
INT CANR-28; MTCW

Sadakichi
See Hartmann, Sadakichi

Sade, Donatien Alphonse Francois Comte
1740-1814 . . . . **NCLC 47**

Sadoff, Ira 1945- . . . . **CLC 9**
See also CA 53-56; CANR 5, 21; DLB 120

Saetone
See Camus, Albert

Safire, William 1929- . . . . **CLC 10**
See also CA 17-20R; CANR 31, 54

Sagan, Carl (Edward) 1934-1996 . . . . **CLC 30**
See also AAYA 2; CA 25-28R; 155;
CANR 11, 36; MTCW; SATA 58;
SATA-Obit 94

Sagan, Francoise . . . . **CLC 3, 6, 9, 17, 36**
See also Quoirez, Francoise
See also DLB 83

Sahgal, Nayantara (Pandit) 1927- . . . **CLC 41**
See also CA 9-12R; CANR 11

Saint, H(arry) F. 1941- . . . . **CLC 50**
See also CA 127

St. Aubin de Teran, Lisa 1953-
See Teran, Lisa St. Aubin de
See also CA 118; 126; INT 126

Sainte-Beuve, Charles Augustin
1804-1869 . . . . **NCLC 5**

Saint-Exupery, Antoine (Jean Baptiste Marie Roger) de
1900-1944 . . . . **TCLC 2, 56; DAM NOV;**
WLC
See also CA 108; 132; CLR 10; DLB 72;
MAICYA; MTCW; SATA 20

St. John, David
See Hunt, E(verette) Howard, (Jr.)

Saint-John Perse
See Leger, (Marie-Rene Auguste) Alexis
Saint-Leger

Saintsbury, George (Edward Bateman)
1845-1933 . . . . **TCLC 31**
See also CA 160; DLB 57, 149

Sait Faik . . . . **TCLC 23**
See also Abasiyanik, Sait Faik

Saki . . . . **TCLC 3; SSC 12**
See also Munro, H(ector) H(ugh)

Sala, George Augustus . . . . **NCLC 46**

Salama, Hannu 1936- . . . . **CLC 18**

Salamanca, J(ack) R(ichard)
1922- . . . . **CLC 4, 15**
See also CA 25-28R

Sale, J. Kirkpatrick
See Sale, Kirkpatrick

Sale, Kirkpatrick 1937- . . . . **CLC 68**
See also CA 13-16R; CANR 10

Salinas, Luis Omar
1937- . . . . . **CLC 90; DAM MULT; HLC**
See also CA 131; DLB 82; HW

Salinas (y Serrano), Pedro
1891(?)-1951 . . . . **TCLC 17**
See also CA 117; DLB 134

Salinger, J(erome) D(avid)
1919- . . . . . . **CLC 1, 3, 8, 12, 55, 56; DA;**
DAB; DAC; DAM MST, NOV, POP;
SSC 2, 28; WLC
See also AAYA 2; CA 5-8R; CANR 39;
CDALB 1941-1968; CLR 18; DLB 2, 102,
173; MAICYA; MTCW; SATA 67

Salisbury, John
See Caute, David

Salter, James 1925- . . . . **CLC 7, 52, 59**
See also CA 73-76; DLB 130

Saltus, Edgar (Everton)
1855-1921 . . . . **TCLC 8**
See also CA 105

Saltykov, Mikhail Evgrafovich
1826-1889 . . . . **NCLC 16**

Samarakis, Antonis 1919- . . . . **CLC 5**
See also CA 25-28R; CAAS 16; CANR 36

Sanchez, Florencio 1875-1910 . . . . . **TCLC 37**
See also CA 153; HW

Sanchez, Luis Rafael 1936- . . . . **CLC 23**
See also CA 128; DLB 145; HW

Sanchez, Sonia
1934- . . . . . . **CLC 5; BLC; DAM MULT;**
PC 9
See also BW 2; CA 33-36R; CANR 24, 49;
CLR 18; DLB 41; DLBD 8; MAICYA;
MTCW; SATA 22

Sand, George
1804-1876 . . . . **NCLC 2, 42, 57; DA;**
DAB; DAC; DAM MST, NOV; WLC
See also DLB 119

Sandburg, Carl (August)
1878-1967 . . . . **CLC 1, 4, 10, 15, 35; DA;**
DAB; DAC; DAM MST, POET; PC 2;
WLC
See also CA 5-8R; 25-28R; CANR 35;
CDALB 1865-1917; DLB 17, 54;
MAICYA; MTCW; SATA 8

Sandburg, Charles
See Sandburg, Carl (August)

Sandburg, Charles A.
See Sandburg, Carl (August)

Sanders, (James) Ed(ward) 1939- . . . **CLC 53**
See also CA 13-16R; CAAS 21; CANR 13,
44; DLB 16

Sanders, Lawrence
1920- . . . . **CLC 41; DAM POP**
See also BEST 89:4; CA 81-84; CANR 33,
62; MTCW

Sanders, Noah
See Blount, Roy (Alton), Jr.

Sanders, Winston P.
See Anderson, Poul (William)

Sandoz, Mari(e Susette)
1896-1966 . . . . **CLC 28**
See also CA 1-4R; 25-28R; CANR 17;
DLB 9; MTCW; SATA 5

Saner, Reg(inald Anthony) 1931- . . . . **CLC 9**
See also CA 65-68

Sannazaro, Jacopo 1456(?)-1530 . . . . . . **LC 8**

Sansom, William
1912-1976 . . . . . . **CLC 2, 6; DAM NOV;**
SSC 21
See also CA 5-8R; 65-68; CANR 42;
DLB 139; MTCW

Santayana, George 1863-1952 . . . . . **TCLC 40**
See also CA 115; DLB 54, 71; DLBD 13

Santiago, Danny . . . . **CLC 33**
See also James, Daniel (Lewis)
See also DLB 122

Santmyer, Helen Hoover
1895-1986 . . . . **CLC 33**
See also CA 1-4R; 118; CANR 15, 33;
DLBY 84; MTCW

Santoka, Taneda 1882-1940 . . . . **TCLC 72**

Santos, Bienvenido N(uqui)
1911-1996 . . . . . . **CLC 22; DAM MULT**
See also CA 101; 151; CANR 19, 46

Sapper . . . . **TCLC 44**
See also McNeile, Herman Cyril

Sapphire 1950- . . . . **CLC 99**

Sappho
fl. 6th cent. B.C.- . . . . **CMLC 3;**
DAM POET; PC 5
See also DLB 176

Sarduy, Severo 1937-1993 . . . . **CLC 6, 97**
See also CA 89-92; 142; CANR 58;
DLB 113; HW

Sargeson, Frank 1903-1982 . . . . **CLC 31**
See also CA 25-28R; 106; CANR 38

Sarmiento, Felix Ruben Garcia
See Dario, Ruben

Saroyan, William
1908-1981 ..... **CLC 1, 8, 10, 29, 34, 56;
DA; DAB; DAC; DAM DRAM, MST,
NOV; SSC 21; WLC**
See also CA 5-8R; 103; CANR 30; DLB 7,
9, 86; DLBY 81; MTCW; SATA 23;
SATA-Obit 24

Sarraute, Nathalie
1900- ...... **CLC 1, 2, 4, 8, 10, 31, 80**
See also CA 9-12R; CANR 23; DLB 83;
MTCW

Sarton, (Eleanor) May
1912-1995 .... **CLC 4, 14, 49, 91;
DAM POET**
See also CA 1-4R; 149; CANR 1, 34, 55;
DLB 48; DLBY 81; INT CANR-34;
MTCW; SATA 36; SATA-Obit 86

Sartre, Jean-Paul
1905-1980 .... **CLC 1, 4, 7, 9, 13, 18, 24,
44, 50, 52; DA; DAB; DAC;
DAM DRAM, MST, NOV; DC 3; WLC**
See also CA 9-12R; 97-100; CANR 21;
DLB 72; MTCW

Sassoon, Siegfried (Lorraine)
1886-1967 .... **CLC 36; DAB;
DAM MST, NOV, POET; PC 12**
See also CA 104; 25-28R; CANR 36;
DLB 20; MTCW

Satterfield, Charles
See Pohl, Frederik

Saul, John (W. III)
1942- ...... **CLC 46; DAM NOV, POP**
See also AAYA 10; BEST 90:4; CA 81-84;
CANR 16, 40

Saunders, Caleb
See Heinlein, Robert A(nson)

Saura (Atares), Carlos 1932- .... **CLC 20**
See also CA 114; 131; HW

Sauser-Hall, Frederic 1887-1961.... **CLC 18**
See Cendrars, Blaise
See also CA 102; 93-96; CANR 36, 62;
MTCW

Saussure, Ferdinand de
1857-1913 .... **TCLC 49**

Savage, Catharine
See Brosman, Catharine Savage

Savage, Thomas 1915- .... **CLC 40**
See also CA 126; 132; CAAS 15; INT 132

Savan, Glenn 19(?)- .... **CLC 50**

Sayers, Dorothy L(eigh)
1893-1957 ..... **TCLC 2, 15; DAM POP**
See also CA 104; 119; CANR 60;
CDBLB 1914-1945; DLB 10, 36, 77, 100;
MTCW

Sayers, Valerie 1952- .... **CLC 50**
See also CA 134; CANR 61

Sayles, John (Thomas)
1950- .... **CLC 7, 10, 14**
See also CA 57-60; CANR 41; DLB 44

Scammell, Michael 1935- .... **CLC 34**
See also CA 156

Scannell, Vernon 1922- .... **CLC 49**
See also CA 5-8R; CANR 8, 24, 57;
DLB 27; SATA 59

Scarlett, Susan
See Streatfeild, (Mary) Noel

Schaeffer, Susan Fromberg
1941- .... **CLC 6, 11, 22**
See also CA 49-52; CANR 18; DLB 28;
MTCW; SATA 22

Schary, Jill
See Robinson, Jill

Schell, Jonathan 1943- .... **CLC 35**
See also CA 73-76; CANR 12

Schelling, Friedrich Wilhelm Joseph von
1775-1854 .... **NCLC 30**
See also DLB 90

Schendel, Arthur van 1874-1946... **TCLC 56**

Scherer, Jean-Marie Maurice 1920-
See Rohmer, Eric
See also CA 110

Schevill, James (Erwin) 1920- .... **CLC 7**
See also CA 5-8R; CAAS 12

Schiller, Friedrich
1759-1805 .... **NCLC 39; DAM DRAM**
See also DLB 94

Schisgal, Murray (Joseph) 1926-..... **CLC 6**
See also CA 21-24R; CANR 48

Schlee, Ann 1934-................. **CLC 35**
See also CA 101; CANR 29; SATA 44;
SATA-Brief 36

Schlegel, August Wilhelm von
1767-1845 .... **NCLC 15**
See also DLB 94

Schlegel, Friedrich 1772-1829 .... **NCLC 45**
See also DLB 90

Schlegel, Johann Elias (von)
1719(?)-1749 .... **LC 5**

Schlesinger, Arthur M(eier), Jr.
1917- .... **CLC 84**
See also AITN 1; CA 1-4R; CANR 1, 28,
58; DLB 17; INT CANR-28; MTCW;
SATA 61

Schmidt, Arno (Otto) 1914-1979 .... **CLC 56**
See also CA 128; 109; DLB 69

Schmitz, Aron Hector 1861-1928
See Svevo, Italo
See also CA 104; 122; MTCW

Schnackenberg, Gjertrud 1953-..... **CLC 40**
See also CA 116; DLB 120

Schneider, Leonard Alfred 1925-1966
See Bruce, Lenny
See also CA 89-92

Schnitzler, Arthur
1862-1931 .... **TCLC 4; SSC 15**
See also CA 104; DLB 81, 118

Schoenberg, Arnold 1874-1951 .... **TCLC 75**
See also CA 109

Schonberg, Arnold
See Schoenberg, Arnold

Schopenhauer, Arthur
1788-1860 .... **NCLC 51**
See also DLB 90

Schor, Sandra (M.) 1932(?)-1990 ... **CLC 65**
See also CA 132

Schorer, Mark 1908-1977 .... **CLC 9**
See also CA 5-8R; 73-76; CANR 7;
DLB 103

Schrader, Paul (Joseph) 1946-...... **CLC 26**
See also CA 37-40R; CANR 41; DLB 44

Schreiner, Olive (Emilie Albertina)
1855-1920 .... **TCLC 9**
See also CA 105; DLB 18, 156

Schulberg, Budd (Wilson)
1914- .... **CLC 7, 48**
See also CA 25-28R; CANR 19; DLB 6, 26,
28; DLBY 81

Schulz, Bruno
1892-1942 .... **TCLC 5, 51; SSC 13**
See also CA 115; 123

Schulz, Charles M(onroe) 1922- .... **CLC 12**
See also CA 9-12R; CANR 6;
INT CANR-6; SATA 10

Schumacher, E(rnst) F(riedrich)
1911-1977 .... **CLC 80**
See also CA 81-84; 73-76; CANR 34

Schuyler, James Marcus
1923-1991 ..... **CLC 5, 23; DAM POET**
See also CA 101; 134; DLB 5, 169; INT 101

Schwartz, Delmore (David)
1913-1966 ... **CLC 2, 4, 10, 45, 87; PC 8**
See also CA 17-18; 25-28R; CANR 35;
CAP 2; DLB 28, 48; MTCW

Schwartz, Ernst
See Ozu, Yasujiro

Schwartz, John Burnham 1965- .... **CLC 59**
See also CA 132

Schwartz, Lynne Sharon 1939-..... **CLC 31**
See also CA 103; CANR 44

Schwartz, Muriel A.
See Eliot, T(homas) S(tearns)

Schwarz-Bart, Andre 1928-....... **CLC 2, 4**
See also CA 89-92

Schwarz-Bart, Simone 1938-....... **CLC 7**
See also BW 2; CA 97-100

Schwob, (Mayer Andre) Marcel
1867-1905 .... **TCLC 20**
See also CA 117; DLB 123

Sciascia, Leonardo
1921-1989 .... **CLC 8, 9, 41**
See also CA 85-88; 130; CANR 35;
DLB 177; MTCW

Scoppettone, Sandra 1936-........ **CLC 26**
See also AAYA 11; CA 5-8R; CANR 41;
SATA 9, 92

Scorsese, Martin 1942- .... **CLC 20, 89**
See also CA 110; 114; CANR 46

Scotland, Jay
See Jakes, John (William)

Scott, Duncan Campbell
1862-1947 .... **TCLC 6; DAC**
See also CA 104; 153; DLB 92

Scott, Evelyn 1893-1963.......... **CLC 43**
See also CA 104; 112; DLB 9, 48

Scott, F(rancis) R(eginald)
1899-1985 .... **CLC 22**
See also CA 101; 114; DLB 88; INT 101

Scott, Frank
See Scott, F(rancis) R(eginald)

Scott, Joanna 1960- .... **CLC 50**
See also CA 126; CANR 53

Scott, Paul (Mark) 1920-1978.... **CLC 9, 60**
See also CA 81-84; 77-80; CANR 33;
DLB 14; MTCW

Scott, Walter
1771-1832 .... NCLC 15; DA; DAB;
DAC; DAM MST, NOV, POET; PC 13;
WLC
See also AAYA 22; CDBLB 1789-1832;
DLB 93, 107, 116, 144, 159; YABC 2

Scribe, (Augustin) Eugene
1791-1861 .... NCLC 16; DAM DRAM;
DC 5

Scrum, R.
See Crumb, R(obert)

Scudery, Madeleine de 1607-1701..... LC 2

Scum
See Crumb, R(obert)

Scumbag, Little Bobby
See Crumb, R(obert)

Seabrook, John
See Hubbard, L(afayette) Ron(ald)

Sealy, I. Allan 1951- .... CLC 55

Search, Alexander
See Pessoa, Fernando (Antonio Nogueira)

Sebastian, Lee
See Silverberg, Robert

Sebastian Owl
See Thompson, Hunter S(tockton)

Sebestyen, Ouida 1924- .... CLC 30
See also AAYA 8; CA 107; CANR 40;
CLR 17; JRDA; MAICYA; SAAS 10;
SATA 39

Secundus, H. Scriblerus
See Fielding, Henry

Sedges, John
See Buck, Pearl S(ydenstricker)

Sedgwick, Catharine Maria
1789-1867 .... NCLC 19
See also DLB 1, 74

Seelye, John 1931- .... CLC 7

Seferiades, Giorgos Stylianou 1900-1971
See Seferis, George
See also CA 5-8R; 33-36R; CANR 5, 36;
MTCW

Seferis, George .... CLC 5, 11
See also Seferiades, Giorgos Stylianou

Segal, Erich (Wolf)
1937- .... CLC 3, 10; DAM POP
See also BEST 89:1; CA 25-28R; CANR 20,
36; DLBY 86; INT CANR-20; MTCW

Seger, Bob 1945-................. CLC 35

Seghers, Anna .... CLC 7
See also Radvanyi, Netty
See also DLB 69

Seidel, Frederick (Lewis) 1936-..... CLC 18
See also CA 13-16R; CANR 8; DLBY 84

Seifert, Jaroslav
1901-1986 .... CLC 34, 44, 93
See also CA 127; MTCW

Sei Shonagon c. 966-1017(?) ...... CMLC 6

Selby, Hubert, Jr.
1928- .... CLC 1, 2, 4, 8; SSC 20
See also CA 13-16R; CANR 33; DLB 2

Selzer, Richard 1928-............. CLC 74
See also CA 65-68; CANR 14

Sembene, Ousmane
See Ousmane, Sembene

Senancour, Etienne Pivert de
1770-1846 .... NCLC 16
See also DLB 119

Sender, Ramon (Jose)
1902-1982 .. CLC 8; DAM MULT; HLC
See also CA 5-8R; 105; CANR 8; HW;
MTCW

Seneca, Lucius Annaeus
4B.C.-65...... CMLC 6; DAM DRAM;
DC 5

Senghor, Leopold Sedar
1906- ..... CLC 54; BLC; DAM MULT,
POET
See also BW 2; CA 116; 125; CANR 47;
MTCW

Serling, (Edward) Rod(man)
1924-1975 .... CLC 30
See also AAYA 14; AITN 1; CA 65-68;
57-60; DLB 26

Serna, Ramon Gomez de la
See Gomez de la Serna, Ramon

Serpieres
See Guillevic, (Eugene)

Service, Robert
See Service, Robert W(illiam)
See also DAB; DLB 92

Service, Robert W(illiam)
1874(?)-1958 ...... TCLC 15; DA; DAC;
DAM MST, POET; WLC
See also Service, Robert
See also CA 115; 140; SATA 20

Seth, Vikram
1952- .... CLC 43, 90; DAM MULT
See also CA 121; 127; CANR 50; DLB 120;
INT 127

Seton, Cynthia Propper
1926-1982 .... CLC 27
See also CA 5-8R; 108; CANR 7

Seton, Ernest (Evan) Thompson
1860-1946 .... TCLC 31
See also CA 109; DLB 92; DLBD 13;
JRDA; SATA 18

Seton-Thompson, Ernest
See Seton, Ernest (Evan) Thompson

Settle, Mary Lee 1918- .... CLC 19, 61
See also CA 89-92; CAAS 1; CANR 44;
DLB 6; INT 89-92

Seuphor, Michel
See Arp, Jean

**Sevigne, Marie (de Rabutin-Chantal) Marquise
de** 1626-1696 .... LC 11

Sewall, Samuel 1652-1730.......... LC 38
See also DLB 24

Sexton, Anne (Harvey)
1928-1974 .... CLC 2, 4, 6, 8, 10, 15, 53;
DA; DAB; DAC; DAM MST, POET;
PC 2; WLC
See also CA 1-4R; 53-56; CABS 2;
CANR 3, 36; CDALB 1941-1968; DLB 5,
169; MTCW; SATA 10

Shaara, Michael (Joseph, Jr.)
1929-1988 .... CLC 15; DAM POP
See also AITN 1; CA 102; 125; CANR 52;
DLBY 83

Shackleton, C. C.
See Aldiss, Brian W(ilson)

Shacochis, Bob .... CLC 39
See also Shacochis, Robert G.

Shacochis, Robert G. 1951-
See Shacochis, Bob
See also CA 119; 124; INT 124

Shaffer, Anthony (Joshua)
1926- .... CLC 19; DAM DRAM
See also CA 110; 116; DLB 13

Shaffer, Peter (Levin)
1926- ...... CLC 5, 14, 18, 37, 60; DAB;
DAM DRAM, MST; DC 7
See also CA 25-28R; CANR 25, 47;
CDBLB 1960 to Present; DLB 13;
MTCW

Shakey, Bernard
See Young, Neil

Shalamov, Varlam (Tikhonovich)
1907(?)-1982 .... CLC 18
See also CA 129; 105

Shamlu, Ahmad 1925- .... CLC 10

Shammas, Anton 1951-............ CLC 55

Shange, Ntozake
1948- .... CLC 8, 25, 38, 74; BLC;
DAM DRAM, MULT; DC 3
See also AAYA 9; BW 2; CA 85-88;
CABS 3; CANR 27, 48; DLB 38; MTCW

Shanley, John Patrick 1950-....... CLC 75
See also CA 128; 133

Shapcott, Thomas W(illiam) 1935-.. CLC 38
See also CA 69-72; CANR 49

**Shapiro, Jane..................... CLC 76

Shapiro, Karl (Jay) 1913- .. CLC 4, 8, 15, 53
See also CA 1-4R; CAAS 6; CANR 1, 36;
DLB 48; MTCW

Sharp, William 1855-1905........ TCLC 39
See also CA 160; DLB 156

Sharpe, Thomas Ridley 1928-
See Sharpe, Tom
See also CA 114; 122; INT 122

**Sharpe, Tom..................... CLC 36
See also Sharpe, Thomas Ridley
See also DLB 14

**Shaw, Bernard.................... TCLC 45
See also Shaw, George Bernard
See also BW 1

Shaw, G. Bernard
See Shaw, George Bernard

Shaw, George Bernard
1856-1950 ... TCLC 3, 9, 21; DA; DAB;
DAC; DAM DRAM, MST; WLC
See also Shaw, Bernard
See also CA 104; 128; CDBLB 1914-1945;
DLB 10, 57; MTCW

Shaw, Henry Wheeler
1818-1885 .... NCLC 15
See also DLB 11

Shaw, Irwin
1913-1984 .... CLC 7, 23, 34;
DAM DRAM, POP
See also AITN 1; CA 13-16R; 112;
CANR 21; CDALB 1941-1968; DLB 6,
102; DLBY 84; MTCW

Shaw, Robert 1927-1978 .... CLC 5
See also AITN 1; CA 1-4R; 81-84;
CANR 4; DLB 13, 14

Shaw, T. E.
See Lawrence, T(homas) E(dward)

Shawn, Wallace 1943- .... **CLC 41**
See also CA 112

Shea, Lisa 1953-................. **CLC 86**
See also CA 147

Sheed, Wilfrid (John Joseph)
1930- .... **CLC 2, 4, 10, 53**
See also CA 65-68; CANR 30; DLB 6;
MTCW

Sheldon, Alice Hastings Bradley
1915(?)-1987
See Tiptree, James, Jr.
See also CA 108; 122; CANR 34; INT 108;
MTCW

Sheldon, John
See Bloch, Robert (Albert)

Shelley, Mary Wollstonecraft (Godwin)
1797-1851 .... **NCLC 14, 59; DA; DAB;
DAC; DAM MST, NOV; WLC**
See also AAYA 20; CDBLB 1789-1832;
DLB 110, 116, 159, 178; SATA 29

Shelley, Percy Bysshe
1792-1822 .... **NCLC 18; DA; DAB;
DAC; DAM MST, POET; PC 14; WLC**
See also CDBLB 1789-1832; DLB 96, 110,
158

Shepard, Jim 1956-................ **CLC 36**
See also CA 137; CANR 59; SATA 90

Shepard, Lucius 1947- .... **CLC 34**
See also CA 128; 141

Shepard, Sam
1943- .... **CLC 4, 6, 17, 34, 41, 44;
DAM DRAM; DC 5**
See also AAYA 1; CA 69-72; CABS 3;
CANR 22; DLB 7; MTCW

Shepherd, Michael
See Ludlum, Robert

Sherburne, Zoa (Morin) 1912-...... **CLC 30**
See also AAYA 13; CA 1-4R; CANR 3, 37;
MAICYA; SAAS 18; SATA 3

Sheridan, Frances 1724-1766........ **LC 7**
See also DLB 39, 84

Sheridan, Richard Brinsley
1751-1816 .... **NCLC 5; DA; DAB;
DAC; DAM DRAM, MST; DC 1; WLC**
See also CDBLB 1660-1789; DLB 89

Sherman, Jonathan Marc........... **CLC 55**

Sherman, Martin 1941(?)- .... **CLC 19**
See also CA 116; 123

Sherwin, Judith Johnson 1936-... **CLC 7, 15**
See also CA 25-28R; CANR 34

Sherwood, Frances 1940-.......... **CLC 81**
See also CA 146

Sherwood, Robert E(mmet)
1896-1955 ...... **TCLC 3; DAM DRAM**
See also CA 104; 153; DLB 7, 26

Shestov, Lev 1866-1938.......... **TCLC 56**

Shevchenko, Taras 1814-1861 .... **NCLC 54**

Shiel, M(atthew) P(hipps)
1865-1947 .... **TCLC 8**
See also Holmes, Gordon
See also CA 106; 160; DLB 153

Shields, Carol 1935-......... **CLC 91; DAC**
See also CA 81-84; CANR 51

Shields, David 1956-.............. **CLC 97**
See also CA 124; CANR 48

Shiga, Naoya 1883-1971... **CLC 33; SSC 23**
See also CA 101; 33-36R; DLB 180

Shilts, Randy 1951-1994 .... **CLC 85**
See also AAYA 19; CA 115; 127; 144;
CANR 45; INT 127

Shimazaki, Haruki 1872-1943
See Shimazaki Toson
See also CA 105; 134

Shimazaki Toson 1872-1943 .... **TCLC 5**
See also Shimazaki, Haruki
See also DLB 180

Sholokhov, Mikhail (Aleksandrovich)
1905-1984 .... **CLC 7, 15**
See also CA 101; 112; MTCW;
SATA-Obit 36

Shone, Patric
See Hanley, James

Shreve, Susan Richards 1939-...... **CLC 23**
See also CA 49-52; CAAS 5; CANR 5, 38;
MAICYA; SATA 46, 95; SATA-Brief 41

Shue, Larry
1946-1985 ...... **CLC 52; DAM DRAM**
See also CA 145; 117

Shu-Jen, Chou 1881-1936
See Lu Hsun
See also CA 104

Shulman, Alix Kates 1932- ...... **CLC 2, 10**
See also CA 29-32R; CANR 43; SATA 7

Shuster, Joe 1914- .... **CLC 21**

Shute, Nevil..................... **CLC 30**
See also Norway, Nevil Shute

Shuttle, Penelope (Diane) 1947- ..... **CLC 7**
See also CA 93-96; CANR 39; DLB 14, 40

Sidney, Mary 1561-1621 .... **LC 19, 39**

Sidney, Sir Philip
1554-1586 .... **LC 19, 39; DA; DAB;
DAC; DAM MST, POET**
See also CDBLB Before 1660; DLB 167

Siegel, Jerome 1914-1996 .... **CLC 21**
See also CA 116; 151

Siegel, Jerry
See Siegel, Jerome

Sienkiewicz, Henryk (Adam Alexander Pius)
1846-1916 .... **TCLC 3**
See also CA 104; 134

Sierra, Gregorio Martinez
See Martinez Sierra, Gregorio

Sierra, Maria (de la O'LeJarraga) Martinez
See Martinez Sierra, Maria (de la
O'LeJarraga)

Sigal, Clancy 1926-............... **CLC 7**
See also CA 1-4R

Sigourney, Lydia Howard (Huntley)
1791-1865 .... **NCLC 21**
See also DLB 1, 42, 73

Siguenza y Gongora, Carlos de
1645-1700 .... **LC 8**

Sigurjonsson, Johann 1880-1919... **TCLC 27**

Sikelianos, Angelos 1884-1951 .... **TCLC 39**

Silkin, Jon 1930- .... **CLC 2, 6, 43**
See also CA 5-8R; CAAS 5; DLB 27

Silko, Leslie (Marmon)
1948- .... **CLC 23, 74; DA; DAC;
DAM MST, MULT, POP; WLCS**
See also AAYA 14; CA 115; 122;
CANR 45; DLB 143, 175; NNAL

Sillanpaa, Frans Eemil 1888-1964... **CLC 19**
See also CA 129; 93-96; MTCW

Sillitoe, Alan
1928- .... **CLC 1, 3, 6, 10, 19, 57**
See also AITN 1; CA 9-12R; CAAS 2;
CANR 8, 26, 55; CDBLB 1960 to
Present; DLB 14, 139; MTCW; SATA 61

Silone, Ignazio 1900-1978 .... **CLC 4**
See also CA 25-28; 81-84; CANR 34;
CAP 2; MTCW

Silver, Joan Micklin 1935- .... **CLC 20**
See also CA 114; 121; INT 121

Silver, Nicholas
See Faust, Frederick (Schiller)

Silverberg, Robert
1935-............. **CLC 7; DAM POP**
See also CA 1-4R; CAAS 3; CANR 1, 20,
36; DLB 8; INT CANR-20; MAICYA;
MTCW; SATA 13, 91

Silverstein, Alvin 1933-........... **CLC 17**
See also CA 49-52; CANR 2; CLR 25;
JRDA; MAICYA; SATA 8, 69

Silverstein, Virginia B(arbara Opshelor)
1937-...................... **CLC 17**
See also CA 49-52; CANR 2; CLR 25;
JRDA; MAICYA; SATA 8, 69

Sim, Georges
See Simenon, Georges (Jacques Christian)

Simak, Clifford D(onald)
1904-1988 .... **CLC 1, 55**
See also CA 1-4R; 125; CANR 1, 35;
DLB 8; MTCW; SATA-Obit 56

Simenon, Georges (Jacques Christian)
1903-1989 .... **CLC 1, 2, 3, 8, 18, 47;
DAM POP**
See also CA 85-88; 129; CANR 35;
DLB 72; DLBY 89; MTCW

Simic, Charles
1938-............ **CLC 6, 9, 22, 49, 68;
DAM POET**
See also CA 29-32R; CAAS 4; CANR 12,
33, 52, 61; DLB 105

Simmel, Georg 1858-1918 .... **TCLC 64**
See also CA 157

Simmons, Charles (Paul) 1924-..... **CLC 57**
See also CA 89-92; INT 89-92

Simmons, Dan 1948-... **CLC 44; DAM POP**
See also AAYA 16; CA 138; CANR 53

Simmons, James (Stewart Alexander)
1933-...................... **CLC 43**
See also CA 105; CAAS 21; DLB 40

Simms, William Gilmore
1806-1870 .... **NCLC 3**
See also DLB 3, 30, 59, 73

Simon, Carly 1945-............... **CLC 26**
See also CA 105

Simon, Claude
1913- .... **CLC 4, 9, 15, 39; DAM NOV**
See also CA 89-92; CANR 33; DLB 83;
MTCW

Snodgrass, W(illiam) D(e Witt)
    1926-. . . . . **CLC 2, 6, 10, 18, 68;**
                                    DAM POET
    See also CA 1-4R; CANR 6, 36; DLB 5;
    MTCW

Snow, C(harles) P(ercy)
    1905-1980 . . . . . . **CLC 1, 4, 6, 9, 13, 19;**
                                    DAM NOV
    See also CA 5-8R; 101; CANR 28;
    CDBLB 1945-1960; DLB 15, 77; MTCW

Snow, Frances Compton
    See Adams, Henry (Brooks)

Snyder, Gary (Sherman)
    1930-. . **CLC 1, 2, 5, 9, 32; DAM POET**
    See also CA 17-20R; CANR 30, 60; DLB 5,
    16, 165

Snyder, Zilpha Keatley   1927-. . . . . . **CLC 17**
    See also AAYA 15; CA 9-12R; CANR 38;
    CLR 31; JRDA; MAICYA; SAAS 2;
    SATA 1, 28, 75

Soares, Bernardo
    See Pessoa, Fernando (Antonio Nogueira)

Sobh, A.
    See Shamlu, Ahmad

Sobol, Joshua. . . . . **CLC 60**

Soderberg, Hjalmar   1869-1941 . . . . **TCLC 39**

Sodergran, Edith (Irene)
    See Soedergran, Edith (Irene)

Soedergran, Edith (Irene)
    1892-1923 . . . . **TCLC 31**

Softly, Edgar
    See Lovecraft, H(oward) P(hillips)

Softly, Edward
    See Lovecraft, H(oward) P(hillips)

Sokolov, Raymond   1941-. . . . . **CLC 7**
    See also CA 85-88

Solo, Jay
    See Ellison, Harlan (Jay)

Sologub, Fyodor . . . . **TCLC 9**
    See also Teternikov, Fyodor Kuzmich

Solomons, Ikey Esquir
    See Thackeray, William Makepeace

Solomos, Dionysios   1798-1857 . . . **NCLC 15**

Solwoska, Mara
    See French, Marilyn

Solzhenitsyn, Aleksandr I(sayevich)
    1918-. . . . . . **CLC 1, 2, 4, 7, 9, 10, 18, 26,**
        34, 78; DA; DAB; DAC; DAM MST,
                                    NOV; WLC
    See also AITN 1; CA 69-72; CANR 40;
    MTCW

Somers, Jane
    See Lessing, Doris (May)

Somerville, Edith   1858-1949 . . . . . . **TCLC 51**
    See also DLB 135

Somerville & Ross
    See Martin, Violet Florence; Somerville,
    Edith

Sommer, Scott   1951-. . . . . **CLC 25**
    See also CA 106

Sondheim, Stephen (Joshua)
    1930-. . . . . . **CLC 30, 39; DAM DRAM**
    See also AAYA 11; CA 103; CANR 47

Sontag, Susan
    1933-. . . . . **CLC 1, 2, 10, 13, 31;**
                                    DAM POP
    See also CA 17-20R; CANR 25, 51; DLB 2,
    67; MTCW

Sophocles
    496(?)B.C.-406(?)B.C.. . . . **CMLC 2; DA;**
        DAB; DAC; DAM DRAM, MST; DC 1;
                                    WLCS
    See also DLB 176

Sordello   1189-1269. . . . . **CMLC 15**

Sorel, Julia
    See Drexler, Rosalyn

Sorrentino, Gilbert
    1929-. . . . . **CLC 3, 7, 14, 22, 40**
    See also CA 77-80; CANR 14, 33; DLB 5,
    173; DLBY 80; INT CANR-14

Soto, Gary
    1952-. . . . . . . **CLC 32, 80; DAM MULT;**
                                    HLC
    See also AAYA 10; CA 119; 125;
    CANR 50; CLR 38; DLB 82; HW;
    INT 125; JRDA; SATA 80

Soupault, Philippe   1897-1990 . . . . . . **CLC 68**
    See also CA 116; 147; 131

Souster, (Holmes) Raymond
    1921-. . . **CLC 5, 14; DAC; DAM POET**
    See also CA 13-16R; CAAS 14; CANR 13,
    29, 53; DLB 88; SATA 63

Southern, Terry   1924(?)-1995 . . . . . . **CLC 7**
    See also CA 1-4R; 150; CANR 1, 55;
    DLB 2

Southey, Robert   1774-1843 . . . . **NCLC 8**
    See also DLB 93, 107, 142; SATA 54

Southworth, Emma Dorothy Eliza Nevitte
    1819-1899 . . . . **NCLC 26**

Souza, Ernest
    See Scott, Evelyn

Soyinka, Wole
    1934-. . . . . . . **CLC 3, 5, 14, 36, 44; BLC;**
        DA; DAB; DAC; DAM DRAM, MST,
                                    MULT; DC 2; WLC
    See also BW 2; CA 13-16R; CANR 27, 39;
    DLB 125; MTCW

Spackman, W(illiam) M(ode)
    1905-1990 . . . . **CLC 46**
    See also CA 81-84; 132

Spacks, Barry (Bernard)   1931-. . . . . . **CLC 14**
    See also CA 154; CANR 33; DLB 105

Spanidou, Irini   1946-. . . . . **CLC 44**

Spark, Muriel (Sarah)
    1918-. . . . . **CLC 2, 3, 5, 8, 13, 18, 40, 94;**
        DAB; DAC; DAM MST, NOV; SSC 10
    See also CA 5-8R; CANR 12, 36;
    CDBLB 1945-1960; DLB 15, 139;
    INT CANR-12; MTCW

Spaulding, Douglas
    See Bradbury, Ray (Douglas)

Spaulding, Leonard
    See Bradbury, Ray (Douglas)

Spence, J. A. D.
    See Eliot, T(homas) S(tearns)

Spencer, Elizabeth   1921-. . . . . **CLC 22**
    See also CA 13-16R; CANR 32; DLB 6;
    MTCW; SATA 14

Spencer, Leonard G.
    See Silverberg, Robert

Spencer, Scott   1945-. . . . . **CLC 30**
    See also CA 113; CANR 51; DLBY 86

Spender, Stephen (Harold)
    1909-1995 . . . . . . **CLC 1, 2, 5, 10, 41, 91;**
                                    DAM POET
    See also CA 9-12R; 149; CANR 31, 54;
    CDBLB 1945-1960; DLB 20; MTCW

Spengler, Oswald (Arnold Gottfried)
    1880-1936 . . . . **TCLC 25**
    See also CA 118

Spenser, Edmund
    1552(?)-1599 . . . . . . **LC 5, 39; DA; DAB;**
        DAC; DAM MST, POET; PC 8; WLC
    See also CDBLB Before 1660; DLB 167

Spicer, Jack
    1925-1965 . . . . **CLC 8, 18, 72;**
                                    DAM POET
    See also CA 85-88; DLB 5, 16

Spiegelman, Art   1948-. . . . . **CLC 76**
    See also AAYA 10; CA 125; CANR 41, 55

Spielberg, Peter   1929-. . . . . **CLC 6**
    See also CA 5-8R; CANR 4, 48; DLBY 81

Spielberg, Steven   1947-. . . . . **CLC 20**
    See also AAYA 8; CA 77-80; CANR 32;
    SATA 32

Spillane, Frank Morrison   1918-
    See Spillane, Mickey
    See also CA 25-28R; CANR 28; MTCW;
    SATA 66

Spillane, Mickey . . . . **CLC 3, 13**
    See also Spillane, Frank Morrison

Spinoza, Benedictus de   1632-1677 . . . . **LC 9**

Spinrad, Norman (Richard)   1940-. . . **CLC 46**
    See also CA 37-40R; CAAS 19; CANR 20;
    DLB 8; INT CANR-20

Spitteler, Carl (Friedrich Georg)
    1845-1924 . . . . **TCLC 12**
    See also CA 109; DLB 129

Spivack, Kathleen (Romola Drucker)
    1938-. . . . . **CLC 6**
    See also CA 49-52

Spoto, Donald   1941-. . . . . **CLC 39**
    See also CA 65-68; CANR 11, 57

Springsteen, Bruce (F.)   1949-. . . . . . **CLC 17**
    See also CA 111

Spurling, Hilary   1940-. . . . . **CLC 34**
    See also CA 104; CANR 25, 52

Spyker, John Howland
    See Elman, Richard

Squires, (James) Radcliffe
    1917-1993 . . . . **CLC 51**
    See also CA 1-4R; 140; CANR 6, 21

Srivastava, Dhanpat Rai   1880(?)-1936
    See Premchand
    See also CA 118

Stacy, Donald
    See Pohl, Frederik

Stael, Germaine de
    See Stael-Holstein, Anne Louise Germaine
    Necker Baronn
    See also DLB 119

Sylvia
See Ashton-Warner, Sylvia (Constance)

Symmes, Robert Edward
See Duncan, Robert (Edward)

Symonds, John Addington
1840-1893 .... **NCLC 34**
See also DLB 57, 144

Symons, Arthur 1865-1945 .... **TCLC 11**
See also CA 107; DLB 19, 57, 149

Symons, Julian (Gustave)
1912-1994 .... **CLC 2, 14, 32**
See also CA 49-52; 147; CAAS 3; CANR 3,
33, 59; DLB 87, 155; DLBY 92; MTCW

Synge, (Edmund) J(ohn) M(illington)
1871-1909 .... **TCLC 6, 37;**
DAM DRAM; DC 2
See also CA 104; 141; CDBLB 1890-1914;
DLB 10, 19

Syruc, J.
See Milosz, Czeslaw

Szirtes, George 1948-............ **CLC 46**
See also CA 109; CANR 27, 61

Szymborska, Wislawa 1923-....... **CLC 99**
See also CA 154; DLBY 96

T. O., Nik
See Annensky, Innokenty (Fyodorovich)

Tabori, George 1914-............ **CLC 19**
See also CA 49-52; CANR 4

Tagore, Rabindranath
1861-1941 .... **TCLC 3, 53;**
DAM DRAM, POET; PC 8
See also CA 104; 120; MTCW

Taine, Hippolyte Adolphe
1828-1893 .... **NCLC 15**

Talese, Gay 1932-................ **CLC 37**
See also AITN 1; CA 1-4R; CANR 9, 58;
INT CANR-9; MTCW

Tallent, Elizabeth (Ann) 1954- ..... **CLC 45**
See also CA 117; DLB 130

Tally, Ted 1952-................ **CLC 42**
See also CA 120; 124; INT 124

Tamayo y Baus, Manuel
1829-1898 .... **NCLC 1**

Tammsaare, A(nton) H(ansen)
1878-1940 .... **TCLC 27**

Tam'si, Tchicaya U
See Tchicaya, Gerald Felix

Tan, Amy (Ruth)
1952- .... **CLC 59; DAM MULT, NOV,**
POP
See also AAYA 9; BEST 89:3; CA 136;
CANR 54; DLB 173; SATA 75

Tandem, Felix
See Spitteler, Carl (Friedrich Georg)

Tanizaki, Jun'ichiro
1886-1965 ...... **CLC 8, 14, 28; SSC 21**
See also CA 93-96; 25-28R; DLB 180

Tanner, William
See Amis, Kingsley (William)

Tao Lao
See Storni, Alfonsina

Tarassoff, Lev
See Troyat, Henri

Tarbell, Ida M(inerva)
1857-1944 .... **TCLC 40**
See also CA 122; DLB 47

Tarkington, (Newton) Booth
1869-1946 .... **TCLC 9**
See also CA 110; 143; DLB 9, 102;
SATA 17

Tarkovsky, Andrei (Arsenyevich)
1932-1986 .... **CLC 75**
See also CA 127

Tartt, Donna 1964(?)-............. **CLC 76**
See also CA 142

Tasso, Torquato 1544-1595 .... **LC 5**

Tate, (John Orley) Allen
1899-1979 .... **CLC 2, 4, 6, 9, 11, 14, 24**
See also CA 5-8R; 85-88; CANR 32;
DLB 4, 45, 63; MTCW

Tate, Ellalice
See Hibbert, Eleanor Alice Burford

Tate, James (Vincent) 1943-... **CLC 2, 6, 25**
See also CA 21-24R; CANR 29, 57; DLB 5,
169

Tavel, Ronald 1940-................ **CLC 6**
See also CA 21-24R; CANR 33

Taylor, C(ecil) P(hilip) 1929-1981... **CLC 27**
See also CA 25-28R; 105; CANR 47

Taylor, Edward
1642(?)-1729 .... **LC 11; DA; DAB;**
DAC; DAM MST, POET
See also DLB 24

Taylor, Eleanor Ross 1920-......... **CLC 5**
See also CA 81-84

Taylor, Elizabeth 1912-1975 ... **CLC 2, 4, 29**
See also CA 13-16R; CANR 9; DLB 139;
MTCW; SATA 13

Taylor, Henry (Splawn) 1942-...... **CLC 44**
See also CA 33-36R; CAAS 7; CANR 31;
DLB 5

Taylor, Kamala (Purnaiya) 1924-
See Markandaya, Kamala
See also CA 77-80

Taylor, Mildred D. .... **CLC 21**
See also AAYA 10; BW 1; CA 85-88;
CANR 25; CLR 9; DLB 52; JRDA;
MAICYA; SAAS 5; SATA 15, 70

Taylor, Peter (Hillsman)
1917-1994 ..... **CLC 1, 4, 18, 37, 44, 50,**
71; SSC 10
See also CA 13-16R; 147; CANR 9, 50;
DLBY 81, 94; INT CANR-9; MTCW

Taylor, Robert Lewis 1912-........ **CLC 14**
See also CA 1-4R; CANR 3; SATA 10

Tchekhov, Anton
See Chekhov, Anton (Pavlovich)

Tchicaya, Gerald Felix
1931-1988 .... **CLC 101**
See also CA 129; 125

Tchicaya U Tam'si
See Tchicaya, Gerald Felix

Teasdale, Sara 1884-1933......... **TCLC 4**
See also CA 104; DLB 45; SATA 32

Tegner, Esaias 1782-1846........ **NCLC 2**

Teilhard de Chardin, (Marie Joseph) Pierre
1881-1955 .... **TCLC 9**
See also CA 105

Temple, Ann
See Mortimer, Penelope (Ruth)

Tennant, Emma (Christina)
1937- .... **CLC 13, 52**
See also CA 65-68; CAAS 9; CANR 10, 38,
59; DLB 14

Tenneshaw, S. M.
See Silverberg, Robert

Tennyson, Alfred
1809-1892 .... **NCLC 30; DA; DAB;**
DAC; DAM MST, POET; PC 6; WLC
See also CDBLB 1832-1890; DLB 32

Teran, Lisa St. Aubin de .... **CLC 36**
See also St. Aubin de Teran, Lisa

Terence
195(?)B.C.-159B.C..... **CMLC 14; DC 7**

Teresa de Jesus, St. 1515-1582...... **LC 18**

Terkel, Louis 1912-
See Terkel, Studs
See also CA 57-60; CANR 18, 45; MTCW

Terkel, Studs.................... **CLC 38**
See also Terkel, Louis
See also AITN 1

Terry, C. V.
See Slaughter, Frank G(ill)

Terry, Megan 1932-.............. **CLC 19**
See also CA 77-80; CABS 3; CANR 43;
DLB 7

Tertz, Abram
See Sinyavsky, Andrei (Donatevich)

Tesich, Steve 1943(?)-1996...... **CLC 40, 69**
See also CA 105; 152; DLBY 83

Teternikov, Fyodor Kuzmich 1863-1927
See Sologub, Fyodor
See also CA 104

Tevis, Walter 1928-1984 .... **CLC 42**
See also CA 113

Tey, Josephine................... **TCLC 14**
See also Mackintosh, Elizabeth
See also DLB 77

Thackeray, William Makepeace
1811-1863 .... **NCLC 5, 14, 22, 43; DA;**
DAB; DAC; DAM MST, NOV; WLC
See also CDBLB 1832-1890; DLB 21, 55,
159, 163; SATA 23

Thakura, Ravindranatha
See Tagore, Rabindranath

Tharoor, Shashi 1956-............ **CLC 70**
See also CA 141

Thelwell, Michael Miles 1939- ..... **CLC 22**
See also BW 2; CA 101

Theobald, Lewis, Jr.
See Lovecraft, H(oward) P(hillips)

Theodorescu, Ion N. 1880-1967
See Arghezi, Tudor
See also CA 116

Theriault, Yves
1915-1983 .. **CLC 79; DAC; DAM MST**
See also CA 102; DLB 88

Theroux, Alexander (Louis)
1939- .... **CLC 2, 25**
See also CA 85-88; CANR 20

Tournier, Michel (Edouard)
1924- . . . . **CLC 6, 23, 36, 95**
See also CA 49-52; CANR 3, 36; DLB 83;
MTCW; SATA 23

Tournimparte, Alessandra
See Ginzburg, Natalia

Towers, Ivar
See Kornbluth, C(yril) M.

Towne, Robert (Burton) 1936(?)- . . . . **CLC 87**
See also CA 108; DLB 44

Townsend, Sue 1946- . . **CLC 61; DAB; DAC**
See also CA 119; 127; INT 127; MTCW;
SATA 55, 93; SATA-Brief 48

Townshend, Peter (Dennis Blandford)
1945- . . . . **CLC 17, 42**
See also CA 107

Tozzi, Federigo 1883-1920 . . . . **TCLC 31**
See also CA 160

Traill, Catharine Parr
1802-1899 . . . . **NCLC 31**
See also DLB 99

Trakl, Georg 1887-1914 . . . . **TCLC 5**
See also CA 104

Transtroemer, Tomas (Goesta)
1931- . . . . **CLC 52, 65; DAM POET**
See also CA 117; 129; CAAS 17

Transtromer, Tomas Gosta
See Transtroemer, Tomas (Goesta)

Traven, B. (?)-1969 . . . . **CLC 8, 11**
See also CA 19-20; 25-28R; CAP 2; DLB 9,
56; MTCW

Treitel, Jonathan 1959- . . . . **CLC 70**

Tremain, Rose 1943- . . . . **CLC 42**
See also CA 97-100; CANR 44; DLB 14

Tremblay, Michel
1942- . . **CLC 29, 102; DAC; DAM MST**
See also CA 116; 128; DLB 60; MTCW

Trevanian . . . . **CLC 29**
See also Whitaker, Rod(ney)

Trevor, Glen
See Hilton, James

Trevor, William
1928- . . . . . **CLC 7, 9, 14, 25, 71; SSC 21**
See also Cox, William Trevor
See also DLB 14, 139

Trifonov, Yuri (Valentinovich)
1925-1981 . . . . **CLC 45**
See also CA 126; 103; MTCW

Trilling, Lionel 1905-1975 . . . . **CLC 9, 11, 24**
See also CA 9-12R; 61-64; CANR 10;
DLB 28, 63; INT CANR-10; MTCW

Trimball, W. H.
See Mencken, H(enry) L(ouis)

Tristan
See Gomez de la Serna, Ramon

Tristram
See Housman, A(lfred) E(dward)

Trogdon, William (Lewis) 1939-
See Heat-Moon, William Least
See also CA 115; 119; CANR 47; INT 119

Trollope, Anthony
1815-1882 . . . . . **NCLC 6, 33; DA; DAB;
DAC; DAM MST, NOV; SSC 28; WLC**
See also CDBLB 1832-1890; DLB 21, 57,
159; SATA 22

Trollope, Frances 1779-1863 . . . . . **NCLC 30**
See also DLB 21, 166

Trotsky, Leon 1879-1940 . . . . **TCLC 22**
See also CA 118

Trotter (Cockburn), Catharine
1679-1749 . . . . **LC 8**
See also DLB 84

Trout, Kilgore
See Farmer, Philip Jose

Trow, George W. S. 1943- . . . . **CLC 52**
See also CA 126

Troyat, Henri 1911- . . . . **CLC 23**
See also CA 45-48; CANR 2, 33; MTCW

Trudeau, G(arretson) B(eekman) 1948-
See Trudeau, Garry B.
See also CA 81-84; CANR 31; SATA 35

Trudeau, Garry B. . . . . **CLC 12**
See also Trudeau, G(arretson) B(eekman)
See also AAYA 10; AITN 2

Truffaut, Francois 1932-1984 . . . **CLC 20, 101**
See also CA 81-84; 113; CANR 34

Trumbo, Dalton 1905-1976 . . . . **CLC 19**
See also CA 21-24R; 69-72; CANR 10;
DLB 26

Trumbull, John 1750-1831 . . . . **NCLC 30**
See also DLB 31

Trundlett, Helen B.
See Eliot, T(homas) S(tearns)

Tryon, Thomas
1926-1991 . . . . . . **CLC 3, 11; DAM POP**
See also AITN 1; CA 29-32R; 135;
CANR 32; MTCW

Tryon, Tom
See Tryon, Thomas

Ts'ao Hsueh-ch'in 1715(?)-1763 . . . . **LC 1**

Tsushima, Shuji 1909-1948
See Dazai, Osamu
See also CA 107

Tsvetaeva (Efron), Marina (Ivanovna)
1892-1941 . . . . **TCLC 7, 35; PC 14**
See also CA 104; 128; MTCW

Tuck, Lily 1938- . . . . **CLC 70**
See also CA 139

Tu Fu 712-770 . . . . **PC 9**
See also DAM MULT

Tunis, John R(oberts) 1889-1975 . . . **CLC 12**
See also CA 61-64; CANR 62; DLB 22,
171; JRDA; MAICYA; SATA 37;
SATA-Brief 30

Tuohy, Frank . . . . **CLC 37**
See also Tuohy, John Francis
See also DLB 14, 139

Tuohy, John Francis 1925-
See Tuohy, Frank
See also CA 5-8R; CANR 3, 47

Turco, Lewis (Putnam) 1934- . . . **CLC 11, 63**
See also CA 13-16R; CAAS 22; CANR 24,
51; DLBY 84

Turgenev, Ivan
1818-1883 . . . . **NCLC 21; DA; DAB;
DAC; DAM MST, NOV; DC 7; SSC 7;
WLC**

Turgot, Anne-Robert-Jacques
1727-1781 . . . . **LC 26**

Turner, Frederick 1943- . . . . **CLC 48**
See also CA 73-76; CAAS 10; CANR 12,
30, 56; DLB 40

Tutu, Desmond M(pilo)
1931- . . . . . **CLC 80; BLC; DAM MULT**
See also BW 1; CA 125

Tutuola, Amos
1920-1997 . . . . **CLC 5, 14, 29; BLC;
DAM MULT**
See also BW 2; CA 9-12R; 159; CANR 27;
DLB 125; MTCW

Twain, Mark
. . . . **TCLC 6, 12, 19, 36, 48, 59; SSC 26;
WLC**
See also Clemens, Samuel Langhorne
See also AAYA 20; DLB 11, 12, 23, 64, 74

Tyler, Anne
1941- . . . . **CLC 7, 11, 18, 28, 44, 59, 103;
DAM NOV, POP**
See also AAYA 18; BEST 89:1; CA 9-12R;
CANR 11, 33, 53; DLB 6, 143; DLBY 82;
MTCW; SATA 7, 90

Tyler, Royall 1757-1826 . . . . **NCLC 3**
See also DLB 37

Tynan, Katharine 1861-1931 . . . . **TCLC 3**
See also CA 104; DLB 153

Tyutchev, Fyodor 1803-1873 . . . . . **NCLC 34**

Tzara, Tristan
1896-1963 . . . . **CLC 47; DAM POET**
See also Rosenfeld, Samuel; Rosenstock,
Sami; Rosenstock, Samuel
See also CA 153

Uhry, Alfred
1936- . . . . . **CLC 55; DAM DRAM, POP**
See also CA 127; 133; INT 133

Ulf, Haerved
See Strindberg, (Johan) August

Ulf, Harved
See Strindberg, (Johan) August

Ulibarri, Sabine R(eyes)
1919- . . . . **CLC 83; DAM MULT**
See also CA 131; DLB 82; HW

Unamuno (y Jugo), Miguel de
1864-1936 . . . **TCLC 2, 9; DAM MULT,
NOV; HLC; SSC 11**
See also CA 104; 131; DLB 108; HW;
MTCW

Undercliffe, Errol
See Campbell, (John) Ramsey

Underwood, Miles
See Glassco, John

Undset, Sigrid
1882-1949 . . . . **TCLC 3; DA; DAB;
DAC; DAM MST, NOV; WLC**
See also CA 104; 129; MTCW

Ungaretti, Giuseppe
1888-1970 . . . . **CLC 7, 11, 15**
See also CA 19-20; 25-28R; CAP 2;
DLB 114

Unger, Douglas 1952-............ **CLC 34**
See also CA 130

Unsworth, Barry (Forster) 1930-.... **CLC 76**
See also CA 25-28R; CANR 30, 54

Updike, John (Hoyer)
1932-...... **CLC 1, 2, 3, 5, 7, 9, 13, 15,
23, 34, 43, 70; DA; DAB; DAC;
DAM MST, NOV, POET, POP;
SSC 13, 27; WLC**
See also CA 1-4R; CABS 1; CANR 4, 33,
51; CDALB 1968-1988; DLB 2, 5, 143;
DLBD 3; DLBY 80, 82; MTCW

Upshaw, Margaret Mitchell
See Mitchell, Margaret (Munnerlyn)

Upton, Mark
See Sanders, Lawrence

Urdang, Constance (Henriette)
1922-..................... **CLC 47**
See also CA 21-24R; CANR 9, 24

Uriel, Henry
See Faust, Frederick (Schiller)

Uris, Leon (Marcus)
1924-.... **CLC 7, 32; DAM NOV, POP**
See also AITN 1, 2; BEST 89:2; CA 1-4R;
CANR 1, 40; MTCW; SATA 49

Urmuz
See Codrescu, Andrei

Urquhart, Jane 1949-........ **CLC 90; DAC**
See also CA 113; CANR 32

Ustinov, Peter (Alexander) 1921-.... **CLC 1**
See also AITN 1; CA 13-16R; CANR 25,
51; DLB 13

U Tam'si, Gerald Felix Tchicaya
See Tchicaya, Gerald Felix

U Tam'si, Tchicaya
See Tchicaya, Gerald Felix

Vaculik, Ludvik 1926-............. **CLC 7**
See also CA 53-56

Vaihinger, Hans 1852-1933 .... **TCLC 71**
See also CA 116

Valdez, Luis (Miguel)
1940-..... **CLC 84; DAM MULT; HLC**
See also CA 101; CANR 32; DLB 122; HW

Valenzuela, Luisa
1938-...... **CLC 31, 104; DAM MULT;
SSC 14**
See also CA 101; CANR 32; DLB 113; HW

Valera y Alcala-Galiano, Juan
1824-1905 .... **TCLC 10**
See also CA 106

Valery, (Ambroise) Paul (Toussaint Jules)
1871-1945 .... **TCLC 4, 15;
DAM POET; PC 9**
See also CA 104; 122; MTCW

Valle-Inclan, Ramon (Maria) del
1866-1936 ..... **TCLC 5; DAM MULT;
HLC**
See also CA 106; 153; DLB 134

Vallejo, Antonio Buero
See Buero Vallejo, Antonio

Vallejo, Cesar (Abraham)
1892-1938 .... **TCLC 3, 56;
DAM MULT; HLC**
See also CA 105; 153; HW

Vallette, Marguerite Eymery
See Rachilde

Valle Y Pena, Ramon del
See Valle-Inclan, Ramon (Maria) del

Van Ash, Cay 1918-.............. **CLC 34**

Vanbrugh, Sir John
1664-1726 .... **LC 21; DAM DRAM**
See also DLB 80

Van Campen, Karl
See Campbell, John W(ood, Jr.)

Vance, Gerald
See Silverberg, Robert

Vance, Jack .... **CLC 35**
See also Kuttner, Henry; Vance, John
Holbrook
See also DLB 8

Vance, John Holbrook 1916-
See Queen, Ellery; Vance, Jack
See also CA 29-32R; CANR 17; MTCW

Van Den Bogarde, Derek Jules Gaspard Ulric
Niven 1921-
See Bogarde, Dirk
See also CA 77-80

Vandenburgh, Jane .... **CLC 59**

Vanderhaeghe, Guy 1951- .... **CLC 41**
See also CA 113

van der Post, Laurens (Jan)
1906-1996 .... **CLC 5**
See also CA 5-8R; 155; CANR 35

van de Wetering, Janwillem 1931-.. **CLC 47**
See also CA 49-52; CANR 4, 62

Van Dine, S. S. .... **TCLC 23**
See also Wright, Willard Huntington

Van Doren, Carl (Clinton)
1885-1950 .... **TCLC 18**
See also CA 111

Van Doren, Mark 1894-1972..... **CLC 6, 10**
See also CA 1-4R; 37-40R; CANR 3;
DLB 45; MTCW

Van Druten, John (William)
1901-1957 .... **TCLC 2**
See also CA 104; DLB 10

Van Duyn, Mona (Jane)
1921-....... **CLC 3, 7, 63; DAM POET**
See also CA 9-12R; CANR 7, 38, 60;
DLB 5

Van Dyne, Edith
See Baum, L(yman) Frank

van Itallie, Jean-Claude 1936-....... **CLC 3**
See also CA 45-48; CAAS 2; CANR 1, 48;
DLB 7

van Ostaijen, Paul 1896-1928 ..... **TCLC 33**

Van Peebles, Melvin
1932-....... **CLC 2, 20; DAM MULT**
See also BW 2; CA 85-88; CANR 27

Vansittart, Peter 1920-........... **CLC 42**
See also CA 1-4R; CANR 3, 49

Van Vechten, Carl 1880-1964 ...... **CLC 33**
See also CA 89-92; DLB 4, 9, 51

Van Vogt, A(lfred) E(lton) 1912-..... **CLC 1**
See also CA 21-24R; CANR 28; DLB 8;
SATA 14

Varda, Agnes 1928- .... **CLC 16**
See also CA 116; 122

Vargas Llosa, (Jorge) Mario (Pedro)
1936- .... **CLC 3, 6, 9, 10, 15, 31, 42, 85;
DA; DAB; DAC; DAM MST, MULT,
NOV; HLC**
See also CA 73-76; CANR 18, 32, 42;
DLB 145; HW; MTCW

Vasiliu, Gheorghe 1881-1957
See Bacovia, George
See also CA 123

Vassa, Gustavus
See Equiano, Olaudah

Vassilikos, Vassilis 1933-......... **CLC 4, 8**
See also CA 81-84

Vaughan, Henry 1621-1695 .... **LC 27**
See also DLB 131

Vaughn, Stephanie................. **CLC 62**

Vazov, Ivan (Minchov)
1850-1921 .... **TCLC 25**
See also CA 121; DLB 147

Veblen, Thorstein (Bunde)
1857-1929 .... **TCLC 31**
See also CA 115

Vega, Lope de 1562-1635.......... **LC 23**

Venison, Alfred
See Pound, Ezra (Weston Loomis)

Verdi, Marie de
See Mencken, H(enry) L(ouis)

Verdu, Matilde
See Cela, Camilo Jose

Verga, Giovanni (Carmelo)
1840-1922 .... **TCLC 3; SSC 21**
See also CA 104; 123

Vergil
70B.C.-19B.C...... **CMLC 9; DA; DAB;
DAC; DAM MST, POET; PC 12; WLCS**

Verhaeren, Emile (Adolphe Gustave)
1855-1916 .... **TCLC 12**
See also CA 109

Verlaine, Paul (Marie)
1844-1896 .... **NCLC 2, 51;
DAM POET; PC 2**

Verne, Jules (Gabriel)
1828-1905 .... **TCLC 6, 52**
See also AAYA 16; CA 110; 131; DLB 123;
JRDA; MAICYA; SATA 21

Very, Jones 1813-1880.......... **NCLC 9**
See also DLB 1

Vesaas, Tarjei 1897-1970 .... **CLC 48**
See also CA 29-32R

Vialis, Gaston
See Simenon, Georges (Jacques Christian)

Vian, Boris 1920-1959 .... **TCLC 9**
See also CA 106; DLB 72

Viaud, (Louis Marie) Julien 1850-1923
See Loti, Pierre
See also CA 107

Vicar, Henry
See Felsen, Henry Gregor

Vicker, Angus
See Felsen, Henry Gregor

Wallace, (Richard Horatio) Edgar
1875-1932 . . . . **TCLC 57**
See also CA 115; DLB 70

Wallace, Irving
1916-1990 . . . . . **CLC 7, 13; DAM NOV,**
POP
See also AITN 1; CA 1-4R; 132; CAAS 1;
CANR 1, 27; INT CANR-27; MTCW

Wallant, Edward Lewis
1926-1962 . . . . **CLC 5, 10**
See also CA 1-4R; CANR 22; DLB 2, 28,
143; MTCW

Walley, Byron
See Card, Orson Scott

Walpole, Horace 1717-1797. . . . . **LC 2**
See also DLB 39, 104

Walpole, Hugh (Seymour)
1884-1941 . . . . **TCLC 5**
See also CA 104; DLB 34

Walser, Martin 1927- . . . . **CLC 27**
See also CA 57-60; CANR 8, 46; DLB 75,
124

Walser, Robert
1878-1956 . . . . **TCLC 18; SSC 20**
See also CA 118; DLB 66

Walsh, Jill Paton. . . . . **CLC 35**
See also Paton Walsh, Gillian
See also AAYA 11; CLR 2; DLB 161;
SAAS 3

Walter, Villiam Christian
See Andersen, Hans Christian

Wambaugh, Joseph (Aloysius, Jr.)
1937- . . . . **CLC 3, 18; DAM NOV, POP**
See also AITN 1; BEST 89:3; CA 33-36R;
CANR 42; DLB 6; DLBY 83; MTCW

Wang Wei 699(?)-761(?). . . . . **PC 18**

Ward, Arthur Henry Sarsfield 1883-1959
See Rohmer, Sax
See also CA 108

Ward, Douglas Turner 1930- . . . . **CLC 19**
See also BW 1; CA 81-84; CANR 27;
DLB 7, 38

Ward, Mary Augusta
See Ward, Mrs. Humphry

Ward, Mrs. Humphry
1851-1920 . . . . **TCLC 55**
See also DLB 18

Ward, Peter
See Faust, Frederick (Schiller)

Warhol, Andy 1928(?)-1987. . . . . . . **CLC 20**
See also AAYA 12; BEST 89:4; CA 89-92;
121; CANR 34

Warner, Francis (Robert le Plastrier)
1937- . . . . **CLC 14**
See also CA 53-56; CANR 11

Warner, Marina 1946- . . . . **CLC 59**
See also CA 65-68; CANR 21, 55

Warner, Rex (Ernest) 1905-1986. . . . **CLC 45**
See also CA 89-92; 119; DLB 15

Warner, Susan (Bogert)
1819-1885 . . . . **NCLC 31**
See also DLB 3, 42

Warner, Sylvia (Constance) Ashton
See Ashton-Warner, Sylvia (Constance)

Warner, Sylvia Townsend
1893-1978 . . . . **CLC 7, 19; SSC 23**
See also CA 61-64; 77-80; CANR 16, 60;
DLB 34, 139; MTCW

Warren, Mercy Otis 1728-1814. . . **NCLC 13**
See also DLB 31

Warren, Robert Penn
1905-1989 . . . . **CLC 1, 4, 6, 8, 10, 13, 18,**
39, 53, 59; DA; DAB; DAC; DAM MST,
NOV, POET; SSC 4; WLC
See also AITN 1; CA 13-16R; 129;
CANR 10, 47; CDALB 1968-1988;
DLB 2, 48, 152; DLBY 80, 89;
INT CANR-10; MTCW; SATA 46;
SATA-Obit 63

Warshofsky, Isaac
See Singer, Isaac Bashevis

Warton, Thomas
1728-1790 . . . . **LC 15; DAM POET**
See also DLB 104, 109

Waruk, Kona
See Harris, (Theodore) Wilson

Warung, Price 1855-1911. . . . . **TCLC 45**

Warwick, Jarvis
See Garner, Hugh

Washington, Alex
See Harris, Mark

Washington, Booker T(aliaferro)
1856-1915 . . . . **TCLC 10; BLC;**
DAM MULT
See also BW 1; CA 114; 125; SATA 28

Washington, George 1732-1799. . . . . . **LC 25**
See also DLB 31

Wassermann, (Karl) Jakob
1873-1934 . . . . **TCLC 6**
See also CA 104; DLB 66

Wasserstein, Wendy
1950- . . . . **CLC 32, 59, 90;**
DAM DRAM; DC 4
See also CA 121; 129; CABS 3; CANR 53;
INT 129; SATA 94

Waterhouse, Keith (Spencer)
1929- . . . . **CLC 47**
See also CA 5-8R; CANR 38; DLB 13, 15;
MTCW

Waters, Frank (Joseph)
1902-1995 . . . . **CLC 88**
See also CA 5-8R; 149; CAAS 13; CANR 3,
18; DLBY 86

Waters, Roger 1944- . . . . **CLC 35**

Watkins, Frances Ellen
See Harper, Frances Ellen Watkins

Watkins, Gerrold
See Malzberg, Barry N(athaniel)

Watkins, Gloria 1955(?)-
See hooks, bell
See also BW 2; CA 143

Watkins, Paul 1964- . . . . **CLC 55**
See also CA 132; CANR 62

Watkins, Vernon Phillips
1906-1967 . . . . **CLC 43**
See also CA 9-10; 25-28R; CAP 1; DLB 20

Watson, Irving S.
See Mencken, H(enry) L(ouis)

Watson, John H.
See Farmer, Philip Jose

Watson, Richard F.
See Silverberg, Robert

Waugh, Auberon (Alexander) 1939- . . **CLC 7**
See also CA 45-48; CANR 6, 22; DLB 14

Waugh, Evelyn (Arthur St. John)
1903-1966 . . . . . . **CLC 1, 3, 8, 13, 19, 27,**
44; DA; DAB; DAC; DAM MST, NOV,
POP; WLC
See also CA 85-88; 25-28R; CANR 22;
CDBLB 1914-1945; DLB 15, 162; MTCW

Waugh, Harriet 1944- . . . . **CLC 6**
See also CA 85-88; CANR 22

Ways, C. R.
See Blount, Roy (Alton), Jr.

Waystaff, Simon
See Swift, Jonathan

Webb, (Martha) Beatrice (Potter)
1858-1943 . . . . **TCLC 22**
See also Potter, (Helen) Beatrix
See also CA 117

Webb, Charles (Richard) 1939- . . . . . **CLC 7**
See also CA 25-28R

Webb, James H(enry), Jr. 1946- . . . . **CLC 22**
See also CA 81-84

Webb, Mary (Gladys Meredith)
1881-1927 . . . . **TCLC 24**
See also CA 123; DLB 34

Webb, Mrs. Sidney
See Webb, (Martha) Beatrice (Potter)

Webb, Phyllis 1927- . . . . **CLC 18**
See also CA 104; CANR 23; DLB 53

Webb, Sidney (James)
1859-1947 . . . . **TCLC 22**
See also CA 117

Webber, Andrew Lloyd. . . . . **CLC 21**
See also Lloyd Webber, Andrew

Weber, Lenora Mattingly
1895-1971 . . . . **CLC 12**
See also CA 19-20; 29-32R; CAP 1;
SATA 2; SATA-Obit 26

Weber, Max 1864-1920 . . . . **TCLC 69**
See also CA 109

Webster, John
1579(?)-1634(?) . . . . . . **LC 33; DA; DAB;**
DAC; DAM DRAM, MST; DC 2; WLC
See also CDBLB Before 1660; DLB 58

Webster, Noah 1758-1843 . . . . **NCLC 30**

Wedekind, (Benjamin) Frank(lin)
1864-1918 . . . . . . **TCLC 7; DAM DRAM**
See also CA 104; 153; DLB 118

Weidman, Jerome 1913- . . . . **CLC 7**
See also AITN 2; CA 1-4R; CANR 1;
DLB 28

Weil, Simone (Adolphine)
1909-1943 . . . . **TCLC 23**
See also CA 117; 159

Weinstein, Nathan
See West, Nathanael

Weinstein, Nathan von Wallenstein
See West, Nathanael

Weir, Peter (Lindsay) 1944- . . . . **CLC 20**
See also CA 113; 123

Weiss, Peter (Ulrich)
1916-1982 . . . . CLC 3, 15, 51;
DAM DRAM
See also CA 45-48; 106; CANR 3; DLB 69,
124

Weiss, Theodore (Russell)
1916- . . . . CLC 3, 8, 14
See also CA 9-12R; CAAS 2; CANR 46;
DLB 5

Welch, (Maurice) Denton
1915-1948 . . . . TCLC 22
See also CA 121; 148

Welch, James
1940- . . . . . CLC 6, 14, 52; DAM MULT,
POP
See also CA 85-88; CANR 42; DLB 175;
NNAL

Weldon, Fay
1933- . . . . CLC 6, 9, 11, 19, 36, 59;
DAM POP
See also CA 21-24R; CANR 16, 46;
CDBLB 1960 to Present; DLB 14;
INT CANR-16; MTCW

Wellek, Rene 1903-1995. . . . . CLC 28
See also CA 5-8R; 150; CAAS 7; CANR 8;
DLB 63; INT CANR-8

Weller, Michael 1942- . . . . CLC 10, 53
See also CA 85-88

Weller, Paul 1958- . . . . CLC 26

Wellershoff, Dieter 1925- . . . . CLC 46
See also CA 89-92; CANR 16, 37

Welles, (George) Orson
1915-1985 . . . . CLC 20, 80
See also CA 93-96; 117

Wellman, Mac 1945- . . . . CLC 65

Wellman, Manly Wade 1903-1986 . . CLC 49
See also CA 1-4R; 118; CANR 6, 16, 44;
SATA 6; SATA-Obit 47

Wells, Carolyn 1869(?)-1942 . . . . . . TCLC 35
See also CA 113; DLB 11

Wells, H(erbert) G(eorge)
1866-1946 . . . . TCLC 6, 12, 19; DA;
DAB; DAC; DAM MST, NOV; SSC 6;
WLC
See also AAYA 18; CA 110; 121;
CDBLB 1914-1945; DLB 34, 70, 156, 178;
MTCW; SATA 20

Wells, Rosemary 1943- . . . . CLC 12
See also AAYA 13; CA 85-88; CANR 48;
CLR 16; MAICYA; SAAS 1; SATA 18,
69

Welty, Eudora
1909- . . . . . . CLC 1, 2, 5, 14, 22, 33; DA;
DAB; DAC; DAM MST, NOV; SSC 1,
27; WLC
See also CA 9-12R; CABS 1; CANR 32;
CDALB 1941-1968; DLB 2, 102, 143;
DLBD 12; DLBY 87; MTCW

Wen I-to 1899-1946 . . . . TCLC 28

Wentworth, Robert
See Hamilton, Edmond

Werfel, Franz (V.) 1890-1945 . . . . . . TCLC 8
See also CA 104; DLB 81, 124

Wergeland, Henrik Arnold
1808-1845 . . . . NCLC 5

Wersba, Barbara 1932- . . . . CLC 30
See also AAYA 2; CA 29-32R; CANR 16,
38; CLR 3; DLB 52; JRDA; MAICYA;
SAAS 2; SATA 1, 58

Wertmueller, Lina 1928- . . . . CLC 16
See also CA 97-100; CANR 39

Wescott, Glenway 1901-1987. . . . . . . CLC 13
See also CA 13-16R; 121; CANR 23;
DLB 4, 9, 102

Wesker, Arnold
1932- . . . . CLC 3, 5, 42; DAB;
DAM DRAM
See also CA 1-4R; CAAS 7; CANR 1, 33;
CDBLB 1960 to Present; DLB 13;
MTCW

Wesley, Richard (Errol) 1945-. . . . . . CLC 7
See also BW 1; CA 57-60; CANR 27;
DLB 38

Wessel, Johan Herman 1742-1785 . . . . LC 7

West, Anthony (Panther)
1914-1987 . . . . CLC 50
See also CA 45-48; 124; CANR 3, 19;
DLB 15

West, C. P.
See Wodehouse, P(elham) G(renville)

West, (Mary) Jessamyn
1902-1984 . . . . CLC 7, 17
See also CA 9-12R; 112; CANR 27; DLB 6;
DLBY 84; MTCW; SATA-Obit 37

West, Morris L(anglo) 1916-. . . . . CLC 6, 33
See also CA 5-8R; CANR 24, 49; MTCW

West, Nathanael
1903-1940 . . . . . TCLC 1, 14, 44; SSC 16
See also CA 104; 125; CDALB 1929-1941;
DLB 4, 9, 28; MTCW

West, Owen
See Koontz, Dean R(ay)

West, Paul 1930- . . . . CLC 7, 14, 96
See also CA 13-16R; CAAS 7; CANR 22,
53; DLB 14; INT CANR-22

West, Rebecca 1892-1983 . . CLC 7, 9, 31, 50
See also CA 5-8R; 109; CANR 19; DLB 36;
DLBY 83; MTCW

Westall, Robert (Atkinson)
1929-1993 . . . . CLC 17
See also AAYA 12; CA 69-72; 141;
CANR 18; CLR 13; JRDA; MAICYA;
SAAS 2; SATA 23, 69; SATA-Obit 75

Westlake, Donald E(dwin)
1933- . . . . CLC 7, 33; DAM POP
See also CA 17-20R; CAAS 13; CANR 16,
44; INT CANR-16

Westmacott, Mary
See Christie, Agatha (Mary Clarissa)

Weston, Allen
See Norton, Andre

Wetcheek, J. L.
See Feuchtwanger, Lion

Wetering, Janwillem van de
See van de Wetering, Janwillem

Wetherell, Elizabeth
See Warner, Susan (Bogert)

Whale, James 1889-1957 . . . . TCLC 63

Whalen, Philip 1923- . . . . CLC 6, 29
See also CA 9-12R; CANR 5, 39; DLB 16

Wharton, Edith (Newbold Jones)
1862-1937 . . . . . . TCLC 3, 9, 27, 53; DA;
DAB; DAC; DAM MST, NOV; SSC 6;
WLC
See also CA 104; 132; CDALB 1865-1917;
DLB 4, 9, 12, 78; DLBD 13; MTCW

Wharton, James
See Mencken, H(enry) L(ouis)

Wharton, William (a pseudonym)
. . . . CLC 18, 37
See also CA 93-96; DLBY 80; INT 93-96

Wheatley (Peters), Phillis
1754(?)-1784 . . . . LC 3; BLC; DA; DAC;
DAM MST, MULT, POET; PC 3; WLC
See also CDALB 1640-1865; DLB 31, 50

Wheelock, John Hall 1886-1978 . . . . CLC 14
See also CA 13-16R; 77-80; CANR 14;
DLB 45

White, E(lwyn) B(rooks)
1899-1985 . . CLC 10, 34, 39; DAM POP
See also AITN 2; CA 13-16R; 116;
CANR 16, 37; CLR 1, 21; DLB 11, 22;
MAICYA; MTCW; SATA 2, 29;
SATA-Obit 44

White, Edmund (Valentine III)
1940- . . . . CLC 27; DAM POP
See also AAYA 7; CA 45-48; CANR 3, 19,
36, 62; MTCW

White, Patrick (Victor Martindale)
1912-1990 . . CLC 3, 4, 5, 7, 9, 18, 65, 69
See also CA 81-84; 132; CANR 43; MTCW

White, Phyllis Dorothy James 1920-
See James, P. D.
See also CA 21-24R; CANR 17, 43;
DAM POP; MTCW

White, T(erence) H(anbury)
1906-1964 . . . . CLC 30
See also AAYA 22; CA 73-76; CANR 37;
DLB 160; JRDA; MAICYA; SATA 12

White, Terence de Vere
1912-1994 . . . . CLC 49
See also CA 49-52; 145; CANR 3

White, Walter F(rancis)
1893-1955 . . . . TCLC 15
See also White, Walter
See also BW 1; CA 115; 124; DLB 51

White, William Hale 1831-1913
See Rutherford, Mark
See also CA 121

Whitehead, E(dward) A(nthony)
1933- . . . . CLC 5
See also CA 65-68; CANR 58

Whitemore, Hugh (John) 1936-. . . . . CLC 37
See also CA 132; INT 132

Whitman, Sarah Helen (Power)
1803-1878 . . . . NCLC 19
See also DLB 1

Whitman, Walt(er)
1819-1892 . . . . . NCLC 4, 31; DA; DAB;
DAC; DAM MST, POET; PC 3; WLC
See also CDALB 1640-1865; DLB 3, 64;
SATA 20

Whitney, Phyllis A(yame)
1903- . . . . CLC 42; DAM POP
See also AITN 2; BEST 90:3; CA 1-4R;
CANR 3, 25, 38, 60; JRDA; MAICYA;
SATA 1, 30

Whittemore, (Edward) Reed (Jr.)
1919- .... **CLC 4**
See also CA 9-12R; CAAS 8; CANR 4;
DLB 5

Whittier, John Greenleaf
1807-1892 .... **NCLC 8, 59**
See also DLB 1

Whittlebot, Hernia
See Coward, Noel (Peirce)

Wicker, Thomas Grey 1926-
See Wicker, Tom
See also CA 65-68; CANR 21, 46

Wicker, Tom .... **CLC 7**
See also Wicker, Thomas Grey

Wideman, John Edgar
1941- .... **CLC 5, 34, 36, 67; BLC;**
DAM MULT
See also BW 2; CA 85-88; CANR 14, 42;
DLB 33, 143

Wiebe, Rudy (Henry)
1934- .... **CLC 6, 11, 14; DAC;**
DAM MST
See also CA 37-40R; CANR 42; DLB 60

Wieland, Christoph Martin
1733-1813 .... **NCLC 17**
See also DLB 97

Wiene, Robert 1881-1938........ **TCLC 56**

Wieners, John 1934-............... **CLC 7**
See also CA 13-16R; DLB 16

Wiesel, Elie(zer)
1928- ...... **CLC 3, 5, 11, 37; DA; DAB;**
DAC; DAM MST, NOV;
WLCS 2:855-57, 854
See also AAYA 7; AITN 1; CA 5-8R;
CAAS 4; CANR 8, 40; DLB 83;
DLBY 87; INT CANR-8; MTCW;
SATA 56

Wiggins, Marianne 1947-........... **CLC 57**
See also BEST 89:3; CA 130; CANR 60

Wight, James Alfred 1916-
See Herriot, James
See also CA 77-80; SATA 55;
SATA-Brief 44

Wilbur, Richard (Purdy)
1921- ... **CLC 3, 6, 9, 14, 53; DA; DAB;**
DAC; DAM MST, POET
See also CA 1-4R; CABS 2; CANR 2, 29;
DLB 5, 169; INT CANR-29; MTCW;
SATA 9

Wild, Peter 1940-............... **CLC 14**
See also CA 37-40R; DLB 5

Wilde, Oscar (Fingal O'Flahertie Wills)
1854(?)-1900 .... **TCLC 1, 8, 23, 41; DA;**
DAB; DAC; DAM DRAM, MST, NOV;
SSC 11; WLC
See also CA 104; 119; CDBLB 1890-1914;
DLB 10, 19, 34, 57, 141, 156; SATA 24

Wilder, Billy .... **CLC 20**
See also Wilder, Samuel
See also DLB 26

Wilder, Samuel 1906-
See Wilder, Billy
See also CA 89-92

Wilder, Thornton (Niven)
1897-1975 ...... **CLC 1, 5, 6, 10, 15, 35,**
82; DA; DAB; DAC; DAM DRAM,
MST, NOV; DC 1; WLC
See also AITN 2; CA 13-16R; 61-64;
CANR 40; DLB 4, 7, 9; MTCW

Wilding, Michael 1942-........... **CLC 73**
See also CA 104; CANR 24, 49

Wiley, Richard 1944-............ **CLC 44**
See also CA 121; 129

Wilhelm, Kate .... **CLC 7**
See also Wilhelm, Katie Gertrude
See also AAYA 20; CAAS 5; DLB 8;
INT CANR-17

Wilhelm, Katie Gertrude 1928-
See Wilhelm, Kate
See also CA 37-40R; CANR 17, 36, 60;
MTCW

Wilkins, Mary
See Freeman, Mary Eleanor Wilkins

Willard, Nancy 1936-........... **CLC 7, 37**
See also CA 89-92; CANR 10, 39; CLR 5;
DLB 5, 52; MAICYA; MTCW;
SATA 37, 71; SATA-Brief 30

Williams, C(harles) K(enneth)
1936- .... **CLC 33, 56; DAM POET**
See also CA 37-40R; CAAS 26; CANR 57;
DLB 5

Williams, Charles
See Collier, James L(incoln)

Williams, Charles (Walter Stansby)
1886-1945 .... **TCLC 1, 11**
See also CA 104; DLB 100, 153

Williams, (George) Emlyn
1905-1987 ...... **CLC 15; DAM DRAM**
See also CA 104; 123; CANR 36; DLB 10,
77; MTCW

Williams, Hugo 1942-............ **CLC 42**
See also CA 17-20R; CANR 45; DLB 40

Williams, J. Walker
See Wodehouse, P(elham) G(renville)

Williams, John A(lfred)
1925- ... **CLC 5, 13; BLC; DAM MULT**
See also BW 2; CA 53-56; CAAS 3;
CANR 6, 26, 51; DLB 2, 33;
INT CANR-6

Williams, Jonathan (Chamberlain)
1929- .... **CLC 13**
See also CA 9-12R; CAAS 12; CANR 8;
DLB 5

Williams, Joy 1944-.............. **CLC 31**
See also CA 41-44R; CANR 22, 48

Williams, Norman 1952- .... **CLC 39**
See also CA 118

Williams, Sherley Anne
1944- ..... **CLC 89; BLC; DAM MULT,**
POET
See also BW 2; CA 73-76; CANR 25;
DLB 41; INT CANR-25; SATA 78

Williams, Shirley
See Williams, Sherley Anne

Williams, Tennessee
1911-1983 ..... **CLC 1, 2, 5, 7, 8, 11, 15,**
19, 30, 39, 45, 71; DA; DAB; DAC;
DAM DRAM, MST; DC 4; WLC
See also AITN 1, 2; CA 5-8R; 108;
CABS 3; CANR 31; CDALB 1941-1968;
DLB 7; DLBD 4; DLBY 83; MTCW

Williams, Thomas (Alonzo)
1926-1990 .... **CLC 14**
See also CA 1-4R; 132; CANR 2

Williams, William C.
See Williams, William Carlos

Williams, William Carlos
1883-1963 .... **CLC 1, 2, 5, 9, 13, 22, 42,**
67; DA; DAB; DAC; DAM MST, POET;
PC 7
See also CA 89-92; CANR 34;
CDALB 1917-1929; DLB 4, 16, 54, 86;
MTCW

Williamson, David (Keith) 1942-.... **CLC 56**
See also CA 103; CANR 41

Williamson, Ellen Douglas 1905-1984
See Douglas, Ellen
See also CA 17-20R; 114; CANR 39

Williamson, Jack................... **CLC 29**
See also Williamson, John Stewart
See also CAAS 8; DLB 8

Williamson, John Stewart 1908-
See Williamson, Jack
See also CA 17-20R; CANR 23

Willie, Frederick
See Lovecraft, H(oward) P(hillips)

Willingham, Calder (Baynard, Jr.)
1922-1995 .... **CLC 5, 51**
See also CA 5-8R; 147; CANR 3; DLB 2,
44; MTCW

Willis, Charles
See Clarke, Arthur C(harles)

Willy
See Colette, (Sidonie-Gabrielle)

Willy, Colette
See Colette, (Sidonie-Gabrielle)

Wilson, A(ndrew) N(orman) 1950- .. **CLC 33**
See also CA 112; 122; DLB 14, 155

Wilson, Angus (Frank Johnstone)
1913-1991 .. **CLC 2, 3, 5, 25, 34; SSC 21**
See also CA 5-8R; 134; CANR 21; DLB 15,
139, 155; MTCW

Wilson, August
1945- .... **CLC 39, 50, 63; BLC; DA;**
DAB; DAC; DAM DRAM, MST,
MULT; DC 2; WLCS
See also AAYA 16; BW 2; CA 115; 122;
CANR 42, 54; MTCW

Wilson, Brian 1942-.............. **CLC 12**

Wilson, Colin 1931- .... **CLC 3, 14**
See also CA 1-4R; CAAS 5; CANR 1, 22,
33; DLB 14; MTCW

Wilson, Dirk
See Pohl, Frederik

Wilson, Edmund
1895-1972 .... **CLC 1, 2, 3, 8, 24**
See also CA 1-4R; 37-40R; CANR 1, 46;
DLB 63; MTCW

Wilson, Ethel Davis (Bryant)
    1888(?)-1980 . . . . CLC 13; DAC;
                                        DAM POET
    See also CA 102; DLB 68; MTCW

Wilson, John 1785-1854. . . . . NCLC 5

Wilson, John (Anthony) Burgess 1917-1993
    See Burgess, Anthony
    See also CA 1-4R; 143; CANR 2, 46; DAC;
        DAM NOV; MTCW

Wilson, Lanford
    1937- . . . . . CLC 7, 14, 36; DAM DRAM
    See also CA 17-20R; CABS 3; CANR 45;
        DLB 7

Wilson, Robert M. 1944-. . . . . CLC 7, 9
    See also CA 49-52; CANR 2, 41; MTCW

Wilson, Robert McLiam 1964- . . . . . CLC 59
    See also CA 132

Wilson, Sloan 1920-. . . . . CLC 32
    See also CA 1-4R; CANR 1, 44

Wilson, Snoo 1948-. . . . . CLC 33
    See also CA 69-72

Wilson, William S(mith) 1932- . . . . . CLC 49
    See also CA 81-84

Wilson, Woodrow 1856-1924. . . . . . TCLC 73
    See also DLB 47

Winchilsea, Anne (Kingsmill) Finch Counte
    1661-1720 . . . . LC 3

Windham, Basil
    See Wodehouse, P(elham) G(renville)

Wingrove, David (John) 1954-. . . . . . CLC 68
    See also CA 133

Wintergreen, Jane
    See Duncan, Sara Jeannette

Winters, Janet Lewis . . . . CLC 41
    See also Lewis, Janet
    See also DLBY 87

Winters, (Arthur) Yvor
    1900-1968 . . . . CLC 4, 8, 32
    See also CA 11-12; 25-28R; CAP 1;
        DLB 48; MTCW

Winterson, Jeanette
    1959- . . . . CLC 64; DAM POP
    See also CA 136; CANR 58

Winthrop, John 1588-1649. . . . . LC 31
    See also DLB 24, 30

Wiseman, Frederick 1930-. . . . . CLC 20
    See also CA 159

Wister, Owen 1860-1938 . . . . TCLC 21
    See also CA 108; DLB 9, 78; SATA 62

Witkacy
    See Witkiewicz, Stanislaw Ignacy

Witkiewicz, Stanislaw Ignacy
    1885-1939 . . . . TCLC 8
    See also CA 105

Wittgenstein, Ludwig (Josef Johann)
    1889-1951 . . . . TCLC 59
    See also CA 113

Wittig, Monique 1935(?)-. . . . . CLC 22
    See also CA 116; 135; DLB 83

Wittlin, Jozef 1896-1976 . . . . CLC 25
    See also CA 49-52; 65-68; CANR 3

Wodehouse, P(elham) G(renville)
    1881-1975 . . . CLC 1, 2, 5, 10, 22; DAB;
                    DAC; DAM NOV; SSC 2
    See also AITN 2; CA 45-48; 57-60;
        CANR 3, 33; CDBLB 1914-1945;
        DLB 34, 162; MTCW; SATA 22

Woiwode, L.
    See Woiwode, Larry (Alfred)

Woiwode, Larry (Alfred) 1941-. . . CLC 6, 10
    See also CA 73-76; CANR 16; DLB 6;
        INT CANR-16

Wojciechowska, Maia (Teresa)
    1927- . . . . CLC 26
    See also AAYA 8; CA 9-12R; CANR 4, 41;
        CLR 1; JRDA; MAICYA; SAAS 1;
        SATA 1, 28, 83

Wolf, Christa 1929- . . . . CLC 14, 29, 58
    See also CA 85-88; CANR 45; DLB 75;
        MTCW

Wolfe, Gene (Rodman)
    1931-. . . . . CLC 25; DAM POP
    See also CA 57-60; CAAS 9; CANR 6, 32,
        60; DLB 8

Wolfe, George C. 1954-. . . . . CLC 49
    See also CA 149

Wolfe, Thomas (Clayton)
    1900-1938 . . . . . TCLC 4, 13, 29, 61; DA;
            DAB; DAC; DAM MST, NOV; WLC
    See also CA 104; 132; CDALB 1929-1941;
        DLB 9, 102; DLBD 2, 16; DLBY 85;
        MTCW

Wolfe, Thomas Kennerly, Jr. 1931-
    See Wolfe, Tom
    See also CA 13-16R; CANR 9, 33;
        DAM POP; INT CANR-9; MTCW

Wolfe, Tom . . . . CLC 1, 2, 9, 15, 35, 51
    See also Wolfe, Thomas Kennerly, Jr.
    See also AAYA 8; AITN 2; BEST 89:1;
        DLB 152

Wolff, Geoffrey (Ansell) 1937- . . . . . CLC 41
    See also CA 29-32R; CANR 29, 43

Wolff, Sonia
    See Levitin, Sonia (Wolff)

Wolff, Tobias (Jonathan Ansell)
    1945-. . . . . CLC 39, 64
    See also AAYA 16; BEST 90:2; CA 114;
        117; CAAS 22; CANR 54; DLB 130;
        INT 117

Wolfram von Eschenbach
    c. 1170-c. 1220 . . . . CMLC 5
    See also DLB 138

Wolitzer, Hilma 1930-. . . . . CLC 17
    See also CA 65-68; CANR 18, 40;
        INT CANR-18; SATA 31

Wollstonecraft, Mary 1759-1797. . . . . LC 5
    See also CDBLB 1789-1832; DLB 39, 104,
        158

Wonder, Stevie . . . . CLC 12
    See also Morris, Steveland Judkins

Wong, Jade Snow 1922-. . . . . CLC 17
    See also CA 109

Woodberry, George Edward
    1855-1930 . . . . TCLC 73
    See also DLB 71, 103

Woodcott, Keith
    See Brunner, John (Kilian Houston)

Woodruff, Robert W.
    See Mencken, H(enry) L(ouis)

Woolf, (Adeline) Virginia
    1882-1941 . . . . TCLC 1, 5, 20, 43, 56;
            DA; DAB; DAC; DAM MST, NOV;
                                    SSC 7; WLC
    See also CA 104; 130; CDBLB 1914-1945;
        DLB 36, 100, 162; DLBD 10; MTCW

Woollcott, Alexander (Humphreys)
    1887-1943 . . . . TCLC 5
    See also CA 105; DLB 29

Woolrich, Cornell 1903-1968. . . . . . . CLC 77
    See also Hopley-Woolrich, Cornell George

Wordsworth, Dorothy
    1771-1855 . . . . NCLC 25
    See also DLB 107

Wordsworth, William
    1770-1850 . . . . NCLC 12, 38; DA; DAB;
        DAC; DAM MST, POET; PC 4; WLC
    See also CDBLB 1789-1832; DLB 93, 107

Wouk, Herman
    1915- . . CLC 1, 9, 38; DAM NOV, POP
    See also CA 5-8R; CANR 6, 33; DLBY 82;
        INT CANR-6; MTCW

Wright, Charles (Penzel, Jr.)
    1935-. . . . . CLC 6, 13, 28
    See also CA 29-32R; CAAS 7; CANR 23,
        36, 62; DLB 165; DLBY 82; MTCW

Wright, Charles Stevenson
    1932- . . . . CLC 49; BLC 3;
                            DAM MULT, POET
    See also BW 1; CA 9-12R; CANR 26;
        DLB 33

Wright, Jack R.
    See Harris, Mark

Wright, James (Arlington)
    1927-1980 . . . . CLC 3, 5, 10, 28;
                                    DAM POET
    See also AITN 2; CA 49-52; 97-100;
        CANR 4, 34; DLB 5, 169; MTCW

Wright, Judith (Arandell)
    1915-. . . . . CLC 11, 53; PC 14
    See also CA 13-16R; CANR 31; MTCW;
        SATA 14

Wright, L(aurali) R. 1939-. . . . . CLC 44
    See also CA 138

Wright, Richard (Nathaniel)
    1908-1960 . . . . CLC 1, 3, 4, 9, 14, 21, 48,
        74; BLC; DA; DAB; DAC; DAM MST,
                        MULT, NOV; SSC 2; WLC
    See also AAYA 5; BW 1; CA 108;
        CDALB 1929-1941; DLB 76, 102;
        DLBD 2; MTCW

Wright, Richard B(ruce) 1937- . . . . . . CLC 6
    See also CA 85-88; DLB 53

Wright, Rick 1945-. . . . . CLC 35

Wright, Rowland
    See Wells, Carolyn

Wright, Stephen Caldwell 1946- . . . . CLC 33
    See also BW 2

Wright, Willard Huntington 1888-1939
    See Van Dine, S. S.
    See also CA 115; DLBD 16

Wright, William 1930-. . . . . CLC 44
    See also CA 53-56; CANR 7, 23

Wroth, LadyMary 1587-1653(?) ..... **LC 30**
See also DLB 121

Wu Ch'eng-en 1500(?)-1582(?) .... **LC 7**

Wu Ching-tzu 1701-1754 .... **LC 2**

Wurlitzer, Rudolph 1938(?)- ... **CLC 2, 4, 15**
See also CA 85-88; DLB 173

Wycherley, William
1641-1715 ..... **LC 8, 21; DAM DRAM**
See also CDBLB 1660-1789; DLB 80

Wylie, Elinor (Morton Hoyt)
1885-1928 .... **TCLC 8**
See also CA 105; DLB 9, 45

Wylie, Philip (Gordon) 1902-1971... **CLC 43**
See also CA 21-22; 33-36R; CAP 2; DLB 9

Wyndham, John................... **CLC 19**
See also Harris, John (Wyndham Parkes
Lucas) Beynon

Wyss, Johann David Von
1743-1818 .... **NCLC 10**
See also JRDA; MAICYA; SATA 29;
SATA-Brief 27

Xenophon
c. 430B.C.-c. 354B.C. .... **CMLC 17**
See also DLB 176

Yakumo Koizumi
See Hearn, (Patricio) Lafcadio (Tessima
Carlos)

Yanez, Jose Donoso
See Donoso (Yanez), Jose

Yanovsky, Basile S.
See Yanovsky, V(assily) S(emenovich)

Yanovsky, V(assily) S(emenovich)
1906-1989 .... **CLC 2, 18**
See also CA 97-100; 129

Yates, Richard 1926-1992 ..... **CLC 7, 8, 23**
See also CA 5-8R; 139; CANR 10, 43;
DLB 2; DLBY 81, 92; INT CANR-10

Yeats, W. B.
See Yeats, William Butler

Yeats, William Butler
1865-1939 ..... **TCLC 1, 11, 18, 31; DA;**
DAB; DAC; DAM DRAM, MST,
POET; WLC
See also CA 104; 127; CANR 45;
CDBLB 1890-1914; DLB 10, 19, 98, 156;
MTCW

Yehoshua, A(braham) B.
1936- .... **CLC 13, 31**
See also CA 33-36R; CANR 43

Yep, Laurence Michael 1948- ...... **CLC 35**
See also AAYA 5; CA 49-52; CANR 1, 46;
CLR 3, 17; DLB 52; JRDA; MAICYA;
SATA 7, 69

Yerby, Frank G(arvin)
1916-1991 .... **CLC 1, 7, 22; BLC;**
DAM MULT
See also BW 1; CA 9-12R; 136; CANR 16,
52; DLB 76; INT CANR-16; MTCW

Yesenin, Sergei Alexandrovich
See Esenin, Sergei (Alexandrovich)

Yevtushenko, Yevgeny (Alexandrovich)
1933- .... **CLC 1, 3, 13, 26, 51;**
DAM POET
See also CA 81-84; CANR 33, 54; MTCW

Yezierska, Anzia 1885(?)-1970 ..... **CLC 46**
See also CA 126; 89-92; DLB 28; MTCW

Yglesias, Helen 1915- .... **CLC 7, 22**
See also CA 37-40R; CAAS 20; CANR 15;
INT CANR-15; MTCW

Yokomitsu Riichi 1898-1947 ...... **TCLC 47**

Yonge, Charlotte (Mary)
1823-1901 .... **TCLC 48**
See also CA 109; DLB 18, 163; SATA 17

York, Jeremy
See Creasey, John

York, Simon
See Heinlein, Robert A(nson)

Yorke, Henry Vincent 1905-1974 ... **CLC 13**
See also Green, Henry
See also CA 85-88; 49-52

Yosano Akiko 1878-1942 .. **TCLC 59; PC 11**

Yoshimoto, Banana .... **CLC 84**
See also Yoshimoto, Mahoko

Yoshimoto, Mahoko 1964-
See Yoshimoto, Banana
See also CA 144

Young, Al(bert James)
1939- ..... **CLC 19; BLC; DAM MULT**
See also BW 2; CA 29-32R; CANR 26;
DLB 33

Young, Andrew (John) 1885-1971.... **CLC 5**
See also CA 5-8R; CANR 7, 29

Young, Collier
See Bloch, Robert (Albert)

Young, Edward 1683-1765 .... **LC 3, 40**
See also DLB 95

Young, Marguerite (Vivian)
1909-1995 .... **CLC 82**
See also CA 13-16; 150; CAP 1

Young, Neil 1945- .... **CLC 17**
See also CA 110

Young Bear, Ray A.
1950- .... **CLC 94; DAM MULT**
See also CA 146; DLB 175; NNAL

Yourcenar, Marguerite
1903-1987 .... **CLC 19, 38, 50, 87;**
DAM NOV
See also CA 69-72; CANR 23, 60; DLB 72;
DLBY 88; MTCW

Yurick, Sol 1925- .... **CLC 6**
See also CA 13-16R; CANR 25

Zabolotskii, Nikolai Alekseevich
1903-1958 .... **TCLC 52**
See also CA 116

Zamiatin, Yevgenii
See Zamyatin, Evgeny Ivanovich

Zamora, Bernice (B. Ortiz)
1938- ..... **CLC 89; DAM MULT; HLC**
See also CA 151; DLB 82; HW

Zamyatin, Evgeny Ivanovich
1884-1937 .... **TCLC 8, 37**
See also CA 105

Zangwill, Israel 1864-1926. ...... **TCLC 16**
See also CA 109; DLB 10, 135

Zappa, Francis Vincent, Jr. 1940-1993
See Zappa, Frank
See also CA 108; 143; CANR 57

Zappa, Frank.................... **CLC 17**
See also Zappa, Francis Vincent, Jr.

Zaturenska, Marya 1902-1982.... **CLC 6, 11**
See also CA 13-16R; 105; CANR 22

Zeami 1363-1443.................. **DC 7**

Zelazny, Roger (Joseph)
1937-1995 .... **CLC 21**
See also AAYA 7; CA 21-24R; 148;
CANR 26, 60; DLB 8; MTCW;
SATA 57; SATA-Brief 39

Zhdanov, Andrei A(lexandrovich)
1896-1948 .... **TCLC 18**
See also CA 117

Zhukovsky, Vasily 1783-1852 .... **NCLC 35**

Ziegenhagen, Eric .... **CLC 55**

Zimmer, Jill Schary
See Robinson, Jill

Zimmerman, Robert
See Dylan, Bob

Zindel, Paul
1936- ..... **CLC 6, 26; DA; DAB; DAC;**
DAM DRAM, MST, NOV; DC 5
See also AAYA 2; CA 73-76; CANR 31;
CLR 3, 45; DLB 7, 52; JRDA; MAICYA;
MTCW; SATA 16, 58

Zinov'Ev, A. A.
See Zinoviev, Alexander (Aleksandrovich)

Zinoviev, Alexander (Aleksandrovich)
1922- .... **CLC 19**
See also CA 116; 133; CAAS 10

Zoilus
See Lovecraft, H(oward) P(hillips)

Zola, Emile (Edouard Charles Antoine)
1840-1902 ...... **TCLC 1, 6, 21, 41; DA;**
DAB; DAC; DAM MST, NOV; WLC
See also CA 104; 138; DLB 123

Zoline, Pamela 1941- .... **CLC 62**

Zorrilla y Moral, Jose 1817-1893 .. **NCLC 6**

Zoshchenko, Mikhail (Mikhailovich)
1895-1958 .... **TCLC 15; SSC 15**
See also CA 115; 160

Zuckmayer, Carl 1896-1977........ **CLC 18**
See also CA 69-72; DLB 56, 124

Zuk, Georges
See Skelton, Robin

Zukofsky, Louis
1904-1978 .... **CLC 1, 2, 4, 7, 11, 18;**
DAM POET; PC 11
See also CA 9-12R; 77-80; CANR 39;
DLB 5, 165; MTCW

Zweig, Paul 1935-1984........ **CLC 34, 42**
See also CA 85-88; 113

Zweig, Stefan 1881-1942 .... **TCLC 17**
See also CA 112; DLB 81, 118

Zwingli, Huldreich 1484-1531 .... **LC 37**
See also DLB 179

Literary Criticism Series
Cumulative Topic Index

This index lists all topic entries in Gale's *Classical and Medieval Literature Criticism, Contemporary Literary Criticism, Literature Criticism from 1400 to 1800, Nineteenth-Century Literature Criticism,* and *Twentieth-Century Literary Criticism.*

Topic Index

Topic Index

LC Cumulative Nationality Index

AFGHAN
Babur **18**

AMERICAN
Bradstreet, Anne **4, 30**
Edwards, Jonathan **7**
Eliot, John **5**
Franklin, Benjamin **25**
Hathorne, John **38**
Hopkinson, Francis **25**
Knight, Sarah Kemble **7**
Mather, Cotton **38**
Mather, Increase **38**
Munford, Robert **5**
Penn, William **25**
Sewall, Samuel **38**
Stoughton, William **38**
Taylor, Edward **11**
Washington, George **25**
Wheatley (Peters), Phillis **3**
Winthrop, John **31**

BENINESE
Equiano, Olaudah **16**

CANADIAN
Marie de l'Incarnation **10**

CHINESE
Lo Kuan-chung **12**
P'u Sung-ling **3**
Ts'ao Hsueh-ch'in **1**
Wu Ch'eng-en **7**
Wu Ching-tzu **2**

DANISH
Holberg, Ludvig **6**
Wessel, Johan Herman **7**

DUTCH
Erasmus, Desiderius **16**
Lipsius, Justus **16**
Spinoza, Benedictus de **9**

ENGLISH
Addison, Joseph **18**
Andrewes, Lancelot **5**
Arbuthnot, John **1**
Aubin, Penelope **9**
Bacon, Francis **18, 32**
Beaumont, Francis **33**
Behn, Aphra **1, 30**
Boswell, James **4**
Bradstreet, Anne **4, 30**
Brooke, Frances **6**
Bunyan, John **4**
Burke, Edmund **7, 36**
Butler, Samuel **16**
Carew, Thomas **13**
Cary, Elizabeth, Lady Falkland **30**
Cavendish, Margaret Lucas **30**
Caxton, William , **17**
Chapman, George **22**
Charles I **13**
Chatterton, Thomas **3**
Chaucer, Geoffrey **17**
Churchill, Charles **3**
Cleland, John **2**
Collier, Jeremy **6**
Collins, William **4, 40**
Congreve, William **5, 21**
Crashaw, Richard **24**
Daniel, Samuel **24**
Davys, Mary **1**
Day, Thomas **1**
Dee, John **20**
Defoe, Daniel **1**

Dekker, Thomas **22**
Delany, Mary (Granville Pendarves) **12**
Dennis, John **11**
Devenant, William **13**
Donne, John **10, 24**
Drayton, Michael **8**
Dryden, John **3, 21**
Elyot, Sir Thomas **11**
Equiano, Olaudah **16**
Fanshawe, Ann **11**
Farquhar, George **21**
Fielding, Henry **1**
Fielding, Sarah **1**
Fletcher, John **33**
Foxe, John **14**
Garrick, David **15**
Gray, Thomas **4, 40**
Hakluyt, Richard **31**
Hawes, Stephen **17**
Haywood, Eliza (Fowler) **1**
Henry VIII **10**
Herbert, George **24**
Herrick, Robert **13**
Hobbes, Thomas **36**
Howell, James **13**
Hunter, Robert **7**
Johnson, Samuel **15**
Jonson, Ben(jamin) **6, 33**
Julian of Norwich **6**
Kempe, Margery **6**
Killigrew, Anne **4**
Kyd, Thomas **22**
Langland, William **19**
Lanyer, Aemilia **10, 30**
Lilly, William **27**
Locke, John **7**
Lovelace, Richard **24**
Lyttelton, George **10**

487

LC Cumulative Title Index

Title Index

Title Index

Title Index

Title Index

Title Index

Title Index

Title Index

Title Index

Title Index

Title Index

Title Index

Title Index

Title Index

Title Index

Title Index